T0191702

Lecture Notes in Computer Science 12506

Jeff Z. Pan · Valentina Tamma ·
Claudia d'Amato · Krzysztof Janowicz ·
Bo Fu · Axel Polleres · Oshani Seneviratne ·
Lalana Kagal (Eds.)

The Semantic Web – ISWC 2020

19th International Semantic Web Conference
Athens, Greece, November 2–6, 2020
Proceedings, Part I

Editors
Jeff Z. Pan
University of Edinburgh
Edinburgh, UK

Claudia d'Amato
University of Bari
Bari, Italy

Bo Fu
California State University, Long Beach
Long Beach, CA, USA

Oshani Seneviratne
Rensselaer Polytechnic Institute
Troy, NY, USA

Valentina Tamma
University of Liverpool
Liverpool, UK

Krzysztof Janowicz
University of California, Santa Barbara
Santa Barbara, CA, USA

Axel Polleres
Vienna University of Economics
and Business
Vienna, Austria

Lalana Kagal
Massachusetts Institute of Technology
Cambridge, MA, USA

ISSN 0302-9743 ISSN 1611-3349 (electronic)
Lecture Notes in Computer Science
ISBN 978-3-030-62418-7 ISBN 978-3-030-62419-4 (eBook)
https://doi.org/10.1007/978-3-030-62419-4

LNCS Sublibrary: SL3 – Information Systems and Applications, incl. Internet/Web, and HCI

This Springer imprint is published by the registered company Springer Nature Switzerland AG
The registered company address is: Gewerbestrasse 11, 6330 Cham, Switzerland

Preface

Throughout the years, the International Semantic Web Conference (ISWC) has firmly established itself as the premier international forum to discuss and present the latest advances in fundamental research, innovative technology, and applications of the Semantic Web, Linked Data, Knowledge Graphs, and Knowledge Processing on the Web. Now in its 19th edition, ISWC 2020 aims to bring together researchers and practitioners to present new approaches and findings, share ideas, and discuss experiences. The conference involves researchers with diverse skills and interests, thanks to the increased adoption of semantic technologies. Furthermore, knowledge-driven technologies have become increasingly synergetic in many subfields of artificial intelligence, such as natural language processing and machine learning, and this year's call for papers for the main conference tracks was broadened to include such topics to acknowledge these cooperative research efforts.

This year, the submission process and the conference planning were heavily affected by the COVID-19 pandemic outbreak. Despite the myriad of challenges faced, ISWC has maintained its excellent reputation as a premier scientific conference. As a means of recognizing the difficulties experienced by the community, the submission deadline was postponed by five weeks, and the decision was made to run the conference as a virtual event. We received submissions from 51 different countries with Germany, the USA, China, Italy, and France featuring prominently in the submissions list.

Across the conference, we witnessed a real effort by the community – authors, Senior Program Committee (SPC) members, Program Committee (PC) members, and additional reviewers – all of whom were all incredibly supportive of the changes we had to make to the conference organization, demonstrating remarkable dedication and energy during the whole process. We also saw the pandemic become an opportunity to support the scientific community at large, with multiple papers related to COVID-19 research submitted to the conference.

The Research Track, chaired by Jeff Pan and Valentina Tamma, received 170 submissions and ultimately accepted 38 papers, resulting in an acceptance rate of 22.3%. Continuing with the approach taken last year, we adopted a double-blind review policy, i.e., the authors' identity was not revealed to the reviewers and vice versa. Furthermore, reviewers assigned to a paper were not aware of the identity of their fellow reviewers. We strengthened the composition of the PC, which comprised 34 SPC and 244 regular PC members. An additional 66 sub-reviewers were recruited to support the review process further.

ISWC has traditionally had a very rigorous reviewing process, which was again reflected this year. For every submission, several criteria were assessed by the PC members, including originality, novelty, relevance, and impact of the research contributions; soundness, rigor, and reproducibility; clarity and quality of presentation; and the positioning to the literature. This year, the vast majority of papers were reviewed by four reviewers and an SPC member. All of the reviewers engaged in lively and thorough discussions once the initial reviews had been submitted, and later after the authors' responses were made available. Each paper was then discussed among the Research Track PC chairs and the SPC members to reach a consensus on the final list of accepted papers. As a further measure to recognize the COVID-19 pandemics' challenges, some papers were conditionally accepted, with the SPC members overseeing them and kindly agreeing to shepherd the papers to address the concerns raised by the reviewers. The PC chairs would like to express their gratitude to all SPC members, PC members, and external reviewers for the time, the dedication, and energy they put into the reviewing process, despite these very challenging circumstances.

The In-Use Track continues the tradition to showcase and learn from the growing adoption of Semantic Web technologies in concrete and practical settings, demonstrating the crucial roles that Semantic Web technologies often play in supporting more efficient, effective interoperable solutions in a range of real-world contexts. This year, the track chairs Bo Fu and Axel Polleres received 47 paper submissions, and they accepted 21 papers, leading to an acceptance rate of 44.7%, which reflects a continued increase in the number of submissions as well as acceptances compared to previous years, which indicates a growing maturity and adoption of Semantic Web technologies. The In-Use Track PC consisted of 50 members who engaged in extensive discussions to ensure a high-quality program, where the committee assessed each submission following review criteria including novelty and significance of the application, acceptance and uptake, scalability and technical soundness, as well as the generalizability of the lessons learned regarding the benefits, risks, and opportunities when adopting Semantic Web technologies. Each paper received at least three reviews. The final accepted papers describe successful applications of technologies, including ontologies, Knowledge Graphs, and Linked Data in a diverse range of domains (e.g., digital humanities, pharmaceutics, manufacturing, taxation, and transportation) and highlight the suitability of Semantic Web methods to advance solutions in various challenging areas (e.g., adaptive systems, data integration, collaborative knowledge management, machine learning, and recommendations).

The Resources Track solicited contributions ranging from ontologies and benchmarks to workflows and datasets over software, services, and frameworks. Many of these contributions are research enablers. For instance, ontologies are used to lift data semantically, datasets become core hubs of the Linked Data cloud, and benchmarks enable others to evaluate their research more systematically. In this year's edition, track chairs Claudia d'Amato and Krzysztof Janowicz received 71 submissions, out of which they decided to accept 22. These submissions are well representative of the spirit of the track and the variety of Semantic Web research. They include knowledge graphs related to COVID-19, benchmarks for OWL2 ontologies, web crawlers, and ontologies. The track chairs are incredibly thankful for the timely and high-quality reviews they received and would like to express their gratitude towards the SPC members who provided excellent meta-reviews and engaged in discussions to ensure fair evaluation of all papers.

In light of the reproducibility crisis in natural sciences, we believe that sharing experimental code, data, and setup will benefit scientific progress, foster collaboration, and encourage the exchange of ideas. We want to build a culture where sharing results, code, and scripts are the norm rather than an exception. To highlight the importance in this area, Valentina Ivanova and Pasquale Minervini chaired the second edition of the reproducibility initiative at ISWC. The track's focus was to evaluate submissions from the ISWC Research and Resources Tracks' accepted papers. This year, the ISWC Reproducibility Track extended the evaluation scope, which now includes two assessment lines: Reproducibility Line of Assessment for reproducing systems set ups and computational experiments and Replicability Line of Assessment for evaluating quantitative laboratory experiments with users. For the Reproducibility Line of Assessment, two independent members of the PC interacted with the authors to check the data's availability, source code, documentation, configuration requirements, and reproduce the paper's most important results. For the Replicability Line of Assessment, one member of the PC interacted with the authors to assess if the authors supplied enough materials about their work so an interested researcher could re-run the experiments in question. We received 10 submissions from the Resources Track in the Reproducibility Line of Assessment.

The Industry Track provides industry adopters an opportunity to highlight and share the key learnings and challenges of applying Semantic Web technologies in real-world and scalable implementations. This year, the track chairs Freddy Lecue and Jun Yan received 22 submissions from a wide range of companies of different sizes, and 15 submissions were accepted. The submissions were assessed in terms of quantitative and qualitative value proposition provided, innovative aspects, impact, and lessons learned, as well as business value in the application domain; and the degree to which semantic technologies are critical to their offering. Each paper got one review from an industry Semantic Web expert, which was checked and validated by the Industry Track chairs. The final decision was based on the evidence and impact of industrial applications using/based on Semantic Web technologies.

The Sister Conference Track has been designed as a forum for presentations of significant Semantic Web-related research results that have been recently presented at very well-established conferences other than the ISWC. The goal is to give visibility of these results to the ISWC audience and promote discussions concerning such results. For this first issue, chaired by Jérôme Euzenat and Juanzi Li, we decided to adopt a dual strategy, issuing an open call for papers and actively looking for relevant papers to invite. We invited 22 papers, out of which five applied. Four Additional papers replied to the call for papers. The authors of one other paper asked to submit, but were discouraged. Of these, we retained 8 papers. These were published in the past two year editions of the European Conference on Artificial Intelligence (ECAI), the Association for the Advancement of Artificial Intelligence (AAAI) conference, the International Joint Conferences on Artificial Intelligence (IJCAI), the International Conference on Autonomous Agents and Multi-Agent Systems (AAMAS), and the World Wide Web (WWW) conference. These papers did not undergo a further peer review, nor are they republished in the ISWC proceedings. They complemented and added value to the ISWC 2020 program.

The workshop program, chaired by Sabrina Kirrane and Satya Sahoo, included a mix of established and relatively new topics. Workshops on established topics included ontology matching, ontology design and patterns, scalable knowledge base systems, semantic statistics, querying and benchmarking, evolution and preservation, profiling, visualization, and Semantic Web for health data management. Workshops on relatively new topics included contextualized knowledge graphs, semantics for online misinformation detection, semantic explainability, natural language interfaces, research data management, artificial intelligence technologies for legal documents, the Semantic Web in practice, and Wikidata. Tutorials on a variety of topics such as knowledge graph construction, common sense knowledge graphs, pattern-based knowledge base construction, building large knowledge graphs efficiently, scalable RDF analytics, SPARQL endpoints, Web API, data science pipelines, semantic explainability, shape applications and tools, and building mobile Semantic Web applications complemented the workshop program.

As of ISWC 2020, the Semantic Web Challenges mark their 17th appearance at the conference. Since last year, all proposed challenges need to provide a benchmarking platform, on which participants can have their solution validated using objective measures against fixed datasets. Three exciting challenges were open for submissions: the SeMantic AnsweR Type prediction task (SMART), the Semantic Web Challenge on Tabular Data to Knowledge Graph Matching (SemTab), and the Mining the Web of HTML-embedded Product Data. For SMART, participants focus on predicting the type of answers to English questions, which is essential to the topic of question answering within the natural language processing and information retrieval domain. For SemTab, participants aimed to convert tables into knowledge graphs to better exploit the information contained in them. For the Product Data challenge, participants had to address tasks in the domain of e-commerce data integration, specifically product matching, and product classification. Challenge entries and lessons learned were discussed at ISWC 2020.

The Posters and Demos Track is one of the most vibrant parts of every ISWC. This year, the track was chaired by Kerry Taylor and Rafael Gonçalves, who received a total of 97 submissions: 58 posters and 39 demos. The PC consisting of 97 members and the track chairs, accepted 43 posters and 35 demos. The decisions were primarily based on relevance, originality, and clarity of the submissions.

The conference also included a Doctoral Consortium (DC) Track, chaired by Elena Simperl and Harith Alani. The DC Track was designed to enable PhD students to share their work and initial results with fellow students and senior researchers from the Semantic Web community, gain experience in presenting scientific research, and receive feedback in a constructive and informal environment. This year, the PC accepted 6 papers for oral presentations out of 11 submissions. The DC program focused on allowing the students to work together during multiple activity sessions on joint tasks, such as articulating research questions or forming an evaluation plan. The aim was to increase their interactions and receive hands-on guidance from the ISWC community's senior members. DC Tracks also included a fantastic invited talk, delivered by Prof. Payam Barnaghi.

This year, ISWC offered Student Grant Awards to support the full conference's registration cost. We acknowledge the Semantic Web Science Association (SWSA) and the *Artificial Intelligence Journal* (AIJ) for generously funding this year's student grants. The applications were solicited from students attending a higher education institution, having either an ISWC 2020 paper accepted or just intending to participate in the conference. Preference was given to the students having a first-authored paper in either the main conference, the doctoral consortium, a workshop, the poster/demo session, or the Semantic Web challenge. This year, given the conference's virtual nature and the challenge of increasing student engagement, we planned a unique program for the Student Engagement and Mentoring Session that was open to all the student attendees of the conference. The session included three main parts. First, we hosted career-advising panels, consisting of senior researchers (mentors) with an open Q&A session on research and career advice. Second, a brainstorming group activity was planned to engage students in participatory design to creatively combine and articulate their research ideas for the Semantic Web's future vision. Lastly, a fun-filled social virtual party took place to help students socially engage with their peers.

Our thanks go to Elmar Kiesling and Haridimos Kondylakis, our publicity chairs, and Ioannis Chrysakis and Ioannis Karatzanis, our Web chairs. Together they did an amazing job of ensuring that all conference activities and updates were made available on the website and communicated across mailing lists and on social media. Gianluca Demartini and Evan Patton were the metadata chairs this year, and they made sure that all relevant information about the conference was available in a format that could be used across all applications, continuing a tradition established at ISWC many years ago. We are especially thankful to our proceedings chair, Oshani Seneviratne, who oversaw the publication of this volume alongside a number of CEUR proceedings for other tracks.

Sponsorships are essential to realizing a conference and were even more important this year as additional funds were necessary to put together the virtual conference. Despite numerous hurdles caused by the unusual situation, our highly committed trio of sponsorship chairs, Evgeny Kharlamov, Giorgios Stamou, and Veronika Thost, went above and beyond to find new ways to engage with sponsors and promote the conference to them.

Finally, our special thanks go to the members of the Semantic Web Science Association (SWSA), especially Ian Horrocks, the SWSA President, for their continuing support and guidance and to the organizers of previous ISWC conferences who were a constant source of knowledge, advice, and experience.

September 2020

Jeff Z. Pan
Valentina Tamma
Claudia d'Amato
Krzysztof Janowicz
Bo Fu
Axel Polleres
Oshani Seneviratne
Lalana Kagal

Organization

Organizing Committee

General Chair

Lalana Kagal	Massachusetts Institute of Technology, USA

Local Chairs

Manolis Koubarakis	University of Athens, Greece
Dimitris Plexousakis	ICS-FORTH, University of Crete, Greece
George Vouros	University of Piraeus, Greece

Research Track Chairs

Jeff Z. Pan	The University of Edinburgh, UK
Valentina Tamma	The University of Liverpool, UK

Resources Track Chairs

Claudia d'Amato	University of Bari, Italy
Krzysztof Janowicz	University of California, Santa Barbara, USA

In-Use Track Chairs

Bo Fu	California State University, Long Beach, USA
Axel Polleres	Vienna University of Economics and Business, Austria

Reproducibility Track Chairs

Valentina Ivanova	RISE Research Institutes of Sweden, Sweden
Pasquale Minervini	University College London, UK

Industry Track Chairs

Freddy Lecue	Inria, France, and CortAIx Thales, Canada
Jun Yan	Yidu Cloud Technology Company Ltd., China

Sister Conference Paper Track Chairs

Jérôme Euzenat	Inria, Université Grenoble Alpes, France
Juanzi Li	Tsinghua University, China

Workshop and Tutorial Chairs

Sabrina Kirrane	Vienna University of Economics and Business, Austria
Satya S. Sahoo	Case Western Reserve University, USA

Semantic Web Challenges Track Chairs

Anna Lisa Gentile	IBM Research, USA
Ruben Verborgh	Ghent University – imec, Belgium

Poster and Demo Track Chairs

Rafael Gonçalves	Stanford University, USA
Kerry Taylor	The Australian National University, Australia, and University of Surrey, UK

Doctoral Consortium Chairs

Harith Alani	KMI, The Open University, UK
Elena Simperl	University of Southampton, UK

Student Coordination Chairs

Maribel Acosta	Karlsruhe Institute of Technology, Germany
Hemant Purohit	George Mason University, USA

Virtual Conference Chairs

Mauro Dragoni	Fondazione Bruno Kessler, Italy
Juan Sequada	data.world, Austin, USA

Proceedings Chair

Oshani Seneviratne	Rensselaer Polytechnic Institute, USA

Metadata Chairs

Gianluca Demartini	The University of Queensland, Australia
Evan Patton	CSAIL MIT, USA

Publicity Chairs

Elmar Kiesling	Vienna University of Economics and Business, Austria
Haridimos Kondylakis	ICS-FORTH, Greece

Web Site Chairs

Ioannis Chrysakis	ICS-FORTH, Greece, and Ghent University, IDLab, imec, Belgium.
Ioannis Karatzanis	ICS-FORTH, Greece

Vision Track Chairs

Natasha Noy	Google Research, USA
Carole Goble	The University of Manchester, UK

Sponsorship Chairs

Evgeny Kharlamov	Bosch Center for Artificial Intelligence, Germany, and University of Oslo, Norway
Giorgios Stamou	AILS Lab, ECE NTUA, Greece
Veronika Thost	MIT, IBM Watson AI Lab, USA

Research Track Senior Program Committee

Eva Blomqvist	Linköping University, Sweden
Gianluca Demartini	The University of Queensland, Australia
Mauro Dragoni	Fondazione Bruno Kessler, Italy
Achille Fokoue	IBM, USA
Naoki Fukuta	Shizuoka University, Japan
Anna Lisa Gentile	IBM, USA
Birte Glimm	Universität Ulm, Germany
Jose Manuel Gomez-Perez	Expert System, Spain
Olaf Hartig	Linköping University, Sweden
Laura Hollink	Vrije Universiteit Amsterdam, The Netherlands
Andreas Hotho	University of Würzburg, Germany
Wei Hu	Nanjing University, China
Mustafa Jarrar	Birzeit University, Palestine
Ernesto Jimenez-Ruiz	City, University of London, UK
Kang Liu	National Laboratory of Pattern Recognition, Chinese Academy of Sciences, China
Vanessa Lopez	IBM, Ireland
Markus Luczak-Roesch	Victoria University of Wellington, New Zealand
David Martin	Nuance Communications, USA
Thomas Meyer	University of Cape Town, CAIR, South Africa
Boris Motik	University of Oxford, UK
Raghava Mutharaju	IIIT-Delhi, India
Francesco Osborne	The Open University, UK
Matteo Palmonari	University of Milano-Bicocca, Italy
Bijan Parsia	The University of Manchester, UK
Terry Payne	The University of Liverpool, UK
Guilin Qi	Southeast University, China
Simon Razniewski	Max Planck Institute for Informatics, Germany
Marta Sabou	Vienna University of Technology, Austria
Elena Simperl	King's College London, UK
Daria Stepanova	Bosch Center for Artificial Intelligence, Germany
Hideaki Takeda	National Institute of Informatics, Japan
Tania Tudorache	Stanford University, USA
Maria-Esther Vidal	Universidad Simón Bolívar, Venezuela
Kewen Wang	Griffith University, Australia

Research Track Program Committee

Ibrahim Abdelaziz	IBM, USA
Maribel Acosta	Karlsruhe Institute of Technology, Germany
Panos Alexopoulos	Textkernel B.V., The Netherlands
Muhammad Intizar Ali	Insight Centre for Data Analytics, National University of Ireland Galway, Ireland
José-Luis Ambite	University of Southern California, USA
Reihaneh Amini	Wright State University, USA
Grigoris Antoniou	University of Huddersfield, UK
Hiba Arnaout	Max Planck Institute for Informatics, Germany
Luigi Asprino	University of Bologna, STLab, ISTC-CNR, Italy
Nathalie Aussenac-Gilles	IRIT, CNRS, France
Carlos Badenes-Olmedo	Universidad Politécnica de Madrid, Spain
Pierpaolo Basile	University of Bari, Italy
Valerio Basile	University of Turin, Italy
Sumit Bhatia	IBM, India
Christian Bizer	University of Mannheim, Germany
Carlos Bobed	Everis, NTT Data, University of Zaragoza, Spain
Alex Borgida	Rutgers University, USA
Paolo Bouquet	University of Trento, Italy
Zied Bouraoui	CRIL, CNRS, Artois University, France
Alessandro Bozzon	Delft University of Technology, The Netherlands
Anna Breit	Semantic Web Company, Austria
Carlos Buil Aranda	Universidad Técnica Federico Santa María, Chile
Davide Buscaldi	LIPN, Université Paris 13, Sorbonne Paris Cité, France
David Carral	TU Dresden, Germany
Giovanni Casini	ISTI-CNR, Italy
Irene Celino	Cefriel, Italy
Vinay Chaudhri	SRI International, USA
Wenliang Chen	Soochow University, China
Jiaoyan Chen	University of Oxford, UK
Yubo Chen	Institute of Automation, Chinese Academy of Sciences, China
Gong Cheng	Nanjing University, China
Cuong Xuan Chu	Max Planck Institute for Informatics, Germany
Philipp Cimiano	Bielefeld University, Germany
Pieter Colpaert	Ghent University – imec, Belgium
Mariano Consens	University of Toronto, Canada
Olivier Corby	Inria, France
Oscar Corcho	Universidad Politécnica de Madrid, Spain
Luca Costabello	Accenture Labs, Ireland
Isabel Cruz	University of Illinois at Chicago, USA
Philippe Cudre-Mauroux	University of Fribourg, Switzerland
Bernardo Cuenca Grau	University of Oxford, UK
Victor de Boer	Vrije Universiteit Amsterdam, The Netherlands

Daniele Dell'Aglio	University of Zurich, Switzerland
Elena Demidova	L3S Research Center, Germany
Ronald Denaux	Expert System, Spain
Grit Denker	SRI International, USA
Danilo Dessì	University of Cagliari, Italy
Tommaso Di Noia	Politecnico di Bari, Italy
Stefan Dietze	GESIS - Leibniz Institute for the Social Sciences, Germany
Djellel Difallah	New York University, USA
Anastasia Dimou	Ghent University, Belgium
Dejing Dou	University of Oregon, USA
Jianfeng Du	Guangdong University of Foreign Studies, China
Michel Dumontier	Maastricht University, The Netherlands
Shusaku Egami	Electronic Navigation Research Institute, Japan
Fajar J. Ekaputra	Vienna University of Technology, Austria
Alessandro Faraotti	IBM, Italy
Michael Färber	Karlsruhe Institute of Technology, Germany
Catherine Faronzucker	Université Nice Sophia Antipolis, France
Yansong Feng	The University of Edinburgh, UK
Alba Fernandez	Universidad Politécnica de Madrid, Spain
Miriam Fernandez	Knowledge Media Institute, UK
Javier D. Fernández	F. Hoffmann-La Roche AG, Switzerland
Besnik Fetahu	L3S Research Center, Germany
Valeria Fionda	University of Calabria, Italy
Fabian Flöck	GESIS Cologne, Germany
Luis Galárraga	Inria, France
Fabien Gandon	Inria, France
Huan Gao	Microsoft, USA
Raúl García-Castro	Universidad Politécnica de Madrid, Spain
Andrés García-Silva	Expert System
Daniel Garijo	Information Sciences Institute, USA
Manas Gaur	KNO.E.SIS Josh Research Center, Wright State University, USA
Pouya Ghiasnezhad Omran	The Australian National University, Australia
Shrestha Ghosh	Max Planck Institute for Informatics, Germany
Jorge Gracia	University of Zaragoza, Spain
Alasdair Gray	Heriot-Watt University, UK
Dagmar Gromann	University of Vienna, Austria
Paul Groth	University of Amsterdam, The Netherlands
Kalpa Gunaratna	Samsung Research, USA
Peter Haase	metaphacts, Germany
Mohand-Said Hacid	Université Claude Bernard Lyon 1, France
Tom Hanika	Knowledge and Data Engineering, University of Kassel, Germany
Andreas Harth	University of Erlangen-Nuremberg, Fraunhofer IIS-SCS, Germany

Mounira Harzallah	LS2N, France
Oktie Hassanzadeh	IBM, USA
Rinke Hoekstra	University of Amsterdam, The Netherlands
Katja Hose	Aalborg University, Denmark
Lei Hou	Tsinghua University, China
Pan Hu	University of Oxford, UK
Renfen Hu	Beijing Normal University, China
Linmei Hu	Beijing University of Posts and Telecommunications, China
Luis Ibanez-Gonzalez	University of Southampton, UK
Ryutaro Ichise	National Institute of Informatics, Japan
Prateek Jain	Nuance Communications, USA
Tobias Käfer	Karlsruhe Institute of Technology, Germany
Lucie-Aimée Kaffee	University of Southampton, UK
Maulik R. Kamdar	Elsevier Inc., USA
Ken Kaneiwa	The University of Electro-Communications, Japan
Tomi Kauppinen	Department of Computer Science, Aalto University, Finland
Takahiro Kawamura	National Agriculture and Food Research Organization, Japan
Mayank Kejriwal	Information Sciences Institute, USA
Ilkcan Keles	Aalborg University, Denmark
Carsten Keßler	Aalborg University, Denmark
Sabrina Kirrane	Vienna University of Economics and Business, Austria
Pavel Klinov	Stardog Union Inc., USA
Matthias Klusch	DFKI, Germany
Boris Konev	The University of Liverpool, UK
Egor V. Kostylev	University of Oxford, UK
Kouji Kozaki	Osaka Electro-Communication University, Japan
Adila A. Krisnadhi	Universitas Indonesia, Indonesia
Markus Krötzsch	TU Dresden, Germany
Sreenivasa Kumar	Indian Institute of Technology Madras, India
Jose Emilio Labra Gayo	Universidad de Oviedo, Spain
Agnieszka Ławrynowicz	Poznan University of Technology, Poland
Danh Le Phuoc	TU Berlin, Germany
Maurizio Lenzerini	Sapienza University of Rome, Italy
Ru Li	Shanxi University, China
Yuan-Fang Li	Monash University, Australia
Matteo Lissandrini	Aalborg University, Denmark
Ming Liu	Harbin Institute of Technology, China
Carsten Lutz	Universität Bremen, Germany
Ioanna Lytra	Enterprise Information Systems, University of Bonn, Germany
Gengchen Mai	University of California, Santa Barbara, USA
Bassem Makni	IBM, USA
Ioana Manolescu	Inria, Institut Polytechnique de Paris, France

Marieke van Erp	KNAW Humanities Cluster, The Netherlands
Miel Vander Sande	Meemoo, Belgium
Jacco Vanossenbruggen	CWI, Vrije Universiteit Amsterdam, The Netherlands
Serena Villata	CNRS, Laboratoire d'Informatique, Signaux et Systèmes de Sophia-Antipolis, France
Domagoj Vrgoc	Pontificia Universidad Católica de Chile, Chile
Hai Wan	Sun Yat-sen University, China
Meng Wang	Southeast University, China
Peng Wang	Southeast University, China
Xin Wang	Tianjin University, China
Zhe Wang	Griffith University, Australia
Haofen Wang	Intelligent Big Data Visualization Lab, Tongji University, China
Weiqing Wang	Monash University, Australia
Gregory Todd Williams	J. Paul Getty Trust, USA
Frank Wolter	The University of Liverpool, UK
Tianxing Wu	Southeast University, China
Honghan Wu	King's College London, UK
Josiane Xavier Parreira	Siemens AG, Austria
Guohui Xiao	KRDB Research Centre, Free University of Bozen-Bolzano, Italy
Yanghua Xiao	Fudan University, China
Bo Xu	Donghua University, China
Ikuya Yamada	Studio Ousia Inc., Japan
Veruska Zamborlini	University of Amsterdam, The Netherlands
Fadi Zaraket	American University of Beirut, Lebanon
Haifa Zargayouna	Université Paris 13, France
Xiaowang Zhang	Tianjin University, China
Yuanzhe Zhang	Institute of Automation, Chinese Academy of Sciences, China
Xin Zhao	Renmin University of China, China
Kenny Zhu	Shanghai Jiao Tong University, China
Antoine Zimmermann	École des Mines de Saint-Étienne, France
Aya Zoghby	Mansoura University, Egypt

Research Track Additional Reviewers

George Baryannis
Sotiris Batsakis
Alberto Benincasa
Akansha Bhardwaj
Russa Biswas
Julia Bosque-Gil
Janez Brank
Tanya Braun
Christoph Braun
Maxime Buron
Ling Cai
Muhao Chen
Francesco Corcoglioniti
Marco Cremaschi
Vincenzo Cutrona
Jiwei Ding

Hang Dong
Dominik Dürrschnabel
Cristina Feier
Maximilian Felde
Herminio García González
Yuxia Geng
Simon Gottschalk
Peiqin Gu
Ryohei Hisano
Fabian Hoppe
Elena Jaramillo
Pavan Kapanipathi
Christian Kindermann
Benno Kruit
Felix Kuhr
Sebastian Lempert
Qiuhao Lu
Maximilian Marx
Qaiser Mehmood
Sylvia Melzer
Stephan Mennicke
Sepideh Mesbah
Payal Mitra
Natalia Mulligan
Anna Nguyen
Kristian Noullet
Erik Novak
Romana Pernischová
Md Rashad Al Hasan Rony
Paolo Rosso
Tarek Saier
Md Kamruzzaman Sarker
Bastian Schäfermeier
Thomas Schneider
Matteo Antonio Senese
Lucia Siciliani
Rita Sousa
Ahmet Soylu
Maximilian Stubbemann
Víctor Suárez-Paniagua
S. Subhashree
Nicolas Tempelmeier
Klaudia Thellmann
Vinh Thinh Ho
Rima Türker
Sahar Vahdati
Amir Veyseh
Gerhard Weikum
Xander Wilcke
Huayu Zhang

Resources Track Senior Program Committee

Irene Celino Cefriel, Italy
Olivier Curé Université Paris-Est, LIGM, France
Armin Haller The Australian National University, Australia
Yingjie Hu University at Buffalo, USA
Ernesto Jimenez-Ruiz City, University of London, UK
Maxime Lefrançois MINES Saint-Etienne, France
Maria Maleshkova University of Bonn, Germany
Matteo Palmonari University of Milano-Bicocca, Italy
Vojtěch Svátek University of Economics Prague, Czech Republic
Ruben Verborgh Ghent University, Belgium

Resources Track Program Committee

Benjamin Adams University of Canterbury, New Zealand
Mehwish Alam FIZ Karlsruhe - Leibniz Institute for Information Infrastructure, AIFB Institute, KIT, Germany
Francesco Antoniazzi École des Mines de Saint-Etienne, France

Christoph Lange	Fraunhofer, Technology FIT, RWTH Aachen University, Germany
Paea Le Pendu	University of California, Riverside, USA
Martin Leinberger	Universität Koblenz-Landau, Germany
Weizhuo Li	Southeast University, China
Albert Meroño-Peñuela	Vrije Universiteit Amsterdam, The Netherlands
Pascal Molli	University of Nantes, LS2N, France
Summaya Mumtaz	University of Oslo, Norway
Lionel Médini	LIRIS, University of Lyon, France
Hubert Naacke	Sorbonne Université, UPMC, LIP6, France
Raul Palma	Poznań Supercomputing and Networking Center, Poland
Heiko Paulheim	University of Mannheim, Germany
Catia Pesquita	LaSIGE, Universidade de Lisboa, Portugal
Alina Petrova	University of Oxford, UK
Rafael Peñaloza	University of Milano-Bicocca, Italy
Giuseppe Pirrò	Sapienza University of Rome, Italy
María Poveda-Villalón	Universidad Politécnica de Madrid, Spain
Blake Regalia	University of California, Santa Barbara, USA
Giuseppe Rizzo	LINKS Foundation, Italy
Sergio José Rodríguez Méndez	The Australian National University, Australia
Maria Del Mar Roldan-Garcia	Universidad de Malaga, Spain
Marco Rospocher	Università degli Studi di Verona, Italy
Ana Roxin	University of Burgundy, France
Michael Röder	Paderborn University, Germany
Tzanina Saveta	ICS-FORTH, Greece
Mark Schildhauer	NCEAS, USA
Stefan Schlobach	Vrije Universiteit Amsterdam, The Netherlands
Patricia Serrano Alvarado	LS2N, University of Nantes, France
Cogan Shimizu	Kansas State University, USA
Blerina Spahiu	University of Milano-Bicocca, Italy
Kavitha Srinivas	IBM, USA
Pedro Szekely	USC, Information Sciences Institute, USA
Ruben Taelman	Ghent University, Belgium
Hendrik Ter Horst	CITEC, Bielefeld University, Germany
Matthias Thimm	Universität Koblenz-Landau, Germany
Tabea Tietz	FIZ Karlsruhe, Germany
Jacopo Urbani	Vrije Universiteit Amsterdam, The Netherlands
Ricardo Usbeck	Paderborn University, Germany
Maria-Esther Vidal	Universidad Simón Bolívar, Venezuela
Tobias Weller	Karlsruhe Institute of Technology, Germany
Bo Yan	University of California, Santa Barbara, USA

Ziqi Zhang	The University of Sheffield, UK
Qianru Zhou	University of Glasgow, UK
Rui Zhu	University of California, Santa Barbara, USA

In-Use Track Program Committee

Renzo Angles	Universidad de Talca, Chile
Carlos Buil Aranda	Universidad Técnica Federico Santa María, Chile
Stefan Bischof	Siemens AG, Austria
Irene Celino	Cefriel, Italy
Muhao Chen	University of Pennsylvania, USA
James Codella	IBM, USA
Oscar Corcho	Universidad Politécnica de Madrid, Spain
Philippe Cudre-Mauroux	University of Fribourg, Switzerland
Brian Davis	Dublin City University, Ireland
Christophe Debruyne	Trinity College Dublin, Ireland
Djellel Difallah	New York University, USA
Luis Espinosa-Anke	Cardiff University, UK
Achille Fokoue	IBM, USA
Daniel Garijo	Information Sciences Institute, USA
Jose Manuel Gomez-Perez	Expert System, Spain
Damien Graux	ADAPT Centre, Trinity College Dublin, Ireland
Paul Groth	University of Amsterdam, The Netherlands
Daniel Gruhl	IBM, USA
Peter Haase	metaphacts, Germany
Armin Haller	The Australian National University, Australia
Nicolas Heist	University of Mannheim, Germany
Aidan Hogan	Universidad de Chile, Chile
Tobias Käfer	Karlsruhe Institute of Technology, Germany
Maulik Kamdar	Elsevier Health Markets, USA
Tomi Kauppinen	Aalto University, Finland
Mayank Kejriwal	Information Sciences Institute, USA
Elmar Kiesling	Vienna University of Economics and Business, Austria
Sabrina Kirrane	Vienna University of Economics and Business, Austria
Vanessa Lopez	IBM, USA
Beatrice Markhoff	LI, Université François Rabelais Tours, France
Sebastian Neumaier	Vienna University of Economics and Business, Austria
Andriy Nikolov	AstraZeneca, Germany
Alexander O'Connor	Autodesk, Inc., USA
Declan O'Sullivan	Trinity College Dublin, Ireland
Francesco Osborne	The Open University, UK
Matteo Palmonari	University of Milano-Bicocca, Italy
Josiane Xavier Parreira	Siemens AG, Austria
Catia Pesquita	LaSIGE, Universidade de Lisboa, Portugal
Artem Revenko	Semantic Web Company, Austria
Mariano Rico	Universidad Politécnica de Madrid, Spain

Petar Ristoski	IBM, USA
Dumitru Roman	SINTEF, Norway
Melike Sah	Near East University, Cyprus
Miel Vander Sande	Meemoo, Belgium
Dezhao Song	Thomson Reuters, Canada
Anna Tordai	Elsevier B.V., The Netherlands
Tania Tudorache	Stanford University, USA
Svitlana Vakulenko	Vienna University of Economics and Business, Austria
Xuezhi Wang	Google, USA
Matthäus Zloch	GESIS - Leibniz Institute for the Social Sciences, Germany

In-Use Track Additional Reviewers

Robert David	Semantic Web Company, Austria
Kabul Kurniawan	Vienna University of Economics and Business, Austria
Michael Luggen	eXascale Infolab, Switzerland
Maria Lindqvist	Aalto University, Finland
Nikolay Nikolov	SINTEF, Norway
Mario Scrocca	Cefriel, Italy
Ahmet Soylu	SINTEF, Norway

Sponsors

Platinum Sponsors

http://www.ibm.com

https://inrupt.com

https://www.metaphacts.com

Gold Sponsors

https://google.com

https://www.oracle.com/goto/rdfgraph

Silver Sponsors

https://coinform.eu

https://www.ebayinc.com/careers

https://sirius-labs.no

https://www.accenture.com

Best Resource Paper Sponsor

https://www.springer.com/gp/computer-science/lncs

Student Support and Grants Sponsor

https://www.journals.elsevier.com/artificial-intelligence

Doctoral Consortium Track Sponsor

https://www.heros-project.eu

Contents – Part I

Research Track

Contents – Part II

Resources Track

Research Track

Computing Compliant Anonymisations of Quantified ABoxes w.r.t. $\mathcal{EL}$ Policies

Franz Baader[1(✉)], Francesco Kriegel[1], Adrian Nuradiansyah[1], and Rafael Peñaloza[2]

[1] TU Dresden, Dresden, Germany
{franz.baader,francesco.kriegel,adrian.nuradiansyah}@tu-dresden.de
[2] University of Milano-Bicocca, Milano, Italy
rafael.penaloza@unimib.it

Abstract. We adapt existing approaches for privacy-preserving publishing of linked data to a setting where the data are given as Description Logic (DL) ABoxes with possibly anonymised (formally: existentially quantified) individuals and the privacy policies are expressed using sets of concepts of the DL $\mathcal{EL}$. We provide a chacterization of compliance of such ABoxes w.r.t. $\mathcal{EL}$ policies, and show how optimal compliant anonymisations of ABoxes that are non-compliant can be computed. This work extends previous work on privacy-preserving ontology publishing, in which a very restricted form of ABoxes, called instance stores, had been considered, but restricts the attention to compliance. The approach developed here can easily be adapted to the problem of computing optimal repairs of quantified ABoxes.

1 Introduction

Before publishing data concerned with persons, one may want to or be legally required to hide certain private information [15]. For example, a shady politician may not want the public to know that he is not only a politician, but also a businessman, and that he is additionally related to someone who is both a politician and a businessman. Before they publish data about their boss, his aids thus need to remove or modify certain information, but being honest themselves, they want to keep the changes minimal, and they do not want to invent incorrect information. This poses the question of how to change a given data set in a minimal way such that all the information to be published follows from the original one, but certain privacy constraints are satisfied. Basically the same question is asked in ontology repair [4], with the difference that the information to be removed is deemed to be erroneous rather than private.

A survey on privacy-preserving data publishing in general is given in [15]. In the context of ontologies, two different approaches for preserving privacy constraints have been investigated. In the controlled query evaluation framework, the source data are left unchanged, but an additional layer, called censor, is

Funded by the Deutsche Forschungsgemeinschaft (DFG) – 430150274.

J. Z. Pan et al. (Eds.): ISWC 2020, LNCS 12506, pp. 3–20, 2020.
https://doi.org/10.1007/978-3-030-62419-4_1

introduced, which decides whether and how queries are answered [9,11,16]. In contrast, anonymisation approaches modify the source data in a minimal way such that secrets that should be preserved can no longer be derived [3,12–14]. We use the approach for privacy-preserving publishing of linked data introduced in [12,13] as a starting point, where the information to be published is a relational dataset, possibly with (labelled) null values, and the privacy constraints (called *policy*) are formulated as conjunctive queries. A dataset is *compliant* with such a policy if the queries have no answers. In our example, the dataset consists of

$$\{\mathit{Politician}(d), \mathit{Businessman}(d), \mathit{related}(d,g), \mathit{Politician}(g), \mathit{Businessman}(g)\},$$

and the policy of the two conjunctive queries $\mathit{Politician}(x) \wedge \mathit{Businessman}(x)$ and $\exists y.\mathit{related}(x,y) \wedge \mathit{Politician}(y) \wedge \mathit{Businessman}(y)$. Since the first query has d and g, and the second has d as answers, the dataset does not comply with this policy. The only anonymisation operation provided in [12,13] for making the given dataset compliant is to replace constants (naming known individuals, like d and g) or null values by new null values. In our example, we can achieve compliance by renaming one occurrence of d and one occurrence of g:

$$\{\mathit{Politician}(d), \mathit{Businessman}(n_1), \mathit{related}(d,g), \mathit{Politician}(n_2), \mathit{Businessman}(g)\}.$$

Basically, this has the effect of removing $\mathit{Businessman}(d)$ and $\mathit{Politician}(g)$ from the dataset. While this is one of the optimal anonymisations (w.r.t. minimal loss of information) that can be obtained with the anonymisation operation allowed in [12,13], it is not optimal without this restriction. In fact, if we add $\mathit{related}(d,n_2)$ to this anonymisation, then the resulting dataset is still compliant, and it retains the information that d is related to some politician. The main difference of our approach to the one in [12,13] is that there only certain operations are available for anonymising ABoxes, whereas we consider all possible ABoxes that are implied by the given one. Optimality in [12,13] looks only at the range of ABoxes that can be obtained using the anonymisation operations defined there. Thus, optimal anonymisations obtained by the approach in [12,13] may not be optimal in our sense, as illustrated by the example above.

The aim of this paper is to determine a setting where optimal compliant anonymisations exist and can effectively be computed. To this purpose, we restrict the datasets with labelled null values of [12,13] to unary and binary relations, as usually done in DL ABoxes. In order to express the labelled null values, we consider an extension of ABoxes, called quantified ABoxes, in which some of the object names occurring in the ABox are existentially quantified. The main restriction is, however, that policies are expressed as concepts of the DL $\mathcal{EL}$, which can be seen as restricted form of conjunctive queries. The policy in our example can be expressed by the $\mathcal{EL}$ concepts $\mathit{Politician} \sqcap \mathit{Businessman}$ and $\exists \mathit{related}.(\mathit{Politician} \sqcap \mathit{Businessman})$.

In this setting, we characterise compliance of quantified ABoxes, and use this characterisation to show how to compute the set of all optimal compliant anonymisations of a non-compliant quantified ABox by a deterministic algorithm with access to an NP oracle that runs in exponential time. We also show that a certain (non-empty) subset of this set can be computed in deterministic exponential time without oracle. If we are only interested in answers to instance queries (i.e., which instance relationships follow from the given ABox), we can replace classical logical entailment by IQ-entailment when defining the notion of an optimal compliant anonymisation. In this case, the full set of all optimal compliant anonymisations can be computed in deterministic exponential time, and the sizes of the anonymisations can be reduced as well.

These results improve on the ones in [3], where a severely restricted form of ABoxes, called instance stores, was investigated. The ABox in our example is not an instance store, due to the role assertion between the individuals d and g. Note that, even in this restricted case, the set of optimal compliant anonymisations may be exponentially large, which demonstrates that the exponential complexity of our algorithms cannot be avoided.

In [12,13] and [3], *safety* is introduced as a strengthening of compliance. Basically, safety means that the hidden facts should not be derivable even if additional compliant information is added. The compliant anonymisation in the above example is not safe since adding *Businessman*(d) would make it non-compliant. Due to the space restrictions, we cannot present results for safety here, though the methods developed in this paper can be extended to deal also with safety [6].

2 Formal Preliminaries

In this section, we first introduce the logical formalisms considered in this paper, and then recall some definitions and known results for them.

From a logical point of view, we consider only formulas in the so-called *primitive positive (pp) fragment* of first-order logic (FO) [20], which consists of existentially quantified conjunctions of atomic relational formulas. Atomic relational formulas are of the form $R(x_1, \ldots, x_n)$, where R is an n-ary relation symbol and the x_i are variables. Not all variables occurring in the conjunction need to be existentially quantified, i.e., a pp formula may contain both quantified and free variables. We say that the pp formula $\exists \vec{x}.\varphi_1(\vec{x}, \vec{z_1})$ *entails* $\exists \vec{y}.\varphi_2(\vec{y}, \vec{z_2})$ if the following is a valid FO formula: $\forall \vec{z_1}.\forall \vec{z_2}.(\exists \vec{x}.\varphi_1(\vec{x}, \vec{z_1}) \rightarrow \exists \vec{y}.\varphi_2(\vec{y}, \vec{z_2}))$.

From a database point of view, pp formulas are conjunctive queries (CQs), where the free variables are usually called answer variables [1]. Entailment of pp formulas corresponds to CQ *containment*, which is a well-known NP-complete problem [10].[1] The relational datasets with labelled null values (which generalize RDF graphs) considered in [12,13] can also be viewed as pp formulas, where the quantified variables are the labelled null values.

Following the tradition in DL, we consider a signature that contains only unary and binary relation symbols, respectively called concept names and role names. Basically, a quantified ABox is just a pp formula over such a signature, but defined in line with the notation usually employed in the DL community.

[1] NP-hardness holds even if only unary and binary relation symbols are available.

Definition 1. *Let Σ be a* signature, *given by pairwise disjoint, countably infinite sets Σ_O, Σ_C, and Σ_R of* object-, concept-, *and* role names, *respectively. A* quantified ABox $\exists X.\mathcal{A}$ *consists of*

- *the* quantifier prefix $\exists X.$, *where X is a finite subset of Σ_O whose elements are called* variables, *and*
- *the* matrix $\mathcal{A}$, *which is a set of assertions of the form $A(u)$ (*concept assertions*) and $r(u, v)$ (*role assertions*), for $A \in \Sigma_\mathsf{C}$, $r \in \Sigma_\mathsf{R}$, and $u, v \in \Sigma_\mathsf{O}$.*

We denote the set of elements of $\Sigma_\mathsf{O} \setminus X$ occurring in $\mathcal{A}$ as $\Sigma_\mathsf{I}(\exists X.\mathcal{A})$, and call them individual names.

An interpretation $\mathcal{I} = (\Delta^\mathcal{I}, \cdot^\mathcal{I})$ of Σ consists of a non-empty set $\Delta^\mathcal{I}$, called the domain, *and an* interpretation function *mapping each object name $u \in \Sigma_\mathsf{O}$ to an element $u^\mathcal{I} \in \Delta^\mathcal{I}$, each concept name $A \in \Sigma_\mathsf{C}$ to a subset $A^\mathcal{I} \subseteq \Delta^\mathcal{I}$, and each role name $r \in \Sigma_\mathsf{R}$ to a binary relation $r^\mathcal{I}$ over $\Delta^\mathcal{I}$. It is a* model *of the quantified ABox $\exists X.\mathcal{A}$ if there is an interpretation $\mathcal{J} = (\Delta^\mathcal{I}, \cdot^\mathcal{J})$ such that*

- *$\cdot^\mathcal{J}$ coincides with $\cdot^\mathcal{I}$ on Σ_C, Σ_R, and $\Sigma_\mathsf{O} \setminus X$, and*
- *$u^\mathcal{J} \in A^\mathcal{J}$ for all $A(u) \in \mathcal{A}$ and $(u^\mathcal{J}, v^\mathcal{J}) \in r^\mathcal{J}$ for all $r(u, v) \in \mathcal{A}$.*

Given two quantified ABoxes $\exists X.\mathcal{A}$ and $\exists Y.\mathcal{B}$, we say that $\exists X.\mathcal{A}$ entails *$\exists Y.\mathcal{B}$ (written $\exists X.\mathcal{A} \models \exists Y.\mathcal{B}$) if every model of $\exists X.\mathcal{A}$ is a model of $\exists Y.\mathcal{B}$. Two quantified ABoxes are* equivalent *if they entail each other.*

Any quantified ABox $\exists X.\mathcal{A}$ can be expressed by a pp formula, which existentially quantifies (in arbitrary order) over the variables in X and conjoins all the assertions from $\mathcal{A}$. The individual names in $\Sigma_\mathsf{I}(\exists X.\mathcal{A})$ are the free variables of this pp formula and the variables in X are the quantified variables. Entailment of quantified ABoxes corresponds to entailment of the corresponding pp formulas, and thus to containment of conjunctive queries. Consequently, the *entailment problem for quantified ABoxes* is NP-complete. It is well known [1,10] that containment of conjunctive queries can be characterised using homomorphisms. This characterisation can be adapted to quantified ABoxes as follows.

Henceforth, when considering two quantified ABoxes, say $\exists X.\mathcal{A}$ and $\exists Y.\mathcal{B}$, we assume without loss of generality that they are *renamed apart* in the sense that X is disjoint with $Y \cup \Sigma_\mathsf{I}(\exists Y.\mathcal{B})$ and Y is disjoint with $X \cup \Sigma_\mathsf{I}(\exists X.\mathcal{A})$. This also allows us to assume that the two ABoxes are built over the same set of individuals $\Sigma_\mathsf{I} := \Sigma_\mathsf{I}(\exists X.\mathcal{A}) \cup \Sigma_\mathsf{I}(\exists Y.\mathcal{B})$. A *homomorphism* from $\exists X.\mathcal{A}$ to $\exists Y.\mathcal{B}$ is a mapping $h\colon \Sigma_\mathsf{I} \cup X \to \Sigma_\mathsf{I} \cup Y$ that satisfies the following conditions:

1. $h(a) = a$ for each individual name $a \in \Sigma_\mathsf{I}$;
2. $A(h(u)) \in \mathcal{B}$ if $A(u) \in \mathcal{A}$ and $r(h(u), h(v)) \in \mathcal{B}$ if $r(u, v) \in \mathcal{A}$.

Proposition 2. *Let $\exists X.\mathcal{A}, \exists Y.\mathcal{B}$ be quantified ABoxes that are renamed apart. Then, $\exists X.\mathcal{A} \models \exists Y.\mathcal{B}$ iff there exists a homomorphism from $\exists Y.\mathcal{B}$ to $\exists X.\mathcal{A}$.*

Traditional DL ABoxes are not quantified. Thus, an *ABox* is a quantified ABox where the quantifier prefix is empty. Instead of $\exists\emptyset.\mathcal{A}$ we simply write $\mathcal{A}$. The *matrix* $\mathcal{A}$ of a quantified ABox $\exists X.\mathcal{A}$ is such a traditional ABox. Note, however, that one can draw fewer consequences from $\exists X.\mathcal{A}$ than from its matrix $\mathcal{A}$.

Example 3. Consider the ABox $\mathcal{A} := \{r(a, x), A(x)\}$, which entails $A(x)$ (where we view $A(x)$ as a singleton ABox). In contrast, the quantified ABox $\exists\{x\}.\mathcal{A}$ does not entail $A(x)$ since, due to the existential quantification, the x in $\exists\{x\}.\mathcal{A}$ stands for an arbitrary object instead of a specific one with name x. This shows that the quantification allows us to hide information about certain individuals. We can, however, still derive from $\exists\{x\}.\mathcal{A}$ that a (which is not quantified) is related with some individual that belongs to A.

Such properties of individuals can be expressed using concept descriptions of the DL $\mathcal{EL}$.

Definition 4. *Given two pairwise disjoint, countably infinite sets Σ_C and Σ_R of concept and role names, we define $\mathcal{EL}$ atoms and $\mathcal{EL}$ concept descriptions by simultaneous induction as follows.*

- *An $\mathcal{EL}$* atom *is either a concept name $A \in \Sigma_\mathsf{C}$ or an* existential restriction *$\exists r.C$, where $r \in \Sigma_\mathsf{R}$ and C is an $\mathcal{EL}$ concept description.*
- *An $\mathcal{EL}$* concept description *is a* conjunction *$\bigsqcap \mathcal{C}$, where $\mathcal{C}$ is a finite set of $\mathcal{EL}$ atoms.*

Given an interpretation $\mathcal{I} = (\Delta^\mathcal{I}, \cdot^\mathcal{I})$ of a signature Σ containing Σ_C and Σ_R (see Definition 1), we extend the interpretation function $\cdot^\mathcal{I}$ to $\mathcal{EL}$ atoms and concept descriptions as follows:

- *$(\exists r.C)^\mathcal{I} := \{\delta \mid$ there exists some γ such that $(\delta, \gamma) \in r^\mathcal{I}$ and $\gamma \in C^\mathcal{I}\}$,*
- *$(\bigsqcap \mathcal{C})^\mathcal{I} := \bigcap_{C \in \mathcal{C}} C^\mathcal{I}$, where the intersection over the empty set $\mathcal{C} = \emptyset$ is $\Delta^\mathcal{I}$.*

Given $\mathcal{EL}$ concept descriptions C, D and a quantified ABox $\exists X.\mathcal{A}$, we say that

- *C* is subsumed by *D (written $C \sqsubseteq_\emptyset D$) if $C^\mathcal{I} \subseteq D^\mathcal{I}$ holds for all interpretations $\mathcal{I}$, and C* is equivalent to *D (written $C \equiv_\emptyset D$) if $C \sqsubseteq_\emptyset D$ and $D \sqsubseteq_\emptyset C$. We write $C \sqsubset_\emptyset D$ to express that $C \sqsubseteq_\emptyset D$, but $C \not\equiv_\emptyset D$.*
- *the object $u \in \Sigma_\mathsf{O}$ is an* instance of *C w.r.t. $\exists X.\mathcal{A}$ (written $\exists X.\mathcal{A} \models C(u)$) if $u^\mathcal{I} \in C^\mathcal{I}$ holds for all models $\mathcal{I}$ of $\exists X.\mathcal{A}$.*

To make the syntax introduced above more akin to the one usually employed for $\mathcal{EL}$, we denote the empty conjunction $\bigsqcap \emptyset$ as $\top$ (*top concept*), singleton conjunctions $\bigsqcap\{C\}$ as C, and conjunctions $\bigsqcap \mathcal{C}$ for $|\mathcal{C}| \geq 2$ as $C_1 \sqcap \ldots \sqcap C_n$, where $C_1, \ldots, C_n$ is an enumeration of the elements of $\mathcal{C}$ in an arbitrary order. Given an $\mathcal{EL}$ concept description $C = \bigsqcap \mathcal{C}$, we sometimes denote the set of atoms $\mathcal{C}$ as $\mathsf{Conj}(C)$. The set $\mathsf{Sub}(C)$ of *subconcepts* of an $\mathcal{EL}$ concept description C is defined in the usual way, i.e., $\mathsf{Sub}(A) := \{A\}$, $\mathsf{Sub}(\exists r.C) := \{\exists r.C\} \cup \mathsf{Sub}(C)$, and $\mathsf{Sub}(\bigsqcap \mathcal{C}) := \{\bigsqcap \mathcal{C}\} \cup \bigcup_{D \in \mathcal{C}} \mathsf{Sub}(D)$. We denote the set of atoms occurring in $\mathsf{Sub}(C)$ with $\mathsf{Atoms}(C)$. The subscript $\emptyset$ in $\sqsubseteq_\emptyset$ indicates that no terminological axioms are available, i.e., we consider subsumption w.r.t. the empty TBox.

It is well-known that $\mathcal{EL}$ concept descriptions C can be translated into semantically equivalent pp formulas $\phi_C(x)$ with one free variable x. For example, the $\mathcal{EL}$ concept description $C := \bigsqcap\{A, \exists r.\bigsqcap\{B, \exists r.\bigsqcap\{A, B\}\}\}$, which we can also write as $A \sqcap \exists r.(B \sqcap \exists r.(A \sqcap B))$, translates into the pp formula $\phi_C(x) = \exists y.\exists z.(A(x) \wedge r(x,y) \wedge B(y) \wedge r(y,z) \wedge A(z) \wedge B(z))$. The subsumption and the instance problems thus reduce to entailment of pp formulas:

$$C \sqsubseteq_\emptyset D \text{ iff } \phi_C(x) \text{ entails } \phi_D(x) \quad \text{and} \quad \exists X.\mathcal{A} \models C(u) \text{ iff } \exists X.\mathcal{A} \text{ entails } \phi_C(u).$$

Thus, the homomorphism characterisation of entailment applies to subsumptions and instances as well. However, since the pp formulas obtained from $\mathcal{EL}$ concept descriptions are *tree-shaped*, the existence of a homomorphism can be checked in polynomial time. Thus, the subsumption and the instance problem are in P [7,19]. The fact that $\mathcal{EL}$ concept descriptions can be translated into pp formulas (and thus quantified ABoxes) also shows that quantified ABoxes can express $\mathcal{EL}$ ABoxes with concept assertions of the form $C(u)$ for complex $\mathcal{EL}$ concepts C.

The homomorphism characterisation of subsumption also yields the following recursive characterisation of subsumption [8].

Lemma 5. *Let C, D be $\mathcal{EL}$ concept descriptions. Then $C \sqsubseteq_\emptyset D$ holds iff the following two statements are satisfied:*

1. *$A \in \mathsf{Conj}(D)$ implies $A \in \mathsf{Conj}(C)$ for each concept name A;*
2. *for each existential restriction $\exists r.F \in \mathsf{Conj}(D)$, there is an existential restriction $\exists r.E \in \mathsf{Conj}(C)$ such that $E \sqsubseteq_\emptyset F$.*

An analogous characterisation can be given for the instance problem w.r.t. (unquantified) ABoxes.

Lemma 6. *Let $\mathcal{A}$ be an ABox, D an $\mathcal{EL}$ concept description, and $u \in \Sigma_\mathsf{O}$. Then $\mathcal{A} \models D(u)$ holds iff the following two statements are satisfied:*

1. *for each concept name $A \in \mathsf{Conj}(D)$, the ABox $\mathcal{A}$ contains $A(u)$,*
2. *for each existential restriction $\exists r.E \in \mathsf{Conj}(D)$, the ABox $\mathcal{A}$ contains a role assertion $r(u,v)$ such that $\mathcal{A} \models E(v)$.*

Regarding the effect that the existential quantification in quantified ABoxes has on the instance problem, we generalise the observations made in Example 3.

Lemma 7. *If $\exists X.\mathcal{A}$ be a quantified ABox, C an $\mathcal{EL}$ concept description, $x \in X$, and $a \in \Sigma_\mathsf{I}(\exists X.\mathcal{A})$, then $\exists X.\mathcal{A} \models C(a)$ iff $\mathcal{A} \models C(a)$, and $\exists X.\mathcal{A} \models C(x)$ iff $C = \top$.*

Note that, according to our definition of the syntax of $\mathcal{EL}$, the only $\mathcal{EL}$ concept description equivalent to $\top = \bigsqcap \emptyset$ is $\top$ itself. We also need the reduced form C^r of an $\mathcal{EL}$ concept description C [18], which is defined inductively as follows.

- For atoms, we set $A^r := A$ for $A \in \Sigma_\mathsf{C}$ and $(\exists r.C)^r := \exists r.C^r$.
- To obtain the reduced form of $\bigsqcap \mathcal{C}$, we first reduce the elements of $\mathcal{C}$, i.e., construct the set $\mathcal{C}^r := \{C^r | C \in \mathcal{C}\}$. Then we build $\mathsf{Min}(\mathcal{C}^r)$ by removing all elements D that are not subsumption minimal, i.e., for which there is an E in the set such that $E \sqsubset_\emptyset D$. We then set $(\bigsqcap \mathcal{C})^r := \bigsqcap \mathsf{Min}(\mathcal{C}^r)$.

Adapting the results in [18], one can show that $C \equiv_\emptyset C^r$ and that $C \equiv_\emptyset D$ implies $C^r = D^r$. In particular, this implies that, on reduced $\mathcal{EL}$ concept descriptions, subsumption is a partial order and not just a pre-order.

3 Compliant Anonymisations w.r.t. Classical Entailment

A *policy* is a finite set of $\mathcal{EL}$ concept descriptions. Intuitively, a policy says that one should not be able to derive that any of the individuals of a quantified ABox belongs to a policy concept.

Definition 8. *Let $\exists X.\mathcal{A}, \exists Y.\mathcal{B}$ be quantified ABoxes and $\mathcal{P}$ a policy. Then*

1. *$\exists X.\mathcal{A}$ is* compliant with $\mathcal{P}$ at object $u \in \Sigma_{\mathsf{O}}$ *if $\mathcal{A} \not\models P(u)$ for each $P \in \mathcal{P}$;*
2. *$\exists X.\mathcal{A}$ is* compliant with $\mathcal{P}$ *if it is compliant with $\mathcal{P}$ at each element of $\Sigma_{\mathsf{I}} = \Sigma_{\mathsf{I}}(\exists X.\mathcal{A})$;*
3. *$\exists Y.\mathcal{B}$ is a $\mathcal{P}$-compliant anonymisation of $\exists X.\mathcal{A}$ if $\exists X.\mathcal{A} \models \exists Y.\mathcal{B}$ and $\exists Y.\mathcal{B}$ is compliant with $\mathcal{P}$;*
4. *$\exists Y.\mathcal{B}$ is an* optimal *$\mathcal{P}$-compliant anonymisation of $\exists X.\mathcal{A}$ if it is a $\mathcal{P}$-compliant anonymisation of $\exists X.\mathcal{A}$, and $\exists X.\mathcal{A} \models \exists Z.\mathcal{C} \models \exists Y.\mathcal{B}$ implies $\exists Y.\mathcal{B} \models \exists Z.\mathcal{C}$ for every $\mathcal{P}$-compliant anonymisation $\exists Z.\mathcal{C}$ of $\exists X.\mathcal{A}$.*

We require that an anonymisation of a quantified ABox is entailed by it, and also compare different anonymisations using entailment. Later on, we will look at a setting where a weaker notion than classical entailment is employed. In the following we assume without loss of generality that all concepts in a given policy are reduced and incomparable w.r.t. subsumption. In fact, given a policy $\mathcal{P}$, we can first reduce the elements of $\mathcal{P}$, i.e., construct the set $\mathcal{P}^r := \{P^r \mid P \in \mathcal{P}\}$, and then build $\mathsf{Max}(\mathcal{P}^r)$ by removing all elements that are not subsumption maximal. Any quantified ABox is compliant with $\mathcal{P}$ iff it is compliant with $\mathsf{Max}(\mathcal{P}^r)$. We call such a policy *reduced.*

Since the instance problem in $\mathcal{EL}$ is in P, compliance can obviously be tested in polynomial time. However, our main purpose is not to test for compliance of a given quantified ABox, but to compute compliant anonymisations of it in case it is not compliant. For this purpose, we need an appropriate characterisation of compliance. The following lemma is an easy consequence of Lemma 6. Its formulation uses the notion of a hitting set. Given a set of sets $\{\mathcal{P}_1, \ldots, \mathcal{P}_n\}$, a *hitting set* of this set is a set $\mathcal{H}$ such that $\mathcal{H} \cap \mathcal{P}_i \neq \emptyset$ for $i \in \{1, \ldots, n\}$.

Lemma 9. *The quantified ABox $\exists X.\mathcal{A}$ is compliant with the policy $\mathcal{P}$ at $u \in \Sigma_{\mathsf{O}}$ iff there is a hitting set $\mathcal{H}$ of $\{\mathsf{Conj}(P) | P \in \mathcal{P}\}$ such that*

- *$\exists X.\mathcal{A}$ is compliant with $\mathcal{H} \cap \Sigma_{\mathsf{C}}$ at u, i.e., $A \notin \mathcal{H}$ for each concept assertion $A(u)$ in $\mathcal{A}$, and*
- *$\exists X.\mathcal{A}$ is compliant with $\{Q | \exists r.Q \in \mathcal{H}\}$ at v for each role assertion $r(u, v)$ in $\mathcal{A}$.*

Computing Compliant Anonymisations. We assume that $\Sigma_{\mathsf{I}}(\exists X.\mathcal{A}) \neq \emptyset$ since otherwise $\exists X.\mathcal{A}$ is trivially compliant, and additionally that the policy $\mathcal{P}$ does not contain $\top$ since otherwise no compliant anonymisation exists.

If a quantified ABox is not compliant with $\mathcal{P}$, then the characterisation of compliance in Lemma 9 tells us that, for some of the individuals $a \in \Sigma_{\mathsf{I}}$, the required hitting sets do not exist. To overcome this problem, one needs to remove some of the (implied) instance relationships for these individuals. Compliance seed functions tell us which ones to remove.

Definition 10. *A* compliance seed function *(abbrv.* csf*) on $\exists X.\mathcal{A}$ for $\mathcal{P}$ is a mapping $s\colon \Sigma_{\mathsf{I}} \to \wp(\mathsf{Atoms}(\mathcal{P}))$ such that the following holds for each $a \in \Sigma_{\mathsf{I}}$:*

1. *the set $s(a)$ contains only atoms C where $\mathcal{A} \models C(a)$,*
2. *for each $P \in \mathcal{P}$ with $\mathcal{A} \models P(a)$, the set $s(a)$ contains an atom subsuming P, i.e., there is some $C \in s(a)$ such that $P \sqsubseteq_\emptyset C$, and*
3. *the set $s(a)$ does not contain $\sqsubseteq_\emptyset$-comparable atoms.*

Assuming that $\top \notin \mathcal{P}$, a compliance seed function always exists because $\mathsf{Conj}(P)$ is non-empty for every $P \in \mathcal{P}$; thus one can take as atom C an arbitrary element of $\mathsf{Conj}(P)$ to satisfy Property 2. Property 3 avoids redundancies in seed functions, and thus reduces their overall number. If it does not hold for the set of atoms chosen to satisfy Property 2, we can simply remove the atoms that are not subsumption-maximal from this set.

We show that each compliance seed function induces a compliant anonymisation. For concept names $A \in s(a)$, we simply remove the concept assertion $A(a)$ from $\mathcal{A}$. For atoms of the form $\exists r.C \in s(a)$, we need to modify the role successors of a such that $\exists r.C(a)$ is no longer entailed. To avoid losing more information than required, we will not just remove assertions from the objects in $\mathcal{A}$, but also split such objects into several objects by introducing new variables, as motivated by the simple example in the introduction.

To be more precise, we will use the elements of the following set as variables.

$$Y := \left\{ y_{u,\mathcal{K}} \;\middle|\; \begin{array}{l} u \in \Sigma_{\mathsf{I}} \cup X, \mathcal{K} \subseteq \{C \in \mathsf{Atoms}(\mathcal{P}) | \mathcal{A} \models C(u)\}, \\ \mathcal{K} \text{ does not contain } \sqsubseteq_\emptyset \text{-comparable atoms, and} \\ \text{if } u \in \Sigma_{\mathsf{I}}, \text{ then } \mathcal{K} \neq s(u) \end{array} \right\}$$

For $a \in \Sigma_{\mathsf{I}}$, there is *no* variable $y_{a,s(a)}$ in Y. To simplify the following definition, we will, however, use $y_{a,s(a)}$ as a synonym for the individual a, i.e., in this definition the object names $y_{u,\mathcal{K}}$ and $y_{v,\mathcal{L}}$ range over the elements of Y and these synonyms for individual names.

Definition 11. *Consider a quantified ABox $\exists X.\mathcal{A}$ that is not compliant with the policy $\mathcal{P}$, a compliance seed function s on $\exists X.\mathcal{A}$ for $\mathcal{P}$, and Y as defined above. The* canonical compliant anonymisation $\mathsf{ca}(\exists X.\mathcal{A}, s)$ of $\exists X.\mathcal{A}$ induced by *s is the quantified ABox $\exists Y.\mathcal{B}$, where $\mathcal{B}$ consists of the following assertions:*

1. *$A(y_{u,\mathcal{K}}) \in \mathcal{B}$ if $A(u) \in \mathcal{A}$ and $A \notin \mathcal{K}$;*
2. *$r(y_{u,\mathcal{K}}, y_{v,\mathcal{L}}) \in \mathcal{B}$ if $r(u,v) \in \mathcal{A}$ and, for each existential restriction $\exists r.Q \in \mathcal{K}$ with $\mathcal{A} \models Q(v)$, the set $\mathcal{L}$ contains an atom subsuming Q, i.e., there is $D \in \mathcal{L}$ such that $Q \sqsubseteq_\emptyset D$.*

We illustrate this definition by an abstract and slightly modified version of the example from the introduction.

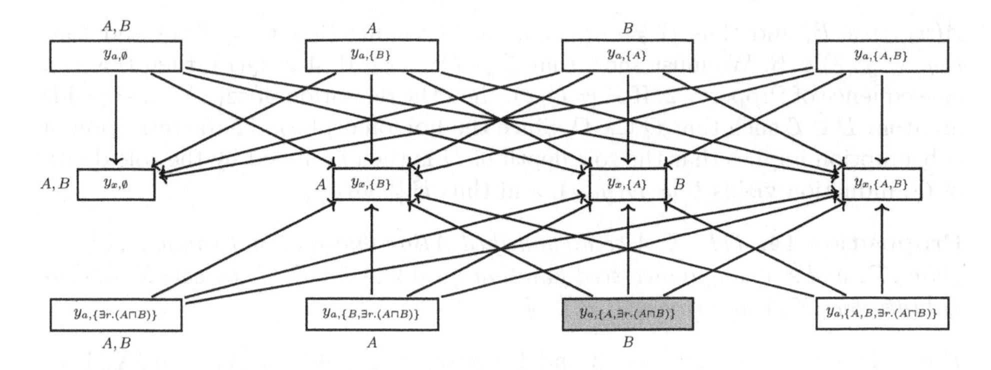

Fig. 1. Canonical anonymisation induced by the seed function s in Example 12.

Example 12. The ABox

$$\exists\{x\}.\{A(a), B(a), A(x), B(x), r(a, x)\}$$

is not compliant with the policy $\mathcal{P} := \{A \sqcap B, \exists r.(A \sqcap B)\}$. In fact, it entails both $(A \sqcap B)(a)$ and $(\exists r.(A \sqcap B))(a)$. There exist only two csfs s and t, where $s(a) = \{A, \exists r.(A \sqcap B)\}$ and $t(a) = \{B, \exists r.(A \sqcap B)\}$. Figure 1 shows the canonical anonymisation induced by s. The gray node represents the individual a, and all other nodes are variables introduced by the construction. Since there is only one role name r, we did not label the edges connecting objects with it. The canonical anonymisation induced by t differs from the one shown in Fig. 1 in that a then corresponds to $y_{a,\{B,\exists r.(A\sqcap B)\}}$.

We want to show that $\mathsf{ca}(\exists X.\mathcal{A}, s)$ is a compliant anonymisation of $\exists X.\mathcal{A}$. This is an easy consequence of the following lemma.

Lemma 13. *Let $\mathsf{ca}(\exists X.\mathcal{A}, s) = \exists Y.\mathcal{B}$ be the canonical compliant anonymisation of $\exists X.\mathcal{A}$ induced by the compliance seed function s, and consider an $\mathcal{EL}$ concept description Q and an $\mathcal{EL}$ atom C. The following properties hold:*

1. *The mapping $h\colon \Sigma_\mathsf{I} \cup Y \to \Sigma_\mathsf{I} \cup X : y_{u,\mathcal{K}} \mapsto u$ is a homomorphism from $\mathsf{ca}(\exists X.\mathcal{A}, s)$ to $\exists X.\mathcal{A}$.*
2. *If $\mathcal{A} \not\models Q(u)$, then $\mathcal{B} \not\models Q(y_{u,\mathcal{K}})$ for all objects $u \in \Sigma_\mathsf{I} \cup X$ and $y_{u,\mathcal{K}} \in \Sigma_\mathsf{I} \cup Y$.*
3. *If $C \in \mathcal{K}$, then $\mathcal{B} \not\models C(y_{u,\mathcal{K}})$ for all objects $y_{u,\mathcal{K}} \in \Sigma_\mathsf{I} \cup Y$.*

Proof. **1.** It is easy to verify that the mapping h defined in the formulation of the lemma is a homomorphism. In particular, since $y_{a,s(a)}$ is synonym for a, this mapping maps every individual $a \in \Sigma_\mathsf{I}$ to itself.
2. It is an easy consequence of the homomorphism characterization of the instance problem that $\mathcal{B} \models C(y_{u,\mathcal{K}})$ implies $\mathcal{A} \models C(h(y_{u,\mathcal{K}}))$. Since $h(y_{u,\mathcal{K}}) = u$, the second property stated in the lemma is the contrapositive of this fact.
3. The third property can be shown by induction on the role depth of C, using the definition of $\mathsf{ca}(\exists X.\mathcal{A}, s)$ and Property 2. If $C = A \in \Sigma_\mathsf{C}$, then $A \in \mathcal{K}$ implies

$A(y_{u,\mathcal{K}}) \notin \mathcal{B}$, and thus $\mathcal{B} \not\models A(y_{u,\mathcal{K}})$. Now, assume that $C = \exists r.Q$ and that $r(y_{u,\mathcal{K}}, y_{v,\mathcal{L}}) \in \mathcal{B}$. We must show that $\mathcal{B} \not\models Q(y_{v,\mathcal{L}})$. If $\mathcal{A} \not\models Q(v)$, then this is a consequence of Property 2. If $\mathcal{A} \models Q(v)$, then the definition of $\mathsf{ca}(\exists X.\mathcal{A}, s)$ yields an atom $D \in \mathcal{L}$ such that $Q \sqsubseteq_\emptyset D$. Since the homomorphism characterisation of subsumption implies that the role depth of D is then bounded by the role depth of Q, induction yields $\mathcal{B} \not\models D(y_{v,\mathcal{L}})$, and thus $\mathcal{B} \not\models Q(y_{v,\mathcal{L}})$. □

Proposition 14. *Let $\exists X.\mathcal{A}$ be a quantified ABox that does not comply with the policy $\mathcal{P}$, and s a compliance seed function on $\exists X.\mathcal{A}$ for $\mathcal{P}$. Then $\mathsf{ca}(\exists X.\mathcal{A}, s)$ is entailed by $\exists X.\mathcal{A}$ and complies with $\mathcal{P}$.*

Proof. Property 1 of Lemma 13 and Proposition 2 yield $\exists X.\mathcal{A} \models \mathsf{ca}(\exists X.\mathcal{A}, s)$. For compliance of $\mathsf{ca}(\exists X.\mathcal{A}, s) = \exists Y.\mathcal{B}$ with $\mathcal{P}$, let $P \in \mathcal{P}$ and $a = y_{a,s(a)} \in \Sigma_\mathsf{I}$. If $\mathcal{A} \not\models P(a)$, then Property 2 of Lemma 13 yields $\mathcal{B} \not\models P(a)$. Otherwise, there is an atom $C \in s(a)$ such that $P \sqsubseteq_\emptyset C$, by the definition of a csf. Then Property 3 of Lemma 13 yields $\mathcal{B} \not\models C(a)$, and thus $\mathcal{B} \not\models P(a)$. □

This proposition shows that the set

$$\mathsf{CA}(\exists X.\mathcal{A}, \mathcal{P}) := \{\mathsf{ca}(\exists X.\mathcal{A}, s) | s \text{ is a csf on } \exists X.\mathcal{A} \text{ for } \mathcal{P}\}$$

contains only compliant anonymisations of $\exists X.\mathcal{A}$. This set actually covers all compliant anonymisations of $\exists X.\mathcal{A}$ in the following sense.

Proposition 15. *If $\exists Z.\mathcal{C}$ is a $\mathcal{P}$-compliant anonymisation of $\exists X.\mathcal{A}$, then there exists a csf s such that $\mathsf{ca}(\exists X.\mathcal{A}, s) \models \exists Z.\mathcal{C}$.*

Proof. Since $\exists X.\mathcal{A} \models \exists Z.\mathcal{C}$, Proposition 2 implies the existence of a homomorphism h from $\exists Z.\mathcal{C}$ to $\exists X.\mathcal{A}$. We define the mapping $f\colon \Sigma_\mathsf{I} \cup Z \to \wp(\mathsf{Atoms}(\mathcal{P}))$:

$$f(u) := \mathsf{Max}_{\sqsubseteq_\emptyset}(\{C \in \mathsf{Atoms}(\mathcal{P}) | \mathcal{C} \not\models C(u) \text{ and } \mathcal{A} \models C(h(u))\}).$$

We claim that the restriction s of f to Σ_I is a csf. Assume that $a \in \Sigma_\mathsf{I}$ and $P \in \mathcal{P}$ with $\mathcal{A} \models P(a)$. Since $\exists Z.\mathcal{C}$ complies with $\mathcal{P}$, there is an atom $C \in \mathsf{Conj}(P)$ such that $\mathcal{C} \not\models C(a)$. Thus, $h(a) = a$ yields that either $C \in f(a)$ or there is $C' \in f(a)$ with $C \sqsubseteq_\emptyset C'$. In both cases, Property 2 of Definition 10 is satisfied. Since the subsumption-maximal elements of a set of reduced atoms are incomparable w.r.t. subsumption,[2] Property 3 is satisfied as well.

Let $\exists Y.\mathcal{B} := \mathsf{ca}(\exists X.\mathcal{A}, s)$. To show that $\exists Y.\mathcal{B} \models \exists Z.\mathcal{C}$, we prove that the mapping $k\colon \Sigma_\mathsf{I} \cup Z \to \Sigma_\mathsf{I} \cup Y$ where $k(u) := y_{h(u),f(u)}$ is a homomorphism. If $A(u) \in \mathcal{C}$, then $A(h(u)) \in \mathcal{A}$ since h is a homomorphism, but $A \notin f(u)$. Thus $A(y_{h(u),f(u)}) \in \mathcal{B}$. If $r(u,v) \in \mathcal{C}$, we must show that $r(y_{h(u),f(u)}, y_{h(v),f(v)}) \in \mathcal{B}$. Assume that $\exists r.Q \in f(u)$ and $\mathcal{A} \models Q(h(v))$. The former yields $\mathcal{C} \not\models (\exists r.Q)(u)$, and thus $\mathcal{C} \not\models Q(v)$. Thus, there is an atom $D \in \mathsf{Conj}(Q)$ with $\mathcal{A} \models D(h(v))$ and $\mathcal{C} \not\models D(v)$. This implies that either D itself or an atom subsuming D belongs to $f(v)$. In both cases, we obtain $r(y_{h(u),f(u)}, y_{h(v),f(v)}) \in \mathcal{B}$. □

[2] Recall that we assume that policies are reduced, which implies that the elements of $\mathsf{Atoms}(\mathcal{P})$ are reduced, and thus subsumption is a partial order on them.

The next theorem is a straightforward consequence of the last two propositions.

Theorem 16. *The set* $\mathsf{CA}(\exists X.\mathcal{A}, \mathcal{P})$ *is a set of* $\mathcal{P}$*-compliant anonymisations of* $\exists X.\mathcal{A}$ *that contains (up to equivalence) all optimal* $\mathcal{P}$*-compliant anonymisations of* $\exists X.\mathcal{A}$*. It can be computed in (deterministic) exponential time. There is a (deterministic) algorithm with access to an NP oracle that computes the set of all optimal* $\mathcal{P}$*-compliant anonymisations of* $\exists X.\mathcal{A}$ *and runs in exponential time.*

Proof. There are exponentially many csfs, which can be computed in exponential time. For each csf, the canonical anonymisation induced by it can also be computed in exponential time. Assume now that $\exists Z.\mathcal{C}$ is an optimal $\mathcal{P}$-compliant anonymisation of $\exists X.\mathcal{A}$. By Proposition 15, there exists a csf s such that $\mathsf{ca}(\exists X.\mathcal{A}, s) \models \exists Z.\mathcal{C}$. Since $\exists Z.\mathcal{C}$ is optimal, $\exists Z.\mathcal{C}$ and $\mathsf{ca}(\exists X.\mathcal{A}, s)$ are equivalent. The non-optimal elements of $\mathsf{CA}(\exists X.\mathcal{A}, \mathcal{P})$ can be removed from this set by applying entailment tests. These tests can be realised using an NP oracle. □

Note that this complexity result considers *combined complexity*, where the policy $\mathcal{P}$ is assumed to be part of the input. For *data complexity*, where the policy is assumed to be fixed, our approach shows that all optimal compliant anonymisations can be computed in polynomial time with an NP oracle.

At the moment, it is not clear whether the set of optimal compliant anonymisations of a quantified ABox can be computed in exponential time. The reason why our approach does not run in exponential time without an NP oracle is that the elements of $\mathsf{CA}(\exists X.\mathcal{A}, \mathcal{P})$ to which the oracle is applied may be exponentially large in the size of $\exists X.\mathcal{A}$. Thus, one may ask whether one can design an approach that only generates optimal compliant anonymisations. We answer this question affirmatively in the rest of this section, but unfortunately the approach we introduce does not produce all of them.

Computing Optimal Compliant Anonymisations. The main idea underlying our approach is to define an appropriate partial order on csfs.

Definition 17. *Let* $\exists X.\mathcal{A}$ *be a quantified ABox that does not comply with the policy* $\mathcal{P}$*, and* s, t *csfs on* $\exists X.\mathcal{A}$ *for* $\mathcal{P}$*. We say that* s is covered by t *(written* $s \leq t$*) if for each* $a \in \Sigma$ *and* $C \in s(a)$ *there is an atom* $D \in t(a)$ *s.t.* $C \sqsubseteq_\emptyset D$*.*

It is easy to see that this relation is a partial order. Reflexivity and transitivity are trivial. To show anti-symmetry, assume that $s \leq t$ and $t \leq s$. It suffices to prove that $s(a) \subseteq t(a)$ holds for all $a \in \Sigma_\mathsf{I}$; the inclusion in the other direction can be shown symmetrically. Assume that $C \in s(a)$. Since $s \leq t$, this implies that there is an atom $D \in t(a)$ with $C \sqsubseteq_\emptyset D$. But then $t \leq s$ yields an atom $C' \in s(a)$ such that $D \sqsubseteq_\emptyset C'$. Since the elements of $s(a)$ are incomparable w.r.t. subsumption, this yields $C = C'$, and thus $C \equiv_\emptyset D$. Since both atoms are assumed to be reduced, we obtain $C = D$, which yields $C \in t(a)$.

To show that entailment between canonical anonymisations implies covering for the compliance seed functions inducing them, we need the following lemma.

Lemma 18. *Let* $\mathsf{ca}(\exists X.\mathcal{A}, s) = \exists Y.\mathcal{B}$ *be the canonical compliant anonymisation of* $\exists X.\mathcal{A}$ *induced by the csf* s, $C \in \mathsf{Atoms}(\mathcal{P})$, *and* $y_{u,\mathcal{K}} \in Y$ *a variable. If* $\mathcal{A} \models C(u)$ *and* $\mathcal{B} \not\models C(y_{u,\mathcal{K}})$, *then* $\mathcal{K}$ *contains an atom subsuming* C.

Proof. We prove the lemma by *induction* on the role depth of C. In the *base case*, $C = A \in \Sigma_\mathsf{C}$. Thus, $\mathcal{A} \models C(u)$ implies that $A(u) \in \mathcal{A}$, and thus $A \notin \mathcal{K}$ would yield $A(y_{u,\mathcal{K}}) \in \mathcal{B}$, contradicting the assumption that $\mathcal{B} \not\models C(y_{u,\mathcal{K}})$.

Induction step: if $C = \exists r.D$, then $\mathcal{A} \models C(u)$ implies that there is an object v such that $r(u, v) \in \mathcal{A}$ and $\mathcal{A} \models D(v)$. Assume that $\mathcal{K}$ does not contain an atom subsuming $\exists r.D$. We claim that this implies the existence of a variable $y_{v,\mathcal{L}} \in Y$ such that $r(y_{u,\mathcal{K}}, y_{v,\mathcal{L}}) \in \mathcal{B}$. Since $\mathcal{K}$ does not contain an atom subsuming $\exists r.D$, we know that, for every existential restriction $\exists r.Q \in \mathcal{K}$, we have $D \not\sqsubseteq_\emptyset Q$, and thus $\mathsf{Conj}(Q)$ must contain an atom C_Q such that $D \not\sqsubseteq_\emptyset C_Q$. Let $\mathcal{L}$ consist of the subsumption-maximal elements of the set $\{C_Q | \exists r.Q \in \mathcal{K} \text{ and } \mathcal{A} \models Q(v)\}$. Then we have $y_{v,\mathcal{L}} \in Y$ and $r(y_{u,\mathcal{K}}, y_{v,\mathcal{L}}) \in \mathcal{B}$. Since $\mathcal{B} \not\models C(y_{u,\mathcal{K}})$, this implies that $\mathcal{B} \not\models D(y_{v,\mathcal{L}})$, and thus there is an atom $C' \in \mathsf{Conj}(D)$ with $\mathcal{A} \models C'(v)$ and $\mathcal{B} \not\models C'(y_{v,\mathcal{L}})$. Induction yields an atom $C'' \in \mathcal{L}$ such that $C' \sqsubseteq_\emptyset C''$. Together with $C' \in \mathsf{Conj}(D)$, this shows that $D \sqsubseteq_\emptyset C''$. However, by construction, $\mathcal{L}$ contains only atoms C_Q such that $D \not\sqsubseteq_\emptyset C_Q$. This contradiction shows that our assumption that $\mathcal{K}$ does not contain an atom subsuming $C = \exists r.D$ cannot hold. □

Proposition 19. *Let* s *and* t *be csfs on* $\exists X.\mathcal{A}$ *for* $\mathcal{P}$. *Then the entailment* $\mathsf{ca}(\exists X.\mathcal{A}, s) \models \mathsf{ca}(\exists X.\mathcal{A}, t)$ *implies that* $s \leq t$.

Proof. Let $\exists Y.\mathcal{B} = \mathsf{ca}(\exists X.\mathcal{A}, s)$ and $\exists Z.\mathcal{C} = \mathsf{ca}(\exists X.\mathcal{A}, t)$, and assume that $\exists Y.\mathcal{B} \models \exists Z.\mathcal{C}$. We must show for all $a \in \Sigma_\mathsf{I}$ that $C \in s(a)$ implies the existence of an atom $D \in t(a)$ with $C \sqsubseteq_\emptyset D$. By the definition of csfs and Property 3 of Lemma 13, $C \in s(a)$ implies $\mathcal{A} \models C(a)$ and $\mathcal{B} \not\models C(a)$. Since $\exists Y.\mathcal{B} \models \exists Z.\mathcal{C}$, the latter yields $\mathcal{C} \not\models C(a)$. By Lemma 18, $t(a)$ contains an atom subsuming C. □

As an easy consequence, this proposition shows that the set

$$\mathsf{CA}_{min}(\exists X.\mathcal{A}, \mathcal{P}) := \{\mathsf{ca}(\exists X.\mathcal{A}, s) | s \text{ is a } \leq\text{-minimal csf on } \exists X.\mathcal{A} \text{ for } \mathcal{P}\}$$

contains only *optimal* compliant anonymisations of $\exists X.\mathcal{A}$.

Theorem 20. *The set* $\mathsf{CA}_{min}(\exists X.\mathcal{A}, \mathcal{P})$ *is non-empty, contains only optimal* $\mathcal{P}$*-compliant anonymisation of* $\exists X.\mathcal{A}$*, and can be computed in exponential time.*

Proof. Since policies are assumed not to contain $\top$, the set of all csfs is non-empty. Since it is a finite set, it must contain minimal elements w.r.t. the partial order $\leq$. Assume the $\mathsf{ca}(\exists X.\mathcal{A}, s) \in \mathsf{CA}_{min}(\exists X.\mathcal{A}, \mathcal{P})$ is not optimal. Then there is a compliant anonymisation $\exists Z.\mathcal{C}$ of $\exists X.\mathcal{A}$ such that $\exists Z.\mathcal{C} \models \mathsf{ca}(\exists X.\mathcal{A}, s)$, but $\exists Z.\mathcal{C}$ and $\mathsf{ca}(\exists X.\mathcal{A}, s)$ are not equivalent. By Proposition 15, there exists a csf t such that $\mathsf{ca}(\exists X.\mathcal{A}, t) \models \exists Z.\mathcal{C}$. But then we have $\mathsf{ca}(\exists X.\mathcal{A}, t) \models \mathsf{ca}(\exists X.\mathcal{A}, s)$, which yields $t \leq s$ by Proposition 19. Since $s = t$ would imply that $\exists Z.\mathcal{C}$ and

$\mathsf{ca}(\exists X.\mathcal{A}, s)$ are equivalent, we actually have $t < s$, which contradicts the minimality of s. The set $\mathsf{CA}_{min}(\exists X.\mathcal{A}, \mathcal{P})$ can be computed in exponential time, by first generating all csfs, then removing the non-minimal ones, and finally generating the induced canonical anonymisations. □

A simple consequence of this theorem is that *one* optimal compliant anonymisation can always be computed in exponential time w.r.t. combined complexity, and polynomial time w.r.t. data complexity. One simply needs to compute a minimal csf s, and then build $\mathsf{ca}(\exists X.\mathcal{A}, s)$. In contrast to computing *all* optimal compliant anonymisations, this process does not need an NP oracle. In general, however, not all optimal compliant anonymisations of $\exists X.\mathcal{A}$ are contained in $\mathsf{CA}_{min}(\exists X.\mathcal{A}, \mathcal{P})$. Technically, the reason is that the converse of Proposition 19 need not hold. The following gives a concrete example where $\mathsf{CA}_{min}(\exists X.\mathcal{A}, \mathcal{P})$ is not complete.

Example 21. Consider the policy $\mathcal{P} := \{\exists r.A\}$ and the non-compliant ABox $\exists\emptyset.\mathcal{A}$, with $\mathcal{A} := \{r(a,b), A(b)\}$. The only minimal csf is the function s defined as $s(a) := \{\exists r.A\}$ and $s(b) := \emptyset$. In $\mathsf{ca}(\exists\emptyset.\mathcal{A}, s)$, the individual b still belongs to A, but the role assertions $r(a,b)$ is no longer there.

Consider the (non-minimal) csf t defined as $t(a) := \{\exists r.A\}$ and $t(b) := \{A\}$. In $\mathsf{ca}(\exists\emptyset.\mathcal{A}, t)$, the individual b does not belong to A, but the role assertions $r(a,b)$ is still there. Thus, $\mathsf{ca}(\exists\emptyset.\mathcal{A}, s)$ and $\mathsf{ca}(\exists\emptyset.\mathcal{A}, t)$ are incomparable w.r.t. entailment, although $s < t$. We claim that $\mathsf{ca}(\exists\emptyset.\mathcal{A}, t)$ is optimal. Otherwise, we can use Proposition 15 to obtain a csf $t' < t$ such that $\mathsf{ca}(\exists\emptyset.\mathcal{A}, t') \models \mathsf{ca}(\exists\emptyset.\mathcal{A}, t)$. However, the only csf smaller than t is s, which yields a contradiction.

4 Compliant Anonymisations w.r.t IQ-Entailment

Since we are only interested in *instance queries* (i.e., checking which instance relationships $C(a)$ hold for individuals a in a quantified ABox), it makes sense to consider a different notion of entailment and equivalence based on which instance relationships are implied by the ABox. Switching to this alternative notion of entailment allows us to improve on the results shown in the previous section.

Definition 22. *Let $\exists X.\mathcal{A}$ and $\exists Y.\mathcal{B}$ be quantified ABoxes. We say that $\exists X.\mathcal{A}$* IQ-entails *$\exists Y.\mathcal{B}$ (written $\exists X.\mathcal{A} \models_{\mathsf{IQ}} \exists Y.\mathcal{B}$) if $\exists Y.\mathcal{B} \models C(a)$ implies $\exists X.\mathcal{A} \models C(a)$ for all $\mathcal{EL}$ concept descriptions C and all $a \in \Sigma_{\mathsf{I}}$. Two quantified ABoxes are* IQ-equivalent *if they IQ-entail each other.*

Obviously, $\exists X.\mathcal{A} \models \exists Y.\mathcal{B}$ implies $\exists X.\mathcal{A} \models_{\mathsf{IQ}} \exists Y.\mathcal{B}$, but the converse need not be true. Whereas entailment can be characterised using homomorphisms, IQ-entailment is characterised using simulations. Similar results have been shown in the context of interpolation and separability, but for interpretations rather than ABoxes (see, e.g., Lemma 4 in [21]). A *simulation* from $\exists X.\mathcal{A}$ to $\exists Y.\mathcal{B}$ is a relation $\mathfrak{S} \subseteq (\Sigma_{\mathsf{I}} \cup X) \times (\Sigma_{\mathsf{I}} \cup Y)$ that satisfies the following properties:

1. $(a,a) \in \mathfrak{S}$ for each individual name $a \in \Sigma_{\mathsf{I}}$;

2. if $(u, v) \in \mathfrak{S}$ and $A(u) \in \mathcal{A}$, then $A(v) \in \mathcal{B}$;
3. if $(u, v) \in \mathfrak{S}$ and $r(u, u') \in \mathcal{A}$, then there exists an object $v' \in \Sigma_\mathsf{I} \cup Y$ such that $(u', v') \in \mathfrak{S}$ and $r(v, v') \in \mathcal{B}$.

Proposition 23. *Let $\exists X.\mathcal{A}$ and $\exists Y.\mathcal{B}$ be quantified ABoxes that are renamed apart. Then, $\exists Y.\mathcal{B} \models_\mathsf{IQ} \exists X.\mathcal{A}$ iff there exists a simulation from $\exists X.\mathcal{A}$ to $\exists Y.\mathcal{B}$.*

Proof. To prove the *only-if* direction, we define an appropriate relation $\mathfrak{S}$ and show that it is a simulation:

$$\mathfrak{S} := \{(u, v) | \mathcal{A} \models C(u) \text{ implies } \mathcal{B} \models C(v) \text{ for each } \mathcal{EL} \text{ concept description } C\}$$

1. Since $\exists Y.\mathcal{B}$ IQ-entails $\exists X.\mathcal{A}$, $\mathfrak{S}$ contains the pair (a, a) for each $a \in \Sigma_\mathsf{I}$.
2. Let $(u, v) \in \mathfrak{S}$ and $A(u) \in \mathcal{A}$. Then $\mathcal{A} \models A(u)$, which yields $\mathcal{B} \models A(v)$ by the definition of $\mathfrak{S}$. By Lemma 6, this implies that $\mathcal{B}$ contains $A(v)$.
3. Let $(u, v) \in \mathfrak{S}$ and consider a role assertion $r(u, u') \in \mathcal{A}$. It follows that $\mathcal{A}$ entails $\exists r.\top(u)$ and so $\mathcal{B}$ entails $\exists r.\top(v)$, i.e., v has at least one r-successor in $\mathcal{B}$. Since $\mathcal{B}$ is finite, v can only have finite number of r-successors in $\mathcal{B}$. We use a diagonalization argument. Assume that, for each $r(v, v') \in \mathcal{B}$, there is an $\mathcal{EL}$ concept description $C_{v'}$ such that $\mathcal{A} \models C_{v'}(u')$ and $\mathcal{B} \not\models C_{v'}(v')$. Define $C := \bigsqcap\{C_{v'} | r(v, v') \in \mathcal{B}\}$, which is a well-defined $\mathcal{EL}$ concept description since v has only finitely many r-successors. Then $\mathcal{A} \models C(u')$, and so $\mathcal{A} \models \exists r.C(u)$. We conclude that $\mathcal{B} \models \exists r.C(v)$, and so there must exist $r(v, v') \in \mathcal{B}$ such that $\mathcal{B} \models C(v')$, which contradicts our construction of C. It follows that there must exist an r-successor v' of v in $\mathcal{B}$ such that $\mathcal{A} \models C(u')$ implies $\mathcal{B} \models C(v')$ for all $\mathcal{EL}$ concept descriptions C, and thus the pair (v, v') is in $\mathfrak{S}$ and the role assertion $r(u', v')$ is in $\mathcal{B}$.

For the *if* direction, assume that $\mathfrak{S}$ is a simulation from $\exists X.\mathcal{A}$ to $\exists Y.\mathcal{B}$. If $\exists X.\mathcal{A} \models C(a)$, then there is a homomorphism from the pp formula $\phi_C(a)$ corresponding to $C(a)$ to $\exists X.\mathcal{A}$ such that a is mapped to a. The composition of this homomorphism with $\mathfrak{S}$ yields a simulation from $\phi_C(a)$ to $\exists Y.\mathcal{B}$. Since $\phi_C(a)$ is tree-shaped, the existence of such a simulation implies the existence of a homomorphism from $\phi_C(a)$ to $\exists Y.\mathcal{B}$, which yields $\exists Y.\mathcal{B} \models C(a)$. □

Since the existence of a simulation can be decided in polynomial time [17], this proposition implies that *IQ-entailment can be decided in polynomial time.* We redefine the notions "compliant anonymisation" and "optimal compliant anonymisation" by using IQ-entailment rather than entailment.

Definition 24. *Let $\exists X.\mathcal{A}, \exists Y.\mathcal{B}$ be quantified ABoxes and $\mathcal{P}$ a policy. Then*

1. *$\exists Y.\mathcal{B}$ is a $\mathcal{P}$-*compliant IQ-anonymisation *of $\exists X.\mathcal{A}$ if $\exists X.\mathcal{A} \models_\mathsf{IQ} \exists Y.\mathcal{B}$ and $\exists Y.\mathcal{B}$ is compliant with $\mathcal{P}$;*
2. *$\exists Y.\mathcal{B}$ is an* optimal $\mathcal{P}$-compliant IQ-anonymisation *of $\exists X.\mathcal{A}$ if it is a $\mathcal{P}$-compliant IQ-anonymisation of $\exists X.\mathcal{A}$, and $\exists X.\mathcal{A} \models_\mathsf{IQ} \exists Z.\mathcal{C} \models_\mathsf{IQ} \exists Y.\mathcal{B}$ implies $\exists Y.\mathcal{B} \models_\mathsf{IQ} \exists Z.\mathcal{C}$ for every $\mathcal{P}$-compliant IQ-anonymisation $\exists Z.\mathcal{C}$ of $\exists X.\mathcal{A}$.*

We can show that $\mathsf{CA}(\exists X.\mathcal{A},\mathcal{P})$ covers all compliant IQ-anonymisations of $\exists X.\mathcal{A}$ w.r.t. IQ-entailment. The proof of this result is similar to the proof of Proposition 15 (see [5] for an explicit proof).

Proposition 25. *If $\exists Z.\mathcal{C}$ is a $\mathcal{P}$-compliant IQ-anonymisation of $\exists X.\mathcal{A}$, then there exists a csf s such that* $\mathsf{ca}(\exists X.\mathcal{A}, s) \models_{\mathsf{IQ}} \exists Z.\mathcal{C}$.

As in Sect. 3, this implies that $\mathsf{CA}(\exists X.\mathcal{A},\mathcal{P})$ contains (up to IQ-equivalence) all optimal compliant IQ-anonymisations. Since IQ-entailment can be decided in polynomial time, removing non-optimal elements from $\mathsf{CA}(\exists X.\mathcal{A},\mathcal{P})$ can now be realised in exponential time without NP oracle.

Theorem 26. *Up to IQ-equivalence, the set of all optimal $\mathcal{P}$-compliant IQ-anonymisations of $\exists X.\mathcal{A}$ can be computed in exponential time.*

This theorem shows that using IQ-entailment improves the complexity of our algorithm for computing optimal compliant anonymisations. For data complexity, it is even in P. Moreover, in the setting of IQ-entailment the set $\mathsf{CA}_{min}(\exists X.\mathcal{A},\mathcal{P})$ turns out to be complete. Indeed, the converse of Proposition 19 holds as well in this setting (see [5] for a detailed proof).

Proposition 27. *Let s and t be compliance seed functions on $\exists X.\mathcal{A}$ for $\mathcal{P}$. Then we have* $\mathsf{ca}(\exists X.\mathcal{A}, s) \models_{\mathsf{IQ}} \mathsf{ca}(\exists X.\mathcal{A}, t)$ *iff* $s \leq t$.

Proof sketch. The *only-if* direction is analogous to the proof of Proposition 19. Conversely, we can show that the relation $\mathfrak{S}$ consisting of the pairs $(y_{u,\mathcal{K}}, y_{u,\mathcal{L}})$ such that, for each $C \in \mathcal{L}$, there is some $D \in \mathcal{K}$ with $C \sqsubseteq_{\emptyset} D$, is a simulation (see [5] for details). □

As a consequence, we obtain the following improvement over Theorem 26.

Theorem 28. *Up to IQ-equivalence, the set $\mathsf{CA}_{min}(\exists X.\mathcal{A},\mathcal{P})$ consists of all optimal $\mathcal{P}$-compliant IQ-anonymisations of $\exists X.\mathcal{A}$, and it can be computed in exponential time.*

Thus, it is not necessary to compute the whole set $\mathsf{CA}(\exists X.\mathcal{A},\mathcal{P})$ first and then remove non-optimal elements. One can directly compute the set $\mathsf{CA}_{min}(\exists X.\mathcal{A},\mathcal{P})$. Using IQ-entailment also allows us to reduce the sizes of the elements of this set. In fact, it is easy to see that removing variables not reachable by a role path from an individual results in a quantified ABox that is IQ-equivalent to the original one. For the canonical anonymisation depicted in Fig. 1, this yields an ABox that, in addition to the individual a (i.e., the grey node) contains only the three variables $y_{x,\{B\}}$, $y_{x,\{A\}}$, and $y_{x,\{A,B\}}$ that are directly reachable from a. In practice, one would not first generate all variables and then remove the unreachable ones, but generate only the reachable ones in the first place.

5 Conclusions

We have developed methods to hide private information (as expressed by a policy $\mathcal{P}$) while modifying the knowledge base (given by a quantified ABox $\exists X.\mathcal{A}$) in a minimal way. More formally, we have shown how to compute the set of all optimal $\mathcal{P}$-compliant anonymisations of $\exists X.\mathcal{A}$. In general, this set contains exponentially many anonymisations that may be of exponential size. As already shown in [3] for the restricted case of an $\mathcal{EL}$ instance store, this exponential blow-up cannot be avoided in the worst case, both regarding the number and the size of the anonymisations. These exponential lower bounds hold both for the case of classical entailment and of IQ-entailment (since for instance stores this does not make a difference). Nevertheless, we have shown that using IQ-entailment leads to a more efficient algorithm (exponential time instead of exponential time with NP oracle), and may result in considerably smaller anonymisations. One may ask why we did not restrict our attention to IQ-entailment altogether. The reason is that, even if one considers only policies expressed by $\mathcal{EL}$ concepts, one may still want to query the ABoxes using general conjunctive queries. ABoxes that are IQ-equivalent, but not equivalent, may yield different answers to CQs. An interesting topic for future research is to see whether our approach can be extended to policies expressed by CQs rather than $\mathcal{EL}$ concepts. A first step in this direction could be to extend the policy language to $\mathcal{ELI}$ or acyclic CQs.

There is a close connection between computing a compliant anonymisation of and repairing an ABox [4]. Basically, if $C \in \mathcal{P}$, then we want to avoid conclusions of the form $C(a)$ for *all* individuals a, whereas repairs want to get rid of conclusions $C(a)$ for a *specific* individual a. It is easy to see how to adapt our notion of a compliance seed function to the repair setting. By making small modifications to our framework, we can thus also compute optimal repairs [5].

As mentioned in the introduction, achieving compliance of a knowledge base is not always sufficient. Instead, one sometimes wants to ensure the more stringent requirement of safety [3,12,13]. Currently, we investigate how to extend the results presented in this paper from compliance to safety. Although adapting our approach to deal with the case of safety is not trivial, and requires the development of new methods, the basic formal setup for both problems remains unchanged. In particular, the results for compliance presented here are important stepping-stones since our approach basically reduces safety to compliance w.r.t. a modified policy [6]. Another interesting topic for future research is to consider compliance and safety of ABoxes w.r.t. terminological knowledge. Without additional restrictions, optimal compliant anonymisations (repairs) need no longer exist [4], but we conjecture that our methods can still be applied if the terminological knowledge is cycle-restricted in the sense introduced in [2].

References

1. Abiteboul, S., Hull, R., Vianu, V.: Foundations of Databases. Addison Wesley Publ. Co., Massachussetts (1995)
2. Baader, F., Borgwardt, S., Morawska, B.: Extending unification in $\mathcal{EL}$ towards general TBoxes. In: Proceedings of KR 2012, pp. 568–572. AAAI Press (2012)
3. Baader, F., Kriegel, F., Nuradiansyah, A.: Privacy-preserving ontology publishing for $\mathcal{EL}$ instance stores. In: Calimeri, F., Leone, N., Manna, M. (eds.) JELIA 2019. LNCS (LNAI), vol. 11468, pp. 323–338. Springer, Cham (2019). https://doi.org/10.1007/978-3-030-19570-0_21
4. Baader, F., Kriegel, F., Nuradiansyah, A., Peñaloza, R.: Making repairs in description logics more gentle. In: Proceedings of KR 2018, pp. 319–328. AAAI Press (2018)
5. Baader, F., Kriegel, F., Nuradiansyah, A., Peñaloza, R.: Computing compliant anonymisations of quantified ABoxes w.r.t. $\mathcal{EL}$ policies (Extended Version). LTCS-Report 20–08, TU Dresden, Germany (2020)
6. Baader, F., Kriegel, F., Nuradiansyah, A., Peñaloza, R.: Computing safe anonymisations of quantified ABoxes w.r.t. $\mathcal{EL}$ policies (Extended Version). LTCS-Report 20–09, TU Dresden, Germany (2020)
7. Baader, F., Küsters, R., Molitor, R.: Computing least common subsumers in description logics with existential restrictions. In: Proceedings of IJCAI 1999, pp. 96–101. Morgan Kaufmann (1999)
8. Baader, F., Morawska, B.: Unification in the description logic $\mathcal{EL}$. Logical Methods Comput. Sci. **6**(3) (2010). https://doi.org/10.2168/LMCS-6(3:17)2010
9. Bonatti, P.A., Sauro, L.: A confidentiality model for ontologies. In: Alani, H., Kagal, L., Fokoue, A., Groth, P., Biemann, C., Parreira, J.X., Aroyo, L., Noy, N., Welty, C., Janowicz, K. (eds.) ISWC 2013. LNCS, vol. 8218, pp. 17–32. Springer, Heidelberg (2013). https://doi.org/10.1007/978-3-642-41335-3_2
10. Chandra, A.K., Merlin, P.M.: Optimal implementation of conjunctive queries in relational data bases. In: Proceedings of STOC 1977, pp. 77–90. ACM (1977)
11. Cima, G., Lembo, D., Rosati, R., Savo, D.F.: Controlled query evaluation in description logics through instance indistinguishability. In: Proceedings of IJCAI 2020, pp. 1791–1797. ijcai.org (2020)
12. Grau, B.C., Kostylev, E.V.: Logical foundations of privacy-preserving publishing of linked data. In: Proceedings of AAAI 2016, pp. 943–949. AAAI Press (2016)
13. Grau, B.C., Kostylev, E.V.: Logical foundations of linked data anonymisation. J. Artif. Intell. Res. **64**, 253–314 (2019)
14. Delanaux, R., Bonifati, A., Rousset, M.-C., Thion, R.: Query-based linked data anonymization. In: Vrandečić, D., Bontcheva, K., Suárez-Figueroa, M.C., Presutti, V., Celino, I., Sabou, M., Kaffee, L.-A., Simperl, E. (eds.) ISWC 2018. LNCS, vol. 11136, pp. 530–546. Springer, Cham (2018). https://doi.org/10.1007/978-3-030-00671-6_31
15. Fung, B.C.M., Wang, K., Chen, R., Yu, P.S.: Privacy-preserving data publishing: a survey of recent developments. ACM Comput. Surv. **42**(4), 14:1–14:53 (2010)
16. Grau, B.C., Kharlamov, E., Kostylev, E.V., Zheleznyakov, D.: Controlled query evaluation for datalog and OWL 2 profile ontologies. In: Proceedings of IJCAI 2015, pp. 2883–2889. AAAI Press (2015)
17. Henzinger, M.R., Henzinger, T.A., Kopke, P.W.: Computing simulations on finite and infinite graphs. In: FOCS 1995, pp. 453–462. IEEE Computer Society Press (1995)

18. Küsters, R. (ed.): Non-Standard Inferences in Description Logics. LNCS (LNAI), vol. 2100. Springer, Heidelberg (2001). https://doi.org/10.1007/3-540-44613-3
19. Küsters, R., Molitor, R.: Approximating most specific concepts in description logics with existential restrictions. In: Baader, F., Brewka, G., Eiter, T. (eds.) KI 2001. LNCS (LNAI), vol. 2174, pp. 33–47. Springer, Heidelberg (2001). https://doi.org/10.1007/3-540-45422-5_4
20. Libkin, L.: Elements of Finite Model Theory. Texts in Theoretical Computer Science. An EATCS Series. Springer (2004)
21. Lutz, C., Seylan, I., Wolter, F.: An automata-theoretic approach to uniform interpolation and approximation in the description logic $\mathcal{EL}$. In: Proceedings of KR 2012, pp. 286–296. AAAI Press (2012)

PNEL: Pointer Network Based End-To-End Entity Linking over Knowledge Graphs

Debayan Banerjee[1(✉)], Debanjan Chaudhuri[2], Mohnish Dubey[2], and Jens Lehmann[2,3]

[1] Language Technology Group, Universität Hamburg, Hamburg, Germany
banerjee@informatik.uni-hamburg.de
[2] Fraunhofer IAIS, Bonn/Dresden, Germany
{debanjan.chaudhuri,mohnish.dubey}@iais.fraunhofer.de
[3] Smart Data Analytics Group, University of Bonn, Bonn, Germany
jens.lehmann@cs.uni-bonn.de

Abstract. Question Answering systems are generally modelled as a pipeline consisting of a sequence of steps. In such a pipeline, Entity Linking (EL) is often the first step. Several EL models first perform span detection and then entity disambiguation. In such models errors from the span detection phase cascade to later steps and result in a drop of overall accuracy. Moreover, lack of gold entity spans in training data is a limiting factor for span detector training. Hence the movement towards end-to-end EL models began where no separate span detection step is involved. In this work we present a novel approach to end-to-end EL by applying the popular Pointer Network model, which achieves competitive performance. We demonstrate this in our evaluation over three datasets on the Wikidata Knowledge Graph.

Keywords: Entity Linking · Question Answering · Knowledge Graphs · Wikidata

1 Introduction

Knowledge Graph based Question Answering (KGQA) systems use a background Knowledge Graph to answer queries posed by a user. Let us take the following question as an example (Fig. 1): *Who founded Tesla?*. The standard sequence of steps for a traditional Entity Linking system is as follows: The system tries to identify *Tesla* as a span of interest. This task is called Mention Detection (MD) or Span Detection. Then an attempt is made to link it to the appropriate entity in the Knowledge Base. In this work we focus on Knowledge Bases in the

D. Chaudhuri and M. Dubey—Equal contribution.

J. Z. Pan et al. (Eds.): ISWC 2020, LNCS 12506, pp. 21–38, 2020.
https://doi.org/10.1007/978-3-030-62419-4_2

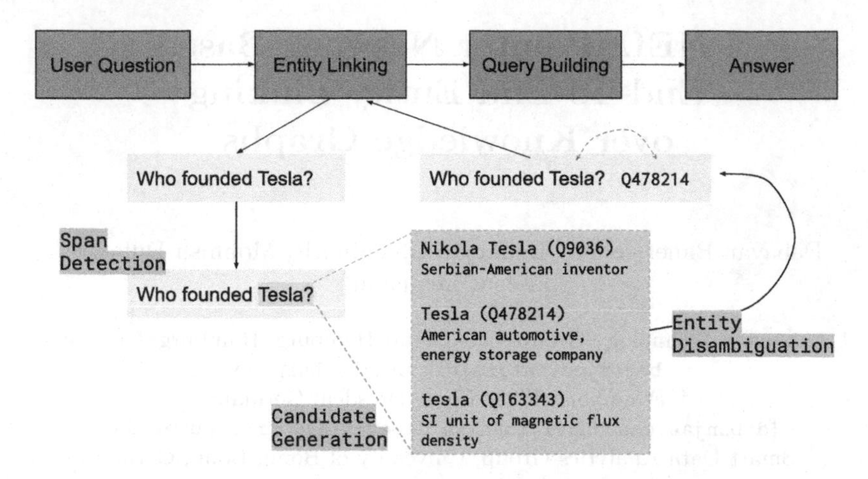

Fig. 1. Illustrating the use of Entity Linking in KGQA system.

form of graphs, hence the entity linker in this case tries to link *Tesla* to the appropriate node in the graph. For a human, it is evident that the question is looking for a person's name who created an organisation named *Tesla*, since the text contains the *relation* `founded`. Hence, it is important that the entity linker understands the same nuance and ignores other entity nodes in the Knowledge Graph which also contain *Tesla* in their labels, e.g., `Nikola Tesla (Q9036, Serbian-American inventor)`, `tesla (Q163343, SI unit)` when considering the example of the Wikidata knowledge graph. The task of ignoring the wrong candidate nodes, and identifying the right candidate node instead, is called *Entity Disambiguation (ED)*. The cumulative process involving Mention Detection and Entity Disambiguation is called *Entity Linking* (EL).

Typically, the MD and ED stages are implemented by different machine learning models which require separate training. Especially for the MD part, sentences with marked entity spans are a requirement. In practice, such data is not easily available. Moreover, errors introduced by the MD phase cascade on to the ED phase. Hence, a movement towards end-to-end Entity Linkers began [11,26]. Such systems do not require labelled entity spans during training. In spite of the benefits of end-to-end models some challenges remain: Due to the lack of a span detector at the initial phase, each word of the sentence needs to be considered as an entity candidate for the disambiguation which leads to the generation of a much larger number of entity candidates. To re-rank these candidates a large amount of time is consumed, not just in processing the features of the candidates, but also in compiling their features.

In this work, we remain cognizant of these challenges and design a system that completely avoids querying the Knowledge Graph during runtime. PNEL (Pointer Network based Entity Linker) instead relies on pre-computed and pre-indexed TransE embeddings and pre-indexed entity label and description text as the only set of features for a given candidate entity. We demonstrate that this produces competitive performance while maintaining lower response times when compared to another end-to-end EL system, VCG [26].

While there is a wide variety of KG embeddings to choose from, we confine our experiments to pre-computed TransE over Wikidata supplied by PyTorch-BigGraph [13]. Our choice was based on the popularity and ease of availability of these embeddings.

Traditionally, the Knowledge Graphs of choice for Question Answering research have been DBpedia [12], Freebase [2] and YAGO [27]. However, in recent times Wikidata [30] has received significant attention owing to the fact that it covers a large number of entities (DBpedia 6M[1], Yago 10M[2], Freebase 39M[3], Wikidata 71M[4]). DBpedia, YAGO and Wikidata source their information from Wikipedia, however DBpedia and YAGO filter out a large percentage of the original entities, while Wikidata does not. While Wikidata has a larger number of entities it also adds to noise which is a challenge to any EL system. Wikidata also allows direct edits leading to up-to-date information, while DBpedia depends on edits performed on Wikipedia. Freebase has been discontinued and a portion of it is merged into Wikidata [19]. Moreover DBpedia now extracts data directly from Wikidata, apart from Wikipedia[5] [8]. Hence, we decide to base this work on the Wikidata knowledge graph and the datasets we evaluate on are all based on Wikidata.

In this work our **contributions** are as follows:

1. PNEL is the first approach that uses the Pointer Network model for solving the End-to-End Entity Linking problem over Knowledge Graphs, inspired by the recent success of pointer networks for convex hull and generalised travelling salesman problems.
2. We are the first work to present baseline results for the entire LC-QuAD 2.0 [5] test set.
3. Our approach produces state-of-the-art results on the LC-QuAD 2.0 and SimpleQuestions datasets.

The paper is organised into the following sections: (2) Related Work, outlining some of the major contributions in entity linking used in question answering; (3) PNEL, where we discuss the pointer networks and the architecture of PNEL (4) Dataset used in the paper (5) Evaluation, with various evaluation criteria, results and ablation test (6) Error Analysis (7) Discussion and future direction.

[1] https://wiki.dbpedia.org/develop/datasets/latest-core-dataset-releases.
[2] https://www.mpi-inf.mpg.de/departments/databases-and-information-systems/research/yago-naga/yago/.
[3] https://developers.google.com/freebase/guide/basic_concepts#topics.
[4] https://www.wikidata.org/wiki/Wikidata:Statistics.
[5] https://databus.dbpedia.org/dbpedia/wikidata.

2 Related Work

DBpedia Spotlight [16] is one of the early works for entity linking over DBpedia. It first identifies a list of surface forms and then generates entity candidates. It then disambiguates the entity based on the surrounding context. In spite of being an early solution, it still remains one of the strongest candidates in our own evaluations, at the same time it has low response times. Compared to PNEL it lags behind in precision significantly. S-MART [31] generates multiple regression trees and then applies sophisticated structured prediction techniques to link entities to resources. S-MART performs especially well in recall on WebQSP in our evaluations and the reason seems to be that they perform more complex information extraction related tasks during entity linking, e.g., "Peter Parker" span fetches "Stan Lee"[6]. However compared to PNEL it has low precision.

The journey towards end-to-end models which combine MD and ED in one model started with attempts to build feedback mechanisms from one step to the other so that errors in one stage can be recovered by the next stage. One of the first attempts, Sil et al. [25], use a popular NER model to generate extra number of spans and let the linking step take the final decisions. Their method however depends on a good mention spotter and the use of hand engineered features. It is also unclear how linking can improve their MD phase. Later, Luo et al. [15] developed competitive joint MD and ED models using semi-Conditional Random Fields (semi-CRF). However, the basis for dependency was not robust, using only type-category correlation features. The other engineered features used in their model are either NER or ED specific. Although their probabilistic graphical model allows for low complexity learning and inference, it suffers from high computational complexity caused by the usage of the cross product of all possible document spans, NER categories and entity assignments. Another solution J-NERD [18] addresses the end-to-end task using engineered features and a probabilistic graphical model on top of sentence parse trees. EARL [6] makes some rudimentary attempts towards a feedback mechanism by allowing the entity and relation span detector to make a different choice based on classifier score in the later entity linking stage, however it is not an End-to-End model.

Sorokin et al. [26] is possibly the earliest work on end-to-end EL. They use features of variable granularities of context and achieve strong results on Wikidata that we are yet unable to surpass on WebQSP dataset. More recently, Kolitsas et al. [11] worked on a truly end-to-end MD (Mention Detection) and ED (Entity Disambiguation) combined into a single EL (Entity Linking) model. They use context-aware mention embeddings, entity embeddings and a probabilistic mention - entity map, without demanding other engineered features. Additionally, there are a few recent works on entity linking for short text on Wikidata [30], which is also the area of focus of PNEL. OpenTapioca [4] works on a limited number of classes (humans, organisations and locations) when compared to PNEL, but is openly available both as a demo and as code and is

[6] https://github.com/UKPLab/starsem2018-entity-linking/issues/8#issuecomment-566469263.

lightweight. Falcon 2.0 [22] is a rule based EL solution on Wikidata which is openly available and fast, but it requires manual feature engineering for new datasets. Sevigli et al. [24] performs ED using KG entity embeddings (DeepWalk [20]) on Wikidata, but they rely on an external MD solution. PNEL and Sorokin et al. both use TransE entity embeddings and also perform MD and ED end-to-end in a single model. Sorokin et al. has a more complex architecture when compared to PNEL. Apart from using TransE embeddings, they fetch neighbouring entities and relations on the fly during EL, which is a process PNEL intentionally avoids to maintain lower response times. KBPearl [14] is a recent work on KG population which also targets entity linking as a task for Wikidata. It uses dense sub-graphs formed across the document text to link entities. It is not an end-to-end model but is the most recent work which presents elaborate evaluation on Wikidata based datasets, hence we include it in evaluations.

We also include QKBFly [17] and TagME [7] in our evaluations because KBPearl includes results for these systems on a common dataset (LC-QuAD 2.0). QKBFly performs on-the-fly knowledge base construction for ad-hoc text. It uses a semantic-graph representation of sentences that captures per-sentence clauses, noun phrases, pronouns, as well as their syntactic and semantic dependencies. It retrieves relevant source documents for entity centric text from multiple sources like Wikipedia and other news websites. TagME is an older system that spots entity spans in short text using a Lucene index built out of anchor text in Wikipedia. It then performs a mutual-voting based disambiguation process among the candidates and finishes with a pruning step.

3 PNEL

PNEL stands for Pointer Network based Entity Linker. Inspired by the use case of Pointer Networks [29] in solving the convex hull and the generalised travelling salesman problems, this work adapts the approach to solving entity linking. *Conceptually, each candidate entity is a point in an euclidean space, and the pointer network finds the correct set of points for the given problem.*

3.1 Encoding for Input

The first step is to take the input sentence and vectorise it for feeding into the pointer network. We take varying length of n-grams, also called n-gram tiling and vectorise each such n-gram.

Given an input sentence $S = \{s_1, s_2 ... s_n\}$ where s_k is a token (word) in the given sentence, we vectorise s_k to v_k, which is done in the following manner:

1. Take the following 4 n-grams: $[s_k], [s_{k-1}, s_k], [s_k, s_{k+1}], [s_{k-1}, s_k, s_{k+1}]$.
2. For each such n-gram find the top L text matches in the entity label database. We use the OKAPI BM25 algorithm for label search.
3. For each such candidate form a candidate vector comprising of the concatenation of the following features

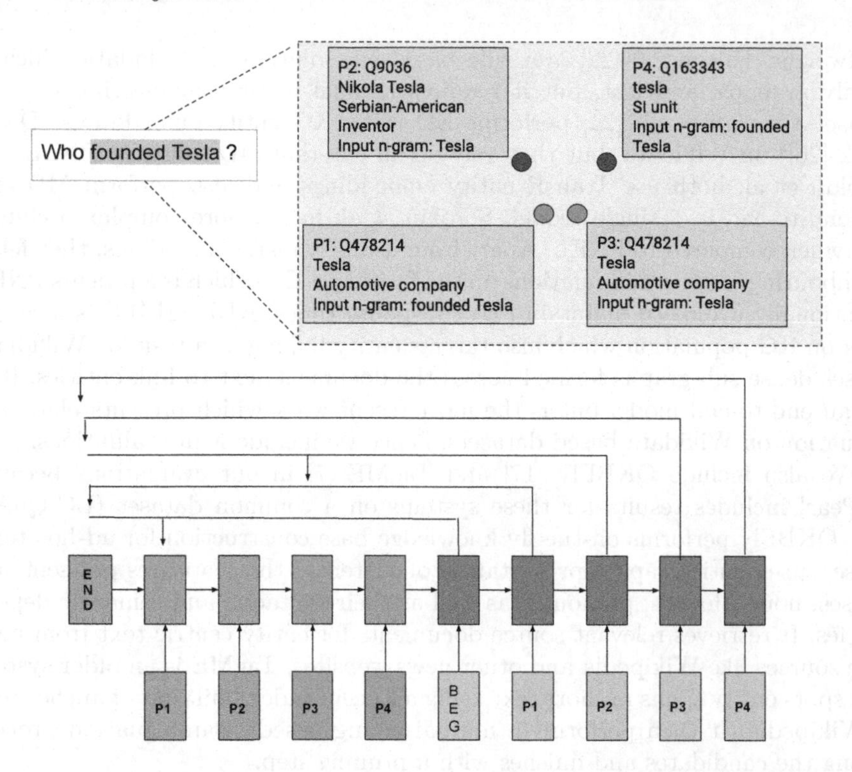

Fig. 2. The red and green dots represent entity candidate vectors for the given question. The green vectors are the correct entity vectors. Although they belong to the same entity they are not the same dots because they come from different n-grams. At each time step the Pointer Network points to one of the input candidate entities as the linked entity, or to the END symbol to indicate no choice. (Color figure online)

(a) R_{kl} = Rank of entity candidate in text search (length 1), where $1 \leq l \leq L$.
(b) $ngramlen$ = The number of words in the current n-gram under consideration where $1 \leq ngramlen \leq 3$ (length 1).
(c) k = The index of the token s_k (length 1).
(d) pos_k = A one-hot vector of length 36 denoting the PoS tag of the word under consideration. The 36 different tags are as declared in the Penn Treebank Project [23] (length 36).
(e) $EntEmbed_{kl}$ = TransE Entity Embedding (length 200).
(f) $SentFTEmbed$ = fastText embedding of sentence S (length 300), which is a mean of the embeddings of the tokens of S. In some sense this carries within it the problem statement.
(g) $TokFTEmbed_k$ = fastText embedding of token s_k (length 300). Addition of this feature might seem wasteful considering we have already added the sentence vector above, but as shown in the ablation experiment in Table 6, it results in an improvement.
(h) $DescriptionEmbed_{kl}$ = fastText embedding of the Wikidata description for entity candidate kl (length 300).

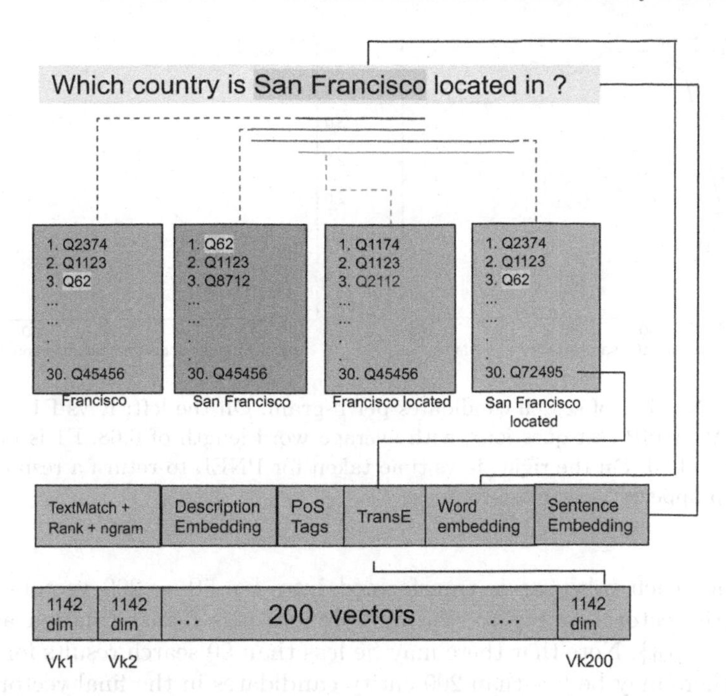

Fig. 3. The word "Francisco" is vectorised in the following manner: 4 n-grams represented by the underlines are considered and searched against an entity label database. The top 50 search results are depicted for each of the n-grams resulting in 200 candidates. For the entity Q72495, for example, we fetch its TransE embedding, add its text search rank, n-gram length, word index position as features. Additionally we also append the fastText embedding for "Francisco" and the entire fastText embedding for the sentence (average of word vectors) to the feature. We then append the fastText embeddings for the label and description for this entity. Hence we get a 1142 dimensional vector V_{k120} **corresponding to entity candidate Q72495**. For all 200 candidate entities for "Francisco", we have a sequence of two hundred 1142 dimensional vectors as input to the pointer network. For the sentence above which has 7 words, this results in a final sequence of $7 \times 200 = 1400$ vectors each of length 1142 as input to our pointer network. Any one or more of these vectors could be the correct entities.

(i) $TextMatchMetric_{kl}$ = This is a triple of values, each ranging from 0 to 100, that measures the degree of text match between the token under consideration s_k and the label of the entity candidate kl. The three similarity matches are *simple ratio, partial ratio, and token sort ratio.* In case of *simple ratio* the following pair of text corresponds to perfect match: `"Elon Musk"` and `"Elon Musk"`. In case of *partial ratio* the following pair of text corresponds to a perfect match: `"Elon Musk"` and `"Musk"`. In case of *token sort ratio* the following pair of text corresponds to a perfect match: `"Elon Musk"` and `"Musk Elon"` (length 3).

For each token s_k we have an expanded sequence of token vectors, comprising of 4 n-grams, upto 50 candidates per n-gram, where each vector is of length

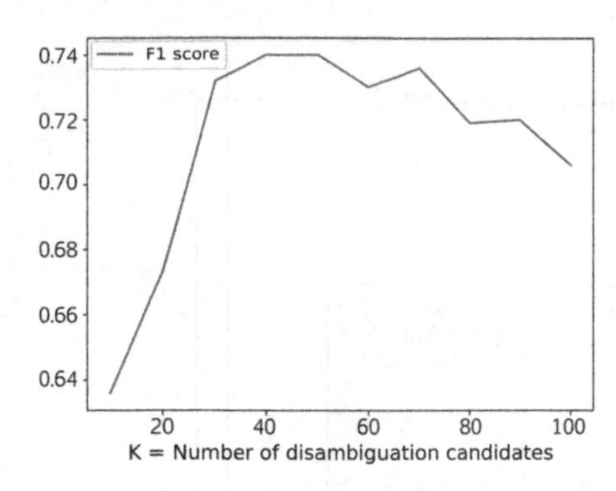

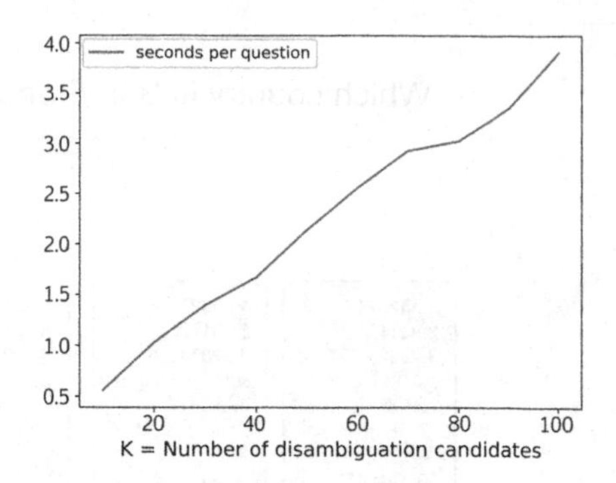

Fig. 4. K = Number of search candidates per n-gram. On the left: K vs F1 score on a set of 100 WebQSP test questions, with average word length of 6.68. F1 is maximum for K = 40 and 50. On the right: K vs time taken for PNEL to return a response. The relationship appears to be close to linear.

1142. Hence each token s_k is transformed into $4 \times 50 = 200$ vectors, each a 1142 length vector (see Fig. 3). We may denote this transformation as $s_k \rightarrow \{v_{k1}, v_{k2}....v_{k200}\}$. Note that there may be less than 50 search results for a given token so there may be less than 200 entity candidates in the final vectorisation. Each of these v_k vectors is an entity candidate (Fig. 3).

3.2 Training

For the entire sentence, a sequence of such vectors is provided as input to the pointer network. During training the labels for the given input sequence are the index numbers of the correct entities in the input sequence. Note that the same entity appears multiple times because of n-gram tiling. During each decoding time step the decoder produces a softmax distribution over the input sequence (see Fig. 2), which in our implementation has a maximum sequence length of 3000. Additionally the `BEGIN`, `END`, `PAD` symbols add to a total of 3003 symbols to softmax over. The cross entropy loss function is averaged over the entire output sequence of labels and is considered the final loss for the entire input sequence.

3.3 Network Configuration

We use a single layer bi-LSTM [9] pointer network with 512 hidden units in a layer and an attention size of 128. Addition of an extra layer to the network did not result in an improvement. The Adam optimizer [10] was used with an initial learning rate of 0.001. A maximum input sequence length of 3000 and a maximum output length of 100 were enforced.

4 Datasets

For reasons explained in Sect. 1 we evaluate on Wikidata based datasets. We use the following:

- **WebQSP:** We use the dataset released by Sorokin et al. [26] where the original WebQSP dataset by Yih et al. [32], which was based on Freebase, has been adapted and all Freebase IDs converted to their respective Wikidata IDs. WebQSP contains questions that were originally collected for the WebQuestions dataset from web search logs (Berant et al. [1]). WebQSP is a relatively small dataset consisting of 3098 train 1639 test questions which cover 3794 and 2002 entities respectively. The dataset has a mixture of simple and complex questions. We found some questions in the test set that had failed Freebase to Wikidata entity ID conversions. We skipped such questions during PNEL's evaluation.
- **SimpleQuestions:** To test the performance of PNEL on simple questions, we choose SimpleQuestions [3], which as the name suggests, consists only of Simple Questions. The training set has more than 30,000 questions while the test set has close to 10,000 questions. This dataset was also originally based on Freeebase and later the entity IDs were converted to corresponding Wikidata IDs. However out of the 10,000 test questions only about half are answerable on the current Wikidata.
- **LC-QuAD 2.0:** Unlike the first two datasets, LC-QuAD 2.0 [5] is based on Wikidata since its inception and is also the most recent dataset of the three. It carries a mixture of simple and complex questions which were verbalised by human workers on Amazon Mechanical Turk. It is a large and varied dataset comprising of 24180 train questions and 6046 test questions which cover 33609 and 8417 entities respectively.

5 Evaluation

In this section we evaluate our proposed model(s) against different state-of-the-art methods for KGQA. As notations, PNEL-L stands for PNEL trained on LC-QuAD 2.0. PNEL-W and PNEL-S stand for PNEL trained on WebQSP and SimpleQuestions respectively.

5.1 Experiment 1: EL over KBPearl Split of LC-QuAD 2.0 Test Set

Objective: The purpose of this experiment is to benchmark PNEL against a large number of EL systems, not just over Wikidata, but also other KBs.

Method: The results are largely taken from KBPearl. PNEL is trained on the LC-QuAD 2.0 training set. For a fair comparison, the systems are tested on the 1294 questions split of test set provided by KBPearl. We train PNEL for 2 epochs.

Remarks: Results for Falcon 2.0 and OpenTapioca were obtained by accessing their live API. The original Falcon 2.0 paper provides an F1 of 0.69 on 15% of randomly selected questions from a combination of the train and test splits of the dataset. Several systems in the table below do not originally produce Wikidata entity IDs, hence the authors of KBpearl have converted the IDs to corresponding Wikidata IDs.

Analysis: As observed from the results in Table 1, PNEL outperforms all other systems on this particular split of LC-QuAD 2.0 dataset.

Table 1. Evaluation on KBPearl split of LC-QuAD 2.0 test set

Entity linker	Precision	Recall	F1
Falcon [21]	0.533	0.598	0.564
EARL [6]	0.403	0.498	0.445
Spotlight [16]	0.585	0.657	0.619
TagMe [7]	0.352	**0.864**	0.500
OpenTapioca [4]	0.237	0.411	0.301
QKBfly [17]	0.518	0.479	0.498
Falcon 2.0	0.395	0.268	0.320
KBPearl-NN	0.561	0.647	0.601
PNEL-L	**0.803**	0.517	**0.629**

5.2 Experiment 2: EL over Full LC-QuAD 2.0 Test Set

Objective: The objective of this experiment is to compare systems that return Wikidata IDs for the EL task.

Method: We train PNEL on LC-QuAD 2.0 train set and test on all 6046 questions in test set. PNEL was trained for 2 epochs.

Remarks: Results for competing systems were obtained by accessing their live APIs. We choose systems that return Wikidata IDs.

Analysis: As seen in Table 2, similar to the previous experiment, PNEL performs the best on the LC-QuAD 2.0 test set.

5.3 Experiment 3: EL over WebQSP Test Set

Objective: Benchmark against an end-to-end model that returns Wikidata IDs.

Table 2. Evaluation on LC-QuAD 2.0 test set

Entity linker	Precision	Recall	F1
VCG [26]	0.516	0.432	0.470
OpenTapioca [4]	0.237	0.411	0.301
Falcon 2.0	0.418	0.476	0.445
PNEL-L	**0.688**	**0.516**	**0.589**

Method: Train and test PNEL on WebQSP train and test sets respectively. PNEL is trained for 10 epochs.

Remarks: Results for the competing systems were taken from Sorokin et al. [26].

Table 3. Evaluation on WebQSP

Entity linker	Precision	Recall	F1
Spotlight	0.704	0.514	0.595
S-MART [31]	0.666	**0.772**	0.715
VCG [26]	0.826	0.653	**0.730**
PNEL-L	0.636	0.480	0.547
PNEL-W	**0.886**	0.596	0.712

Analysis: As seen in Table 3 PNEL comes in third best in this experiment, beaten by VCG and S-MART. S-MART has high recall because it performs semantic information retrieval apart from lexical matching for candidate generation, as explained in Sect. 2. VCG is more similar to PNEL in that it is also an end-to-end system. It has higher recall but lower precision than PNEL.

5.4 Experiment 4: EL over SimpleQuestions Test Set

Objective: Benchmark systems on the SimpleQuestions Dataset.

Method: Train and test PNEL on SimpleQuestions train and test sets respectively. PNEL is trained for 2 epochs.

Remarks: We extended the results from Falcon 2.0 [22].

Table 4. Evaluation on SimpleQuestions

Entity linker	Precision	Recall	F1
OpenTapioca [4]	0.16	0.28	0.20
Falcon 2.0	0.38	0.44	0.41
PNEL-L	0.31	0.25	0.28
PNEL-S	**0.74**	**0.63**	**0.68**

Analysis: As seen in Table 4, PNEL outperforms the competing systems both in precision and recall for SimpleQuestions dataset. As observed, PNEL has the best precision across all datasets, however, recall seems to be PNEL's weakness.

5.5 Experiment 5: Candidate Generation Accuracy

Objective: The purpose of this experiment is to see what percentage of correct entity candidates were made available to PNEL after the text search phase. This sets a limit on the maximum performance that can be expected from PNEL.

Remarks: PNEL considers each token a possible correct entity, but since it only considers top-K text search matches for each token, it also loses potentially correct entity candidates before the disambiguation phase. The results in Table 5 are for K = 30.

Table 5. Entity Candidates available post label search

Dataset	PNEL (%)
WebQSP	73
LC-QuAD 2.0	82
SimpleQuestions	90

5.6 Experiment 6: Ablation of Features Affecting Accuracy

Objective: We present an ablation study on the WebQSP dataset to understand the importance of different feature vectors used in the model.

Analysis: As seen in Table 6 it appears that the most important feature is the TransE entity embedding, which implicitly contains the entire KG structure information. On removing this feature there is drop in F1 score from 0.712 to 0.221. On the other hand the least important feature seem to be the description embedding. Removal of this feature merely leads to a drop in F1 from 0.712 to 0.700. A possible reason is that the Text Search Rank potentially encodes

Table 6. Ablation test for PNEL on WebQSP test set features

Sentence embed.	Word embed.	Descript. embed.	TransE	PoS tags	Text rank	n-gram length	Text match metric	F1 score
✓	✓	✓	✓	✓	✓	✓	✓	0.712
	✓	✓	✓	✓	✓	✓	✓	0.554
✓		✓	✓	✓	✓	✓	✓	0.666
✓	✓		✓	✓	✓	✓	✓	0.700
✓	✓	✓		✓	✓	✓	✓	**0.221**
✓	✓	✓	✓		✓	✓	✓	0.685
✓	✓	✓	✓	✓		✓	✓	0.399
✓	✓	✓	✓	✓	✓		✓	0.554
✓	✓	✓	✓	✓	✓	✓		0.698

significant text similarity information, and TransE potentially encodes other type and category related information that description often adds. Removal of the Text Search Rank also results in a large drop in F1 reaching to 0.399 from 0.712.

5.7 Experiment 7: Run Time Evaluation

Objective: We look at a comparison of run times across the systems we have evaluated on

Table 7. Time taken per question on the WebQSP dataset of 1639 questions

System	Seconds	Target KG
VCG	8.62	Wikidata
PNEL	3.14	Wikidata
Falcon 2.0	1.08	Wikidata
EARL	0.79	DBpedia
TagME	0.29	Wikipedia
Spotlight	0.16	DBpedia
Falcon	0.16	DBpedia
OpenTapioca	0.07	Wikidata

Analysis: QKBFly and KBPearl are off-line systems, requiring separate steps for entity candidate population and entity linking, hence they are not evaluated in Table 7. VCG and PNEL are end-to-end systems while the others are modular systems. VCG and PNEL were installed locally on a machine with the following configuration: 256 GB RAM, 42 core E5-2650 Intel Xeon v4@2.2 GHz. No GPU was present on the system during run time. For VCG and PNEL, the times taken for first runs were recorded, where the corresponding databases such as Virtuoso and Elasticsearch, were started just before the evaluation. This was done so that the times were not affected by caching from previous runs. For systems except PNEL and VCG, the times mentioned in the table were collected from API calls to their hosted services. It must be considered that, due to network latency, and other unknown setup related configurations at the service end, the times may not be comparably directly. PNEL performs faster than VCG since it avoids querying the KG during runtime, and instead relies on pre-computed KG embeddings. PNEL also uses lesser number of features than VCG. A visible trend is that the more accurate system is slower, however Spotlight is an exception, which performs well in both speed and accuracy.

6 Error Analysis

A prominent feature of PNEL is high precision and low recall. We focus on loss in recall in this section. For LC-QuAD 2.0 test set consisting of 6046 questions, the precision, recall and F-score are 0.688, 0.516 and 0.589 respectively. We categorise the phases of loss in recall in two sections 1) Failure in the candidate generation phase 2) Failure in re-ranking/disambiguation phase. When considering the top 50 search candidates during text label search, it was found that 75.3% of the correct entities were recovered from the entity label index. This meant that before re-ranking we had already lost 24.7% recall accuracy. During re-ranking phase, a further 23.7% in absolute accuracy was lost, leading to our recall of 0.516. We drill down into the 23.7% absolute loss in accuracy during re-ranking, attempting to find the reasons for such loss, since this would expose the weaknesses of the model. In the plots below, we consider all those questions which contained the right candidate entity in the candidate generation phase. Hence, we discard those questions for our analysis, which already failed in the candidate generation phase.

Table 8. Comparison of PNEL's performance with respect to number of entities in a question.

Entity count	Questions count	Precision	Recall	F1
1	3311	0.687	0.636	0.656
2	1981	0.774	0.498	0.602
3	88	0.666	0.431	0.518

It is observed in Table 8 that recall falls as the number of entities per question rises. It must not be concluded however, that PNEL fails to recognise more than an entity per question. There were 375 questions with multiple entities where PNEL was able to link all the entities correctly. In Fig. 5 we observe that the recall does not exhibit significant co-relation with either the length of the question, or the length of entity label. The recall remains stable. There seems to be some co-relation between the amount of data available for a given length of question, and the recall on it. It appears that the model performs better on question lengths it has seen more often during training.

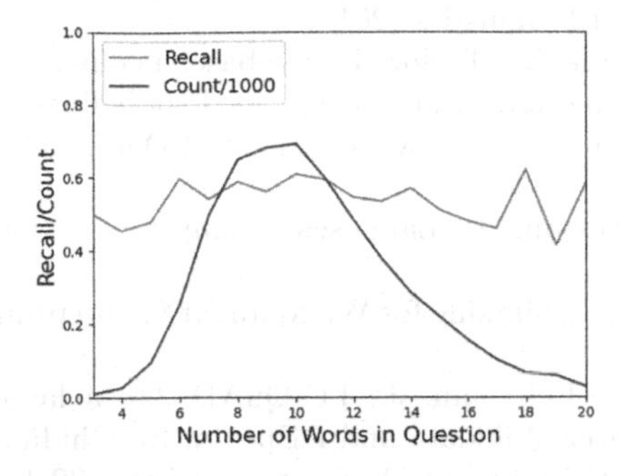

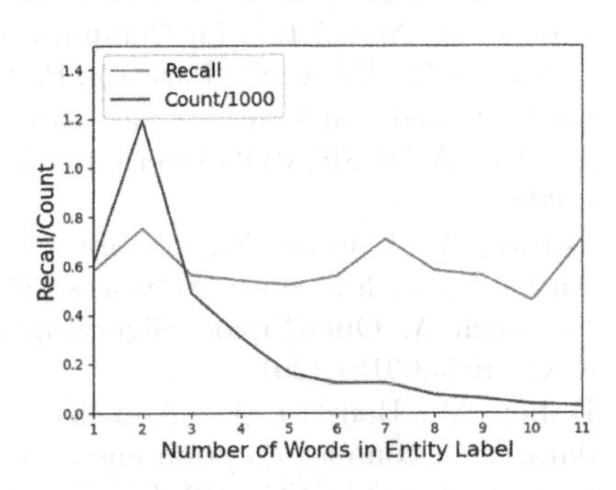

Fig. 5. Plots of recall variation versus 1) Length of Question 2) Length of entity span 3) Frequency of questions with the given lengths in the dataset (scaled down by a factor of 1000)

7 Discussion and Future Work

In this work we have proposed PNEL, an end-to-end Entity Linking system based on the Pointer Network model. We make no modifications to the original Pointer Network model, but identify its utility for the problem statement of EL, and successfully model the problem so the Pointer Network is able to find the right set of entities. We evaluate our approach on three datasets of varying complexity and report state of the art results on two of them. On the third dataset, WebQSP, we perform best in precision but lag behind in recall. We select such features that require no real time KG queries during inference. This demonstrates that the Pointer Network model, and the choice of features presented in this work, result in a practical and deployable EL solution for the largest Knowledge Graph publicly available - Wikidata.

For future work: PNEL being based on the LSTM cell inevitably processes tokens sequentially increasing the response times. This limitation could be overcome by using some variant of the Transformer model [28] instead, which is not only a powerful model but also able to process tokens in parallel. As a future work we would also like to explore different entity embedding techniques and investigate which characteristics make an embedding suitable for the entity linking task.

Acknowledgement. We would like to thank Prof. Dr. Chris Biemann of the Language Technology Group, University of Hamburg, for his valuable suggestions towards improving this work.

References

1. Berant, J., Chou, A., Frostig, R., Liang, P.: Freebase from question-answer pairs. In: Proceedings of the 2013 Conference on Empirical Methods in Natural Language Processing. Association for Computational Linguistics (2013)
2. Bollacker, K., Evans, C., Paritosh, P., Sturge, T., Taylor, J.: Freebase: a collaboratively created graph database for structuring human knowledge. In: Proceedings of the 2008 ACM SIGMOD International Conference on Management of Data. ACM (2008)
3. Bordes, A., Usunier, N., Chopra, S., Weston, J.: Large-scale Simple Question Answering with Memory Networks (2015)
4. Delpeuch, A.: OpenTapioca: lightweight entity linking for Wikidata. arXiv preprint arXiv:1904.09131 (2019)
5. Dubey, M., Banerjee, D., Abdelkawi, A., Lehmann, J.: LC-QuAD 2.0: a large dataset for complex question answering over Wikidata and DBpedia. In: Ghidini, C., et al. (eds.) ISWC 2019. LNCS, vol. 11779, pp. 69–78. Springer, Cham (2019). https://doi.org/10.1007/978-3-030-30796-7_5
6. Dubey, M., Banerjee, D., Chaudhuri, D., Lehmann, J.: EARL: joint entity and relation linking for question answering over knowledge graphs. In: Vrandečić, D., et al. (eds.) ISWC 2018. LNCS, vol. 11136, pp. 108–126. Springer, Cham (2018). https://doi.org/10.1007/978-3-030-00671-6_7
7. Ferragina, P., Scaiella, U.: TAGME: on-the-fly annotation of short text fragments (by Wikipedia entities). In: Proceedings of the 19th ACM International Conference on Information and Knowledge Management (2010)
8. Frey, J., Hofer, M., Obraczka, D., Lehmann, J., Hellmann, S.: DBpedia FlexiFusion the best of Wikipedia > Wikidata > your data. In: Ghidini, C., et al. (eds.) ISWC 2019. LNCS, vol. 11779, pp. 96–112. Springer, Cham (2019). https://doi.org/10.1007/978-3-030-30796-7_7
9. Graves, A., Fernández, S., Schmidhuber, J.: Bidirectional LSTM networks for improved phoneme classification and recognition. In: Duch, W., Kacprzyk, J., Oja, E., Zadrożny, S. (eds.) ICANN 2005, Part II. LNCS, vol. 3697, pp. 799–804. Springer, Heidelberg (2005). https://doi.org/10.1007/11550907_126
10. Kingma, D.P., Ba., J.: Adam: a method for stochastic optimization. arXiv preprint arXiv:1412.6980 (2014)
11. Kolitsas, N., Ganea, O.-E., Hofmann, T.: End-to-end neural entity linking. In: Proceedings of the 22nd Conference on Computational Natural Language Learning (2018)
12. Lehmann, J., et al.: DBpedia – A Large-Scale, Multilingual Knowledge Base Extracted from Wikipedia. Semantic Web (2015)
13. Lerer, A., et al.: PyTorch-BigGraph: a large-scale graph embedding system. In: Proceedings of the 2nd SysML Conference (2019)
14. Lin, X., Li, H., Xin, H., Li, Z., Chen, L.: KBPearl: a knowledge base population system supported by joint entity and relation linking. Proc. VLDB Endow. **13**, 1035–1049 (2020)

15. Luo, G., Huang, X., Lin, C.-Y., Nie, Z.: Joint entity recognition and disambiguation. In: Proceedings of the 2015 Conference on Empirical Methods in Natural Language Processing. Association for Computational Linguistics (2015)
16. Mendes, P.N., Jakob, M., García-Silva, A., Bizer, C.: DBpedia spotlight: shedding light on the web of documents. In: Proceedings the 7th International Conference on Semantic Systems (2011)
17. Nguyen, D.B., Abujabal, A., Tran, K., Theobald, M., Weikum, G.: Query-driven on-the-fly knowledge base construction. Proc. VLDB Endow. **11**, 66–79 (2017)
18. Nguyen, D.B., Theobald, M., Weikum, G.: NERD: joint named entity recognition and disambiguation with rich linguistic features. Trans. Assoc. Comput. Ling. **4**, 215–229 (2016)
19. Pellissier Tanon, T., Vrandečić, D., Schaffert, S., Steiner, T., Pintscher, L.: From freebase to Wikidata: the great migration. In: Proceedings of the 25th International Conference on World Wide Web. International World Wide Web Conferences Steering Committee (2016)
20. Perozzi, B., Al-Rfou, R., Skiena, S.: DeepWalk. In: Proceedings of the 20th ACM SIGKDD International Conference on Knowledge Discovery and Data Mining - KDD 2014 (2014)
21. Sakor, A., et al.: Old is gold: linguistic driven approach for entity and relation linking of short text. In: Proceedings of the 2019 Conference of the North American Chapter of the Association for Computational Linguistics: Human Language Technologies, Volume 1 (Long and Short Papers). Association for Computational Linguistics (2019)
22. Sakor, A., Singh, K., Patel, A., Vidal, M.-E.: FALCON 2.0: an entity and relation linking tool over Wikidata (2019)
23. Santorini, B.: Part-of-speech tagging guidelines for the Penn Treebank Project (1990)
24. Sevgili, Ö., Panchenko, A., Biemann, C.: Improving neural entity disambiguation with graph embeddings. In: Proceedings of the 57th Annual Meeting of the Association for Computational Linguistics: Student Research Workshop. Association for Computational Linguistics (2019)
25. Sil, A., Yates, A.: Re-ranking for joint named-entity recognition and linking. In: Proceedings of the 22nd ACM International Conference on Information and Knowledge Management. Association for Computing Machinery (2013)
26. Sorokin, D., Gurevych, I.: Mixing context granularities for improved entity linking on question answering data across entity categories. In: Proceedings of the Seventh Joint Conference on Lexical and Computational Semantics. Association for Computational Linguistics (2018)
27. Suchanek, F.M., Kasneci, G., Weikum, G.: Yago: a core of semantic knowledge. In: Proceedings of the 16th International Conference on World Wide Web. ACM (2007)
28. Vaswani, A., et al.: Attention is all you need. In: Guyon, I., et al. (eds.) Advances in Neural Information Processing Systems, vol. 30, pp. 5998–6008. Curran Associates Inc. (2017)
29. Vinyals, O., Fortunato, M., Jaitly, N.: Pointer networks. In: Cortes, C., Lawrence, N.D., Lee, D.D., Sugiyama, M., Garnett, R. (eds.) Advances in Neural Information Processing Systems, vol. 28. Curran Associates Inc. (2015)
30. Vrandečić, D., Krötzsch, M.: Wikidata: a free collaborative knowledge base. Commun. ACM **57**, 78–85 (2014)

31. Yang, Y., Chang, M.-W.: S-MART: novel tree-based structured learning algorithms applied to tweet entity linking. In: ACL 2015 (2015)
32. Yih, W.-T., Richardson, M., Meek, C., Chang, M.-W., Suh, J.: The value of semantic parse labeling for knowledge base question answering. In: Proceedings of the 54th Annual Meeting of the Association for Computational Linguistics (Volume 2: Short Papers). Association for Computational Linguistics (2016)

Explainable Link Prediction for Emerging Entities in Knowledge Graphs

Rajarshi Bhowmik[1(✉)] and Gerard de Melo[2]

[1] Rutgers University, Piscataway, New Brunswick, NJ, USA
rajarshi.bhowmik@rutgers.edu
[2] Hasso Plattner Institute, University of Potsdam, Potsdam, Germany
gdm@demelo.org

Abstract. Despite their large-scale coverage, cross-domain knowledge graphs invariably suffer from inherent incompleteness and sparsity. Link prediction can alleviate this by inferring a target entity, given a source entity and a query relation. Recent embedding-based approaches operate in an uninterpretable latent semantic vector space of entities and relations, while path-based approaches operate in the symbolic space, making the inference process explainable. However, these approaches typically consider static snapshots of the knowledge graphs, severely restricting their applicability for evolving knowledge graphs with newly emerging entities. To overcome this issue, we propose an inductive representation learning framework that is able to learn representations of previously unseen entities. Our method finds reasoning paths between source and target entities, thereby making the link prediction for unseen entities interpretable and providing support evidence for the inferred link.

Keywords: Explainable link prediction · Emerging entities · Inductive representation learning

1 Introduction

Recent years have seen a surge in the usage of large-scale cross-domain knowledge graphs [17] for various tasks, including factoid question answering, fact-based dialogue engines, and information retrieval [2]. Knowledge graphs serve as a source of background factual knowledge for a wide range of applications [6]. For example, Google's knowledge graph is tightly integrated into its search engine, while Apple adopted Wikidata as a source of background knowledge for its virtual assistant Siri. Many such applications deal with queries that can be transformed to a structured relational query of the form $(e_s, r_q, ?)$, where e_s is the source entity and r_q is the query relation. For example, the query "*Who is the director of World Health Organization?*" can be mapped to the structured query *(World Health Organization, director, ?)* while executing it on a knowledge graph. Unfortunately, due to the inherent sparsity and incompleteness of knowledge graphs, answers to many such queries cannot be fetched directly from the existing data, but instead need to be inferred indirectly.

J. Z. Pan et al. (Eds.): ISWC 2020, LNCS 12506, pp. 39–55, 2020.
https://doi.org/10.1007/978-3-030-62419-4_3

Furthermore, with the ever-increasing volume of the knowledge graphs, the number of emerging entities also increases. Many of these emerging entities have a small number of known facts at the time they are integrated into the knowledge graphs. Therefore, their connectivity to pre-existing entities in the knowledge graph is often too sparse (Fig. 1).

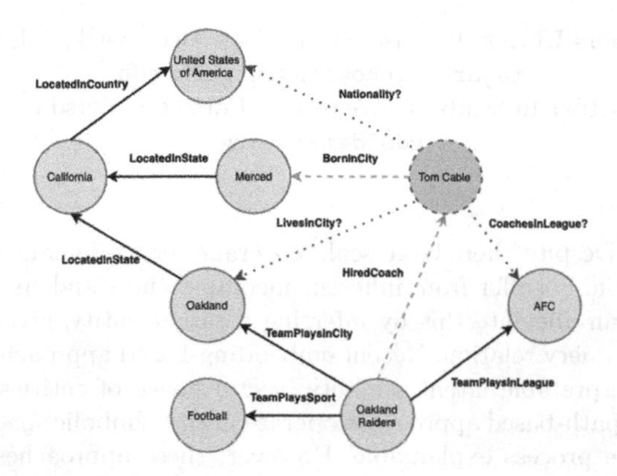

Fig. 1. A subgraph of NELL with *Tom Cable* as an emerging entity. The solid-lined circles and arrows represent the existing entities and relations. The dashed-lined circles and arrows denote an emerging entity and some of its known relationships to other existing entities. The unknown relationships that need to be inferred through inductive representation learning and explainable reasoning are shown as dotted arrows.

In recent years, embedding-based models [28] have widely been adopted to infer missing relationships in a knowledge graph. In such embedding-based models, distributed vector representations of entities and relations in the knowledge graph are used to learn a scoring function $f(e_s, r_q, e_o)$ in a latent embedding space to determine the plausibility of inferring a new fact. However, these models are lacking in terms of the interpretability and explainability of the decisions they make. One does not obtain any clear explanation of why a specific inference is warranted. For example, from the embeddings of facts *(A, born_in, California)* and *(California, located_in, US)*, the fact *(A, born_in, US)* could be deduced. But logical composition steps like this one are learned implicitly by knowledge graph embeddings. This means that this approach cannot offer such logical inference paths as support evidence for an answer.

In contrast, path-based reasoning approaches operate in the symbolic space of entities and relations, leveraging the symbolic compositionality of the knowledge graph relations, thus making the inference process explainable. This means that the user can inspect the inference path, consisting of existing edges in the knowledge graph, as support evidence. To this end, purely symbolic and fast rule-mining systems, e.g., PRA [22], AMIE+ [9], and AnyBURL [25] may attain a level of performance that is comparable to embedding-based methods, but neglect many of the statistical signals exploited by the latter. To leverage the advantages of both path-based and embedding-based models, some neural-symbolic approaches [10,11,13,16,26] have as well been proposed. Some recent path-based reasoning approaches [4,23] formulate the path-finding problem as a Partially Observable Markov Decision Process (POMDP), in which the model learns a policy to find an inference path from the source entity to the target entity using REINFORCE [41], a policy gradient based reinforcement learning algorithm.

However, most of these approaches are studied with static snapshots of the knowledge graphs, thus severely restricting their applicability for a dynamically evolving knowledge graph with many emerging entities. Except for the purely symbolic rule-mining systems mentioned above, most existing approaches that depend on learning latent representations of entities require that all entities are present during training. Therefore, these models are incapable of learning representations of arbitrary newly emerging entities not seen during training. Some recent approaches such as HyTE [5] and DyRep [34] have considered dynamically evolving temporal knowledge graphs. However, similar to embedding-based models, these models are not explainable.

To overcome this issue, we propose a joint framework for representation learning and reasoning in knowledge graphs that aims at achieving inductive node representation learning capabilities applicable to a dynamic knowledge graph with many emerging entities while preserving the unique advantage of the path-based approaches in terms of explainability. For inductive node representation learning, we propose a variant of *Graph Transformer* encoder [21,47] that aggregates neighborhood information based on its relevance to the query relation. Furthermore, we use policy gradient-based reinforcement learning (REINFORCE) to decode a reasoning path to the answer entity. We hypothesize that the inductively learned embeddings provide prior semantic knowledge about the underlying knowledge environment to the reinforcement learning agent.

We summarize the contributions of this paper as follows: (1) We introduce a joint framework for inductive representation learning and explainable reasoning that is capable of learning representations for unseen emerging entities during inference by leveraging only a small number of known connections to the other pre-existing entities in the knowledge graph. Our approach can not only infer new connections between an emerging entity and any other pre-existing entity in the knowledge graph, but also provides an explainable reasoning path as support evidence for the inference. (2) We introduce new train/development/test set splits of existing knowledge graph completion benchmark datasets that are appropriate for inductive representation learning and reasoning.

2 Related Work

2.1 Embedding-Based Methods

Knowledge graph completion can be viewed as an instance of the more general problem of link prediction in a graph [39]. Due to advances in representation learning, embedding-based methods have become the most popular approach.

Such methods learn d-dimensional distributed vector representations of entities and relations in a knowledge graph. To this end, the translation embedding model TransE [3] learns the embedding of a relation as a simple translation vector from the source entity to the target entity such that $\mathbf{e}_s + \mathbf{e}_r \approx \mathbf{e}_o$. Its variants, e.g., TransH [40], TransR [24], TransD [18] consider similar objectives. Tri-linear models such as DistMult [45], along with its counterpart ComplEx [35] in the complex embedding space, use a multiplicative scoring function $f(s, r, o) = \mathbf{e}_s^{\intercal}\mathbf{W}_r\mathbf{e}_o$, where $\mathbf{W}_r$ is a diagonal matrix representing the embedding of relation r. Convolutional neural network models such as ConvE [7] and ConvKB [27] apply convolutional kernels over entity and relation embeddings to capture the interactions among them across different dimensions. These models obtain state-of-the-art results on the benchmark KBC datasets. However, none of the above-mentioned approaches deliver the full reasoning paths that license specific multi-hop inferences, and hence they either do not support multi-hop inference or do not support it in an interpretable manner. Moreover, these approaches assume a static snapshot of the knowledge graph to train the models and are not straightforwardly extensible to inductive representation learning with previously unseen entities.

2.2 Path-Based Methods

An alternative stream of research has explored means of identifying specific paths of inference, which is the task we consider in this paper. To this end, the Path Ranking Algorithm (PRA) [22] uses random walks with restarts for multi-hop reasoning. Following PRA, other approaches [10,11,13,26] also leverage random walk based inference. However, the reasoning paths that these methods follow are gathered by random walks independently of the query relation.

Recent approaches have instead adopted policy gradient based reinforcement learning for a more focused exploration of reasoning paths. Policy gradient based models such as DeepPath [44], MINERVA [4], MINERVA with Reward Shaping and Action Dropout [23], and M-Walk [31] formulate the KG reasoning task as a Partially Observable Markov Decision Process and learn a policy conditioned on the query relation. Such reasoning techniques have also been invoked for explainable recommendation [8,42,43] and explainable dialogue systems [46]. Although the inference paths are explainable in these models (if reward shaping is omitted), there may be a substantial performance gap in comparison with embedding-based models.

Another sub-category of path-based methods, e.g., AMIE+ [9], AnyBURL [25], and RuleS [16] proceed by mining Horn rules from the the existing knowledge graphs for link prediction. The body of a Horn rule provides the reasoning path. Although these approaches are capable of fast rule mining and can easily be applied to unseen emerging entities, the quality of the learned rules are affected by the sparsity of the knowledge graph.

2.3 Graph Convolution-Based Methods

Graph Convolution Networks (GCNs) can be used for node classification in a homogeneous graph [20]. They are an instance of Message Passing Neural Networks (MPNN), in which the node representations are learned by aggregating information from the nodes' local neighborhood. GraphSAGE [15] attempts to reduce the memory footprint of GCN by random sampling of the neighborhood. Graph Attention Networks (GAT) [38] are a variant of GCN that learn node representations as weighted averages of the neighborhood information. However, GCN and its variants such as GAT and GraphSAGE are not directly applicable for link prediction in knowledge graphs, as they ignore the edge (relation) information for obtaining the node embeddings. To alleviate this issue, R-GCNs operate on relational multi-graphs [29], but, similar to GCNs, R-GCNs also need all nodes of the graphs to be present in memory and therefore are not scalable to large-scale knowledge graphs. Hamaguchi et al. [14] proposed a model for computing representations for out-of-KG entities using graph neural networks. The recent models such as SACN [30] and CompGCN [36] leverage the graph structure by inductively learning representations for edges (relations) and nodes (entities). However, unlike our model, these methods are not explainable.

3 Model

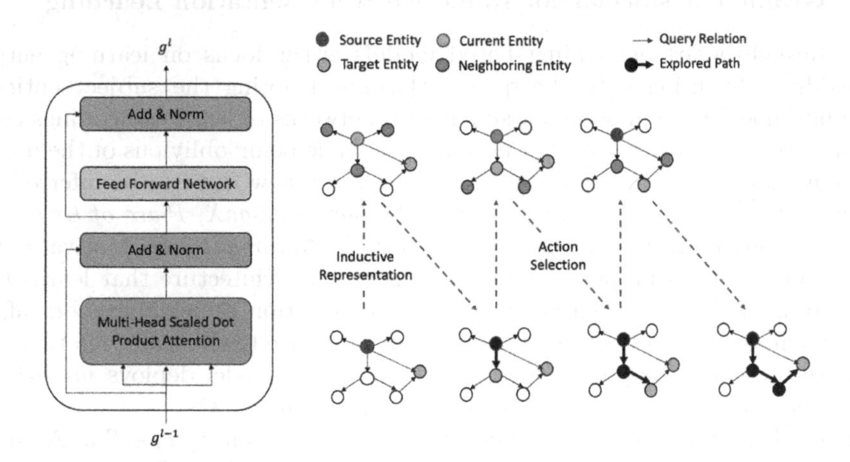

Fig. 2. A schematic diagram of a Graph Transformer block, along with an illustration of the workflow of our model, demonstrating successive applications of inductive node representation learning and action selection to find a reasoning path.

Our model consists of two modules that are subject to joint end-to-end training. The encoder module learns inductive entity embeddings while accounting for the query relation and the local neighborhood of an entity (Sect. 3.2). The decoder module operates on this learned embedding space of entities and relations. By leveraging the embeddings of the source entity and the query relation, the decoder module infers a reasoning path to the target entity using policy gradient-based reinforcement learning (Sect. 3.3). Before describing these components in more detail, Sect. 3.1 first provides preliminary definitions.

3.1 Problem Statement

Formally, we consider knowledge graphs $\mathcal{G}(\mathcal{E}, \mathcal{R}, \mathcal{F})$ defined as directed multigraphs such that each node $e \in \mathcal{E}$ represents an entity, each $r \in \mathcal{R}$ represents a unique relation, and each directed edge $(e_\mathrm{s}, r, e_\mathrm{o}) \in \mathcal{F}$ represents a fact about the subject entity e_s.

Given a structured relational query $(e_\mathrm{s}, r_\mathrm{q}, ?)$, where e_s is the source entity, r_q is the query relation, and $(e_\mathrm{s}, r_\mathrm{q}, e_\mathrm{o}) \notin \mathcal{F}$, the goal is to find a set of plausible answer entities $\{e_\mathrm{o}\}$ by navigating paths through the existing entities and relations in $\mathcal{G}$ leading to answer entities. Note that, unlike previous methods that consider transductive settings with a static snapshot of the knowledge graph, we allow for dynamic knowledge graphs, where e_s may be an emerging entity, and therefore, previously unseen. Moreover, while embedding-based methods only deliver candidate answer entities, we here also seek the actual paths, i.e., sequences of nodes and edges for better interpretability.[1]

3.2 Graph Transformer for Inductive Representation Learning

The state-of-the-art embedding based models either focus on learning entity embeddings by using only the query relations, ignoring the subject entity's neighborhood, or use message passing neural networks to learn embeddings conditioned on neighboring entities and relations while being oblivious of the query relation. However, we observe that in many cases a new fact can be inferred by using another existing fact. For example, the fact *(PersonX, Place of Birth, Y)* can often help to answer to the query *(PersonX, Nationality, ?)*. Motivated by this observation, we propose a Graph Transformer architecture that learns the embedding of the source entity by iterative aggregation of neighborhood information (messages) that are weighted by their relevance to the query relation. To learn the relevance weights, our Graph Transformer model deploys *multi-head scaled dot product attention*, also known as *self-attention* [37].

Formally, we denote the local neighborhood for each entity $e_i \in \mathcal{E}$ as $\mathcal{N}_i$ such that $\mathcal{N}_i = \{e_j \mid e_j \in \mathcal{E} \wedge (e_i, r, e_j) \in \mathcal{F} \wedge r \in \mathcal{R}_{ij}\}$, where $\mathcal{R}_{ij}$ is the set of relations between entities e_i and e_j.

Each neighboring entity $e_j \in \mathcal{N}_i$ connected to e_i by a relation r sends in a message to entity e_i. The message $\mathbf{m}_{ijr}$ is a linear transformation of the fact (e_i, r, e_j) followed by the application of a non-linear function, specifically, the

[1] From here onwards, we will use the terms *node* and *entity*, as well as *edge* and *relation(ship)* interchangeably.

leaky rectified linear unit (LeakyReLU) function with a negative slope of 0.01. Formally,

$$\mathbf{m}_{ijr} = \text{LeakyReLU}(\mathbf{W}_f[\mathbf{e_i}; \mathbf{r}; \mathbf{e_j}]), \tag{1}$$

where $\mathbf{W}_f \in \mathbb{R}^{d \times 3d}$ is a shared parameter for the linear transformation and [;] is the concatenation operator.

To compute an attention head, our model performs linear projections of the query relation r_q, the neighborhood relations $r \in \mathcal{R}_{ij}$, and the neighborhood messages $\mathbf{m}_{ijr}$ to construct queries Q, keys K, and values V, respectively, such that $Q = \mathbf{W}_Q\mathbf{r}_\text{q}$, $K = \mathbf{W}_K\mathbf{r}$, and $V = \mathbf{W}_V\mathbf{m}_{ijr}$, where $\mathbf{W}_Q, \mathbf{W}_K, \mathbf{W}_V \in \mathbb{R}^{d' \times d}$ are learnable parameters.

Next, we use the queries Q to perform a dot-product attention over the keys K. Formally,

$$\alpha_{ijr} = \frac{\exp((\mathbf{W}_Q\mathbf{r}_\text{q})^\intercal(\mathbf{W}_K\mathbf{r}))}{\sum\limits_{z \in \mathcal{N}_i}\sum\limits_{r' \in \mathcal{R}_{ij}} \exp((\mathbf{W}_Q\mathbf{r}_\text{q})^\intercal(\mathbf{W}_K\mathbf{r}'))} \tag{2}$$

We adopt the common procedure of scaling the dot products of Q and K by a factor of $\frac{1}{\sqrt{d'}}$ [37].

The attention weights are then used to aggregate the neighborhood messages. Note that *self-attention* deploys multiple attention heads, each having its own query, key, and value projectors. The aggregated messages from N attention heads are concatenated and added to the initial embedding $\mathbf{e_i}$ through a residual connection to obtain new intermediate representation

$$\hat{\mathbf{e}}_i = \mathbf{e_i} + \|_{n=1}^{N} \left(\sum_{j \in \mathcal{N}_i} \sum_{r \in \mathcal{R}_{ij}} \alpha_{ijr}^n \mathbf{W}_V^n \mathbf{m}_{ijr} \right), \tag{3}$$

where $\|$ is the concatenation operator.

Layer normalization (LN) [1] is applied to the intermediate representation $\hat{\mathbf{e}}_i$, followed by a fully connected two-layer feed forward network (FFN) with a non-linear activation (ReLU) in between. Finally, the output of the feed forward network is added to the intermediate representation through another residual connection. The resulting embedding is again layer normalized to obtain the new representation $\mathbf{g_i}^l$ for e_i. Formally,

$$\mathbf{g_i}^l = \text{LN}(\text{FFN}(\text{LN}(\hat{\mathbf{e}}_i)) + \text{LN}(\hat{\mathbf{e}}_i)) \tag{4}$$

This pipeline is called a *Transformer block.* Figure 2 represents a schematic diagram of a Transformer block in Graph Transformers. We stack L layers of Transformer blocks to obtain the final embedding $\mathbf{g_i}^L$ for e_i.

3.3 Policy Gradient for Explainable Reasoning

To infer the answer entity, we could leverage the entity representations obtained by the Graph Transformers. However, our goal is not only to infer the answer entity, but to find a symbolic reasoning path to support the inference. Following previous work [4,23], we formulate the reasoning task as a finite horizon, deterministic partially observable Markov Decision Process (POMDP). A knowledge graph can be seen as a partially observable environment with out-going relations at each entity node corresponding to a set of discrete actions that an agent can explore to reach the target answer from the source entity.

Knowledge Graph Environment. Formally, a Markov Decision Process is defined by a 4-tuple $(\mathcal{S}, \mathcal{A}, \mathcal{P}, \mathcal{R})$, where $\mathcal{S}$ is a finite set of states, $\mathcal{A}$ is a finite set of actions, $\mathcal{P}$ captures state transition probabilities, and $\mathcal{R}$ is the reward function. In a knowledge graph environment, the state space is defined as a set of tuples $s_t = (e_t, r_\mathrm{q}) \in \mathcal{S}$, where e_t is an entity node in the knowledge graph, and r_q is the query relation. The action space $A_t \in \mathcal{A}$ for a state s_t is defined as the set of outgoing edges from entity node e_t in the knowledge graph. Formally, $A_t = \{(r_{t+1}, s_{t+1}) \mid (e_t, r_{t+1}, s_{t+1}) \in \mathcal{G}\}$. Since state transitions in a KG environment are deterministic, the transition probabilities $P(s_{t+1} \mid s_t, a_t) = 1\ \forall P \in \mathcal{P}$. The agent receives a terminal reward of 1 if it arrives at the correct answer entity at the end.

Graph Search Policy. To find a plausible path to the answer entity, the model must have a policy to choose the most promising action at each state. Note that in the KG environment, the decision of choosing the next action is not only dependent on the current state, but also on the sequence of observations and actions taken so far in the path. We use a multi-layer LSTM as a sequence encoder to encode the path history.

Formally, each state s_t is represented by a vector $\mathbf{s}_t = [\mathbf{e}_t; \mathbf{r}_q] \in \mathbb{R}^{2d}$ and each possible action $a_t \in A_t$ is represented by $\mathbf{a}_t = [\mathbf{e}_{t+1}; \mathbf{r}_{t+1}] \in \mathbb{R}^{2d}$, where $\mathbf{e}_t$, $\mathbf{e}_{t+1} \in \mathbb{R}^d$ are the embeddings of the entity nodes at timesteps t and $t+1$, respectively, that are obtained from Graph Transformer encoders. $\mathbf{r}_{t+1} \in \mathbb{R}^d$ is the embedding of an out-going relation from entity e_t, and $\mathbf{r}_q \in \mathbb{R}^d$ corresponds to the embedding of the query relation r_q. Each of these embeddings is also obtained from the Graph Transformer encoder. The path history is encoded as $\mathbf{h}_t = \mathrm{LSTM}(\mathbf{h}_{t-1}, \mathbf{a}_{t-1})$. Given the embedded action space $\mathbf{A}_t \in \mathbb{R}^{2|A_t|}$, i.e., the stacked embeddings of actions $a_t \in A_t$, and the path history $\mathbf{h}_t$, we define the parameterized policy as:

$$\pi_\theta(a_t \mid s_t) = \mathrm{Softmax}(\mathbf{A}_t(\mathbf{W_2}\mathrm{ReLU}(\mathbf{W_1}[\mathbf{h}_t; \mathbf{e}_t; \mathbf{r}_q])))$$

Policy Optimization. The policy network is trained to maximize the expected reward for all $(e_\mathrm{s}, r_\mathrm{q}, e_\mathrm{o})$ triples in the training sub-graph. The agent learns an optimal policy π_θ by exploring a state space of all possible actions. The objective of the agent is to take actions to maximize the expected end reward. Formally:

$$J(\theta) = \mathbb{E}_{(e_\mathrm{s}, r_\mathrm{q}, e_\mathrm{o})}\left[\mathbb{E}_{a_1,\ldots,a_{T-1}\sim\pi_\theta}[R(s_T | e_\mathrm{s}, r_\mathrm{q})]\right] \quad (5)$$

Table 1. Evaluation datasets for inductive setting

Dataset	$\lvert\mathcal{E}\rvert$	$\lvert\mathcal{R}\rvert$	$\lvert\mathcal{U}\rvert$	$\lvert\mathcal{F}\rvert$			
				train	dev	test	aux
FB15k-237-Inductive	13,119	237	1,389	227,266	17,500	32,197	61,330
WN18RR-Inductive	35,928	11	4,029	67,564	3,000	11,015	19,395
NELL-995-Inductive	71,578	200	776	137,221	500	1,679	2,267

Since policy gradient uses gradient-based optimization techniques, the estimated gradient of the objective function can be derived as follows:

$$\nabla_\theta J(\theta) = \mathbb{E}_{a_{1:T}\sim\pi_\theta}[\nabla_\theta \log \pi_\theta(a_{1:T}|e_s, r_q) R(s_T|e_s, r_q)] \tag{6}$$

$$\approx \frac{1}{N}\sum_{n=1}^{N} \nabla_\theta \log \pi_\theta(a_{1:T}^n|e_s, r_q) R \tag{7}$$

Here, N is the number of policy rollouts.

Each policy rollout explores a sequence of actions $a_{1:T}$. At each timestep $t \in \{1 : T\}$, the agent selects an action a_t conditioned on the current state s_t. Therefore, the gradient of the log-likelihood in Eq. 6 can be expressed as

$$\nabla_\theta \log \pi_\theta(a_{1:T}|e_s, r_q) = \sum_{t=1}^{T} \nabla_\theta \log \pi_\theta(a_t|s_t, e_s, r_q) \tag{8}$$

Reward Shaping. Previous work [23] observed that a soft reward for the target entities is more beneficial than a binary reward. Following their work, we use pre-trained ConvE [7] embeddings for the observed entities and relations to shape the reward function. If the agent reaches the correct answer entity, it receives reward 1. Otherwise, the agent receives a reward estimated by the scoring function of the pre-trained ConvE. Note that the ConvE model is trained only on the training sub-graph of seen entities. ConvE plays no role during inference. Its only purpose is to provide *soft reward* signals during training to help the model in learning a better policy.

4 Evaluation

4.1 Datasets

We evaluate our model based on three standard benchmark knowledge graph completion datasets. (1) FB15k-237 [33], introduced as a replacement for the FB15k dataset [3]. In FB15k-237, the reverse relations are removed, rendering the dataset more challenging for inference. (2) WN18RR [7] is a subset of the WN18 benchmark dataset. Similar to FB15k-237, the reverse relations are removed for this dataset. (3) NELL-995 [44] is a subset of the 995-th iteration of NELL.

To test the effectiveness of our model for inductive representation learning and reasoning, we create new splits of training, development, and test sets for each of the three benchmark datasets mentioned above. This new split of the data is necessary, as in an inductive setting, the subject entities in the test set must not be present anywhere in the training subgraph. To satisfy this requirement, we first sample 10% of all the entities present in each of the benchmark datasets. We denote this as the set of *unseen entities* $\mathcal{U}$, while the remaining entities are denoted as *seen entities* $\mathcal{E}$. Then, we proceed to split the triples in the datasets into three disjoint sets. The first set contains the triples in which both the head and the tail entities are in $\mathcal{E}$. The second set consists of the triples with head entities belonging to $\mathcal{U}$, but tail entities in $\mathcal{E}$. In the third set, the head entities belong to $\mathcal{E}$, but the tail entities are in $\mathcal{U}$. We further split the first set into *train* and *dev* triples. The second set becomes the *test* triples, and the union of the second and the third set is denoted as *auxiliary* data. Auxiliary triples are required to obtain the local neighborhood of a source entity at inference time. Note that an emerging entity in the test set is not disconnected from the training graph. It has at least one seen entity in its neighborhood. This ensures that our model can find a path to the target entity during inference. If the emerging entity were completely disconnected from the training graph (i.e. all neighboring nodes were in $\mathcal{U}$), finding a path to the target entity would not be possible.

We append the suffix *"-Inductive"* to distinguish these newly derived datasets from their original counterparts. A summary of these datasets is presented in Table 1. To help with the reproducibility for future research on this topic, we make the datasets and our source code publicly available at: https://github.com/kingsaint/InductiveExplainableLinkPrediction

4.2 Baselines

Embedding Methods. We compare our model to a set of embedding based models that perform well under the transductive setting of link prediction. Although these models are particularly unsuitable for the inductive setting, we include them to better demonstrate the challenges of applying such algorithms in an inductive setting. In particular, we compare our model to ConvE [7], TransH [40], TransR [24], and RotatE [32]. For these experiments, we adapted the PyKEEN[2] implementations of these models.

Graph Convolution Methods. We choose a state-of-the-art graph convolution-based method CompGCN [36] as a baseline. Our choice is motivated by two factors: (1) CompGCN performs strongly in the transductive setting by outperforming the other baselines for most of the datasets, and (2) since its encoder module deploys neighborhood integration through Graph Convolution Networks, it has similar characteristics to our model, and therefore, is a good candidate for inductive representation learning. We also compare our model to R-GCN [29]

[2] https://github.com/pykeen/pykeen.

and SACN [30], which also leverage the graph structure to learn node representations by aggregating neighborhood information. For CompGCN and SACN, we adapted the source code made available by the authors to make them suitable for inductive representation learning and link prediction. For R-GCN, we adapted the source code available in the DGL library[3].

Symbolic Rule Mining. We compare our model with AnyBURL [25], a purely symbolic rule mining system. AnyBURL is capable of extremely fast rule mining, has outperformed other rule mining approaches including AMIE+ [9], and produces comparable results to existing embedding-based models.

Path-Based Model. Finally, we compare our model to a policy gradient-based multihop reasoning approach [23] that is similar to the decoder module of our model. We modified the source code[4] of this model to adapt it to our task.

4.3 Experimental Details

Training Protocol. Since the benchmark knowledge graph completion datasets contain only unidirectional edges (e_s, r_q, e_o), for all methods, we augment the training sub-graph with the reverse edges (e_o, r_q^{-1}, e_s). During the Graph Transformer based inductive representation learning, $n\%$ of local neighboring entities are randomly selected and masked. During training, we mask 50%, 50%, and 30% of neighboring nodes, respectively, for the FB15k-237, WN188RR, and NELL-995 datasets. Neighborhood masking helps in learning robust representations and reduces the memory footprint, and has been shown to be effective [15]. Following previous work [4,23], during training of the policy network, we also retain the top-k outgoing edges for each entity that are ranked by the PageRank scores of the neighboring entities. We set the value of k for each dataset following Lin et al. [23]. Such a cut-off threshold is necessary to prevent memory overflow. Finally, we adopt the false-negative masking technique in the final timestep of the policy rollouts to guide the agent to the correct answer entities as described in previous work [4,23], where it was found helpful when multiple answer entities are present in the training graph.

Hyperparameters. For a fair comparison to the baselines, we keep the dimensionality of the entity and relation embeddings at 200. For our model, we deploy one layer of a Transformer block ($L = 1$) and 4 attention heads ($N = 4$). We choose a minibatch size of 64 during training due to limited GPU memory. We rely on Adam [19] stochastic optimization with a fixed learning rate of 0.001 across all training epochs. Additionally, we adopt entropy regularization to improve the learning dynamics of the policy gradient method. The regularizer is weighted by a hyperparameter β set to a value within $[0, 0.1]$. We apply dropout to the entity and relation embeddings, the feedforward networks, and the residual connections. The policy rollout is done for $T = 3$ timesteps for every dataset.

[3] https://github.com/dmlc/dgl/tree/master/examples/pytorch/rgcn.
[4] https://github.com/salesforce/MultiHopKG.

Table 2. Evaluation results of our model as compared to alternative baselines on inductive variants of the WN18RR, FB15K-237, and NELL-995 datasets. The Hits@N and MRR metrics are multiplied by 100.

Model	WN18RR-Inductive				FB15K-237-Inductive				NELL-995-Inductive			
		Hits@N				Hits@N				Hits@N		
	MRR	@1	@3	@10	MRR	@1	@3	@10	MRR	@1	@3	@10
TransR [24]	0.8	0.6	0.7	0.9	5.0	4.0	5.2	6.6	5.3	4.9	5.3	6.5
TransH [40]	0.0	0.0	0.0	0.0	6.2	5.4	6.3	8.0	3.6	3.4	3.6	3.6
RotatE [32]	0.0	0.0	0.0	0.0	0.0	0.0	0.0	0.0	0.0	0.0	0.0	0.0
ConvE [7]	1.9	1.1	2.1	3.5	26.3	20.0	28.7	38.8	43.4	32.5	50.3	60.9
R-GCN [29]	14.7	11.4	15.1	20.7	19.1	11.5	20.9	34.3	58.4	50.9	62.9	71.6
SACN [30]	17.5	9.7	20.3	33.5	29.9	20.5	32.8	50.0	42.4	37.0	42.9	53.2
CompGCN [36]	2.2	0.0	2.2	5.2	26.1	19.2	28.5	39.2	42.8	33.1	47.9	61.0
AnyBURL [25]	–	**48.3**	50.9	53.9	–	28.3	43.0	56.5	–	8.7	11.0	12.3
MultiHopKG [23]	45.5	39.4	49.2	56.5	38.6	29.3	43.4	56.7	74.7	69.1	78.3	84.2
Our Model w/ RS	**48.8**	42.1	**52.2**	**60.6**	**39.8**	**30.7**	**44.5**	**57.6**	**75.2**	**69.7**	**79.1**	**84.4**

Evaluation Protocol. Following previous work [23], we adopt beam search decoding during inference with a beam width of 512 for NELL-995 and 256 for the other datasets. If more than one path leads to the same target entity, then the path with the maximum log-likelihood is chosen over the others. During evaluation, the auxiliary graph augments the training graph to construct the KG environment with unseen entities and their relations to the seen entities. For our model and the baselines, the embeddings of all unseen entities are initialized with Xavier normal initialization [12] at inference time.

Evaluation Metrics. We adopt the ranking based metrics *Mean Reciprocal Rank* and *Hits@k* that are also used by prior work for evaluation. We follow the *filtered setting* [3] adopted by prior approaches. In the filtered setting, the scores for the false negative answer entities are masked to facilitate correct ranking of the target entity.

4.4 Results

We present the experimental results of our method and the baselines in Table 2. The results of the embedding-based models TransH, TransR, and RotatE across all datasets demonstrates their inability to deal with entities that are unseen during training. These models are thus rendered as ineffective for inductive representation learning and reasoning. ConvE performs better than other embedding-based models we consider. Still, the much inferior performance of ConvE compared to our model shows that ConvE is not particularly suitable for inductive representation learning.

We observe that our model significantly outperforms the graph convolution network baselines CompGCN, SACN, and R-GCN across all datasets. Although these models use the neighborhood information for learning representations,

Table 3. Ablation study. The Hits@N and MRR metrics are multiplied by 100.

Model	WN18RR-Inductive				FB15K-237-Inductive				NELL-995-Inductive			
		Hits@N				Hits@N				Hits@N		
	MRR	@1	@3	@10	MRR	@1	@3	@10	MRR	@1	@3	@10
Our Model w/ RS	**48.8**	42.1	**52.2**	**60.6**	**39.8**	**30.7**	**44.5**	**57.6**	**75.2**	**69.7**	**79.1**	**84.4**
Our Model w/o RS	48.2	40.1	53.0	62.2	37.8	29.4	42.6	54.0	71.1	65.3	75.0	79.9
GT + ConvTransE	1.1	0.6	1.1	1.8	22.9	17.3	24.9	33.3	47.9	40.6	51.1	61.9

unlike our method, their neighborhood integration methods do not explicitly consider the query relations.

We find AnyBURL and MultiHopKG to be the most competitive methods to ours. AnyBURL performs adequately for the WN18RR and FB15K-237 dataset while performing poorly on the NELL-995 dataset. MultiHopKG adapts surprisingly well to our dataset despite the unseen entities being initialized with Xavier normal initialization. We conjecture that the learned representations of the query and the outgoing edges (relations) have enough semantic information encoded in them to navigate to the target entity by simply exploiting the edge (relation) information. However, our proposed model holds an edge over this model with 7.2%, 3.1%, and 0.7% gains in the MRR metric for the WN18RR, FB15K-237, and NELL-995 datasets respectively.

5 Analysis

In this section, we perform further analysis of our proposed model. First, we conduct a set of ablation studies (Table 3). Then, we qualitatively analyze our model's ability to provide reasoning paths as supporting evidence for inference. Finally, we analyze the effect of the cardinality of relation types on the inference process.

5.1 Ablation Study

To better understand the contribution of reward shaping in our model, we perform an ablation study, where our model is deprived of the *soft reward* signals provided by ConvE. In general, we observe that replacing reward shaping with hard binary reward deteriorates the performance of our model across all datasets. Note that our ablated version still mostly outperforms the other baseline methods.

Additionally, we experiment with a non-explainable variant of our model, in which we retain the Graph Transformer (GT) encoder, but we replace the policy gradient-based decoder with an embedding-based decoder called ConvTransE, which is also used in SACN as a decoder module. With this model, we observe a significant drop in performance. Thus, we conjecture that the policy gradient-based decoder not only provides explainability, but also is crucial for decoding.

Table 4. Example queries from the NELL-995 test set with unseen source entities. The answers are supported by the explainable reasoning paths derived by our model.

Query	(William Green, worksFor, ?)
Answer	Accenture
Explanation	William Green $\xrightarrow{\text{personLeadsOrganization}}$ Accenture
Query	(Florida State, organizationHiredPerson, ?)
Answer	Bobby Bowden
Explanation	Florida State $\xleftarrow{\text{worksFor}}$ Bobby Bowden
Query	(Messi, athleteHomeStadium, ?)
Answer	Camp Nou
Explanation	Messi $\xrightarrow{\text{athletePlaysForTeam}}$ Barcelona $\xrightarrow{\text{teamHomeStadium}}$ Camp Nou
Query	(Adrian Griffin, athleteHomeStadium, ?)
Answer	United Center
Explanation	Adrian Griffin $\xrightarrow{\text{athletePlaysForTeam}}$ Knicks $\xleftarrow{\text{athletePlaysForTeam}}$ Eddy Curry $\xrightarrow{\text{athleteHomeStadium}}$ United Center
Query	(Bucks, teamPlaysInLeague, ?)
Answer	NBA
Explanation	Bucks $\xrightarrow{\text{organizationHiredPerson}}$ Scott Stiles $\xleftarrow{\text{organizationHiredPerson}}$ Chicago Bulls $\xrightarrow{\text{teamPlaysInLeague}}$ NBA

Table 5. MRR for the test triples in inductive setting with *to-Many* and *to-1* relation types. The % columns show the percentage of test triples for each relation type.

Dataset	to-Many		to-1	
	%	MRR	%	MRR
FB15k-237-Inductive	77.4	31.6	22.6	75.5
WN18RR-Inductive	48.1	60.8	51.9	30.1
NELL-995-Inductive	7.6	41.4	92.4	78.5

5.2 Qualitative Analysis of Explainability

Since explainability is one of the key objectives of our model, we provide examples of explainable reasoning paths for queries that involve previously unseen source entities at inference time. Table 4 contains examples of 1-hop, 2-hop, and 3-hop reasoning paths. These examples demonstrate our model's effectiveness in learning inductive representations for the unseen entities, which helps to infer the reasoning paths.

5.3 Effect of Relation Types

Following Bordes et al. [3], we categorize the relations in the seen snapshot of the knowledge graph into Many-to-1 and 1-to-Many relations. The categorization is done based on the ratio of the cardinality of the target answer entities to the source entities. If the ratio is greater than 1.5, we categorize the relation as *to-Many*, otherwise as *to-1*. We analyzed the results of the test set for these two types of relations. We report the percentage of triples with these two types of relations and the corresponding MRR achieved by our model in Table 5. For FB15k-237 and NELL-995, our model performs better for *to-1* relations than for *to-many* relations. On the contrary, we observe a reverse trend for the WN18RR dataset. Note however that *to-many* relations have alternative target entities. In the current evaluation protocol, our model is punished for predicting any alternative target entity other than the ground truth target.

6 Conclusion

The ever-expanding number of entities in knowledge graphs warrants the exploration of knowledge graph completion methods that can be applied to emerging entities without retraining the model. While prior approaches assume a static snapshot of the knowledge graph, we introduce a joint framework for inductive representation learning to predict missing links in a dynamic knowledge graph with many emerging entities. Additionally, our method provides explainable reasoning paths for the inferred links as support evidence. Through experiments we demonstrate that our model significantly outperforms the baselines across the new inductive benchmark datasets introduced in this paper.

Acknowledgement. We thank Diffbot for their grant support to Rajarshi Bhowmik's work. We also thank Diffbot and Google for providing the computing infrastructure required for this project.

References

1. Ba, J., Kiros, J.R., Hinton, G.E.: Layer normalization. ArXiv, vol. 1607, p. 06450 (2016)
2. Bhowmik, R., de Melo, G.: Be concise and precise: synthesizing open-domain entity descriptions from facts. In: Proceedings of The Web Conference 2019, pp. 116–126. ACM, New York (2019)
3. Bordes, A., Usunier, N., García-Durán, A., Weston, J., Yakhnenko, O.: Translating embeddings for modeling multi-relational data. Adv. Neural Inform. Process. Syst. **26**, 2787–2795 (2013)
4. Das, R., et al.: Go for a walk and arrive at the answer: reasoning over paths in knowledge bases using reinforcement learning. arXiv 1711.05851 (2017)
5. Dasgupta, S.S., Ray, S.N., Talukdar, P.: HyTE: hyperplane-based temporally aware knowledge graph embedding. In: Proceedings of EMNLP 2018 (2018)
6. van Erp, M., et al. (eds.): ISWC 2016. LNCS, vol. 10579. Springer, Cham (2017). https://doi.org/10.1007/978-3-319-68723-0
7. Dettmers, T., Minervini, P., Stenetorp, P., Riedel, S.: Convolutional 2D knowledge graph embeddings. In: Proceedings of the Thirty-Second AAAI Conference on Artificial Intelligence (AAAI 2018), pp. 1811–1818. AAAI Press (2018)
8. Fu, Z., et al.: Fairness-aware explainable recommendation over knowledge graphs. In: Proceedings of the 43rd SIGIR 2020. ACM (2020)
9. Galárraga, L., Teflioudi, C., Hose, K., Suchanek, F.M.: Fast rule mining in ontological knowledge bases with AMIE++. VLDB J. **24**(6), 707–730 (2015)

10. Gardner, M., Talukdar, P.P., Kisiel, B., Mitchell, T.M.: Improving learning and inference in a large knowledge-base using latent syntactic cues. In: Proceedings of EMNLP 2013, pp. 833–838. ACL (2013)
11. Gardner, M., Talukdar, P.P., Krishnamurthy, J., Mitchell, T.M.: Incorporating vector space similarity in random walk inference over knowledge bases. In: Proceedings of EMNLP 2014, pp. 397–406. ACL (2014)
12. Glorot, X., Bengio, Y.: Understanding the difficulty of training deep feedforward neural networks. In: Proceedings of the Thirteenth International Conference on Artificial Intelligence and Statistics, Proceedings of Machine Learning Research, vol. 9, pp. 249–256. PMLR, 13–15 May 2010
13. Guu, K., Miller, J., Liang, P.: Traversing knowledge graphs in vector space. In: Proceedings of EMNLP 2015, pp. 318–327. ACL (2015)
14. Hamaguchi, T., Oiwa, H., Shimbo, M., Matsumoto, Y.: Knowledge transfer for out-of-knowledge-base entities: a graph neural network approach. In: Proceedings of IJCAI, pp. 1802–1808. AAAI Press (2017)
15. Hamilton, W.L., Ying, R., Leskovec, J.: Inductive representation learning on large graphs. In: Advances in Neural Information Processing (2017)
16. Ho, V.T., Stepanova, D., Gad-Elrab, M.H., Kharlamov, E., Weikum, G.: Rule learning from knowledge graphs guided by embedding models. In: Vrandečić, D., et al. (eds.) ISWC 2018. LNCS, vol. 11136, pp. 72–90. Springer, Cham (2018). https://doi.org/10.1007/978-3-030-00671-6_5
17. Hogan, A., et al.: Knowledge graphs. ArXiv, vol. 2003, p. 02320 (2020)
18. Ji, G., He, S., Xu, L., Liu, K., Zhao, J.: Knowledge graph embedding via dynamic mapping matrix. In: Proceedings of ACL-IJCNLP 2015, pp. 687–696. ACL (2015)
19. Kingma, D.P., Ba, J.: Adam: a method for stochastic optimization (2014). http://arxiv.org/abs/1412.6980
20. Kipf, T.N., Welling, M.: Semi-supervised classification with graph convolutional networks. In: International Conference on Learning Representations (ICLR) (2017)
21. Koncel-Kedziorski, R., Bekal, D., Luan, Y., Lapata, M., Hajishirzi, H.: Text generation from knowledge graphs with graph transformers. In: Proceedings of NAACL 2019, pp. 2284–2293. ACL, June 2019
22. Lao, N., Mitchell, T.M., Cohen, W.W.: Random walk inference and learning in a large scale knowledge base. In: Proceedings of EMNLP 2011, pp. 529–539. ACL (2011)
23. Lin, X.V., Socher, R., Xiong, C.: Multi-hop knowledge graph reasoning with reward shaping. arXiv abs/1808.10568 (2018). http://arxiv.org/abs/1808.10568
24. Lin, Y., Liu, Z., Sun, M., Liu, Y., Zhu, X.: Learning entity and relation embeddings for knowledge graph completion. In: AAAI Conference on Artificial Intelligence (2015)
25. Meilicke, C., Chekol, M.W., Ruffinelli, D., Stuckenschmidt, H.: An introduction to AnyBURL. In: Benzmüller, C., Stuckenschmidt, H. (eds.) KI 2019. LNCS (LNAI), vol. 11793, pp. 244–248. Springer, Cham (2019). https://doi.org/10.1007/978-3-030-30179-8_20
26. Neelakantan, A., Roth, B., McCallum, A.: Compositional vector space models for knowledge base completion. In: Proceedings of ACL 2015. ACL (2015)
27. Nguyen, D.Q., Nguyen, T.D., Nguyen, D.Q., Phung, D.: A novel embedding model for knowledge base completion based on convolutional neural network. In: Proceedings of NAACL, vol. 2018, pp. 327–333 (2018)
28. Nguyen, D.Q.: An overview of embedding models of entities and relationships for knowledge base completion. arXiv 1703.08098 (2017)

29. Schlichtkrull, M., Kipf, T.N., Bloem, P., van den Berg, R., Titov, I., Welling, M.: Modeling Relational Data with Graph Convolutional Networks. In: Gangemi, A., Navigli, R., Vidal, M.-E., Hitzler, P., Troncy, R., Hollink, L., Tordai, A., Alam, M. (eds.) ESWC 2018. LNCS, vol. 10843, pp. 593–607. Springer, Cham (2018). https://doi.org/10.1007/978-3-319-93417-4_38
30. Shang, C., Tang, Y., Huang, J., Bi, J., He, X., Zhou, B.: End-to-end structure-aware convolutional networks for knowledge base completion. In: Proceedings of AAAI (2019)
31. Shen, Y., Chen, J., Huang, P.S., Guo, Y., Gao, J.: M-Walk: Learning to walk over graphs using Monte Carlo tree search. In: Advances in Neural Information Processing Systems 31, pp. 6786–6797. Curran Associates, Inc. (2018)
32. Sun, Z., Deng, Z.H., Nie, J.Y., Tang, J.: RotatE: knowledge graph embedding by relational rotation in complex space. In: International Conference on Learning Representations (2019)
33. Toutanova, K., Lin, V., Yih, W., Poon, H., Quirk, C.: Compositional learning of embeddings for relation paths in knowledge base and text. In: Proceedings of ACL 2016. ACL (2016). http://aclweb.org/anthology/P/P16/P16-1136.pdf
34. Trivedi, R., Farajtabar, M., Biswal, P., Zha, H.: DyRep: learning representations over dynamic graphs. In: ICLR (2019)
35. Trouillon, T., Welbl, J., Riedel, S., Gaussier, É., Bouchard, G.: Complex embeddings for simple link prediction. In: Proceedings of the 33nd International Conference on Machine Learning. (ICML 2016), vol. 48, pp. 2071–2080 (2016)
36. Vashishth, S., Sanyal, S., Nitin, V., Talukdar, P.: Composition-based multi-relational graph convolutional networks. In: International Conference on Learning Representations (2020)
37. Vaswani, A., et al.: Attention is all you need. In: Advances in Neural Information Processing Systems 30, pp. 5998–6008. Curran Associates, Inc. (2017)
38. Veličković, P., Cucurull, G., Casanova, A., Romero, A., Liò, P., Bengio, Y.: Graph Attention Networks. In: International Conference on Learning Representations (2018)
39. Wang, L., et al.: Link prediction by exploiting network formation games in exchangeable graphs. In: Proceedings of IJCNN 2017, pp. 619–626 (2017). https://ieeexplore.ieee.org/document/7965910/
40. Wang, Z., Zhang, J., Feng, J., Chen, Z.: Knowledge graph embedding by translating on hyperplanes. In: Proceedings of AAAI 2014, pp. 1112–1119. AAAI Press (2014)
41. Williams, R.J.: Simple statistical gradient-following algorithms for connectionist reinforcement learning. Mach. Learn. **8**(3–4), 229–256 (1992)
42. Xian, Y., Fu, Z., Muthukrishnan, S., de Melo, G., Zhang, Y.: Reinforcement knowledge graph reasoning for explainable recommendation. In: Proceedings of SIGIR 2019, pp. 285–294. ACM, New York (2019)
43. Xian, Y., et al.: CAFE: coarse-to-fine knowledge graph reasoning for e-commerce recommendation. In: Proceedings of CIKM 2020. ACM (2020)
44. Xiong, W., Hoang, T., Wang, W.Y.: DeepPath: a reinforcement learning method for knowledge graph reasoning. In: Proceedings of EMNLP 2017. ACL (2017)
45. Yang, B., Yih, W., He, X., Gao, J., Deng, L.: Embedding entities and relations for learning and inference in knowledge bases. CoRR abs/1412.6575 (2014)
46. Yang, K., Xinyu, K., Wang, Y., Zhang, J., de Melo, G.: Reinforcement learning over knowledge graphs for explainable dialogue intent mining. IEEE Access **8**, 85348–85358 (2020). https://ieeexplore.ieee.org/document/9083954
47. Yun, S., Jeong, M., Kim, R., Kang, J., Kim, H.J.: Graph Transformer networks. Adv. Neural Inform. Process. Syst. **32**, 11983–11993 (2019)

Tentris – A Tensor-Based Triple Store

Alexander Bigerl[1](✉), Felix Conrads[1], Charlotte Behning[2], Mohamed Ahmed Sherif[1], Muhammad Saleem[3], and Axel-Cyrille Ngonga Ngomo[1]

[1] DICE Group, CS Department, Paderborn University, Paderborn, Germany
{alexander.bigerl,felix.conrads,mohamed.sherif}@uni-paderborn.de, axel.ngonga@upb.de

[2] Department of Medical Biometry, Informatics and Epidemiology, University Hospital Bonn, Bonn, Germany
behning@imbie.uni-bonn.de

[3] CS Department, University of Leipzig, Leipzig, Germany
saleem@informatik.uni-leipzig.de
https://dice-research.org/

Abstract. The number and size of RDF knowledge graphs grows continuously. Efficient storage solutions for these graphs are indispensable for their use in real applications. We present such a storage solution dubbed TENTRIS. Our solution represents RDF knowledge graphs as sparse order-3 tensors using a novel data structure, which we dub hypertrie. It then uses tensor algebra to carry out SPARQL queries by mapping SPARQL operations to Einstein summation. By being able to compute Einstein summations efficiently, TENTRIS outperforms the commercial and open-source RDF storage solutions evaluated in our experiments by at least 1.8 times with respect to the average number of queries it can serve per second on three datasets of up to 1 billion triples. Our code, evaluation setup, results, supplementary material and the datasets are provided at https://tentris.dice-research.org/iswc2020.

1 Introduction

A constantly increasing amount of data is published as knowledge graphs. Over 149 billion facts are published in the 2973 datasets of the Linked Open Data (LOD) Cloud [9], including large datasets such as UniProt[1] (55.3 billion facts) and LinkedTCGA [22] (20.4 billion facts). Even larger knowledge graphs are available in multinational organisations, including Google, Microsoft, Uber and LinkedIn [18]. Proposing scalable solutions for storing and querying such massive amount of data is of central importance for the further uptake of knowledge graphs. This has motivated the development of a large number of solutions for their storage and querying [4,8,10,12,15,19,24,27–29].

We present TENTRIS, a new in-memorytriple store for the efficient storage and querying of RDF data. Two innovations are at the core of our triple store. First, TENTRIS represents RDF data as sparse order-3 tensors using a novel in-memorytensor data structure dubbed *hypertrie*, which we also introduce in this paper. This data structure facilitates the representation of SPARQL queries as (sequences of) operations on tensors. A hypertrie combines multiple indexes into a single data structure, thus eliminating

[1] https://www.uniprot.org/downloads.

J. Z. Pan et al. (Eds.): ISWC 2020, LNCS 12506, pp. 56–73, 2020.
https://doi.org/10.1007/978-3-030-62419-4_4

some of the redundancies of solutions based on multiple indexes (see, e.g., [15]). As a result, TENTRIS can store whole knowledge graphs and corresponding indexes into a single unified data structure.

Our second innovation lies in the way we process SPARQL[2] queries: To query the RDF data stored in TENTRIS, SPARQL queries are mapped to Einstein Summations. As a result, query optimization is delegated to the implementation of an Einstein summation operator for hypertries. Since the proposed tensor data structure offers precise statistics, the order for tensor operations is computed online, thus further speeding up the query execution.

The rest of the paper is organized as follows: Sect. 2 gives an overview of related work. In Sect. 3 notations are defined and backgrounds on tensors are provided. In Sect. 4 the mapping of RDF graphs to tensors is defined and in Sect. 5 we introduce our new tensor data structure. In Sect. 6 the querying approach is described. The evaluation is presented in Sect. 7, and in Sect. 8 we conclude and look at future prospects. Examples for definitions and concepts are provided throughout the paper. For an extended, comprehensive example, see the supplementary material.

2 Related Work

Several commercial and open-source triple stores have been developed over recent years and used in a number of applications. In the following, we briefly introduce the most commonly used triple stores that are documented and freely available for benchmarking. We focus on these triple stores because they are candidates for comparison with our approach. We do not consider distributed solutions (see [1] for an overview), as a distributed version of TENTRIS will be the subject of future work. Throughout our presentation of these approaches, we sketch the type of indexes they use for storing and querying RDF, as this is one of the key differences across triple stores.[3]

RDF-3X [15] makes extensive use of indexes. This triple store builds indexes for all full collation orders SPO (Subject, Predicate, Object), SOP, OSP, OPS, PSO, POS, all aggregated indexes SP, PS, SO, OS, PO, OP and all one-value indexes S, P and O. It uses a B^+-tree as index data structure that is extended by LZ77 compression to reduce the memory footprint. Virtuoso [8] uses "2 full indexes over RDF quads plus 3 partial indexes" [8], i.e., PSOG (Predicate, Subject, Object, Graph), POGS, SP, OP and GS. Apache Jena TDB2 [10] uses three indexes to store the triples in the collation orders SPO, POS, and OSP. The indexes are loaded via memory mapped files. GraphDB [19] uses PSO and POS indexes to store RDF statements. BlazeGraph [24] uses B^+-trees as data structure for its indexes. Statements are stored in the collation orders SPO,

[2] At the moment TENTRIS supports the same fragment of SPARQL as [4,12,26,27] which includes basic graph patterns and projections with or without DISTINCT.

[3] Note that indexes for different collation orders are crucial for the performance of triple stores. They determine which join orders are possible and which triple patterns are cheap to resolve. However, building indexes comes at a cost: each index takes additional time to build and update. It also requires additional memory. Consequently, there is always a trade-off between querying speed on the one hand and memory consumption and maintenance cost on the other hand.

POS, and OSP. gStore [29] uses a signature-based approach to store RDF graphs and to answer SPARQL queries. An RDF graph is stored in an extended signature tree, called VS*-tree. Additionally, it generates materialized views to speed up star queries. In contrast to most other triple stores, gStore derives signatures from RDF terms instead of using unique IDs. gStore is a in-memory system, i.e., it holds all data in main memory.

Another in-memory triple store, RDFox [14], uses a triple table with three additional rows which store linked lists of triples with equal subjects, predicates and object respectively. The elements of the subjects and objects lists are grouped by predicates. Indices on the triple table are maintained for collation orders S, P, and O as arrays, and for collation orders SP, OP and SPO as hashtables.

The idea of using matrices or tensors to build triple stores has been described in a few publications. BitMat [4], like TENTRIS, uses an order-3 Boolean tensor as an abstract data structure for an RDF graph. The actual implementation stores the data in collation orders PSO and POS. The subindexes for SO and OS are stored using Boolean matrices. Join processing is done using a multi-way join approach. However, BitMat is unable to answer queries that use variables for predicates in triple patterns, i.e., `SELECT ?p WHERE {a ?p b.}`. A similar approach was chosen by the authors of TripleBit [28]. For each predicate, this approach stores an SO and OS index based on a custom column-compressed matrix implementation. This results in two full indexes—PSO and POS. In contrast to BitMat, TripleBit supports variables for predicates in triple patterns. A more generic approach is used for MagiQ [12]. The authors define a mapping of RDF and SPARQL to algebraic structures and operations that may be implemented with different linear algebra libraries as a backend. The RDF graph is encoded into a sparse matrix. A statement is represented by using predicates as values and interpreting the column and row number as subject and object IDs. Basic graph patterns are translated to general linear algebra operations. The approach does not support variables for predicates in triple patterns. A similar mapping was also chosen by the authors of TensorRDF [27] using Mathematica as a backend for executing matrix operations. All mentioned triple stores except gStore use unique IDs to represent each resource. They store the mapping in an index for query translation and result serialization. Further, all of them except gStore apply column-oriented storage.

Like most stores above, TENTRIS adopts the usage of unique IDs for resources and column-oriented storage. However, it does not use multiple independent indexes or materialized views. Instead, TENTRIS relies on the novel hypertrie tensor data structure that unifies multiple indexes into a single data structure. Like gStore and RDFox, it holds all data in-memory. In contrast to some of the other tensor-based solutions, TENTRIS can process queries which contain unbound predicates.

3 Background

3.1 Notation and Conventions

Let $\mathbb{B}$ be the set of Boolean values, i.e., $\{true, false\}$ and $\mathbb{N}$ be the set of the natural numbers including 0. We map *true* to 1 and *false* to 0. The natural numbers from 1 to n are shorthanded by $\mathbb{I}_n := \{i \in \mathbb{N} \mid 1 \leq i \leq n\}$. The set of functions $\{f \mid f : X \to Y\}$ is denoted Y^X or $[X \to Y]$. The domain of a function f is written as $\operatorname{dom}(f)$ and the target (also called codomain) is denoted by cod (f). A function which maps x_1 to y_1 and x_2 to y_2 is denoted by $[x_1 \rightarrow y_1, x_2 \rightarrow y_2]$. Sequences with a fixed order are delimited by angle brackets like $l = \langle a, b, c \rangle$. Their elements are accessible via subscript, e.g., $l_1 = a$. Bags are delimited by curly-pipe brackets, e.g., $\{\!|a, a, b|\!\}$. The number of times an element e is contained in any bag or sequence C is denoted by $count(e, C)$; for example, $count(a, \{\!|a, a, b|\!\}) = 2$. We denote the Cartesian product of S with itself i times with $S^i = \underbrace{S \times S \times \dots S}_{i}$.

3.2 Tensors and Tensor Operations

In this paper, we limit ourselves to tensors that can be represented as finite n-dimensional arrays.[4] An order-n tensor T is defined as a mapping from a finite multi-index $\mathbf{K} = \mathbf{K}_1 \times \cdots \times \mathbf{K}_n$ to some codomain V. We only use multi-indexes with $\mathbf{K}_1 = \cdots = \mathbf{K}_n \subset \mathbb{N}$. In addition, we consider exclusively tensors T with $\mathbb{B}$ or $\mathbb{N}$ as codomain. We call $\mathbf{k} \in \mathbf{K}$ a key with key parts $\langle \mathbf{k}_1, \dots, \mathbf{k}_n \rangle$. Values v in a tensor are accessed in array style, e.g., $T[\mathbf{k}] = v$.

Example 1. An example of an order-3 tensor $T \in [(\mathbb{I}_8)^3 \rightarrow \mathbb{B}]$ is given in Fig. 1. Only those entries given by the points in the figure are set to 1.

Slices. Slicing is an operation on a tensor T that returns a well-defined portion of T in the form of a lower-order tensor. Slicing is done by means of a slice key $\mathbf{s} \in \mathbf{S} := \mathbf{K}_1 \cup \{:\} \times \dots \times \mathbf{K}_n \cup \{:\}$ with: $\notin \mathbf{K}_1, \dots, \mathbf{K}_n$. When applying $\mathbf{s}$ to a tensor T (denoted $T[\mathbf{s}]$), the dimensions marked with : are kept. A slice key part $\mathbf{s}_i \neq :$ removes all entries with other key parts at position i and removes $\mathbf{K}_i$ from the result's domain. The sequence brackets may be omitted from the notation, e.g., $T[:, 2, :]$ for $T[\langle :, 2, : \rangle]$.

Example 2. Let T be the tensor from Example 1. The slice $T[\mathbf{s}]$ with the slice key $\mathbf{s} = \langle :, 2, : \rangle$ is an order-2 tensor with 1 at keys $\langle 1, 3 \rangle$, $\langle 1, 4 \rangle$, $\langle 3, 4 \rangle$, $\langle 3, 5 \rangle$, $\langle 4, 3 \rangle$ and $\langle 4, 5 \rangle$.

Definition 1. *Assume T, $\mathbf{K}$, V, n, $\mathbf{S}$ and $\mathbf{s}$ to be defined as above. Let P be the sequence of positions in $\mathbf{s}$ which are set to :. For $\mathbf{s} = \langle :, 2, : \rangle$, P would be $\langle 1, 3 \rangle$. A sub-multi-index is defined by $\mathbf{K}' := \times_{i \in P} \mathbf{K}_i$. Keys from the sub-multi-index are mapped to the original multi-index by $\varphi_{\mathbf{s}} : \mathbf{K}' \rightarrow \mathbf{K}$ with*

$$\varphi_{\mathbf{s}} : \mathbf{k}' \mapsto \mathbf{k} \text{ with } \mathbf{k}_i = \begin{cases} \mathbf{k}'_j & \text{if } i = P_j, \\ \mathbf{s}_i & \text{otherwise.} \end{cases}$$

A slice $T' = T[\mathbf{s}]$ can now be defined formally as follows: $T' \in V^{\mathbf{K}'} : \mathbf{k}' \mapsto T[\varphi_{\mathbf{s}}(\mathbf{k}')]$.

[4] Tensors can be defined in a more general manner than provided herein, see [2] for details.

Table 1. Example RDF Graph. Resources are printed alongside their integer IDs. The integer IDs are enclosed in brackets and are not part of the resource.

Subject	Predicate	Object
:e1 (1)	foaf:knows (2)	:e2 (3)
:e1 (1)	foaf:knows (2)	:e3 (4)
:e2 (3)	foaf:knows (2)	:e3 (4)
:e2 (3)	foaf:knows (2)	:e4 (5)
:e3 (4)	foaf:knows (2)	:e2 (3)
:e3 (4)	foaf:knows (2)	:e4 (5)
:e2 (3)	rdf:type (6)	dbr:Unicorn (7)
:e4 (5)	rdf:type (6)	dbr:Unicorn (7)

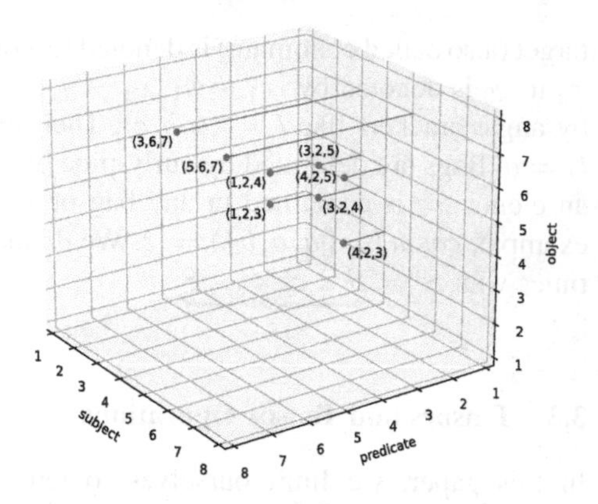

Fig. 1. 3D plot of the tensor that represents the RDF graph from Table 1. Every 1 is indicated by a point at the corresponding position. Points are orthogonally connected to the subject-object-plane for better readability.

Einstein Summation. We define Einstein summation in a manner akin to [13]. Einstein summation is a variable-input operation that makes the combination of multiple operations on vectors, matrices and tensors in a single expression possible [7,20]. Einstein summation is available in many modern tensor and machine learning frameworks [11,13,25,26]. It supports, amongst others, inner products, outer products, contractions and scalar multiplications. "The notation uses [subscript labels] to relate each [dimension] in the result to the [dimension] in the operands that are combined to produce its value." [13, p. 77:3]

Example 3. Consider the tensor T from Example 2 and slices $T^{(1)} := T[1,2,:]$, $T^{(2)}[:,2,:]$ and $T^{(3)} := T[:,6,7]$. An exemplary Einstein summation is given by $R_f \leftarrow T^{(1)}_f \times T^{(2)}_{f,u} \times T^{(3)}_u$. The result R is an order-1 tensor, which is calculated as $R[f \in \mathbb{I}_8] = \sum_{u \in \mathbb{I}_8} T^{(1)}[f] \cdot T^{(2)}[f,u] \cdot T^{(3)}[u]$, and results in $R = \langle \underset{1}{0}, \underset{2}{0}, \underset{3}{1}, \underset{4}{2}, \underset{5}{0}, \underset{6}{0}, \underset{7}{0}, \underset{8}{0} \rangle$.

We use Einstein notation expressions on the semiring $(\mathbb{N}, +, 0, \cdot, 1)$ to support bag semantics for SPARQL results. We also implement set semantics for `DISTINCT` queries using $(\mathbb{B}, \vee, 0, \wedge, 1)$ as semiring. All corresponding definitions are analogous to those presented in the paper for bag semantics and are hence not detailed any further.

4 RDF Graphs as Tensors

Our mapping of RDF graphs to order-3 tensors extends the model presented in [17] by adding a supplementary index, which serves to map undefined variables in SPARQL solution mappings. By adopting the same representation for RDF graphs and bags of solution mappings, we ensure that graphs and bags of mappings are compatible and can hence conjoint in tensor operations. Informally, the tensor $T(g)$ of an RDF graph g with α resources is hence an element of $[(\mathbb{I}_{\alpha+1})^3 \rightarrow \mathbb{B}]$ such that $T[i, j, k] = 1$ holds iff the i-th resource of g is connected to the k-th resource of g via the j-th resource (which must be a predicate) of the same graph. Otherwise, $T[i, j, k] = 0$.

Example 4. Consider the triples of the RDF graph g' shown in Table 1. Each RDF term of g' is printed alongside an integer identifier that is unique to each term. All entries shown in Fig. 1 are set to 1. All other entries are 0.

Formally, we define the tensor $T(g)$ for an RDF graph g:

Definition 2. *Let g be an RDF graph and $r(g)$ the set of RDF terms used in g. We define id as a fixed bijection that maps RDF terms $r(g)$ and ϵ, a placeholder for undefined variables in SPARQL solution mapping, to integer identifiers $\mathbb{I} := \mathbb{I}_{|r(g)|+1}$. The inverse of id is denoted id^{-1}. With respect to g and id, an RDF term $\langle s, p, o\rangle$ is represented by a key $\langle id(s), id(p), id(o)\rangle$. The tensor representation of g is given by $t(g) \in [\mathbb{I}^3 \rightarrow \mathbb{B}]$. The entries of $t(g)$ map a key $\mathbf{k}$ to 1 if the RDF statement corresponding to $\mathbf{k}$ is in g; otherwise $\mathbf{k}$ is mapped to 0:*

$$\forall \mathbf{k} \in \mathbb{I}^3 : t(g)[\mathbf{k}] := count\,(\langle id^{-1}(\mathbf{k}_1), id^{-1}(\mathbf{k}_2), id^{-1}(\mathbf{k}_3)\rangle, g).$$

The results of a SPARQL query on g is a bag of solution mappings Ω with variables U. Let $\langle u_1, \ldots, u_{|U|}\rangle$ be an arbitrary but fixed sorting of U. A solution mapping $[u_1 \rightarrow w_1, \ldots, u_{|U|} \rightarrow w_{|U|}]$ with $w_i \in r(g) \cup \{\epsilon\}$ is represented by a key $\langle id(w_1), \ldots, id(w_{|U|})\rangle$.[5] *The tensor representation of Ω is an order-$|U|$ tensor $t(\Omega)$ where each variable $u \in U$ is mapped to a separate dimension. $t(\Omega)$ maps a key $\mathbf{k}$ to the count of the represented solution mapping in Ω:*

$$\forall \mathbf{k} \in \mathbb{I}^{|U|} : t(\Omega)[\mathbf{k}] := count\,([u_1 \rightarrow id^{-1}(\mathbf{k}_1), \ldots, u_{|U|} \rightarrow id^{-1}(\mathbf{k}_{|U|})], \Omega).$$

5 Hypertries – A Data Structure for Tensors

Using tensors for RDF graphs requires a data structure that fulfills the following requirements: (R1) the data structure must be memory-efficient and (R2) must allow efficient slicing (R3) by any combination of dimensions (also see Sect. 6.1). Additionally, (R4) such a data structure must provide an efficient way to iterate the non-zero slices of any of its dimensions.

A trie [6] with a fixed depth is a straightforward sparse tensor representation that fulfills (R1) and (R2). A key consisting of consecutive key parts is stored by adding a path labeled with these key parts from the root node of the trie. Existing labeled edges are reused, introducing a moderate amount of compression (R1). Further, the trie sparsely encodes a Boolean-valued tensor by only storing those keys that map to 1 (R1). Descending by an edge, representing a key part k, is equal to slicing the tensor with the first key part fixed to k. The descending is efficient (R2) if a hashtable or a search tree is used to store the children of a node. However, to support efficient slicing by any other dimension except the first, a new trie with another collation order must be populated. The same holds true for iterating non-zero slices as required for joins (see (R4)).

[5] Technically, SPARQL semantics define solution mappings as partial functions f. Our formal model is equivalent and simply maps all variables for which f is not defined to ϵ.

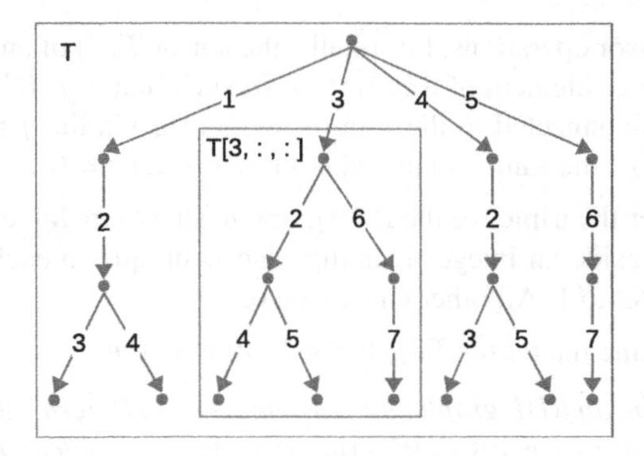

Fig. 2. Trie representation of a tensor **T** depicting the data from Table 1. A slice $\mathbf{T}[\mathbf{3}, :, :]$ by the first dimension with 3 is shown in the red box. (Color figure online)

Example 5. Figure 2 shows an order-3 Boolean tensor stored in a trie. Each leaf encodes a 1 value for the key that is encoded on the path towards it. The slice for the key $\langle 3, :, : \rangle$ is shown in the red box, resulting in an order-2 tensor.

These limitations are overcome by *hypertries*, a generalization of fixed-depth tries. A hypertrie permits the selection of a key part at an arbitrary position to get a (sub-) hypertrie that holds the concatenations of the corresponding key prefixes and suffixes. To achieve this goal, a node holds not only a set of edges for resolving the first key part, but also a set for every other dimension. This allows for slicing by any dimension as required by condition (R3) above. By storing each dimension's edges and children in a hashmap or search tree, iterating the slices by any dimension is accomplished implicitly. Hence, hypertries fulfill (R4).

Formally, we define a hypertrie as follows:

Definition 3. *Let $H(d, A, E)$ with $d \geq 0$ be the set of all hypertries with depth d, alphabet A and values E. If A and E are clear from the context, we use $H(d)$. We set $H(0) = E$ per definition. A hypertrie $h \in H(1)$ has an associated partial function $c_1^{(h)} : A \nrightarrow E$ that specifies outgoing edges by mapping edge labels to children. For $h' \in H(n), n > 1$, partial functions $c_i^{(h')} : A \nrightarrow H(d-1), i \in \mathbb{I}_n$ are defined. Function $c_i^{(h')}$ specifies the edges for resolving the part equivalent to depth i in a trie by mapping edge labels to children. For a hypertrie h, $z(h)$ is the size of the set or mapping it encodes.*

An example of a hypertrie is given in Fig. 3. A naive implementation of a hypertrie would require as much memory as tries in every collation order. However, we can take advantage of the fact that the slicing order relative to the original hypertrie does not matter when chaining slices. For example, consider a hypertrie h of depth 3. It holds that $h[3, :, :][:, 4] = h[:, :, 4][3, :]$. Consequently, such equivalent slices should be stored only once and linked otherwise. By applying this technique, the storage bound is reduced from $\mathcal{O}(d! \cdot d \cdot z(h))$ for tries in any collation order to $\mathcal{O}(2^{d-1} \cdot d \cdot z(h))$ for a hypertrie (for proof see supplementary material). Given that d is fixed to 3 for RDF graphs, this

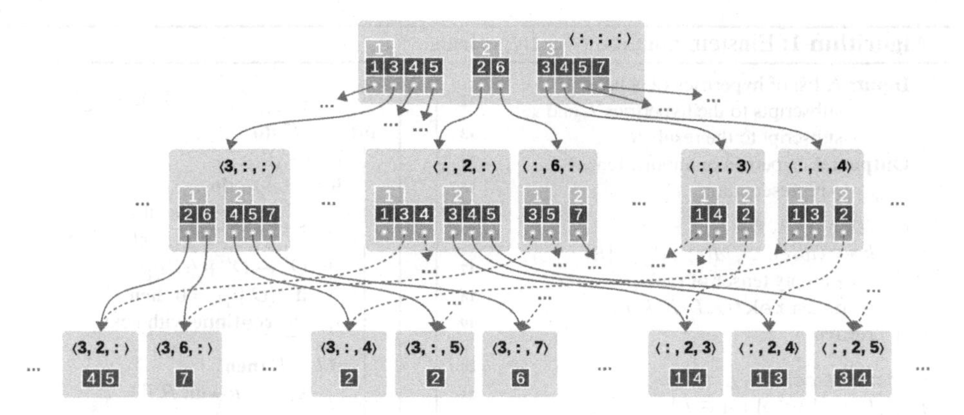

Fig. 3. A hypertrie storing the IDs from Table 1. Most nodes are left out for better readability. Each node represents a non-empty slice of the parent node. The slice key relative to the root node is printed in the node. The orange numbers indicate slice key positions, the mapping below them link all non-empty slices by that position to the nodes encoding the slice result.

results in a data structure that takes at most 4 times more memory than storing the triples in a list. Note that storing all tries for all six collation orders (see, e.g., [15]) requires 6 times as much memory as storing the triples in a list.

6 Querying

6.1 From SPARQL to Tensor Algebra

Triple Pattern. Let g be an RDF graph with the tensor representation T and index function id as defined in Definition 2. Let Q be a triple pattern with variables U and let $Q(g)$ be the bag of solutions that results from applying Q to g. The slice key $\mathbf{k}^{(Q)}$ which serves to execute Q on T is given by

$$\mathbf{k}_i^{(Q)} := \begin{cases} : & \text{if } Q_i \in U, \\ id(Q_i), & \text{otherwise.} \end{cases}$$

If $\mathbf{k}^{(Q)}$ is defined,[6] it holds true that $T[\mathbf{k}^{(Q)}] \in [\mathbb{I}^{|U|} \to \mathbb{B}]$ is a tensor representation for the set of solution mappings $Q(g)$. Otherwise, the set is empty and thus represented by the empty tensor which has all values set to 0.

Basic Graph Pattern. Consider a BGP $B = \{B^{(1)}, \dots, B^{(r)}\}$ and its set of used variables U. Let g and T be defined as above. A tensor representation of applying B to g, i.e., $B(g)$, is given by T' with $T'_{\langle l \in U \rangle} \leftarrow \times_{i \in \mathbb{I}_r} T[\mathbf{k}^{B^{(i)}}]_{\langle l \in B^{(i)} | l \in U \rangle}$.

[6] It may not be defined if t contains any resource that is not in dom (id).

Algorithm 1: Einstein notation over hypertries

Input: A list of hypertries O, a list of subscripts to the hypertries L and a subscript to the result R
Output: A hypertrie or another tensor representation

1 `einsum`(O, L, R)
2 $k \leftarrow \langle id(\epsilon), \dots, id(\epsilon)\rangle, |k| = |R|$
3 $r \leftarrow$ empty tensor of rank $|R|$
4 `einsum_rek`(O, L, R, k, r)
5 **return** r

6 `einsum_rek`(O, L, R, k, r)
7 $U \leftarrow \{\lambda \in \Lambda \mid \Lambda \in L\}$
8 **if** $U \neq \emptyset$ **then**
9 $l \leftarrow$ any label from U
10 $L' \leftarrow \langle \Lambda \setminus l \mid \Lambda \in L\rangle$
11 $\mathcal{P} \leftarrow \langle \{i \mid \Lambda[i] = l\} \mid \Lambda \in L\rangle$
12 $K \leftarrow \bigcap_{j \in \mathbb{I}_{|O|}} \bigcap_{i \in \mathcal{P}[i]} \mathrm{dom}\left(c_i^{O[j]}\right)$
13 **for** $\kappa \in K$ **do**
14 $O' \leftarrow \langle\rangle$
15 **for** $i \in \mathbb{I}_{|O|}$ **do**
16 $s \leftarrow s[i] := \begin{cases} \kappa, & \text{if } i \in \mathcal{P}[i] \\ :, & \text{otherwise} \end{cases}$
17 $O' \leftarrow O' + \langle O[i][s]\rangle$
18 **if** $z(O'[i]) = 0$ **then**
19 **continue** with next κ
20 **if** $l \in R$ **then**
21 $k[i] \leftarrow \kappa$ with $R[i] = l$
22 `einsum_rek`(O', L', R, k, r)
23 **else**
24 $r[k] {+}{\leftarrow} \prod_{o \in O} o$

Projection. Let B, r, U, g, and T be as above; consider $U' \subseteq U$. The projection $\Pi_{U'}(B(g))$ is represented by the tensor $T''_{\langle l \in U' \rangle} \leftarrow \times_{i \in \mathbb{I}_r} T[\mathbf{k}^{B^{(i)}}]_{\langle l \in B^{(i)} | l \in U \rangle}$.

With this mapping, we can now implement the key operations of the SPARQL algebra using hypertries.

6.2 Tensor Operations on Hypertries

Hypertries support both slices and Einstein summation efficiently. The efficient evaluation of slices was described in Sect. 5. An algorithm to evaluate Einstein summation based on a worst-case optimal multi-join algorithm by [16] is given by Algorithm 1 and discussed in this section. The algorithm is structured in two functions, a recursion starter and a recursion. The *recursion starter* (ll. 1–5) takes a list O of hypertrie operands, a list L of subscripts for the operands and a subscript R for the result as input and returns the resulting tensor r. A subscript is represented by a sequence of labels. The recursion starter prepares the key k and the result tensor r, calculates the result by calling the recursion `einsum_rek` and returns the result.

The recursion (ll. 6–24) additionally takes k and r as parameters. It first selects a label l that is used in L (ll. 7+9). If there is such a label (l. 8), a new operand's subscript L' is calculated by removing l from L (l. 10). It is to be used in the next recursion level. Next, the intersection K (l. 12) of edge labels by all those dimensions of the hypertries O (l. 11) that are subscripted by l is calculated. Note that operand subscripts with repeating labels, e.g., $\langle ?x, ?x\rangle$ for a TP `?x :pred ?x`, are implicitly covered by the construction of $\mathcal{P}$ which stores for each operand all positions that are subscripted with l. For each $\kappa \in K$ (l. 13) the l-subscripted dimensions of operands in O are resolved by κ and the new operands stored to O' (ll. 14–17). If any of the new operands is empty, the current κ is skipped (ll. 18–19). Operands that are not subscripted by l are just copied. If R contains l, k is set to κ at the corresponding position (ll. 20–21).

A recursive call is issued with the modified operands O' and operands' subscript L' (l. 22). If there is no label left in L, the break condition is reached (ll. 23–24). At this point the operands are scalars. The product of the operands is calculated and added to the entry at k in the result tensor r (l. 24).

6.3 Processing Order

The Einstein summation encapsulates all joins into a single operation. Thus, join ordering is not required. Nonetheless, the order in which labels are selected in line 9 of Algorithm 1 is crucial for the actual processing time. Clearly, the worst-case search space for the result is a subset to the Cartesian product of all operands' non-zero entries' keys. Evaluating a label that occurs more than once at operands reduces the search space if the size of the cut K in line 12 of Algorithm 1 is smaller than its inputs. Assuming equal distribution in the subhypertries, an upper bound to the reduction factor by a label is given by the ratio of the size of K to the maximum number of children of dimensions subscripted with the label. Given a sequence of operands O and their sequences of labels L, we define the reduction factor for a label l, an operand $o \in O$ and its labels $\Lambda \in L$ by

$$\psi_{o,\Lambda}(l) = \begin{cases} \frac{\mathrm{m}^{-}_{O,L}(l)}{\mathrm{m}^{+}_{o,\Lambda}(l)} & \text{if } l \in \Lambda, \\ 1 & \text{otherwise.} \end{cases}$$

where, $\mathrm{m}^{-}_{O,L}(l) = \min\left(|\operatorname{dom}(c^{O[i]}_j)| \;\middle|\; L[i][j] = l\right)$ is the minimal cardinality of dimensions of any operand subscripted with l and $\mathrm{m}^{+}_{o,\Lambda}(l) = \max\left(|\operatorname{dom}(c^o_j)| \;\middle|\; \Lambda[j] = l\right)$ is the maximum cardinality of dimensions of o subscripted with l. Thus, the full guaranteed reduction factor for l is given by $\Psi_{O,L}(l) = \prod_i \psi_{O[i],L[i]}(l)$. To reflect the observation that in practice K is mostly smaller than $\mathrm{m}^{-}_{O,L}(l)$, we additionally divide $\Psi_{O,L}(l)$ by the number of sets of different sizes used in the cut. We hereby assume two such sets to be equal if they have the same size. As $\Psi_{O,L}(l)$ can be computed efficiently, it is calculated in each recursive call for all label candidates l. The label with the smallest factor is chosen.

7 Evaluation

7.1 Experimental Setup

All experiments[7] were executed on a server machine with an AMD EPYC 7742, 1 TB RAM and two 3 TB NVMe SSDs in RAID 0 running Debian 10 and OpenJDK 11.0.6. Each experiment was executed using the benchmark execution framework IGUANA v3.0.0-alpha2 [5], which we chose because it is open-source and thus ensures that our experiments can be repeated easily.

Benchmarks. We chose WatDiv [3] to generate a synthetic benchmark, and FEASIBLE [23] – a benchmark generation framework which uses query logs – to generate

[7] The full setup is available as Ansible playbook at https://github.com/dice-group/tentris-paper-benchmarks/releases/tag/v1.0.

a benchmark on real-world data. We used datasets of varied sizes and structures (see Table 2) by choosing the 1 billion-triple dataset from WatDiv as well as the real datasets English DBpedia 2015-10[8] (681 M triples) and Semantic Web Dog Food SWDF (372K triples). We used all query templates for WatDiv.[9] The benchmark queries for DBpedia and SWDF were generated by using FEASIBLE on real-world query logs contained in LSQ [21]. FEASIBLE was configured to generate `SELECT` queries with BGPs and optional `DISTINCT`. Queries with more than 2^{20} results were excluded from all benchmarks to ensure a fair comparison.[10] Statistics on the queries[11] used are given in Table 3.

Table 2. Numbers of distinct triples (T), subjects (S), predicates (P) and objects (O) of each dataset. Additionally, Type classifies the datasets as real-world or synthetic.

Dataset	#T	#S	#P	#O	Type
SWDF	372 k	32 k	185	96 k	Real-world
DBpedia	681 M	40 M	63 k	178 M	Real-world
WatDiv	1 G	52 M	186	92 M	Synthetic

Table 3. Statistics on the queries used for each dataset. #Q stands for the number of queries used in our evaluation. The average and the min-max range in brackets are given for the number of triple patterns (#TP), the number of results (#R), and the average join-vertex degree (avg JVD). The absolute and relative frequencies (in brackets) are given for the number of distinct queries (#D) and for the number of queries with large results (>5000 results).

Dataset	#Q	#TP	#R	#D	avg JVD	>5000 results
SWDF	203	1.74 (1–9)	5.5 k (1–304 k)	124 (61%)	0.75 (0–4)	18 (8.9%)
DBpedia	557	1.84 (1–14)	13.2 k (0–843 k)	222 (40%)	1.19 (0–4)	73 (13.1%)
WatDiv	45	6.51 (2–10)	3.7 k (0–34 k)	2 (4%)	2.61 (2–9)	9 (20.0%)

Triple Stores. We chose triple stores that were openly available and supported at least `SELECT` queries with or without `DISTINCT` and BGPs. All triple stores were required to be able to load the three benchmarking datasets. Triple stores which were not able to load all experimental datasets had to be excluded from our experiments. The following triple stores were used in our evaluation: a) TENTRIS 1.0.4, b) Virtuoso Open-Source Edition 7.2.5.1, c) Fuseki (Jena TDB) 3.14.0, d) Blazegraph v2.1.4, e) GraphDB Free v9.1.1, f) TripleBit [28],[12] which uses matrices to store triples similar to TENTRIS's

[8] We used this version because of query logs being available for FEASIBLE.

[9] For each template one query was generated. Additionally, queries not projecting all variables were included with and without `DISTINCT`.

[10] Virtuoso has a limit of 2^{20} results for queries answered via HTTP (see issue https://github.com/openlink/virtuoso-opensource/issues/700).

[11] All queries can be found in the supplementary material.

[12] We extended TripleBit to support entering SPARQL queries via command-line interface directly. This modification was necessary to use TripleBit with IGUANA. Code available at: https://github.com/dice-group/TripleBit/releases/tag/2020-03-03.

tensor, g) RDF-3X 0.3.8 [15], which uses many indices similar to the hypertrie used by TENTRIS, and e) gStore commit 3b4fe58-mod[13] which stores all data in-memory like TENTRIS. All triple stores were allocated the same amount of RAM.

Benchmark Execution. We used two evaluation setups to cater for the lack of HTTP endpoints in TripleBit and RDF-3X. In the first setup, we executed a HTTP-based benchmark. Here, five stress tests with 1, 4, 8, 16 and 32 users were executed using the HTTP SPARQL endpoints of the triple stores TENTRIS, Virtuoso, Fuseki, Blazegraph, and gStore. For GraphDB we executed only the stress tests with one user because it does not support more than two parallel users in the free version. The second setup covered triple stores with a command-line interface (CLI). This benchmark simulated a single user because CLI does not support multiple concurrent users. The second setup was executed against TENTRIS, RDF3X and TripleBit. Like in previous works [5,22], we set the runtime of all benchmarks to 60 min with a 3-min. timeout. The performance of each triple store was measured using Queries per Second (QpS) for each client. In addition, we assessed the overall performance of each triple store by using an average penalized QpS (avg pQpS) per client: If a triple store failed to answer a query before the timeout or returned an error, then said query was assigned a runtime of 3 min.

7.2 Evaluation of Join Implementation

The performance of TENTRIS depends partially on the approach used to process joins. In our first series of experiments, we hence compared our default join implementation (see Sect. 6.3) with two other possible join implementations: 2-way joins (T2j) and a random label selection strategy (Tr). We used the HTTP-based benchmarks with one user. The results of this series of experiments is shown in Fig. 7. Our join implementation based on multi-way joins and label ordering strategy contributes substantially to the performance of TENTRIS. Our default TENTRIS is the fastest w.r.t. avg pQpS and median QpS on all datasets. T2j and Tr time out on several queries through the benchmarks and answer several queries from each benchmark more than an order of magnitude slower than the default TENTRIS. Hence, we use the default implementation of TENTRIS throughout the rest of the experiments.

7.3 Comparison with Other Approaches

Figure 4 shows the results of our HTTP evaluation on SWDF, DBpedia and WatDiv. For each number of clients tested in the HTTP evaluation, two vertically aligned plots are given: the first shows a boxplot of QpS and the mean QpS for single queries as points, while the second reflects the avg pQpS. Please note the log-scale of the boxplots. For a better comparison between the number of clients tested, Fig. 5 shows a plot for each dataset with the avg pQpS depending on the number of clients. Analogous

[13] As IGUANA requires SPARQL Protocol conformance, we fixed the HTTP request handling of gStore, i.e., parsing requests, naming of parameters, and response content-type. With respect to benchmark execution, we set the timeout to 3 min, and the thread limit to 32 and raised the total memory limit to 800 GB. Code available at: https://github.com/dice-group/gStore-1/releases/tag/3b4fe58-mod.

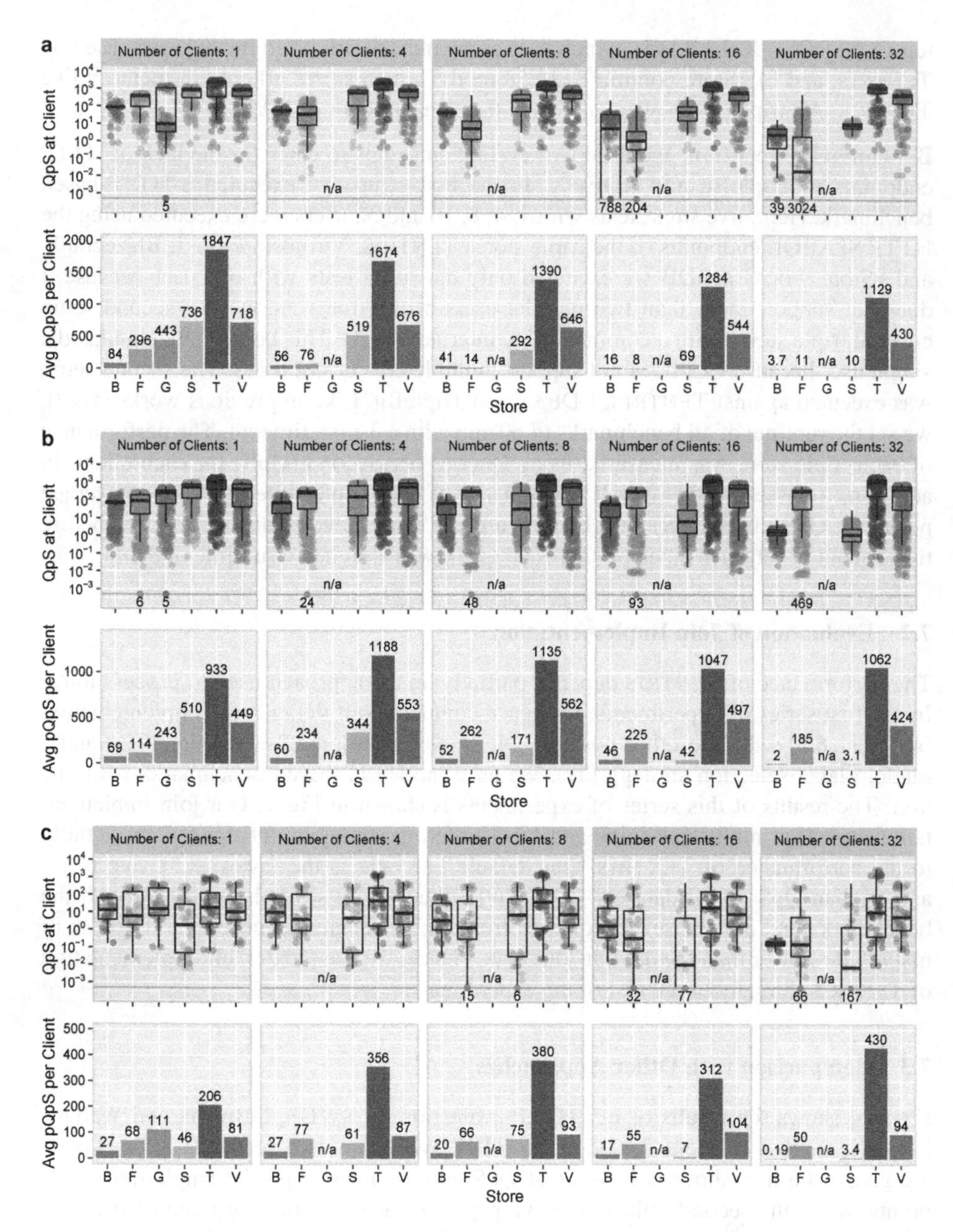

Fig. 4. Benchmark results on SWDF (a), DBpedia (b) and WatDiv (c) using HTTP with triple stores Blazegraph (B), Fuseki (F), GraphDB (G), gStore (S), TENTRIS (T) and Virtuoso (V): For each dataset, the first row shows boxplots for evaluations with 1, 4, 8, 16 and 32 clients respectively. Each point represents QpS for each single query, or mean QpS for a single query type for more than one client. For better readability we log-scaled the first line of the graphics. If queries with 0 QpS were present, those values were converted to $5 \cdot 10^{-4}$ QpS and the number of occurrences are shown as values on the bottom line. The second row shows avg pQpS per client.

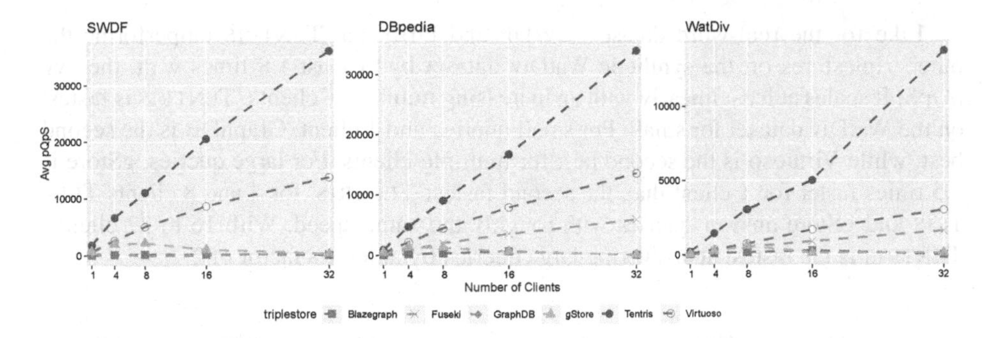

Fig. 5. The plots show for SWDF, DBpedia and WatDiv the avg pQpS for each triple store with increasing number of clients.

to Fig. 4, Fig. 6 provides the results of the CLI evaluation. Figure 7 shows the results of the comparison of different TENTRIS versions. For a comparison of the time and space requirements for loading the datasets into the triple stores see the supplementary material.

HTTP Results. Overall, TENTRIS outperforms all other triple stores for all datasets clearly with respect to avg pQpS. For a single client, our approach achieves a 1.83 to 2.51 times higher avg pQpS than the second best triple store, i.e., gStore or GraphDB. The avg pQpS of our approach is even 7.62 to 21.98 times higher than that of the slowest framework. With multiple users, TENTRIS scales almost linearly with the number of clients (see Fig. 5). TENTRIS is the only triple store in our evaluation that completed each query of all benchmarks at least once. Virtuoso succeeded on nearly all queries, with only a single failed query in the DBpedia benchmark with 32 users. The other triple stores failed on several queries across benchmark configurations.

As shown in Fig. 4a, TENTRIS is the fastest triple store for SWDF. It achieves avg pQpS that are at least 2 times higher than the second best and the median of its QpS lies above all values of all other stores. TENTRIS scales up the best to 32 users. The QpS per client drops from 1 to 32 clients by just 39%. Only Virtuoso shows a similar behavior, with a drop of 41%. The other triple stores are orders of magnitude slower when queried with multiple clients. Looking further into detail, TENTRIS outperforms the other stores for small queries which produce less then 5000 results (see Table 3) and Virtuoso is second best. For the 9% large queries with more than 5000 results, Blazegraph and gStore are about 1.5 times faster than TENTRIS for 1 client, but do not not scale with the number of clients; such that TENTRIS is 10 times faster than Blazegraph and 3 times faster than gStore for 32 clients.

For the DBpedia dataset, TENTRIS is the fastest store w.r.t. the avg pQpS and the median QpS. The result plots in Fig. 4b show that TENTRIS is almost two times faster than the second best triple store with respect to avg pQpS. It scales at least linearly with an increasing number of clients. When dividing the queries by small and large results, TENTRIS is always the fastest for DBpedia on small queries and only outperformed by gStore on large queries with 1–8 clients. Again, TENTRIS scales better and is fastest for 16–32 clients.

Like for the real-word datasets SWDF and DBpedia, TENTRIS outperforms the other triplestores on the synthetic WatDiv dataset by at least 1.8 times w.r.t. the avg pQpS. It scales at least linearly with an increasing number of clients. TENTRIS is fastest on the WatDiv dataset for small. For small queries and 1 client, GraphDB is the second best, while Virtuoso is the second best for multiple clients. For large queries, gStore is 1.5 times faster for 1 client than the second fastest TENTRIS, for 4 and 8 clients TENTRIS and gStore answer queries with roughly the same speed. With 16 to 32 clients, TENTRIS is the fastest at answering large queries by at least a factor of 2.

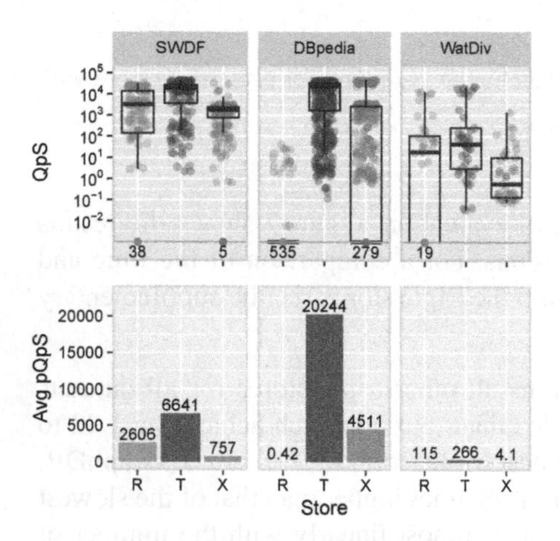

Fig. 6. Benchmarks on SWDF, DBpedia and WatDiv using a CLI with triple stores TripleBit (R), TENTRIS (T) and RDF-3X (X). A description of the layout is given in Fig. 4.

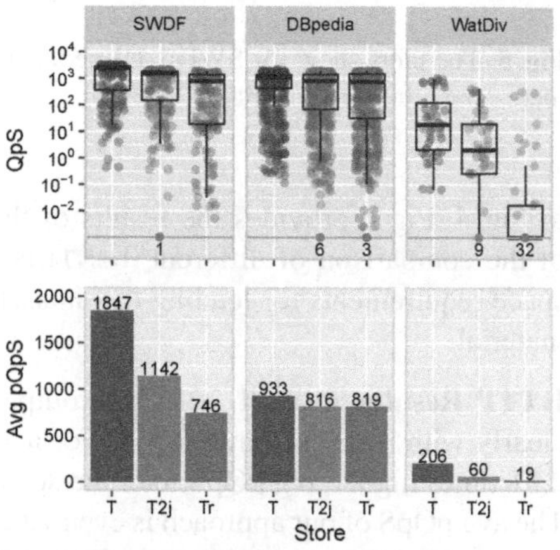

Fig. 7. Benchmarks on SWDF, DBpedia and WatDiv using different configurations of TENTRIS, i.e., the default configuration (T), using two-way joins (T2j) and using a random label order for the Einstein summation (Tr). A description of the layout is given at Fig. 4

CLI Results. The results of the CLI evaluation plotted in Fig. 6 show that TENTRIS clearly outperforms TripleBit and RDF-3X on all datasets. TripleBit and RDF-3X fail on 38 resp. 5 out of 203 queries for SWDF and 535 resp. 279 out of 557 queries for DBpedia. For the SWDF dataset, TENTRIS is at least 2.5 times faster with respect to pQpS. For DBpedia, the margin is even higher with 4.4-48,200 times higher pQpS. The scatterplot shows that TENTRIS answers more than 75% of the queries faster than TripleBit answers any query and than RDF-3X answers most queries. For the WatDiv dataset TENTRIS outperforms TripleBit and RDF-3X by at least 2.3 times w.r.t. pQpS.

Summary. Overall, TENTRIS outperforms all other approaches in the HTTP benchmarks client w.r.t. the average QpS per client across all datasets. The CLI experiments lead to a similar picture. While TENTRIS is always best for small queries with up to 5000 results, gStore is faster for large queries with more than 5000 results with up to 8 clients. This difference in performance seems to be due to the current result serialization of TENTRIS and will be addressed in future versions of the framework. The additional better scalability of the approach w.r.t. the number of clients suggests that TENTRIS is a viable alternative to existing solutions for querying RDF knowledge graphs. An analysis of our results suggests that the selection of the sequence of operations in the Einstein summation can be improved further by using heuristics (e.g., star joins vs. path joins) or by using function approximators ranging from regression-based solutions to deep learning.

8 Conclusion and Outlook

With TENTRIS, we present a time-efficient triple store for RDF knowledge graphs. We define a new mapping of RDF and SPARQL to tensors and tensor operations like slicing and Einstein summation. Our experimental results show that TENTRIS outperforms established triple stores with respect to QpS within experimental settings with up to 32 concurrent users. This improvement is the result of a novel tensor data structure, called hypertrie, that is designed to store low-rank tensors efficiently and allows the efficient evaluation of slices and Einstein summation. We show that hypertries allow for constant time slices on any combination of dimensions. An efficient evaluation of Einstein summation expressions on hypertries is achieved by an adaption of a worst-case optimal multi-join algorithm. TENTRIS will be extended in future works to be a fully-fledged triple store. Further improvements will include the data-driven improvement of the processing order for Einstein summation labels. Moreover, we will develop domain-specific versions of TENTRIS, e.g., geo-spatial extensions.

Acknowledgments. The authors would like to thank Lennart Austenfeld for automating the evaluation setup. This work has been supported by the German Federal Ministry for Economic Affairs and Energy (BMWi) within the project RAKI under the grant no 01MD19012D, by the German Federal Ministry of Education and Research (BMBF) within the project DAIKIRI under the grant no 01IS19085B, and by the EU H2020 Marie Skłodowska-Curie project KnowGraphs under the grant agreement no 860801.

References

1. Abdelaziz, I., Harbi, R., Khayyat, Z., Kalnis, P.: A survey and experimental comparison of distributed SPARQL engines for very large RDF data. Proc. VLDB Endow. **10**(13), 2049–2060 (2017)
2. Abraham, R., Marsden, J.E., Ratiu, T.: Manifolds, Tensor Analysis, and Applications. Springer, New York (1988)
3. Aluç, G., Hartig, O., Özsu, M.T., Daudjee, K.: Diversified stress testing of RDF data management systems. In: Mika, P., et al. (eds.) ISWC 2014. LNCS, vol. 8796, pp. 197–212. Springer, Cham (2014). https://doi.org/10.1007/978-3-319-11964-9_13
4. Atre, M., Chaoji, V., Zaki, M.J., Hendler, J.A.: Matrix "bit" loaded: a scalable lightweight join query processor for RDF data. In: WWW, pp. 41–50 (2010)

5. Conrads, F., Lehmann, J., Saleem, M., Morsey, M., Ngonga Ngomo, A.-C.: IGUANA: a generic framework for benchmarking the read-write performance of triple stores. In: d'Amato, C., et al. (eds.) ISWC 2017. LNCS, vol. 10588, pp. 48–65. Springer, Cham (2017). https://doi.org/10.1007/978-3-319-68204-4_5
6. De La Briandais, R.: File searching using variable length keys. In: Western Joint Computer Conference, IRE-AIEE-ACM 1959 (Western), pp. 295–298 (1959)
7. Einstein, A.: Die Grundlage der allgemeinen Relativitätstheorie. Annalen der Physik **354**, 769–822 (1916)
8. Erling, O.: Virtuoso, a hybrid RDBMS/graph column store. http://vos.openlinksw.com/owiki/wiki/VOS/VOSArticleVirtuosoAHybridRDBMSGraphColumnStore. Accessed 17 Mar 2018
9. Ermilov, I., Lehmann, J., Martin, M., Auer, S.: LODStats: the data web census dataset. In: Groth, P., et al. (eds.) ISWC 2016. LNCS, vol. 9982, pp. 38–46. Springer, Cham (2016). https://doi.org/10.1007/978-3-319-46547-0_5
10. Apache Software Foundation: Apache Jena documentation - TDB - store parameters (2019). https://jena.apache.org/documentation/tdb/store-parameters. Accessed 25 Apr 2019
11. Google Ireland Limited: tf.einsum — TensorFlow core r2.0 — TensorFlow (2019). https://pytorch.org/docs/stable/torch.html#torch.einsum. Accessed 06 Aug 2019
12. Jamour, F., Abdelaziz, I., Chen, Y., Kalnis, P.: Matrix algebra framework for portable, scalable and efficient query engines for RDF graphs. In: Proceedings of the Fourteenth EuroSys Conference 2019, EuroSys 2019. ACM (2019)
13. Kjolstad, F., Kamil, S., Chou, S., Lugato, D., Amarasinghe, S.: The tensor algebra compiler. In: Proceedings of the ACM on Programming Languages, 1(OOPSLA), October 2017
14. Motik, B., Nenov, Y., Piro, R., Horrocks, I., Olteanu, D.: Parallel materialisation of datalog programs in centralised, main-memory RDF systems. In: Proceedings of the Twenty-Eighth AAAI Conference on Artificial Intelligence, AAAI 2014, pp. 129–137. AAAI Press (2014)
15. Neumann, T., Weikum, G.: RDF-3X: a RISC-style engine for RDF. Proc. VLDB Endow. **1**(1), 647–659 (2008)
16. Ngo, H.Q., Ré, C., Rudra, A.: Skew strikes back: new developments in the theory of join algorithms. SIGMOD Rec. **42**, 5–16 (2013)
17. Nickel, M., Tresp, V., Kriegel, H.-P.: Factorizing YAGO: scalable machine learning for linked data. In: WWW, pp. 271–280 (2012)
18. Noy, N., Gao, Y., Jain, A., Narayanan, A., Patterson, A., Taylor, J.: Industry-scale knowledge graphs: lessons and challenges. Queue **17**(2), 48–75 (2019)
19. Inc. Ontotext USA: Storage – GraphDB free 8.9 documentation. http://graphdb.ontotext.com/documentation/free/storage.html#storage-literal-index. Accessed 16 Apr 2019
20. MMG Ricci and Tullio Levi-Civita: Méthodes de calcul différentiel absolu et leurs applications. Mathematische Annalen **54**(1–2), 125–201 (1900)
21. Saleem, M., Ali, M.I., Hogan, A., Mehmood, Q., Ngomo, A.-C.N.: LSQ: the linked SPARQL queries dataset. In: Arenas, M., et al. (eds.) ISWC 2015. LNCS, vol. 9367, pp. 261–269. Springer, Cham (2015). https://doi.org/10.1007/978-3-319-25010-6_15
22. Saleem, M., Kamdar, M.R., Iqbal, A., Sampath, S., Deus, H.F., Ngomo Ngomo, A.-C.: Big linked cancer data: Integrating linked TCGA and PubMed. JWS (2014)
23. Saleem, M., Mehmood, Q., Ngonga Ngomo, A.-C.: FEASIBLE: a feature-based SPARQL benchmark generation framework. In: Arenas, M., et al. (eds.) ISWC 2015. LNCS, vol. 9366, pp. 52–69. Springer, Cham (2015). https://doi.org/10.1007/978-3-319-25007-6_4
24. SYSTAP, LLC. Bigdata Database Architecture - Blazegraph (2013). https://blazegraph.com/docs/bigdata_architecture_whitepaper.pdf. Accessed 29 Nov 2019
25. The SciPy community: numpy.einsum – NumPy v1.17 manual (2019). https://docs.scipy.org/doc/numpy/reference/generated/numpy.einsum.html. Accessed 6 Aug 2019

26. Torch Contributors: torch – PyTorch master documentation (2018). https://pytorch.org/docs/stable/torch.html#torch.einsum. Accessed 06 Aug 2019
27. De Virgilio, R.: A linear algebra technique for (de)centralized processing of SPARQL queries. In: Conceptual Modeling, pp. 463–476, October 2012
28. Pingpeng Yuan, P., Liu, B.W., Jin, H., Zhang, W., Liu, L.: TripleBit: a fast and compact system for large scale RDF data. Proc. VLDB Endow. **6**(7), 517–528 (2013)
29. Zou, L., Özsu, M.T., Chen, L., Shen, X., Huang, R., Zhao, D.: gStore: a graph-based SPARQL query engine. VLDB J. **23**(4), 565–590 (2014)

Refining Node Embeddings via Semantic Proximity

Melisachew Wudage Chekol[1] and Giuseppe Pirrò[2](✉)

[1] Department of Information and Computing Sciences, Utrecht University, Utrecht, Netherlands
m.w.chekol@uu.nl

[2] Department of Computer Science, Sapienza University of Rome, Via Salaria 113, 00198 Rome, Italy
pirro@di.uniroma1.it

Abstract. There is a variety of available approaches to learn graph node embeddings. One of their common underlying task is the generation of (biased) random walks that are then fed into representation learning techniques. Some techniques generate biased random walks by using structural information. Other approaches, also rely on some form of semantic information. While the former are purely structural, thus not fully considering knowledge available in semantically rich networks, the latter require complex inputs (e.g., metapaths) or only leverage node types that may not be available. The goal of this paper is to overcome these limitations by introducing **NESP** (**N**ode **E**mbeddings via **S**emantic **P**roximity), which features two main components. The first provides four different ways of biasing random walks by leveraging semantic relatedness between predicates. The second component focuses on refining (existing) embeddings by leveraging the notion of semantic proximity. This component iteratively refines an initial set of node embeddings imposing the embeddings of semantic neighboring nodes of a node to lie within a sphere of fixed radius. We discuss an extensive experimental evaluation and comparison with related work.

1 Introduction

Nowadays there is abundant graph data on the Web; from friendship graphs in social networks to knowledge graphs [6]. These graphs can be used for several tasks such as link prediction–whether any two nodes are connected by some edge/relation, node classification–identifying the type of a node, node clustering–grouping the same type nodes into the same category, and so on. Recently, graph embeddings have become a popular means to accomplish those tasks.

The idea is to project nodes or triples [7] of a given graph into a low dimensional vector space while maintaining its structure; as an example, nodes sharing an edge will be nearby in the vector space [2]. Research on graph embeddings focuses on two main types of graphs: homogeneous, having a single type of both nodes and edges (e.g., social relationships of bloggers aka. BlogCatalog [27])–and

J. Z. Pan et al. (Eds.): ISWC 2020, LNCS 12506, pp. 74–91, 2020.
https://doi.org/10.1007/978-3-030-62419-4_5

heterogeneous, having different types of nodes and edges (e.g., DBpedia [20]). Homogeneous graph embeddings such as LINE [24], node2vec [9], and Deepwalk [17] learn node embeddings by using *random walks* to encode node proximity. While random walk based approaches perform well in several embedding tasks, this result does not directly apply to heterogeneous information networks (HINs) aka knowledge graphs (KGs), partly due to the difficulty to precisely take into account the different kinds of node and edge types in the graph.

Some approaches find biased random walks in HIN by leveraging edge weights (e.g., based on TF-IDF in predicates) that are derived from structural information (e.g., Biased-RDF2Vec [16]). Other approaches, besides the structure, also rely on some form of semantic information (e.g., [5,8]) either as an additional input (e.g, metapaths [5], that is, sequences of node types) or implicit (e.g., alternating the node types [12] traversed during the walk generation according to some likelihood probability). A survey of related literature can be found in [2,25].

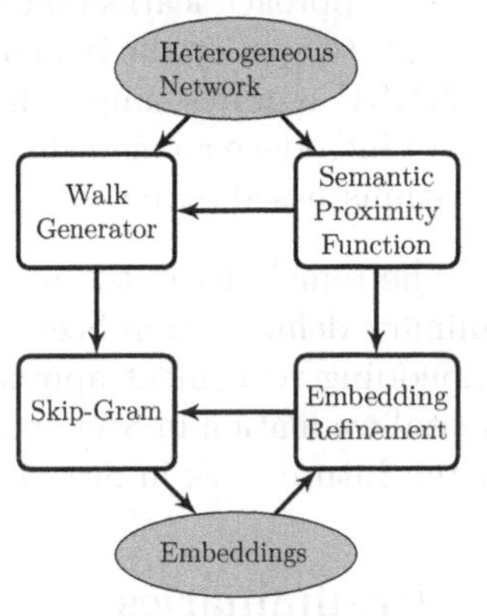

Fig. 1. The **NESP** framework.

While the former are mainly structural-based, thus not fully considering the knowledge available in semantically rich networks (e.g., KGs or HIN), the latter require complex inputs (e.g., it is not clear how to find meaningful metapaths) or only leverage node types where, besides the fact that these may not be available, there is also the need to precisely define the initial stay probability and the number of memorized domains whose optimal values may vary from dataset to dataset. Moreover, none of these approaches can learn (or refine) embeddings where the embeddings of semantic neighbors, even if not directly connected, are constrained to be close together in the vector space.

The goal of this paper is to fill these gaps by introducing a framework called **NESP** (**N**ode **E**mbeddings via **S**emantic **P**roximity), shown in Fig. 1 which *contributes two main components. The first provides four different ways of biasing random walks by leveraging semantic information.* Differently, from approaches using metapaths or similar, where one needs, for instance, to understand the schema-compatibility of the sequence of node types, **NESP** allows to find domain-driven walks when optionally specifying a set of predicates related to a domain of interest. After generating the walks, **NESP** employs the Skip-gram model [15] to learn the node embeddings. *The second component focuses on the notion of semantic proximity,* which identifies the semantic neighborhood of a node that may be different from the structural neighborhood (e.g., considering (directly) connected nodes). For instance, the semantic neighbor of the node (entity) S. Kubrick in DBpedia can be the node M. Forman, which is some hops away from S. Kubrick or another node, which is, for instance of the same type. This second component can be used to refine embeddings found by any existing system. Concretely, it leverages penalty functions [1] to iteratively refine an initial set of embeddings so that embeddings of the semantic neighbor of a node lie within a sphere of fixed radius centered at the node's embedding. Overall, the contributions of this paper are summarized as follows:

- We introduce a novel approach that leverages edge relatedness to drive the embedding construction. It is much simpler to use edges than nodes (in meta paths) as one needs to guarantee compatibility between node sequences.
- Our approach learns domain-specific embeddings by using some input predicates to specify the domain.
- **NESP** requires simpler input than related approaches (e.g., metapath2vec).
- We introduce an embedding refinement strategy for existing embedding algorithms based on penalty functions and semantic proximity.

The remainder of the paper is organized as follows. We introduce some preliminary definitions in Sect. 2. The **NESP** system is introduced in Sect. 3. Our embedding refinement approach is presented in Sect. 4. We discuss the experimental evaluation in Sect. 5. Related work is treated in Sect. 6. We conclude and sketch future work in Sect. 7.

2 Preliminaries

Heterogeneous Networks. A graph $G = (V, E)$ has a set of nodes V and edges E as well as a function τ that maps nodes and edges into their respective types, formally, $\tau : V \to T_V$ and $\tau : E \to T_E$. A Graph G is called *heterogeneous* if nodes (resp. edges) of the graph have different types, i.e., $|T_V| > 1$ (resp. $|T_E| > 1$). When all nodes (resp. edges) of the graph have one type of nodes and one type of edges, i.e., $|T_V| = |T_E| = 1$, then the graph is *homogeneous.* In this work, we are mainly interested in a type of heterogeneous graphs called *knowledge graphs* (KGs) aka heterogeneous information networks (HINs). A knowledge graph is a directed node and edge labeled multi-graph $G = (V, E, U)$ where V is a set of vertices that represent entities, E is a set of predicates and U is a set of triples of the form (s, p, o) representing directed labeled edges where $s, o \in V$ and $p \in E$.

Graph Embedding. A graph embedding model $h : v \to \mathbb{R}^d$ projects nodes into a low dimensional vector space, where $d \ll |V|$–number of nodes, so that neighboring nodes are nearby in the vector space. At the simplest level, an input to an embedding model consists of an adjacency matrix of a given graph and its output is a vector embedding of each node in the graph so that the distance between two neighboring nodes is much smaller than the ones that are far apart. The dot product between two node embeddings approximates an edge existence between them. After producing an embedding model of a given graph, the model can be used for accomplishing several tasks such as node clustering, node classification, recommendation, and so on. Given their wide array of advantages, graph embeddings have been well researched, we refer the reader to [2] for a survey. A graph embedding model is defined based on a node similarity and an objective function. Broadly, graph embedding approaches can be divided into two, homogeneous and heterogeneous, based on the kind of graphs they focus on. In this study, we propose an embedding model for heterogeneous networks based on predicate relatedness to find biased random walks and an embedding refinement model based on semantic proximity.

Predicate Relatedness. To find biased random walks **NESP** leverages an existing predicate relatedness measure [18]. Given a knowledge graph $G = (V, E, U)$ and a pair of predicates $(p_i, p_j) \in E$, the relatedness measure is based on the Triple Frequency defined as $TF(p_i, p_j) = \log(1 + C_{i,j})$, where $C_{i,j}$ counts the number of times the predicates p_i and p_j link the same subjects and objects. Moreover, it uses the Inverse Triple Frequency defined as $ITF(p_j, E) = \log \frac{|E|}{|\{p_i : C_{i,j} > 0\}|}$. Based on TF and ITF, for each pair of predicates p_i and p_j we can build a (symmetric) matrix C_M where each element is $C_M(i,j) = TF(p_i, p_j) \times ITF(p_j, E)$. The final predicate relatedness matrix M_R can be constructed such that $Rel(p_i, p_j) = Cosine(W_i, W_j)$, where W_i (resp., W_j) is the row of p_i (resp., p_j) in C_M. We refer to $Rel(p_i, p_j)$ as the relatedness score.

3 NESP: Relatedness-Driven Walk Generation

Unlike previous heterogeneous network embedding approaches that use the types of nodes and metapaths, we use predicates (i.e., edge labels) and their relatedness, to guide walk generation. The input to the walk generator is a graph $G = (V, E, U)$, a predicate relatedness matrix C_M, and a set of input predicates $\mathcal{R}$ that may be used to generate *domain-driven embeddings*, that is, embeddings where some edges are preferred to others during the walk generation. This set if not specified includes all the available predicates. Let $u \in V$ be the current node in a walk, $N(u)$ is the set of its neighbors, $v \in N(u)$ is the *next* node in a walk, $\mathcal{E}(u, v)$ is the set of all predicates linking u and one of its neighbor $v \in N(u)$. Moreover, let $Rel(p_i, p_j)$ be the relatedness score for predicates p_i and p_j. To pick the next node $v \in N(u)$ starting from u we define the following approaches.

Semantic Relatedness Driven Walk. For a given node u and its neighbors $N(u)$, we collect the set of all predicates $\mathcal{E}(u, v)$ between u and its neighbors $\{v \in N(u)\}$. Then, the relatedness between each predicate $p_{uv} \in \mathcal{E}(u, v)$ and all the input predicates $p_j \in \mathcal{R}$ is computed. Once having a relatedness score for each edge (resp. neighbor) this strategy picks as the next node v the one linked to u via the highest relatedness score. When two or more edges have the same relatedness score, one will be selected uniformly at random. The approach is summarized in the following equation:

$$P(v|u,\mathcal{R}) = \begin{cases} 0 \text{ if } |\mathcal{E}(u,v)| = 0 \\ 1 \text{ if } |\mathcal{E}(u,v)| = 1 \\ \varphi(\mathcal{R},\mathcal{E}(u,v)) \text{ otherwise} \end{cases}$$
$$\varphi(\mathcal{R},\mathcal{E}(u,v)) = \max_{p_j \in \mathcal{R}, p_{uv} \in \mathcal{E}(u,v)} Rel(p_j, p_{uv}) \quad (1)$$

Relatedness Driven Jump and Stay Walk. The walks generated by the above approach tend to be biased, indeed, it always picks the node linked via the predicate having the highest relatedness score, thus introducing a form of determinism. To overcome this aspect, we propose relatedness driven jump and stay. For the first M steps of a walk and when the probability of picking the next node is larger than some threshold α, we choose the next node according to Eq. 1 (corresponding to staying); otherwise, we choose a random neighbor (corresponding to jump). We use two parameters: a threshold α for the relatedness score and a step counter M to track the number of nodes visited so far. For each walk, the neighbor v of u is selected according to α and M. For the first M steps (nodes), we choose a node having $\varphi(\mathcal{R},\mathcal{E}(u,v)) > \alpha$. Starting from the $(M+1)$th step, the next node is randomly chosen. By denoting with m the current step, the next node is selected according to the following equation:

$$P(v|u,\mathcal{R},\alpha,m) = \begin{cases} P(v|u,\mathcal{R}) \text{ if } P(v|u,\mathcal{R},\alpha,m) > \alpha \text{ and } m < M \\ x \leftarrow \mathcal{U}(0,1) \text{ otherwise,} \end{cases} \quad (2)$$

x is a random number chosen from a uniform distribution $\mathcal{U}(0,1)$.

Randomized Relatedness Driven Walk. In this approach, we use a parameter K to specify the percentage of nodes to choose from. As in the previous strategy, we compute the relatedness scores between the input edges and the edges linking the current node u to each of its neighbors v. However, we only consider the top-k highest values that single out a subset of all neighbors (those linked via these top-k predicates). The next node v is selected at random among them. In particular, the higher the relatedness score of an edge, the more likely that it will be selected. Formally v is chosen according to the following distribution:

$$P(v|u,\mathcal{R},K) = \begin{cases} \frac{\varphi(\mathcal{R},p_{uv})}{\sum_{w \in P_r(u,\mathcal{R},K)} w} \text{ if } |\mathcal{E}(u,v)| > 1 \\ P(v|u,\mathcal{R}) \text{ otherwise} \end{cases}$$
$$P_r(u,\mathcal{R},K) = \underset{X' \subseteq \mathcal{X}(u,\mathcal{R}), |X'|=K}{argmax} \sum_{x \in X'} x \quad (3)$$
$$\mathcal{X}(u,\mathcal{R}) \leftarrow \{\varphi(\mathcal{R},p_j) | \forall p_j \in \mathcal{E}(u,v') \text{ and } \forall v' \in V\}$$

In the denominator of the above equation, we consider only the top-k ranked edges to choose from. To elaborate, $\mathcal{X}()$ contains the set of all relatedness scores between u and its neighbors; and the function $P_r()$ selects the top-k relatedness scores using the *argmax*. Note that if the number of neighbors of u is less than K, then K is changed to the number of its neighbors.

Probabilistic Relatedness Driven Walk. This approach is a variation of the above approach in which instead of considering the top-k neighbors, we choose randomly one of them. In particular, the next node v is sampled from the non-uniform discrete distribution corresponding to the relatedness score according to the following equation:

$$P_t(v|u,\mathcal{R}) = \begin{cases} \frac{\varphi(\mathcal{R},p_{uv})}{\sum_{v' \in V, p_j \in \mathcal{E}(u,v')} \varphi(\mathcal{R},p_j)} & \text{if } |\mathcal{E}(u,v)| > 1 \\ P(v|u,\mathcal{R}) & \text{otherwise} \end{cases} \quad (4)$$

Note that all the above approaches provide much simpler ways of guiding the walks than metapath-based approaches. This is because one has to have precise domain knowledge in picking meaningful metapaths. Not to mention the fact that in schema-rich graphs, it can be the case that no path in the graph satisfies the input metapath. Hence, approaches based on metapaths can only work on graphs that have a simple schema, i.e., a few edge and node types. Moreover, we underline the fact that some of the walk generation strategies are refinements (for instance, probabilistic relatedness driven walk is a variation of randomized relatedness driven walk). The choice of the walk generation strategy depends on many factors including how rich in semantics is the graph, how big is the graph, etc. As an example, if there are node types one can use relatedness driven jump and stay walk. For large graphs, one can pick the semantic relatedness driven walk, which is generally faster as observed in the experiments.

3.1 Learning Node Embeddings

In this section, we describe how nodes of heterogeneous graphs are mapped into vectors in a d-dimensional vector space. For a graph $G = (V, E, U)$ and node $u \in V$, the function h maps nodes into vectors, i.e., $h : u \rightarrow \mathbb{R}^d$ where $d \ll |V|$. Similar to previous approaches, we use the Skip-gram model to learn latent representations of nodes by making use of the walks generated. Skip-gram maximizes the co-occurrence probability among nodes that appear within a given walk of length L. The co-occurrence probability of two nodes u and v in a set of walks W is given by the Softmax function using their vector embeddings e_u and e_v:

$$P((e_u, e_v) \in W) = \sigma(e_u \cdot e_v) \quad (5)$$

In the above equation, σ is the softmax function and $e_u \cdot e_v$ is the dot product of the vectors e_u and e_v. Likewise, the probability that a node u and a randomly chosen node v_j that does not appear in a walk starting from u is given by:

$$P((e_{v_j}, e_u) \notin W) = \sigma(-e_u \cdot e_{v_j}) \quad (6)$$

The negative sampling objective of the Skip-gram model, that needs to be maximized, is given by the following objective function:

$$\mathcal{O}(\theta) = \log \sigma(e_u \cdot e_v) + \sum_{n \in \Gamma} \mathbb{E}_{e_n}[\log \sigma(-e_u \cdot e_n)], \quad (7)$$

where θ denotes the set of all parameters and Γ is the set of negative samples. We use the asynchronous stochastic gradient descent (ASGD) algorithm in parallel to optimize the objective function [12,19].

4 NESP: Embedding Refinement via Semantic Proximity

In this section, we describe the second strategy included in **NESP**. Its goal is to refine node embeddings that have been learned by any existing mechanism both semantic (e.g., JUST [12]) and structural based (e.g., node2vec [10], Deepwalk [17]). The core of the approach is the notion of *semantic proximity*, which for a node identifies a set of semantic neighbors. This definition is very general; the semantic neighbors can be nodes having the same node type (but not necessarily connected), nodes having a similar degree, the edge types, they can be top-k neighbors and so on. The goal of this strategy is to use information about the semantic neighbors (and their initial embeddings) of each node so that *the refined node embeddings are nearby in the vector space.* To elaborate, the refinement strategy allows to modify an initial embedding that may have placed nodes that are semantically neighbors far apart in the vector space.

Semantic Proximity. We mentioned that semantic proximity defines the neighborhood of a node. As mentioned, the notion of neighborhood is general and allows to identify semantically close nodes according to different strategies. We see semantic proximity as a mapping from a node into its semantic neighbors, i.e., $N_K : V \rightarrow 2^{|V|}$. Concretely, an instantiation of N_K can be a function based on semantic relatedness. Given a node u, and a set of input predicates $\mathcal{R}$, describing a domain of interest, N_K can be defined as follows:

$$N_K(u) = P_r(u, \mathcal{R}, K) \tag{8}$$

The definition of $P_r()$ is given in Eq. 3.

Embedding Refinement. Once $N_K(u)$ has been defined, to implement embedding refinement for each node u we consider a sphere with a small radius $r \in \mathbb{R}$ and then constrain the embeddings of the semantic neighbor nodes of u to lie within this sphere. Thus, any two node embeddings within the sphere are at a maximum of $2r$ distance. A small r would place the embeddings of neighboring nodes as close as possible. We mentioned that the initial embeddings to be refined can be computed with any mechanism, which is one of the benefits of our refinement approach. To summarize, under a given semantic proximity, the embedding of u and $v \in N_K(u)$ must be close to each other. Hence, the objective is to minimize the sum of all radii for all v, given the center u, by using Eq. 7 and the cost function given in [1,9].

$$\begin{aligned}
\min_{R,C} \quad & \sum_{v \in N_K(u)} \sum_{b \in V} \Big[\log \sigma(e_v \cdot e_b) + \sum_{n \in \Gamma} \mathbb{E}_{e_n}[\log \sigma(-e_v \cdot e_n)] \Big] + \\
& \alpha \sum_{u \in V} r_u^2 + \varphi(u, v, r_u) \qquad (9) \\
\text{subject to} \quad & ||e_v - e_u||_2^2 \leq r_u^2,\ r_u \geq 0,\ \forall v \in N_K(u) \text{ and } \forall u \in V
\end{aligned}$$

Table 1. Statistics of the datasets used in our experiments.

Graph	$\|V\|$	$\|E\|$	$\|T_V\|$	$\|T_E\|$	#labels
DBLP [11]	∼2M	∼276M	3	4	4
Foursquare [11]	∼30K	∼83K	4	4	10
Yago movies [11]	∼7K	∼89K	4	5	5
PubMed [25]	∼63K	∼245K	10	4	8
AIFB [20]	∼2.4K	∼16K	21	18	4
BGS [20]	∼12K	∼1423K	2	15	3

In the above equation, Γ is the set of negative samples, α denotes a positive weight, the constraint $||e_v - e_u||_2^2 \leq r_u^2$ ensures that (the embeddings of) nodes that have the same semantic proximity as u belong to the sphere of radius r_u and centered at e_u, and R and C denote set of all radii and center embeddings respectively. Besides, $\varphi(u, v, r_u)$ is the penalty function given in Eq. 10. Note that Eq. 9 is a non-convex constrained optimization problem. To convert into an unconstrained optimization problem, we add the following penalty function to the formulation as done in [1].

$$\varphi(u, v, r_u) = \lambda \sum_{u \in V} \sum_{v \in N(u)} f(||e_v - e_u||_2^2 - r_u^2) + \sum_{u \in V} \rho(u) f(-r_u) \qquad (10)$$

In the above formula $\lambda, \rho(u) \in \mathbb{Z}^+$ are parameters which are gradually increased depending on the violation of the constraint. f is a penalty function defined as $f(t) = max(t, 0)$ and controls the violations of the constraints in Eq. 9. We use ASGD to solve the unconstrained optimization problem corresponding to Eq. 9. The optimized solution gives the refined node embedding of v.

5 Experiments

In this section, we report on an empirical evaluation of our approach and comparison with related work. **NESP** has been implemented in Python. Experiments were run on a MacBook P2.7 GHz quad-core processor with 16 GB RAM. The reported results are the average of 5 runs. We used six datasets (see Table 1) from different domains for which the ground truth results were already available.

5.1 Competitors and Parameter Setting

We consider a sample of the most popular and well-performing approaches to compute embeddings in (knowledge) graphs.

- **Deepwalk:** designed for homogeneous graphs, it generates random walks and then feeds them into the Skip-gram model. We set the number of walks per node to $n = 10$, the maximum walk length to $L = 100$ and the window size (necessary for the notion of context in the Skip-gram model) to $w = 10$.

- **node2vec:** this approach improves upon Deepwalk in both the way random walks are generated (by balancing the breadth-first search (BFS) and depth first search (DFS) strategies) and in the objective function optimization (it uses negative sampling). We set the parameter values for n, L, and w to the same values as Deepwalk. Moreover, we also set the parameters p and q, which defines probability of returning to source node and of moving to a node away from the source node, to the best values reported in [9].
- **Metapath2vec:** it takes as input one or more metapaths and generates walks to be fed into the Skip-gram model. We consider the same metapaths used in the evaluation of JUST [12]. For DBLP, Π_1^{DBLP} = A-P-A and Π_2^{DBLP} = A-P-V-P-A linking authors to papers and authors to papers and venues respectively. For Yago movies (mov), Π_1^{mov} = A-M-D-M-A and Π_2^{mov} = A-M-C-M-A representing actors starring in movies with common directors and composers, respectively. For Foursquare (4SQ), Π_1^{4SQ} = U-C-P-C-U representing users checking-in at the same point of interest, and Π_2^{4SQ} = P-C-T-C-P representing points of interest having check-ins at the same timestamp.
- **JUST:** this approach was designed to get rid of metapaths. In doing so, the authors consider probabilities of jump or stay based on the kinds of domains (node types) visited during the generation of a random walk. We set the algorithm parameters to the best values reported in [12].
- **RDF2Vec:** this approach uses graph kernels, extracted using the Weisfeiler-Lehman, to guide walk generation; it assumes equal weights for all edges [20].
- **Biased-RDF2Vec:** this approach focuses on finding domain-specific embeddings by providing a set of input predicates.
- **NESP$_{\mathbf{red}}$:** with this we considered specific subsets of edge labels in the computation of embeddings to evaluate the domain-driven approach. For the DBLP dataset, we considered $\mathcal{R}_1 = \{author\}$ linking a paper to an author, and $\mathcal{R}_2 = \{author, venue\}$ including edges to link a paper to its authors and to the venue it was published. For Foursquare we used $\mathcal{R}_1 = \{perform, locate\}$ and $\mathcal{R}_2 = \{locate, happenedAt\}$ including edges linking users to check-in locations and edges to link the time of checking and the location. For the Yago dataset we used $\mathcal{R}_1 = \{actedIn, directed\}$ and $\mathcal{R}_2 = \{actedIn, coDirector\}$ linking actors to movies and directors and actors to movies co-directed. In these datasets, the set of edges were picked to mimic the link between nodes in the metapaths discussed above. For the datasets AIFB and BGS we use the same predicates used to evaluate *biased-RDF2Vec* [16].

For **NESP**, we considered all the edge types and set the values of n, L, and w as for the other approaches. For each system, we used d=128 as dimension of the node embeddings, and the number of negative samples Γ is set to 10 for all methods in all experiments. For **NESP**, the notion of semantic proximity N_K used in the experiment about embedding refinement is defined as top-k most related nodes via Eq. 8. We only report the best walk strategy, i.e., *probabilistic relatedness driven walk*; the others were slightly worse even though we noticed that *semantic relatedness driven walk* was generally faster. In Table 2, we highlight a summary of the features of the considered systems.

5.2 Node Classification

The goal of this task is to give the label of some test nodes based on the labels of some training nodes. In order to predict the node labels, we use the node embeddings obtained by training **NESP**, node2vec, Deepwalk, JUST, and metapath2vec. Node labels are predicted by using the embeddings as a training input to a one-vs-rest logistic regression classifier. The results of this experiment are given in Fig. 2, where the average (of 5 rounds) Micro-F1 and Macro-F1 scores for classification is shown. For all the datasets and performance metrics (Micro-F1 and Macro-F1), **NESP**'s results are comparable with the baseline, slightly superior in some cases. We observe that as the percentage of training data increases, the performance of all the systems improves, in general. We also observe that when the percentage of training input is above 75%, **NESP** outperforms all the baselines, including $\mathbf{NESP}_{red}$, which makes usage of a subset of predicates. In general, we observe that this variant of **NESP** performs relatively well, especially in the PubMed and AIFB datasets. Unlike all the other systems, JUST's performance slightly decreases as more training input is provided on DBLP. On the other hand, on the datasets PubMed, AIFB and BGS, **NESP** outperforms all the other methods by a higher margin. Note that the results of methpath2vec are not reported for some datasets since metapaths were unavailable and it was difficult to identify meaningful ones. In addition, on the BGS dataset, although not visible from the plot, increasing the size of the samples increases the accuracy. For instance, when we use 10% of the samples, the Micro-F1 is 0.9983 and when we use 20%, it rises to 0.9986, i.e., we obtain a 0.0003 improvement.

Table 2. Walk generation techniques adopted by state of the art systems.

Network type	Approach	Walk guiding		Metapath
		Node type	Edge type	
Homogeneous	Deepwalk	No	No	/
	Node2vec	No	No	/
Heterogeneous	metapath2vec	Yes	No	Yes
	JUST	Yes	No	No
	RDF2Vec	No	No	No
	Biased-RDF2Vec	No	Yes	No
	$\mathbf{NESP}_{\mathbf{red}}$	No	Yes	No
	NESP	No	Yes	No

5.3 Node Clustering

The goal of this task is to investigate how similar nodes can be grouped to form communities. We follow the methodology described in Hussein et al. [12]. For each of the graphs, we consider nodes having the same label as being part of the

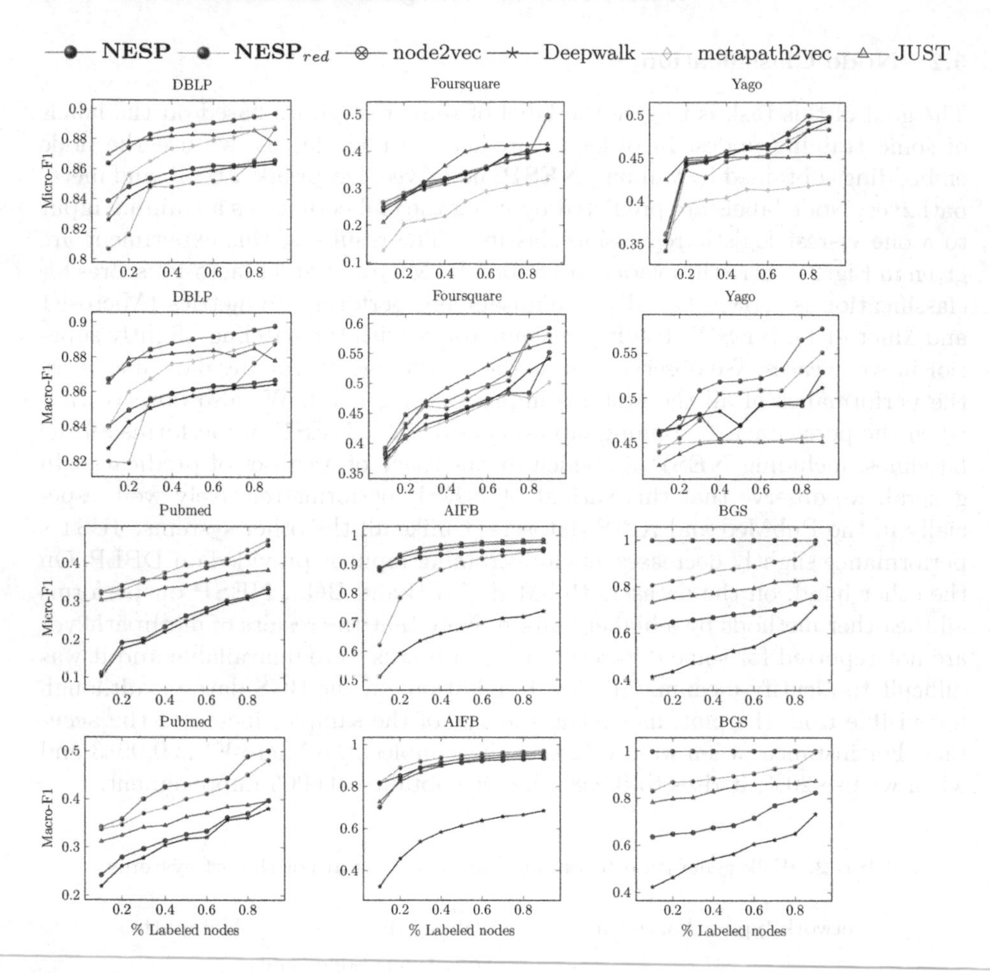

Fig. 2. Node classification results in terms of micro and macro F1.

same community. Then, we fed the node embeddings to the k-means algorithm and evaluated cluster quality by computing the Normalized Mutual Information (NMI). As in the Yago dataset, each movie could be part of more than a class, we provided a classification such that each movie belongs only to one label. This increases the number of possible labels. The results of this experiment are given in Fig. 3. As can be seen, **NESP** outperforms all the baselines on all the datasets. JUST comes second best in terms of clustering performance. Both **NESP** and JUST provide a good indication that one does not need metapaths to outperform state of the art heterogeneous embedding models. In fact, this is clearly visible in the results over the Yago dataset. Interestingly, the performance of homogeneous embedding models, node2vec and Deepwalk is very competitive over the graphs, DBLP and Foursquare. However, on the more schema-rich Yago, their performance degrades showing that they are not well suited for heterogeneous

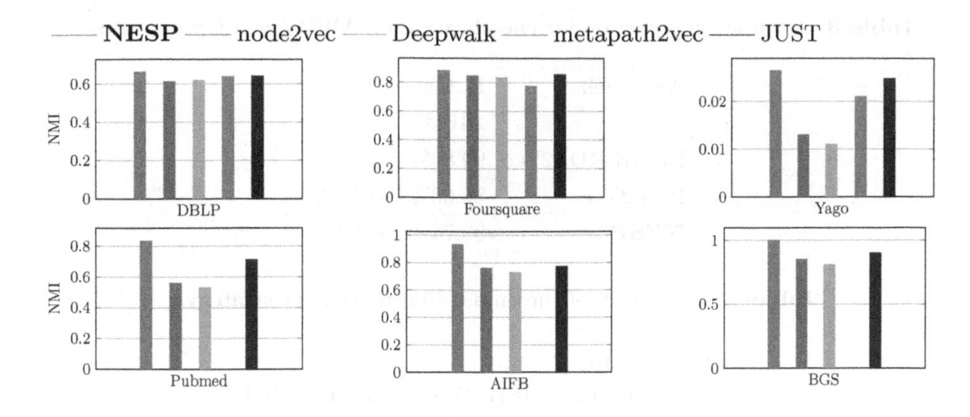

Fig. 3. Clustering results.

graph embedding tasks. In both PubMed and AIFB datasets, which are richer than the other datasets, **NESP** outperforms all the other methods by a very high margin. We also observe that on BGS all approaches performed relatively well with **NESP** reaching the maximum value. For metapath2vec results are not reported for some datasets since metapaths were unavailable and it was difficult to identify meaningful ones.

5.4 Comparison with Domain-Driven Embedding Approaches

In this section we focus on a comparison with *Biased-RDF2Vec* [16], another approach, which focuses on learning domain-driven embeddings. There are crucial differences with our approach. First, *Biased-RDF2Vec* is based on two fixed edge weights; one high, for predicates that *exactly match* the input predicates specifying a domain of interest and one low for the others. On the other hand, **NESP**, relying on the notion of predicate relatedness, covers a more general edge weighting approach. As an example for the input predicate *director*, while *biased-RDF2Vec* matches only this predicate, **NESP** can also assign a high weight to the semantically related predicate like *editor*. In this experiment, we use the same setting (parameters and datasets) used to evaluate *Biased-RDF2Vec* [16]. In particular, we use k-NN (Nearest Neighbor) for node classification with the settings $k = 4$ for AIFB and $k = 10$ for BGS. Below, we also include the results of RDF2Vec [20] that were reported for those datasets. RDF2vec is used as a baseline. Table 3 shows the results of classification accuracy for domain-driven approaches (*biased-RDF2Vec* and **NESP**) as well as structural-driven approach RDF2Vec. The results reported for RDF2Vec are obtained using k-NN. However, higher results were achieved by using SVM (support vector machine), respectively, 93.41% for AIFB and 96.33% for BGS. **NESP** reports a slighter lower value on AIFB and a slightly higher value on BGS with respect to the direct competitor *biased-RDF2Vec*. However, these two datasets were quite specific and limited in the variety of edge types. While Biased-RDF2Vec only assigns

Table 3. Accuracy comparison for classification on AIFB and BGS datasets.

Approach	Dataset	
	AIFB	BGS
Biased-RDF2Vec	99.86%	93.10%
RDF2Vec	88.66%	93.19%
NESP	99.74%	94.04%

Table 4. Evaluation of the embedding refinement strategy.

Approach	Dataset			
	DBLP	AIFB	Foursquare	PubMed
Deepwalk	8%	12%	6%	16%
Node2vec	9%	16%	7%	18%
JUST	4%	8%	4%	6%
NESP	5%	3%	5%	4%

two edge weights (high to the chosen predicate and low to the other) **NESP** offers a broader spectrum of edge weights thus implicitly been able to smooth the difference between predicates of interest for the domain and the others.

5.5 Embedding Refinement

In this set of experiments, the goal was to investigate whether the embedding refinement strategy coupled with some definition of semantic proximity can bring some benefit to embeddings computed by any existing mechanism. We considered embeddings found by: (i) the semantic approaches **NESP** and JUST and (ii) the non-semantic approaches node2vec and Deepwalk. We report experimental results on DBLP, AIFB, Foursquare, and PubMed. The evaluation was carried out as follows. Given a method and a dataset, we computed the initial embeddings, the walks used to learn these embeddings and the set of semantic neighbors $N_K(u)$ for each node u according to Eq. 8. Then, we fed these three inputs and the hyperparameter values to the refinement strategy described in Sect. 4. The output is an updated set of embeddings for each approach and dataset considered. In what follows we focus on the variation of performance in the clustering experiment (see Fig. 3). The results, depicted in Table 4, show the percentage of improvement for each system.

We observe two interesting things. First, the approaches that benefit more from the refinement strategy are Deepwalk and node2vec that completely disregard the semantics of nodes and edges in a graph when computing node embeddings. It shows that refining the embeddings originally found by these approaches by incorporating the notion of semantic proximity is a viable strategy. Second, JUST and **NESP** obtain some improvement, with JUST obtaining a higher margin than **NESP**. This comes as no surprise since the walk generation technique used by **NESP** (Eq. 4) shares commonalities with the definition of semantic proximity used in the refinement (Eq. 3).

5.6 Parameter Sensitivity

In this section, we investigate the impact of the algorithm parameters related to the Skip-gram model. In particular, we consider the context window size w. We fixed the other parameters to their best values and vary the context window size w from 2 to 12. The results are shown in Fig. 4. We observe that larger values of w lead to better performance. This can be explained by the fact that a larger context window allows to better characterize the notion of neighbors and thus place nodes having a similar neighborhood closer in the embedding space. Nevertheless, when the value of w increases above 10, the benefits are lost, as too long node proximity does not reflect into node similarity. Therefore, we considered $w = 10$ in all previous experiments. We want to stress the fact that **NESP** can capture semantic proximity by favoring the traversal of edge types that are most semantically related to the input edges.

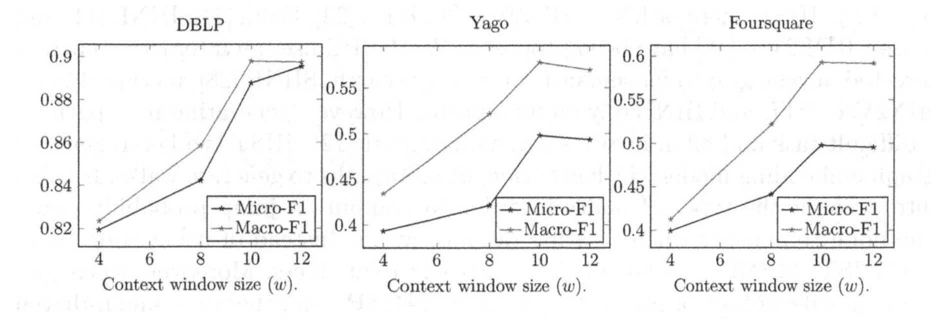

Fig. 4. Impact of the parameter w (context size) for the classification task.

5.7 Discussion

We have observed in the experimental evaluation that **NESP** offers performance comparable or higher than the state of the art in the datasets considered. There are some aspects that make the system more flexible than its competitors. First, **NESP** can be used to learn both domain-specific and general relatedness-driven embeddings. The usage of relatedness allows to implement a sort of semantic proximity during the construction of the walks, which favorably reflects in the fact that nodes with similar neighbors (relatedness-wise) will have closer representations in the embedding space. Second, differently from metapath2vec, **NESP** when used to build domain-specific embeddings, requires a much simpler input, that is, an edge set instead of a complex metapath. We also mention the fact that an input metapath may not even have a counterpart in the underlying data. As compared to domain-driven approaches like biased-RDF2Vec, **NESP** is more flexible as it considers a broader range of edge weights than the only two weights considered by the former. Another important aspect is that **NESP** (besides those necessary for Word2vec) does not require to set any parameter while biased-RDF2Vec needs to manually assign the two weights and JUST requires to input both the number of domain to memorize (parameter m) and the initial stay probability (parameter α), the choice of which affects the overall quality of the walks generated as well as the embeddings. Finally, the embedding refinement strategy showed to be potentially very useful in combination with simpler approaches like Deepwalk and node2vec besides providing some improvement to the embeddings found by other systems too.

6 Related Work

There are two broad directions in the area of graph representation learning: homogeneous and heterogeneous graph embeddings. Homogeneous graph embedding models include DeepWalk, node2vec, LINE and others. Recently, there is a growing interest in adapting random walk generation techniques from these models to heterogeneous graphs. As a result, IPE [13] (and an earlier version ProxEmbed [14]), JUST, metapath2vec, HIN2Vec [8], PTE [23], ESim [21], HINE [11] and biased-RDF2Vec [16] have been proposed. While IPE uses an interactive path (a directed acyclic graph) for semantic proximity search, SHNE [28], metapath2vec, HIN2Vec, PTE and HINE rely on metapaths. However, generating metapaths is a difficult task and often involves a domain expert [12]. JUST is a heterogeneous graph embedding model which gets ride off metapaths to generate walks. It takes into account the types of nodes in order to compute a jump probability from one node to another when creating random walks. Instead of using node types like JUST, **NESP** uses edge types and their relatedness. Moreover, when giving a specific subset of predicates as input, **NESP** can generate domain-driven embeddings. The approach of [16] also generates domain-specific embeddings. However, it is based on the manual assignment of weights for the predicates given as input while for the others weights are assigned using different strategies (e.g., predicate frequency). **NESP** is more general, domain-independent and does not require an expert for weight assignment as weights are automatically derived from the co-occurrences of predicates in the graph considered.

MetaGraph2Vec [29] uses metagraphs instead of metapaths in order to guide walk generation. However, similar to metapaths, building metagraphs is challenging. Along the same line, RDF2Vec [20] extracts subtree graph kernels from RDF graphs using the Weisfeiler-Lehman method. For each node in a given RDF graph, a subtree up to some depth k is extracted and this subtree is used as a walk to learn node embeddings of RDF graphs using two models: continuous bag of words (CBOW) and Skip-gram. In addition, RDF2Vec provides an alternative way of walk generation using a breadth-first algorithm. Unlike **NESP**, which takes into account the semantics of edges, RDF2Vec picks the next node relying on structural information. Other relevant literature in the area of heterogeneous embeddings [11,22,26]. There exist also semi-supervised approaches that leverage user feedback to improve the learned embeddings for heterogeneous networks [3]. Away from approaches that are based on local patterns (graph walks, subgraphs and kernels), RDF vector embeddings based on the GloVe (Global Vectors) model have been proposed in [4]. Glove-RDF embedding method creates a global co-occurrence matrix from graphs instead of random walks. For a more detailed discussion on heterogeneous and homogeneous embeddings, we refer the reader to the survey [2,25].

Finally, our notion of semantic proximity, used for embedding refinement, has been inspired by the notion of collective homophily from social networks. In particular [1] used collective homophily to refine embeddings of edges from social networks (including only one edge type). However, our formulation is based on a general notion of semantic neighborhood.

7 Concluding Remarks and Future Work

We described **NESP** a novel approach to heterogeneous graph embeddings including two components. The first features four different walk generation approaches based on predicate relatedness and not only structural information. **NESP** does not require metapaths, node types or other parameters to generate such walks. The second features an embedding refinement strategy that can be applied to embeddings learned by any existing system. It is based on the notion of semantic proximity, which first identifies the semantic neighbors of each node according to any notion of neighborhood (e.g., nodes sharing the same type, nodes linked by specific paths, etc.) and then strive to arrange the positions of a node and those of its neighbor as close as possible in the vector space. The experimental evaluations show that **NESP** is competitive and that the embedding refinement strategy is a viable solution, especially for approaches originally designed for homogeneous networks. Further investigating the refinement strategy and performing experiments on other domains is in our research agenda.

References

1. Bandyopadhyay, S., Biswas, A., Murty, M., Narayanam, R.: Beyond node embedding: a direct unsupervised edge representation framework for homogeneous networks. arXiv preprint arXiv:1912.05140 (2019)
2. Cai, H., Zheng, V.W., Chang, K.C.C.: A comprehensive survey of graph embedding: problems, techniques, and applications. IEEE Trans. Knowl. Data Eng. **30**(9), 1616–1637 (2018)
3. Chen, X., Yu, G., Wang, J., Domeniconi, C., Li, Z., Zhang, X.: ActiveHNE: active heterogeneous network embedding. In: Proceedings of the 28th International Joint Conference on Artificial Intelligence (IJCAI), pp. 2123–2129 (2019)
4. Cochez, M., Ristoski, P., Ponzetto, S.P., Paulheim, H.: Global RDF vector space embeddings. In: d'Amato, C., et al. (eds.) ISWC 2017. LNCS, vol. 10587, pp. 190–207. Springer, Cham (2017). https://doi.org/10.1007/978-3-319-68288-4_12
5. Dong, Y., Chawla, N.V., Swami, A.: metapath2vec: scalable representation learning for heterogeneous networks. In: Proceedings of the 23rd International Conference on Knowledge Discovery and Data Mining (KDD), pp. 135–144 (2017)

6. Fionda, V., Pirrò, G.: Querying graphs with preferences. In: Proceedings of the 22nd International Conference on Information and Knowledge Management (CIKM), pp. 929–938 (2013)
7. Fionda, V., Pirrò, G.: Learning triple embeddings from knowledge graphs. In: Proceedings of the 34th Conference on Artificial Intelligence (AAAI), pp. 3874–3881 (2020)
8. Fu, T., Lee, W.C., Lei, Z.: Hin2vec: explore meta-paths in heterogeneous information networks for representation learning. In: Proceedings of the Conference on Information and Knowledge Management (CIKM), pp. 1797–1806 (2017)
9. Grover, A., Leskovec, J.: node2vec: scalable feature learning for networks. In: Proceedings of International Conference on Knowledge Discovery and Data Mining (KDD), pp. 855–864 (2016)
10. Hamilton, W., Ying, Z., Leskovec, J.: Inductive representation learning on large graphs. In: Proceedings of Advances in Neural Information Processing Systems (NIPS), pp. 1024–1034 (2017)
11. Huang, Z., Mamoulis, N.: Heterogeneous information network embedding for meta path based proximity. arXiv preprint arXiv:1701.05291 (2017)
12. Hussein, R., Yang, D., Cudré-Mauroux, P.: Are meta-paths necessary?: revisiting heterogeneous graph embeddings. In: Proceedings of the 27th International Conference on Information and Knowledge Management (CIKM), pp. 437–446 (2018)
13. Liu, Z., et al.: Interactive paths embedding for semantic proximity search on heterogeneous graphs. In: Proceedings of the 24th ACM SIGKDD International Conference on Knowledge Discovery & Data Mining, pp. 1860–1869. ACM (2018)
14. Liu, Z., et al.: Semantic proximity search on heterogeneous graph by proximity embedding. In: Proceedings of 31st Conference on Artificial Intelligence (AAAI) (2017)
15. Mikolov, T., Chen, K., Corrado, G., Dean, J.: Efficient estimation of word representations in vector space. In: Proceedings of the 1st International Conference on Learning Representations (ICLR) (2013)
16. Mukherjee, S., Oates, T., Wright, R.: Graph node embeddings using domain-aware biased random walks. arXiv preprint arXiv:1908.02947 (2019)
17. Perozzi, B., Al-Rfou, R., Skiena, S.: DeepWalk: online learning of social representations. In: Proceedings of the 20th International Conference on Knowledge Discovery and Data Mining (KDD), pp. 701–710 (2014)
18. Pirrò, G.: Building relatedness explanations from knowledge graphs. Semant. Web **10**(6), 963–990 (2019)
19. Recht, B., Re, C., Wright, S., Niu, F.: HOGWILD: a lock-free approach to parallelizing stochastic gradient descent. In: Proceedings of Advances in Neural Information Processing Systems (NIPS), pp. 693–701 (2011)
20. Ristoski, P., Rosati, J., Di Noia, T., De Leone, R., Paulheim, H.: RDF2Vec: RDF graph embeddings and their applications. Semant. Web **10**(4), 721–752 (2019)
21. Shang, J., Qu, M., Liu, J., Kaplan, L.M., Han, J., Peng, J.: Meta-path guided embedding for similarity search in large-scale heterogeneous information networks. arXiv preprint arXiv:1610.09769 (2016)
22. Shi, Y., Zhu, Q., Guo, F., Zhang, C., Han, J.: Easing embedding learning by comprehensive transcription of heterogeneous information networks. In: Proceedings of International Conference on Knowledge Discovery & Data Mining (KDD), pp. 2190–2199 (2018)
23. Tang, J., Qu, M., Mei, Q.: PTE: predictive text embedding through large-scale heterogeneous text networks. In: Proceedings of 21st International Conference on Knowledge Discovery and Data Mining, pp. 1165–1174 (2015)

24. Tang, J., Qu, M., Wang, M., Zhang, M., Yan, J., Mei, Q.: LINE: large-scale information network embedding. In: Proceedings of 24th International Conference on World Wide Web (WWW), pp. 1067–1077 (2015)
25. Yang, C., Xiao, Y., Zhang, Y., Sun, Y., Han, J.: Heterogeneous network representation learning: survey, benchmark, evaluation, and beyond. arXiv preprint arXiv:2004.00216 (2020)
26. Lu, Y., Shi, C., Hu, L., Liu, Z.: Relation structure-aware heterogeneous information network embedding. In: Proceedings of 33rd Conference on Artificial Intelligence (AAAI) (2019)
27. Zafarani, R., Liu, H.: Social computing data repository at ASU (2009)
28. Zhang, C., Swami, A., Chawla, N.V.: SHNE: representation learning for semantic-associated heterogeneous networks. In: Proceedings of 12th International Conference on Web Search and Data Mining (WSDM), pp. 690–698 (2019)
29. Zhang, D., Yin, J., Zhu, X., Zhang, C.: MetaGraph2Vec: complex semantic path augmented heterogeneous network embedding. In: Proceedings of Pacific-Asia Conference on Knowledge Discovery and Data Mining, pp. 196–208 (2018)

Learning Short-Term Differences and Long-Term Dependencies for Entity Alignment

Jia Chen[1], Zhixu Li[1,2,3](✉), Pengpeng Zhao[1], An Liu[1], Lei Zhao[1], Zhigang Chen[3], and Xiangliang Zhang[4]

[1] School of Computer Science and Technology, Soochow University, Suzhou, China
jchen0812@stu.suda.edu.cn, {zhixuli,ppzhao,anliu,zhaol}@suda.edu.cn
[2] IFLYTEK Research, Suzhou, China
[3] State Key Laboratory of Cognitive Intelligence, iFLYTEK, Hefei, People's Republic of China
zgchen@iflytek.com
[4] King Abdullah University of Science and Technology, Thuwal, Saudi Arabia
xiangliang.zhang@kaust.edu.sa

Abstract. We study the problem of structure-based entity alignment between knowledge graphs (KGs). The recent mainstream solutions for it apply KG embedding techniques to map entities into a vector space, where the similarity between entities could be measured accordingly. However, these methods which are mostly based on TransE and its variants treat relation triples in KGs independently. As a result, they fail to capture some advanced interactions between entities that are implicit in the surrounding and multi-hop entities: One is the differences between the one-hop and two-hop neighborhood of an entity, which we call as short-term differences, while the other is the dependencies between entities that are far apart, which we call as long-term dependencies. Based on the above observations, this paper proposes a novel approach learning to capture both the short-term differences and the long-term dependencies in KGs for entity alignment using graph neural networks and self-attention mechanisms respectively. Our empirical study conducted on four couples of real-world datasets shows the superiority of our model, compared with the state-of-the-art methods.

Keywords: Knowledge graph · Entity alignment · KG embedding

1 Introduction

Entity alignment (EA) aims at associating entities across different knowledge graphs (KGs) if they refer to the same real-world object. As numerous KGs have been constructed and applied in recent years, it is necessary to connect or merge them to comprehensively represent the knowledge in one domain or a specific cross-domain. To measure the similarity between entities across different

J. Z. Pan et al. (Eds.): ISWC 2020, LNCS 12506, pp. 92–109, 2020.
https://doi.org/10.1007/978-3-030-62419-4_6

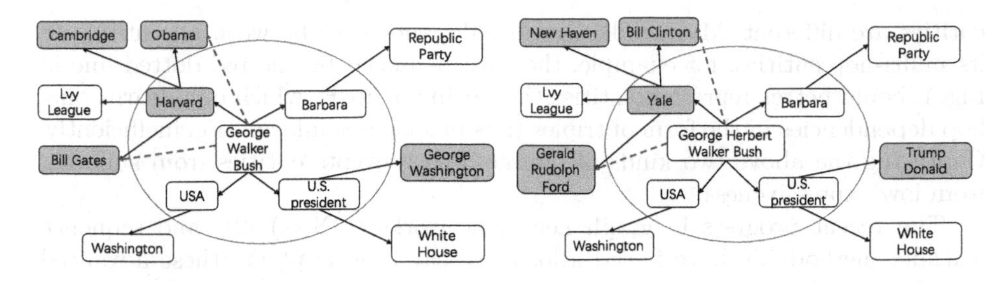

Fig. 1. Two implicit advanced interactions between entities in the EA scenario (Color figure online)

KGs, traditional methods mainly rely on designing proper features [12,14] which are labor-intensive and hard to transfer, while recent work [4,16] focus on applying various kinds of KG embedding models, which have shown their effectiveness on entity alignment. Although much other information such as the attributes, attribute values, and descriptions of entities could be utilized to enhance the embedding results for entity alignment, the mainstream studies always concentrate on using structure information, i.e., the relation triples in KGs.

The key idea of embedding-based methods is to encode entities and relations into vector spaces and then find alignment between entities according to their embedding similarities. Most embedding-based methods are developed from TransE [2], a seminal work in the KG embedding field, encoding entities and relations into vector spaces and making them satisfy some specific mathematical operations. MTransE [4] and SEA [16] are extensions of the TransE model for entity alignment task, they encode two KGs via TransE separately and learn transitions to map an entity's embedding in one KG to its counterpart in the other one. Different from adjusting entities using mapping functions, IPTransE [25] and BootEA [18] propose to swap aligned entities to calibrate the embeddings of entities in two KGs into a unified embedding space and generate more aligned entities during the process of iteration. JAPE [17], KDcoE [3], AttrE [19] and MultiKE [24] combine structure-based TransE with other external embeddings, such as attribute-based TransE, name-based TransE and entity description embeddings to get better representations for entities.

However, TransE and its variants learn embeddings from triples independently and thus fail to capture some advanced interactions between entities that are implicit in the surrounding and multi-hop entities. One implicit complex interaction between entities is the differences between the one-hop and two-hop neighborhood of an entity, which we call as **short-term differences**, while the other is the dependencies between entities that are far apart, which we call as **long-term dependencies**. As the example illustrated in Fig. 1, the traditional embedding results of "Geroge Walker Bush" and "Geroge Herbert Walker Bush" learned from their one-hop neighbors (i.e., those within the blue circle) may hardly distinguish them, but the short-term differences of the two entities could let them be better represented and distinguished as many of their two-hop entities are different. Meanwhile, learning dependencies between an entity and its multi-hop entities, for example, the entities linked by the red dotted line in Fig. 1, could better represent entities than using TransE, which only learns one-hop dependencies in the form of triples thus propagates information inefficiently. Capturing the above two kinds of interactions prevents entities from suffering from low expressiveness.

The recent progress in graph neural networks (GNNs) [21] and sequence learning methods [5] have fueled a lot of research on applying these advanced models to entity alignment. GCN-Align [22] is the first to train graph convolutional networks (GCNs) on KGs, it quantifies relations in triples and embeds entities of each KG into a unified space. However, like the TransE-based methods, it also overlooks the differences in the surrounding entities and the dependencies between multi-hop entities. Instead of directly modeling triples or neighbors, RSNs [8] is proposed to learn from relational paths through an RNN-based sequence model where long-term dependencies between entities can be captured. Nevertheless, its sequence model precludes parallelization and the generated paths are biased to entities and relations of high degree. Besides, it is also not sensitive to short-term differences.

In this paper, we propose a novel model that can capture both the short-term differences and long-term dependencies. First, we leverage the self-attention mechanism [20] to model dependencies between entities without regard to the distance between items in the sequences generated by a well-designed degree-aware random walk. Second, unlike GCNs that update nodes' vectors by incorporating first-order neighbors, we capture short-term differences of entities by repeatedly mixing neighborhood information aggregated at various distances [1]. Then, a linear combination is used to concatenate embeddings learned from the above two modules as the final representation. Finally, we find alignments by calculating their embedding similarities.

In summary, our main contributions are listed as follows:

- This work is the first attempt to captures both the long-term dependencies and the short-term differences in KGs for entity alignment.
- We propose to utilize the self-attention mechanism instead of RNN to model long-term dependencies between entities and devise a degree-aware random walk to generate high-quality sequences in KGs.
- To obtain the representation of the short-term differences of entities, we introduce a new graph neural network, from which we can better interpret the short-term semantics of an entity from its surrounding neighbors.
- Our extensive empirical study conducted on four real-world datasets shows the superiority and efficacy of our method, compared with the state-of-the-art structure-based methods.

2 Related Work

KG embedding techniques have evolved rapidly in recent years and their usefulness has been demonstrated in entity alignment. The current methods for embedding-based entity alignment models fall into the following three categories:

2.1 TransE-Based Entity Alignment

TransE [2] is the most representative model in KG embedding approaches. It holds the assumption that when mapping a triple (h, r, t) in KGs into a vector space, the triple should satisfy $\mathbf{h} + \mathbf{r} \approx \mathbf{t}$, where $\mathbf{h}$, $\mathbf{r}$ and $\mathbf{t}$ are the corresponding vectors of h, r, t in the vector space. MTransE [4] encodes triples of each KG in a separated embedding space via TransE, and makes use of seed alignments to learn transitions for each embedding vector to its counterpart in the other space. IPTransE [25] and BootEA [18] learn to map embeddings of different KGs into the same space and perform iterative entity alignment to update the joint embeddings and provide more training samples. Instead of utilizing the limited aligned entities, SEA [16] is proposed to learn transitions from both labeled and unlabeled data. It also mitigates the effect of degree differences in the existing KG embedding methods by adversarial training. Further, several works, such as JAPE [17] and AttrE [19], considers to learn representations from the structure and attribute information in KGs while KDcoE [3] and MultiKE [24] leverage descriptions, names and attributes to enhance the structure-based embedding methods. All the methods above focus on the utilization of existing TransE-based methods that treat triples separately, including MultiKE, which learns comprehensive entity embeddings from different views. However, the hidden complex information involved in the surrounding and multi-hop entities is neglected and thus remained to be exploited.

2.2 GNN-Based Entity Alignment

As entities can be seen as nodes in graphs, GNN is then proposed for entity alignment. GCN-Align [22] is the first attempt to generate node-level embeddings by encoding information about the nodes' neighborhoods via GCN, which is a type of convolutional network that directly operates on graph data. It assumes that equivalent entities are usually neighbored by some other equivalent entities and they tend to have similar attributes, so when GCN produces neighborhood-aware embeddings of entities, alignment can be predicted by a pre-defined distance function. Inga [15] introduces an iterative training mechanism on GCN-Align and improves the initial attribute feature by considering local and global attribute information. Unlike the above node-level matching, [23] formulates the alignment task as a graph matching problem. It proposes a topic graph structure and matches all entities in two topic entity graphs by attentive node-level matching. However, none of them considers the importance of differences in the surrounding entities of an entity. Besides, although high-order dependency information, i.e., long-term dependencies, can be captured by increasing the number of GNN propagation layers, embeddings tend to be the same for different nodes and the noise introduced can not be ignored, as reported in [11].

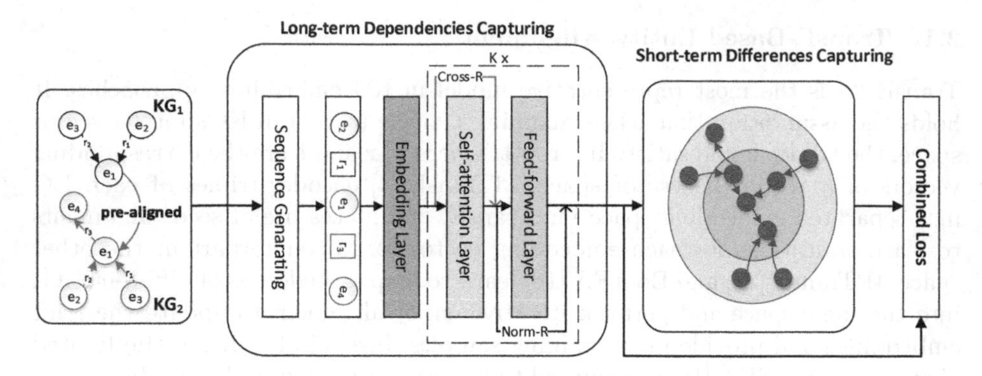

Fig. 2. The architecture of our proposed model

2.3 Sequence-Based Entity Alignment

Sequence is a ubiquitous data structure, employed extensively in natural language processing and related fields. RSNs [8] is the first to investigate long-term relational dependencies in KGs. It uses biased random walk to sample paths in KGs which are composed of entities and relations alternately and then models relational paths through recurrent skipping networks rather than recurrent neural networks due to the unique triple structure in KGs. In specific, RSNs makes the output hidden states of relations learn a residual from their direct former entities in the sequences. Though it achieves a significant performance improvement and outperforms TransE-based and GCN-based methods, it is also unaware of the short-term differences of entities and unable to capture long-term dependencies between entities well enough. As pointed out in a recent study of machine translation [20], without any recurrent or convolutional structures, long-term dependencies between words in sequences can be captured effectively by solely using self-attention mechanisms. Therefore, we seek to propose a model that can capture both the long-term dependencies and the short-term differences in KGs for entity alignment using self-attention mechanisms and graph neural networks, respectively.

3 Our Proposed Model

In this section, we introduce the proposed model for entity alignment. We first formulate the problem of entity alignment in KGs and then describe the proposed model in detail.

3.1 Problem Formulation

In this paper, we consider structure-based entity alignment between KGs, which aims to learn entity embeddings merely based on structure information in KGs (i.e., relation triples). A KG can be noted as a 3-tuple $G = (E, R, T)$, where E,

R, and T denote the set of entities, relations and triples, respectively. Triples have three components: head entity h, relation r and tail entity t. A triple is always presented as (h, r, t).

Our problem is formulated as follows: Given two KGs $G_1 = (E_1, R_1, T_1)$, $G_2 = (E_2, R_2, T_2)$ and some pre-aligned entity pairs $S = \{(e_i, e_j)|e_i \in E_1, e_j \in E_2\}$, entity alignment is aimed at discovering new equivalent entities $N = \{(e_{i'}, e_{j'})|e_{i'} \in E_1, e_{j'} \in E_2\}$ based on S.

3.2 Capturing Long-Term Dependencies

The overview of our model is presented in Fig. 2. The first part is designed to facilitate the learning of long-term dependencies between entities. It first connects two KGs as one joint KG by pre-aligned entities and adds reverse relations between entities to enhance connectivity. Then, after generating entity-relation sequences for each triple through a degree-aware random walk method, leverages a self-attention based sequence predicting model to capture the long-term dependencies.

Sequence Generating. Sequence generating takes two KGs and a set of pre-aligned entities as input to produce sequences $P = \{p_1, p_2, \cdots p_i, \ldots, p_l\}$, where $p_i = (e_{i_1}, r_{i_2}, \ldots, e_{i_m})$, made up of entities and relations alternately. To obtain desired sequences, inspired by random walk which is widely used in networks [6], we propose a degree-aware random walk for KG to maintain a balanced collection of information between long-tail entities and frequent entities. More specifically, we leverage the idea of node2vec [7] and introduce a depth bias and a degree bias to reduce the likelihood of revisiting an entity's one-hop neighbors and increase the likelihood of visiting entities of low-degree, respectively. To formalize, when the current entity is e_i, the transition probability to the next entity e_{i+1}, denoted as $P(e_{i+1}|e_i)$, is calculated as follows:

$$P(e_{i+1}|e_i) = \alpha_{dp}(e_i, e_{i+1}) \cdot \beta_{dg}(e_i, e_{i+1}) \tag{1}$$

where $\alpha_{dp}(e_i, e_{i+1})$ is the depth bias and $\beta_{dg}(e_i, e_{i+1})$ is the degree bias. They are defined as follows:

$$\alpha_{dp}(e_i, e_{i+1}) = \begin{cases} q & d(e_{i-1}, e_{i+1}) = 2 \\ 1-q & d(e_{i-1}, e_{i+1}) \neq 2 \end{cases} \tag{2}$$

where q is a hyperparameter ranging from 0 to 1 controlling the depths, e_{i-1} is the previous entity of e_i and $d(e_{i-1}, e_{i+1})$ denotes the shortest distance from e_{i-1} to e_{i+1}.

$$\beta_{dg}(e_i, e_{i+1}) = \begin{cases} \frac{1}{d_{e_{i+1}}+f_r} & \exists r \in R, (e_i, r, e_{i+1}) \in T \\ 0 & otherwise \end{cases} \tag{3}$$

where $d_{e_{i+1}}$ gains the number of entities linked with e_{i+1}, and we name it the degree of entity e_{i+1}. f_r indicates the occurrence number of relation r in all triples.

It is noticeable that the bias we designed favor entities that haven't appeared in a specific sequence and have a low degree, which ensures the high quality of the generated sequences.

Self-attention-Based Sequence Predicting. The inputs of this module are sequences P and the goal of it is to effectively capture the long-term dependencies between items in P. The beginning of this module consists of three kinds of embeddings: entity embedding $\boldsymbol{E}$, relation embedding $\boldsymbol{R}$, and position embedding $\boldsymbol{P}$. After adding the embeddings of items in sequences to their corresponding positional embeddings, the output of the embedding layer $\hat{\boldsymbol{E}}$ is obtained and fed to the self-attention layer.

$$\begin{aligned} \boldsymbol{S} &= Concat(head_1, \ldots, head_h) \\ where\, head_h &= softmax(\frac{(\hat{\boldsymbol{E}}\boldsymbol{W}_h^Q)(\hat{\boldsymbol{E}}\boldsymbol{W}_h^K)^T}{\sqrt{d}})(\hat{\boldsymbol{E}}\boldsymbol{W}_h^V) \end{aligned} \tag{4}$$

where $\boldsymbol{W}_h^Q$, $\boldsymbol{W}_h^K$, and $\boldsymbol{W}_h^V$ are projection matrices of $head_h$, and the output of self-attention layer is the simple concatenation of multiple heads.

Hereafter, distinct from the normal residual connection (Norm-R) in [20], we use a specific crossed residual (Cross-R) connection $\boldsymbol{C}$ to better optimize the model due to the unique triple structure in KGs. It means that when capturing long-term dependencies, the importance of tripe structure should be reflected, so when the input is a relation, a residual from its previous entity is needed.

$$\boldsymbol{C}_i = \begin{cases} \boldsymbol{S}_i & \frac{i+1}{2} \in \mathbb{N}^+ \\ \boldsymbol{S}_i + \hat{\boldsymbol{E}}_{\frac{i}{2}} & \frac{i}{2} \in \mathbb{N}^+ \end{cases} \tag{5}$$

Then, we employ a point-wise feed-forward network and a normal residual connection (Norm-R) to allow interactions within different latent dimensions inspired by [20].

$$\boldsymbol{F} = \boldsymbol{C} + ReLU(\boldsymbol{C}\boldsymbol{W}_1 + b_1)\boldsymbol{W}_2 + b_2 \tag{6}$$

where $ReLU$ is activation function, $\boldsymbol{W}_1$ and $\boldsymbol{W}_2$ are trainable matrices and b_1 and b_2 are bias vectors.

We can further stack more layers to explore different types of dependencies. Formally, for the *k-th* layer, we recursively formulate the representation as:

$$\hat{\boldsymbol{E}}^{(k)} = SA(\hat{\boldsymbol{E}}^{(k-1)}) \tag{7}$$

where $k > 1$, $\hat{\boldsymbol{E}}^{(1)} = \hat{\boldsymbol{E}}$ and SA is made up of the above self-attention layer with crossed residual connection and feed-forward layer with normal residual connection.

After performing k layers, we obtain representations of long-term dependencies for entities and relations. We optimize the embeddings of items in sequences by adopting the sequence predicting method and leverage the idea used in [13] to accelerate training. The prediction loss of one sequence is defined as follows:

$$\mathcal{L}_{LD}^{(1)} = -\sum_{i=1}^{m-1}\Big(\log\sigma(\hat{\boldsymbol{E}}_i\cdot\boldsymbol{y}_i) + \sum_{j=1}^{n}\mathbb{E}_{y'_j\sim P(y')}\big[\log\sigma(-\hat{\boldsymbol{E}}_i\cdot\boldsymbol{y}'_j)\big]\Big) \quad (8)$$

where m is the number of items in the sequence, σ is an activation function, $\boldsymbol{y}_i$ is the object of the i-th item while y'_j is the j-th negative sample of it. n is the number of negative samples and $P(y')$ is the noise distribution where only items whose frequencies appear in the first three-quarters can be found, it changes according to the current item is entity or relation, which indicates that the object and its corresponding negative examples come from the same type. Adding the prediction loss of all l sequences is the whole loss of the long-term dependencies capturing model.

$$\mathcal{L}_{LD} = \sum_{i=1}^{l}\mathcal{L}_{LD}^{(i)} \quad (9)$$

3.3 Capturing Short-Term Differences

Next, we build upon the architecture of graph neural networks to capture short-term differences of entities. The major difference to [10] lies in that our graph convolutional network encodes neighborhood information at various distances rather than first-order neighborhood features, as such, short-term semantics of an entity can be augmented.

Formally, this module takes the vectors learned from the above self-attention based layers as input to produce embeddings of short-term differences for each entity as follows:

$$\boldsymbol{H}^{(i)} = \begin{cases} \hat{\boldsymbol{E}}^{(k)} & \text{if} \, i = 0 \\ \big\Vert_{j\in A}\ \sigma(\hat{\boldsymbol{A}}^{j}\boldsymbol{H}^{(i-1)}\boldsymbol{W}_j^{(i)}) & \text{if} \, i \in [1..t] \end{cases} \quad (10)$$

where $\Vert$ denotes column-wise concatenation, A is the hyperparameter containing a set of integer adjacency powers, σ denotes an element-wise activation function, $\hat{\boldsymbol{A}}^{j}$ represents the self-defined adjacency matrix $\hat{\boldsymbol{A}}$ that is multiplied by itself j times and $\boldsymbol{W}_j^{(i)}$ is the weight matrix when gathering the j-order neighborhood information in the i-th layer. Note that, different from the commonly used adjacency matrix in GNNs: $\hat{\boldsymbol{A}} = \boldsymbol{D}^{-\frac{1}{2}}(\boldsymbol{A}+\boldsymbol{I}_n)\boldsymbol{D}^{-\frac{1}{2}}$, where $\boldsymbol{D}$ is the degree matrix, $\boldsymbol{A}$ is the connectivity matrix indicating the graph structure and $\boldsymbol{I}_n$ is the $n\times n$ identity matrix making $\hat{\boldsymbol{A}}$ symmetrically normalized with self-connections, we remove I_n from $\hat{\boldsymbol{A}}$ since our goal is to capture short-term differences surrounding an entity. In addition, we set $\boldsymbol{W}_j^{(1)}$ to be identity matrix because there is

Table 1. Statistics of datasets

Datasets	Source KGs	#Entity	#Norm-R	#Norm-T	#Dense-R	#Dense-T
DBP-WD	DBPdeia (English)	15,000	253	38,421	220	68,598
	Wikidata (English)	15,000	144	40,159	135	75,465
DBP-YG	DBPdeia (English)	15,000	219	33,571	206	71,257
	YAGO3 (English)	15,000	30	34,660	30	97,131
EN-FR	DBPdeia (English)	15,000	221	36,508	217	71,929
	DBPdeia (French)	15,000	177	33,532	174	66,760
EN-DE	DBPdeia (English)	15,000	225	38,281	207	56,983
	DBPdeia (German)	15,000	118	37,069	117	59,848

no need to transform the input features which have already captured long-term dependencies into higher-level features.

The short-term differences for equivalent entities are expected to be alike, hence we train the GNN model to encode equivalent entities as close as possible in the embedding space by using the pre-aligned entity pairs. We use the following loss function to measure its plausibility:

$$\mathcal{L}_{SD} = \sum_{(e_i,e_j)\in S} \sum_{(e'_i,e'_j)\in S'} \left[\|\boldsymbol{e}_i - \boldsymbol{e}_j\| + \gamma - \|\boldsymbol{e}'_i - \boldsymbol{e}'_j\|\right]_+ \tag{11}$$

where $[x]_+ = \max\{0, x\}$, $\|\cdot\|$ denotes either L_1 or L_2 vector norm, γ is a margin hyperparameter which is greater than 0, and S' denotes the set of negative-sampled entity alignments by replacing e_i or e_j in S.

3.4 Combined Loss

To preserve both the long-term and short-term complex information of entities, we jointly minimize the following loss function:

$$\mathcal{L}_{joint} = \mathcal{L}_{LD} + \mathcal{L}_{SD} \tag{12}$$

Considering the complementarity between the embeddings of long-term dependencies captured by the self-attention-based sequence model and that of short-term differences captured by GNNs, we concatenate them linearly and use the combined embeddings as entities' final representations.

$$\boldsymbol{e}_i^f = \left[\theta \boldsymbol{e}_i^{ld}; (1-\theta)\boldsymbol{e}_i^{sd}\right] \tag{13}$$

where θ is a parameter balancing the distribution between $\boldsymbol{e}_i^{ld}$ and $\boldsymbol{e}_i^{sd}$, which are the embedding of long-term dependencies and the embedding of short-term differences, respectively.

4 Experiments

This section covers four parts. We start by considering datasets and details of the model in the experimental setup and then introduce baselines briefly. Ultimately, experiments and analyses are shown to validate the proposed model.

4.1 Experimental Setup

Datasets. To evaluate the effectiveness of our proposed model comprehensively, we reuse four couples of real-world datasets, namely DBP-WD, DBP-YG, EN-FR and EN-DE, recently proposed in [8]. It is worth mentioning that each dataset is sampled from real-world KGs: DBPedia (DBP), YAGO3 (YG) and Wikidata (WD) by the PageRank algorithm to ensure that their entity distributions keep consistent with original KGs, and each has two kinds of entity distributions: a normal one and a dense one. DBP-WD and DBP-YG are mono-lingual KGs while EN-FR and EN-DE are cross-lingual KGs. The statistics of the datasets are shown in Table 1 where #Norm-R denotes the number of relations in the normal datasets while #Norm-T denotes that of triples in them, and similar notations for the dense datasets. For both the normal and dense datasets, each KG contains 15,000 entities.

Implementation Details. Our model is implemented with TensorFlow. We use an embedding dimension of 256 for all methods compared in 4.2 on all datasets. Adam [9] is adopted to optimize $\mathcal{L}_{LD}$ and $\mathcal{L}_{SD}$ in turn. For the sequence generating part, we set $q = 0.9$, $m = 15$ and for the sequence predicting phase, we use 8 head in the self-attention layer and set $k = 3$. When aggregate neighborhood information, i and A in Eq. (10) are set to 2 and $\{0, 1, 2\}$, respectively and the non-linearity function σ is tanh. Besides, dropout and layer normalization are adopted to stabilize the training. For fair comparison, we sample 30% of the aligned entity set as the training set and the rest for testing for all approaches. We choose Hits@1, Hits@10 and MRR to evaluate the alignment results, where Hits@k indicates the proportion of correctly aligned entities ranked in the top k and MRR is the abbreviation of mean reciprocal rank measuring the average reciprocal values of testing entities.

4.2 Baselines

We include the following methods for performance comparison, which have been thoroughly discussed in Sect. 2:

- **MTransE** [4]**:** This is the first to leverage KG embeddings to cross-lingual knowledge alignment. It explores different kinds of mapping functions between two KGs to find alignment in an efficient way.
- **IPTranE** [25]**:** It jointly encodes different KGs into the same space and improves alignment performance by iteration strategy.
- **JAPE** [17]**:** As the first attempt to learn embeddings of cross-lingual KGs while preserving their attribute information, this model achieves a certain improvement by updating its embeddings through attribute correlations which comes from attribute type similarity.
- **BootEA** [18]**:** It introduces a bootstrapping approach to iteratively generate more likely training data for alignment-oriented KG embedding and employs an editing method to weaken error accumulation caused by iteration.

Table 2. Results on the normal and mono-lingual datasets

Datasets	DBP-WD			DBP-YG		
Metrics	Hits@1	Hits@10	MRR	Hits@1	Hits@10	MRR
MTransE	22.3	50.1	0.32	24.6	54.0	0.34
IPTransE	23.1	51.7	0.33	22.7	50.0	0.32
JAPE	21.9	50.1	0.31	23.3	52.7	0.33
BootEA	32.3	63.1	0.42	31.3	62.5	0.42
GCN-Align	17.7	37.8	0.25	19.3	41.5	0.27
SEA	31.0	51.9	0.38	30.3	45.9	0.36
RSNs	38.8	65.7	0.49	40.0	67.5	0.50
Ours w/o LD	24.4	54.9	0.34	29.8	58.9	0.40
Ours w/o SD	44.1	70.7	0.53	44.5	71.0	0.53
Ours	**46.8**	**75.3**	**0.56**	**46.5**	**74.0**	**0.56**
%Improv	20.62%	14.61%	14.29%	16.25%	9.63%	12.00%

Table 3. Results on the normal and cross-lingual datasets

Datasets	EN-FR			EN-DE		
Metrics	Hits@1	Hits@10	MRR	Hits@1	Hits@10	MRR
MTransE	25.1	55.1	0.35	31.2	58.6	0.40
IPTransE	25.5	55.7	0.36	31.3	59.2	0.41
JAPE	25.6	56.2	0.36	32.0	59.9	0.41
BootEA	31.3	62.9	0.42	44.2	70.1	0.53
GCN-Align	15.5	34.5	0.22	25.3	46.4	0.33
SEA	25.8	40.0	0.31	42.5	59.6	0.49
RSNs	34.7	63.1	0.44	48.7	72.0	0.57
Ours w/o LD	22.0	51.1	0.32	37.1	62.7	0.46
Ours w/o SD	38.3	65.8	0.47	51.3	73.4	0.59
Ours	**41.1**	**70.6**	**0.51**	**53.9**	**77.8**	**0.62**
%Improv.	18.44%	11.89%	15.91%	10.68%	8.06%	8.77%

- **GCN-Align** [22]: It proposes a novel approach for cross-lingual KG alignment, whose core is graph convolutional networks. This GNN-based method takes relations in triples as edges with weights and produces neighborhood-aware embeddings of entities to discover entity alignments.
- **SEA** [16]: An extension of the MTransE-based alignment model, whose purpose is to design a semi-supervised entity alignment model to leverage abundant unlabeled data leaving unused before and improve the original KG embedding with awareness of degree difference by an adversarial framework.

Table 4. Results on the dense and mono-lingual datasets

Datasets	DBP-WD			DBP-YG		
Metrics	Hits@1	Hits@10	MRR	Hits@1	Hits@10	MRR
MTransE	38.9	68.7	0.49	22.8	51.3	0.32
IPTransE	43.5	74.5	0.54	23.6	51.3	0.33
JAPE	39.3	70.5	0.50	26.8	57.3	0.37
BootEA	67.8	91.2	0.76	68.2	89.8	0.76
GCN-Align	43.1	71.3	0.53	31.3	57.5	0.40
SEA	67.2	85.2	0.74	68.1	84.1	0.74
RSNs	76.3	92.4	0.83	82.6	95.8	0.87
Ours w/o LD	53.5	84.7	0.64	65.4	88.2	0.74
Ours w/o SD	79.9	93.7	0.85	85.6	96.5	0.89
Ours	**81.8**	**95.9**	**0.87**	**86.9**	**97.4**	**0.91**
%Improv.	7.21%	3.79%	4.82%	5.21%	1.67%	4.60%

Table 5. Results on the dense and cross-lingual datasets

Datasets	EN-FR			EN-DE		
Metrics	Hits@1	Hits@10	MRR	Hits@1	Hits@10	MRR
MTransE	37.7	70.0	0.49	34.7	62.0	0.44
IPTransE	42.9	78.3	0.55	34.0	63.2	0.44
JAPE	40.7	72.7	0.52	37.5	66.1	0.47
BootEA	64.8	91.9	0.74	66.5	87.1	0.73
GCN-Align	37.3	70.9	0.49	32.1	55.2	0.40
SEA	62.3	85.7	0.71	65.2	79.4	0.70
RSNs	75.6	92.5	0.82	73.9	89.0	0.79
Ours w/o LD	51.6	86.0	0.63	60.9	82.2	0.68
Ours w/o SD	80.6	94.2	0.85	77.6	91.2	0.82
Ours	**83.6**	**97.2**	**0.89**	**79.4**	**93.0**	**0.84**
%Improv.	10.58%	5.08%	8.54%	7.44%	4.49%	6.33%

- **RSNs** [8]: It is a state-of-the-art structure-based alignment model, which learns embeddings from relational paths instead of triples. It captures long-term dependencies between KGs by a sequence model integrating recurrent neural networks with residual learning.

4.3 Comparisons of Performance

The experimental results on the mono-lingual and cross-lingual datasets are presented in Table 2, 3, 4 and 5, respectively. Table 2 and 3 are results on normal

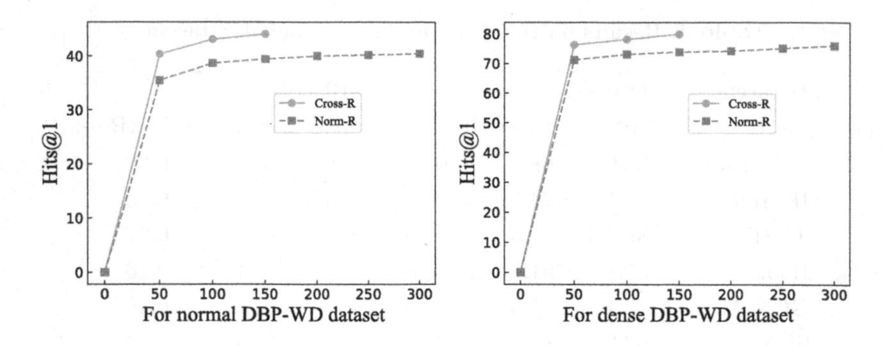

Fig. 3. Effect of the proposed Cross-R.

datasets while Table 4 and 5 are that on dense datasets. The best results are shown in bold, along with the percentage of improvement when comparing our method with the best baseline method. Ours w/o LD and Ours w/o SD denote our model without capturing long-term dependencies and short-term differences, respectively, and they are disabled by ignoring the loss. From the results, we have the following findings:

For the baseline methods, TransE-based models perform better than GNN-based GCN-Align in most cases. One possible reason is that GCN-Align weakens the role of relations and only expresses them numerically in the adjacency matrix. Among the TransE-based methods, BootEA always achieves better performance than SEA as it finds alignments in an efficient and iterative manner while SEA prevents entities of similar degree from being aggregated into the same region in the embedding space without discovering more alignments. It is noticeable that the sequence-based method RSNs outperforms all the other baselines, whether it is a TransE-based or GNN-based, on both the normal and dense datasets, which verifies the effectiveness and significance of capturing long-term relational dependencies between entities in KGs.

Compared to RSNs, the performance of Ours w/o SD demonstrates that introducing the self-attention mechanism is of importance to enhance the long-term dependency representations of entities. Ours w/o LD outperforms GCN-Align by a large margin and achieves comparable performance to some TransE-based approaches mainly because its multi-hop neighborhood concatenating layers allows GNN to capture the complex and hidden interactions existing in the surrounding entities. By considering both the long-term dependencies and short-term differences in KGs, our complete method consistently yields the best performance on all datasets in terms of all evaluation metrics, especially on Hits@1 and MRR, indicating the complementarity between the self-attention-based sequence model and the GNN-based model. In particular, our model improves over the best baseline RSNs w.r.t. Hits@1 by more than 10% and 5% on the normal and dense datasets, respectively. The superiority is more evident on the normal and monolingual datasets with more than 15% improvement. One possible reason is that cross-lingual datasets are extracted from one KG with different languages.

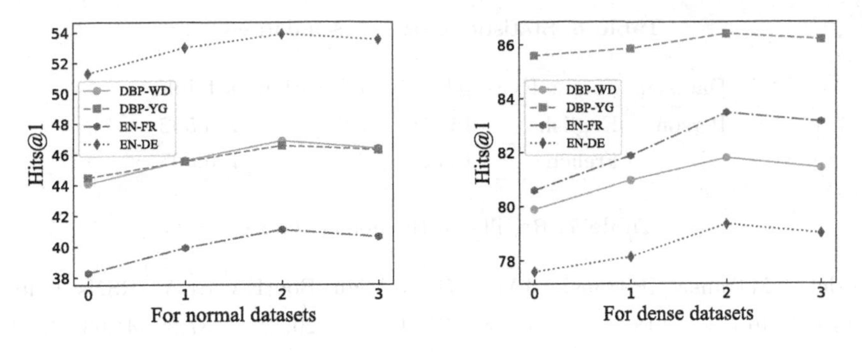

Fig. 4. Effect of the number of GNN layers t.

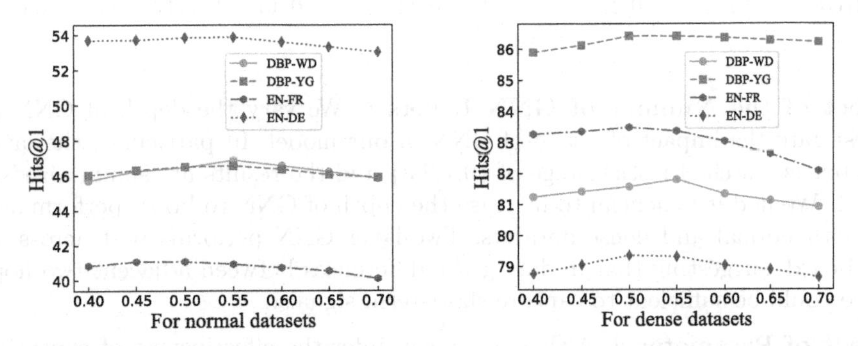

Fig. 5. Effect of parameter θ.

Hence they are less heterogeneous than monolingual datasets and thus easier to be represented. Moreover, compared with our model without long-term dependencies and short-term differences, the results justify the validity and efficacy of the complete model.

4.4 Model Analyses

In this subsection, we take a deep insight into the model to further understand the proposed architecture. As Hits@1 is the preferable metric, we only show the results on it. To evaluate the feasibility of our proposed crossed residual connection (Cross-R), we conduct experiments to compare it with the original norm residual connection (Norm-R). Both of them are under the same settings of long-term dependencies capturing model and disabled loss of short-term differences. Besides, we select two representative parameters for in-depth discussion.

Effect of the Crossed Residual Connection. Figure 3 shows the results of different residual connections on normal and dense DBP-WD dataset. Our proposed Cross-R achieves better performance with less epoch on both of them, which indicates that considering the unique triple structure is vital for learning long-term dependencies in KGs.

Table 6. Statistics of the person dataset

Datasets	Source KGs	#Entity	#Relation	#Triple
Person	English	15,170	2,228	203,502
	French	15,393	2,442	170,605

Table 7. Results on the person dataset

Model	MTransE	IPTransE	JAPE	GCN-Align	BootEA	SEA	RSNs	Ours
Hits@1	16.77	18.21	15.68	17.24	29.72	37.28	44.63	49.13
Hits@10	25.35	27.41	28.69	31.16	61.19	63.56	70.10	76.87
MRR	0.20	0.21	0.21	0.22	0.40	0.47	0.57	0.63

Effect of the Number of GNN Layers t**.** We vary the depth of GNN to investigate the impact of usage of GNN in our model. In particular, the layer number is searched in the range of {0,1,2,3} and the results are summarized in Fig. 4. We find it beneficial to increase the depth of GNN to boost performance on both normal and dense datasets. Two-layer GNN performs best across all the board, suggesting that updating the differences between adjacent two hops twice could be sufficient to capture short-term signals.

Effect of Parameter θ**.** Although we can infer the effectiveness of capturing long-term dependencies and short-term differences implicitly from Table 2, 3, 4 and 5, we would like to see how the two different modules contribute to our complete model. As depicted in Fig. 5, the parameter θ, which controls the contribution of the long-term dependency representations, is capable of balancing between the long-term dependencies and short-term differences. Jointly analyzing Table 2, 3, 4 and 5 with Fig. 5, we find that adaptively combining these two kinds of embeddings outperforms a single model and the best results are always achieved at $\theta = 0.55$. It indicates that the sequence model is of crucial significance and the GNN model is indispensable to enable the model with short-term differences capturing ability. Both of them play important roles in improving entity alignment performance.

4.5 Case Study

In this subsection, we perform an extra experimental evaluation on a specific domain provided in [16] to comprehensively evaluate the performance of our approach. The statistics of this person dataset is given in Table 6, which includes KGs in English and French, each of which contains more than 15,000 entities and 2,000 relations. There are 10,108 aligned entities between the two KGs.

The evaluation results are presented in Table 7. Our proposed model still outperforms other baselines on all metrics with about 10% improvement on Hits@1 and MRR compared to the second best method, which is consistent with the previous experiments and demonstrates the effectiveness of our model.

5 Conclusions

In this paper, short-term differences and long-term dependencies in KGs for entity alignment are illustrated for the first time. We propose a novel approach to manage to capture both short-term differences and long-term dependencies in KGs for our task. Specifically, we utilize and adapt the self-attention mechanism instead of RNN to model long-term dependencies between entities and devise a degree-aware random walk to generate high-quality sequences in KGs for learning. Next, to acquire the representation of the short-term differences of entities, we introduce a new graph neural network to treat triples as a graph, from which we can better interpret the short-term semantics of an entity by repeatedly mixing neighborhood information aggregated at various distances. Eventually, embeddings of entities can be obtained by combining short-term and long-term semantics in a linear way. Extensive experiments and analyses on four couples of real-world datasets demonstrate that our model consistently outperformed the state-of-the-art methods.

Acknowledgments. This research is partially supported by National Key R&D Program of China (No. 2018AAA0101900), the Priority Academic Program Development of Jiangsu Higher Education Institutions, Natural Science Foundation of Jiangsu Province (No. BK20191420), National Natural Science Foundation of China (Grant No. 62072323, 61632016), Natural Science Research Project of Jiangsu Higher Education Institution (No. 17KJA520003, 18KJA520010).

References

1. Abu-El-Haija, S., et al.: MixHop: higher-order graph convolution architectures via sparsified neighborhood mixing. In: Proceedings of the 36th International Conference on Machine Learning, vol. 97, pp. 21–29. PMLR, Long Beach (2019)
2. Bordes, A., Usunier, N., Garcia-Duran, A., Weston, J., Yakhnenko, O.: Translating embeddings for modeling multi-relational data. In: 27th Annual Conference on Neural Information Processing Systems 2013, Nevada, United States, pp. 2787–2795 (2013)
3. Chen, M., Tian, Y., Chang, K.W., Skiena, S., Zaniolo, C.: Co-training embeddings of knowledge graphs and entity descriptions for cross-lingual entity alignment. In: Proceedings of the Twenty-Seventh International Joint Conference on Artificial Intelligence, Stockholm, Sweden, pp. 3998–4004 (2018)
4. Chen, M., Tian, Y., Yang, M., Zaniolo, C.: Multilingual knowledge graph embeddings for cross-lingual knowledge alignment. In: Proceedings of the Twenty-Sixth International Joint Conference on Artificial Intelligence, Melbourne, Australia, pp. 1511–1517 (2017)
5. Devlin, J., Chang, M.W., Lee, K., Toutanova, K.: BERT: pre-training of deep bidirectional transformers for language understanding. In: Proceedings of the 2019 Conference of the North American Chapter of the Association for Computational Linguistics: Human Language Technologies, pp. 4171–4186 (2019)
6. Goyal, P., Ferrara, E.: Graph embedding techniques, applications, and performance: a survey. Knowl.-Based Syst. **151**, 78–94 (2018)

7. Grover, A., Leskovec, J.: node2vec: scalable feature learning for networks. In: Proceedings of the 22nd International Conference on Knowledge Discovery and Data Mining, pp. 855–864. ACM, San Francisco (2016)
8. Guo, L., Sun, Z., Hu, W.: Learning to exploit long-term relational dependencies in knowledge graphs. In: Proceedings of the 36th International Conference on Machine Learning, vol. 97, pp. 2505–2514. PMLR, Long Beach (2019)
9. Kingma, D.P., Ba, J.: Adam: a method for stochastic optimization. In: 3rd International Conference on Learning Representations, San Diego, California (2015)
10. Kipf, T.N., Welling, M.: Semi-supervised classification with graph convolutional networks. In: 5th International Conference on Learning Representations, Toulon, France (2017)
11. Li, Q., Han, Z., Wu, X.M.: Deeper insights into graph convolutional networks for semi-supervised learning. In: Proceedings of the Thirty-Second AAAI Conference on Artificial Intelligence, New Orleans, Louisiana, pp. 3538–3545 (2018)
12. Mahdisoltani, F., Biega, J., Suchanek, F.M.: YAGO3: a knowledge base from multilingual Wikipedias. In: Seventh Biennial Conference on Innovative Data Systems Research, Asilomar, California (2015)
13. Mikolov, T., Sutskever, I., Chen, K., Corrado, G.S., Dean, J.: Distributed representations of words and phrases and their compositionality. In: 27th Annual Conference on Neural Information Processing Systems, Lake Tahoe, Nevada, pp. 3111–3119 (2013)
14. Ngomo, A.C.N., Auer, S.: LIMES-a time-efficient approach for large-scale link discovery on the web of data. In: Twenty-Second International Joint Conference on Artificial Intelligence, Catalonia, Spain, pp. 2312–2317 (2011)
15. Pang, N., Zeng, W., Tang, J., Tan, Z., Zhao, X.: Iterative entity alignment with improved neural attribute embedding. In: Proceedings of the Workshop on Deep Learning for Knowledge Graphs, vol. 2377, pp. 41–46. CEUR-WS.org, Portoroz (2019)
16. Pei, S., Yu, L., Hoehndorf, R., Zhang, X.: Semi-supervised entity alignment via knowledge graph embedding with awareness of degree difference. In: The World Wide Web Conference, pp. 3130–3136. ACM, San Francisco (2019)
17. Sun, Z., Hu, W., Li, C.: Cross-lingual entity alignment via joint attribute-preserving embedding. In: d'Amato, C., et al. (eds.) ISWC 2017. LNCS, vol. 10587, pp. 628–644. Springer, Cham (2017). https://doi.org/10.1007/978-3-319-68288-4_37
18. Sun, Z., Hu, W., Zhang, Q., Qu, Y.: Bootstrapping entity alignment with knowledge graph embedding. In: Proceedings of the Twenty-Seventh International Joint Conference on Artificial Intelligence, Stockholm, Sweden, pp. 4396–4402 (2018)
19. Trisedya, B.D., Qi, J., Zhang, R.: Entity alignment between knowledge graphs using attribute embeddings. In: The Thirty-Third AAAI Conference on Artificial Intelligence, Honolulu, Hawaii, pp. 297–304 (2019)
20. Vaswani, A., et al.: Attention is all you need. In: Advances in Neural Information Processing Systems 30: Annual Conference on Neural Information Processing Systems, Long Beach, California, pp. 5998–6008 (2017)
21. Velickovic, P., Cucurull, G., Casanova, A., Romero, A., Liò, P., Bengio, Y.: Graph attention networks. In: 6th International Conference on Learning Representations, Vancouver, Canada (2018)
22. Wang, Z., Lv, Q., Lan, X., Zhang, Y.: Cross-lingual knowledge graph alignment via graph convolutional networks. In: Proceedings of the 2018 Conference on Empirical Methods in Natural Language Processing, pp. 349–357. Association for Computational Linguistics, Brussels (2018)

23. Xu, K., et al.: Cross-lingual knowledge graph alignment via graph matching neural network. In: Proceedings of the 57th Conference of the Association for Computational Linguistics, pp. 3156–3161. Association for Computational Linguistics, Florence (2019)
24. Zhang, Q., Sun, Z., Hu, W., Chen, M., Guo, L., Qu, Y.: Multi-view knowledge graph embedding for entity alignment. In: Proceedings of the Twenty-Eighth International Joint Conference on Artificial Intelligence, Macao, China, pp. 5429–5435 (2019)
25. Zhu, H., Xie, R., Liu, Z., Sun, M.: Iterative entity alignment via joint knowledge embeddings. In: Proceedings of the Twenty-Sixth International Joint Conference on Artificial Intelligence, Melbourne, Australia, pp. 4258–4264 (2017)

Generating Compact and Relaxable Answers to Keyword Queries over Knowledge Graphs

Gong Cheng[1(✉)], Shuxin Li[1], Ke Zhang[1], and Chengkai Li[2]

[1] State Key Laboratory for Novel Software Technology, Nanjing University, Nanjing, China
gcheng@nju.edu.cn, {sxli,161120169}@smail.nju.edu.cn
[2] Department of Computer Science and Engineering, University of Texas at Arlington, Arlington, USA
cli@uta.edu

Abstract. Keyword search has been a prominent approach to querying knowledge graphs. For exploratory search tasks, existing methods commonly extract subgraphs that are group Steiner trees (GSTs) as answers. However, a GST that connects all the query keywords may not exist, or may inevitably have a large and unfocused graph structure in contrast to users' favor to a compact answer. Therefore, in this paper, we aim at generating compact but relaxable subgraphs as answers, i.e., we require a computed subgraph to have a bounded diameter but allow it to only connect an incomplete subset of query keywords. We formulate it as a new combinatorial optimization problem of computing a minimally relaxed answer with a compactness guarantee, and we present a novel best-first search algorithm. Extensive experiments showed that our approach efficiently computed compact answers of high completeness.

Keywords: Keyword search · Knowledge graph · Query relaxation

1 Introduction

Non-expert users have difficulty in querying a knowledge graph (KG) without a prior knowledge of the specialized query language. Keyword search provides users with convenient access to KGs, by automatically matching keyword queries with KGs. For a lookup task where there is a specific search target that can be represented as a precise formal query such as a SPARQL query over RDF-based KGs, existing methods commonly transform the keyword query into a formal query to execute [10,22,25]. For exploratory search [19] where the keyword query and the underlying search target are vague and cannot be precisely interpreted as a formal query, e.g., searching for relationships between a set of entities [2], one promising solution is to directly extract subgraphs from KGs that contain query keywords as answers [7,16,18,23]. The extracted subgraphs should satisfy certain constraints and have high quality. For example, it has been standard to

J. Z. Pan et al. (Eds.): ISWC 2020, LNCS 12506, pp. 110–127, 2020.
https://doi.org/10.1007/978-3-030-62419-4_7

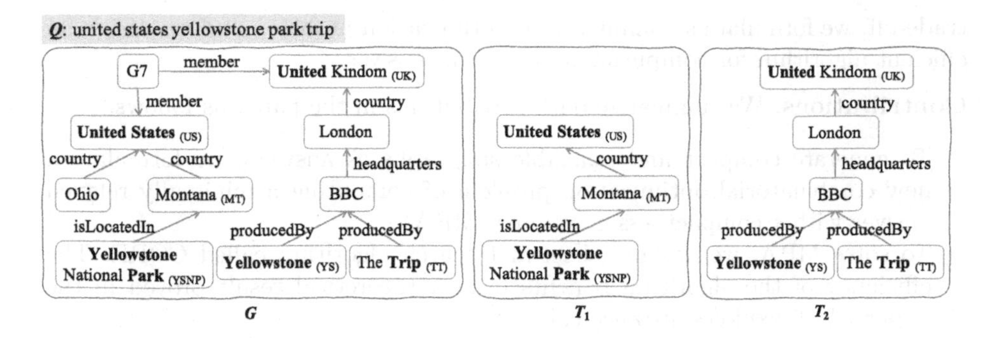

Fig. 1. A keyword query Q over a KG G with two answers T_1 and T_2.

extract a *group Steiner tree* (GST) [13]. By assigning weights to vertices and/or edges of KGs to represent salience, a GST is a tree of minimum total weight that connects as least one matching vertex for each query keyword.

Motivation. The effectiveness of GST-based answers to human users in exploratory search was recently challenged by the results of an extensive user study [5]. Several popular weighting schemes were evaluated in [5] but, surprisingly, none of them were assessed to be useful for shaping a favourable answer. Instead, the study showed that users strongly favor answers that are structurally *compact* subgraphs having a small diameter, thereby suggesting extracting such subgraphs as answers. However, when some query keywords are absent, disconnected, or only connected by long paths in the KG, one cannot find any structurally compact subgraph that connects all the query keywords. To address this problem, we proposed to extract compact but *relaxable* subgraphs that have a small diameter to ensure compactness but are not required to connect all the query keywords, i.e., allowing query relaxation [17]. The preliminary search algorithm we designed in [17], called CertQR+, has several limitations that will be addressed in this paper.

Our Approach. We aim at computing *co*mpact and *re*laxable subgraphs as answers to exploratory keyword search over KGs. Our algorithm is abbreviated to **CORE** and is open source.[1] To help understanding our approach, consider the example in Fig. 1. For keyword query "united states yellowstone park trip", a traditional GST-based answer has to contain the long path between `Yellowstone National Park` and `The Trip` in the KG. This unfocused path is not interesting to the user but prevents structurally compact subgraphs as answers. In comparison, CORE can compute answers like T_1 that is more compact and meaningful though drops a keyword "trip" in the query. Answer completeness (i.e., covering all the query keywords) and compactness (i.e., having a small diameter) are conflicting objectives. CORE achieves the following trade-off: computing a minimally relaxed answer (i.e., covering the largest number of query keywords) with a compactness guarantee (i.e., having a bounded diameter). To model this

[1] https://github.com/nju-websoft/CORE.

trade-off, we formulate a combinatorial optimization problem, and we design an efficient algorithm for computing an optimum answer.

Contributions. We summarize our contributions in the paper as follows.

- To generate compact and relaxable subgraphs as answers, we formulate a new combinatorial optimization problem of computing a minimally relaxed answer with a compactness guarantee (MRA).
- To solve MRA, we design a best-first search algorithm called CORE. The efficiency of the algorithm benefits from a theoretical result proved in the paper which exploits distance calculation.
- With public KGs and keyword queries, we demonstrate the necessity of trading off answer completeness for compactness, and we show that CORE performs significantly faster than CertQR+.

The remainder of the paper is organized as follows. Section 2 formulates MRA. Section 3 discusses related work. Section 4 describes CORE. Section 5 presents experiments. Finally we conclude the paper in Sect. 6.

2 Problem Formulation

2.1 Preliminaries

Below we define necessary terms used in the paper.

Knowledge Graph. A *knowledge graph* (KG) represents a set of linked and annotated entities. We formulate it as a directed graph $G = \langle V, E \rangle$, where V is a set of n annotated vertices representing entities, and $E \subseteq V \times V$ is a set of m annotated edges representing relations between entities. We keep edge directions, but the edges in a path/tree can be oriented in different directions.

Keyword Query. Let $\mathbb{K}$ be the set of all keywords. A retrieval function $\texttt{hits} : \mathbb{K} \mapsto 2^V$ maps keywords to subsets of vertices from V. The concrete implementation of hits, i.e., the exact way of matching keywords with entity annotations, is not our research focus. For simplicity, edge matching is omitted from our formulation but is supported by our approach. Indeed, we can subdivide an edge (u, v) by yielding a new vertex w with the annotations of the edge (u, v) and then replacing (u, v) by two new edges (u, w) and (w, v). A *keyword query* $Q \subseteq \mathbb{K}$ is a non-empty set of g keywords $Q = \{k_1, \ldots, k_g\}$. For the ease of notation we write $\texttt{hits}(k_i)$ as K_i for $1 \leq i \leq g$ and call them *keyword vertices*.

Query Answer. A *complete answer* to Q is a subgraph $T = \langle V_T, E_T \rangle$ such that: (1) T is connected, (2) T covers all the query keywords, i.e., $V_T \cap K_i \neq \emptyset$ for $1 \leq i \leq g$, and (3) T is minimal, i.e., none of its proper subgraphs satisfy both (1) and (2). Minimality indicates T's tree structure where leaves are keyword vertices. For example, in Fig. 1, T_1 is a complete answer to "united states yellowstone park", and T_2 is a complete answer to "united yellowstone trip".

Graph Terminology. $\mathtt{N}(u)$ is the set of vertex u's *neighbors*, i.e., vertices adjacent from/to u. The *degree* of a vertex is the number of incident edges. We define *path* in a standard way, except that the edges can be oriented differently. The *length* ($\mathtt{len}$) of a path is the number of edges. The *distance* ($\mathtt{d}$) between two vertices is the length of a shortest path connecting them. The *eccentricity* of vertex u is the greatest distance between u and other vertices. The *radius* ($\mathtt{rad}$) and *diameter* ($\mathtt{diam}$) of a graph are the minimum and maximum eccentricity of the vertices, respectively. A *central vertex* is a vertex of minimum eccentricity.

2.2 Problem Statement

We assess the quality of an answer by its degrees of relaxation and compactness.

Degree of Relaxation. We allow an answer to cover an incomplete subset of Q. For $\emptyset \subset Q' \subset Q$, a complete answer to Q' is called a *partial answer* to Q. Complete and partial answers are collectively called *answers*. We measure the *degree of relaxation* (dor) of answer T to Q as follows:

$$\mathtt{dor}(T) = |Q \setminus \mathtt{CQ}(T)|\,, \quad \mathtt{CQ}(T) = \{k_i \in Q : K_i \cap V_T \neq \emptyset\}\,, \tag{1}$$

where $\mathtt{CQ}(T)$ represents the subset of keywords in Q that are covered by T. For example, T_1 and T_2 in Fig. 1 are partial answers to "united states yellowstone park trip" with $\mathtt{dor}(T_1) = 1$ and $\mathtt{dor}(T_2) = 2$.

Degree of Compactness. Following [3–5], we measure the *degree of compactness* (doc) of an answer by its diameter:

$$\mathtt{doc}(T) = \mathtt{diam}(T)\,. \tag{2}$$

For example, in Fig. 1 we have $\mathtt{doc}(T_1) = 2$ and $\mathtt{doc}(T_2) = 3$.

MRA Problem. To achieve a trade-off between answer completeness and compactness, we aim at computing a *m*inimally *r*elaxed *a*nswer with a compactness guarantee, abbreviated to the **MRA** problem. Such an answer has a bounded degree of compactness and the smallest degree of relaxation:

$$\mathop{\arg\min}_{T\,:\,\mathtt{doc}(T) \leq D} \mathtt{dor}(T)\,, \tag{3}$$

where $D \geq 0$ is a predetermined integer bound.

3 Related Work

Our work is related to but different from the following research in the literature.

Semantic Parsing. One way to interpret a keyword query over a KG is to turn it into a formal query such as a SPARQL query to be executed using a standard back end [10,22,25]. Such methods are suitable for lookup tasks where there is a specific search target that can be formally and precisely represented.

Some of these methods support representing as a basic graph pattern while other methods support expressive constructs. However, they are not very suitable for exploratory search with a vague search target.

Answer Extraction. Methods in the style of subgraph extraction are flexible, thus suitable for exploratory search. Their effectiveness relies on the scoring function used to rank subgraphs. In theory, all the functions for ranking candidate formal queries in semantic parsing can be adapted here to take account of the semantics of a keyword query. However, existing methods commonly extract GSTs [13] using exact [7,16,18] or approximation algorithms [23]. The weighting schemes used are simple and seem not very effective [5]. The computed min-weight subgraphs are not necessarily structurally compact as favored by human users [5]. Therefore, we are motivated to compute structurally compact subgraphs as answers, leaving the incorporation of weights for future work.

Answer Compactness. We follow [3–5,12] to bound the diameter of an answer. As we will see in Sect. 4, our MRA problem based on such a bound admits a polynomial-time solution. Alternatively, if we bound the number of vertices as in [1,14,24], the problem will be intractable because one can easily reduce to it from the GST problem with unit weights. In [8,15], all possible radius-bounded answers are offline extracted and indexed. They allow fast online retrieval of answers but their bounds cannot be online tuned as in our approach.

Answer Completeness. Our CORE extends CertQR+ [17] by overcoming several limitations. First, CORE is a more general approach. It supports keyword search where a keyword is mapped to a set of vertices, whereas CertQR+ only supports entity relationship search [2] where a keyword is mapped to a single vertex. Second, CORE has a better overall performance. It directly computes a minimally relaxed answer, whereas CertQR+ only computes a minimally relaxed query which needs further execution. Third, as we will see in Sect. 4, the depth of search $\lfloor \frac{D}{2} \rfloor$ in CORE is smaller than $\lceil \frac{D}{2} \rceil$ in CertQR+ when D is odd. There are other studies of query relaxation in the Semantic Web community such as [9,21,26]. They relax SPARQL queries, e.g., by making some triple patterns optional. These methods could not directly apply to our MRA problem.

4 Approach

In this section, we firstly give some theoretical foundations, and then we design and analyze our algorithm CORE.

4.1 Theoretical Foundations

In the following proposition, we establish a necessary and sufficient condition for the existence of a compactness-bounded complete answer to a keyword query. It describes the existence of a vertex v that is fairly close to all the query keywords. Later in the paper we will employ this proposition to design CORE.

Proposition 1. *A complete answer* $T = \langle V_T, E_T \rangle$ *to* Q *with* $\mathtt{diam}(T) \leq D$ *exists if and only if a vertex* $v \in V$ *exists such that*

1. $\forall 1 \leq i \leq g,\ \exists u \in K_i,\ \mathtt{d}(u, v) \leq \lceil \frac{D}{2} \rceil$;
2. *if* D *is odd and* $\widehat{Q} = \{k_i \in Q : \min_{u \in K_i} \mathtt{d}(u, v) = \lceil \frac{D}{2} \rceil\} \neq \emptyset$, *then* $\exists v' \in \mathtt{N}(v),\ \forall k_i \in \widehat{Q},\ \exists u \in K_i,\ \mathtt{d}(u, v') = \lfloor \frac{D}{2} \rfloor$;
3. $\exists 1 \leq i \leq g,\ \exists u \in K_i,\ \mathtt{d}(u, v) \leq \lfloor \frac{D}{2} \rfloor$.

Proof. We present a constructive proof.

Necessity. Let v be an arbitrary central vertex of T. Below we will show that v satisfies all the three conditions in the proposition.

For Condition 1, since T is a tree, graph theory tells us that

$$\mathtt{rad}(T) = \left\lceil \frac{\mathtt{diam}(T)}{2} \right\rceil \leq \left\lceil \frac{D}{2} \right\rceil . \tag{4}$$

Let $\mathtt{d}$ and $\mathtt{d}_T$ be the distances between two vertices in G and in T, respectively. Since T is a complete answer to Q, we have $\mathtt{CQ}(T) = Q$, i.e., $\forall 1 \leq i \leq g,\ \exists u \in (K_i \cap V_T)$. Because T is a subgraph of G, and v is a central vertex of T, we have

$$\mathtt{d}(u, v) \leq \mathtt{d}_T(u, v) \leq \mathtt{rad}(T) \leq \left\lceil \frac{D}{2} \right\rceil . \tag{5}$$

For Condition 2, if D is odd and $|\widehat{Q}| \neq \emptyset$, we choose an arbitrary $k_i \in \widehat{Q}$ and $u_i = \arg\min_{u' \in (K_i \cap V_T)} \mathtt{d}(u', v)$, i.e., $\mathtt{d}(u_i, v) \geq \lceil \frac{D}{2} \rceil$. Since T is a tree, consider the unique path P_i between u_i and v in T. We have $\mathtt{len}(P_i) = \mathtt{d}_T(u_i, v)$, and

$$\mathtt{d}_T(u_i, v) \leq \mathtt{rad}(T) \leq \left\lceil \frac{D}{2} \right\rceil \quad \text{and} \quad \mathtt{d}_T(u_i, v) \geq \mathtt{d}(u_i, v) \geq \left\lceil \frac{D}{2} \right\rceil . \tag{6}$$

Therefore, $\mathtt{len}(P_i) = \mathtt{d}_T(u_i, v) = \mathtt{d}(u_i, v) = \lceil \frac{D}{2} \rceil$ and hence P_i is a shortest path between u_i and v in G. Let $v' \in \mathtt{N}(v)$ be the unique neighbor of v in P_i. Below we show that v and v' satisfy Condition 2. We trivially have $\mathtt{d}(u_i, v') = \lfloor \frac{D}{2} \rfloor$. Then $\forall k_j \in (\widehat{Q} \setminus \{k_i\})$, let $u_j = \arg\min_{u' \in (K_j \cap V_T)} \mathtt{d}(u', v)$. Similar to the above proof, we know $\mathtt{d}(u_j, v) = \lceil \frac{D}{2} \rceil$ and the unique path P_j between u_j and v in T is their shortest path in G with $\mathtt{len}(P_j) = \lceil \frac{D}{2} \rceil$. This path has to pass through v' and hence $\mathtt{d}(u_j, v') = \lfloor \frac{D}{2} \rfloor$ because otherwise

$$\mathtt{d}_T(u_i, u_j) = \mathtt{len}(P_i) + \mathtt{len}(P_j) = \left\lceil \frac{D}{2} \right\rceil + \left\lceil \frac{D}{2} \right\rceil = D + 1 , \tag{7}$$

which contradicts $\mathtt{diam}(T) \leq D$.

For Condition 3, when D is even, it is easily derived from Condition 1. When D is odd, we prove by contradiction and assume: $\forall 1 \leq i \leq g,\ \forall u \in K_i,\ \mathtt{d}(u, v) > \lfloor \frac{D}{2} \rfloor$. Combined with Condition 1 we obtain $\forall 1 \leq i \leq g,\ \min_{u \in K_i} \mathtt{d}(u, v) = \lceil \frac{D}{2} \rceil$ and hence $Q = \widehat{Q}$. Now we discuss the cardinality of $|Q|$. When $|Q| = 1$, T is a trivial graph, and Condition 3 is satisfied. When $|Q| = |\widehat{Q}| \geq 2$, if we consider v' in Condition 2 as a new v, the above assumption will be contradicted as one can easily verify that this new v satisfies all the conditions.

Sufficiency. If D is even, we call GenAnsEven(G, Q, D, v) in Algorithm 3 to construct T. If D is odd, we call GenAnsOdd$(G, Q, D, v, v', \widehat{Q})$ in Algorithm 4. We will detail these algorithms later in the paper.

□

Certificate Vertex. In Proposition 1, vertex v is a certificate of the existence of a compactness-bounded complete answer to Q. We refer to v as a *certificate vertex* for Q. For example, in Fig. 1, under $D = 2$, $v =$ `Montana` is a certificate vertex for "united states yellowstone park". Under $D = 3$, $v =$ `London` is a certificate vertex with $v' =$ `BBC` for "united yellowstone trip".

Proposition 1 helps to solve the MRA problem in two aspects. First, if we want to decide the existence of a compactness-bounded complete answer to Q or to some $Q' \subset Q$, we can avoid actually searching for an answer which would be an expensive process. Instead, we only need to calculate a few distances. Distance calculation can be efficiently implemented based on the proper graph indexes. Second, once the above existence of an answer is confirmed, i.e., a certificate vertex v is found, we will be able to easily construct such an answer using v. These two benefits form the foundation of our algorithms.

4.2 Algorithm Design

Below we overview and then detail CORE, and finally show a running example.

Overview. Under a compactness bound D, our main algorithm CORE adopts a best-first search strategy. Iteratively, the most promising search direction is explored, which may update the current best (i.e., minimally relaxed) answer. The search process will be terminated if it is guaranteed that unexplored answers cannot exceed the current best answer. In the search process, rather than directly searching for a better (i.e., less relaxed) answer, our subroutine FindAns firstly searches for a certificate vertex for a larger subset of Q, and then constructs a complete answer to this sub-query using the subroutine GenAnsEven or GenAnsOdd, depending on the parity of D. These two steps in FindAns are both supported by Proposition 1.

Algorithm 1: CORE

```
   Input: G = ⟨V, E⟩,
          Q = {k_1, ..., k_g}, D.
   Output: An optimum answer T_opt.
1  T_opt ← null;
   /* CQ(null) = ∅, dor(null) = |Q| */
2  foreach u ∈ ⋃_{i=1}^{g} K_i do
3  |  visited[u][u] ← true;
4  |  foreach w ∈ (V \ {u}) do
5  |  |  visited[u][w] ← false;
6  PQ ← an empty min-priority queue
   of ordered pairs of vertices;
7  foreach u ∈ ⋃_{i=1}^{g} K_i do
8  |  PQ.Insert(⟨u, u⟩);
9  foreach u ∈ V do
10 |  checked[u] ← false;
11 while PQ is not empty do
12 |  ⟨u, v⟩ ← PQ.Pull();
13 |  if pri(u, v) ≥ dor(T_opt) then
14 |  |  break the while loop;
15 |  if checked[v] is false then
16 |  |  T ←
   |  |  FindAns(G, Q, D, v, T_opt);
17 |  |  checked[v] ← true;
18 |  |  if T is not null then
19 |  |  |  T_opt ← T;
20 |  if d(u, v) < ⌊D/2⌋ then
21 |  |  foreach w ∈ N(v) do
22 |  |  |  if visited[u][w] is false
   |  |  |  then
23 |  |  |  |  visited[u][w] ← true;
24 |  |  |  |  PQ.Insert(⟨u, w⟩);
25 return T_opt;
```

Algorithm CORE. Our main algorithm is presented in Algorithm 1. T_{opt} represents the current best answer (line 1). We run one independent search starting from each keyword vertex in $\bigcup_{i=1}^{g} K_i$. Each search maintains a separate set of visited vertices; *visited*$[u][w]$ represents whether w has been visited in the search starting from u (lines 2–5). The frontiers of all these searches are kept in a shared priority queue *PQ* where each element is an ordered pair of vertices $\langle u, v\rangle$ representing a vertex v to be explored in the search starting from u (line 6). Initially, *PQ* is fed with all the keyword vertices (lines 7–8). A vertex can be visited multiple times, at most one time in each search, but is checked using the subroutine FindAns at most once; *checked*$[u]$ represents whether u has been checked (lines 9–10). We will describe the implementation of FindAns later. Briefly, for vertex v, FindAns either returns an answer better than T_{opt}, which is a compactness-bounded complete answer to the largest subset of Q which v is a certificate vertex for, or returns null if such a better answer does not exist.

Iteratively, vertices that are at most $\lfloor \frac{D}{2} \rfloor$ hops away from each keyword vertex are searched and checked in a best-first manner (lines 11–24). In each iteration, the pair $\langle u, v\rangle$ in *PQ* with the minimum priority $\mathtt{pri}(u, v)$ is pulled out of *PQ* (line 12). We will compute $\mathtt{pri}(u, v)$ later in the paper; it represents a lower bound on the number of keywords dropped by subsets of Q which v or its descendant in the search starting from u is a certificate vertex for. If this lower bound is not better than the $\mathtt{dor}$ of T_{opt}, the algorithm will be terminated because T_{opt} is guaranteed to be optimum (lines 13–14). Otherwise, v or some of its descendants may be a certificate vertex for a larger subset of Q and hence a better answer may exist. So if v has not been checked in other searches, it will be checked using FindAns which either returns a better answer T and updates T_{opt}, or returns null (lines 15–19). The search starting from u continues, and the unvisited neighbors of v are expanded (lines 20–24). By requiring $\mathtt{d}(u, v) < \lfloor \frac{D}{2} \rfloor$, the search is restricted to vertices that are at most $\lfloor \frac{D}{2} \rfloor$ hops away from u.

Algorithm 2: FindAns

```
   Input: G, Q = {k_1, ..., k_g}, D, v, T_opt.
   Output: An answer T better than T_opt,
           or null if not found.
 1 for i ← 1 to g do
 2 |   U[1][i] ← {u ∈ K_i : d(u, v) ≤ ⌈D/2⌉};
 3 |   U[2][i] ← {u ∈ K_i : d(u, v) = ⌈D/2⌉};
 4 Q_1 ← {k_i ∈ Q : U[1][i] ≠ ∅};
 5 Q_2 ← {k_i ∈ Q : U[1][i] = U[2][i] ≠ ∅};
 6 if D is even then
 7 |   if |Q_1| > |CQ(T_opt)| then
 8 |   |   return GenAnsEven(G, Q_1, D, v);
 9 if D is odd then
10 |   Q̂_max ← ∅, v'_max ← null;
11 |   foreach v' ∈ N(v) do
12 |   |   Q̂ ← ∅;
13 |   |   foreach k_i ∈ Q_2 do
14 |   |   |   if ∃u ∈ U[2][i], d(u, v') = ⌊D/2⌋ then
15 |   |   |   |   Q̂ ← Q̂ ∪ {k_i};
16 |   |   if |Q̂| > |Q̂_max| then
17 |   |   |   Q̂_max ← Q̂, v'_max ← v';
18 |   Q_max ← (Q_1 \ Q_2) ∪ Q̂_max;
19 |   if |Q_max| > |CQ(T_opt)| then
20 |   |   return GenAnsOdd(G, Q_max, D, v, v'_max, Q̂_max);
21 return null;
```

Subroutine FindAns. This subroutine is presented in Algorithm 2. It employs Proposition 1 to find the largest subset of Q which v is a certificate vertex for, and then construct a compactness-bounded complete answer to this sub-query. The answer will be returned only if it is better than T_{opt}. According to Condition 1 in the proposition, Q_1 (line 4) represents the largest possible subset of Q which v can be a certificate vertex for. Q_2 (line 5) represents the largest possible $\widehat{Q}$ in Condition 2.

When D is even (line 6), Q_1 is indeed the largest subset of Q which v is a certificate vertex for. If Q_1 is larger than the set of query keywords covered by T_{opt}, we will return T constructed by the subroutine GenAnsEven (lines 7–8).

When D is odd (line 9), the vertices in Q_2 may not all satisfy Condition 2 for the same $v' \in \mathtt{N}(v)$. We look for $\widehat{Q}_{\max}$, the largest subset of Q_2 that can satisfy Condition 2 for the same neighbor of v, denoted by $v'_{\max}$ (line 10). We compute $\widehat{Q}_{\max}$ and $v'_{\max}$ by going over all the neighbors of v (lines 11–17). Finally, $Q_{\max}$ (line 18) is the largest subset of Q which v is a certificate vertex for. If $Q_{\max}$ is larger than the set of query keywords covered by T_{opt}, we will return T constructed by the subroutine GenAnsOdd (lines 19–20).

Subroutine GenAnsEven. This subroutine is presented in Algorithm 3. It employs Proposition 1 to construct a complete answer to Q_1 using its certificate vertex v under an even D. Following Condition 1 in the proposition, for each $k_i \in Q_1$, we find $u_i \in K_i$ and a shortest path P_i between u_i and v in G such that $\mathtt{len}(P_i) \leq \lceil \frac{D}{2} \rceil$ (lines 2–4). All such $|Q_1|$ shortest paths are merged into a connected subgraph T (line 5), which covers all the keywords in Q_1 and satisfies $\mathtt{diam}(T) \leq D$. Here, to ensure that T has a tree structure, when there are multiple shortest paths between two vertices, we consistently choose one throughout our algorithm, e.g., the alphabetically smallest shortest path in terms of vertex identifiers. Still, T may not be minimal when some u_i covers not only keyword k_i but also some $k_j \neq k_i$ so that u_j should be removed from T for the minimality of T. To handle this, we repeatedly remove an unnecessary leaf from T until T is minimal and hence is a complete answer to Q_1 (lines 6–7).

Subroutine GenAnsOdd. This subroutine is presented in Algorithm 4. It employs Proposition 1 to construct a complete answer to $Q_{\max}$ using its certificate vertex v and a neighbor $v'_{\max}$ thereof under an odd D. The difference between GenAnsEven and GenAnsOdd is that, following Condition 2 in the proposition, for each $k_i \in \widehat{Q}_{\max}$, we find $u_i \in K_i$ and a shortest path P'_i between u_i and $v'_{\max}$ such that $\mathtt{len}(P'_i) = \lfloor \frac{D}{2} \rfloor$ (lines 3–5), and then we extend P'_i from $v'_{\max}$ to v by adding one edge to form P_i (line 6); furthermore, for each $k_i \in (Q_{\max} \setminus \widehat{Q}_{\max})$, we find $u_i \in K_i$ such that P_i connecting u_i and v satisfies $\mathtt{len}(P_i) \leq \lfloor \frac{D}{2} \rfloor$ (lines 7–9). These modifications ensure that $\mathtt{diam}(T) \leq D$.

Algorithm 3: GenAnsEven

```
  Input: G, Q_1, D, v.
  Output: A complete answer T to Q_1.
1 T ← a null graph;
2 foreach k_i ∈ Q_1 do
3   | ∃u_i ∈ K_i, d(u_i, v) ≤ ⌈D/2⌉;
4   | P_i ← a shortest path between u_i
    | and v in G;
5   | T ← T merged with P_i;
6 while T is not minimal do
7   | Remove an unnecessary leaf from T;
8 return T;
```

Algorithm 4: GenAnsOdd

```
   Input: G, Q_max, D, v, v'_max, Q̂_max.
   Output: A complete answer T to Q_max.
1  T ← a null graph;
2  foreach k_i ∈ Q_max do
3    | if k_i ∈ Q̂_max then
4    |   | ∃u_i ∈ K_i, d(u_i, v'_max) = ⌊D/2⌋;
5    |   | P'_i ← a shortest path between u_i
     |   | and v'_max in G;
6    |   | P_i ← P'_i extended by adding the
     |   | edge between v'_max and v;
7    | else
8    |   | ∃u_i ∈ K_i, d(u_i, v) ≤ ⌊D/2⌋;
9    |   | P_i ← a shortest path between u_i
     |   | and v in G;
10   | T ← T merged with P_i;
11 while T is not minimal do
12   | Remove an unnecessary leaf from T;
13 return T;
```

Priority Computation. Priority $\mathtt{pri}(u, v)$ represents a lower bound on the number of keywords dropped by subsets of Q which v or its descendant in the search starting from u is a certificate vertex for. A complete answer to such a sub-query satisfies $\mathtt{diam} \leq D$ and should contain u. It inspires us to define the following heuristic lower bound:

$$\mathtt{pri}(u, v) = |\mathtt{UQ}(u, v)|, \quad \mathtt{UQ}(u, v) = \{k_i \in Q : \forall u_i \in K_i,\ \mathtt{d}(u, v) + \mathtt{d}(v, u_i) > D\}. \quad (8)$$

We will later prove that this heuristic guarantees the optimality of T_{opt} returned at the end of Algorithm 1.

Further, observe that $\mathtt{pri}(u, v)$ is an integer. There can be ties in the priority queue. We break ties based on the degree of v. If multiple vertices have the same value of $\mathtt{pri}$, we will give priority to one that has the smallest degree because the cost of expanding its neighbors in Algorithm 1 (lines 21–24) is minimal.

Running Example. In Fig. 2 we illustrate the process of CORE using the example in Fig. 1 under $D = 2$. Initially, PQ is fed with five keyword vertices. In the first iteration, ⟨YSNP, YSNP⟩ has the smallest priority; in particular, YSNP has a smaller degree than US. For YSNP, it is checked using FindAns which computes an answer that consists of a single vertex YSNP and assigns this answer to T_{opt}. The only neighbor of YSNP, namely MT, is then expanded. In the second iteration,

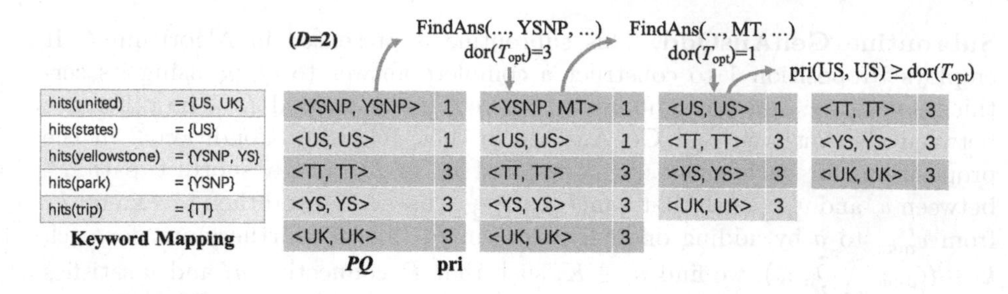

Fig. 2. A running example where vertices are written in abbreviations.

MT is checked using FindAns which computes T_1 in Fig. 1 and updates T_{opt}. In the third iteration, we terminate the search process because the priority of the head of PQ is not better than $\texttt{dor}(T_{\text{opt}})$. Therefore, T_1 is returned.

4.3 Algorithm Analysis

We analyze the correctness and time complexity of CORE.

Correctness. The following proposition gives the correctness of CORE.

Proposition 2. *CORE returns an optimum solution to the MRA problem.*

Proof. We prove by contradiction.

Assume CORE returns a suboptimal answer T_{opt} whose dor is larger than that of an optimum answer T^*. Below we will show that when CORE is terminated, T^* should have been found, leading to a contradiction.

Let v be a certificate vertex for $\texttt{CQ}(T^*)$. Without loss of generality, assume that T^* is composed of shortest paths between keyword vertices and v in G, i.e., T^* can be constructed by calling subroutine GenAnsEven or GenAnsOdd. Following Condition 3 in Proposition 1, let u be a keyword vertex in T^* that satisfies $\texttt{d}(u, v) \leq \lfloor \frac{D}{2} \rfloor$, and let P_{uv} be the unique path between u and v in T^*, which is a shortest path in G and hence satisfies $\texttt{len}(P_{uv}) \leq \lfloor \frac{D}{2} \rfloor$.

Following Condition 1 in Proposition 1, $\forall k_i \in \texttt{CQ}(T^*)$ that is not covered by u, $\exists u_i \in K_i$ such that u_i is in T^* and $\texttt{d}(u_i, v) \leq \lceil \frac{D}{2} \rceil$. Let P_{vu_i} be the unique path between v and u_i in T^*, which is a shortest path in G and hence satisfies $\texttt{len}(P_{vu_i}) \leq \lceil \frac{D}{2} \rceil$. For every vertex w in P_{uv}, we have

$$\texttt{d}(u, w) + \texttt{d}(w, u_i) \leq \texttt{len}(P_{uv}) + \texttt{len}(P_{vu_i}) \leq \left\lfloor \frac{D}{2} \right\rfloor + \left\lceil \frac{D}{2} \right\rceil = D\,. \tag{9}$$

Therefore, $k_i \notin \texttt{UQ}(u, w)$ and hence $\texttt{CQ}(T^*) \cap \texttt{UQ}(u, w) = \emptyset$. It gives us

$$\texttt{pri}(u, w) = |\texttt{UQ}(u, w)| \leq |Q \setminus \texttt{CQ}(T^*)| = \texttt{dor}(T^*) < \texttt{dor}(T_{\text{opt}})\,. \tag{10}$$

Due to the best-first search strategy, it is impossible that CORE returns T_{opt} before checking each w in P_{uv} from u to v using subroutine FindAns, which would have found T^* when checking v, leading to a contradiction.

□

Time Complexity. Recall that $|V| = n$, $|E| = m$, $|Q| = g$. We precompute a hub labeling [23]; this index structure supports computing distance in $O(n)$ and computing a shortest path in $O(n \log n)$. The run time of CORE consists of

- $O(ng)$ for collecting query vertices,
- $O(n(n+m))$ for $O(n)$ searches starting from different keyword vertices,
- $O(n^4 g)$ for computing priority for $O(n)$ vertices in $O(n)$ searches,
- $O(n^2 \log n)$ for $O(n^2)$ insert/pull operations over a Fibonacci heap for priority queue, and
- $O(n^2(n+m)g)$ for $O(n)$ calls of FindAns, including $O(n^3 g)$ for computing U, $O(n^2 mg)$ for computing distances to v', and $O(n^2 g \log n)$ for calling GenAnsEven or GenAnsOdd.

Therefore, the total run time of CORE is in $O(n^4 g)$, i.e., the MRA problem admits a polynomial-time solution. As we will see in the next section, the run time in practice is much faster than $O(n^4 g)$ because: g is commonly much smaller than n, distance and shortest path computation based on a hub labeling is nearly in constant time, and the search process is usually terminated early.

5 Experiments

We carried out experiments to verify three research hypotheses (RH). First, compared with traditional GST-based answers, our approach trades off answer completeness for compactness. We showed the necessity of this trade-off (**RH1**). We did not evaluate the effectiveness of compact answers to human users in exploratory search because it has been demonstrated in [5]. Still, we showed that the completeness of our computed answers is very high (**RH2**), thereby having little influence on effectiveness. Last but not least, we demonstrated the efficiency of CORE and showed that it significantly outperformed CertQR+ [17] (**RH3**).

Table 1. KGs and keyword queries.

	KG		Keyword query		
	Vertices (n)	Edges (m)	Quantity	Size (g): avg;	Max
MONDIAL (about geography)	8,478	34,868	40	2.03;	4
LinkedMDB (about movies)	1,326,784	2,132,796	200	5.38;	10
DBpedia (an encyclopedia)	5,356,286	17,494,749	438	3.92;	10

5.1 Experiment Setup

We used a 3.10 GHz CPU with 80 GB memory for Java programs.

KGs. We used three popular KGs in RDF format: MONDIAL,[2] LinkedMDB,[3] and DBpedia.[4] Their sizes (n and m) are shown in Table 1.

Keyword Queries. We used public queries. For MONDIAL we reused 40 keyword queries in [6]. For LinkedMDB we randomly sampled 200 natural language questions from [20] and transformed each question into a keyword query by removing stop words and punctuation marks. For DBpedia we reused 438 keyword queries in [11]. Their sizes (g) are shown in Table 1.

Keyword Mapping. Our retrieval function `hits` maps each keyword k to vertices K whose human-readable names (`rdfs:label`) contain k. To test scalability, we set the maximum allowable number of keyword vertices retrieved by `hits` to different values: $|K| \leq 1$, $|K| \leq 10$, and $|K| \leq 100$.

Compactness Bound. Following [3,4], we used two settings: $D \in \{3, 4\}$.

Other experiment settings, e.g., using more advanced `hits` functions, would be left for the future work.

5.2 Baselines

We implemented two baseline methods for comparison. We did not compare with semantic parsing such as [10,22,25] since we focused on exploratory search tasks.

CertQR+. CORE is the first algorithm for the MRA problem. However, we could adapt CertQR+ [17] to MRA. CertQR+ originally addresses a special case of MRA where each keyword is mapped to a single vertex, and it only computes a minimally relaxed query rather than an answer. In our adaptation, for $Q = \{k_1, \ldots, k_g\}$ in MRA, we: (1) for each combination of keyword vertices in $K_1 \times \cdots \times K_g$, feed the combined set of keyword vertices as input into CertQR+, which outputs a minimally relaxed set of keyword vertices, (2) choose the maximum output set over all the combinations, and (3) find a complete answer to connect the chosen set of keyword vertices using a state-of-the-art search algorithm [3,4]. Therefore, we remark that the performance of this baseline relies on the search algorithm used, which may affect the fairness of its comparison with CORE.

GST-Based Answers. We implemented an algorithm [16] to compute traditional GST-based answers. We assigned unit weights to the edges of KGs. We also tried several other weighting schemes [5] but obtained similar findings.

5.3 Experiment 1: Compactness of GST-Based Answers (RH1)

To show the necessity of trading off answer completeness for compactness (RH1), we computed the degree of compactness (`doc`) of traditional GST-based answers

[2] http://www.dbis.informatik.uni-goettingen.de/Mondial/Mondial-RDF/mondial.rdf.

[3] http://www.cs.toronto.edu/~oktie/linkedmdb/linkedmdb-latest-dump.zip.

[4] http://downloads.dbpedia.org/2016-10/core-i18n/en/mappingbased_objects_en.tql.bz2.

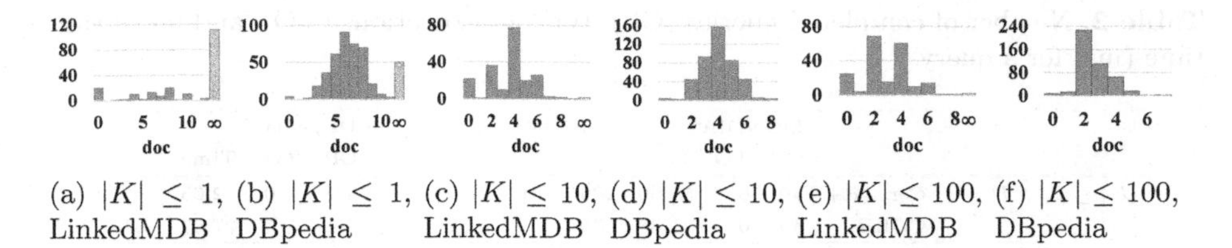

(a) $|K| \leq 1$, LinkedMDB (b) $|K| \leq 1$, DBpedia (c) $|K| \leq 10$, LinkedMDB (d) $|K| \leq 10$, DBpedia (e) $|K| \leq 100$, LinkedMDB (f) $|K| \leq 100$, DBpedia

Fig. 3. Distribution of doc of GST-based answers for all the queries.

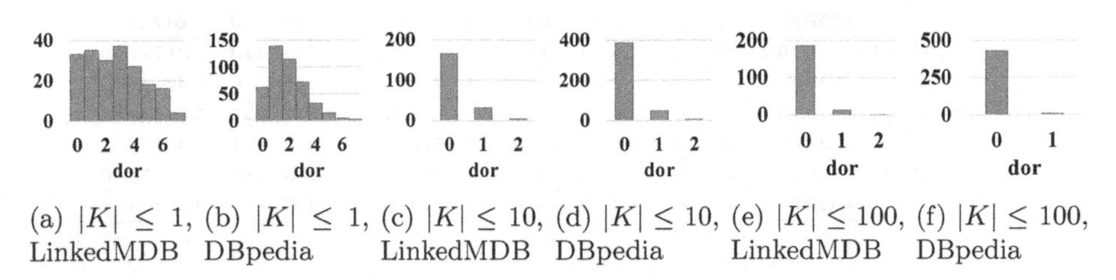

(a) $|K| \leq 1$, LinkedMDB (b) $|K| \leq 1$, DBpedia (c) $|K| \leq 10$, LinkedMDB (d) $|K| \leq 10$, DBpedia (e) $|K| \leq 100$, LinkedMDB (f) $|K| \leq 100$, DBpedia

Fig. 4. Distribution of dor of relaxable answers for all the queries under $D = 4$.

according to Eq. (2). The distributions of doc (i.e., diameter) of answers for all the queries over two large KGs are presented in Fig. 3. When $|K| \leq 1$, GST-based answers cannot be found (i.e., doc $= \infty$) for 56% of queries over LinkedMDB and for 11% on DBpedia because keyword vertices are not pairwise connected. Even for $|K| \leq 100$, it happens for a few queries over LinkedMDB. Apart from that, doc is as large as up to 8 on LinkedMDB and to 7 on DBpedia. When $|K| \leq 10$, we observe doc > 4 for 27% of queries over LinkedMDB and for 32% on DBpedia. These many failing queries and structurally large answers are not favored by human users [5], thereby demonstrating the necessity of trading off answer completeness for compactness (RH1).

5.4 Experiment 2: Completeness of Relaxable Answers (RH2)

To show the completeness of our relaxable answers (RH2), we computed their degree of relaxation (dor) according to Eq. (1). The distributions of dor (i.e., number of dropped query keywords) of answers for all the queries over two large KGs under $D = 4$ are presented in Fig. 4. Only in the extreme case of $|K| \leq 1$, the dor of our answers is not satisfying due to the disconnectivity between keyword vertices. At least 3 keywords have to be dropped (i.e., dor ≥ 3) in more than half of the queries over LinkedMDB, and at least 2 (i.e., dor ≥ 2) on DBpedia. With $|K|$ increased to 10 and 100, relaxation is not needed (i.e., dor $= 0$) for over 80% and 90% of the queries, respectively. When relaxation takes place (i.e., dor > 0), typically only 1 and very rarely 2 keywords are dropped. These results show that the completeness of our relaxable answers is very high in normal cases (RH2).

Table 2. Number of completed queries (CP), timeout exceptions (TO), and mean run time (ms) for a query.

			MONDIAL			LinkedMDB			DBpedia		
			CP	TO	Time	CP	TO	Time	CP	TO	Time
$\lvert K\rvert \leq 1$	$D = 3$	CertQR+	40	0	55.60	200	0	30.91	438	0	62.65
		CORE	40	0	1.88	200	0	5.38	438	0	27.87
	$D = 4$	CertQR+	40	0	15.13	200	0	127.36	438	0	221.68
		CORE	40	0	2.80	200	0	96.33	438	0	193.47
$\lvert K\rvert \leq 10$	$D = 3$	CertQR+	40	0	85.10	125	75	436,566.95	321	117	327,641.86
		CORE	40	0	3.95	200	0	23.45	438	0	1,017.26
	$D = 4$	CertQR+	40	0	6.80	113	87	475,926.77	319	119	319,777.02
		CORE	40	0	2.23	200	0	179.17	438	0	4,181.92
$\lvert K\rvert \leq 100$	$D = 3$	CertQR+	40	0	39.23	82	118	611,297.51	211	227	547,598.42
		CORE	40	0	5.15	200	0	506.62	437	1	6,107.36
	$D = 4$	CertQR+	40	0	5.70	90	110	561,819.84	253	185	453,752.70
		CORE	40	0	4.13	200	0	324.22	437	1	4,307.86

5.5 Experiment 3: Efficiency of CORE (RH3)

To show the efficiency of CORE (RH3), we compared the run time of CORE and CertQR+. We set a timeout of 1,000 s. Each run of an algorithm for a query that reached timeout was terminated, and its run time was defined to be the timeout value. Therefore, the longest run time reported below is at most 1,000 s. The overall results are presented in Table 2. When $|K| \leq 1$, CertQR+ and CORE complete all the queries before timeout. CORE is faster because it fuses query relaxation and answer generation into a single search process. When $|K| \leq 10$, CertQR+ is called up to 10^g times for each query. On LinkedMDB and DBpedia, it reaches timeout for many queries and uses several hundred seconds. CORE never reaches timeout and performs at least two orders of magnitude faster because it fuses at most $10g$ searches into a single best-first search process. For $|K| \leq 100$, the comparison is similar.

Furthermore, we visualize the distributions of run time for all the queries as box plots in Fig. 5. CORE uses less than 1 s for most queries, except for a small number of outliers. Comparing the median run time of CORE and CertQR+ represented by vertical lines going through boxes, on large KGs (LinkedMDB and DBpedia), for non-trivial settings of the retrieval function ($|K| \leq 10$ and $|K| \leq 100$), CORE is about 2–4 orders of magnitude faster than CertQR+. All the above results demonstrate the efficiency of CORE, which significantly outperforms CertQR+ (RH3).

5.6 Experiment 4: Effectiveness in Lookup Tasks

Although our approach is mainly developed for supporting exploratory search, one may be interested in its effectiveness in lookup tasks. We conducted the following experiment to accommodate such interests. Since CORE only returns an optimum answer, we computed the precision at 1 (P@1) of the answers returned

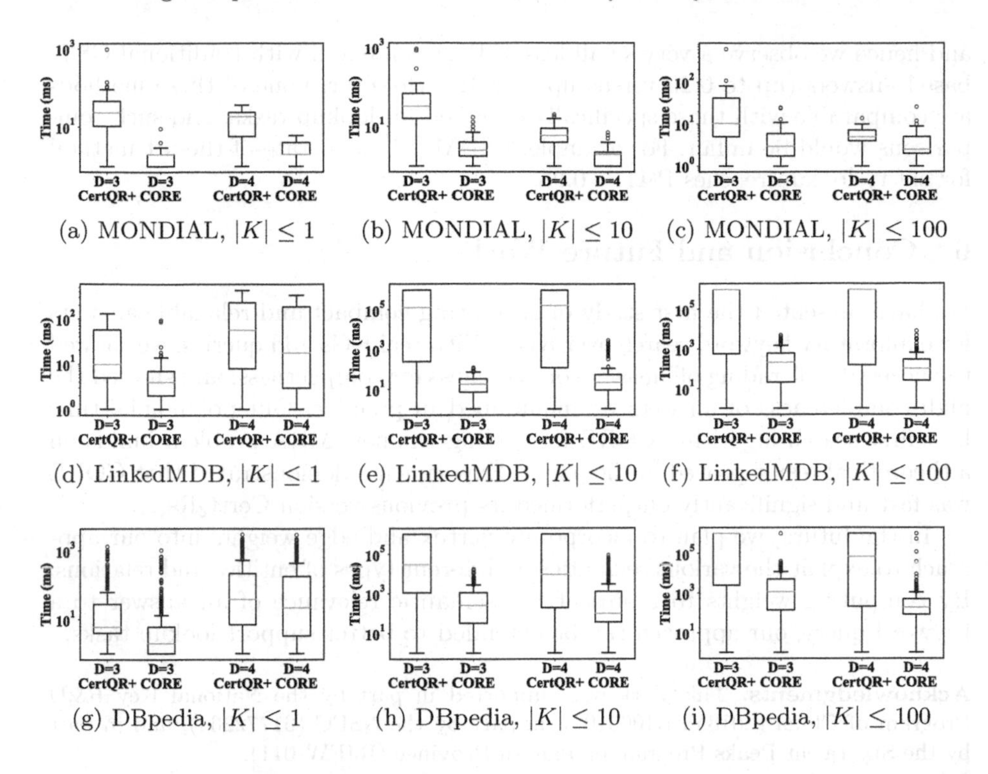

(a) MONDIAL, $|K| \leq 1$ (b) MONDIAL, $|K| \leq 10$ (c) MONDIAL, $|K| \leq 100$

(d) LinkedMDB, $|K| \leq 1$ (e) LinkedMDB, $|K| \leq 10$ (f) LinkedMDB, $|K| \leq 100$

(g) DBpedia, $|K| \leq 1$ (h) DBpedia, $|K| \leq 10$ (i) DBpedia, $|K| \leq 100$

Fig. 5. Distribution of run time for all the queries.

Table 3. Mean P@1 for a lookup query on DBpedia.

		CertQR+	CORE	GST-Based Answers	FSDM
$\lvert K\rvert \leq 1$	$D = 3$	0.17	0.17	0.27	0.98
	$D = 4$	0.23	0.23		
$\lvert K\rvert \leq 10$	$D = 3$	0.21	0.23	0.31	
	$D = 4$	0.24	0.28		
$\lvert K\rvert \leq 100$	$D = 3$	0.17	0.29	0.30	
	$D = 4$	0.21	0.23		

by each algorithm. We compared CORE with CertQR+ and traditional GST-based answers. We conducted this experiment on DBpedia since the keyword queries we used for this dataset were originally extracted from entity lookup tasks with gold-standard answers [11] so that we could compute precision. Specifically, we defined P@1 = 1 if a computed answer contained a gold-standard answer entity, otherwise P@1 = 0. The mean P@1 for a lookup query over DBpedia is presented in Table 3. CORE and CertQR+ show similar results since they essentially aim at the same goal. For compactness, they trade off answer completeness and hence we observe a very small loss of P@1 compared with traditional GST-based answers (up to 0.29 versus up to 0.31). However, none of these methods are comparable with those specifically designed for lookup tasks, and such comparisons would be unfair. For example, FSDM [27] as a state-of-the-art method for entity lookup reaches P@1 = 0.98.

6 Conclusion and Future Work

We have presented the first study of generating compact and relaxable answers for exploratory keyword search over KGs. With real KGs and queries, we showed the necessity of trading off answer completeness for compactness, and showed the high completeness of answers we maintained in practice. Our polynomial-time best-first search algorithm CORE for solving the new MRA problem builds on a theoretical result proved in the paper. Experiments demonstrated that CORE was fast and significantly outperformed its previous version CertQR+.

In the future, we plan to incorporate vertex and edge weights into our approach to exploit the various semantics of different types of entities and relations. By computing weights to represent the semantic relevance of an answer to a keyword query, our approach can be extended to better support lookup tasks.

Acknowledgments. This work was supported in part by the National Key R&D Program of China (2018YFB1005100), in part by the NSFC (61772264), and in part by the Six Talent Peaks Program of Jiangsu Province (RJFW-011).

References

1. Chen, C., Wang, G., Liu, H., Xin, J., Yuan, Y.: SISP: a new framework for searching the informative subgraph based on PSO. In: CIKM, pp. 453–462 (2011)
2. Cheng, G.: Relationship search over knowledge graphs. ACM SIGWEB Newsl. **2020**(Summer), 3 (2020)
3. Cheng, G., Liu, D., Qu, Y.: Efficient algorithms for association finding and frequent association pattern mining. In: Groth, P., et al. (eds.) ISWC 2016. LNCS, vol. 9981, pp. 119–134. Springer, Cham (2016). https://doi.org/10.1007/978-3-319-46523-4_8
4. Cheng, G., Liu, D., Qu, Y.: Fast algorithms for semantic association search and pattern mining. IEEE Trans. Knowl. Data Eng. Early Access, 1–13 (2019). https://doi.org/10.1109/TKDE.2019.2942031
5. Cheng, G., Shao, F., Qu, Y.: An empirical evaluation of techniques for ranking semantic associations. IEEE Trans. Knowl. Data Eng. **29**(11), 2388–2401 (2017)
6. Coffman, J., Weaver, A.C.: An empirical performance evaluation of relational keyword search techniques. IEEE Trans. Knowl. Data Eng. **26**(1), 30–42 (2014)
7. Ding, B., Yu, J.X., Wang, S., Qin, L., Zhang, X., Lin, X.: Finding top-k min-cost connected trees in databases. In: ICDE, pp. 836–845 (2007)
8. Dosso, D., Silvello, G.: A scalable virtual document-based keyword search system for RDF datasets. In: SIGIR, pp. 965–968 (2019)
9. Elbassuoni, S., Ramanath, M., Weikum, G.: Query relaxation for entity-relationship search. In: Antoniou, G., et al. (eds.) ESWC 2011. LNCS, vol. 6644, pp. 62–76. Springer, Heidelberg (2011). https://doi.org/10.1007/978-3-642-21064-8_5

10. Fu, H., Anyanwu, K.: Effectively interpreting keyword queries on RDF databases with a rear view. In: ISWC, pp. 193–208 (2011)
11. Hasibi, F., et al.: DBpedia-entity v2: a test collection for entity search. In: SIGIR, pp. 1265–1268 (2017)
12. Huang, Z., Li, S., Cheng, G., Kharlamov, E., Qu, Y.: MiCRon: making sense of news via relationship subgraphs. In: CIKM, pp. 2901–2904 (2019)
13. Ihler, E.: The complexity of approximating the class Steiner tree problem. In: Schmidt, G., Berghammer, R. (eds.) WG 1991. LNCS, vol. 570, pp. 85–96. Springer, Heidelberg (1992). https://doi.org/10.1007/3-540-55121-2_8
14. Kasneci, G., Elbassuoni, S., Weikum, G.: MING: mining informative entity relationship subgraphs. In: CIKM, pp. 1653–1656 (2009)
15. Li, G., Ooi, B.C., Feng, J., Wang, J., Zhou, L.: EASE: an effective 3-in-1 keyword search method for unstructured, semi-structured and structured data. In: SIGMOD, pp. 903–914 (2008)
16. Li, R., Qin, L., Yu, J.X., Mao, R.: Efficient and progressive group steiner tree search. In: SIGMOD, pp. 91–106 (2016)
17. Li, S., Cheng, G., Li, C.: Relaxing relationship queries on graph data. J. Web Semant. **61–62**, 100557 (2020)
18. Lu, X., Pramanik, S., Roy, R.S., Abujabal, A., Wang, Y., Weikum, G.: Answering complex questions by joining multi-document evidence with quasi knowledge graphs. In: SIGIR, pp. 105–114 (2019)
19. Marchionini, G.: Exploratory search: from finding to understanding. Commun. ACM **49**(4), 41–46 (2006)
20. Miller, A.H., Fisch, A., Dodge, J., Karimi, A., Bordes, A., Weston, J.: Key-value memory networks for directly reading documents. In: EMNLP, pp. 1400–1409 (2016)
21. Poulovassilis, A., Selmer, P., Wood, P.T.: Approximation and relaxation of semantic web path queries. J. Web Semant. **40**, 1–21 (2016)
22. Shekarpour, S., Ngomo, A.N., Auer, S.: Question answering on interlinked data. In: WWW, pp. 1145–1156 (2013)
23. Shi, Y., Cheng, G., Kharlamov, E.: Keyword search over knowledge graphs via static and dynamic hub labelings. In: WWW, pp. 235–245 (2020)
24. Tong, H., Faloutsos, C.: Center-piece subgraphs: problem definition and fast solutions. In: KDD, pp. 404–413 (2006)
25. Tran, T., Herzig, D.M., Ladwig, G.: SemSearchPro - using semantics throughout the search process. J. Web Semant. **9**(4), 349–364 (2011)
26. Wang, M., Wang, R., Liu, J., Chen, Y., Zhang, L., Qi, G.: Towards empty answers in SPARQL: approximating querying with RDF embedding. In: Vrandečić, D., et al. (eds.) ISWC 2018. LNCS, vol. 11136, pp. 513–529. Springer, Cham (2018). https://doi.org/10.1007/978-3-030-00671-6_30
27. Zhiltsov, N., Kotov, A., Nikolaev, F.: Fielded sequential dependence model for ad-hoc entity retrieval in the web of data. In: SIGIR, pp. 253–262 (2015)

Controlled Query Evaluation in Ontology-Based Data Access

Gianluca Cima[1], Domenico Lembo[1(✉)], Lorenzo Marconi[1], Riccardo Rosati[1], and Domenico Fabio Savo[2]

[1] Sapienza Università di Roma, Rome, Italy
{cima,lembo,marconi,rosati}@diag.uniroma1.it
[2] Università degli Studi di Bergamo, Bergamo, Italy
domenicofabio.savo@unibg.it

Abstract. In this paper we study the problem of information disclosure in ontology-based data access (OBDA). Following previous work on Controlled Query Evaluation, we introduce the framework of Policy-Protected OBDA (PPOBDA), which extends OBDA with data protection policies specified over the ontology and enforced through a *censor*, i.e., a function that alters answers to users' queries to avoid the disclosure of protected data. We consider PPOBDA systems in which the ontology is expressed in OWL 2 QL and the policies are denial constraints, and show that query answering under censors in such a setting can be reduced to standard query answering in OBDA (without data protection policies). The basic idea of our approach is to compile the policies of a PPOBDA system into the mapping of a standard OBDA system. To this aim, we analyze some notions of censor proposed in the literature, show that they are not suited for the above-mentioned compilation, and provide a new definition of censor that enables the effective realization of our idea. We have implemented our technique and evaluated it over the NPD benchmark for OBDA. Our results are very promising and show that controlled query evaluation in OBDA can be realized in the practice by using off-the-shelf OBDA engines.

Keywords: Ontology-based data access · Information disclosure · Data protection · First-order rewritability

1 Introduction

Controlled Query Evaluation (CQE) is an approach to privacy-preserving query answering that recently has gained attention in the context of ontologies [7,13,14,20]. In this paper, we consider the more general Ontology-based

This work was partly supported by the EU within the H2020 Programme under the grant agreement 834228 (ERC WhiteMec) and the grant agreement 825333 (MOSAICrOWN), by Regione Lombardia within the Call Hub Ricerca e Innovazione under the grant agreement 1175328 (WATCHMAN), and by the Italian MUR (Ministero dell'Università e della Ricerca) through the PRIN project HOPE (prot. 2017MMJJRE).

J. Z. Pan et al. (Eds.): ISWC 2020, LNCS 12506, pp. 128–146, 2020.
https://doi.org/10.1007/978-3-030-62419-4_8

Data Access (OBDA) framework, where an ontology is coupled to external data sources via a declarative mapping [23,26], and extend OBDA with CQE features. In this new framework, which we call *Policy-Protected Ontology-based Data Access (PPOBDA)*, a data protection policy is specified over the ontology of an OBDA system in terms of logical statements declaring confidential information that must not be revealed to the users. As an example, consider the following formula:

$$\forall x, y. OilComp(x) \wedge IssuesLic(x, y) \wedge Comp(y) \rightarrow \bot$$

which says that the existence of an oil company issuing a license to another company (to operate over its properties) is a private information.

More formally, we define a PPOBDA specification $\mathcal{E}$ as a quadruple $\langle \mathcal{T}, \mathcal{S}, \mathcal{M}, \mathcal{P} \rangle$, where $\mathcal{T}$ is a Description Logic (DL) TBox [2], formalizing intensional domain knowledge, $\mathcal{S}$ is the relational schema at the sources, $\mathcal{M}$ is the mapping between the two, i.e., a set of logical assertions defining the semantic correspondence between $\mathcal{T}$ and $\mathcal{S}$, and $\mathcal{P}$ is the data protection policy expressed over $\mathcal{T}$. The components $\mathcal{T}$, $\mathcal{S}$, and $\mathcal{M}$ are exactly as in OBDA specifications, and, as in standard OBDA, a user can only ask queries over the TBox $\mathcal{T}$. Then, query answering is filtered through a *censor*, i.e., a function that alters the answers to queries, in such a way that no data are returned that may lead a malicious user to infer knowledge declared confidential by the policy, even in case he/she accumulates the answers he/she gets over time. Among possible censors, *optimal* ones are preferred, i.e., those altering query answers in a minimal way.

Within this framework, we initially consider two different notions of censor, called censor in **CQ** and censor in **GA**, previously defined for CQE over DL ontologies [14,20], and which can be naturally extended to PPOBDA. More precisely, given a PPOBDA specification $\mathcal{E} = \langle \mathcal{T}, \mathcal{S}, \mathcal{M}, \mathcal{P} \rangle$, an optimal censor in **CQ** (resp., **GA**) for $\mathcal{E}$ is a function that, taken as input a database instance D for the source schema $\mathcal{S}$, returns a maximal subset $\mathcal{C}$ of the set of Boolean conjunctive queries (resp., ground atoms) inferred by $\langle \mathcal{T}, \mathcal{S}, \mathcal{M} \rangle$ and D, such that $\mathcal{C} \cup \mathcal{T}$ does not entail information protected by the policy. Since in general, for such notions of censor, several of these maximal sets (incomparable to each other) exist, for both cases we define *query answering under optimal censors* in PPOBDA as a form of skeptical reasoning over all such sets, in the same spirit of [20].

Our basic idea to solve query answering under censors is to transform a PPOBDA specification $\mathcal{E}$ into a classical OBDA specification $\mathcal{J}$ (i.e., without policies), in such a way that, whatever database D instantiates the source schema $\mathcal{S}$, query answering under censors in $\mathcal{E}$ over D is equivalent to standard query answering in $\mathcal{J}$ over D. In this transformation, we require that $\mathcal{J}$ has the same TBox of $\mathcal{E}$, so that this reduction is transparent to the user, who can continue asking to $\mathcal{J}$ exactly the same queries he/she could ask to $\mathcal{E}$. We also impose that $\mathcal{J}$ maintains the same source schema as $\mathcal{E}$, since, as typical in OBDA, the data sources to be accessed are autonomous, and cannot be modified for OBDA purposes. Moreover, we aim at a transformation that is independent from the underlying data and from the user queries, so that it can be computed only once, at design-time. This enables us to use off-the-shelf OBDA engines, like MASTRO[1] or Ontop[2] to realize CQE in OBDA. The problem we study can be thus summarized as follows: Given a PPOBDA specification $\mathcal{E} = \langle \mathcal{T}, \mathcal{M}, \mathcal{S}, \mathcal{P} \rangle$, construct an OBDA specification $\mathcal{J} = \langle \mathcal{T}, \mathcal{S}, \mathcal{M}' \rangle$ such that, for any database D for $\mathcal{S}$, conjunctive query answering under censors in $\mathcal{E}$ over D is equivalent to standard conjunctive query answering in $\mathcal{J}$ over D.

We investigate the above problem for the relevant case in which the TBox is expressed in *DL-Lite*$_\mathcal{R}$, the DL underpinning OWL 2 QL [21], the standard profile of OWL 2 designed for ontology-based data management and prominently used in OBDA, and the policy is a set of denial assertions, i.e., conjunctive queries for which an empty answer is imposed due to confidential reasons (as in our initial example). Our contributions are as follows.

- We show that the above problem has in general no solution when censors in either **CQ** or **GA** are considered. We in fact prove this result for an empty TBox, and thus it holds for TBoxes in any DL, and not only for OWL 2 QL ones.
- To overcome this issue, we propose a further, semantically well-founded approximated notion of censor, which we call IGA censor. Intuitively, an IGA censor for a PPOBDA specification $\mathcal{E}$ is a function that, for any database D instantiating the source schema $\mathcal{S}$ of $\mathcal{E}$, returns the intersection of the sets of ground atoms computed by the optimal censors in **GA** for $\mathcal{E}$ applied to D.
- We provide an algorithm that solves our problem for OWL 2 QL PPOBDA specifications under IGA censors.
- We provide an experimental evaluation of our approach. We have implemented our algorithm in Java, and tested it over the OBDA NPD benchmark [18], whose TBox has been suitably approximated from OWL 2 to OWL 2 QL. We have compared query answering in the case in which no data protection policy is specified (i.e., in standard OBDA) with query answering under IGA censors for an increasing number of policy assertions. We have used MASTRO as OBDA engine. Our results show that the cost of the off-line transformation performed by our tool is negligible, and answering queries in the presence of a data protection policy in our approach does not cause a significant overhead with respect to the case without policy.

We remark that our main objective was to devise a practical, though theoretically well-founded, approach to policy-protected query answering in OBDA, allowing for the exploitation of existing OBDA engines. We believe that the pipeline we have realized and the experimental results we have obtained show the achievement of our goal.

The rest of the paper is organized as follows. In Sect. 2 we discuss some related work. In Sect. 3 we provide preliminaries. In Sect. 4 we present our framework

[1] http://obdasystems.com/mastro.
[2] https://ontop-vkg.org/.

for PPOBDA. In Sect. 5 we show that query answering under censors in both **CQ** and **GA** cannot be reduced to standard query answering in OBDA. In Sect. 6 we give the notion of IGA censor and provide our algorithm for reducing conjunctive query answering under IGA censors to query answering in OBDA. In Sect. 7 we describe our experiments, and in Sect. 8 we conclude the paper.

2 Related Work

Existing OBDA solutions do not provide any explicit support to the protection of confidential data, and the research has so far produced only initial theoretical contributions in this direction. In [4], the authors study the problem of determining whether information that is declared confidential at the sources through a protection policy, as in CQE, can be inferred by a user on the basis of the answers to the queries posed over the OBDA system, assuming that he/she is knowledgeable about the OBDA specification. Both [4] and the present paper focus on the role of the mapping in filtering data coming from the sources with respect to a declarative data protection policy. However, we consider the policy expressed over the TBox of the OBDA specification and look at the mapping as a means to enforce data protection, whereas in [4] the policy is declared at the source level and the mapping is seen as a potential cause for secret disclosure. Possible disclosure of confidential source-level information has also been studied in [3,9,22], in the context of data integration or exchange, possibly in the presence of integrity constraints at the sources. In these works, the integrated target schema is a flat relational one, thus not an expressive TBox, as in OBDA, and secrets are specified in terms of queries over the sources, thus not policies over the target schema, as in our framework. Also, the focus is on disclosure analysis and not confidentiality enforcement.

Initially, CQE has been studied in the context of propositional theories under closed world assumption (see, e.g., [5,24]), thus in a framework substantially different from ours. The more recent works on CQE over DL ontologies are instead closer to our research. In [7], the authors propose a method for computing secure knowledge views over DL ontologies in the presence of user background knowledge and investigate the computational complexity of the approach for ontologies and policies specified in various expressive DLs. In [13], the authors generalize the CQE paradigm for incomplete databases proposed in [6], and study CQE for OWL 2 RL ontologies and policies represented by a set of ground atoms. The same authors continued their investigation in [14], for ontologies and policies specified in Datalog or in one of the OWL 2 profiles [21], mainly focusing on the problem of the existence of a censor under two incomparable different notions of censors. In [20], the authors revisited CQE as the problem of computing the answers to a query that are returned by all optimal censors, which is also the approach we adopt in this paper. However, like all the above mentioned papers on CQE over ontologies, [20] does not consider OBDA mappings to external data sources.

We finally point out that forms of privacy-preserving query answering over DL ontologies have been studied also, e.g., in [12,25], but not according to the CQE approach, or in an OBDA context.

3 Preliminaries

We use standard notions of function-free first-order (FO) logic and relational databases. We assume to have the pairwise disjoint countably infinite sets Σ_R, Σ_T, Σ_C, and Σ_V for relational database predicates, ontology predicates, constants (a.k.a. individuals), and variables, respectively. Given a symbol $p \in \Sigma_R \cup \Sigma_T$, with p/n we denote that p has arity n, i.e., n is the number of arguments of r.

Ontologies. With **FO** we indicate the language of all FO sentences over Σ_T, Σ_C, and Σ_V. An FO ontology $\mathcal{O}$ is a finite set of FO sentences, i.e., $\mathcal{O} \subseteq \mathbf{FO}$. With $Mod(\mathcal{O})$ we denote the set of the models of $\mathcal{O}$, i.e., the FO interpretations $\mathcal{I}$ such that $\phi^{\mathcal{I}}$ (i.e., the interpretation of ϕ in $\mathcal{I}$) evaluates to true, for each sentence $\phi \in \mathcal{O}$. We say that $\mathcal{O}$ is consistent if $Mod(\mathcal{O}) \neq \emptyset$, inconsistent otherwise, and that $\mathcal{O}$ entails an FO sentence ϕ, denoted $\mathcal{O} \models \phi$, if $\phi^{\mathcal{I}}$ is true in every $\mathcal{I} \in Mod(\mathcal{O})$. The set of logical consequences of an ontology $\mathcal{O}$ in a language $\mathcal{L} \subseteq \mathbf{FO}$, denoted $\mathsf{cl}_{\mathcal{L}}(\mathcal{O})$, is the set of sentences in $\mathcal{L}$ entailed by $\mathcal{O}$.

Queries. A query q is a (possibly open) FO formula $\phi(\boldsymbol{x})$, where $\boldsymbol{x}$ are the free variables of q. The number of variables in $\boldsymbol{x}$ is the *arity* of q. We consider queries over either relational databases or ontologies. Given a query q of arity n over a database D, we use $Eval(q, D)$ to denote the evaluation of q over D, i.e., the set of tuples $\boldsymbol{t} \in \Sigma_C^n$ such that $D \models \phi(\boldsymbol{t})$, where $\phi(\boldsymbol{t})$ is the sentence obtained by substituting $\boldsymbol{x}$ with $\boldsymbol{t}$ in q.

A conjunctive query (CQ) q is an FO formula of the form $\exists \boldsymbol{y}.\alpha_1(\boldsymbol{x}, \boldsymbol{y}) \wedge \ldots \wedge \alpha_n(\boldsymbol{x}, \boldsymbol{y})$, where $n \geq 1$, $\boldsymbol{x}$ is the sequence of free variables, $\boldsymbol{y}$ is the sequence of existential variables, and each $\alpha_i(\boldsymbol{x}, \boldsymbol{y})$ is an atom (possibly containing constants) with predicate α_i and variables in $\boldsymbol{x} \cup \boldsymbol{y}$. Each variable in $\boldsymbol{x} \cup \boldsymbol{y}$ occurs in at least one atom of q. Boolean CQs (BCQs) are queries whose arity is zero (i.e., BCQs are sentences). The length of a CQ q is the number of its atoms. The set of *certain answers* to a CQ q of arity n over an ontology $\mathcal{O}$ is the set $cert(q, \mathcal{O})$ of tuples $\boldsymbol{c} \in \Sigma_C^n$ such that $\mathcal{O}$ entails the sentence $\exists \boldsymbol{y}.\alpha_1(\boldsymbol{c}, \boldsymbol{y}) \wedge \ldots \wedge \alpha_n(\boldsymbol{c}, \boldsymbol{y})$. As usual [1], when a BCQ q is entailed by $\mathcal{O}$, i.e., $\mathcal{O} \models q$, we may also say $cert(q, \mathcal{O}) = \{\langle\rangle\}$, i.e., the set of certain answers contains only the empty tuple, $cert(q, \mathcal{O}) = \emptyset$, otherwise.

For ease of exposition, in our technical development we will focus on the entailment of BCQs from DL ontologies. However, our results can be straightforwardly extended to non-Boolean CQs through a standard encoding of open formulas into closed ones.

In the following, we denote by **CQ** the languages of BCQs, and by **GA** the language of ground atoms, i.e., BCQs with only one atom and no variables, both specified over Σ_T, Σ_C, and Σ_V.

OWL 2 QL and *DL-Lite*$_\mathcal{R}$. We consider ontologies expressed in *DL-Lite*$_\mathcal{R}$ [8], i.e., the DL that provides the logical underpinning of OWL 2 QL [21]. DLs are decidable FO languages using only unary and binary predicates, called concepts and roles, respectively [2]. Concepts denote sets of objects, whereas roles denote binary relationships between objects. A DL ontology $\mathcal{O}$ is a set $\mathcal{T} \cup \mathcal{A}$, where $\mathcal{T}$ is the *TBox* and $\mathcal{A}$ is the *ABox*, specifying intensional and extensional knowledge, respectively.

A TBox $\mathcal{T}$ in *DL-Lite*$_\mathcal{R}$ is a finite set of axioms of the form: $B_1 \sqsubseteq B_2$, $B_1 \sqsubseteq \neg B_2$, $R_1 \sqsubseteq R_2$, and $R_1 \sqsubseteq \neg R_2$, where each R_i, with $i \in \{1, 2\}$ is an atomic role Q (i.e, $Q/2 \in \Sigma_T$), or its inverse Q^-; each B_i, with $i \in \{1, 2\}$ is an atomic concept A (i.e., $A/1 \in \Sigma_T$), or a concept of the form $\exists Q$ or $\exists Q^-$, i.e., unqualified existential restrictions, which denote the set of objects occurring as first or second argument of Q, respectively. Assertions of the form $B_1 \sqsubseteq B_2$ and $R_1 \sqsubseteq R_2$ indicate subsumption between predicates, those of the form $B_1 \sqsubseteq \neg B_2$ and $R_1 \sqsubseteq \neg R_2$ indicate disjointness between predicates.

An ABox $\mathcal{A}$ is a finite set of ground atoms, i.e., assertions of the form $A(a)$, $Q(a, b)$, where $A/1, Q/2 \in \Sigma_T$, and $a, b \in \Sigma_C$. The semantics of a *DL-Lite*$_\mathcal{R}$ ontology $\mathcal{O}$ is given in terms of FO models over the signature of $\mathcal{O}$ in the standard way [8].

OBDA. An *OBDA specification* is a triple $\mathcal{J} = \langle \mathcal{T}, \mathcal{S}, \mathcal{M} \rangle$, where $\mathcal{T}$ is a DL TBox over the alphabet Σ_T, $\mathcal{S}$, called *source schema*, is a relational schema over the alphabet Σ_R, and $\mathcal{M}$ is a *mapping* between $\mathcal{S}$ and $\mathcal{T}$.

The mapping $\mathcal{M}$ is a finite set of *mapping assertions* from $\mathcal{S}$ to $\mathcal{T}$. Each of these assertions m has the form $\phi(\boldsymbol{x}) \rightsquigarrow \psi(\boldsymbol{x})$, where $\phi(\boldsymbol{x})$, called the *body of* m, and $\psi(\boldsymbol{x})$, called the *head of* m, are queries over (the signature of) $\mathcal{S}$ and $\mathcal{T}$, respectively, both with free variables $\boldsymbol{x}$. We consider the case in which $\phi(\boldsymbol{x})$ is an FO query, and $\psi(\boldsymbol{x})$ is a single-atom query without constants and existential variables (i.e., each m is a GAV mapping assertion [17]). This is the form of mapping commonly adopted in OBDA, and a special case of the W3C standard R2RML [15].

In the above definition, for ease of exposition, we have assumed that the source database directly stores the identifiers (e.g., the URIs) of the instances of the ontology predicates. However, all our results hold also when such identifiers are constructed in the mapping using the database values, as usual in OBDA [23] and in R2RML.

The semantics of $\mathcal{J}$ is given with respect to a database instance for $\mathcal{S}$, called source database for $\mathcal{J}$. Given one such database D, the *retrieved ABox* for $\mathcal{J}$ w.r.t. D, denoted *ret*$(\mathcal{J}, D)$, is the ABox that contains all and only the facts $\psi(\boldsymbol{t})$ such that $\psi(\boldsymbol{x})$ occurs in the head of some mapping assertion $m \in \mathcal{M}$, and $\boldsymbol{t}$ is a tuple of constants such that $\boldsymbol{t} \in$ *Eval*$(\phi(\boldsymbol{x}), D)$, where $\phi(\boldsymbol{x})$ is the body of m. Then, a *model* for $\mathcal{J}$ w.r.t. D is a model of the ontology $\mathcal{T} \cup$ *ret*$(\mathcal{J}, D)$. The set of models of $\mathcal{J}$ w.r.t. D is denoted by *Mod*$(\mathcal{J}, D)$. Also, we call $(\mathcal{J}, D)$ an *OBDA setting* and say that $(\mathcal{J}, D)$ *is inconsistent* if *Mod*$(\mathcal{J}, D) = \emptyset$, and denote by $(\mathcal{J}, D) \models \alpha$ the entailment of a sentence α by $(\mathcal{J}, D)$, i.e., the fact that $\alpha^\mathcal{I}$ is true in every $\mathcal{I} \in$ *Mod*$(\mathcal{J}, D)$.

4 Framework

We start by introducing the formal notion of policy-protected OBDA specification. Our framework is a generalization to the OBDA context of the CQE framework for DL ontologies provided in [10,20].

First thing, we define a *denial assertion* (or simply a denial) as an FO sentence of the form $\forall \boldsymbol{x}.\phi(\boldsymbol{x}) \rightarrow \bot$, such that $\exists \boldsymbol{x}.\phi(\boldsymbol{x})$ is a BCQ. Given one such denial δ and a DL ontology $\mathcal{O}$, then $\mathcal{O} \cup \{\delta\}$ is a consistent FO theory if $\mathcal{O} \not\models \exists \boldsymbol{x}.\phi(\boldsymbol{x})$, and is inconsistent otherwise. We then give the following definition.

Definition 1 (PPOBDA specification). *A* policy-protected ontology-based data access (PPOBDA) *specification is a quadruple* $\mathcal{E} = \langle \mathcal{T}, \mathcal{S}, \mathcal{M}, \mathcal{P} \rangle$ *such that* $\langle \mathcal{T}, \mathcal{S}, \mathcal{M} \rangle$ *is an OBDA specification, and* $\mathcal{P}$ *is a* policy, *i.e., a set of denial assertions over the signature of* $\mathcal{T}$*, such that* $\mathcal{T} \cup \mathcal{P}$ *is a consistent FO theory.*

Example 1. Consider the following PPOBDA specification $\mathcal{E} = \langle \mathcal{T}, \mathcal{S}, \mathcal{M}, \mathcal{P} \rangle$, where

$$\begin{aligned}
\mathcal{T} = \{ & \mathit{OilComp} \sqsubseteq \mathit{Comp},\ \exists \mathit{IssuesLic}^- \sqsubseteq \mathit{Comp}, \\
& \exists \mathit{PipeOp} \sqsubseteq \mathit{Pipeline},\ \exists \mathit{PipeOp}^- \sqsubseteq \mathit{Comp} \}
\end{aligned}$$

$$\mathcal{S} = \{ \mathsf{company}/2, \mathsf{license}/2, \mathsf{operator}/2 \}$$

$$\begin{aligned}
\mathcal{M} = \{ & m_1\colon \exists y.\mathsf{company}(x,y) \rightsquigarrow \mathit{Comp}(x), \\
& m_2\colon \mathsf{company}(x, \text{'oil'}) \rightsquigarrow \mathit{OilComp}(x), \\
& m_3\colon \mathsf{license}(x,y) \rightsquigarrow \mathit{IssuesLic}(x,y), \\
& m_4\colon \mathsf{operator}(x,y) \rightsquigarrow \mathit{PipeOp}(x,y) \}
\end{aligned}$$

$$\begin{aligned}
\mathcal{P} = \{ & d_1\colon \forall x,y.\mathit{OilComp}(x) \land \mathit{IssuesLic}(x,y) \land \mathit{Comp}(y) \rightarrow \bot, \\
& d_2\colon \forall x,y.\mathit{PipeOp}(x,y) \land \mathit{OilComp}(y) \rightarrow \bot \}
\end{aligned}$$

In words, the TBox $\mathcal{T}$ specifies that oil companies (concept *OilComp*) are a special kind of companies (concept *Comp*), individuals (e.g., companies) can issue licenses (role *IssuesLic*) to companies (over the properties of the issuer), and companies can be operators (role *PipeOp*) of pipelines (concept *Pipeline*). The schema $\mathcal{S}$ has three tables: company, which contains data about companies and their type, license, which contains data about license issuance, and operator, which contains operators of pipelines. The policy $\mathcal{P}$ specifies as confidential the fact that an oil company issues a license to a company, and the fact that an oil company is the operator of a pipeline. □

The semantics of a PPOBDA specification $\mathcal{E} = \langle \mathcal{T}, \mathcal{S}, \mathcal{M}, \mathcal{P} \rangle$ coincides with that of the OBDA specification $\langle \mathcal{T}, \mathcal{S}, \mathcal{M} \rangle$, and thus we naturally extend to PPOBDA the notion of source database D, retrieved ABox (denoted $\mathit{ret}(\mathcal{E}, D)$), set of models (denoted $\mathit{Mod}(\mathcal{E}, D)$), and setting (denoted $(\mathcal{E}, D)$).

We now give a notion of censor in PPOBDA that is parametric with respect to the language $\mathcal{L}$ used for enforcing the policy (similarly to [20]). In the following, given a TBox $\mathcal{T}$, with $\mathcal{L}(\mathcal{T})$ we denote the subset of $\mathcal{L}$ containing all and only the sentences specified only over the predicates occurring in $\mathcal{T}$ and the constants in Σ_C. For instance, with $\mathbf{FO}(\mathcal{T})$ we denote the set of FO sentences having the above mentioned characteristics. Moreover, given a database D, with $\mathcal{L}_D$ we denote the formulas in $\mathcal{L}$ mentioning only constants in D.

Definition 2 (censor in $\mathcal{L}$). *Given a PPOBDA specification $\mathcal{E} = \langle \mathcal{T}, \mathcal{S}, \mathcal{M}, \mathcal{P} \rangle$ and a language $\mathcal{L} \subseteq \mathbf{FO}(\mathcal{T})$, a* censor *for $\mathcal{E}$ in $\mathcal{L}$ is a function* $\mathsf{cens}(\cdot)$ *such that, for each source database D for $\mathcal{E}$, returns a set* $\mathsf{cens}(D) \subseteq \mathcal{L}_D$ *such that:*

(i) $(\langle \mathcal{T}, \mathcal{S}, \mathcal{M} \rangle, D) \models \phi$*, for each* $\phi \in \mathsf{cens}(D)$*, and*
(ii) $\mathcal{T} \cup \mathcal{P} \cup \mathsf{cens}(D)$ *is a consistent FO theory.*

We call $\mathcal{L}$ the censor language.

Given two censors $\mathsf{cens}(\cdot)$ and $\mathsf{cens}'(\cdot)$ for $\mathcal{E}$ in $\mathcal{L}$, we say that $\mathsf{cens}'(\cdot)$ is *more informative* than $\mathsf{cens}(\cdot)$ if:

(*i*) for every database instance D for $\mathcal{E}$, $\mathsf{cens}(D) \subseteq \mathsf{cens}'(D)$, and
(*ii*) there exists a database instance D' for $\mathcal{E}$ such that $\mathsf{cens}(D') \subset \mathsf{cens}'(D')$.

Then, a censor $\mathsf{cens}(\cdot)$ for $\mathcal{E}$ in $\mathcal{L}$ is *optimal* if there does not exist a censor $\mathsf{cens}'(\cdot)$ for $\mathcal{E}$ in $\mathcal{L}$ such that $\mathsf{cens}'(\cdot)$ is more informative than $\mathsf{cens}(\cdot)$. The set of all optimal censors in $\mathcal{L}$ for a PPOBDA specification $\mathcal{E}$ is denoted by $\mathcal{L}$-$\mathsf{OptCens}_{\mathcal{E}}$.

In this paper we consider censors in the languages $\mathbf{CQ}(\mathcal{T})$ and $\mathbf{GA}(\mathcal{T})$, i.e., we instantiate $\mathcal{L}$ in Definition 2 to either the language of Boolean conjunctive queries or the language of ground atoms, respectively, both over the predicates occurring in $\mathcal{T}$. These are the censor languages studied in [20] over DL ontologies. In the following, when $\mathcal{T}$ is clear from the context, we simply denote them as **CQ** and **GA**, respectively.

Example 2. Consider the PPOBDA specification $\mathcal{E}$ of Example 1, and let cens_1 be the function such that, given a source database D for $\mathcal{E}$, $\mathsf{cens}_1(D)$ is the set of ground atoms $\mathsf{cl}_{\mathbf{GA}}(\mathcal{T} \cup \mathcal{A}_1)$, where $\mathcal{A}_1$ is the ABox obtained from $ret(\mathcal{E}, D)$ by adding the assertion $Comp(c)$ and removing the assertion $OilComp(c)$, for each individual c such that $\mathcal{T} \cup ret(\mathcal{E}, D) \models (OilComp(c) \wedge \exists x.IssuesLic(c, x) \wedge Comp(x)) \vee (\exists x.PipeOp(x, c) \wedge OilComp(c))$. It is easy to verify that cens_1 is an optimal censor for $\mathcal{E}$ in **GA**, i.e. $\mathsf{cens}_1 \in \mathbf{GA}$-$\mathsf{OptCens}_{\mathcal{E}}$. □

In answering users' queries, one might choose to select a single optimal censor. However, as already pointed out in [10,20], in the lack of further meta-information about the application domain, picking up just one optimal censor may end up in arbitrary behaviour. Thus, following the approach studied in [10,20], we prefer to reason about *all* the optimal censors. In particular, for the censor languages **CQ** and **GA**, we define the following entailment problems.

Definition 3. *Given a PPOBDA specification $\mathcal{E} = \langle \mathcal{T}, \mathcal{S}, \mathcal{M}, \mathcal{P} \rangle$, a database instance D for $\mathcal{S}$, and a BCQ q, we consider the following decision problems:*

(CQ-Cens-Entailment)*: decide whether* $\mathcal{T} \cup \mathsf{cens}(D) \models q$ *for every* $\mathsf{cens} \in \mathbf{CQ}$-$\mathsf{OptCens}_{\mathcal{E}}$*. If this is the case, we write* $(\mathcal{E}, D) \models^{cqe}_{\mathbf{CQ}} q$*.*

***(GA-Cens-Entailment)**: decide whether* $\mathcal{T} \cup \mathsf{cens}(D) \models q$ *for every* $\mathsf{cens} \in \mathbf{GA}\text{-}\mathsf{OptCens}_{\mathcal{E}}$. *If this is the case, we write* $(\mathcal{E}, D) \models^{cqe}_{\mathbf{GA}} q$.

Our ultimate goal is to solve the above problems by reducing them to classical entailment of BCQs in OBDA. To this aim, we define below the notion of query equivalence under censor between PPOBDA and OBDA specifications.

Definition 4 (query equivalence). *Given a PPOBDA specification* $\mathcal{E} = \langle \mathcal{T}, \mathcal{S}, \mathcal{M}, \mathcal{P} \rangle$ *and an OBDA specification* $\mathcal{J} = \langle \mathcal{T}, \mathcal{S}, \mathcal{M}' \rangle$, *we say that* $\mathcal{E}$ *and* $\mathcal{J}$ *are* query-equivalent under censors in **CQ** (resp. **GA**) *if for every database instance* D *for* $\mathcal{S}$ *and every BCQ* q, $(\mathcal{E}, D) \models^{cqe}_{\mathbf{CQ}} q$ *(resp.* $(\mathcal{E}, D) \models^{cqe}_{\mathbf{GA}} q$*) iff* $(\mathcal{J}, D) \models q$.

Based on the above definition, we can decide **CQ**-cens-entailment of a BCQ q from a PPOBDA $\mathcal{E}$ coupled with a source database D for $\mathcal{S}$ by constructing an OBDA specification $\mathcal{J}$ such that $\mathcal{E}$ and $\mathcal{J}$ are query-equivalent under censors in **CQ** and checking whether $(\mathcal{J}, D) \models q$ (analogously for **GA**-cens-entailment). We remark that, besides the policy, the mapping is the only component in which $\mathcal{E}$ and $\mathcal{J}$ differ (see also Sect. 1). Intuitively, $\mathcal{M}'$ in $\mathcal{J}$ implements a censor (in either **CQ** or **GA**) for $\mathcal{E}$.

5 Inexpressibility Results

In this section, we start investigating how to reduce query entailment in PPOBDA to query entailment in OBDA, based on the query equivalence definition given in the previous section.

Before proceeding further, we notice that, given a PPOBDA specification $\mathcal{E} = \langle \mathcal{T}, \mathcal{S}, \mathcal{M}, \mathcal{P} \rangle$, a natural question is whether the OBDA specification $\mathcal{J} = \langle \mathcal{T}, \mathcal{S}, \mathcal{M} \rangle$, i.e., obtained by simply eliminating the policy $\mathcal{P}$ from $\mathcal{E}$, is query-equivalent to $\mathcal{E}$ under censors in either **CQ** or **GA**. In other terms, one might wonder whether the mapping $\mathcal{M}$ is already realizing a filter on the data such that denials in $\mathcal{P}$ are never violated by the underlying data retrieved through $\mathcal{M}$, whatever source database for $\mathcal{J}$ is considered[3]. If this would be the case, the entailment problems we are studying would become trivial. However, since the bodies of mapping assertions are FO queries, to answer the above question we should decide entailment in FO, which is an undecidable problem.

The following result says that, under censors in **CQ**, constructing an OBDA specification query-equivalent to $\mathcal{E}$ is in general not possible, already for the case of an empty TBox, i.e., a TBox that does not contain axioms. As a consequence, entailment of BCQs under censors in **CQ** cannot be solved through transformation in a query-equivalent OBDA specification, whatever logic is used for the TBox.

Theorem 1. *There exists a PPOBDA specification* $\mathcal{E} = \langle \mathcal{T}, \mathcal{S}, \mathcal{M}, \mathcal{P} \rangle$ *with* $\mathcal{T} = \emptyset$ *for which there does not exist an OBDA specification* $\mathcal{J}$ *such that* $\mathcal{E}$ *and* $\mathcal{J}$ *are query-equivalent under censors in* **CQ**.

[3] Note that this is not the problem studied in [4] (see also the discussion in Sect. 2).

Proof. Consider the PPOBDA specification $\mathcal{E} = \langle \mathcal{T}, \mathcal{S}, \mathcal{M}, \mathcal{P} \rangle$ such that $\mathcal{T} = \emptyset$, $\mathcal{S}$ contains the relation $T/2$, where $T \in \Sigma_R$, $\mathcal{M} = \{T(x, y) \rightsquigarrow Q(x, y)\}$, where $Q/2 \in \Sigma_T$, and $\mathcal{P}$ is as follows:

$$\mathcal{P} = \{\forall x \,.\, Q(a, x) \rightarrow \bot, \;\; \forall x \,.\, Q(x, a) \rightarrow \bot\},$$

where a belongs to Σ_C. Assume that $\mathcal{J}$ is an OBDA specification such that $\mathcal{E}$ and $\mathcal{J}$ are query-equivalent under censors in **CQ**, and let $\mathcal{M}'$ be the mapping of $\mathcal{J}$. Consider now the case when the source database D consists of the fact $T(a, a)$. First, it is immediate to see that, given the policy $\mathcal{P}$, no BCQ mentioning the individual a can belong to any censor $\mathsf{cens}(\cdot)$ in $\mathbf{CQ}$-$\mathsf{OptCens}_{\mathcal{E}}$. Then, since a is the only individual appearing in D, it follows that no BCQ mentioning any individual can belong to any censor $\mathsf{cens}(\cdot)$ in $\mathbf{CQ}$-$\mathsf{OptCens}_{\mathcal{E}}$. This implies that the mapping $\mathcal{M}'$ of $\mathcal{J}$ cannot retrieve any instance from D, i.e., $ret(\mathcal{J}, D)$ is empty, and therefore no BCQ is entailed by $(\mathcal{J}, D)$. On the other hand, the OBDA setting $(\langle \mathcal{T}, \mathcal{S}, \mathcal{M} \rangle, D)$ infers purely existential BCQs. For instance, all the BCQs expressing existential cycles of any length over the role Q, that is all the queries of the form

$$\exists x_0, \ldots, x_n \,.\, Q(x_0, x_1) \wedge Q(x_1, x_2) \wedge \ldots \wedge Q(x_n, x_0)$$

where $n \in \mathbb{N}$. All such queries can be positively answered by the PPOBDA setting $(\mathcal{E}, D)$ without revealing a secret: so, all such queries belong to every censor $\mathsf{cens}(\cdot)$ in $\mathbf{CQ}$-$\mathsf{OptCens}_{\mathcal{E}}$. Since they are not entailed by $(\mathcal{J}, D)$, this contradicts the hypothesis that $\mathcal{E}$ and $\mathcal{J}$ are query-equivalent under censors in **CQ**, thus proving the theorem. □

Hereinafter, we focus on *DL-Lite*$_{\mathcal{R}}$ PPOBDA specifications, i.e., whose TBox is expressed in the logic *DL-Lite*$_{\mathcal{R}}$. The following theorem states that the same issue of Theorem 1 arises also under censors in **GA**.

Theorem 2. *There exists a DL-Lite*$_{\mathcal{R}}$ *PPOBDA specification* $\mathcal{E}$ *for which there does not exist an OBDA specification* $\mathcal{J}$ *such that* $\mathcal{E}$ *and* $\mathcal{J}$ *are query-equivalent under censors in* **GA**.

Proof. From Theorem 6 in [20], it follows that, for *DL-Lite*$_{\mathcal{R}}$ PPOBDA specifications, **GA**-Cens-Entailment is coNP-hard in data complexity. Instead, standard conjunctive query entailment for OBDA specifications with a *DL-Lite*$_{\mathcal{R}}$ TBox is in AC^0 in data complexity [23]. This clearly shows the thesis. □

6 Embedding a Policy into the Mapping

Towards the identification of a notion of censor that allows us to always transform a PPOBDA specification $\mathcal{E}$ into a query-equivalent OBDA one, we define below a new notion of censor that suitably approximates censors for $\mathcal{E}$ in **GA**.

Definition 5 (Intersection GA censor). *Given a PPOBDA specification* $\mathcal{E} = \langle \mathcal{T}, \mathcal{S}, \mathcal{M}, \mathcal{P} \rangle$, *the* intersection GA (IGA) censor *for* $\mathcal{E}$ *is the function* $\mathsf{cens}_{IGA}(\cdot)$ *such that, for every database instance* D *for* $\mathcal{S}$, $\mathsf{cens}_{IGA}(D) = \bigcap_{\mathsf{cens} \in \mathbf{GA}\text{-}\mathsf{OptCens}_{\mathcal{E}}} \mathsf{cens}(D)$.

Example 3. Let $\mathcal{E}$ be the PPOBDA specification of Example 1, and let $D = \{\mathsf{company}(c_1, \textit{`oil'}), \mathsf{company}(c_2, \textit{`oil'}), \mathsf{company}(c_3, \textit{`oil'}), \mathsf{license}(c_1, c_4), \mathsf{operator}(p_1, c_2)\}$ be a source database for $\mathcal{E}$. One can verify that $\mathsf{cens}_{IGA}(D) = \{Comp(c_1), Comp(c_2), Comp(c_3), OilComp(c_3), Comp(c_4), Pipeline(p_1)\}$. □

Notice that, differently from the previous notions of censors, the IGA censor is unique. Then, given a source database instance D for $\mathcal{E}$ and a BCQ q, *IGA-Cens-Entailment* is the problem of deciding whether $\mathcal{T} \cup \mathsf{cens}_{IGA}(D) \models q$. If this is the case, we write $(\mathcal{E}, D) \models_{IGA}^{cqe} q$.

The following proposition, whose proof is straightforward, says that IGA-Cens-Entailment is a sound approximation of GA-Cens-Entailment.

Proposition 1. *Given a PPOBDA specification* $\mathcal{E}$, *a source database* D *for* $\mathcal{E}$ *and a BCQ* q, *if* $(\mathcal{E}, D) \models_{IGA}^{cqe} q$ *then* $(\mathcal{E}, D) \models_{\mathbf{GA}}^{cqe} q$.

We now naturally extend Definition 4 to IGA censors. Given a PPOBDA specification $\mathcal{E} = \langle \mathcal{T}, \mathcal{S}, \mathcal{M}, \mathcal{P} \rangle$ and an OBDA specification $\mathcal{J} = \langle \mathcal{T}, \mathcal{M}', \mathcal{S} \rangle$, we say that $\mathcal{E}$ and $\mathcal{J}$ are *query-equivalent under IGA censor* if for every source database D for $\mathcal{E}$ and every BCQ q, $(\mathcal{E}, D) \models_{IGA}^{cqe} q$ iff $(\mathcal{J}, D) \models q$.

We point out that we could in principle consider a counterpart of Definition 5 also for censors in **CQ**. However, BCQ entailment under a censor that for every source database D returns the intersection of all the sets of BCQs returned by censors in **CQ** applied to D coincides with CQ-Cens-Entailment, and thus Theorem 1 says that a query-equivalent PPOBDA to OBDA transformation is not possible in this case.

In the rest of this section, we prove that every *DL-Lite*$_\mathcal{R}$ PPOBDA specification $\mathcal{E}$ admits an OBDA specification $\mathcal{J}$ that is query-equivalent under IGA censor to $\mathcal{E}$, and provide an algorithm to build $\mathcal{J}$. The intuition behind our algorithm is as follows. For any source database D, we want that $ret(\mathcal{J}, D)$ does not contain all those facts of $ret(\mathcal{E}, D)$ that together with the TBox $\mathcal{T}$ lead to the violation of the policy $\mathcal{P}$. At the same time, we want this elimination of facts to be done in a minimal way, according to our definition of IGA censor. Thus only "really dangerous" facts have to be dropped from $ret(\mathcal{E}, D)$. These facts actually belong to at least one minimal (w.r.t. set containment) ABox $\mathcal{A}$ such that $\mathcal{T} \cup \mathcal{A} \cup \mathcal{P}$ is inconsistent. Note that in this case, for each fact $\alpha \in \mathcal{A}$ there is at least a censor $\mathsf{cens}(\cdot) \in \mathbf{GA}\text{-}\mathsf{OptCens}_{\mathcal{E}}$ such that $\mathsf{cens}(D)$ does not contain α. Therefore α does not belong to the set $\mathsf{cens}_{IGA}(D)$, where $\mathsf{cens}_{IGA}(\cdot)$ is the IGA censor for $\mathcal{E}$.

Identifying such facts is easier if we can reason on each denial in isolation. For this to be possible, the policy $\mathcal{P}$ must enjoy the following property: for every denial $\delta \in \mathcal{P}$, every minimal (w.r.t. set containment) ABox $\mathcal{A}$ such that $\{\delta\} \cup \mathcal{T} \cup \mathcal{A}$ is inconsistent is also a minimal ABox such that $\mathcal{P} \cup \mathcal{T} \cup \mathcal{A}$ is inconsistent.

This is, however, not always the case. Consider, e.g., the policy $\mathcal{P} = \{\forall x.A(x) \land B(x) \to \bot; \forall x.A(x) \to \bot\}$. The ABox $\{A(d), B(d)\}$ is a minimal ABox violating the first denial, but is not a minimal ABox violating $\mathcal{P}$, since $\{A(d)\}$ violates the second denial (in this example $\mathcal{T} = \emptyset$). We thus first transform $\mathcal{P}$ into a policy $\mathcal{P}'$ enjoying the above property.

To this aim we introduce the notion of *extended denial assertion* (or simply extended denial), which is a formula of the form $\forall \boldsymbol{x}.\phi(\boldsymbol{x}) \land \neg\pi(\boldsymbol{x}) \to \bot$ such that $\exists \boldsymbol{x}.\phi(\boldsymbol{x})$ is a BCQ and $\pi(\boldsymbol{x})$ is a (possibly empty) disjunction of conjunctions of equality atoms of the form $t_1 = t_2$, where t_1 and t_2 are either variables in $\boldsymbol{x}$ or constants in Σ_C. An extended policy is a finite set of extended denials.

Definition 6. *Given a policy $\mathcal{P}$ and an extended policy $\mathcal{P}'$. We say that $\mathcal{P}'$ is a* non-redundant representation *of $\mathcal{P}$ if the following conditions hold: (i) for every ABox $\mathcal{A}$, $\mathcal{P} \cup \mathcal{A}$ is inconsistent iff $\mathcal{P}' \cup \mathcal{A}$ is inconsistent; (ii) for every extended denial δ' occurring in $\mathcal{P}'$, every minimal ABox $\mathcal{A}$ such that $\{\delta'\} \cup \mathcal{A}$ is inconsistent is also a minimal ABox such that $\mathcal{P} \cup \mathcal{A}$ is inconsistent.*

One might think that computing a non-redundant representation of $\mathcal{P}$ means simply eliminating from $\mathcal{P}$ each denial δ such that $\mathcal{P} \setminus \{\delta\} \cup \mathcal{T} \models \delta$. In fact, only eliminating denials that are (fully) logically inferred by other denials (and the TBox) is not sufficient, since some redundancies can occur for specific instantiations of the denials. For example, $\delta_1 = \forall x, y.Q(x, y) \land C(y) \to \bot$ is not inferred by $\delta_2 = \forall x.Q(x, x) \to \bot$, but it becomes inferred when $x = y$. This implies that a minimal violation of δ_1 where the two arguments of Q are the same (e.g., $\{Q(a, a), C(a)\}$) is not a minimal violation of $\{\delta_1, \delta_2\}$ (since $Q(a, a)$ alone is already a violation of δ_2). A non-redundant representation of this policy would be $\{\delta_1', \delta_2\}$, where $\delta_1' = \forall x, y.Q(x, y) \land C(y) \land \neg(x = y) \to \bot$. Our algorithm to compute a non-redundant policy $\mathcal{P}'$, called policyRefine, takes into account also this situation, applying a variant of the saturate method used in [19] to solve a similar problem in the context of consistent query answering over ontologies.

Hereinafter, we assume that $\mathcal{P}$ has been *expanded* w.r.t. $\mathcal{T}$, that is, $\mathcal{P}$ contains every denial δ such that $\mathcal{P} \cup \mathcal{T} \models \delta$. In this way, to establish non-redundancy we can look only at $\mathcal{P}$, getting rid of $\mathcal{T}$. To expand the policy, we use the rewriting algorithm perfectRef of [8] to reformulate (the premise of) denials in $\mathcal{P}$ with respect to the assertions in $\mathcal{T}$.

Example 4. Consider the same PPOBDA specification $\mathcal{E}$ of Example 1. By rewriting each denial in $\mathcal{P}$ w.r.t. $\mathcal{T}$ through perfectRef[4], we obtain the following set of denials.

d_1: $\forall x, y.OilComp(x) \land IssuesLic(x, y) \land Comp(y) \to \bot$
d_2: $\forall x, y.PipeOp(x, y) \land OilComp(y) \to \bot$
d_3: $\forall x, y.OilComp(x) \land IssuesLic(x, y) \land OilComp(y) \to \bot$
d_4: $\forall x, y.OilComp(x) \land IssuesLic(x, y) \to \bot$
d_5: $\forall x, y, z.OilComp(x) \land IssuesLic(x, y) \land PipeOp(z, y) \to \bot$

[4] For details on perfectRef, we refer the reader to [8].

Algorithm 1: PolicyEmbed

input: a *DL-Lite*$_\mathcal{R}$ TBox $\mathcal{T}$, a mapping $\mathcal{M}$, a policy $\mathcal{P}$;
output: a mapping $\mathcal{M}'$;
(1) let $\hat{\mathcal{P}}$ be the expansion of the policy $\mathcal{P}$ w.r.t $\mathcal{T}$;
(2) $\mathcal{P}' \rightarrow \mathsf{policyRefine}(\hat{\mathcal{P}})$;
(3) $\mathcal{M}' \leftarrow \emptyset$;
(4) **for each** atomic concept C **do**
(5) $\quad \psi \leftarrow \mathsf{addPolicyConditions}(C(x), \mathcal{P}')$;
(6) $\quad \phi_p \leftarrow \mathsf{expand}(C(x), \mathcal{T})$;
(7) $\quad \phi_n \leftarrow \mathsf{expand}(\psi, \mathcal{T})$;
(8) $\quad \mathcal{M}' \leftarrow \mathcal{M}' \cup \{\mathsf{unfold}(\phi_p \wedge \neg\phi_n, \mathcal{M}) \rightsquigarrow C(x)\}$
(9) **for each** atomic role Q **do**
(10) $\quad \psi \leftarrow \mathsf{addPolicyConditions}(Q(x,y), \mathcal{P}')$;
(11) $\quad \phi_p \leftarrow \mathsf{expand}(Q(x,y), \mathcal{T})$;
(12) $\quad \phi_n \leftarrow \mathsf{expand}(\psi, \mathcal{T})$;
(13) $\quad \mathcal{M}' \leftarrow \mathcal{M}' \cup \{\mathsf{unfold}(\phi_p \wedge \neg\phi_n, \mathcal{M})) \rightsquigarrow Q(x,y)\}$
(14) **return** $\mathcal{M}'$;

Intuitively, perfectRef adds to the original denials d_1 and d_2 the new denials d_3, d_4 and d_5, obtained by rewriting the atom $Comp(y)$ in d_1 according to the inclusions $OilComp \sqsubseteq Comp$, $\exists IssuesLic^- \sqsubseteq Comp$, and $\exists PipeOp^- \sqsubseteq Comp$, respectively (for d_4, perfectRef also unifies two atoms having $IssuesLic$ as predicate). It is easy then to verify that d_1, d_3 and d_5 are implied by d_4, and thus must be discarded. So the non-redundant policy $\mathcal{P}'$ in this case contains only d_2 and d_4. □

We recall that the only means we have to avoid retrieving the "dangerous facts" is to embed suitable conditions in the mapping assertions of $\mathcal{M}'$. Algorithm 1 shows our overall procedure, called PolicyEmbed.

Step 1 expands the input policy $\mathcal{P}$ into the policy $\hat{\mathcal{P}}$ by using $\mathsf{perfectRef}(\mathcal{P}, \mathcal{T})$. Step 2 produces the non-redundant policy $\mathcal{P}'$ by means of $\mathsf{policyRefine}(\hat{\mathcal{P}})$. Then, the algorithm constructs one mapping assertion for each ontology predicate. We discuss steps 4–8 for concepts (steps 9–13 for roles are analogous).

The algorithm $\mathsf{addPolicyConditions}(C(x), \mathcal{P}')$ constructs an FO query ψ expressing the disjunction of all CQs corresponding to the premise of a denial $\delta \in \mathcal{P}'$ such that $C(x)$ unifies with an atom of δ. For instance, if $\mathcal{P}'$ contains $\forall x.C(x) \wedge D(x) \rightarrow \bot$ and $\forall x, y.C(x) \wedge Q(x,y) \wedge E(y) \rightarrow \bot$, $\mathsf{addPolicyConditions}(C(x), \mathcal{P}')$ returns $((C(x) \wedge D(x)) \vee (\exists y.C(x) \wedge Q(x,y) \wedge E(y)))$. This is actually the union of all the conditions that lead to the generation of dangerous facts for C.

Then, the algorithm $\mathsf{expand}(\varphi, \mathcal{T})$ rewrites every positive atom α occurring in the formula φ according to the TBox $\mathcal{T}$. More precisely, the expansion $\mathsf{expand}(C(x), \mathcal{T})$ of a positive concept atom is the disjunction of the atoms of the form $A(x)$ (resp. $\exists y.Q(x,y)$, $\exists y.Q(y,x)$), where A is an atomic concept (resp. Q is an atomic role), such that $\mathcal{T} \models A \sqsubseteq C$ (resp. $\mathcal{T} \models \exists Q \sqsubseteq C$, $\mathcal{T} \models \exists Q^- \sqsubseteq C$).

For example, if $\mathcal{T}$ infers $A \sqsubseteq C$ and $\exists Q \sqsubseteq C$, then $\mathsf{expand}(C(x), \mathcal{T})$ returns $C(x) \vee A(x) \vee \exists y.Q(x,y)$. The expansion $\mathsf{expand}(Q(x,y), \mathcal{T})$ of a role atom is defined analogously. Finally, the expansion $\mathsf{expand}(\varphi, \mathcal{T})$ of an arbitrary formula φ is obtained by replacing each occurrence of a positive atom α in φ with the formula $\mathsf{expand}(\alpha, \mathcal{T})$.

At step 8, the mapping is incremented with the mapping assertion for C. The function unfold realizes a typical unfolding for GAV mapping [26], i.e., it substitutes each atom a with the union of the body of all mapping assertions having a in their heads. The presence of (the expansion of) the subformula ψ in $\neg\phi_n$ guarantees that no fact causing a violation of a denial involving C is retrieved.

Example 5. In our ongoing example, $\mathsf{PolicyEmbed}(\mathcal{T}, \mathcal{M}, \mathcal{P})$ returns

$$\begin{aligned}\mathcal{M}' = \{\ & m'_1\colon \exists y.\mathsf{company}(x,y) \vee \mathsf{company}(x,\text{'oil'}) \vee \exists y.\mathsf{license}(y,x) \vee \\ & \quad\quad \exists y.\mathsf{operator}(y,x) \rightsquigarrow \mathit{Comp}(x), \\ & m'_2\colon \mathsf{company}(x,\text{'oil'}) \wedge \neg((\exists y.\mathsf{company}(x,\text{'oil'}) \wedge \mathsf{license}(x,y)) \vee \\ & \quad\quad (\exists z.\mathsf{operator}(z,x) \wedge \mathsf{company}(x,\text{'oil'}))) \rightsquigarrow \mathit{OilComp}(x), \\ & m'_3\colon \mathsf{license}(x,y) \wedge \neg(\mathsf{license}(x,y) \wedge \mathsf{company}(x,\text{'oil'})) \rightsquigarrow \mathit{IssuesLic}(x,y) \\ & m'_4\colon \mathsf{operator}(x,y) \wedge \neg(\mathsf{operator}(x,y) \wedge \mathsf{company}(x,\text{'oil'})) \rightsquigarrow \mathit{PipeOp}(x,y) \\ & m'_5\colon \exists y.\mathsf{operator}(x,y) \rightsquigarrow \mathit{Pipeline}(x)\ \}\end{aligned}$$

For the database instance D for $\mathcal{S}$ provided in Example 3, one can verify that $\mathsf{cens}_{IGA}(D) = \mathit{ret}(\langle \mathcal{T}, \mathcal{S}, \mathcal{M}' \rangle, D)$. □

PolicyEmbed can be used to realize a PPOBDA-OBDA transformation, as stated below.

Theorem 3. *Let $\mathcal{E} = \langle \mathcal{T}, \mathcal{S}, \mathcal{M}, \mathcal{P} \rangle$ be a DL-Lite$_\mathcal{R}$ PPOBDA specification, and let $\mathcal{J}$ be the OBDA specification $\langle \mathcal{T}, \mathcal{S}, \mathcal{M}' \rangle$, where $\mathcal{M}'$ is the mapping returned by* $\mathsf{PolicyEmbed}(\mathcal{T}, \mathcal{M}, \mathcal{P})$. *Then, $\mathcal{J}$ is query-equivalent to $\mathcal{E}$ under IGA censor.*

Proof. Let D be a source database for $\mathcal{S}$. We prove the theorem by showing that $\mathit{ret}(\mathcal{J}, D)$ is equal to $\mathsf{cens}_{IGA}(D)$, where $\mathsf{cens}_{IGA}(\cdot)$ is the IGA censor for $\mathcal{E}$.

We start by showing a lemma that is crucial for this proof. From now on, we denote by $\mathcal{A}$ the ABox $\mathit{ret}(\langle \mathcal{T}, \mathcal{S}, \mathcal{M} \rangle, D)$, i.e., the ABox retrieved from D through the initial mapping $\mathcal{M}$. Moreover, we denote by $\mathcal{A}''$ the ABox $\mathit{ret}(\langle \mathcal{T}, \mathcal{S}, \mathcal{M}'' \rangle, D)$, where $\mathcal{M}''$ is the mapping obtained from the algorithm by discarding the formulas ϕ_n, i.e., when $\mathsf{unfold}(\phi_p \wedge \neg\phi_n, \mathcal{M})$ is replaced with $\mathsf{unfold}(\phi_p, \mathcal{M})$ in steps 8 and 13 of the algorithm.

The next lemma follows immediately from the definition of the algorithm expand:

Lemma 1. $\mathcal{A}'' = \mathit{cl}_{\mathbf{GA}}(\mathcal{T} \cup \mathcal{A})$.

Informally, the lemma states that the "positive" part of the mapping computed by the algorithm retrieves from D exactly the set of ground atoms derivable by the TBox $\mathcal{T}$ from the ABox $\mathcal{A}$ retrieved from D through the initial mapping $\mathcal{M}$.

In the following, we prove that every concept assertion $C(a)$ belongs to $ret(\mathcal{J}, D)$ iff $C(a)$ belongs to $\mathsf{cens}_{IGA}(D)$ (the proof for role assertions is analogous). From now on, let ϕ_p be the formula computed for $C(x)$ at step 6 of the algorithm, and let ϕ_n be the formula computed for $C(x)$ at step 7 of the algorithm.

First, assume that the concept assertion $C(a)$ belongs to $ret(\mathcal{J}, D)$ but does not belong to $\mathsf{cens}_{IGA}(D)$. Then, there exists a censor $\mathsf{cens}'(\cdot)$ in $\mathbf{GA}$ for $\mathcal{E}$ such that $C(a) \notin \mathsf{cens}'(D)$. Now, there are two possible cases:

(i) $C(a) \notin \mathsf{cl}_{\mathbf{GA}}(\mathcal{T} \cup \mathcal{A})$. In this case, by Lemma 1 it follows that $C(a) \notin \mathcal{A}''$, hence $\mathsf{unfold}(\phi_p, \mathcal{M})$ (that is, the positive part of the mapping for the concept C in $\mathcal{M}'$) is false in D for $x = a$, and therefore $C(a)$ does not belong to $ret(\mathcal{J}, D)$;
(ii) $C(a)$ belongs to a minimal violation of $\mathcal{P}$ in $\mathsf{cl}_{\mathbf{GA}}(\mathcal{T} \cup \mathcal{A})$: then, from Definition 6 it follows that there exists a denial δ in $\mathcal{P}'$ such that $C(a)$ belongs to a minimal violation of δ in $\mathsf{cl}_{\mathbf{GA}}(\mathcal{T} \cup \mathcal{A})$. Consequently, from the definition of the algorithms addPolicyConditions and expand it follows that $\mathsf{unfold}(\phi_n, \mathcal{M})$ (that is, the negative part of the mapping for the concept C in $\mathcal{M}'$) is true in D for $x = a$, and therefore $C(a)$ does not belong to $ret(\mathcal{J}, D)$.

Conversely, assume that the concept assertion $C(a)$ belongs to $\mathsf{cens}_{IGA}(D)$ but does not belong to $ret(\mathcal{J}, D)$. Then, the mapping for the concept C in $\mathcal{M}'$ is false for $x = a$. Now, there are two possible cases:

(i) $\mathsf{unfold}(\phi_p, \mathcal{M})$ is false in D for $x = a$. This immediately implies by Lemma 1 that $C(a) \notin \mathsf{cl}_{\mathbf{GA}}(\mathcal{T} \cup \mathcal{A})$: hence, in every censor cens' in $\mathbf{GA}$ for $\mathcal{E}$, $C(a) \notin \mathsf{cens}'(D)$, and therefore $C(a) \notin \mathsf{cens}_{IGA}(D)$;
(ii) $\mathsf{unfold}(\phi_n, \mathcal{M})$ is true in D for $x = a$. From the definition of the algorithms addPolicyConditions and expand, this immediately implies that there exists $\delta \in \mathcal{P}'$ such that $C(a)$ belongs to a minimal violation of δ in $\mathsf{cl}_{\mathbf{GA}}(\mathcal{T} \cup \mathcal{A})$: then, from Definition 6 it follows that $C(a)$ belongs to a minimal violation of $\mathcal{P}$ in $\mathsf{cl}_{\mathbf{GA}}(\mathcal{T} \cup \mathcal{A})$. Consequently, there exists a censor cens' in $\mathbf{GA}$ for $\mathcal{E}$ such that $C(a) \notin \mathsf{cens}'(D)$, and therefore $C(a) \notin \mathsf{cens}_{IGA}(D)$. □

7 Experiments

In this section, we report the results of the experimentation we carried out using the NPD benchmark for OBDA [18]. The benchmark is based on real data coming from the oil industry: the Norwegian Petroleum Directorate (NPD) FactPages. It provides an OWL 2 ontology, the NPD database, the mapping between the ontology and the database, an RDF file specifying the instances of the ontology predicates, i.e., the retrieved ABox of the OBDA setting, and a set of 31 SPARQL queries. We remark that we tested non-Boolean CQs adapted from this set (details later on).

For our experimentation, we produced an approximation [11] in OWL 2 QL of the OWL 2 benchmark ontology. Moreover, we made use of the benchmark RDF file containing the retrieved ABox to populate a relational database constituted by unary and binary tables (a unary table for each concept of the ontology and a binary table for each role and each attribute). Finally, we specified a mapping between the ontology and this database. In this case, the mapping in simply a set of one-to-one mapping assertions, i.e., every ontology predicate is mapped to the database table containing its instances. This kind of OBDA specification, with the simplest possible form of mapping assertions, allowed us to verify the feasibility of our technique for data protection, leaving aside the impact of more complex queries in the mapping.

In the resulting OBDA setting, the TBox comprises 1377 axioms over 321 atomic concepts, 135 roles, and 233 attributes. There are in total 2 millions of instances circa, which are stored in a MySQL database of 689 tables.

For the experiments, we specified a policy $\mathcal{P}$ constituted by the following denials:

d_1: $\forall d, l. \mathit{DevelopmentWellbore}(d) \land \mathit{developmentWellboreForLicence}(d, l) \land$
$\mathit{ProductionLicence}(l) \rightarrow \bot$

d_2: $\forall d, t, w, b, q, f. \mathit{Discovery}(d) \land \mathit{dateIncludedInField}(d, t) \land \mathit{containsWellbore}(b, w) \land$
$\mathit{wellboreForDiscovery}(w, d) \land \mathit{ExplorationWellbore}(w) \land \mathit{quadrantLocation}(b, q) \land$
$\mathit{explorationWellboreForField}(w, f) \rightarrow \bot$

d_3: $\forall c, w. \mathit{WellboreCore}(c) \land \mathit{coreForWellbore}(c, w) \land \mathit{DevelopmentWellbore}(w) \rightarrow \bot$

d_4: $\forall c, f, d. \mathit{Company}(c) \land \mathit{currentFieldOperator}(f, c) \land \mathit{Field}(f) \land$
$\mathit{includedInField}(d, f) \land \mathit{Discovery}(d) \rightarrow \bot$

d_5: $\forall w, e, f, l. \mathit{belongsToWell}(w, e) \land \mathit{wellboreAgeHc}(w, l) \land \mathit{drillingFacility}(w, f) \land$
$\mathit{ExplorationWellbore}(w) \rightarrow \bot$

d_6: $\forall f, p, l. \mathit{Field}(f) \land \mathit{currentFieldOwner}(f, p) \land \mathit{ProductionLicence}(p)$
$\land \mathit{licenseeForLicence}(l, p) \rightarrow \bot$.

As queries, we considered nine (non-Boolean) CQs from the ones provided with the NPD benchmark. Strictly speaking, some of these queries in the benchmark are not CQs, since they use aggregation operators, but we have extracted from them their conjunctive subqueries. The resulting queries are reported below.

q_3 : $\exists li. \mathit{ProductionLicence}(li) \land \mathit{name}(li, ln) \land \mathit{dateLicenceGranted}(li, d) \land$
$\mathit{isActive}(li, a) \land \mathit{licensingActivityName}(li, an)$

q_4 : $\exists li, w. \mathit{ProductionLicence}(li) \land \mathit{name}(li, n) \mathit{explorationWellboreForLicence}(w, li) \land$
$\mathit{dateWellboreEntry}(w, e)$

q_5 : $\exists le, li, c. \mathit{licenseeForLicence}(le, li) \land \mathit{ProductionLicence}(li) \land \mathit{name}(li, ln) \land$
$\mathit{licenceLicensee}(le, c) \land \mathit{name}(c, n) \land \mathit{dateLicenseeValidFrom}(le, d)$

q_9 : $\exists li, w. \mathit{ProductionLicence}(li) \land \mathit{name}(li, n) \land \mathit{belongsToWell}(w, we) \land$
$\mathit{explorationWellboreForLicence}(w, li) \land \mathit{name}(we, wn)$

q_{12} : $\exists w, lu, c. \mathit{wellboreStratumTopDepth}(w, st) \land \mathit{wellboreStratumBottomDepth}(w, sb) \land$
$\mathit{stratumForWellbore}(w, u) \land \mathit{name}(u, n) \land \mathit{inLithostratigraphicUnit}(w, lu) \land$
$\mathit{name}(lu, un) \land \mathit{WellboreCore}(c) \land \mathit{coreForWellbore}(c, u) \land \mathit{coreIntervalTop}(c, ct) \land$
$\mathit{coreIntervalBottom}(c, cb)$

q_{13} : $\exists wc, we, c. \mathit{WellboreCore}(wc) \land \mathit{coreForWellbore}(wc, we) \land \mathit{name}(we, wn) \land$
$\mathit{Wellbore}(we) \land \mathit{wellboreCompletionYear}(we, y) \land \mathit{drillingOperatorCompany}(we, c) \land$
$\mathit{name}(c, cn)$

q_{14} : $\exists we, c. \mathit{Wellbore}(we) \land \mathit{name}(we, n) \land \mathit{wellboreCompletionYear}(we, y) \land$
$\mathit{drillingOperatorCompany}(we, c) \land \mathit{name}(c, cn)$

$q_{18}: \exists p, m, f, op.productionYear(p, \text{'2010'}) \wedge productionMonth(p, m) \wedge$
$producedGas(p, g) \wedge producedOil(p, o) \wedge productionForField(p, f) \wedge name(f, fn) \wedge$
$currentFieldOperator(f, op) \wedge Field(f) \wedge shortName(op, \text{'statoil petroleum as'})$
$q_{44}: \exists y, f, c.wellboreAgeTD(w, a) \wedge explorationWellboreForField(w, f) \wedge$
$wellboreEntryYear(w, y) \wedge Field(f) \wedge name(f, fn) \wedge coreForWellbore(c, w)$

We executed each query in seven different settings, in each of which we considered an incremental number of denials in the policy among those given above. For each setting, we computed a new mapping through a Java implementation of the algorithm illustrated in Sect. 6. So, in the first setting, we used the mapping computed by considering the empty policy $\mathcal{P}_{\emptyset}$; in the second one, we considered the policy $\mathcal{P}_1$ containing only the denial d_1; in the third one, we considered the policy $\mathcal{P}_2$ containing the denials d_1 and d_2; and so on. For each query, we report in Table 1 the size of the result and the query evaluation time, columns "res" and columns "time" in the table, respectively. The number in square brackets near each query name indicates the length of the query.

Table 1. CQE test results. The "res" columns contain the size of the results while the "time" columns contain the query evaluation times in milliseconds.

Policy	q_3 [5]		q_4 [4]		q_5 [6]		q_9 [5]		q_{12} [10]		q_{13} [7]		q_{14} [5]		q_{18} [9]		q_{44} [6]	
	res	time	res	time	res	time	res	time	res	time	res	time	res	time	res	time	res	time
$\mathcal{P}_{\emptyset}$	910	4789	1558	4625	17254	4545	1566	4648	96671	7368	22541	6410	141439	20150	339	6933	5078	4179
$\mathcal{P}_1$	910	3871	1558	4111	17254	4782	1566	4401	96671	7133	22541	6886	130341	15544	339	6128	5078	4078
$\mathcal{P}_2$	910	4154	880	4078	17254	4628	888	4204	96671	6852	22541	5007	126679	16566	339	5887	12	4413
$\mathcal{P}_3$	910	4080	880	4189	17254	4902	888	3953	96641	7746	15340	5623	124248	16807	339	5873	12	4653
$\mathcal{P}_4$	910	4419	880	4089	17254	5015	888	4487	96641	7836	15340	6011	124248	17393	339	6893	12	4318
$\mathcal{P}_5$	910	5548	880	4373	17254	6224	888	4422	96641	8683	15340	6499	123816	20116	339	7201	12	4491
$\mathcal{P}_6$	910	4309	880	4029	14797	5189	888	4785	96641	8297	15340	6796	123816	17513	339	6176	12	4475

For our experiments, we used the OBDA MASTRO system [16], and a standard laptop with Intel i5 @1.6 GHz processor and 8 Gb of RAM.

Values in Table 1 show the effect of the policy on the size of the result of the queries. Specifically, we have that the queries q_0, q_3, and q_{18} are not censored in any of the considered settings. The answers to the queries q_4, q_9, and q_{44} are affected by the introduction of the denial d_2 in the policy, while the denial d_3 alters the answers of the queries q_{12} and q_{13}. Some answers to the query q_5 are cut away by the introduction of the denial d_6 in the policy. Moreover, the query q_{14} is affected by the denials d_1, d_2, d_3, and d_5. Finally, the denial d_4 alters no queries. Notably, although the policy alters the query results, one can see that the execution time is only slightly affected. This suggests that our proposed technique can be effectively used for protecting data in OBDA setting.

8 Conclusions

Our current research is mainly focused on modifying the user model formalized in our framework in order to capture richer data protection scenarios. In particular, the user model we adopted (which we inherited from previous works on CQE over ontologies) assumes that an attacker has only the ability of making standard inference reasoning on the ontology and the query answers. Under these assumptions, data declared as confidential are certainly protected in our framework.

We are also investigating more expressive forms of policy to improve the abilities of our framework in the enforcement of confidentiality. Finally, while our experimental evaluation clearly shows the practical feasibility of our approach, we still have to consider the issue of optimization of our algorithms and implementation.

References

1. Abiteboul, S., Hull, R., Vianu, V.: Foundations Boston of Databases. Addison Wesley Publishing Company, Boston (1995)
2. Baader, F., Calvanese, D., McGuinness, D., Nardi, D., Patel-Schneider, P.F. (eds.): The Description Logic Handbook: Theory, Implementation and Applications, 2nd edn. Cambridge University Press, Cambridge (2007)
3. Benedikt, M., Bourhis, P., Jachiet, L., Thomazo, M.: Reasoning about disclosure in data integration in the presence of source constraints. In: Proceedings of IJCAI, pp. 1551–1557 (2019)
4. Benedikt, M., Grau, B.C., Kostylev, E.V.: Logical foundations of information disclosure in ontology-based data integration. AIJ **262**, 52–95 (2018)
5. Biskup, J., Bonatti, P.A.: Controlled query evaluation for known policies by combining lying and refusal. AMAI **40**(1–2), 37–62 (2004)
6. Biskup, J., Weibert, T.: Keeping secrets in incomplete databases. Int. J. of Inf. Secur. **7**(3), 199–217 (2008)
7. Bonatti, P.A., Sauro, L.: A confidentiality model for ontologies. In: Alani, H., et al. (eds.) ISWC 2013. LNCS, vol. 8218, pp. 17–32. Springer, Heidelberg (2013). https://doi.org/10.1007/978-3-642-41335-3_2
8. Calvanese, D., De Giacomo, G., Lembo, D., Lenzerini, M., Rosati, R.: Tractable reasoning and efficient query answering in description logics: the DL-Lite family. J. Autom. Reason. **39**(3), 385–429 (2007)
9. Chirkova, R., Yu, T.: Exact detection of information leakage: decidability and complexity. Trans. Large Scale Data Knowl. Cent. Syst. **32**, 1–23 (2017)
10. Cima, G., Lembo, D., Rosati, R., Savo, D.F.: Controlled query evaluation in description logics through instance indistinguishability. In: Proceedings of IJCAI, pp. 1791–1797 (2020)
11. Console, M., Mora, J., Rosati, R., Santarelli, V., Savo, D.F.: Effective computation of maximal sound approximations of description logic ontologies. In: Mika, P., et al. (eds.) ISWC 2014. LNCS, vol. 8797, pp. 164–179. Springer, Cham (2014). https://doi.org/10.1007/978-3-319-11915-1_11
12. Grau, B.C., Horrocks, I.: Privacy-preserving query answering in logic-based information systems. In: Proceedings of ECAI, pp. 40–44 (2008)
13. Cuenca Grau, B., Kharlamov, E., Kostylev, E.V., Zheleznyakov, D.: Controlled query evaluation over OWL 2 RL ontologies. In: Alani, H., et al. (eds.) ISWC 2013. LNCS, vol. 8218, pp. 49–65. Springer, Heidelberg (2013). https://doi.org/10.1007/978-3-642-41335-3_4

14. Grau, B.C., Kharlamov, E., Kostylev, E.V., Zheleznyakov, D.: Controlled query evaluation for datalog and OWL 2 profile ontologies. In: Proceedings of IJCAI, pp. 2883–2889 (2015)
15. Das, S., Sundara, S., Cyganiak, R.: R2RML: RDB to RDF mapping language. W3C Recommendation, W3C, September 2012. http://www.w3.org/TR/r2rml/
16. De Giacomo, G., et al.: MASTRO: a reasoner for effective ontology-based data access. In: Proceedings of ORE (2012)
17. Doan, A., Halevy, A.Y., Ives, Z.G.: Principles of Data Integration. Morgan Kaufmann, Burlington (2012)
18. Lanti, D., Rezk, M., Xiao, G., Calvanese, D.: The NPD benchmark: reality check for OBDA systems. In: Proceedings of EDBT, pp. 617–628 (2015)
19. Lembo, D., Lenzerini, M., Rosati, R., Ruzzi, M., Savo, D.F.: Inconsistency-tolerant query answering in ontology-based data access. J. Web Semant. **33**, 3–29 (2015)
20. Lembo, D., Rosati, R., Savo, D.F.: Revisiting controlled query evaluation in description logics. In: Proceedings of IJCAI, pp. 1786–1792 (2019)
21. Motik, B., et al.: OWL 2 Web Ontology Language profiles (second edn.). W3C Recommendation, W3C, December 2012. http://www.w3.org/TR/owl2-profiles/
22. Nash, A., Deutsch, A.: Privacy in GLAV information integration. In: Schwentick, T., Suciu, D. (eds.) ICDT 2007. LNCS, vol. 4353, pp. 89–103. Springer, Heidelberg (2006). https://doi.org/10.1007/11965893_7
23. Poggi, A., Lembo, D., Calvanese, D., De Giacomo, G., Lenzerini, M., Rosati, R.: Linking data to ontologies. In: Spaccapietra, S. (ed.) Journal on Data Semantics X. LNCS, vol. 4900, pp. 133–173. Springer, Heidelberg (2008). https://doi.org/10.1007/978-3-540-77688-8_5
24. Sicherman, G.L., de Jonge, W., van de Riet, R.P.: Answering queries without revealing secrets. ACM Trans. Database Syst. **8**(1), 41–59 (1983)
25. Stouppa, P., Studer, T.: Data privacy for $\mathcal{ALC}$ knowledge bases. In: Artemov, S., Nerode, A. (eds.) LFCS 2009. LNCS, vol. 5407, pp. 409–421. Springer, Heidelberg (2008). https://doi.org/10.1007/978-3-540-92687-0_28
26. Xiao, G., et al.: Ontology-based data access: a survey. In: Proceedings of IJCAI, pp. 5511–5519 (2018)

Linked Credibility Reviews for Explainable Misinformation Detection

Ronald Denaux(✉) and Jose Manuel Gomez-Perez

Expert System, Madrid, Spain
{rdenaux,jmgomez}@expertsystem.com

Abstract. In recent years, misinformation on the Web has become increasingly rampant. The research community has responded by proposing systems and challenges, which are beginning to be useful for (various subtasks of) detecting misinformation. However, most proposed systems are based on deep learning techniques which are fine-tuned to specific domains, are difficult to interpret and produce results which are not machine readable. This limits their applicability and adoption as they can only be used by a select expert audience in very specific settings. In this paper we propose an architecture based on a core concept of Credibility Reviews (CRs) that can be used to build networks of distributed bots that collaborate for misinformation detection. The CRs serve as building blocks to compose graphs of (i) web content, (ii) existing credibility signals –fact-checked claims and reputation reviews of websites–, and (iii) automatically computed reviews. We implement this architecture on top of lightweight extensions to Schema.org and services providing generic NLP tasks for semantic similarity and stance detection. Evaluations on existing datasets of social-media posts, fake news and political speeches demonstrates several advantages over existing systems: extensibility, domain-independence, composability, explainability and transparency via provenance. Furthermore, we obtain competitive results without requiring finetuning and establish a new state of the art on the Clef'18 CheckThat! Factuality task.

Keywords: Disinformation detection · Credibility signals · Explainability · Composable semantics

1 Introduction

Although misinformation is not a new problem, the Web –due to the pace of news cycles combined with social media, and the information bubbles it creates– has increasingly evolved into an ecosystem where misinformation can thrive [8] with various societal effects. Tackling misinformation[1] is not something that can be achieved by a single organization –as evidenced by struggling efforts by the

[1] https://ec.europa.eu/digital-single-market/en/tackling-online-disinformation.

J. Z. Pan et al. (Eds.): ISWC 2020, LNCS 12506, pp. 147–163, 2020.
https://doi.org/10.1007/978-3-030-62419-4_9

major social networks– as it requires decentralisation, common conceptualisations, transparency and collaboration [3].

Technical solutions for computer-aided misinformation detection and fact-checking have recently been proposed [1,6] and are essential due to the scale of the Web. However, a lack of hand-curated data, maturity and scope of current AI systems, means assessing *veracity* [12] is not feasible. Hence the value of the current systems is not so much their accuracy, but rather their capacity of retrieving potentially relevant information that can help human fact-checkers, who are the main intended users of such systems, and are ultimately responsible for verifying/filtering the results such systems provide. Therefore, a main challenge is developing automated systems which can help the *general public*, and influencers in particular, to assess the credibility of web content, which requires explainable results by AI systems. This points towards the need for hybrid approaches that enable the use of the best of deep learning-based approaches, but also of symbolic knowledge graphs to enable better collaboration between large platforms, fact-checkers, the general public and other stakeholders like policy-makers, journalists, webmasters and influencers.

In this paper, we propose a design on how to use semantic technologies to aid in resolving such challenges. Our contributions are:

- a datamodel and architecture of distributed agents for composable credibility reviews, including a lightweight extension to `schema.org` to support provenance and explainability (Sect. 3)
- an implementation of the architecture demonstrating feasibility and value (Sect. 4)
- an evaluation on various datasets establishing state-of-the-art in one dataset (Clef'18 CheckThat! Factuality task) and demonstrating capabilities and limitations of our approach, as well as paths for improvements (Sect. 5).

2 Related Work

The idea of automating (part of) the fact-checking process is relatively recent [1]. ClaimBuster [6] proposed the first automated fact-checking system and its architecture is mostly still valid, with a database of fact-checks and components for monitoring web sources, spotting claims and matching them to previously fact-checked claims. Other similar services and projects include Truly media[2], invid[3] and CrowdTangle[4]. These systems are mainly intended to be used by professional fact-checkers or journalists, who can evaluate whether the retrieved fact-check article is relevant for the identified claim. These automated systems rarely aim to predict the accuracy of the content; this is (rightly) the job of the journalist or fact-checker who uses the system. Many of these systems provide valuable REST APIs to access their services, but as they use custom schemas,

[2] https://www.truly.media/ https://www.disinfobservatory.org/.

[3] https://invid.weblyzard.com/.

[4] https://status.crowdtangle.com/.

they are difficult to compose and inspect as they are not machine-interpretable or explainable.

Besides full-fledged systems for aiding in fact-checking, there are also various strands of research focusing on specific computational tasks needed to identify misinformation or assess the accuracy or veracity of web content based on ground credibility signals. Some low-level NLP tasks include check-worthiness [11] and stance detection [14,15], while others aim to use text classification as a means of detecting deceptive language [13]. Other tasks mix linguistic and social media analysis, for example to detect and classify rumours [20]. Yet others try to assess veracity of a claim or document by finding supporting evidence in (semi)structured data [18]. These systems, and many more, claim to provide important information needed to detect misinformation online, often in some very specific cases. However without a clear conceptual and technical framework to integrate them, the signals such systems provide are likely to go unused and stay out of reach of users who are exposed to misinformation.

The Semantic Web and Linked Data community has also started to contribute ideas and technical solutions to help in this area: perhaps the biggest impact has been the inclusion in Schema.org [5] of the `ClaimReview` markup[5], which enables fact-checkers to publish their work as machine readable structured data. This has enabled aggregation of such data into knowledge graphs like ClaimsKG [17], which also performs much needed normalisation of labels, since each fact-checker uses its own set of labels. A conceptual model and RDF vocabulary was proposed to distinguish between the utterance and propositional aspects of claims [2]. It allows expressing fine-grained provenance (mainly of annotations on the text of the claim), but still relies on `ClaimReview` as the main accuracy describing mechanism. It is unclear whether systems are actually using this RDF model to annotate and represent claims as the model is heavyweight and does not seem to align well with mainstream development practices. In this paper, we build on these ideas to propose a lightweight model which focuses on the introduction of a new type of Schema.org. Review that focuses on *credibility* rather than *factuality*[6].

The focus on credibility, defined as an estimation of factuality based on available signals or evidence, is inspired by MisinfoMe [9,10] which borrows from social science, media literacy and journalism research. MisinfoMe focuses on credibility of sources, while we expand this to credibility of any web content and integrate some of MisinfoMe's services in our implementation to demonstrate how our approach enables composition of such services. There is also ongoing work on W3C Credibility Signals[7], which aims to define a vocabulary to specify *credibility indicators* that may be relevant for assessing the credibility of some

[5] https://www.blog.google/products/search/fact-check-now-available-google-search-and-news-around-world/.
[6] In our opinion, current AI systems cannot truly assess veracity since this requires human skills to access and interpret new information and relate them to the world.
[7] https://credweb.org/signals-beta/.

web content. To the best of our knowledge, this is still work in progress and no systems are implementing the proposed vocabularies.

3 Linked Credibility Reviews

This section presents *Linked Credibility Reviews* (LCR), our proposed linked data model for composable and explainable misinformation detection. As the name implies, *Credibility Reviews* (CR) are the main resources and outputs of this architecture. We define a CR as a tuple $\langle d, r, c, p \rangle$, where the CR:

- reviews a *data item* d, this can be any linked-data node but will typically refer to articles, claims, websites, images, social media posts, social media accounts, people, publishers, etc.
- assigns a *credibility rating* r to the *data item* under review and qualifies that rating with a *rating confidence* c.
- *provides provenance information* p about:
  - *credibility signals* used to derive the credibility rating. Credibility Signals (CS) can be either (i) CRs for data items relevant to the data item under review or (ii) *ground credibility signals* (GCS) resources (which are not CRs) in databases curated by a trusted person or organization.
  - the *author* of the review. The author can be a person, organization or bot. Bots are automated agents that produce CRs for supported data items based on a variety of strategies, discussed below.

The credibility rating is meant to provide a subjective (from the point-of-view of the author) measure of how much the credibility signals support or refute the content in data item. Provenance information is therefore crucial as it allows humans—e.g. end-users, bot developers—to retrace the CRs back to the ground credibility signals and assess the accuracy of the (possibly long) chain of bots (and ultimately humans) that were involved in reviewing the initial data item. It also enables the generation of explanations for each step of the credibility review chain in a composable manner as each bot (or author) can describe its own strategy to derive the credibility rating based on the used credibility signals.

Bot Reviewing Strategies. CR bots are developed to be able to produce CRs for specific data item types. We have identified a couple of generic strategies that existing services seem to implement and which can be defined in terms of CRs (these are not exhaustive, though see Fig. 2 for a depiction of how they can collaborate):

- **ground credibility signal lookup** from some trusted source. CR bots that implement this strategy will (i) generate a query based on d and (ii) convert the retrieved ground credibility signal into a CR;
- **linking** the item-to-review d with n other data items d'_i *of the same type*, for which a $\text{CR}_{d'_i}$ is available. These bots define functions f_r, f_c and f_{agg}. The first two, compute the new values r_i and c_i based on the original values

and the relation or similarity between d and d'_i i.e. $r_i = f_r(\text{CR}_{d'_i}, d, d')$. These produce n credibility reviews, CR^i_d, which are then aggregated into $\text{CR}_d = f_{\text{agg}}(\{CR^i_d \mid 0 \leq i < n\})$.
- **decomposing** whereby the bot identifies relevant parts d'_i of the item-to-review d and requests CRs for those parts $CR_{d'_i}$. Like the linking bots, these require deriving new credibility ratings CR_{d_i} and confidences based on the relation between the whole and the parts; and aggregating these into the CR for the whole item. The main difference is that the parts can be items of different types.

Representing and Aggregating Ratings. For ease of computation, we opt to represent credibility ratings and their confidences as follows:

- $r \in \Re$, must be in the range of $[-1.0, 1.0]$ where -1.0 means not credible and 1.0 means credible
- $c \in \Re$, must be in the range of $[0.0, 1.0]$ where 0.0 means no confidence at all and 1.0 means full confidence in the accuracy of r, based on the available evidence in p.

This representations makes it possible to define generic, relatively straightforward aggregation functions like:

- $f^{\text{mostConfident}}$ which selects CR_i which has the highest confidence value c
- $f^{\text{leastCredible}}$ which selects the CR_i which has the lowest value r

3.1 Extending `schema.org` for LCR

While reviewing existing ontologies and vocabularies which could be reused to describe the LCR model, we noticed that `schema.org` [5] was an excellent starting point since it already provides suitable schema types for data items on the web for which credibility reviews would be beneficial (essentially any schema type that extends `CreativeWork`). It already provides suitable types for `Review`, `Rating`, as well as properties for expressing basic provenance information and meronymy (`hasPart`). Some basic uses and extensions compliant with the original definitions are:

- Define `CredibilityReview` as an extension of `schema:Review`, whereby the `schema:reviewAspect` is `credibility`[8]
- use `schema:ratingValue` to encode r.
- add a `confidence` property to `schema:Rating` which encodes the rating confidence c.
- use `isBasedOn` to record that a CR was computed based on other CRs. We also use this property to describe dependencies between CR Bots, even when those dependencies have not been used as part of a CR.
- use `author` to link the CR with the bot that produced it.

[8] Note that `ClaimReview` is not suitable since it is overly restrictive: it can only review `Claims` (and it assumes the review aspect is, implicitly, `accuracy`).

The main limitation we encountered with the existing definitions was that `CreativeWorks` (including `Reviews`) are expected to be created only by `Persons` or `Organizations`, which excludes reviews created by bots. We therefore propose to extend this definition by:

- introducing a type `Bot` which extends `SoftwareApplication`
- allowing `Bots` to be the `authors` of `CreativeWorks`.

Finally, in this paper we focus on *textual* misinformation detection and found we were missing a crucial type of `CreativeWork`, namely `Sentences`. Recently, a `Claim` type was proposed, to represent factually-oriented sentences and to work in tandem with the existing `ClaimReview`, however, automated systems still have trouble determining whether a sentence is a claim or not, therefore, CR bots should be able to review the credibility of `Sentences` and relevant aspects between pairs of sentences such as their stance and similarity. The overall `schema.org` based data model is depicted in Fig. 1, focused on CRs for textual web content (we leave other modalities as future work).

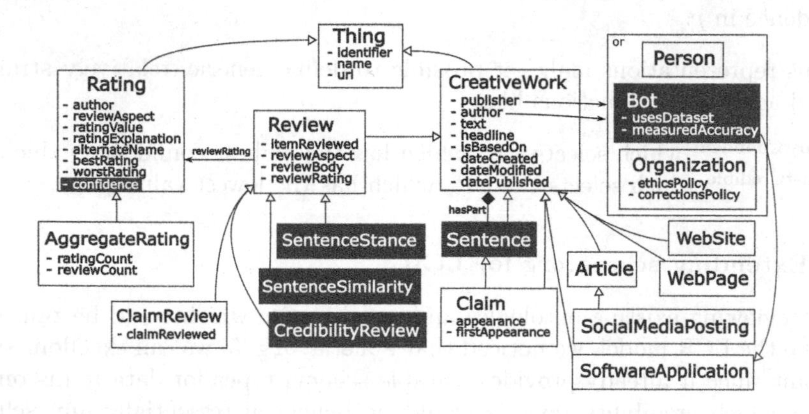

Fig. 1. Linked credibility review data model, extending schema.org.

4 acred – Deep Learning-Based CR Bots

To demonstrate the potential of the Linked Credibility Review architecture, we have implemented a series of CR bots capable of collaborating to review articles, tweets, sentences and websites.[9] We present the conceptual implementation in Sects. 4.1 to 4.4 and provide further details in Sect. 4.5.

[9] The source code is available at https://github.com/rdenaux/acred.

4.1 Ground Credibility Signal Sources

Ultimately we rely on two ground credibility signal sources:

- A database of `ClaimReviews` which provide accuracy ratings for factual claims by a variety of fact-checkers.
- Third-party, well-established services for validating `WebSites`, such as NewsGuard and Web Of Trust[10], which rely on either expert or community-based ratings.

4.2 GCS Lookup Bots

The two GCS sources are mediated via two GCS lookup bots.

The $\texttt{LookupBot}_{\texttt{ClaimReview}}$ returns a CR for a `Claim` based on a `ClaimReview` from the database. In order to derive a CR from a `ClaimReview`, the accuracy rating in the `ClaimReview` need to be converted into equivalent credibility ratings. The challenge here is that each fact-checker can encode their review rating as they see fit. The final review is typically encoded as a textual `alternateName`, but sometimes also as a numerical `ratingValue`. ClaimsKG already performs this type of normalisation into a set of "veracity" labels, but for other `ClaimReviews` we have developed a list of simple heuristic rules to assign a credibility and confidence score.

The $\texttt{LookupBot}_{\texttt{WebSite}}$ returns a CR for a `WebSite`. This is a simple wrapper around the existing MisinfoMe aggregation service [10], which already produces credibility and confidence values.

4.3 Linking Bots

Although the GCS lookup bots provide access to the basic credibility signals, they can only provide this for a relatively small set of claims and websites. Misinformation online often appears as variations of fact-checked claims and can appear on a wide variety of websites that may not have been reviewed yet by a human. Therefore, to increase the number of sentences which can be reviewed, we developed the following linking bots (see Sect. 4.5 for further details).

The $\texttt{LinkBot}^{\texttt{PreCrawled}}_{\texttt{Sentence}}$ uses a database of pre-crawled sentences extracted from a variety of websites. A proprietary NLP system[11] extracts the most relevant sentences that may contain factual information in the crawled documents. This is done by identifying sentences that (i) are associated with a topic (e.g. Politics or Health) and (ii) mentions an entity (e.g. a place or person). The CR for the extracted sentence is assigned based on the website where the sentence was found (i.e. by using the $\texttt{LookupBot}_{\texttt{WebSite}}$). Since not all sentences published by a website are as credible as the site, the resulting CR for the sentence has a lower confidence than the CR for the website itself.

[10] https://www.newsguardtech.com/, https://www.mywot.com/.
[11] http://expert.ai.

The $\texttt{LinkBot}^{\texttt{SemSim}}_{\texttt{Sentence}}$ is able to generate CRs for a wide variety of sentences by linking the input sentence s_i to sentences s_j for which a CR is available (via other bots). This linking is achieved by using a neural sentence encoder $f_{\text{enc}} : S \mapsto \Re^d$ –where S is the set of sentences and $d \in N^+$–, that is optimised to encode semantically similar sentences close to each other in an embedding space. The bot creates an index by generating embeddings for all the sentences reviewed by the $\texttt{LookupBot}_{\texttt{ClaimReview}}$ and the $\texttt{LinkBot}^{\texttt{PreCrawled}}_{\texttt{Sentence}}$. The incoming sentence, s_i is encoded and a nearest neighbor search produces the closest matches along with a similarity score based on a similarity function $f_{\text{sim}} : \Re^d \times \Re^d \mapsto \Re^{[0,1]}$. Unfortunately, most sentence encoders are not polarity aware so that negations of a phrase are considered similar to the original phrase; therefore we use a second neural model for stance detection $f_{\text{stance}} : S \times S \mapsto \text{SL}$, where SL is a set of stance labels. We then define $f_{\text{polarity}} : \text{SL} \mapsto \{1, -1\}$, which we use to invert the polarity of r_j if s_i disagrees with s_j. We also use the predicted stance to revise the similarity score between s_i and s_j by defining a function $f_{\text{reviseSim}} : \text{SL}, \Re^{[0,1]} \mapsto \Re^{[0,1]}$. For example, stances like *unrelated* or *discuss* may reduce the estimated similarity, which is used to revise the confidence of the original credibility. In summary, the final CR for s_i is selected via $f^{\text{mostConfident}}$ from a pool of $\text{CR}_{i,j}$ for the matching s_j; where the rating and confidences for each $\text{CR}_{i,j}$ are given by:

$$r_i = r_j \times f_{\text{polarity}}(f_{\text{stance}}(s_i, s_j))$$

$$c_i = c_j \times f_{\text{reviseSim}}\Big(f_{\text{stance}}(s_i, s_j), f_{\text{sim}}\big(f_{\text{enc}}(s_i), f_{\text{enc}}(s_j)\big)\Big)$$

4.4 Decomposing Bots

By combining linking and GCS lookup bots we are already capable of reviewing a wide variety of sentences. However, users online encounter misinformation in the form of high-level `CreativeWorks` like social media posts, articles, images, podcasts, etc. Therefore we need bots which are capable of (i) dissecting those CreativeWorks into relevant parts for which CRs can be calculated and (ii) aggregating the CRs for individual parts into an overall CR for the whole `CreativeWork`. In acred, we have defined two main types:

- $\texttt{DecBot}_{\texttt{Article}}$ reviews `Articles`, and other long-form textual `CreativeWorks`
- $\texttt{DecBot}_{\texttt{SocMedia}}$ reviews `SocialMediaPosts`

In both bots, decomposition works by performing NLP and content analysis on the title and textual content of the `CreativeWork` d_i. This results in a set of parts $P = \{d_j\}$ which include `Sentences`, linked `Articles` or `SocialMediaPosts` and metadata like the `WebSite` where d was published. Each of these can be analysed either recursively or via other bots, which results in a set of reviews $\{\text{CR}_j\}$ for the identified parts. We define a function f_{part} which maps CR_j onto $\text{CR}_{\text{i,j}}$, which takes into account the relation between d_i and d_j as well as the provenance of CR_j to derive the credibility rating and confidence. The final CR_i is selected from all $\text{CR}_{i,j}$ via $f^{\text{leastCredible}}$.

Figure 2 shows a diagram depicting how the various CR bots compose and collaborate to review a tweet.

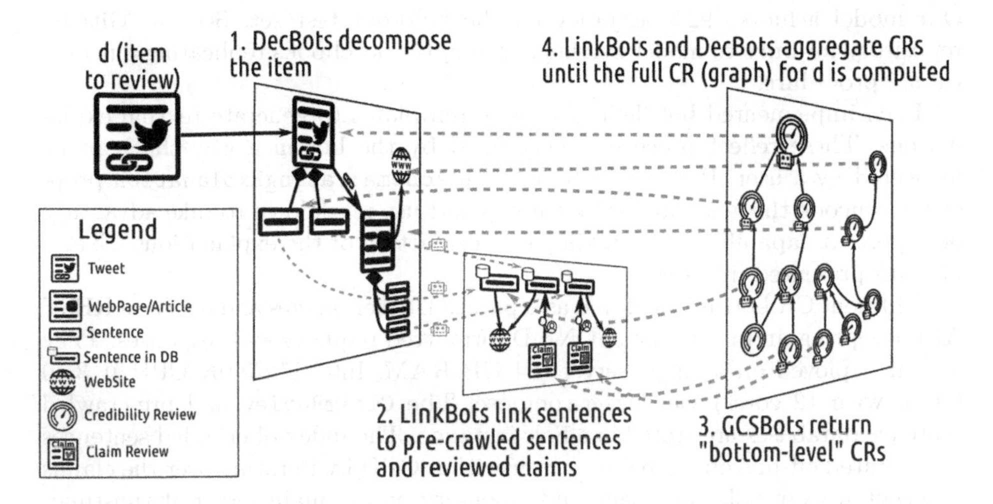

Fig. 2. Depiction of acred bots collaborating to produce a CR for a tweet.

4.5 Implementation Details

Our database of `ClaimReviews` contains 45K claims and was based on public resources such as ClaimsKG [17] (32K), data-commons (9.6K) and our in-house developed crawlers (4K). The database of pre-crawled sentences contained 40K sentences extracted from a variety of generic news sites on-line between april 2019 and april 2020. It consisted primarily in relatively well-regarded news sites like `expressen.se`, `krone.at`, `zdf.de`, which combined for about 35K of the sentences, and a long tail of other sites including `theconversation.com` and `heartland.org`. For reproducibility, we will publish the list of sentences along associated URLs.

Our heuristic rules to normalise `ClaimReviews` are implemented in about 50 lines of python to map numeric `ratingValues` (in context of specified `bestRating` and `worstRating` values) and 150 lines of python to map about 100 `alternateName` values (e.g. "inaccurate", "false and misleading", "this is exaggerated") and about 20 patterns (e.g. "wrong.*", "no, *") into estimated c, r values.

The sentence encoder, f_{enc} in $\texttt{LinkBot}^{\texttt{SemSim}}_{\texttt{Sentence}}$ is implemented as a RoBERTa-base [7] model finetuned on STS-B [4]. We employ a siamese structure as this enables us to perform encoding of the claims off-line (slow) and comparison on-line (fast) at the cost of some accuracy. Our model achieves 83% Pearson correlation on STS-B dev.

The stance detector, f_{stance}, is also a RoBERTa-base model trained on FNC-1 [14], which assigns a stance label (either "agree", "disagree", "discuss" or "unrelated") to pairs of texts: about 50K for training and about 25K for testing. Our model achieves 92% accuracy on the held-out test set. See our GitHub repository for links to model weights and jupyter notebooks replicating our fine-tuning procedure.

Each implemented bot defines a set of templates to generate textual explanations. These reflect processing performed by the bot in a way that can be inspected by a user. Produced CRs use the `schema:ratingExplanation` property to encode the generated explanations and use markdown to take advantage of hypertext capabilities like linking and formatting of the explanations. Examples are presented in Table 1.

Different CR bots are deployed as separate Docker images and expose a REST API accepting and returning JSON-LD formatted requests and responses. They are all deployed on a single server (64 GB RAM, Intel i7-8700K CPU @ 3.70 GHzn with 12 cores) via docker-compose. The `ClaimReview` and pre-crawled sentence databases are stored in a Solr instance. The index of encoded sentences is generated off-line on a separate server with a GPU by iterating over the claims and sentences in Solr, and loaded into memory on the main server at run-time.

5 Evaluation

One of the main characteristics of the LCR architecture is that CR bots can be distributed across different organizations. This has the main drawback that it can be more difficult to fine-tune bots to specific domains since top-level bots do not have direct control on how lower-level bots are implemented and fine-tuned. Therefore in this paper we first evaluated our `acred` implementation, described above, on a variety of datasets covering social media posts, news articles and political speeches. Our rationale is that existing, non-distributed fact-checking approaches have an edge here as they can fine-tune their systems based on training data and therefore provide strong baselines to compare against. We used the explanations, along with the provenance trace, to perform error analysis[12] on the largest dataset, described in Sect. 5.2. This showed `acred` was overly confident in some cases. To address this, we introduced a modified version, `acred`$^+$ with custom functions to reduce the confidence and rating values of two bots under certain conditions: $\texttt{DecBot}_{\texttt{Article}}$ when based only on a website credibility; $\texttt{LinkBot}^{\texttt{SemSim}}_{\texttt{Sentence}}$ when the stance is "unrelated" or "discuss".

5.1 Datasets

The first dataset we use is the Clef'18 CheckThat! Factuality Task [11] (`clef18`). The task consists in predicting whether a check-worthy claim is either `true`,

[12] Note that usability evaluation of the generated explanations is not in the scope of this paper.

Table 1. Example explanations generated by our bots.

Bot	Example explanation
$\texttt{LookupBot}_{\texttt{ClaimRev}}$	Claim `'Ford is moving all of their small-car productin to Mexico.'` is *mostly not credible* based on a fact-check by politifact with normalised numeric ratingValue 2 in range [1–5]
$\texttt{LookupBot}_{\texttt{WebSite}}$	Site www.krone.at seems *mostly credible* based on 2 review(s) by external rater(s) NewsGuard or Web Of Trust
$\texttt{LinkBot}^{\texttt{PreCrawled}}_{\texttt{Sentence}}$	Sentence `Now we want to invest in the greatest welfare program in modern times.` seems *credible* as it was published in site www.expressen.se. (Explanation for WebSite omitted)
$\texttt{LinkBot}^{\texttt{SemSim}}_{\texttt{Sentence}}$	Sentence `When Senator Clinton or President Clinton asserts that I said that the Republicans had better economic policies since 1980, that is not the case.` seems *not credible* as it agrees with sentence: `Obama said that 'since 1992, the Republicans have had all the good ideas...'` that seems *not credible* based on a fact-check by politifact with textual rating 'false'. Take into account that the sentence appeared in site www.cnn.com that seems *credible* based on 2 review(s) by external rater(s) NewsGuard or Web Of Trust
$\texttt{LinkBot}^{\texttt{SemSim}}_{\texttt{Sentence}}$	Sentence `Can we reduce our dependence on foreign oil and by how much in the first term, in four years?` is similar to and discussed by: `Drilling for oil on the Outer Continental Shelf and in parts of Alaska will 'immediately reduce our dangerous dependence on foreign oil.'` that seems *not credible*, based on a fact-check by politifact with textual rating 'false'
$\texttt{DecBot}_{\texttt{Article}}$	Article "Part 1 of CNN Democratic presidential debate" seems *not credible* based on its least credible sentence. (explanation for sentence CR omitted)
$\texttt{DecBot}_{\texttt{SocMedia}}$	Sentence `Absolutely fantastic, there is know difference between the two facist socialist powers of today's EU in Brussels, and the yesteryears of Nazi Germany` in tweet agrees with: `'You see the Nazi platform from the early 1930s ... look at it compared to the (Democratic Party) platform of today, you're saying, 'Man, those things are awfully similar.''` that seems *not credible* based on a fact-check by politifact with textual claim-review rating 'false"'

half-true or false. The dataset was derived from fact-checked political debates and speeches by factcheck.org. For our evaluation we only use the English part of this dataset[13] which contains 74 and 139 claims for training and testing.

FakeNewsNet [16] aims to provide a dataset of fake and real news enriched with social media posts and context sharing those news. In this paper we only use the fragment derived from articles fact-checked by Politifact that have textual content, which consists of 420 *fake* and 528 *real* articles. The articles were retrieved by following the instructions on the Github page[14].

Finally, coinform250[15] is a dataset of 250 annotated tweets. The tweets and original labels were first collected by parsing and normalising ClaimReviews from datacommons and scraping fact-checker sites using the MisinfoMe data collector [9,10]. Note that acred's collection system is **not** based on MisinfoMe[16]. The original fact-checker labels were mapped onto six labels (see Table 2) by 7 human raters achieving a Fleiss κ score of 0.52 (moderate agreement). The fine-grained labels make this a challenging but realistic dataset.

For each dataset our prediction procedure consisted in steps to (i) read samples, (ii) convert them to the appropriate schema.org data items (Sentence, Article or SocialMediaPost), (iii) request a review from the appropriate acred CR bot via its REST API; (iv) map the produced CR onto the dataset labels and (v) optionally store the generated graph of CRs. For clef18 we set $t = 0.75$, so that $r \geq t$ has label TRUE, $r \leq -0.75$ has label FALSE and anything in between is HALF-TRUE. See Table 2 for coinform250 threshold definitions.

Table 2. Mapping of credibility ratingValue r and confidence c for coinform250.

Label	r	c
Credible	$r \geq 0.5$	$c > 0.7$
Mostly credible	$0.5 > r \geq 0.25$	$c > 0.7$
Uncertain	$0.25 > r \geq -0.25$	$c > 0.7$
Mostly not credible	$-0.25 > r \geq -0.5$	$c > 0.7$
Not credible	$-0.5 > r$	$c > 0.7$
Not verifiable	Any	$c \leq 0.7$

5.2 Results

On clef18, acred establishes a new state-of-the-art result as shown in Table 3, achieving 0.6835 in MAE, the official metric in the competition [11]. This result is noteworthy as, unlike the other systems, acred did not use the training set of clef18 at all to finetune the underlying models. With acred$^+$, we further improved our results achieving 0.6475 MAE.

[13] Our implementation has support for machine translation of sentences, however this adds a confounding factor hence we leave this as future work.

[14] https://github.com/KaiDMML/FakeNewsNet, although we note that text for many of the articles could no longer be retrieved, making a fair comparison difficult.

[15] https://github.com/co-inform/Datasets.

[16] acred's data collector is used to build the ClaimReview database described in Sect. 4; it does not store the itemReviewed URL values; only the claimReviewed strings.

Table 3. Results on `clef18` English test dataset compared to baselines. The bottom rows shows results on the English training set.

System	MAE	Macro MAE	Acc	Macro F1	Macro AvgR
`acred`	0.6835	0.6990	**0.4676**	**0.4247**	0.4367
`acred`$^+$	**0.6475**	**0.6052**	0.3813	0.3741	0.4202
Copenhagen [19]	0.7050	0.6746	0.4317	0.4008	**0.4502**
Random [11]	0.8345	0.8139	0.3597	0.3569	0.3589
`acred` "training"	0.6341	0.7092	0.4878	0.4254	0.4286
`acred`$^+$ "training"	0.6585	0.6386	0.4024	0.3943	0.4020

On FakeNewsNet, `acred`$^+$ obtained state of the art results and `acred` obtained competitive results in line with strong baseline systems reported in the original paper [16], shown in Table 4. We only consider as baselines systems which only use the article content, since acred does not use credibility reviews based on social context yet. Note that baselines used 80% of the data for training and 20% for testing, while we used the full dataset for testing.

Table 4. Results on FakeNewsNet Politifact compared to baselines that only use article content.

System	Accuracy	Precision	Recall	F1
`acred`	0.586	0.499	**0.823**	0.622
`acred`$^+$	**0.716**	0.674	0.601	**0.713**
CNN	0.629	**0.807**	0.456	0.583
SAF/S	0.654	0.600	0.789	0.681

We performed a manual error analysis on the `acred` results for FakeNewsNet[17]:

- 29 errors of fake news predicted as highly credible ($r \geq 0.5$): 16 cases (55%) were due to acred finding pre-crawled sentence matches in that appeared in `snopes.com`, but not `ClaimReviews` for that article. A further 7 cases (24%) were due to finding `unrelated` sentences and using the `WebSiteCR` where those sentences appeared, while being over-confident about those credibilities.
- 41 errors of fake news predicted with low-confidence ($c \leq 0.7$). 30 of these cases (73%) are due to the FakeNewsNet crawler as it fails to retrieve valid content for the articles: GDPR or site-for-sale messages instead of the original article content. In these cases, acred is correct in having low-confidence credibility ratings. In the remaining 27% of cases, acred indeed failed to find evidence to decide on whether the article was credible or not.
- 264 real articles were rated as being highly not credible ($r < -0.5$). This is by far the largest source of errors. We manually analysed 26 of these, chosen at random. In 13 cases (50%), the real stance should be *unrelated*, but is predicted as *discussed* or even *agrees*; often the sentences are indeed about a closely related topics, but still about unrelated entities or events. In a further 7 cases (27%) the stance is correctly predicted to be *unrelated*, but

[17] As stated above, we used the results of this analysis to inform the changes implemented in `acred`$^+$.

the confidence still passess the threshold. Hence 77% of these errors are due to incorrect or overconfident linking by the $\texttt{LinkBot}^{\texttt{SemSim}}_{\texttt{Sentence}}$.
- 48 real articles were rated as being somewhat not credible ($-0.25 < r \leq 0.25$), in a majority of these cases, the r was obtained from $\texttt{LinkBot}^{\texttt{PreCrawled}}_{\texttt{Sentence}}$ rather than from $\texttt{LinkBot}^{\texttt{SemSim}}_{\texttt{Sentence}}$.

Finally, for the `coinform250` dataset, `acred`$^+$ obtains 0.279 accuracy which is well above a baseline of random predictions, which obtains 0.167 accuracy. The confusion matrix shown in Fig. 3f shows that the performance is in line with that shown for FakeNewsNet (Fig. 3d) and `clef18` (Fig. 3e). It also shows that `acred` tends to be overconfident in its predictions, while `acred`$^+$ is more cautious.

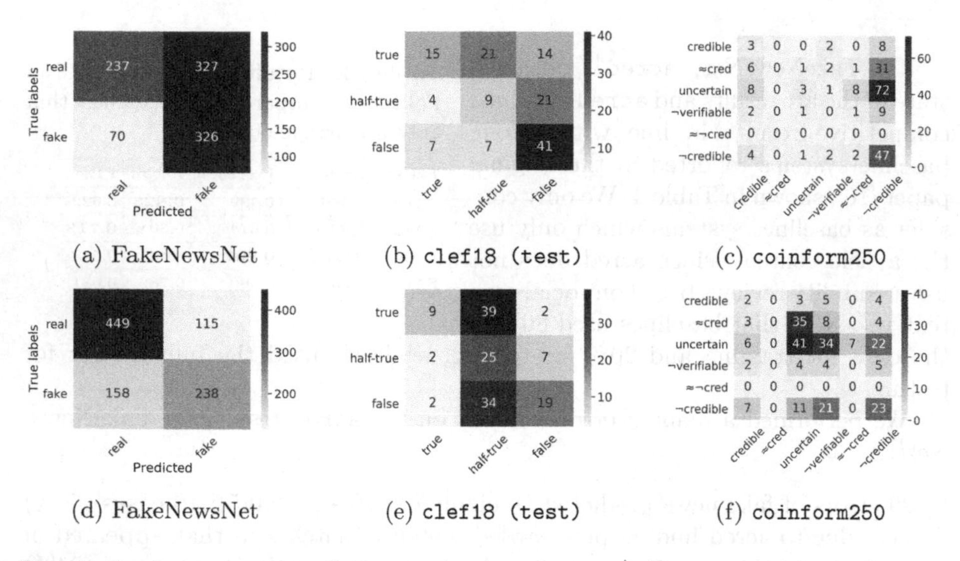

(a) FakeNewsNet (b) `clef18 (test)` (c) `coinform250`

(d) FakeNewsNet (e) `clef18 (test)` (f) `coinform250`

Fig. 3. Confusion matrices for `acred` (top) and `acred`$^+$ (bottom row) in evaluation datasets. We use ≈ for *mostly* and ¬ for *not* in the `coinform250` labels.

5.3 Discussion

The Good. Our approach obtains competitive results in challenging datasets; these results are especially impressive when you take into account that we do not train or fine-tune our underlying models on these datasets. With `acred`$^+$, we also showed we can substantially improve results by performing some simple optimization of aggregation functions; however doing this in a systematic manner is not in the scope of this paper where we are focusing on validating the LCR design. Since the results were consistent across the different datasets, this shows that our network of bots have certain domain independence and validate our design for composable CR bots as our lookup and linking bots can successfully be reused by the high-level decomposing bots. We think this is largely due to our choice of generic deep-learning models for linguistic tasks like semantic similarity and stance detection where fairly large datasets are available.

We obtain state of the art results in all datasets. This shows that our approach excels at identifying misinformation, which is arguably the primary task of these kinds of systems. Furthermore, in many cases, our system correctly matches the misinforming sentence to a previously fact-checked claim (and article). Even when no exact match is found, often the misinforming sentence is linked to a similar claim that was previously reviewed and that is indicative of a recurring misinforming narrative. Such cases can still be useful for end-users to improve their awareness of such narratives.

The Bad. The `acred` implementation is overly sceptical, which resulted in poor precision for data items which are (mostly) accurate or not verifiable. This is an important type of error preventing real-world use of this technology. As prevalent as misinformation is, it still only represents a fraction of the web content and we expected such errors to undermine confidence in automated systems. The presented error analysis shows that this is largely due to (i) errors in the stance-detection module or (ii) incorrect weighting of predicted stance and semantic similarity. The former was surprising as the stance prediction model obtained 92% accuracy on FNC-1. This seems to be due to the fact that FNC-1 is highly unbalanced, hence errors in under-represented classes are not reflected in the overall accuracy. Note that we addressed this issue to a certain extent with `acred`$^{+}$, which essentially `compensates` for errors in the underlying semantic similarity and stance prediction modules.

The poor precision on real news is especially apparent in FakeNewsNet and `coinform250`. We think this is due to our naive implementation of our pre-crawled database of sentences extracted from websites. First, the relevant sentence extractor does not ensure that the sentence is a factual claim, therefore introducing significant noise. This suggests that the system can benefit from adding a check-worthiness filter to address this issue. The second source of noise is our selection of pre-crawled article sources which did not seem to provide relevant matches in most cases. We expect that a larger and more balanced database of pre-crawled sentences, coming from a wider range of sources, should provide a better pool of credibility signals and help to improve accuracy.

The Dubious. Fact-checking is a recent phenomenon and publishing fact-checked claims as structured data even more so. It is also a laborious process that requires specialist skills. As a result, the pool of machine-readable high-quality reviewed data items is relatively small. Most of the datasets being used to build and evaluate automated misinformation detection systems are therefore ultimately based on this same pool of reviews. A percentage of our results may be based on the fact that we have exact matches in our database of ClaimReviews. On manual inspection, this does not appear to occur very often; we estimate low, single digit, percentage of cases.

Although we did a systematic error analysis, presented in the previous section, we have not yet done a systematic success analysis. Cursory inspection of the successful cases shows that in some cases, we predicted the label correctly, but the explanation itself is incorrect; this tends to happen when a sentence is matched but is deemed to be *unrelated* to a matched sentence. Note that other systems based on machine learning may suffer of the same issue, but unlike our approach they behave as black boxes making it difficult to determine whether the system correctly identified misinforming content for the wrong reasons.

6 Conclusion and Future Work

In this paper we proposed a simple data model and architecture for using semantic technologies (linked data) to implement composable bots which build a graph of Credibility Reviews for web content. We showed that `schema.org` provides most of the building blocks for expressing the necessary linked data, with some crucial extensions. We implemented a basic fact-checking system for sentences, social media posts and long-form web articles using the proposed LCR architecture and validated the approach on various datasets. Despite not using the training sets of the datasets, our implementations obtained state of the art results on the `clef18` and FakeNewsNet datasets.

Our experiments have demonstrated the capabilities and added value of our approach such as human-readable explanations and machine aided navigation of provenance paths to aid in error analysis and pinpointing of sources of errors. We also identified promising areas for improvement and further research. We plan to (i) further improve our stance detection model by fine-tuning and testing on additional datasets [15]; (ii) perform an ablation test on an improved version of acred to understand the impact of including or omitting certain bots and datasets; (iii) perform crowdsourcing to evaluate both the understandability, usefulness and accuracy of the generated explanations. Beside our own plans, it is clear that a single organization or team cannot tackle all the issues which need to be resolved to achieve high-accuracy credibility analysis of web content. This is exactly why we propose the Linked Credibility Review, which should enable the distributed collaboration of fact-checkers, deep-learning service developers, database curators, journalists and citizens in building an ecosystem where more advanced, multi-perspective and accurate credibility analyses are possible.

Acknowledgements. Work supported by the European Commission under grant 770302 – Co-Inform – as part of the Horizon 2020 research and innovation programme. Thanks to Co-inform members for discussions which helped shape this research and in particular to Martino Mensio for his work on MisInfoMe. Also thanks to Flavio Merenda and Olga Salas for their help implementing parts of the pipeline.

References

1. Babakar, M., Moy, W.: The state of automated factchecking. Technical report (2016)
2. Boland, K., Fafalios, P., Tchechmedjiev, A.: Modeling and contextualizing claims. In: 2nd International Workshop on Contextualised Knowledge Graphs (2019)

3. Cazalens, S., Lamarre, P., Leblay, J., Manolescu, I., Tannier, X.: A content management perspective on fact-checking. In: The Web Conference (2018)
4. Cer, D., Diab, M., Agirre, E., Lopez-Gazpio, I., Specia, L.: SemEval-2017 task 1: semantic textual similarity multilingual and cross-lingual focused evaluation. In: Proceedings of the 10th International Workshop on Semantic Evaluation, pp. 1–14 (2018)
5. Guha, R.V., Brickley, D., Macbeth, S.: Schema.org: evolution of structured data on the web. Commun. ACM **59**(2), 44–51 (2016)
6. Hassan, N., et al.: ClaimBuster: the first-ever end-to-end fact-checking system. In: Proceedings of the VLDB Endowment, vol. 10, pp. 1945–1948 (2017)
7. Liu, Y., et al.: RoBERTa: a robustly optimized BERT pretraining approach. Technical report (2019)
8. Marwick, A., Lewis, R.: Media Manipulation and Disinformation Online. Data & Society Research Institute, New York (2017)
9. Mensio, M., Alani, H.: MisinfoMe: who's interacting with misinformation? In: 18th International Semantic Web Conference: Posters & Demonstrations (2019)
10. Mensio, M., Alani, H.: News source credibility in the eyes of different assessors. In: Conference for Truth and Trust Online (2019, in press)
11. Nakov, P., et al.: Overview of the CLEF-2018 CheckThat! Lab on automatic identification and verification of political claims. In: Bellot, P., et al. (eds.) CLEF 2018. LNCS, vol. 11018, pp. 372–387. Springer, Cham (2018). https://doi.org/10.1007/978-3-319-98932-7_32
12. Papadopoulos, S., Bontcheva, K., Jaho, E., Lupu, M., Castillo, C.: Overview of the special issue on trust and veracity of information in social media. ACM Trans. Inf. Syst. (TOIS) **34**(3), 1–5 (2016)
13. Pérez-Rosas, V., Kleinberg, B., Lefevre, A., Mihalcea, R.: Automatic detection of fake news. In: COLING (2018)
14. Pomerleau, D., Rao, D.: The fake news challenge: exploring how artificial intelligence technologies could be leveraged to combat fake news (2017)
15. Schiller, B., Daxenberger, J., Gurevych, I.: Stance detection benchmark: how robust is your stance detection? (2020)
16. Shu, K., Mahudeswaran, D., Wang, S., Lee, D., Liu, H.: FakeNewsNet: a data repository with news content, social context and spatialtemporal information for studying fake news on social media. Technical report (2018)
17. Tchechmedjiev, A., et al.: ClaimsKG: a knowledge graph of fact-checked claims. In: Ghidini, C., et al. (eds.) ISWC 2019. LNCS, vol. 11779, pp. 309–324. Springer, Cham (2019). https://doi.org/10.1007/978-3-030-30796-7_20
18. Thorne, J., Vlachos, A., Cocarascu, O., Christodoulopoulos, C., Mittal, A.: The FEVER 2.0 shared task. In: Proceedings of the Second Workshop on Fact Extraction and VERification (FEVER), pp. 1–6 (2019)
19. Wang, D., Simonsen, J.G., Larsen, B., Lioma, C.: The Copenhagen team participation in the factuality task of the competition of automatic identification and verification of claims in political debates of the CLEF-2018 fact checking lab. CLEF (Working Notes) 2125 (2018)
20. Zubiaga, A., Aker, A., Bontcheva, K., Liakata, M., Procter, R.: Detection and resolution of rumours in social media: a survey. ACM Comput. Surv. **51**(2), 1–36 (2018)

A Novel Path-Based Entity Relatedness Measure for Efficient Collective Entity Linking

Cheikh Brahim El Vaigh[1], François Goasdoué[2](✉), Guillaume Gravier[3], and Pascale Sébillot[4]

[1] Inria, IRISA, Rennes, France
cheikh-brahim.el-vaigh@inria.fr
[2] Univ. Rennes, IRISA, Lannion, France
fg@irisa.fr
[3] CNRS, IRISA, Rennes, France
guig@irisa.fr
[4] INSA Rennes, IRISA, Rennes, France
pascale.sebillot@irisa.fr

Abstract. Collective entity linking is a core natural language processing task, which consists in jointly identifying the entities of a knowledge base (KB) that are mentioned in a text exploiting existing relations between entities within the KB. State-of-the-art methods typically combine local scores accounting for the similarity between mentions and entities, with a global score measuring the coherence of the set of selected entities. The latter relies on the structure of a KB: the hyperlink graph of Wikipedia in most cases or the graph of an RDF KB, e.g., BaseKB or Yago, to benefit from the precise semantics of relationships between entities. In this paper, we devise a novel RDF-based entity relatedness measure for global scores with important properties: (*i*) it has a clear semantics, (*ii*) it can be calculated at reasonable computational cost, and (*iii*) it accounts for the transitive aspects of entity relatedness through existing (bounded length) property paths between entities in an RDF KB. Further, we experimentally show on the TAC-KBP2017 dataset, both with BaseKB and Yago, that it provides significant improvement over state-of-the-art entity relatedness measures for the collective entity linking task.

Keywords: Collective entity linking · Entity relatedness measure · RDF KBs

1 Introduction

Entity linking is a crucial task for textual document engineering in both natural language processing and information retrieval, with applications such as semantic search [2] and information extraction [16]. It aims at identifying the mentions of

J. Z. Pan et al. (Eds.): ISWC 2020, LNCS 12506, pp. 164–182, 2020.
https://doi.org/10.1007/978-3-030-62419-4_10

entities in a document and linking each mention to a unique referential such as a URI in Wikipedia or in an RDF knowledge base (KB). Entity linking is thus instrumental for semantic search and retrieval [2,16].

The literature on entity linking distinguishes two main approaches, depending on whether mentions within a single document are linked to entities independently one from another [10,12,20] or collectively [5,11,13,19,24,27]. The former uses the KB at hand to generate and select candidate entities independently for each entity mention in the text, while collective linking further uses the KB to select the best global mapping between mentions and candidate entities based on the entity interrelationships recorded in the KB. State-of-the-art methods for this collective linking step typically combine within a classifier a local score accounting for the string similarity between the mention and an entity's name, with a global score that measures the coherence of the set of selected entities. In particular, the cornerstone of global score computation is a *measure of relatedness between two entities* that indicates to which extent these entities may co-occur in a document.

In this paper, we focus on improving collective entity linking performance by devising a novel entity relatedness measure. Notably, we advocate that, in addition to showing significant performance improvement on standard benchmarks w.r.t. state-of-the-art competitors, a *well-founded* measure should meet the following three requirements to the extent possible: **(R1)** it must have a *clear semantics* so that linking decisions can be easily understood or explained, in particular it must build on a knowledge base with formal semantics (e.g., an RDF or OWL one, as opposed to Wikipedia) and avoid tuning parameters or knobs that are hard to set by end-users, **(R2)** it must be calculated at *reasonable computational cost* to be of practical interest and **(R3)** it must consider relatedness as a *transitive relation*, to capture that entities may be related within the KB either directly or indirectly, i.e., through *paths*. The last requirement **(R3)** is crucial as it allows encoding implicit links between entities. For instance, if *X worksFor Y* and *Y isLocatedIn Z* then, the path from *X* to *Z* implicitly encodes *X worksIn Z*, which is an information not stored in the KB that can be captured by measures meeting **(R3)**.

To the best of our knowledge, no entity relatedness measure in the literature meets all three requirements. Approaches making use of Wikipedia, e.g., [1,4,6,11,13,17,24], consider Wikipedia's web page URIs as entities, web pages as textual entity descriptions, and hyperlinks between web pages as generic relations between entities. It is worth noting that, although a hyperlink from an entity to another states a direct relation between them, it carries very loose semantics: it solely indicates that the target entity somehow occurs in the description of the source one, be it central to this description or unimportant. Hence, Wikipedia-based entity relatedness measures do not meet **(R1)**, at least. A few other approaches [14,15,22,26] rely on RDF KBs, like BaseKB, DBpedia or Yago, instead of Wikipedia. Such KBs encode in a formal knowledge graph model, the precise semantics of entities (e.g., types) and of their direct relations called *properties* (e.g., property names and cardinalities). While the Ref measure [1,18] just provides a binary indicator of whether or not a relation exists between two entities in the RDF KB, the recent WSRM measure [9], which can be viewed as an extension of Ref, further considers the amount of relations between two entities. Though they both have (simple) clear semantics **(R1)** and are cheap to calculate with edge lookups **(R2)**, they only consider properties between entities to compute relatedness, thus do not meet **(R3)**. By contrast, the rel^k_{Excl} relatedness measure [15] exploits the top-k property paths between two entities (more details in Sect. 2), hence meets **(R3)**. However, it does not fully meet **(R1)** because though its definition has a clear semantics, its relies on user-defined constants that are non-trivial to set due to their unforeseeable consequences on the measure results. Also, rel^k_{Excl} does not meet **(R2)** because it requires computing all paths between entity pairs so as to select the top-k ones; this is not feasible in general in the setting of entity linking, which relies on large encyclopedic RDF KBs. Finally, the cosine similarity is used as an entity relatedness measure in approaches based on RDF KB embeddings [3,25], i.e., when entities are mapped into coordinates of a multidimensional space. Though the cosine similarity itself has a clear semantics **(R1)** and is not costly to compute **(R2)**, the machine learning-based computation of embeddings cannot guarantee that cosine similar entities within the multidimensional space are indeed related in the KB, hence does not meet **(R3)**.

Our main contribution is the novel ASRMP$_m$ entity relatedness measure for RDF KBs, which satisfies the three requirements stated above. In particular, for two entities e_1 and e_2, it uses the fuzzy logic AND and OR operators [7] to compute, respectively, the score of every e_1-to-e_2 path of length up to m within the KB, by aggregating the WSRM values between the entity pairs found along the path, the final measure being obtained by aggregating over all paths of length m between e_1 and e_2. In particular, ASRMP$_1$ boils down to WSRM. Importantly, ASRMP$_m$ is not tied to WSRM (i.e., another measure could have been used like Ref). We adopt it here because, in addition to satisfying **(R1)** and **(R2)**, it is currently the relatedness measure showing best performance for collective entity linking in the literature [9]. Our fuzzy logic-based aggregation scheme allows ASRMP$_m$ to inherit both **(R1)** and **(R2)** from WSRM. Further, while computing the paths of length up to m between entities rapidly becomes unfeasible as m grows, **(R3)** is met by the need for considering low m values only. Indeed, it has been widely observed (e.g., in [15] for rel^k_{Excl} that also consider paths) that the longer the path between two entities, the less significant the relation it encodes. To evaluate ASRMP$_m$ for entity linking, we first define a collective entity linking system within which we experimentally show on the TAC-KBP2017 dataset, both with the BaseKB and Yago RDF KBs, that ASRMP$_m$ with $m > 1$ improves linking performance w.r.t. the above-mentioned relatedness measures from the literature. We also show significant improvement over popular collective linking techniques using standard entity linking benchmarks.[1]

The paper is organized as follows. We first present in Sect. 2 the main entity relatedness measures used for collective entity linking. In Sect. 3, we define the

[1] https://gitlab.inria.fr/celvaigh/celasrmp.

ASRMP_m entity relatedness measure. In Sect. 4, we describe our collective entity linking system with which ASRMP_m is experimentally compared to state-of-the-art competitors in Sect. 5. Finally, we conclude and discuss perspectives in Sect. 6.

2 Related Work

Most of the entity relatedness measures proposed so far in the context of collective entity linking rely on Wikipedia's hyperlink structure [1,4,6,11,13,17,24]. As pointed out above, such hyperlinks do not encode the precise semantics of the relations between entities they model, hence can hardly be used within well-founded entity relatedness measures, i.e., that meet the three requirements stated above.

A handful of measures rely on RDF KBs [1,3,9,15,18,25]. Such KBs model both data (facts) and knowledge (ontological description of the application domain) using explicit and implicit triples; the latter can be derived through reasoning based on an RDF-specific consequence relation, a.k.a. entailment. In particular, within RDF KBs, the precise relation (a.k.a. *property*) r that directly relates an entity e_i to another entity e_j is encoded by the triple (e_i, r, e_j). The use of RDF KBs can therefore be seen as an important step towards devising well-founded entity relatedness measures. We recall below the few relatedness measures that use RDF KBs, and discuss to which extent they meet the three requirements of well-foundedness introduced above: **(R1)**, **(R2)** and **(R3)**.

The Binary Indicator. Ref [1,18] is defined between two entities e_i and e_j as:

$$\text{Ref}(e_i, e_j) = \begin{cases} 1 & \exists r \; s.t. \; (e_i, r, e_j) \in \text{KB}; \\ 0 & \text{otherwise.} \end{cases}$$

The above definition shows that Ref has a clear semantics **(R1)** and a low computational cost **(R2)** since it can be computed using edge lookups. We however remark that, though clear, its semantics is *very simple*: it does not take into account the various properties between e_i and e_j, nor those that e_i and e_j may have with other entities. Further, Ref does not allow entities to be related through a property path within the RDF KB, hence does not meet **(R3)**: they can only be related through a *single* property, i.e., a single edge or triple.

The Weighted Semantic Relatedness Measure. WSRM [9] improves on Ref by not only accounting for the existence of some property between two entities using a Boolean value, but also by *weighting* how related they are in the [0,1] interval, assuming that the more properties between them, the stronger their relatedness. Formally, WSRM is defined between two entities e_i and e_j as

$$\text{WSRM}(e_i, e_j) = \frac{|\{r \mid (e_i, r, e_j) \in \text{KB}\}|}{\sum_{e' \in E} |\{r' \mid (e_i, r', e') \in \text{KB}\}|}, \tag{1}$$

where E denotes the set of entities in the KB and $|S|$ the cardinality of the set S.

In spirit, WSRM is comparable to the *Wikipedia popularity* often used in local entity linking scores, e.g., [8,10], as the probability that a mention m is used as the text (anchor) of a hyperlink referring to an entity e. WSRM is however conceptually different, being applied between two entities rather than between a mention and an entity. It can be interpreted as the probability that e_i is directly related to e_j through some property.

The above definition shows that WSRM has a clear and more fine-grained semantics than Ref **(R1)**. Also, clearly, it can be computed at low computational cost **(R2)** based on edge lookups. However, like Ref, it does not allow entities to be related through property paths within the RDF KB, hence does not meet **(R3)**.

The Path-Based Semantic Relatedness Measure. [15] between two entities, denoted $rel^{(k)}_{Excl}$, is an aggregation of *path weights* for the top-k paths with highest weights between those entities; path weights are computed using the so-called *exclusivity* measure

$$\text{exclusivity}(x \xrightarrow{\tau} y) = \frac{1}{|x \xrightarrow{\tau} *| + |* \xrightarrow{\tau} y| - 1}, \tag{2}$$

where $|x \xrightarrow{\tau} *|$ is the number of outgoing τ relations for x, while $|* \xrightarrow{\tau} y|$ is the number of incoming τ relations for y; 1 is subtracted to avoid counting the relation $|x \xrightarrow{\tau} y|$ twice. Given a path $\mathtt{P} = x_1 \xrightarrow{\tau_1} x_2 \xrightarrow{\tau_2} \ldots \xrightarrow{\tau_{k-1}} x_k$ within the KB, its weight is

$$\text{weight}(\mathtt{P}) = \frac{1}{\sum_{i=1}^{k-1} 1/\text{exclusivity}(x_i \xrightarrow{\tau_i} x_{i+1})}. \tag{3}$$

Finally $rel^{(k)}_{Excl}$ is defined as the weighted sum of the top-k paths with highest weight between x and y

$$rel^{(k)}_{Excl}(x, y) = \sum_{\mathtt{P} \in P^k_{xy}} \alpha^{\text{length}(\mathtt{P})} \text{weight}(\mathtt{P}) \tag{4}$$

where P^k_{xy} denotes the top-k paths with highest weight between x and y, and $\alpha \in [0, 1]$ is a constant length decay factor introduced to give preference to shorter paths.

We remark that the above definition relies on paths between entities to measure their relatedness **(R3)**. However, we note that the semantics of $rel^{(k)}_{Excl}$ is controlled with parameters whose "good" values are hard to guess, though $k = 5$ and $\alpha = 0.25$ are recommended default values based on empirical observations. Thus $rel^{(k)}_{Excl}$ hardly meets **(R1)**. Further, the above definition requires to compute all the paths within the KB, which may not be computationally feasible since in large KBs, like the encyclopedic ones used for entity linking, the number of paths blows up as the considered path length increases; hence $rel^{(k)}_{Excl}$ does not meet **(R2)**.

Cosine Similarity. [3,25] is used to measure the semantic relatedness between two entities in entity linking systems based on embeddings, e.g., [5,19,22,24]: entities are mapped into coordinates of a multidimensional space, in which the closer two entities are, the more related they are. Several kernels exist for computing such embeddings, e.g., [3,23,25]. While the cosine similarity itself has a clear semantics **(R1)** and is not costly to compute **(R2)**, the machine learning-based construction of the entity embeddings cannot guarantee that cosine similar entities are indeed somehow related through some path in the KB, hence does not meet **(R3)**.

Table 1. Entity relatedness measures in the light of well-foundedness requirements: × indicates the requirement is met, while ∼ indicates it is only partially met.

Measure	(R1)	(R2)	(R3)	Measure	(R1)	(R2)	(R3)
Ref [1,18]	×	×		$rel^{(k)}_{Excl}$ [15]	∼		×
WSRM [9]	×	×		cosine [3,25]	×	×	

Table 1 recaps the above discussion and highlights that none of the entity relatedness measures used so far in the entity linking literature meets the three requirements of well-foundedness. Devising a measure that meets them all is a contribution of this paper, which we present next.

3 The Path-Based Weighted Semantic Relatedness Measure

Our approach to define a novel entity relatedness measure that meets all the well-foundedness requirements extends a measure from the literature that only considers properties (direct relations) between entities, to a measure that considers paths between entities. In the sequel, we chose to rely on WSRM to capitalize (*i*) on properties **(R1)** and **(R2)** that WSRM verifies and (*ii*) on its state-of-the-art performance for collective entity linking, in particular w.r.t. Ref [9].

A straightforward extension of WSRM to take into account paths between entities would consist in counting the paths between the entities e_i, e_j and e_i, e', instead of the properties r and r' respectively in Eq. 1. However, the resulting measure would loose **(R2)** as it would require to compute all the paths between the entities in the KB. To circumvent this issue and retain **(R2)**, one may be tempted to only count paths up to some typically small length, as it is well-known (e.g., [15]) that the longer a path between two entities, the weaker the semantics of the relation it encodes. Still, in this case, though clear, the semantics of the resulting measure is poor as it does not account for the strength of the paths between entities.

Instead, in addition to bounding the length of the paths we consider, we do aggregate the WSRM values of the successive entity pairs found along a path between two entities, so that the resulting value reflects how related these entities are through this particular path. Further, since many paths (with same or different lengths) may relate two entities, we also aggregate the individual relatedness values of these paths into a final entity relatedness score. Hereafter, the aggregation operator for the WSRM values found along a path is denoted $\otimes$, while the one for path scores is denoted $\oplus$. Tough typical candidate operators for $\otimes$ and $\oplus$ are either min and max, or product and sum, we chose fuzzy logic operators (discussed shortly) modeling the counterparts of the Boolean logical AND and OR operators in the [0, 1] interval (recall that WSRM values are also within this interval). We now discuss three strategies to combine path relatedness values, yielding a family of entity relatedness measures.

The first strategy consists in aggregating all paths of length m separately, and aims at showing the contribution of paths with different lengths when considered separately. Formally, we define the weighted semantic relatedness measure for path of length m between entities e_i and e_j as

$$\text{ASRMP}^a_m(e_i, e_j) = \oplus_{p \in e_i \rightsquigarrow e_j, |p|=m} \otimes_{k=1}^{|p|} \text{WSRM}(p_k, p_{k+1}), \tag{5}$$

where $e_i \rightsquigarrow e_j$ denotes the set of paths between e_i and e_j, here limited to paths of length m, and p_k is the kth entity along path p (hence $p_1 = e_i$ and $p_{|p|+1} = e_j$). The inner $\otimes$ operator aggregates the WSRM scores along the edges of a given path; the outer $\oplus$ operator aggregates scores obtained for different paths of length m between the two entities. The cost of the different aggregations is low, so $\text{ASRMP}^a_m(e_i, e_j)$ meets both **(R2)** and **(R3)**. It however only roughly meets **(R1)**, because the semantics is deteriorated by combining separately the paths of different lengths at a subsequent stage, e.g., in the entity linking process.

A second strategy consists in aggregating all paths of length less or equal m, as opposed to limiting ourselves to paths of a given length, extending Eq. 5 as

$$\text{ASRMP}^b_m(e_i, e_j) = \oplus_{p \in e_i \rightsquigarrow e_j, |p| \leq m} \otimes_{k=1}^{|p|} \text{WSRM}(p_k, p_{k+1}). \tag{6}$$

This measure provides a first approach to combining paths of different lengths, however assuming equal weight for all of them. This assumption seems unrealistic: intuitively, direct relations are expected to account for strong relations, while indirect ones are weaker, where the longer the path, the weaker the relation. We thus introduce a weight depending on the path length according to

$$\text{ASRMP}^c_m(e_i, e_j) = \sum_{l=1}^{m} \sum_{p \in e_i \rightsquigarrow e_j, |p|=l} w_l \otimes_{k=1}^{|p|} \text{WSRM}(p_k, p_{k+1}), \tag{7}$$

where w_l is a length-dependent weight roughly corresponding to the percentage of useful paths of length l and optimized by grid search. Thus, $\text{ASRMP}^b_m(e_i, e_j)$

meets the three requirements while $\text{ASRMP}^c_m(e_i, e_j)$ does not meet **(R1)**, because the semantics is once again deteriorated by the introduced weight.

Finally, all measures are made symmetrical according to

$$\psi^x_m(e_i, e_j) = \frac{1}{2}\left(\text{ASRMP}^x_m(e_i, e_j) + \text{ASRMP}^x_m(e_j, e_i)\right) \qquad x \in \{a, b, c\}. \quad (8)$$

The rationale for symmetrization is that in an RDF KB, if a triple (e_i, r, e_j) exists, the symmetric triple (e_j, r^-, e_i) may not exist at the same time, e.g., for r, r^- the symmetric properties 'hasWritten', 'writtenBy' respectively. This depends on the modeling choices adopted for the KB at design time.

Aggregating Scores with Fuzzy Logic. The score aggregators used in the definition of ASRMP^x_m are crucial: they have to be chosen so as to preserve the semantics of the relations between entities without introducing noise, i.e., semantic drift. The longer a path between two entities, the smaller should be the relatedness value because the link between the entities may become meaningless. Typically, a product of WSRM values along a path will quickly decrease, resulting into useless scores; the average score can be noisy. For two given entities with a direct link and indirect links, the average can also result in scores for paths of length $m > 1$ larger than the score for the direct link, which we assume to be semantically incorrect. Hence we advocate for fuzzy logic operators which provide a wide range of aggregators, such as the equivalent of the AND/OR logic operators for real values in the $[0, 1]$ interval. The semantics of the fuzzy operators is also important because it allows to explain the linking decisions and ensures **(R1)**.

Fuzzy logic, especially triangular norm fuzzy logic (*t-norm*) which guarantees triangular inequality in probabilistic spaces, generalizes intersection in a lattice and conjunction in logic, offering many aggregation operators to define conjunction for values within $[0, 1]$. Each t-norm operator is associated with an s-norm (t-conorm) with respect to De Morgan's law: $S(x, y) = 1 - T(1 - x, 1 - y)$. The t-norm is the standard semantics for conjunction in fuzzy logic and thus the couple t-norm/s-norm acts as AND/OR operators on real values in $[0, 1]$. Thus using fuzzy logic to define our relatedness measure allows to ensure its transitivity by definition and avoids the introduction of arbitrary weighting parameters like in $rel^{(k)}_{Excl}$.

As $\text{WSRM}(e, e') \in [0, 1]$, any t-norm/s-norm couple can be used to aggregate values along one path of length m and across all paths between two entities. We experimented with several couples of fuzzy operators: beside the classical min/max, we also consider the family of Hamacher t-norms (Hamacher product) defined for $\lambda \geq 0$ as

$$T_{\text{H},\lambda}(x, y) = \frac{xy}{\lambda + (1 - \lambda)(x + y - xy)}, \quad (9)$$

the family of Yager t-norms defined for $\lambda > 0$ as

$$T_{\text{Y},\lambda}(x, y) = \max \begin{cases} 0 \\ 1 - \sqrt[\lambda]{(1 - x)^\lambda + (1 - y)^\lambda} \end{cases} \quad (10)$$

and the Einstein sum

$$T_{\mathrm{E}}(x,y) = \frac{xy}{1+(1-x)(1-y)}. \tag{11}$$

The two families of t-norm used here are not exhaustive but generalize many t-norms: one can easily see that $T_{\mathrm{H},2}(x,y) = T_{\mathrm{E}}(x,y)$; $T_{\mathrm{H},1}(x,y)$ is known as the product t-norm; $T_{\mathrm{Y},1}(x,y)$ is the Łukasiewicz t-norm. We studied a large body of those operators and chose the one maximizing the accuracy of the collective linking system described hereunder.

4 Linking with Entity Relatedness Measure

We study the interest of the entity relatedness measure in the context of entity linking. In a general collective entity linking pipeline, semantic relatedness measures between entities are used at the end of the process to globally select the best candidate entity for each mention. They are typically used within a classifier along with features describing the mapping between the mention and the entity, to predict whether an entity is a good match (1) for a mention or not (0). The classifier operates independently on each mention-entity pair, and allows an ensemble of local classifications based on the relatedness of the entity to candidate entities of other mentions.

We briefly review the entity linking pipeline that we adopted. As in many previous pieces of work, e.g., [5,9,11,22,24], we do not consider the initial named entity recognition step, assuming perfect entity mention detection. The next step is the candidate entity generation stage, which consists in determining for each mention a reduced set of plausible entities that the mention could refer to. The final stage is the candidate selection stage, a.k.a. disambiguation, in which the best candidate is selected for each mention taking into account possible relations to candidates from other mentions.

In the remainder of this section, a document D is represented by its set of entity mentions, $D = (m_1, \ldots, m_n)$. For each mention m_i, $C(m_i) = (e_{i1}, \ldots, e_{ik})$ denotes the set of its candidate entities.

4.1 Knowledge Base

In this paper, we focus on two RDF KBs, namely Yago[2] and BaseKB[3], but however make use of Wikipedia for candidate generation for practical reasons, since the names of Wikipedia pages are meaningful unique identifiers unlike entities' labels in KB. BaseKB, derived from Freebase, contains over one billion facts (i.e., triples) about more than 40 millions subjects. Yago, derived from Wikipedia, WordNet and GeoNames, currently has knowledge of more than 10

[2] https://www.mpi-inf.mpg.de/departments/databases-and-information-systems/research/yago-naga/yago.

[3] http://basekb.com/.

million subjects and contains more than 120 million facts. Within those two KBs, interrelationships between entities bear precise semantics as specified by their schema. Contrary to Yago, BaseKB is saturated, i.e., all facts are made explicit with property instances thus circumventing the need for reasoning mechanisms. As, for practical reasons, we take advantage of Wikipedia in the candidate generation step, a mapping between Wikipedia and Yago or BaseKB entities is maintained. We also limit ourselves to entities appearing both in Wikipedia and in the RDF KB, resulting in approximately 2.5M entities in BaseKB and 3M entities in Yago.

Note that while BaseKB and Yago are used in this paper, there are no conceptual limitations to those KBs, ASRMP_m being able to account for any RDF KB schema.

4.2 Candidate Entity Generation

The generation of the candidate entities e_{ij} for each mention m_i in a document relies on Cross-Wiki, a dictionary computed from a Google crawl of the web that stores the frequency with which a mention links to a particular entity within Wikipedia. We used the same Cross-Wiki dictionary as in [12]. Each entry of the dictionary corresponds to a possible entity mention and provides a list of Wikipedia entities to which the mention points to, along with popularity scores. This list is directly used for candidate generation whenever a mention appears in the dictionary. The dictionary entries are normalized by removing all punctuation marks and converting to lower case. For mentions absent from Cross-Wiki, a query on Wikipedia was performed using the text of the mention, and the resulting Wikipedia pages were collected as the candidate entities.

4.3 Supervised Entity Selection

To select the best candidate entity $e_{i\hat{\jmath}}$ for each entity mention m_i in a document in a collective manner, we adopted a supervised approach similar to [9,22,27], where a classifier is trained to predict whether a mention and a candidate entity are related (1) or not (0). We used a binary logistic regression, denoted logreg(), applied independently on each mention-candidate entity pair, selecting for a mention m_i the candidate entity with the highest response from the classifier, i.e., $\hat{\jmath} = \arg\max_j \text{logreg}(m_i, e_{ij})$. We also experimented with different classifiers–see Sect. 5.3 for details–and the choice of a binary logistic regression is motivated by its simplicity and the fact that it turned out the best classification strategy. In our collective setting, the classifier relies on features describing the similarity between the mention and the entity on the one hand, and, on the other hand, the relatedness of the candidate entity under consideration with the candidate entities from other mentions in the document. The latter accounts for the context and ensures the collective aspect of the linking.

For the similarity between the mention and the candidate entity, we considered two features namely the cosine similarity between the vectors representations of the mention and of the entity name within Wikipedia, as obtained with word2vec [21], and the Wikipedia popularity as provided by Cross-Wiki.

For the relatedness of the candidate entity e_{ij} with candidate entities from other mentions, i.e., e_{kl} with $k \neq i$, we relied on an aggregation of the scores $\phi(e_{ij}, e_{kl})$ over the set of candidate entities $\cup_{k \neq i} C(m_k)$, where $\phi()$ is an entity relatedness measure (e.g., $rel^{(k)}_{Excl}$, WSRM, ASRMP), thus providing a global measure of how e_{ij} relates to other entity propositions in D. This aggregation is different from the one used to design our relatedness measure. We used sum and maximum aggregation, which has proven efficient in previous work. Formally, considering an entity relatedness $\phi()$, we define the sum aggregator as

$$S(e_{ij}; D) = \sum_{k=1, k \neq i}^{n} \sum_{e \in C(m_k)} \phi(e_{ij}, e), \tag{12}$$

and the maximum aggregators as

$$M^k(e_{ij}; D) = \max_{k=1, k \neq i}^{n} @\mathrm{k} \max_{e \in C(m_k)} \phi(e_{ij}, e) \tag{13}$$

where max @k is an operator returning the kth highest value. Note that the two aggregators are complementary: the sum provides a global averaged view while the max values emphasize good matches. We observed that retaining the sum, max@1, max@2 and max@3 aggregators as global features for the logistic regression worked best for the relatedness measure $\psi^a_1()$. We therefore retained the same strategy for $\psi^a_2()$, and $\psi^a_3()$ resulting in a total of 12 global features—namely S_m, $M^{(1)}_m$, $M^{(2)}_m$ and $M^{(3)}_m$ for $m = 1, 2, 3$—to represent the relatedness of a candidate entity with other possible entities in D. Experiments with $\psi^x_m()$ with $x \in \{b, c\}$, i.e., where different path lengths are already aggregated within ASRMP^x_m, involve only 4 global features, i.e., sum, max@1, max@2 and max@3. Thus ASRMP^a_m leverages 12 global features while ASRMP^b_m and ASRMP^c_m only use 4.

5 Experiments

In the remainder of the paper, we report on a set of experiments conducted to assess the benefit of our entity relatedness measure in a collective entity linking task. We are using different entity relatedness measures, within the same collective entity linking pipeline as described per Sect. 4. Experiments are mostly carried out on the TAC-KBP Entity Discovery and Linking (EDL) 2016–2017 datasets, two newswire and forum-discussion sets of documents originally collected for the TAC Knowledge Base Population Entity Discovery and Linking 2016 and 2017 international evaluation campaigns [16], which constitute the reference for the task of entity linking. Results are reported in terms of F1-score, where precision $P = \frac{|G \cap S|}{|S|}$ and recall $R = \frac{|G \cap S|}{|G|}$ are calculated between the linking in the gold-standard (G) and the linking given by a system (S). The 2016 version was used to learn the classifiers while the 2017 one served as test set. As the collective entity linking system is trained while only changing the entity relatedness measure, the linking accuracy can be used to evaluate the quality of the entity relatedness measure.

After providing implementation details in Sect. 5.1, selecting the best fuzzy aggregator in Sect. 5.2 and the best classification strategy in Sect. 5.3, we compare in Sect. 5.4 the various flavors of ASRMP_m seeking for the best one. The latter is compared to the entity relatedness measures used for entity linking in the literature in Sect. 5.5. Finally, we compare in Sect. 5.6 our collective entity linking system to a series of competing systems.

5.1 Implementation Details

Computing *all* the paths of length m between *every* pair of entities in the KB can be computationally expensive. For instance, in BaseKB, and after data cleansing, there are approximately 13M paths of length one and 46B paths of length two. We designed an efficient way of doing so, taking advantage of a relational database management system—which offers today much more tuning opportunities than RDF data management systems, e.g., various indices, clustered tables, etc.—to store edges and their semantic relatedness weights.

In PostgreSQL 11.2[4], a table $\texttt{edges}(\texttt{e}_1, \texttt{e}_2, \texttt{v})$ is used to store the pairs of entities (e_1, e_2) directly connected through some property in the KB, along with the corresponding WSRM value v. This table is dictionary-encoded (entity names are replaced by integers) to save space and speed up value comparisons, indexed by (e_1, e_2) and (e_2, e_1) values to offer many options to the PostgreSQL optimizer. Limiting ourselves to path lengths $m \leq 4$, the four tables $\texttt{path1}(\texttt{e}_1, \texttt{e}_2, \texttt{v}_1)$, $\texttt{path2}(\texttt{e}_1, \texttt{e}_2, \texttt{v}_1, \texttt{v}_2)$, $\texttt{path3}(\texttt{e}_1, \texttt{e}_2, \texttt{v}_1, \texttt{v}_2, \texttt{v}_3)$ and $\texttt{path4}(\texttt{e}_1, \texttt{e}_2, \texttt{v}_1, \texttt{v}_2, \texttt{v}_3, \texttt{v}_4)$ are efficiently created from the edge table using SQL queries, to represent paths of length 1, 2, 3 and 4 respectively. The entities e_1 and e_2 are restricted to the candidate entities for the entity mentions found in the TAC-KBP2016-2017 datasets: entities along the paths may however not be candidate entities. The values v_i are the WSRM values along the path.

In BaseKB, we obtained 53K one-, 11M two- and 2B three-edges paths, from which we computed the various ASRMP_m, relatedness values. We were not able to compute paths of length four, as the number of paths exploded. The same process was applied to Yago and we obtained 28K one-, 845K two-, 25M three- and 679M four-edges paths. Paths of length four could be computed due to the cleanliness and the higher structure of Yago.

5.2 Comparing Fuzzy Logic Aggregators

One crucial issue for paths of length $m > 1$ lies in the aggregation of the semantic relatedness measure of each edge along the path and of the relatedness measure over multiple paths between two entities. ASRMP_m reflects entity relatedness

[4] https://www.postgresql.org.

in the KB at hand: obviously, an aggregation of its values should reflect similar properties. Moreover, and in order to avoid a semantic drift, the resulting value of the aggregation for one path of length m must be smaller than that of a path of length $m - 1$ since the latter bears stronger semantics. Finally, because there can be many paths between two entities, one needs also to aggregate the values of the different paths connecting two given entities.

Experimental results (not reported here for lack of space) show that $T_{\text{H},0}(x, y)$ is the best aggregator with the collective linking setting in this paper. We however experimentally observed only minor differences between the Hammacher and Yager t-norms and various values of λ. In the remainder, $T_{\text{H},0}(x, y)$ with its associated s-norm is used for the aggregation of paths of length $m \in \{2, 3, 4\}$ between two entities.

5.3 Comparing Classifiers

We compared several classifiers within our collective entity linking system. In addition to popular classification techniques such as k-nearest neighbours (KNN), decision trees (DT), logistic regression (REG) or support vector machines (SVM), we also experimented with gradient boosting (GB). The latter was used in previous work on entity relatedness for entity linking [27,28]. Results reported in Table 2 for ASRMP^a_m, $m \in \{1, 2, 3, 4\}$, on the TAC-KBP dataset using either BaseKB or (saturated) Yago as KB, clearly show that the logistic regression classification strategy turns out to be the best option overall, in particular when considering paths of length 2 or more.

Table 2. F1-scores for various classifiers within the entity linking system for TAC-KBP.

Approach	BaseKB					Yago					Yago + Saturation				
	KNN	DT	GB	SVM	REG	KNN	DT	GB	SVM	REG	KNN	DT	GB	SVM	REG
ASRMP_1	49.58	47.71	79.59	79.19	**80.03**	49.64	47.51	79.67	79.75	**79.88**	50.46	47.58	**80.05**	79.60	79.94
ASRMP^a_2	50.00	47.10	79.75	79.82	**80.79**	49.13	47.02	**80.93**	79.52	80.71	49.46	46.99	79.09	80.15	**80.78**
ASRMP^a_3	50.02	47.24	80.20	80.12	**80.60**	49.48	46.79	80.36	79.66	**80.40**	50.33	46.74	79.42	79.62	**80.67**
ASRMP^a_4	–	–	–	–	–	50.20	46.78	78.56	80.40	**80.98**	49.43	46.79	80.51	80.78	**81.34**

5.4 Comparing Aggregation Strategies

We also compared the aggregation strategies described in Sect. 3, reporting in Fig. 1 the F1-score as a function of m for the various strategies: distinct ASRMP^a_m measures for each value of m (including length four for Yago) aggregated by the classifier; aggregation with fuzzy logic as defined by ASRMP^b_m; explicit weighting as in ASRMP^c_m optimized by grid search. In most cases, better performance is achieved for $m = 2$, diminishing for $m > 2$, which confirms that paths longer than 2 mostly bring noise because of a semantic drift. This is particularly visible in Fig. 1b. Classifier-based fusion, Fig. 1a, however

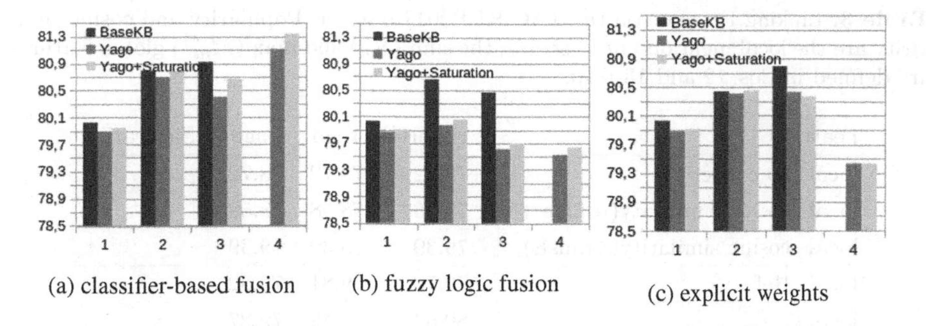

(a) classifier-based fusion (b) fuzzy logic fusion (c) explicit weights

Fig. 1. Linking F1-score for various aggregation strategies. (Color figure online)

seems to keep increasing for $m = 3$ on BaseKB, but the gain is only minimal between $m = 2$ and $m = 3$ and is counterbalanced by the computational cost (see Sect. 5.5), specially for BaseKB. Interestingly, for explicit weighting, the weights w_l can be seen as the strength of the paths with length l. We found that the optimal values of w_l decrease when l increases, i.e., $w_2 = 1$, $w_3 = 0.1$ and $w_4 = 0.1$ for Yago. These different aggregation studies show that fuzzy aggregator (Fig. 1b) and explicit weights (Fig. 1c) are more robust for combining paths of different lengths, while the classifier-based fusion (Fig. 1a) is more accurate though it introduces noise for paths of length > 2. For example, in both Fig. 1b and c paths of length four are always adding noise, when considered with Yago and Yago saturated. With respect to the entity linking task, ASRMP_m^a with classifier-based fusion appears the best strategy. In all generality and contrary to ASRMP_m^b, this strategy only loosely verifies **(R1)** as classifier-based fusion can be difficult to interpret. In this regard, logistic regression nevertheless offers interesting properties, with coefficients and intercepts that can be interpreted to some extent.

5.5 Comparisons of Entity Relatedness Measures

We now concentrate on the study of (the different components of) ASRMP_m^a, $m > 1$, with classifier-based fusion, and how it compares with other relatedness measures, namely WSRM [9], cosine similarity [3,25] and Ref [1,18]. All measures are used within the same collective entity linking system as input features to the classifier, thus providing fair comparison of the entity relatedness measures. Results are gathered in Table 3 for BaseKB, Yago and Yago saturated, reporting linking accuracy (F1-score). The different measures compared are:

- Local performs linking using only the two local features depicting the adequacy of the mention and the entity—see Sect. 4.3—thus not considering entity relatedness
- Cosine similarity(kernel), the kernel being either rdf2vec [25] or TransE [3], measures entity relatedness as the cosine similarity between the entities embedded in a high-dimension space with the given kernel
- Ref [1,18] considers the Ref entity relatedness measure as defined in Eq. 1

Table 3. Linking F1-score on the TAC-KBP2017 dataset. Popularity and cosine similarity are the local mention-entity scores; the sum (S_m) and max ($M_m^{(k)}$) global features are defined in Eqs. 12 and 13 resp.

Features	BaseKB	Yago	Yago + Saturation
local (no collective)	78.72	78.72	78.72
local+cosine similarity(rdf2vec)	78.58	78.58	78.58
local+cosine similarity(TransE)	79.39	79.39	79.39
local+Ref	79.70	79.81	79.82
local+$rel_{Excl}^{(5)}$	80.54	80.49	79.27
$\text{ASRMP}_1 = \text{local} + S_1 + M_1^{(k)}$	80.03	79.88	79.94
$\text{ASRMP}_1 + S_2$	80.02	80.02	80.12
$\text{ASRMP}_1 + M_2^{(k)}$	80.68	80.69	**80.78**
$\text{ASRMP}_2^a = \text{ASRMP}_1 + S_2 + M_2^{(k)}$	80.79	80.71	**80.78**
$\text{ASRMP}_2^a + S_3$	**80.92**	**80.77**	80.77
$\text{ASRMP}_2^a + M_3^{(k)}$	80.55	80.35	80.76
$\text{ASRMP}_3^a = \text{ASRMP}_2^a + S_3 + M_3^{(k)}$	80.60	80.40	80.67
$\text{local} + S_2 + M_2^{(k)}$	80.16	80.60	80.52
$\text{local} + S_3 + M_3^{(k)}$	80.42	79.46	79.27

- $Rel_{Excl}^{(5)}$ [15] uses entity relatedness as defined in Eq. 4 with $k = 5$
- WSRM [9], which is equivalent to ASRMP_1, where only direct paths are used to measure entity relatedness
- ASRMP_m^a which embed basic reasoning mechanisms accounting for paths of length $m > 1$.

Adding paths of length 2 allows a slight increase of the linking accuracy, where the best score for ASRMP_2^a is obtained using both S_2 and $M_2^{(k)}$ for $k = 1, 2, 3$ (row ASRMP_2^a). Looking separately at the benefit of the aggregators S_2 and $M_2^{(k)}$ across couples of candidate entities, we see that considering only the maximum increases the accuracy of the ASRMP_1 system but, as it reflects the predominant topic, mentions that are far from that general topic can be incorrectly linked. Meanwhile, using S_2 can be slightly worse than ASRMP_1 only (e.g., on BaseKB, not on Yago) because this aggregator reflects choosing the mean topic which can be very vague. Combining both seems to be a compromise between the two extreme cases. On the other hand, ASRMP_2^a is better than both WSRM [9] and $Rel_{Excl}^{(5)}$ [15] showing the interest of using a well founded entity relatedness measure along with property paths.

Paths of length 3 can further be successfully combined with the features used for ASRMP_2^a when S_3 is considered; while using $M_3^{(k)}$, either alone or with S_3, seems to introduce noise in the linking decision. This counter-intuitive result can be explained by the fact that introducing path of length three adds limited relevant semantics into the relatedness measure. As an outcome, considering

Table 4. Time in (min.) for different entity relatedness measures.

	$TransE$	$rel^{(5)}_{Excl}$	Ref	$\mathrm{ASRMP}_1 = \mathrm{WSRM}$	ASRMP^a_2	ASRMP^a_3
BaseKB	15.29	1680	13.33	13.85	20,94	418,85
Yago	0.84	507	0.58	0.59	6.75	9.17
Yago + Saturation	0.79	403	0.57	0.69	6.14	8.60

the predominant entities only (max aggregators) tends to take strong linking decision and can be more drastic than adding vague links, mostly for entities that were not linked with the aggregation of ASRMP_1 and ASRMP^a_2.

From the complexity point of view, relatedness measures are computed offline for a static KB (a given version of Yago or BaseKB). Meanwhile ASRMP^x_m can easily be computed for lower values of m making it tractable and more suitable for dynamic scenario where entities are added to or removed from the KB, unlike rel^k_{Excl} where top-k path has to be computed, or cosine similarity where the kernel embedding has to be retrained. Table 4 shows the computation time for the different entity relatedness measures, including the offline part. For small values of m, which are required in practice, Ref, ASRMP^a_m, and $TransE$ have low computation cost, while rel^k_{Excl} has high computation cost due to the need to compute top-k best paths. Thus we can conclude that ASRMP^a_m meets **(R2)**, and more generally that ASRMP^x_m with $x \in \{a, b, c\}$ meets **(R2)**. They indeed have similar computation times: most of the time is spent in computing paths of length up to m, while aggregating path scores is very fast.

We also studied the impact of the saturation of the KB using Yago. As shown in Table 3 (columns 3 and 4) and in Fig. 1 (red and yellow bars), the gain is very limited in the case of TAC-KBP2017 dataset. In practice, this result saves the explicit computation of the implicit triples in the RDF KB.

5.6 Comparison of Entity Linking Systems

We finally compared the collective entity linking system based on ASRMP^a_m with prominent state-of-the-art methods over standard benchmarks: NCEL [5], AIDA [13], PHoH [11] and CEL-WSRM [9]. All follow the classical three stage architecture for collective entity linking. CEL-WSRM [9] is based on the WSRM entity relatedness measure (Eq. 1), equivalent to ASRMP_1. Results of the entity linking process, evaluated in terms of micro-averaged F1 classification scores, are reported in Table 5. These results were obtained with the Yago KB that allows considering paths of length up to 4. Similar results are obtained when the Yago KB is saturated. On all four datasets, the proposed method CEL-ASRMP^a_m, $m \in \{2, 3, 4\}$, does outperform the NCEL, AIDA and PBoH collective linking approaches by a large margin. The proposed method is better than CEL-WSRM on the four datasets, with small improvement on the RSS-500 dataset. Moreover, we observe the same conclusion as before: paths of length two improve the accuracy of the linking, while longer paths may add noise.

Table 5. Micro-averaged F1 score for different collective entity linking systems on four standard datasets.

Approach	AIDA-A	AIDA-B	Reuters128	RSS-500
NCEL [5]	79.0	80.0	–	–
AIDA [13]	74.3	76.5	56.6	65.5
PBoH [11]	79.4	80.0	68.3	55.3
CEL-ASRMP$_1$ =CEL-WSRM	90.6	87.7	76.6	76.4
CEL-ASRMP$_2^a$	**93.8**	**91.0**	77.5	**76.6**
CEL-ASRMP$_3^a$	93.4	90.6	**78.5**	**76.6**
CEL-ASRMP$_4^a$	93.1	90.3	76.6	74.6

6 Conclusions

In summary, we extended previous measures of entity relatedness within a knowledge base to account for indirect relations between entities through the consideration of property paths. The measure that we proposed is the first to satisfy the three good properties that such measures should have: clear semantics, reasonable computational cost and transitivity. We experimentally showed its benefit in a collective entity linking task, where paths of length 2 and 3 bring improvement over the state of the art in collective entity linking, using either only direct connections between entities [9] or previous work on path-based relatedness measures [15]. In theory, the scalability of ASRMP$_m$ varies in inverse proportion with the length of the paths. We however proved it to be still tractable for reasonable sized datasets with paths of length up to 3, which is sufficient in practice as longer paths add noise.

This contribution opens up new horizons towards fully exploiting the semantics of RDF knowledge bases for entity linking, when only relatedness measures are used. Taking a historical perspective, this task was first conventionally addressed leveraging entity relatedness measures based on Wikipedia hyperlinks counts between two pages and on the presence of one relation between two entities in the KB. WSRM (=ASRMP$_1$) made use of KB semantics by weighting the relatedness between entities exploiting the basic properties within the KB. The ASRMP$_m$ extension proposed here further introduces (basic) reasoning mechanisms that exploit the graph-structure of the KB alongside robust aggregators for paths of arbitrary length. In this work, all paths were considered regardless of their precise semantics. In specific application contexts, this could be improved by selecting paths between two entities that are semantically meaningful in this context, e.g., using ontological knowledge and reasoning.

References

1. Alhelbawy, A., Gaizauskas, R.: Graph ranking for collective named entity disambiguation. In: 52nd Annual Meeting of the Association for Computational Linguistics, Baltimore, Maryland, USA, vol. 2, pp. 75–80 (2014)

2. Blanco, R., Ottaviano, G., Meij, E.: Fast and space-efficient entity linking for queries. In: 8th ACM International Conference on Web Search and Data Mining, Shanghai, China, pp. 179–188 (2015)
3. Bordes, A., Usunier, N., Garcia-Duran, A., Weston, J., Yakhnenko, O.: Translating embeddings for modeling multi-relational data. In: 27th Advances in Neural Information Processing Systems, Lake Tahoe, Nevada, USA, pp. 2787–2795 (2013)
4. Bunescu, R., Paşca, M.: Using encyclopedic knowledge for named entity disambiguation. In: 11th Conference of the European Chapter of the Association for Computational Linguistics, Trento, Italy, pp. 9–16 (2006)
5. Cao, Y., Hou, L., Li, J., Liu, Z.: Neural collective entity linking. In: 27th International Conference on Computational Linguistics, Santa Fe, New Mexico, USA, pp. 675–686 (2018)
6. Cucerzan, S.: Large-scale named entity disambiguation based on Wikipedia data. In: Joint Conference on Empirical Methods in Natural Language Processing and Computational Natural Language Learning, Prague, Czech Republic, pp. 708–716 (2007)
7. Detyniecki, M.: Mathematical aggregation operators and their application to video querying. Ph.D. thesis, Univ. Paris 6 (2000)
8. Durrett, G., Klein, D.: A joint model for entity analysis: coreference, typing, and linking. Trans. Assoc. Comput. Linguist. **2**, 477–490 (2014)
9. El Vaigh, C.B., Goasdoué, F., Gravier, G., Sébillot, P.: Using knowledge base semantics in context-aware entity linking. In: ACM Symposium on Document Engineering 2019, Berlin, Germany, pp. 8:1–8:10 (2019)
10. Francis-Landau, M., Durrett, G., Klein, D.: Capturing semantic similarity for entity linking with convolutional neural networks. In: 15th Annual Conference of the North American Chapter of the Association for Computational Linguistics: Human Language Technologies, San Diego, CA, USA, pp. 1256–1261 (2016)
11. Ganea, O.E., Ganea, M., Lucchi, A., Eickhoff, C., Hofmann, T.: Probabilistic bag-of-hyperlinks model for entity linking. In: 25th International Conference on World Wide Web, Montréal, Québec, Canada, pp. 927–938 (2016)
12. Gupta, N., Singh, S., Roth, D.: Entity linking via joint encoding of types, descriptions, and context. In: 2017 Conference on Empirical Methods in Natural Language Processing, Copenhagen, Denmark, pp. 2681–2690 (2017)
13. Hoffart, J., et al.: Robust disambiguation of named entities in text. In: 2011 Conference on Empirical Methods in Natural Language Processing, Edinburgh, Scotland, UK, pp. 782–792 (2011)
14. Huang, H., Heck, L., Ji, H.: Leveraging deep neural networks and knowledge graphs for entity disambiguation. arXiv preprint arXiv:1504.07678 (2015)
15. Hulpuş, I., Prangnawarat, N., Hayes, C.: Path-based semantic relatedness on linked data and its use to word and entity disambiguation. In: Arenas, M., et al. (eds.) ISWC 2015. LNCS, vol. 9366, pp. 442–457. Springer, Cham (2015). https://doi.org/10.1007/978-3-319-25007-6_26
16. Ji, H., et al.: Overview of TAC-KBP2017 13 languages entity discovery and linking. In: Text Analysis Conference, Gaithersburg, Maryland, USA (2017)
17. Le, P., Titov, I.: Improving entity linking by modeling latent relations between mentions. In: 56th Annual Meeting of the Association for Computational Linguistics, Melbourne, Australia, pp. 1595–1604 (2018)
18. Ling, X., Singh, S., Weld, D.S.: Design challenges for entity linking. Trans. Assoc. Comput. Linguist. **3**, 315–328 (2015)
19. Liu, M., Gong, G., Qin, B., Liu, T.: A multi-view-based collective entity linking method. ACM Trans. Inf. Syst. **37**(2), 23:1–23:29 (2019)

20. Mendes, P.N., Jakob, M., García-Silva, A., Bizer, C.: DBpedia spotlight: shedding light on the web of documents. In: 7th International Conference on Semantic Systems, Graz, Austria, pp. 1–8 (2011)
21. Mikolov, T., Sutskever, I., Chen, K., Corrado, G.S., Dean, J.: Distributed representations of words and phrases and their compositionality. In: Advances in Neural Information Processing Systems, Lake Tahoe, Nevada, USA, pp. 3111–3119 (2013)
22. Moreno, J.G., et al.: Combining word and entity embeddings for entity linking. In: Blomqvist, E., Maynard, D., Gangemi, A., Hoekstra, R., Hitzler, P., Hartig, O. (eds.) ESWC 2017. LNCS, vol. 10249, pp. 337–352. Springer, Cham (2017). https://doi.org/10.1007/978-3-319-58068-5_21
23. Pennington, J., Socher, R., Manning, C.: GloVe: global vectors for word representation. In: 2014 Conference on Empirical Methods in Natural Language Processing, Doha, Qatar, pp. 1532–1543 (2014)
24. Phan, M.C., Sun, A., Tay, Y., Han, J., Li, C.: Pair-linking for collective entity disambiguation: two could be better than all. IEEE Trans. Knowl. Data Eng. **31**, 1383–1396 (2018)
25. Ristoski, P., Rosati, J., Di Noia, T., De Leone, R., Paulheim, H.: RDF2Vec: RDF graph embeddings and their applications. Semant. Web **10**(4), 721–752 (2019)
26. Wang, H., Zheng, J.G., Ma, X., Fox, P., Ji, H.: Language and domain independent entity linking with quantified collective validation. In: 2015 Conference on Empirical Methods in Natural Language Processing, Lisbon, Portugal, pp. 695–704 (2015)
27. Yamada, I., Shindo, H., Takeda, H., Takefuji, Y.: Joint learning of the embedding of words and entities for named entity disambiguation. In: 20th SIGNLL Conference on Computational Natural Language Learning, Berlin, Germany, pp. 250–259 (2016)
28. Yang, Y., İrsoy, O., Rahman, K.S.: Collective entity disambiguation with structured gradient tree boosting. In: 2018 Conference of the North American Chapter of the Association for Computational Linguistics: Human Language Technologies, New Orleans, Louisiana, USA, pp. 777–786 (2018)

Enhancing Online Knowledge Graph Population with Semantic Knowledge

Dèlia Fernàndez-Cañellas[1,2](✉), Joan Marco Rimmek[1], Joan Espadaler[1], Blai Garolera[1], Adrià Barja[1], Marc Codina[1], Marc Sastre[1], Xavier Giro-i-Nieto[2], Juan Carlos Riveiro[1], and Elisenda Bou-Balust[1]

[1] Vilynx, Inc., Barcelona, Spain
delia@vilynx.com

[2] Universitat Politecnica de Catalunya (UPC), Barcelona, Spain

Abstract. Knowledge Graphs (KG) are becoming essential to organize, represent and store the world's knowledge, but they still rely heavily on humanly-curated structured data. Information Extraction (IE) tasks, like disambiguating entities and relations from unstructured text, are key to automate KG population. However, Natural Language Processing (NLP) methods alone can not guarantee the validity of the facts extracted and may introduce erroneous information into the KG. This work presents an end-to-end system that combines Semantic Knowledge and Validation techniques with NLP methods, to provide KG population of novel facts from clustered news events. The contributions of this paper are two-fold: First, we present a novel method for including entity-type knowledge into a Relation Extraction model, improving F1-Score over the baseline with TACRED and TypeRE datasets. Second, we increase the precision by adding data validation on top of the Relation Extraction method. These two contributions are combined in an industrial pipeline for automatic KG population over aggregated news, demonstrating increased data validity when performing online learning from unstructured web data. Finally, the TypeRE and AggregatedNewsRE datasets build to benchmark these results are also published to foster future research in this field.

Keywords: Knowledge Graph · Relation extraction · Data validation

1 Introduction

Knowledge Graphs (KG) play a crucial role for developing many intelligent industrial applications, like search, question answering or recommendation systems. However, most of KG are incomplete and need continuous enrichment and data curation in order to keep up-to-date with world's dynamics. Automatically detecting, structuring and augmenting a KG with new facts from text is therefore essential for constructing and maintaining KGs. This is the task of Knowledge Graph Population, which usually encompasses two main Information

J. Z. Pan et al. (Eds.): ISWC 2020, LNCS 12506, pp. 183–200, 2020.
https://doi.org/10.1007/978-3-030-62419-4_11

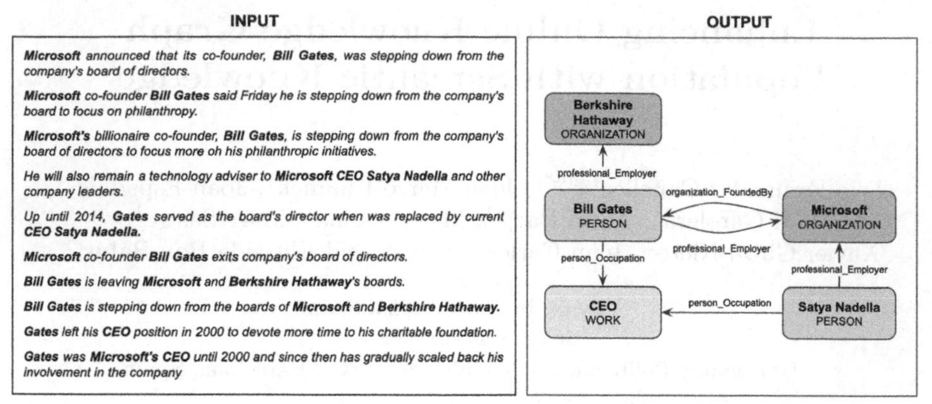

Fig. 1. Example of graph constructed from sentences from aggregated news articles.

Extraction (IE) sub-tasks: (1) Named Entity Recognition and Disambiguation (NERD) [16,29], consisting on identifying entities from a KG in unstructured texts; and (2) Relation Extraction [13,39], which seeks to extract semantic relations between the detected entities in the text. Over the last years, the Natural Language Processing (NLP) community has accomplished great advances regarding these IE tasks [3,28]. However, the information extracted by these systems is imperfect, and may compromise KGs data veracity and integrity when performing a population task. On the other hand, the Semantic Web community has provided semantic technologies to express how the world is structured. For example, ontology languages like OWL[1] represent complex knowledge and relations between things, and constraint mechanisms like SHACL[2] specify rules and can detect data constraints violations. When building ontology-driven IE systems, these semantic techniques can be applied to asses data veracity and detect false positives before adding erroneous information into the KG.

In this work, we explore opportunities in the intersection between NLP and Semantic technologies, and demonstrate how combining both modalities can provide improved data quality. Semantic technologies are applied both at subsystem level (by introducing entity-type knowledge in a relation extraction model), as well as at system level (by adding data validation techniques to an end-to-end KG population system from clustered news events).

We propose a novel KG population approach, which learns over aggregated news articles to keep up to date an industrial KG based on mass media. Aggregated news are clusters of news articles describing the same story. While web-based news aggregators such as *Google News* or *Yahoo! News* present these events with headlines and short descriptions, we aim towards presenting this information as relational facts that can facilitate relational queries. As shown in Fig. 1,

[1] https://www.w3.org/TR/owl-ref/.
[2] https://www.w3.org/TR/shacl/.

the system ingests unstructured text from these news stories as input and produces an RDF[3] graph as output. We propose learning from aggregated news as a more reliable way to learn from unstructured web data than from free crawled data. This approach also achieves triple redundancy, which is later exploited by the validation techniques.

The contributions of this work can be summarized as: a) A method to introduce entity-type knowledge into a deep relation extraction model, which shows strong performance on TACRED [1,40] benchmark and on TypeRE[4], a new relation extraction dataset presented in this work. b) The addition of a validation module into an automatic KG population system, which exploits the context and redundancy from aggregated news. We show how this validation highly increases overall data quality on the new AggregatedNewsRE[5] dataset presented.

The paper is organized as follows. Section 2 presents related work. In Sect. 3, we provide an overview of the aforementioned automatic KG population system. Section 4 describes the approaches taken to add entity-types knowledge on the relation extraction model. In Sect. 5 we explain the validation techniques added to the system in order to provide increased accuracy in automatic KG population from aggregated news. Experimental evaluation and datasets made public are described in Sect. 6. Finally, Sect. 7 includes conclusions and future work.

2 Related Work

In this work, we present an end-to-end system which automatically populates a KG using unstructured text from aggregated news. To implement this system, we study how to exploit semantic knowledge to improve data quality, in conjunction with a relation extraction model. Following our contributions, in this section we will overview literature on automatic KG population (Sect. 2.1), relation extraction (Sect. 2.2), and data validation (Sect. 2.3).

2.1 Automatic KG Population

Information Extraction (IE) fills the gap between machine understandable languages (e.g. RDF, OWL), used by Semantic Web technologies, and natural language (NL), used by humans [27]. Literature differentiates between two main IE approaches: (1) *Open IE*, when extraction is not constrained to any ontology, e.g. Reverb [7], OLLIE [28] or PRISMATIC [8]; and (2) *Closed IE*, when extraction is constrained to a fixed ontology or schema, e.g. NELL [22] or Knowledge Vault [6]. Our system is similar to methods from the second group, which extract facts in the form of disambiguated triples. However, all mentioned methods learn from web crawling, while our system performs population from aggregated news. Similar approaches are taken by event-encoding systems, like ICEWS[6]

[3] https://www.w3.org/RDF/.
[4] https://figshare.com/articles/dataset/TypeRE_Dataset/12850154.
[5] https://figshare.com/articles/dataset/AggregatedNewsRE_Dataset/12850682.
[6] https://www.icews.com/.

and GDELT[7]. These systems extract international political incidents from news media and update their knowledge graphs online, making them applicable to real-time conflict analysis. Other news-based systems are: RDFLiveNews [12], which extracts triples from unstructured news streams and maps the relations found to DBPedia properties; and VLX-Stories [10], which, like our system, performs automatic population from aggregated news, but focus on detecting emerging entities, instead of new triples.

2.2 Relation Extraction

One of the main tasks when populating a KG is relation extraction, which consists on extracting semantic relationships from text. Closed IE approaches treat this task as a classification problem: given a pair of entities co-occurring in a text segment, we want to classify its relation into one of the predefined relation types. Recent improvements in pre-trained language models (LM), like BERT [5], have established a new trend when solving this task. R-BERT [36] presents an architecture that uses markers to indicate entity spans in the input and incorporates a neural architecture on top of BERT to add information from the target entities. A similar input configuration is presented in Soares et al. [30], by using *Entity Markers*. Moreover, they test different output configurations and obtain state-of-the-art results when training with *Matching the Blanks* (MTB) method. Inspired by these previous works, SpanBERT [17] has been proposed as an extension of BERT that uses a pre-training configuration which masks spans instead of tokens. Other works like ERNIE [41], KG-BERT [37] or KnowBert [24] propose enhanced language representations by incorporating external knowledge from KGs.

2.3 RDF Validation

When constructing a KG, its data is only valuable if it is accurate and without contradictions. Requirements for evaluating data quality may differ across communities, fields, and applications, but nearly all systems require some form of data validation. Following this approach, different works analyzed the consequences of errors in KGs and established recommendations [15,32]. The detection of inconsistencies and errors in public KGs has also become the subject of various studies during the past years. Many works analyzed errors in public semantic resources like DBPedia and Wikidata, and proposed automatic methods to detect them [31,33]. There are different RDF validation languages to define these constraints, but shape approaches like ShEx [11], SHACL [18] and ReSh [26] are the ones receiving the greatest community support and advanced features [32]. In particular, SHACL (Shapes Constraint Language), has become the latest standard and the W3C recommended system for validation of RDF graphs. Following these recommendations and to maintain a high level of data integrity in our KG, in this work we will describe the integration of a SHACL validation module into our KG population system.

[7] https://www.gdeltproject.org/.

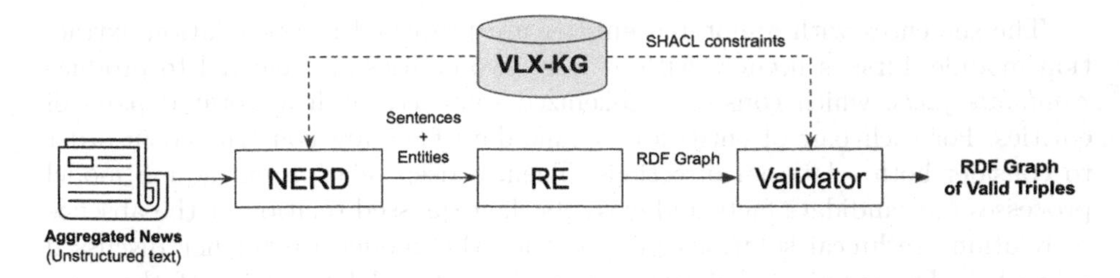

Fig. 2. KG Population framework. The system ingests unstructured text from aggregated news and extracts an RDF graph of valid triples. It is composed by three modules: Named Entity Recognition and Disambiguation (NERD), Relation Extraction (RE) and a Triple Validator.

3 System Overview

This section describes the proposed end-to-end KG population framework, displayed in Fig. 2. The system transforms unstructured text from aggregated news articles to a structured knowledge representation. The architecture is composed by a KG and three main processing components: 1) Named Entity Recognition and Disambiguation (NERD), 2) Relation Extraction (RE), and 3) Validator.

The input of the system are aggregated news. In this work, we understand as aggregated news a set of clustered articles that discuss the same event or story. These clusters are created by VLX-Stories [10] news aggregator. This external system provides unified text consisting on the aggregated articles.

The KG integrated into the current population system is the *Vilynx's*[8] *Knowledge Graph.* (VLX-KG) [9,10]. This KG contains encyclopedic knowledge, as it is constructed by merging different public knowledge resources: Freebase [2], Wikidata [35] and Wikipedia[9]. Its schema is inspired by Wikidata, and consists on 160 entity-types with 21 root-types, and 126 different relations. It also provides multilingual alias for over 3M entities, and 9M relations between entities. In the presented system, VLX-KG is used to disambiguate entities in the NERD module, define the possible relations to extract in the relation extractor and the SHACL constrains used in the validator.

The NERD module splits the input text, coming from the news aggregator, in sentences and detects KG entities appearing in these sentences. The output of this module are sentences with annotated entities. In this work we are using Vilynx's NERD, which combines Spacy's[10] library and models for Name Entity Recognition (NER) and Part of Speech Tagging (POST), with an Entity Disambiguation algorithm based ino our previous work, ViTS citech11fernandez2017vits. However, any NERD system could be adapted for this task.

[8] https://www.vilynx.com/.
[9] https://www.wikipedia.org/.
[10] https://spacy.io/.

The sentences with annotated entities are processed in the relation extraction module. First, sentences with at least two entities are selected to produce *candidate facts*, which consist of tokenized sentences with annotated pairs of entities. For each pair of entities two candidate facts are constructed in order to consider both relational directions. Then, a deep relation extraction model processes the candidate facts and extracts the expressed relation or the absence of relation. Technical solutions proposed for this model are further discussed in Sect. 4. The extracted relations are expressed as RDF triples of the form ⟨*subject, predicate, object*⟩, and interconnected into an RDF graph.

Finally, the extracted RDF graph is validated with our SHACL constraints, in the Validator module. During validation, we enhance results thanks to the redundancy and contextual information from aggregated news. In Sect. 5 we give a detailed description of the constraints applied and the validation process. The output of this module and the whole pipeline is an RDF graph of valid triples.

4 Relation Extraction

Relation extraction is the task of predicting the relations or properties expressed between two entities, directly from the text. Semantics define different types of entities and how these may relate to each other. Previous works [4,25] have already shown that entity-type information is useful for constraining the possible categories of a relation. For instance, family-related relations like *Parents* or *Siblings* can only occur between entities of type *Person*, while *Residence* relation must occur between entities of type *Person* and a *Location*. Recent advances in NLP have shown strong improvements on relation extraction when using deep models, specially deep transformers [34]. In this section, we explore different input configurations for adding entity-type information when predicting relations with BERT [5], a pre-trained deep transformer model which is currently giving state-of-the-art results when adapted for relation extraction. The remainder of the section starts by defining the relation extraction task (Sect. 4.1). Later we introduce *Type Markers* (Sect. 4.2), our novel proposal to encode the root type of the entities. We finish the section by presenting the different input model configurations proposed to add *Type Markers* (Sect. 4.3).

4.1 Task Definition

In the relation extraction task we want to learn mappings from candidate facts to relation types $r \in R$, where R is a fixed dictionary of relation types. We add the no-relation category, to denote lack of relation between the entities in the candidate fact. In our particular implementation, a candidate fact $(\mathbf{x}, \mathbf{e}_1, \mathbf{e}_2)$ is composed by a set of tokens $\mathbf{x} = [x_0 ... x_n]$ from a sentence s, with a pair of entity mentions located at $\mathbf{e}_1 = (i, j)$ and $\mathbf{e}_2 = (k, l)$, being pairs of integers such that $0 < i \leq j$, $j < n$, $k \leq l$ and $l < n$. Start and end markers, $x_0 = [CLS]$ and $x_n = [SEP]$ respectively, are added to indicate the beginning and end of

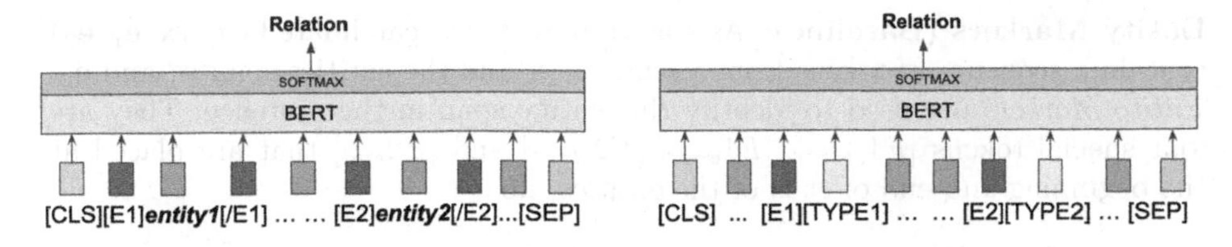

Fig. 3. Entity Markers [30]

Fig. 4. Type Markers only

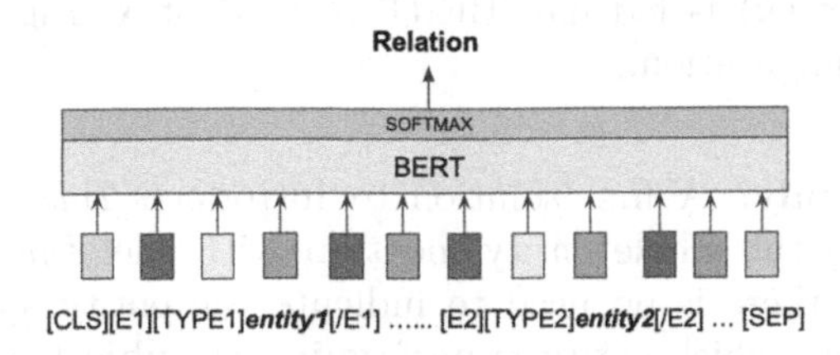

Fig. 5. Entity and Type Markers

the sentence tokens. Our goal is, thus, to learn a function $r = f(\mathbf{x}, \mathbf{e}_1, \mathbf{e}_2)$ that maps the candidate fact to the relation type expressed in $\mathbf{x}$ between the entities marked by $\mathbf{e}_1$ and $\mathbf{e}_2$.

4.2 Introducing Type Markers

In this work, we present the novel concept of *Type Markers*, to add entity-type background knowledge into the relation extraction model. This markers are special tokens representing the root type of an entity, e.g. [PERSON], [LOCATION], [ORGANIZATION], [WORK], etc. These new tokens are added into BERT embeddings, and its representation will be learned when fine-tuning our model. For each entity in a candidate fact, its type can be extracted from the KG. However, as KG are often incomplete, type information may be missing for some entities. In this case, the entity-type extracted by a Named Entity Recognition (NER) [20,23] system can be used. In the next section we propose two methods to include this tokens into the model input.

4.3 Models

This subsection presents different input configurations for the relation extraction model. Following the work from Soares et al. [30], we will take BERT [5] pre-trained model and adapt it to solve our relation extraction task. On top of BERT we add a Softmax classifier, which will predict the relation type (r). As baseline for comparison we use Soares et al. [30] configuration of BERT with *Entity Markers*. We will start by briefly overviewing their method, and continue with our two configurations proposed to add *Type Markers*.

Entity Markers (Baseline): As stated in Sect. 4.1, candidate facts $(\mathbf{x}, \mathbf{e}_1, \mathbf{e}_2)$ contain a sequence of tokens from a sentence $\mathbf{x}$ and the entities span $\mathbf{e}_1$ and $\mathbf{e}_2$. *Entity Markers* are used to identify this entity span in the sentence. They are four special tokens $[E1_{start}]$, $[E1_{end}]$, $[E2_{start}]$ and $[E2_{end}]$ that are placed at the beginning and end of each of the entities, i.e.:

$$\hat{\mathbf{x}} = [x_0 \ldots [E1_{start}]x_i \ldots x_j[E1_{end}] \ldots [E2_{start}]x_k \ldots x_l[E2_{end}] \ldots x_n]$$

this token sequence ($\hat{\mathbf{x}}$) is fed into BERT instead of $\mathbf{x}$. Figure 3 displays the described input configuration.

Type Markers Only: A first solution to introduce *Type Markers* into the system is replacing the whole entity mention with the *Type Marker*. In this new configuration, there is no need to indicate the entity span. However, we still need to indicate which entity is performing as subject or object, because relations are directed. Thus, an *Entity Marker* for each entity is still needed: $[E1]$, $[E2]$. Figure 4 displays the model configuration, we use $[Type_{e_m}]$ to refer to each entity *Type Marker*. The modified $\mathbf{x}$ which will be fed into BERT looks like:

$$\hat{\mathbf{x}} = [x_0 \ldots [E1][Type_{e_1}] \ldots [E2][Type_{e_2}] \ldots x_n]$$

Entity and Type Markers: Finally we propose a combination of both previous models. It consists on adding *Type Marker* tokens without removing entity mentions nor any *Entity Marker*. The resulting input $\hat{\mathbf{x}}$, displayed in Fig. 5, is:

$$\hat{\mathbf{x}} = [x_0 \ldots [E1_{start}][Type_{e_1}]x_i \ldots x_j[E1_{end}] \ldots [E2_{start}][Type_{e_2}]x_k \ldots x_l[E2_{end}] \ldots x_n]$$

This model keeps the whole contextual information from the entity mentions, while adding the semantic types of the entities.

5 Triple Validation Within Aggregated News

When building KGs from unstructured or semi-structured data, information extracted is specially vulnerable to quality issues [19]. To enhance extracted triples quality, we propose KG population on aggregated news over free crawled data, and a validation method that exploits this information. On one hand, the fact that articles come from verified sources and have been clustered on news story events, increases the trustfulness of the text and ensures that the content from which we learn is relevant. On the other hand, the aggregated articles talk about the same agents and events, adding redundancy and context to the predictions. In the example from Fig. 1, we can see how many of the sentences in the input text are expressing the same relations, e.g. sentences "*Microsoft announced that its co-founder, Bill Gates..*", "*Microsoft's billionaire co-founder, Bill Gates...*", and "*Microsoft co-founder Bill Gates said...*" can all be synthesized with the triple ⟨*Microsoft, FoundedBy, Bill Gates*⟩. The validation system takes advantage of this redundancy, as well as other extracted triples, to detect contradicting information while verifying against our ontology and the KG.

In this section we overview the SHACL constraints applied in our system (Sect. 5.1) and describe the validation module methodology (Sect. 5.2) to exploit aggregated news context and redundancy.

5.1 Constraints Overview

We divided the validation rules applied in two main groups: *type constraints*, where validation is based on rules from the pre-defined ontology concerning the entity-types a relation can connect; and *data constraints*, where validation relies on data from other triples in the KG.

Type Constraints: When defining an ontology, *domain* and *ranges* are associated to the different kinds of relations. These properties describe if a relation can link a subject to an object, based on its associated type classes. The *domain* defines the types of entities which can have certain property, while the *range* defines the entity types which can work as an object. Domain and range properties also apply to types sub-classes defined in the ontology hierarchy. As an example, if the relation "*FoundedBy*" is applied from a root domain "*Organization*" to a root range "*Person*", this means entities with types or sub-types of this domain and range can be linked by this property. However, if we restrict the relation "*MemberOfSportsTeam*" to the domain "*sportsPerson*" and range "*sportOrganization*", only the entities with these sub-types will be linked by this relation. For all relations in our ontology we defined their respective domains and ranges, which will be used for validation.

Notice that when applying this rule we will discard false positives, but if we are missing entity-types relations in the KG, we will also discard some true positives. For example, we may know some entity is type "*Person*", but if we do not have the association of this entity with the sub-type "*Politician*", we will discard triples of this entity involving the relation "*MemberOfPoliticalPary*" or "*HeadOfGovernment*". While this will cause a decrease in recall, it is also an indicator of missing entity-type relations that should be populated. Nevertheless, this problem is currently not analyzed, and in this work these triples will be discarded.

Data Constraints: We define two kinds of data constraints: *cardinality* and *disjoint*. Cardinality constrains refer to the number of times a property can be assigned to an entity of a given domain. For example, an entity of type "*Person*" can have at most one "*BirthDate*". This constraint can also be applied considering time range statements, to guarantee e.g. that a country does not have two presidents at the same time. Disjoint rules guarantee that entities have to be disassociated for a set of properties. For example, if two entities are known to be related as *Siblings*, they can not be associated as *Parent* or *Child*. We apply this kind of restriction to relations concerning the *Person* domain in connection to family relation properties like *Parent*, *Child*, *Sibling* and *Partner*. Moreover, we consider inverse predicates when applying these constraints.

5.2 RDF Graph Validation Methodology

In this sub-section we are describing the validation preformed to an RDF graph extracted from an aggregated news content. We will start describing the nomenclature used, and continue with the algorithm.

An RDF graph G is constructed by a finite set of triples $\mathbf{t} = [t_0, ..., t_n]$, where $0 \leq n$. Triples are of the form (s, p, o), where s is the subject, p the predicate and o the object. s and o are the *nodes* elements in the graph G, and p the *edge*. Particularly, given a set of RDF triples $\mathbf{t}_{AN}$, extracted from an aggregated news (AN) content, and composing an RDF graph G_{AN}, our triple validator follows the next methodology:

Algorithm 1. Triple validation algorithm

1: Repeated triples in G_{AN} are merged in a graph of unique triples $\hat{G}_{AN}$, where $\hat{G}_{AN} \leq G_{AN}$.
2: The occurrence count for each unique triple is stored in a counter $\mathbf{c} = [c_{\hat{t}_0}, ..., c_{\hat{t}_m}]$, where $c_{\hat{t}_j}$ is an integer ≥ 1 with the number of occurrences of a unique triple $\hat{t}_j$.
3: A second graph (G_{KG}) is constructed with all KG triples from entities appearing in the same aggregated news content.
4: $\hat{G}_{AN}$ is extended with G_{KG}, being $G = \hat{G}_{AN} \cap G_{KG}$.
5: SHACL constraints are applied to G.
6: The SHACL validator outputs a set of a valid triple $\mathbf{t}_v$, invalid triples by type $\mathbf{t}_{it}$ and a list of alternative sets of incompatible triples by data constraints $\mathbf{T}_d = [\mathbf{t}_{d_1}, ..., \mathbf{t}_{d_k}]$ where each set $\mathbf{t}_{d_l}$ is composed by a valid triple t_{vd} followed by the triple that would be incompatible with the previous one t_{id}.
7: **if** triples are invalidated by type constraints ($\mathbf{t}_{it}$) **then**
8:     Discard triple
9: **end if**
10: **for** each set of incompatible triples by data constraints ($\mathbf{t}_{d_l}$) **do**
11:     **if** triple $t_{vd_l} \in G_{KG}$ **then**
12:         Correct Set. The invalid triple (t_{id_l}) in the set is discarded.
13:     **else**
14:         **if** $c_{\hat{t}_{vd_l}} > c_{\hat{t}_{id_l}} + \alpha$, (being $\alpha \in \mathbb{R}$ and $\alpha \geq 0$), **then**
15:             Correct Set. Discard invalid triple t_{id_l}.
16:         **else**
17:             Incorrect Set. Discard all triples in $\mathbf{t}_{dl}$
18:         **end if**
19:     **end if**
20: **end for**
21: Final output consists in an RDF graph of valid and unique triples extracted from the aggregated news content, $\hat{G}_{AN_v}$

6 Experiments

The presented contributions for relation extraction and validation have been tested in an experimental set up. In this section we provide description and analytical results on these experiments. First, we compare the different configurations proposed for the relation extraction module (Sect. 6.1). Second, we evaluate the validation step, and how working with aggregated news helps this validation (Sect. 6.2). Finally, we present representative metrics from the automatic KG population system (Sect. 6.3).

6.1 Relation Extraction

The different variations of the relation extraction model, presented in Sect. 4 have been compared considering two datasets: the well known TACRED [39] dataset, and the new TypeRE dataset introduced in this work.

Datasets: TACRED is used with the purpose of comparing our system with other works. This dataset provides entity spans and relation category annotations for 106k sentences. Moreover, entity-types annotations for the subject and object entities are included. There are 41 different relation categories, plus the no-relation label, and 17 entity-types.

In this work we present the TypeRE dataset. This dataset is aligned with our ontology to be able to integrate the relation extraction model into our KG population system. As manually annotating a whole corpus is an expensive task, we generated the new dataset by aligning three public relation extraction datasets with our ontology. The datasets used are: Wiki80 [14], KBP37 [38] and KnowledgeNet[11] [21]. The entities from all three datasets were disambiguated to Freebase [2] identifiers. For Wiki80 and KnowledgeNet datasets, Wikidata identifiers are already provided, so the linking was solved mapping identifiers. For KBP37 we disambiguated the annotated entities to Freebase ids using Vilynx's NERD system [9], as no identifiers are provided. For the three datasets, when an entity could not be disambiguated or mapped to a Freebase identifier, the whole sentence was discarded. For each entity, its root type is also added into the dataset. The included types are: "*Person*", "*Location*", "*Organization*", "*Work*", "*Occupation*" and "*Sport*". Sentences with entities with not known types were discarded. Regarding relations, we manually aligned relational categories from the datasets to our ontology relations. In order to make sure external dataset relations are correctly matched to ours, we validated that all triples in the dataset had valid root domain and range given the relation, and discarded the sentences otherwise. Sentences from relations not matching our ontology and from relations with less than 100 annotated sentences, were discarded.

The dataset metrics are presented in Table 1, in comparison with the origin datasets. Type-RE is composed by 30.923 sentences expressing 27 different relations, plus the no-relation label, being a 73.73% of the total data from Wiki80,

[11] Only training data annotations are publicly available.

19.85% from KBP37 and 6.42% from KnowledgeNet. The partition between train, develop and test sets was made in order to preserve an 80-10-10% split for each category.

Results: In this section we compare the proposed input configurations to combine *Type Markers* (TM) and *Entity Markers* (EM), against the baseline model, BERT_{EM}[30]. For all variants, we performed fine-tuning from $\text{BERT}_{\text{BASE}}$ model. Fine-tuning was configured with the next hyper-parameters: 10 epochs, a learning rate of 3e-5 with Adam, and a batch size of 64.

Table 1. Relation extraction datasets metrics comparison. For each dataset we display the total number of sentences (Total), the number of sentences in each partition (Train, Dev and Test), the number of relational categories, and the number of unique entities labeled.

Dataset	#Total	#Train	#Dev	#Test	#Relations	#Entities
TypeRE	30.923	24.729	3.095	3.099	27	29.730
KnowledgeNet [21]	13.000	10.895	2.105	-	15	3.912
Wiki80 [14]	56.000	50.400	5.600	-	80	72.954
KBP37 [38]	20.832	15.765	3.364	1.703	37	-

Table 2. Test performance on the TACRED relation extraction benchmark.

	Dev			Test		
	P	**R**	**F1**	**P**	**R**	**F1**
ERNIE [41]	-	-	-	69.9	66.1	67.9
SpanBERT [17]	-	-	-	-	-	68.1
$\textbf{BERT}_{\textbf{EM}}$ [30]	65.8	68.4	67.1	67.8	65.3	65.5
$\textbf{BERT}_{\textbf{TM}}$	66.3	**71.0**	68.6	67.8	**69.4**	68.5
$\textbf{BERT}_{\textbf{EM+TM}}$	**69.6**	69.0	**69.3**	**70.3**	67.3	**68.8**

Table 2 presents the performance on the TACRED dataset. Our configuration combining *Entity* and *Type Markers*, $\text{BERT}_{\text{EM+TM}}$, exceeds the baseline ($\text{BERT}_{\text{EM}}$) by a 3.3% F1 and BERT_{TM} exceeds it by a 3% F1, on the test set. The two proposed implementations also obtain better F1 score than ERNIE [41] and SpanBERT [17], when trained with base model. Some works [17,30] have reported higher F1 scores with a larger $\text{BERT}_{\text{LARGE}}$ language model. The very high computational requirements of this model prevented us from providing results with them. However, published results [30] on our baseline configuration (BERT_{EM}) show promising possibilities to beat state-of-the-art when training our proposed models on $\text{BERT}_{\text{LARGE}}$.

Table 3 shows performance for the three input configurations on the TypeRE dataset. Our proposed configuration, $\text{BERT}_{\text{EM+TM}}$, achieves the best scores of the three configurations with a 2.2% F1 improvement over the baseline. However, BERT_{TM} decreases overall performance in comparison to the baseline, while for the TACRED dataset it performed better. We believe this difference is because the granularity on the types given in TACRED (17 types) is higher than in TypeRE (6 types). This increased detail on types taxonomy helps on a better representation an thus improved classification.

Regarding individual relations evaluation, we observed type information helps improving detection of relations with less training samples, as it helps generalization: e.g. "*PER:StateOrProvinceOfDeath*" and "*ORG:numberOfEmployees*", some of the relations with less data samples in the TACRED dataset, improve the F1-score by a 32% and 13% correspondingly when using $\text{BERT}_{\text{EM+TM}}$.

Table 3. Test performance on the TypeRE relation extraction benchmark.

	Dev				Test			
	P	R	F1	Acc	P	R	F1	Acc
$\textbf{BERT}_{\textbf{EM}}$ [30]	84.3	86.9	85.6	90.9	87.0	88.3	87.6	92.1
$\textbf{BERT}_{\textbf{TM}}$	80.4	86.6	83.4	89.1	81.5	88.5	84.8	89.7
$\textbf{BERT}_{\textbf{EM+TM}}$	**88.4**	**87.0**	**87.7**	**93.2**	**90.2**	**89.5**	**89.9**	**93.7**

Table 4. Metrics of the AggregatedNewsRE dataset.

Dataset	#Total	#Relations	#Entities	#Aggregated News
AggregatedNewsRE	400	17	91	11

6.2 Triple Validation Within Aggregated News

The effects of each step from the validation algorithm presented in Sect. 5 are analyzed in this subsection. We want to see the capabilities of this module to detect erroneous triples and evaluate validation in the aggregated news context.

Datasets: We generated a manually annotated corpus of candidate facts extracted from aggregated news collected by our system, which we call AggregatedNewsRE. This dataset is used to evaluate the contribution of the presented validation module and analyze the applied constraints. Sentences from aggregated news were annotated by our NERD module, and candidate facts were constructed for each sentence where entity pairs were identified. After this preprocessing, the relations in this candidate facts were manually annotated by one expert annotator. The resulting dataset contains a total of 11 aggregated news stories and 400 candidate facts. Diverse topics were selected for these news, in order to cover different kinds of relations. The final aggregated news corpus includes 17 from the 27 relations in the TypeRE dataset. Table 4 shows the AggregatedNewsRE dataset metrics.

Table 5. Comparison on the validation contribution when using contextual information of all RDF graph extracted from aggregated news (AN). We compare the output from the RE model (Base), type constraints (Type), all constraints validated against our KG (Type+Data), and all constraints validated against the KG and the triples in the RDF graph extracted from the aggregated news (Type+Data in AN).

	P	R	F1	Acc
Base	54.5	85.5	66.6	62.3
Type	60.0	85.1	70.4	67.6
Type+Data	62.8	85.1	72.3	70.0
Type+Data in AN	**70.1**	**81.7**	**75.5**	**75.0**

Results: We extract triples for all the candidate facts in the AggregatedNewsRE dataset, using the previously trained relation extraction model, $\text{BERT}_{\text{EM+TM}}$. On top of these results we perform three different levels of validation, that we analyzed. Results are presented in Table 5. Notice the performance on the base result is low in comparison to scores presented in Table 3. This is because the sentences in the TypeRE dataset, used to train the model, are from Wikipedia articles, while sentences in AggregatedNewsRE dataset are from news articles, where language expressions follow a different distribution.

Our experiments compare different levels of validations. First, we apply Type Constraints, which discarded 35 triples and improved precision by a 5.5%. Second, we test the validation of each individual triple using the SHACL constraints. This applies both Type and Data Constraints, and discards a total of 50 triples, increasing precision an 8.3%. Finally, we validate the RDF graph extracted for each group of aggregated news. This last validations uses the redundant information from the aggregated news, discarding a total of 95 triples and improving precision by a 15.6%, with respect to the baseline. For this last experiment, α was set to 2. As can be seen, the main effect of validation is an increase in precision, thanks to the detection of false positives. As expected, recall is lowered down by the Type Constraint due to incomplete entity-type information. When the validation process uses all aggregated news RDF graph, some true positives are discarded due to contradictions between extracted triples. Nevertheless, notice that only a 3.8% of recall is lost, while accuracy increases 12.7%.

6.3 Automatic KG Population System Analytics

Finally, we study the quantity and quality of the generated triples on the online KG population system under study. We analyze triples extracted from 171 aggregated news, collected during a period of time of 24h. From these news stories 706 triples have been obtained, setting an average of 4.12 triples/content. However, if we aggregate repeated triples extracted from the same content, we have a total of 447 triples. These values show high redundancy on these data.

The final population system not only validates triples with SHACL constraints, but also filters out triples with a prediction confidence lower than α=0.85. This threshold has been chosen to prioritize precision over recall in order to boost data quality. From the 447 triples extracted, 29.98% are valid, while 70.02% are invalid. Among the invalid triples, 56.23% were discarded by the confidence threshold, 35.46% because of type constraints, and 3.68% for data constraints. From the remaining 134 valid triples: 72.5% are new. We manually evaluated these new triples and stated that an 88.6% of them are correct.

7 Conclusions

This paper studies opportunities for enhancing the quality of an automatic KG population system by combining IE techniques with Semantics. We present a novel framework, which automatically extracts novel facts from aggregated news articles. This system is composed by a NERL module, followed by a relation extractor and a SHACL validator. The contributions presented in this paper are focused on the relation extraction and validation parts.

The relation extractor model proposed improves performance with respect to the baseline, by adding entity-types knowledge. To introduce types information, we have presented *Type Markers* and proposed two novel input configurations to add these markers when fine-tuning BERT. The proposed models have been tested with the widely known relation extraction benchmark, TACRED, and the new TypeRE dataset, presented and released in this work. For both datasets, our models outperform the baseline and show strong performance in comparison to other state-of-the-art models.

On top of the relation extraction we have built a SHACL validator module that ensures coherence and data integrity to the output RDF graph. This module enforces restrictions on relations to maintain a high level of overall data quality. The novelty in this module resides in exploiting context and redundancy from the whole RDF graph extracted from aggregated news. Finally, we provided metrics on the system performance and shown how this validation is capable to discard almost all erroneous triples.

As future work, we plan to study novel relation extraction architectures which integrate KG information into the language model representation, inspired by [24]. Other future works include extending the KG population framework by adding a co-reference resolution module and analyzing triples invalidated by type to infer missing entity-types automatically.

Acknowledgements. This work was partially supported by the Government of Catalonia under the industrial doctorate 2017 DI 011.

References

1. TACRED corpus ldc2018t24. Web download file. Linguistic Data Consortium, Philadelphia (2002). Accessed 20 May 2020
2. Bollacker, K., Evans, C., Paritosh, P., Sturge, T., Taylor, J.: Freebase: a collaboratively created graph database for structuring human knowledge. In: Proceedings of the 2008 ACM SIGMOD International Conference on Management of Data, pp. 1247–1250 (2008)
3. Carlson, A., Betteridge, J., Kisiel, B., Settles, B., Hruschka, E.R., Mitchell, T.M.: Toward an architecture for never-ending language learning. In: Twenty-Fourth AAAI Conference on Artificial Intelligence (2010)
4. Chan, Y.S., Roth, D.: Exploiting background knowledge for relation extraction. In: Proceedings of the 23rd International Conference on Computational Linguistics, pp. 152–160. Association for Computational Linguistics (2010)
5. Devlin, J., Chang, M.W., Lee, K., Toutanova, K.: BERT: pre-training of deep bidirectional transformers for language understanding. arXiv preprint arXiv:1810.04805 (2018)
6. Dong, X., et al.: Knowledge vault: a web-scale approach to probabilistic knowledge fusion. In: Proceedings of the 20th ACM SIGKDD International Conference on Knowledge Discovery and Data Mining, pp. 601–610 (2014)
7. Fader, A., Soderland, S., Etzioni, O.: Identifying relations for open information extraction. In: Proceedings of the Conference on Empirical Methods in Natural Language Processing, pp. 1535–1545. Association for Computational Linguistics (2011)
8. Fan, J., Ferrucci, D., Gondek, D., Kalyanpur, A.: Prismatic: inducing knowledge from a large scale lexicalized relation resource. In: Proceedings of the NAACL HLT 2010 First International Workshop on Formalisms and Methodology for Learning by Reading, pp. 122–127. Association for Computational Linguistics (2010)
9. Fernández, D., et al.: ViTS: video tagging system from massive web multimedia collections. In: Proceedings of the IEEE International Conference on Computer Vision Workshops, pp. 337–346 (2017)
10. Fernàndez-Cañellas, D., et al.: Vlx-stories: building an online event knowledge base with emerging entity detection. In: Ghidini, C., et al. (eds.) The Semantic Web – ISWC 2019. Lecture Notes in Computer Science, vol. 11779, pp. 382–399. Springer, Cham2019 (2019). https://doi.org/10.1007/978-3-030-30796-7_24
11. Gayo, J.E.L., Prud'hommeaux, E., Solbrig, H.R., Rodríguez, J.M.Á.: Validating and describing linked data portals using RDF shape expressions. In: LDQ@ SEMANTICS (2014)
12. Gerber, D., Hellmann, S., Bühmann, L., Soru, T., Usbeck, R., Ngomo, A.C.N.: Real-time RDF extraction from unstructured data streams. In: Alani, H., et al. (eds.) The Semantic Web – ISWC 2013. Lecture Notes in Computer Science, vol. 8218, pp. 135–150. Springer, Berlin, Heidelberg (2013). https://doi.org/10.1007/978-3-642-41335-3_9
13. Han, X., Gao, T., Yao, Y., Ye, D., Liu, Z., Sun, M.: OpenNRE: an open and extensible toolkit for neural relation extraction. In: Proceedings of EMNLP-IJCNLP: System Demonstrations, pp. 169–174 (2019). https://doi.org/10.18653/v1/D19-3029. https://www.aclweb.org/anthology/D19-3029
14. Han, X., et al.: FewRel: a large-scale supervised few-shot relation classification dataset with state-of-the-art evaluation. arXiv preprint arXiv:1810.10147 (2018)

15. Hogan, A., Harth, A., Passant, A., Decker, S., Polleres, A.: Weaving the pedantic web (2010)
16. Ji, H., et al.: Overview of TAC-KBP2017 13 languages entity discovery and linking. In: TAC (2017)
17. Joshi, M., Chen, D., Liu, Y., Weld, D.S., Zettlemoyer, L., Levy, O.: Spanbert: improving pre-training by representing and predicting spans. Trans. Assoc. Comput. Linguist. **8**, 64–77 (2020)
18. Knublauch, H., Kontokostas, D.: Shapes constraint language (SHACL). In: W3C Candidate Recommendation, vol. 11, p. 8 (2017)
19. Kontokostas, D., Zaveri, A., Auer, S., Lehmann, J.: TripleCheckMate: a tool for crowdsourcing the quality assessment of linked data. In: Klinov, P., Mouromtsev, D. (eds.) Knowledge Engineering and the Semantic Web (KESW 2013). Communications in Computer and Information Science, vol. 394, pp. 265–272. Springer, Berlin, Heidelberg (2013). https://doi.org/10.1007/978-3-642-41360-5_22
20. Lample, G., Ballesteros, M., Subramanian, S., Kawakami, K., Dyer, C.: Neural architectures for named entity recognition. arXiv preprint arXiv:1603.01360 (2016)
21. Mesquita, F., Cannaviccio, M., Schmidek, J., Mirza, P., Barbosa, D.: KnowledgeNet: a benchmark dataset for knowledge base population. In: Proceedings of the 2019 Conference on Empirical Methods in Natural Language Processing and the 9th International Joint Conference on Natural Language Processing (EMNLP-IJCNLP), pp. 749–758 (2019)
22. Mitchell, T., Cohen, W., Hruschka, E., Talukdar, P., Yang, B., Betteridge, J., Carlson, A., Dalvi, B., Gardner, M., Kisiel, B., et al.: Never-ending learning. Commun. ACM **61**(5), 103–115 (2018)
23. Nadeau, D., Sekine, S.: A survey of named entity recognition and classification. Lingvisticae Investigationes **30**(1), 3–26 (2007)
24. Peters, M.E., et al.: Knowledge enhanced contextual word representations. In: EMNLP/IJCNLP (2019)
25. Roth, D., Yih, W.T.: Global inference for entity and relation identification via a linear programming formulation. In: Introduction to Statistical Relational Learning, pp. 553–580 (2007)
26. Ryman, A.G., Le Hors, A., Speicher, S.: OSLC resource shape: a language for defining constraints on linked data. LDOW **996** (2013)
27. Sarawagi, S., et al.: Information extraction. Found. Trends® in Databases **1**(3), 261–377 (2008)
28. Schmitz, M., Bart, R., Soderland, S., Etzioni, O., et al.: Open language learning for information extraction. In: Proceedings of the 2012 Joint Conference on Empirical Methods in Natural Language Processing and Computational Natural Language Learning, pp. 523–534. Association for Computational Linguistics (2012)
29. Shen, W., Wang, J., Han, J.: Entity linking with a knowledge base: Issues, techniques, and solutions. IEEE Trans. Knowl. Data Eng. **27**(2), 443–460 (2014)
30. Soares, L.B., FitzGerald, N., Ling, J., Kwiatkowski, T.: Matching the blanks: distributional similarity for relation learning. In: Proceedings of the 57th Annual Meeting of the Association for Computational Linguistics, pp. 2895–2905 (2019)
31. Spahiu, B., Maurino, A., Palmonari, M.: Towards improving the quality of knowledge graphs with data-driven ontology patterns and SHACL. In: ISWC (Best Workshop Papers), pp. 103–117 (2018)

32. Tomaszuk, D.: RDF validation: a brief survey. In: Kozielski, S., Mrozek, D., Kasprowski, P., Małysiak-Mrozek, B., Kostrzewa, D. (eds.) International Conference: Beyond Databases, Architectures and Structures. Communications in Computer and Information Science, vol. 716, pp. 344–355. Springer, Cham (2017). https://doi.org/10.1007/978-3-319-58274-0_28
33. Töpper, G., Knuth, M., Sack, H.: DBpedia ontology enrichment for inconsistency detection. In: Proceedings of the 8th International Conference on Semantic Systems, pp. 33–40 (2012)
34. Vaswani, A., et al.: Attention is all you need. In: Advances in Neural Information Processing Systems, pp. 5998–6008 (2017)
35. Vrandečić, D., Krötzsch, M.: Wikidata: a free collaborative knowledgebase. Commun. ACM **57**(10), 78–85 (2014)
36. Wu, S., He, Y.: Enriching pre-trained language model with entity information for relation classification. In: Proceedings of the 28th ACM International Conference on Information and Knowledge Management, pp. 2361–2364 (2019)
37. Yao, L., Mao, C., Luo, Y.: KG-BERT: BERT for knowledge graph completion. arXiv preprint arXiv:1909.03193 (2019)
38. Zhang, D., Wang, D.: Relation classification via recurrent neural network. arXiv preprint arXiv:1508.01006 (2015)
39. Zhang, Y., Zhong, V., Chen, D., Angeli, G., Manning, C.D.: Position-aware attention and supervised data improve slot filling. In: Proceedings of the 2017 Conference on Empirical Methods in Natural Language Processing, pp. 35–45 (2017)
40. Zhang, Y., Zhong, V., Chen, D., Angeli, G., Manning, C.D.: Position-aware attention and supervised data improve slot filling. In: Proceedings of the 2017 Conference on Empirical Methods in Natural Language Processing (EMNLP 2017), pp. 35–45 (2017). https://nlp.stanford.edu/pubs/zhang2017tacred.pdf
41. Zhang, Z., Han, X., Liu, Z., Jiang, X., Sun, M., Liu, Q.: ERNIE: enhanced language representation with informative entities. In: Proceedings of ACL 2019 (2019)

Extending SPARQL with Similarity Joins

Sebastián Ferrada(✉), Benjamin Bustos, and Aidan Hogan

Department of Computer Science, Universidad de Chile,
Millenium Institute for Foundational Research on Data, Santiago, Chile
{sferrada,bebustos,ahogan}@dcc.uchile.cl

Abstract. We propose techniques that support the efficient computation of multidimensional similarity joins in an RDF/SPARQL setting, where similarity in an RDF graph is measured with respect to a set of attributes selected in the SPARQL query. While similarity joins have been studied in other contexts, RDF graphs present unique challenges. We discuss how a similarity join operator can be included in the SPARQL language, and investigate ways in which it can be implemented and optimised. We devise experiments to compare three similarity join algorithms over two datasets. Our results reveal that our techniques outperform DBSimJoin: a PostgreSQL extension that supports similarity joins.

Keywords: Similarity joins · SPARQL

1 Introduction

RDF datasets are often made accessible on the Web through a SPARQL endpoint where users typically write queries requesting *exact* matches on the content. For instance, in Wikidata [27], a SPARQL query may request *the names of Nobel laureates that have fought in a war*. However, there are times when users need answers to a *similarity query*, such as requesting *the Latin American country with the most similar population and GDP to a European country*. The potential applications for efficient similarity queries in SPARQL are numerous, including: entity comparison and linking [23,24], multimedia retrieval [9,15], similarity graph management [7,10], pattern recognition [4], query relaxation [12], as well as domain-specific use-cases, such as protein similarity queries [2].

An important feature for similarity queries are *similarity joins* $X \bowtie_{\mathfrak{s}} Y$, which obtain all pairs (x, y) from the (natural) join $X \bowtie Y$ such that $x \in X$, $y \in Y$, and additionally, x is similar to y according to similarity criteria $\mathfrak{s}$. Similarities are often measured in terms of distance functions between pairs of objects in a d-dimensional vector space, with two objects being more similar the closer they are in that space. A distance function $\delta : \mathbb{R}^d \times \mathbb{R}^d \to \mathbb{R}$ is called a *metric* when it is non-negative, reflexive, symmetric and satisfies the triangle inequality. There are two main types of similarity criteria $\mathfrak{s}$ considered in practice: *a)* in a *range-based* similarity join, $\mathfrak{s}$ specifies a range r such that the distance between output pairs must be below r; and *b)*, in a *k-nearest neighbours* (k-nn)

J. Z. Pan et al. (Eds.): ISWC 2020, LNCS 12506, pp. 201–217, 2020.
https://doi.org/10.1007/978-3-030-62419-4_12

similarity join, $\mathfrak{s}$ specifies an integer k such that the pair (x, y) will be output if and only if there are fewer than k other elements in Y with lower distance to x.

Similarity joins for some metrics (e.g., Manhattan distance) can be expressed in SPARQL using built-in numeric operators, order-by, limit, etc. Other metrics can at best be approximated; for example, SPARQL offers no direct way to compute a square root for Euclidean distance. Even when similarity joins can be expressed, a SPARQL engine will typically evaluate these queries by computing distances for all pairs and then filtering by the specific criteria. Conversely, a variety of algorithms and indexes have been proposed to evaluate similarity joins in a more efficient manner than processing all pairs, where the available optimisations depend on the precise definition of $\mathfrak{s}$. Compiling similarity joins expressed in vanilla SPARQL into optimised physical operators would require showing equivalence of the SPARQL expression to the similarity join supported by the physical operator, which is not even clear to be decidable. Thus, dedicated query operators for similarity joins address both usability and efficiency.

Though similarity joins have been well-studied, a key challenge arising in the RDF/SPARQL setting is that of *dimensionality*, where we allow the user to select any number of dimensions from the data, including dynamic dimensions computed from the data (through functions, aggregations, etc.). Being dimension-agnostic introduces various complications; for example, indexing on all combinations of d dimensions would naively result in $O(2^d)$ different indexes, and would not support dynamic dimensions. Such challenges distinguish the problem of supporting similarity queries in SPARQL from typical usage in multimedia databases (based on fixed descriptors), and also from works on supporting domain-specific distances in query languages, such as geographic distances [1,29].

In this paper, we propose to extend SPARQL with multidimensional similarity joins in metric spaces, and investigate optimised techniques for evaluating such queries over RDF graphs. Most works thus far on extending SPARQL with similarity features have either focused on (1) unidimensional similarity measures that consider similarity with respect to one attribute at a time [14,26], or (2) domain-specific fixed-dimensional similarity measures, such as geographic distance [1,29]. Other approaches rather pre-compute and index similarity scores as part of the RDF graphs [7,12,20] or support metric distances measures external to a query engine [19,24]. To the best of our knowledge, our proposal is the first to consider multidimensional similarity queries in the context of SPARQL, where the closest proposal to ours is DBSimJoin [25]: a PostgreSQL extension, which – though it lacks features we argue to be important for the RDF/SPARQL setting (namely k-nn semantics) – we will consider as a baseline for experiments.

Section 2 discusses literature regarding efficient similarity join evaluation, and proposals to include such joins in database systems. In Sect. 3 we propose the syntax and semantics of a SPARQL extension that supports similarity joins. Section 4 presents our implementation, shows use-case queries and discusses possible optimisations. In Sect. 5 we perform experiments over two real datasets; we compare different evaluation algorithms, further adopting DBSimJoin as a baseline system. We conclude and outline future directions in Sect. 6.

2 Related Work

In this section we first describe works addressing the efficient evaluation of similarity joins. Thereafter, we discuss works on similarity queries and distance computation in SPARQL and other query languages for database systems.

Similarity Joins: The brute force method for computing a similarity join between X and Y is to use a *nested loop*, which computes for each $x \in X$ the distance to each $y \in Y$, outputting the pair if it satisfies the similarity condition, thus performing $|X| \cdot |Y|$ distance computations. For range or nearest-neighbour queries over metric distances, there are then three main strategies to improve upon the brute force method: *indexing*, *space partitioning*, and/or *approximation*.

A common way to optimise similarity joins is to index the data using tree structures that divide the space in different ways (offline), then pruning distant pairs of objects from comparison (online). Among such approaches, we highlight *vantage-point Trees* (*vp-Trees*) [28], which make recursive ball cuts of space centred on selected points, attempting to evenly distribute objects inside and outside the ball. vp-Trees have an average-case search time of $O(n^\alpha)$ on n objects, where $0 \leq \alpha \leq 1$ depends on the distance distribution and dimensionality of the space, among other factors [17], thus having an upper bound of $O(n^{2\alpha})$ for a similarity join. Other tree indexes, such as the D-Index [6] and the List of Twin Clusters [21], propose to use clustering techniques over the data.

Other space partitioning algorithms are not used for indexing but rather for evaluating similarity joins online. The Quickjoin (QJ) algorithm [13] was designed to improve upon grid-based partition algorithms [3,5]; it divides the space into ball cuts using random data objects as pivots, splitting the data into the vectors inside and outside the ball, proceeding recursively until the groups are small enough to perform a nested loop. It keeps window partitions in the boundaries of the ball in case there are pairs needed for the result with vectors assigned to different partitions. QJ requires $O(n(1+w)^{\lceil \log n \rceil})$ distance computations, where w is the average fraction of elements within the window partitions. QJ was intended for range-based similarity joins and extending QJ to compute a k-nn similarity join appears far from trivial, since its simulation with a range-based join would force most of the data to fall within the window partitions, thus meaning that QJ will reach its quadratic worst case.

Another alternative is to apply approximations to evaluate similarity joins, trading the precision of results for more efficient computation. FLANN [16] is a library that provides several approximate k-nn algorithms based on randomised k-d-forests, k-means trees, locality-sensitive hashing, etc.; it automatically selects the best algorithm to index and query the data, based, for example, on a target precision, which can be traded-off to improve execution time.

Similarity in Databases: Though similarity joins do not form part of standard query languages, such as SQL or SPARQL, a number of systems have integrated variations of such joins within databases. In the context of SQL, DBSimJoin [25] implements a range-based similarity join operator for PostgreSQL. This implementation claims to handle any metric space, thus supporting various metric distances; it is based on the aforementioned index-free QJ algorithm.

A number of works have proposed online computation of similarity joins in the context of domain-specific measures. Zhai et al. [29] use OWL to describe the spatial information of a map of a Chinese city, enabling geospatial SPARQL queries that include the computation of distances between places. The Parliament SPARQL engine [1] implements an OGC standard called GeoSPARQL, which aside from various geometric operators, also includes geospatial distance. Works on link discovery may also consider specific forms of similarity measures [24], often string similarity measures over labels and descriptions [26].

Other approaches pre-materialise distance values that can then be incorporated into (standard) SPARQL queries. IMGpedia [7] pre-computes a k-nn self similarity join offline over images and stores the results as part of the graph. Similarity measures have also been investigated for the purposes of SPARQL query relaxation, whereby, in cases where a precise query returns no or few results, relaxation finds queries returning similar results [12,20].

Galvin et al. [8] propose a multiway similarity join operator for RDF; however, the notion of similarity considered is based on semantic similarity that tries to match different terms referring to the same real-world entity. Closer to our work lies iSPARQL [14], which extends SPARQL with `IMPRECISE` clauses that can include similarity joins on individual attributes. A variety of distance measures are proposed for individual dimensions/attributes, along with aggregators for combining dimensions. However, in terms of evaluation, distances are computed in an attribute-at-a-time manner and input into an aggregator. For the multidimensional setting, a (brute-force) nested loop needs to be performed; the authors leave optimisations in the multidimensional setting for future work [14].

Novelty: To the best of our knowledge, the two proposals most closely related to our work are DBSimJoin [25] and iSPARQL [14]. Unlike DBSimJoin, our goal is to introduce similarity joins to the RDF/SPARQL setting. Unlike both systems, we support k-nn semantics for similarity join evaluation, thus obviating the need for users to explicitly specify range values, which can be unintuitive within abstract metric spaces. We further outperform both systems (including under range semantics) by incorporating more efficient similarity join algorithms than the nested-loop joins of iSPARQL [14] and the Quickjoin of DBSimJoin [25]. Without the proposed extension, queries attempting to generate some kind of similarity search in SPARQL would be a) too verbose and b) too costly, since there is no clear strategy to avoid nested-loop executions.

3 Syntax and Semantics

In this section, we define the desiderata, concrete syntax and semantics for our proposed extension of SPARQL for supporting similarity joins.

3.1 Desiderata

We consider the following list of desiderata for the similarity join operator:

- *Closure*: Similarity joins should be freely combinable with other SPARQL query operators in the same manner as other forms of joins.
- *Extensibility*: There is no one-size-fits-all similarity metric [14]; hence the operator should allow for custom metrics to be defined.
- *Robustness*: The similarity join should make as few assumptions as possible about the input data in terms of comparability, completeness, etc.
- *Usability*: The feature should be easy for SPARQL users to adopt.

With respect to *closure*, we define a similarity join analogously to other forms of joins that combine graph patterns in the `WHERE` clause of a SPARQL query; furthermore, we allow the computed distance measure to be bound to a variable, facilitating its use beyond the similarity join. With respect to *extensibility*, rather than assume one metric, we make the type of distance metric used explicit in the semantics and syntax, allowing other types of distance metric to be used in future. Regarding *robustness*, we follow the precedent of SPARQL's error-handling when dealing with incompatible types or unbound values. Finally, regarding *usability*, we support syntactic features for both range-based semantics and k-nn semantics, noting that specifying particular distances for ranges can be unintuitive in abstract, high-dimensional metric spaces.

3.2 Syntax

In defining the syntax for similarity joins, we generally follow the convention of SPARQL for other binary operators present in the standard that allow for combining the solutions of two SPARQL graph patterns [11], such as `OPTIONAL` and `MINUS`. Besides stating the two graph patterns that form the operands of the similarity join, it is necessary to further define at least the following: the attributes from each graph pattern with respect to which the distance is computed, the distance function to be used, a variable to bind the distance value to, and a similarity parameter (search radius or number of nearest neighbours).

We propose the following extension to the SPARQL 1.1 EBNF Grammar [11], adding one new production rule (for `SimilarityGraphPattern`) and extending one existing production rule (`GraphPatternNotTriples`). All other non-terminals are interpreted per the standard EBNF Grammar [11].

```
SimilarityGraphPattern ::= 'SIMILARITY JOIN ON (' Var+ ')('Var+')'
                           ( 'TOP' INTEGER | 'WITHIN' DECIMAL ) 'DISTANCE' iri 'AS' Var
                           GroupGraphPattern
GraphPatternNotTriples ::= GroupOrUnionGraphPattern | [···] | SimilarityGraphPattern
```

The keyword `ON` is used to define the variables in both graph patterns upon which the distance is computed; the keywords `TOP` and `WITHIN` denote a k-nn query and an r-range query respectively; the keyword `DISTANCE` specifies the IRI of the distance function to be used for the evaluation of the join, whose result will be bound to the variable indicated with `AS`, which is expected to be *fresh*, i.e., to not appear elsewhere in the `SimilarityGraphPattern` (similar to `BIND`). The syntax may be extended in future to provide further customisation, such as supporting different normalisation functions, or to define default parameters.

Depending on the metric, we could, in principle, express such queries as vanilla SPARQL 1.1 queries, taking advantage of features such as variable binding, numeric expressions, sub-selects, etc. However, there are two key advantages of the dedicated syntax: (1) similarity join queries in vanilla syntax are complex to express, particularly in the case of k-nn queries or metrics without the corresponding numeric operators in SPARQL; (2) optimising queries written in the vanilla syntax (beyond nested-loop performance) would be practically infeasible, requiring an engine that can prove equivalence between the distance metrics and semantics for which similarity join algorithms are optimised and the plethora of ways in which they can be expressed in vanilla syntax. We rather propose to make similarity joins for multidimensional distances a first class feature, with dedicated syntax and physical operators offering sub-quadratic performance.

3.3 Semantics

Pérez et al. [22] define the semantics of SPARQL operators in terms of their evaluation over an RDF graph, which results in a set of *solution mappings*. We follow their formulation and define the semantics of a similarity join in terms of its evaluation. Letting $\mathbf{V}$, $\mathbf{I}$, $\mathbf{L}$ and $\mathbf{B}$ denote the set of all variables, IRIs, literals and blank nodes, respectively, then a solution mapping is a partial mapping $\mu : \mathbf{V} \to \mathbf{I} \cup \mathbf{L} \cup \mathbf{B}$ defined for a set of variables called its *domain*, denoted $\text{dom}(\mu)$. We say that two mappings μ_1, μ_2 are compatible, denoted $\mu_1 \sim \mu_2$, if and only if for all $v \in \text{dom}(\mu_1) \cap \text{dom}(\mu_2)$ it holds that $\mu_1(v) = \mu_2(v)$. Now we can define the following core operators on sets of mappings:

$$X \bowtie Y := \{\mu_1 \cup \mu_2 \mid \mu_1 \in X \wedge \mu_2 \in Y \wedge \mu_1 \sim \mu_2\}$$
$$X \cup Y := \{\mu \mid \mu \in X \vee \mu \in Y\} \qquad \sigma_f(X) := \{\mu \in X \mid f(\mu) = \text{true}\}$$
$$X \setminus Y := \{\mu \in X \mid \nexists \mu' \in Y : \mu \sim \mu'\} \quad X ⟕ Y := (X \bowtie Y) \cup (X \setminus Y)$$

where f denotes a filter condition that returns true, false or error for a mapping.

The *similarity join expression* parsed from the aforementioned syntax is defined as $\mathfrak{s} := (\mathcal{V}, \delta, v, \phi)$, where $\mathcal{V} \subseteq \mathbf{V} \times \mathbf{V}$ contains pairs of variables to be compared; δ is a distance metric that accepts a set of pairs of RDF terms and returns a value in $[0, \infty)$ or an error (interpreted as ∞) for incomparable inputs; $v \in \mathbf{V}$ is a fresh variable to which distances will be bound; and $\phi \in \{\mathtt{rg}_r, \mathtt{nn}_k\}$ is a filter expression based on range or k-nn. Given two solution mappings $\mu_1 \sim \mu_2$, we denote by $[\![\mathcal{V}]\!]^{\mu_1}_{\mu_2}$ the set of pairs $\{((\mu_1 \cup \mu_2)(x), (\mu_1 \cup \mu_2)(y)) \mid (x, y) \in \mathcal{V}\}$ (note: $[\![\mathcal{V}]\!]^{\mu_1}_{\mu_2} = [\![\mathcal{V}]\!]^{\mu_2}_{\mu_1}$). We say that $[\mu_1, \ldots, \mu_n] \in X_1 \bowtie \ldots \bowtie X_n$ if and only if $\mu_1 \in X_1$, ..., $\mu_n \in X_n$, and $\mu_i \sim \mu_j$ (for $1 \leq i \leq n$, $1 \leq j \leq n$). We can also interpret $\mu = [\mu_1, \ldots, \mu_n]$ as the mapping $\bigcup_{i=1}^{n} \mu_i$. We denote by $X_{\sim\mu} := \{\mu' \in X \mid \mu \sim \mu'\}$ the solution mappings of X compatible with μ. We define $\text{udom}(X) = \bigcup_{\mu \in X} \text{dom}(\mu)$ and $\text{idom}(X) = \bigcap_{\mu \in X} \text{dom}(\mu)$. Finally we use v/d to denote a mapping μ such that $\text{dom}(\mu) = \{v\}$ and $\mu(v) = d$.

Definition 1. *Given two sets of solution mappings X and Y, we define the evaluation of range and k-nn similarity joins, respectively, as:*

$$\underset{(\mathcal{V},\delta,v,rg_r)}{X \bowtie Y} := \{[\mu_1, \mu_2, \mu_v] \in X \bowtie Y \bowtie \{v/\delta(\llbracket \mathcal{V} \rrbracket^{\mu_1}_{\mu_2})\} \mid \mu_v(v) \leq r\}$$

$$\underset{(\mathcal{V},\delta,v,nn_k)}{X \bowtie Y} := \{[\mu_1, \mu_2, \mu_v] \in X \bowtie Y \bowtie \{v/\delta(\llbracket \mathcal{V} \rrbracket^{\mu_1}_{\mu_2})\} \mid \mu_v(v) \leq \kappa^{\delta,k}_{\mu_1,Y}\}$$

when $v \notin \text{udom}(X) \cup \text{udom}(Y)$ *or error otherwise, where:*

$$\kappa^{\delta,k}_{\mu_1,Y} := \min\left\{\delta(\llbracket \mathcal{V} \rrbracket^{\mu_1}_{\mu_2}) \mid \mu_2 \in Y_{\sim\mu_1} \wedge |\{\mu'_2 \in Y_{\sim\mu_1} \mid \delta(\llbracket \mathcal{V} \rrbracket^{\mu_1}_{\mu'_2}) < \delta(\llbracket \mathcal{V} \rrbracket^{\mu_1}_{\mu_2})\}| < k\right\}.$$

We return an error when $v \notin \text{udom}(X) \cup \text{udom}(Y)$ to emulate a similar behaviour to `BIND` in SPARQL. Per the definition of $\kappa^{\delta,k}_{\mu_1,Y}$, more than k results can be returned for μ_1 in the case of ties, which keeps the semantics deterministic.

We define bag semantics for similarity joins in the natural way, where the multiplicity of $\mu \in X \bowtie_{\mathfrak{s}} Y$ is defined to be the product of the multiplicities of the solutions $\mu_1 \in X$ and $\mu_2 \in Y$ that produce it.

3.4 Algebraic Properties

We now state some algebraic properties of the similarity join operators. We use $\bowtie_{\mathfrak{r}}$, $\bowtie_{\mathfrak{n}}$, $\bowtie_{\mathfrak{s}} \in \{\bowtie_{\mathfrak{r}}, \bowtie_{\mathfrak{n}}\}$ to denote range, k-nn and similarity joins, respectively.

Proposition 1. $\bowtie_{\mathfrak{r}}$ *is commutative and distributive over* $\cup$.

Proof. Assume $\mathfrak{r} = (\mathcal{V}, \delta, v, \mathtt{rg}_r)$. For any pair of sets of mappings X and Y:

$$\begin{aligned} X \bowtie_{\mathfrak{r}} Y &:= \{[\mu_1, \mu_2, \mu_v] \in X \bowtie Y \bowtie \{[v/\delta(\llbracket \mathcal{V} \rrbracket^{\mu_1}_{\mu_2})]\} \mid \mu_v(v) \leq r\} \\ &\equiv \{[\mu_2, \mu_1, \mu_v] \in Y \bowtie X \bowtie \{[v/\delta(\llbracket \mathcal{V} \rrbracket^{\mu_2}_{\mu_1})]\} \mid \mu_v(v) \leq r\} \equiv \quad Y \bowtie_{\mathfrak{r}} X \end{aligned}$$

Which proves the commutativity. For left-distributivity over $\cup$:

$$\begin{aligned} X \bowtie_{\mathfrak{r}} (Y \cup Z) &:= \{[\mu_1, \mu_2, \mu_v] \in X \bowtie (Y \cup Z) \bowtie \{v/\delta(\llbracket \mathcal{V} \rrbracket^{\mu_1}_{\mu_2})\} \mid \mu(v) \leq r\} \\ &\equiv \{[\mu_1, \mu_2, \mu_v] \in X \bowtie Y \bowtie \{v/\delta(\llbracket \mathcal{V} \rrbracket^{\mu_1}_{\mu_2})\} \mid \mu(v) \leq r\} \cup \\ &\qquad \{[\mu_1, \mu_2, \mu_v] \in X \bowtie Z \bowtie \{v/\delta(\llbracket \mathcal{V} \rrbracket^{\mu_1}_{\mu_2})\} \mid \mu(v) \leq r\} \\ &\equiv (X \bowtie_{\mathfrak{r}} Y) \cup (X \bowtie_{\mathfrak{r}} Z) \end{aligned}$$

Commutativity and left-distributivity over $\cup$ imply distributivity over $\cup$. □

Proposition 2. $\bowtie_{\mathfrak{n}}$ *is not commutative nor distributive over* $\cup$.

Proof. As counterexamples for commutativity and distributivity, note that there exist sets of mappings X, Y, Z with $|X| = n$, $|Y| = |Z| = 2n$, $n \geq k$ such that:

- Commutativity: $|X \bowtie_{\mathfrak{n}} Y| = nk$ and $|Y \bowtie_{\mathfrak{n}} X| = 2nk$.
- Distributivity: $|X \bowtie_{\mathfrak{n}} (Y \cup Z)| = nk$ and $|(X \bowtie_{\mathfrak{n}} Y) \cup (X \bowtie_{\mathfrak{n}} Z)| = 2nk$. □

Proposition 3. $\bowtie_{\mathfrak{n}}$ *is right-distributive over* $\cup$.

Proof. Assume $\mathfrak{n} = (\mathcal{V}, \delta, v, \mathrm{nn}_k)$. We see that:

$$\begin{aligned}(X \cup Y) \bowtie_{\mathfrak{n}} Z &:= \{[\mu_1, \mu_2, \mu_v] \in (X \cup Y) \bowtie Z \bowtie \{v/\delta([\![\mathcal{V}]\!]^{\mu_1}_{\mu_2})\} \mid \mu_v(v) \leq \kappa^{\delta,k}_{\mu_1,Z}\} \\ &\equiv \{[\mu_1, \mu_2, \mu_v] \in X \bowtie Z \bowtie \{v/\delta([\![\mathcal{V}]\!]^{\mu_1}_{\mu_2})\} \mid \mu_v(v) \leq \kappa^{\delta,k}_{\mu_1,Z}\} \cup \\ &\quad\ \{[\mu_1, \mu_2, \mu_v] \in Y \bowtie Z \bowtie \{v/\delta([\![\mathcal{V}]\!]^{\mu_1}_{\mu_2})\} \mid \mu_v(v) \leq \kappa^{\delta,k}_{\mu_1,Z}\} \\ &\equiv (X \bowtie_{\mathfrak{n}} Z) \cup (Y \bowtie_{\mathfrak{n}} Z)\end{aligned}$$
□

Proposition 4. $(X \bowtie_{\mathfrak{s}} Y) \bowtie_{\mathfrak{s}'} Z \not\equiv X \bowtie_{\mathfrak{s}} (Y \bowtie_{\mathfrak{s}'} Z)$ *holds.*

Proof. As a counter example, consider that $\mathfrak{s}$ and $\mathfrak{s}'$ bind distance variables v and v' respectively such that $v' \in \mathrm{udom}(X)$, $v' \notin \mathrm{udom}(Y) \cup \mathrm{udom}(Z)$ and $v \notin \mathrm{udom}(X) \cup \mathrm{udom}(Y) \cup \mathrm{udom}(Z)$. Now $(X \bowtie_{\mathfrak{s}} Y) \bowtie_{\mathfrak{s}'} Z$ returns an error as the left operand of $\bowtie_{\mathfrak{s}'}$ assigns v but $X \bowtie_{\mathfrak{s}} (Y \bowtie_{\mathfrak{s}'} Z)$ will not. □

Finally, we discuss how the defined operators relate to other key SPARQL operators. The condition in claim 3 is analogous to well-designed queries [22].

Proposition 5. *Let* $\mathfrak{s} = (\mathcal{V}, \delta, v, \phi)$. *If each mapping in* $X \bowtie Y$ *binds all variables in* $\mathcal{V}$ *and* $v \notin \mathrm{udom}(X) \cup \mathrm{udom}(Y) \cup \mathrm{udom}(Z)$, *then the following hold:*

1. $(X \bowtie_{\mathfrak{s}} Y) \bowtie Z \equiv (X \bowtie Z) \bowtie_{\mathfrak{s}} Y$
2. $(X \bowtie_{\mathfrak{s}} Y) \setminus Z \equiv (X \setminus Z) \bowtie_{\mathfrak{s}} Y$ *if* $\mathrm{udom}(Z) \cap (\mathrm{udom}(Y) - \mathrm{idom}(X)) = \emptyset$
3. $(X \bowtie_{\mathfrak{s}} Y) ⟕ Z \equiv (X ⟕ Z) \bowtie_{\mathfrak{s}} Y$ *if* $\mathrm{udom}(Z) \cap (\mathrm{udom}(Y) - \mathrm{idom}(X)) = \emptyset$
4. $\sigma_f(X \bowtie_{\mathfrak{s}} Y) \equiv \sigma_f(X) \bowtie_{\mathfrak{s}} Y$ *if* f *is scoped to* $\mathrm{idom}(X)$.

Proof. We prove each claim in the following:

1. The third step here is possible as ϕ does not rely on Z (per the assumptions).

$$\begin{aligned}(X \bowtie_{\mathfrak{s}} Y) \bowtie Z &:= \{[\mu_1, \mu_2, \mu_v] \in X \bowtie Y \bowtie \{v/\delta([\![\mathcal{V}]\!]^{\mu_1}_{\mu_2})\} \mid \phi(\mu_v)\} \bowtie Z \\ &\equiv \{[\mu_1, \mu_1', \mu_2, \mu_v] \in X \bowtie Z \bowtie Y \bowtie \{v/\delta([\![\mathcal{V}]\!]^{\mu_1}_{\mu_2})\} \mid \phi(\mu_v)\} \\ &\equiv \{[\mu_1, \mu_2, \mu_v] \in (X \bowtie Z) \bowtie Y \bowtie \{v/\delta([\![\mathcal{V}]\!]^{\mu_1}_{\mu_2})\} \mid \phi(\mu_v)\} \\ &\equiv (X \bowtie Z) \bowtie_{\mathfrak{s}} Y\end{aligned}$$

2. For a mapping $\mu = [\mu_1, \mu_2]$ such that $\mathrm{udom}(Z) \cap (\mathrm{dom}(\mu_2) - \mathrm{dom}(\mu_1)) = \emptyset$, there does not exist $\mu' \in Z$ such that $\mu \sim \mu'$ if and only if there does not exist $\mu' \in Z$ such that $\mu_1 \sim \mu'$. Taking $\mu_1 \in X$ and $\mu_2 = [\mu_2', \mu_2''] \in Y \bowtie \{v/\delta([\![\mathcal{V}]\!]^{\mu_1}_{\mu_2})$ from $X \bowtie_{\mathfrak{s}} Y$, the result then holds per the given assumptions.
3. The second step here uses the previous two results. The third step uses the right-distributivity of $\bowtie_{\mathfrak{r}}$ and $\bowtie_{\mathfrak{n}}$ over $\cup$ proven in previous propositions.

$$\begin{aligned}(X \bowtie_{\mathfrak{s}} Y) ⟕ Z &:= ((X \bowtie_{\mathfrak{s}} Y) \bowtie Z) \cup ((X \bowtie_{\mathfrak{s}} Y) \setminus Z) \\ &\equiv ((X \bowtie Z) \bowtie_{\mathfrak{s}} Y) \cup ((X \setminus Z) \bowtie_{\mathfrak{s}} Y) \\ &\equiv ((X \bowtie Z) \cup (X \setminus Z)) \bowtie_{\mathfrak{s}} Y \qquad \equiv (X ⟕ Z) \bowtie_{\mathfrak{s}} Y\end{aligned}$$

4. For a mapping $\mu = [\mu_1, \mu_2]$ and filter f scoped to $\mathrm{dom}(\mu_1)$, $f(\mu)$ is true if and only if $f(\mu_1)$ is true. Taking $\mu_1 \in X$ and $\mu_2 = [\mu_2', \mu_2''] \in Y \bowtie \{v/\delta([\![\mathcal{V}]\!]^{\mu_1}_{\mu_2})\}$ from $X \bowtie_{\mathfrak{s}} Y$, the result then holds per the given assumptions. □

```
SELECT ?c1 ?c2 ?d WHERE {
  { ?c1 wdt:P31 wd:Q6256 ;                               # Countries
        wdt:P2250 ?lifex1 ; wdt:P2131 ?ngdp1 ;           # Life expectancy, Nominal GDP
        wdt:P4010 ?gdp1 ; wdt:P2219 ?growth1 ;           # GDP, GDP growth rate
        wdt:P1081 ?hdi1 ; wdt:P361 wd:Q12585 }           # HDI, Latin America
  SIMILARITY JOIN
    ON (?lifex1 ?ngdp1 ?gdp1 ?growth1 ?hdi1)
       (?lifex2 ?ngdp2 ?gdp2 ?growth2 ?hdi2)
    TOP 1 DISTANCE sim:manhattan AS ?d                   # 1-nn using Manhattan
  { ?c2 wdt:P31 wd:Q6256 ;                               # Countries
        wdt:P2250 ?lifex2 ; wdt:P2131 ?ngdp2 ;           # Life expectancy, Nominal GDP
        wdt:P4010 ?gdp2 ; wdt:P2219 ?growth2 ;           # GDP, GDP growth rate
        wdt:P1081 ?hdi2 ; wdt:P30 wd:Q46 }}              # HDI, Europe
```

?c1	?c2	?d
wd:Q419 [Peru]	wd:Q218 [Romania]	0.129
wd:Q298 [Chile]	wd:Q45 [Portugal]	0.134
wd:Q96 [Mexico]	wd:Q43 [Turkey]	0.195

Fig. 1. Query for European countries most similar to Latin American countries in terms of a variety of economic indicators, with sample results

4 Use-Cases, Implementation and Optimisation

Having defined the syntax and semantics of the similarity join operator, we now illustrate how the operator can be used, implemented and optimised.

4.1 Use-Case Queries

To illustrate the use of similarity joins in SPARQL, we will now present three use-case queries, demonstrating different capabilities of the proposal. All three queries are based on real-world data from Wikidata [27] and IMGpedia [7].

Similar Countries: In Fig. 1 we present a similarity query for Wikidata [27] that, for each Latin American country, will return the European country with the most similar welfare indicators to it, considering life expectancy, Gross Domestic Product (GDP), nominal GDP, GDP growth rate and Human Development Index (HDI).[1] The query performs a 1-nn similarity join between both sets of countries based on the Manhattan distance over the given dimensions. The figure also presents three sample pairs of results generated by the query (though not returned by the query, we add English labels for illustration purposes).

Similar Elections: In Fig. 2, we present a more complex similarity query over Wikidata to find the four most similar elections to the 2017 German Federal Election in terms of the number of candidates, parties and ideologies involved. The query involves the use of aggregates and paths in the operand graph patterns of the similarity join. The figure also presents the results of the query.

[1] We use prefixes as defined in http://prefix.cc.

```
SELECT ?e2 ?c1 ?c2 ?p1 ?p2 ?d
WHERE {
  { SELECT (wd:Q15062956 AS ?e1)
      (COUNT(DISTINCT ?candidate) AS ?c1)
      (COUNT(DISTINCT ?party) AS ?p1)
      (COUNT(DISTINCT ?ideology) AS ?i1) WHERE {
        wd:Q15062956 wdt:P726 ?candidate .                  # candidates
        ?candidate wdt:P102 ?party . ?party wdt:P1387 ?ideology.}}# parties, ideologies
  SIMILARITY JOIN ON (?c1 ?p1 ?i1) (?c2 ?p2 ?i2)
    TOP 4 DISTANCE sim:manhattan AS ?d                      # 4-nn using Manhattan
  { SELECT ?e2
      (COUNT(DISTINCT ?candidate) AS ?c2)
      (COUNT(DISTINCT ?party) AS ?p2)
      (COUNT(DISTINCT ?ideology) AS ?i2) WHERE {
        ?e2 wdt:P31/wdt:P279* wd:Q40231 ; wdt:P726 ?candidate .   # elections, candidates
        ?candidate wdt:P102 ?party . ?party wdt:P1387 ?ideology . # parties and ideologies
    } GROUP BY ?e2 }}
```

?e2	?c1	?c2	?p1	?p2	?d
wd:Q15062956 [2017 German Federal Election]	10	10	8	8	0.000
wd:Q1348890 [2000 Russian Presidential Election]	10	10	8	7	0.220
wd:Q1505420 [2004 Russian Presidential Election]	10	6	8	8	0.240
wd:Q19818995 [2017 Saarland State Election]	10	7	8	7	0.293

Fig. 2. Query for elections similar to the 2017 German Federal Election in terms of number of candidates, parties and ideologies participating, with results

Similar Images: Figure 3 presents a similarity query over IMGpedia [7]: a multimedia Linked Dataset. The query retrieves images of the Capitol Building in the US, and computes a 3-nn similarity join for images of cathedrals based on a pre-computed Histogram of Oriented Gradients (HOG) descriptor, which extracts the distribution of edge directions of an image. The figure further includes a sample of results for two images of the Capitol Building, showing for each, the three most similar images of cathedrals that are found based on edge directions.

4.2 Implementation

The implementation of the system extends ARQ – the SPARQL engine of Apache Jena[2] – which indexes an RDF dataset and receives as input a (similarity) query in the syntax discussed in Section 3.2. The steps of the evaluation of an extended SPARQL query follow a standard flow, namely PARSING, ALGEBRA OPTIMISATION, ALGEBRA EXECUTION, and RESULT ITERATION. The PARSING stage receives the query string defined by a user, and outputs the algebraic representation of the similarity query. Parsing is implemented by extending Jena's Parser through JavaCC[3], wherein the new keywords and syntax rules are defined. The ALGEBRA OPTIMISATION can then apply rewriting rules (discussed presently) over the query, further turning logical operators (e.g., knnsimjoin) into physical operators (e.g., nestedloop). Next, ALGEBRA EXECUTION begins to evaluate

[2] http://jena.apache.org.

[3] https://javacc.github.io/javacc/.

the physical operators, with low-level triple/quad patterns and path expression operators feeding higher-level operators. Finally, RESULT ITERATION streams the final results from the evaluation of the top-level physical operator. All physical similarity-join operators follow the same lazy evaluation strategy used for the existing join operators in Jena.

```
SELECT ?img1 ?img2 WHERE {
  { ?img1 imo:associatedWith wd:Q54109 .                              # Capitol Building
    ?vector1 a imo:HOG ; imo:describes ?img1 ; imo:value ?hog1 .}     # HOG descriptor
  SIMILARITY JOIN ON (?hog1) (?hog2) TOP 3 DISTANCE sim:manhattan AS ?d # 3nn w/ Manhattan
  { ?cathedral wdt:P31 wd:Q2977 .                                     # Cathedrals
    ?img2 imo:associatedWith ?cathedral .
    ?vector2 a imo:HOG ; imo:describes ?img2 ; imo:value ?hog2 .}}    # HOG descriptor
```

Fig. 3. Query for the three images of cathedrals most similar to each image of the US Capitol Building in terms of the HOG visual descriptor

4.3 Similarity Join Optimisation and Query Planning

The PARSING phase will output either a knnsimjoin or rangesimjoin logical operator for the similarity join. The ALGEBRA OPTIMISATION phase must then select an algorithm with which to instantiate these operators. As previously discussed, for a similarity join $X \bowtie_{\mathfrak{s}} Y$, the naive strategy of computing a nested-loop join will require $|X| \cdot |Y|$ distance computations. The algorithms we include with our implementation of similarity joins are: nested loops, vp-Trees[4] and QJ for range queries; and nested loops, vp-Trees and FLANN[5] for k-nn.

Nested loops constitute a baseline for evaluating similarity joins without optimisation, as would be applied for similarity queries written in vanilla SPARQL syntax or in iSPARQL [14]. On the other hand, QJ is used in DBSimJoin [25],

[4] We use the library provided by Chambers at https://github.com/jchambers/jvptree.
[5] We use the Java implementation provided by Stavrev at https://gitlab.com/jadro-ai-public/flann-java-port.git.

and thus we also include it as a baseline measure, although it does not support k-nn, which we previously argued to be an important feature in this setting.

In initial experiments we noted that the results of similarity queries as defined herein sometimes gave unintuitive results when the magnitude of values in one dimension was naturally much greater or much smaller than that of other dimensions. Taking the query of Fig. 1, for example, while the values for GDP tends to be in the order of billions or trillions, the values for HDI fall in $[0, 1]$; as defined, the HDI dimension would have a negligible effect on the results of the similarity join. To address this, we apply pre-normalisation of each dimension such that the values fall in the range $[0, 1]$.

Aside from adopting efficient similarity join algorithms, we can further optimise evaluation by applying query planning techniques over the query as a whole: given an input similarity query, we can try to find an equivalent, more efficient plan through query rewriting rules. While Jena implements techniques for optimising query plans in non-similarity graph patterns, we further explored both rewriting rules and caching techniques to try to further optimise the overall query plan. However, the techniques we have implemented had negligible or negative effect on runtimes, yielding a negative result, because of which further optimisations in this direction are left as future work.

Regarding rewriting rules, in fact there is little opportunity for such rules to optimise queries with similarity joins for two main reasons. One reason is that since similarity joins are a relatively expensive operation, optimally the results returned from the sub-operands should be as small as possible at the moment of evaluation; this often negates the benefit of delaying operations until after the similarity join. Another reason is that for k-nn similarity joins, the operation is not commutative, nor associative (see Sect. 3.3) preventing join reordering. The most promising rewritings from a performance perspective relate to properties 2 and 4 of Proposition 5, as they reduce the size of the similarity join by first applying the negation or filter, respectively, on the left operand; however, we did not encounter such cases (we further believe that queries are more likely to be written by users in the more optimal form).

Since the operands of similarity joins often have significant overlap in terms of triple patterns, an avenue for optimisation is evaluating this overlap once, reusing the results across both sub-operands. As an example, for the query in Fig. 1, both operands have the same graph pattern except the last triple pattern, which distinguishes European and Latin American countries. We implemented such a technique, which we expected would reduce the runtime by avoiding redundant computation. However, experiments contradicted this expectation, where similar or slightly worse performance was found, for the following reasons. First, the overlap may be less selective than the non-overlapping patterns, making it disadvantageous to evaluate first; conversely, if we conservatively identify the maximal overlap maintaining the original selectivity-based ordering, the overlap will often be negligible. Second, even in favourable examples where a significant and selective overlap was present, no effect was seen due to lower-level caching.

5 Evaluation

We now present our evaluation, comparing the performance of different physical operators for similarity joins in the context of increasingly complex SPARQL queries, as well as a comparison with the baseline system DBSimJoin. We conduct experiments with respect to two benchmarks: the first is a benchmark we propose for Wikidata, while the second is an existing benchmark used by DBSimJoin based on colour information. All experiments were run on a Windows 10 machine with a 4-core Intel i7-7700 processor @2.80 GHz and 16 GB RAM. We provide code, queries, etc., online: https://github.com/scferrada/jenasj.

5.1 Wikidata: k-nn Self-similarity Queries

In order to compare the relative performance of the three similarity join algorithms implemented: nested loop, vp-Trees and FLANN, we present performance results for a set of self-similarity join queries extracted from Wikidata[6]. To arrive at these queries, we begin with some data exploration. Specifically, from the dump, we compute the *ordinal/numeric characteristic sets* [18] by: (1) filtering triples with properties that do not take numeric datatype values, or that take non-ordinal numeric datatype values (e.g., Universal Identifiers); (2) extracting the *characteristic sets* of the graph [18] along with their cardinalities, where, specifically, for each subject in the resulting graph, we extract the set of properties for which it is defined, and for each such set, we compute for how many subjects it is defined. Finally, we generate k-nn self-similarity join queries from 1,000 ordinal/numeric characteristic sets containing more than 3 properties that were defined for more than 500 subjects. The values of k used are $1, 4, 8$. The joins were executed several times per algorithm to make a better estimation of the execution time, since vp-Trees and FLANN present randomised stages; we then report average runtimes over the runs.

Figure 4 presents the average execution time for differing *numbers of entities*, defined to be the cardinality of the solutions $|X|$ input to the self-similarity join $X \bowtie_{\mathrm{n}} X'$, where X' rewrites the variables of X in a one-to-one manner. Highlighting that the y-axis is presented in log scale, we initially remark that the value of k appears to have an effect on the execution time roughly comparable with the associated increase in results that can be expected. We can see a general trend that as the number of entities in the input initially increases, so too do the execution times. Comparing the algorithms, we see significant differences in performance depending on the similarity join algorithm, where (as expected) the nested loop strategy performs poorly. On the other hand, vp-Trees and FLANN are competitive with each other, showing similar performance; both see less sharp increases in time as the number of input entities increases. More specifically, FLANN is faster in 54.7% of the queries; however, we remark that, unlike vp-Trees, FLANN computes an approximation of the real result where, in these experiments, it gave 98% precision overall.

[6] We use a truthy dump available in February, 2020.

In terms of absolute times, we find that both FLANN and vp-Trees can compute self-similarity joins $X \bowtie_{\mathrm{n}} X'$ where $|X| < 20000$ and $1 \leq k \leq 8$ in less than one second (nested loops can take minutes on such queries), and can compute most of the queries analysed ($|X| < 120000$) within 10 s for $k = 1$, 40 s for $k = 4$, and 100 s for $k = 8$.

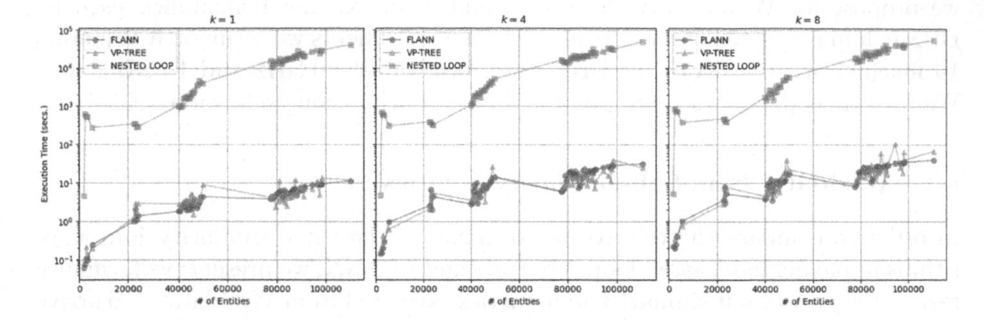

Fig. 4. Average execution time by number of input solutions (entities) for $k = 1, 4, 8$

5.2 Corel Colour Moments: Range Similarity Queries

We compare our system with the closest found in literature, DBSimJoin [25], a PostgreSQL extension that supports range-based similarity joins in metric spaces implementing the QJ algorithm. As DBSimJoin only supports range queries, we compare it with the vp-Tree implementation in Jena (Jena-vp). The DBSimJoin system was originally tested with synthetic datasets and with the Corel Colour Moments (CCM) dataset, which consists of 68,040 records of images, each described with 9 dimensions representing the mean, standard deviation and skewness for the colours of pixels in the image. For CCM, the DBSimJoin paper only reports the effect of the number of QJ pivots on the execution time when $r = 1\%$ of the maximum possible distance in the space [25]. We compare the DBSimJoin implementation with our system for more general performance metrics, using CCM. We converted the CCM dataset to an RDF graph using a direct mapping.

To find suitable distances for the query, we compute a 1-nn self-similarity join on the data, where we take the maximum of minimum distances in the result: 5.9; this distance ensures that each object is paired with at least another object in a range-based query. We compare the runtime of both systems with increasing values of r, using $r = 5.9$ as an upper bound.

Table 1 presents the results: the execution time of DBSimJoin grows rapidly with r because of the quick growth of the size of the window partitions in the QJ algorithm. DBSimJoin crashes with $r \geq 0.4$ so we include results between 0.3 and 0.4 to illustrate the growth in runtime. The runtime of Jena-vp increases slowly with r, where more tree branches need to be visited as the result-set size increases up to almost $4 \cdot 10^8$. Our implementation does not crash with massive results because it fetches the bindings lazily: it obtains all pairs within distance r for a single object and returns them one by one, only computing the next batch when it runs out of pairs; on the other hand, QJ starts piling up window partitions that replicate the data at a high rate, thus causing it to crash.

Considering range-based similarity joins, these results indicate that our system outperforms DBSimJoin in terms of efficiency (our system is faster) and scalability (our system can handle larger amounts of results).

Table 1. Execution times in seconds for range similarity joins over the CCM Dataset.

Distance	# of Results	DBSimJoin (s)	Jena-vp (s)
0.01	68,462	47.22	6.92
0.1	68,498	84.00	7.45
0.3	72,920	775.96	9.63
0.39	92,444	1,341.86	11.17
0.4	121,826	–	11.30
1.0	4,233,806	–	35.01
5.9	395,543,225	–	1,867.86

6 Conclusions

Motivated by the fact that users of knowledge graphs such as Wikidata are sometimes interested in finding similar results rather than crisp results, we have proposed and evaluated an extension of the SPARQL query language with multidimensional similarity joins. Applying similarity joins in the RDF/SPARQL setting implies unique challenges in terms of requiring dimension-agnostic methods (including dimensions that can be computed by the query), as well as data-related issues such as varying magnitudes amongst attributes. We thus present a novel syntax and semantics for multidimensional similarity joins in SPARQL, an implementation based on Apache Jena, a selection of optimised physical operators for such joins, along with use-case queries to illustrate the extension.

We evaluate three different strategies for implementing nearest neighbour joins: a brute-force method (nested loops), an online index-based approach (vp-Trees), and an approximation-based approach (FLANN). Of these, nested loops and vp-Trees can also be applied for range queries. Our experiments show that of these alternatives, vp-Trees emerge as a clear winner, being an exact algorithm that supports both k-nn and range similarity joins, as well as mostly outperforming the other algorithms tested. Our implementation with vp-Trees (and FLANN) outperforms the brute-force nested loop approach – which is how multidimensional distances expressed in vanilla SPARQL queries or queries in iSPARQL are evaluated by default – by orders of magnitude. Compared with the only other system we are aware of that implements multidimensional similarity joins as part of a database query language – DBSimJoin – our approach can handle k-nn queries, as well as much larger distances and result sizes.

Based on our results, we believe that similarity joins are an interesting direction to explore for SPARQL, where they could be used in applications such as entity matching, link prediction, recommendations, multimedia retrieval, query relaxation, etc.; they would also provide novel query functionality for users of SPARQL endpoints, allowing them to find entities in a knowledge graph that are similar within a metric space defined in the query by the user themselves.

Acknowledgements. This work was partly funded by the Millennium Institute for Foundational Research on Data, by FONDECYT Grant No. 1181896 and by CONICYT Grant No. 21170616. We thank the reviewers for their feedback.

References

1. Battle, R., Kolas, D.: Enabling the geospatial Semantic Web with Parliament and GeoSPARQL. Semantic Web **3**(4), 355–370 (2012)
2. Belleau, F., Nolin, M.A., Tourigny, N., Rigault, P., Morissette, J.: Bio2RDF: towards a mashup to build bioinformatics knowledge systems. J. Biomed. Inform. **41**(5), 706–716 (2008)
3. Böhm, C., Braunmüller, B., Krebs, F., Kriegel, H.P.: Epsilon grid order: an algorithm for the similarity join on massive high-dimensional data. SIGMOD Rec. **30**, 379–388 (2001)
4. Böhm, C., Krebs, F.: Supporting KDD applications by the k-nearest neighbor join. In: Mařík, V., Retschitzegger, W., Štěpánková, O. (eds.) DEXA 2003. LNCS, vol. 2736, pp. 504–516. Springer, Heidelberg (2003). https://doi.org/10.1007/978-3-540-45227-0_50
5. Dittrich, J.P., Seeger, B.: GESS: a scalable similarity-join algorithm for mining large data sets in high dimensional spaces. In: Special Interest Group on Knowledge Discovery in Data (SIGKDD), pp. 47–56. ACM (2001)
6. Dohnal, V., Gennaro, C., Savino, P., Zezula, P.: D-index: distance searching index for metric data sets. Multimedia Tools Appl. **21**(1), 9–33 (2003)
7. Ferrada, S., Bustos, B., Hogan, A.: IMGpedia: a linked dataset with content-based analysis of wikimedia images. In: d'Amato, C., et al. (eds.) ISWC 2017. LNCS, vol. 10588, pp. 84–93. Springer, Cham (2017). https://doi.org/10.1007/978-3-319-68204-4_8
8. Galkin, M., Vidal, M.-E., Auer, S.: Towards a multi-way similarity join operator. In: Kirikova, M., Nørvåg, K., Papadopoulos, G.A., Gamper, J., Wrembel, R., Darmont, J., Rizzi, S. (eds.) ADBIS 2017. CCIS, vol. 767, pp. 267–274. Springer, Cham (2017). https://doi.org/10.1007/978-3-319-67162-8_26
9. Giacinto, G.: A nearest-neighbor approach to relevance feedback in content based image retrieval. In: International Conference on Image and Video Retrieval (CIVR), pp. 456–463. ACM, New York (2007)
10. Guerraoui, R., Kermarrec, A., Ruas, O., Taïani, F.: Fingerprinting big data: the case of KNN graph construction. In: International Conference on Data Engineering (ICDE), pp. 1738–1741, April 2019
11. Harris, S., Seaborne, A., Prud'hommeaux, E.: SPARQL 1.1 Query Language. W3C Recommendation, March 2013. https://www.w3.org/TR/sparql11-query/

12. Hogan, A., Mellotte, M., Powell, G., Stampouli, D.: Towards fuzzy query-relaxation for RDF. In: Extended Semantic Web Conference (ESWC), pp. 687–702 (2012)
13. Jacox, E.H., Samet, H.: Metric space similarity joins. ACM TODS **33**(2), 7 (2008)
14. Kiefer, C., Bernstein, A., Stocker, M.: The fundamentals of iSPARQL: a virtual triple approach for similarity-based semantic web tasks. In: Aberer, K., et al. (eds.) ASWC/ISWC -2007. LNCS, vol. 4825, pp. 295–309. Springer, Heidelberg (2007). https://doi.org/10.1007/978-3-540-76298-0_22
15. Li, H., Zhang, X., Wang, S.: Reduce pruning cost to accelerate multimedia kNN search over MBRs based index structures. In: 2011 Third International Conference on Multimedia Information Networking and Security, pp. 55–59, November 2011
16. Muja, M., Lowe, D.G.: Fast approximate nearest neighbors with automatic algorithm configuration. In: International Joint Conference on Computer Vision, Imaging and Computer Graphics Theory and Applications (VISSAPP), pp. 331–340. INSTICC Press (2009)
17. Navarro, G.: Analyzing metric space indexes: what for? In: International Conference on Similarity Search and Applications (SISAP), pp. 3–10. IEEE Computer Society, Washington, DC (2009)
18. Neumann, T., Moerkotte, G.: Characteristic sets: accurate cardinality estimation for RDF queries with multiple joins. In: International Conference on Data Engineering (ICDE), pp. 984–994 (2011)
19. Ngomo, A.N., Auer, S.: LIMES - a time-efficient approach for large-scale link discovery on the web of data. In: International Joint Conference on Artificial Intelligence (IJCAI), pp. 2312–2317 (2011)
20. Oldakowski, R., Bizer, C.: SemMF: a framework for calculating semantic similarity of objects represented as RDF graphs. In: Poster at ISWC (2005)
21. Paredes, R., Reyes, N.: Solving similarity joins and range queries in metric spaces with the list of twin clusters. J. Discrete Algorithms **7**(1), 18–35 (2009)
22. Pérez, J., Arenas, M., Gutiérrez, C.: Semantics and complexity of SPARQL. ACM TODS **34**(3), 16:1–16:45 (2009)
23. Petrova, A., Sherkhonov, E., Cuenca Grau, B., Horrocks, I.: Entity comparison in RDF graphs. In: d'Amato, C., et al. (eds.) ISWC 2017. LNCS, vol. 10587, pp. 526–541. Springer, Cham (2017). https://doi.org/10.1007/978-3-319-68288-4_31
24. Sherif, M.A., Ngomo, A.N.: A systematic survey of point set distance measures for link discovery. Semantic Web **9**(5), 589–604 (2018)
25. Silva, Y.N., Pearson, S.S., Cheney, J.A.: Database similarity join for metric spaces. In: Brisaboa, N., Pedreira, O., Zezula, P. (eds.) SISAP 2013. LNCS, vol. 8199, pp. 266–279. Springer, Heidelberg (2013). https://doi.org/10.1007/978-3-642-41062-8_27
26. Volz, J., Bizer, C., Gaedke, M., Kobilarov, G.: Discovering and maintaining links on the web of data. In: Bernstein, A., et al. (eds.) ISWC 2009. LNCS, vol. 5823, pp. 650–665. Springer, Heidelberg (2009). https://doi.org/10.1007/978-3-642-04930-9_41
27. Vrandečić, D., Krötzsch, M.: Wikidata: a free collaborative knowledgebase. Comm. ACM **57**, 78–85 (2014)
28. Yianilos, P.N.: Data structures and algorithms for nearest neighbor search in general metric spaces. In: Symposium on Discrete Algorithms (SODA), vol. 93, pp. 311–321 (1993)
29. Zhai, X., Huang, L., Xiao, Z.: Geo-spatial query based on extended SPARQL. In: International Conference on Geoinformatics (GEOINFORMATICS), pp. 1–4. IEEE (2010)

ExCut: Explainable Embedding-Based Clustering over Knowledge Graphs

Mohamed H. Gad-Elrab[1,2](✉), Daria Stepanova[2], Trung-Kien Tran[2], Heike Adel[2], and Gerhard Weikum[1]

[1] Max-Planck Institute for Informatics, Saarland Informatics Campus, Saarbrücken, Germany
{gadelrab,weikum}@mpi-inf.mpg.de

[2] Bosch Center for Artificial Intelligence, Renningen, Germany
{daria.stepanova,trungkien.tran,heike.adel}@de.bosch.com

Abstract. Clustering entities over knowledge graphs (KGs) is an asset for explorative search and knowledge discovery. KG embeddings have been intensively investigated, mostly for KG completion, and have potential also for entity clustering. However, embeddings are latent and do not convey user-interpretable labels for clusters. This work presents ExCut, a novel approach that combines KG embeddings with rule mining methods, to compute informative clusters of entities along with comprehensible explanations. The explanations are in the form of concise combinations of entity relations. ExCut jointly enhances the quality of entity clusters and their explanations, in an iterative manner that interleaves the learning of embeddings and rules. Experiments on real-world KGs demonstrate the effectiveness of ExCut for discovering high-quality clusters and their explanations.

1 Introduction

Motivation. Knowledge graphs (KGs) are collections of triples of the form ⟨*subject predicate object*⟩ used for important tasks such as entity search, question answering and text analytics, by providing rich repositories of typed entities and associated properties. For example, Tedros Adhanom is known as a health expert, director of the World Health Organization (`WHO`), alumni of the University of London, and many more.

KGs can support analysts in exploring sets of interrelated entities and discovering interesting structures. This can be facilitated by **entity clustering**, using unsupervised methods for grouping entities into informative subsets. Consider, for example, an analyst or journalist who works on a large corpus of topically relevant documents, say on the Coronavirus crisis. Assume that key entities in this collection have been spotted and linked to the KG already. Then the KG can guide the user in understanding what kinds of entities are most relevant. With thousands of input entities, from health experts, geo-locations, political decision-makers all the way to diseases, drugs, and vaccinations, the user is

J. Z. Pan et al. (Eds.): ISWC 2020, LNCS 12506, pp. 218–237, 2020.
https://doi.org/10.1007/978-3-030-62419-4_13

likely overwhelmed and would appreciate a group-wise organization. This task of computing entity clusters [4,6,16] is the problem we address.

Merely clustering the entity set is insufficient, though. The user also needs to understand the nature of each cluster. In other words, clusters must be explainable, in the form of **user-comprehensible labels.** As entities have types in the KG, an obvious solution is to label each cluster with its prevalent entity type. However, some KGs have only coarse-grained types and labels like "people" or "diseases" cannot distinguish health experts from politicians or virus diseases from bacterial infections. Switching to fine-grained types, such as Wikipedia categories, on the other hand, causes the opposite problem: each entity is associated with tens or hundreds of types, and it is unclear which of these would be a good cluster label. The same holds for an approach where common SPO properties (e.g., *educatedIn* `UK`) are considered as labels. Moreover, once we switch from a single KG to a set of linked open data (LOD) sources as a joint entity repository, the situation becomes even more difficult.

Problem Statement. Given a large set of entities, each with a substantial set of KG properties in the form of categorical values or relations to other entities, our problem is to jointly tackle: (i) **Clustering:** group the entities into k clusters of semantically similar entities; (ii) **Explanation:** generate a user-comprehensible concise labels for the clusters, based on the entity relations to other entities.

State-of-the-Art and Its Limitations. The problem of clustering relational data is traditionally known as conceptual clustering (see, *e.g.*, [25] for overview). Recently, it has been adapted to KGs in the Semantic Web community [6,16]. Existing approaches aim at clustering graph-structured data itself by, *e.g.*, introducing novel notions of distance and similarity directly on the KG [4,5]. Due to the complexity of the data, finding such universally good similarity notions is challenging [5].

Moreover, existing relational learning approaches are not sufficiently scalable to handle large KGs with millions of facts, *e.g.*, YAGO [26] and Wikidata [30]. Clustering entities represented in latent space, *e.g.*, [12,31], helps to overcome this challenge, yet, the resulting clusters are lacking explanations, clustering process is prone to the embedding quality, and hyperparameters are hard to tune [5]. Explaining clusters over KGs, such as [27,28] focus on the discovery of explanations for given perfect clusters. However, obtaining such high-quality clusters in practice is not straightforward.

Approach. To address the above shortcomings, we present **ExCut**, a new method for computing explainable clusters of large sets of entities. The method uses KG embedding as a signal for finding plausible entity clusters, and combines it with logical rule mining, over the available set of properties, to learn interpretable labels. The labels take the form of concise conjunctions of relations that characterize the majority of entities in a cluster. For example, for the above Coronavirus scenario, we aim at mining such labels as $worksFor(X,Y) \wedge type(Y, \texttt{health\_org}) \wedge hasDegreeIn(X, \texttt{life\_sciences})$ for a cluster of health experts, $type(X, \texttt{disease}) \wedge causedBy(X,Y) \wedge type(Y, \texttt{virus})$ for a cluster of virus diseases, and more. A key point in our approach is that these labels can in turn inform the entity embeddings, as they add salient information. Therefore, we interleave and iterate the computation of embeddings and rule mining adapting the embeddings using as feedback the information inferred by the learned rules.

Contributions. Our main contributions can be summarized as follows:

- We introduce ExCut, a novel approach for computing explainable clusters, which combines embedding-based clustering with symbolic rule learning to produce human-understandable explanations for the resulting clusters. These explanations can also serve as new types for entities.
- We propose several strategies to iteratively fine-tune the embedding model to maximize the explainability and accuracy of the discovered clusters based on the feedback from the learned explanations.
- We evaluate ExCut on real-world KGs. In many cases, it out-performs state-of-the-art methods w.r.t. both clustering and explanations quality.

We made the implementation of ExCut and the experimental resources publicly available at https://github.com/mhmgad/ExCut.

2 Preliminaries

Knowledge Graphs. KGs represent interlinked collections of factual information, encoded as a set of ⟨*subject predicate object*⟩ triples, *e.g.*, ⟨`tedros_adhanom` *directorOf* `WHO`⟩. For simplicity, we write triples as in predicate logics format, e.g., *directorOf* (`tedros_adhanom`, `WHO`). A signature of a KG $\mathcal{G}$ is $\Sigma_{\mathcal{G}} = \langle \mathbf{P}, \mathbf{E} \rangle$, where $\mathbf{P}$ is a set of binary predicates and $\mathbf{E}$ is a set of entities, *i.e.*, constants, in $\mathcal{G}$.

KG Embeddings. KG embeddings aim at representing all entities and relations in a continuous vector space, usually as vectors or matrices called *embeddings.* Embeddings can be used to estimate the likelihood of a triple to be true via a scoring function: $f : \mathbf{E} \times \mathbf{P} \times \mathbf{E} \rightarrow \mathbb{R}$. Concrete scoring functions are defined based on various vector space assumptions: (i) The translation-based assumption, *e.g.*, TransE [1] embeds entities and relations as vectors and assumes $\mathbf{v_s} + \mathbf{v_r} \approx \mathbf{v_o}$ for true triples, where $\mathbf{v_s}, \mathbf{v_r}, \mathbf{v_o}$ are vector embeddings for subject s, relation r and object o, resp. (ii) The linear map assumption, *e.g.*, ComplEx [29] embeds entities as vectors and relations as matrices. It assumes that for true triples, the linear mapping $\mathbf{M_r}$ of the subject embedding $\mathbf{v_s}$ is close to the object embedding $\mathbf{v_o} : \mathbf{v_s}\mathbf{M_r} \approx \mathbf{v_o}$. The likelihood that these assumptions of the embedding methods hold should be higher for triples in the KG than for those outside. The learning process is done through minimizing the error induced from the assumptions given by their respective loss functions.

Rules. Let $\mathbf{X}$ be a set of variables. A *rule* r is an expression of the form *head* ← *body*, where *head*, or *head*(r), is an atom over $\mathbf{P} \cup \mathbf{E} \cup \mathbf{X}$ and *body*, or *body*(r), is a conjunction of positive atoms over $\mathbf{P} \cup \mathbf{E} \cup \mathbf{X}$. In this work, we are concerned with *Horn rules*, a subset of first-order logic rules with only

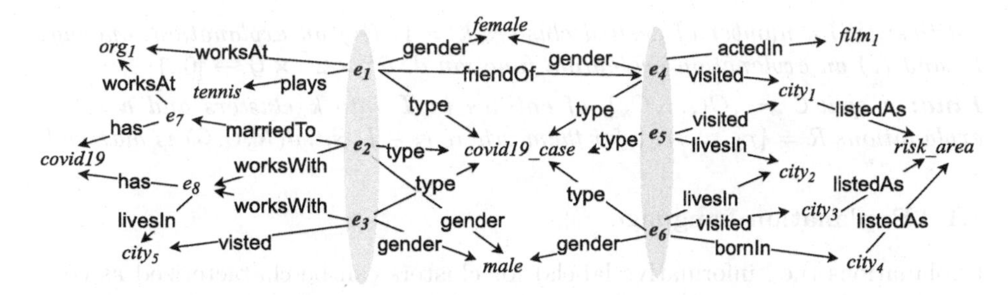

Fig. 1. An example KG with potential COVID-19 cases split into two entity clusters (in green and red). Black edges are relevant for the potential explanations of these clusters.

positive atoms, in which every head variable appears at least once in the body atoms.

Example 1. An example of a rule over the KG in Fig. 1 is r : $has(X,\texttt{covid19}) \leftarrow worksWith(X,Y), has(Y,\texttt{covid19})$ stating that coworkers of individuals with covid19 infection, potentially, also have covid19.

Execution of rules over KGs is defined in the standard way. More precisely, let $\mathcal{G}$ be a KG, r a rule over $\Sigma_{\mathcal{G}}$, and a an atom, we write $r \models_{\mathcal{G}} a$ if there is a variable assignment that maps all atoms of $body(r)$ into $\mathcal{G}$ and $head(r)$ to the atom a. *Rule-based inference* is the process of applying a given rule r on $\mathcal{G}$, which results in the extension $\mathcal{G}_r$ of $\mathcal{G}$ defined as: $\mathcal{G}_r = \mathcal{G} \cup \{a \mid r \models_{\mathcal{G}} a\}$.

Example 2. Application of the rule r from Example 1 on the KG $\mathcal{G}$ from Fig. 1 results in $r \models_{\mathcal{G}} has(\texttt{e}_2, \texttt{covid19})$ and $r \models_{\mathcal{G}} has(\texttt{e}_3, \texttt{covid19})$. Hence, $\mathcal{G}_r = \mathcal{G} \cup \{has(\texttt{e}_2, \texttt{covid19}), has(\texttt{e}_3, \texttt{covid19})\}$.

3 Model for Computing Explainable Clusters

Given a KG, a subset of its entities and an integer k, our goal is to find a "good" split of entities into k clusters and compute explanations for the constructed groups that would serve as informative cluster labels. E.g., consider the KG in Fig. 1, the set of target entities $\{\texttt{e}_1, \ldots, \texttt{e}_6\}$ and the integer $k = 2$. One of the possible solutions is to put $\texttt{e}_{1-3}$ into the first cluster C_1 and the other three entities into the second one C_2. Explanations for this split would be that C_1 includes those who got infected via interacting with their coworkers, while the others were infected after visiting a risk area. Obviously, in general there are many other splits and identifying the criteria for the best ones is challenging.

Formally, we define the problem of *computing explainable entity clusters* as follows:

Definition 1 (Computing Explainable Entity Clusters Problem). ***Given:*** *(i) a knowledge graph* $\mathcal{G}$ *over* $\Sigma_{\mathcal{G}} = \langle \mathbf{P}, \mathbf{E} \rangle$; *(ii) a set* $T \subseteq \mathbf{E}$ *of target*

entities; (iii) a number of desired clusters $k > 1$; (iv) an explanation language L; and (v) an explanation evaluation function $d : 2^L \times 2^T \times \mathcal{G} \rightarrow [0..1]$
Find: *a split $\mathcal{C} = \{C_1, \ldots C_k\}$ of entities in T into k clusters and a set of explanations $\mathcal{R} = \{r_1, \ldots, r_k\}$ for them, where $r_i \in L$, s.t. $d(\mathcal{R}, \mathcal{C}, \mathcal{G})$ is maximal.*

3.1 Explanation Language

Explanations (i.e., informative labels) for clusters can be characterized as conjunctions of common entity properties in a given cluster; for that Horn rules are sufficient. Thus, our explanation language relies on (cluster) explanation rules defined as follows:

Definition 2 (Cluster Explanation Rules). *Let $\mathcal{G}$ be a KG with the signature $\Sigma_\mathcal{G} = \langle \mathbf{P}, \mathbf{E} \rangle$, let $C \subseteq \mathbf{E}$ be a subset of entities in $\mathcal{G}$,* i.e., *a cluster, and $\mathbf{X}$ a set of variables. A* (cluster) explanation rule *r for C over $\mathcal{G}$ is of the form*

$$r : belongsTo(X, e_C) \leftarrow p_1(\boldsymbol{X_1}), \ldots, p_m(\mathbf{X}_m), \qquad (1)$$

where $e_C \notin \mathbf{E}$ is a fresh unique entity representing the cluster C, $belongsTo \notin \mathbf{P}$ is a fresh predicate, and $body(r)$ is a finite set of atoms over $\mathbf{P}$ and $\mathbf{X} \cup \mathbf{E}$.

Example 3. A possible explanation rule for $C_1 = \{\mathtt{e}_1, \mathtt{e}_2, \mathtt{e}_3\}$ in $\mathcal{G}$ from Fig. 1 is

$$r : belongsTo(X, \mathtt{e}_{\mathtt{c}_1}) \leftarrow worksWith(X, Y), has(Y, \mathtt{covid19})$$

which describes C_1 as a set of people working with infected colleagues.

Out of all possible cluster explanation rules we naturally prefer **succinct** ones. Therefore, we put further restrictions on the explanation language L by limiting the number of rule body atoms (an adjustable parameter in our method).

3.2 Evaluation Function

The function d from Definition 1 compares solutions to the problem of explainable entity clustering w.r.t. their quality, and ideally d should satisfy the following two criteria: (i) **Coverage:** Given two explanation rules for a cluster, the one covering more entities should be preferred and (ii) **Exclusiveness:** Explanation rules for different clusters should be (approximately) mutually exclusive.

The coverage measure from data mining is a natural choice for satisfying (i).

Definition 3 (Explanation Rule Coverage). *Let $\mathcal{G}$ be a KG, C a cluster of entities, and r a cluster explanation rule. The* coverage *of r on C w.r.t. $\mathcal{G}$ is*

$$cover(r, C, \mathcal{G}) = \frac{|\{c \in C | r \models_\mathcal{G} belongsTo(c, e_C)\}|}{|C|} \qquad (2)$$

Example 4. Consider clusters $C_1 = \{\mathtt{e}_1, \mathtt{e}_2, \mathtt{e}_3\}$, $C_2 = \{\mathtt{e}_4, \mathtt{e}_5, \mathtt{e}_6\}$ shown in Fig. 1. The set of potential cluster explanation rules along with their coverage scores for C_1 and C_2 respectively, is given as follows:

$r_1 : belongsTo(X, \mathtt{ec}_{i}) \leftarrow type(X, \mathtt{covid19\_case})$	1	1
$r_2 : belongsTo(X, \mathtt{ec}_{i}) \leftarrow gender(X, \mathtt{male})$	0.67	0.33
$r_3 : belongsTo(X, \mathtt{ec}_{i}) \leftarrow worksWith(X, Y), has(Y, \mathtt{covid19})$	0.67	0
$r_4 : belongsTo(X, \mathtt{ec}_{i}) \leftarrow visited(X, Y), listedAs(Y, \mathtt{risk\_area})$	0	1

While addressing (i), the coverage measure does not account for the criteria (ii). Indeed, high coverage of a rule for a given cluster does not imply a low value of this measure for other clusters. For instance, in Example 4 r_1 is too general, as it perfectly covers entities from both clusters. This motivates us to favour (approximately) mutually exclusive explanation rules, *i.e.*, explanation rules with high coverage for a given cluster but low coverage for others (similar to [13]). To capture this intuition, we define the *exclusive explanation coverage* of a rule for a cluster given other clusters as follows.

Definition 4 (Exclusive Explanation Rule Coverage). *Let $\mathcal{G}$ be a KG, let $\mathcal{C}$ be a set of all clusters of interest, $C \in \mathcal{C}$ a cluster, and r an explanation rule. The* exclusive explanation rule coverage *of r for C w.r.t. $\mathcal{C}$ and $\mathcal{G}$ is defined as*

$$exc(r,C,\mathcal{C},\mathcal{G})=\begin{cases} 0, \; if \min\limits_{C'\in\mathcal{C}\setminus C}\{cover(r,C,\mathcal{G})-cover(r,C',\mathcal{G})\}\leq 0 \\ cover(r,C,\mathcal{G})-\frac{\sum_{C'\in\mathcal{C}\setminus C} cover(r,C',\mathcal{G})}{|\mathcal{C}\setminus C|}, \; otherwise. \end{cases} \tag{3}$$

Example 5. Consider $\mathcal{C} = \{C_1, C_2\}, \mathcal{R} = \{r_1, r_2, r_3, r_4\}$ from Example 4 and the KG $\mathcal{G}$ from Fig. 1. We have $exc(r_1, C_1, \mathcal{C}, \mathcal{G}) = exc(r_1, C_2, \mathcal{C}, \mathcal{G}) = 0$, which disqualifies r_1 as an explanation for either of the clusters. For r_2, we have $exc(r_2, C_1, \mathcal{C}, \mathcal{G}) = 0.34$ making it less suitable for the cluster C_1 than r_3 with $exc(r_3, C_1, \mathcal{C}, \mathcal{G}) = 0.67$. Finally, r_4 perfectly explains C_2, since $exc(r_4, C_2, \mathcal{C}, \mathcal{G}) = 1$.

Similarly, we can measure the *quality* of a collection of clusters with their explanations by averaging their per-cluster exclusive explanation rule coverage.

Definition 5 (Quality of Explainable Clusters). *Let $\mathcal{G}$ be a KG, $\mathcal{C} = \{C_1, \ldots, C_k\}$ a set of entity clusters, and $\mathcal{R} = \{r_1, \ldots, r_k\}$ a set of cluster explanation rules, where each r_i is an explanation for C_i, $1 \leq i \leq k$. The* explainable clustering quality *q of $\mathcal{R}$ for $\mathcal{C}$ w.r.t. $\mathcal{G}$ is defined as follows:*

$$q(\mathcal{R}, \mathcal{C}, \mathcal{G}) = \frac{1}{|\mathcal{C}|} \sum_{i=1}^{|\mathcal{C}|} exc(r_i, C_i, \mathcal{C}, \mathcal{G}) \tag{4}$$

Realizing the function d in Definition 1 by the above measure allows us to conveniently compare the solutions of the explainable clusters discovery problem.

Example 6. Consider $\mathcal{G}$ from Fig. 1, the set of target entities $T = \{\mathtt{e}_1, \ldots, \mathtt{e}_6\}$, $k = 2$, language L of cluster explanation rules with at most 2 body atoms, and the evaluation function d given as q from Definition 5. The best solution to the respective problem of computing explainable entity clusters is $\mathcal{C} = \{C_1, C_2\}$, $\mathcal{R} = \{r_3, r_4\}$, where C_1, C_2, r_3, r_4 are from Example 4. We have that $q(\mathcal{R}, \mathcal{C}, \mathcal{G})$=0.83.

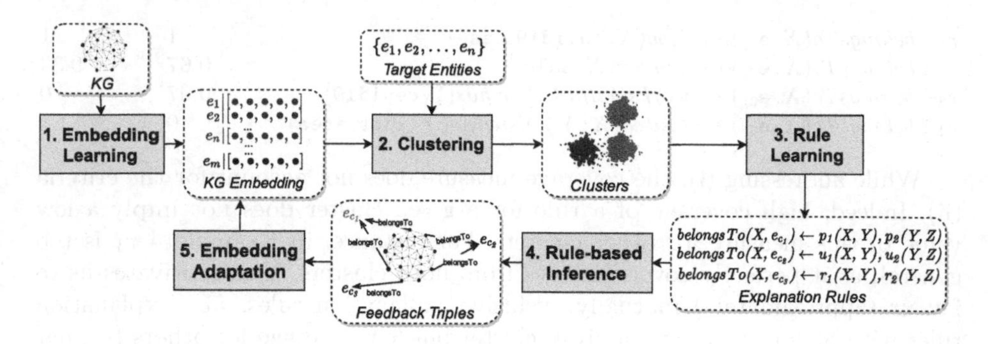

Fig. 2. ExCut pipeline overview.

4 Method

We now present our method ExCut, which iteratively utilizes KG *Embedding-based Clustering* and *Rule Learning* to compute explainable clusters. More specifically, as shown in Fig. 2, ExCut starts with (1) *Embedding Learning* for a given KG. Then, it performs (2) *Clustering* of the entities in the target set over the learned embeddings. Afterwards, (3) *Rule Learning* is utilized to induce explanation rules for the constructed clusters, which are ranked based on the exclusive coverage measure. Using the learned explanation rules, we perform (4) *Rule-based Inference* to deduce new entity-cluster assignment triples reflecting the learned structural similarities among the target entities. Then, ExCut uses the rules and the inferred assignment triples in constructing feedback to guide the clustering in the subsequent iterations. We achieve that by fine-tuning the embeddings of the target entities in Step (5) *Embedding Adaptation.*

In what follows we present the detailed description of ExCut's components.

4.1 Embedding Learning and Clustering

Embedding Learning. ExCut starts with learning vector representations of entities and relations. We adopt KG embeddings in this first step, as they are well-known for their ability to capture semantic similarities among entities, and thus could be suited for defining a robust similarity function for *clustering relational data* [5]. Embeddings are also effective for dealing with data incompleteness, *e.g.*, predicting the potentially missing fact *worksWith*(e_1, e_7) in Fig. 1. Moreover, embeddings facilitate the inclusion of unstructured external sources during training, *e.g.*, textual entity descriptions [33].

Conceptually, any embedding method can be used in our approach. We experimented with TransE [1] and ComplEx [29] as prominent representatives of translation-based and linear map embeddings. To account for the context surrounding the target entities, we train embeddings using the whole KG.

Clustering. The *Clustering* step takes as input the trained embedding vectors of the target entities and the number k of clusters to be constructed. We perform

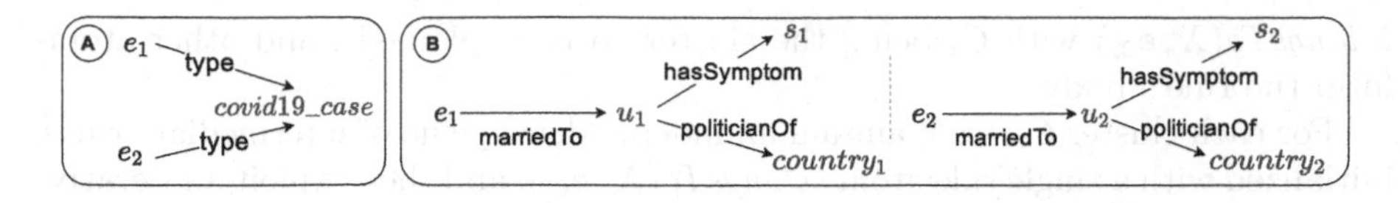

Fig. 3. KG fragments.

clustering relying on the embeddings as features to compute pairwise distances among the target entities using standard distance functions, *e.g.*, *cosine distance*. Various classical clustering approaches or more complex embedding-driven clustering techniques [31] could be exploited here too. In this paper, we rely on the traditional *Kmeans* method [17] as a proof of concept.

For KGs with types, the majority of embedding models [1,29] would map entities of a certain type to similar vectors [31]. For example, e_1 and e_2 in Fig. 3A are likely to be close to each other in the embedding space, and thus have a high chance of being clustered together. An ideal embedding model for explainable clustering should follow the same intuition even if types in the KG are missing. In other words, it should be capable of assigning similar vectors to entities that belong to structurally similar subgraphs of certain pre-specified complexity. For instance, in Fig. 3B, both e_1 and e_2 belong to subgraphs reflecting that these entities are married to politicians with some `covid19` symptom, and hence should be mapped to similar vectors.

Despite certain attempts to consider specific graph patterns (*e.g.*, [15]), to the best of our knowledge none of the existing embedding models is general enough to capture patterns of arbitrary complexity. We propose to tackle this limitation (see Sect. 4.3) by passing to the embedding model feedback created using cluster explanation rules learned in the Step 3 of ExCut.

4.2 Explanation Mining

KG-Based Explanations. KG embeddings and the respective clusters constructed in Steps 1 and 2 of our method are not interpretable. However, since KG embeddings are expected to preserve semantic similarities among entities, the clusters in the embedding space should intuitively have some meaning. Motivated by this, in ExCut, we aim at decoding these similarities by learning rules over the KG extended by the facts that reflect the cluster assignments computed in the *Clustering* step.

Rule Learning Procedure. After augmenting $\mathcal{G}$ with *belongsTo*$(\mathsf{e}, \mathsf{e}_{\mathsf{C}_i})$ facts for all entities e clustered in C_i, we learn Horn rules of the form (1) from Definition 2. There are powerful rule-learning tools such as AMIE+ [8], AnyBurl [18], RLvLR [20,21] and RuDiK [22]. Nevertheless, we decided to develop our own rule learner so that we could have full control over our specific scoring functions and their integration into the learner's search strategy. Following [8], we model rules as sequences of atoms, where the first atom is the head of the rule (*i.e.*,

$belongsTo(X, \mathtt{e}_{\mathtt{C}_i})$ with C_i being the cluster to be explained), and other atoms form the rule's body.

For each cluster C_i, we maintain an independent queue of intermediate rules, initialized with a single rule atom $belongsTo(X, \mathtt{e}_{\mathtt{C}_i})$, and then exploit an iterative breadth-first search strategy. At every iteration, we expand the existing rules in the queue using the following *refinement operators*: (i) *add a positive dangling atom*: add a binary positive atom with one fresh variable and another variable appearing in the rule, *i.e.*, *shared variable* , *e.g.*, adding $worksAt(X, Y)$, where Y is a fresh variable not appearing in the current rule; (ii) *add a positive instantiated atom*: add a positive atom with one argument being a constant and the other one a shared variable , *e.g.*, adding $locatedIn(X, usa)$, where usa is a constant, and X appears elsewhere in the rule constructed so far.

These operators produce a set of new rule candidates, which are then filtered relying on the given explanation language L. Suitable rules with a minimum coverage of 0.5, *i.e.*, rules covering the majority of the respective cluster, are added to the output set. We refine the rules until the maximum length specified in the language bias is reached. Finally, we rank the constructed rules based on the *exclusive explanation coverage* (Definition 4), and select the top m rules for each cluster.

Example 7. Assume that for $\mathcal{G}$ in Fig. 1, and $T = \{\mathtt{e}_1, \ldots, \mathtt{e}_6\}$, the embedding-based clustering resulted in the following clusters $C_1 = \{\mathtt{e}_1, \mathtt{e}_2, \underline{\mathtt{e}_4}\}$ and $C_2 = \{\mathtt{e}_5, \mathtt{e}_6, \underline{\mathtt{e}_3}\}$, where $\mathtt{e}_4$ and $\mathtt{e}_3$ are incorrectly placed in wrong clusters. The top cluster explanation rules for C_2 ranked based on exc measure from Definition 4 are:

$r_1 : belongsTo(X, \mathtt{e}_{\mathtt{C}_2}) \leftarrow visited(X, Y)$ 0.67
$r_2 : belongsTo(X, \mathtt{e}_{\mathtt{C}_2}) \leftarrow gender(X, \mathtt{male})$ 0.33
$r_3 : belongsTo(X, \mathtt{e}_{\mathtt{C}_2}) \leftarrow visited(X, Y), listedAs(Y, \mathtt{risk\_area})$. 0.33

Inferring Entity-Clusters Assignments. In the *Rule-based Inference* (Step 4 in Fig. 2), we apply the top-m rules obtained in the *Rule Learning* step on the KG to predict the assignments between the target entities and the discovered clusters over *belongsTo* relation using standard deductive reasoning techniques. The computed assignment triples are ranked and filtered based on the exc score of the respective rules that inferred them.

Example 8. Application of the rules from Example 7 on $\mathcal{G}$ w.r.t. the target entities $\mathtt{e}_{1-6}$ results in the cluster assignment triples: $\{belongsTo(\mathtt{e}_3, \mathtt{e}_{\mathtt{C}_2}), belongsTo(\mathtt{e}_4, \mathtt{e}_{\mathtt{C}_2}), belongsTo(\mathtt{e}_2, \mathtt{e}_{\mathtt{C}_2})\}$. Note that based on r_1, $\mathtt{e}_4$ is assigned to C_2 instead of C_1.

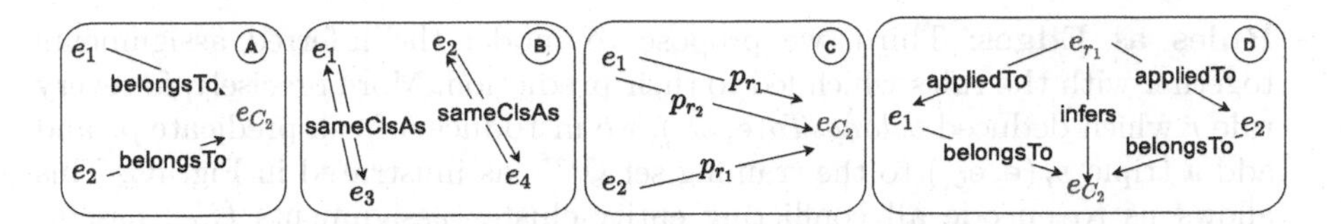

Fig. 4. Inferred clusters assignment triples modeling options.

4.3 Embedding Adaptation

Learned explanation rules capture explicit structural similarities among the target entities. We propose to utilize them to create feedback to guide the embedding-based clustering towards better explainable clusters. This feedback is passed to the embedding model in the form of additional training triples reflecting the assignments inferred by the learned rules. Our intuition is that such added triples should potentially help other similarities of analogous nature to be discovered by the embeddings, compensating for the embedding-based clustering limitation discussed in Sect. 4.1.

Specifically, the embedding adaptation (Step 5 in Fig. 2) is summarized as follows: (a) From the *Rule Learning* and *Rule-based Inference* steps, described above, we obtain a set of *cluster assignment triples* of the form $belongsTo(e, e_C)$ together with rules inferring them, where e is an entity in the input KG $\mathcal{G}$ and e_C is a new entity uniquely representing the cluster C. (b) We then model the cluster assignments from (a) and rules that produce them using one of our four strategies described below and store the results in $\mathcal{G}^{inf}$. (c) A subset $\mathcal{G}^{context}$ of $\mathcal{G}$ consisting of triples that surround the target entities is then constructed. (d) Finally, we fine-tune the embedding model by training it further on the data compiled from $\mathcal{G}^{inf}$ and $\mathcal{G}^{context}$.

Modeling Rule-Based Feedback. Determining the adequate structure and amount of training triples required for fine-tuning the embedding model is challenging. On the one hand, the training data should be rich enough to reflect the learned structure, but on the other hand, it should not corrupt the current embedding. We now present our proposed four strategies for representing the inferred cluster-assignments along with the corresponding rules as a set of triples $\mathcal{G}^{inf}$ suitable for adapting the embedding. The strategies are listed in the ascending order of their complexity.

- **Direct**: As a straightforward strategy, we directly use the inferred entity-cluster assignment triples in $\mathcal{G}^{inf}$ as shown in Fig. 4A, *e.g.*, $belongsTo(\mathsf{e}_1, \mathsf{e}_{\mathsf{C}_2})$.
- **Same-Cluster-as**: In the second strategy, we model the inferred assignments as edges only. As shown in Fig. 4B, we compile $\mathcal{G}^{inf}$ using triples of *sameClsAs* relations between every pair of entities belonging to the same cluster as the learned rules suggest, *e.g.*, $sameClsAs(\mathsf{e}_1, \mathsf{e}_2)$. Modeling the cluster assignments using fresh relations allows us to stress the updates related to the target entities, as no extra entities are added to the KG in this strategy.

- **Rules as Edges**: Third, we propose to model the inferred assignments together with the rules which led to their prediction. More precisely, for every rule r which deduced $belongsTo(\mathtt{e}, \mathtt{e}_{\mathtt{C}_i})$, we introduce a fresh predicate p_r and add a triple $p_r(\mathtt{e}, \mathtt{e}_{\mathtt{C}_i})$ to the training set $\mathcal{G}^{inf}$, as illustrated in Fig. 4C. This allows us to encode all conflicting entity-cluster assignments (*i.e.*, assignments, in which an entity belongs to two different clusters) and supply the embedding model with richer evidence about the rules that predicted these assignments.
- **Rules as Entities**: Rules used in the deduction process can also be modeled as entities. In the fourth strategy, we exploit this possibility by introducing additional predicates *infers* and *appliedTo*, and for every rule r a fresh entity $\mathtt{e}_r$. Here, each $belongsTo(\mathtt{e}, \mathtt{e}_{\mathtt{C}_i})$ fact deduced by the rule r is modeled in $\mathcal{G}^{inf}$ with two triples $infers(\mathtt{e_r}, \mathtt{e}_{\mathtt{C}_i})$ and $appliedTo(\mathtt{e_r}, \mathtt{e})$ as shown in Fig. 4D.

Embedding Fine-Tuning. At every iteration i of ExCut, we start with the embedding vectors obtained in the previous iteration $i-1$ and train the embedding further with a set of adaptation triples $\mathcal{G}^{adapt}$. The set $\mathcal{G}^{adapt}$ is composed of the union of all $\mathcal{G}_j^{inf}$ for $j = 1 \dots i$ and a set of context triples $\mathcal{G}^{context}$. For $\mathcal{G}^{context}$, we only consider those directly involving the target entities as a subject or object. E.g., among the facts in the surrounding context of $\mathtt{e}_1$, we have $worksAt(\mathtt{e}_1, \mathtt{org}_1)$ and $plays(\mathtt{e}_1, \mathtt{tennis})$.

Our empirical studies (see the technical report[1]) showed that including assignment triples from previous iterations $j < i$ leads to better results; thus, we include them in $\mathcal{G}^{adapt}$, but distinguish entity and relation names from different iterations. Additionally, considering the context subgraph helps in regulating the change caused by the cluster assignment triples by preserving some of the characteristics of the original embeddings.

5 Experiments

We evaluate the effectiveness of ExCut for computing explainable clusters. More specifically, we report the experimental results covering the following aspects: (i) the quality of the clusters produced by ExCut compared to existing clustering approaches; (ii) the quality of the computed cluster explanations; (iii) the usefulness and understandability of the explanations for humans based on a user study; (iv) the benefits of interleaving embedding and rule learning for enhancing the quality of the clusters and their explanations; and (v) the impact of using different embedding paradigms and our strategies for modeling the feedback from the rules.

5.1 Experiment Setup

ExCut Configurations. We implemented ExCut in Python and configured its components as follows: (i) *Embedding-based Clustering:* We extended the

[1] Code, data and the technical report are available at https://github.com/mhmgad/ExCut.

Table 1. Datasets statistics.

	UWCSE	WebKB	Terror.	IMDB	Mutag.	Hepatitis	LUBM	YAGO
Target Entities	209	106	1293	268	230	500	2850	3900
Target Clusters	2	4	6	2	2	2	2	3
KG Entities	991	5906	1392	578	6196	6511	242558	4295825
Relations	12	7	4	4	14	19	22	38
Facts	2216	72464	17117	1231	30805	77585	2169451	12430700

implementation of *TransE* and *ComplEx* provided by Ampligraph [3] to allow embedding fine-tuning. We set the size of the embeddings to 100, and trained a base model with the whole KG for 100 epochs, using stochastic gradient descent with a learning rate of 0.0005. For fine-tuning, we trained the model for 25 epochs with a learning rate of 0.005. *Kmeans* is used for clustering. (ii) *Rule Learning:* We implemented the algorithm described in Sect. 4.2. For experiments, we fix the language bias of the explanations to paths of length two, *e.g.*, $belongsTo(x, \mathrm{ec}_i) \leftarrow p(x, y), q(y, z)$, where z is either a free variable or bind to a constant. (iii) *Modeling Rule-based Feedback:* We experiment with the four strategies from Sect. 4.3: direct (*belongToCl*), same cluster as edges (*sameClAs*), rules as edges (*entExplCl*), and rules as entities (*followExpl*).

Datasets. We performed experiments on six datasets (Tab. 1) with a prespecified set of target entities, which are widely used for relational clustering [4]. Additionally, we considered the following large-scale KGs: (i) *LUBM-Courses*: a subset of entities from LUBM syntactic KG [9] describing the university domain, where target entities are distributed over *graduate* and *undergraduate courses*; and (ii) *YAGO-Artwork* KG with a set of target entities randomly selected from *YAGO* [26]. The entities are uniformly distributed over three types, *book*, *song*, and *movie*. To avoid trivial explanations, type triples for target entities were removed from the KG. Table 1 reports the dataset statistics.

Baselines. We compare ExCut to the following clustering methods: (i) *ReCeNT* [4], a state-of-the-art relational clustering approach, that clusters entities based on a similarity score computed from entity neighborhood trees; (ii) *Deep Embedding Clustering (DEC)* [32], an embedding-based clustering method that performs dimensionality reduction jointly with clustering and (iii) Standard *Kmeans* applied directly over embeddings: *TransE (Kmeans-T)* and *ComplEx (Kmeans-C)*. This baseline is equivalent to a single iteration of our system ExCut. Extended experiments with clustering algorithms that automatically detect the number of clusters can be found in the technical report.

Clustering Quality Metrics. We measure the clustering quality w.r.t. the ground truth with three standard metrics: *Accuracy (ACC)*, *Adjusted Rand Index (ARI)*, and *Normalized Mutual Information (NMI)* (the higher, the better).

Explanation Quality Metrics. The quality of the generated explanations is measured using the coverage metrics defined in Sect. 3.2, namely, *per cluster coverage (Cov)* and *exclusive coverage (Exc)*. In addition, we adapted the “novelty” metric *Weighted Relative Accuracy (WRA)* [14], which represents a trade-off

Table 2. Clustering results of ExCut compared to the baselines.

	Methods	UWCSE			IMDB			Hepatitis			Mutagenesis			WebKB			Terrorist		
		ACC	ARI	NMI	ACC	ARI	NMI	ACC	ARI	NMI	ACC	ARI	NMI	ACC	ARI	NMI	ACC	ARI	NMI
Baselines	ReCeNT	0.90	0.60	0.54	0.61	0.02	0.01	0.51	-0.01	0.01	**0.77**	0.30	0.24	**0.52**	0.00	-0.25	0.37	0.10	0.13
	DEC	0.67	0.17	0.12	0.54	0.00	0.01	0.55	0.01	0.01	0.51	0.00	0.00	0.31	0.03	0.05	0.37	0.16	0.26
	Kmeans-T	0.91	0.66	0.51	0.58	0.03	0.08	0.51	0.00	0.00	0.52	0.00	0.00	0.33	0.01	0.06	0.53	0.33	0.44
	Kmeans-C	0.54	0.00	0.01	0.53	0.00	0.00	0.52	0.00	0.00	0.73	0.21	0.18	0.49	0.21	0.34	0.51	0.23	0.28
ExCut-T	belongToCl	0.99	0.96	0.92	**1.00**	1.00	1.00	**0.83**	0.43	0.35	0.68	0.12	0.13	0.43	0.13	0.17	0.52	0.27	0.31
	sameClAs	**1.00**	1.00	1.00	**1.00**	1.00	1.00	0.56	0.01	0.01	0.65	0.08	0.08	0.36	0.06	0.08	0.35	0.03	0.06
	entExplCl	**1.00**	1.00	1.00	**1.00**	1.00	1.00	0.82	0.41	0.33	0.64	0.07	0.08	0.43	0.13	0.20	0.45	0.17	0.23
	followExpl	**1.00**	1.00	1.00	**1.00**	1.00	1.00	0.82	0.41	0.33	0.64	0.08	0.08	0.44	0.15	0.22	0.45	0.16	0.22
Excut-C	belongToCl	0.96	0.85	0.77	**1.00**	1.00	1.00	0.63	0.07	0.05	0.73	0.21	0.18	0.51	0.23	0.37	**0.54**	0.26	0.29
	sameClAs	0.98	0.91	0.86	**1.00**	1.00	1.00	0.58	0.02	0.02	0.73	0.21	0.18	0.38	0.08	0.17	0.34	0.03	0.08
	entExplCl	0.97	0.88	0.81	0.65	0.08	0.19	0.69	0.15	0.11	0.73	0.21	0.19	**0.52**	0.24	0.36	0.53	0.25	0.29
	followExpl	0.99	0.97	0.94	**1.00**	1.00	1.00	0.66	0.10	0.08	0.73	0.20	0.18	0.51	0.22	0.34	0.52	0.24	0.29

between the coverage and the accuracy of the discovered explanations. We compute the average of the respective quality of the top explanations for all clusters. To assess the quality of the solution to the explainable clustering problem from Definition 1 found by ExCut, we compare the computed quality value to the quality of the explanations computed over the ground truth.

All experiments were performed on a Linux machine with 80 cores and 500 GB RAM. The average results over 5 runs are reported.

User Study. To assess the human-understandability and usefulness of the explanation rules, we analyze whether ExCut explanations are the best fitting labels for the computed clusters based on the user opinion. The study was conducted on Amazon MTurk.

More specifically, based on the YAGO KG, we provided the user study participants with: (i) Three clusters of entities, each represented with three entities pseudo-randomly selected from these clusters along with a brief summary for each entity, and a link to its Wikipedia page; (ii) A set of 10 potential explanations composed of the top explanations generated by ExCut and other explanations with high *Cov* but low *Exc*. Explanations were displayed in natural language for the ease of readability. We asked the participants to match each explanation to all relevant clusters.

A *useful* explanation is the one that is *exclusively matched* to the correct cluster by the participants. To detect useful explanations, for every *explanation-cluster* pair, we compute the ratio of responses where the pair is *exclusively matched*. Let $match(r_i, c_m) = 1$ if the user *matched* explanation r_i to the cluster c_m (otherwise 0). Then, r_i is *exclusively matched* to c_m if additionally, $match(r_i, c_j) = 0$ for all $j \neq m$.

5.2 Experiment Results

In seven out of eight datasets, our approach outperforms the baselines with regard to the overall clustering and explanation quality metrics. Additionally, the quality of the computed explanations increases after few iterations.

Table 3. Quality of Clusters Explanations by ExCut compared to the baselines.

	Methods	UWCSE			IMDB			Hepatitis			Mutagenesis			WebKB			Terrorist		
		Cov	Exc	WRA	Cov	Exc	WRA	Cov	Exc	WRA	Cov	Exc	WRA	Cov	Exc	WRA	Cov	Exc	WRA
Baselines	ReCeNT	0.91	0.88	0.14	1.00	0.04	0.01	1.00	0.00	0.00	1.00	0.00	0.00	1.00	1.00	0.00	0.93	0.42	0.06
	DEC	0.73	0.31	0.07	1.00	0.03	0.01	1.00	0.01	0.00	1.00	0.00	0.00	1.00	0.06	0.01	0.60	0.13	0.02
	Kmeans-T	0.83	0.76	0.16	0.74	0.11	0.01	0.81	0.09	0.02	0.75	0.11	0.03	0.75	0.11	**0.03**	0.49	0.17	0.02
	Kmeans-C	0.59	0.06	0.01	0.73	0.04	0.01	0.61	0.09	0.02	0.87	0.30	0.08	0.98	0.04	0.01	0.64	0.28	0.02
ExCut-T	belongToCl	0.89	0.89	**0.19**	1.00	1.00	**0.11**	0.76	0.64	0.13	0.94	0.39	0.09	0.98	0.12	0.01	0.68	0.26	0.03
	sameClAs	0.90	0.90	**0.19**	1.00	1.00	**0.11**	0.94	0.45	0.09	0.96	0.50	**0.12**	0.99	0.04	0.01	0.87	0.49	0.06
	entExplCl	0.90	0.90	**0.19**	1.00	1.00	**0.11**	0.75	0.64	0.13	0.99	0.48	0.12	0.99	0.10	0.01	0.94	0.80	**0.11**
	followExpl	0.90	0.90	**0.19**	1.00	1.00	**0.11**	0.75	0.63	0.13	0.98	0.46	0.11	0.99	0.09	0.01	0.95	0.79	**0.11**
ExCut-C	belongToCl	0.88	0.86	0.18	1.00	1.00	**0.11**	0.73	0.50	0.12	0.87	0.31	0.08	0.98	0.08	0.01	0.68	0.32	0.02
	sameClAs	0.91	0.89	**0.19**	1.00	1.00	**0.11**	0.80	0.45	0.11	0.87	0.30	0.08	0.98	0.10	0.01	0.85	0.61	0.07
	entExplCl	0.88	0.88	**0.19**	0.73	0.18	0.01	0.85	0.73	**0.18**	0.87	0.31	0.08	0.97	0.08	0.01	0.68	0.33	0.03
	followExpl	0.90	0.89	**0.19**	1.00	1.00	**0.11**	0.81	0.66	0.12	0.87	0.31	0.08	0.97	0.07	0.01	0.67	0.30	0.03
Ground truth		0.92	0.90	0.19	1.00	1.00	0.11	0.92	0.57	0.14	1.00	0.16	0.04	1.00	0.04	0.01	0.64	0.33	0.03

Clustering Quality. Table 2 presents the quality of the clusters computed by the baselines, in the first 4 rows, followed by ExCut with the four feedback strategies, where *ExCut-T* and *ExCut-C* stand for ExCut with TransE and ComplEx respectively.

For all datasets except for *Mutagensis*, ExCut achieved, in general, better results w.r.t. the *ACC* value than the state-of-the-art methods. Furthermore, ExCut-T results in significantly better clusters on all datasets apart from *Terrorists* compared to Kmeans-T, *i.e.*, the direct application of *Kmeans* on the TransE embedding model. Since the *Terrorists* dataset contains several attributed predicates (e.g., facts over numerical values), a different language bias for the explanation rules is required.

Our system managed to fully re-discover the ground truth clusters for the two datasets: *UWCSE* and *IMDB.* The accuracy enhancement by ExCut-T compared to the respective baseline (Kmeans-T) exceeds 30% for *IMDB* and *Hepatitis.* Other quality measurements indicate similar increments.

Explanation Quality. Table 3 shows the average quality of the top explanations for the discovered clusters, where the average per cluster coverage (*Cov*) and exclusive coverage (*Exc*) are intrinsic evaluation metrics used as our optimization functions, while the *WRA* measure is the extrinsic one.

The last row presents the quality of the learned explanations for the ground truth clusters; these values are not necessarily 1.0, as perfect explanations under the specified language bias may not exist. We report them as reference points.

ExCut enhances the average *Exc* and *WRA* scores of the clusters' explanations compared to the ones obtained by the baselines. These two measures highlight the exclusiveness of the explanations; making them more representative than *Cov.* Thus, the decrease in the *Cov,* as in *Terrorist,* is acceptable, given that it is in favor of increasing them.

Similar to the clustering results, for *UWCSE* and *IMDB* our method achieved the explanations quality of the ground truth. For other datasets, our method obtained higher explanations quality than the respective baselines. This demon-

Table 4. Quality of the clusters and the explanations found in Large-scale KGs.

	Methods	LUBM Courses						Yago Artwork					
		ACC	ARI	NMI	Cov	Exc	WRA	ACC	ARI	NMI	Cov	Exc	WRA
Baselines	DEC	0.92	0.70	0.66	0.96	0.95	0.19	0.56	0.44	0.57	0.92	0.49	0.11
	Kmeans-T	0.50	0.00	0.00	0.46	0.03	0.01	0.52	0.42	0.58	0.92	0.42	0.11
ExCut-T	belongToCl	1.00	1.00	1.00	1.00	1.00	0.25	0.82	0.63	0.59	0.85	0.70	0.16
	sameClAs	0.88	0.57	0.53	0.91	0.79	0.19	0.97	0.91	0.90	0.95	0.93	0.21
	entExplCl	**1.00**	**1.00**	**1.00**	**1.00**	**1.00**	**0.25**	**0.97**	**0.92**	**0.91**	**0.95**	**0.93**	**0.21**
	followExpl	1.00	1.00	1.00	1.00	1.00	0.25	0.88	0.73	0.70	0.86	0.78	0.17
Ground truth		-	-	-	1.00	1.00	0.25	-	-	-	0.95	0.93	0.21

Table 5. Explanations of clusters *song*, *book*, and *movie* from Yago KG. ($\forall X \in C_i$)

	Kmeans-T				ExCut-T			
	Explanations	Cov	Exc	WRA	Explanations	Cov	Exc	WRA
C_1	$\mathit{created}(Y,X), \mathit{bornIn}(Y,Z)$	0.94	0.55	0.13	$\mathit{created}(Y,X), \mathit{type}(Y,\texttt{artist})$	0.99	0.96	**0.21**
	$\mathit{created}(Y,X), \mathit{type}(Y,\texttt{artist})$	0.49	0.45	0.10	$\mathit{created}(Y,X), \mathit{won}(Y,\texttt{grammy})$	0.57	0.57	**0.12**
	$\mathit{created}(Y,X), \mathit{type}(Y,\texttt{writer})$	0.52	0.44	0.10	$\mathit{created}(Y,X), \mathit{type}(Y,\texttt{person})$	0.84	0.48	**0.11**
C_2	$\mathit{directed}(Y,X)$	0.92	0.56	0.11	$\mathit{created}(Y,X), \mathit{type}(Y,\texttt{writer})$	0.99	0.91	**0.19**
	$\mathit{directed}(Y,X), \mathit{gender}(Y,\texttt{male})$	0.89	0.54	**0.10**	$\mathit{created}(Y,X), \mathit{diedIn}(Y,Z)$	0.46	0.20	0.04
	$\mathit{created}(Y,X), \mathit{type}(Y,\texttt{person})$	0.71	0.52	**0.06**	$\mathit{created}(Y,X)$	1.00	0.00	0.05
C_3	$\mathit{actedIn}(Y,X), \mathit{type}(Y,\texttt{person})$	0.58	0.30	0.07	$\mathit{actedIn}(Y,X)$	0.81	0.81	**0.19**
	$\mathit{locatedIn}(X,Y), \mathit{hasLang}(Y,Z)$	0.60	0.29	0.07	$\mathit{actedIn}(Y,X), \mathit{bornIn}(Y,Z)$	0.79	0.79	**0.18**
	$\mathit{locatedIn}(X,Y), \mathit{currency}(Y,Z)$	0.60	0.29	0.07	$\mathit{actedIn}(Y,X), \mathit{type}(Y,\texttt{person})$	0.78	0.78	**0.18**

strates the effectiveness of the proposed feedback mechanism in adapting the embedding model to better capture the graph structures in the input KGs.

Results on Large-Scale KGs. Table 4 presents quality measures for clustering and explainability of ExCut running with TransE on *LUBM* and *YAGO*. ExCut succeeds to compute the ground truth clusters on *LUBM*. Despite the noise in *YAGO*, it achieves approximately 40% enhancement of the clustering accuracy. The explanation quality is also improved. ReCent did not scale on *LUBM* and *YAGO* due to memory requirements.

Human-Understanbility. For illustration in Table 5, we present the top-3 explanations for each cluster computed by ExCut along with their quality on the *YAGO* KG. In the ground truth, C_1, C_2, C_3 are clusters for entities of the type *Songs*, *Books*, and *Movies* respectively. One can observe that the explanations generated by ExCut-T are more intuitive and of higher quality than those obtained using Kmeans-T. The correlation between the explanation relevance and the used quality metrics can also be observed.

Figure 5 summarizes the results of the 50 responses collected via the user-study. Each bar shows the ratio of responses exclusively matching explanation r_i to each of the provided clusters. The results show that the majority of the participants exclusively matched explanations r_3 and r_{10} to *movies*; r_7 and r_9 to *books*; and r_6 and r_8 to *songs*. The explanations r_3, r_6, and r_9 have been learned by ExCut. The high relative exclusive matching ratio to the correspond-

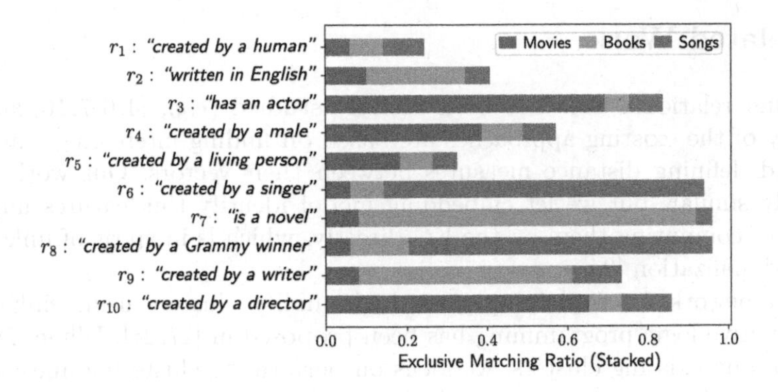

Fig. 5. Ratio of explanation-to-cluster pairs exclusively matched.

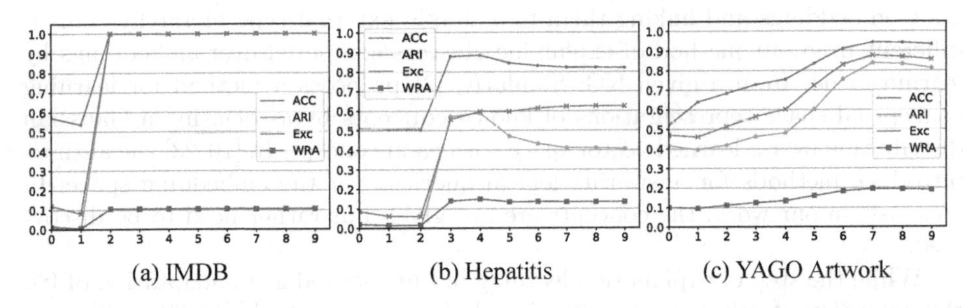

Fig. 6. ExCut-T clustering and explanations quality over the iterations(x-axis).

ing correct cluster for the ExCut explanations demonstrates their usefulness in differentiating between the given clusters.

Results Analysis. In Fig. 6, we present a sample for the quality of the clusters and the aggregated quality of their top explanations over 10 iterations of ExCut-T using the *followExpl* configuration. In general, clustering and explanations qualities consistently improved over iterations, which demonstrates the advantage of the introduced embedding fine-tuning procedure. For *IMDB*, the qualities drop at the beginning, but increase and reach the highest values at the third iteration. This highlights the benefit of accumulating the auxiliary triples for enhancing the feedback signal, thus preventing the embedding tuning from diverging. The charts also show a correlation between the clustering and explanation quality, which proves our hypothesis that the introduced exclusive coverage measure (*Exc*) is useful for computing good clusters.

With respect to the effects of different embeddings and feedback modeling, as shown in Tables 2 and 3, we observe that ExCut with *TransE* is more robust than with *ComplEx* regardless of the feedback modeling method. Furthermore, modeling the feedback using *followExpl* strategy leads to better results on the majority of the datasets, especially for large-scale KGs. This reflects the benefit of passing richer feedback to the embedding, as it allows for better entity positioning in the latent space.

6 Related Work

Clustering relational data has been actively studied (*e.g.*, [4,6,7,16,25]). The majority of the existing approaches are based on finding interesting features in KGs and defining distance measures between their vectors. Our work is conceptually similar, but we let embedding model identify the features implicitly instead of computing them on the KG directly, which is in spirit of linked data propositionalization [24].

A framework for explaining given high-quality clusters using linked data and inductive logic programming has been proposed in [27,28]. While [28] aims at explaining existing clusters, we focus on performing clustering and explanation learning iteratively to discover high-quality clusters with explanations. The work [12] targets interpreting embedding models by finding concept spaces in node embeddings and linking them to a simple external type hierarchy. This is different from our method of explaining clusters computed over embeddings by learning rules from a given KG. Similarly, [2] proposes a method for learning conceptual space representations of known concepts by associating a Gaussian distribution over a learned vector space with each concept. In [10,23] the authors introduce methods for answering logical queries over the embedding space. In contrast, in our work, the concepts are not given but rather need to be discovered.

While the step of explanation learning in our method is an adaptation of [8], the extension of other exact symbolic rule learning methods [18,22] is likewise possible. In principle, one can also employ neural-based rule learners for our needs, such as [20,21,34]; however the integration of our exclusive rule coverage scoring function into such approaches is challenging, and requires further careful investigation.

Several methods recently focused on combining [11,35] and comparing [5,19] rule learning and embedding methods. The authors of [11] propose to rank rules learned from KGs by relying both on their embedding-based predictive quality and traditional rule measures, which is conceptually different from our work. In [35] an iterative method for joint learning of linear-map embeddings and OWL axioms (without nominals) has been introduced. The triples inferred by the learned rukes are injected into the KG, before the embedding is re-trained from scratch in the subsequent iteration. In contrast, the rule-based feedback generated by ExCut is not limited to only fact predictions, but encodes further structural similarities across entities. Furthermore, we do not re-train the whole model from scratch, but rather adapt the embedding of target entities accounting for the feedback. Finally, unlike [35], the rules that we learn support constants, which allow to capture a larger variety of explanations.

7 Conclusion

We have proposed ExCut, an approach for explainable KG entity clustering, which iteratively utilizes embeddings and rule learning methods to compute accurate clusters and human-readable explanations for them. Our approach is flexible, as any embedding model can be used. Experiments show the effectiveness of ExCut on real-world KGs.

There are several directions for future work. Considering more general rules (*e.g.*, with negations) in the *Rule Learning* component of our method or exploiting several embedding models instead of a single one in the *Embedding-based Clustering* step should lead to cleaner clusters. Further questions to study include the analysis of how well our method performs when the number of clusters is very large, and how the feedback from the rules can be used to determine the number of clusters automatically.

References

1. Bordes, A., Usunier, N., Garcia-Duran, A., Weston, J., Yakhnenko, O.: Translating embeddings for modeling multi-relational data. In: NeurIPS, pp. 2787–2795 (2013)
2. Bouraoui, Z., Schockaert, S.: Learning conceptual space representations of interrelated concepts. In: IJCAI, pp. 1760–1766 (2018)
3. Costabello, L., Pai, S., Van, C.L., McGrath, R., McCarthy, N., Tabacof, P.: AmpliGraph: a library for representation learning on knowledge graphs (2019)
4. Dumancic, S., Blockeel, H.: An expressive dissimilarity measure for relational clustering over neighbourhood trees. MLJ (2017)
5. Dumancic, S., García-Durán, A., Niepert, M.: On embeddings as an alternative paradigm for relational learning. CoRR arXiv:abs/1806.11391v2 (2018)
6. Fanizzi, N., d'Amato, C., Esposito, F.: Conceptual clustering and its application to concept Drift and Novelty Detection. In: Bechhofer, S., Hauswirth, M., Hoffmann, J., Koubarakis, M. (eds.) ESWC 2008. LNCS, vol. 5021, pp. 318–332. Springer, Heidelberg (2008). https://doi.org/10.1007/978-3-540-68234-9_25
7. Fonseca, N.A., Costa, V.S., Camacho, R.: Conceptual clustering of multi-relational data. In: ILP, pp. 145–159 (2011)
8. Galárraga, L., Teflioudi, C., Hose, K., Suchanek, F.M.: Fast rule mining in ontological knowledge bases with AMIE+. VLDB J. **24**(6), 707–730 (2015)
9. Guo, Y., Pan, Z., Heflin, J.: LUBM: a benchmark for OWL knowledge base systems. J. Web Semant. **3**(2–3), 158–182 (2005)
10. Hamilton, W.L., Bajaj, P., Zitnik, M., Jurafsky, D., Leskovec, J.: Embedding logical queries on knowledge graphs. In: NeurIPS, pp. 2030–2041 (2018)
11. Ho, V.T., Stepanova, D., Gad-Elrab, M.H., Kharlamov, E., Weikum, G.: Rule learning from knowledge graphs guided by embedding models. In: Vrandečić, D., et al. (eds.) ISWC 2018. LNCS, vol. 11136, pp. 72–90. Springer, Cham (2018). https://doi.org/10.1007/978-3-030-00671-6_5
12. Idahl, M., Khosla, M., Anand, A.: Finding interpretable concept spaces in node embeddings using knowledge bases. In: Cellier, P., Driessens, K. (eds.) ML/KDD, pp. 229–240 (2020)
13. Knobbe, A.J., Ho, E.K.Y.: Pattern teams. In: PKDD, pp. 577–584 (2006)
14. Lavrač, N., Flach, P., Zupan, B.: Rule evaluation measures: a unifying view. In: ILP, pp. 174–185 (1999)
15. Lin, Y., Liu, Z., Luan, H., Sun, M., Rao, S., Liu, S.: Modeling relation paths for representation learning of knowledge bases. In: EMNLP, pp. 705–714 (2015)

16. Lisi, F.A.: A pattern-based approach to conceptual clustering in FOL. In: Schärfe, H., Hitzler, P., Øhrstrøm, P. (eds.) ICCS-ConceptStruct 2006. LNCS (LNAI), vol. 4068, pp. 346–359. Springer, Heidelberg (2006). https://doi.org/10.1007/11787181_25
17. MacQueen, J., et al.: Some methods for classification and analysis of multivariate observations. In: Proceedings of the fifth Berkeley Symposium on Mathematical Statistics and Probability, vol. 1, pp. 281–297 (1967)
18. Meilicke, C., Chekol, M.W., Ruffinelli, D., Stuckenschmidt, H.: Anytime bottom-up rule learning for knowledge graph completion. In: IJCAI, pp. 3137–3143 (2019)
19. Meilicke, C., Fink, M., Wang, Y., Ruffinelli, D., Gemulla, R., Stuckenschmidt, H.: Fine-grained evaluation of rule- and embedding-based systems for knowledge graph completion. In: Vrandečić, D., et al. (eds.) ISWC 2018. LNCS, vol. 11136, pp. 3–20. Springer, Cham (2018). https://doi.org/10.1007/978-3-030-00671-6_1
20. Omran, P.G., Wang, K., Wang, Z.: An embedding-based approach to rule learning in knowledge graphs. IEEE Trans. Knowl. Data Eng. 1–1 (2019)
21. Omran, P.G., Wang, K., Wang, Z.: Scalable rule learning via learning representation. In: IJCAI, pp. 2149–2155 (2018)
22. Ortona, S., Meduri, V.V., Papotti, P.: Robust discovery of positive and negative rules in knowledge bases. In: ICDE, pp. 1168–1179. IEEE (2018)
23. Ren, H., Hu, W., Leskovec, J.: Query2box: Reasoning over knowledge graphs in vector space using box embeddings. In: ICLR (2020)
24. Ristoski, P., Paulheim, H.: A comparison of propositionalization strategies for creating features from linked open data. In: 1st Linked Data for Knowledge Discovery Workshop at ECML/PKDDAt: Nancy, France (2014)
25. Pérez-Suárez, A., Martínez-Trinidad, J.F., Carrasco-Ochoa, J.A.: A review of conceptual clustering algorithms. Artif. Intell. Rev. **52**(2), 1267–1296 (2018). https://doi.org/10.1007/s10462-018-9627-1
26. Suchanek, F.M., Kasneci, G., Weikum, G.: Yago: A core of semantic knowledge. In: Proceedings of WWW, pp. 697–706 (2007)
27. Tiddi, I., d'Aquin, M., Motta, E.: Dedalo: Looking for clusters explanations in a labyrinth of linked data. In: Presutti, V., d'Amato, C., Gandon, F., d'Aquin, M., Staab, S., Tordai, A. (eds.) The Semantic Web: Trends and Challenges (ESWC 2014). Lecture Notes in Computer Science, vol. 8465, pp. 333–348. Springer, Cham (2014). https://doi.org/10.1007/978-3-319-07443-6_23
28. Tiddi, I., d'Aquin, M., Motta, E.: Data patterns explained with linked data. In: Bifet, A., et al. (eds.) Machine Learning and Knowledge Discovery in Databases (ECML PKDD 2015). Lecture Notes in Computer Science, vol. 9286, pp. 271–275. Springer, Cham (2015). https://doi.org/10.1007/978-3-319-23461-8_28
29. Trouillon, T., Welbl, J., Riedel, S., Gaussier, É., Bouchard, G.: Complex embeddings for simple link prediction. In: ICML, pp. 2071–2080 (2016)
30. Vrandecic, D., Krötzsch, M.: Wikidata: a free collaborative knowledgebase. Commun. ACM **57**(10), 78–85 (2014)
31. Wang, C., Pan, S., Hu, R., Long, G., Jiang, J., Zhang, C.: Attributed graph clustering: a deep attentional embedding approach. In: IJCAI, pp. 3670–3676 (2019)
32. Xie, J., Girshick, R.B., Farhadi, A.: Unsupervised deep embedding for clustering analysis. In: ICML, pp. 478–487 (2016)
33. Xie, R., Liu, Z., Jia, J., Luan, H., Sun, M.: Representation learning of KGs with entity descriptions. In: AAAI, pp. 2659–2665 (2016)

34. Yang, F., Yang, Z., Cohen, W.W.: Differentiable learning of logical rules for knowledge base reasoning. In: NeurIPS, pp. 2319–2328 (2017)
35. Zhang, W., et al.: Iteratively learning embeddings and rules for knowledge graph reasoning. In: WWW, pp. 2366–2377 (2019)

Cost- and Robustness-Based Query Optimization for Linked Data Fragments

Lars Heling(✉) and Maribel Acosta

Institute AIFB, Karlsruhe Institute of Technology (KIT), Karlsruhe, Germany
{heling,acosta}@kit.edu

Abstract. Client-side SPARQL query processing enables evaluating queries over RDF datasets published on the Web without producing high loads on the data providers' servers. Triple Pattern Fragment (TPF) servers provide means to publish highly available RDF data on the Web and clients to evaluate SPARQL queries over them have been proposed. For clients to devise efficient query plans that minimize both the number of requests submitted to the server as well as the overall execution time, it is key to accurately estimate join cardinalities to appropriately place physical join operators. However, collecting accurate and fine-grained statistics from remote sources is a challenging task, and clients typically rely on the metadata provided by the TPF server. Addressing this shortcoming, we propose CROP, a cost- and robust-based query optimizer to devise efficient plans combining both cost and robustness of query plans. The idea of robustness is determining the impact of join cardinality estimation errors on the cost of a query plan and to avoid plans where this impact is very high. In our experimental study, we show that our concept of robustness complements the cost model and improves the efficiency of query plans. Additionally, we show that our approach outperforms existing TPF clients in terms of overall runtime and number of requests.

1 Introduction

Different means to publish RDF and Linked Data on the web have been proposed ranging from data dumps with no support to directly query the data to SPARQL endpoints which allow for executing complex SPARQL queries over the data [17]. Motivated by the low availability and high server-side cost of SPARQL endpoints, Triple Pattern Fragments (TPFs) have been proposed as a lightweight triple pattern-based query interface [17]. The goal is to increase the availability of data by reducing server-side costs and shifting the cost for evaluating large queries to the client. Given a triple pattern, the TPF server returns all matching triples split into pages as well as additional metadata on the estimated number of total matching triples and the page size. Evaluating SPARQL queries over datasets published via TPF server requires a specific client with query processing capabilities. A key challenge of such clients is devising efficient query plans able to minimize both the overall query execution time as well as the number of requests submitted to the TPF server. Different clients implement

J. Z. Pan et al. (Eds.): ISWC 2020, LNCS 12506, pp. 238–257, 2020.
https://doi.org/10.1007/978-3-030-62419-4_14

heuristics based on the provided metadata to devise efficient query plans over TPF servers [1,16,17]. However, a major drawback of the heuristics implemented by those clients is the fact that they fail to adapt to different classes of queries which can lead to long runtimes and produce large numbers of requests. This can be attributed to the following reasons. First, they follow a greedy planning strategy and do not explore and compare alternative query plans. Second, they only rely on basic cardinality estimation functions to estimate the cost of query plans and to place physical join operators. To overcome these limitations, a more flexible way of query planning in TPF clients can be realized by implementing both a cost model to estimate the cost of query plans and a query planner that explores alternative plans.

To this end, we propose a new cost model incorporating both the cost at the client (execution time) as well as the cost induced at the server (number of requests) to devise efficient query plans. Our cost model relies on a basic estimation function to estimate the number of intermediate results and join cardinalities of sub-queries based on the TPF metadata. Due to the limited statistics, we additionally propose the concept of robustness for query plans to avoid query plans which are very susceptive to errors in the estimations. Therefore, the robustness of a query plan is determined by the ratio of its best-case cost and its average-case cost. A higher ratio indicates that the best-case cost deviates less from the average case cost and the plan is considered more robust. Finally, we present a query plan optimizer that combines both the cost model and the concept of robustness to select the most appropriate query plan which ideally minimizes the overall evaluation runtime and the number of requests submitted to the TPF server. In summary, our contributions are

- a cost model for executing query plans over TPF servers,
- the concept of robustness for SPARQL query plans,
- a query plan optimizer using iterative dynamic programming to explore alternative query plans with the goal to obtain both cheap and robust query plans, and
- an implementation of the approach evaluated in an extensive experimental study.

The remainder of this paper is structured as follows. First, we present a motivating example in Sect. 2. In Sect. 3, we present our approach and evaluate it in Sect. 4 by analyzing the results of our experimental study. Next, we discuss related work in Sect. 5. Finally, we summarize our work in Sect. 6 and point to future work.

2 Motivating Example

Consider the query from Listing 1.1 to *obtain persons with "Stanford University" as their alma mater, the title of their thesis, and their doctoral advisor* using the TPF for the English version of DBpedia[1] with a page size of 100. The estimated

[1] http://fragments.dbpedia.org/2014/en.

triples per triple pattern provided as metadata from the TPF server are indicated in Listing 1.1.

Listing 1.1. Query to get persons with "Stanford University" as their alma mater, the title of their thesis and their doctoral advisor. Prefixes are used as in http://prefix.cc/.

```
0 SELECT * WHERE {
1 ?u rdfs:label "Stanford University"@en .      # Count: 2
2 ?s dbo:almaMater ?u .                          # Count: 86088
3 ?s dbp:thesisTitle ?t .                        # Count: 1187
4 ?s dbo:doctoralAdvisor ?d . }                  # Count: 4885
```

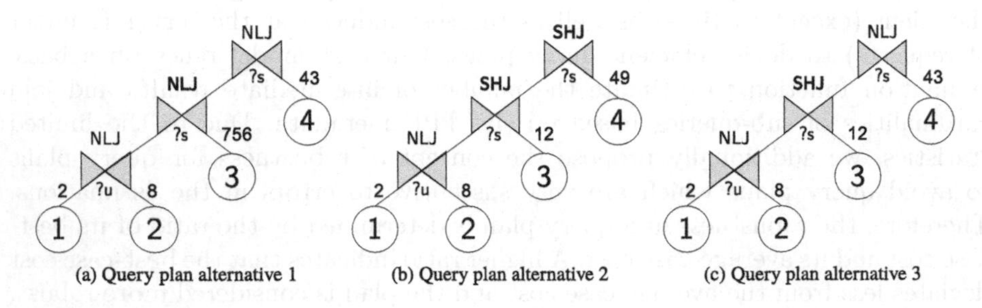

Fig. 1. Three alternative query plans for the SPARQL query from Listing 1.1. Indicated on the edges are the number of requests to be performed according to the corresponding join operators: nested loop join (NLJ) and symmetric hash join (SHJ).

We now want to investigate the query plans produced by the recent TPF clients Comunica and nLDE. When executing the query using comunica-sparql[2], the client produces 813 requests to obtain the 29 results of the query. The heuristics first sorts the triple patterns according to the number of triples they match. They are then placed in ascending order in the query plan with Nested Loop Joins (NLJs) as the physical operators [16]. The corresponding physical plan is shown in Fig. 1a, where the number of requests is indicated on the edges. First, 4 requests are performed to obtain the statistics on the triple patterns, and thereafter, the plan is executed with 809 requests. Executing the query using nLDE[3] results in a total of 75 requests. First, 4 requests are performed to receive the triple patterns' statistics. Next, by placing two Symmetric Hash Join (SHJ) instead of NLJs only, the number of requests for executing the plan is reduced to a total of 71. In the heuristic of the nLDE query planner, the number of results produced by a join, i.e., the join cardinality estimations, are computed as the sum of the incoming cardinalities of the join. Based on these estimations the planner places either an NLJ or an SHJ [1]. The corresponding query plan is shown in Fig. 1b. Taking a closer look at the query, we observe that neither

[2] https://github.com/comunica/comunica/tree/master/packages/actor-init-sparql.
[3] https://github.com/maribelacosta/nlde.

comunica-sparql nor nLDE find the query plan which minimizes the number of requests to be performed. The optimal plan is shown in Fig. 1c and it requires a total of 69 requests only. This is achieved by placing an NLJ at first and third join operator, and an SHJ at the second join operator. This example emphasizes the challenge for heuristics to devise efficient query plans based on only the count statistic provided by the TPF servers. In this example, the subject-object join of triple patterns 1 and 2 yields 756 results. This can be difficult to estimate relying on the TPF metadata alone. On the one hand, an optimistic heuristic assuming low join cardinalities (for example the minimum) can lead to sub-optimal query plans as the query plan in Fig. 1a shows. On the other hand this also true for more conservative cardinality estimation models that assume the higher join cardinalities, for example the sum, which may lead to overestimating cardinalities and too conservative query plans.

The motivating example illustrates the challenge of query planning in the absence of fine-grained statistics in client-side SPARQL query evaluation over remote data sources such as TPF servers. In such scenarios, query plans should ideally consider not only the estimated cost of the query plans but also its robustness with respect to errors in the join cardinality estimations. Therefore, we investigate how query planning for TPFs can be improved by considering not only the cost of a given query plan but also its robustness. Furthermore, we investigate for which class of queries the concept of robustness is most beneficial and whether such queries can be identified by our robustness metric.

3 Our Approach

We propose CROP, a Cost- and Robustness-based query plan Optimizer to devise efficient plans for SPARQL queries over Triple Pattern Fragment (TPF) servers. The key components of our approach are: (Sect. 3.1) **a cost model** to estimate the cost of executing a query plan over a TPF server, (Sect. 3.2) **the concept of plan robustness** to assess how robust plans are with respect to join cardinality estimation errors, and (Sect. 3.3) **a query plan optimizer** combining both cost and robustness to obtain efficient query plans.

3.1 Cost Model

We present a cost model for estimating the cost of query plans for conjunctive SPARQL queries, i.e. Basic Graph Patterns (BGPs). Given a query plan P for a conjunctive query $\mathcal{Q} = \{tp_1, \ldots, tp_n\}$ with $|\mathcal{Q}| = n$ triple patterns, the cost of P is computed as

$$Cost(P) := \begin{cases} 0 & \text{if } P \text{ is a leaf } tp_i \\ Cost(P_1 \bowtie P_2) + Cost(P_1) + Cost(P_2) & \text{if } P = P_1 \bowtie P_2. \end{cases} \quad (1)$$

where $Cost(P_1 \bowtie P_2)$ is the cost of joining sub-plans P_1 and P_2 using the physical join operator $\bowtie$. Note that the cost for a leaf is 0 as its cost is accounted for as part of the join cost $Cost(P_i \bowtie P_j)$. In our model, the cost of joining two sub-plans is comprised of two aspects: (i) *request cost*, the cost for submitting HTTP requests to the TPF server if necessary; and (ii) *processing cost*, the cost for processing the results on the client side. Hence, the cost of joining sub-plans P_1 and P_2 using the join operator $\bowtie$ is given by:

$$Cost(P_1 \bowtie P_2) := Proc(P_1 \bowtie P_2) + Req(P_1 \bowtie P_2) \quad (2)$$

where *Proc* are the processing cost and *Req* the request cost. Note that both components depend on the physical join operator. First, we distinguish the processing cost joining sub-plans P_1 and P_2 using the physical operator Symmetric Hash Join ($\bowtie_{SHJ}$) and Nested Loop Join ($\bowtie_{NLJ}$) as

$$Proc(P_1 \bowtie P_2) := \begin{cases} \phi_{SHJ} \cdot card(P_1 \bowtie P_2), & \text{if } \bowtie = \bowtie_{SHJ} \\ \phi_{NLJ} \cdot (card(P_1 \bowtie P_2) + card(P_2)), & \text{if } \bowtie = \bowtie_{NLJ} \end{cases} \quad (3)$$

Note the first parameter of the cost model $\phi \in [0, \infty)$ allows for weighting the local processing cost with respect to the request cost. For instance, $\phi = 1$ indicates that processing a single tuple locally is equally expensive as one HTTP request. The impact of processing cost and request cost on the query execution time depends on the scenario in which the TPF server and client are deployed. In a local scenario, where network latency and the load on the TPF server are low, the impact of the processing cost on the execution time might be higher than in a scenario with high network latency, where the time for submitting requests has a larger share on the execution time. Furthermore, including $card(P_2)$ in the processing cost for the NLJ allows the optimizer to estimate the cost of alternative plans more accurately. For instance, if we assume the minimum as the estimation function and do not consider the cardinality of the inner relation, a plan $(A \bowtie_{NLJ} B)$ could be chosen over $(A \bowtie_{NLJ} C)$ even if B has a higher cost than C.

The expected number of requests to be performed for joining two sub-plans depends on the physical operator and the estimated number of results produced by the sub-plans. Therefore, we introduce the request cost function for two common physical join operators. In the following, we denote $|P_i|$ as the number of triples in sub-plan P_i.

Nested Loop Join. The cost of a Nested Loop Join (NLJ) combines the cost induced by the requests for obtaining the tuples of the outer plan P_1 and then probing the instantiations in the inner plan P_2. Therefore, the request costs are computed as

$$\begin{aligned} Req(P_1 \bowtie_{NLJ} P_2) &:= [\![|P_1| = 1]\!] \cdot \left\lceil \frac{card(P_1)}{p} \right\rceil \\ &+ d(P_1, P_2) \cdot \max \left\{ card(P_1), \left\lceil \frac{card(P_1 \bowtie P_2)}{p} \right\rceil \right\}, \end{aligned} \quad (4)$$

[4]where p is the page size of the TPF server, and $d(P_1, P_2)$ computes a discounting factor. In this work, we restrict the inner plan in the NLJs to be triple patterns only, i.e. $|P_2| = 1$, as it allows for more accurate request cost estimations. The first summand calculates the number of requests for obtaining solution mappings for P_1. In case P_1 is a triple pattern, the number of requests is given the cardinality of P_1 divided by the page size. The second summand is the estimated number of requests to be performed on the inner plan multiplied by a discount factor. The minimum number of requests that need to be performed is given by the cardinality for P_1, i.e. one request per binding. However, in the case the join produces more results per binding than the page size, such that paginating is required to obtain all solutions for one binding in the inner relation, we need to consider this in the maximum as well. The discounting factor is computed using the parameter $\delta \in [0, \infty)$ and the maximum height of the sub-plans as

$$d(P_1, P_2) := (\max\{1, \delta \cdot height(P_1), \delta \cdot height(P_2)\})^{-1}.$$

The rationale for including a discount factor for the requests on the inner plan of the NLJ is twofold. First, since the join variables are bound by the terms obtained from the outer plan, the number of variables in the triple pattern is reduced and as the empirical study by Heling et al. [10] indicates, this also leads to a reduction in response times of the TPF server. Second, for star-shaped queries, typically the number of results reduces with an increasing number of join operations and, therefore, the higher an NLJ is placed in the query plan, the more likely it is that it needs to perform fewer requests in the inner plan than the estimated cardinality of the outer relation suggests. The discount factor $d(P_1, P_2)$ allows for considering these aspects and its parameter $\delta \in [0, \infty)$ allows for setting the magnitude of the discount factor. With $\delta = 0$, there is no discount and with increasing δ, placing NLJs higher in the query plan becomes increasingly cheaper.

Symmetric Hash Join. The request cost is computed based on the number of requests that need to be performed if either or both sub-plans are triple patterns.

$$Req(P_1 \bowtie_{SHJ} P_2) := [\![|P_1| = 1]\!] \cdot \left\lceil \frac{card(P_1)}{p} \right\rceil + [\![|P_2| = 1]\!] \cdot \left\lceil \frac{card(P_2)}{p} \right\rceil. \quad (5)$$

Note that the request cost can be computed accurately as it only depends on the metadata provided by the TPF server, with $card(P_i) = count(P_i)$ if $|P_i| = 1$.

Cardinality Estimation. The previous formulas for computing the cost rely on the expected number of intermediate results produced by the join operators, which is determined by recursively applying a join cardinality estimation function. Given two sub-plans P_1 and P_2, we estimate the cardinality as the minimum of the sub-plans' cardinalities:

$$card(P_1 \bowtie P_2) := \min(card(P_1), card(P_2)), \quad (6)$$

[4] $[\![\cdot]\!]$ denote Iverson brackets that evaluate to 1 if its logical proposition is true and to 0 otherwise.

where the cardinality for a single triple pattern is obtain from the metadata provided by the TPF server $card(P_i) = count(P_i), \forall |P_i| = 1$. In our cost model, we choose the minimum as the cardinality estimation function since it showed good results in our preliminary analysis. Next, we will show how the concept of robustness helps to avoid choosing the cheapest plan merely based on these optimistic cardinality estimations.

3.2 Robust Query Plans

Accurate join cardinality estimations aid to find a suitable join order and to properly place physical operators in the query plan to minimize the number of requests. However, estimating the cardinalities is challenging, especially when only basic statistics about the data are available. To address this challenge, we propose the concept of robustness for SPARQL query plans to determine how strongly the cost of a plan is impacted when using alternative cardinality estimations. The core idea is comparing the *best-case* cost of a query plan to the *average-case* cost. To obtain the average-case cost, the cost of the query plan is computed using different cardinality estimation functions for joining sub-plans. The results are several cost values for the query plan under different circumstances which can be aggregated to an averaged cost value. Consequently, a robust query plan is a query plan in which the best-case cost only slightly differs from the average-case cost.

Example 1. Let us revisit the query from the motivating example. For the sake of simplicity, we only consider the sub-plan $P = ((tp_1 \bowtie tp_2) \bowtie tp_3)$ and request cost with $\delta = 0$. Let us consider the alternative query plans $P_1 = ((tp_1 \bowtie_{NLJ} tp_2) \bowtie_{NLJ} tp_3)$ and $P_2 = ((tp_1 \bowtie_{NLJ} tp_2) \bowtie_{SHJ} tp_3)$. For comparing the robustness of P_1 and P_2, we not only use the cardinality estimation of the cost model (the minimum, cf. Eq. 6) but compute the cost using different cardinality estimation functions, for example using the maximum and mean as alternatives. The resulting cost values allow for deriving the average-case cost and thus the robustness of P_1 and P_2. Depending on the cardinality estimation function, we obtain the following cost for the query plans P_1 and P_2:

	Cardinality Estimation Function		
	minimum	mean	maximum
$Cost(P_1)$	5	43,477.45	86,950.88
$Cost(P_2)$	15	444.45	874.88

Query plan P_1 yield the lowest *best-case* cost. However, we observe that the cost for query plan P_2 is not as strongly impacted by different estimation functions. Hence, its average-case cost does not deviate as strongly from its best-case cost in comparison to P_1. As a result, query plan P_2 is considered a more robust query plan.

Definition 1 (Query Plan Robustness). *Let P be a physical query plan for query $\mathcal{Q}$, $Cost^*(P)$ the best-case and $\overline{Cost}(P)$ the average-case cost for P. The* *query plan robustness for P is defined as*

$$Robustness(P) := \frac{Cost^*(P)}{\overline{Cost}(P)}.$$

Namely, the robustness of a plan is the ratio between the cost in the *best-case* $Cost^*$ and the cost in the *average-case* $\overline{Cost}$. A higher ratio indicates a more robust query plan since its expected average-case cost are not as strongly affected by changes in the cardinality estimations with respect to its best-case cost. Next, we extend the definition of our $Cost$ function to formalize the average-case cost of a query plan. Let $O = \{o_1, \ldots, o_{n-1}\}$ be the set of binary join operators for plan P ($|P| = n$) for a conjunctive query $\mathcal{Q}$, and $E = [e_1, \ldots, e_{n-1}]$ a vector of estimation functions with e_i the cardinality estimation function applied at join operator o_i. A cardinality estimation function $e_i : \mathbb{N}_0^2 \to \mathbb{N}_0$ maps the cardinalities of a join operators' sub-plans $a = card(P_1)$ and $b = card(P_2)$ to an estimated join cardinality value. We then denote the cost for a query plan P computed using the cardinality estimation function given by E as $Cost_E(P)$.

Definition 2 (Best-case Cost). *The best-case cost for a query plan P is defined as*

$$Cost^*(P) := Cost_E(P), \text{ with } e_i = f, \forall e_i \in E, \text{ and } f : (a, b) \mapsto \min\{a, b\}.$$

In other words, at every join operator in the query plan, we use the minimum cardinality of the sub-plans to estimate the join cardinality. This is identical to the estimations used in our cost model. The computation of the average-case cost requires applying different combinations of such estimation functions at the join operators.

Definition 3 (Average-case Cost) *Let $F = \{f_1, \ldots, f_m\}$ be a set of m estimation functions with $f : \mathbb{N}_0^2 \to \mathbb{N}_0$, $\forall f \in F$. The average-case cost for a query plan P is defined as the median of its cost when applying all potential combinations of estimation functions $E \in F^{n-1}$ for the operators of the query plan:*

$$\overline{Cost}(P) := \text{median}\{Cost_E(P) \mid \forall E \in F^{n-1}\}.$$

We empirically tested different sets of estimation functions in F and found that the following produce suitable results for the average-case cost: $F = \{f_1, f_2, f_3, f_4\}$ with

$$f_1 : (a, b) \mapsto \min\{a, b\}, \quad f_2 : (a, b) \mapsto \max\{a, b\},$$
$$f_3 : (a, b) \mapsto a + b, \quad f_4 : (a, b) \mapsto \max\{a/b, b/a\}.$$

Furthermore, we observed that for subject-object (s-o) and object-object (o-o) joins the cardinalities were more frequently misestimated in the original cost model, while for all other types of joins, such as star-shaped groups, it provided adequate estimations. Therefore, we only consider alternative cardinality estimation function e_i for a join operator o_i, if the join performed at o_i is either of type s-o or o-o.

3.3 Query Plan Optimizer

The idea of robust query plans yields two major questions: (i) when should a more robust plan be chosen over the cheapest plan, and (ii) which alternative plan should be chosen instead? To this end, we propose a query plan optimizer combining cost and robustness to devise efficient query plans. Its parameters define when a robust plan is chosen and which alternative plan is chosen instead. The main steps of the query plan optimizer are:

1. Obtain a selection of query plans based on Iterative Dynamic Programming (IDP).
2. Assess the robustness of the cheapest plan.
3. If the cheapest plan is not robust enough, find an alternative more robust query plan.

The process is detailed in Algorithm 1. The inputs are a SPARQL Query $\mathcal{Q}$, block size $k \in [2, \infty)$, the number of top $t \in \mathbb{N}$ cheapest plans, the robustness threshold $\rho \in [0, 1]$ and the cost threshold $\gamma \in [0, 1]$. The first step is to obtain a selection of alternative query plans using IDP. We adapted the original "$IDP_1 - standard - bestPlan$" algorithm presented by Kossmann and Stocker [11] in the following way. Identical to the original algorithm, we only consider select-project-join queries, i.e. BGP queries, and each triple pattern $tp_i \in \mathcal{Q}$ is considered a *relation* in the algorithm. Given a subset of triple patterns $S \subset \mathcal{Q}$, the original algorithm considers the single optimal plan for S according to the cost model in $optPlan(S)$ by applying the $prunePlans$ function to the potential candidate plans. However, as we do want to obtain alternative plans, we keep the top t cheapest plans for S in $optPlan(S)$ for $|S| > 2$. When joining two triple patterns ($|S| = 2$), we always chose the physical join operator with the lowest cost for the following reasons: We expect accurate cost estimations for joining two triple patterns as the join estimation error impact is low and it reduces the number of plans to be evaluated in the IDP.

Example 2. Consider the query for the motivating example and $S_1 = \{tp_1, tp_2\}$. According to the cost model, the cheapest plan is $optPlan(S_1) = \{(tp_1 \bowtie_{NLJ} tp_2)\}$. However, for $|S| > 2$ we need to place at least two join operators where the cost of at least one join operator relies on the estimated cardinality of the other. Therefore, we need to keep alternative plans in case a robust alternative plan is required. For instance with $S_2 = \{tp_1, tp_2, tp_3\}$, the optimal plan according to the cost model is $P_1 = ((tp_1 \bowtie_{NLJ} tp_2) \bowtie_{NLJ} tp_3)$, however as it turns out, the true optimal plan for S is $P_2 = ((tp_1 \bowtie_{NLJ} tp_2) \bowtie_{SHJ} tp_3)$. As a result, the algorithm cannot prune all but one plan such that it can choose an alternative robust plan if necessary. Combining the latter observations, we can set $optPlan(S_2) = \{P_1, P_2\}$.

Given the set of t candidate query plans $\mathcal{P}$ from IDP, the overall cheapest plan P^* is determined (Line 2). If the cheapest plan P^* is considered robust enough according to the robustness threshold ρ, it becomes the final plan and is returned

Algorithm 1: CROP Query Plan Optimizer

Input: BGP query $\mathcal{Q}$, block size k, top t, robustness threshold ρ, cost threshold γ

1 $\mathcal{P} = \texttt{IDP}(\mathcal{Q}, k, t)$
2 $P^* = \arg\min_{P \in \mathcal{P}} \texttt{Cost}(P)$
3 **if** $\texttt{Robustness}(P^*) < \rho$ *and* $|\mathcal{P}| > 1$ **then**
4 $\quad \mathcal{R} = \{R \mid R \in \mathcal{P} \wedge \texttt{Robustness}(R) \geq \rho\}$
5 $\quad$ **if** $\mathcal{R} == \emptyset$ **then**
6 $\quad\quad \mathcal{R} = \mathcal{P} \setminus \{P^*\}$
7 $\quad R^* = \arg\min_{R \in \mathcal{R}} \texttt{Cost}(R)$
8 $\quad$ **if** $\frac{\texttt{Cost}(P^*)}{\texttt{Cost}(R^*)} > \gamma$ **then**
9 $\quad\quad P^* = R^*$
10
11 **return** P^*

(Line 10). However, if the plan is not robust enough with respect to ρ and there are alternative plans to chose from (Line 3), the query plan optimizer tries to obtain a more robust alternative plan. First, the planner selects all plans which are above the robustness threshold as $\mathcal{R}$. If no such plans exist, it will consider all alternative plans except the cheapest plan. If the ratio of best-case cost of the cheapest plan P^* to the best-case cost of the alternative plan R^* is higher than the cost threshold γ, the alternative plan R^* is selected as the final plan P^*. For instance, for $\rho = 0.1$ and $\gamma = 0.2$, a robust plan is chosen over the cheapest plan if (i) for the cheapest plan P^*, $\overline{Cost}(P^*)$ is 10 times higher than $Cost^*(P^*)$ and (ii) for alternative robust plan R^*, $Cost^*(R^*)$ is no more than 5 times $(1/\gamma)$ higher than $Cost^*(P^*)$. Hence, smaller robustness threshold values lead to selecting alternative plans when the cheapest plan is less robust, and smaller cost threshold values lead to less restriction on the alternative robust plan with respect to its cost. The combination of both parameters allows for exploring alternative robust plans (ρ) but does not require to chose them at any cost (γ) and therefore limit the *performance degradation risk* [19]. Next, we investigate the time complexity of the proposed optimizer.

Theorem 1. *With the number top plans t and the set of estimation functions F constant, the time complexity of the query plan optimizer is in the order of*

Case 1: *$\mathcal{O}(2^n)$, for $2 \leq k < n$,*
Case 2: *$\mathcal{O}(3^n)$, for $k = n$.*

Proof. The time complexity of the query plan optimizer is given by the IDP algorithm and computing the average-case cost in the robustness computation. Kossmann and Stocker [11] provide the proofs for the former. For the latter, given $|F| = m$ different estimation functions and the top t query plans, the upper bound for the number of alternative cardinality estimations per query plan is $t \cdot m \cdot 2^{n-1}$. As t and m are considered constants, the time complexity of the robustness computation is in the order of $\mathcal{O}(2^n)$. Combining these complexity results, we have:

Case 1: For $k < n$, the time complexity of computing the robustness exceeds the time complexity of IDP, which is $\mathcal{O}(n^2)$, for $k = 2$ and $\mathcal{O}(n^k)$, for $2 < k < n$. As a result, the time complexity is in the order of $\mathcal{O}(2^n)$.

Case 2: For $k = n$, the time complexity of IDP exceeds the time complexity of the robustness computation and therefore, we have that the time complexity of the query plan optimizer is in the order of $\mathcal{O}(3^n)$.

4 Experimental Evaluation

We empirically evaluate the query plan optimizer with the proposed cost model and the concept of robust query plans. First, we study how the parameters of the cost model and the IDP algorithm impact on the efficiency of the query plans. Thereafter, we study different robustness and cost thresholds in the query plan optimizer to find a good combination of both. Finally, we compare our implementation with the found parameters to state of the art TPF clients: `comunica-sparql` (See footnote 2) (referred to as Comunica) and nLDE (See footnote 3).

Datasets and Queries. We use the datasets used in previous evaluations: DBpedia 2014 (nLDE) and WatDiv [3] (Comunica). For DBpedia, we choose a total of 35 queries including Q1-Q10 from the nLDE Benchmark 1 and all from Benchmark 2. For WatDiv, we generated a dataset with scale factor = 100 and the corresponding default queries with query-count = 5 resulting in a total of 88 distinct queries.[5] The resulting 123 queries are used for our experimental study. In addition, to showcase the benefits of including the robustness in the query plan optimizer on a variety of datasets, we designed an additional benchmark with 10 queries for 3 datasets (DBpedia 2014, GeoNames 2012[6], DBLP 2017 (See footnote 6)) that include either a `s-o` and or an `o-o` join and 3–4 triple patterns.[7]

Implementation. CROP is implemented based on the nLDE source code (See footnote 3). We additionally implemented our cost model, robustness computation and the query plan optimizer.[8] No routing adaptivity features, i.e. routing policies, are used in our implementation. The engine was implemented in Python 2.7.13 and we used the `Server.js` v2.2.3[9] to deploy the TPF server with HDT backend for all datasets. Experiments were executed on a Debian Jessie 64 bit machine with CPU: 2x Intel(R) Xeon(R) CPU E5-2670 2.60 GHz (16 physical cores), and 256 GB RAM. The timeout was set to 900 s. After a warm-up run, the queries were executed three times in all experiments.

---

[5] Complex queries do not contain placeholders, leading to one distinct query in `C1`, `C2`, and `C3`.

[6] http://www.rdfhdt.org/datasets/.

[7] https://github.com/Lars-H/crop_analysis.

[8] https://github.com/Lars-H/crop.

[9] https://github.com/LinkedDataFragments/Server.js.

Evaluation Metrics. The following metrics are computed: (i) *Runtime*: Elapsed time spent by a query engine to complete the evaluation of a query. For our implementation, we measure both the *optimization time* to obtain the query plan and the *execution time* to execute the plan separately. (ii) *Number of Requests*: Total number of requests submitted to the server during the query execution. (iii) *Number of Answers*: Total number of answers produced during query execution. If not stated otherwise, we report mean values for all three runs. All raw results are provided in the supplemental material.

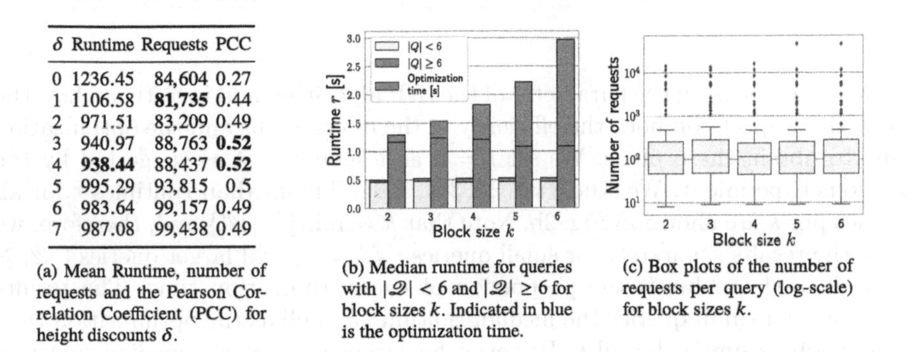

δ	Runtime	Requests	PCC
0	1236.45	84,604	0.27
1	1106.58	**81,735**	0.44
2	971.51	83,209	0.49
3	940.97	88,763	**0.52**
4	**938.44**	88,437	**0.52**
5	995.29	93,815	0.5
6	983.64	99,157	0.49
7	987.08	99,438	0.49

(a) Mean Runtime, number of requests and the Pearson Correlation Coefficient (PCC) for height discounts δ.

(b) Median runtime for queries with $|\mathcal{Q}| < 6$ and $|\mathcal{Q}| \geq 6$ for block sizes k. Indicated in blue is the optimization time.

(c) Box plots of the number of requests per query (log-scale) for block sizes k.

Fig. 2. Experimental results for the parameters of the cost model and IDP.

4.1 Experimental Results

Cost Model and IDP Parameters. First, we investigate how the parameters of the cost model impact runtime and the number of requests. In the optimizer, we disable robust plan selection ($\rho = 0.00$), set the default block size to $k = 3$, and select the top $t = 5$ plans. We focus on the parameter δ which we set to $\delta \in \{0, 1, 2, 3, 4, 5, 6, 7\}$. We do not investigate different processing cost parameters and set $\phi_{NLJ} = \phi_{SHJ} = 0.001$, as they are more relevant when considering different deployment scenarios, where network delays have a stronger impact on the cost. Figure 2a shows the mean runtime, the mean number of requests per run, and the Pearson Correlation Coefficient (PCC) between the cost and the number of requests. The latter provides an indication of how well the estimated cost of a query plan reflects the actual number of requests to be performed. The best runtime results are observed for $\delta = 4$, even though the number requests are about 8% higher than for $\delta = 1$. Furthermore, the highest positive correlation between the estimated cost and the number of requests of a plan are observed for $\delta \in \{3, 4\}$ with $PCC = 0.52$. The worst runtime results are observed for $\delta = 0$, which is equal to no height discount at all. This shows that the parameter allows for adjusting the cost model such that the estimated cost better reflects the number of requests resulting in more efficient query plans. Based on the findings, we set $\delta = 4$ in the following experiments.

Table 1. Mean runtime (r), mean number of requests (Req.) and the number of robust plans ($|R^*|$) selected by the query plan optimizer. Indicate in bold are best overall runtime and minimum number of requests.

	$\rho = 0.05$			$\rho = 0.10$			$\rho = 0.15$			$\rho = 0.20$			$\rho = 0.25$		
γ	r	Req.	$\|R^*\|$	r	Req.	$\|R^*\|$	r	Req.	$\|R^*\|$	r	Req.	$\|R^*\|$	r	Req.	$\|R^*\|$
0.1	556.86	64,167	16	534.16	82,657	17	2048	99,015	28	2094	103,709	31	2784	124,070	38
0.3	552.44	**64,157**	16	**533.7**	82,629	17	930	105,337	10	937	105,537	10	940	105,728	11
0.5	957.0	86,640	6	911.71	90,932	6	910	91,175	9	908	91,388	9	911	91,511	9
0.7	950.98	86,634	6	909.64	90,962	6	910	91,161	8	913	91,173	5	909	91,298	5
0.9	947.87	86,627	6	915.23	90,934	6	909	90,937	7	907	90,939	4	910	90,986	2

Next, we focus on the parameter of the IDP algorithm and investigate how the block size impacts on both the efficiency of the query plans and the optimization time to obtain these plans. We set $t = 5$ and keep $\delta = 4$ as suggested by the previous experiment. We study $k \in \{2, 3, 4, 5, 6\}$. The median runtimes $\widetilde{r}$ for all queries per k are shown in Fig. 2b. Note that $k = \min\{k, |\mathcal{Q}|\}$ and, therefore, we show the results separately for small queries ($|\mathcal{Q}| < 6$) and larger queries ($|\mathcal{Q}| \geq 6$). Indicated in blue is the proportion of the optimization time. The results show that for small queries the median runtime, as well as the optimization time proportion, is similar for all k. However, for larger queries, the median runtimes increase with k. Interestingly, this increase is due to an increased proportion of optimization time spent on obtaining *ideally* better plans. At the same time the execution time (lower part of the bars) is similar ($k = 4$) or slightly lower ($k \in \{5, 6\}$). The box plots for the number of requests for the query plans per k are shown in Fig. 2c. The results show that the median number of requests is minimal for $k = 4$ and the $25 - 75\%$ quantile is most compact for $k = 4$ as well. Moreover, the most extreme outliers are observed with $k = 5$ and $k = 6$. Based on these observations to avoid disproportionate optimization times but still explore the space of possible plans sufficiently, we set k in a dynamic fashion with: $k = 4$ if $|\mathcal{Q}| < 6$ and $k = 2$ otherwise.

Robustness and Cost Threshold. After determining appropriate parameters for the cost model and IDP, we investigate the parameters that impact the decision when an alternative robust plan should be chosen over the cheapest

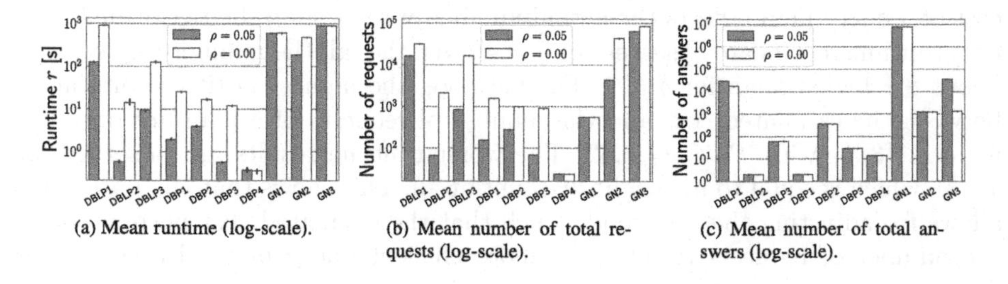

(a) Mean runtime (log-scale).

(b) Mean number of total requests (log-scale).

(c) Mean number of total answers (log-scale).

Fig. 3. Results for the 10 queries of the custom benchmark.

plan. The robustness threshold ρ determines *when* an alternative plan should be considered, while the cost threshold γ limits the alternative plans to those which are not considered too expensive. We tested all 25 combinations of $\rho \in \{0.05, 0.10, 0.15, 0.20, 0.25\}$ and $\gamma \in \{0.1, 0.3, 0.5, 0.7, 0.9\}$ and run all queries for each combination three times. The averaged results of the total runtimes and the number of requests per run for all 25 parameter configurations are listed in Table 1. Also included is the number of queries for which an alternative robust query plan was selected over the cheapest plan as $|R^*|$. Lowest runtime and number of requests are indicated in bold. The parameters configuration $\rho = 0.10$, $\gamma = 0.3$ yield the best runtime results while the lowest number of requests are performed with the configuration $\rho = 0.05$, $\gamma = 0.3$. Taking a closer look at the two configurations, we find that the runtime is only about 3.5% higher for $\rho = 0.05$, $\gamma = 0.3$, but the number of requests is about 22% lower. Moreover, when comparing the values for $\rho = 0.05$ to $\rho = 0.10$ for all cost threshold values, we find that the runtimes and the total number of requests for $\rho = 0.05$ (388,227) is substantially lower than for $\rho = 0.10$ (438,116) while the total runtime is just slightly higher for $\rho = 0.05$ (3965.16 s) than for $\rho = 0.1$ (3804.43 s). Following these findings, we set the cost threshold to $\gamma = 0.3$ and the robustness threshold $\rho = 0.05$ in the following experiments. The results in Table 1 show that for the parameter configuration $\rho = 0.05$, $\gamma = 0.3$, for 16 out of 123 queries the robust alternative query plan R^* is chosen over the cheapest plan. And 15 out of the 16 queries stem from the WatDiv L2, L5, and S7 queries. To show that other classes of queries for which the more efficient alternative robust query plan can be identified using our approach, we investigate the experimental results for our benchmark with 10 queries over the three datasets DBpedia (DBP), GeoNames (GN), DBLP (DBLP). We keep the same parameters that we obtained from the previous experimental evaluation on the other benchmarks. In Fig. 3, the results of always choosing the cheapest query plans ($\rho = 0.00$) and the results when enabling robust query plans to be chosen with $\rho = 0.05$ and $\gamma = 0.3$ are shown. It can be observed that in 8 queries (DBLP1-3, DBP1-3, GN2-3) robustness allows for obtaining more efficient query plans. For these queries, the runtime and total number of requests are lower and at the same time, the robust alternative query plans produce the same number of answers or even more. Even though the runtime of the robust query plan for query GN3 reaches the timeout, it produces more answers with fewer requests during the time. The results show that our approach devises efficient query plans even for queries where the cost model produces high cardinality estimation errors. The low robustness of the cheapest plans drives our optimizer to choose more robust plans which reduce the query execution times as well as the number of requests.

Comparison to the State of the Art. Given the parameters determined by the previous experiments, we want to compare the performance of the proposed approach to existing TPF clients, namely nLDE and Comunica. Analogously to the previous experiments, we run the 123 queries from both the nLDE Benchmark and WatDiv with all three engines. In Fig. 4a the mean runtimes for all three clients are shown for the WatDiv queries. The results show that our

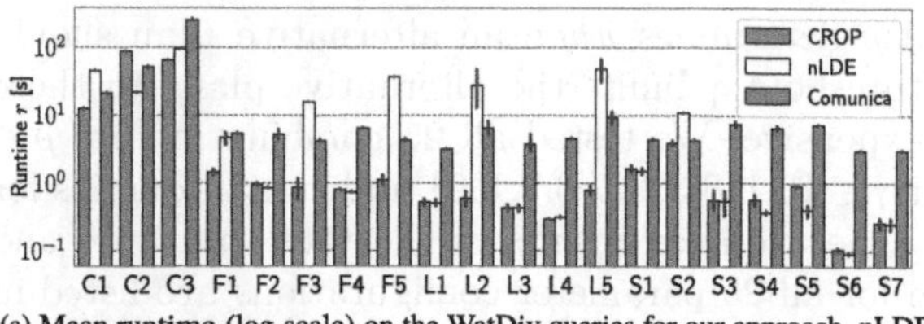

(a) Mean runtime (log-scale) on the WatDiv queries for our approach, nLDE and comunica.

	CROP	nLDE	Comunica
$\sum r$	**540.69**	2815.3	1087.3
$\widetilde{r}$	0.71	**0.7**	2.71
Req.	**64,155**	151,594	204,453
Ans.	**456,090**	438,056	456,054
$\frac{\text{Ans.}}{\text{Req.}}$	**1.18**	0.79	0.22

(b) Summarized results for all TPF clients for all queries.

Fig. 4. Experimental results: comparison to state-of-the-art clients.

proposed approach has a similar performance to the existing engines nLDE and Comunica. Only for the complex query C2 our approach yields the highest average runtime, while for 6 query types (C1, C3, F1, F3, F5, L5) it outperforms the other engines. The results for all queries are summarized in Fig. 4b. Regarding the runtime, our approach yields the lowest overall runtime ($\sum r$) while Comunica has the second-highest and nLDE the highest overall runtime. Taking a closer look, we find that nLDE reaches the timeout (900 s) for queries Q5 and Q8 in the nLDE Benchmark 1, explaining the highest overall runtime. In contrast, nLDE has the lowest the median runtime $\widetilde{r}$. Our approach produces the highest number of answers while Comunica only produces a few answers less. The fewest answers are produced by nLDE, likely due to the queries where the timeout is reached. Next, we consider the mean ratio of answers and requests per query (Ans./Req.) as a measure of productivity. It can be observed that our approach on average produces the most answers per request, followed by nLDE and then Comunica with the fewest answers per request. Increasing this productivity can have two key benefits: (i) it reduces query runtimes at the client, and (ii) reduces the load on the TPF server. Finally, we additionally investigated the diefficiency [2] to evaluate the continuous efficiency of the clients. The highest *dief@t* (where t is set to the maximum execution time across all engines per query) is observed in 39% of all queries for CROP, 54% of all queries for nLDE and 7% of all queries for Comunica. The results suggest that even though the overall runtimes for CROP are the lowest, nLDE is outperforming the approach with respect to its continuous behavior of producing answers. Additional results for queries Q11-Q20 of the nLDE Benchmark 1 are provided as part of our supplemental material online (See footnote 7). For those queries, we observe that all engines time out more often, yet CROP outperforms nLDE and Comunica in the remaining queries.

Concluding our findings, the results show that the proposed approach is competitive with existing TPF clients and on average produces more efficient query plans minimizing both the runtime and the number of requests to be performed. Nonetheless, it must be pointed out that in contrast to heuristics, the proposed cost model and query optimizer rely on parameters that need to be chosen appropriately. On one side, this allows for adapting these parameters to the specifics of different types of datasets to be queried. On the other side, it might require preliminary testing to optimize the parameter settings.

5 Related Work

We start by discussing cost model-based decentralized SPARQL query processing approaches and approaches for querying different Linked Data Fragments (LDF). An overview of these approaches with their main features is presented in Table 2.

The first group of approaches [7,8,13–15] consists of engines that evaluate queries over federations of SPARQL endpoints. These approaches rely on statistics to perform query decomposition, source selection, and estimate the intermediate results of sub-queries which is the basis for their cost model. The contents and granularity of these statistics vary across the approaches. While the specific computation of cost, supported physical join operators and sub-query cardinality estimations differ for all these approaches, their commonality is factoring in the cost of transferring the result tuples. SPLENDID [8], SemaGrow [7] and Odyssey [13] rely on Dynamic Programming (DP) while DARQ [14] implements Iterative Dynamic Programming (IDP) and CostFed [15] implements a greedy heuristic to find an efficient plan. However, all of the aforementioned approaches rely on dataset statistics for accurate cardinality estimations and they do not consider the concept of robust query plans with respect to errors in the estimations.

With the advent of Triple Pattern Fragments (TPFs), different approaches for decentralized SPARQL query processing over this Web interface have been introduced. The TPF Client proposed by Verborgh et al. [17] evaluates conjunctive SPARQL queries (BGPs) over TPF server. The TPF Client intertwines query planning and evaluation based on the metadata provided by the TPF server to minimize the number of requests: the triple pattern with the smallest estimated number of matches is evaluated and the resulting solution mappings are used to instantiate variables in the remaining triple patterns. This procedure is executed continuously until all triple patterns have been evaluated. Comunica [16] is a meta query engine supporting SPARQL query evaluation over heterogeneous interfaces including TPF servers. The authors propose and evaluate two heuristic-based configurations of the engine. The *sort* configuration sorts all triple patterns according to the metadata and joins them in that order, while the *smallest* configuration does not sort the entire BGP, but starts by selecting the triple pattern with the smallest estimated count on each evaluation call. The network of Linked Data Eddies (nLDE) [1] is a client for adaptive SPARQL query processing over TPF servers. The query optimizer in nLDE builds star-shaped groups (SSG) and joins the triple patterns by ascending number of estimated matches. The optimizer places physical operators to minimize the expected number of requests that need to be performed. Furthermore, nLDE realizes adaptivity by adjusting the routing of result tuples according to changing runtime conditions and data transfer rates based. Different from the existing clients, our query plan optimizer relies on a cost model, the concept of robust query plans, and IDP to generate alternative, potentially efficient plans.

Table 2. Overview and features of decentralized SPARQL query processing approaches over different Linked Data Fragment (LDF) interfaces.

Approach	Federation	LDF	Query Planner Cost	Robustness	Statistics	Strategy
DARQ [14]	✓	SPARQL	✓	✗	Service descriptions	IDP
SPLENDID [8]	✓	SPARQL	✓	✗	VOID descriptions	DP
SemaGrow [7]	✓	SPARQL	✓	✗	TP-based statistics	DP
Odyssey [13]	✓	SPARQL	✓	✗	Characteristic sets	DP
CostFed [15]	✓	SPARQL	✓	✗	Data summaries	Heuristic
TPF Client [17]	✓	TPF	✗	✗	TPF metadata	Heuristic
nLDE [1]	✗	TPF	✓	✗	TPF metadata	Heuristic
Comunica [16]	✓	TPF, SPARQL	✗	✗	TPF metadata	Heuristic
brTPF Client [9]	✗	BRTPF	✗	✗	TPF metadata	Heuristic
SaGe [12]	✗	SAGE-SERVER	✗	✗	–	Heuristic
smart-KG [4]	✗	SMART-KG	✗	✗	TPF metadata	Heuristic
CROP	✗	TPF	✓	✓	TPF metadata	IDP

Other LDF interfaces include brTPF, smart-KG, and SaGe. Hartig et al. [9] propose bindings-restricted Triple Pattern Fragments (brTPF), an extension of the TPF interface that allows for evaluating a given triple pattern with a sequence of bindings to enable bind-join strategies. To this end, the authors propose a heuristic-based client that builds left-deep query plans which aims to reduce the number of requests and data transferred. Smart-KG [4] is a hybrid shipping approach proposed to balance the load between client and server when evaluating SPARQL queries over remote sources. The smart-KG server extends the TPF interface by providing access to compressed partitions of the graph. The smart-KG client determines which subqueries are evaluated locally over the partitions and which triple pattern requests should be evaluated at the server. SaGe [12] is a SPARQL query engine that supports Web preemption by combining a preemptable server and a corresponding client. The server supports the fragment of full SPARQL which can be evaluated in a preemptable fashion. As a result, the evaluation of BGPs is carried out at the server using a heuristic-based query planner. Our client focuses on the TPF interface and can be adapted to support additional LDF interfaces. For instance, by extending the cost model with bind joins to support brTPF or implementing our concept of robustness as part of the query planner in the smart-KG client or the SaGe server.

In the realm of relational databases, various approaches addressing uncertainty in statistics and parameters of cost models have been suggested. In their survey, Yin et al. [19] classify robust query optimization methods with respect to estimation errors, which can lead to sub-optimal plans as the error propagates through the plan. One class of strategies they present are *Robust Plan Selection* approaches in which not the "optimal" plan but rather a "robust" plan that is less sensitive to estimation errors are chosen. For instance, robust approaches may use a probability density function for cardinality estimations instead of single-point values [5]. Other approaches define cardinality estimation intervals where the size of the intervals indicate the uncertainty of the optimizer [6]. In a recent paper, Wolf et al. [18] propose robustness metrics for query plans and the core idea is considering the cost for a query plan as a function of the cardinality and selectivity estimations at all edges in the plan. Similar to our work, the authors propose computing the k-cheapest plans and selecting the estimated most robust plan. These works rely on fine-grained statistics to assess the selectivity of joins, however, in a decentralized scenario, it is not possible to obtain such detailed dataset information. Therefore, we propose a robust plan selection approach and introduce a new concept of robustness for SPARQL query plans based on the TPF metadata.

6 Conclusion and Future Work

We have proposed CROP, a novel cost model-based robust query plan optimizer to devise efficient query plans. CROP implements a cost-model and incorporates the concept of robustness for query plans with respect to cardinality estimations errors. Our proposed concept of robust query plans is based on comparing the best-case to the average-case cost of query plans and could be combined with other existing cost models as well. Combining these concepts, CROP uses iterative dynamic programming (IDP) to determine alternative plans and decides when a more robust query plan should be chosen over the cheapest query plan. In our experimental study, we investigated how the parameters of the cost model and IDP impact the efficiency of the query plans. Thereafter, we studied different combinations of the robustness and the cost thresholds in the query plan optimizer. The parameters allow for finding a good balance between choosing alternative robust plans over the cheapest plan but not at any cost. Therefore, our concept of robustness complements the cost model in helping to find better query plans. Finally, we compared our approach to existing TPF clients. The results show that our approach is competitive with these clients regarding runtime performance. Moreover, the query plans of our query plan optimizer require fewer requests to produce the same number of results and, thus, reduce the load on the TPF server. Future work can focus on alternative strategies to IDP for exploring the space of plans more efficiently and extending the optimizer to apply the concept of robustness in federated querying. Our robust query planning approach may be implemented in Linked Data Fragment clients such as Comunica or smart-KG and the cost model may be further extended to include bind joins supported by brTPF. Besides, Linked Data Fragment interfaces, such as SaGe (HDT) may also benefit from including the notion of query plan robustness.

Acknowledgement. This work is funded by the German BMBF in QUOCA, FKZ 01IS17042.

References

1. Acosta, M., Vidal, M.-E.: Networks of Linked Data Eddies: an adaptive web query processing engine for RDF data. In: Arenas, M., et al. (eds.) ISWC 2015. LNCS, vol. 9366, pp. 111–127. Springer, Cham (2015). https://doi.org/10.1007/978-3-319-25007-6_7
2. Acosta, M., Vidal, M.-E., Sure-Vetter, Y.: Diefficiency metrics: measuring the continuous efficiency of query processing approaches. In: d'Amato, C., et al. (eds.) ISWC 2017. LNCS, vol. 10588, pp. 3–19. Springer, Cham (2017). https://doi.org/10.1007/978-3-319-68204-4_1
3. Aluç, G., Hartig, O., Özsu, M.T., Daudjee, K.: Diversified stress testing of RDF data management systems. In: Mika, P., et al. (eds.) ISWC 2014. LNCS, vol. 8796, pp. 197–212. Springer, Cham (2014). https://doi.org/10.1007/978-3-319-11964-9_13
4. Azzam, A., Fernández, J.D., Acosta, M., Beno, M., Polleres, A.: SMART-KG: hybrid shipping for SPARQL querying on the web. In: WWW 2020: The Web Conference 2020 (2020)
5. Babcock, B., Chaudhuri, S.: Towards a robust query optimizer: a principled and practical approach. In: ACM SIGMOD International Conference on Management of Data (2005)
6. Babu, S., Bizarro, P., DeWitt, D.J.: Proactive re-optimization. In: ACM SIGMOD International Conference on Management of Data (2005)
7. Charalambidis, A., Troumpoukis, A., Konstantopoulos, S.: SemaGrow: optimizing federated SPARQL queries. In: SEMANTICS 2015 (2015)
8. Görlitz, O., Staab, S.: SPLENDID: SPARQL endpoint federation exploiting VOID descriptions. In: COLD 2011 (2011)
9. Hartig, O., Buil-Aranda, C.: Bindings-restricted triple pattern fragments. In: Debruyne, C., et al. (eds.) OTM 2016. LNCS, vol. 10033, pp. 762–779. Springer, Cham (2016). https://doi.org/10.1007/978-3-319-48472-3_48
10. Heling, L., Acosta, M., Maleshkova, M., Sure-Vetter, Y.: Querying large knowledge graphs over triple pattern fragments: an empirical study. In: Vrandečić, D., et al. (eds.) ISWC 2018. LNCS, vol. 11137, pp. 86–102. Springer, Cham (2018). https://doi.org/10.1007/978-3-030-00668-6_6
11. Kossmann, D., Stocker, K.: Iterative dynamic programming: a new class of query optimization algorithms. ACM Trans. Database Syst. **25**(1), 43–82 (2000)
12. Minier, T., Skaf-Molli, H., Molli, P.: Sage: web preemption for public SPARQL query services. In: WWW 2019: The Web Conference 2019 (2019)
13. Montoya, G., Skaf-Molli, H., Hose, K.: The *Odyssey* approach for optimizing federated SPARQL queries. In: d'Amato, C., et al. (eds.) ISWC 2017. LNCS, vol. 10587, pp. 471–489. Springer, Cham (2017). https://doi.org/10.1007/978-3-319-68288-4_28
14. Quilitz, B., Leser, U.: Querying distributed RDF data sources with SPARQL. In: Bechhofer, S., Hauswirth, M., Hoffmann, J., Koubarakis, M. (eds.) ESWC 2008. LNCS, vol. 5021, pp. 524–538. Springer, Heidelberg (2008). https://doi.org/10.1007/978-3-540-68234-9_39
15. Saleem, M., Potocki, A., Soru, T., Hartig, O., Ngomo, A.N.: CostFed: cost-based query optimization for SPARQL endpoint federation. In: SEMANTICS 2018 (2018)
16. Taelman, R., Van Herwegen, J., Vander Sande, M., Verborgh, R.: Comunica: a modular SPARQL query engine for the web. In: Vrandečić, D., et al. (eds.) ISWC 2018. LNCS, vol. 11137, pp. 239–255. Springer, Cham (2018). https://doi.org/10.1007/978-3-030-00668-6_15

17. Verborgh, R., et al.: Triple pattern fragments: a low-cost knowledge graph interface for the web. J. Web Semant. **37**, 184–206 (2016)
18. Wolf, F., Brendle, M., May, N., Willems, P.R., Sattler, K., Grossniklaus, M.: Robustness metrics for relational query execution plans. PVLDB **1**(11), 1360–1372 (2018)
19. Yin, S., Hameurlain, A., Morvan, F.: Robust query optimization methods with respect to estimation errors: a survey. SIGMOD Rec. **44**(3), 25–36 (2015)

GeoSPARQL+: Syntax, Semantics and System for Integrated Querying of Graph, Raster and Vector Data

Timo Homburg[1(✉)], Steffen Staab[3,4], and Daniel Janke[2]

[1] Mainz University of Applied Sciences, DE, Mainz, Germany
timo.homburg@hs-mainz.de
[2] Universität Koblenz, DE, Mainz, Germany
danijank@uni-koblenz.de
[3] Universität Stuttgart, DE, Stuttgart, Germany
steffen.staab@ipvs.uni-stuttgart.de
[4] WAIS Research Group, University of Southampton, Southampton, UK

Abstract. We introduce an approach to semantically represent and query raster data in a Semantic Web graph. We extend the GeoSPARQL vocabulary and query language to support raster data as a new type of geospatial data. We define new filter functions and illustrate our approach using several use cases on real-world data sets. Finally, we describe a prototypical implementation and validate the feasibility of our approach.

Keywords: GeoSPARQL · Raster data · Geospatial semantics

1 Introduction

The Geospatial Semantic Web [9,16] has grown in size and importance in the last decade. It is estimated that about 80% of all data has a geospatial relation [19]. Therefore, GeoSPARQL [6] has been developed and became an OGC[1] and W3C[2] recommendation allowing for the representation and querying of geospatial data in the semantic web. GeoSPARQL and comparable approaches [22,24] only provide support for geospatial vector data. However, geospatial data may also take the shape of a raster. It may, e.g., be obtained from aerial imagery or from simulation data to support tasks such as city planning and risk assessment as shown by the examples depicted in Fig. 1.

Raster data must not be represented as vector geometries, because vector representations of raster data

1. are inefficient implying overconsumption of data storage. Raster data can be large and may be compressed efficiently.
2. are ineffective representations as they lack operations needed to query raster data e.g. raster algebra operations that transform raster data in ways not applicable to vector data.

[1] https://www.opengeospatial.org.
[2] https://www.w3.org.

J. Z. Pan et al. (Eds.): ISWC 2020, LNCS 12506, pp. 258–275, 2020.
https://doi.org/10.1007/978-3-030-62419-4_15

3. lack the semantics needed to appropriately represent raster data. Raster data is often visualized with RGB values, such as varying shades of blue for different flood altitudes. A semantic representation, however, should not represent color shades, but rather the underlying semantics, which should refer to data from the actual nominal, ordinal, interval or ratio scales and what they stand for.

We propose GeoSPARQL+, an extension of the GeoSPARQL query language, and the GeoSPARQL+ ontology in order to integrate geospatial raster data into the Semantic Web.

Let us consider the analysis of a flood as our running example. Our running example is depicted in Fig. 1a showing the overlay of two related datasets:

1. Vector data representing the roads of Cologne
2. Raster data representing the altitudes of a simulated flood

A query in one of our real-world use cases asks for all the road sections not covered by more than 10cm of water. This is only possible if the data model can represent raster data, vector data, semantics (road, water, depth, 10cm) and allows for joint querying of these representations. Existing geographical information systems lack the explicit representation of semantics and require the user to manually adapt his high-level information need into a query of the low-level representation. The GeoSPARQL standard [6] and systems that currently support geographic information in the Semantic Web [6,10,14,15,22,24,26] do not represent raster data, thus, they do not allow for asking such questions.

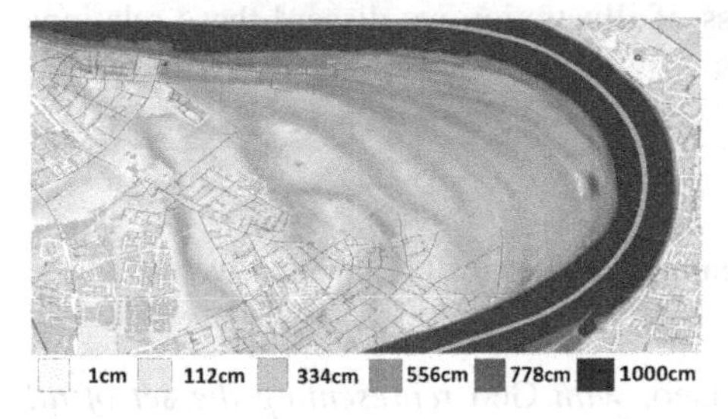

(a) Floodmap depicting the flood altitude and a road network. The map legend informally describes the semantics of colors in terms of a fractional scale of flood altitudes.

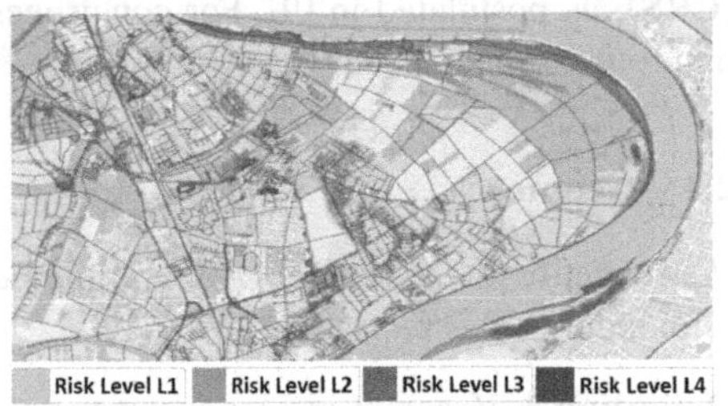

(b) Fire hazard risks displayed in different shades of red with darker shades implying higher risk levels. The map legend informally describes the risks using an ordinal scale.

Fig. 1. Visualizations of two sources of risk in Cologne

In the remainder of this paper, we will assume that there are data sources that contain vector data (e.g. roads in Fig. 1) and raster data (e.g. flood altitudes Fig. 1a or fire hazards Fig. 1b). We describe a GeoSPARQL+ ontology which allows a data engineer to integrate these data into an RDF graph. A user may issue a semantic query against the RDF graph using GeoSPARQL+. To allow for these capabilities, this paper makes the following contributions:

1. *Semantic Representation of Raster Data:* A data model that allows for representing raster data and its semantics (Sect. 4).
2. *GeoSPARQL Vocabulary Extension:* This vocabulary extension defines how to relate the raster data to semantic descriptions (Sect. 5.1).
3. *GeoSPARQL Query Language Extension:* A SPARQL extension which allows the interoperable use of semantic graph data, semantic vector geometries, and semantic raster data and uses map algebra [35] to combine and modify rasters (Sects. 5.2 and 5.3).
4. *Prototypical Implementation:* An open source implementation of the proposed approach for geospatial vector and raster data (Sect. 6).
5. *Requirements and Feasibility Check:* Deriving requirements of GeoSPARQL+ by discussing relevant use cases (Sect. 3), assessing their feasibility and conducting a performance check of the implemented system (Sect. 7).

The tasks of data integration and visualization of query results are beyond the focus of this paper. More technical details about the supported functions may be found in our companion technical report [18].

2 Foundations for Extending GeoSPARQL

In this publication we limit ourselves to 2D representations in order to remain concise. We see no major issue in extending our approach to higher dimensional representations. We assume that all geographical representations relate to coordinate reference systems (CRS), as postulated in [9]. For conciseness of illustration we discard these relations and transformations between CRSs.

2.1 Geometry

We formally define several OGC Simple Feature geometries [17], which we use in the remainder of this paper.

Definition 1 (*Geometry*). *A geometry $g \in \mathrm{Geo}$, with* Geo *representing the set of all geometries, is an instantiation of one of the following data structures:*

1. *A geometry g may be a* Point $p = (x, y), p \in \mathbb{R}^2$, *or*
2. *A* LineString *defined as a list of at least two different points denoted as* $g = (p_0, p_1, \ldots, p_n), p_i \in \mathbb{R}^2$, *or*
3. *A* Polygon *g represented as a LineString with* $g = (p_0, p_1, \ldots, p_n)$, $p_0 = p_n, p_i \in \mathbb{R}^2$ *and all other points being unique. We further restrict ourselves to valid Polygons. In valid Polygons lines do not cross each other. A Polygon includes the encompassed area.*
4. *A geometry g may also be a* Rectangle, *which is a special polygon comprised of four LineStrings with the angles between connected LineStrings being* 90°. $\mathrm{Rect} \subset \mathrm{Geo}$ *is the set of all rectangles.*
5. *Finally, a geometry may be a* GeometryCollection *g, which itself is a finite set of geometries* $g = \{g_1, \ldots, g_k\}, g_i \in \mathrm{Geo}$.

MultiPolygons *and* MultiLineStrings *are examples of GeometryCollections.*

We assume that the function geom2pset : $Geo \rightarrow 2^{\mathbb{R}^2}$ exists which converts a geometry to a PointSet representation.

2.2 RDF, SPARQL and GeoSPARQL

In order to semantically describe and query raster data we build upon the following standard definitions of SPARQL 1.1 [12,27]. We provide the first formal definitions of the operators and filter functions which GeoSPARQL [6] adds to the SPARQL query language and describe the resulting modified definitions of SPARQL 1.1 in the following. In order to keep the definitions concise enough for this paper, we formalize syntax and semantics with 3 exemplary operators and 2 exemplary filter functions. We pick GeoSPARQL specific elements such that they are representative for the most common types of signatures. The differences between SPARQL 1.1 and the GeoSPARQL extensions are marked in blue fonts.

Definition 2 (*RDF Triple and RDF Graph*). *Let I, B and L be disjoint sets of IRIs, blank nodes and literals, respectively. An element of the set $(I \cup B) \times I \times (I \cup B \cup L)$ is called a* triple *$t \in T$ with T denoting the set of all triples. $G \in 2^{(I \cup B) \times I \times (I \cup B \cup L)}$ is called an* RDF graph. *$GL \subset L$ is the set of all geometry literals.*

In an RDF triple (s, p, o), s, p and o are called *subject*, *predicate* and *object*, respectively. Geometry literals (GL) are serialized according to the GeoSPARQL standard either as Well-Known-Text (WKT) [36] literals or as Geography Markup Language (GML) [29] literals.

Definition 3 (*Triple Pattern*). *Let V be a set of variables that is disjoint to I, B and L. An element of $(I \cup B \cup L \cup V) \times (I \cup V) \times (I \cup B \cup L \cup V)$ is called a* triple pattern.

The set of variables occurring in a triple pattern tp is abbreviated as $\text{var}(tp)$.

Definition 4 (*Expression*). *An* expression *is*

$Expression ::= ?X$	*with $?X \in V$*
$\mid c$	*with constant $c \in L \cup I$.*
$\mid E_1 \cap E_2$	*with E_1, E_2 being expressions.*
$\mid \text{geof}:\text{buffer}(E_1, E_2, E_3)$	*with E_1, E_2, E_3 being expressions*
$\mid \text{geof}:\text{distance}(E_1, E_2)$	*with E_1, E_2 being expressions*

Definition 5 (*Filter Condition*). *A* filter condition *is*

$FilterCondition ::= ?X = c$	*with $?X \in V$ and $c \in I \cup L$*
$\mid ?X = ?Y$	*with $?X, ?Y \in V$*
$\mid \neg F$	*with filter condition F*
$\mid F_1 \vee F_2$	*with filter conditions F_1 and F_2*
$\mid F_1 \wedge F_2$	*with filter conditions F_1 and F_2*
$\mid E_1 \circleddash E_2$	*with E_1, E_2 being expressions*
$\mid E_1 \textcircled{$\cap$} E_2$	*with E_1, E_2 being expressions*

$\cap$, $\circleddash$, $\textcircled{\cap}$ correspond to the GeoSPARQL operators geof : intersection, geof : equals and geof : intersects respectively [11]. We provide complete list of all GeoSPARQL functions in our technical report that extends this paper [18].

Definition 6 (*Basic Graph Pattern*). *A* basic graph pattern *(BGP) is*

$BGP ::= \mathrm{tp}$	*a triple pattern* tp
$\mid \{B\}$	*a block of a basic graph pattern B*
$\mid B_1.B_2$	*a conjunction of two basic graph patterns B_1 and B_2*
$\mid B\ \texttt{FILTER}\ F$	*a filter pattern with BGP B and filter condition F*
$\mid B\ \texttt{BIND}\ (E\ \texttt{AS}\ \texttt{?X})$	*a bind with BGP B, expression E and variable* ?X.

Definition 7 (*Select Query*). *A* select query *is defined as* SELECT *W* WHERE *B with $W \subseteq V$ and basic graph pattern B.*

Definition 8 (*Variable Binding*). *A* variable binding *is a partial function $\mu : V \nrightarrow I \cup B \cup L$. The set of all variable bindings is Φ.*

The abbreviated notation $\mu(tp)$ means that variables in triple pattern *tp* are substituted according to μ.

Definition 9 (*Compatible Variable Binding*). *Two variable bindings μ_1 and μ_2 are* compatible, *denoted by $\mu_1 \sim \mu_2$, if*

$$\forall \texttt{?X} \in \mathrm{dom}(\mu_1) \cup \mathrm{dom}(\mu_2) : \mu_1(\texttt{?X}) = \mu_2(\texttt{?X})$$

Thereby $\mathrm{dom}(\mu)$ *refers to the set of variables of variable binding μ.*

Definition 10 (*Join*). *The* join *of two sets of variable bindings Φ_1, Φ_2 is defined as*

$$\Phi_1 \bowtie \Phi_2 = \{\mu_1 \cup \mu_2 | \mu_1 \in \Phi_1 \wedge \mu_2 \in \Phi_2 \wedge \mu_1 \sim \mu_2\}$$

Definition 11 (*Expression Evaluation*). *The* evaluation *of an expression E over a variable binding μ, denoted by $[\![E]\!]_\mu$, is defined recursively as follows:*

$[\![\texttt{?X}]\!]_\mu := \mu(\texttt{?X})$	*with* $\texttt{?X} \in V$.
$[\![c]\!]_\mu := c$	*with c being a constant, literal or IRI.*
$[\![E_1 \cap E_2]\!]_\mu := [\![E_1]\!]_\mu \cap [\![E_2]\!]_\mu$	*retrieves a geometry $g \in$ Geo that represents all Points in the intersection of $[\![E_1]\!]_\mu, [\![E_2]\!]_\mu \in$ Geo [6]*
$[\![\mathrm{geof:buffer}(E_1, E_2, E_3)]\!]_\mu := g$	*retrieves a bounding box $g \in$ Rect of radius $[\![E_2]\!]_\mu \in \mathbb{R}$ around $[\![E_1]\!]_\mu \in$ Geo using the unit given in $[\![E_3]\!]_\mu \in I$ [6]*
$[\![\mathrm{geof:distance}(E_1, E_2)]\!]_\mu := c$	*returns the minimum distance $c \in \mathbb{R}$ between $[\![E_1]\!]_\mu \in$ Geo and $[\![E_2]\!]_\mu \in$ Geo [6]*

Definition 12 (*Filter Condition Satisfaction*). *Whether variable binding μ* satisfies a filter condition *F, denoted by $\mu \models F$, is defined recursively as follows:*

$\mu \models ?X = c$ *holds if* $?X \in \mathrm{dom}(\mu)$ *and* $\mu(?X) = c$.
$\mu \models ?X = ?Y$ *holds if* $?X \in \mathrm{dom}(\mu)$, $?Y \in \mathrm{dom}(\mu)$ *and* $\mu(?X) = \mu(?Y)$.
$\mu \models \neg F$ *holds if it is not the case that* $\mu \models F$.
$\mu \models F_1 \vee F_2$ *holds if* $\mu \models F_1$ *or* $\mu \models F_2$.
$\mu \models F_1 \wedge F_2$ *holds if* $\mu \models F_1$ *and* $\mu \models F_2$
$\mu \models E_1 \circleddash E_2$ *holds if* $[\![E_1]\!]_\mu \in \mathrm{Geo}$, $[\![E_2]\!]_\mu \in \mathrm{Geo}$ *and* $\mathrm{geom2pset}([\![E_1]\!]_\mu) = \mathrm{geom2pset}([\![E_2]\!]_\mu)$
$\mu \models E_1 \textcircled{\cap} E_2$ *holds if* $[\![E_1]\!]_\mu \in \mathrm{Geo}$, $[\![E_2]\!]_\mu \in \mathrm{Geo}$ *and* $\mathrm{geom2pset}([\![E_1]\!]_\mu) \cap \mathrm{geom2pset}([\![E_2]\!]_\mu) \neq \emptyset$.

Definition 13 (*SPARQL Evaluation*). *The* evaluation *of a SPARQL query Q over an RDF graph G, denoted by* $[\![Q]\!]_G$, *is defined recursively as follows:*

$[\![\mathrm{tp}]\!]_G := \{\mu \mid \mathrm{dom}(\mu) = \mathrm{var}(\mathrm{tp}) \wedge \mu(\mathrm{tp}) \in G\}$ *with triple pattern* tp.
$[\![\{B\}]\!]_G := [\![B]\!]_G$ *with basic graph pattern B.*
$[\![B_1.B_2]\!]_G := [\![B_1]\!]_G \bowtie [\![B_2]\!]_G$ *with basic graph patterns* B_1 *and* B_2.
$[\![B\ \mathtt{FILTER}\ F]\!]_G := \{\mu \mid \mu \in [\![B]\!]_G \wedge \mu \models F\}$ *with basic graph pattern B and filter condition F.*
$[\![B\ \mathtt{BIND}\ (E\ \mathtt{AS}\ ?X)]\!]_G :=$ $\{\mu \cup \{?X \mapsto [\![E]\!]_\mu\} \mid \mu \in [\![B]\!]_G \wedge ?X \notin \mathrm{dom}(\mu)\}$ *with basic graph pattern B, expression E and variable* $?X$.
$[\![\mathtt{SELECT}\ W\ \mathtt{WHERE}\ B]\!]_G := \{\mu_{|W} \mid \mu \in [\![B]\!]_G\}$ *with basic graph pattern B and* $W \subseteq V$

Thereby $\mu_{|W}$ *means that the domain of* μ *is restricted to the variables in W.*

3 Use Case Requirements

We now define requirements for use cases we have encountered when collaborating with companies developing geographical information systems.

U1 *Client: Rescue Forces; Use case: Emergency rescue routing*
Rescue vehicles and routing algorithms guiding them need to know which roads are passable in case of flooding.
Example query: *"Give me all roads which are not flooded by more than 10 cm"*

U2 *Client: Insurance; Use case: Risk assessment*
Insurances evaluate the hazard risk for str'eets and buildings in order to calculate the insurance premium.
Example query: *"Assess the combined risk of fire and flood hazards for all buildings in the knowledge base"*

U3 *Client: Disaster Management Agency; Use case: Rescue capacity planning*
In case of disasters, the number of people present at a specified time and place needs to be estimated to prepare hospitals for casualties.
' Example query: *"Give me the roads which contain elements at risk which are open to the public at 23rd May 2019 10.20am"* Note: An *element at risk* is a term in disaster management describing a class of buildings affected by certain disasters [18].

U4 *Client: City Planning Agency; Use case: Rescue facility location planning*
Rescue forces should be stationed in a way that they can react fast to possible hazards and city planners should position rescue stations accordingly.
Example query: *"Give me the percentage of served hazardous areas, i.e. areas within a bounding box of 10km around a to-be-built rescue station at a given geo-coordinate"*

These example queries can currently not be expressed using GeoSPARQL. Abstracting from the given natural language query examples we have defined a graph data model for raster data and the syntax and semantics of GeoSPARQL+ that allow us to respond to these queries.

4 Modeling Raster Data

We have analyzed the requirements for representing raster data using examples like the ones depicted in Fig. 1 and use cases in Sect. 3. These examples show that we need to transform the following visual elements into semantic representations:

1. Raster geometry: A raster covers a geometrical area. In this paper, we limit ourselves to rectangular areas though other geometries might be supported in the future.
2. Atomic values: In visualizations of raster data, atomic values are mapped onto pixel values. In simple cases this is a one-to-one mapping. Depending on the resolution of the raster and the rendered picture, it may also be a n:1 or 1:n or even an n:m mapping.
3. Atomic value geometry: Each atomic value represents the situation in a geometry area, typically in a rectangular area.
4. Raster legend: A raster legend is a description of the semantic interpretation of the raster's atomic values. This description includes a categorical, ordinal, interval or fractional scale.

We formally define a raster following [20] as:

Definition 14 (*Raster*). *Let R be the set of all rasters and $\mathbb{S}$ the set of all scales. A* Raster *$r \in R$ is a partial function $r : \mathbb{R}^2 \nrightarrow S$ which maps positions onto a scale $S \in \mathbb{S}$. We define a scale as a partially ordered set. In addition, every scale defines a NODATA value, a unique value which is not to be used elsewhere in the scale definition. The domain of a raster $dom(r)$ is the closed, rectangular region represented by its raster geometry for which its atomic values are defined.*

dom(r) can be represented by a rectangle defined by its four corners (p_l, p_b, p_r, p_t), where $p_i = (x_i, y_i)$ and $x_l \leq x_r, x_l \leq x_t, x_l \leq x_b, x_r \geq x_t, x_r \geq x_b$ and $y_l \geq y_b, y_t \geq y_r, y_l \leq y_t, y_b \leq y_r$.

Figure 2 shows an example of a raster. In order to execute geometric operations on raster data and geometries we assume a function raster2geom(r) returning dom(r) as a geometric object. In order to compare rasters to other rasters we assume an equality function. rastervaleq(r,r) compares the rasters atomic values and its domains.

Definition 15 (*Raster Literal*). *The set* RL $\subset L$ *with* GL $\cap$ RL $= \emptyset$ *represents the set of all raster literals.*

We use the CoverageJSON format [8] to serialize rasters to raster literals, but many other textual serializations or even binary serializations are possible. These representations assume that the raster geometry is divided uniformly into rectangular cell geometries (atomic value geometries in our previous definition). A cell c is a pair $(g,s) \in \text{Rect} \times S$. We relate a cell c to a raster r via a pair of indexes (i,j). $r_{i,j}$ refers to a specific cell indexed by (i,j) in a raster r. $r_{i,j}(x,y)$ is undefined for values outside of the cell and has the identical value for all positions within the cell. Thus, given x,y such that $r_{i,j}(x,y)$ is defined, c may be defined as $(raster2geom(r_{i,j}), r_{i,j}(x,y))$.

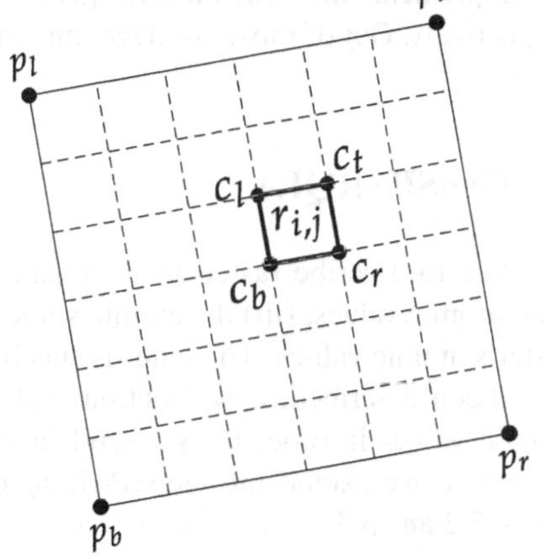

Fig. 2. Raster representation: The raster r is represented using a raster geometry $dom(r)$, a subdivision in cells and a scale $S \in \mathbb{S}$.

The function cellval : $R \times \mathbb{R} \times \mathbb{R} \rightarrow \mathbb{R}$ retrieves the atomic value of a given raster cell. The function cellval2 : $R \rightarrow \{\mathbb{R}\}$ retrieves atomic values of all raster cells.

Raster Algebra or map algebra is a set based algebra to manipulate raster data. Following [35] we assume the definition of scale-dependent raster algebras with operations $\ominus$, $\oplus$ and $\otimes$ defined for the following signatures:

$$(1)\ \ominus : R \rightarrow R,\ (2)\ \oplus : R \times R \rightarrow R.\ (3)\ \otimes : R \times \mathbb{R} \rightarrow R$$

The three operations we indicate here, their formal definitions given in [35], are examples for a broader set of possible raster algebra operations. Most other algebraic operators exhibit the same signatures as one of these three example operations. Hence, syntax and semantics of other operators can be integrated into GeoSPARQL+ taking the integration of example operators as templates.

The $\ominus$ function converts each atomic value different from 0 to 0, all 0 values to 1 and does not change NODATA values. The $\oplus$ function creates a new raster with the domain of the first raster. The resulting raster contains all values of the first raster which have no correspondence with the atomic values of the second raster (i.e. not map to the same position). All values with a correspondence are added together or ignored if one of the input values is the NODATA value of either of the two rasters. This function can be used to combine risks of fire and flood hazards given in two different rasters representing the same area.

The ⊘ function takes one raster and one constant. It returns a new raster with the domain of the given raster. Atomic values smaller than the given constant are kept, all other values become the NODATA value. One application of this function is to only keep the flood altitude values displayed in Fig. 1a which signify an altitude value smaller than a given constant.

Implementations like PostGIS [31] and JAI [32] provide 26 and 108 raster functions respectively. Out of those we have implemented 14 in our system which we describe in [18].

5 GeoSPARQL+

In order to describe raster data semantically,we must define (i) their geometries, (ii) their atomic values, (iii) the atomic value geometries, and (iv) the semantic meaning of raster's atomic values. The latter is specified in this section. When the raster's contents have been described, new functions are needed to filter, relate or modify the raster's atomic values in order to be useful in the application cases we would like to solve. Therefore we extend the GeoSPARQL query language to include such functions in Sects. 5.2 and 5.3

5.1 The GeoSPARQL+ Vocabulary

We define the new GeoSPARQL+ vocabulary (cf. Fig. 3).

A raster is described by its semantic class (*geo2:Raster*), and a scale which describes the semantic content of its atomic values. In Fig. 3, we depict the example of a semantic class *ex:FloodArea* which is assigned an instance of *geo2:Raster* with a CoverageJSON literal (Listing 1.1) including the raster's type, a CRS, the raster's atomic values and their description. In order to re-use the representations of the CoverageJSON format, we model rasters in a concept hierarchy of OGC coverage types. By the OGC definition, a raster is a special type of coverage which is rectangular, i.e. a grid, and is georeferenced. This definition is reflected in Fig. 3 in the given concept hierarchy. The instance of *geo:Raster* connects to an instance of *om:Scale* describing its legend and unit of measurement derived from the units of measurements ontology (UOM) as well as the scales NODATA value.

```
1 {"type" : "Coverage","domain" : { "type" : "Domain", "domainType" : "Grid",
  "axes": { "x" : { "values": [−10,−5,0] },"y" : { "values": [40,50] }
3 "referencing": [{"coordinates": ["y","x"],"system": {
  "type": "GeographicCRS","id": "http://www.opengis.net/def/crs/EPSG/0/4979"}}]},
5 "observedProperty" : {
  "ranges" : { "FloodAT" : { "type" : "NdArray", "dataType": "float",
7 "axisNames": ["y","x"], "shape": [2, 2], "values" : [ 0.5, 0.6, 0.4, 0.6 ]}}}
```

Listing 1.1. Coverage JSON Literal example

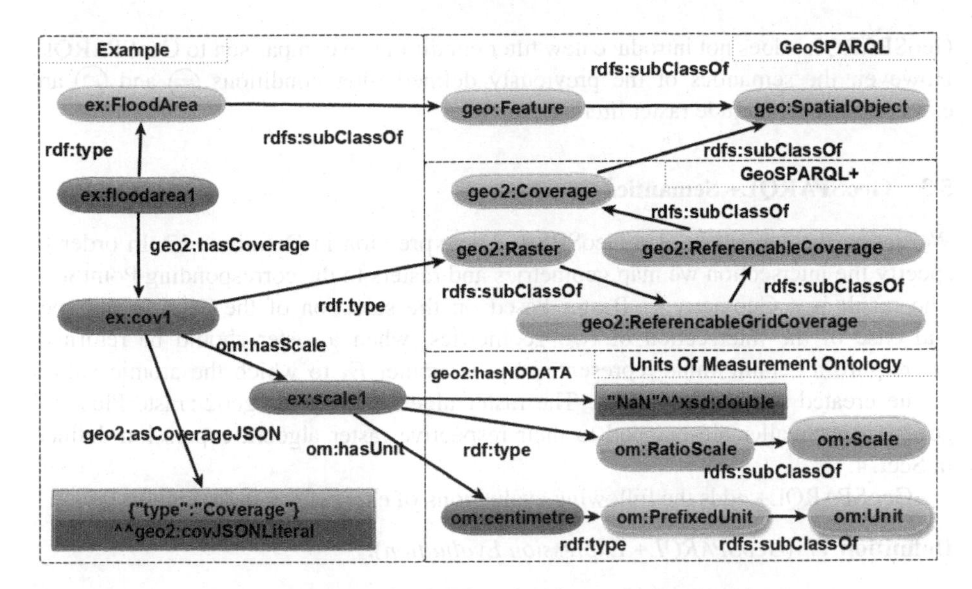

Fig. 3. We use vocabularies of three different ontologies: The GeoSPARQL ontology describes the concepts *geo:SpatialObject* and *geo:Feature*, the OGC coverage hierarchy describes the abstract concepts of coverages and the unit of measurement vocabulary describes legends of raster data.

5.2 GeoSPARQL+ Syntax

We added several new operators to the GeoSPARQL+ query language that allow to filter, modify and combine rasters as well as polygons. Due to space limitations, we present only one example for each of the three possibilites. A full list of the implemented functions is provided in [18]. geometryIntersection calculates intersections between arbitrary combinations of Geometries and Rasters, returning a Geometry. To get a raster as result instead, the rasterIntersection can be used. $\boxed{+}$ and $\boxed{<}$ provide two examples of raster algebra expressions.
GeoSPARQL+ defines the following new expressions to replace Definition 4:

Definition 16 (*GeoSPARQL+ Expression*).

Expression ::= $?X$	*with* $?X \in V$
$\mid c$	*with constant* $c \in L \cup I$.
$\mid$ geometryIntersection(E_1, E_2)	*with* E_1, E_2 *being expressions*
$\mid$ rasterIntersection(E_1, E_2)	*with* E_1, E_2 *being expressions*
$\mid E_1 \boxed{+} E_2$	*with* E_1, E_2 *being expressions*
$\mid E_1 \boxed{<} E_2$	*with* E_1, E_2 *being expressions*
$\mid \boxed{\neg} E$	*with* E *being an expression*
$\mid$ raster2geom(E)	*with* E *being an expression*
$\mid$ rastervaleq(E_1, E_2)	*with* E_1, E_2 *being expressions*
$\mid$ geom2raster(E_1, E_2)	*with* E_1, E_2 *being expressions*

GeoSPARQL+ does not introduce new filter conditions in comparison to GeoSPARQL. However, the semantics of the previously defined filter conditions $\circleddash$ and $\textcircled{\cap}$ are extended to also include raster literals.

5.3 GeoSPARQL+ Semantics

We define the semantics of a GeoSPARQL+ expression in Definition 17. In order to specify the intersection we map geometries and rasters to the corresponding PointSets. The result is a Geometry or Raster based on the selection of the user. In the special case of the intersection of two geometries, when a raster should be returned, we require a default value represented by parameter E_3 to which the atomic values of the created raster are mapped. The raster algebra functions geo2 : rasterPlus and geo2 : rasterSmaller are mapped to their respective raster algebra expression defined in Sect. 4.

GeoSPARQL+ adds the following evaluations of expressions to Definition 11:

Definition 17 (*GeoSPARQL+ Expression Evaluation*).

$$
\begin{aligned}
&[\![\text{geometryIntersection}(E_1,E_2)]\!]_\mu := [\![E_1]\!]_\mu \cap [\![E_2]\!]_\mu \\
&\qquad\qquad \textit{if } [\![E_1]\!]_\mu \textit{ and } [\![E_2]\!]_\mu \in \textit{Geo} \\
&[\![\text{geometryIntersection}(E_1,E_2)]\!]_\mu := [\![E_1]\!]_\mu \cap \text{raster2geom}([\![E_2]\!]_\mu) \\
&\qquad\qquad \textit{if } [\![E_1]\!]_\mu \in \textit{Geo and } [\![E_2]\!]_\mu \in R \\
&[\![\text{geometryIntersection}(E_1,E_2)]\!]_\mu := [\![\text{geometryIntersection}(E_2,E_1)]\!]_\mu \\
&\qquad\qquad \textit{if } [\![E_1]\!]_\mu \in R \textit{ and } [\![E_2]\!]_\mu \in \text{Geo} \\
&[\![\text{rasterIntersection}(E_1,E_2)]\!]_\mu := r \in R \textit{ with } \forall i,j : r_{i,j} = r1_{i,j} \\
&\qquad\qquad \textit{if } [\![E_1]\!]_\mu = r1, [\![E_2]\!]_\mu = r2 \in R \\
&\qquad\qquad \textit{and } \text{dom}(r1_{i,j}) \cap \text{dom}(r2_{i,j}) \neq \emptyset \\
&[\![\text{rasterIntersection}(E_1,E_2)]\!]_\mu := r \in R \textit{ with } \forall i,j : r_{i,j} = r1_{i,j} \\
&\qquad\qquad \textit{if } [\![E_1]\!]_\mu = r1 \in R \textit{ and } [\![E_2]\!]_\mu = g \in \text{Geo} \\
&\qquad\qquad \textit{and } \text{dom}(r1_{i,j}) \cap g \neq \emptyset \\
&[\![\text{rasterIntersection}(E_1,E_2)]\!]_\mu := [\![\text{rasterIntersection}(E_2,E_1)]\!]_\mu \\
&\qquad\qquad \textit{if } [\![E_1]\!]_\mu = r1 \in R \textit{ and } [\![E_2]\!]_\mu = g \in \text{Geo} \\
&[\![\text{rastervaleq}(E_1,E_2)]\!]_\mu := r \in R \quad \textit{with } \forall i,j : \text{dom}(r1_{i,j}) \cap \text{dom}(r2_{i,j}) \neq \emptyset \\
&\qquad\qquad \textit{and } \text{cellval}(r1_{i,j}) == \text{cellval}(r2_{i,j}) \\
&\qquad\qquad \textit{if } [\![E_1]\!]_\mu = r1, [\![E_2]\!]_\mu = r2 \in R \\
&[\![\boxed{\neg} E]\!]_\mu := r \in R \quad \textit{with } \forall i,j : r_{i,j} = \circleddash r1_{i,j} \textit{ if } [\![E]\!]_\mu = r1 \in R \\
&[\![E_1 \boxed{+} E_2]\!]_\mu := [\![E_1]\!]_\mu \oplus [\![E_2]\!]_\mu \quad \textit{if } [\![E_1]\!]_\mu, [\![E_2]\!]_\mu \in R \\
&[\![E_1 \boxed{<} E_2]\!]_\mu := [\![E_1]\!]_\mu \textcircled{<} [\![E_2]\!]_\mu \quad \textit{if } [\![E_1]\!]_\mu, [\![E_2]\!]_\mu \in R \\
&[\![\text{geom2raster}(E_1,E_2,E_3,E_4)]\!]_\mu := r \in R \textit{ with} \\
&\qquad\qquad \forall (x,y) \in \text{geof} : \text{buffer}([\![E_1]\!]_\mu, 1, \text{uom} : \text{meter}) \\
&\qquad\qquad r(x,y) = [\![E_2]\!]_\mu \\
&\qquad\qquad \textit{if } [\![E_1]\!]_\mu \in \textit{Geo}, [\![E_2]\!]_\mu, [\![E_3]\!]_\mu, [\![E_4]\!]_\mu \in \mathbb{R} \\
&\qquad\qquad \textit{with } [\![E_3]\!]_\mu \cdot [\![E_4]\!]_\mu \textit{ indicating the number of cells}
\end{aligned}
$$

We define the semantics of a GeoSPARQL+ filter condition in Definition 18. The geo2:equals method returns true if two Raster or two Geometries are identical. The geo2 : intersects method returns true if the PointSets of two Raster or Geometries overlap. GeoSPARQL+ replaces the evaluation of the filter condition from Definition 12 as follows:

Definition 18 (*GeoSPARQL+ Filter Condition Satisfaction*).

$\mu \models E_1 \textcircled{=} E_2$ *holds if* $[\![E_1]\!]_\mu, [\![E_2]\!]_\mu \in \text{Geo}$ *and* $\text{geom2pset}([\![E_1]\!]_\mu) = \text{geom2pset}([\![E_2]\!]_\mu)$.

$\mu \models E_1 \textcircled{=} E_2$ *holds if* $[\![E_1]\!]_\mu \in R$ *and* $[\![E_2]\!]_\mu \in \text{Geo}$ *and* $\text{geom2pset}(\text{raster2geom}([\![E_1]\!]_\mu)) = \text{geom2pset}([\![E_2]\!]_\mu)$

$\mu \models E_1 \textcircled{=} E_2$ *holds if* $[\![E_1]\!]_\mu \in \text{Geo}$ *and* $[\![E_2]\!]_\mu \in R$ *and* $\mu \models E_2 \textcircled{=} E_1$

$\mu \models E_1 \textcircled{=} E_2$ *holds if* $[\![E_1]\!]_\mu, [\![E_2]\!]_\mu \in R$ *and* $\text{geom2pset}(\text{raster2geom}([\![E_1]\!]_\mu)) = \text{geom2pset}(\text{raster2geom}([\![E_2]\!]_\mu))$

$\mu \models E_1 \textcircled{\cap} E_2$ *holds if* $[\![E_1]\!]_\mu \in R, [\![E_2]\!]_\mu \in R$ *and* $\text{geom2pset}(\text{raster2geom}([\![E_1]\!]_\mu)) \cap \text{geom2pset}(\text{raster2geom}([\![E_2]\!]_\mu)) \neq \varnothing$

$\mu \models E_1 \textcircled{\cap} E_2$ *holds if* $[\![E_1]\!]_\mu \in \text{Geo}, [\![E_2]\!]_\mu \in R$ *and* $\text{geom2pset}([\![E_1]\!]_\mu) \cap \text{geom2pset}(\text{raster2geom}([\![E_2]\!]_\mu)) \neq \varnothing$

$\mu \models E_1 \textcircled{\cap} E_2$ *holds if* $[\![E_1]\!]_\mu \in R, [\![E_2]\!]_\mu \in \text{Geo}$ *and* $\mu \models E_2 \textcircled{\cap} E_1$

Further Functions. We have provided a couple of example functions and their signatures in order to show the principles of working with raster data. In practice, one needs a much larger set of functions and signatures. In particular the signatures *geo:area*: $Geo \rightarrow \mathbb{R}$, *geo2:max*: $R \rightarrow \mathbb{R}$ are used. *geo:area* is a GeoSPARQL function calculating the area of a Geometry, *geo2:max* calculates the maximum atomic value of a raster. We also use the additional raster algebra functions *geo2:isGreater*: $Rx\mathbb{R} \rightarrow \mathbb{R}$ and *geo2:rasterUnion* $RxR \rightarrow \mathbb{R}$. The first one returns a raster which only includes atomic values greater than a given constant and the second one is the complement of the *geo2:rasterIntersection* function.

6 Implementation

The implementation[3] is built on Apache Jena [22] and geosparql-jena [3] and extends the ARQ query processor of Apache Jena with the GeoSPARQL+ functions defined in Sect. 5. ARQ registers functions in an internal function registry which maps URIs to function implementations. The implementations were done in Java and used the Java Topology Suite library to implement vector geometry related functions, Apache SIS[4] to represent rasters in Java and the Java Advanced Imaging Library (JAI) [21] to implement raster algebra operations. In addition, new literal types needed to be implemented in ARQ. geosparql-jena already provides support for vector literals (WKT and GML). To represent rasters we implemented CoverageJSON and Well-Known-Binary (WKB)

[3] https://github.com/i3mainz/jena-geo.

[4] http://sis.apache.org.

literals with appropriate parsers for (de)serialization. In addition we implemented further functions defined in the SQL/MM standard [34]. These functions help to prepare/-modify vector geometries before they are compared or combined with rasters. Finally, we combined our implementation to work with a Apache Jena Fuseki triple store used for the feasibility study in Sect. 7.

7 Feasibility

We work with the following datasets:

1. A vector dataset (GeoJSON): Road network of Cologne from OpenStreetMap
2. A vector dataset (GeoJSON) of elements at risk extracted from OpenStreetMap
3. Two rasters (flood altitude and fire hazards) of Cologne provided by a company simulating hazards

The RDF graph contains the classes *ex:Road*, classes for elements at risk and the classes *ex:FloodRiskArea*, *ex:FireRiskArea* for the rasters described in Sect. 5.

7.1 GeoSPARQL+ Queries

The feasibility check includes the four use cases defined in Sect. 3 and defines two queries per application case in GeoSPARQL+ and an equivalent query in SQL/MM [34]. The GeoSPARQL+ query is executed on our prototypical implementation, the second query is executed on a POSTGIS implementation. For brevity we only illustrate the GeoSPARQL+ queries in Listings 1.2 to 1.5.

The first query (Listing 1.2) solves usecase U1 and uses the raster algebra function *geo:rasterSmaller* ($\boxed{<}$) (line 5) to filter those parts of a flood raster where roads that are still passable.

```
1 SELECT ?road WHERE {
  ?road a ex:Road ; geo:hasGeometry ?roadseg . ?roadseg geo:asWKT ?roadseg_wkt .
3 ?floodarea a ex:FloodRiskArea ; geo2:asCoverage ?floodarea_cov .
  ?floodarea_cov geo2:asCoverageJSON ?floodarea_covjson .
5 BIND(geo2:rasterSmaller(?floodarea_covjson,10) AS ?relfloodarea)
  FILTER(geo2:intersects(?roadseg_wkt,?relfloodarea))}
```

Listing 1.2. Use Case 1: Flood Altitude

The second query (Listing 1.3) solving use case U2 adds the values of two different rasters (fire and floodhazard) of the same area together (*geo2:rasterPlus* ($\boxed{+}$) line 8) and extracts atomic values of the combined raster to assign a risk value to each given building. The maximum risk value per building is returned.

```
1 SELECT ?building (MAX(?riskvalue) AS ?riskmax) WHERE {
  ?building a ex:Building ; geo:hasGeometry ?building_geom .
3 ?building_geom geo:asWKT ?building_wkt .
  ?floodarea a ex:FloodRiskArea ; geo2:hasCoverage ?floodcov.
5 ?floodcov geo2:asCoverageJSON ?floodcov_covjson .
  ?firearea rdf:type ex:FireRiskArea ; geo2:hasCoverage ?firecov.
7 ?firecov geo2:asCoverageJSON ?firecov_covjson .
  BIND (geo2:rasterPlus(?firecov_covjson,?floodcov_covjson) AS ?riskarea)
9 BIND (geo2:cellval2(geo2:rasterIntersection(?building_wkt,?riskarea)) AS ?riskvalue)
  FILTER(geo2:intersects(?building_wkt,?riskarea))}
```

Listing 1.3. Use case 2: Risk assessment

The third query (Listing 1.4) solving use case U3 combines the assessment of properties of vector geometries (line 10) with assessments gained from rasters (line 7) and GeoSPARQL functions like geo:buffer and geo:intersects (line 11–12) to evaluate roads with a higher priority to be evacuated.

```
1  SELECT ?road WHERE{
   ?road a ex:Road ; geo:hasGeometry ?roadgeom . ?roadgeom geo:asWKT ?road_wkt .
3  ?ear a ear:ElementAtRisk ; geo:hasGeometry ?eargeom ; ex:openTime ?earopen ; ex:closeTime ?earclose .
   ?eargeom geo:asWKT ?ear_wkt .
5  ?floodarea a ex:FloodRiskArea ; geo2:hasCoverage ?floodcov. ?floodcov geo2:asCoverageJSON ?floodcov_covjson
   .
   ?firearea rdf:type ex:FireRiskArea ; geo2:hasCoverage ?firecov. ?firecov geo2:asCoverageJSON ?firecov_covjson .
7  BIND (geo2:rasterPlus(?firecov_covjson,?floodcov_covjson) AS ?riskarea)
   BIND("2019-05-23T10:20:13+05:30"^^xsd:dateTime AS ?givendate)
9  FILTER(?givendate>?earopen AND ?givendate<?earclose)
   FILTER(geo:intersects(geo:buffer(?road_wkt,2,uom:meter),?ear))
11 FILTER(!geo:intersects(?road_wkt,?riskarea))}
```

Listing 1.4. Use case 3: Rescue Capacity Planning

Roads with a higher priority are near elements at risk for which we provide an ontology model in the appended technical report. The element at risk definition simplifies this query in comparison to an equivalent POSTGIS query, as the semantics are already explicitly stated.

Finally, the query for use case U4 (Listing 1.5) combines the GeoSPARQL functions *geo:area* (line 8) and *geo:buffer* (line 7) with GeoSPARQL+ functions to intersect geometries and rasters (line 7–8) and to return a rasters geometry (line 8).

```
   SELECT ?hazardcoveragepercentage WHERE {
2  ?floodarea a ex:FloodRiskArea; geo2:hasCoverage ?floodcov.
   ?floodcov geo2:asCoverageJSON ?floodcov_covjson .
4  ?firearea rdf:type ex:FireRiskArea ; geo2:hasCoverage ?firecov.
   ?firecov geo2:asCoverageJSON ?firecov_covjson .
6  BIND(geo2:rasterUnion(?firecov_covjson,?floodcov_covjson) AS ?hazardriskarea)
   BIND(geo2:geometryIntersection(?hazardriskarea,geo:buffer(?locationtocheck,10,uom:km)) AS ?intersectarea)
8  BIND(geo:area(?intersectarea)/geo2:raster2geom(?hazardriskarea) AS ?hazardcoveragepercentage)
   BIND("POINT(49.2,36.2)"^^geo:wktLiteral AS ?locationtocheck)}
```

Listing 1.5. Use case 4: City Planning

7.2 Results

We measured the execution times of the introduced GeoSPARQL+ queries in comparison to equivalent SQL/MM [36] queries run on a POSTGIS implementation. The results are shown in Table 1.
Table 1 shows that the execution time of our prototype is significantly longer than that of the native POSTGIS implementation.

7.3 Discussion

In Sect. 5 have shown that the query solutions for use cases U1-U4 exploit different elements of GeoSPARQL+. Use case U1 relates a raster to a vector data set, use case U2 showcases the need of raster algebra operators to solve questions of combined risks, use

Table 1. Execution times of the given queries in the GeoSPARQL+ prototype vs. the comparison implementation in POSTGIS.

Use case	GeoSPARQL+	POSTGIS
Use case 1	112,423 ms	86,817 ms
Use case 2	164,865 ms	108,357 ms
Use case 3	134,865 ms	112,817 ms
Use case 4	184,865 ms	140,357 ms

case U3 combines values gained from rasters with attributes gained from vector data at the same geographic location. Both use case U2 and U3 make use of raster-aware filter functions. Finally, the query to solve use case U4 utilizes the raster to geometry function to create intersections between rasters with certain characteristics. We therefore illustrated the usefulness of GeoSPARQL+. Our prototypical implementation exhibits a slight performance decay between 23% and 34% for various example queries. We speculate that this degradation comes from overhead of dealing with semantics, lack of geospatial indices for rasters and further caches as well as a lack of technical optimizations that POSTGIS as a mature well-used system comes with. Considering that our implementation merely constitutes a proof of concepts, we consider this a graceful degradation and an acceptable result. Future work may consider an improvement of its performance.

8 Related Work

[23] and [28] proposed stSPARQL and SPARQL-ST, which extend SPARQL with spatiotemporal query capabilities for vector data. Spatiotemporal aspects for raster data and vector data are not considered by our approach but we see no major issues to combine the ideas of stSPARQL with our work. This is relevant as not only rasters with spatiotemporal aspects exist, but the content of raster data may also change over time.

Some approaches like LinkedGeoData [5] convert SPARQL queries to SQL queries in order to execute them on a native geospatial-aware SQL database. Similarly, hybrid systems such as Virtuoso [15] add a semantic layer on top of a relational database such as POSTGIS [31]. In principle, this would allow for accessing raster data, but has only been used to store and distribute vector data (cf. [5]). We attribute this to a lack of semantic description of raster data which we address in this publication. Furthermore, we provide a solution independent of SQL datatabases and independent of the need for query conversions from SPARQL to SQL.

Relational spatial databases like POSTGIS [31] or OGC geospatial webservices [25] along with software suites such as QGIS[5] and their accompanying libraries can handle, import, modify and query raster data, in particular with raster algebra. None of the aforementioned systems combines the advantages of linked data with the ability to semantically describe or access raster data information.

[5] https://qgis.org/de/site/.

In addition to the previously mentioned work, there is a line of work that represents raster data as linked data ([13,30,33]). These works do not consider how to query raster data. Hence, they lack the expressiveness required to cover our use cases. Similarly, [7] wrap raster data from a POSTGIS database and make it available as vector data that can be queried with GeoSPARQL. Because GeoSPARQL has no means for asking raster-specific queries (e.g. raster algebra), this work also lacks the expressiveness that our approach provides.

Another line of work includes representing and querying multi-dimensional arrays, SciSPARQL [4]. While there is an overlap between managing raster data and arrays, raster data has geometric aspects that our approach supports (e.g. raster cell geometries, intersections and conversions between rasters and polygons, semantic descriptions of scales) that are not available when the underlying data model is restricted to arrays of real numbers. Hence, [4] can not support our use cases, e.g. lacking intersecting street data and flooding data as we illustrate in Fig. 1a.

9 Conclusion

We presented GeoSPARQL+ a novel approach that allows for the semantic description and querying of raster data in the semantic web. We expect these new capabilities to make publishing geospatial data in the geospatial semantic web more attractive and consider contributing this work to the currently discussed revision of GeoSPARQL [1, 2]. Future work could explore the semantic description of further OGC coverage types such as trajectories or even point clouds. Also, non-grid-based raster types should be investigated, as well as the representation of 3D rasters.

Acknowledgements. Work by Steffen Staab was partially supported by DFG through the project LA 2672/1, Language-integrated Semantic Querying (LISeQ).

References

1. Abhayaratna, J., et al.: OGC benefits of representing spatial data using semantic and graph technologies (2020). https://github.com/opengeospatial/geosemantics-dwg/raw/master/white_paper/wp.pdf
2. Abhayaratna, J., van den Brink, L., Car, N., Homburg, T., Knibbe, F.: OGC GeoSPARQL SWG charter (2020). https://github.com/opengeospatial/geosemantics-dwg/tree/master/geosparql_2.0_swg_charter
3. Albiston, G.L., Osman, T., Chen, H.: GeoSPARQL-Jena: Implementation and benchmarking of a GeoSPARQL graphstore. Semant. Web J. (2019)
4. Andrejev, A., Misev, D., Baumann, P., Risch, T.: Spatio-temporal gridded data processing on the semantic web. In: 2015 IEEE International Conference on Data Science and Data Intensive Systems, pp. 38–45. IEEE (2015)
5. Auer, S., Lehmann, J., Hellmann, S.: LinkedGeoData: adding a spatial dimension to the web of data. In: Bernstein, A., et al. (eds.) ISWC 2009. LNCS, vol. 5823, pp. 731–746. Springer, Heidelberg (2009). https://doi.org/10.1007/978-3-642-04930-9_46
6. Battle, R., Kolas, D.: Enabling the geospatial semantic web with parliament and GeoSPARQL. Semant. Web **3**(4), 355–370 (2012)

7. Bereta, K., Stamoulis, G., Koubarakis, M.: Ontology-based data access and visualization of big vector and raster data. In: 2018 IEEE International Geoscience and Remote Sensing Symposium, IGARSS 2018, pp. 407–410. IEEE (2018)
8. Blower, J., Riechert, M., Roberts, B.: Overview of the CoverageJSON format (2017)
9. Van den Brink, L., Barnaghi, P., et al.: Best practices for publishing, retrieving, and using spatial data on the web. Semant. Web **10**(1), 95–114 (2019)
10. Cerans, K., Barzdins, G., et al.: Graphical schema editing for StarDog OWL/RDF databases using OWLGrEd/S In: OWLED, vol. 849 (2012)
11. Consortium, O.G., et al.: OGC GeoSPARQL-a geographic query language for RDF data. OGC Candidate Implementation Standard (2012)
12. World Wide Web Consortium: Sparql 1.1 overview (2013)
13. World Wide Web Consortium: The RDF data cube vocabulary (2014)
14. Eclipse Foundation Contributor: Rdf4j (2020). rdf4j.org
15. Erling, O.: Virtuoso, a hybrid RDBMS/graph store. IEEE Data Eng. **35**(1), 3–8 (2012)
16. Fonseca, F.: Geospatial semantic web. In: Shekhar, S., Xiong, H. (eds.) Encyclopedia of GIS, pp. 388–391. Springer, Boston (2008). https://doi.org/10.1007/978-0-387-35973-1_513
17. Herring, J., et al.: Opengis® implementation standard for geographic information-simple feature access-part 1: Common architecture [corrigendum] (2011)
18. Homburg, T., Staab, S., Janke, D.: GeoSPARQL+: syntax, semantics and system for integrated querying of graph, raster and vector data. extended version. technical report (2020) (at arXiv.org). Technical report, Mainz University of Applied Sciences (2020)
19. Huxhold, W.E., et al.: An introduction to urban geographic information systems. OUP Catalogue (1991)
20. ISO 19123:2005: Geographic information–schema for coverage geometry and functions. The International Organization for Standardization, Geneva, Switzerland (2005)
21. Jaiswal, D., Dey, S., Dasgupta, R., Mukherjee, A.: Spatial query handling in semantic web application: an experience report. In: 2015 Applications and Innovations in Mobile Computing (AIMoC), pp. 170–175. IEEE (2015)
22. Jena, A.: A free and open source java framework for building semantic web and linked data applications (2019)
23. Koubarakis, M., Kyzirakos, K.: Modeling and querying metadata in the semantic sensor web: the model stRDF and the query language stSPARQL. In: Aroyo, L., et al. (eds.) ESWC 2010. LNCS, vol. 6088, pp. 425–439. Springer, Heidelberg (2010). https://doi.org/10.1007/978-3-642-13486-9_29
24. Kyzirakos, K., Karpathiotakis, M., Koubarakis, M.: Strabon: a Semantic Geospatial DBMS. In: Cudré-Mauroux, P., et al. (eds.) ISWC 2012. LNCS, vol. 7649. Springer, Heidelberg (2012). https://doi.org/10.1007/978-3-642-35176-1_19
25. Nogueras-Iso, J., Zarazaga-Soria, F.J., Béjar, R., Álvarez, P., Muro-Medrano, P.R.: OGC catalog services: a key element for the development of spatial data infrastructures. Comput. Geosci. **31**(2), 199–209 (2005)
26. Ontotext: Graphdb (2020). graphdb.ontotext.com
27. Pérez, J., Arenas, M., Gutierrez, C.: Semantics and complexity of SPARQL. In: Cruz, I., et al. (eds.) ISWC 2006. LNCS, vol. 4273, pp. 30–43. Springer, Heidelberg (2006). https://doi.org/10.1007/11926078_3
28. Perry, M., Jain, P., Sheth, A.P.: SPARQL-ST: extending SPARQL to support spatiotemporal queries. In: Ashish, N., Sheth, A. (eds.) Geospatial Semantics and the Semantic Web. ADSW, vol. 12, pp. 61–86. Springer, Boston (2011). https://doi.org/10.1007/978-1-4419-9446-2_3
29. Portele, C.: OpenGIS® geography markup language (GML) encoding standard. Open Geospatial Consortium (2007)

30. Quintero, R., Torres, M., Moreno, M., Guzmán, G.: Towards a semantic representation of raster spatial data. In: Janowicz, K., Raubal, M., Levashkin, S. (eds.) GeoS 2009. LNCS, vol. 5892, pp. 63–82. Springer, Heidelberg (2009). https://doi.org/10.1007/978-3-642-10436-7_5
31. Ramsey, P., et al.: PostGIS Manual, p. 17. Refractions Research Inc. (2005)
32. Santos, R.: Java advanced imaging API: a tutorial. Revista de Informática Teórica e Aplicada **11**(1), 93–124 (2004)
33. Scharrenbach, T., Bischof, S., Fleischli, S., Weibel, R.: Linked raster data. In: Xiao, N., Kwan, M.P., Goodchild, M.F., Shekhar, S. (eds.) Geographic Information Science. LNCS, vol. 7478. Springer, Heidelberg (2012)
34. Stolze, K.: SQL/MM spatial: The standard to manage spatial data in a relational database system. In: BTW 2003-Datenbanksysteme für Business, Technologie und Web, Tagungsband der 10. BTW Konferenz. Gesellschaft für Informatik eV (2003)
35. Tomlin, C.D.: Map algebra: one perspective. Landsc. Urban Plan. **30**, 3–12 (1994)
36. Wirz, D.: OGC Simple Features (for SQL and XML/GML). University of Zurich, Department Geography, Zurich (2004)

FunMap: Efficient Execution of Functional Mappings for Knowledge Graph Creation

Samaneh Jozashoori[1(✉)], David Chaves-Fraga[2], Enrique Iglesias[1,3], Maria-Esther Vidal[1], and Oscar Corcho[2]

[1] TIB Leibniz Information Center for Science and Technology and L3S, Hannover, Germany
{samaneh.jozashoori,maria.vidal}@tib.eu

[2] Ontology Engineering Group, Universidad Politécnica de Madrid, Madrid, Spain
{dchaves,ocorcho}@fi.upm.es

[3] University of Bonn, Bonn, Germany
s6enigle@uni-bonn.de

Abstract. Data has exponentially grown in the last years, and knowledge graphs constitute powerful formalisms to integrate a myriad of existing data sources. Transformation functions – specified with function-based mapping languages like FunUL and RML+FnO – can be applied to overcome interoperability issues across heterogeneous data sources. However, the absence of engines to efficiently execute these mapping languages hinders their global adoption. We propose FunMap, an interpreter of function-based mapping languages; it relies on a set of lossless rewriting rules to push down and materialize the execution of functions in initial steps of knowledge graph creation. Although applicable to any function-based mapping language that supports joins between mapping rules, FunMap feasibility is shown on RML+FnO. FunMap reduces data redundancy, e.g., duplicates and unused attributes, and converts RML+FnO mappings into a set of equivalent rules executable on RML-compliant engines. We evaluate FunMap performance over real-world testbeds from the biomedical domain. The results indicate that FunMap reduces the execution time of RML-compliant engines by up to a factor of 18, furnishing, thus, a scalable solution for knowledge graph creation.

Keywords: Knowledge graph creation · Mapping rules · Functions

1 Introduction

Knowledge graphs (KGs) have gained momentum due to the explosion of available data and the demand for expressive formalisms to integrate factual knowledge spread across various data sources [14]. KG creation requires the description of schema alignments among data sources and an ontology, as well as the specification of methods to curate and transform data collected from the input sources into a unified format. A rich spectrum of mapping languages has been proposed to specify schema-ontology alignments across data sources implemented in a

J. Z. Pan et al. (Eds.): ISWC 2020, LNCS 12506, pp. 276–293, 2020.
https://doi.org/10.1007/978-3-030-62419-4_16

variety of semi-structured and structured formats; exemplar approaches include R2RML [6], RML [10], and xR2RML [21]. Furthermore, function-based mapping languages [7,8,17,26] are equipped with abstractions that enable interoperable and reusable specifications of data transformations by means of user-defined functions. Moreover, formalisms like RML+FnO [7] combine the Function ontology and RML, enabling declarative specification of the schema-ontology alignments and data transformations that define the process of KG creation. Albeit expressive, existing mapping languages lack efficient interpreters able to scale up to complex KG creation scenarios. The incoming data avalanche urges KG creation approaches capable of integrating large and diverse data, and efficiently transforming this data to comply with application-specific KG formats.

Problem and Objectives: We tackle the problem of scaled-up KG creation from functional mapping rules and study the impact of functions when applied to large data sources with a high data duplication rate. A KG creation process is defined as a data integration system [19]. Mappings among data sources and the system ontology are expressed using the RDF mapping language (RML) [7] and the Function Ontology (FnO); they define how the ontology concepts are populated with data from the sources in the resulting KG. We aim at transforming complex data integration systems composed of large data sources and mappings with functions into equivalent ones that generates the same KG but in less time.

Our Proposed Approach: We present FunMap, an interpreter of RML+FnO, that converts a data integration system defined using RML+FnO into an equivalent one where RML mappings are function-free. FunMap resembles existing mapping translation proposals (e.g., [2,5,17]) and empowers a KG creation process with optimization techniques to reduce execution time. Transformations of data sources include the projection of the attributes used in the RML+FnO mappings. They are supported on well-known properties of the relational algebra, e.g., the pushing down of projections and selections into the data sources, and enable not only the reduction of the size of data sources but also the elimination of duplicates. Additionally, FunMap materializes functions –expressed in FnO– and represents the results as data sources of the generated data integration system; the translation of RML+FnO into RML mappings that integrate the materialization of functions is performed using joins between the generated RML mappings. The combination of data source and function transformations results in data integration systems where only the data required to execute the RML mappings are retained. The computation of the functions used in the original data integration system is performed once. As a result, the new data integration system's execution is sped up while the same knowledge graph is generated.

Contributions. i) FunMap, an interpreter of RML+FnO that resorts to syntax-based translation [1] to push down projections and selections, and materialize functions. **ii)** Empirical evaluations of the performance of FunMap in real-world testbeds with data of various formats (CSV and Relational), sizes, and degrees of duplication that show reductions in KG creation time by up to a factor of 18.

The remainder of this paper is structured as follows: Section 2 motivates our work using a use case from the biomedical domain. Section 3 describes the set of rewriting and optimization rules that assemble FunMap, while the experimental results are reported in Sect. 4. Finally, Sect. 5 presents the related work and Sect. 6 outlines the main conclusions of the paper and future lines of work.

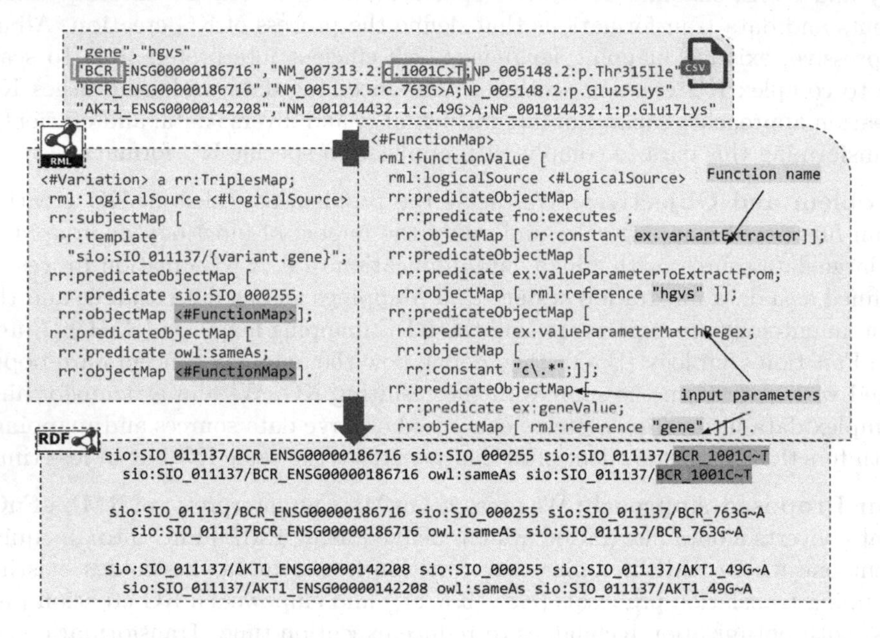

Fig. 1. Motivating example. Knowledge graph construction using RML+FnO mapping rules for the biomedical domain. The input source in the top is transformed to RDF output (at the bottom) through the processing of the mapping (middle) where the transformation functions are defined. Repeated computations of a function negatively impacts on the performance of an RML engine.

2 Preliminaries and Motivating Example

2.1 Preliminaries

The RDF Mapping Language (RML) extends the W3C-standard mapping language R2RML with logical sources (a.k.a. `logicalSource`) in heterogeneous formats (e.g., CSV, Relational, JSON, and XML). As the W3C-standard R2RML, `TriplesMap` corresponds to mapping rules where the resources (a.k.a. `subjectMap`) of an RDF class and their properties (a.k.a. `predicateMap`) are assigned to values (a.k.a. `objectMap`) based on logical data sources. An `objectMap` can be also defined as a reference or a join with the `subjectMap` in another `TriplesMap` (a.k.a. `RefObjectMap` and `joinCondition`, respectively). `subjectMap`, `predicateMap`, and `objectMap` are also referred as `TermMap` in general; they generate RDF terms. FnO is an ontology for describing transformation functions declaratively; FnO and RML relationship is described in [7]. Accordingly, the `FunctionMap` class is introduced in RML; it defines transformation functions in any part of the `TriplesMap` (`subjectMap`, `predicateMap`, or `objectMap`). These concepts are illustrated in the next example and highlighted in Fig. 1.

2.2 A Real-World Example from the Biomedical Domain

Our work is motivated by the challenges revealed during genomic variant reconciliation while creating a biomedical knowledge graph. Although the vast majority of the single variations in the genome of a person causes no disease, benign variants can appear in sequenced genomic data repeatedly. In addition to the large heterogeneous volumes generated during genome sequencing and analysis, high-frequency of genomic variants impose data integration challenges while collecting genomic data from different sources. Additionally, genomic variants are expressed in diverse standard formats [9] and reported at DNA, RNA, or protein level. Moreover, this representation can be done according to any of the accepted terminologies and genomic reference versions. Unified representations for variants are required to semantically recognize and integrate equivalent variants residing in different data sources. Variant representations can result from a composition of several factors, such as gene name, genomic position, and residue alteration. Pre-processing functions (e.g., FnO functions) are needed to extract and compose values from different attributes from each data source and generate such a combined representation of variants. These functions are part of the data integration system's mapping rules that define the KG creation process.

Figure 1 depicts a mapping rule in RML+FnO where the `FunctionMap` class is utilized. Consider that according to the `LogicalSource` provided in this example, a `FunctionMap` is defined in the mapping rules to create a unified representation for a variant by extracting the values of "gene name" (e.g., BCR) from the attribute `gene` and "coding alteration" (e.g., c.1001C>T) from the attribute named `hgvs` and combine them (e.g., BCR_1001C~T). Current approaches evaluate `FunctionMap` for each `variant`, which can be expensive in presence of large data sources. Nevertheless, the large number of redundant values leaves room for the scalable transformations to execute functional mappings.

3 The FunMap Approach

FunMap is an interpreter of data integration systems $DIS_G = \langle O, S, M \rangle$, where O stands for a unified ontology, and S and M represent sets of sources and mapping rules, respectively [19]. The evaluation of DIS_G (a.k.a. *RDFize*(DIS_G)) results into a knowledge graph G that integrates data from S according to the mapping rules in M; entities and properties in G are described in terms of O. A complex data integration system DIS_G consists of large data sources with high-duplicated data and mapping rules including functions for both schema-ontology alignments and data transformations. FunMap converts DIS_G into an

Table 1. Summary of the notation used for defining FunMap

Notation	Explanation
$DIS_G = \langle O, S, M\rangle$	Data Integration System which creates a KG G
O	Unified Ontology of $DIS_G = \langle O, S, M\rangle$
S	Finite set of Data Sources S_i of $DIS_G = \langle O, S, M\rangle$
M	Finite set of `TriplesMaps` T_i in $DIS_G = \langle O, S, M\rangle$
$RDFize(.)$	A function producing RDF triples from a data integration system
T_i' and T_k'	`TriplesMaps` resulting of applying MTRs
F_i	A Transformation Function in a `TriplesMap` in M
S'	Finite set of Data Sources S_i' resulting of applying DTRs
M'	Finite set of Mapping Rules M_i' resulting of applying MTRs
S_i^{output}	Data source resulting of applying DTR1, with attributes o_i' and a_i' representing the materialization of a transformation function F_i
$S_i^{project}$	Data source resulting of applying DTR2

equivalent data integration system that creates the same knowledge graph but in less time. Table 1 summarizes the notation utilized in the FunMap approach.

Problem Statement: Given a data integration system $DIS_G = \langle O, S, M\rangle$, the problem of scaled-up knowledge graph creation from functional mappings requires the generation of a data integration system $DIS_G' = \langle O, S', M'\rangle$:

- The knowledge graphs resulting of the evaluations of both data integration systems are the same, i.e., $RDFize(DIS_G' = \langle O, S', M'\rangle) = RDFize(DIS_G = \langle O, S, M\rangle)$ where $RDFize(.)$ is a function producing RDF triples utilizing the input data integration system.
- The execution time of $RDFize(DIS_G' = \langle O, S', M'\rangle)$ is *less than* the execution time of $RDFize(DIS_G = \langle O, S, M\rangle)$.

Solution: FunMap implements a heuristic-based approach; it relies on the assumption that eliminating duplicates, maintaining in the data sources only the attributes mentioned in the mappings, and materializing the functions in the mappings, reduces the execution time of knowledge graph creation process. FunMap receives a data integration system $DIS_G = \langle O, S, M\rangle$ where the mappings M are expressed in RML+FnO. FunMap interprets the mappings in M and converts DIS into the data integration system DIS_G' in which the mappings M' are function free and duplicates in the data sources S' are reduced. Figure 2 depicts the FunMap approach; it performs a syntax-based translation of the mappings in M and ensures that each redundant function is evaluated exactly once on the same data values. FunMap transforms S to S' by means of data transformation rules (DTR1 and DTR2). For each F_i over a given S_i, DTR1 creates a temporal source S'_i that includes the attributes from S_i that correspond to the input of F_i; it also generates a source S_i^{output} that contains the attributes in S'_i and attributes representing the output of F_i. For each `FunctionMap` defined over a source S_i, DTR2 creates a source $S_i^{project}$ that includes all attributes of S_i used in the `FunctionMap`. Additionally, FunMap converts mapping rules that include functions by using mapping transformation rules (MTRs); a `FunctionMap` is transformed into `FunctionMaps` without functions while connected by `joinConditions`; initially, S' and S are equal, as well as M' and M. Properties 1, 2, and 3 state the pre- and post-conditions of DTRs and MTRs.

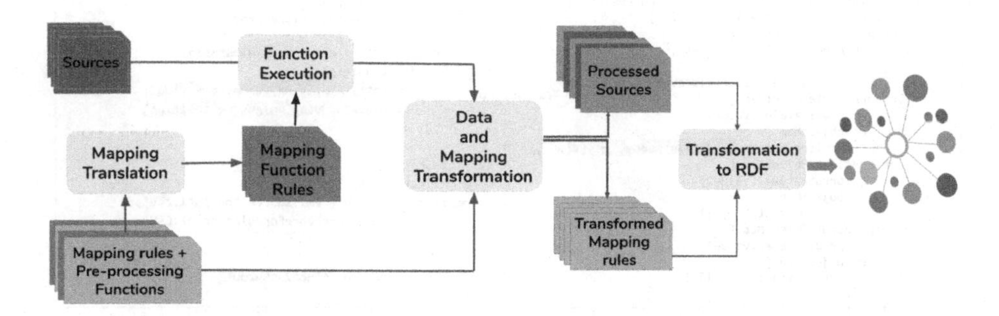

Fig. 2. The FunMap approach

3.1 Transformation Rules in FunMap

The FunMap syntax-based translation component parses `FunctionMaps` exactly once, i.e., `FunctionMaps` repeated in various mappings are not evaluated more than once. Given `FunctionMaps`, original data sources, and mappings, FunMap executes transformation rules on data sources and mappings, accordingly. Meanwhile, given the transformed data sources, FunMap detects that a `FunctionMap` has been computed for a given value and avoids repeating this computation. As an outcome, FunMap provides **a)** a new set of data sources S' consisting of the original ones in conjunction with transformed data sources, and **b)** a set M' of transformed function-free mappings. FunMap is loyal to the formats of data sources and mappings. Thus, any RDF mapping language is compatible with the process implemented in FunMap, as far as the language enables the definition of joins between mapping rules. Next, we present the transformation rules.

Data Source Transformation Rules (DTRs): Considering the fact that a `TriplesMap` may only be used some attributes of a dataset, FunMap relies on the properties of the relational algebra and performs DTRs to project only the attributes mentioned in the `TriplesMap`. DTRs are followed by transformation rules (MTRs) that update mappings defined over the transformed data sources.

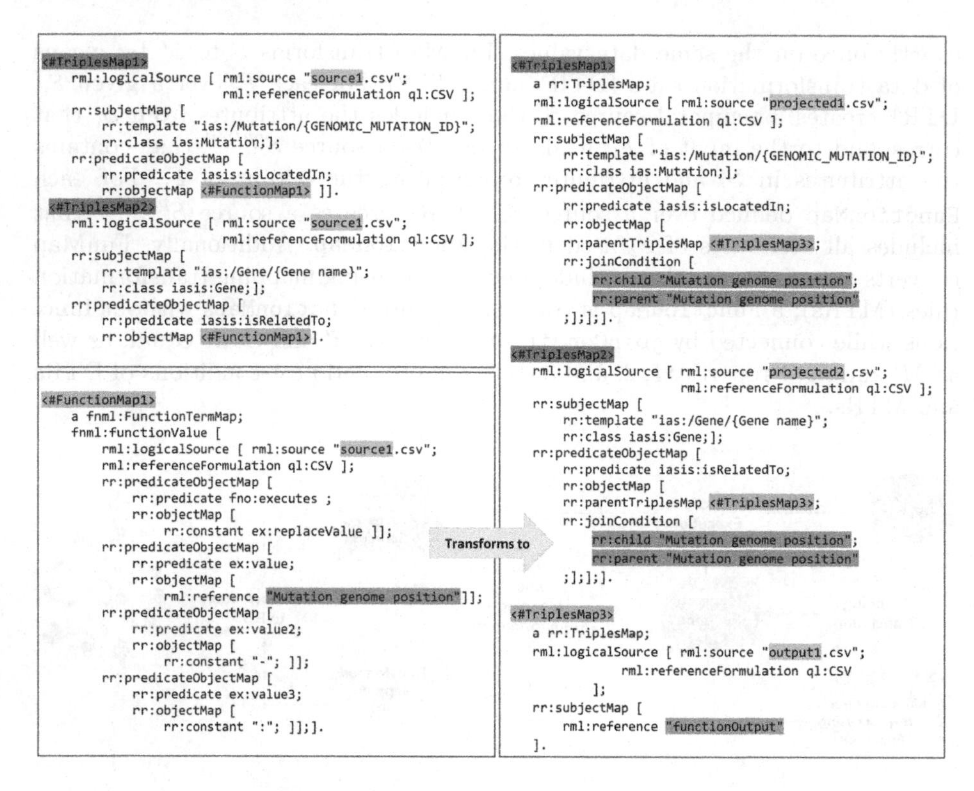

Fig. 3. Example of DTR and Object-based MTR. On the left, an exemplary mapping including two TriplesMaps and a FunctionMap provided by the original data integration system. On the right side, the mappings are transformed by FunMap including two new TriplesMaps and one new TriplesMap.

DTR1: Projection of Functional Attributes: For each transformation function F_i over a given source S_i in the set of data sources S, FunMap projects all attributes a'_i in S_i that are input attributes of F_i, into a temporal data source S'_i followed by duplicate removal. Subsequently, it evaluates F_i over S'_i and stores the results into the attribute o_i. Lastly, it creates a new data source S_i^{output} with the attributes a'_i and o_i; S_i^{output} is added to S'.

DTR2: Projection of Non-functional Attributes: FunMap provides an additional DTR to further optimize the knowledge graph creation process. Exploiting transformation rules that are proposed in [16], FunMap projects all attributes in S_i that are needed by `TriplesMap` including those that are received by `FunctionMap` as input into a new data source $S_i^{project}$ which is added to S'. To better conceive DTRs, consider the original mappings in Fig. 3 (left-side) and corresponding data source `source1.csv` that can be seen in Fig. 4. As shown in Fig. 3, `FunctionMap1` receives `Mutation genome position` as input. According to DTR1, FunMap projects `Mutation genome position` from `source1` into a new data source named `output1.csv` which is shown in Fig. 5c. The rows number

ID	Gene name	GRCh	Mutation genome position	Mutation CDS	Primary site	GENOMIC_MUTATION_ID	...
1	DGCR6L	37	22:20302597-20302597	c.514-250C>A	Liver	COSV50619134	...
2	HMCN1	37	1:186072702-186072702	c.10672C>T	lung	COSV54901969	...
3	SLC5A10_ET0000039564	37	17:18874996-18874996	c.597+465T>A	Skin	COSV58755801	...
4	HMCN1_ET00000367492	37	1:186072702-186072702	c.10672C>T	Skin	COSV54901969	...
5	COL21A1_ET0000037081	37	6:56246049-56246049	c.-39+12720G>A	Prostate	COSV63690608	...
6	AKT3	37	1:243692781-243692781	c.1251+16031C>G	Pancreas	COSV55606438	...
7	WDFY4_ET00000413659	37	10:50044166-50044166	c.*1825+3412G>A	Oesophagus	COSV55433638	...
...	...		...	...	...	...	...

Fig. 4. Original data source for KG creation. The data source includes many attributes among which only a few are required by the transformation function or function-free mappings in the process of knowledge graph creation.

2 and 4 have the same value for attribute `Mutation genome posit-ion` which leads FunMap to remove the duplicated value from `output1.csv`. Afterwards, `FunctionMap1` is evaluated given `output1.csv` as input and the output values are inserted as a new attribute named `functionOutput` into the `output1.csv` data source. Moreover, attributes `GENOMIC_MUTATION_ID` and `Primary site` from `source1.csv` that are in `TriplesMap1` are projected into the new data source that is shown in Fig. 5a and duplicated values are removed. Similarly, `Projected2.csv` is created based on the attributes of `TriplesMap2`.

Mapping Transformation Rules (MTRs). Mappings are transformed to create the same knowledge graph utilizing the transformed data sources. MTRs are defined considering the role of a transformation function F_i in each `TriplesMap` T_i. **I)** F_i as an `ObjectMap`: We refer to the MTRs that are required in this case as `Object-based`. First of all, for each F_i, a new `TriplesMap` T_i' is created; it refers to the data source generated as the outcome of F_i, i.e., S_i^{output}. Accordingly, the `SubjectMap` of T_i' refers to the output attributes o_i in S_i^{output}. Afterwards, in `TriplesMap` T_i where F_i is presented as an `ObjectMap`, F_i is replaced by a `joinCondition` which joins T_i and T_i' over attributes a_i', i.e., the input attributes of F_i. Moreover, the `logicalSource` of T_i is changed to $S_i^{project}$, i.e., the corresponding projected data source provided as an outcome of DTR2. **II)** F_i as a `SubjectMap`: Contrary to the `Object-based`, in this set of MTR - we refer to as `Subject-based`- for each `predicateObjectMap` that follows a F_i of the type `SubjectMap`, a new `TriplesMap` T_i' refers to the data source $S_i^{project}$ which is generated as an outcome of DTR2 by projecting the attribute a_i' from S_i that are referenced as `objectMap` in the original `predicateObjectMap`. The `subjectMap` of T_k' –the transformed T_i – refers to the o_i and its `logicalSource` is S_i^{output}. Note that `subjectMap` of T_i' is by definition a `TermMap`, which means that its value can be any RDF term according to the RML specification. Each `objectMap` in T_i that is a `FunctionMap` is replaced by a `joinCondition` between

ID	Mutation genome position	GENOMIC_MUTATION_ID
1	22:20302597-20302597	COSV50619134
3	17:18874996-18874996	COSV58755801
4	1:186072702-186072702	COSV54901969
5	6:56246049-56246049	COSV63690608
6	1:243692781-243692781	COSV55606438
7	10:50044166-50044166	COSV55433638
...	...	...

(a) Projected1

ID	Mutation genome position	Gene name
1	22:20302597-20302597	DGCR6L
2	1:186072702-186072702	HMCN1
3	17:18874996-18874996	SLC5A10_ET0000039564
4	1:186072702-186072702	HMCN1_ET00000367492
5	6:56246049-56246049	COL21A1_ET0000037081
6	1:243692781-243692781	AKT3
7	10:50044166-50044166	WDFY4_ET00000413659
...	...	...

(b) Projected2

ID	Mutation genome position	functionOutput
1	22:20302597-20302597	22:20302597:20302597
3	17:18874996-18874996	17:18874996:18874996
4	1:186072702-186072702	1:186072702:186072702
5	6:56246049-56246049	6:56246049:56246049
6	1:243692781-243692781	1:243692781:243692781
7	10:50044166-50044166	10:50044166:50044166
...	...	...

(c) Output1

Fig. 5. Transformed sources generated by FunMap. The DTR2 generates a new source by projecting attributes for each TripleMap (a and b) while DTR1 projects input and output attributes of each FunctionMap into a new source (c). Both remove the generated duplicates.

T_i and corresponding T'_i over input attributes a'_i of F_i. In both cases, the transformed T_i– denoted as T'_k– and T'_i are added to M' and T_i is removed from M'. Figures 3 and 6 illustrate two examples of rewritten mappings based on DTRs and MTRs. In the left side of both figures, the original mappings are presented while the transformed mappings are depicted on the right side. In the transformed mappings in Fig. 3, `TriplesMap3` is created for `FunctionMap1`; it refers to the attribute `functionOutput` in the projected data source `output1.csv`– shown in Fig. 5c. Then, `FunctionMap1` is replaced in both `TriplesMap1` and `TriplesMap2` by a join condition over the attribute `Mutation genome position` which is the input attribute of `FunctionMap` in the original mapping file as it is highlighted by the same color. Accordingly, data sources -highlighted- of `TriplesMaps` are also transformed to refer to the projected data sources. Consider Fig. 6 where `FunctionMap` is a `subjectMap`. In both `predicateObjectMa-ps` of `TriplesMap1`, `FunctionMap1` is replaced by a `joinCondition` over the attribute `Mutation genome position` that is the input of `FunctionMap1`. To better clarify the performed transformation, consider the first `predicateObjectMap` in `TripleMap1` in the original mappings; the `predicate` is represents and the `ObjectMap` refers to the attribute Mutation. After the transformation, the first `predicateObjectMap` has the same `predicate` represents and through the `joinCondition` refers to the same attribute Mutation in `projected1.csv`.

Pre- and post-conditions of Data Source Transformation Rules (DTRs) and Mapping Transformation Rules (MTRs) are stated in the following properties:

Property 1 (Lossless Function). Given data integration systems $DIS_G = \langle O, S, M \rangle$ and $DIS'_G = \langle O, S', M \rangle$ such that DIS'_G is the result of applying

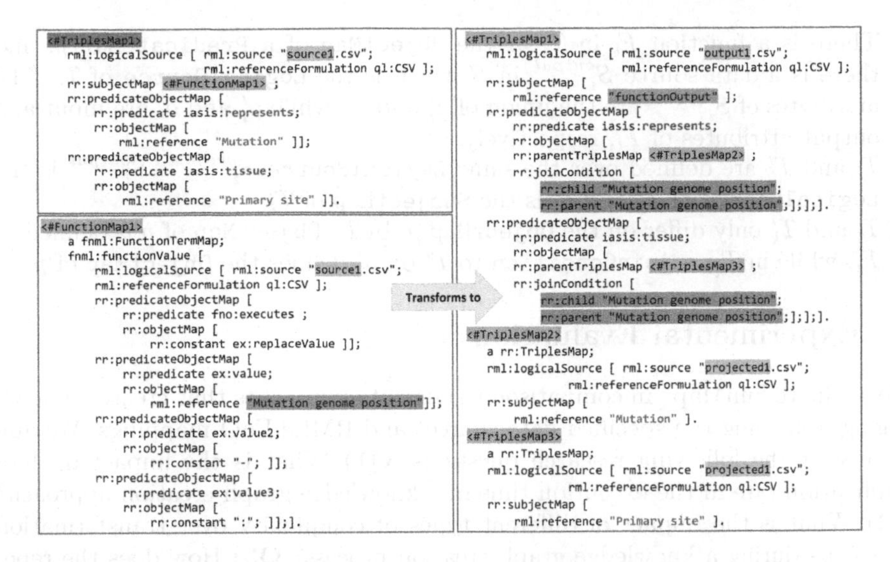

Fig. 6. Example of Subject-based MTR. An example of mappings including a TriplesMaps and FunctionMap are illustrated on the left and their transformed version including three TriplesMap are shown on the right side.

one DTR1 transformation to DIS_G. Then, there are data sources S_i and S_i^{output} in S and S', respectively, and the following statements hold:

- $S' - S = \{S_i^{output}\}$, there is a mapping T_i in M with a function F_i, and $Attrs$ contains the attributes a_i' of F_i in S_i and the output attributes o_i of F_i.
- S_i^{output} comprises the attributes $Attrs$ and $\pi_{a_i'}(S_i^{output}) = \pi_{a_i'}(S_i)$.
- For each tuple $t_{i,j}$ in S_i^{output}, the values of the attributes o_i in $t_{i,j}$ correspond to the result of F_i over the values of a_i' in $t_{i,j}$, i.e., $t_{i,j}.o_i = F_i(t_{i,j}.a_i')$.

Property 2 (Lossless Projection). Given data integration systems $DIS_G = \langle O, S, M \rangle$ and $DIS_G' = \langle O, S', M \rangle$ such that DIS_G' is the result of applying one DTR2 transformation to DIS_G. Then, there are data sources S_i and $S_i^{project}$ in S and S', respectively, and the following statements hold:

- $S' - S = \{S_i^{project}\}$, and there is a mapping T_i in M defined over the attributes $Attrs$ from S_i, and $S_i^{project} = \pi_{Attrs}(S_i)$.

Property 3 (Lossless Schema-Ontology Alignments).[1] Given data integration systems $DIS_G = \langle O, S, M \rangle$ and $DIS_G' = \langle O, S, M' \rangle$ such that DIS_G' is the result of applying one MTR transformation to DIS_G. Then, there are `TriplesMaps` T_i in M, and T_i' and T_k' in M', and the following statements hold:

- $M - M' = \{T_i\}$ and $M' - M = \{T_i', T_k'\}$.

[1] Similarly, this property can be stated for the result of applying MTR over the subject position of a property in a mapping of a data integration system.

- There is a function F_i in T_i as the `ObjectMap` of a `PredicateMap` p, and there is a data source S_i^{output} in S which is the `LogicalSource` of T_i. The attributes of S_i^{output} are the union of a_i' and o_i, while a_i' and o_i are input and output attributes of F_i, respectively.
- T_i and T_k' are defined over the same `LogicalSource` $S_i^{project}$. S_i^{output} is the `LogicalSource` of T_i' and o_i is the `SubjectMap` of T_i'.
- T_i and T_k' only differ on the `ObjectMap` p. In T_i, `ObjectMap` of p is defined as F_i, while in T_k', a `joinCondition` to T_i' on a_i' defines the `ObjectMap` of p.

4 Experimental Evaluation

We evaluate FunMap[2] in comparison to current approaches that create a knowledge graph using the specified data sources and RML+FnO mappings. We aim to answer the following research questions: **Q1)** What is the impact of data duplication rate in the execution time of a knowledge graph creation approach? **Q2)** What is the impact of different types of complexity over transformation functions during a knowledge graph creation process? **Q3)** How does the repetition of a same function in different mappings affect the existing RML engines? **Q4)** What is the impact of relational data sources in the knowledge graph creation process? All the resources used to perform this evaluation are available in our Github repository[3]. The experimental configuration is as follows:

Datasets and Mappings. To the best of our knowledge, there are no testbeds to evaluate the performance of a knowledge graph construction approach that applies functional mappings. Consequently, following the real-world scenario that initially motivated this research, we create our testbed from the biomedical domain. We generate a baseline dataset by randomly selecting 20,000 records from the coding point mutation dataset in COSMIC[4] database. We keep all 39 attributes of the original dataset in the baseline dataset, while only five to seven of them are utilized in mappings. In total, four different mapping files are generated consisting of one `FunctionMap` and four, six, eight, or ten `TriplesMaps` with a `predicateObjectMap` linked to the function. To additionally validate FunMap in case of large-sized data, we create another dataset following the same criteria, with 4,000,000 records and the size of about 1.3 GB.

Engines. The baselines of our study are three different open source RML-complaint engines that are able to execute RML+FnO mappings and have been extensively utilized in multiple applications and tested by the community: SDM-RDFizer v3.0 [15], RMLMapper[5] v4.7, and RocketRML[6] v1.1.[7]. In order to evaluate the impact of transformation rules, we implement FunMap v1.0 on the top

[2] https://doi.org/10.5281/zenodo.3993657.
[3] https://github.com/SDM-TIB/FunMap.
[4] https://cancer.sanger.ac.uk/cosmic GRCh37, version90, released August 2019.
[5] https://github.com/RMLio/rmlmapper-java.
[6] https://github.com/semantifyit/RocketRML/.
[7] We name them SDM-RDFizer**(RML+FnO), RMLMapper**(RML+FnO), and RocketRML**(RML+FnO).

of the aforementioned engines with DTR2 optimization as an optional parameter. We refer to the approach which applies FunMap excluding DTR2 as FunMap^{-}[8]. We created a docker image per tested engine for reproducibility.

Metrics. *Execution time:* Elapsed time spent by an engine to complete the creation of a knowledge graph and also counts FunMap pre-processing; it is measured as the absolute wall-clock system time as reported by the `time` command of the Linux operating system. Each experiment was executed five times and average is reported. The experiments were executed on an Ubuntu 16.04 machine with Intel(R) Xeon(R) Platinum 8160, CPU 2.10 GHz and 700 Gb RAM.

Experimental Setups. Based on our research questions, we set up in overall 198 experiments as the combinations of the following scenarios. We create two datasets from our baseline with 25% and 75% duplicates which means in the 25% duplicate dataset, 25% and in the 75% duplicate dataset, 75% of the records are duplicated. Additionally, two functions with different levels of complexity are created. We describe the complexity level of the functions based on the number of required input attributes and operations to be performed. Accordingly, "simple" function is defined to receive one input attribute and perform one operation, while a "complex" function receives two input attributes and completes five operations. In total, we create eight mapping files including four, six, eight, and ten `TriplesMap` and one `FunctionMap` to be either "simple" or "complex". Additionally, six experiments using 75% duplicate datasets of 20,000 and 4,000,000 records and a mapping file including ten complex functions are set up in order to be run over a relational database (RDB) implemented in MySQL 8.0[9].

4.1 Discussion of Observed Results

In this section, we describe the outcomes of our experimental evaluation. Figure 7 reports on the execution time of the different testbeds in which the functions are considered to be "simple" whereas Fig. 8 shows the experiments involving "complex" functions. Both figures represent the total execution time for constructing the knowledge graph applying selected engines (i.e., SDM-RDFizer, RMLMapper, and RocketRML) in three different configurations: a) the current version of the engine that is able to directly interpret RML+FnO mappings in the engine (e.g., RMLMapper**(RML+FnO)); b) FunMap^{-} in conjunction with the engine (e.g., FunMap^{-}+RMLMapper); and c) FunMap together with the engine (e.g., FunMap+RMLMapper). In the case of all the configuration of RocketRML, we only provide the results for the execution of simple functions because the engine does not execute joins with multiple conditions[10] correctly,

[8] We name these combined engines as follows: a) FunMap: FunMap+SDM-RDFizer, FunMap+RMLMapper, and FunMap+RocketRML; b) FunMap^{-}: FunMap^{-}+SDM-RDFizer, FunMap^{-}+RMLMapper, and FunMap^{-}+RocketRML.

[9] https://www.mysql.com/.

[10] Check an example in the zip file of the supplementary material.

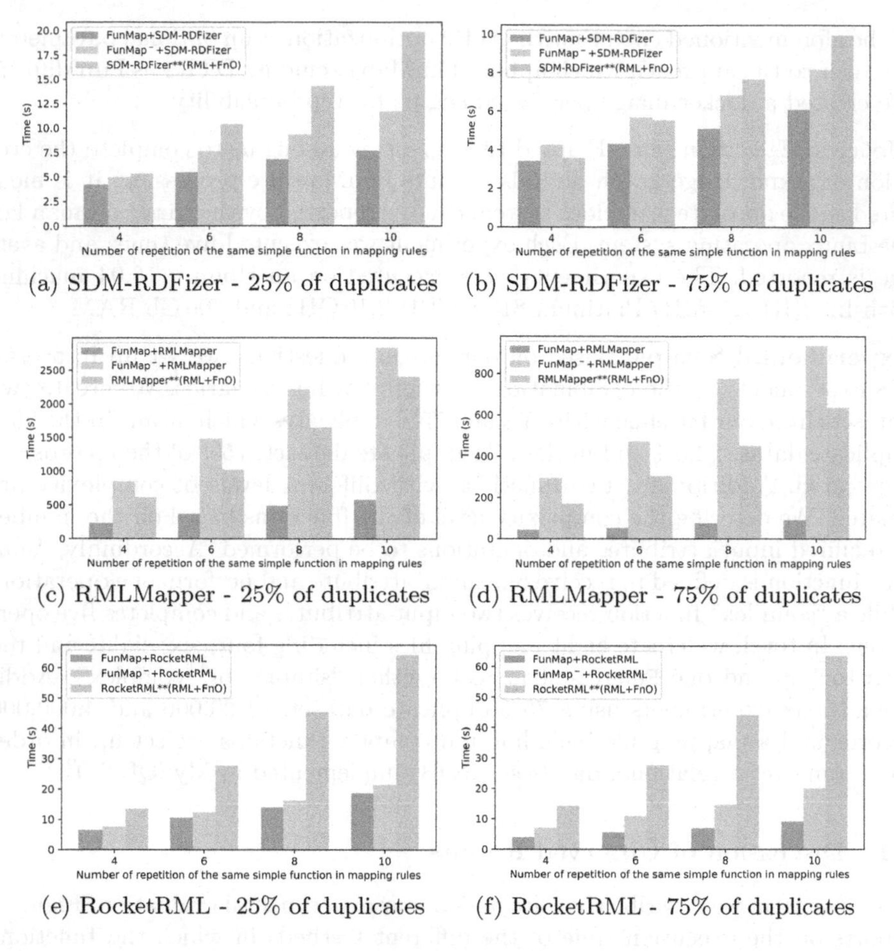

(a) SDM-RDFizer - 25% of duplicates (b) SDM-RDFizer - 75% of duplicates

(c) RMLMapper - 25% of duplicates (d) RMLMapper - 75% of duplicates

(e) RocketRML - 25% of duplicates (f) RocketRML - 75% of duplicates

Fig. 7. Total execution time of experiments with simple functions 25–75% of duplicates. SDM-RDFizer, RMLMapper and RocketRML executing simple functions in RML+FnO mappings and with FunMap and FunMap$^-$.

hence, the proposed optimizations cannot be applied. For the rest of the experiments, we have verified that the results are the same for all the approaches in terms of cardinality and correctness. The results obtained by the application of SDM-RDFizer with the repetition of simple functions (Figs. 7a and 7b) reflect an improvement of the execution time when FunMap is applied in the process. With the growth of number of duplicates and repeated functions, the difference between the performance of SDM-RDFizer**(RML+FnO) and FunMap+SDM-RDFizer increases. Using this engine, FunMap$^-$ shows the same behavior as FunMap, however, in the case of having a large number of duplicates and a few repeated functions FunMap$^-$ does not improve the performance of SDM-RDFizer**(RML+FnO). In the case of using RMLMapper (Figs. 7c and 7d), we observe that the results obtained together with FunMap$^-$ (i.e., DTR1 optimization) do not show better performance than RMLMapper**(RML+FnO). DTR1 which only focuses on transforming functions, delegates the removal of the duplicates to the engine which is not accomplished efficiently by RMLMapper. However, in FunMap+RMLMapper, that includes DTR1 and DTR2 optimizations, duplicates are removed before the execution of the RML mappings and leads to obtain the results that clearly show improvements with respect to the baseline. In the same manner as the SDM-RDFizer, the number of repetitions of the functions affects the execution time of the RMLMapper**(RML+FnO), while FunMap maintains similar execution times. Finally, RocketRML (Figs. 7e and 7f) seems not to be affected by the number of duplicates over the input data, obtaining similar execution times for 25% and 75% rate for RocketRML**(RML+FnO). However, the number of repetitions over functions impacts the performance of RocketRML**(RML+FnO), increasing the total execution time. The incorporation of DTR1 (i.e., FunMap$^-$+RocketRML) and DTR2 (i.e., FunMap+RocketRML) enhances the performance and scalability during the construction of the knowledge graph, obtaining a similar behavior as the other two tested engines.

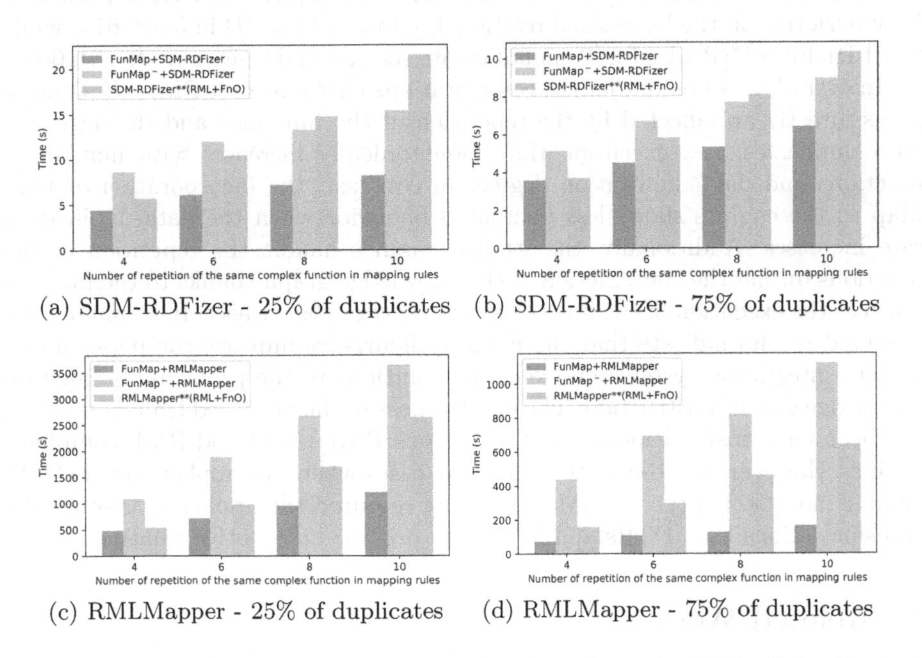

(a) SDM-RDFizer - 25% of duplicates (b) SDM-RDFizer - 75% of duplicates

(c) RMLMapper - 25% of duplicates (d) RMLMapper - 75% of duplicates

Fig. 8. Total execution time for complex functions 25–75% of duplicates. SDM-RDFizer and RMLMapper executing complex functions in RML+FnO mappings and with FunMap and FunMap$^-$.

The effect of function complexity over SDM-RDFizer can be observed in Figs. 8a and 8b. Whenever the number of repetitions is low (4–6), the join with multiple conditions affects FunMap$^-$+SDM-RDFizer, obtaining worse results than SDM-RDFizer**(RML+FnO). However, if repetitions increase (8–10), DTR1 empowers SDM-RDFizer**(RML+FnO) due the reduction of repeated operations during the evaluation of the mappings. Conversely, FunMap+SDM-RDFizer exhibits better results than SDM-RDFizer**(RML+FnO) in all the testbeds. Finally, the behavior of RMLMapper – when it has to execute complex transformation functions (Figs. 8c and 8d) – is affected in terms of execution time for the configuration FunMap$^-$+RMLMapper in comparison to the case of simple functions. As similar as SDM-RDFizer, the join with several conditions is impacting the performance. However, together with data transformation optimizations, FunMap+RMLMapper outperforms the baseline.

The experimental results on RDBs show even more significant improvement in the performance of both RMLMapper and SDM-RDFizer in the presence of FunMap. In FunMap+RMLMapper, applying `joins` in the SQL queries that define the `logicalSources` instead of using `joinConditions` reduces execution time by up to a factor of 18. These results evidence that `joinConditions` are not efficiently implemented by RMLMapper, and explain why FunMap+RMLMapper is showing less improvement compared to FunMap+SDM-RDFizer in Fig. 8. Moreover, FunMap+SDM-RDFizer successfully performs on the large-sized relational dataset of 1.3 GB in 5,670.67 s, while SDM-RDFizer**(RML+FnO) cannot create the KG and times out after 10,000 s.

In overall, we observe that the configurations that interpret RML+FnO mappings directly are affected by the repetition of the functions and the degree of data duplicates, i.e., execution time monotonically increases with number of functions and data duplication degree. In contrast, the incorporation of FunMap to the engines shows less fluctuated behavior when the data duplication rate increases. Additionally, the studied engines handle the repetition of the functions during the construction of the knowledge graph thanks to the pushing down of the execution of the functions directly over the dataset. In summary, the observed results indicate that the FunMap heuristics improve the performance of data integration systems and generate solutions to the problem of scaled-up knowledge graph construction. The effectiveness of the proposed transformations has been empirically demonstrated on various RML+FnO and RML-compliant engines. However, we observe that there are cases where the application of DTR1 alone is not enough (i.e., FunMap$^-$), being required the applications of all the transformations (i.e., DTRs and MTRs) to provide an effective solution.

5 Related Work

Solutions provided to the problem of KG creation from (semi)-structured data are gaining momentum in practitioners and users [5]. The seminal paper by Lenzerini [19] provides a formal framework for solving this problem and represents a pivot for Ontology-Based Data Access/Integration (OBDA/I) [22] and the corresponding optimization approaches. Gawriljuk et al. [12] present a framework for incremental knowledge graph creation. While optimized SPARQL-to-SQL query translation techniques [4] are implemented to support virtual knowledge graph creation [3,23]. Albeit efficient, these approaches do not support data transformations (i.e., functions), preventing an efficient evaluation of declarative knowledge graph creation processes. Although FunMap is focused on customized transformation functions for materialized KGs, it can be applied on top of these OBDA approaches. However, this would require the definition of new transformation rules able to push down the corresponding functions into SQL engines.

Rahm and Do [24] have reported the relevance of data transformations expressed with functions during data curation and integration. Grounding on this statement, different approaches have been proposed for facilitating the definition of functions to enhance data curation (e.g., [11,13,25]). Similarly, declarative languages have been proposed to allow for the definition of functions in the mappings; exemplar approaches include R2RML-F [8], FunUL [17], RML+FnO [7], and D-REPR [26]. Moreover, mapping engines enable to interpret functions in declarative mappings (e.g., Squerall [20], RMLStreamer[11] and CARML[12] for RML+FnO), as well as in non-declarative formalisms [18]. FunMap optimizations currently are performed over static data and require the implementation of the `joinCondition` by a KG creation engine. However, RMLStreamer works over streaming data, while CARML does not entirely cover RML joins. Additionally, Squerall is a SPARQL query engine over heterogeneous data able to process RML+FnO on the fly, but Squerall does not implement RML joins. Despite the rich repertory of these approaches, optimizing the declarative description of complex data integration systems remains still open. The absence of frameworks capable of efficiently execute complex data integration systems negatively impacts on the global adoption of existing formalisms in real-world applications of knowledge graphs. FunMap aims at bridging this gap and offering an alternative of evaluating RML+FnO over existing RML-compliant engines.

6 Conclusions and Future Work

We addressed the problem of scaled-up KG creation in complex data integration systems, i.e., systems with large data sources, high data duplication rate, and functional mappings. We presented a heuristic-based approach for efficiently evaluating data integration systems with data sources in diverse formats (e.g., CSV or relational). The proposed heuristics are implemented in FunMap, an interpreter of RML+FnO, that converts data integration systems in RML+FnO into equivalent data integration systems specified in RML. Besides shaping an RML-engine independent interpreter of RML+FnO, FunMap generates data integration systems that enhance RML-compliant engines whenever transformation functions are repeatedly used, and data sources are large and have highly-duplicated data. Empirical evaluations of the combination of FunMap with RML-compliant engines suggest that the execution time of RML+FnO can be reduced by up to a factor of 18. Thus, FunMap widens the repertory of tools to scale up knowledge graphs to the enormous increase of incoming data and

[11] https://github.com/RMLio/RMLStreamer.

[12] https://github.com/carml/carml.

ease the development of real-world KG applications. As the main limitation, FunMap can only be applied with an RML-compliant engine which supports either `joinCondition` or RDB on the backend. We plan to devise cost-based optimization approaches that, together with the proposed heuristics, allow for the generation of the best solution for a complex data integration system in RML+FnO.

Acknowledgments. This work has been partially supported by the EU H2020 project iASiS No. 727658, the ERAMed project P4-LUCAT No. 53000015, Ministerio de Economía, Industria y Competitividad, and EU FEDER funds under the DATOS 4.0: RETOS Y SOLUCIONES - UPM Spanish national project (TIN2016-78011-C4-4-R) and by the FPI grant (BES-2017-082511).

References

1. Aho, A.V., Sethi, R., Ullman, J.D.: Compilers, Principles, Techniques, vol. 7, no, 8. Addison Wesley, Boston (1986)
2. Ali, S.M.F., Wrembel, R.: Towards a cost model to optimize user-defined functions in an ETL workflow based on user-defined performance metrics. In: Advances in Databases and Information Systems, ADBIS (2019)
3. Calvanese, D., et al.: Ontop: answering SPARQL queries over relational databases. Semant. Web **8**(3), 471–487 (2017)
4. Chebotko, A., Lu, S., Fotouhi, F.: Semantics preserving SPARQL-to-SQL translation. Data Knowl. Eng. **68**(10), 973–1000 (2009)
5. Corcho, O., Priyatna, F., Chaves-Fraga, D.: Towards a new generation of ontology based data access. Semant. Web J. **11**(1), 153–160 (2020)
6. Das, S., Sundara, S., Cyganiak, R.: R2RML: RDB to RDF Mapping Language, W3C Recommendation 27 September 2012. W3C (2012)
7. De Meester, B., Maroy, W., Dimou, A., Verborgh, R., Mannens, E.: Declarative data transformations for linked data generation: the case of DBpedia. In: Blomqvist, E., Maynard, D., Gangemi, A., Hoekstra, R., Hitzler, P., Hartig, O. (eds.) ESWC 2017. LNCS, vol. 10250, pp. 33–48. Springer, Cham (2017). https://doi.org/10.1007/978-3-319-58451-5_3
8. Debruyne, C., O'Sullivan, D.: R2RML-F: towards sharing and executing domain logic in R2RML mappings. In: LDOW Workshop (2016)
9. den Dunnen, J.T., et al.: HGVS recommendations for the description of sequence variants: 2016 update. Hum. Mutat. **37**(6), 564–569 (2016)
10. Dimou, A., Vander Sande, M., Colpaert, P., Verborgh, R., Mannens, E., Van de Walle, R.: RML: a generic language for integrated RDF mappings of heterogeneous data. In: 7th Workshop on Linked Data on the Web (2014)
11. Galhardas, H., Florescu, D., Shasha, D., Simon, E., Saita, C.: Declarative data cleaning: Language, model, and algorithms (2001)
12. Gawriljuk, G., Harth, A., Knoblock, C.A., Szekely, P.: A scalable approach to incrementally building knowledge graphs. In: Fuhr, N., Kovács, L., Risse, T., Nejdl, W. (eds.) TPDL 2016. Lecture Notes in Computer Science, vol. 9819. Springer, Cham (2016). https://doi.org/10.1007/978-3-319-43997-6_15
13. Gupta, S., Szekely, P., Knoblock, C.A., Goel, A., Taheriyan, M., Muslea, M.: Karma: a system for mapping structured sources into the semantic web. In: Simperl, E., et al. (eds.) ESWC 2012. LNCS, vol. 7540. Springer, Heidelberg (2015). https://doi.org/10.1007/978-3-662-46641-4_40

14. Hogan, A., et al.: Knowledge graphs. CoRR, abs/2003.02320 (2020)
15. Iglesias, E., Jozashoori, S., Chaves-Fraga, D., Collarana, D., Vidal, M.-E.: SDM-RDFizer: an RML interpreter for the efficient creation of RDF knowledge graphs. In ACM International Conference on Information and Knowledge Management, CIKM (2020)
16. Jozashoori, S., Vidal, M.-E.: MapSDI: a scaled-up semantic data integration framework for knowledge graph creation. In: Panetto, H., Debruyne, C., Hepp, M., Lewis, D., Ardagna, C.A., Meersman, R. (eds.) OTM 2019. LNCS, vol. 11877, pp. 58–75. Springer, Cham (2019). https://doi.org/10.1007/978-3-030-33246-4_4
17. Junior, A.C., Debruyne, C., Brennan, R., O'Sullivan, D.: FunUL: a method to incorporate functions into uplift mapping languages. In: International Conference on Information Integration and Web-based Applications and Services (2016)
18. Lefrançois, M., Zimmermann, A., Bakerally, N.: Flexible RDF generation from RDF and heterogeneous data sources with SPARQL-generate. In: Ciancarini, P., et al. (eds.) EKAW 2016. LNCS (LNAI), vol. 10180, pp. 131–135. Springer, Cham (2017). https://doi.org/10.1007/978-3-319-58694-6_16
19. Lenzerini, M.: Data integration: a theoretical perspective. In: ACM Symposium on Principles of Database Systems (2002)
20. Mami, M.N., Graux, D., Scerri, S., Jabeen, H., Auer, S., Lehmann, J.: Squerall: virtual ontology-based access to heterogeneous and large data sources. In: Ghidini, C., et al. (eds.) ISWC 2019. LNCS, vol. 11779, pp. 229–245. Springer, Cham (2019). https://doi.org/10.1007/978-3-030-30796-7_15
21. Michel, F., Djimenou, L., Faron-Zucker, C., Montagnat, J.: Translation of relational and non-relational databases into RDF with xR2RML. In: WEBIST, pp. 443–454. SciTePress (2015)
22. Poggi, A., Lembo, D., Calvanese, D., De Giacomo, G., Lenzerini, M., Rosati, R.: Linking data to ontologies. In: Spaccapietra, S. (ed.) Journal on Data Semantics X. LNCS, vol. 4900, pp. 133–173. Springer, Heidelberg (2008). https://doi.org/10.1007/978-3-540-77688-8_5
23. Priyatna, F., Corcho, O., Sequeda, J.F.: Formalisation and experiences of R2RML-based SPARQL to SQL query translation using morph. In: International Conference on World Wide Web, WWW 2014 (2014)
24. Rahm, E., Do, H.H.: Data cleaning: problems and current approaches. IEEE Data Eng. Bull. **23**(4), 3–13 (2000)
25. Raman, V., Hellerstein, J.M.: Potter's wheel: an interactive data cleaning system. In: VLDB, vol. 1 (2001)
26. Vu, B., Pujara, J., Knoblock, C.A.: D-REPR: a language for describing and mapping diversely-structured data sources to RDF. In: International Conference on Knowledge Capture (2019)

KnowlyBERT - Hybrid Query Answering over Language Models and Knowledge Graphs

Jan-Christoph Kalo(✉), Leandra Fichtel, Philipp Ehler, and Wolf-Tilo Balke

Institut Für Informationssysteme, Technische Universität Braunschweig, Mühlenpfordtstraße 23, 38106 Braunschweig, Germany
{kalo,balke}@ifis.cs.tu-bs.de, {l.fichtel,p.ehler}@tu-bs.de

Abstract. Providing a plethora of entity-centric information, Knowledge Graphs have become a vital building block for a variety of intelligent applications. Indeed, modern knowledge graphs like Wikidata already capture several billions of RDF triples, yet they still lack a good coverage for most relations. On the other hand, recent developments in NLP research show that neural language models can easily be queried for relational knowledge without requiring massive amounts of training data. In this work, we leverage this idea by creating a hybrid query answering system on top of knowledge graphs in combination with the masked language model BERT to complete query results. We thus incorporate valuable structural and semantic information from knowledge graphs with textual knowledge from language models to achieve high precision query results. Standard techniques for dealing with incomplete knowledge graphs are either (1) relation extraction which requires massive amounts of training data or (2) knowledge graph embeddings which have problems to succeed beyond simple baseline datasets. Our hybrid system KnowlyBERT requires only small amounts of training data, while outperforming state-of-the-art techniques by boosting their precision by over 30% in our large Wikidata experiment.

Keywords: Query answering · Language models · Knowledge graphs

1 Introduction

Large Knowledge Graphs (KG) like Wikidata [17], DBpedia [2], YAGO [15] and the Google Knowledge Graph [5] have become an essential component in data-intensive applications, like Web search, information retrieval or for adding an additional value to machine learning techniques. Most of these knowledge graphs contain entity-centric knowledge that is either manually curated like in Wikidata, extracted from structured sources like tables for DBpedia or also extracted from natural language text by relation extraction techniques [5].

J. Z. Pan et al. (Eds.): ISWC 2020, LNCS 12506, pp. 294–310, 2020.
https://doi.org/10.1007/978-3-030-62419-4_17

Still, modern knowledge graphs like Wikidata lack important information about entities which drastically hampers its application. As an example, only 36% of all persons in the current Wikidata version have a birthplace. To overcome problems with the incompleteness, several ways to complete knowledge graphs are investigated: (1) Knowledge graph completion techniques, as for example relational learning techniques [10], are employed for learning statistical regularities in knowledge graph data to infer new facts. However, current benchmarks, only comprising several thousand entities, show that existing techniques are far from being able to deliver reliable results [1]. (2) On the other hand, relation extraction method use existing triples as training data for NLP machine learning techniques to extract similar facts from textual data automatically. These techniques need large amounts of training data and also only achieve low quality results [13].

Very recently Petroni et al. have proposed a third idea for dealing with the incompleteness of structured knowledge graphs: utilizing masked language models as a knowledge graph [13]. Masked language models are a technique that lead to a quantum leap in almost all natural language processing tasks. It is a machine learning technique, that is able to complete sentences, based on massive amounts of text that it was trained on. The language model is even able to complete sentences correctly, if the information was not present in the training data, since it is able to infer new knowledge. Therefore, Petroni et al. came up with the idea of extracting relational knowledge (i. e; triples) directly from the model. As an example, we could figure out the birthplace of Albert Einstein by a sentence completion task as follows: "*Albert Einstein is born in ...*", would be completed by the language model with the word *Ulm*. Hence, we could infer the valid triple (*Albert Einstein*, `born in`, *Ulm*) to directly answer basic SPARQL queries on the language model. Some follow up works [3,12], have shown that we easily extract relational knowledge from such language model, with good quality for a variety of semantic and syntactic relations. However, this idea still shows several problems: In contrast to knowledge graphs, language models work on words and not on IRIs for entities as it is common in knowledge graphs. This leaves the open question on how to map the language model result to the correct knowledge graph entity. Existing works, are only considering entities whose label consists of a single word. Multi-word entities cannot be found. So far, only first experiments on how triples are extracted from a language model have been shown.

Here, instead of just extracting knowledge from the language model, we overcome existing problems and present - KnowlyBERT - the first read-to-use hybrid query answering system for knowledge graphs incorporating masked language models on the fly at query time. Our system is able to answer entity-centric SPARQL queries on incomplete knowledge graphs, using state-of-the-art language models to complete the results. Furthermore, we incorporate existing semantic information from the knowledge graph in multiple ways to improve the accuracy of the hybrid system: We developed a typing system, filtering language model results based on knowledge graphs fine-grained class hierarchies.

As an additional filtering step, our system uses existing answers to further filter out incorrect answer candidates. We also use the knowledge graphs information to automatically find good natural language sentence for the language model prediction task [3].

We present the first ready-to-use query answering system for Wikidata combined with the language model BERT [4]. In a large real-world evaluation on Wikidata, we compare our system for various queries on an incomplete knowledge graph against a state-of-the-art relation extraction system ([14]) and the knowledge base completion system HoLE [11].

The main contributions of this paper can be summarized as follows:

- We develop a system integrating the advantages of knowledge graphs and large-scale masked language models to answer entity-centric SPARQL queries efficiently.
- We perform several large-scale experiments with around 6500 queries of KnowlyBERT on the real-world knowledge graph Wikidata against two state-of-the-art baselines.
- Our implementation and all our experimental data is openly available for easy reproducibility of our work[1].

2 Related Work

Knowledge Graph Completion is used to learn statistical regularities in the data to predict new triples connecting existing entities in incomplete knowledge graphs. Thus, similar to our system, such techniques may be used to complete query results, by finding missing triples in a first step and use these triples additionally, to existing ones to answer queries.

Basically, two approaches for knowledge graph completion are common. Rule-based approaches, such as AMIE+ [7] are used to learn closed Horn rules from knowledge graphs. These rules infer new triples with high precision. However, rule induction algorithms have performance problems when it comes to large knowledge graphs with hundreds of millions of triples such as Wikidata.

To overcome the performance problem, knowledge embedding-based techniques have been proposed. These techniques have in common that they learn high-dimensional vector representations of entities and relationships and use these to predict new triples [10]. In practice, knowledge embeddings are hardly used yet because their result quality for real-world knowledge graphs is poor and it is not desirable to introduce low quality triples into a high-quality knowledge graph [1]. Furthermore, state-of-the-art benchmarks rely on a well-chosen subset of the knowledge graph Freebase, only comprising 15,000 entities. The prediction quality in these benchmarks is acceptable, but mainly because of the small and well-chosen datasets.

Overall, existing techniques for knowledge graph completion cannot work properly with large-scale knowledge graphs and achieve high quality predictions

[1] https://github.com/JanKalo/KnowlyBERT.

at the same time. In contrast to both techniques, our approach makes use of pre-trained language models without the need of massive computing resources and still can predict new triples with high quality or high recall.

To provide a comparison, we also evaluate the state-of-the-art KG embedding technique HoLE [11] against our system in the evaluation section.

Relation Extraction is about extracting triples from natural language text using automatic machine learning techniques. State-of-the-art techniques are based on so called *distant supervision*. Existing knowledge graph triples are used to generate training data for a classification algorithm that decides for a given sentence whether it contains a triple or not. Systems achieve a precision between 50% and 90% on small Wikidata corpora [14,16]. In contrast to our work, relation extraction systems need large amounts of training data to train a classifier for each relation independently. Furthermore, they cannot be directly used in an on-the fly querying answering system. Relation extraction has to be performed upfront on large text collections to cover all possible queries, because due to its runtime it cannot be used for on-the-fly query answering. To provide a comparison to relation extraction, in our evaluation, we compare to the open source system provided by Sorokin et al. [14].

Masked Language Models have recently shown great results in a plethora of different NLP tasks. Petroni et al. have shown that knowledge graph facts can be directly extracted from pre-trained language models, instead performing a complex relation extraction process [13]. In their work, they have manually built sentence templates for several relationships from knowledge graphs. These templates are then used to complete a sentence and predict a word to complete a triple, as demonstrated in the introduction. This work is only able to predict entity labels consisting of a single word, excluding almost all persons from being a query answer. Furthermore, it only provides words as answers, but not KG IRIs. An entity linking step is not performed yet. They evaluate on several relations from Wikidata, but also on a variety of other relation datasets. They achieve a high accuracy of 32% on the T-Rex datasets [6], comprising 41 different Wikidata relations. We evaluate our system on the same relations from T-Rex, but a larger dataset also comprising multi-word entities.

In an extension, it was shown that the quality of these predictions is highly dependent on the input sentence. Therefore Bouraoui et al. have proposed to automatically generate templates for relationships that achieve high quality results [3]. They show that indeed they can double the accuracy of triple inference for some relations. Still, this approach is also restricted, since it cannot predict entities consisting of more than a single word.

Another work in this direction circumvents the restriction to single-word entities, by defining a new fine-tuning task on masked language models [18]. They directly include entity knowledge from the knowledge graph to train masked language models. However, in their work they restrict to a small amount of most popular entities from Wikidata only. Covering a large amount of entities, including rare entities would dramatically increase the computational effort for training. Thus, this approach is not suitable for general query answering in knowledge graphs.

In contrast, our present work builds upon existing systems and further refines their ideas to create a query answering system for incomplete knowledge graphs without any restrictions on the type of entities or relations.

3 Preliminaries

KnowlyBERT is a query answering system for RDF-based knowledge graphs. RDF information is expressed in the form of subject, predicate, object triples $(s, \mathtt{p}, o) \in E \times P \times E \cup L$, whereas s represents an entity from the real-world E, p represents a relation from the set of all relations P that can be mapped to real-world relations and o represents an entity from E or a literal value from L. Entities and predicates in RDF are represented by Internationalized Resource Identifiers (IRIs). Furthermore, each entity from E and each relation from P has a natural language text label. For readability reasons in this work, we use these labels instead of IRIs. As an example, the triple (*Albert Einstein*, `bornIn`, *Ulm*) states that the entity Albert Einstein is in a `born in` relation with the entity *Ulm*. Entities may have multiple types from the set of classes $C \subseteq E$. A type relation can also be formulated in a triple as follows: (*Albert Einstein*, `type`, *Scientist*) The set of all triples in a knowledge graphs defined as $KG \subseteq E \times P \times E \cup L$.

Queries against a KG can be performed by the query language SPARQL. In this work, we restrict to the most prominent part of SPARQL: basic graph pattern (BGP) queries. The simplest basic graph pattern query consists of a single triple pattern with variables that are indicated by a leading ?. As an example, a BGP query $Q = (\textit{Albert Einstein}, \mathtt{bornIn}, ?x)$ is asking for the `birthplace` of *Albert Einstein*. To answer the query, we need to match this triple against the knowledge graph, whereas a variable can be matched to an arbitrary entity. In the example case, $?x$ could be matched to the entity *Ulm*. In the present work, we restrict to entity-centric SPARQL queries. They have one triple pattern with a single variable either in subject or object position.

A language model is a statistical model providing the probability of an upcoming word, given a sequence of words. Usually, it is used to complete natural language sentences, by learning the parameters of the model from large text corpora. In this work, we work with the masked language model BERT, a neural network-based language model, which is based on the transformer model [4]. This model is created in a pre-training step, where the model learns to complete arbitrary sentences and predict next sentences in a self-supervised fashion using large input text corpora, e.g. Wikipedia. Thus it, for example, learns how to complete the sentence: "*The birthplace of Albert Einstein is....*" with the word *Ulm*. Therefore, masked language models, as BERT, may be used to answer simple basic graph pattern queries, as demonstrated by Petroni et al. [13]. As an example, we could translate the query $Q = (AlbertEinstein, \mathtt{bornIn}, ?x)$ to the sentence "*Albert Einstein is born in ...*", which would be completed with the word *Ulm*. In most masked language models, the word to be predicted is represented by a so-called mask token "[MASK]". The input to the language model is a sentence including a mask token: "*The birthplace of Albert Einstein is* [MASK]". The model's output is a list of words from its vocabulary, accompanied with a prediction probability for each of them.

Finding appropriate translations from triples to sentences, so that the language model is able to answer the query is an open problem that has gained recent interest [3,9,12]. We further investigate this problem in the present work by comparing different schemes for sentence generation. As an additional problem, masked language models, as they are available today, are only able to predict words, but not entities. So, to answer a query, we need to map natural language words to an entity from our knowledge graph in E. Because of that, some language model extensions have been developed to include entity knowledge. As described in our related work section, this leads to problems, which is why we stick to masked language models and develop an entity disambiguation technique on top. Existing works for extracting relational knowledge from language models have focused on entities having labels consisting of a single word only. We will extend the technique to multi-word entities (entities whose label consists of more than a single word). More details of these step will be described in the next section.

4 KnowlyBERT - Query Answering with Language Models and Knowledge Graphs

In this section, we describe KnowlyBERT, a hybrid query answering system using a knowledge graph and the masked language model BERT to complete queries over an incomplete knowledge graph. We start with an overview of the system and shortly describe all components, while we go into the details of the different components in the following subsections.

The overview is sketched in Fig. 1. As an input for KnowlyBERT, a user can pose an entity-centric SPARQL query to our system. First, the language model is queried (a). Then we pose the query to the incomplete knowledge graph and get the existing results (b). The SPARQL query is translated into multiple natural language sentences that are completed by the language model in the Relation Template Generation step. As a result, the language model returns multiple lists of words together with a confidence value for each word (c). These lists are then combined into a single list (d) and filtered using our semantic filtering step based on knowledge graph type information (e). Furthermore, we perform a thresholding, cutting of irrelevant results (f). As a final step, the results of the language model and the knowledge graph are combined (g) and returned to the user.

4.1 Relation Template Generation

As a first step to query a language model for relational knowledge, a SPARQL query needs to be translated into a natural language sentence with [MASK]

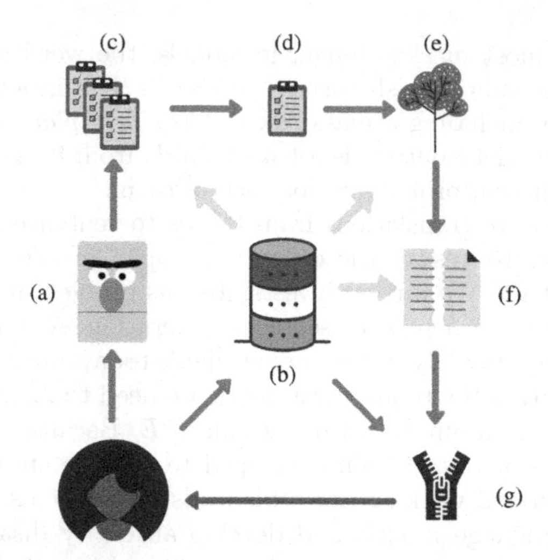

Fig. 1. An overview of the query answering system KnowlyBERT. A user query is distributed to BERT using the generated templates from Sect. 4.1 (a) and the KG (b). BERT outputs several result lists (c) with information from the KG. The results are integrated and filtered as described in Sect. 4.2 (d). A semantic type filter (Sect. 4.3) is applied (e) and later we employ thresholding methods to cut off incorrect results (f), which is described in Sect. 4.4. Finally, results from the LM and KG are integrated (g) and returned to the user.

tokens. Bouraoui et al. showed in [3] that automatically generated sentences outperform manually build templates as presented by Petroni et al. [13]. Therefore, in this work, we adapt the idea and automatically extract and rate sentence candidates for each relation of a knowledge graph to generate relation sentence templates in a pre-processing step. Such a template may have the format: "*[S] is born in [O]*", for the `birthplace` relation whereas [S] is replaced by the subject entity of a query or the [O] by the object. Generating sentence templates is not performed at query time, but is a pre-processing step.

To demonstrate this procedure, we continue with our artificial running example from Sect. 3: (*Albert Einstein*, `bornIn`, $?x$). For the relation `birthplace`, we use all subject, object pairs (s, o) such that $(s, \texttt{bornIn}, o) \in KG$. An example is the subject, object pair $(GottfriedLeibniz, Leipzig)$. We use pre-annotated Wikipedia abstracts (T-REx), where entity recognition and disambiguation as well as relation linking have been performed already [6]. As sentence candidates, we extract all sentences containing exactly one (s, o) pair for the `bornIn` relation. For example, the sentence *"Gottfried Leibniz was born in the city of Leipzig, Germany"*. for the respective entity pair. As template sentences, we use sentences with at most 15 words and exactly 2 tagged entities. Longer sentences often are too specific or consist of multiple subordinate clauses from different contexts. Hence, choosing different parameters here, may decrease the performance of the predictions. In contrast to the idea in [3], our input sentences have also been processed by basic co-reference resolution in sentences, replacing pronouns by the respective entity names as provided by the T-REx dataset [6].

As an additional new technique, we perform a string similarity check between the different sentences for the `bornIn` relation and only pick sentences that are different to each other to end up with a diverse set of sentence templates for each relation. We use a basic sequence pattern matching method finding the longest sub-sequence between every two template sentences. When the similarity of such a pair is above 0.8, it is put into the same sentence cluster. After performing similarity checks among all sentences, we obtain a set of sentence template clusters comprising similar sentences. From each cluster only a single sentence template is picked as a representative.

In a final step, we rate sentence template, using the language model and valid (s, o) pairs from the KG similar to Bouraoui et al. [3]. We rate the extracted `birthplace` sentence in the following way. The sentence *"Gottfried Leibniz was born in the city of Leipzig".* is instantiated by subjects and objects, so that we can check the language model's predictions and compare to the correct `bornIn` pairs from the KG. For example, we create the sentence *"Gottfried Leibniz was born in the city of [MASK]"* using the existing pair (*Gottfried Leibniz, Leipzig*). We have a look at the top predictions of the language model and check, whether they have an overlap with existing objects of the `birthplace` relation in the KG. The size overlap of these object predictions with the KG objects and size of the overlap of the respective subject predictions are summed up and used as a weight of the sentence template. In the end, we take the top five sentence templates for our predictions.

Additional Context Paragraphs. An additional boost in the prediction quality of language models is achieved by providing additional context information to the query sentences [12]. Petroni et al. have shown that instead of only giving a query template sentence as the input to the language model, providing additional sentences about the entity of interest increases the precision of predictions by around 30%. Following their description, for each entity in a query, we have extracted the first five sentences from the respective Wikipedia abstract and added them to the generate templates using a [SEP] token of BERT. We provide context with the first sentences of Einstein's Wikipedia article as follows:

> *Albert Einstein was born in the city of* [MASK].[SEP]
> *Albert Einstein was a German-born theoretical physicist who developed the theory of relativity, one of the two pillars of modern physics (alongside quantum mechanics).*

In contrast to existing works, we combine automatic template generation and context paragraph retrieval, which in combination boost the result quality. We use five template sentences for each query, each annotated with a five sentence long context paragraph.

Template generation for relations and also context paragraph retrieval can be performed in a pre-processing step. The information for all relations and entities in the KG is indexed properly for fast access at query time.

4.2 Querying the Language Model and Combining the Results

For the Einstein query, we now use multiple sentence templates together with the respective context paragraph to get possible answers from the language model. Since possible answer entity labels might consist of more than a single word, we have to pose queries with a single [MASK] token for returning possible single-word entities, but also queries with multiple [MASK] tokens. Changing our example query to (?x, `bornIn`, Ulm), would require us to find (among others) Albert Einstein, an entity with a label of two words, as a correct answer. To predict such entities, we provide two or more [MASK] tokens in the query sentence as follows: "[MASK] [MASK] *was born in the city of Ulm*" for a template returning two tokens and "[MASK] [MASK] [MASK] *was born in the city of Ulm*" if we want to find answer entities with three tokens. This leads to independent result list for each [MASK], so that we have to check for valid word combinations. We join all possible word combinations from the result lists and check whether a valid entity label from the knowledge graph is created. This is a very important step, since it enables us to filter out a large proportion of predicted words which cannot be mapped to any entity. Valid word combinations are weighted by the average of the words output probabilities. The output is a list of single and multi-token entity labels with the correctness probabilities assigned by the masked language model. We present an artificial result set as an example for the query containing one correct entity in the top position and two locations below:

1. *Ulm - 0.95*
2. *Princeton, New Jersey - 0.45*
3. *Munich - 0.22*

Note that in this work we restrict the system to a maximum of three [MASK] tokens. This number may be increased with small increases in the query answering time.

Aggregating Results from Multiple Templates. Different sentence templates for a single query lead to independent result lists with different probability values for each result entity. In our case, we obtain 5 entity lists. To combine these lists into a single list, we stick to the idea from [3]. The lists are first simply merged. If an entity occurs in multiple lists the maximum probability is chosen. Furthermore, the maximum probability and the minimum probability for each entity occurring in multiple lists are compared. If their difference exceeds a threshold of 0.6, the entity is not taken into the final result list. 0.6 has been chosen as a good compromise between precision- or recall-oriented behavior. This excludes entities, where the language model shows unstable predictions, leading to a higher overall precision. Increasing this threshold increases the overall precision of the results.

4.3 Semantic Type Filtering

Most knowledge graphs provide a very detailed type hierarchy for its entities which we employ for further filtering the language model results. For every relation in the knowledge graph, we create frequency distributions over the classes of the subject and objects entities. A class of an entity is determined by using the `instance of` relation (P31) of Wikidata, but we also consider the first level of super classes (P279) of these classes, so that the type filter is not too specific. Using the created frequency distributions, we only define the most frequently occurring classes as valid types for a relation. These can be called the expected types of a relation. Based on the expected types, we are able to filter out answer candidates that do not fit these types, employing a semantic type filter. This way, we are more restrictive, possibly filtering out some correct entities, but increase the systems precision.

Entity Disambiguation. After the semantic type filtering step, we still could end up with multiple possible answer entities, having the same entity label. Such a homonym could for example be another entity with the name *Ulm*. In Germany as an example, one large city, but also several smaller villages called *Ulm* are known. For such rare cases, we need to perform an additional entity disambiguation step. As a first simple pre-processing step, we exclude extremely rare entities using a popularity filter. Concretely, entities are excluded when they never occur as an object entity in the whole knowledge graph. If multiple homonyms exist, the most popular entity is returned as an answer. Further filtering steps using knowledge graph embeddings are possible here. However, our evaluation has shown no benefits in precision without large losses in recall here.

4.4 Thresholding

As a last step before returning the result list, we perform a thresholding procedure to guarantee that only high-quality results are returned to the user. We perform two different thresholding mechanisms. The first threshold is dynamically chosen for each query by a statistical outlier analysis among the prediction values. If after several top prediction values (e.g. 0.95, 0.45, 0.22), the next prediction value is significantly lower (e.g. 0.45), we pick a threshold in the gap between 0.95 and 0.45. If no correct answer is returned by the language model, the dynamic threshold methods do not work. Therefore, we pick an additional static threshold that is valid for all queries. This threshold is learned automatically by averaging the probabilities of known results that are already in the incomplete knowledge graph and that are also in the language model's result list. Using our example result list from above, we end up with the following list only comprising the correct answer Ulm:

1. *Ulm - 0.95*

Finally, we join the result lists of the incomplete knowledge graph with the result list of our language model-based pipeline and eliminate duplicates.

5 Evaluation

In this section, we describe the evaluation of KnowlyBERT on the large real-world knowledge graph Wikidata and the language model BERT. We evaluate precision and recall for 41 different relations similar to other language model-based systems [3,12,13] and compare against a state-of-the-art relation extraction technique using distant supervision [14] and a technique for knowledge graph completion which uses high dimensional embeddings [11]. In detail, we provide an overview of the performance on different relations and provide an extensive discussion on the drawbacks and advantages of language model-based techniques for on-the-fly query answering in contrast to existing techniques which are particularly trained for inducing new triples in incomplete knowledge graphs.

5.1 Experimental Setup

Baselines. KnowlyBERT performs query answering on incomplete knowledge graphs, which may be seen as an on-the-fly knowledge graph completion method. Since no directly comparable baselines are available, we compare to standard knowledge graph completion techniques that work in an offline setting. Here, inferring new triples using external knowledge by relation extraction from text and triple induction by structural methods purely on the knowledge graph are the most popular methods being used today.

Therefore as a first baseline, we use a recent distant supervised relation extraction system from [14] with available pre-trained models for Wikipedia triple extraction. This baseline has already been used by Petroni et al. [13] to compare to their language model-based approach. We have used their pre-trained Wikipedia model for extracting triples from natural language text and performed relation extraction from T-Rex [6]. T-Rex links Wikidata entities and triples to Wikipedia abstracts. These linked entities in text are used as an input for the relation extraction framework, to extract triples from sentences.

As a second baseline, we have compared to another state-of-the-art technique for coping with incomplete knowledge graphs [10]. Knowledge graph embeddings are latent machine learning models for knowledge graph completion. High dimensional vector representations of entities and relations are learned from an existing knowledge graph. Arithmetic operations between these vector representations enable giving a correctness probability to every possible subject, predicate, object-combination. Hence, it is also possible to find most likely substitutions for subject-predicate-pairs or predicate-object pairs. In our case, we use HoLE as a baseline, which has shown good results in benchmark datasets, and also is scalable to the size of our large Wikidata sample [11]. Due to the size of Wikidata, we trained HoLE using 50 dimensions for 200 epochs. Since HoLE itself only provides a top-k list of newly inferred triples ordered by their prediction probability, we only took the predictions with the best possible prediction value of HoLE. This may also include several predictions showing the same prediction value.

Dataset. Our experiments are performed on the Wikidata Truthy dump from February 6th, 2020. We evaluate only on triples where subject and object are entities having an `rdf:label` relation. For simplicity reasons, we also restrict to labels consisting of at most three words. We restrict to the 41 different relations that are used in the LAMA probe [13]. But we use different queries, since they were restricted to entities consisting of single word labels only.

We have sampled queries for each of these 41 relations by randomly choosing triples from the Wikidata. We remove the subject, creating an entity-centric SPARQL query, asking for a subject entity (?x, p, o), or removing the object respectively to ask for the object (s, p, ?x). We name the query type asking for subjects, *subject queries* and the others *object queries.* Hence, we created 100 subject and 100 object queries for each relation, if possible. For some relations, we could only generate fewer queries. Overall, this leads to 6649 queries.

For all queries we assume that the current Wikidata version as the ideal knowledge graph. The incomplete knowledge graph is simulated by leaving out existing triples by performing a *leave k out* evaluation, deleting at least 1 and at most 100 answers from the answer set of each query. To be comparable to the relation extraction baseline which extracts triples from text, we have restricted the deleted triples to triples that actually occur in the text corpus we use. This gives an advantage to this baseline system since it ensures that it is possible to achieve 100% recall which is not necessarily valid for our system. The ideal knowledge graph has 54,056,746 triples and the incomplete knowledge graph has 125,213 fewer triples deleted for the 6,649 queries. Thus, the incomplete knowledge graph comprises 53,931,533 triples.

Evaluation Metrics. We have evaluated every query separately by querying the language model and removing the answer triples that already were in the incomplete KG. For the remaining additional results, we computed precision and recall values. The reported results are average precision and recall values over all queries that returned additional results.

Implementation Details. Our system KnowlyBERT is implemented in Python 3 and is openly available on Github[2]. We also make scripts for reproducing these results available. Our system is based on the masked language model BERT from Google [4]. We use the large and cased model pre-trained by Google comprising 340 m parameters. Since our system is built on the LAMA framework by Petroni et al, we are able to include arbitrary language models[3]. For the relation extraction baseline, we use the original implementation also available on Github[4]. The knowledge graph embedding HoLE is implemented in OpenKE [8].

5.2 Experimental Results

An overview of precision and recall of KnowlyBERT and the two baseline systems is presented in Table 1. First, we have a look at the total precision and recall values depicted in the last row. KnowlyBERT outperforms the two other approaches with regard to precision by more than 30% by achieving an average precision of 47.5%. In contrast to the relation extraction baseline (RE), we

[2] https://github.com/JanKalo/KnowlyBERT.
[3] https://github.com/facebookresearch/LAMA.
[4] https://github.com/UKPLab/emnlp2017-relation-extraction.

Table 1. Precision (Prec) and Recall (Rec) from KnowlyBERT against two baseline systems in percent. Relation extraction (RE) and the knowledge graph embedding technique HoLE (KE) on 41 relations. We evaluate different query parameters.

Evaluation	Parameter	Statistics		RE		KE		KnowlyBERT	
		#Queries	#Rel	Prec	Rec	Prec	Rec	Prec	Rec
Cardinality	1-1	400	2	5.5	5.5	<0.1	**20.2**	**16.9**	3.0
	1-n	3756	23	18.8	**17.4**	<0.1	11.5	**55.0**	13.7
	n-m	2493	16	16.4	19.8	<0.1	**22.6**	**36.0**	5.9
Query type	$(s, p, ?x)$	4029	41	37.5	17.3	<0.1	**20.5**	**51.0**	16.5
	$(?x, p, o)$	2620	41	6.9	**17.9**	<0.1	9.5	**10.5**	0.3
Words	single	2474	41	39.6	13.9	<0.1	21.1	**59.6**	**25.9**
	multi	4175	41	**13.0**	**19.7**	<0.1	13.2	11.4	0.8
#Results	1	3497	41	40.5	13.2	<0.1	15.8	**51.3**	**17.4**
	2–10	1367	39	18.7	**20.5**	<0.1	20.4	**37.0**	4.9
	11–100	796	37	7.4	**30.7**	0.2	24.7	**15.8**	0.1
	>100	989	37	**5.7**	**18.2**	<0.1	4.8	<0.1	<0.1
Total		6649	41	17.5	**17.6**	<0.1	16.2	**47.5**	10.1

improve the precision drastically, however the recall of our approach is slightly lower with 10.1% in comparison to 17.6% of the RE baseline.

HoLE (KE) is showing good results with regard to the recall, but its precision is extremely low at around 0.03%. This very low precision, but high recall value is due to a high number of false positives all having top prediction values. The result for a knowledge graph embedding technique confirms recent research results that it is not ready for completion tasks in real-world knowledge graphs [1]. We present the results here anyways for completeness reasons, but will not discuss them in detail. Our main focus in this evaluation will compare the RE baseline with KnowlyBERT.

In the first rows, we present the results ordered by the cardinality of the relations in the query. We have analyzed two 1-1 relations[5], 23 1-n relations and 16 n-m relations. KnowlyBERT show its best results for 1-n relations with a precision of 55.0% and recall of 13.7%. Similarly, the two baselines show there best precision here.

We also present an evaluation of subject vs. object-based queries. Here, we observe something particularly interesting. KnowlyBERT achieves an extremely high precision for (s, p, ?x) queries asking for the object, but low precision and recall for queries asking for the subject of a triple. Also, the RE baseline shows a much smaller precision here, but at least shows good recall values.

[5] We follow the categorization of Petroni et al. [13]. Note that some queries for 1-1 relations have more than a single result.

Table 2. Precision (Prec) and Recall (Rec) of KnowlyBERT and the baseline systems for a variety of relations from Wikidata in percent.

Relation	Label	Statistics	RE		KE		KnowlyBERT	
		#Queries	Prec	Rec	Prec	Rec	Prec	Rec
P17	`country`	145	16.6	16.7	<0.1	21.6	**97.4**	**51.0**
P19	`birthplace`	191	21.8	**19.4**	<0.1	13.7	**73.3**	11.5
P31	`instance of`	152	**11.9**	15.0	<0.1	**17.3**	<0.1	<0.1
P36	`capital`	200	5.5	11.1	<0.1	**23.0**	**15.4**	3.0
P101	`field of work`	174	11.0	9.3	<0.1	**12.1**	**45.1**	7.8
P103	`native language`	117	<0.1	<0.1	<0.1	31.5	**100**	**74.3**
P108	`employer`	173	17.1	3.2	<0.1	**17.3**	**100**	0.6
P159	`headquarter`	190	19.6	**26.8**	<0.1	9.5	**56.8**	13.2
P279	`subclass of`	197	6.8	**28.8**	<0.1	13.5	16.7	<0.1
P1303	`instrument`	128	**35.0**	**43.4**	<0.1	15.8	<0.1	<0.1
P1412	`language spoken`	124	6.4	2.5	<0.1	**21.9**	**45.8**	17.7

The next part of our evaluation presents on how well the different approaches deal with multi word entities. We analyze whether the respective results of queries who only return single word entities against queries which correct answers comprise also multi-word entities. Here, we observe that KnowlyBERT works best for single-word entities, as does the RE baseline. Multi-word entities are often much harder to find using a language model-based approach. One reason is that queries asking for persons are often multi-word queries. Answering such person queries, is extremely difficult, since the set of possibly correct answers is often huge. Details will be evaluated in the next category in Table 1.

The next evaluation clusters queries by the number of results they have in the ideal KG. Here, we see that queries with few results generally show much better results. The precision and recall of KnowlyBERT for queries with a single result is over 50% with a recall of over 17% achieving the best results. Queries with large result sets are only answered with a low result quality. If they have more than 100 answers, we hardly find any correct answer, resulting in a poor precision. The RE baseline also has worse results for queries with many results, but at least returns some results.

In Table 2, we present the results for some particularly good working and badly working relations. We see that for some relations we achieve a precision of over 90% and a recall also above 70%. We see that many of the well working relations are about locations or languages. On the other hand, we also have several relations with an extremely low recall near to 0%. Particularly bad were the `instance of` and `subclass of` relations. Which implies that type information is hardly represented in the language model. But also the `instrument` relation shows extremely bad results. In contrast, the RE baseline shows its best results here.

5.3 Discussion

The evaluation of KnowlyBERT in comparison to other techniques for coping with incomplete knowledge graphs has shown us, that none of the existing techniques is ready to deal with all problems that come with missing information. While the knowledge graph embedding-based technique has shown poor results in the real-world scenario as already shown in recent research on the evaluation of such techniques [1], the state-of-the-art relation extraction technique has shown a consistently moderate result quality with a precision and recall around 17%.

In contrast, a language model-based approach shows a much higher precision with a small loss in recall. We have seen that the language model BERT has very different quality depending on the relation used in the queries. In some cases, we achieve almost perfect results with a precision of over 90% and high recall values, whereas for other relations we cannot find any correct results at all. Particularly geographic relations show good results, outperforming the baselines by far. Queries with single-word entities are also showing good quality. However, multi-word entities are very difficult to predict. Multi-word queries strongly correlate to queries with large result sets and subject-queries. One possible problem is that subject queries and multi-word queries often ask for long-tail entities. For these, the language model is rarely able to provide correct answers. All of these problems are reflected by our lower recall in contrast to the baselines. Particularly the relation extraction baseline still achieves an acceptable recall for these difficult query types.

Note that queries with large result sets are substantially more difficult to solve. Due to the fact that we do not count predicted result entities that already are in the incomplete KG, we add another difficulty. Even though a technique finds correct results, its precision for such queries might be 0%.

6 Conclusion

In this work, we have presented a hybrid query answering system for knowledge graphs using language models to cope with the incompleteness of real-world knowledge graphs. We have seen a plethora of different techniques to find missing triples in a knowledge graph completion task in a pre-processing step. Such techniques would introduce a lot of new and often incorrect triples into the knowledge graph, since they are not producing high quality results. Knowledge graph embedding techniques only show high precision in standard benchmark datasets, but fail in large real-world knowledge graphs [1]. On the other hand, NLP methods, that extract triples from natural language text in a binary classification task, require massive amounts of training data and a high quality entity linking step up front. The quality of relation extraction is under 20%, which would introduce massive amounts of incorrect data.

In contrast, we have presented a precision-oriented method that does not extract triples in a pre-processing step to be inserted into the knowledge graph, but an on-the-fly query answering system. This way, we do not contaminate the high quality of a knowledge graph and still can help to provide complete results, if necessary. KnowlyBERT has shown that a language model is a promising way to reduce the gap between incomplete knowledge graphs and complete result sets when used in combination with the KG itself. The KG can help to filter many incorrect results from the language model and helps us to also return multi-word entities, enabling us to be used as a full-fledged query answering system. As a drawback, we have seen that some relations could not be answered at all by KnowlyBERT, since the language model did not return correct results.

So far, KnowlyBERT is restricted to basic entity-centric queries. Existing question answering datasets could be used to learn natural language query templates to feature more complex queries with multiple triples. Furthermore, we plan to further investigate the boundaries of language models in representing relational knowledge to further characterize its benefits in knowledge graph tasks. Additionally, the suitability of general purpose language models in more specific domains should be investigated. In specific domains, choosing a domain-specific language model (e.g. BioBERT, SciBERT) and different method for retrieving contextual paragraphs would be interesting fields of research.

References

1. Akrami, F., Saeef, M., Zhang, Q., Hu, W., Li, C.: Realistic re-evaluation of knowledge graph completion methods: an experimental study. In: Proceedings of the 2020 International Conference on Management of Data, SIGMOD Conference 2020, Portland, OR, USA, 14–19 June 2020, March 2020
2. Auer, S., Bizer, C., Kobilarov, G., Lehmann, J., Cyganiak, R., Ives, Z.: DBpedia: a nucleus for a web of open data. In: Aberer, K., et al. (eds.) ASWC/ISWC -2007. LNCS, vol. 4825, pp. 722–735. Springer, Heidelberg (2007). https://doi.org/10.1007/978-3-540-76298-0_52
3. Bouraoui, Z., Camacho-Collados, J., Schockaert, S.: Inducing relational knowledge from BERT. In: Proceedings of the Thirty-Fourth Conference on Artificial Intelligence, AAAI 2020 (2020)
4. Devlin, J., Chang, M.W., Lee, K., Toutanova, K.: BERT: pre-training of deep bidirectional transformers for language understanding. In: Proceedings of the 2019 Conference of the North American Chapter of the Association for Computational Linguistics: Human Language Technologies, vol. 1, pp. 4171–4186, Jun 2019
5. Dong, X., et al.: Knowledge vault: a web-scale approach to probabilistic knowledge fusion. In: Proceedings of the 20th International Conference on Knowledge Discovery and Data Mining, SIGKDD 2014, pp. 601–610 (2014)
6. Elsahar, H., et al.: T-REx: a large scale alignment of natural language with knowledge base triples. In: Proceedings of the Eleventh International Conference on Language Resources and Evaluation (LREC 2018), Miyazaki, Japan. European Language Resources Association (ELRA), May 2018
7. Galárraga, L., Teflioudi, C., Hose, K., Suchanek, F.M.: Fast rule mining in ontological knowledge bases with AMIE+. VLDB J. **24**(6), 707–730 (2015)
8. Han, X., et al.: OpenKE: an open toolkit for knowledge embedding. In: EMNLP (2018)
9. Jiang, Z., Xu, F.F., Araki, J., Neubig, G.: How can we know what language models know? Trans. Assoc. Comput. Linguist. (TACL) **8**, 423–438 (2020)

10. Nickel, M., Murphy, K., Tresp, V., Gabrilovich, E.: A review of relational machine learning for knowledge graphs. In: Proceedings of the IEEE, vol. 104, no. 1, pp. 11–33, January 2016
11. Nickel, M., Rosasco, L., Poggio, T.: Holographic embeddings of knowledge graphs. In: Proceedings of the 30 AAAI Conference on Artificial Intelligence, AAAI 2016, pp. 1955–1961. AAAI Press (2016)
12. Petroni, F., et al.: How context affects language models' factual predictions. In: Automatic Knowledge Base Construction (AKBC) (2020)
13. Petroni, F., et al.: Language models as knowledge bases? In: Proceedings of the 2019 Conference on Empirical Methods in Natural Language Processing and the 9th International Joint Conference on Natural Language Processing (EMNLP-IJCNLP), pp. 2463–2473, November 2019
14. Sorokin, D., Gurevych, I.: Context-aware representations for knowledge base relation extraction. In: Proceedings of the 2017 Conference on Empirical Methods in Natural Language Processing, pp. 1784–1789, September 2017
15. Suchanek, F.M., Kasneci, G., Weikum, G.: YAGO: a core of semantic knowledge. In: Proceedings of the 16th International Conference on World Wide Web, WWW 2007, p. 697 (2007)
16. Trisedya, B.D., Weikum, G., Qi, J., Zhang, R.: Neural relation extraction for knowledge base enrichment. In: Proceedings of the 57th Annual Meeting of the Association for Computational Linguistics, pp. 229–240, July 2019
17. Vrandečić, D.: Wikidata: a new platform for collaborative data collection. In: Proceedings of the 21st International Conference Companion on World Wide Web, WWW 2012 Companion, p. 1063 (2012)
18. Xiong, W., Du, J., Wang, W.Y., Stoyanov, V.: Pretrained encyclopedia: weakly supervised knowledge-pretrained language model. In: International Conference on Learning Representations (ICLR) (2020)

Generating Referring Expressions from RDF Knowledge Graphs for Data Linking

Armita Khajeh Nassiri[1(✉)], Nathalie Pernelle[1,2(✉)], Fatiha Saïs[1(✉)], and Gianluca Quercini[1(✉)]

[1] LRI, CNRS 8623, Paris Saclay University, 91405 Orsay, France
{armita.khajeh_nassiri,nathalie.pernelle,fatiha.sais, gianluca.quercini}@lri.fr

[2] LIPN, CNRS (UMR 7030), University Sorbonne Paris Nord, Villetaneuse, France

Abstract. The generation of referring expressions is one of the most extensively explored tasks in natural language generation, where a description that uniquely identifies an instance is to be provided. Some recent approaches aim to discover referring expressions in knowledge graphs. To limit the search space, existing approaches define quality measures based on the intuitiveness and simplicity of the discovered expressions. In this paper, we focus on referring expressions of interest for data linking task and present *RE-miner*, an algorithm tailored to automatically discover minimal and diverse referring expressions for all instances of a class in a knowledge graph. We experimentally demonstrate on several benchmark datasets that, compared to existing data linking tools, referring expressions for data linking substantially improve the results, especially the recall without decreasing the precision. We also show that the RE-miner algorithm can scale to datasets containing millions of facts.

Keywords: Knowledge graphs · Referring expressions · Data linking

1 Introduction

A *referring expression* (*RE*) is a description in natural language or a logical formula that can uniquely identify an entity. For instance, the statement "president of the United States who was born in Hawaii" is a referring expression that unambiguously characterizes Barack Obama. There may potentially exist many logical expressions for uniquely identifying an entity. Referring expressions find applications in disambiguation, data anonymization, query answering, and data linking. The generation of referring expressions is a well-studied task in natural language generation [22], and various algorithms with different objectives have been proposed to discover REs automatically. These approaches vary depending on the expressivity of the logical formulas they can generate. For instance, in [8,21], REs are created as conjunctions of atoms, while [27] presents an approach that discovers more complex REs represented in description logics that can involve the universal quantifier. To ensure efficiency and reduce the search

J. Z. Pan et al. (Eds.): ISWC 2020, LNCS 12506, pp. 311–329, 2020.
https://doi.org/10.1007/978-3-030-62419-4_18

space, some of these methods focus on the minimality of the expression they discover and others on predicate preferences [16]. However, most of these methods are neither able to scale to large knowledge graphs such as YAGO or DBpedia with millions of instances nor are suited for the data linking task.

This paper embarks on automatically discovering REs for each entity within a class of a knowledge graph. These REs are conjunctions of atoms, e.g., $isPresident(x) \wedge isPoliticianOf(x, \texttt{\#USA}) \wedge bornIn(x, \texttt{\#Hawaii})$[1], and can also contain existentially quantified variables, e.g., $isPresident(x) \wedge marriedTo(x, y) \wedge hasName(y, \text{“}Michelle\text{”})$. Such conjunctions of atoms are not all relevant when they are exploited in a data linking task. As knowledge graphs are built independently and autonomously, individual IRIs are rarely reused in different knowledge graphs. This is the reason why a referring expression that involves a specified IRI may not be useful for the task of linking instances. Additionally, since data are usually incomplete and generally several referring expressions can be associated with an individual, to foster the utility of REs, it is preferable to diversify the sets of properties that are involved in the referring expressions of a given individual.

In order to reduce the enormous search space of referring expressions, our approach relies on defining types of graph patterns and quality measures that focus on REs that are more suitable in a data linking task. Moreover, we direct our attention to REs that cannot be found by instantiating the keys. As a reminder, the keys of a class are sets of properties whose values can uniquely identify one entity of that class. Hence, if the properties for the keys are instantiated, they can each be considered as a referring expression. For instance, take the class “book” and imagine that ISBN is key to this class. If we instantiate the books with their corresponding ISBNs, we can be sure to find them each uniquely. Recent approaches in the literature can efficiently discover keys in knowledge graphs [28,30,31], some of which do so by first finding the maximal non-keys [30,31]. Hence, our proposed RE-miner algorithm is based on the search space defined by these non-keys. Furthermore, we use the discovered REs in a data linking task and evaluate our approach on three benchmark datasets.

More precisely, our contributions are as follows:

- Defining graph patterns and several quality criteria that set forth REs, potentially relevant for data linking, discovered by our algorithm.
- Proposing an efficient algorithm, RE-miner, that computes complementary REs with regards to those REs that correspond to instantiated OWL2 keys.
- An extensive set of experiments showing that: (i) the approach scales to datasets consisting of millions of facts; (ii) the discovered REs, when used in a data linking task, can significantly increase the recall when compared to other approaches.

The remainder of this paper is organized as follows. We discuss the related work in Sect. 2. Section 3 details the formal problem statement. Section 4

[1] `#USA` and `#Hawaii` are IRIs (Internationalized Resource Identifier) that refer to the country USA and to the state of Hawaii, respectively.

describes the RE-miner algorithm, and Sect. 5 outlines how REs can be used for the data linking task. Section 6 shows our quantitative and data linking experiments, and finally, Sect. 7 concludes the paper.

2 Related Work

Both the generation of referring expressions and link discovery has been an area of active research in past years. The task of generating referring expressions, also known as REG, finds applications in fundamental fields such as natural language generation, text summarization, and query generation. Link discovery is rooted in record linkage, deduplication, and data integration. Existing methods for link discovery alleviate this task by matching the schema, instances, or both. In this paper, we focus on rule-based instance matching.

Referring Expression Generation. Robert Dale is first to frame REG as the problem of determining the properties that must be used to identify an entity [7]. The *Full Brevity* algorithm, outputs the shortest possible description by incrementally testing all combinations of properties to find the RE for the target. Later, acknowledging that finding the shortest RE is NP-hard, Dale approximated *Full Brevity* into a greedy algorithm that generates a RE by iteratively adding to an empty expression the property with the most discriminative power [8]. This algorithm does not necessarily produce the shortest RE but is much more efficient than *Full Brevity*.

As much as the length of a RE is important (people tend to prefer short ones), at times, a slightly longer and more informative RE is preferable. The *Incremental Algorithm* adds properties to an expression based on a preference order and does not necessarily produce the shortest RE [9]. Although logic optimization techniques are used to shorten the resulting REs, in some cases this algorithm might produce overly lengthy REs; a problem addressed in further research [17,19]. Incremental algorithms do not lend themselves well to generating *relational REs* [22], that identify a target through a relation to another entity (e.g., "the dog near the house"). Relational REs are best modelled with a graph (the *scene graph*), where relations between entities are represented as edges that link the corresponding nodes; the generation of referring expressions reduces to searching a subgraph (the *description graph*) that uniquely identifies the target [21]. Croitoru and van Deemter take this graph approach a step further and propose the use of *conceptual graphs*, a logic-based knowledge representation model that enriches the *factual knowledge* with *ontological knowledge* (i.e., background knowledge, e.g., "a cup is a vessel") [6]. The ontological knowledge is particularly useful to perform automatic inference. Other approaches turn to description logics as an alternative knowledge representation model [2,26]. Similar to conceptual graphs, description logics can model background knowledge and apply reasoning.

Nevertheless, the approaches discussed earlier have difficulties scaling to today's knowledge graphs. Galárraga et al. introduced an algorithm named

REMI that mines intuitive REs from a knowledge base [16]. The intuitiveness of a RE is computed with the Kolmogorov distance as a trade-off between its length and the use of properties which people are familiar with (e.g., Paris is better described as the capital of France than the birth place of Voltaire). REMI represents expressions that describe a target entity x in a tree that represents conjunctions of atoms (e.g., cityIn(x,y) ∧ officialLanguage(y, z) ∧ langFamily(z, Romance)) and identifies the RE that has the least cost in terms of intuitiveness through a depth first search with backtracking. Our proposed *RE-miner* algorithm differs from the previous ones by addressing some of the challenges in the field. It discovers not just one, but all referring expressions complementary to those that can be obtained by instantiating key properties. Moreover, to the best of our knowledge, this is the first work that exerts REs that are useful for linking instances of two knowledge graphs.

Link Discovery. Schema matching is the task of deriving alignments between classes and relation in two different knowledge graphs [11]. Instance matching, or data linking, is the ability to determine – with a certain degree of confidence – that two individuals refer to the same real-world object [15]. Many different approaches for schema matching and instance matching have been proposed [11, 25]. These link discovery approaches can fall into 3 different categories regarding how they include schema and instance matching in their workflow.

Some systems only focus on instance matching. Among these systems, some depend on declared linkage rules that can be used to logically infer identity links [1,12] while others compute a similarity score thanks to complex rules that can involve simple similarity measures and aggregation functions, like LIMES or Silk [24,34]. Such rules are generally based on sets of discriminative properties or more complex graph patterns, such as OWL2 keys, and schema mappings. Since such properties are not so easy to specify, some approaches aim to discover discriminative properties using one or several knowledge graphs, assuming that the mappings are known [30–32], or allowing to discover keys that involve property mappings [4]. Other approaches can efficiently discover linkage points which are related property paths sharing values between heterogeneous data sources. Indeed, it has been shown that such properties can enhance the performance of linkage algorithms [18]. However, the efficiency of such rule-based approaches is strongly related to the quality of the discriminative properties and to the proportion of instances that can be covered by them. Some approaches have defined the quality of a key with respect to a specified linking task. In [32], keys obtained in two datasets can be merged to generate valid keys on both datasets, while in [13], keys that involve syntactically similar literals in both datasets are chosen. Nevertheless, no approach has been defined to discover and exploit linkage rules that are based on REs. Other systems only focus on schema matching. These systems usually exploit terminological similarities, structural similarities, similarity of instances, external resources, or logical axioms to discover more or less complex schema mappings (e.g., [5,10]).

Finally, some systems do instance and schema matching in their ontology matching processes (e.g., [14,20,29,33]). Some of these systems like PARIS and ILIADS perform interleaved schema matching and instance matching in iterations where the mappings from one task help refine those of the other task [29,33].

In this paper, we focus on the instance matching task, and more precisely, we aim to discover REs that can be useful for data linking. We assume that a link discovery approach has provided a subset of class and property mappings. It's worth mentioning that in data linking approaches where schema matching is to be known, the mappings do not necessarily have to be the complete set of mappings between properties and classes, and very simple approaches can be used. For instance, in the Knowledge Graph track of OAEI 2019[2], the baseline solution adopting a terminological approach, and using only schema labels, has achieved an F-measure of 0.79 for mapping properties.

3 Problem Statement

Knowledge Graph. A knowledge graph $\mathcal{G}$ is defined by a couple $(\mathcal{O}, \mathcal{F})$ where: the ontology $\mathcal{O} = (\mathcal{C}, \mathcal{DP}, \mathcal{OP}, \mathcal{A})$ is defined by a set of classes $\mathcal{C}$, a set of *owl:DataTypeProperty* $\mathcal{DP}$, a set of *owl:ObjectProperty* $\mathcal{OP}$, and a set of axioms $\mathcal{A}$; $\mathcal{F}$ is a collection of triples (subject, property, object) $\in (\mathcal{I} \cup \mathcal{B}) \times (\mathcal{OP} \cup \mathcal{DP}) \times (\mathcal{I} \cup \mathcal{C} \cup \mathcal{L} \cup \mathcal{B})$[3] where $\mathcal{I}$ is a set of individuals, $\mathcal{B}$ is a set of blank nodes, and $\mathcal{L}$ is a set of Literals.

In this work, we consider referring expressions that are valid for an individual u of a class C in a knowledge graph G, that are defined as follows:

Definition 1 ***(Referring Expression).*** *A referring expression, denoted by $RE_k(u)$ for the kth RE of a given individual u, of a class C can be expressed by the following first order logic formula:*

$$C(x) \bigwedge_{p_i \in \mathcal{OP} \cup \mathcal{DP}} p_i(w, y)$$

such that the formula, existentially closed, is restricted to those conjunctions of atoms that form a connected graph pattern rooted at x with the leaves being either an individual in $\mathcal{I}$ or a literal in $\mathcal{L}$, and the other nodes being variables.

Definition 2 ***(Referring Expression Validity).*** *A referring expression $RE_k(u)$ is valid in a dataset D if it holds when x is instantiated by u and does not hold for any other individual $v \neq u$ of C in D.*

[2] http://ceur-ws.org/Vol-2536/oaei19_paper0.pdf.
[3] We do not consider blank nodes in this work.

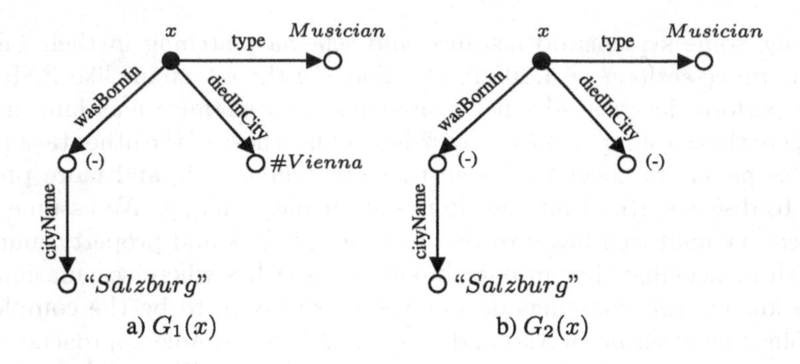

Fig. 1. Two graph patterns. $G_1(x)$ is compliant with Definition 1 and $G_2(x)$ is not.

Example. Two graph patterns $G_1(x)$ and $G_2(x)$ are shown in Fig. 1 where $(-)$ indicates a variable. $G_1(x)$ is compliant with Definition 1 and is a valid referring expression for Mozart: a **musician** who was born in a city named Salzburg and who died in Vienna. $Musician(x) \wedge wasBornIn(x, c) \wedge cityName(c, \text{"}Salzburg\text{"}) \wedge diedInCity(x, \#Vienna)$ Nevertheless, $G_2(x)$ is not compliant with Definition 1, since in this work we do not consider referring expressions that include variables appearing in the leaves of the graph pattern; hence, the following cannot be discovered as a RE.

$$Musician(x) \wedge wasBornIn(x, c) \wedge cityName(c, \text{"}Salzburg\text{"}) \wedge diedInCity(x, z)$$

Propelled by data linking, we aim to discover **minimal** referring expressions; that are the simplest graph patterns allowing to distinguish one individual from all the others.

Definition 3 ***(Referring Expression Minimality).*** *A referring expression $RE_k(u)$ is minimal iff:*

$$\nexists\, RE_j(u) \ s.t. \ (RE_k(u) \cup \mathcal{F} \cup \mathcal{A}) \models RE_j(u)$$

To focus on REs that are of interest to link data when datasets are incomplete, we exploit various properties while limiting the number of REs and their complexity. Hence, we do not construct REs that involve different instantiations of the same property, and we only consider **diversified** REs, simply meaning that when a valued property appears in a RE for an individual, it cannot reappear in another RE for the same individual having more atoms. This should not be confused with the notion of minimality.

Example. Take the valid $RE_1(u)$ for the film *Ocean's Eleven*: $Film(x) \wedge hasActor(x, \#George\_Clooney) \wedge wasCreatedOnYear(x, \text{"2001"})$. Then the following $RE_2(u)$, although valid for this movie and minimal, will not be discovered. $Film(x) \wedge hasActor(x, \#Julia\_Roberts) \wedge wasCreatedOnYear(x, \text{"2001"}) \wedge editedBy(x, \#Stephen\_Mirrione)$. Because $RE_2(u)$ is not diversified; since it has more atoms than $RE_1(u)$ while sharing the subgraph pattern $wasCreatedOnYear(x, \text{"2001"})$ with it.

Definition 4 ***(Diversified Referring Expression).*** *A referring expression $RE_i(u)$ is* **diversified** *if there is no $RE_j(u)$ with fewer number of atoms that contains a subgraph $p1(x,t_1) \wedge \ldots \wedge p_i(t_{i-1},t_i) \wedge p_m(t_{m-1},v_m)$ of $RE_i(u)$, where $v_m \in \mathcal{L} \cup \mathcal{I}$.*

Additionally, in the data linking task, one might argue that graph patterns that involve mostly IRIs of individuals are not relevant. Indeed, individuals that are described in two knowledge graphs are rarely represented with the same IRI. This is why we also consider Expanded REs that are not minimal but where the individuals' IRIs in a RE are replaced by a description constructed from instantiated key properties.

Definition 5 ***(Referring Expression Expansion).*** *The expansion $exp(RE_k(u))$ of a referring expression $RE_k(u)$ is a set of referring expressions in which, each leaf node n_i of $RE_k(u)$ that represents an individual i is replaced by an existential variable x_j. These variables are recursively expanded by a subgraph G rooted by n_i representing one possible instantiation of a key K for the class typing i, such that $exp(RE_k(u))$ leads to a graph pattern whose leaves are only literals.*

Example. Consider the following referring expression for Marie Curie: $Scientist(x) \wedge wasBornOnYear(x, \text{“1867”}) \wedge isCitizenOf(x, \#Poland)$. We observe that Poland is a leaf node representing an individual, thus we can expand it by creating keys for the class country (range of the property $isCitizenOf$). Suppose it has two sets of keys, namely $\{hasName\}$ and $\{hasArea,\ isLocatedIn\}$. We obtain the following RE when $\#Poland$ is replaced by an instantiation of the first key set: $Scientist(x) \wedge wasBornOnYear(x, \text{“1867”}) \wedge isCitizenOf(x,y) \wedge hasName(y, \text{“Poland”})$. And the following RE, when using the second set of key for country, and subsequently expanding $\#europe$ by considering $\{hasName\}$ as a key for the class location (range of the property $isLocatedIn$): $Scientist(x) \wedge wasBornOnYear(x, \text{“1867”}) \wedge isCitizenOf(x,y) \wedge hasArea(y, \text{“312,696} < km2 > \text{”})$ $\wedge isLocatedIn(y,z) \wedge hasName(z, \text{“europe”})$.

4 Referring Expression Generation Approach

In this section, we present an approach to automatically discover minimal and diversified REs for each instance within a class of a knowledge graph.

Our generation approach is composed of two successive steps. We first generate the set of minimal and diversified REs for each instance using the algorithm *RE-miner*. Since recent approaches have been developed to discover keys, we focus on complementary REs that do not represent an instantiated key. In a second step, we can generate the expansion of each RE.

4.1 Keys, Non-keys and Complementary REs

In a knowledge graph, an OWL2 key can be defined as follows:

Definition 6 ***(Key).*** *A key* $\{p_1, \ldots, p_n\}$ *for a class* C *expresses that:*

$$\forall x \forall y \forall z_1 ... z_n (C(x) \wedge C(y) \wedge \bigwedge_{i=1}^{n} (p_i(x, z_i) \wedge p_i(y, z_i)) \rightarrow x = y)$$

By definition, each instantiation of the key properties for a class $\mathcal{C}$ will uniquely identify an individual present in $\mathcal{C}$. This instantiation will potentially yield many REs. Nevertheless, this does not represent the complete set of possible minimal REs that can be discovered. We are thus interested in enriching this set with those REs that only involve non-key properties. To this end, we will only exploit sets of properties that are included in one of the maximal non-keys of class $\mathcal{C}$ to construct complementary REs.

Definition 7 ***(Maximal Non-Key).*** *A maximal non-key for a class* $\mathcal{C}$ *in a knowledge graph* $\mathcal{G}$ *is a set of properties* P *such that* P *is not a key, but the addition of any property to* P *makes it a key for that class.*

4.2 RE-miner Algorithm

We outline the procedure of mining the complete set of complementary, minimal, and diversified REs in Algorithm 1. To retain a reasonable search space and to prevent the REs from becoming too complex for data linking, the depth of the aimed REs is restricted to 2. Nevertheless, this restriction can be dropped by applying a recursive adaptation of the function $existentialRE(\mathcal{G}, RE_{new})$ (see line 10 of Algorithm 1). The algorithm takes as input a knowledge graph $\mathcal{G}$, a class $\mathcal{C}$, and a Boolean E which is set to True if we aim to mine REs at depth 2 (i.e., REs that contain at least an existential quantifier). If the E is False, the REs will not contain any existential quantifiers.

To generate the set of REs for a given class $\mathcal{C}$ of knowledge graph $\mathcal{G}$, we first create the dataset for that class. This dataset will serve as the search space SS (line 1), and is created by keeping all the facts (s, p, o) in $\mathcal{G}$ whose subjects s belong to $\mathcal{C}$. Then using SAKey [30], a key discovery approach, we create the maximal non-key sets NK of the dataset $\mathcal{SS}$ (line 2). We build the powerset, excluding the empty set, of each set in NK, and group them based on their cardinality (line 3). For instance, imagine that NK $= \{\{p_1, p_2\}, \{p_3, p_4, p_5\}\}$; then level 1, includes subsets of cardinality 1, composed of $\{\{p_1\}, \{p_2\}, \{p_3\}, \{p_4\}, \{p_5\}\}$, level 2 composed of $\{\{p_1, p_2\}, \{p_3, p_4\}, \{p_3, p_5\}, \{p_4, p_5\}\}$, and level 3 containing $\{\{p_3, p_4, p_5\}\}$.

Since we desire to find minimal REs, the algorithm proceeds level by level (line 4), starting from level 1, which results in REs containing only one atom. To mine REs at level l, we take one set of properties P within that level at a time (line 6). The algorithm generates subgraph patterns from the search space with instantiated properties P (e.g. $p_1(x, v)$ for level 1 and $p_1(x, y) \wedge p_2(x, z)$ for level 2) as candidate expressions (line 7). We keep the valid REs, among the candidates in RE_{new} (line 8); these expressions are compliant with Definition 2 and hence uniquely identify an individual of the class $\mathcal{C}$. If we also aim to find REs of depth 2, i.e., if E is True, the *existentialRE* algorithm detailed in 2 is called on the knowledge graph $\mathcal{G}$ and REs found at level l with properties P (line 10). We add all the recently discovered REs composed of properties P, to RE_{level} (line 12), and reiterate until all sets of properties at this level are covered. Then RE_{level} is added to the resulting REs (line 14), and all the facts (s, p, o) involved in these referring expressions are removed from the search space; to ensure both minimality and diversity (line 14).

Algorithm 1: RE-miner

```
   Input: A knowledge graph: G, a class: C, a Boolean:E
   Output: The set of minimal REs for instances of type C: RE_set
 1 SS ← createData (G, C) // serves as the search space
 2 NK ← generateNK(SS)
 3 createRankedPowerset(NK) // Dictionary level to props
 4 for level = 1 to |longestNonKey| do
 5 |   RE_level = ∅
 6 |   foreach P ∈ props.level do
 7 |   |   RE_candidates ← constructSubgraphs (SS, P)
 8 |   |   RE_new = validSubgraphs(RE_candidates)
 9 |   |   if E = True then
10 |   |   |   RE_new.add(existentialRE(G), RE_new)
11 |   |   end
12 |   |   RE_level.add(RE_new)
13 |   end
14 |   RE_set.add(RE_level)
15 |   SS ← suppressFacts (SS, RE_level) // reduce the search space to
   |   preserve minimality and diversity
16 end
17 return RE_set
```

As stated in Algorithm 1, we can mine more complex REs containing the existential quantifier where the depth of the subgraph patterns will be 2. To do so, all the REs at a level l composed of properties P, are passed to the *existentialRE* algorithm. The output of this algorithm will be a set of referring expressions, each containing one or more existential quantifiers. The details are sketched in Algorithm 2.

This algorithm starts by keeping a copy of RE_{new} in the RE existential candidate set (line 1). This candidate set will grow as the algorithm proceeds. We iterate over each property p in P (line 2) and get its range using $\mathcal{G}$'s schema (line 3). Let the range of p be the class $\mathcal{C}'$. If not all the instances of the class $\mathcal{C}'$ are literals, we can expand the leaf node with a subgraph pattern; else, we move on to the next property (line 4). These subgraph patterns should be chosen such that when replaced, the whole pattern remains a valid RE. To this end, using RE-miner, Algorithm 1, we construct REs of depth 1, by setting E to False, for the class $\mathcal{C}'$ (line 5). It should be noted that to have the complete and minimal resulting $RE_{existential}$, when creating the dataset for $\mathcal{C}'$ (line 1 of Algorithm 1), we only keep those instances $o \in \mathcal{C}'$ that are involved in such facts $(s, p, o)|s \in \mathcal{C}$. The resulting REs from RE-miner are kept in *inducedSubgraphs* (line 5). Then for each referring expression in the candidate set (line 6), we replace the applicable node, based on p, with the appropriate subgraph in *inducedSubgraphs* (line 7). In the end, we remove the REs of depth one RE_{new} we had added initially to the existential candidate set (line 10), and return the unique subgraphs, which are valid referring expressions having depth 2 (line 11).

Algorithm 2: existentialRE

```
   Input: A knowledge graph: G, a set of REs having properties P: RE_new
   Output: The set of REs with existential variable : RE_existential
 1 RE_existentialCands = RE_new.copy()
 2 foreach p ∈ P do
 3     C' ← getRange(G, p)
 4     if exists an instance of C' ∈ I then
 5         inducedSubgraphs ← RE-miner(G, C', E= False)
 6         foreach RE ∈ RE_existentialCands do
 7             RE_existentialCands.add(replaceNodeSubgraph(RE, p,
               inducedSubgraphs))
 8         end
 9     end
10     RE_existentialCands.remove(RE_new)
11     RE_existential = validSubgraphs(RE_existentialCands)
12 end
13 return RE_existential
```

4.3 RE Expansion

We have developed a post-processing step to obtain the expansion of referring expressions discovered by *RE-miner*, as defined in Definition 5. To do so, given a *RE*, for every IRI u appearing in the leaves of *RE*, we exploit the set of minimal keys of the class u belongs to and expand the *RE* by instantiating properties of every minimal key. If the keys involve object properties, this step is re-performed recursively on the generated IRIs until either reaches a maximum depth d specified beforehand, or the leaves only correspond to literal values. The sets of minimal keys are generated each time a new class is considered, and are stored on the disk so that there's no need to regenerate them to expand another RE. The graphs resulting from the expansion of one IRI are then combined to other IRI expansions to finally construct expanded REs.

5 Data Linking with REs

Each $RE(u)$ declared for an individual u in the source dataset D_1 can be expressed by a linking rule as follows:

$$\forall x RE(x) \rightarrow sameAs(x, u)$$

where $RE(x)$ can be rewritten using the classes and properties of a target dataset D_2 at the linking step. These rules can be represented in SWRL[4]. Hence, to discover identity links between individuals described in two given datasets, we focus on referring expressions that only involve mapped properties, and individuals belonging to classes that have been aligned. Such mappings can be obtained using existing schema matching techniques discussed in Sect. 2.

The linkage rules introduced above can be used either logically to deduce identity links, or by linking tools where simple similarity measures and aggregation functions can be introduced. Since available existing linking tools like [23,24,34] do not consider such intricate graph patterns (i.e., not just paths of properties), we have developed a simple bottom-up approach explained in Fig. 2, where normalizations or classical similarity measures can be declared and applied to datatype properties.

We consider a data linking problem between a source dataset in which the REs are discovered and other target datasets that have a non-empty set of properties mapped to the source dataset (that can be obtained using ontology alignment tools [11]). The linking process is comprised of exploiting for every individual u in the source dataset, the set of distinct $RE(u)$s to find all the individuals x in the target datasets that check $RE(u)$. When a RE is discovered in the source dataset, it cannot necessarily be assumed valid for other target datasets. Indeed, even if the source dataset is voluminous, several distinct individuals that can instantiate a RE may exist in the other dataset. Theoretically, when the unique name assumption (UNA) is fulfilled, only one $sameAs(u, x)$ link can be found for a given $RE(u)$ in the target dataset. If this is the case, the quality of $RE(u)$ has to be weakened. Therefore, we assign to every $RE(u)$ a confidence degree inverse proportional to the number of distinct links the $RE(u)$ finds.

To pick the best identity link(s), we adopt a voting strategy that assigns a weight to each link. This weight is the sum of the RE confidence degrees that can be instantiated to generate the link. Eventually, the instance(s) associated with the link(s) having the highest score is selected. The RE confidence degrees can then be stored and updated when another data linking task is performed on the source dataset.

---

[4] https://www.w3.org/Submission/SWRL/.

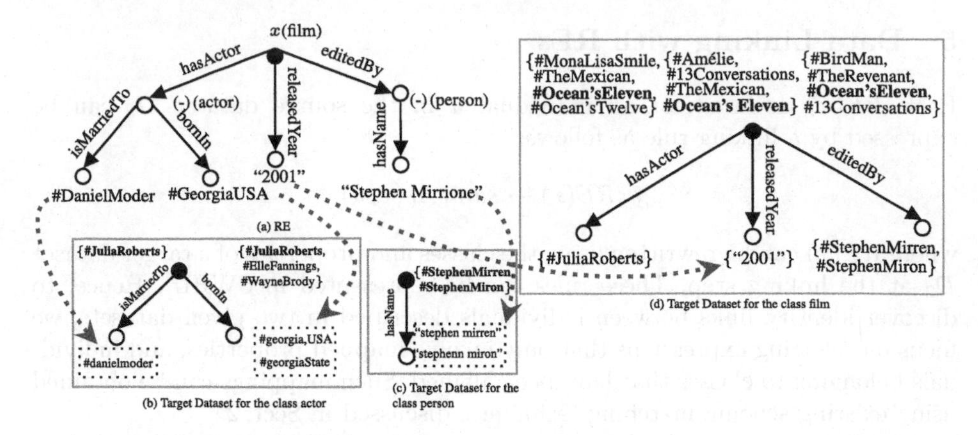

Fig. 2. Bottom-up linking with $RE_k(u)$. (a) is a valid RE for the film *Ocean's Eleven* in the source dataset. We adopt a bottom-up approach where the traversal begins from leaf nodes. (b,c) For each of the RE's leaf nodes n_i in (x, p, n_i), verifies the matches (s, p, o) in the target dataset for the class of x; such that o has a high similarity with n_i. (d) The matches are intersected at the internal nodes, until those intersections at the root are reported as the links.

6 Experimental Evaluation

To evaluate *RE-miner*, we conducted two series of experiments. The first is quantitative that is dedicated to studying the scalability of the proposed algorithm. In the second series of experiments, we explored how REs can contribute to the data linking task.

All experiments are run on a single machine with processor 2.7 GHz, 8 cores, and 16 GB of RAM that runs Mac OS X 10.13. The source code of our approach is publicly available[5].

6.1 Datasets

We summarize the characteristics of the 3 datasets on which we did our experiments.

DBpedia-YAGO.[6] We use 10 different classes of YAGO and DBpedia knowledge graphs. The data for these 10 classes are the same data used in VICKEY [31], where the properties of the two knowledge graphs have been aligned manually. Moreover, the properties of YAGO have been rewritten using their DBpedia counterparts. This dataset contains 206,736 ground truth entity pairs.

[5] https://github.com/iswc2020/REGeneratipnAndLinking.
[6] https://github.com/lgalarra/vickey.

IM@OAEI2019.[7] We use the Sandbox SPIMBENCH dataset of the instance matching track at OAEI 2019, its gold standard is available and consists of 300 entity pairs. This dataset is composed of a Tbox and an Abox for each of the source and target ontologies. The goal of the task is to match instances describing the same *Creative Work*, which can be a news item, blog post, or a program.

IM@OAEI2011.[8] We use IIMB (ISLab Instance Matching Benchmark) dataset which consists of a set of interlinking tasks used by the instance matching track of OAEI 2011. The source dataset (File 000) describes movies, locations, actors, etc. Files 001 to 080 are generated by applying several transformations to the source dataset. For each of these files, a gold standard containing around 12.3k identity links has been provided.

6.2 Quantitative Results

Here, we study the scalability of our approach and will report the number of REs found on average for each individual in the considered knowledge graph, as well as the average number of nodes in the graphs representing the discovered REs; first at depth 1 and then at depth 2.

Initially, we run *RE-miner* on the 10 classes of YAGO at depth 1, i.e., without allowing for any existential variables. Table 1 details the characteristics of each of these 10 classes. Furthermore, this table shows the number of discovered referring expressions for each class as well as their run time. We can observe that the process takes less than 2 min for all classes except for organization, which took more than 3 hours to complete[9]. On average, there are less than 7 REs per individual for all classes, except for the most voluminous class organization with almost 158 REs for each individual. Without having limited the number of discovered REs' atoms, these expressions do not tend to be complex; the maximum number of atoms among all 10 classes is 4 and on average, each RE has 2 atoms or less[10].

Example. The following examples translated to natural language, have been chosen among the REs of depth 1: (i) Yellow Submarine is an album created by the Beatles on date 1966-05-26. (ii) MIT university's motto is *mind and hand.* (iii) Charles Louis Alphonse Laveran is a scientist who was born on year 1845 in Paris, graduated from university of Strasbourg and has won the Nobel prize in Physiology or Medicine.

Similar results have been obtained on OAEI2011 and OAEI2019 datasets with 1.19 and 3.75 average atoms and a maximum of 4 and 8 atoms, respectively (see Table 4).

---

[7] https://project-hobbit.eu/challenges/om2019/.

[8] http://oaei.ontologymatching.org/2011/instance/index.html.

[9] Note that the non-key sets had been computed beforehand in all experiments.

[10] Note that the rdf: type properties are not being counted in number of atoms.

Table 1. Class statistics, number of non-keys (#NKs), number of discovered REs at depth 1 (#REs), runtime, and size of the REs

Class	#triples	#instances	#properties	#NKs	#REs	runtime	max#atoms	avg#atoms
Museum	81.6k	21.1k	7	5	53.5k	2.6 s	3	1.23
Mountain	116.7k	32.9k	6	4	59.2k	1.4 s	3	1.28
Book	123.6k	41.8k	7	6	66.3k	3.5 s	3	1.27
University	131.8k	23.3k	9	9	161.8k	17.7 s	3	1.62
Scientist	335.6k	93.1k	18	92	309.9k	64.0 s	4	1.58
Album	381.1k	137.1k	5	2	212.1k	14.7 s	3	1.30
Actor	514.7k	108.4k	16	69	725.6k	95.1 s	3	1.74
Film	533.5k	123.9k	9	7	690.9k	102.3 s	4	1.77
City	1.1M	83.5k	17	29	1.2M	109.7 s	3	1.23
Organization	2.2M	430.3k	17	43	68.3M	3.48 h	4	2.05

To show how many more REs can be found at depth 2 (i.e., REs that contain at least an existential quantifier), we run *RE-miner* with the Boolean E set to True, on the 3 classes of YAGO having the least number of referring expressions at depth 1. As described in Sect. 4.2, the algorithm should create the dataset for the class the variable belongs to. To this end, we use instances of this class and all its sub-classes in the non-saturated (i.e., no OWL2 entailment rule has been applied) YAGO version 3.1[11] to ensure having a dataset with at least 1000 instances whenever possible.

Table 2 shows that as expected, many additional REs can be generated at depth 2. However, the proportion of REs that have only literals values at leaf nodes is rather small, and we can use those REs for data linking. On average, these referring expressions have 2 atoms more than REs of depth 1.

Table 2. Number of additional REs detected at depth 2 (#REs), runtime, percentage of REs having only literals in leaf nodes, maximum and average number of atoms.

Class	#REs	runtime	%AllLiterals	max#atoms	avg#atoms
Mountain	150.8k	3006 s	13.4%	6	3.03
Museum	1.4M	3143 s	5.2%	5	3.57
Book	1.3M	1.2 h	2.50%	6	3.47

6.3 Data Linking

Here, we evaluate data linking on the 3 datasets, each time comparing the results with the previous works in the literature that used the same datasets. We study the advantage of using REs of depth 1 and 2, REs plus keys (i.e., the complete set of referring expressions), and expanded REs. For each of the datasets, we

[11] http://resources.mpi-inf.mpg.de/yago-naga/yago3.1/yago3.1_entire_tsv.7z.

compare the results with a baseline approach that picks random subgraph patterns (i.e., random expressions) and uses them for linking just as it is done with referring expressions. To be fair when comparing the random baseline results to that of REs for data linking, for each dataset, a) the number of generated random expressions is the same as that of discovered REs. b) the size of the random baseline's subgraphs comes from the same distribution as the discovered referring expressions. In other words, the same number of random subgraphs and referring expressions with n atoms exist. c) the results for the random baseline are averaged over three runs.

DBpedia-YAGO. We report our linking results on those 8 classes of this dataset for which other approaches had previously published results. We have used all REs of depth 1 whose statistics were delineated in Table 1, with strict string equality. The quality of linking results is reported in terms of precision, recall and F-measure, and is compared to the results of linking with keys (Ks), keys and conditional keys (Ks+CKs) reported in [31], ontological graph keys (OGK) reported in [23], and the random baseline (RBL). A conditional key is a valid key for a specified part of a class's instances [31]. Ontological graph keys defined in [23] are a variant of keys defined by a graph pattern extended by ontological pattern matching. Table 3 shows that RE-miner outperforms the other approaches in terms of recall and F-measure on all classes except book. More precisely, only using REs of depth 1, we can detect much more correct links without having a significant change to the precision. We also observe that the baseline solution – taking thousands to million of random subgraphs, depending on the dataset, and using them for linking – results in much lower scores than REs; showcasing that using the referring expressions discovered through RE-miner are indeed effective for linking.

Table 3. Linking results with keys (Ks), conditional keys and keys (Ks+CKs), ontological graph keys (OGK), random baseline (RBL), and REs of depth 1.

Class	Recall					Precision					F1				
	Ks	Ks+CKs	OGK	RBL	REs	Ks	Ks+CKs	OGK	RBL	REs	Ks	Ks+CKs	OGK	RBL	REs
Actor	0.27	0.60	0.66	0.19	**0.69**	0.99	0.99	1.00	0.37	0.99	0.43	0.75	0.79	0.25	**0.81**
Album	0.00	0.15	–	0.35	**0.65**	1.00	0.99	–	0.22	0.98	0.00	0.26	–	0.27	**0.78**
Book	0.03	0.13	**0.85**	0.12	0.80	1.00	0.99	0.97	0.38	0.98	0.06	0.23	**0.90**	0.18	0.88
Film	0.04	0.39	–	0.30	**0.73**	0.99	0.98	–	0.73	0.94	0.08	0.55	–	0.43	**0.82**
Mountain	0.00	0.29	–	0.05	**0.78**	1.00	0.99	–	0.08	0.99	0.00	0.45	–	0.06	**0.87**
Museum	0.00	0.29	0.42	0.20	**0.85**	1.00	0.99	0.99	0.34	0.99	0.00	0.45	0.58	0.25	**0.91**
Scientist	0.00	0.29	0.67	0.24	**0.70**	1.00	0.99	0.99	0.14	0.99	0.00	0.45	0.80	0.18	**0.82**
University	0.09	0.25	0.50	0.29	**0.68**	0.99	0.99	0.96	0.64	0.98	0.16	0.40	0.66	0.40	**0.80**

IM@OAEI2011. We first evaluate our data linking results on the entire IIMB dataset. IIMB is made of 13 different classes (e.g., person, actor, location, etc.); 5 of which are at the top of the ontology according to the schema. We create the saturated dataset for these 5 classes and discover all minimal and diversified REs of depth 1 and 2 on the source file 000. We use these REs to find identity links in each of the files 001 to 010. The accuracy measures reported in Table 4 are averaged over these 10 files to compare to the results of the Combinatorial Optimization for Data Integration (CODI) system [20], which reformulates the alignment problem as a maximum-a-posteriori optimization problem. We can observe that *RE-miner* outperforms CODI by a large margin of 12% to 7% in recall and F-measure. Also the baseline solution, which generates 1.3 M random expressions regardless of being RE or not, exhibits poor results. Similar to the previous datasets, this performance reassures us that RE-miner algorithm is indeed beneficial for linking. We also investigated the effects of using expanded RE and observed that it helps increase the recall by 5.1% on average, over REs of depth 1.

Moreover, we compare data linking results using the discovered REs, on the class Film, against data linking with keys reported in [3]. We obtained a high F-measure of 99% and gained about 70% increase in the recall.

Table 4. Class statistics and linking results of REs+keys, random baseline (RBL), and other systems compared to results with REs of depth 1 and 2 on IM@OAEI2011 dataset and the class Film of IM@OAEI2011, and with REs of depth 1 on IM@OAEI2019 dataset.

Dataset	#classes	#triples	#properties	#NKs	#REs	System	Precision	Recall	F-measure
IIMB OAEI 2011	13	87.3k	23	17	1.3M	REs	0.92	0.87	0.90
						REs+Ks	0.93	**0.88**	**0.91**
						CODI	**0.94**	0.76	0.84
						RBL	0.69	0.29	0.41
Film OAEI 2011	1	11.8k	13	4	1.2M	REs	0.99	**0.98**	**0.99**
						Ks	**1.00**	0.27	0.43
						REs+Ks	0.99	**0.98**	**0.99**
						RBL	0.89	0.03	0.06
SPIMBENCH OAEI 2019	1	6.2k	18	3	1.6k	REs	0.98	0.84	0.91
						REs+Ks	**0.99**	0.99	**0.99**
						Lily	0.84	**1.00**	0.91
						AML	0.83	0.89	0.86
						FTRLIM	0.85	**1.00**	0.92
						RBL	0.78	0.87	0.82

IM@OAEI2019. We report the linking results using the discovered REs of depth 1 for the *Creative Work* class on the source dataset of SPIMBENCH; as the datasets were not saturated, we could not mine and use REs of depth 2 for linking. We compare our results to the 3 systems with the best performances in the competition[12]: Lily, AML, and FTRLIM, as well as the baseline solution. Looking at Table 4, we observe that the random baseline approach is the least effective and that REs alone have comparable performance to the other 3

[12] http://ceur-ws.org/Vol-2536/oaei19_paper0.pdf.

systems. However, when combined with the instantiation of keys, resulting in the full set of REs, they outperform all other systems achieving an F-measure of 99%. The average confidence of the discovered links is 85.5%, whereas this number increases to 97.9% among the links that are picked through the voting strategy described in Sect. 5.

Relevancy of Diversity. We also performed another set of experiments to observe the effects discovering diversified REs brings to the data linking task. By modifying the RE-miner algorithm, we discovered all minimal REs on the same 3 classes of DBpedia-YAGO dataset presented in Table 2. We observed a considerable increase in the number of discovered REs (e.g., it almost doubled for the class book); whereas the recall and F-measure of the linking task either remained the same or slightly decreased (e.g., for the class book, it dropped by 2%). These results support that the use of diversity as a quality criterion for referring expressions proves beneficial in limiting the number of REs while preserving the quality of data linking.

To sum, we showed that using REs improves data linking results compared to previous works and the random baseline. The results were verified on different datasets containing classes with 5 to 23 properties and 300 to 137k instances.

7 Conclusion

In this paper, we proposed an approach that efficiently discovers referring expressions by reducing the search space thanks to the use of maximal non-keys. The generated REs are adapted to a data linking task through the notions of minimality and diversification and the post-processing step of expansion.

We showed that *RE-Miner* can scale to classes consisting of millions of triples and that the defined REs can significantly improve the performance of instance matching and increase the recall of rule-based data linking methods.

As future work, we aim to refine REs by virtue of data linking, whereby if a RE finds more than one match in the target dataset, we can deduce that some information had been missing in the source dataset and hence can add the new relevant facts to the source knowledge graph.

Acknowledgements. This work has been supported by the project PSPC AIDA: 2019-PSPC-09 funded by BPI-France.

References

1. Al-Bakri, M., Atencia, M., Lalande, S., Rousset, M.: Inferring same-as facts from linked data: an iterative import-by-query approach. In: Proceedings of the Twenty-Ninth AAAI Conference on Artificial Intelligence, Texas, USA, pp. 9–15. AAAI Press (2015)
2. Areces, C., Koller, A., Striegnitz, K.: Referring expressions as formulas of description logic. In: Fifth International Natural Language Generation Conference, pp. 42–49. ACL (2008)

3. Atencia, M., et al.: Defining key semantics for the RDF datasets: experiments and evaluations. In: Hernandez, N., Jäschke, R., Croitoru, M. (eds.) ICCS 2014. LNCS (LNAI), vol. 8577, pp. 65–78. Springer, Cham (2014). https://doi.org/10.1007/978-3-319-08389-6_7
4. Atencia, M., David, J., Euzenat, J., Napoli, A., Vizzini, J.: Link key candidate extraction with relational concept analysis. Discrete Appl. Math. **273**, 2–20 (2019)
5. Aumueller, D., Do, H.H., Massmann, S., Rahm, E.: Schema and ontology matching with coma++. In: Proceedings of the 2005 ACM SIGMOD International Conference on Management of Data, pp. 906–908. Association for Computing Machinery (2005)
6. Croitoru, M., Van Deemter, K.: A conceptual graph approach for the generation of referring expressions. In: IJCAI, pp. 2456–2461 (2007)
7. Dale, R.: Cooking up referring expressions. In: 27th Annual Meeting of the association for Computational Linguistics, pp. 68–75 (1989)
8. Dale, R.: Generating Referring Expressions: Constructing Descriptions in a Domain of Objects and Processes. The MIT Press, Cambridge (1992)
9. Dale, R., Reiter, E.: Computational interpretations of the Gricean maxims in the generation of referring expressions. Cogn. Sci. **19**(2), 233–263 (1995)
10. Doan, A., Domingos, P., Levy, A.: Learning source description for data integration. In: Proceedings of the Third International Workshop on the Web and Databases, in Conjunction with ACM PODS/SIGMOD 2000, pp. 81–86, January 2000
11. Euzenat, J., Shvaiko, P.: Ontology Matching, 2nd edn. Springer, Heidelberg (2013). https://doi.org/10.1007/978-3-642-38721-0
12. Fan, W., Fan, Z., Tian, C., Dong, X.L.: Keys for graphs. PVLDB **8**(12), 1590–1601 (2015)
13. Farah, H., Symeonidou, D., Todorov, K.: KeyRanker: automatic RDF key ranking for data linking. In: Proceedings of the Knowledge Capture Conference, K-CAP 2017, TX, USA, 4–6 December 2017, pp. 7:1–7:8. ACM (2017)
14. Faria, D., Pesquita, C., Santos, E., Palmonari, M., Cruz, I.F., Couto, F.M.: The AgreementMakerLight ontology matching system. In: Meersman, R., et al. (eds.) OTM 2013. LNCS, vol. 8185, pp. 527–541. Springer, Heidelberg (2013). https://doi.org/10.1007/978-3-642-41030-7_38
15. Ferrara, A., Nikolov, A., Scharffe, F.: Data linking for the semantic web. Int. J. Semant. Web Inf. Syst. (IJSWIS) **7**(3), 46–76 (2011)
16. Galárraga, L., Delaunay, J., Dessalles, J.: REMI: mining intuitive referring expressions on knowledge bases. In: Proceedings of the 23nd International Conference on Extending Database Technology, EDBT 2020, Denmark, pp. 387–390. OpenProceedings.org (2020)
17. Gardent, C.: Generating minimal definite descriptions. In: Proceedings of the 40th Annual Meeting on Association for Computational Linguistics, pp. 96–103. ACL (2002)
18. Hassanzadeh, O., et al.: Discovering linkage points over web data. Proc. VLDB Endow. **6**(6), 445–456 (2013)
19. Horacek, H.: On referring to sets of objects naturally. In: Belz, A., Evans, R., Piwek, P. (eds.) INLG 2004. LNCS (LNAI), vol. 3123, pp. 70–79. Springer, Heidelberg (2004). https://doi.org/10.1007/978-3-540-27823-8_8
20. Huber, J., Sztyler, T., Noessner, J., Meilicke, C.: CODI: combinatorial optimization for data integration - results for OAEI 2011. In: Proceedings of the 6th International Conference on Ontology Matching, vol. 814. pp. 134–141. CEUR-WS.org (2011)
21. Krahmer, E., Erk, S.V., Verleg, A.: Graph-based generation of referring expressions. Comput. Linguist. **29**(1), 53–72 (2003)

22. Krahmer, E., Van Deemter, K.: Computational generation of referring expressions: a survey. Comput. Linguist. **38**(1), 173–218 (2012)
23. Ma, H., Alipourlangouri, M., Wu, Y., Chiang, F., Pi, J.: Ontology-based entity matching in attributed graphs. Proc. VLDB Endow. **12**(10), 1195–1207 (2019)
24. Ngonga Ngomo, A.C., Auer, S.: Limes - a time-efficient approach for large-scale link discovery on the web of data. In: IJCAI 2011, Proceedings of the 22nd International Joint Conference on Artificial Intelligence, Barcelona, Catalonia, Spain, pp. 2312–2317, January 2011
25. Rahm, E., Bernstein, P.: A survey of approaches to automatic schema matching. VLDB J. **10**, 334–350 (2001)
26. Ren, Y., Van Deemter, K., Pan, J.Z.: Charting the potential of description logic for the generation of referring expressions. In: Proceedings of the 6th International Natural Language Generation Conference, pp. 115–123. ACL (2010)
27. Ren, Y., Van Deemter, K., Pan, J.Z.: Generating referring expressions with OWL2. In: 23rd International Workshop on Description Logics DL2010, p. 420 (2010)
28. Soru, T., Marx, E., Ngonga Ngomo, A.C.: Rocker: a refinement operator for key discovery. In: Proceedings of the 24th International Conference on WWW, pp. 1025–1033 (2015)
29. Suchanek, F.M., Abiteboul, S., Senellart, P.: Paris: probabilistic alignment of relations, instances, and schema. Proc. VLDB Endow. **5**(3), 157–168 (2011)
30. Symeonidou, D., Armant, V., Pernelle, N., Saïs, F.: SAKey: scalable almost key discovery in RDF data. In: Mika, P., et al. (eds.) ISWC 2014. LNCS, vol. 8796, pp. 33–49. Springer, Cham (2014). https://doi.org/10.1007/978-3-319-11964-9_3
31. Symeonidou, D., Galárraga, L., Pernelle, N., Saïs, F., Suchanek, F.: VICKEY: mining conditional keys on knowledge bases. In: d'Amato, C., et al. (eds.) ISWC 2017. LNCS, vol. 10587, pp. 661–677. Springer, Cham (2017). https://doi.org/10.1007/978-3-319-68288-4_39
32. Symeonidou, D., Pernelle, N., Saïs, F.: KD2R: a key discovery method for semantic reference reconciliation. In: Meersman, R., Dillon, T., Herrero, P. (eds.) OTM 2011. LNCS, vol. 7046, pp. 392–401. Springer, Heidelberg (2011). https://doi.org/10.1007/978-3-642-25126-9_51
33. Udrea, O., Getoor, L., Miller, R.J.: Leveraging data and structure in ontology integration. In: Proceedings of the 2007 ACM SIGMOD International Conference on Management of Data, SIGMOD 2007, pp. 449–460. Association for Computing Machinery (2007)
34. Volz, J., Bizer, C., Gaedke, M., Kobilarov, G.: Silk - a link discovery framework for the web of data. In: LDOW (2009)

Prevalence and Effects of Class Hierarchy Precompilation in Biomedical Ontologies

Christian Kindermann(✉), Bijan Parsia, and Uli Sattler

University of Manchester, Manchester M13 9PL, UK
{christian.kindermann,bijan.parsia,uli.sattler}@manchester.ac.uk

Abstract. It is sometimes claimed that adding inferred axioms, e.g. the inferred class hierarchy (ICH), to an ontology can improve reasoning performance or an ontology's usability in practice. While such beliefs may have an effect on how ontologies are published, there is no conclusive empirical evidence to support them. To develop an understanding of the impact of this practice, both for ontology curators as well as tools, we survey to what extent published ontologies in BioPortal already contain their ICH and most specific class assertions (MSCA). Furthermore, we investigate how added inferred axioms from these sets can affect the performance of standard reasoning tasks such as classification and realisation. We find that axioms from the ICH and MSCA are highly prevalent in published biomedical ontologies. Our reasoning evaluation indicates that added inferred axioms are likely to be inconsequential for reasoning performance. However, we observe instances of both positive as well as negative effects that seem to depend on the used reasoner for a given ontology. These results suggest that the practice of adding inferred axioms during the release process of ontologies should be subject to a task-specific analysis that determines whether desired effects are obtained.

Keywords: Ontology engineering · Reasoning performance · OWL · Web ontology language · BioPortal · Class hierarchy · Concept hierarchy

1 Introduction

In the biomedical domain, there seems to be a belief that adding certain kinds of inferred axioms to an ontology, e.g., its inferred class hierarchy (ICH), may improve the ontology's usability in practice. This is even said to be a fundamental step in the release process of ontologies and is supported by automation tools [7]. However, there are also arguments claiming that redundant subsumption axioms can negatively affect the maintenance burden for ontology curators [13]. Overall, there appears to be a lot of folk-wisdom about the benefits and drawbacks of materialising entailed axioms.

To develop an understanding of the possible impact of this practice, we introduce the notion of *precompilation* to distinguish between substantive and

J. Z. Pan et al. (Eds.): ISWC 2020, LNCS 12506, pp. 330–348, 2020.
https://doi.org/10.1007/978-3-030-62419-4_19

redundant materialisations of entailment sets. We survey to what extent published biomedical ontologies materialise entailment sets derived from the ICH, and how this practice affects reasoning performance. Our results indicate that axioms of such sets are often materialised. While many ontologies contain redundant axioms from the ICH, their relative proportion is often low. We find that precompiling the ICH can positively impact the performance of reasoning tasks. However, this does not hold in general and depends on the reasoning task, the reasoner, and the given ontology itself.

2 Preliminaries

We assume the reader to be familiar with OWL, in particular OWL 2 [3], and only fix some terminology. Let N_C, N_I, and N_P be sets of *class names*, *individual names*, and *property names*. A *class* is either a class name or a *complex class* built using OWL class constructors. In the following, we use DL notation for increased readability; in particular, we use $\mathsf{A} \sqsubseteq \mathsf{B}$ for a subclass axiom between A and B, $\mathsf{A} \equiv \mathsf{B}$ for an equivalence axiom between A and B, $\bot, \top$ for `owl:Thing`, `owl:Nothing`, $\mathsf{A}(a)$ for a class assertion between an individual a and a class A, and write $\mathcal{O} \models \alpha$ to denote that the ontology $\mathcal{O}$ entails the axiom α. We also use $\equiv(\mathsf{A}_1, \ldots, \mathsf{A}_n)$ to denote the n-ary equivalence axiom between the classes A_i and take the OWL view that its parameters are a set, i.e, $\equiv(\mathsf{A}_1, \mathsf{A}_2) = \equiv(\mathsf{A}_2, \mathsf{A}_1)$. In particular, we say that the axioms $\mathsf{A} \sqsubseteq \mathsf{B}$, $\equiv(\mathsf{A}_1, \ldots, \mathsf{A}_n)$ are *atomic* if $\mathsf{A}, \mathsf{B}, \mathsf{A}_1, \ldots, \mathsf{A}_n \in N_C \cup \{\bot, \top\}$. Similarly, we say that the assertion $\mathsf{A}(a)$ is *atomic* if $\mathsf{A} \in N_C \cup \{\bot, \top\}$. Other axioms are called *complex*.

Furthermore, we use $[\mathsf{A}]$ to denote the set $\{\mathsf{A}_i \mid \mathcal{O} \models \mathsf{A} \equiv \mathsf{A}_i\}$ for a class name A in ontology $\mathcal{O}$. By abuse of notation we write $[\mathsf{A}] \sqsubseteq [\mathsf{B}]$ to denote the set of axioms $\{\mathsf{A}' \sqsubseteq \mathsf{B}' \mid \mathsf{A}' \in [\mathsf{A}], \mathsf{B}' \in [\mathsf{B}]\}$ and $[\mathsf{A}](a)$ to denote the set $\{\mathsf{A}_i(a) \mid \mathsf{A} \equiv \mathsf{A}_i\}$.

An *ontology* is a set of axioms. An ontology is *logically empty* if it entails only tautologies. We write $\mathcal{O}_1 \equiv \mathcal{O}_2$ to denote that $\mathcal{O}_1$ and $\mathcal{O}_2$ are equivalent, i.e., have the same models, and use $\mathcal{O}$ for an ontology and $\widetilde{\mathcal{O}}$ for the set of class, property, and individual names in $\mathcal{O}$. Finally, since we are concerned with entailments, we only consider consistent ontologies.

3 Precompilation

We introduce the notion of *precompilation* to capture the idea of systematically adding inferred axioms to an ontology. The characteristics of related axioms are defined in terms of *entailment sets*.

Definition 1 (Entailment Set, Materialisation). *Let $\mathcal{O}$ be an ontology. An* entailment set *of $\mathcal{O}$ is a set of axioms $\mathcal{E}$ such that $\mathcal{O} \models \alpha$ for each $\alpha \in \mathcal{E}$. An entailment set $\mathcal{E}$ is* materialised *in $\mathcal{O}$ if $\mathcal{E} \subseteq \mathcal{O}$.*

Note that an axiom in a materialised entailment set is not necessarily entailed by the remainder of the ontology. For example, consider an ontology $\mathcal{O}$ with a single axiom α. Clearly, the set $\{\alpha\}$ is an entailment set of $\mathcal{O}$ and is materialised. However, unless α is a tautology, removing it from $\mathcal{O}$ changes $\mathcal{O}$'s meaning. Hence, a materialisation may in fact be a substantive part of the ontology as opposed to a semantically redundant addition.

Definition 2 (Redundancy). *An entailment set $\mathcal{E}$ of an ontology $\mathcal{O}$ is* redundant in $\mathcal{O}$ *if $\mathcal{E}$ is also an entailment set of $\mathcal{O} \setminus \mathcal{E}$.*

In the following, we often call an axiom α redundant in $\mathcal{O}$ as a shorthand for $\{\alpha\}$ being redundant in $\mathcal{O}$. Of course, adding entailed axioms to an ontology adds redundancy. To capture the idea of purposefully adding sets of entailed axioms as a form of preprocessing, we propose the notion of *precompilation* as redundant materialisations.

Definition 3 (Precompilation). *An entailment set $\mathcal{E}$ of an ontology $\mathcal{O}$ is* precompiled in $\mathcal{O}$ *if $\mathcal{E}$ is materialised and redundant in $\mathcal{O}$.*

Any entailment set can be partitioned into three (possibly empty) subsets of precompiled, materialised but not redundant, and non-materialised axioms. Note that such a partition is not necessarily unique as we will explain in Sect. 4.

A standard OWL reasoning service is *classification*, i.e., the computation of the entailment set of all atomic subsumption axioms. As discussed in [1], fixing reasonable sets of even atomic entailments is tricky.

Definition 4 (Inferred Class Hierarchy). *The* inferred class hierarchy $\mathsf{ICH}(\mathcal{O})$ *of $\mathcal{O}$ is defined as follows:*

$$\begin{aligned}\mathsf{ICH}(\mathcal{O}) = {} & \{\mathsf{A} \sqsubseteq \mathsf{B} \mid \mathsf{A}, \mathsf{B} \in N_C \cup \{\bot, \top\}, \mathcal{O} \models \mathsf{A} \sqsubseteq \mathsf{B}\} \cup \\ & \{\equiv(\mathsf{A}_1, \ldots, \mathsf{A}_n) \mid \mathsf{A}_1, \ldots, \mathsf{A}_n \in N_C \cup \{\bot, \top\}, \mathcal{O} \models {\equiv}(\mathsf{A}_1, \ldots, \mathsf{A}_n)\}.\end{aligned}$$

While the inferred class hierarchy of an ontology is a well understood and widely used (finite) entailment set, it has been noted that informal references to this set are often understood as some more restrictive subset [1]. In our case, we include redundant versions of equivalence axioms, e.g., if $\equiv(\mathsf{A}_1, \mathsf{A}_2, \mathsf{A}_3) \in \mathsf{ICH}(\mathcal{O})$, then $\equiv(\mathsf{A}_1, \mathsf{A}_2) \in \mathsf{ICH}(\mathcal{O})$. In practice, the ICH is most commonly represented by some form of a transitive *reduct* and may include or exclude tautologies, e.g., $\mathsf{A} \sqsubseteq \top$ or $\bot \sqsubseteq \mathsf{A}$. Therefore, we distinguish between four distinct entailment sets that capture different aspects of an ontology's ICH.

Definition 5 (Transitive Reduct). *A* transitive reduct *of $\mathsf{ICH}(\mathcal{O})$, written $\mathsf{TR}(\mathcal{O})$, is*

1. *a subset of $\mathsf{ICH}(\mathcal{O})$ that is equivalent to $\mathsf{ICH}(\mathcal{O})$ and*
2. *cardinality minimal, i.e., if $\mathcal{O}' \subseteq \mathsf{ICH}(\mathcal{O})$ and $\mathcal{O}' \equiv \mathcal{O}$, then $|\mathsf{TR}(\mathcal{O})| \leq |\mathcal{O}'|$.*

Note that a transitive reduct is not necessarily unique in the presence of equivalences. Consider $\mathcal{O}_{ex} = \{\mathsf{AlaskanMoose} \sqsubseteq \mathsf{Moose}, \mathsf{Moose} \equiv \mathsf{Elk}, \mathsf{Elk} \sqsubseteq \mathsf{Deer}\}$ as an example. Here, $\mathsf{TR}(\mathcal{O}_{ex}) = \mathcal{O}_{ex}$ is only one of four transitive reducts. Also, the transitive reduct mentions $\bot$ iff the ontology contains unsatisfiable classes (which are all gathered in a single maximal equivalence axiom that includes $\bot$). Dually, it mentions $\top$ iff the ontology contains global classes (which are all gathered in a single maximal equivalence axiom that includes $\top$). In case there is only a single global class, this leads to two reducts, one with an equivalence class and one with a subclass axiom with/of $\top$.

Second, we define the set of tautologies that would be included in the transitive reduction of an ontology's class hierarchy if $\bot$ and $\top$ were "normal" class names.

Definition 6 (Tautological Completion). *The* tautological completion $\top\bot\text{-}\mathsf{TR}(\mathcal{O})$ *of* $\mathcal{O}$ *is defined as follows:*

$$\begin{aligned}\top\bot\text{-}\mathsf{TR}(\mathcal{O}) = &\{\mathsf{A} \sqsubseteq \top \mid \mathsf{A} \in N_C \setminus [\top] \textit{ and } \mathcal{O} \models \mathsf{A} \sqsubseteq \mathsf{B} \textit{ implies } \mathsf{B} \in [\mathsf{A}] \cup [\top]\} \cup \\ &\{\bot \sqsubseteq \mathsf{A} \mid \mathsf{A} \in N_C \setminus [\bot] \textit{ and } \mathcal{O} \models \mathsf{B} \sqsubseteq \mathsf{A} \textit{ implies } \mathsf{B} \in [\mathsf{A}] \cup [\bot]\}.\end{aligned}$$

In this definition, $\mathsf{TR}(\mathcal{O})$ occurs unquantified as it does not matter which one we pick in case there are more than one: they only differ in subclass axioms to and from equivalent classes and do not contain tautologies, hence $\top\bot\text{-}\mathsf{TR}(\mathcal{O})$ always contains all subclass axioms between top-level classes (not equivalent to $\top$) and $\top$ and between $\bot$ and bottom-level classes (not equivalent to $\bot$). Continuing our example $\mathcal{O}_{ex}$, we have $\top\bot\text{-}\mathsf{TR}(\mathcal{O}_{ex}) = \{\bot \sqsubseteq \mathsf{AlaskanMoose}, \mathsf{Deer} \sqsubseteq \top\}$.

Third, we define short-cuts in the class hierarchy, i.e., non-tautological but inferred subsumption axioms that are not in any transitive reduction of an ontology's class hierarchy.

Definition 7 (Short Cut). *The set of* short cuts $\mathsf{SC}(\mathcal{O})$ *is an defined as follows:*

$$\mathsf{SC}(\mathcal{O}) = \mathsf{ICH}(\mathcal{O}) \setminus \bigcup_{\mathsf{TR}(\mathcal{O})} (\mathsf{TR}(\mathcal{O}) \cup \top\bot\text{-}\mathsf{TR}(\mathcal{O})).$$

Please note that short cuts can also contain equivalence axioms. For example, consider $\mathcal{O}' = \mathcal{O}_{ex} \cup \{\mathsf{Elk} \equiv \mathsf{AlcesAlces}\}$. Then we have $\mathsf{Moose} \equiv \mathsf{Elk}, \mathsf{Elk} \equiv \mathsf{AlcesAlces} \in \mathsf{SC}(\mathcal{O}')$ because $\equiv(\mathsf{Moose}, \mathsf{Elk}, \mathsf{AlcesAlces}) \in \mathsf{TR}(\mathcal{O}')$ (for all transitive reducts of $\mathcal{O}'$). Also note that short cut axioms are not necessarily redundant in an ontology as demonstrated by the example. Lastly, we define short cut tautologies in an ontology's class hierarchy that are not in the tautological completion of its transitive reduction.

Definition 8 (Short Cut Tautologies). *The set of* short cut tautologies, *written* $\top\bot\text{-}\mathsf{SC}(\mathcal{O})$, *is defined as follows:*

$$\begin{aligned}\top\bot\text{-}\mathsf{SC}(\mathcal{O}) = &\{\mathsf{A} \sqsubseteq \top \mid \mathsf{A} \in \widetilde{\mathcal{O}}, \mathsf{A} \sqsubseteq \top \notin \top\bot\text{-}\mathsf{TR}(\mathcal{O})\} \cup \\ &\{\bot \sqsubseteq \mathsf{A} \mid \mathsf{A} \in \widetilde{\mathcal{O}}, \bot \sqsubseteq \mathsf{A} \notin \top\bot\text{-}\mathsf{TR}(\mathcal{O})\} \cup \\ &\{\mathsf{A} \sqsubseteq \mathsf{A} \mid \mathsf{A} \in N_C \cup \{\bot, \top\}\}.\end{aligned}$$

In the case of our example $\mathcal{O}_{ex}$, we have for instance $\mathsf{AlaskanMoose} \sqsubseteq \top \in \top\bot\text{-}\mathsf{SC}(\mathcal{O}_{ex})$. The distinction between atomic axioms in (i) transitive reducts, (ii) the tautological completion of transitive reducts, (iii) non-tautological short cuts, and (iv) short cut tautologies results in a unique partition of the $\mathsf{ICH}(\mathcal{O})$ for a given transitive reduct.

In addition to $\mathsf{ICH}(\mathcal{O})$, which only captures the terminological knowledge about named class, another important entailment set in practice is the set of *class assertions* for individuals contained in an ontology.

Definition 9 (Inferred Class Hierarchy Assertions). *The set of* inferred class hierarchy assertions *of* $\mathcal{O}$ *is defined as follows:*

$$\mathsf{ICHA}(\mathcal{O}) = \{\mathsf{A}(a) \mid \mathsf{A} \in \widetilde{\mathcal{O}}, a \in N_I, \mathcal{O} \models \mathsf{A}(a)\}$$

As for $\mathsf{ICH}(\mathcal{O})$, there may be some variance in terms of how $\mathsf{ICHA}(\mathcal{O})$ is understood. Therefore we define the set of *most specific* class assertions as the smallest entailment set that still captures the $\mathsf{ICHA}(\mathcal{O})$, which is realised as another standard OWL reasoning service called *realisation.*

Definition 10 (Most Specific Class Assertions). *A set of* most specific class assertions *of* $\mathcal{O}$*, written* $\mathsf{MSCA}(\mathcal{O})$*, is a (cardinality) minimal set* $\mathsf{MSCA}(\mathcal{O}) \subseteq \mathsf{ICHA}(\mathcal{O})$ *such that* $\mathsf{MSCA}(\mathcal{O}) \cup \mathsf{ICH}(\mathcal{O}) \models \mathsf{ICHA}(\mathcal{O})$.

Extending $\mathcal{O}_{ex}$ with $\{\mathsf{Elk}(a), \mathsf{Deer}(a), \mathsf{hasCalf}(a, b)\}$, yields $\mathsf{MSCA}(\mathcal{O}_{ex}) = \{\mathsf{Elk}(a)\}$.

Analogously to what we did for the ICH, we define the (unique) tautological completion for MSCAs:

Definition 11 (Tautological Completion). *The* tautological completion *of* $\mathsf{MSCA}(\mathcal{O})$ *is defined as follows:*

$$\top\bot\text{-}\mathsf{MSCA}(\mathcal{O}) = \{\top(a) \mid a \in \widetilde{\mathcal{O}} \textit{ and there is no } \mathsf{A}(a) \in \mathsf{MSCA}(\mathcal{O})\}.$$

In case of our extended example $\mathcal{O}_{ex}$, we have $\top\bot\text{-}\mathsf{MSCA}(\mathcal{O}_{ex}) = \{\top(b)\}$.

Similarly, we define a notion for short-cuts w.r.t. class assertions:

Definition 12 (Short Cut Assertions). *The set of* short cut assertions *of* $\mathsf{SCA}(\mathcal{O})$ *is defined as follows:*

$$\mathsf{SCA}(\mathcal{O}) = \mathsf{ICHA}(\mathcal{O}) \setminus \bigcup_{\mathsf{MSCA}(\mathcal{O})} (\mathsf{MSCA}(\mathcal{O}) \cup \top\bot\text{-}\mathsf{MSCA}(\mathcal{O})).$$

Continuing our extended example $\mathcal{O}_{ex}$, we find $\mathsf{Deer}(a) \in \mathsf{SCA}(\mathcal{O}_{ex})$.

And finally, we define a notion for short-cut assertion tautologies:

Definition 13 (Short Cut Assertion Tautologies). *The set of* short cut assertion tautologies $\top\bot\text{-}\mathsf{SCA}(\mathcal{O})$ *is defined as follows:*

$$\top\bot\text{-}\mathsf{SCA}(\mathcal{O}) = \{\top(a) \mid \mathcal{O} \models \top(a)\} \setminus \top\bot\text{-}\mathsf{MSCA}(\mathcal{O}).$$

Analogously to the case of the ICH, the Definitions 10–13 give rise to a unique partition of the ICHA into four sets for a given set of most specific class assertions.

4 Determining the Extent of Precompilation

In this section, we discuss how we can determine the extent of precompilation in an ontology. Given an entailment set $\mathcal{E}$ of an ontology $\mathcal{O}$, we check whether it is materialised in $\mathcal{O}$ by simply checking whether $\mathcal{E} \subseteq \mathcal{O}$ holds. To determine whether $\mathcal{E}$ is precompiled, we simply test whether $\mathcal{O} \setminus \mathcal{E} \models \mathcal{E}$ holds. This straightforward way of determining precompilation suffers, however, from two issues: firstly, it is insensitive to different but equivalent representations of an entailment set. For example, a subsumption entailed from an equivalence axiom is not necessarily a precompiled axiom. Secondly, it considers the entailment set as a whole: if a single axiom of a large entailment set is not precompiled, then the whole entailment set is not precompiled. Therefore, instead of searching for precompiled entailment sets, it is more appropriate to search for maximal precompiled subsets of a given entailment set in an ontology.

Identifying sets of redundant axioms in ontologies is known to be challenging in practice [6,13]. While it is straightforward to identify a single axiom α in an ontology $\mathcal{O}$ as redundant by testing whether $\mathcal{O} \setminus \{\alpha\} \models \alpha$ holds, such axioms do not, in general, form redundant subsets when grouped together. As an example, consider the ontology $\mathcal{O} = \{\mathsf{A} \sqsubseteq \mathsf{B}, \mathsf{A} \sqsubseteq \mathsf{C}, \mathsf{A} \sqsubseteq \mathsf{B} \sqcap \mathsf{C}\}$. Then for all axioms $\alpha \in \mathcal{O}$, we have $\mathcal{O} \setminus \{\alpha\} \models \alpha$. However, all three axioms taken together, i.e. $\mathcal{O}$ itself, does not constitute a redundant set. As a consequence of this, removing redundant axioms from an ontology comes down to a choice between a number of alternatives. This also means, that for a given ontology, there may exist several irredundant equivalent ontologies.

Since we are interested in identifying redundant axioms with respect to some entailment set, we define a notion of irredundancy for ontologies accordingly.

Definition 14 (Reduced Ontology). *Let $\mathcal{O}$ be an ontology and $\mathcal{E}$ an entailment set of $\mathcal{O}$. An ontology $\mathcal{O}^- \subseteq \mathcal{O}$ is a* reduction of $\mathcal{O}$ with respect to $\mathcal{E}$, *if*

(i) $\mathcal{O} \setminus \mathcal{O}^- \subseteq \mathcal{E}$,
(ii) $\mathcal{O}^- \equiv \mathcal{O}$,
(iii) there exists no $\alpha \in \mathcal{E}$ such that $\{\alpha\}$ is redundant in $\mathcal{O}^-$.

Each reduction $\mathcal{O}^-$ of $\mathcal{O}$ can be associated with its corresponding precompiled subset of $\mathcal{E}$, namely $\mathcal{O} \setminus \mathcal{O}^-$. With this, we can elaborate on the statement made in Sect. 3 with respect to possible partitions of an entailment set into subsets of precompiled, materialised but not redundant, and non-materialised axioms.

Proposition 1. *A reduction $\mathcal{O}^-$ of an ontology $\mathcal{O}$ wrt. an entailment set $\mathcal{E}$ uniquely identifies a partition of $\mathcal{E}$ into three subsets defined as follows:*

1. $P = \mathcal{O} \setminus \mathcal{O}^-$ *precompiled axioms in $\mathcal{O}$,*
2. $M = \mathcal{O}^- \cap \mathcal{E} = (\mathcal{O} \cap \mathcal{E}) \setminus P$ *of materialised but not redundant axioms in $\mathcal{O}^-$,*
3. $N = \mathcal{E} \setminus \mathcal{O}$ *non-materialised axioms in $\mathcal{O}$.*

5 Methods

5.1 Materials

Ontology Corpus. We use a publicly available snapshot of BioPortal from 2017.[1] The data set of ontologies with their imports closure merged in encompasses a total of 438 ontologies. We select ontologies for individual reasoners according to the following criteria: (i) can be processed using the OWL API, (ii) contains logical axioms, (iii) is found to be consistent by a reasoner, and (iv) can be classified by a reasoner within one hour. The last criterion is chosen primarily for practical reasons owing to the large scale of our empirical investigation. This choice is justified by empirical evidence that most ontologies can be classified well within one hour [5].

No ontologies have been excluded based on criterion (i). A total of 13 ontologies were excluded based on criterion (ii). As for criteria (iii) and (iv), note that an ontology is not necessarily deemed consistent or classifiable by all reasoners. In particular, HermiT found three ontologies to be inconsistent, Pellet five, JFact eight, and Konclude seven. Likewise, 352 ontologies of the remaining ontologies could by classified by HermiT, 319 by Pellet, 381 by JFact, and 406 by Konclude. Any statements involving a reasoner will be made w.r.t. these the reasoner's respective ontologies.

In experiments, we distinguish between ontologies that consist of atomic axioms only, axioms expressible in $\mathcal{EL}^{++}$, and rich otherwise. We refer to these three kinds of ontologies as *atomic*, $\mathcal{EL}^{++}$, and *rich* ontologies respectively.

Experimental Environment. Ontologies in this study are processed using the OWL API (version 4.5.13). With the exception of Konclude[2] (version 0.6.2), all reasoning tasks are orchestrated via a reasoner's OWL API support. The used reasoners are HermiT[3] (version 1.3.8.413), JFact[4] (version 4.0.4), and Pellet[5] (version 2.3.3). Konclude is used via its command line interface.

All reasoning performance experiments are run on a machine with an Intel Core i5-3470 Quad-Core processor at 3.2 GHz with 8 GB of RAM. The reasoners were given 5 GB of RAM and the remaining 3 GB were reserved for the operating system (Ubuntu 16.04.04 LTS). The installed Java runtime environment was "OpenJDK Runtime Environment AdoptOpenJDK (build 11.0.4+11)".

Source code used for this work is available online.[6]

5.2 Research Questions

The notion of precompilation raises a number of research questions. Here, we distinguish between two broad categories of such questions. On the one hand, we

1 https://zenodo.org/record/439510#.XoR4Td-YVhF.
2 https://www.derivo.de/en/produkte/konclude.html.
3 http://www.hermit-reasoner.com/.
4 http://jfact.sourceforge.net/.
5 https://github.com/stardog-union/pellet.
6 https://github.com/ckindermann/precompilation.

are interested in the *prevalence* of precompiled entailment sets in practice. On the other hand, we are interested in the *implications* of precompiled entailment sets for practitioners.

To develop a first understanding of precompilation in practice, we focus on entailment sets that are related to entailment sets of standard OWL reasoning services. In particular, we investigate entailment sets revolving around the class hierarchy and class assertions (cf. Sect. 3). We determine to what degree such entailment sets are materialised and to what extent they are redundant and precompiled. Furthermore, we qualify the size of materialised entailment sets relative to an ontology overall size and draw comparisons w.r.t. an ontology's reduction (w.r.t. said entailment set).

Lastly, we shed some light on the practical impact of precompilation by evaluating its effects on reasoning performance. In particular, we investigate reasoning performance with respect to the standard reasoning tasks (i) classification and (ii) realisation.

5.3 Experimental Design

The notion of precompilation is partially predicated on the materialisation of entailment sets and partially on their redundancy. Hence, both the extent of materialisation and redundancy are partial indicators for precompilation. In this work, we investigate precompilation w.r.t. entailment sets revolving around an ontology's class hierarchy (c.f. Sect. 3). Our investigation consists of four distinct experiments that we run over biomedical ontologies as described in Sect. 5.1. The four experiments concern the extent of *materialisation*, *redundancy*, and *precompilation* of entailment sets, as well as the impact of precompilation on *reasoning performance*. In the following, we give a brief description for each of these experiments.

Materialisation. We determine to what extent an ontology consists of atomic axioms and what kinds of atomic axioms are most prevalent. We analyse an ontology's TBox and ABox in the same fashion according to their respective sets defined in Sect. 3. As the entailment sets of transitive reducts and most specific class assertions are of special interest, we shed light on both their materialised and non-materialised proportions. As already mentioned these sets are, in general, not uniquely determined, which makes counting their axioms rather difficult. To avoid over-counting axioms in transitive reducts due to their non-determinism, we adopt the following approach: first, we take an injective function r that returns a representative element $r([\mathsf{A}])$ for each equivalence class $[\mathsf{A}]$. The transitive reduct induced by r is called $r\mathsf{TR}(\mathcal{O})$, and we consider the axiom $r([\mathsf{A}]) \sqsubseteq r([\mathsf{B}]) \in r\mathsf{TR}(\mathcal{O})$ to be materialised in $\mathcal{O}$ if some axiom in $[\mathsf{A}] \sqsubseteq [\mathsf{B}]$ is materialised. Analogously, r induces most specific class assertions $r\mathsf{MSCA}(\mathcal{O})$, and a class assertion $r([\mathsf{A}])(a) \in r\mathsf{MSCA}(\mathcal{O})$ is considered to be materialised if some axiom in $[\mathsf{A}](a)$ is materialised.

For this experiment, we use Konclude to compute an ontology's classification and realisation.[7] When analysing TBoxes, we exclude ontologies with empty TBoxes or empty transitive reducts (TR) of their inferred class hierarchy. Likewise, when analysing ABoxes, we exclude ontologies with empty ABoxes or an empty set of most specific class assertions (MSCA).

Redundancy. We determine to what extent atomic axioms are redundantly contained in ontologies. We test for each axiom α in an ontology $\mathcal{O}$ whether $\mathcal{O} \setminus \{\alpha\} \models \alpha$ holds. As we work with a large number of ontologies that may include many axioms expressed in very expressive DLs, testing atomic axioms individually for redundancy is an expensive operation. Therefore, we configure two timeouts. One timeout, set to two minutes, limits the time a reasoner has to answer an individual redundancy test. A second timeout, set to one hour, limits the time a reasoner has to test all atomic axioms in an ontology. We run this experiment for all three reasoners supported by the OWL API (HermiT, JFact, and Pellet) separately.

Precompilation. We investigate the impact of precompilation on published ontologies by drawing a threefold comparison. We distinguish between the cases of (i) published ontology, (ii) no precompilation, and (iii) minimal precompilation.

For atomic TBox axioms, these three cases are defined as follows: for a given (i) published ontology $\mathcal{O}$ we compute its (ii) reduction $\mathcal{O}^-$ w.r.t. $\mathsf{ICH}(\mathcal{O})$, and (iii) a minimally precompiled ontology defined by $\mathcal{O}^+ = \mathcal{O}^- \cup \mathsf{TR}(\mathcal{O})$ for a transitive reduct that results in a minimal number of added axioms. For atomic ABox axioms, define conditions (i)–(iii) analogously w.r.t. $\mathsf{ICHA}(\mathcal{O})$ and $\mathsf{MSCA}(\mathcal{O})$.

Using Proposition 1, we compare $\mathcal{O}^-$ with $\mathcal{O}$ and $\mathcal{O}^+$ under set difference to measure the impact of precompiling class hierarchy entailment sets on an ontology's size in practice.

Reductions are computed brute-force by iteratively removing redundant axioms. We configure two timeouts as in the redundancy experiment to limit individual reasoning calls and the overall computation. We run this experiment for all three reasoners supported by the OWL API (HermiT, JFact, and Pellet) separately.

Reasoning Performance. We investigate the impact of precompilation on reasoning performance w.r.t. class hierarchy entailment sets. In particular, we time the standard reasoning tasks classification and realisation under three experimental conditions respectively. The three experimental conditions distinguish between the cases of (i) published ontology, (ii) no precompilation, and

[7] Konclude does not compute the realisation of an ontology as it is defined in Sect. 3. Instead, Konclude's `realization` command returns *all* inferable atomic class assertions for an ontology. However, given the inferred class hierarchy of an ontology, one can easily determine the *most specific* class assertions.

(iii) precompilation as defined in the precompilation experiment. We time the classification of $\mathcal{O}$, $\mathcal{O}^-$, and $\mathcal{O}^+$ w.r.t. $\mathsf{ICH}(\mathcal{O})$ and $\mathsf{TR}(\mathcal{O})$ and the realisation w.r.t. $\mathsf{ICHA}(\mathcal{O})$ and $\mathsf{MSCA}(\mathcal{O})$.

In the classification experiment, we remove ABoxes from ontologies to control for confounding effects due to large ABoxes. As there is no analogous operation for the realisation experiment we will discuss confounding factors and limitations in Sect. 7. We run this experiment for all three reasoners supported by the OWL API (HermiT, JFact, and Pellet) separately.

6 Results

6.1 Experiment 1: Materialisation

The experimental conditions as specified in Sect. 5.3 resulted in a total of 394 ontologies (65 atomic, 55 $\mathcal{EL}^{++}$, 274 rich) in the case of TBoxes and 132 (6 atomic, 2 $\mathcal{EL}^{++}$, 124 rich) in the case of ABoxes.

We begin the presentation of results with the materialisation of the transitive reduct (TR)[8] and most specific class assertions (MSCA).

In the case of the TR, we find that 274 (65 atomic, 53 $\mathcal{EL}^{++}$, 156 rich) of the 394 ontologies materialise TR in its entirety. An additional 38 ontologies materialise their TR to at least 99%. Overall, there are only 30 (one $\mathcal{EL}^{++}$, 29 rich) ontologies that materialise their TR to less than 90%. Only 4 of which materialise their TR to less than 50% (the smallest percentage of materialisation is 27%).

In the case of the MSCA, we find that 94 (6 atomic, one $\mathcal{EL}^{++}$, 87 rich) of the 132 ontologies materialise their MSCA in its entirety. An additional 6 ontologies materialise their MSCA to at least 90%. There are only 7 (rich) ontologies that materialise their MSCA to less than 50%; two of which do not materialise any axiom of the MSCA.

While most ontologies materialise their TR and MSCA to generally high percentages, it is important to relate these percentages to absolute counts. Figure 1A shows absolute counts for the number of axioms in an ontology's TBox, materialised TR axioms, and non-materialised TR axioms. While the total number of non-materialised axioms is below 1000 for most ontologies, there are exceptions. For example, the "The Drug Ontology", shown on index 391, materialises 97% of the TR. Yet, the corresponding number of non-materialised axioms is 12,883.

Figure 1B shows absolute counts for the number of axioms in an ontology's ABox, materialised MSCA axioms, and non-materialised MSCA axioms. We note that ontologies with the huge ABoxes tend to contain a large (absolute) number of axioms from MSCA and materialise their MSCA to 100%; e.g., the RadLex ontology (shown at index 131 in Fig. 1B) has an ABox with 398,016 axioms which includes 46,936 axioms of a materialised MSCA.

[8] Here, we use TR and MSCA as the more abstract concepts that stand for all $\mathsf{TR}(\mathcal{O})$ and $\mathsf{MSCA}(\mathcal{O})$, and remind the reader that we use $r\mathsf{TR}(\mathcal{O})$ and $r\mathsf{MSCA}(\mathcal{O})$ and suitable counting to avoid over-counting these entailments.

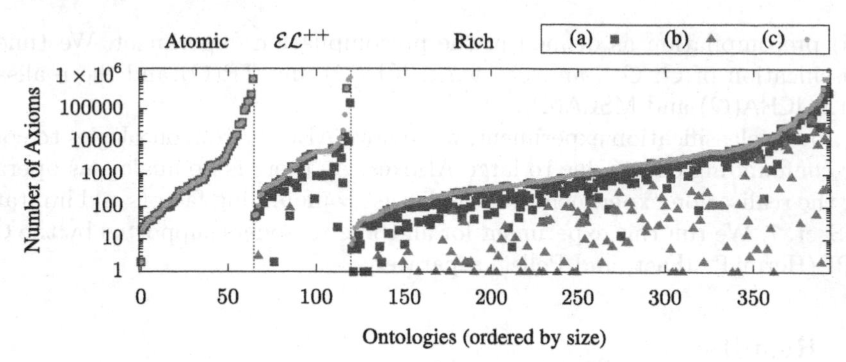

(A) Absolute counts for materialised axioms of the TR (a), non-materialised axioms for the TR (b), TBox axioms (c).

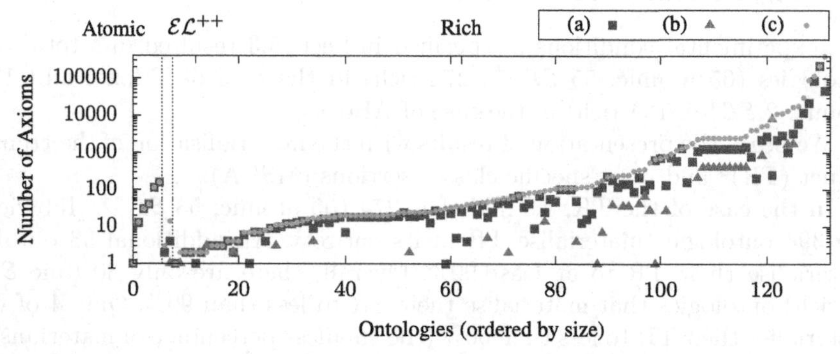

(B) Absolute counts for materialised MSCA axioms (a), non-materialised MSCA axioms (b), and ABox axioms (c).

Fig. 1. Size comparison between an ontology's TR and TBox (A), and MSCA and ABox. The legend indicates the drawing order. This order ensures that purple squares (a) cannot hide green triangles (b) nor blue dots (c). Also, a blue dot cannot hide green triangles (b) or purple squares due to its smaller size. (Color figure online)

Figure 1 suggests that the absolute size of materialised TR axioms and MSCA axioms correlate with the size of an ontology's TBox and ABox respectively. However, the logarithmic scale makes it hard to determine visually whether these axioms from the TR and MSCA make up a large proportion of an ontology's TBox or ABox. Figure 2 shows the relative proportions of atomic axioms w.r.t. an ontology's TBox and ABox respectively. It also shows to what extent these axioms are TR axioms or MSCA axioms, short cut axioms, or tautologies.

For TBoxes of non-atomic ontologies, we note that there are both TBoxes with a very small proportion of atomic axioms and TBoxes that consist almost exclusively of atomic axioms. Instances of ontologies with a low proportion of atomic axioms, e.g., at index 112, 118, 212, 275, contain a large number of axioms involving properties (which are non-atomic by our definitions). Interestingly, the proportions of atomic axioms in rich ontologies seem to be almost uniformly distributed in our experimental corpus. We also note, that in most cases, atomic

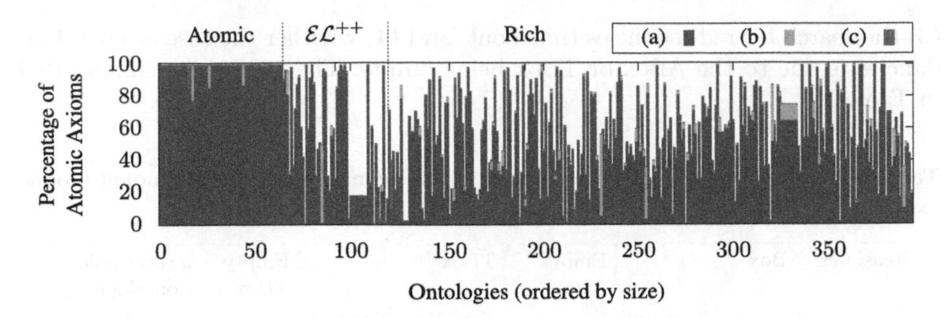

(A) Percentages are shown for axioms of the TR (a), shot cut axioms (b), and tautologies (c).

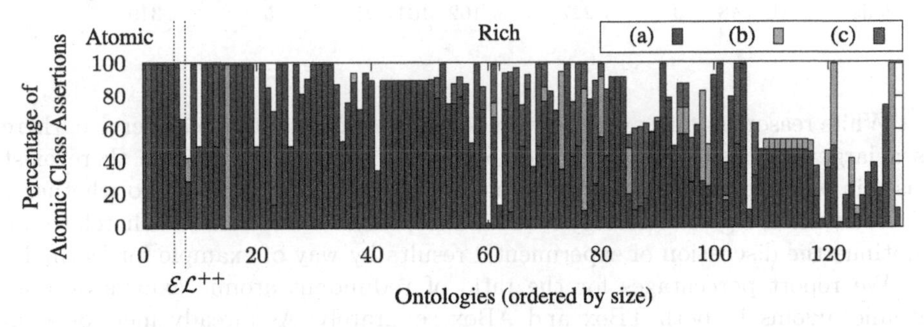

(B) Percentages are shown for axioms of the MSCA (a), shot cut axioms (b), and tautologies (c).

Fig. 2. Relative size comparison between an ontology's atomic axioms and TBox (A) and ABox (B).

TBox axioms are indeed TR axioms. However, there are examples where short cuts and tautologies dominate, e.g. at index 121 or 230. While almost all ontologies include a few tautological subclass axioms involving $\top$, the vast majority of axioms from the tautological completion of the TR are not materialised in ontologies.

For ontologies with ABoxes of more than 100 axioms (starting at index 80), we note that the proportion of atomic class assertions tends to decrease. Furthermore, we note that atomic class assertions often contain relatively large numbers of both short cut axioms and tautologies. In particular, we find example ontologies, e.g. at index 77, that materialise all inferred class hierarchy assertions.

6.2 Experiment 2: Redundancy

We report the results of our redundancy experiments for each reasoner by distinguishing for each ontology's ABox and TBox whether (1) redundant atomic axioms could be identified, (2) no redundant atomic axioms could be identified,

(3) the search for redundancies timed out, and (4) whether the case of no redundancies is due to the ABox or TBox being empty. The results are summarised in Table 1.

Table 1. Number of ontologies that contain/do not contain (yes/no) redundant atomic axioms.

Reasoner	ABox			Empty ABox	TBox			Empty TBox	Servicable ontologies
	Yes	No	Timeout		Yes	No	Timeout		
HermiT	59	47	5	241	190	133	24	5	352
JFact	56	46	24	255	200	136	40	5	381
Pellet	41	48	3	227	162	131	21	5	319

While reasoners differ with respect to what ontologies they can service, there is a large overlap of 295 ontologies between all three. Also, while there exist cases in which different reasoners come to different conclusions as to whether a given axiom in a given ontology is redundant, these cases are rare. Therefore, we continue the discussion of experimental results by way of example for HermiT.

We report percentages for the ratio of redundant atomic axioms over all atomic axioms in both TBox and ABox separately. As already mentioned in Sect. 6.1, such percentages may not always give an accurate account of absolute numbers. However, we will defer the discussion of absolute numbers to the experiment on precompilation where ontology reductions are computed.

In TBoxes, the percentage of redundant atomic axioms is rather small for most ontologies. In Fig. 3, on the upward-directed axis, we show to what extent atomic axioms in an ontology's TBox are redundant. For 50 of the 190 ontologies we report that at least 10% of all atomic axioms are redundant. For eight of these ontologies the percentage even surpasses 50%. On the downward-directed axis, we show to what degree redundant axioms are transitive reduct axioms, short cut axioms, or tautologies. We notice that $\mathcal{EL}^{++}$ ontologies contain predominantly redundant short cut axioms. However, in rich ontologies all three kinds of atomic axioms occur as redundant to varying proportions.

In ABoxes, we report comparatively high percentages of redundant atomic axioms. For 31 of the 59 ontologies at least 80% of their atomic class assertions are redundant. Only 20 ontologies contain less than 50% of redundant atomic class assertions. We note, that all three reasoners find redundant atomic class assertions almost exclusively in rich ontologies. In case of Hermit, 57 of the 59 ontologies with redundant atomic class assertions are rich. Lastly, we note that the majority of redundant atomic class assertions are axioms from the MSCA or tautologies. Redundant short cuts occur in 13 ontologies and only make up more than 50% of all redundant atomic axioms in three ontologies.

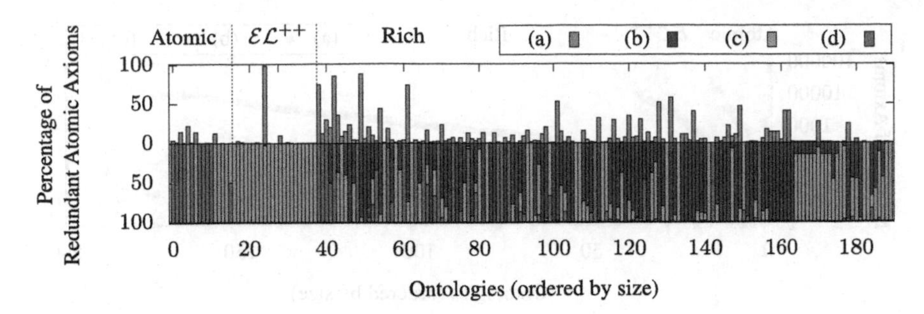

Fig. 3. Prevalence of redundant atomic TBox axioms. Percentages in the upward direction show the ratio of redundant atomic axioms over all atomic axioms of an ontology's TBox (a). Percentages in the downward direction show to what extent redundant atomic axioms are transitive reduct axioms (b), short cut axioms (c), or tautologies (d). Ontologies are ordered by the size of their atomic axioms.

6.3 Experiment 3: Precompilation

We report the results of our precompilation experiment by building on the findings of our materialisation and redundancy experiments. In light of the large proportions of atomic axioms in many ontologies of reasonably large size, removing or adding even small percentages of redundant entailment sets may have a significant impact in practice. For example, in the "FoodOn" ontology, we identified a precompiled set of atomic axioms in its TBox that makes up only 1% of all its atomic axioms. Removing this set from the ontology changed the ontology's overall size only by 0.6%. Yet, more than 100 axioms have been removed.

The results of our precompilation experiment show that such cases are not uncommon. Figure 4 shows absolute counts for the number of axioms in an ontology's TBox, the number of removed axioms in comparison with its reduction (as computed by HermiT), the minimal number of axioms required to add to the reduction so that the TR is materialised in its entirety. We note that 34 of the 190 ontologies (c.f. Fig. 3 in Sect. 6.2) contain precompiled sets of more than 100 atomic axioms.[9] We also note, that there are quite a number of ontologies for which $\mathcal{O}^+ \setminus \mathcal{O}^-$ is rather large. For example, in case of the "Non-coding RNA Ontology", adding a minimal number of axioms to its reduction amounts to the addition of 7659 axioms.

Lastly, we mention that the results of the precompilation experiment for ABoxes are similar to the results we report for TBoxes.

[9] We remind the reader of Proposition 1 according to which a reduction of an ontology w.r.t. an entailment set uniquely identifies a precompiled set of axioms in that ontology.

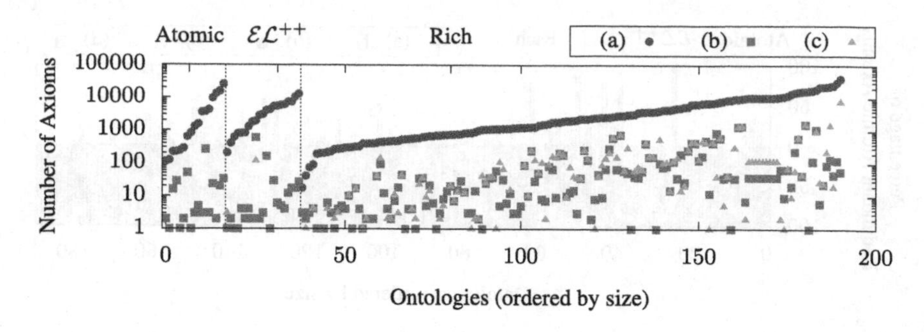

Fig. 4. Size comparison between $\mathcal{O}, \mathcal{O}^-$, and $\mathcal{O}^+$ w.r.t. TBox changes. Absolute counts for axioms of an ontology $\mathcal{O}$'s TBox (a), axioms of $\mathcal{O}$'s precompiled set associated with $\mathcal{O}^-$ (b), the minimal number of axioms to add to $\mathcal{O}^-$ so as to fully materialise its TR (c).

6.4 Experiment 4: Reasoning Performance

We report the results of our reasoning performance in relation to ontologies for which a reasoner spent more than 10 s to solve a reasoning task. For HermiT there are 12 such ontologies for classification and 21 for realisation. For JFact we have 11 and 2 respectively, and for Pellet we have 3 and 4. All results were found for rich ontologies.

Our experiments indicate that precompilation can affect classification times both positively as well as negatively depending on which reasoner is used on what ontology.

HermiT is either consistently unaffected by precompilation of an ontology's TR or seems to benefit. Table 2 summarises the classification times for four of five cases in which the classification times noticeably improve as a result of precompilation. The table also includes the one exception, namely the Immunogenetics Ontology (imgt), for which HermiT's performance suffers under the effect of precompilation.

JFact on the other hand is consistently affected negatively by precompilation. For 8 of the 11 ontologies, JFact's classification time increases considerably. In one case the time increases from 3 min to more than 15 – in another case, the time increases from 16 min to more than 40. There is only one ontology that did not incur performance degradation with JFact under precompilation.

Pellet shows improved reasoning times for one ontology, no effect for another, and yet slightly more volatile behaviour in terms of minimal and maximal classification times that produce similar averages as the no-precompilation condition.

Reasoning behaviour with respect to realisation appears to be largely unaffected by precompilation of the MSCA. JFact was negatively affected by precompilation for one ontology resulting in an increased time from 10 s (no-precompilation) to 30 s (precompilation). Pellet's reasoning time, on the other hand, improved for one ontology from 20 s (no-precompilation) down to 4 s (precompilation).

Table 2. HermiT Classification time for five experimental runs

Ontology	bt-biotop			fb-cv			imgt			ntdo			stato		
Condition	Min.	Avg.	Max.	Min.	Avg.	Max.	Min.	Avg.	Max.	Min.	Avg.	Max.	Min.	Avg.	Max.
$\mathcal{O}^-$	146 s	171 s	206 s	38 s	46 s	52 s	19 s	19 s	20 s	190 s	259 s	322 s	415 s	438 s	456 s
$\mathcal{O}$	96 s	116 s	152 s	11 s	13 s	16 s	77 s	79 s	82 s	142 s	174 s	224 s	276 s	290 s	305 s
$\mathcal{O}^+$	84 s	102 s	131 s	12 s	13 s	15 s	72 s	77 s	80 s	137 s	144 s	155 s	283 s	300 s	306 s

7 Discussion

We find that a good portion of ontologies indexed in BioPortal contains their TR in its entirety. However, consistent with the hypothesis of low redundancy formulated in [6], we find that most materialised axioms from the ICH are indeed not redundant and hence not precompiled. Yet, in case of large ontologies, it is important to keep in mind that even small percentages of redundant axioms may in fact correspond to a large absolute number of axioms. Concerns about such redundancies have been raised on the grounds of their informational value for ontology curators as well as tools [10,13].

Furthermore, the observed differences in reasoning times by a factor of three or more may be of practical relevance. Even in case of only a few seconds, such differences may become noticeable if ontologies need to be classified frequently or in bulk.

Limitations. We have limited the scope of our investigation to the biomedical domain. This design choice is primarily motivated by the view that precompilation of entailment sets is a "fundamental step in the release process for biomedical ontologies [7]." While the notion of precompilation is independent of a particular domain, we are unaware of strong beliefs about precompilation in other domains. Apart from this, BioPortal is a large corpus of actively maintained ontologies that are highly heterogeneous in terms of size and complexity [5,9]. Thus, the generally small effect size of precompilation w.r.t. BioPortal is unlikely to change w.r.t. other corpora of comparable size and complexity.

By using a one-hour timeout in combination with a straightforward method to identify redundancies and computing ontology reductions, we may have systematically excluded computationally challenging ontologies from our reasoning evaluation. Note, however, that our chosen approach proves to be sufficient for the majority of ontologies in our corpus. For example, in the case of HermiT, we only exclude 24 out of 352, i.e., less than 7% of serviceable ontologies. Also note, that a successful treatment of these excluded ontologies would not change the quintessence of our two primary observations. Namely, that precompilation has no effect for the vast majority of ontologies and that precompilation can have both positive as well as negative effects in specific instances.

Lastly, we need to point out that our reasoning experiments were primarily designed to investigate the *impact* of precompilation *in practice*. We did not investigate the *potential* of precompilation to affect reasoning performance *in general*. Although we controlled for long classification times due to large ABoxes, we did not control for factors that could (in theory) interact with precompilation. For example, it is conceivable that realisation times depend on both precompilation of the MSCA as well as precompilation of the TR. Similarly, one can speculate that different kinds of precompiled entailment sets would affect each others impact w.r.t. reasoning performance.

Future Work. Given the observed effects of precompilation on reasoning performance in a few instances, an understanding of cause and effect would be valuable. For this purpose, we plan a study on computationally challenging ontologies (not restricted to a domain). Here, we give a brief description of crucial points for future experimentation.

To investigate the potential impact of precompilation, ontology reductions w.r.t. to the whole ontology need to be considered. Since the number of such reductions is (in theory) exponential, stochastic sampling for exploring this search space may be sensible. Similarly, different precompilations of an entailment set, e.g., via minimal but non-unique representations, need to be analysed (also possibly by stochastic sampling).

A straightforward approach to compute ontology reductions is unlikely to be sufficient for a study on computationally challenging ontologies. Thus, optimisations and approximation techniques are needed; especially for large scale experiments.

A detailed analysis of used algorithms and concrete implementations of reasoners is necessary to develop an understanding of reasoner specific behaviour. Software profiling techniques may provide useful information for pinpointing implementation-specific factors contributing to effects of precompilation on reasoning time.

Ultimately, the potential impact of precompilation on reasoning performance involves three independent factors: an ontology, an entailment set, and a reasoner. Thus, a full investigation of this impact will need to examine all three factors as well as their potential interactions.

Related Work. Precompilation and materialisation of entailment sets is discussed in a range of settings. First, related but different precompilation approaches involve rewriting an ontology into a certain normal form to make subsequent tasks, including reasoning, easier [2,4]. Here, we focus on *extending* an ontology with entailed axioms.

Second, materialisation is used to compensate for shortcomings of tools. In [12], the materialisation of entailment sets is proposed to mitigate limitations of incomplete reasoners. The main idea is to determine entailment sets $\mathcal{R}$ that function as a *repair* without which an incomplete reasoner would fail to derive answers to some queries.

Third, materialisation is used to preserve an ontology's entailments when it is translated into a less expressive description logic in [11]. We could say that materialisation, in this setting, compensates for lack of expressive power which, in turn, can be motivated by reasoner or tool performance requirements or other reasons like readability.

Fourth, materialisation of TBox entailments has been used to improve the performance of (ABox) query answering in a range of settings, e.g., in [8].

Finally, while there are numerous surveys of properties of existing ontologies, there are none—to the best of our knowledge—that investigate the extent of materialisation.

8 Conclusion

We find that biomedical ontologies materialise class hierarchy entailment sets in both their TBox and Abox. While these entailment sets are to large proportions a substantive part of the ontology and cannot be removed without changing the ontology's meaning, there exist redundant subsets in ontologies that are of non-trivial size. Likewise, adding the TR to an ontology may result in a non-trivial increase in size. While our experiments on reasoning performance suggest that precompilation is inconsequential in most cases, there are instances where this practice can have a noticeable impact, both positive as well as negative, that depends on the used reasoner for a given ontology.

Overall, we conclude that the practice of precompilation has to be treated with due diligence. Adding entailment sets in an automated manner can have a significant impact on both an ontology's size and its usability in practice. Whether the precompilation of an entailment set provides its desired beneficial effects needs to be tested on a case by case basis. Tool support to facilitate such testing will be of great value moving forward.

References

1. Bail, S., Parsia, B., Sattler, U.: Extracting finite sets of entailments from OWL ontologies. In: Description Logics. CEUR Workshop Proceedings, vol. 745. CEUR-WS.org (2011)
2. Bienvenu, M.: Prime implicate normal form for ALC concepts. In: AAAI, pp. 412–417. AAAI Press (2008)
3. Cuenca Grau, B., Horrocks, I., Motik, B., Parsia, B., Patel-Schneider, P.F., Sattler, U.: OWL 2: the next step for OWL. J. Web Semant. **6**(4), 309–322 (2008)
4. Furbach, U., Günther, H., Obermaier, C.: A knowledge compilation technique for ALC Tboxes. In: FLAIRS Conference. AAAI Press (2009)
5. Gonçalves, R.S., Matentzoglu, N., Parsia, B., Sattler, U.: The empirical robustness of description logic classification. In: Description Logics. CEUR Workshop Proceedings, vol. 1014, pp. 197–208. CEUR-WS.org (2013)
6. Grimm, S., Wissmann, J.: Elimination of redundancy in ontologies. In: Antoniou, G., et al. (eds.) ESWC 2011. LNCS, vol. 6643, pp. 260–274. Springer, Heidelberg (2011). https://doi.org/10.1007/978-3-642-21034-1_18
7. Jackson, R.C., Balhoff, J.P., Douglass, E., Harris, N.L., Mungall, C.J., Overton, J.A.: ROBOT: a tool for automating ontology workflows. BMC Bioinform. **20**(1), 407:1–407:10 (2019)

8. Liu, Y., McBrien, P.: SPOWL: spark-based OWL 2 reasoning materialisation. In: Proceedings of the 4th ACM SIGMOD Workshop on Algorithms and Systems for MapReduce and Beyond, pp. 3:1–3:10. ACM (2017)
9. Matentzoglu, N., Bail, S., Parsia, B.: A snapshot of the OWL web. In: Alani, H., et al. (eds.) ISWC 2013. LNCS, vol. 8218, pp. 331–346. Springer, Heidelberg (2013). https://doi.org/10.1007/978-3-642-41335-3_21
10. Mougin, F.: Identifying redundant and missing relations in the gene ontology. In: MIE. Studies in Health Technology and Informatics, vol. 210, pp. 195–199. IOS Press (2015)
11. Pan, J.Z., Thomas, E.: Approximating OWL-DL ontologies. In: AAAI, pp. 1434–1439. AAAI Press (2007)
12. Stoilos, G., Grau, B.C.: Repairing incomplete reasoners. In: Description Logics. CEUR Workshop Proceedings, vol. 745. CEUR-WS.org (2011)
13. Xing, G., Zhang, G., Cui, L.: FEDRR: fast, exhaustive detection of redundant hierarchical relations for quality improvement of large biomedical ontologies. BioData Min. **9**, 31 (2016)

Tab2Know: Building a Knowledge Base from Tables in Scientific Papers

Benno Kruit[1,2](✉), Hongyu He[1], and Jacopo Urbani[1]

[1] Department of Computer Science,
Vrije Universiteit Amsterdam, Amsterdam, The Netherlands
b.b.kruit@cwi.nl, hongyu.he@vu.nl, jacopo@cs.vu.nl

[2] Centrum Wiskunde & Informatica, Amsterdam, The Netherlands

Abstract. Tables in scientific papers contain a wealth of valuable knowledge for the scientific enterprise. To help the many of us who frequently consult this type of knowledge, we present Tab2Know, a new end-to-end system to build a Knowledge Base (KB) from tables in scientific papers. Tab2Know addresses the challenge of automatically interpreting the tables in papers and of disambiguating the entities that they contain. To solve these problems, we propose a pipeline that employs both statistical-based classifiers and logic-based reasoning. First, our pipeline applies weakly supervised classifiers to recognize the type of tables and columns, with the help of a data labeling system and an ontology specifically designed for our purpose. Then, logic-based reasoning is used to link equivalent entities (via *sameAs* links) in different tables. An empirical evaluation of our approach using a corpus of papers in the Computer Science domain has returned satisfactory performance. This suggests that ours is a promising step to create a large-scale KB of scientific knowledge.

1 Introduction

Often, scientific advancement requires an extensive analysis of pre-existing techniques or a careful comparison with previous experimental results. For instance, it is common for researchers in Artificial Intelligence (AI) to ask questions like "Which are the most popular datasets used for graph embeddings?" or "What is the F1 of BERT on TACRED?". Finding the answers obliges the researchers to spend much time in perusing existing literature, looking for experimental results, techniques, or other valuable resources.

The answers to such questions can be frequently found in tabular form, especially the ones that describe the output of experiments. Unfortunately, tables in papers are made for human consumption; thus, their layout can be irregular or contain specific abbreviations that are hard to disambiguate automatically. It would be very useful if their content were copied into a clean Knowledge Base (KB) where tables are disambiguated and connected using a single standardized vocabulary. This KB could assist the users in finding those answers without accessing the papers or could be used for many other purposes, like categorizing papers, finding inconsistencies or plagiarized content.

J. Z. Pan et al. (Eds.): ISWC 2020, LNCS 12506, pp. 349–365, 2020.
https://doi.org/10.1007/978-3-030-62419-4_20

To build such a KB, we present Tab2Know, an end-to-end system designed to interpret the tables in scientific papers. The main challenge tackled by Tab2Know lies in the interpretation of the table, which is a necessary step to build a KB. In this context, the peculiarities of tables in scientific literature make our domain quite different from previous work (e.g., [3,23,32]), which mainly focused on Web tables. First, the interpretation of Web tables benefits from the existence of large, curated KBs (e.g., DBPedia [5]), which allows the linking of many entities. In our case, there is no such KB. Second, a large number of Web tables can be categorized as *entity-attribute* tables, i.e., tables where each row describes one entity, and the columns represent attributes [23,32,39]. In our context, we observed that many tables are of different types, namely they express n-ary relations, such as the results of experiments. For such tables, existing techniques designed for entity-attribute tables cannot be reused.

With Tab2Know, we propose a pipeline for knowledge extraction that includes both weakly supervised learning methods and logical reasoning. Tab2Know is designed to 1) detect the type of the table; 2) disambiguate the types of columns, and 3) link the entities between tables. The first operation is applied to distinguish, for instance, tables that report experiments from tables that report examples. The second operation recognizes the rows that contain the headers of the table and disambiguates the columns, linking them to classes of an ontology. The third operation links entities in different tables.

We implement the first two operations using statistical-based classifiers trained with bag-of-words and context-based features. These classifiers have an accuracy that largely depends on the quality and amount of training data. Unfortunately, labeling training data is increasingly the largest bottleneck as it often requires an expensive manual effort and/or expertise that might not be readily available. To counter this problem, we propose a weakly supervised method that relies on SPARQL queries and Snorkel [30]. The SPARQL queries are used to automatically retrieve samples of a given class, type, etc., while Snorkel resolves potential conflicts in the prediction with a sophisticated voting mechanism.

After the first two operations are completed, we transform the tables into an RDF KB and apply reasoning with existentially quantified rules to identify and link entities in different tables. Reasoning with existentially quantified rules is a well-known technology for data integration and wrangling [22]. For our problem, we designed a set of rules that considers the types of columns and string similarities to establish links using the *sameAs* relation. Then, we used VLog [8] to materialize the derivations and link the entities across the tables.

We evaluated our approach considering open access CS papers. In particular, we evaluated the performance of our pipeline using gold standards and compared it to another state-of-the-art method. We also applied our method to a larger corpus with 73k scientific tables. In these tables, we found 312k entities, which are linked to the table structure and metadata in our large-scale KB.

We release the datasets, gold standards, and resulting KB as an open resource for the research community at https://doi.org/10.5281/zenodo.3983012.

The code, ruleset, and instructions to replicate our experiments are also publicly available at https://github.com/karmaresearch/tab2know.

2 Related Work

Extracting knowledge from tables is a process that can be divided into *three* main tasks: *table extraction*, *structure detection*, and *table interpretation*. Once a set of tables is interpreted, another problem consists of recognizing whether multiple tables mention the same entities. We call this task *entity linking*, but this is also known as *entity resolution* [28], *record linkage* [10], or *entity matching* [6].

Table Extraction. This task consists of recognizing the parts of a PDF/image which contain a table. Existing methods can be categorized either as heuristic (e.g., [11,27]) or supervised (e.g., [29]). In this paper, we use the system *PDFFigures* [11], which is a recent approach based on heuristics with very high precision and recall ($\geq 90\%$) that is used in Semantic Scholar [1].

Structure Detection. Given as input an image-like representation of a table, some systems focus on recognizing the table's structure so that it can be correctly extracted. A popular system is *Tabula* (https://tabula.technology/), which recognizes the table's structure using rules. More recently, some deep learning methods based on Convolutional Neural Networks (CNN) [34], Conditional Generative Adversarial Networks (CGAN) [37], and a combination of a CNN, saliency and graphical models [20] have been evaluated. The performance of these methods is good ($F_1 \geq 0.95$), but not much different from Tabula, which returns a F_1 between 0.86 and 0.96 and has the advantage that is unsupervised.

Table Interpretation. The goal of table interpretation consists of linking the content of the table to a KB so that new knowledge can be extracted from the table [24]. In this context, most of the previous work has focused on tables that represent *entity-attribute* relations [23]. These tables have rows that describe entities and columns that describe attributes. Thus, their interpretation consists of mapping each row to an entity in the KB, and linking each column to a relation in the KB. Some work has focused only on the first task (e.g., [3]) while others on the second (e.g., [9,14,25]). The work at [9], in particular, is similar to ours as it also uses SPARQL queries to create training data. The difference is that in [9], SPARQL is used to query a rich KB automatically, whereas in our case, we let users specify queries since we lack such a KB. In terms of methodology, current work in this field either relies on statistical models, like PGMs [3,24], or introduces an iterative process that filters out candidates [32,33,39].

As far as we know, the only systems that offer a end-to-end table interpretation are *T2K* [32], *TableMiner+* [39], and *TAKCO* [23], but these are designed for Web tables and rely on a rich KB like DBPedia [5], which we do not have.

The only work that has focused on the interpretation of tables from scientific literature is [38]. The authors describe an approach to automatically extract experimental data from tables based on ensemble learning. Although we view this work as the most relevant to our problem, there are several important differences between our work and theirs. First, our approach employs a different set of technologies and performs entity linking, which is not considered in [38]. Then, our approach is more general. In fact, [38] focuses only on the extraction of tuples (*method*, *dataset*, *metric*, *score*, *source*) while ours extracts a larger variety of knowledge. Finally, our approach yields a better accuracy (see Sect. 6).

Entity Linking. The problem of resolving entities in tables has received considerable attention in database research (96+ papers in VLDB, KDD, etc. in 2009–2014) [10,21,28]. One of the most popular systems is Magellan [21]. Magellan is a tool to help users to perform entity matching, providing different implementations of matching and blocking algorithms. Recently, Mudgal et al. [26] have studied the application of deep learning for entity matching, but concluded that it does not outperform existing methods on structured data. Other works have explored the usage of embeddings for this task: For instance, Cappuzzo et al. [7] have shown how we can construct embeddings from tabular data. Another line of work has been focusing on crowds, e.g., [12] and citations therein, while other works have focused on entity resolution using knowledge bases (e.g., LINDA [6]). Our work differs from the ones above because they either focus on highly structured table sets or require the existence of KBs (which we do not have). Moreover, another important difference is that we take a declarative approach with rules. Rules are useful because they can be easily debugged/extended directly by domain experts, and they can be integrated with ontological reasoning.

Other Related Works. We mention, as further related work, the systems by [13] and *TableNet* [17] which focus on *searching* for tables related to a given query. Other, less relevant works focus on extracting and searching for figures on papers [35,36]. These works complement our approach and can further assist the user to find relevant knowledge in papers.

3 Overview

Our goal is to construct a clean and large KB from the content of tables in scientific papers stored as PDFs. To do so, we need to address two main challenges: first, we must resolve the ambiguities that might arise during the noisy extraction process and reduce the error rate as much as possible. Second, we must counter the problem that we lack both: 1) a pre-existing KB that can guide the extraction process and 2) a large amount of training data. We must, in other words, find a way to build a KB from scratch.

Our proposal is a pipeline with three main tasks, as shown in Fig. 1:

- **Task 1: Table Extraction.** The system receives as input an image-like representation of a table, recognizes its structure, and returns its content as a CSV file. For this task, we use external tools. We provide more details below;
- **Task 2: Table Interpretation.** The system processes the CSV to recognize the headers and the type of the table. Then, it disambiguates the columns by mapping them to ontological classes. We describe this task in Sect. 4;

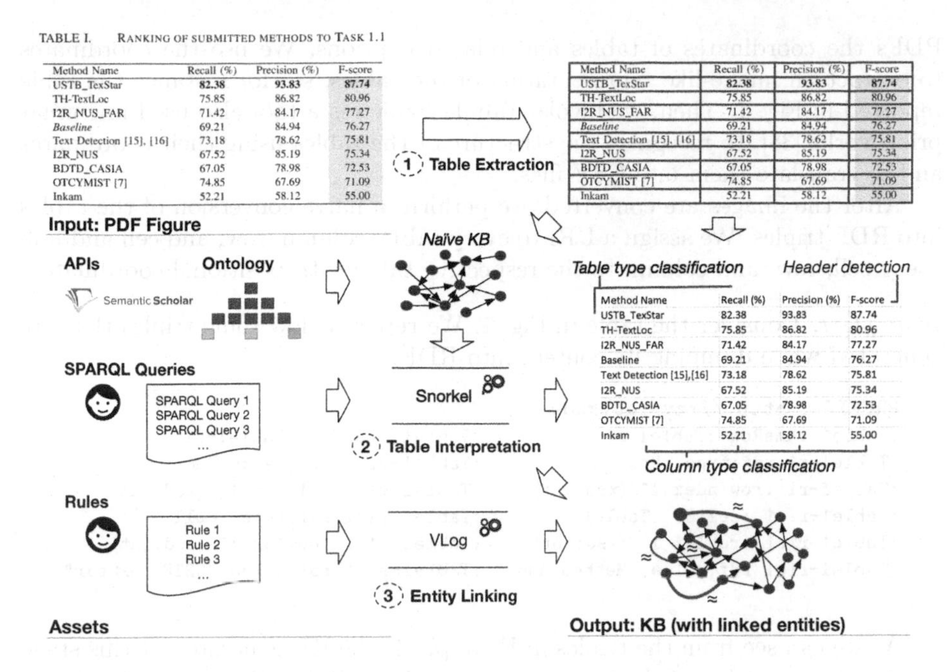

Fig. 1. Tab2Know: system overview

- **Task 3: Entity Linking.** Finally, the system performs logical-based reasoning to link the entities across tables. We describe this task in Sect. 5.

While in principle our method can be applied to scientific papers in any domain, we restrict our analysis to papers in Computer Science, which is our area of expertise. In particular, we consider Open Access papers and have been published in top-tier venues in subfields like AI, semantic web, databases, etc.

Before we describe the components, we describe *two* additional assets that we use for different purposes. The first one is an ontology constructed annotating a sample of random tables. A first version of this ontology contained 44 classes organized in a hierarchy with a maximum depth of 6. After further annotations, we decided to simplify it to a set of 27 classes (depth 3) for which we had substantial evidence in our corpus. The final ontology has 4 root classes: **Example**, **Input**, **Observation**, and **Other**. These classes define general table types. Then, the subclasses describe column types, e.g., **Dataset**, **Runtime**, or **Mean**. As an example, one of the longest chains is **Recall** $\sqsubseteq$ **Metric** $\sqsubseteq$ **Observation** with $\sqsubseteq$ denoting the subclass relation. The ontology is serialized in OWL using WebProtégé [19] and is publicly available as resource.

The second asset is an external KB that contains metadata of the papers, namely Semantic Scholar [1]. We access it using the provided APIs to retrieve the list of authors, the venue, and other contextual data.

Table Extraction. Our input consists of a collection of papers in PDF format. The first operation consists of launching PDFFigures [11] to extract from the

PDFs the coordinates of tables and related captions. We use the coordinates to extract an image-like representation of the tables, see for instance the table reported in Fig. 1. Then, we invoke Tabula, which is a tool also used in similar prior works [38], to recognize the structure of the tables using their coordinates and to translate them into CSV files.

After the images are converted, we perform a naïve conversion of the tables into RDF triples. We assign a URI to every table, column, row, and cell and link every cell, row, and column to the respective table with positional coordinates.

Example 1. Consider the table in Fig. 1. We report below some triples that are generated while dumping its content into RDF.

```
PREFIX : http://xzy/tab2know
:Table1 :hasRow :Table1-r1                :Table1 :hasCol :Table1-c1
:Table1-r1 rdf:type :Row                  :Table1-c1 rdf:type :Column
:Table1-r1 :rowIndex 1^^⟨xsd:int⟩         :Table1-c1 :colIndex 1^^⟨xsd:int⟩
:Table1-r1c1 :cellOf :Table1              :Table1-r1c1 rdf:type :Cell
:Table1-r1c1 :rowIdx 1^^⟨xsd:int⟩         :Table1-r1c1 :colIdx 1^^⟨xsd:int⟩
:Table1-r1c1 rdf:value "Method name" :Table1-r2c1 rdf:value "USTB_TexStar"
                                    ...
```

As we can see from the triples in Example 1, the KB generated at this stage is a direct conversion of the tabular structure into triples. Despite its simplicity, however, such a KB is already useful because it can be used to query the n-ary relations expressed in the tables in combination with the papers' metadata. For instance, we can write a SPARQL query to retrieve all the tables created by one author with a caption containing the word "results", or to retrieve the tables containing "F1" and which appear as proceedings of a certain venue.

The main problem at this stage is that we can only query using string similarities, which severely reduces the recall. For instance, a query could miss a column titled `Prec.` if it searches for `Precision`. The next operation, described below, attempts to disambiguate the tables to create a KB that is more robust against the syntactic diversity of the surface form of their content.

4 Table Interpretation

Tab2Know performs three main operations to interpret the tables. First, it identifies the rows with the table's header (Sect. 4.2). Then, it detects the type of the table (Sect. 4.3). Finally, it maps each column to an ontological class (Sect. 4.4). First, we describe the procedure to obtain training data.

4.1 Training Data Generation

Statistical models are ideal for implementing a table interpretation that is robust against noise. However, their accuracy depends on high-quality training data, which we do not have (and it is expensive to obtain such data with human annotators). We counter this problem following the paradigm of *weak supervision.*

The idea is to employ many annotators, which are much cheaper than a human expert but also much noisier. These annotators can deliver a large volume of labeled data, but the labels might be incorrect or conflicting. To resolve these problems, we can either rely on procedures like majority voting or train a dedicated model to computed the most likely correct label. In the second case, we can use Snorkel, one of the most popular models for this purpose [30].

Snorkel's goal is to facilitate the learning of a model θ that, given a data point $x \in \mathcal{X}$, predicts its label $y \in \mathcal{Y}$. Instead of training θ by fitting it to a set of pre-labeled data points, as it would happen in a traditional supervised approach, Snorkel trains an additional generative model with unlabeled data and uses pre-labeled data only for validation and testing. For these two tasks, the amount of pre-labeled data can be much smaller, and thus cheaper to obtain. Then, the generative model can be used to train θ.

Snorkel introduces the term *labeling function* to indicate a data annotator with possibly low accuracy. A labeling function $\lambda : \mathcal{X} \rightarrow \mathcal{Y} \cup \{\emptyset\}$ can encode a heuristic or be a simple predictor. It receives a data point x in input and either returns a label in $\mathcal{Y}$ or *abstains*, i.e., returns $\emptyset$. Given m unlabeled data points and n labeling functions, Snorkel applies the labeling functions to the data points and computes a matrix $M \in (\mathcal{Y} \cup \{\emptyset\})^{m \times n}$.

Then, Snorkel processes M to compute, for each x_i where $i \in \{1, \ldots, m\}$, a *probabilistic training label* $\tilde{y}_i$. The processing consists of creating a generative model using a matrix completion-style algorithm over the covariance matrix of the labels [31]. Then, this model can be used to generate labeled data for training θ. In this work, we considered models such as Naïve Bayes (NB), Support Vector Machine (SVM), and Logistic Regression (LR) [4] to implement θ. We have also experimented with deeper learning models, but we did not obtain improvements because such models are more prone to overfitting if training data is scarce.

The effectiveness of Snorkel largely depends on the number and quality of the labeling functions. In our context, we implemented them using SPARQL queries, which are supposed to be entered by a (human) user. SPARQL queries are ideal because they can assign labels to many data points at once. For each query Q, we create a labeling function that receives in input a column/table x and returns an assigned class label (e.g., a table type, or the class of a column) if x is among the answers of Q. Otherwise, the function abstains.

Example 2. We show below an example of a SPARQL query that labels columns with the class $\mathbf{F_1}$ if they have a header cell with value "f1" and contain any cell with a numeric type.

```
select distinct ?column where {
      ?table :column ?column ; :cell ?cell .
      ?column :hasTitle "f1" . ?cell rdf:type xsd:decimal . }
```

Clearly, this query is not a good predictor if taken alone, but if we combine its output with the ones of many other functions, then the resulting predictive power is likely to be superior. This is the key observation used by Snorkel.

l_1-l_2	#S	#l_1-W	#l_2-W	#l_1-V	#l_2-V
en-de	1.9M	55M	52M	40k	50k
en-fr	2.0M	50M	51M	40k	50k
en-es	1.9M	49M	51M	40k	50k

(a) Input

Models	Rerank size	Beam size	GMV	Latency
miDNN	50	-	2.91%	9%
miRNN	50	5	5.03%	58%
miRNN+att.	50	5	5.82%	401%

(b) Observation

Type	Example Words
Offensive	disgusting, filthy, nasty, rude, horrible, terrible, aw-ful, worst, idiotic, stupid, dumb, ugly, etc.
Non-offensive	help, love, respect, believe, congrats, hi, like, great, fun, nice, neat, happy, good, best, etc.

(c) Example

α_c	DP concentration parameter for each $c \in V$
$P_0(e\|c)$	CFG base distribution
$\boldsymbol{x}$	Set of non-terminal nodes in the treebank
$\mathcal{S}$	Set of sampling sites (one for each $x \in \boldsymbol{x}$)
S	A block of sampling sites, where $S \subseteq \mathcal{S}$
$\boldsymbol{b} = \{b_s\}_{s \in S}$	Binary variables to be sampled ($b_s = 1 \rightarrow$ frontier node)
$\boldsymbol{z}$	Latent state of the segmented treebank
m	Number of sites $s \in S$ s.t. $b_S = 1$
$\boldsymbol{n} = \{n_{c,e}\}$	Sufficient statistics of $\boldsymbol{z}$
$\Delta n^{S:m}$	Change in counts by setting m sites in S

(d) Other

Fig. 2. Examples of tables of each category

In our pipeline, we execute all the user-provided SPARQL queries and then use their outputs to build the matrix M for a large number of data points. Next, we train the final discriminative model θ. We compute two different θ: One to generate training data for predicting the tables' types (Sect. 4.3) while the other is for predicting the columns' types (Sect. 4.4).

4.2 Table Header Detection

First, we identify the rows that define the headers. To this end, we can either always select the first row as header or employ more sophisticated methods to recognize multi-row headers, like [16]. We observed that a simplified unsupervised version of [16] yields a good accuracy on our dataset. We describe it below.

Our procedure exploits the observation that header rows differ significantly from the rest of the table with respect to character-based statistics. Hence, we categorize characters either as *numeric*, *uppercase*, *lowercase*, *space*, *non-alphanumeric*, or *other*. Then, for each column, we count how many characters of each class (e.g., numeric) appear in its cell. We compute the average count per class across the column and use these values to determine the standard deviation for each cell. The *outlier score* of a row r is determined as the average of the standard deviations of all classes of its cells. If the outlier score or r is greater than τ (default value is 1, set after cross-validation), then r is marked as header.

4.3 Table Type Detection

In scientific papers, tables are used for various reasons. We classified them in the classes **Observation**, **Input**, **Example**, and **Other** (See Fig. 2 for examples).

Knowing the class of a table is useful for reducing the search space when the user is interested in some specific content (e.g., The F_1 measure is typically not mentioned in tables of type **Example**). Moreover, we can also use this information as a feature for the column disambiguation.

We predict the table type with a statistical classifier. As features for the classifier, we selected bags-of-ngrams of lengths 1 to 3 that occurred more than once, weighted by their TF-IDF score. Tables often contain abbreviations and domain-specific symbols that address an audience of experts. These provide strong hints for determining the type of the table; thus we consider the ngram in the content of the cells and the table caption. We also included other numerical features. In particular, we use the fraction of numeric cells in the table and the minimum, maximum, median, mean and standard deviation of numerical columns. This resulted in a total of 5804 features.

To train the models, we first ask the users to specify some SPARQL queries which will be used by Snorkel to create a large volume of training data. Then, we experimented with three well-known types of classifiers: NB, SVM, and LR. Eventually, we selected LR because it returned the best performance on the noisiest dataset.

4.4 Column Type Detection

Finally, the interpretation procedure attempts at linking the columns to one of the available classes in our ontology. The ontology includes popular classes that we identified while annotating a sample (e.g., **Dataset**, **Runtime**,...), while infrequent classes with very few columns are mapped to the class **Other**. In general, we assume that a column is *untyped* if it is mapped to **Other**.

For this task, we also used bag-of-ngram features of lengths 1 to 3, extracted from the table caption, the column header cells, the header cells of the other columns, and the column body. We restricted the set of ngrams to only the top 1000 most frequent per extraction source. Additionally, we added features about the numerical columns, identical to those in Sect. 4.3. This resulted in a total of 3076 features.

Similarly as before, we first rely on user-provided SPARQL queries to generate training data. Then, we considered NB, SVM, and LR as classifiers. Once the models for the table and column types are trained, we use them to predict the types of every table and column in our corpus. Finally, we use the predicted class to annotate the table/column in the KB with a semantic type.

5 Entity Linking

Rationale. Predicting the types of tables and columns is useful to map the table schema into a meaningful n-ary relation. The last operation in our pipeline consists of associating cells to entities so that we can populate the n-ary relations with new instances.

We start by assuming that every non-numerical cell contains an entity mention, which implies the existence of one entity. This assumption is not unrealistic. Indeed, if we look at the table in Fig. 1, then we see that every non-numerical cell that is not in the table's header refers to an entity (e.g., the cell "USTB_TextStar" refers to an algorithm to detect text inside images).

In practice, it is likely that some entities are mentioned multiple times. This consideration motivates us to discover whether two entity mentions (possibly on different tables) refer to the same entity. When we do so, then we gain more knowledge about the entity and reduce the number of entities in the target KB. We call this task *entity linking* because we are linking, with the *sameAs* relation, equivalent entities across tables.

With this goal in mind, we start by assuming that every entity has the content of the corresponding cell as label. For instance, the entity mentioned in the cell with "USTB_TextStar" has "USTB_TextStar" as label. Using the labels to determine equality can be surprisingly effective in practice, but it is not an operation without risks. In fact, there are cases where different entities have the same label, or the same entity has multiple labels. These cases call for a more sophisticated procedure to discover equalities.

Reasoning. Reasoning with existentially quantified rules is an ideal tool to establish non-trivial equalities between entities since it was already previously used for data integration problems [15,18]. For our purposes, we are interested in applying two types of rules: *Tuple Generating Dependencies (TGDs)* and *Equality Generating Dependencies (EGDs)*. We describe those below.

Consider a vocabulary consisting of infinite and mutually disjoint sets of predicates $\mathcal{P}$, constants $\mathcal{C}$, null values $\mathcal{N}$, and variables $\mathcal{V}$. A *term* is either a constant, a variable, or a null value. An *atom* is an expression of the form $p(\vec{x})$ where $p \in \mathcal{P}$, $\vec{x}$ is a tuple of terms of length equal to the arity of p, which is fixed. A *fact* is an atom without variables. A TGD is a rule of the form:

$$\forall \vec{x}, \vec{y}.(B \rightarrow \exists \vec{z}.H) \tag{1}$$

where B is a conjunction of atoms over $\vec{x}$ and $\vec{y}$ while H is a conjunctions of atoms over $\vec{y}$ and $\vec{z}$. Let $x, y \in \vec{x}$. A EGD is a rule of the form:

$$\forall \vec{x}.(B \rightarrow x \approx y) \tag{2}$$

Intuitively, TGDs are used to infer new facts from an existing set of facts (i.e., the database). Their execution consists of finding in the database suitable replacements for the variables in $\vec{x}$ and $\vec{y}$ that render B a set of facts in the database. Then, these replacements and mappings from $\vec{z}$ to fresh values in $\mathcal{N}$ are used to map H into a set of facts, which is the set of *inferred* facts.

EGDs are used to establish the equivalence between terms. Their execution is similar to the one of TGDs, with the difference that whenever they infer that $a \approx b$, where a and b are terms and $a < b$ according to a predefined ordering, then every occurrence of b in the database is replaced with a.

The *chase* [15] is a class of forward-chaining procedures that exhaustively apply TGDs and EGDs to infer new knowledge with the rules. A formal definition of various chase procedures is available at [2]. In this work, we apply the restricted chase, one of the most popular variants. It is known that sometimes the chase may not terminate, but this is not our case since we use an *acyclic* ruleset [15].

We first map the content of the KB extracted from the tables into a set of facts. For example, the first two RDF triples in Example 1 map to the facts `hasRow(Table1,Table1-r1)` and `hasCol(Table1,Table1-c1)` respectively.

Then, we use the two TGDs

$$type(X, \texttt{Column}) \rightarrow \exists Y.colEntity(X, Y) \quad (r_1)$$

$$type(X, \texttt{Cell}) \rightarrow \exists Y.cellEntity(X, Y) \quad (r_2)$$

to introduce fresh entities for every column and cell in the tables. The predicates *colEntity* and *cellEntity* link entities (Y) to the columns and cells respectively. Note that we use null values to represent entities, thus we are simply stating their existence with some placeholders. To reason and discover whether two different entities are equivalent, we employ EGDs. In particular, we use five EGDs, reported below:

$$ceNoTypLabel(X, L), ceNoTypLabel(Y, L) \rightarrow X \approx Y \quad (r_3)$$

$$eNoTypLabel(X, C, L), eNoTypLabel(Y, C, L) \rightarrow X \approx Y \quad (r_4)$$

$$eTableLabel(X, T, L), eTableLabel(Y, T, L) \rightarrow X \approx Y \quad (r_5)$$

$$eTypLabel(X, S, L), eTypLabel(Y, S, M), STR\_EQ(L, M) \rightarrow X \approx Y \quad (r_6)$$

$$eAuthLabel(X, A, L), eAuthLabel(Y, A, M), STR\_EQ(L, M) \rightarrow X \approx Y \quad (r_7)$$

where $ceNoTypLabel$, $eNoTypLabel$, $eTableLabel$, $eTypLabel$, and $eAuthLabel$ are auxiliary predicates that we introduce for improving the readability. We describe their intended meaning as follows. The fact $ceNoTypeLabel(X, L)$ is true if $colEntity(Y, X)$ is true and Y is an untyped column with header value L; $eNoTypeLabel(X, C, L)$ is true if X is an entity with a label L that appears in a cell inside an untyped column associated to entity C; $eTableLabel(X, T, L)$ is true if entity X with label L appears in table T; $eTypeLabel(X, S, L)$ is true if entity X with label L appears in a column with type S; $eAuthLabel(X, A, L)$ is true if entity X with label L appears in a table authored by author A.

The rationale behind each EGD is the following:

- **Rule $\mathbf{r_3}$** : This rule is introduced to disambiguate untyped columns. Since we were unable to discover the columns' types and assigned them to the class `Other`, we use the value of the header to determine whether they contain the same type of entities. Thus, the rule will infer that their associated entities are equal if they share the same header.
- **Rule $\mathbf{r_4}$** : This rule infers that two entities are equal if they appear in the same group of columns (created by r_3), and they share the same label.
- **Rule $\mathbf{r_5}$** : This rule encodes a simple heuristics, namely that if two entities with the same label appear in the same table, then they should be equal, irrespective of the type of columns where they appear.
- **Rule $\mathbf{r_6}$** : This rule disambiguates entities in columns of the same type. Here, we no longer consider the header of the column (as done by r_3 and r_4) but

compare the entities' labels. After experimenting with approximate string similarity measures, like the Levenshtein distance, we decided to use a case insensitive string equality (STR_EQ) to reduce the number of false positives. Case-insensitive similarity is more expensive than an exact string match because it requires dictionary lookups. We use it here and not in r_3, r_4, and r_5 because the comparisons are done only between entities of the same type.

- **Rule $\mathbf{r_7}$** : This rule implements another heuristic which takes into account the authors of the paper. It assumes that two entities are equal if they appear in two tables authored by the same author (we used the IDs provided by Semantic Scholar to disambiguate authors) and have the same label.

Once the reasoning has terminated, we introduce a new entity for each different null value and add RDF triples that link them to the corresponding cells and columns. Notice that the list of presented rules is not meant to be exhaustive. The ones that we describe show how we can exploit the predictions computed in the previous step (r_6) and external knowledge (r_7) relying on string similarity when no extra knowledge is available. We believe that additional EGDs, possibly designed to capture some specific cases, can further improve the performance.

6 Evaluation

Inputs. We considered two datasets: A corpus of tables that we manually constructed, and the dataset by [38], which is called *Tablepedia*.

Our corpus of tables contains 142,966 open-access PDFs distributed by Semantic Scholar. These papers appear in the proceedings of top venues in CS (the full list of venues is reported in our data repository). From these papers, we extracted 73,236 tables with PDFFigures and Tabula. These tables have 6.23 rows on average (SD = 6.58), and they have 7.11 columns (SD = 6.27). We converted the tables into RDF, resulting in a KB with 23M triples. We used Blazegraph to execute the SPARQL queries. After adding the table types and column types, we loaded the KB into VLog [8] to perform rule-based reasoning.

Tablepedia contains 451 tables, which have the columns annotated only with three classes: **Method**, **Dataset**, and **Metric**. To use this dataset in our pipeline, we created a graph representation of the tables without the annotations. Then, we translate the 15 *seed concepts* that are used in [38] to create the tables into labelling queries, so that we could apply Snorkel using both datasets. In contrast to Tablepedia, our annotated dataset maps to a much larger number of classes. Notice that the most frequent column types in our dataset (**Observation**, **Accuracy**, and **Count**), do not occur in Tablepedia.

Training Data. To create the training data for weak supervision, two human annotators (one PhD and one bachelor CS student) wrote SPARQL queries for labeling with the aid of a web interface designed for this purpose. The annotators examined the results of these queries on a sample of 400 tables, ensuring that the queries represented heuristics that covered a reasonable amount of the data. The quality of the SPARQL queries is fundamental to produce a good training

Method	Acc.
1st Row	0.71
Ours	**0.76**

(a) Header detection

Model	Prec.	Recall	F1	AUC
SVM	0.71	0.79	0.74	0.86
LR	0.72	0.79	0.74	0.84
NB	**0.80**	**0.82**	**0.79**	**0.91**

(b) Table type prediction on our corpus

Task	MV	Snorkel
Table Types	0.50	**0.71**
Column Types (Our corpus)	**0.56**	0.49
Column Types (Tablepedia)	0.39	**0.65**

(c) MV vs. Snorkel

Model	Prec.	Recall	F1	AUC
NB	0.52	0.48	0.47	**0.87**
SVM	**0.58**	**0.56**	**0.53**	0.83
LR	**0.58**	**0.56**	**0.53**	**0.85**

(d) Column type prediction on our corpus

Model	Prec.	Recall	F1	AUC
Yu et al. [38]	0.82	0.81	0.81	0.90
NB	0.84	0.82	0.81	0.96
SVM	0.90	0.89	0.89	0.97
LR	**0.92**	**0.91**	**0.91**	**0.98**

(e) Column type prediction on Tablepedia

Fig. 3. Table interpretation with Naïve Bayes (NB), Support Vector Machine (SVM), Logistic Regression (LR). MV is Majority Voting, AUC is area under the curve

dataset, and hence return good predictions. It is crucial that the queries have *large coverage* to avoid introducing a bias and to increase the training data size. For instance, if the queries label only a few tables, then the model will not receive enough evidence. To this end, we encouraged them to write queries which also matched a large number of items on the entire set of tables, and that did not excessively overlap. This resulted in 39 queries for labeling 98,570 tables with the corresponding type and 55 queries for labeling 165,302 columns.

Gold Standards. To test the performance, the same human annotators as before manually annotated 400 random tables. The tables in this sample have, on average, 9.92 rows (SD 7.28) and 5.07 columns (SD 3.20). These tables were annotated with the number of header rows, and table and column types. This process resulted in 321 table type and 873 column type annotations (excluding **Other**). Most tables were annotated with the **Observation** class (258), followed by **Input** (50); the smallest class was **Example** (13). The human annotators have annotated the table and column types looking at the images of the tables, the table captions, and possibly the full paper in case it was still not clear. The annotators have annotated the tables independently and resolved the conflicts together whenever they disagreed. After the first round of annotation using the first version of the ontology (44 classes), we marked as infrequent all classes with fewer than 10 annotations. These classes were removed from the ontology and the annotations were redirected to **Other**. For the Tablepedia dataset, we used the annotations provided by the original authors.

We highlight two aspects of our gold standard that have a direct impact on the evaluation. First, in contrast to [38], we decided not to filter out tables that were incorrectly extracted by Tabula. This makes our corpus more challenging because it might contain errors due to incorrect parsing. Second, our choice of merging infrequent column types into the type **Other** ensures that for each type there is always some evidence, but it has the downside that some classes in the long tail are ignored. Interpreting such types is an additional challenge that deserves a thorough study in future work.

6.1 Table Interpretation

Figure 3a reports the accuracy of our header detection heuristic compared to the baseline that consists of always selecting the 1st row. We observe that our technique has superior performance, although it still makes some mistakes.

In Fig. 3b, we report the performance of our table type detection models on our gold standard. In general, we observe that all three models return reasonably high performance. Naïve Bayes (NB) outperformed the others, especially in terms of F_1 and AUC. Thus, we decided to select this as the default one for this task.

In Fig. 3d, we report the classifiers' performance for the column types on our gold standard, while Fig. 3e reports the same for Tablepedia. In both cases, we see that LR performs best, likely due to the combined importance of textual and numeric features for this task. Additionally, we observe that our model significantly outperforms the model of [38] on their dataset. If we compare the scores between the two datasets, then we see that they are significantly lower with our dataset. The reason is two-fold: First, the authors of Tablepedia have manually removed much noise from the extracted tables while no pre-processing took place on our dataset. Second, our dataset contains many more classes than Tablepedia, which makes it more challenging to predict.

Finally, we studied the added value of using Snorkel and compared it with a simpler majority voting (MV), i.e., labeling a data point using the most frequently predicted class. In Fig. 3c, we report both the accuracy obtained with majority voting and with Snorkel with various types of predictions. While Snorkel outperforms MV for the table type detection and column type detection in Tablepedia, MV is better when detecting the column types of our corpus. This was expected because, in this last case, our labeling functions (i.e., SPARQL queries) have frequently abstained. Consequently, M has a low label density, and whenever this occurs, Snorkel is unable to compute optimal weights that diverge from MV [30].

6.2 Entity Linking

Figure 4a reports the number of entities before and after the execution of the EGD rules. The left side compares the number of entities that refer to columns before and after r_3 was executed. As we can see, r_3 merged many entities, and this reduced the number of distinct entities of 65%. The right side shows the decrease of entities that refer to cells after the execution of rules $r_4, \ldots, r_7$. Here, the bar titled r_i reports the number of entities if only r_i is executed while the right-most column indicates the number of entities when all rules are included. We observe that every EGD contributes to merge some entities, but the best results are obtained when all EGDs are activated: here, the EGDs merged about 55% of the entities.

To evaluate the quality of entity links, we manually evaluated a sample of 100 merged entities. For each sampled entity, we first determined whether the entity was a meaningful one. From this analysis, we discovered that 65% of the entities are correct while the remaining have either nonsensical labels or some

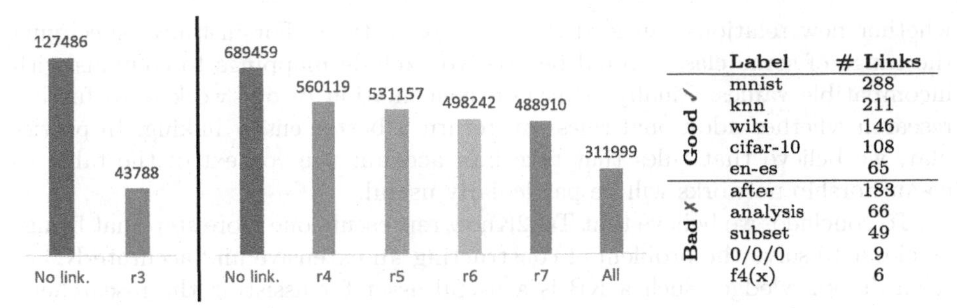

	Label	# Links
Good ✓	mnist	288
	knn	211
	wiki	146
	cifar-10	108
	en-es	65
Bad ✗	after	183
	analysis	66
	subset	49
	0/0/0	9
	f4(x)	6

(a) Ablation study. The bar marked with r_i reports the number of entities when only EGD r_i is included in the rule set

(b) Examples

Fig. 4. Analysis of the performance of entity linking

text resulted from errors of Tabula. In Fig. 4b, we report examples of good and bad entities with their number of links.

Then, we looked at the cells which referred to the entity, which were 541 in total. Since the rules could make a mistake and link two cells to the same entity although they meant different ones, we evaluated, for each entity, the precision of its links. Given the set of n cells that link to the same entity, the precision is computed by taking the cardinality of the largest subset of cells that refer to the same concept and divide it by n. For instance, consider an entity X with label Y which is linked to $n = 4$ cells. Three of these cells contain the text Y but refer to a dataset while one cell contains Y but refers to something else. In this case, the precision for X is $\frac{3}{4}$. In our sample, the average precision over the meaningful entities was about 97%, which is a relatively high value. This indicates that reasoning produced an accurate entity linking.

7 Conclusion

Summary. We presented Tab2Know, an end-to-end system for building a KB from the knowledge in scientific tables. One distinctive feature of Tab2Know is the usage of SPARQL queries for weak supervision to counter the lack of training data. Another distinctive feature is the usage of existentially quantified rules to link the entities without the help of a pre-existing KB.

Our pipeline effectively combines statistical-based classification and logical reasoning, exploiting SPARQL and remote KBs like Semantic Scholar. Therefore, we believe that ours is an excellent example of how semantic web technologies, statistical- and logic-based AI can be used side-by-side.

Future Work. Although our results are encouraging, and the current KB is already able to answer some non-trivial queries, future work is required to improve the performance. First, a more accurate table extraction procedure is needed to improve the accuracy of table interpretation and entity linking. Moreover, our current ontology links classes only via $\sqsubseteq$. It is interesting to study whether new relations can lead to better extractions. For instance, specifying the range of some classes could be used to exclude mappings to columns with incompatible values. Finally, a natural continuation of our work is to further research whether additional rules can return a better entity linking. In particular, we believe that rules that take into account the context of the table or co-authorship networks will be particularly useful.

To conclude, we believe that Tab2Know represents one more step that brings us closer to solve the problem of constructing an extensive and accurate KB of scientific knowledge. Such a KB is a useful asset for assisting the researchers, and it can play a crucial role in turning the vision of open science into a reality.

References

1. Ammar, W., et al.: Construction of the Literature Graph in Semantic Scholar. In: NAACL, pp. 84–91 (2018)
2. Benedikt, M., et al.: Benchmarking the chase. In: PODS, pp. 37–52 (2017)
3. Bhagavatula, C.S., Noraset, T., Downey, D.: TabEL: entity linking in web tables. In: Arenas, M., et al. (eds.) ISWC 2015. LNCS, vol. 9366, pp. 425–441. Springer, Cham (2015). https://doi.org/10.1007/978-3-319-25007-6_25
4. Bishop, C.M.: Pattern Recognition and Machine Learning. Springer, New York (2006)
5. Bizer, C., et al.: DBpedia-a crystallization point for the web of data. J. Web Semant. **7**(3), 154–165 (2009)
6. Böhm, C., de Melo, G., Naumann, F., Weikum, G.: LINDA: distributed web-of-data-scale entity matching. In: CIKM, pp. 2104–2108 (2012)
7. Cappuzzo, R., Papotti, P., Thirumuruganathan, S.: Creating embeddings of heterogeneous relational datasets for data integration tasks. In: SIGMOD, pp. 1335–1349 (2020)
8. Carral, D., Dragoste, I., González, L., Jacobs, C., Krötzsch, M., Urbani, J.: VLog: a rule engine for knowledge graphs. In: ISWC, pp. 19–35 (2019)
9. Chen, J., Jiménez-Ruiz, E., Horrocks, I., Sutton, C.A.: ColNet: embedding the semantics of web tables for column type prediction. In: AAAI, pp. 29–36 (2019)
10. Christen, P.: A survey of indexing techniques for scalable record linkage and deduplication. TKDE **24**(9), 1537–1555 (2012)
11. Clark, C., Divvala, S.: PDFFigures 2.0: mining figures from research papers. In: JCDL, pp. 143–152 (2016)
12. Das, S., et al.: Falcon: scaling up hands-off crowdsourced entity matching to build cloud services. In: SIGMOD, pp. 1431–1446 (2017)
13. Das Sarma, A., et al.: Finding related tables. In: SIGMOD, pp. 817–828 (2012)
14. Efthymiou, V., Hassanzadeh, O., Rodriguez-Muro, M., Christophides, V.: Matching web tables with knowledge base entities: from entity lookups to entity embeddings. In: d'Amato, C., et al. (eds.) ISWC 2017. LNCS, vol. 10587, pp. 260–277. Springer, Cham (2017). https://doi.org/10.1007/978-3-319-68288-4_16
15. Fagin, R., Kolaitis, P.G., Miller, R.J., Popa, L.: Data exchange: semantics and query answering. Theoret. Comput. Sci. **336**(1), 89–124 (2005)
16. Fang, J., Mitra, P., Tang, Z., Giles, C.L.: Table header detection and classification. In: AAAI, pp. 599–605 (2012)
17. Fetahu, B., Anand, A., Koutraki, M.: TableNet: an approach for determining fine-grained relations for wikipedia tables. In: WWW, pp. 2736–2742 (2019)

18. Geerts, F., Mecca, G., Papotti, P., Santoro, D.: That's all folks! LLUNATIC goes open source. PVLDB **7**(13), 1565–1568 (2014)
19. Horridge, M., Gonçalves, R.S., Nyulas, C.I., Tudorache, T., Musen, M.A.: Webprotégé: A cloud-based ontology editor. In: WWW, pp. 686–689 (2019)
20. Kavasidis, I., et al.: A saliency-based convolutional neural network for table and chart detection in digitized documents. In: ICIAP, pp. 292–302 (2019)
21. Konda, P., et al.: Magellan: toward building entity matching management systems. PVLDB **9**(12), 1197–1208 (2016)
22. Konstantinou, N., et al.: VADA: an architecture for end user informed data preparation. J. Big Data **6**(1), 1–32 (2019). https://doi.org/10.1186/s40537-019-0237-9
23. Kruit, B., Boncz, P., Urbani, J.: Extracting novel facts from tables for knowledge graph completion. In: Ghidini, C., et al. (eds.) ISWC 2019. LNCS, vol. 11778, pp. 364–381. Springer, Cham (2019). https://doi.org/10.1007/978-3-030-30793-6_21
24. Limaye, G., Sarawagi, S., Chakrabarti, S.: Annotating and searching web tables using entities, types and relationships. PVLDB **3**(1–2), 1338–1347 (2010)
25. Luo, X., Luo, K., Chen, X., Zhu, K.Q.: Cross-lingual entity linking for web tables. In: AAAI, pp. 362–369 (2018)
26. Mudgal, S., et al.: Deep learning for entity matching: a design space exploration. In: SIGMOD, pp. 19–34 (2018)
27. Oro, E., Ruffolo, M.: PDF-TREX: an approach for recognizing and extracting tables from PDF documents. In: ICDAR, pp. 906–910 (2009)
28. Papadakis, G., Ioannou, E., Palpanas, T.: Entity resolution: Past, present and yet-to-come. In: EDBT, pp. 647–650 (2020)
29. Pinto, D., McCallum, A., Wei, X., Croft, W.B.: Table extraction using conditional random fields. In: SIGIR, pp. 235–242 (2003)
30. Ratner, A., Bach, S.H., Ehrenberg, H., Fries, J., Wu, S., Ré, C.: Snorkel: rapid training data creation with weak supervision. VLDB J. **29**(2), 709–730 (2020)
31. Ratner, A., Hancock, B., Dunnmon, J., Sala, F., Pandey, S., Ré, C.: Training complex models with multi-task weak supervision. In: AAAI, pp. 4763–4771 (2019)
32. Ritze, D., Lehmberg, O., Bizer, C.: Matching HTML tables to DBpedia. In: WIMS, pp. 1–6 (2015)
33. Ritze, D., Lehmberg, O., Oulabi, Y., Bizer, C.: Profiling the potential of web tables for augmenting cross-domain knowledge bases. In: WWW, pp. 251–261 (2016)
34. Schreiber, S., Agne, S., Wolf, I., Dengel, A., Ahmed, S.: DeepDeSRT: deep learning for detection and structure recognition of tables in document images. In: ICDAR, pp. 1162–1167 (2017)
35. Siegel, N., Horvitz, Z., Levin, R., Divvala, S., Farhadi, A.: FigureSeer: parsing result-figures in research papers. In: Leibe, B., Matas, J., Sebe, N., Welling, M. (eds.) ECCV 2016. LNCS, vol. 9911, pp. 664–680. Springer, Cham (2016). https://doi.org/10.1007/978-3-319-46478-7_41
36. Siegel, N., Lourie, N., Power, R., Ammar, W.: Extracting scientific figures with distantly supervised neural networks. In: JCDL, pp. 223–232 (2018)
37. Vine, N.L., Zeigenfuse, M., Rowan, M.: Extracting tables from documents using conditional generative adversarial networks and genetic algorithms. In: IJCNN, pp. 1–8 (2019)
38. Yu, W., Peng, W., Shu, Y., Zeng, Q., Jiang, M.: Experimental evidence extraction system in data science with hybrid table features and ensemble learning. In: WWW, pp. 951–961 (2020)
39. Zhang, Z.: Effective and efficient semantic table interpretation using TableMiner+. Semant. Web **8**(6), 921–957 (2017)

Deciding SHACL Shape Containment Through Description Logics Reasoning

Martin Leinberger[1(✉)], Philipp Seifer[2], Tjitze Rienstra[1], Ralf Lämmel[2], and Steffen Staab[3,4]

[1] Institute for Web Science and Technologies, University of Koblenz-Landau, Koblenz, Germany
{mleinberger,rienstra}@uni-koblenz.de

[2] The Software Languages Team, University of Koblenz-Landau, Koblenz, Germany
{pseifer,laemmel}@uni-koblenz.de

[3] Institute for Parallel and Distributed Systems, University of Stuttgart, Stuttgart, Germany
steffen.staab@ipvs.uni-stuttgart.de

[4] Web and Internet Science Research Group, University of Southampton, Southampton, England

Abstract. The Shapes Constraint Language (SHACL) allows for formalizing constraints over RDF data graphs. A shape groups a set of constraints that may be fulfilled by nodes in the RDF graph. We investigate the problem of containment between SHACL shapes. One shape is contained in a second shape if every graph node meeting the constraints of the first shape also meets the constraints of the second. To decide shape containment, we map SHACL shape graphs into description logic axioms such that shape containment can be answered by description logic reasoning. We identify several, increasingly tight syntactic restrictions of SHACL for which this approach becomes sound and complete.

1 Introduction

RDF has been designed as a flexible, semi-structured data format. To ensure data quality and to allow for restricting its large flexibility in specific domains, the W3C has standardized the *Shapes Constraint Language (SHACL)*[1]. A set of SHACL shapes are represented in a *shape graph*. A shape graph represents constraints that only a subset of all possible RDF data graphs *conform* to. A SHACL processor may validate whether a given RDF data graph conforms to a given SHACL shape graph.

A shape graph and a data graph that act as a running example are presented in Fig. 1. The shape graph introduces a `PaintingShape` (line 1–4) which constrains all instances of the class (Painting). It requires the presence of at least one —exhibitedAt→ property (line 3) as well as that each node reachable via the —creator→ property from a (Painting) conforms to the `PainterShape` (line 4). The

[1] https://www.w3.org/TR/shacl/.

J. Z. Pan et al. (Eds.): ISWC 2020, LNCS 12506, pp. 366–383, 2020.
https://doi.org/10.1007/978-3-030-62419-4_21

```
1  :PaintingShape a sh:NodeShape;
2      sh:targetClass :Painting;
3      sh:property [ sh:path :exhibitedAt; sh:minCount 1; ];
4      sh:property [ sh:path :creator; sh:node :PainterShape; ].
5
6  :PainterShape a sh:NodeShape;
7      sh:property [ sh:inversePath :creator; sh:node :PaintingShape; ];
8      sh:property [ sh:path :birthdate; sh:minCount 1; sh:maxCount 1;
           ];
9
10 :CubistShape a sh:NodeShape
11     sh:property [ sh:path ( [sh:inversePath :creator] :style );
12         sh:minCount 1; sh:value :cubism; ].
```

(a) Example for a SHACL shape graph.

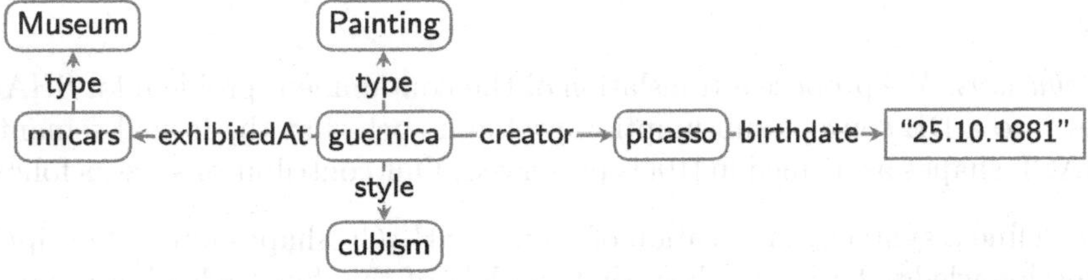

(b) Example for a data graph that conforms to the shape graph.

Fig. 1. Example of a shape graph (a) and a data graph (b).

PainterShape (lines 5–8) requires all incoming -creator→ properties to conform to PaintingShape (line 6) as well as the presence of exactly one -birthdate→ property. Lastly, the shapes define a CubistShape (lines 9–11) which must have an incoming -creator→ property from a node that has an outgoing -style→ property to the node (cubism). The graph shown in Fig. 1 conforms to this set of shapes as it satisfies the constraints imposed by the shape graph.

In this paper, we investigate the problem of *containment* between shapes: Given a shape graph S including the two shapes s and s', intuitively s is contained in s' if and only if every data graph node that conforms to s is also a node that conforms to s'. An example of a containment problem is the question whether CubistShape is contained in PainterShape for all possible RDF graphs. While containment is not directly used in the validation of RDF graphs with SHACL, it offers means to tackle a broad range of other problems such as SHACL constraint debugging, query optimization [1,5] or program verification [16]. As an example of query optimization, assume that CubistShape is contained in PainterShape and that the graph being queried conforms to the shapes. A query querying for ?X and ?Y such that ?X -style→(cubism),, ?X -creator→ ?Y and ?X -exhibitedAt→ ?Z can be optimized. Since nodes that are results for ?Y must conform to CubistShape and CubistShape is contained in PainterShape, nodes that are results for ?X must conform to PaintingShape.

Subsequently, the pattern ?X -exhibitedAt→ ?Z can be removed without consequence.

Given a set of shapes S, checking whether a shape s is contained in another shape s' involves checking whether there is no counterexample. That means, searching for a graph that conforms to S, but in which a node exists that conforms to s' but not to s. A similar problem is concept subsumption in description logics (DL). For DL, efficient tableau-based approaches [4] are known that either disprove concept subsumption by constructing a counterexample or prove that no counterexample can exist. Despite the fundamental differences between the Datalog-inspired semantics of SHACL [10] and the Tarski-style semantics used by description logics, we leverage concept subsumption by translating SHACL shapes into description logic knowledge bases such that the shape containment problem can be answered by performing a subsumption check.

Contributions. We propose a translation of the containment problem for SHACL shapes into a DL concept subsumption problem such that the formal semantics of SHACL shapes as defined in [10] is preserved. Our contributions are as follows:

1. We define a syntactic translation of a set of SHACL shapes into a description logic knowledge base and show that models of this knowledge base and the idea of faithful assignments for RDF graphs in SHACL can also be mapped into each other.
2. We show that by using the translation, the containment of SHACL shapes can be decided using DL concept subsumption.
3. Based on the translation and the resulting description logic, we identify syntactic restrictions of SHACL for which the approach is sound and complete.

Organization. The paper first recalls the basic syntax and semantics of SHACL and description logics in Sect. 2. We describe how sets of SHACL shapes are translated into a DL knowledge base in Sect. 3. Section 4 investigates how to use standard DL entailment for deciding shape containment. Finally, we discuss related work in Sect. 5 and summarize our results. An extended version of this paper including full proofs and additional explanations is available on Arxiv[2].

2 Preliminaries

2.1 Shape Constraint Language

The Shapes Constraint Language (SHACL) is a W3C standard for validating RDF graphs. For this, SHACL distinguishes between the *shape graph* that contains the schematic definitions (e. g., Fig. 1a) and the *data graph* that is being

[2] https://arxiv.org/abs/2008.13603.

validated (e.g., Fig. 1b). A shape graph consists of *shapes* that group *constraints* and provide so called *target nodes.* Target nodes specify which nodes of the data graph have to be valid with respect to the constraints in order for the graph to be valid. In the following, we rely on the definitions presented by [10].

Data Graphs. We assume familiarity with RDF. We abstract away from concrete RDF syntax, representing an RDF Graph G as a labeled oriented graph $G = (V_G, E_G)$ where V_G is the set of nodes of G and E_G is a set of triples of the form (v_1, p, v_2) meaning that there is an edge in G from v_1 to v_2 labeled with the property p. We use $\mathcal{V}$ to denote the set of all possible graph nodes and $\mathcal{E}$ to denote the set of all possible triples. A subset $\mathcal{V}_C \subseteq \mathcal{V}$ represents the set of possible RDF classes. We use $\mathcal{G}$ to denote the set of all possible RDF graphs.

Constraints. While shape graphs and constraints are typically given as RDF graphs, we use a logical abstraction in the following. We use $\mathcal{N}_S$ to refer to the set of all possible shape names. A constraint ϕ from the set of all constraints Φ is then constructed as follows:

$$\phi ::= \top \mid s \mid v \mid \phi_1 \wedge \phi_2 \mid \neg\phi \mid \geqslant_n \rho.\phi \tag{1}$$

$$\rho ::= p \mid \hat{}\rho \mid \rho_1/\rho_2 \tag{2}$$

where $\top$ represents a constraint that is always true, $s \in \mathcal{N}_S$ references a shape name, $v \in \mathcal{V}$ is a graph node, $\neg\phi$ represents a negated constraint and $\geqslant_n \rho.\phi$ indicates that there must be at least n successors via the path expression ρ that satisfy the constraint ϕ. For simplicity, we restrict ourselves to path expressions ρ comprising of either standard properties p, inverse of path $\hat{}\rho$, and concatenations of two paths ρ_1/ρ_2. We therefore leave out operators for transitive closure and alternative paths. We use $\mathcal{P}$ to indicate the set of all possible path expressions. A number of additional syntactic constructs can be derived from these basic constructors, including $\phi_1 \vee \phi_2$ for $\neg(\neg\phi_1 \wedge \neg\phi_2)$, $\leqslant_n \rho.\phi$ for $\neg(\geqslant_{n+1} \rho.\phi)$,$=_n \rho.\phi$ for $(\leqslant_n \rho.\phi) \wedge (\geqslant_n \rho.\phi)$, and $\forall \rho.\phi$ for $\leq_0 \rho.\neg\phi$. As an example, the constraint of `CubistShape` (see Fig. 1) can be expressed as $\geqslant_1$(`^creator/style`).`cubism`.

Evaluation of constraints is rather straightforward with the exception of reference cycles. To highlight this issue, consider a shape name `Local` with its constraint $\forall$ `knows.Local`. In order to fulfill the constraint, any graph node reachable through –knows→ must conform to `Local`. Consider a graph with a single vertex (b_1) whose –knows→ property points to itself Intuitively, there are two possible solutions. If (b_1) is assumed to conform to `Local`, then the constraint is satisfied and it is correct to say that (b_1) conforms to `Local`. If (b_1) is assumed to not conform to `Local`, then the constraint is violated and it is correct to say that (b_1) does not conform to `Local`. We follow the proposal of [10] and ground evaluation of constraints using *assignments.* An assignment σ maps graph nodes v to shape names s. Evaluation of constraints takes an assignment as a parameter and evaluates the constraints with respect to the given assignment. The case above is therefore represented through two different assignments—one in which `Local` $\in \sigma(\boxed{b_1})$ and a different one where `Local` $\notin \sigma(\boxed{b_1})$. We require assignments to be total, meaning that they map all graph nodes to the set of all shapes that the node supposedly conforms to. This disallows certain combinations of reference cycles and negation in constraints, in essence requiring them to be stratified. In contrast, [10] also defines partial assignments, lifting this restriction. Due to the lack of space, we refer to [10] for an in depth discussion on the differences of total and partial assignments.

Definition 1 (Assignment). *Let $G = (V_G, E_G)$ be an RDF graph and S a set of shapes with its set of shape names* $\text{Names}(S)$. *An assignment σ is a total function $\sigma : V_G \rightarrow 2^{\text{Names}(S)}$ mapping graph nodes $v \in V_G$ to subsets of shape names. If a shape name $s \in \sigma(v)$, then v is assigned to the shape name s. For all $s \notin \sigma(v)$, the node v is not assigned to the shape s.*

Evaluating whether a node v in G satisfies a constraint ϕ, written $[\![\phi]\!]^{v,G,\sigma}$, is defined as shown in Fig. 2.

$$[\![\top]\!]^{v,G,\sigma} = \text{true} \qquad [\![\neg\phi]\!]^{v,G,\sigma} = \begin{cases} \text{true if } [\![\phi]\!]^{v,G,\sigma} = \text{false} \\ \text{false otherwise} \end{cases}$$

$$[\![\phi_1 \wedge \phi_2]\!]^{v,G,\sigma} = \begin{cases} \text{true if } [\![\phi_1]\!]^{v,G,\sigma} = \text{true} \wedge \\ \quad [\![\phi_2]\!]^{v,G,\sigma} = \text{true} \\ \text{false otherwise} \end{cases} \qquad [\![v']\!]^{v,G,\sigma} = \begin{cases} \text{true if } v = v' \\ \text{false otherwise} \end{cases}$$

$$[\![\geqslant_n \rho.\phi]\!]^{v,G,\sigma} = \begin{cases} \text{true if } |\{v_2 \mid (v_1, v_2) \in [\![r]\!]^G \wedge \\ \quad [\![\phi]\!]^{v_2,G,\sigma} = \text{true}\}| \geq n \\ \text{false otherwise} \end{cases} \qquad [\![s]\!]^{v,G,\sigma} = \begin{cases} \text{true if } s \in \sigma(v) \\ \text{false otherwise} \end{cases}$$

$$\begin{aligned} [\![p]\!]^G &= \{(v_1, v_2) \mid \exists p : (v_1, p, v_2) \in E_G\} \\ [\![{}^\wedge\rho]\!]^G &= \{(v_2, v_1) \mid (v_1, v_2) \in [\![\rho]\!]^G\} \\ [\![\rho_1/\rho_2]\!]^G &= \{(v_1, v_2) \mid \exists v : (v_1, v) \in [\![\rho_1]\!]^G \wedge (v, v_2) \in [\![\rho_2]\!]^G\} \end{aligned}$$

Fig. 2. Evaluation rules for constraints and path expressions.

Shapes and Validation. A shape is modelled by a triple (s, ϕ, q). It consists of a shape name s, a constraint ϕ and a query for target nodes q. Target nodes denote those nodes which are expected to fulfill the constraint associated with the shape. Queries for target nodes are built according to the following grammar:

$$q ::= \bot \mid \{v_1, \ldots, v_n\} \mid \texttt{class}\ v \mid \texttt{subjectsOf}\ p \mid \texttt{objectsOf}\ p \tag{3}$$

where $\bot$ represents a query that targets no nodes, $\{v_1 \ldots v_n\}$ targets all explicitly listed nodes with $v_1, \ldots, v_n \in \mathcal{V}$, `class` v targets all instances of the class represented by v where $v \in \mathcal{V}_C$, `subjectsOf` p targets all subjects of the property p and `objectsOf` p targets all objects of p. We use $\mathcal{Q}$ to refer to the set of all possible queries and $[\![q]\!]_G$ to denote the set of nodes in the RDF graph G targeted by the query q (c.f. Fig. 3).

$$[\![\bot]\!]_G = \emptyset \qquad [\![\mathtt{class}\ v_2]\!]_G = \{v_1 \mid (v_1, \mathtt{type}, v_2) \in E_G\}$$
$$[\![\{v_1, \ldots, v_n\}]\!]_G = \{v_1, \ldots, v_n\} \qquad [\![\mathtt{subjectsOf}\ p]\!]_G = \{v_1 \mid \exists v_2 : (v_1, p, v_2) \in E_G\}$$
$$[\![\mathtt{objectsOf}\ p]\!]_G = \{v_2 \mid \exists v_1 : (v_1, p, v_2) \in E_G\}$$

Fig. 3. Evaluation of target node queries.

A shape graph is then represented by a set of shapes S whereas $\mathcal{S}$ represents the set of all possible sets of shapes. We assume for each $(s, \phi, q) \in S$ that, if a shape name s' appears in ϕ, then there also exists a $(s', \phi', q') \in S$. Similar to [10], we refer to the language represented by the definitions above as $\mathcal{L}$. As an example, Fig. 4 shows the shape graph defined in Fig. 1a as a set of shapes.

$$\begin{array}{ll} S_1 = \{ & \\ (\mathtt{PaintingShape}, \geqslant_1 \mathtt{exhibitedAt}.\top \wedge \forall \mathtt{creator.PainterShape}, \mathtt{class\ Painting}), & \\ (\mathtt{PainterShape}, \ =_1 \mathtt{birthdate}.\top \wedge \forall {}^\wedge\mathtt{creator.PaintingShape}, & \bot), \\ (\mathtt{CubistShape}\ \ , \geqslant_1 {}^\wedge\mathtt{creator/style.cubism}, & \bot) \\ \} & \end{array}$$

Fig. 4. Representation of the shape graph shown in Fig. 1a as a set of shapes.

Validating an RDF graph means finding a *faithful assignment*. That is, finding an assignment for which two conditions hold: First, if a node is a target node of a shape, then the assignment must assign that shape to the node. Second, if an assignment assigns a shape to a graph node, the constraint of the shape must evaluate to true. Third, when a constraint evaluates to true (false) on a node, that node must (not) be assigned to the corresponding shape.

Definition 2 (Faithful assignment). *An assignment σ for a graph $G = (V_G, E_G)$ and a set of shapes S is faithful, iff for each $(s, \phi, q) \in S$ and for each graph node $v \in V_G$, it holds that:*

- $s \in \sigma(v) \Leftrightarrow [\![\phi]\!]^{v,G,\sigma}$.
- $v \in [\![q]\!]_G \Rightarrow s \in \sigma(v)$.

A graph that is valid with respect to a set of shapes is said to *conform* to the set of shapes.

Definition 3 (Conformance). *An RDF graph G conforms to a set of shapes S iff there is at least one faithful assignment σ for G and S. We write* Faith(G, S) *to denote the set of all faithful assignments for G and S.*

For the data graph shown in Fig. 1b, there is a faithful assignment σ_1 that maps `PaintingShape` to guernica and both `PainterShape` and `CubistShape` to

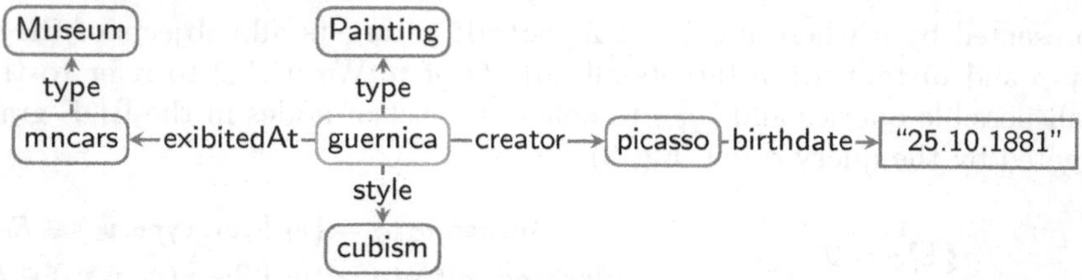

Museum Painting
type type
mncars ← exibitedAt – guernica – creator → picasso – birthdate → "25.10.1881"
style
cubism

$\sigma_1(\bigcirc) = \emptyset \quad \sigma_1(\bigcirc) = \{\texttt{PaintingShape}\} \quad \sigma_1(\bigcirc) = \{\texttt{PainterShape}, \texttt{CubistShape}\}$

Fig. 5. Faithful assignment σ_1 for S_1 and the data graph shown in Fig. 1b.

picasso (see Fig. 5). The assignment is faithful because all instances of Painting are assigned to `PaintingShape` and all nodes that are assigned to a shape satisfy the constraints of the shape.

2.2 Description Logics

We focus on the highly-expressive DL $\mathcal{ALCOIQ}(\circ)$ as well as decidable subsets of this logic. We follow routine syntax and interpretation-based semantics (c. f. [3,4, 13]). $\text{Sig}(K) = (N_A, N_P, N_O)$ is the signature of a knowledge base K comprising of a set of atomic concept names N_A that is a subset of the set of all possible atomic concept names $\mathcal{N}_A$, a set of atomic property names N_P (a subset of $\mathcal{N}_P$) and a set of object names N_O (a subset of $\mathcal{N}_O$). From these, more complex role expressions, denoted by r, and concept expressions, denoted by C and D, are built (see Fig. 6) whereby $\mathcal{C}$ denotes the set of all possible concept expressions and $\mathcal{R}$ the set of all possible role expressions.

Constructor Name	Syntax	Semantics
atomic property name	p	$p^I \subseteq \Delta^I \times \Delta^I$
inverse role	r^-	$\{(o_2, o_1) \mid (o_1, o_2) \in r^I\}$
role composition	$r_1 \circ r_2$	$\{(o_1, o_2) \mid (o_1, o) \in {r_1}^I \wedge (o, o_2) \in {r_2}^I\}$
atomic concept name	A	$A^I \subseteq \Delta^I$
nominal concept	$\{o_1, \dots o_n\}$	$\{o_1^I, \dots, o_n^I\}$
top	$\top$	Δ^I
negation	$\neg C$	$\Delta^I \setminus C^I$
conjunction	$C \sqcap D$	$C^I \cap D^I$
qualified number restriction	$\geq_n r.C$	$\{o_1 \mid \lvert\{o_1 \mid (o_1, o_2) \in r^I \wedge o_2 \in C^I\}\rvert \geq n\}$

Fig. 6. Syntax and semantics of roles r (above the line) and concept expressions C, D (below the line).

Axioms are either concept inclusions, concept assertions or role assertions (see Fig. 7). We use $C \equiv D$ as a shorthand for the two axioms $C \sqsubseteq D$ and $D \sqsubseteq C$. In a given interpretation $I = (\Delta, \cdot^I)$ comprised of a universe Δ and an interpretation function $\cdot^I$, an axiom ψ is either true or false. An interpretation in which all

Name	Syntax	Semantics
concept inclusion	$C \sqsubseteq D$	$C^I \subseteq D^I$
concept assertion	$o : C$	$o^I \in C^I$
role assertion	$(o_1, o_2) : r$	$(o_1^I, o_2^I) \in r^I$

Fig. 7. Syntax and semantics of axioms.

axioms of K are true is a model of K. We use $\text{Mod}(K)$ to denote the set of all models of K. An axiom ψ is entailed by K written $K \models \psi$ if it is true in all models of K. Lastly, we use $\mathcal{K}$ for the set of all possible knowledge bases.

3 From SHACL Shape Containment to Description Logic Concept Subsumption

Given two shapes s and s' that are elements of the same set of shapes S, we say that s is contained in s' if any node that conforms to s will also conform to s' for any given RDF data graph G as well as any given faithful assignment for S and G.

Definition 4 (Shape Containment). *Let S be a set of shapes with $s, s' \in \text{Names}(S)$. The shape s is contained in shape s' if:*

$$\forall G \in \mathcal{G} : \forall \sigma \in \text{Faith}(G, S) : \forall v \in V_G : s \in \sigma(v) \Rightarrow s' \in \sigma(v) \textit{ with } s, s' \in \text{Names}(S)$$

We use $s <:_S s'$ to indicate that shape s is contained in s' with respect to S.

Both SHACL and description logics use syntactic formulas inspired by first-order logic. However, their semantics are fundamentally different. For SHACL, we follow the Datalog-inspired semantics introduced by [10]. Description logics on the other hand adopt Tarskian-style semantics. To decide shape containment, we map sets of shapes syntactically into description logic knowledge bases such that the difference in semantics can be overcome.

The function τ_{shapes} maps a set of shapes S to a description logic knowledge base $K^{<S>}$ using four auxiliary functions (see Fig. 8): First, τ_{name} maps shape names, RDF classes as well as properties and graph nodes onto atomic concept names, atomic property names and object names. Second, τ_{role} maps SHACL path expressions to DL role expressions. Third, τ_{constr} maps constraints to concept expressions. Fourth, τ_{target} maps queries for target nodes to concept expressions. The function τ_{shapes} maps a set of shapes S to a set of axioms such that $s <:_S s'$ is true if $K^{<S>} \models \tau_{\text{name}}(s) \sqsubseteq \tau_{\text{name}}(s')$.

To prove this property, we show that every finite model of $K^{<S>}$ can be used to construct an RDF graph G and an assignment that is faithful with respect to G and S. Likewise, a model of $K^{<S>}$ can be constructed from an assignment that is faithful with respect to S and any given RDF graph G.

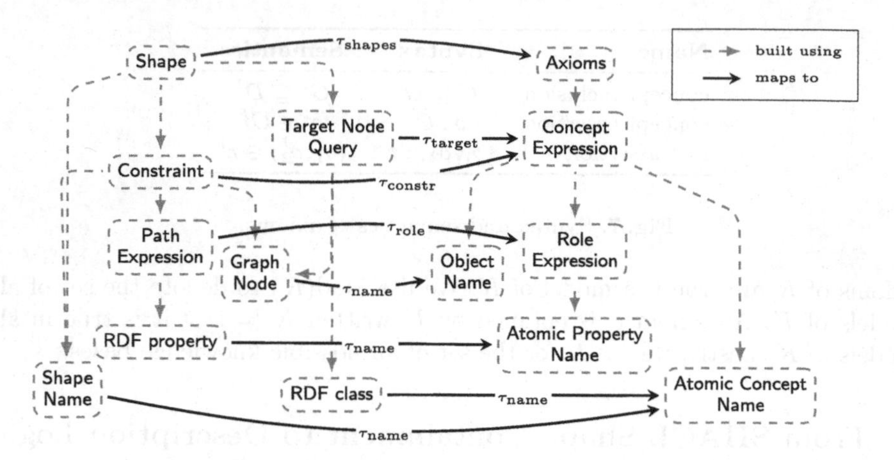

Fig. 8. Syntactic translation of SHACL to description logics.

3.1 Syntactic Mapping

We map the set of shapes S into a knowledge base $K^{<S>}$ by constraints and target node queries of each shape using the functions τ_{role}, τ_{constr}, τ_{target}, and τ_{shapes}. All those functions rely on τ_{name} which maps atomic elements used in SHACL to atomic elements of a DL knowledge base:

Definition 5 (Mapping atomic elements). *The function* $\tau_{\text{name}} : \mathcal{N}_S \cup \mathcal{V}_C \cup \mathcal{V} \cup \mathcal{E} \to \mathcal{N}_A \cup \mathcal{N}_P \cup \mathcal{N}_O$ *is an injective function mapping shape names and RDF classes onto atomic concept names, graph nodes onto object names as well as properties onto atomic property names.*

Definition 6 (Mapping path expressions to DL roles). *The* path mapping *function* $\tau_{\text{role}} : \mathcal{P} \to \mathcal{R}$, *is defined as follows:*

$$\begin{aligned}
\tau_{\text{role}}(p) &= \tau_{\text{name}}(p)\\
\tau_{\text{role}}(\hat{}\rho) &= \tau_{\text{role}}(\rho)^{-}\\
\tau_{\text{role}}(\rho_1/\rho_2) &= \tau_{\text{role}}(\rho_1) \circ \tau_{\text{role}}(\rho_2)
\end{aligned}$$

Definition 7 (Mapping constraints to DL concept expressions). *The* constraint mapping $\tau_{\text{constr}} : \Phi \to \mathcal{C}$ *is defined as follows:*

$$\begin{aligned}
\tau_{\text{constr}}(\top) &= \top\\
\tau_{\text{constr}}(s) &= \tau_{\text{name}}(s)\\
\tau_{\text{constr}}(v) &= \{\tau_{\text{name}}(v)\}\\
\tau_{\text{constr}}(\phi_1 \wedge \phi_2) &= \tau_{\text{constr}}(\phi_1) \sqcap \tau_{\text{constr}}(\phi_2)\\
\tau_{\text{constr}}(\neg\phi) &= \neg\tau_{\text{constr}}(\phi)\\
\tau_{\text{constr}}(\geqslant_n \rho.\phi) &= \geq_n \tau_{\text{role}}(\rho).\tau_{\text{constr}}(\phi)
\end{aligned}$$

Definition 8 (Mapping target node queries to DL concept expressions). *The* target node mapping $\tau_{\text{target}} : \mathcal{Q} \rightarrow \mathcal{C}$ *is defined as follows:*

$$\begin{aligned}
\tau_{\text{target}}(\bot) &= \bot\\
\tau_{\text{target}}(\{v_1,\ldots,v_n\}) &= \{\tau_{\text{name}}(v_1),\ldots,\tau_{\text{name}}(v_n)\}\\
\tau_{\text{target}}(\texttt{class}\ v) &= \tau_{\text{name}}(v)\\
\tau_{\text{target}}(\texttt{subjectsOf}\ p) &= \exists\, \tau_{\text{name}}(p).\top\\
\tau_{\text{target}}(\texttt{objectsOf}\ p) &= \exists\, \tau_{\text{name}}(p)^{-}.\top
\end{aligned}$$

The mapping $\tau_{\text{target}}(q)$ of a target query q is defined such that querying for the instances of q returns exactly the same nodes from the data graph. Likewise, the mapping $\tau_{\text{constr}}(\phi)$ is defined such that it contains those nodes for which ϕ evaluates to true and τ_{role} that the interpretation of the role expression contains those nodes that are also in the evaluation of the path expression. τ_{shapes} generalizes the construction to sets of shapes:

Definition 9 (Mapping sets of shapes to DL axioms). *The* shape mapping *function* $\tau_{\text{shapes}} : \mathcal{S} \rightarrow \mathcal{K}$ *is defined as follows:*

$$\tau_{\text{shapes}}(S) = \bigcup_{(s,\phi,q)\in S} \{\tau_{\text{target}}(q) \sqsubseteq \tau_{\text{name}}(s), \tau_{\text{constr}}(\phi) \equiv \tau_{\text{name}}(s)\}$$

To illustrate the function τ_{shapes}, the translation of the set of shapes $\tau_{\text{shapes}}(S_1) = K^{<S_1>}$ is shown in Fig. 9.

$$\begin{aligned}
K^{S_1} = \{\, & \textbf{Painting} \sqsubseteq \textbf{PaintingShape},\\
& \geq_1 \textbf{exhibitedAt}.\top \sqcap \forall\, \textbf{creator.PainterShape} \equiv \textbf{PaintingShape},\\
& \bot \sqsubseteq \textbf{PainterShape},\\
& \geq_1 \textbf{birthdate}.\top \sqcap \forall\, \textbf{creator}^{-}.\textbf{PaintingShape} \equiv \textbf{PainterShape},\\
& \bot \sqsubseteq \textbf{Cubist},\\
& \geq_1 \textbf{creator}^{-} \circ \textbf{style}.\{\textbf{cubism}\} \equiv \textbf{CubistShape} \quad \}
\end{aligned}$$

Fig. 9. Translation $\tau_{\text{shapes}}(S_1) = K^{<S_1>}$ of the set of shapes S_1.

3.2 Construction of Faithful Assignments and Models

Given our translation, we now show that the notion of faithful assignments of SHACL and *finite models* in description logics coincide.

Definition 10 (Finite model). *Let K be a knowledge base and $I \in \text{Mod}(K)$ a model of K. The model I is finite, if its universe Δ^I is finite [7]. We use* $\text{Mod}^{\text{fin}}(K)$ *to refer to the set of all finite models of K.*

Given an RDF data graph G, a set of shapes S and an assignment σ that is faithful with respect to S and G, we construct an interpretation $I^{G,\sigma}$ that is a finite model for the knowledge base $K^{<S>}$.

Definition 11 (Construction of the finite model $I^{G,\sigma}$). *Let S be a set of shapes, $G = (V_G, E_G)$ an RDF data graph and σ an assignment that is faithful with respect to S and G. Furthermore, let τ_{node} be the inverse of the function τ_{name}. The finite model $I^{G,\sigma}$ for the knowledge base $\tau_{\text{shapes}}(S) = K^{<S>}$ is constructed as follows:*

1. *All objects are interpreted as themselves:* $\forall o \in N_O : o^I = o$.
2. *A pair of objects is contained in the interpretation of a relation if the two objects are connected in the RDF data graph:*
   $\forall p \in N_P : \forall o_1, o_2 \in N_O : (o_1^{I^{G,\sigma}}, o_2^{I^{G,\sigma}}) \in p^{I^{G,\sigma}}$ *if* $(\tau_{\text{node}}(o_1), p, \tau_{\text{node}}(o_2)) \in (E_G \setminus \{(v_1, \texttt{type}, v_2) \in E_G\})$.
3. *Objects are in the interpretation of a concept if this concept is a class used in the RDF data graph and the object is an instance of this class according to the graph:*
   $\forall A_v \in N_A : \forall o \in N_O : o^{I^{G,\sigma}} \in A_v^{I^{G,\sigma}}$ *if* $(\tau_{\text{node}}(o), \texttt{type}, \tau_{\text{node}}(A_v)) \in E_G$.
4. *Objects are in the interpretation of a concept if the concept is a shape name and the assignment σ assigns the shape to the object:*
   $\forall A_s \in N_A : \forall o \in N_O : o^{I^{G,\sigma}} \in A_s^{I^{G,\sigma}}$ *if* $\tau_{\text{node}}(A_s) \in \sigma(\tau_{\text{node}}(o))$.

The interpretation $I^{G,\sigma}$ is a model of the knowledge base $K^{<S>}$. Before we show this, it is important to notice that the interpretation of role expressions constructed through τ_{role} contains the same nodes in the interpretation $I^{G,\sigma}$ as the evaluation of the path expression.

Lemma 1. *Let S be a set of shapes, G an RDF data graph and σ an assignment that is faithful with respect to S and G. Furthermore, let $I^{G,\sigma}$ be an interpretation for $K^{<S>}$. It holds that $\forall (o_1, o_2) \in \tau_{\text{role}}(\rho)^{I^{G,\sigma}} \Rightarrow (\tau_{\text{node}}(o_1), \tau_{\text{node}}(o_2)) \in [\![\rho]\!]^G$ for any path expression ρ.*

Proof. The interpretation $I^{G,\sigma}$ contains all properties of the RDF graph. The result is then immediate from the evaluation rules of path expressions (c. f. Fig. 2) and semantics of role expressions (c. f. Fig. 6). □

Theorem 1. *Let S be a set of shapes, G an RDF data graph and σ an assignment that is faithful with respect to S and G. Furthermore, let $K^{<S>}$ be a knowledge base that is constructed through $\tau_{\text{shapes}}(S)$. The interpretation $I^{G,\sigma}$ is a finite model of $K^{<S>}$ ($I^{G,\sigma} \models K^{<S>}$).*

Proof (Sketch). $I^{G,\sigma}$ is finite because the RDF graph G has only a finite number of graph nodes. Furthermore, $I^{G,\sigma}$ satisfying the axioms created by τ_{shapes} can be shown via induction over the mapping rules for τ_{constr} and τ_{target}. □

Furthermore, we show that any finite model I of a knowledge base $K^{<S>}$ built from a set of shapes S can be transformed into an RDF graph G^I and an assignment σ^I such that σ^I is faithful with respect to S and G^I. We construct G^I and σ^I in the following manner:

Definition 12 (Construction of G^I and σ^I). *Let S be a set of shapes and $K^{<S>}$ a knowledge base constructed via $\tau_{\text{shapes}}(S)$. Furthermore, let $I \in \text{Mod}^{\text{fin}}(K^{<S>})$ be a finite model of $K^{<S>}$. The RDF graph $G^I = (V_G^I, E_G^I)$ and the assignment σ^I can then be constructed as follows:*

1. *The interpretations of all relations are interpreted as relations between graph nodes in the RDF graph:* $\forall p \in N_P : (o^I, o'^I) \in p^I \Rightarrow (\tau_{\text{node}}(o), p, \tau_{\text{node}}(o')) \in E_G^I$.
2. *The interpretations of all concepts that are not shape names are triples indicating an instance in the RDF graph:* $\forall A \in N_A : (o^I \in A^I \wedge A \notin \text{Names}(S)) \Rightarrow (\tau_{\text{node}}(o), \texttt{type}, \tau_{\text{node}}(A)) \in E_G^I$.
3. *The interpretations of all concept names that are shape names are used to construct the assignment* $\sigma^I : \forall A \in N_A : (o^I \in A^I \wedge A \in \text{Names}(S)) \Rightarrow \tau_{\text{node}}(A) \in \sigma^I(\tau_{\text{node}}(o))$.

An assignment σ^I constructed in this manner is faithful with respect to the constructed RDF graph G^I and the set of shapes S.

Theorem 2. *Let S be a set of shapes and $K^{<S>}$ be a knowledge base constructed through $\tau_{\text{shapes}}(S)$. Furthermore, let $I \in \text{Mod}^{\text{fin}}(K^{<S>})$ be a finite model for $K^{<S>}$. The assignment σ^I is faithful with respect to S and G^I.*

Proof (Sketch). The two axioms that are generated by τ_{shapes} coincide with the two conditions for faithful assignments (c. f. Definitions 2 and 9). This can be shown by induction over the translation rules. □

3.3 Deciding Shape Containment Using Concept Subsumption

Given the translation rules and semantic equivalence between finite models of a description logic knowledge base and assignments for SHACL shapes, we can leverage description logics for deciding shape containment. Assume a set of shapes S containing definitions for two shapes s and s'. Those shapes are represented by atomic concepts in the knowledge base $K^{<S>}$. As the following theorem proves, deciding whether the shape s is contained in the shape s' is equivalent to deciding concept subsumption between s and s' in $K^{<S>}$ using finite models.

Theorem 3 (Shape containment and concept subsumption). *Let S be a set of shapes and $K^{<S>}$ the knowledge base constructed via $\tau_{\text{shapes}}(S)$. Let $\models_{\text{fin}}$ indicate that an axiom is true in all finite models. It holds that:*

$$s <:_S s' \Leftrightarrow K^{<S>} \models_{\text{fin}} \tau_{\text{name}}(s) \sqsubseteq \tau_{\text{name}}(s')$$

Proof (Sketch). Using Theorems 1 and 2, any counterexample for one side can always be translated to a counterexample for the other side. □

As an example, reconsider the translation of the set of shapes $\tau_{\text{shapes}}(S_1) = K^{<S_1>}$ (see Fig. 9). From $K^{<S_1>}$ follows that $K^{<S_1>} \not\models$ `CubistShape` $\sqsubseteq$ `PainterShape`

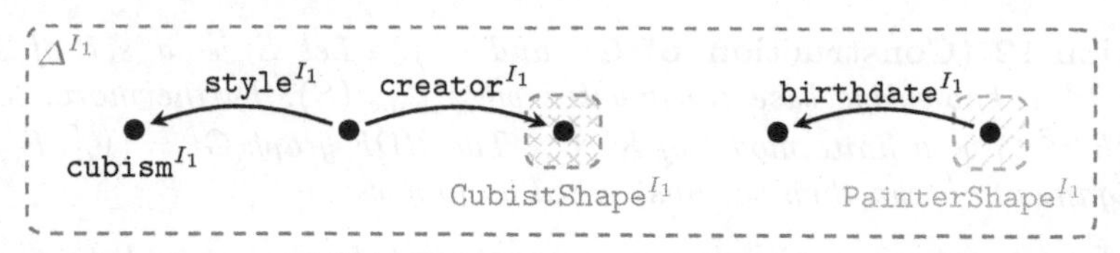

(a) Model of $K^{<S_1>}$ showing that `CubistShape` $\not\sqsubseteq$ `PainterShape`.

cubism ←style— b_2 —creator→ b_1 "..." ←birthdate— b_4

$\sigma_1(\bigcirc) = \emptyset$ $\sigma_1(\bigcirc) = \{$`CubistShape`$\}$ $\sigma_1(\bigcirc) = \{$`PainterShape`$\}$

(b) Graph and assignment showing that `CubistShape` is not contained in `PainterShape`.

Fig. 10. Counterexamples for `CubistShape` $<:_{S_1}$ `PainterShape`.

as there is a finite model $I_1 \in \text{Mod}^{\text{fin}}(K^{<S_1>})$ in which the concept expression `CubistShape` $\sqcap \neg$`PainterShape` is satisfiable (see Fig. 10).

An important observation is that it is possible to express arbitrary concept subsumptions $C \sqsubseteq D$ despite the syntactic restrictions of τ_{shapes}.

Lemma 2. *For any axiom $C \sqsubseteq D$, one can define some $(s, \phi, q) \in S$ and $(s', \phi', q') \in S$ such that $\tau_{\text{constr}}(\phi) = C$ and $\tau_{\text{constr}}(\phi') = D$ and $\tau_{\text{shapes}}(S) \models C \sqsubseteq D$.*

Proof (Sketch). Given constraints ϕ and ϕ', it is possible to introduce unique shape names s_C and s_D as well as an RDF class v_C. Constraint ϕ is then extended with v_C, allowing shape s_D to target v_C. □

For shapes belonging to the language $\mathcal{L}$, the corresponding description logic is $\mathcal{ALCOIQ}(\circ)$. To the best of our knowledge, finite satisfiability has not yet been investigated for $\mathcal{ALCOIQ}(\circ)$. Path concatenation can be restricted such that the fragment of SHACL corresponds to the description logic $\mathcal{SROIQ}$. The fragment for which constraints map to syntactical elements of $\mathcal{SROIQ}$, called $\mathcal{L}^{\text{restr}}$, uses the following constraint grammar:

$$\phi^{\text{restr}} ::= \top \mid s \mid v \mid \phi_1{}^{\text{restr}} \wedge \phi_2{}^{\text{restr}} \mid \neg\phi^{\text{restr}} \mid \exists\, p.\phi^{\text{restr}} \mid \geqslant_n p.\phi^{\text{restr}}$$

Finite satisfiability is known to be decidable for $\mathcal{SROIQ}$ [14] and all its sublogics such as $\mathcal{ALCOIQ}$ which completely removes role concatenation.

4 Deciding Shape Containment Using Standard Entailment

While shape containment can be decided using finite model reasoning (c.f. Theorem 3), practical usability of our approach depends on whether existing reasoner implementations can be leveraged. Implementations that are readily-available rely on standard entailment which includes infinitely large models. We therefore now focus on the soundness and completeness of our approach using the standard entailment relation.

Using standard entailment, the description logic $\mathcal{ALCOIQ}(\circ)$ which corresponds to the language $\mathcal{L}$, satisfiability of concepts, and thus concept subsumption, is undecidable [13]. First-order logic is semi-decidable. As $\mathcal{ALCOIQ}(\circ)$ can be translated to first-order logic through a straightforward extension of the translation rules for $\mathcal{SROIQ}$ [21], $\mathcal{ALCOIQ}(\circ)$ is also semi-decidable. Therefore, a decision procedure can verify whether a formula is entailed in finite time, but may not terminate for non-entailed formula. More restricted description logics such as $\mathcal{SROIQ}$, which corresponds to $\mathcal{L}^{\text{restr}}$, are decidable, meaning that an answer by the decision procedure is guaranteed in finite time. However, the question arises whether the satisfiability of a concept implies the existence of a finite model.

Definition 13. (Finite Model Property). *A description logic has the* finite model property *if every concept that is satisfiable with respect to a knowledge base has a finite model [4].*

If C is a concept expression that is satisfiable with respect to some knowledge base K that belongs to a description logic having the finite model property, then there must be a finite model of K that shows the satisfiability of C. Thus, finite entailment and standard entailment are the same if a description logic has the finite model property.

Proposition 1. *The finite model property does not hold for the description logic $\mathcal{ALCOIQ}$ [7] or more expressive description logics such as $\mathcal{ALCOIQ}(\circ)$ and $\mathcal{SROIQ}$. If a concept expression C is satisfiable with respect to a knowledge base K written in $\mathcal{ALCOIQ}$ or a more expressive description logic, then it may be that there are only models with an infinitely large universe.*

Given Proposition 1, it may be that there are only models with an infinitely large universe that show the satisfiability of a concept expression. There are three different possibilities: (1) $\tau_{\text{name}}(s) \sqcap \neg\tau_{\text{name}}(s')$ is neither finitely nor infinitely satisfiable, meaning that $K^{<S>} \models \tau_{\text{name}}(s) \sqsubseteq \tau_{\text{name}}(s')$. It follows that $s <:_S s'$ is true, as there is no counterexample. (2) $\tau_{\text{name}}(s) \sqcap \neg\tau_{\text{name}}(s')$ is not finitely, but only infinitely satisfiable. It follows that $K^{<S>} \not\models \tau_{\text{name}}(s) \sqsubseteq \tau_{\text{name}}(s')$, but $s <:_S s'$ is true since the infinitely large model has no corresponding RDF graph. (3) $\tau_{\text{name}}(s) \sqcap \neg\tau_{\text{name}}(s')$ is both, finitely and infinitely, satisfiable. It follows that $K^{<S>} \not\models \tau_{\text{name}}(s) \sqsubseteq \tau_{\text{name}}(s')$ and indeed $s <:_S s'$ is false since the finite model can be translated into an RDF graph and a faithful assignment. Deciding shape containment for the shape languages that are translatable into $\mathcal{ALCOIQ}(\circ)$, $\mathcal{SROIQ}$ or $\mathcal{ALCOIQ}$ is therefore sound, if the decision procedure terminates.

Theorem 4. *Let S be a set of shapes of the language $\mathcal{L}^{restr}$. It then holds that:*

$$s <:_S s' \Leftarrow \tau_{\text{shapes}}(S) \models \tau_{\text{name}}(s) \sqsubseteq \tau_{\text{name}}(s')$$

Proof. For $\mathcal{L}^{\text{restr}}$, the corrseponding DL is $\mathcal{SROIQ}$ for which the finite model property does not hold. If $K^{<S>} \models \tau_{\text{name}}(s) \sqsubseteq \tau_{\text{name}}(s')$, then there is neither a finitely nor an infinitely large model in which $\tau_{\text{name}}(s) \sqcap \neg\tau_{\text{name}}(s')$ is satisfiable. The shape s must therefore be contained in the shape s' as there is no RDF graph and assignment that acts as a counterexample. □

However, the approach is incomplete as it may be that $s <:_S s'$ but $K^{<S>} \not\models \tau_{\text{name}}(s) \sqsubseteq \tau_{\text{name}}(s')$ because due to an infinitely large model in which $\tau_{\text{name}}(s) \sqcap \neg\tau_{\text{name}}(s')$ is satisfiable.

To restore the finite model property, inverse path expressions have to be removed. That is, the set of SHACL shapes S must belong to the language fragment $\mathcal{L}^{\text{non-inv}}$ that uses the following grammar:

$$\phi^{\text{non-inv}} ::= \top \mid v \mid s \mid {\phi_1}^{\text{non-inv}} \wedge {\phi_2}^{\text{non-inv}} \mid \neg\phi^{\text{non-inv}} \mid \geqslant_n p.\phi^{\text{non-inv}}$$

$$q^{\text{non-inv}} ::= \bot \mid \{v_1, \ldots, v_n\} \mid \texttt{class}\ v \mid \texttt{subjectsOf}\ p$$

As a result, the description logic that corresponds to $\mathcal{L}^{\text{non-inv}}$ is $\mathcal{ALCOQ}$.

Proposition 2. *The description logic $\mathcal{ALCOQ}$ has the finite model property [17].*

Subsequently, for SHACL shapes that belong to $\mathcal{L}^{\text{non-inv}}$ shape containment and concept subsumption in the knowledge base constructed from the set of shapes are equivalent.

Theorem 5. *Let S be a set of shapes belonging to $\mathcal{L}^{\text{non-inv}}$. Let $K^{<S>}$ be the knowledge base constructed through $\tau_{\text{shapes}}(S)$. Then it holds that*

$$s <:_S s' \Leftrightarrow K^{<S>} \models \tau_{\text{name}}(s) \sqsubseteq \tau_{\text{name}}(s')$$

Proof (Sketch). Due to $\mathcal{ALCOQ}$ having the finite model property, it is always possible to construct counterexamples for either side (c. f. Theorem 3). □

In summary, using standard entailment our approach is sound and complete for the fragment of SHACL not using path concatenation or inverse path expressions. If inverse path expressions are used, then the approach is still sound although completeness is lost. Once arbitrary path concatenation is added, the resulting DL becomes semi-decidable. While an answer is not guaranteed in finite time, shape containment is still sound.

5 Related Work

SHACL containment has also been studied by [19], whereas this work studies theoretical shape satisfiability (and thus containment) by defining an equisatisfiable FOL language. In contrast, our approach focuses on practical applicability by leveraging standard entailment of description logic reasoners. Before SHACL, several constraint-based schema languages for RDF have been proposed before SHACL. Among those are [2,12]. To the best of our knowledge, containment has not been investigated for those languages. Additionally, SPIN[3] proposed the usage of SPARQL queries as constraints. Then, the containment problem for constraints is equivalent to query containment. ShEx [6] is a constraint language for RDF that is inspired by XML schema languages. While SHACL and ShEx are similar approaches, the semantics of the latter is rooted in regular bag expressions. Validation of an RDF graph with ShEx therefore constructs a single assignment whereas the SHACL semantics used in this papers deals with multiple possible assignments. The containment problem of ShEx shapes has been investigated in [22]. Due to the specific definition of recursion in ShEx, any graph that conforms to the ShEx shapes will also conform to an equivalent SHACL definition. However, not all graphs that conform to SHACL shapes conform to equivalent ShEx shapes.

Similar to dedicated constraint languages, there have been proposals for the extension of description logics with constraints. While standard description logics adopts an open-world assumption not suited for data validation, extensions include special constraint axioms [18,23], epistemic operators [11], and closed predicates [20]. Constraints constitute T-Box axioms in these approaches, making constraint subsumption a routine problem.

Lastly, containment problems have been investigated for queries [8,15]. The query containment problem is slightly different as result sets of queries are typically sets of tuples whereas in SHACL we deal with conformance relative to faithful assignments. Given an RDF graph and a set of shapes there may be several, different faithful assignments. Operators available for SHACL are more expressive than operators found in query languages for which subsumption has been investigated. In particular, recursion is not part of most query languages. There is a non-recursive subset of SHACL that is known to be expressible as SPARQL queries [9]. When constraints are expressed as queries, containment of SHACL shapes becomes equivalent to query containment. Recursive fragments of SHACL, however, cannot be expressed as SPARQL queries.

6 Summary

In this paper, we have presented an approach for deciding SHACL shape containment by translating the problem into a description logic subsumption problem. Our translation allows for using efficient and well-known DL reasoning implementations when deciding shape containment. Thus, shape containment can be used, for example, in query optimization. We defined a syntactic translation of a set of shapes into a description logic knowledge base. We then showed that finite models of this knowledge base and faithful assignments of RDF graphs can be mapped onto each other. Using finite model reasoning, this provides a sound and complete decision procedure for deciding SHACL shape containment, although the decidability of finite satisfiability in $\mathcal{ALCOIQ}(\circ)$ is still an open issue. As part of future work, we plan to adapt the proof used by [14], which comprises of a translation of $\mathcal{SROIQ}$ into a fragment of first-order logic for which finite

[3] http://spinrdf.org/.

satisfiability is known. To ensure practical applicability, we also investigated the soundness and completeness of our approach using standard entailment. Our findings are summarized in Fig. 11. Our approach is sound and complete for the SHACL fragment $\mathcal{L}^{\text{non-inv}}$ that uses neither path concatenation nor inverse roles, as the finite model property holds for the corresponding description logic $\mathcal{ALCOQ}$. Thus, finite entailment and standard entailment are the same for this description logic. The finite model property is lost as soon as inverse roles are added. Using standard entailment, our procedure is still sound for the fragment $\mathcal{L}^{\text{restr}}$ which translates into $\mathcal{SROIQ}$ knowledge bases, but is incomplete due to the possibility of a knowledge base having only infinitely large models. Lastly, the SHACL fragment $\mathcal{L}$ translates into $\mathcal{ALCOIQ}(\circ)$ knowledge bases. Our approach is sound, but incomplete. However, due to the semi-decidability of the description logic, it may be that the decision procedure does not terminate.

SHACL Fragment	**DL**	*Sound*	*Complete*	*Terminates*
$\mathcal{L}$	$\mathcal{ALCOIQ}(\circ)$	Yes	No	Not guaranteed
$\mathcal{L}^{\text{restr}}$	$\mathcal{SROIQ}$	Yes	No	Yes
$\mathcal{L}^{\text{non-inv}}$	$\mathcal{ALCOQ}$	Yes	Yes	Yes

Fig. 11. Soundness and completeness for deciding shape containment through description logics reasoning using standard entailment.

Acknowledgements. The authors gratefully acknowledge the financial support of project LISeQ (LA 2672/1-1) by the German Research Foundation (DFG).

References

1. Abbas, A., Genevès, P., Roisin, C., Layaïda, N.: SPARQL query containment with ShEx constraints. In: Kirikova, M., Nørvåg, K., Papadopoulos, G.A. (eds.) ADBIS 2017. LNCS, vol. 10509, pp. 343–356. Springer, Cham (2017). https://doi.org/10.1007/978-3-319-66917-5_23
2. Akhtar, W., Cortés-Calabuig, Á., Paredaens, J.: Constraints in RDF. In: Schewe, K.-D., Thalheim, B. (eds.) SDKB 2010. LNCS, vol. 6834, pp. 23–39. Springer, Heidelberg (2011). https://doi.org/10.1007/978-3-642-23441-5_2
3. Baader, F., Calvanese, D., McGuinness, D.L., Nardi, D., Patel-Schneider, P.F. (eds.): The Description Logic Handbook: Theory, Implementation, and Applications. Cambridge University Press, Cambridge (2003)
4. Baader, F., Horrocks, I., Lutz, C., Sattler, U.: An Introduction to Description Logic. Cambridge University Press, New York (2017)
5. Beneventano, D., Bergamaschi, S., Sartori, C.: Semantic query optimization by subsumption in OODB. In: Proceedings of the Flexible Query-Answering Systems (FQAS), pp. 167–187. Roskilde University (1996)
6. Boneva, I., Labra Gayo, J.E., Prud'hommeaux, E.G.: Semantics and validation of shapes schemas for RDF. In: d'Amato, C., et al. (eds.) ISWC 2017. LNCS, vol. 10587, pp. 104–120. Springer, Cham (2017). https://doi.org/10.1007/978-3-319-68288-4_7

7. Calvanese, D.: Finite model reasoning in description logics. In: Proceedings of the KR, pp. 292–303. Morgan Kaufmann (1996)
8. Chaudhuri, S., Vardi, M.: Optimization of real conjunctive queries. In: Proceedings of the PODS, pp. 59–70. ACM (1993)
9. Corman, J., Florenzano, F., Reutter, J.L., Savković, O.: Validating SHACL constraints over a SPARQL endpoint. In: Ghidini, C., Hartig, O., Maleshkova, M., Svátek, V., Cruz, I., Hogan, A., Song, J., Lefrançois, M., Gandon, F. (eds.) ISWC 2019. LNCS, vol. 11778, pp. 145–163. Springer, Cham (2019). https://doi.org/10.1007/978-3-030-30793-6_9
10. Corman, J., Reutter, J.L., Savković, O.: Semantics and validation of recursive SHACL. In: Vrandečić, D., Bontcheva, K., Suárez-Figueroa, M.C., Presutti, V., Celino, I., Sabou, M., Kaffee, L.-A., Simperl, E. (eds.) ISWC 2018. LNCS, vol. 11136, pp. 318–336. Springer, Cham (2018). https://doi.org/10.1007/978-3-030-00671-6_19
11. Donini, F.M., Nardi, D., Rosati, R.: Description logics of minimal knowledge and negation as failure. ACM TOCL **3**(2), 177–225 (2002)
12. Fischer, P.M., Lausen, G., Schätzle, A., Schmidt, M.: RDF constraint checking. In: Proceedings of the EDBT/ICDT, pp. 205–212. CEUR-WS.org (2015)
13. Grandi, F.: On expressive description logics with composition of roles in number restrictions. In: Baaz, M., Voronkov, A. (eds.) LPAR 2002. LNCS (LNAI), vol. 2514, pp. 202–215. Springer, Heidelberg (2002). https://doi.org/10.1007/3-540-36078-6_14
14. Kazakov, Y.: RIQ and SROIQ are harder than SHOIQ. In: Proceedings of the KR, pp. 274–284. AAAI Press (2008)
15. Klug, A.: On conjunctive queries containing inequalities. J. ACM **35**, 146–160 (1988)
16. Leinberger, M., Seifer, P., Schon, C., Lämmel, R., Staab, S.: Type checking program code using SHACL. In: Ghidini, C., Hartig, O., Maleshkova, M., Svátek, V., Cruz, I., Hogan, A., Song, J., Lefrançois, M., Gandon, F. (eds.) ISWC 2019. LNCS, vol. 11778, pp. 399–417. Springer, Cham (2019). https://doi.org/10.1007/978-3-030-30793-6_23
17. Lutz, C., Areces, C., Horrocks, I., Sattler, U.: Keys, nominals, and concrete domains. J. Artif. Intell. Res. **23**, 667–726 (2004)
18. Motik, B., Horrocks, I., Sattler, U.: Adding integrity constraints to OWL. In: Proceedings of the OWLED. CEUR Workshop Proceedings, vol. 258. CEUR-WS.org (2007)
19. Pareti, P., Konstantinidis, G., Magavero, F., Norman, T.J.: SHACL satisfiability and containment. In: Proceedings of the ISWC. LNCS. Springer (2020)
20. Patel-Schneider, P.F., Franconi, E.: Ontology constraints in incomplete and complete data. In: Cudré-Mauroux, P., Heflin, J., Sirin, E., Tudorache, T., Euzenat, J., Hauswirth, M., Parreira, J.X., Hendler, J., Schreiber, G., Bernstein, A., Blomqvist, E. (eds.) ISWC 2012. LNCS, vol. 7649, pp. 444–459. Springer, Heidelberg (2012). https://doi.org/10.1007/978-3-642-35176-1_28
21. Rudolph, S.: Foundations of description logics. In: Polleres, A., et al. (eds.) Reasoning Web 2011. LNCS, vol. 6848, pp. 76–136. Springer, Heidelberg (2011). https://doi.org/10.1007/978-3-642-23032-5_2
22. Staworko, S., Wieczorek, P.: Containment of shape expression schemas for RDF. In: Proceedings of the PODS, pp. 303–319. ACM (2019)
23. Tao, J., Sirin, E., Bao, J., McGuinness, D.L.: Integrity constraints in OWL. In: Proceedings of the AAAI. AAAI Press (2010)

Rule-Guided Graph Neural Networks for Recommender Systems

Xinze Lyu, Guangyao Li, Jiacheng Huang, and Wei Hu(✉)

State Key Laboratory for Novel Software Technology, Nanjing University, Nanjing, China
xinzelyu@outlook.com, gyli.nju@gmail.com, jchuang.nju@gmail.com, whu@nju.edu.cn

Abstract. To alleviate the cold start problem caused by collaborative filtering in recommender systems, knowledge graphs (KGs) are increasingly employed by many methods as auxiliary resources. However, existing work incorporated with KGs cannot capture the explicit long-range semantics between users and items meanwhile consider various connectivity between items. In this paper, we propose RGRec, which combines rule learning and graph neural networks (GNNs) for recommendation. RGRec first maps items to corresponding entities in KGs and adds users as new entities. Then, it automatically learns rules to model the explicit long-range semantics, and captures the connectivity between entities by aggregation to better encode various information. We show the effectiveness of RGRec on three real-world datasets. Particularly, the combination of rule learning and GNNs achieves substantial improvement compared to methods only using either of them.

Keywords: Recommender system · Rule learning · Graph neural network · Knowledge graph

1 Introduction

Recommender systems play an important role in modern society. They provide users convenient access to the needed resources out of massive information on the Internet. For services offering content to users like YouTube [3] and Alibaba [25], recommender systems are almost a necessity. Collaborative filtering is a widely-used and effective solution, which recommends items by exploring existing user-item interactions. However, collaborative filtering often suffers from the so-called *cold start* problem. It may perform poorly for recommending brand new items or suggesting items to new users. To alleviate this problem, many efforts [1,27] have been devoted to designing methods for using auxiliary resources like user or item profiles. In recent years, knowledge graphs (KGs) are increasingly selected. KGs contain structural data of high quality, which provide a wealth of relations between items. Thus, brand new items, which are rarely interacted with users, can be better recommended by the relations recorded in KGs.

J. Z. Pan et al. (Eds.): ISWC 2020, LNCS 12506, pp. 384–401, 2020.
https://doi.org/10.1007/978-3-030-62419-4_22

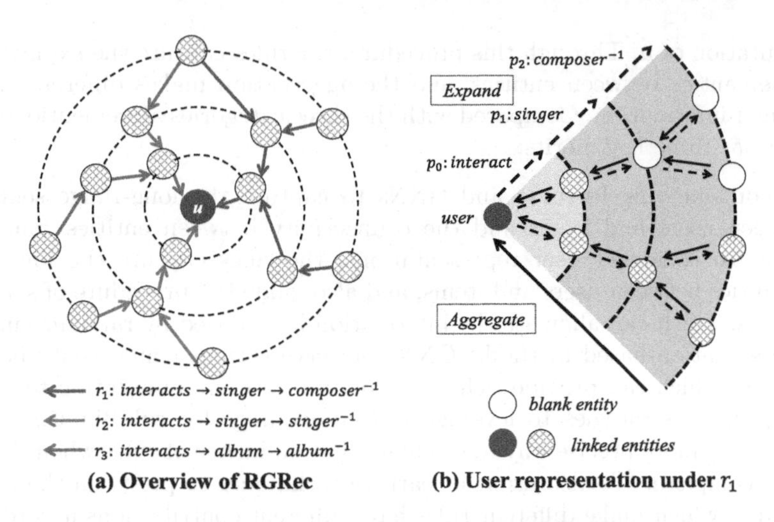

Fig. 1. Overview of RGRec. Expansion is denoted by dashed arrows, which means that we search the connected entities of *user* based on each rule. Aggregation is denoted by solid arrows, which means that we combine the representations of *user* and the entities connected to it.

Existing works incorporated with KGs can be roughly divided into three categories: embedding-based, path-based and aggregation-based. The embedding-based methods [32] often model the direct relations between entities only; they lack the capability of capturing the long-range semantics between entities. A few path-based methods [31] leverage experts to manually construct (meta)paths between users and items, while others [18,28] learn rules automatically but ignore various relations between different entities; they only consider the relations presented in rules. Aggregation-based methods [24,26] model relations between different entities by the attention mechanism. They can preserve rich information around a central entity (i.e. the entity that we want to obtain its representation) by aggregating the representations of its directly or indirectly connected entities. However, it is usually hard to model the explicit relations between the central entity and its indirectly connected entities. Thus, the explicit long-range semantics is still not fully explored in aggregation-based methods.

In this paper, we design RGRec, a method integrating automatic rule learning and graph neural network (GNN)-based aggregation for recommendation. As shown in Fig. 1(a), we model the users, items, and entities by a graph, where rules present relation paths between them. Taking u as an example, at first, we extract the entities for u along a rule. Then, we aggregate the representations of entities in the relation path to form the representation of u, which can be regarded as the representation on one dimension. We repeat the step on different rules, and form the representations of u on multiple dimensions which corresponds to different rules. Furthermore, different rules have different strengths to extract entities, which corresponds to rules with different confidence. So, the generated multi-dimensional representations are gathered selectively to construct the final representation of u. Through this procedure, the rules capture the explicit long-range semantics between entities, and the aggregation makes different entities share their information. Compared with the three categories aforementioned, our method has three key merits:

1. We combine rule learning and GNNs to capture the long-range semantics between users and items and the connectivity between entities simultaneously. To construct user representations, the rules capture the long-range semantics between users and items, and also guide the procedure of sampling entities, which can alleviate the information loss caused by random sampling in aggregation-based methods. GNNs preserve various connectivity between entities, which can provide richer information to users in addition to rules.
2. We propose strategies to leverage KG embeddings for rule filtering, which provides a more precise way to calculate the confidence of rules when the KGs are incomplete. We also use rule learning techniques to pre-train the weights of rules, which make different rules have different contributions according to their importance.
3. We conduct experiments on three real-world datasets and compare with a number of methods in all the three categories mentioned above. Our results demonstrate the effectiveness of the combination of rule learning and GNNs.

2 Related Work

Recommender systems incorporated with KGs can be generally classified into three categories. The first category borrows the idea from KG embedding. MKR [23] designs a cross-and-compress unit to share latent features between items in the recommendation task and entities in the KG embedding task. CKE [32] generates embeddings for structural knowledge with TransR [13] and combines the embeddings of structural, textual and visual knowledge for collaborative filtering. DKN [21] incorporates KG embeddings into news recommendation. It designs a multi-channel and word-entity-aligned knowledge-aware convolutional neural network that fuses word-level and knowledge-level representations of news. These works only consider the direct relations between entities, so they cannot model the long-range semantics between entities.

The second category is based on paths. A part of works uses metapaths, which are defined as the sequences of entity types between users and items, e.g., $user \rightarrow song \rightarrow singer \rightarrow song$. PER [31] introduces metapath-based latent features to represent the connectivity between users and items along different types of paths. It defines recommendation models at both global (same for all users) and personalized levels. FMG [34] incorporates more complex semantics between users and items by introducing metagraphs, which are composed of many different metapaths. HERec [16] and metapath2vec [4] use metapaths to sample entities and generate embeddings. MEIRec [5] presents the metapath-guided neighbors to aggregate rich neighbor information. It needs users, items, and queries (a.k.a. intents) as input, and studies the intent recommendation problem, which means that the recommendation for a user is personalized queries rather than items. The performance of metapath-based methods depends heavily on the quality of handcrafted metapaths. To resolve this problem, several works like RKGE [18] and KPRN [28] mine paths (rules) automatically. Although they can capture the long-range semantics between users and items, their strategies to use rules can be improved. For all rules about a user-item pair, the released code of RKGE[1] and KPRN[2] shows that they only sample a very small amount of rules randomly. These strategies may omit much useful information. We think that a better way is to delete low-quality rules and save high-quality rules by designing rule filtering algorithms. Generally speaking, modeling with rules is precise because the information is collected by the control of predicates presented in rules, but this also makes the rule-based methods weak in capturing the various connectivity between entities and insufficient in generalization ability.

The third category is characterized by iterative aggregation. RippleNet [20] classifies the entities around one entity as 1-hop, 2-hop, ..., k-hop neighbors, and aggregates the representations of all these neighbors from different hops in a weighted manner. Differently, KGCN [24] and KGAT [26] are inspired by GNN architectures like GCN [9], GraphSage [7], GAT [19] and HAN [29] to aggregate the representations of only 1-hop neighbors around one entity, and the entity will get the information of k-hop neighbors by repeating the aggregation k times. Note that, different GNN architectures are designed to capture the information of a graph more precisely, and they are often evaluated on the classification and clustering tasks; while KGCN and KGAT just utilize GNNs to build recommender systems. In these methods, when we choose neighbors for a central entity, we usually cannot know the explicit relations between the central entity and its indirectly connected neighbors. So, less informative neighbors may be collected as noises. Contrary to the path-based methods, the aggregation-based methods are strong in generalization ability because they can capture various connectivity between entities, but weak in precision because the quality of sample entities cannot be guaranteed.

3 Problem Formulation

In this paper, we define a KG $\mathcal{G}$ as a set of RDF triples. An RDF triple, denoted by (s, p, o), consists of three components: subject s, predicate p and object o. According to the common recommendation scenario, we refer to subjects and objects in $\mathcal{G}$ as entities, and the set of entities is denoted by $\mathcal{E} = \{e_0, \ldots, e_{n_e}\}$. Predicates represent the relations between entities, and the set of predicates is denoted by $\mathcal{P} = \{p_1, \ldots, p_{n_p}\}$.

A typical recommender system contains a set of users $\mathcal{U} = \{u_1, \ldots, u_{n_u}\}$, a set of items $\mathcal{M} = \{m_1, \ldots, m_{n_m}\}$, and the interactions between them (usually modeled as an interaction matrix $\mathcal{H}$). To link $\mathcal{U}$ and $\mathcal{M}$ to KGs, we map an item m in $\mathcal{M}$ to a corresponding entity e in $\mathcal{E}$, then a new triple $(u, \textit{interacts}, e)$ is

[1] https://github.com/sunzhuntu/Recurrent-Knowledge-Graph-Embedding.
[2] https://github.com/eBay/KPRN.

added in $\mathcal{G}$, where u is regarded as a new entity and the relation between u and e is denoted by *interacts*. This newly-supplemented $\mathcal{G}$ is denoted by $\mathcal{G}_{\mathcal{H}}$.

A rule specifically refers to an inference rule of predicate *interacts*. So, the rules are means to reason whether a user-item pair instantiates predicate *interacts*. We define the set of rules as $\mathcal{R} = \{r_1, \ldots, r_{n_r}\}$, where a rule r in $\mathcal{R}$ is composed by a set of predicates $\{p, p_1, \ldots, p_h\}$, written as $r : p \Leftarrow p_1 \wedge \ldots \wedge p_h$. p on the left of $\Leftarrow$ is called rule head, the part on the right of $\Leftarrow$ is called rule body, and the number of predicates in the rule body is the rule length. When a user u and an item m instantiate a rule r, it means that there are entities $\{e_1, e_2, \ldots, e_{h-1}\}$ connecting u and m as $u \xrightarrow{p_1} e_1 \xrightarrow{p_2} \ldots \xrightarrow{p_{h-1}} e_{h-1} \xrightarrow{p_h} m$, which is recorded as $(u, r, m) \in \mathcal{G}_{\mathcal{H}}$. We distinguish directly connected entities (rule length $= 1$) and indirectly connected entities (rule length ≥ 2). We believe that rules of length over 1 can help reflect the explicit relations between those indirectly connected entities.

Definition 1 (Problem definition). *Given a KG $\mathcal{G}$ and the interaction matrix $\mathcal{H}$ between users $\mathcal{U}$ and items $\mathcal{M}$, our goal is to learn a function $\mathcal{F}(u, m \mid \Theta, \mathcal{R}, \mathcal{G}_{\mathcal{H}})$ that can predict the probability of each user-item pair (u, m) instantiating predicate interacts, where $u \in \mathcal{U}, m \in \mathcal{M}, \Theta$ denotes the parameter to learn, $\mathcal{R}$ is the set of rules and $\mathcal{G}_{\mathcal{H}}$ is the KG supplemented with $\mathcal{H}$.*

4 RGRec

RGRec imitates the ways that humans recommend things and focuses on expressing user features precisely and completely. Taking songs for example, we may consider several aspects when we want to recommend songs to a user u. Assume that u likes song m_1. We may consider songs that are composed by the singer of m_1, or have the same singer as m_1, or are recorded in the same album as m_1. These three linear modes of thinking can be expressed by r_1, r_2 and r_3, respectively:

$$r_1 : \textit{interacts}(u, m_1) \Leftarrow \textit{interacts}(u, m_2) \wedge \textit{singer}(m_2, c_1) \wedge \textit{composer}^{-1}(c_1, m_1), \tag{1}$$

$$r_2 : \textit{interacts}(u, m_1) \Leftarrow \textit{interacts}(u, m_2) \wedge \textit{singer}(m_2, s_1) \wedge \textit{singer}^{-1}(s_1, m_1), \tag{2}$$

$$r_3 : \textit{interacts}(u, m_1) \Leftarrow \textit{interacts}(u, m_2) \wedge \textit{album}(m_2, a_1) \wedge \textit{album}^{-1}(a_1, m_1), \tag{3}$$

where p^{-1} denotes the inverse predicate of p, e.g., $\textit{composer}^{-1}(c_1, m_1)$ expresses the same meaning as $\textit{composer}(m_1, c_1)$.

KGs contain various entities and rich connections, which provide a wealth of resources to generate the representations of users. To construct a user representation, we leverage the rules that can capture the long-range semantics between entities as the guidance. Different rules lead to different user representations, which can be regarded as the representations from various dimensions. A complete user representation is formed by aggregating the collected representations selectively. In Fig. 1(a), user u is expanded with three rules, and the expanded entities converge to u in the opposite direction (from outside to inside) iteratively to generate the representation of u. To achieve this, we face three challenges:

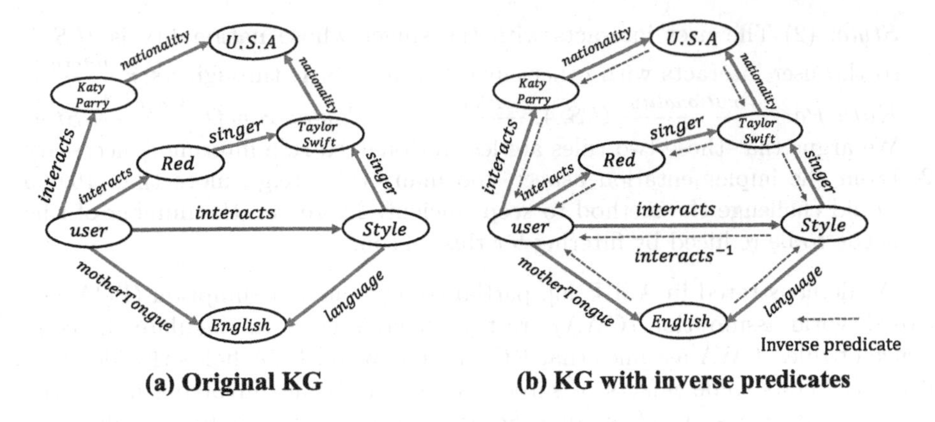

Fig. 2. A KG fragment

1. How to learn rules of high quality?
2. How to model the user representation with a single rule?
3. How to aggregate various representations collected under different rules?

We describe our method in detail in the rest of this section.

4.1 Rule Learning

In this paper, we aim to find high-quality inference rules for predicate *interacts*, which express users like some things. We divide our rule learning process into two steps: rule finding and rule filtering.

For **rule finding**, we define that each candidate inference rule of *interacts* is a connected path from a user to an item, where the user and the item instantiate predicate *interacts* and the direction of predicates in the path is omitted. For example, in Fig. 2(a), a user interacts with a song called *Style*, the connected paths between the user and *Style* can be regarded as candidate rules. These rules can represent the reasons why this user likes *Style*. For instance, we may infer that the user likes *Style* because the singer of *Style* is the same as a song interacted with the user, through $user \xrightarrow{interacts} Red \xrightarrow{singer} Taylor\ Swift \xrightarrow{singer^{-1}} Style.$

To facilitate path finding, we add an inverse predicate to every edge in the KG like Fig. 2(b) to make the KG undirected, i.e. adding an inverse triple (o, p^{-1}, s) in the KG for every (s, p, o). With the triple $(s, interacts, o)$ as input, we use bidirectional breadth-first search to find connected paths between s and o of length at most I as the candidate rules of *interacts*.

For **rule filtering**, there are two reasons to adopt it:

1. Getting rid of low-quality rules that are harmful. In Fig. 2(b), in addition to the path passing *Red*, two other paths between the user and *Style* are: (1) The mother tongue of the user is English, *Style* is an English song, so the user interacts with *Style* through $user \xrightarrow{motherTongue} English \xrightarrow{language^{-1}}$

Style; (2) The user interacts with the singer whose nationality is *U.S.A.*, so the user interacts with other singers from U.S.A. through $user \xrightarrow{interacts}$ $Katy\ Parry \xrightarrow{nationality} U.S.A. \xrightarrow{nationality^{-1}} Taylor\ Swift \xrightarrow{singer^{-1}} Style.$ We argue that these two rules are less rational, so rule filtering is necessary.
2. From the implementation aspect, too many rules (e.g., more than 10,000) would challenge the method to keep efficient. Therefore, the number of rules needs to be reduced by filtering for this reason.

As demonstrated in AMIE [6], partial completeness assumption (PCA) and closed world assumption (CWA) are two effective ways to calculate the confidence of rules. CWA assumes that KGs are complete. PCA holds the idea that, if a KG knows some p-facts of subject s, i.e. the triples involving predicate p of s, then it knows all p-facts of s. So, it neglects the inferred (s, o) whose s is not involved in any p-facts. Since users interact with at least one item in our scenario, PCA is identical to CWA for predicate *interacts*. Also, *interacts* is assumed to be very incomplete in recommendation tasks, i.e. there are many potential items that may interact with users. Consequently, the confidence calculated under CWA may have a great loss. On the other hand, the embeddings of a KG have the ability to complete the graph [2]. Thus, it can make up the shortcomings of CWA. We design an efficient algorithm to filter rules based on a KG embedding model called RotatE [17]. Below, we briefly describe it. For a triple (s, p, o), RotatE maps s, p and o into a complex vector space and defines p as the rotation from s to o. It expects $\boldsymbol{o} = \boldsymbol{s} \circ \boldsymbol{p}$, where $\boldsymbol{s}, \boldsymbol{p}, \boldsymbol{o} \in \mathbb{C}^{d_{re}}$ denote the embeddings, $\circ$ is the Hadamard (a.k.a. element-wise) product, and the modulus of each element of $\boldsymbol{p}$ is 1. RotatE can infer the composition pattern of predicates, e.g., $\boldsymbol{p} = \boldsymbol{p_1} \circ \ldots \circ \boldsymbol{p_h}$ holds if the rule $r : p \Leftarrow p_1 \wedge \ldots \wedge p_h$ is absolutely correct. So, the distance between $\boldsymbol{p_1} \circ \ldots \circ \boldsymbol{p_h}$ and $\boldsymbol{p}$ can reflect the confidence of r, which is calculated as follows:

$$conf(r) = -||\boldsymbol{p} - f(\boldsymbol{p})||_2, \tag{4}$$

$$f(\boldsymbol{p}) = \boldsymbol{p_1} \circ \ldots \circ \boldsymbol{p_h}, \tag{5}$$

where $||\cdot||_2$ represents the L_2-norm of a complex vector. Taking r_1 in Eq. (1) as an example, we denote *interacts*, *singer*, *composer*$^{-1}$ by p_t, p_s and p_c^{-1}, respectively. If r_1 is correct, i.e. $\boldsymbol{m_1} = \boldsymbol{u} \circ \boldsymbol{p_t}, \boldsymbol{m_2} = \boldsymbol{u} \circ \boldsymbol{p_t}, \boldsymbol{c_1} = \boldsymbol{m_2} \circ \boldsymbol{p_s}$ and $\boldsymbol{m_1} = \boldsymbol{c_1} \circ \boldsymbol{p_c^{-1}}$ hold, $\boldsymbol{p_t} = \boldsymbol{p_t} \circ \boldsymbol{p_s} \circ \boldsymbol{p_c^{-1}}$ can be inferred by $\boldsymbol{u} \circ \boldsymbol{p_t} = \boldsymbol{c_1} \circ \boldsymbol{p_c^{-1}} = (\boldsymbol{m_2} \circ \boldsymbol{p_s}) \circ \boldsymbol{p_c^{-1}} = ((\boldsymbol{u} \circ \boldsymbol{p_t}) \circ \boldsymbol{p_s}) \circ \boldsymbol{p_c^{-1}}$.

Finally, we reserve top-L rules with the highest confidence as output.

In addition to RotatE, DistMult [30] and RLvLR [14] can also use the composition pattern of predicates and embeddings to measure the confidence of rules. However, DistMult, which represents relations by matrices in bilinear transformation, needs special constraints to infer the composition pattern of predicates, but the constraints may not hold in implementation. RotatE points out that DistMult cannot infer the composition pattern of predicates, but TransE [2] and itself can [17]. For RLvLR, by only using the composition pattern, it performs poorly when rules are longer than 2. So, it designs another strategy based on co-occurrence for longer rules. Compared with these two methods, our strategy of using the embeddings trained by RotatE to model the composition pattern of predicates is theoretically reasonable and practical in reality. Still, RotatE has some detrimental effects, such as the fixed composition pattern mentioned in QuatE [33]. This causes the performance of RotatE not particularly good when some predicates participating in a compositional pattern are the same. We will consider other advanced KG embedding models to alleviate this problem in future work.

4.2 User Representation Guided by Single Rule

Inspired by GraphSAGE [7], which is a general inductive framework for graph representation learning, we design a rule-guided GNN model. To learn the representation of a user u along a rule r, we firstly select fixed-size k-hop neighbors of u along r. Then, we aggregate the representations of entities to their directly connected neighbors and apply a non-linear transformation to construct the representations of entities aware of neighbors. Finally, we repeat this process for a few iterations to make u receive the information from all selected neighbors. We take rule r_1 in Eq. (1) as an example to explain how to obtain the representation of a user under the guidance of r_1. As shown in Fig. 1(b), we expand the user along the rule (direction: *Expand*), then we aggregate the representations of the expanded entities to the user reversely (direction: *Aggregate*) to obtain the representation of the user under this rule.

We define the k-hop expanding entity set of user u on r as $\mathcal{D}_u^k(r) = \{o \,|\, (s, p_k, o), s \in \mathcal{D}_u^{k-1}(r)\}$, where $k \in [1, h]$ and $\mathcal{D}_u^0(r) = \{u\}$. When we expand u along r, if there exist entities in $\mathcal{D}_u^{k-1}(r)$ that cannot use the k-th predicate to conduct the k-hop expansion, then it receives a negative feedback that r is infeasible for u to some extent. In practice, we return a blank entity B as the negative feedback for $\{s \,|\, \nexists o, (s, p_k, o) \in \mathcal{G}_\mathcal{H}, s \in \mathcal{D}_u^{k-1}\}$. The blank entities are shown as white circles in Fig. 1(b).

The entity set whose representations to be aggregated is denoted by $\mathcal{J}_i = \{\mathcal{D}_u^0(r) \cup \ldots \cup \mathcal{D}_u^{h-i}(r)\}$, where $i \in [1, h]$, and h is the length of rule r, which is also the total number of aggregation iterations in r. The aggregation proceeds from $\mathcal{J}_1$ to $\mathcal{J}_h$ in turn. The $(i+1)$-th iteration is shown in the upper part of Fig. 3. During this iteration, the state $\boldsymbol{e}$ of entity e (self entity) in $\mathcal{J}_{i+1}$ is transformed from $\boldsymbol{e}^i$ to $\boldsymbol{e}^{i+1}$ (new state) as follows:

$$\boldsymbol{e}^{i+1} = c\Big(\boldsymbol{e}^i \oplus \big(\frac{1}{Y}\sum_{y=1}^{Y} \boldsymbol{e}_y^i\big)\Big), \tag{6}$$

$$c(\boldsymbol{x}) = \sigma(\boldsymbol{W}_{agg}\boldsymbol{x} + \boldsymbol{b}), \tag{7}$$

where the states of entities which should be aggregated to $\boldsymbol{e}^i$ are denoted by $\{\boldsymbol{e}_1^i, \ldots, \boldsymbol{e}_Y^i\}$ (linked entities), $\boldsymbol{e}$ is of size d_r, $\oplus$ means vector concatenation, and σ is a nonlinear function like *Sigmoid*. At each round of iterations, RGRec applies the aggregation operation to entities along the direction of *Expand*,

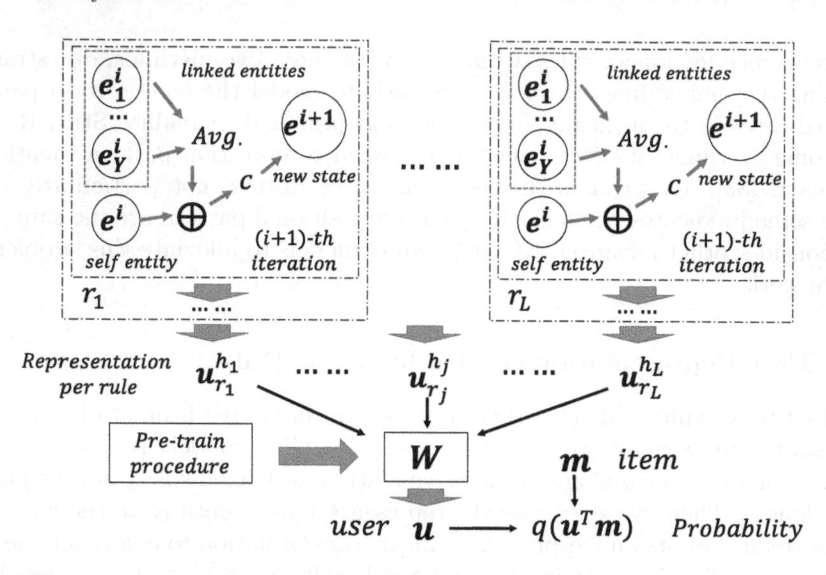

Fig. 3. The framework of RGRec

where *user* is the first entity to be applied the aggregation operation in the first iteration. After h iterations, the final representation of u under r is $\boldsymbol{u}_r^h$.

4.3 Multi-dimensional Representation Aggregation

Given L representations $\{\boldsymbol{u}_{r_1}^{h_1}, \boldsymbol{u}_{r_2}^{h_2}, \ldots, \boldsymbol{u}_{r_L}^{h_L}\}$ of user u under the guidance of L rules $\{r_1, r_2, \ldots, r_L\}$, where h_j denotes the length of r_j, the final representation $\boldsymbol{u}$ of u is aggregated as follows:

$$\boldsymbol{u} = \left[\boldsymbol{u}_{r_1}^{h_1}; \boldsymbol{u}_{r_2}^{h_2}; \ldots; \boldsymbol{u}_{r_L}^{h_L}\right] \boldsymbol{W}, \tag{8}$$

where $\boldsymbol{W}$ is the rule weights of size $(L \times 1)$ and the size of $\left[\boldsymbol{u}_{r_1}^{h_1}; \boldsymbol{u}_{r_2}^{h_2}; \ldots; \boldsymbol{u}_{r_L}^{h_L}\right]$ is $(d_r \times L)$.

The loss function $loss_{\text{RGRec}}$ of RGRec is defined as

$$loss_{\text{RGRec}} = \frac{1}{N} \sum_{i=1}^{N} \left(l_i - q(\boldsymbol{u}_i^T \boldsymbol{m}_i)\right)^2 + \mu ||\boldsymbol{W}||_2, \tag{9}$$

where, for N training data $\{(\boldsymbol{u}_i, \boldsymbol{m}_i, l_i)\}_{i=1}^N$, $\boldsymbol{u}_i$, $\boldsymbol{m}_i$ and l_i are the user representation, item representation and label (1 if the user and the item instantiate predicate *interacts*, and 0 otherwise), respectively. μ is the hyperparameter of L_2-regularization. $\boldsymbol{m}_i$ has size $(d_r \times 1)$. q is a nonlinear function like *Sigmoid*. The idea behind the loss function is that, if a user u and an item m instantiate *interacts*, their label l is 1, and the inner product of their representations is expected to be 1; otherwise, their label is 0, and the inner product is expected to be 0. $\mu||\boldsymbol{W}||_2$ is a regularization term to avoid overfitting.

4.4 Rule Weights Pre-training

Not every rule should play an equal role during the formation of the final representation. However, the confidence of rules calculated by embeddings does not work well here. That confidence only measures whether the rules can interpret predicate *interacts*. It checks rules in isolation and lacks the consideration for the whole rule set. In fact, rules can affect each other, including both positive and negative influences. For example, if r_1 (Eq. (1)) or r_3 (Eq. (3)) hold between user u and item m, m is less likely to be recommended to u just by one rule, but when m has the same composer and belongs to the same album as one song that u interacts, i.e. r_1 and r_3 both hold, the probability of being recommended is higher. In this paper, we design a pre-training procedure to learn rule weights $\boldsymbol{W}$ automatically from a more holistic perspective.

Assume that we have L rules $\mathcal{R} = \{r_1, r_2, \dots, r_L\}$ for *interacts* and N user-item pairs $\{(u_i, m_i)\}_{i=1}^{N}$. For each user-item pair that instantiates *interacts*, we label it with 1, otherwise we label it with 0. The label set for all user-item pairs is denoted by $\{l_i\}_{i=1}^{N}$. Then, we test every user-item pair (u_i, m_i) against every rule r_j, i.e. returning 1 if $(u_i, r_j, m_i) \in \mathcal{G}_{\mathcal{H}}$, and 0 otherwise, which generates the feature set $\{\boldsymbol{X}_i\}_{i=1}^{N}$. $\boldsymbol{X}_i$ is a vector of size L and composed of 0/1.

With training data $\{(\boldsymbol{X}_i, l_i)\}_{i=1}^{N}$, we convert the problem whether the user and the item instantiate *interacts* to a binary classification problem, and the parameters to learn are the rule weights $\boldsymbol{W}$. The loss function is defined as

$$loss_{\text{pre-train}} = \frac{1}{N} \sum_{i=1}^{N} \Big(l_i - z(\boldsymbol{W}^T \boldsymbol{X}_i) \Big)^2 + \lambda ||\boldsymbol{W}||_2, \tag{10}$$

where λ is the hyperparameter of L_2-regularization and z is a nonlinear function like *Sigmoid*. $\boldsymbol{W}$ is pre-trained in Eq. (10) and fine-tuned in Eq. (9) to obtain the representations of users and items. Here, our method to form each feature vector $\boldsymbol{X}_i$ is inspired by PRA [11]. Each dimension feature is corresponding to the probability of the connectivity between the user and the item by the relation path. We simplify the process by assigning 0/1 to each feature, which makes the procedure more efficient.

5 Experiments and Results

We implement RGRec on a workstation with an Intel Core i9-9900K CPU, 64 GB memory and a NVIDIA GeForce RTX 2080 Ti graphics card. The source code is available online[3]. In our experiments, we want to answer the following two research questions:

Q1. Compared to the state-of-the-art rule-based and GNN-based methods, how does RGRec perform? Are rule learning and GNNs both effective? Particularly, does RGRec work well in the cold start scenario?

Q2. How do rule length and number, rule filtering strategy, and rule weights pre-training affect the overall performance?

[3] https://github.com/nju-websoft/RGRec.

Table 1. Statistical data of the datasets

	Last.FM	MovieLens-1M	Dianping-Food
#Users	1,872	6,036	2,298,698
#Items	3,864	2,445	1,362
#Interactions	42,346	753,772	23,416,418
#Entities	9,366	182,011	28,115
#Predicates	60	12	7
#KG triples	15,518	1,241,995	160,519

5.1 Preparation

Datasets. We pick three real-world datasets: Last.FM (released in KGCN [24]), MovieLens-1M (in RippleNet [20]) and Dianping-Food (in KGCN-LS [22]). They all use Microsoft Satori[4] to prepare the corresponding KGs. The statistical data of the three datasets are depicted in Table 1, where "#Entities", "#Predicates" and "#KG triples" denote the numbers before complementing interaction matrix $\mathcal{H}$. Following conventions [22,24], we split all the data to training : validation : testing = 6 : 2 : 2.

Evaluation Metrics. We use two sets of metrics: AUC and F1 under the click through rate scenario, and Hits@k and NDCG@k ($k \in \{5, 10\}$) under the top-k recommendation scenario. To reduce the complexity of measuring Hits@k and NDCG@k during the testing stage, following KPRN [28], we sample 100 negatives for one positive. Also, following KGCN [24], we implement AUC and F1 with the ratio of positives and negatives being 1 : 1. Each experiment is repeated five times and the average results are reported.

Hyperparameters. For RotatE, we select the implementation in [8]. The dimension of predicate embeddings d_{re} is set to 1,024, and other hyperparameters strictly follow the settings in [8]. For RGRec, we perform a grid search. The used hyperparameters are determined by optimizing AUC on the validation set with the early stop strategy, i.e. stopped if not improved in successive three epochs. As a result, we set the maximum length of rules $I = 3$, the maximum number of used rules $L = 30$, the dimension of entity embeddings $d_r = 8$, the number of neighbors for every entity $Y = 4$, the learning rate to 0.05 for Last.FM and to 0.0005 for MovieLens-1M and Dianping-Food, the L_2-regularization parameter $\mu = 0.0001$, and the batch size to 128 for Last.FM and to 64 for MovieLens-1M and Dianping-Food. To pre-train rule weights $\boldsymbol{W}$, we assign the L_2-regularization parameter $\lambda = 0.0001$, the learning rate to 0.0001 and the batch size to 256. For the choices of non-linear functions q, z and σ, we set q and z to *Sigmoid*, and σ to *ReLU* for non-last iterations and to *tanh* for the last iteration.

Competitors. We pick SVD [10], LibFM [15], LibFM+TransE, PER [31], RKGE [18], CKE [32], KGCN [24] and KGAT [26] as our competitors. SVD and

[4] https://searchengineland.com/library/bing/bing-satori.

Table 2. AUC and F1 in the click through rate scenario

	Last.FM		MovieLens-1M		Dianping-Food	
	AUC	F1	AUC	F1	AUC	F1
SVD	0.772	0.683	0.833	0.757	0.787	0.729
LibFM	0.773	0.716	0.830	0.777	0.809	0.766
LibFM+TransE	0.726	0.669	0.825	0.772	0.820	0.761
PER	0.633	0.596	0.712	-	0.746	-
CKE	0.727	0.649	0.771	0.680	0.773	0.703
RKGE	0.745	0.689	0.894	0.825	0.847	0.766
KGCN	0.797	0.719	0.869	0.789	0.842	0.774
KGAT	0.706	0.709	0.906	**0.838**	-	-
RGRec	**0.825**	**0.747**	**0.913**	**0.838**	**0.884**	**0.809**

LibFM are two classical methods for recommendation. LibFM+TransE adds embeddings trained by TransE [2] to LibFM. PER represents those methods using manually constructed metapaths, while RKGE represents those methods mining paths automatically. CKE is a typical embedding-based method. KGAT and KGCN represent the aggregation-based methods. The hyperparameters for the competitors follow the settings in [24] or the settings suggested in their original papers. We develop SVD, LibFM, LibFM+TransE, RKGE and CKE by ourselves, while reuse the source code of KGAT and KGCN. We cannot implement PER because the three datasets do not provide entity types to construct metapaths. The results of PER on Last.FM, MovieLens-1M and Dianping-Food are quoted from [20,22,24], respectively, and the results of KGAT on Dianping-Food is missing due to the scalability issue.

5.2 Results and Analysis

Based on our experimental results, we answer the two research questions as follows. For Q1, as illustrated in Tables 2, 3 and 4, RGRec achieves the overall best AUC, F1, Hits@k and NDCG@k ($k \in \{5, 10\}$) on all the three datasets, except for NDCG@5 and NDCG@10 on Last.FM.

Specifically, we find that (1) for the aggregation-based methods, KGAT achieves competitive AUC and F1 on MovieLens-1M, and KGCN is stable and can be seen as the second best competitor. Compared with them, RGRec shows that rules indeed have the power to guide the aggregation of entity representations. (2) For other methods, PER obtains the worst AUC and F1 on all the three datasets, because it heavily relies on the quality of metapaths manually created. This also demonstrates the advantage of RGRec in learning rules automatically. (3) RKGE has poor Hits@k and NDCG@k ($k \in \{5, 10\}$) due to the fact that, although RKGE uses rules during training, it does not use rules during testing. In fact, it only computes the inner product of user embeddings and item embeddings during testing to resolve the complexity of rule searching. RGRec does not have this problem because rules are searched in advance and the search process is only executed once.

Furthermore, we use 20%, 40% and 60% of the data for training to see the performance of RGRec in the cold start scenario. Limited by the space, we only report the results on the largest Dianping-Food dataset, using AUC and F1 as the metrics. The results on the other two datasets using Hits@k and NDCG@k exhibit a similar phenomenon. As depicted in Table 5, RGRec obtains the best and stable results when 20%, 40% and 60% (i.e. the default setting) of the data for training are used. We can also see that the performance of several competitors (e.g., KGCN) significantly drops with fewer training data. This verifies the capability of RGRec to address the cold start problem.

Table 3. Hits@k ($k \in \{5, 10\}$) in the top-k recommendation scenario

	Last.FM		MovieLens-1M		Dianping-Food	
	Hits@5	Hits@10	Hits@5	Hits@10	Hits@5	Hits@10
SVD	0.357	0.501	0.306	0.511	0.384	0.557
LibFM	0.396	0.539	0.304	0.513	0.380	0.582
LibFM+TransE	0.344	0.453	0.234	0.438	0.355	0.542
CKE	0.188	0.294	0.070	0.134	0.351	0.526
RKGE	0.058	0.122	0.152	0.251	0.090	0.167
KGCN	0.417	0.551	0.333	0.537	0.295	0.479
KGAT	0.284	0.394	0.235	0.340	-	-
RGRec	**0.450**	**0.571**	**0.394**	**0.562**	**0.43**	**0.606**

Table 4. NDCG@k ($k \in \{5, 10\}$) in the top-k recommendation scenario

	Last.FM		MovieLens-1M		Dianping-Food	
	NDCG@5	NDCG@10	NDCG@5	NDCG@10	NDCG@5	NDCG@10
SVD	0.240	0.287	0.186	0.252	0.249	0.305
LibFM	0.267	0.313	0.183	0.250	0.238	0.303
LibFM+TransE	0.244	0.279	0.137	0.203	0.233	0.293
CKE	0.122	0.156	0.042	0.063	0.231	0.288
RKGE	0.033	0.053	0.095	0.126	0.054	0.079
KGCN	**0.325**	**0.373**	0.236	0.306	0.216	0.279
KGAT	0.198	0.233	0.154	0.188	-	-
RGRec	0.324	0.363	**0.271**	**0.325**	**0.298**	**0.354**

For Q2, the maximum length of rules is a sensitive parameter. The length of rules indicates the number of iterations for aggregation, which is also called the depth of GNNs in some methods. Deep GNNs can help central entities get information from farther entities but also lead to the over-smoothing problem [12],

Table 5. AUC and F1 on Dianping-Food in the cold start scenario

	AUC			F1		
	20%	40%	60%	20%	40%	60%
SVD	0.709	0.762	0.787	0.648	0.704	0.729
LibFM	0.812	0.814	0.809	0.761	0.766	0.766
LibFM+TransE	0.798	0.819	0.820	0.747	0.760	0.761
CKE	0.710	0.743	0.773	0.614	0.671	0.703
RKGE	0.703	0.811	0.847	0.628	0.719	0.766
KGCN	0.774	0.807	0.842	0.719	0.742	0.774
RGRec	**0.882**	**0.884**	**0.884**	**0.808**	**0.809**	**0.809**

Table 6. Number of rules w.r.t. different lengths

Lengths	Last.FM	MovieLens-1M	Dianping-Food
2	6	0	1
3	51	54	8
4	335	0	12

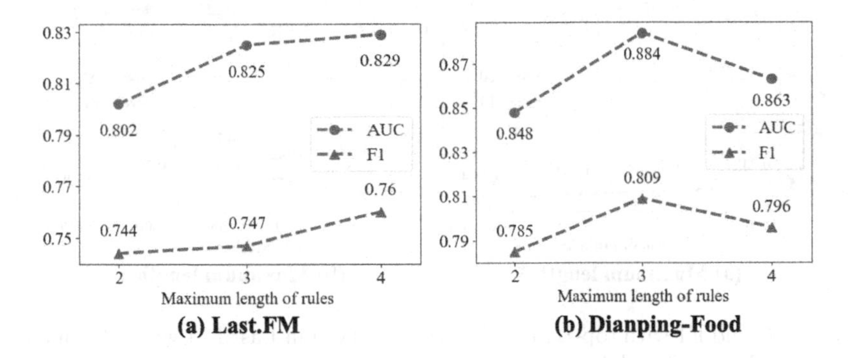

Fig. 4. AUC and F1 varying with the maximum lengths of rules

i.e. the representations of different entities would become indistinguishable. Also, in some aggregation-based methods [20,24,26], the maximum distance between a central entity and its neighbors is four, which corresponds to rules of length four. Thus, we search the rules of maximum length two, three and four on the three datasets and show the statistics in Table 6. Note that, we cannot find the rules of length two and four on MovieLens-1M, so Fig. 4 only shows how the performance of RGRec varies on Last.FM and Dianping-Food. RGRec achieves the best results on Last.FM when the maximum length is four and on Dianping-Food when the maximum length is three. However, the performance difference is pretty subtle. In practice, we prefer to use three. We believe that this length usually makes sense in recommender systems, like r_1 (Eq. (1)), r_2 (Eq. (2)) and r_3 (Eq. (3)).

To explore the effect of rule filtering strategies, RGRec is assessed with different numbers of rules preserved in Last.FM when the maximum lengths of rules are 3 and 4. MovieLens-1M and Dianping-Food have much less number of rules than Last.FM, so they are less suitable than Last.FM for this experiment. The results are shown in Fig. 5. RGRec does not perform the best when using all rules, which demonstrates that some low-quality rules are harmful and must be eliminated. The strategy of rule filtering succeeds in controlling the quality.

Additionally, we assess four strategies for rule filtering: CWA (closed world assumption), RLvLR [14], TransE [2] and RotatE [17], which are denoted by $\text{RGRec}_{\text{CWA}}$, $\text{RGRec}_{\text{RLvLR}}$, $\text{RGRec}_{\text{TransE}}$ and $\text{RGRec}_{\text{RotatE}}$, respectively. We compare them on Last.FM when the maximum length of rules is 3. We show AUC and F1 with top-L reserved rules in Table 7. Considering the best results, the highest AUC and F1 of these four methods are not achieved when all rules are used, which verifies the effectiveness of rule filtering. $\text{RGRec}_{\text{RotatE}}$ performs slightly better than the other three, showing that it is more capable of modeling

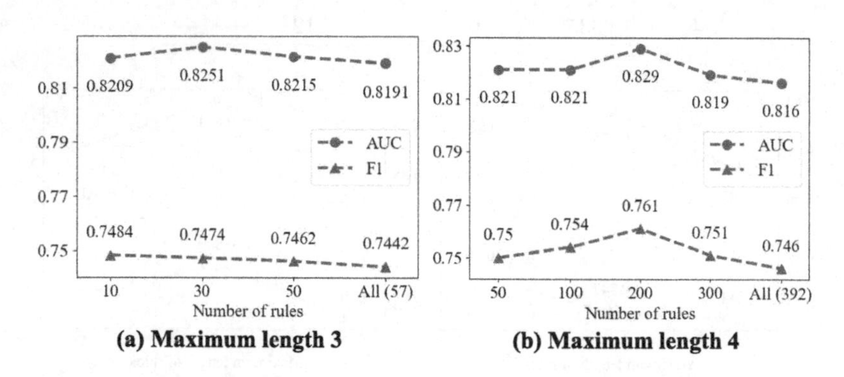

Fig. 5. AUC and F1 with top-L ranked rules preserved in Last.FM when the maximum lengths of rules are 3 and 4

Table 7. AUC and F1 of different filtering strategies on Last.FM

	Top-L	$\text{RGRec}_{\text{CWA}}$	$\text{RGRec}_{\text{RLvLR}}$	$\text{RGRec}_{\text{TransE}}$	$\text{RGRec}_{\text{RotatE}}$
AUC	10	0.8146	0.8204	0.8127	**0.8209**
	30	0.8179	0.8244	0.8202	**0.8251**
	50	0.8195	0.8163	0.8141	**0.8215**
	All (57)	0.8191			
F1	10	0.7408	0.7451	0.7397	**0.7484**
	30	0.7466	**0.7479**	0.7476	0.7474
	50	**0.7470**	0.7419	0.7381	0.7462
	All (57)	0.7442			

Table 8. AUC and F1 of RGRec, $\mathrm{RGRec}_{\mathrm{wo\_}\boldsymbol{W}}$ and the best competitor

	Last.FM		MovieLens-1M		Dianping-Food	
	AUC	F1	AUC	F1	AUC	F1
Best competitor	0.797	0.719	0.906	**0.838**	0.847	0.774
$\mathrm{RGRec}_{\mathrm{wo\_}\boldsymbol{W}}$	0.787	0.703	0.910	0.836	0.879	0.806
RGRec	**0.825**	**0.747**	**0.913**	**0.838**	**0.884**	**0.809**

the composition pattern of predicates. Also, embeddings overcome the incompleteness of KGs to some extent.

To explore the effect of rule weights pre-training, we disable the pre-training procedure and build $\mathrm{RGRec}_{\mathrm{wo\_}\boldsymbol{W}}$. As depicted in Table 8, $\mathrm{RGRec}_{\mathrm{wo\_}\boldsymbol{W}}$ underperforms RGRec on all the three datasets. However, compared with the best competitor, $\mathrm{RGRec}_{\mathrm{wo\_}\boldsymbol{W}}$ is still competitive on MovieLens-1M and Dianping-Food. We conclude that the pre-training procedure can improve the predictive capability of RGRec.

6 Conclusion

In this paper, we propose RGRec, which combines rule learning and GNNs for recommendation. Rules capture the explicit long-range semantics between entities, and GNNs aggregate the information of captured entities along the rules to learn precise representations of users. RGRec achieves superior performance on three real-world datasets. Furthermore, the combination of rule learning and GNNs is better than only using either of them. In future work, we will leverage multi-modal learning to build a more powerful recommender system.

Acknowledgment. This work is supported by the National Natural Science Foundation of China (No. 61872172), the Water Resource Science & Technology Project of Jiangsu Province (No. 2019046), and the Key R&D Program of Jiangsu Science and Technology Department (No. BE2018131).

References

1. Bayer, I., He, X., Kanagal, B., Rendle, S.: A generic coordinate descent framework for learning from implicit feedback. In: WWW, pp. 1341–1350 (2017)
2. Bordes, A., Usunier, N., Garcia-Durán, A., Weston, J., Yakhnenko, O.: Translating embeddings for modeling multi-relational data. In: NIPS, pp. 2787–2795 (2013)
3. Covington, P., Adams, J., Sargin, E.: Deep neural networks for YouTube recommendations. In: RecSys, pp. 191–198 (2016)
4. Dong, Y., Chawla, N.V., Swami, A.: metapath2vec: scalable representation learning for heterogeneous networks. In: KDD, pp. 135–144 (2017)
5. Fan, S., et al.: Metapath-guided heterogeneous graph neural network for intent recommendation. In: KDD, pp. 2478–2486 (2019)

6. Galárraga, L., Teflioudi, C., Hose, K., Suchanek, F.M.: AMIE: association rule mining under incomplete evidence in ontological knowledge bases. In: WWW, pp. 413–422 (2013)
7. Hamilton, W.L., Ying, Z., Leskovec, J.: Inductive representation learning on large graphs. In: NeurIPS, pp. 1024–1034 (2017)
8. Han, X., et al.: OpenKE: an open toolkit for knowledge embedding. In: EMNLP, pp. 139–144 (2018)
9. Kipf, T.N., Welling, M.: Semi-supervised classification with graph convolutional networks. In: ICLR (2017)
10. Koren, Y.: Factorization meets the neighborhood: a multifaceted collaborative filtering model. In: KDD, pp. 426–434 (2008)
11. Lao, N., Mitchell, T., Cohen, W.: Random walk inference and learning in a large scale knowledge base. In: EMNLP, pp. 529–539 (2011)
12. Li, Q., Han, Z., Wu, X.: Deeper insights into graph convolutional networks for semi-supervised learning. In: AAAI, pp. 3538–3545 (2018)
13. Lin, Y., Liu, Z., Sun, M., Liu, Y., Zhu, X.: Learning entity and relation embeddings for knowledge graph completion. In: AAAI, pp. 2181–2187 (2015)
14. Omran, P.G., Wang, K., Wang, Z.: Scalable rule learning via learning representation. In: IJCAI, pp. 2149–2155 (2018)
15. Rendle, S.: Factorization machines with libFM. ACM Trans. Intell. Syst. Technol. **3**(3), 57 (2012)
16. Shi, C., Hu, B., Zhao, W.X., Philip, S.Y.: Heterogeneous information network embedding for recommendation. IEEE Trans. Knowl. Data Eng. **31**(2), 357–370 (2018)
17. Sun, Z., Deng, Z.H., Nie, J.Y., Tang, J.: RotatE: knowledge graph embedding by relational rotation in complex space. In: ICLR (2019)
18. Sun, Z., Yang, J., Zhang, J., Bozzon, A., Huang, L., Xu, C.: Recurrent knowledge graph embedding for effective recommendation. In: RecSys, pp. 297–305 (2018)
19. Velickovic, P., Cucurull, G., Casanova, A., Romero, A., Liò, P., Bengio, Y.: Graph attention networks. In: ICLR (2018)
20. Wang, H., t al.: RippleNet: propagating user preferences on the knowledge graph for recommender systems. In: CIKM, pp. 417–426 (2018)
21. Wang, H., Zhang, F., Xie, X., Guo, M.: DKN: deep knowledge-aware network for news recommendation. In: WWW, pp. 1835–1844 (2018)
22. Wang, H., et al.: Knowledge-aware graph neural networks with label smoothness regularization for recommender systems. In: KDD, pp. 968–977 (2019)
23. Wang, H., Zhang, F., Zhao, M., Li, W., Xie, X., Guo, M.: Multi-task feature learning for knowledge graph enhanced recommendation. In: WWW, pp. 2000–2010 (2019)
24. Wang, H., Zhao, M., Xie, X., Li, W., Guo, M.: Knowledge graph convolutional networks for recommender systems. In: WWW, pp. 3307–3313 (2019)
25. Wang, J., Huang, P., Zhao, H., Zhang, Z., Zhao, B., Lee, D.L.: Billion-scale commodity embedding for e-commerce recommendation in Alibaba. In: KDD, pp. 839–848 (2018)
26. Wang, X., He, X., Cao, Y., Liu, M., Chua, T.: KGAT: knowledge graph attention network for recommendation. In: KDD, pp. 950–958 (2019)
27. Wang, X., He, X., Feng, F., Nie, L., Chua, T.S.: TEM: tree-enhanced embedding model for explainable recommendation. In: WWW, pp. 1543–1552 (2018)
28. Wang, X., Wang, D., Xu, C., He, X., Cao, Y., Chua, T.: Explainable reasoning over knowledge graphs for recommendation. In: AAAI, pp. 5329–5336 (2019)

29. Wang, X., et al.: Heterogeneous graph attention network. In: WWW, pp. 2022–2032 (2019)
30. Yang, B., Yih, W., He, X., Gao, J., Deng, L.: Embedding entities and relations for learning and inference in knowledge bases. In: ICLR (2015)
31. Yu, X., et al.: Personalized entity recommendation: a heterogeneous information network approach. In: WSDM, pp. 283–292 (2014)
32. Zhang, F., Yuan, N.J., Lian, D., Xie, X., Ma, W.Y.: Collaborative knowledge base embedding for recommender systems. In: KDD, pp. 353–362 (2016)
33. Zhang, S., Tay, Y., Yao, L., Liu, Q.: Quaternion knowledge graph embeddings. In: NeurIPS, pp. 2735–2745 (2019)
34. Zhao, H., Yao, Q., Li, J., Song, Y., Lee, D.L.: Meta-graph based recommendation fusion over heterogeneous information networks. In: KDD, pp. 635–644 (2017)

Leveraging Semantic Parsing for Relation Linking over Knowledge Bases

Nandana Mihindukulasooriya(✉), Gaetano Rossiello, Pavan Kapanipathi, Ibrahim Abdelaziz, Srinivas Ravishankar, Mo Yu, Alfio Gliozzo, Salim Roukos, and Alexander Gray

IBM Research, T.J. Watson Research Center, Yorktown Heights, NY, USA
{nandana.m,gaetano.rossiello,ibrahim.abdelaziz1, srini,alexander.gray}@ibm.com,
{kapanipa,yum,gliozzo,roukos}@us.ibm.com

Abstract. Knowledge base question answering systems are heavily dependent on relation extraction and linking modules. However, the task of extracting and linking relations from text to knowledge bases faces two primary challenges; the ambiguity of natural language and lack of training data. To overcome these challenges, we present SLING, a relation linking framework which leverages semantic parsing using Abstract Meaning Representation (AMR) and distant supervision. SLING integrates multiple approaches that capture complementary signals such as linguistic cues, rich semantic representation, and information from the knowledge base. The experiments on relation linking using three KBQA datasets, QALD-7, QALD-9, and LC-QuAD 1.0 demonstrate that the proposed approach achieves state-of-the-art performance on all benchmarks.

Keywords: Relation linking · Semantic parsing · Knowledge bases · Question answering

1 Introduction

Relationship Extraction and Linking (REL) is a necessary task for Knowledge Base Question Answering (KBQA) [20–22]. The goal of REL in KBQA is to identify the relations in input natural language questions and link them to their equivalent relations in a knowledge base, which are then used to construct the corresponding SPARQL query to retrieve answers. For example, we show below the corresponding DBpedia [9] SPARQL query for the question "Who is starring in Spanish movies produced by Benicio del Toro?":

```
SELECT DISTINCT ?result WHERE {
    ?film dbo:starring ?result .
    ?film dbo:country dbr:Spain .
    ?film dbo:producer dbr:Benicio_del_Toro .
    }
```


J. Z. Pan et al. (Eds.): ISWC 2020, LNCS 12506, pp. 402–419, 2020.
https://doi.org/10.1007/978-3-030-62419-4_23

Identifying the relevant relations in the question and linking them to their equivalent DBpedia relationships `dbo:starring`, `dbo:country`, and `dbo:producer` is the primary goal of REL in the context of KBQA.

REL for KBQA faces the following challenges: (1) Knowledge bases such as DBpedia, Wikidata, and Freebase have a large number of relationships which makes it challenging to acquire training data to build data-intensive deep learning models. For instance, DBpedia has thousands of relationships (some of which are generated automatically from *Wikipedia* infobox keys). (2) There is an extensive lexical gap between the surface form of relations in text and how they are represented in the KB, which makes the linking between them challenging. For example, the question above does not explicitly mention any reference to the relationship `dbo:country` which is a required relation to form the SPARQL query that can retrieve the answer. (3) Determining multiple relationships and their source and target concepts in a sentence. The example question above requires three relationships to be linked with their corresponding source and target entities/unbound variables.

In order to address the aforementioned challenges, in this work, we propose our `Semantic LINkinG` system: `SLING`; a distant supervision based approach that leverages semantic parsing such as Abstract Meaning Representation (AMR) for relation extraction and linking. Distant supervision techniques address the challenge of lack of training data, particularly for thousands of relations in KBs such as DBpedia. Transforming the text to a semantic parse such as AMR, provides advantages that include (1) normalising relations to a set of standard `PropBank` predicates, (2) identification of named entities, and (3) entity typing with a predefined type system. These characteristics of AMR help to alleviate the lexical gap by reducing different phrasings of relations to its predicate set. Furthermore, they also help to automatically determine the relationship structure of an input question and extract all relationships useful for forming a SPARQL query, hence addressing the challenge of extracting multiple relationships from questions text.

In summary, the main contributions of this paper are as follows:

- A generic framework integrating different approaches for REL based on statistical predicate alignment, word embedding and neural networks. Furthermore, the framework is modular to allow for integrating more techniques to the pipeline.
- A novel approach that harnesses AMR semantic parses of texts for REL in KBQA. Our novel usage of AMR successfully addresses the lexical gap and multiple relationship problems in REL, and achieves the new state-of-the-art on multiple benchmarks (QALD [21,22] and LC-QuAD 1.0 [20]).
- A distant supervised technique that can generate mappings between text, AMR, and KB relations leveraged for training relation classification models in the absence of task-specific training data.

The rest of the paper is organised as follows: In Sect. 2, we position our work compared to related work in REL, and Sect. 3 provides an overview of the proposed approach including a summary of each sub-module. In Sect. 4 we describe the metadata generated from the question to be used by the relation linking modules. Section 5 describes how the distant supervision data is generated and the two relation linking modules that leverage these data to generate relation linking candidates. Section 6 describes how SLING aggregates the scores from the different relation linking modules and identify the top-k relations. Next, we evaluate our system in comparison with state-of-the-art relation extraction linking approaches in Sect. 7. Finally, we conclude and present our future work in Sect. 8.

2 Related Work

Several KBQA systems have been proposed in the literature which differ according to the traits of the datasets used, such as the amount of training data available, the complexity of the questions, or if the formal queries are provided as ground truth [2,5]. In most KBQA systems, extracting relations from the questions and linking them to the KB is an essential step to generate the structure of the formal queries.

REL has been addressed using deep learning models for KBQA datasets with large number of training examples. These deep learning approaches fall into two main categories: classification-based models [10] and ranking-based models [24]. However, there are drawbacks using end to end neural approaches for REL linking: (1) they are limited only to the questions expressing one single relation in the KB. (2) they cannot be applied in the case of a lack of training data.

QALD [21,22] and LC-QuAD [20], are well-known datasets derived from DBpedia [1], represent a real-world evaluation benchmark in evaluating KBQA systems. The limited amount of training examples of these datasets along with the complex questions involving an arbitrary number of relation types make the task of identifying and linking relations significantly challenging. For KBQA, this is addressed either as a part of an end-to-end question answering system such as GAnswer [6] or by training a model to select the best off the shelf REL system Frankenstein [17]. Our work focuses on building such off the shelf tools, particularly for KBQA.

There are four primary REL works that are geared towards the above mentioned KBQA datasets [4,12,16,18]. ReMatch [12] models every KB relation into a data structure that encapsulates the relation and some enhanced attributes from dependency parsers and WordNet taxonomy. It then applies a number of similarity measures between the question and the KB relations to output a list of candidate relations. EARL [4] jointly links relation and entities from natural language to KGs. It extracts the keywords from the question, identifies them as entity or relation, then gets a list of candidates from the KG. Similarly, Falcon [16] is an approach that jointly links entities and relations in question-like sentences to DBpedia. For a given question, it applies a number of steps to extract candidate entities and relations including POS tagging, tokenization, compounding and n-gram tiling. Falcon is the state-of-the-art approach for REL on the QALD-7 and LC-QuAD 1.0 datasets. Entity Enabled Relation Linking (EERL) [14] introduces entity-based relation expansion to the existing commonly used keyword based relation extraction with the hypothesis that relations that occur in the question should be either properties of the entities in question or of their types.

However, none of the above mentioned REL methods for KBQA have explored the use of semantic parsers, whilst our work is the first to leverage the AMR of the question text as one of the inputs in an effort to reduce the ambiguity of natural language. Furthermore, we train a distantly supervised neural model in order to address the lexical gap issue between the relations expressed in the questions and the relation labels in the KB. This is inspired by the use of distant supervision for standard relation extraction tasks when there is limited or no training data for the target relations [15].

3 System Overview

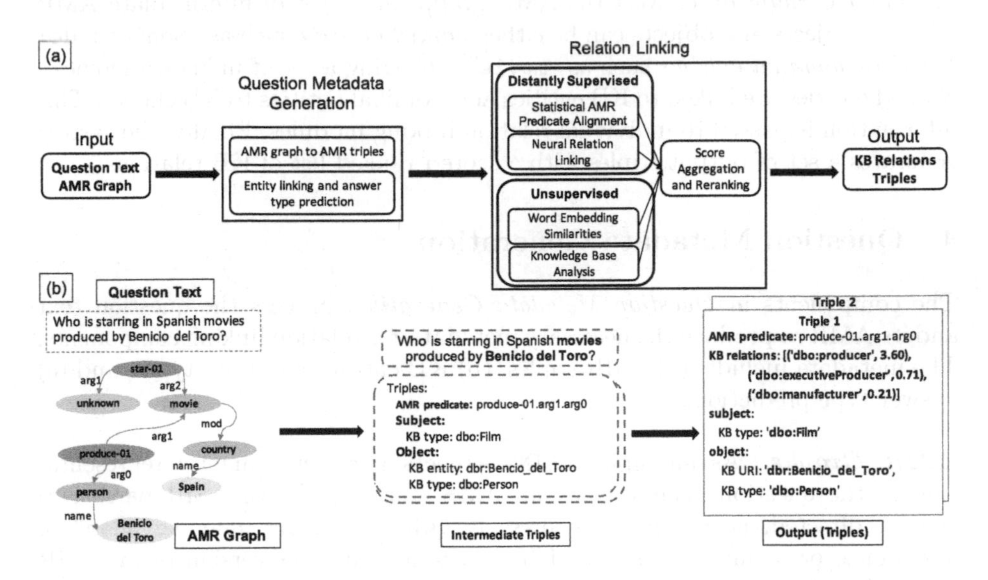

Fig. 1. (a) Overview of SLING. (b) Example driven flow of the approach.

Figure 1 shows an overview of SLING with 1-(a) showing a process-oriented view while 1-(b) illustrating with an example. The input to SLING is a question in natural language along with its corresponding AMR representation. The required output is a ranked list of relations corresponding to every subject-object pair in the sentence. The input is processed by the components in *Question Metadata Generation* (Sect. 4) to extract AMR triples (subject-object pair and their AMR predicate) and generate metadata corresponding to each of them. Each module in *Relationship Linking* produces a ranked list of KB relations with scores for a metadata-enriched AMR triple. These are aggregated to produce the required output. The source code is available at GitHub[1] under Apache 2.0 license.

SLING's design is modular to allow different relation linking modules to be plugged in and used as needed. The motivation for using multiple modules is to capture different signals such as linguistic cues from the question, richer semantic information from the AMR predicates and roles, semantic similarities of terms, and heuristics from the KB itself.

We have implemented four different relation linking modules. The first two are novel relation linking approaches; both rely on distantly supervised data which we create automatically using the DBpedia and Wikipedia documents (see Sect. 5). The other two relation linking modules are unsupervised (see Sect. 6). Each of the four modules provides relations with corresponding scores. We aggregate these scores to output a final ranked list of relations.

An example of the metadata and the output is shown in Fig. 1 (b). The input data includes the question text and its AMR graph. The modules in *Question Metadata Generation* convert the AMR graph into a set of intermediate AMR triples. Subjects and objects can be either *named entities* such as "Benicio del Toro" or *nominal entities* such as "movie" (referring a set of unknown movies). Named entities are linked to KB entities and nominal entities to KB classes. This information is passed to individual relation linking modules. Finally, the system generates a set of output triples with a scored ranked list of KB relations.

4 Question Metadata Generation

The components in *Question Metadata Generation*, process the question text and its AMR to produce the necessary metadata for relation linking components. The metadata include: (a) AMR triples, (b) KB entities and their types, and (c) answer type prediction.

AMR Graphs. As an input, SLING expects a richer semantic representation of the question generated by an AMR parser [13]. An AMR parse is a rooted, directed, acyclic graph expressing "who is doing what to whom" in a sentence or a question. Figure 1(b) shows a simplified version of an AMR graph for the question Who is starring in Spanish movies produced by Benicio del Toro?. Each node in the graph represents a concept, whereas edges represent relations between concepts that include ProbBank frames, nominal entities (types) and named entities. In this work, we rely on AMR graphs for the following reasons: (1) AMR detects named entities and maps them to predefined entity types (normalized) which forms the arguments of relations that have to be mapped to a KB, (2) AMR not only identifies relations in text but also normalises them using *PropBank* frames; (3) It reduces the ambiguity of natural language by converting relation phrases to their corresponding sense and (4) for questions, a special node, *amr-unknown*, is used to represent a placeholder for the answer to the question. Furthermore, the root node of the AMR graph,

[1] https://github.com/IBM/kbqa-relation-linking.

a.k.a the focus node, identifies the main focus of the question. Therefore, by using semantic parsing, we abstract out the syntactic variations and capture the meaning of the question in a more normalised manner.

AMR Graph to AMR Triples. DBpedia has only binary relations (two arguments). However, frames in AMR can have more than two arguments. For example, the `produce-01`[2] frame can have four core roles; `creator` (arg0), `creation` (arg1), `created from` (arg2), and `benefactive` (arg3) and other non-core roles such as time or location whereas on DBpedia there are only binary relations such as `dbo:producer`, `dbp:productionDate`, `dbo:basedOn`, or `dbo:location`. Despite the richer representation, this inherent mismatch between *n-ary* arguments of PropBank [7] frames and *binary* predicates in the KB poses a challenge. Therefore, it is necessary to generate AMR triples with a similar structure to KB triples (subject, predicate, and object) to facilitate their alignment. To resolve this issue, we use an approach that performs combinatorial expansion of all arguments of a frame to create binary relations and then prunes less probable combinations. More details of this process are presented in Sect. 5.2.

Entity/Type Linking and Answer Type Prediction. Once the AMR triples are derived, the next step is to link its subject and object to the KB. Subjects and objects from AMR can either be entities (Fig. 1: Bencio del Toro → `dbr:Bencio_del_Toro`) or classes (Fig. 1: movie → `dbo:Film`) in the KB. Entities are first linked to the KB using a regular entity linking tool that is based on BLINK [8] and DBpedia Lookup.

For classes, the mapping between AMR type system and DBpedia type system are generated semi-automatically. First, for each of 126 types from AMR type system (from AMR spec[3]), their instances are collected from AMR graphs and linked to KB entities. Then KB entity types are collected and they are ranked by frequency. Top 5 types are checked manually to map a KB type to each AMR type. This is a one time process that takes ~2 h. This mapping can be performed against any type system (e.g., DBpedia, Wikidata) given a tool for entity linking is available. For the special node, `amr-unknown`, we map it to a KB-type by using an LSTM-based answer type prediction model. For instance, given a question such as "`Who is starring in Spanish movies produced by Benicio del Toro?`", it predicts `dbo:Actor` as the answer type.

5 Distantly Supervised Relation Linking

The question metadata such as AMR parse, AMR triples with entity and type information (from Sect. 4) are used as input to the four REL modules. Two of the modules that rely on distant supervision data are described below and the other two in the next Sect. 6.

Distantly supervised data is generally used in tasks where there is a lack of training data [11]. The lack of training data is also a significant challenge

[2] http://verbs.colorado.edu/propbank/framesets-english-aliases/produce.html.
[3] https://amr.isi.edu/doc/ne-types.html.

for REL tasks on KBQA datasets. Particularly, if we want to perform REL to DBpedia, we need training data for thousands of DBpedia relations. On the other hand, the KBQA datasets such as QALD and LC-QuAD 1.0 have 408 and 5000 questions covering a small subset of DBpedia relations. In order to address this issue, we collect training data using distant supervision, which eliminates the need for task-specific supervision for relation linking.

5.1 Distant Supervision Dataset

To train our REL models, for each relation, we require training examples (sentence, subject, object) mapped to its corresponding KB relation. For instance, as shown in Fig. 2 (Sentence: `Barack Obama was born in Honolulu, Hawaii`, subject: `Barack Obama`, object: `Honolulu, Hawaii`) mapped to (KB relation: `dbo:birthPlace`).

Corpus Pre-processing and Indexing: As shown in Fig. 2, we begin with the Wikipedia corpus, and perform co-reference resolution on each document. The corpus is then tokenized into sentences, and named entities are identified in each sentence to serve as `ElasticSearch` indices. We also store meta-data such as the document the sentence was extracted from and its position in the document. This meta-data is later used for selecting sentences.

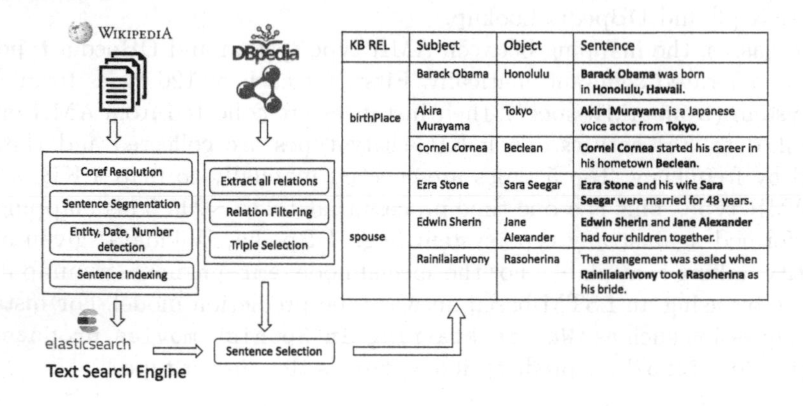

Fig. 2. Distant supervision data generation pipeline

Relation Selection: To address the issue of the large number of relations in KB, we select a manageable subset. DBpedia has a long tail of relations mainly due to uncommon Wikipedia infobox keys that are not widely used in queries. The number of examples that are generated by the distant supervision process depends on the number of triples containing the relation in the KB. While unsupervised modules use all relations in DBpedia, distantly supervised modules require some amount of examples to train the modules; thus the number of relations used by them depends of their frequency of occurrence. The distance supervision process can generate more than 10 examples for ~ 1.3K relations.

Selection of Examples: For each relation, we pick up to 1000 KB triples by ordering them by the sum of subject and object in-degrees. The assumption is that these entities are central and generally their corresponding Wikipedia articles contain more information. Then for each KB triple, we select a single example sentence, which is the first cooccurrence in entity's Wikipedia article. We choose sentences that satisfy the following: 1) subject and object co-occur, 2) have at least 4 tokens, 3) have at least 1 verb and 4) the entity surface forms do not overlap in the text (when one is a multi-word containing other). We observed that these basic heuristics increased the probability that the sentence contains a relation and filtered out accidental co-occurrences in titles, lists, etc.

5.2 Statistical AMR Predicate Alignment

This section presents a relation linking module that leverages the information present in the AMR semantic parses to generates alignments between *PropBank* predicates in AMR graphs and KB ontology relations. We describe below how these alignments are generated and then used to produce candidate relations.

Building PropBank Alignments. One challenge for creating these alignments is the inherent mismatch between frame-based representation and triple-based representation. In AMR graphs, a single frame captures a rich set of information using *n-ary* relations (e.g., who is doing what to whom, when, etc.) while triples in KBs capture simpler atomic facts using *binary* relations. For example, the frame `bear-02`[4], which is used to capture the event of giving birth to a child, has two core roles: `arg0` (mother), `arg1` (child) and several non-core roles including `location` (place of birth), `time` (time of birth) as shown in Fig. 3-A.

To address this mismatch in the number of arguments, we first decompose the AMR graph into a set of AMR triples. This is performed by creating binary relations between all entities participating in different roles of the frame using combinatorial expansion, as shown in Fig. 3-B. The generated binary relations are paths between the two nodes in the graph and follow the structure, <propbank-frame>.<subject-role>.<object-role>. Given a combination of two entities, for example, *Duka Tesla* (with the arg0 role) and *Nikola Tesla* (with the arg1 role), two AMR triples are generated, one with Dula Tesla as subject and Nikola Tesla as object and the other vice-versa as shown below:

```
Duka Tesla       bear02.arg0.arg1     Nikola Tesla
Nikola Tesla     bear02.arg1.arg0     Duka Tesla
```

Nevertheless, this process generates a large number of AMR triples that will not necessarily have their mapping relation in the KB. For example, in DBpedia, the place or the date that a mother gave a birth to a child

[4] http://verbs.colorado.edu/propbank/framesets-english-aliases/bear.html.

Natural Language Sentence: **Duka Tesla** gave birth to **Nikola Tesla** in **Smiljan** on **10th of July 1856.**

(A)

```
(b / bear-02
 :ARG0 (p / person
   :name (n / name
       :op1 "Duka" :op2 " Tesla" ))
 :ARG1 (p / person
   :name (n1 / name
       :op1 " Nikola" :op2 " Tesla" ))
 :location (c2 / city
   :name (n2 / name
       :op1 "Smiljan" ))
 :time (d / date-entity
   :year 1856 :month 07 :day 10 ))
```

AMR Graph (who is doing what to whom)

(B) AMR Triples (combinatorial expansion of roles) / (C) KB relations

(B)			(C)
Duka Tesla	**bear-02.arg0.arg1**	**Nikola Tesla**	**dbo:child**
Duka Tesla	bear-02.arg0.location	Smiljan	
Duka Tesla	bear-02.arg0.time	10/07/1856	
Nikola Tesla	**bear-02.arg1.arg0**	**Duka Tesla**	**dbo:mother**
Nikola Tesla	**bear-02.arg1.location**	**Smiljan**	**dbo:birthPlace**
Nikola Tesla	**bear-02.arg1.time**	**10/07/1856**	**dbo:birthDate**
Smiljan	bear-02.location.arg0	Duka Tesla	
Smiljan	bear-02.location.arg1	Nikola Tesla	
Smiljan	bear-02.location.time	10/07/1856	
10/07/1856	bear-02.time.arg0	Duka Tesla	
10/07/1856	bear-02.time.arg1	Nikola Tesla	
10/07/1856	bear-02.time.location	Smiljan	

Fig. 3. converting AMR graphs to binary relations using combinatorial expansion

(bear02.arg0.location/time) is not represented as an attribute of the mother but only as attributes of the child and consequently there is no equivalent relation for those in the KB. This can be addressed by analysing how often we can align a given AMR triple to a KB triple. For example, out of 12 AMR triples generated (Fig. 3-B), only the four highlighted can be aligned with the existing KB triples in DBpedia.

Because KBs are generally multi-graphs and there are cases where two entities are connected with multiple relations in the KB. For example, if we assume Nikola Tesla was born and died in the same place, two entities (Nicola Tesla and Smijan) will be related both by `birthPlace` and `deathPlace` relations. In such cases with multiple candidates, we use lexical similarity between frame definition/aliases from PropBank (e.g., `bear`, `bear children`, `birth`, `give birth`) and DBpedia relation labels to disambiguate and select the most similar one.

Finally, to accommodate error propagation from both distant supervision dataset and AMR parsing, which could lead to noise in the alignments, we also use type constraints to further refine the alignments. The goal of this step is to induce type constraints for each role in a given frame. This is performed by collecting all entities participating in a given role in a frame (*e.g.*, bear-02.ARG0) and analyzing their types (including data types such as numerics and dates). Using this information, proxy domain and range constraints for AMR binary relations can be generated as in Fig. 4. These constraints are used to filter out any aligned DBpedia relation that does not match with the type constraints.

To summarize, for generating these alignments efficiently, we used the distant supervision dataset, defined as $D = \{(s_i, r_i, o_i, t_i), \dots\}$ where $\{s_i, r_i, o_i\}$ are the subject, relation, object of the KB triple and t_i is the corresponding sentence (see Fig. 2). We parse each t_i and generate an AMR graph a_i. Each a_i is then converted into a set of AMR triples $x_j = \{\grave{s}_j, p_j, \grave{o}_j\}$ where $x_j \in a_i$ and p_j is the AMR binary predicate, $\grave{s}_j$ and $\grave{o}_j$ are the subject and object from the AMR graph. Finally, we check for an AMR triple x_j where $\grave{s}_j = s_i$ and $\grave{o}_j = o_i$ and if found, one alignment between r_i and p_j is created.

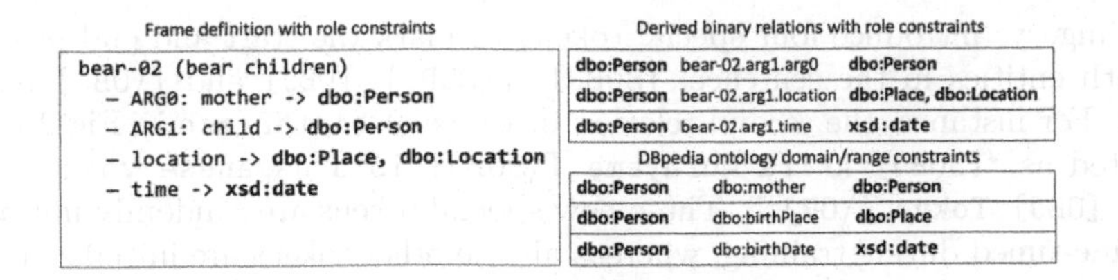

Frame definition with role constraints
bear-02 (bear children)
- ARG0: mother -> dbo:Person
- ARG1: child -> dbo:Person
- location -> dbo:Place, dbo:Location
- time -> xsd:date
Derived binary relations with role constraints
dbo:Person bear-02.arg1.arg0 dbo:Person
dbo:Person bear-02.arg1.location dbo:Place, dbo:Location
dbo:Person bear-02.arg1.time xsd:date
DBpedia ontology domain/range constraints
dbo:Person dbo:mother dbo:Person
dbo:Person dbo:birthPlace dbo:Place
dbo:Person dbo:birthDate xsd:date

Fig. 4. Type constraints for frame roles

Finding Relation Candidates. Once the complete dataset is processed and alignments are filtered using type constraints, for each AMR binary predicate p_j we get a set of cumulative alignments $A(p_j) = \{(r_0, c_0), \ldots, (r_n, c_n)\}$ where each r is a KB relation and c is a alignment count. Using that, for each AMR binary predicate p_j, relation candidate scores are calculated using $relation\_score(p_j, r_n) = [c_n/max(c)] * [1/1 + log(inv\_pred\_count(r_n)]$ where $max(c)$ is highest count in $A(p_j)$ and $inv\_pred\_count(r_n)$ is the inverse predicate count, *i.e.*, number of distinct AMR predicates which r_n is aligned at least once.

5.3 Neural Model for Relation Linking

Statistical AMR mapping has the following drawbacks that can be addressed using a neural approach: (1) mapping generic frames such as `have-01` can be ambiguous. For example for: ``‘‘Did Che Guevara have children?"`` has the frame `have` that needs to be mapped to `dbo:child` (2) lexical gap where the same relation type can be expressed as different linguistic patterns. Therefore, we train a neural model for relation linking by exploiting the distant supervision dataset (Sect. 5.1). The neural model produces dense embedding vectors for input questions, which can learn to project the same relation type's different surface forms close in the latent space. In this section, we describe how to train the neural model on the distant supervision data (*training*) and how to make use of the model for question REL (*inference*).

Training Phase. Leveraging our distant supervision dataset, our training data is defined as $D = \{(x_0, r_0), \ldots, (x_N, r_N)\}$. Here $r_i \in R$ are the relation types, and $x_i = (t_i, s_i, o_i)$ are the relation instances consisting of a textual sentence t_i and the spans of the subject s_i and the object o_i. The set R represents the vocabulary of $K = |R|$ distinct relation types. We train a neural network M on D with the purpose to predict the correct relation type r_k given the instance x_k by minimize the cross-entropy loss regarding the conditional probability $p_M(\cdot|x_k)$ modeled by M, with respect to the true relation r_k.

In order to generate a vector representation of the relation instance x, we adopt the relation encoder inspired by [19]. This encoder is an adaptation of the original Transformer [23] architecture that encodes the given sentence while being aware of the subject and object. To achieve this entity-aware encoding, we introduce four special tokens to mark the start and end positions of both entities in the sentence, [SUBJ], [\SUBJ], [OBJ] and [\OBJ] respectively. For instance, the second relation instance of birthPlace in Fig 2 is represented as "[SUBJ] Akira Murayama [\SUBJ] is a Japanese voice actor from [OBJ] Tokyo [\OBJ]". These new special tokens are randomly initialized and fine-tuned during training, whereas all the other tokens are initialized using the pre-trained BERT-BASE embeddings [3]. We concatenate the vectors of the final-layer hidden states of the start entity markers of subject and object entities, feed them into a fully connected layer to get the finally embedding vector for the relation instance x.

Finally, to estimate $p_M(r_k|x_k)$, we add a further classification layer with the output size K followed by a softmax function.

Inference Phase. There are several challenges to address when applying the trained neural relation linking model M to deal with question relationship linking. In particular, how to mark the missing entities from the question, which consists of two cases: (1) the missing entity is the answer; (2) the missing entity is an intermediate entity when the question requires multiple hops to reach the answer. We exploit the *AMR graph to AMR triples* feature described in Sect. 4 to handle these challenges.

- *Intermediate entities:* Consider the question in Fig. 1 and its generated metadata. The question requires to first find some Spanish movie entities having the dbo:producer relation with Benicio del Toro, e.g.., 7 días en La Habana, then identifies another relation dbo:star from the movie entity. Since the movie name is missing in the question text, when predicting its relationship to Benicio del Toro, we take the surface form of arg2 for star-01.arg2.arg1, i.e., the word "movies" as the object. In this way, we generate the following input relation instance to the neural model M, Who is starring in Spanish [OBJ] movies [\OBJ] produced by [SUBJ] Benicio del Toro [\SUBJ] ?.
- *Unknown (answer) entities:* Consider the same question as above. The predicate star-01.arg2.arg1 has no explicit text for the arg1 since the amr-type is unknown, which refers to the answer. In this case, we mark the question word "Who" for the arg2. Therefore the following format for the relation instance is generated for our neural model: "[OBJ] Who [\OBJ] is starring in Spanish [SUBJ] movies [\SUBJ] produced by Benicio del Toro?".

Finally, with the aforementioned treatments, for each relation instance a ranked list of relation types in DBpedia is generated and sorted by their probability scores produced by our neural model.

6 Unsupervised Relation Linking and Score Aggregation

In the previous section, we have described the 2 distantly supervised modules. In this section, we describe the remaining 2 modules and aggregation of scores to get the final ranked list of KB relations.

6.1 Unsupervised Modules

Lexical Similarity. To derive the score of a relation with respect to an AMR triple, we compute its lexical similarity to the question text and AMR predicate. For each relation candidate, like `dbo:deathPlace`, we consider its label as a word sequence `death place`. We concatenate each question, e.g., `Who was married to Lincoln`, with the AMR predicate of the triple (e.g. `marry` from `marry-01`) to get the other word sequence. We compute the lexical similarity between the two word sequences by first calculating a word-by-word cosine similarity based on word2vec embeddings. If there are m words in one word sequence, and n words in the other, this produces $m \times n$ similarity scores. This is max-pooled to produce a single score as output.

Knowledge Base Connections. In KBQA, the entities from the questions are identified and linked to KB first. Therefore, the task of relation linking also assumes the existence of such linked KB entities and entity types as described in the *Question Metadata Generation* step. Hence, candidate relations that also connect these detected entities can be scored higher, following previous works [16]. For example, given the question "`Who created Family Guy?`", to predict the relation in this question, we score all relations connected to the KB entity (`dbr:Family_Guy`) as the object and a subject of KB type `dbo:Person` or any subclass of it (which is predicted by answer type prediction). We then apply a soft constraint to focus more on the relations that are within this set.[5].

6.2 Score Aggregation

The scores from each module are normalized using min-max normalization. The final score of a relation is the arithmetic sum of its normalized score from each module, and a ranked list of relations is obtained for the AMR triple. This process is repeated for every AMR triple extracted from the question.

7 Evaluation

In this section, we detail our experimental setup and evaluate our approach against the state-of-the-art relation linking approaches for KBQA. We replicate the experimental setup proposed in Falcon [16] in terms of the same datasets and metrics used for a fair comparison, as described below.

[5] Ideally, we can do the hard filtering with the relation connections. However as REL is a component of a whole KBQA pipeline. To mitigate potential error propagation from entity linking, most works adopt a soft approach [6,16].

Table 1. KBQA datasets statistics

Dataset	Questions	Avg constraints
QALD-7	215	1.5
QALD-9	408	1.5
LC-QuAD 1.0	5000	1.7

Table 2. Relation Linking systems comparison

	QALD-7			LC-QuAD 1.0			QALD-9		
System	P	R	F1	P	R	F1	P	R	F1
SIBKB	0.29	0.31	0.30	0.13	0.15	0.14	–	–	–
ReMatch	0.31	0.34	0.33	0.15	0.17	0.16	–	–	–
EARL	0.27	0.28	0.27	0.17	0.21	0.18	–	–	–
Falcon	**0.58**	0.61	0.59	**0.42**	0.44	0.43	0.31	0.34	0.32
SLING	0.57	**0.76**	**0.65**	0.41	**0.58**	**0.48**	**0.50**	**0.64**	**0.56**

7.1 Experimental Setup

We used three KBQA datasets; QALD-7 [22], QALD-9 [21] and LC-QuAD 1.0 [20]. All the datasets comprise of question text, their corresponding SPARQL queries, and answers from DBpedia. Similar to [16], we use the question text and the relations in the SPARQL queries for evaluation[6]. Table 1 shows the number of questions and the average triple constraints in SPARQL queries for each of the datasets. QALD-9 is an evolved version of QALD-7 extending the number of questions from 215 to 408.

We compare SLING against four existing REL approaches for KBQA: (1) SIBKB [18], (2) ReMatch [12], (3) EARL [4], and (4) Falcon [16]. Falcon [16] is the state-of-the-art approach evaluated on QALD-7 and LC-QuAD 1.0 datasets. We use standard metrics such as precision, recall, and F-measure for evaluation and comparisons. The precision measures the capability of a REL system to predict the exact number of expected relations in a given question and the recall measures the capability of a system to cover all the expected relations.

7.2 Results

Table 2 shows the precision, recall, and F-measure of SLING in comparison to state-of-the-art approaches. The results show that our approach consistently achieves a better F1 score than the existing approaches and is robust across datasets, i.e. the results on QALD-7 and QALD-9 are respectively similar compared to those obtained by Falcon[7]. Moreover, SLING provides a remarkably higher recall than the other competing systems.

[6] We exclude `rdf:type`, and `rdfs:label` to follow same setting in [16].

[7] Falcon numbers on QALD-7 and LC-QuAD 1.0 are taken from their paper.

Ablation Study: In order to understand the contribution of each module in the SLING framework, we perform an ablation study by removing the corresponding module from the overall system and comparing its performance. These results reported in Table 3 indicates that every module contributes to the overall performance of the system results. Particularly, removing the statistical AMR mapping approach from the system has the biggest drop in performance. The AMR mapping component provides the strongest contribution of the modules, with the system performance dropping considerably without its usage. AMR provides predicates that are already a strong signal for identifying the relations in a sentence. Moreover, AMR parsers normalize syntactic variations across sentences which have the same meaning. Finally, AMR provides type information about the subject and object of a relation, even when they are unknown. This enables domain and range-derived features to constrain the predicted relation candidates.

Table 3. Ablation study on QALD-7 dataset

	P	R	F1
SLING	0.57	0.76	0.65
w/o AMR Mapping	0.45	0.57	0.51
w/o Neural Relation Linking	0.52	0.66	0.58
w/o Word Embeddings	0.53	0.68	0.59
w/o KB Analysis	0.46	0.61	0.53

Table 4. Relation linking performance with machine generated vs human annotated AMR on a subset of QALD-9 dataset

	P	R	F1
w/ machine generated AMR	0.53	0.76	0.62
w/ human annotated AMR	0.57	0.77	0.66

For relations that are implicit in text, the Neural Relation Linking bridges the lexical gap to map them. For instance, considering the first example in Table 6, the relation type `dbo:country` is implicit in the question, but the neural model is able to identify it nevertheless. Furthermore, the Neural Relation Linking is able to handle questions having more than one relation, where different relations can be predicted given the same question text, but different spans of entities, as described in Sect. 5.3. This insight confirms that the distant supervision technique can be helpful in covering different language phrases to identify and link relations to a KB, especially in setting such as QALD, where only a small training set is provided.

Table 5. Relation linking performance with our entity linking implementation vs annotations from [14] on LC-QuAD dataset.

	P	R	F1
w/ our entity linker implementation	0.41	0.58	0.48
w/ entity annotations from [14]	0.46	0.62	0.53

Based on our analysis we find that the Word Embeddings module is particularly useful when the relation is explicitly mentioned in the question, like `'Who is the mayor of Paris?'`, with the relation being `dbo:mayor`. It provides high-precision estimates about the relations in the question.

Automatic extraction of DBpedia triples from Wikipedia Infoboxes (when mappings are not available) introduces redundant and noisy (`dbp:`) relations. For instance, there are relations such as `dbo:birthPlace`, `dbp:birthPlace`, `dbp:birthLocation` and `dbp:placeOfBirth` that are semantically equivalent and cannot be lexically distinguished based on their labels. In such scenarios KB analysis allows the system to choose the correct relation by considering only the ones connected to the entities of interest. For the question `'What is the birth place of Frank Sinatra?'`, without the KB analysis we find `dbo:birthPlace` and `dbp:placeOfBirth` as the top ranked relations. KB analysis scores `dbp:placeOfBirth` higher because of its association with the entity `dbr:Frank_Sinatra` (Table 5).

Impact of AMR Parser: To understand how the quality of AMR affects the results, we have manually annotated a subset of QALD-9 questions (ids 250 to 408) and the results are presented in Table 4. It shows that human annotated AMRs provide an improvement of 4 points in F1. The state-of-the-art AMR parser [13] has a smatch score of 90% when tested on a subset of QALD-9 dataset.

Impact of Entity Linking: To understand the effect of entity linking, we have performed a similar experiment using entity annotations provided by [14] for LC-QuAD 1.0. We have tested the entity linker implementation we used with QALD-9; it has an F1 of 0.75.

7.3 Qualitative Analysis and Discussion

Table 6 shows five example questions with their gold standard relations compared to what `SLING` predicts for each question. `SLING` was able to find the correct set of relations for the first three questions and partially solves the rest. In the first question, the main challenge is to decompose the question into three triples with correct subject/object combinations. Leveraging AMR allows `SLING` accurately determine the correct triple decomposition including directionality and the number of triples. Once decomposed, all relation linking modules provide strong signals in this example. The second and third questions are lexically

Table 6. Example queries with gold and predicted relations.

ID	Question	Gold standard triple patterns	Predicted relations
1	Who is starring in Spanish movies produced by Benicio del Toro?	?film dbo:starring ?actor . ?film dbo:country res:Spain . ?film dbo:producer res:Benicio_del_Toro	dbo:starring dbo:country dbo:producer
2	Who developed Skype?	res:Skype dbo:developer ?company	dbo:developer
3	Who developed Slack?	?company dbo:product res:Slack	dbo:product
4	Give me the grandchildren of Bruce Lee.	res:Bruce_Lee dbo:child ?child ?child ?dbp:child ?granchild	dbo:child
5	Which organizations were founded in 1950?	{ ?org dbo:formationYear ?date } UNION { ?org dbo:foundingYear ?date } UNION { ?org dbp:foundation ?date } UNION { ?org dbp:formation ?date }	dbo:foundingYear

very similar but their representations in KB are different. The fact that `SLING` creates triples with directionality into account and perform KB analysis allowing it to pick correct relation in each case. The fourth question is challenging because it requires to reason that grand children are children of children. AMR represent this using a single triple. Furthermore, the relation used in each constraint is different (`dbo:child` vs `dbp:child`). `SLING` gets a set of candidates such as `dbo:child`, `dbp:children`, `dbp:grandChilden` and picks `dbo:child` as it is connected to `res:Bruce_Lee`. Nevertheless, it does not decompose this question into two triples. Similarly, some gold standard questions have the `UNION` construct with logically equivalent relations in KB. However, as the relation appears only once in the text, `SLING` only aims to predict one relation.

8 Conclusions and Future Work

In this paper, we presented `SLING`, a framework for relation linking that leverages semantic parsing with AMR and distant supervision. `SLING` is a combination of multiple modules that capture complementary signals both from the AMR representation as well as natural language text. Experimental results show that `SLING` outperforms state-of-the-art approaches on three KBQA datasets; QALD-7, QALD-9, and LC-QuAD 1.0. Furthermore, our ablation study shows that leveraging AMR and the use of distant supervision contributes to outperform the state-of-the-art techniques. As a part of our future work, we are planning to convert all the components as feature generators for an end to end neural approach. Furthermore, we intend to investigate the use of transformer-based architectures for encoding both AMR graphs and the question text for relation linking.

References

1. Auer, S., Bizer, C., Kobilarov, G., Lehmann, J., Cyganiak, R., Ives, Z.: DBpedia: a nucleus for a web of open data. In: Aberer, K., et al. (eds.) ASWC/ISWC -2007. LNCS, vol. 4825, pp. 722–735. Springer, Heidelberg (2007). https://doi.org/10.1007/978-3-540-76298-0_52
2. Chakraborty, N., Lukovnikov, D., Maheshwari, G., Trivedi, P., Lehmann, J., Fischer, A.: Introduction to neural network based approaches for question answering over knowledge graphs. CoRR abs/1907.09361 (2019)
3. Devlin, J., Chang, M., Lee, K., Toutanova, K.: BERT: pre-training of deep bidirectional transformers for language understanding. In: NAACL-HLT 2019, pp. 4171–4186 (2019)
4. Dubey, M., Banerjee, D., Chaudhuri, D., Lehmann, J.: EARL: joint entity and relation linking for question answering over knowledge graphs. In: Vrandečić, D., et al. (eds.) ISWC 2018. LNCS, vol. 11136, pp. 108–126. Springer, Cham (2018). https://doi.org/10.1007/978-3-030-00671-6_7
5. Höffner, K., Walter, S., Marx, E., Usbeck, R., Lehmann, J., Ngomo, A.N.: Survey on challenges of question answering in the semantic web. Semant. Web **8**(6), 895–920 (2017)
6. Hu, S., Zou, L., Yu, J.X., Wang, H., Zhao, D.: Answering natural language questions by subgraph matching over knowledge graphs. IEEE Trans. Knowl. Data Eng. **30**(5), 824–837 (2018)
7. Kingsbury, P., Palmer, M.: PropBank: the next level of treebank. In: Proceedings of Treebanks and lexical Theories, vol. 3. Citeseer (2003)
8. Wu, L., Petroni, F., Josifoski, M., Riedel, S., Zettlemoyer, L.: Zero-shot entity linking with dense entity retrieval. arXiv:1911.03814 (2019)
9. Lehmann, J., et al.: DBpedia-a large-scale, multilingual knowledge base extracted from Wikipedia. Semant. Web **6**(2), 167–195 (2015)
10. Lukovnikov, D., Fischer, A., Lehmann, J.: Pretrained transformers for simple question answering over knowledge graphs. In: Ghidini, C., et al. (eds.) ISWC 2019. LNCS, vol. 11778, pp. 470–486. Springer, Cham (2019). https://doi.org/10.1007/978-3-030-30793-6_27
11. Mintz, M., Bills, S., Snow, R., Jurafsky, D.: Distant supervision for relation extraction without labeled data. In: ACL 2009, pp. 1003–1011 (2009)
12. Mulang, I.O., Singh, K., Orlandi, F.: Matching natural language relations to knowledge graph properties for question answering. In: SEMANTiCS 2017, pp. 89–96 (2017)
13. Naseem, T., Shah, A., Wan, H., Florian, R., Roukos, S., Ballesteros, M.: Rewarding smatch: Transition-based AMR parsing with reinforcement learning. arXiv preprint arXiv:1905.13370 (2019)
14. Pan, J.Z., Zhang, M., Singh, K., Harmelen, F., Gu, J., Zhang, Z.: Entity enabled relation linking. In: Ghidini, C., et al. (eds.) ISWC 2019. LNCS, vol. 11778, pp. 523–538. Springer, Cham (2019). https://doi.org/10.1007/978-3-030-30793-6_30
15. Rossiello, G., Gliozzo, A., Farrell, R., Fauceglia, N.R., Glass, M.R.: Learning relational representations by analogy using hierarchical siamese networks. In: NAACL-HLT (1), pp. 3235–3245. Association for Computational Linguistics (2019)
16. Sakor, A., et al.: Old is gold: linguistic driven approach for entity and relation linking of short text. In: NAACL: HLT 2019, pp. 2336–2346 (2019)

17. Singh, K., Both, A., Sethupat, A., Shekarpour, S.: Frankenstein: a platform enabling reuse of question answering components. In: Gangemi, A., et al. (eds.) ESWC 2018. LNCS, vol. 10843, pp. 624–638. Springer, Cham (2018). https://doi.org/10.1007/978-3-319-93417-4_40
18. Singh, K., et al.: Capturing knowledge in semantically-typed relational patterns to enhance relation linking. In: K-CAP 2017, pp. 1–8 (2017)
19. Soares, L.B., FitzGerald, N., Ling, J., Kwiatkowski, T.: Matching the blanks: distributional similarity for relation learning. In: ACL 2019, pp. 2895–2905 (2019)
20. Trivedi, P., Maheshwari, G., Dubey, M., Lehmann, J.: LC-QuAD: a corpus for complex question answering over knowledge graphs. In: d'Amato, C., et al. (eds.) ISWC 2017. LNCS, vol. 10588, pp. 210–218. Springer, Cham (2017). https://doi.org/10.1007/978-3-319-68204-4_22
21. Usbeck, R., Gusmita, R.H., Ngomo, A.N., Saleem, M.: 9th challenge on question answering over linked data (QALD-9) (invited paper). In: Semdeep/NLIWoD@ISWC. CEUR Workshop Proceedings, vol. 2241, pp. 58–64. CEUR-WS.org (2018)
22. Usbeck, R., Ngomo, A.-C.N., Haarmann, B., Krithara, A., Röder, M., Napolitano, G.: 7th open challenge on question answering over linked data (QALD-7). In: Dragoni, M., Solanki, M., Blomqvist, E. (eds.) SemWebEval 2017. CCIS, vol. 769, pp. 59–69. Springer, Cham (2017). https://doi.org/10.1007/978-3-319-69146-6_6
23. Vaswani, A., et al.: Attention is all you need. In: NIPS, pp. 5998–6008 (2017)
24. Yu, M., Yin, W., Hasan, K.S., dos Santos, C.N., Xiang, B., Zhou, B.: Improved neural relation detection for knowledge base question answering. In: ACL 2017, pp. 571–581 (2017)

NABU – Multilingual Graph-Based Neural RDF Verbalizer

Diego Moussallem[1(✉)], Dwaraknath Gnaneshwar[2], Thiago Castro Ferreira[3,4], and Axel-Cyrille Ngonga Ngomo[1]

[1] Data Science Group, University of Paderborn, Paderborn, Germany
{diego.moussallem,axel-cyrille.ngomo}@upb.de

[2] DL Group, Manipal Institute of Technology, Manipal, India
dwarakasharma@gmail.com

[3] Federal University of Minas Gerais (UFMG), Belo Horizonte, Brazil

[4] Tilburg Center for Cognition and Communication (TiCC), Tilburg University, Tilburg, The Netherlands
tcastrof@tilburguniversity.edu

Abstract. The RDF-to-text task has recently gained substantial attention due to continuous growth of Linked Data. In contrast to traditional pipeline models, recent studies have focused on neural models, which are now able to convert a set of RDF triples into text in an end-to-end style with promising results. However, English is the only language widely targeted. We address this research gap by presenting NABU, a multilingual graph-based neural model that verbalizes RDF data to German, Russian, and English. NABU is based on an encoder-decoder architecture, uses an encoder inspired by Graph Attention Networks and a Transformer as decoder. Our approach relies on the fact that knowledge graphs are language-agnostic and they hence can be used to generate multilingual text. We evaluate NABU in monolingual and multilingual settings on standard benchmarking WebNLG datasets. Our results show that NABU outperforms state-of-the-art approaches on English with 66.21 BLEU, and achieves consistent results across all languages on the multilingual scenario with 56.04 BLEU.

Keywords: Knowledge Graphs · Natural Language Generation · Semantic Web

1 Introduction

Natural Language Generation (NLG) is the process of generating coherent natural language text from non-linguistic data [38]. Despite community agreement on the text and speech output of these systems, there is far less consensus on what

D. Moussallem and D. Gnaneshwar—Equal contribution

D. Moussallem, D. Gnaneshwar and T. Castro Ferreira—This work was carried out under the Google Summer of Code 2019.

J. Z. Pan et al. (Eds.): ISWC 2020, LNCS 12506, pp. 420–437, 2020.
https://doi.org/10.1007/978-3-030-62419-4_24

the input should be [20]. A large number of inputs have hence been employed for NLG systems, including images [48], numeric data [22], and Semantic Web (SW) data [34]. Practical applications can be found in domains such as weather forecasts [30], feedback for car drivers [8], diet management [1].

Presently, the generation of natural language from Resource Description Framework (RDF) data has gained substantial attention [7]. The RDF-to-text task has hence been proposed to investigate the quality of automatically generated texts from RDF Knowledge Graphs (KGs) [11]. With the emergence of neural methods, end-to-end data-to-text models have been introduced to learn input-output mappings directly. These approaches rely much less on explicit intermediate representations compared to rule-based approaches [21].

Although Neural NLG models have been achieving very good results [19], English is the only language that has been widely targeted. In this work, we alleviate this language limitation by proposing a multilingual approach, named NABU. The motivation behind multilingual models lies in several directions, mainly in (1) transfer learning; when low-resource language pairs are trained together with high-resource languages, the translation quality improves; (2) zero-shot translation, where multilingual models are able to translate between language pairs from similar families that were never seen during training; (3) Easy deploy, a multilingual model achieving same performance on many languages in comparison to several separate language-specific models are much more desirable for companies in terms of deployment [24].

Our approach, NABU, is based on the fact that knowledge graphs are language-agnostic and hence can be used on the encoder side to generate multilingual text. NABU consists of an encoder-decoder architecture which incorporates structural information of RDF triples using an encoding mechanism inspired by Graph Attention Network (GAT) [47]. In contrast to recent related work [39], NABU relies on the use of a reification strategy for modeling the graph structure of RDF input. The decoder part is based on the vanilla Transformer model [46] along with an unsupervised tokenization model.

We evaluate NABU on the standard benchmarking WebNLG datasets [18] in three settings: monolingual, bilingual and multilingual. For the monolingual setting, we compare NABU with state-of-the-art English approaches and also perform experiments on Russian and German. The goal of the bilingual setting is to analyze the performance of NABU for language families. To achieve this goal, we train and evaluate bilingual models using NABU on English-German and on English-Russian. In the multilingual setting, we compare NABU with a multilingual Transformer model on English, German and Russian. Our results show that NABU outperforms state-of-the-art approaches on English and achieves 66.21 BLEU. NABU also achieves consistent results across all languages on multilingual settings with 56.04 BLEU. In addition, NABU presents promising results on the bilingual models with 61.99 BLEU. Our findings suggest that NABU is able to generate multilingual text with similar quality to that generated by humans. The main contributions of this paper can be summarized as follows:

- We present a novel approach dubbed NABU based on a GAT-Transformer architecture for generating multilingual text from RDF KGs.
- NABU outperforms English state-of-the-art approaches with consistent average improvements of +10 BLEU, METEOR and chrF3 on the WebNLG datasets.
- NABU exploits the benefits of modeling of language families in the generation task.

The version of NABU used in this paper and also all experimental data are publicly available.[1]

2 Related Work

A significant body of research has investigated the generation of Natural Language (NL) texts from RDF data. A plenty of research is based on template- and rule-based approaches such as [10,14,15,34]. Recently, the WebNLG [11] challenge made this research area more prominent by providing a benchmark corpus of English texts verbalizing RDF triples in 15 different semantic domains. Among the participating models, the works based on sequence-to-sequence Neural Networks (NNs) achieved some of the best results [32,43]. Moreover, RDF has also been showing promising benefits to the generation of benchmarks for evaluating NLG systems [33].

The choice of neural architectures for RDF-to-text has evolved constantly along the last couple of years. All end-to-end models submitted to the WebNLG challenge [19] received the set of triples in a linearized form as input. However, researchers have recently been experimenting with graph-based approaches, which take the RDF input formatted as a graph, with promising results. Marcheggiane and Perez [29] proposed a structured data encoder based on Graph Convolutional Network (GCN) that directly exploits the graph structure and presented better results than Long Short-Term Memories (LSTM) models. Distiawan et al. [13] presented a GTR-LSTM architecture which captures the global information of a KG by encoding the relationships both within a triple and between the triples. Ferreira et al. [17] introduced a systematic comparison between neural pipeline and end-to-end data-to-text approaches for the generation of text from RDF triples. Although Marcheggiane and Perez [29] showed that the linearisation of the input graph has several drawbacks, the authors implemented Gated recurrent unit (GRU) and Transformer architectures which showed results superior to those of the former architecture. Recently, Ribeiro et.al [39] devised an unified graph attention network structure which investigates graph-to-text architectures that combined global and local graph representations to improve fluency in text generation. Their experiments demonstrated significant improvements on seen categories in the WebNLG dataset.

Despite the plethora of graph-based neural approaches on handling RDF data, English is the only language which has been widely targeted. Recent efforts

[1] https://github.com/dice-group/NABU.

were made to create German and Russian language versions of WebNLG [16,42]. However, no work that investigates these languages has been published at the time of writing. To the best of our knowledge, NABU is hence the first approach which tackles multilinguality in the RDF-to-text task.

3 The NABU Approach

NABU tackles RDF-to-text based on the formal description of a translation problem. The RDF-to-text task takes an RDF graph as input and generates an output text which reflects its meaning. Figure 1 depicts an example of a set of 3 RDF triples and the corresponding text. Therefore, the underlying idea behind our approach is as follows: *Given that KGs are language-agnostic and represent facts often extracted from text, we can regard the facts (i.e., RDF triples) as sentences and train a model to translate the facts from a language-agnostic graph representation to several languages.* In the following, we give an overview of GAT architecture and Transformer. Thereafter, we present NABU in detail. Throughout the description of our methodology and our experiments, we use DBpedia [2] as reference Knowledge Base (KB) since the benchmarking datasets are based on this KB.

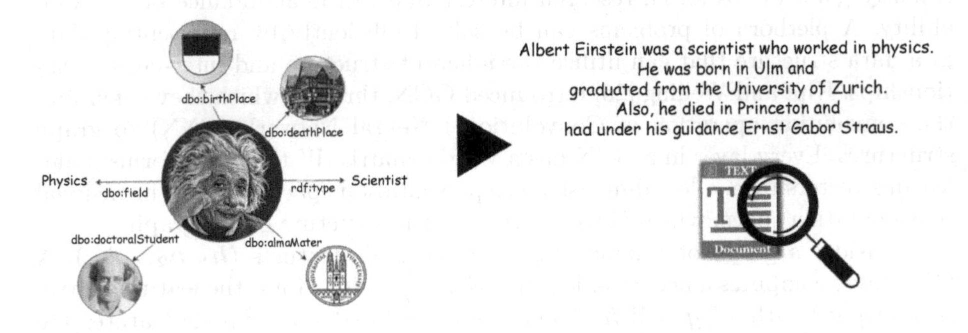

Fig. 1. Example of a set of triples (left) and the corresponding verbalization (right).

3.1 Background

Transformer. Transformer-based models consist of an encoder and a decoder, i.e., a two-tier architecture where the encoder reads an input sequence $x = (x_1, ..., x_n)$ and the decoder predicts a target sequence $y = (y_1, ..., y_n)$. The encoder and decoder interact via a soft-attention mechanism [3,28], which comprises one or multiple attention layers. We follow the notations from Tang et al. [45] in the subsequent sections: Let m stand for the word embedding size and n for the number of hidden units. Further, let K be the vocabulary size of the source language. Then, h_i^l corresponds to the hidden state at step i of layer l. h_{i-1}^l represents the hidden state at the previous step of layer l while

h_i^{l-1} means the hidden state at i of layer $l-1$. $E \in \mathbb{R}^{m \times K}$ is a word embedding matrix, $W \in \mathbb{R}^{n \times m}$, $U \in \mathbb{R}^{n \times n}$ are weight matrices, E_{x_i} refers to the embedding of x_i, and $e_{pos,i}$ indicates a positional embedding at position i.

Transformer models rely deeply on self-attention networks. Each token is connected to every other token in the same sentence directly via self-attention. Thus, the path length between any two tokens is 1. Due to lack of recurrence found in Recurrent Neural Network (RNN), Transformers implement *positional encoding* to input and output. Additionally, these models rely on multi-head attention to feature attention networks, which are more complex in comparison to the 1-head attention mechanism used in RNNs. In contrast to RNN, the positional information is also preserved in positional embeddings. Equation 1 describes the hidden state h_i^l, which is calculated from all hidden states of the previous layer. f represents a feed-forward network with the rectified linear unit (ReLU) as the activation function and layer normalization. The first layer is implemented as $h_i^0 = WE_{x_i} + e_{pos,i}$. Moreover, the decoder has a multi-head attention over the encoder's hidden states:

$$h_i^l = h_i^{l-1} + f(\text{self-attention}(h_i^{l-1})). \tag{1}$$

Graph Attention Networks. Deep Learning on non-euclidean data has recently gained substantial research interest due to the abundance of its availability. A plethora of problems can be solved efficiently by representing data in a data structure that can utilize the inherent structure and inter-entity relationships. Kipf and Welling [26] introduced GCN, through which they generalize the convolution operation of Convolutional Neural Network (CNN) to graph structures. Every layer in a GCN has a weight matrix W that transforms nodes feature vectors from a low-dimensional representation space to high-dimensional representation space, which aims to preserve the structure of the graph.

Consider a graph of z nodes and a set of node features $(\boldsymbol{h_1}, \boldsymbol{h_2}, .., \boldsymbol{h_z})$. A GCN layer computes a net set of features $(\boldsymbol{h_1'}, \boldsymbol{h_2'}, .., \boldsymbol{h_z'})$. First the feature matrix is multiplied with W $\boldsymbol{g} = W\boldsymbol{h}$. Then, the aggregated sum of node features are normalized using normalization constant $\frac{1}{c_{ij}}$ to stabilize the update rule. Finally,

$$\boldsymbol{h_i'} = \sigma\left(\sum_{j \epsilon N_i} \frac{1}{c_{ij}} \boldsymbol{g}_j\right)$$

However, the convolution operation in GCN does not take into account the fact that some nodes are more important than others to generate a particular segment of the target sentence. To alleviate this problem, Velickovic et al. [47] devised GAT, which converts the normalization constant into dynamic attention coefficients. The attention coefficients are calculated by applying *self-attention* over node features. In one forward pass, a GAT layer calculate a score of a given node that quantifies the importance of neighbors to its representation:

$$e_{ij} = a\left(\boldsymbol{h_i}, \boldsymbol{h_j}\right).$$

The attention scores are then normalized using softmax:

$$\alpha_{ij} = \frac{exp(e_{ij})}{\sum_{k \epsilon N_i} exp(e_{ik})}.$$

3.2 Approach

Graph-based NNs have been used successfully to parse and support the generation of natural-language sentences from RDF KG. Although GAT models have shown to alleviate the loss of node information, the network still suffers from parameter explosion depending on the size of the graph structure [5]. To alleviate the parameters explosion problem, we follow the same strategy used in [29], named reification,[2] to slightly modify how the RDF graph is encoded. We describe below how reification is applied. Afterward, we explain the encoder and decoder parts of NABU. An overview of NABU architecture after reification can be found in Fig. 2.

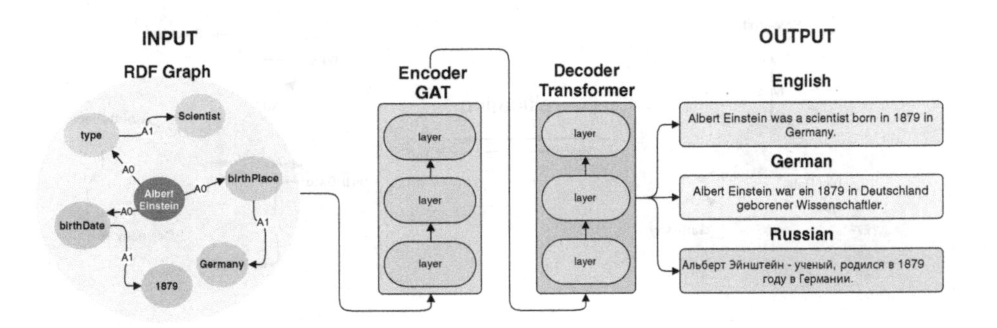

Fig. 2. NABU architecture

Reification. RDF triples are represented as a graph in which (i) the subjects and objects are nodes and (ii) predicates (relationships) between them are labeled edges. For example, `<Albert_Einstein, birthPlace, Germany>` can be seen as a sub-KG in DBpedia where `Albert_ Einstein` and `Germany` are the nodes and `birthPlace` is the edge. However, the edges are encoded as parameters by the GAT, and the parameters explosion problem stated by Beck et al. [5] often occurs.

Therefore, we follow the reification strategy, which maps the relations to nodes in the KG and creates new binary relations for each relation in the RDF triples. We rely on two binary relations, which model the relationship between the subject and predicate (A0) and predicate and object (A1) only. For example, ⟨`Albert_Einstein`, `birthPlace`, `Germany`⟩ becomes ⟨`Albert_Einstein`, `A0`,

[2] Not to be confused with RDFS reification.

birthPlace⟩ and ⟨birthPlace, A1, Germany⟩. Apart from handling the parameter explosion problem, reification is useful in two ways. First, the encoder generates a hidden state for each relation in the input. Second, it allows for modeling an arbitrary number of edges (predicates) efficiently. Figure 3 illustrates the reification strategy for our example.

Encoder. Here, the reified graph is sent as input to the GAT that applies a self-attention mechanism to compute the importance of each node in the graph. The GAT encoder represents nodes in a high-dimensional vector space whilst taking into account the representations of their neighbors. Note that NABU follows the same strategy of recent literature on multilingual Neural Machine Translation (NMT) models in which a special token is used in the encoder to determine to what target language to translate [44]. Figure 4 shows how a single forward step/pass works in NABU approach.

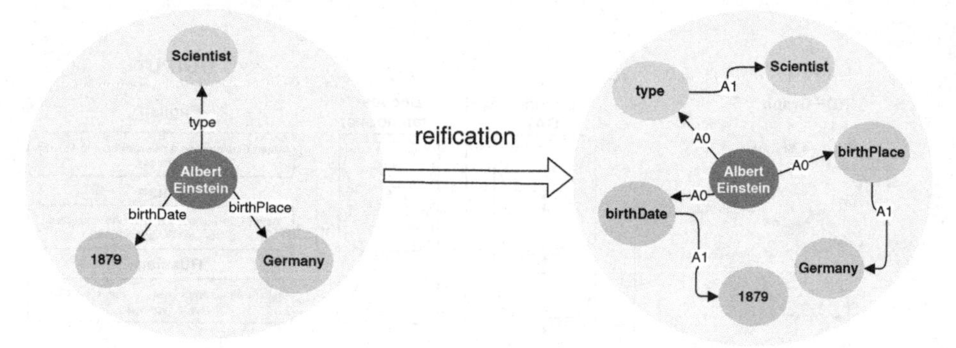

Fig. 3. Reification used on our example.

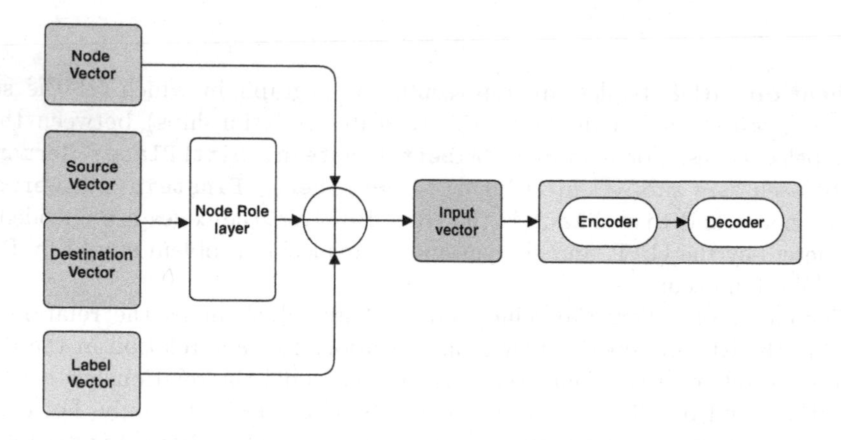

Fig. 4. An overview of a single forward pass in NABU.

In one forward pass of our model, we have four dense vectors as inputs, namely (i) the *node vector* $\boldsymbol{H} = (\boldsymbol{h_1}, \boldsymbol{h_2}, .., \boldsymbol{h_z})$ with embeddings of all nodes in the graphs, (ii) the *source vector*, $\boldsymbol{S} = (\boldsymbol{s_1}, \boldsymbol{s_2}, .., \boldsymbol{s_z})$ with embeddings of source nodes in edges of the graph, (iii) the *destination vector*, $\boldsymbol{D} = (\boldsymbol{d_1}, \boldsymbol{d_2}, .., \boldsymbol{d_z})$ with embeddings of target nodes in edges of the graphs and (iv) the *label vector*, $\boldsymbol{L} = (\boldsymbol{l_1}, \boldsymbol{l_2}, .., \boldsymbol{l_z})$ with embedding labels. The source $\boldsymbol{S}$ and destination $\boldsymbol{D}$ vectors are concatenated and are passed through dense layer which encodes them into a vector of the same shape as the label vector. We call this new vector the *edge vector*, $\boldsymbol{E}$. We then add the edge vector ($\boldsymbol{E}$), node vector ($\boldsymbol{H}$) and label vector ($\boldsymbol{L}$) to form the input vector to our encoder:

$$\boldsymbol{E} = f(\boldsymbol{S}, \boldsymbol{D}), \text{ and}$$

$$\boldsymbol{H}' = \|_{h \in \eta}\, G(\boldsymbol{H} + \boldsymbol{L} + \boldsymbol{E}),$$

where η is the number of heads in the multi-head attention layer.

Decoder. Our decoder follows the standard architecture of the Transformer decoder, which takes into account the intermediate representation generated by the encoder. The decoder gives a probability distribution over the target language's vocabulary. We also rely on an unsupervised tokenizer, which implements yte Pair Encoding (BPE) [41] and unigram language model [27] for handling multilinguality and out-of-vocabulary words. Afterward, we apply a beam search for selecting the most likely word in the output sentence.

4 Evaluation

4.1 Goals

In our evaluation, we address the following research questions:

Q1: How does our multilingual approach compare with state-of-the-art results in English?
Q2: Is NABU able to generate bilingual text while modelling two languages from distinct families?
Q3: How accurate are the multilingual texts generated by NABU?

We designed our evaluation as follows: First, we measured the performance of NABU on English by using the WebNLG dataset and compared it with state-of-the-art approaches. Additionally, we evaluated NABU on two other languages—German and Russian. Second, we evaluated NABU on bilingual models—English-German and English-Russian. Third, we combined all three languages in a multilingual setting and compared it with a multilingual Transformer baseline model. For measuring the quality of our approach, we used the automatic evaluation metrics BLEU, METEOR, and CHRF++.

4.2 Data

The experiments presented in this work were conducted on the WebNLG corpus [18,19], which consists of sets of RDF triples mapped to target texts. In comparison with other popular NLG benchmarks [6,31,35], WebNLG is the most semantically varied corpus. Its English version contains 25,298 texts which describe 9,674 sets of up to 7 RDF triples in 15 domains: Astronaut, University, Monument, Building, Comics Character, Food, Airport, Sports Team, Written Work, City, Athlete, Artist, Means of Transportation, Celestial Body and Politician. Out of these domains, five (Athlete, Artist, MeanOfTransportation, CelestialBody, Politician) are exclusively present in the test set, being unseen during the training and validation processes.

For German and Russian, we relied on the translated versions of WebNLG corpus [9,42]. The German version comprises 20,370 texts describing 7,812 sets of up to 7 RDF triples in 15 domains. Additionally, the German datasets provide gold-standard representations for traditional pipeline steps, such as discourse ordering (i.e., the order in which the source triples are verbalized in the target text), text structuring (i.e., the organization of the triples into paragraph and sentences), lexicalization (i.e., verbalization of the predicates) and referring expression generation (i.e., verbalization of the entities). The Russian datasets contain 20,800 texts describing 5,185 sets of up to 7 RDF triples in 9 domains. Both were automatically created and manually analyzed. The English and Russian datasets abide by the criteria to gold standards as they were manually assessed by several native speakers. The German version can be regarded as a silver standard given that it did not go through the same process and contains some known errors. For the monolingual experiments, we relied on the standard WebNLG parts of train, dev, and test sets across all languages. Note that the German version does not contain a test set originally. Therefore we relied on a k-Fold Cross-Validation technique to create the test set. For the multilingual set of experiments, we concatenated all English, German and Russian datasets and shuffled their training sets randomly to facilitate an end-to-end training of the model.

4.3 Tasks

We designed three tasks for carrying out our evaluation, (1) Monolingual, (2) Bilingual, (3) Multilingual. (1) In the monolingual task, we train our models to work in each language separately. Hence, we generate three models, one for English, one for German, and another for Russian. Each model receives RDF triples from its given DBPedia language version. For example, the German model receives triples from the German DBpedia. Afterward, we evaluate the models on each WebNLG language-specific dataset. (2) The bilingual task was divided into two sets; the first set, we train one English-German model. This model receives RDF triples from the English and German DBpedia versions as input and has to generate text in English and German, as output. For the second set, we trained one English-Russian model that receives RDF triples from the English and Russian DBpedia versions and generates text in English and Russian, respectively. (3) In the third task, we train one multilingual model which receives as input the triples from the English, German, and Russian DBpedia versions. This model has to output text in three languages, English, German, and Russian, respectively. The input relies on WebNLG triples containing resources from the English, German, and Russian DBpedia KGs, all entities are found across the three KGs via `sameAs` relations for the sake of completeness.

4.4 Model Settings

In this section, we describe the parameters and hyper-parameters used to train NABU models. We experimented with two encoder-decoder architectures for RDF verbalization. First, $\text{Transformer}_{baseline}$ which is an encoder-decoder model with a pure transformer architecture used to both encode triples into intermediate representation and decode it into tokens. Second, $\text{NABU}_{GAT-Trans}$, which comprises a GAT encoder and Transformer as the decoder.

For both models, we relied on the same settings. We used a Transformer 6-layer encoder-decoder model with an 8-headed multi-head attention mechanism [46]. The training used a batch size of 32 and Adam optimizer with an initial maximum learning rate of 0.001. We set a source and target word embedding's size of 256, and hidden layers to size 256, dropout = 0.3 (naive). We used a vocabulary of 32000 words for the word based models and a beam size of 5. All our vocabularies were trained using the sentencepiece library.[3] In addition, we used a copy mechanism for investigating the out-of-vocabulary (OOV) words issue. This mechanism first tries to substitute the OOV words with target words that have the highest attention weight according to their source words [28]. If the words are not found, it copies the source words to the position of the not-found target word [23]. Note that we added an extra language token at the beginning of our input sentences for the Transformer model, and a language node to the input graph in our GAT model for performing the bilingual and multilingual experiments. This technique of adding a special language token is in line with [44].

4.5 Evaluation Metrics

We used three automatic Machine Translation (MT) standard metrics to ensure consistent and clear evaluation of the common evaluation datasets of the WebNLG challenge. BLEU [36] uses a modified precision metric for comparing the MT output with the reference (human) translation. The precision is calculated by measuring the n-gram similarity (n = 1,..4) at the word level. BLEU also applies a brevity penalty by comparing the length of the MT output with the reference translation. METEOR [4] was mainly introduced to overcome the semantic weakness of BLEU. To this end, METEOR considers stemming and

[3] https://github.com/google/sentencepiece.

paraphrasing along with exact standard word (or phrase) matching. The synonymy overlap through a shared WordNet synset of the words. Along with exact standard word (or phrase) matching, it has additional features, i.e., stemming and paraphrasing. CHRF++ [37] exploits the use of character n-gram precision and recall (F-score) for automatic evaluation of MT outputs. chrF++ has shown a good correlation with human rankings of different MT outputs and is simple and does not require any additional information. Additionally, chrF++ is language- and tokenization-independent.

4.6 Results

Monolingual. Our experiments report that NABU consistently outperforms state-of-the-art models on English data. Table 1 shows that NABU achieved a BLEU score of 66.21, which is 28.15% higher than the previous state-of-the-art Transformer model [17]. We decided to run our experiments on all WebNLG categories to elucidate the strengths and limitations of NABU. According to [17], the main drawback in current NN models is the incapability of generating text for unseen entities and that the experiments should be on all categories. NABU, in turn, shows that it is capable of predicting correctly both seen and unseen entities and their relations. In addition, NABU shows an improvement in METEOR up to +2 points. We report NABU's chrF++ as our intention is to follow recent literature which has adopted this metric due to its good correlation with human results. We can now answer [Q1] as follows: NABU surpasses state-of-the-art results on WebNLG in English.

Table 2 shows that NABU outperforms the transformer baseline on German and Russian. It is important to note that our Transformer baseline, $\text{Transformer}_{baseline}$, already outperforms the previous state-of-the-art approaches on English. The difference between our $\text{Transformer}_{baseline}$ and the Transformer presented by [17] is that we rely on BPE and character-level tokenizer on the decoder side. Our results suggest that we can refrain from running the related work (see Table 1) on the German and Russian datasets, especially as they were designed and tested to work on English, thus there is currently no baseline for German and Russian. With these results, NABU demonstrates its

Table 1. Results on WebNLG English test set with all categories (seen and unseen), comparison with the state-of-the-art approaches

Model	BLEU	METEOR	chrF++
UPF-FORGe	38.65	39.00	–
Melbourne	45.13	37.00	–
Moryossef et al., (2019)	47.40	39.00	–
Castro et al. (2019)	51.68	32.00	–
$\text{NABU}_{GAT-Trans}$	**66.21**	**41.11**	**71.98**

language agnosticism and presents improvements in German and Russian over the baseline.

Table 2. Monolingual results on WebNLG language testsets

Models	Language	BLEU	METEOR	chrF++
Monolingual				
$\text{Transformer}_{baseline}$	ENG	54.96	38.43	69.11
	GER	50.07	34.51	63.48
	RUS	46.42	27.74	56.80
$\text{NABU}_{GAT-Trans}$	ENG	**66.21**	**41.47**	**71.98**
	GER	**53.08**	**37.42**	**64.57**
	RUS	**46.86**	**28.84**	**58.37**

Bilingual. Table 3 presents the results of $\text{NABU}_{GAT-Trans}$ on two bilingual models. The results show that NABU on English-German outperformed the $\text{Transformer}_{baseline}$ on all metrics. On English-Russian, $\text{NABU}_{GAT-Trans}$ presented worse results on BLEU and METEOR than $\text{Transformer}_{baseline}$. However, $\text{NABU}_{GAT-Trans}$ showed superior results on chrF++ which is the metric that best correlates with human results. On the one hand, we analyzed that the English-German model leveraged both languages properly due to their vocabulary overlap. German and English share a word vocabulary of 33%, thus training both languages with $\text{NABU}_{GAT-Trans}$, which employs a graph representation on the encoder side and a character level on decoder could actually model both languages correctly and generate coherent text. On the other hand, English-Russian presented inconsistent results because both languages are significantly different, and they do not share any vocabulary. We reckoned these conflicting scores are due to the language family of both languages. Looking manually at the results, we concluded that encoding distinct language families requires additional features, and we, therefore, plan to investigate this phenomenon in the future. The results presented herein answer our second research question, [Q2], by showing that NABU is capable of modeling languages from distinct families in a bilingual approach, but a deeper investigation is required.

Table 3. Bilingual results on WebNLG language test sets

Models	Language	BLEU	METEOR	chrF++
Bilingual				
$\text{Transformer}_{baseline}$	ENG-GER	58.30	36.46	66.72
$\text{NABU}_{GAT-Trans}$	ENG-GER	**61.99**	**39.51**	**69.68**
$\text{Transformer}_{baseline}$	ENG-RUS	**55.30**	**37.90**	61.63
$\text{NABU}_{GAT-Trans}$	ENG-RUS	49.15	33.41	**64.00**

Multilingual. Table 4 shows that NABU$_{GAT-Trans}$ performed better than Transformer$_{baseline}$ by presenting consistent improvement of +2 BLEU, METEOR, and chrF++. This result exhibits that NABU can effectively generate multilingual text, thus answering our third research question, [Q3]. Comparing the multilingual results of NABU with its bilingual results on English-Russian, we concluded that the characteristics of the German language, namely its three gender types, contributed to the better alignment of the languages in the decoder side of multilingual NABU model. Russian also contains three genders as German; therefore, NABU made use of it as features for generating coherent texts. We also noticed that the English texts generated by the multilingual NABU model are comparable to those of the English state-of-the-art models. NABU's multilingual model is also better than the previous English state-of-the-art by 4 BLEU and presents comparable results on METEOR. This result also reaffirms the capability of NABU for achieving English state-of-the-art results and contributes to our first research question, [Q1].

Table 4. Multilingual Results on WebNLG language testsets

Models	Language	BLEU	METEOR	chrF++
Multilingual				
Transformer$_{baseline}$	ENG-GER-RUS	53.39	36.86	60.72
NABU$_{GAT-Trans}$	ENG-GER-RUS	**56.04**	**38.34**	**62.04**

Time-Performance. All models were trained on NVIDIA Tesla P100. Both NABU$_{GAT-Trans}$ and Transformer$_{baseline}$ models took the same amount of time since they contain the same number of weights. Therefore, the monolingual models took 6 h to be trained, while the multilingual models took 8 h on average. This difference of 2 h lies in the size of the multilingual training dataset, which contains all English, German, and Russian training sets.

4.7 Error Analysis and Discussion

In this section, we report some of the errors found in NABU's output while carrying out a human evaluation. First, we analyzed the discrepancy between BLEU, METEOR, and chrF++: NABU outperformed the previous state-of-the-art approach for English by roughly 15 BLEU, while the difference in METEOR is considerable smaller. Our analysis shows that some entities contained typos and were not generated correctly by NABU. In addition, we found a low variance in the generated synonyms. BLEU ignores these aspects while METEOR penalizes based on them, thus explaining the discrepancy between the scores.

Additionally, we noticed some wrong verbalization of similar predicates (edges) that were responsible for decreasing NABU scores across all languages. For example, NABU was sometimes not able to generate text correctly in the

Artist domain. The problem lies in the triples which contain both `dbo:artist` or `dbo:producer` relations as predicates. Both predicates are often verbalized to "artist". This happens because the predicates share the same domain and range and therefore have a similar vector representation in the embeddings. We plan to address this issue in future work by using a more appropriate embedding model.

We also analyzed the multilingual texts generated by $\text{NABU}_{GAT-Trans}$ and $\text{Transformer}_{baseline}$. We noticed that the $\text{NABU}_{GAT-Trans}$ performed better at structuring the RDF graph as input and verbalizing a structured set of RDF triples, whereas $\text{Transformer}_{baseline}$ presented better results than $\text{NABU}_{GAT-Trans}$ at ordering (also known as Discourse Ordering step) the triples for a better verbalization. The advantage of $\text{Transformer}_{baseline}$ over $\text{NABU}_{GAT-Trans}$ in Discourse Ordering seems to be related to the linearized form of its input, which explicitly represents in what order the triples have to be verbalized. Additionally, our reification strategy affected the Discourse Ordering, we noticed it by analyzing the generated text from an input with two equal predicates for different subjects. For example, "Albert_Einstein dbo:birthPlace Germany" and "Michael_Jackson dbo:birthPlace USA". $\text{NABU}_{GAT-Trans}$ verbalized this two triples as "Albert Einstein was born in the United States of America and Michael Jackson was born in Germany". This problem occurs because NABU can not identify the subjects of each predicate correctly as they are identical in the encoder side. We plan to address this drawback by investigating new approaches for the structuring and ordering steps.

Another interesting insight is related to the inflections of words in German, similar to [9]. The possessive was often a source of errors when verbalizing into German. The translation "Elliot See's Besatzung war ein Testpilot." is not perfect as the apostrophe ('s) is placed wrongly. However, this problem did not happen when generating the sentence, "Bill Oddies Tochter ist Kate Hardie", where the possessive of "Oddie" is built correctly. Similar insights can be derived pertaining to the preposition "von" (en: of). For example, the entity `Texas_University` was wrongly verbalized as "Universität von Texas" instead of the correct form "Universität Texas". The possessive and related constructions are well-known challenges in MT from English to German. Therefore, we plan to explore this phenomenon in future research deeply.

On the Russian results, we observed that the main challenge was related to the verbalization of unseen entities. In $\text{NABU}_{GAT-Trans}$, some entities were copied from their source sentences due to the use of the copy mechanism in NABU. For example, the entity "Visvesvaraya_Technological_University" was generated as "Visvesvaraya Technical University" in the English form instead of being verbalized in the Russian language. Additionally, we perceived that $\text{NABU}_{GAT-Trans}$ displayed problems similar to those reported in [42] for generating Entities. However, these problems were mostly detected in the unseen category. Our current hypothesis is that the generation of unseen entities in Russian is more challenging than German and English due to the Cyrillic alphabet.

5 Conclusion

We presented a multilingual RDF verbalizer which relies on graph attention NN along with a reification strategy. Our experiments suggest that our approach, named NABU, outperforms state-of-the-art approaches in English. Additionally, NABU presented consistent results across the languages used in our evaluation. NABU is language-agnostic, which means it can be ported easily to languages other than those considered in this paper. To the best of our knowledge, we are the first approach to exploit and achieve the multilinguality successfully in the RDF-to-text task. As future work, we aim to exploit other graph-based neural architecture and other reification approaches for improving NABU's performance. Additionally, we plan to investigate how to deal with the similarity of relations by combining language models and new evaluation metrics [40]. Moreover, we plan to investigate our methodology in the context of low-resource scenarios as well as on different KGs [12,25].

Acknowledgments. Research funded by the German Federal Ministry of Economics and Technology (BMWI) in the project RAKI (no. 01MD19012D) and by the H2020 KnowGraphs (GA no. 860801). This work also has been supported by the German Federal Ministry of Education and Research (BMBF) within the project DAIKIRI under the grant no 01IS19085B as well as by the German Federal Ministry for Economic Affairs and Energy (BMWi) within the project SPEAKER under the grant no 01MK20011U. Finally, we also would like to thank the funding provided by the Coordination for the Improvement of Higher Education Personnel (CAPES) from Brazil under the grant 88887.367980/2019-00.

References

1. Anselma, L., Mazzei, A.: Designing and testing the messages produced by a virtual dietitian. In: Proceedings of the 11th International Conference on Natural Language Generation, Tilburg University, The Netherlands, November 2018, pp. 244–253. Association for Computational Linguistics (2018)
2. Auer, S., Bizer, C., Kobilarov, G., Lehmann, J., Cyganiak, R., Ives, Z.: DBpedia: a nucleus for a web of open data. In: Aberer, K., et al. (eds.) ASWC/ISWC -2007. LNCS, vol. 4825, pp. 722–735. Springer, Heidelberg (2007). https://doi.org/10.1007/978-3-540-76298-0_52
3. Bahdanau, D., Cho, K., Bengio, Y.: Neural machine translation by jointly learning to align and translate. arXiv preprint arXiv:1409.0473 (2014)
4. Banerjee, S., Lavie, A.: METEOR: an automatic metric for MT evaluation with improved correlation with human judgments. In: Proceedings of the ACL Workshop on Intrinsic and Extrinsic Evaluation Measures for MT and/or Summarization, pp. 65–72. ACL (2005)
5. Beck, D., Haffari, G., Cohn, T.: Graph-to-sequence learning using gated graph neural networks. In: Proceedings of the 56th Annual Meeting of the Association for Computational Linguistics (Volume 1: Long Papers), pp. 273–283 (2018)
6. Belz, A., White, M., Espinosa, D., Kow, E., Hogan, D., Stent, A.: The first surface realisation shared task: overview and evaluation results. In: Proceedings of the 13th European Workshop on Natural Language Generation, Nancy, France, pp. 217–226. Association for Computational Linguistics (2011)

7. Bouayad-Agha, N., Casamayor, G., Wanner, L.: Natural language generation in the context of the semantic web. Semant. Web **5**(6), 493–513 (2014)
8. Braun, D., Reiter, E., Siddharthan, A.: SaferDrive: an NLG-based behaviour change support system for drivers. Nat. Lang. Eng. **24**(4), 551–588 (2018)
9. Ferreira, T.C., Moussallem, D., Krahmer, E., Wubben, S.: Enriching the WebNLG corpus. In: Proceedings of the 11th International Conference on Natural Language Generation, pp. 171–176. Association for Computational Linguistics (2018)
10. Cimiano, P., Lüker, J., Nagel, D., Unger, C.: Exploiting ontology lexica for generating natural language texts from RDF data. In: Proceedings of the 14th European Workshop on Natural Language Generation, Sofia, Bulgaria, August 2013, pp. 10–19. ACL (2013)
11. Colin, E., Gardent, C., Mrabet, Y., Narayan, S., Perez-Beltrachini, L.: The WebNLG challenge: generating text from DBPedia data. In: Proceedings of the 9th INLG Conference, pp. 163–167 (2016)
12. Moussallem, D., et al.: RDF2PT: generating Brazilian Portuguese texts from RDF data. In: The 11th Edition of the Language Resources and Evaluation Conference, Miyazaki (Japan), 7–12 May 2018 (2018)
13. Distiawan, B., Qi, J., Zhang, R., Wang, W.: GTR-LSTM: a triple encoder for sentence generation from RDF data. In: Proceedings of the 56th Annual Meeting of the Association for Computational Linguistics (Volume 1: Long Papers), pp. 1627–1637 (2018)
14. Duma, D., Klein, E.: Generating natural language from linked data: unsupervised template extraction. In: IWCS, pp. 83–94 (2013)
15. Ell, B., Harth, A.: A language-independent method for the extraction of RDF verbalization templates. In: INLG, pp. 26–34 (2014)
16. Ferreira, T.C., Moussallem, D., Krahmer, E., Wubben, S.: Enriching the WebNLG corpus. In: Proceedings of the 11th International Conference on Natural Language Generation, pp. 171–176 (2018)
17. Ferreira, T.C., van der Lee, C., van Miltenburg, E., Krahmer, E.: Neural data-to-text generation: a comparison between pipeline and end-to-end architectures. In: Proceedings of the 2019 Conference on Empirical Methods in Natural Language Processing and the 9th International Joint Conference on Natural Language Processing (EMNLP-IJCNLP), pp. 552–562 (2019)
18. Gardent, C., Shimorina, A., Narayan, S., Perez-Beltrachini, L.: Creating training corpora for NLG micro-planners. In: Proceedings of the 55th Annual Meeting of the Association for Computational Linguistics (Volume 1: Long Papers), pp. 179–188. Association for Computational Linguistics (2017)
19. Gardent, C., Shimorina, A., Narayan, S., Perez-Beltrachini, L.: The WebNLG challenge: generating text from RDF data. In: Proceedings of the 10th International Conference on Natural Language Generation, pp. 124–133 (2017)
20. Gatt, A., Krahmer, E.: Survey of the state of the art in natural language generation: core tasks, applications and evaluation. arXiv preprint arXiv:1703.09902 (2017)
21. Gehrmann, S., Dai, F., Elder, H., Rush, A.: End-to-end content and plan selection for data-to-text generation. In: Proceedings of the 11th International Conference on Natural Language Generation, Tilburg University, The Netherlands, November 2018, pp. 46–56. Association for Computational Linguistics (2018)
22. Gkatzia, D., Hastie, H.F., Lemon, O.: Comparing multi-label classification with reinforcement learning for summarisation of time-series data. In: ACL, no. 1, pp. 1231–1240 (2014)

23. Gu, J., Lu, Z., Li, H., Li, V.O.K.: Incorporating copying mechanism in sequence-to-sequence learning. In: Proceedings of the 54th Annual Meeting of the Association for Computational Linguistics, vol. 1, pp. 1631–1640 (2016)
24. Johnson, M., et al.: Google's multilingual neural machine translation system: enabling zero-shot translation. Trans. Assoc. Comput. Linguist. **5**, 339–351 (2017)
25. Kaffee, L.-A., et al.: Mind the (language) gap: generation of multilingual Wikipedia summaries from Wikidata for ArticlePlaceholders. In: Gangemi, A., et al. (eds.) ESWC 2018. LNCS, vol. 10843, pp. 319–334. Springer, Cham (2018). https://doi.org/10.1007/978-3-319-93417-4_21
26. Kipf, T.N., Welling, M.: Semi-supervised classification with graph convolutional networks. arXiv preprint arXiv:1609.02907 (2016)
27. Kudo, T.: Subword regularization: improving neural network translation models with multiple subword candidates. In: Proceedings of the 56th Annual Meeting of the Association for Computational Linguistics (Volume 1: Long Papers), pp. 66–75 (2018)
28. Luong, T., Pham, H., Manning, C.D.: Effective approaches to attention-based neural machine translation. In: Proceedings of the Conference on Empirical Methods in Natural Language Processing, pp. 1412–1421. ACL (2015)
29. Marcheggiani, D., Perez, L.: Deep graph convolutional encoders for structured data to text generation. In: Proceedings of the 11th International Conference on Natural Language Generation, pp. 1–9. Association for Computational Linguistics (2018)
30. Mei, H., Bansal, M., Walter, M.R.: What to talk about and how? Selective generation using LSTMs with coarse-to-fine alignment. In: Proceedings of the 2016 Conference of the North American Chapter of the Association for Computational Linguistics: Human Language Technologies, HLT-NAACL 2016, San Diego, California, pp. 720–730. Association for Computational Linguistics (2016)
31. Mille, S., Belz, A., Bohnet, B., Graham, Y., Pitler, E., Wanner, L.: The first multilingual surface realisation shared task (SR'18): overview and evaluation results. In: Proceedings of the First Workshop on Multilingual Surface Realisation, Melbourne, Australia, July 2018, pp. 1–12. Association for Computational Linguistics (2018)
32. Mrabet, Y., et al.: Aligning texts and knowledge bases with semantic sentence simplification. In: WebNLG 2016 (2016)
33. Ngonga Ngomo, A.-C., Röder, M., Moussallem, D., Usbeck, R., Speck, R.: BENGAL: an automatic benchmark generator for entity recognition and linking. In: Proceedings of the 11th International Conference on Natural Language Generation, pp. 339–349 (2018)
34. Ngonga Ngomo, A.-C., Moussallem, D., Bühman, L.: A holistic natural language generation framework for the semantic web. In: Proceedings of the International Conference Recent Advances in Natural Language Processing, p. 8. ACL (Association for Computational Linguistics) (2019)
35. Novikova, J., Dusek, O., Rieser, V.: The E2E dataset: new challenges for end-to-end generation. In: Proceedings of the 18th Annual SIGDIAL Meeting on Discourse and Dialogue, Saarbrücken, Germany, pp. 201–206 (2017)
36. Papineni, K., Roukos, S., Ward, T., Zhu, W.-J.: BLEU: a method for automatic evaluation of machine translation. In: Proceedings of the 40th Annual Meeting on Association for Computational Linguistics (2002)
37. Popović, M.: chrF++: words helping character n-grams. In: Proceedings of the Second Conference on Machine Translation, pp. 612–618 (2017)
38. Reiter, E., Dale, R.: Building Natural Language Generation Systems. Cambridge University Press, Cambridge (2000)

39. Ribeiro, L.F.R., Zhang, Y., Gardent, C., Gurevych, I.: Modeling global and local node contexts for text generation from knowledge graphs. arXiv preprint arXiv:2001.11003 (2020)
40. Sellam, T., Das, D., Parikh, A.: BLEURT: learning robust metrics for text generation. In: Proceedings of the 58th Annual Meeting of the Association for Computational Linguistics, July 2020, pp. 7881–7892. Association for Computational Linguistics (2020)
41. Sennrich, R., Haddow, B., Birch, A.: Neural machine translation of rare words with subword units. In: Proceedings of the 54th Annual Meeting of the Association for Computational Linguistics (Volume 1: Long Papers), ACL 2016, Berlin, Germany, pp. 1715–1725. Association for Computational Linguistics (2016)
42. Shimorina, A., Khasanova, E., Gardent, C.: Creating a corpus for Russian data-to-text generation using neural machine translation and post-editing. In: Proceedings of the 7th Workshop on Balto-Slavic Natural Language Processing, pp. 44–49 (2019)
43. Sleimi, A., Gardent, C.: Generating paraphrases from DBPedia using deep learning. In: WebNLG 2016, p. 54 (2016)
44. Tan, X., Ren, Y., He, D., Qin, T., Zhao, Z., Liu, T.-Y.: Multilingual neural machine translation with knowledge distillation. arXiv preprint arXiv:1902.10461 (2019)
45. Tang, G., Müller, M., Rios, A., Sennrich, R.: Why self-attention? A targeted evaluation of neural machine translation architectures. In: Proceedings of the 2018 Conference on Empirical Methods in Natural Language Processing, pp. 4263–4272 (2018)
46. Vaswani, A., et al.: Attention is all you need. In: Advances in Neural Information Processing Systems, pp. 5998–6008 (2017)
47. Veličković, P., Cucurull, G., Casanova, A., Romero, A., Lio, P., Bengio, Y.: Graph attention networks. arXiv preprint arXiv:1710.10903 (2017)
48. Xu, K., et al.: Show, attend and tell: neural image caption generation with visual attention. In: International Conference on Machine Learning, pp. 2048–2057 (2015)

Fantastic Knowledge Graph Embeddings and How to Find the Right Space for Them

Mojtaba Nayyeri[1,2](✉), Chengjin Xu[1], Sahar Vahdati[2,3], Nadezhda Vassilyeva[1], Emanuel Sallinger[3,4], Hamed Shariat Yazdi[1], and Jens Lehmann[1,5]

[1] Smart Data Analytics Group (SDA), University of Bonn, Bonn, Germany
{nayyeri,xuc,jens.lehmann}@cs.uni-bonn.de, nadya.vassilyeva@gmail.com, shariatyazdi@gmail.com

[2] InfAI Dresden Lab, Dresden, Germany
vahdati@infai.org

[3] University of Oxford, Oxford, UK
emanuel.sallinger@cs.ox.ac.uk

[4] TU Wien, Wien, Austria

[5] Fraunhofer IAIS Dresden Lab, Dresden, Germany
jens.lehmann@iais.fraunhofer.de

Abstract. During the last few years, several knowledge graph embedding models have been devised in order to handle machine learning problems for knowledge graphs. Some of the models which were proven to be capable of inferring relational patterns, such as symmetry or transitivity, show lower performance in practice than those not allowing to infer those patterns. It is often unknown what factors contribute to such performance differences among KGE models in the inference of particular patterns. We develop the concept of a solution space as a factor that has a direct influence on the practical performance of knowledge graph embedding models as well as their capability to infer relational patterns. We showcase the effect of solution space on a newly proposed model dubbed SpacE^{ss}. We describe the theoretical considerations behind the solution space and evaluate our model against state-of-the-art models on a set of standard benchmarks namely WordNet and FreeBase.

Keywords: Link prediction · Knowledge graph embedding · Relation pattern · Solution space · Knowledge completion

1 Introduction

Knowledge Graphs (KGs) have recently become a crucial part of different AI applications. In its simplest definition, a KG is a set of triples of the form (h, r, t), where h and t refer to entities and r refers to the relation between these entities. Following this structure, a lot of KGs have been published in recent years,

J. Z. Pan et al. (Eds.): ISWC 2020, LNCS 12506, pp. 438–455, 2020.
https://doi.org/10.1007/978-3-030-62419-4_25

such as Freebase [2], WordNet [14], WikiData [23], and DBpedia [11]. Although quantitatively KGs often consist of several thousand entities and relations and millions of triples, this is nowhere near enough to cover the knowledge that exists in the real world – even when restricted to a particular domain. Therefore, KGs often suffer from incompleteness.

One of the common approaches for knowledge graph completion is the *Knowledge Graph embeddings* (KGEs). KGEs assign a latent feature vector to each entity and relation in a KG. Furthermore, a scoring function is used to define the degree to which a relation between two entities is plausible. Relations between entities of a graph often follow particular relational patterns, e.g. symmetric, transitive, inverse patterns. Such patterns are generally given by logical formulas [8,18] and the ability to infer them is broadly considered as expressiveness of a KGE model [25]. However, not every KGE model is designed to infer all kinds of patterns, meaning that characteristics of the patterns are not taken into consideration by the model in the inference of implicit knowledge. Given a logical formula of the form *premise* $\implies$ *conclusion*, a constraint is enforced for the plausibility of the grounding atoms involved in the conclusion when the grounding of atoms in the premise holds. For example, given a symmetric rule, $(e_l, r, e_r) \leftrightarrow (e_r, r, e_l)$, if a grounding (h, r, t) of (e_l, r, e_r) is true, then (t, r, h) is constrained to be true as well. Such a constraint should be followed by KGE models in the associated vector space measuring the correctness of triples.

Already existing models have been majorly designed and evaluated without specifically considering relational patterns. This can lead to two problems: the models are either 1.) not capable of encoding any pattern or 2.) they are only partially capable of encoding patterns, both of which can lead to wrong inferences. For example, when the relation vector is non-zero, one of the baseline KGEs dubbed TransE [3] is not able to infer symmetric relational patterns $((h, r, t) \implies (t, r, h))$. Instead, it only infers the explicit triple (h, r, t) from such a relation and not its symmetrical triple (t, r, h) [13,26]. Yet, "the success of such a task heavily relies on the ability of modeling and inferring the patterns of (or between) the relations" [19]. The ability of encoding relational patterns and expressiveness of KGE models is a property of their *solution space* (SS), i.e., the set of all possible vectors that can be assigned to the entities and relations involved in a particular pattern. This heavily depends on multiple aspects such as *data complexity, model formulation*, and *embedding dimension*. Data complexity in KGs denotes the extent to which the relations between entities are interconnected. A combination of relational patterns results in more constraints which causes higher data complexity. This also enforces constraints in the associated vector space for the KGE model. For example, a cycle (sequence of nodes of a graph connected in a closed path) containing symmetric and anti-symmetric relations causes wrong inference in the RotatE model [19] (see Sect. 3).

The model formulation defines the way entity and relation vectors are optimized in the vector space to measure triple correctness. Constraints caused by patterns in the vector space are dependent on model-formulation and directly limit the solution space of any model. Given a triple (h, r, t) and its embedding vectors $(\mathbf{h}, \mathbf{r}, \mathbf{t})$ where r is symmetric, TransE induces the correctness of the triple as $(\mathbf{h} + \mathbf{r} \approx \mathbf{t})$ and its symmetrical counterpart as $(\mathbf{t} + \mathbf{r} \approx \mathbf{h})$. Therefore, for symmetric relation r, the solution space for the relation is one i.e. $\mathbf{r} = \mathbf{0}$.

Generally, using a higher embedding dimension (values of 1,000 [19] or even 10,000 [6] have been used) is considered as one way of increasing the solution space of a KGE model by increasing the number of possible embeddings satisfying the relational patterns. However, using a very big dimension is not always practical in large scale KGs due to the prohibitive memory requirements. In addition, there are also cases in which increasing the embedding dimension does not necessarily improve the solution space. For example, in the TransE the solution space for encoding symmetric patterns [19] is always only one independent of the embedding dimension.

In this paper, we show a novel approach towards overcoming the problems of KGE models to encode relational patterns. Our goal is to show how the model formulation can extend the *solution space* and improve the ability for encoding relational patterns. To do so, we introduce a new knowledge graph embedding model *SpacE*^{ss}[1] and show that it is capable of expressing each pattern reflexive, symmetric, and inverse patterns individually. *SpacE*^{ss} covers both translation and rotation transformations which enables it to inherit the expressive power of TransE, RotatE, and TransComplEx for encoding *composition, transitivity, equivalence, and implication* [3,16,19]. Compared to RotatE and TransComplEx, SpacE^{ss} provides a bigger solution space when encoding different relation patterns. Finally, we evaluate our model experimentally on several popular KGs to demonstrate our model's performance in practice.

2 Related Work

The aim of a KGE model is to optimize a loss function (denoted by $\mathcal{L}$) in order to embed entities and relations of a KG K into a d-dimensional vector space. Each model also defines a score function $f(h, r, t)$, or $f_{h,t}^{r}$, that measures the probability of correctness of a triple (h, r, t). There are several types of KGE models [24] namely distance-based (TransE, RotatE, TransComplEx), semantic-matching (HolE [17], Distmult [28], complEx [21] and TuckER [22]) and neural network-based (ConvE [4]) models. This section provides a review of popular and prominent score functions used by different embedding models that are distace-based, as they are the main focus of this work.

TransE [3] is one of the early KGE models. The core idea here is to optimize the embedding vectors in real space such that $\mathbf{h} + \mathbf{r} \approx \mathbf{t}$ holds for every valid triple (h, r, t). Intuitively, this means that a relation vector is a translation from head to tail. This restrictive assumption enables TransE to properly infer some, but not all of the relation patterns. For example, the relation vector becomes a zero vector when the model encodes a reflexive relation (as for any h, we have $\mathbf{h} + \mathbf{r} \approx \mathbf{h}$). Thus, if a relation is reflexive, it is enforced by the model to

[1] https://github.com/mojtabanayyeri/KGE-Models/tree/master/SpacESS.

be symmetric as well [10]. TransE is a starting point for a family of different embedding models such as TransR [12], TransH [27] and TransD [9,29]. These works attempted to improve expressiveness of TransE by modifying its score function, which is $f^r_{h,t} = \|\mathbf{h}+\mathbf{r}-\mathbf{t}\|$. However, neither of these models succeeded in solving the aforementioned problem [10].

TransComplEx [16] is an extension of TransE from real space to complex space (i.e. $\mathbf{h}, \mathbf{r}, \mathbf{t} \in \mathcal{C}^d$). Such a space consists of complex numbers shown as $x = Re(x) + i\,Im(x)$. $Re(x)$ and $Im(x)$ refer to the real and imaginary parts of x respectively. TransComplEx represents relation vector $\mathbf{r}$ as a translation from head $\mathbf{h}$ to the complex conjugate of the tail $\bar{\mathbf{t}}$. The score function then becomes $f^r_{h,t} = \|\mathbf{h} + \mathbf{r} - \bar{\mathbf{t}}\|$, where $\|.\|$ is the $L2$ norm of the vector whose elements are the modulus of each complex element of the vector $(\mathbf{h} + \mathbf{r} - \bar{\mathbf{t}})$. TransComplEx encodes reflexive and symmetric relational patterns as well as the ones neither reflexive nor irreflexive. However, later we show the role of the limited space considered by the model and its influences on the performance.

RotatE [19] is a very recent new model that has already garnered a lot of attention as one of the state-of-the-art KGE models. RotatE takes advantage of the Euler formula $e^{i\theta} = \cos(\theta) + i\sin(\theta)$ and requires that for every correct triple (h, r, t) $h_j r_j = t_j$ holds $\forall j \in \{0, \ldots, d\}$ where $|r_j| = \sqrt{Re(r_j)^2 + Im(r_j)^2} = 1$. Setting $|r_j|$ to 1, combined with the Euler formula, means that the model performs a rotation of the j-th element h_j of the head vector $\mathbf{h}$ by the j-th element $r_j = e^{i\theta_{r_j}}$ of a relation vector $\mathbf{r}$ to get the j-th element t_j of the tail vector $\mathbf{t}$, where θ_{r_j} is the phase of the relation r. The score function of RotatE is then defined as $f^r_{h,t} = \|\mathbf{h} \circ \mathbf{r} - \mathbf{t}\|$, where $\circ$ is the Hadamard (element-wise) product of two vectors. RotatE encodes symmetric, inverse, and composition relation patterns. However, the constraints enforced by several patterns restrict the vector space of the embeddings. This restriction indeed causes wrong inferences when the model embeds entities and relations into a vector space (this is discussed with a motivating example in Sect. 3).

To understand the core of the issue, the RotatE model takes a triple (h, r, t) in the KG and returns three vectors $(\mathbf{h}, \mathbf{r}, \mathbf{t})$ and arrange them based on its score function. For symmetric relations, it was shown in [19, Lemma 1] that $\mathbf{r}_j = e^{i0}$ or $e^{i\pi}$, which corresponds to rotation of 0 or π for the j-th element of the relation vector. In this case, the solution space of RotatE has two values of 0 or π per each considered dimension. Therefore, each element of a symmetric relation is either 1 or -1 (e.g. $\mathbf{r} = [1, -1, \ldots, -1]$). Given a vector $\mathbf{h}$, there are only *two* possible options for each element of the tail vector $\mathbf{t}_j$: either $\mathbf{t}_j = \mathbf{h}_j$ or it is the "mirror image" of $\mathbf{h}_j$ (i.e. rotated by π). Later, we raise the attention on an important factor behind this problem explaining the *solution space* in more details. In the next section, we present this problem in an example.

3 Motivating Example

Consider a knowledge graph containing companies with four different relation types between them: two symmetric relations *in a business* (br) relationship

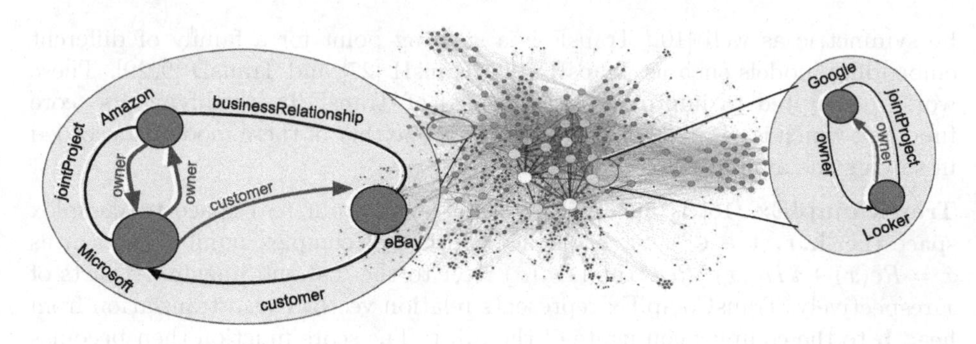

Fig. 1. Motivating Example. The RotatE embedding model infers wrong links (in red) for subgraphs with symmetric and anti-symmetric patterns. (Color figure online)

and in *joint projects* (jp) relationship and two anti-symmetric relationships *is customer of* (c) or *is owner of* (o) of another company. The triples of our concern in the KG are as follow:

$$\begin{cases} eBay \circ r_{br} = Amazon, \\ Amazon \circ r_{jp} = Microsoft, \\ eBay \circ r_c = Microsoft. \end{cases} \qquad \begin{cases} Google \circ r_{jp} = Looker, \\ Google \circ r_o = Looker, \end{cases} \tag{1}$$

In RotatE model, the symmetric relations r_{jp}, r_{br} obtain embedding vectors with elements of either -1 (rotation 0) or 1 (rotation π). The anti-symmetric relations vectors c and o get arbitrary values (except 1 and -1) [19]. Considering the left side of Eq. 1, we substitute Amazon by $eBay \circ \mathbf{r_{br}}$ in the second row. The right side of the equation remains the same. Therefore, we have:

$$\begin{cases} eBay \circ r_{br} \circ r_{jp} = Microsoft, \\ eBay \circ r_c = Microsoft. \end{cases} \qquad \begin{cases} Google \circ r_{jp} = Looker, \\ Google \circ r_o = Looker. \end{cases} \tag{2}$$

These lead to creation of extra constraints $r_{br} \circ r_{jp} = r_c$ and $r_{jp} = r_o$. We already know r_{jp}, r_{br} are symmetric and are represented in vectors with elements of -1 and 1. From the extra constraints created above, r_c is enforced to be symmetric (with elements of -1 and 1). Moreover, r_o will be equivalent with r_{jp}. Thus a set of wrong inferences (shown in Fig. 1 in red) are made by the model, such as $Amazon \circ r_o = Microsoft$, $Microsoft \circ r_o = Amazon$, $Microsoft \circ r_c = eBay$, and $Looker \circ r_o = Google$. This is especially problematic in large scale KGs, where there are many different symmetric relations and millions of entities. In our example, consider just adding the roughly 100 million ownership relations in the EU between companies. As the overwhelming majority are non-symmetric, over 90 million wrong inferences occur.

4 Our Approach

The inference of relational patterns by KGE models heavily depends on the model formulation and causes contradictions between (theoretically proven)

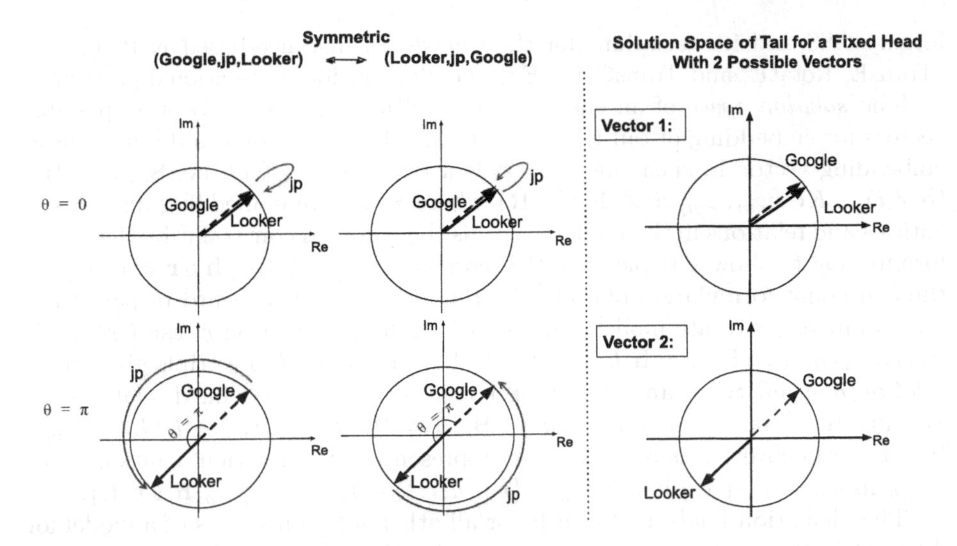

Fig. 2. Solution Space of RotatE for Symmetric. The possible vectors as solutions in SS are shown for symmetric relation of joint project (jp) in RotatE.

expressive power and (practical) performance by the models. When comparing different models, it is often unclear which factors are responsible for this difference and the expressiveness power of such models. Most work focuses on determining whether a model is capable of expressing a relational pattern or not, the most course-grained criterion possible. This course-grained analysis is a good start, but hides a lot of theoretical and practical limitations of models. A more fine-grained understanding of the capability of models is missing so far. Our focused study led us to discover a hidden factor as a cause of this issue namely *solution space*. In this section, we first describe the meaning and formulation of SS and introduce our novel KGE model namely $SpacE^{ss}$ empowered by the SS concept.

4.1 Solution Space - a Cause of Expressiveness in KGEs

Initially, using formulation of RotatE model without enforcing any constraints (patterns) in the KG, the possible solutions for representing embedding vectors of each relation r is an ∞ space. However, by enforcing relational patterns for example symmetric constraint, the SS of r reduces to 2 (i.e., $\{-1, 1\}$) per each dimension (or 2^d for all dimension). This reduction in solution space causes issues (e.g. wrong inference) when additional constraints are added as shown in Eq. 1 and Fig. 2. Generally, such constraints enforced by the definition of the corresponding relation pattern over the score function formula of a KGE builds the *solution space (SS)* of the model. Conceptually, SS is the coverage of all the possible variations for the embeddings of the elements of a triple (h,r,t) in the corresponding geometric space e.g. vector space. Here, we provide the formulation of SS and its variations for the considered distance-based KGE models (TransE, RotatE, and TransComplEx) and the considered relational patterns.

The *solution space* of an entity in tail position t is the set $\mathbf{S}$ of all possible vectors for embedding of tail $\mathbf{t}$ having a fixed relation vector $\mathbf{r}$ and a fixed head embedding vector $\mathbf{h}$, such that (h,r,t) is a triple in the KG, i.e. $\mathbf{S}_{t|r,h} = \{\mathbf{t} \mid (h,r,t) \in KG, \varphi_m, \varphi_{mp}, \mathbf{h} \in \mathbf{E}, \mathbf{r} \in \mathbf{R}\}$ where $\mathbf{E}, \mathbf{R}$, are embedding matrices of entities and relations in the model m. φ_m is the enforced constraint by the model formulation to show a triple (h,r,t) is correct e.g. $\varphi_{RotatE} : \mathbf{h} \circ \mathbf{r} = \mathbf{t}$. φ_{mp} is the constraint formulation obtained by the model m with regard to pattern p. For example, for rotate model and the given reflexive relation r, the formula is $\varphi_{RotatEReflexive} : \mathbf{h} \circ \mathbf{r} = \mathbf{h}, \mathbf{t} \circ \mathbf{r} = \mathbf{t}$. The SS for the *head* of a triple given fixed *relation and tail* $\mathbf{S}_{h|r,t}$ and the SS of a *relation* $\mathbf{S}_{r|h,t}$ are defined analogously. We similarly define the *relation-tail* SS: $\mathbf{S}_{r,t|h} = \{(\mathbf{r}, \mathbf{t}) \mid (h,r,t) \in KG, \varphi_m, \varphi_{mp}, \mathbf{h} \in \mathbf{E}\}$. Moreover, φ is a formulation representing the relation solution space $S_{r|t,h}$ in a vector space V if $\mathbf{S}_{r|t,h} = \{\mathbf{r} \mid (h,r,t) \in KG, \varphi_m, \varphi_{mp}, \mathbf{h}, \mathbf{t} \in \mathbf{E}\}$.

This definition holds analogously for all other solution spaces of a model for different patterns. In our company example, the SS of an element in example triple for Amazon being in joint project relationship with Microsoft is $|\mathbf{S}_{\mathsf{jp|Microsoft,Amazon}}| = 2$ considering all possible cases by RotatE model. In Sect. 4.2, we introduce SpacE^{ss} with considerably larger SS, and show how this improves its ability to represent various relational patterns.

4.2 SpacE^{ss} - A Novel KGE Model Empowered by SS

With a systematic study of SS on already existing models, claimed capable of encoding relational patterns (RotatE, TransComplEx), we concluded that none of the existing models have a proper SS for encoding of relational patterns. The results led us to propose a new embedding model *SpacE^{ss}* considering an extended solution space (SS) compared to existing models. We show the impact of SS encoding different types of relation patterns by our model with its high expressiveness, both theoretically and empirically. The improvement in expressiveness of *SpacE^{ss}* is due the larger space for solutions than RotatE, TransE and TransComplEx.

Given a triple (h,r,t), *SpacE^{ss}* first rotates the head entity counterclockwise and the tail entity clockwise to produce embedding vectors $\mathbf{h}_{\theta_L^r}$ (left rotation) and $\mathbf{t}_{\theta_R^r}$ (right rotation) respectively. It then applies a translation corresponding to the relation vector $\mathbf{r}$ from the relation-specific rotated-head (left rotation) to the relation-specific rotated-tail (right rotation), such that

$$\varphi_{SpacE^{SS}} : \mathbf{h}_{\theta_L^r} + \mathbf{r} = \mathbf{t}_{\theta_R^r}, \tag{3}$$

where $\mathbf{h}_{\theta_L^r}$ and $\mathbf{t}_{\theta_R^r}$ are computed as rotations of $\mathbf{h}_{\theta_L^r} = \mathbf{h}\, e^{i\theta_L^r}$, $\mathbf{t}_{\theta_R^r} = \mathbf{t}\, e^{-i\theta_R^r}$, and, θ_L^r and θ_R^r are the phase vectors for head and tail rotations corresponding to the relation r. The score function that computes the degree of correctness for a triple (h,r,t) is defined as:

$$f_{h,t}^r = \|\mathbf{h}_{\theta_L^r} + \mathbf{r} - \mathbf{t}_{\theta_R^r}\|. \tag{4}$$

Let $\mathbf{h}_i$ and $\mathbf{t}_i$ be the i-th elements (i $= 1, \ldots, d$) of head and tail embedding vectors, and $\theta_{L_i}^r$ and $\theta_{R_i}^r$ be the left and right rotation vectors respectively. The rotation is performed element-wise $\mathbf{h}_{\theta_{L_i}^r} = \mathbf{h}_i e^{i\theta_{L_i}^r}$, and $\mathbf{t}_{\theta_{R_i}^r} = \mathbf{t}_i e^{-i\theta_{R_i}^r}$. Our model is sufficiently expressive to encode different relation patterns including reflexive, symmetric, transitive, inverse, implication, equivalence and composition. Note that SpacE^{ss} only uses simple operators of addition, subtraction, and multiplication over embeddings of dimension d. Therefore, the computational complexity of the model is $O(d)$ which is similar to RotatE and TransComplEx.

4.3 Formulation of SS for Distance-Based KGE Models

The capability of a model to encode a specific relational pattern can be proven through a series of steps namely: 1) the formal definition of the considered relational pattern, 2) the formulation of the score function of the considered KGE model, and 3) the triple correctness condition. The latter is used for the scoring function and requires separate calculations which will be introduced in this part.

Conditions of Triple Correctness. The correctness of triples involved in a relational pattern defines whether the pattern holds. Among the wide range of scores assigned by a KGE model to the triples, a concrete threshold γ is required for deciding the correctness of each triple in a KG. In practice, this threshold is set as a hyper-parameter of the underlying KGE model. In this work, we use simplified thresholds [16] for investigating the capability of models to encode relational patterns, for correct triples: (a) if score $= 0$ then any triple with non-zero score is false, and (b) if score $\leq \gamma$ then any triple with score $> \gamma$ is false. Condition (a) is the most restrictive one and follows the original formulation of translation-based models and applies on the symmetric and inverse relations of all the models in Table 1. In case, the condition (a) does not apply (for example when the SS becomes zero), condition (b) could be considered with a specific γ, and applies on reflexive patterns of all the models in Table 1.

Formulation of Solution Space (SS). Table 1 illustrates the capability of three distance-based KGE models namely SpacE^{ss}, RotatE and TransComplEx in encoding relation patterns namely reflexive, symmetric and inverse. The column *Patterns* specifies each of the investigated relation patterns. The column *Cond.* shows whether threshold condition (a) or (b) is used for the considered pattern. The Table 1 indicates whether the model is capable of encoding the specified pattern under the specified condition or not. The column *Formulation* in Table 1 lists the formula under which the models encode the corresponding relation patterns, thus giving our desired *fine-grained* analysis of the capability. For space reasons, we describe only one cell of Table 1 to show SpacE^{ss} is capable of encoding the relation pattern symmetric under the condition (a). A relation is symmetric if $\forall h, t, (h, r, t) \leftrightarrow (t, r, h)$ holds. In other words, if a triple (h, r, t) is positive, (t, r, h) must also be positive. According to equation (3):

Table 1. A Fine-grained (Formulation) of KGE Models Encoding Relational Patterns. Each column corresponds to a specific model which is capable of encoding a specific relational pattern presented in each row, under a possible triple correctness condition (Cond.) and capability (Formulation).

	SpaceE^{ss} (φ_{mp})	RotatE (φ_{mp})	TransComplEx (φ_{mp})
Ref.	$\Vert\mathbf{h}_i(e^{i\theta^r_{Ri}} + e^{-i\theta^r_{Ri}})$ - $\mathbf{r}_i\Vert = \lambda$	$\Vert\mathbf{h}_i e^{i\theta^r_i} - \mathbf{h}_i\Vert = \lambda$	$\Vert -2\mathbf{h}_i - \mathbf{r}\Vert = \lambda$
Sym.	$(e^{i\theta^r_{Li}} - e^{-i\theta^r_{Ri}}) = 0$	$r_i^2 = 1$	$Re(ri) = 0$ $Re(hi) = Re(ti)$ $Im(\mathbf{h}) + Im(\mathbf{r}) = Im(\mathbf{t})$
Inv.	$\mathbf{h}(e^{i\theta^{r1}_{Li}} + e^{-i\theta^{r2}_{Ri}}) + r_{1i} -$ $r_{2i} = (e^{i\theta^{r1}_{Ri}} - e^{-i\theta^{r2}_{Li}})$	$r_{1i}r_{2i} = 1$	$2(Im(h_i) + Im(t_i)) +$ $Im(r_{1i}) + Im(r_{2i}) = 0$ $Re(r)^1 + Re(r)^2 = 0$

$$\begin{cases} \mathbf{h}_{\theta^r_{Li}} + \mathbf{r}_i = \mathbf{t}_{\theta^r_{Ri}} \\ \mathbf{t}_{\theta^r_{Li}} + \mathbf{r}_i = \mathbf{h}_{\theta^r_{Ri}} \end{cases}, \tag{5}$$

after a set of derivations, the resulting condition turns to be $e^{i\theta^r_{L_i}} + e^{-i\theta^r_{R_i}} = 0$ (see Table 1 for symmetric in SpacE^{ss}). It follows that a relation r is a symmetric relation if the following equations hold for it:

$$\begin{aligned} \cos(\theta^r_{L_i}) &= -\cos(\theta^r_{R_i}) = \cos(\pi - \theta^r_{R_i}), \\ \sin(\theta^r_{L_i}) &= \sin(\theta^r_{R_i}) = \sin(\pi - \theta^r_{R_i}). \end{aligned} \tag{6}$$

Therefore, in order to encode symmetric relation patterns by SpacE^{ss}, the summation of the rotations on the left and right sides ($\theta^r_{Li} + \theta^r_{Ri}$) should be equal to π. There are infinitely many solutions for (6) (e.g. $\{\theta^r_{L_i} = 0, \theta^r_{R_i} = \pi\}, \{\theta^r_{L_i} = \pi/3, \theta^r_{R_i} = 2\pi/3\}, \ldots$). We use the same reasoning to obtain results for each of the models with regard to an underlying relation pattern.

Company Example for Symmetry in SpacE^{ss}. Extending SS in *SpacE^{ss}* enables it to correctly encode all the patterns existed in our company example. Due to a bigger SS, triples are properly encoded in a vector space. This enables SpacE^{ss} to return correct inferences opposite to RotatE. Figure 3 shows how SpacE^{ss} encodes the example from Fig. 1. A left and a right rotation is assigned for each relation, e.g. one out of infinite solutions could be $\theta_{L_{br}} = 45$ and $\theta_{R_{br}} = -135°$. In Sub-figure a and b, the encoding of the positive triples from the symmetric relations are shown, and Sub-figure c represents the correct encoding of non-symmetric relations. In Sub-figure d, we show that SpacE^{ss} does not infer any expected incorrect triple (wrong inferences) from non-symmetric relations r_c, r_o. More precisely, the r_c relation in Sub-figure d is forced by the model formulation to have a different direction than the relation r_c in Sub-figure c. The same applies for r_o. As it contradicts with the actual triple in Sub-figure c, the model concludes that the two triples in Sub-figure d do not hold in the vector space as correct inferences.

The correct embeddings of r_c, r_o are shown in Sub-figure c. Using these vectors, we conclude that $Microsoft + r_c \neq eBay$ and $Looker + r_o \neq Google$.

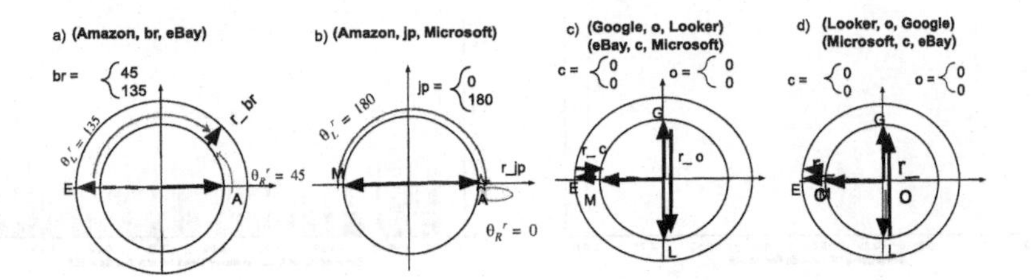

Fig. 3. Company Example in SpacE^{ss}. Encoding of the positive triples as correct inferences (blue vectors for entities and black for relations) and failure in returning wrong inferences (red vectors). (Color figure online)

Sub-figure d shows that the embeddings of r_c, r_o relations are different from their actual embeddings shown in Sub-figure c. Therefore, the model refuses the wrong inference of these symmetric relations which was not the case in RotatE.

Medium-Grained Analysis. So far, we have discussed a very coarse-grained capability, namely "yes"/"no", and a very fine-grained capability, namely the defining formula of the SS (see Table 1). It remains to show a medium-grained analysis that would allow us to easily compare different models. In Table 2, different variations of feasible solution space for three KGE models are shown which exactly gives us this medium-grained understanding. In Table 4 we visualize how theoretic FSS assumption hold in practice.

Table 2. Comparison of Solution SpacE^{ss} for Different KGE Models. An element-wise comparison of different values for SS are shown.

	SpacE^{ss}			Rotate			TransComplEx		
Ref.	$\mathbf{S}_{r\|h}$	$\mathbf{S}_{h\|r}$	-	$\mathbf{S}_{r\|h}$	$\mathbf{S}_{h\|r}$	-	$\mathbf{S}_{r\|h}$	$\mathbf{S}_{h\|r}$	-
	Inf	Inf	-	2	Inf	-	Inf	4	-
Sym.	$\mathbf{S}_{r\|h,t}$	$\mathbf{S}_{h\|r,t}$	$\mathbf{S}_{h,r\|t}$	$\mathbf{S}_{r\|h,t}$	$\mathbf{S}_{h\|r,t}$	$\mathbf{S}_{h,r\|t}$	$\mathbf{S}_{r\|h,t}$	$\mathbf{S}_{h\|r,t}$	$\mathbf{S}_{h,r\|t}$
	Inf	1	Inf	2	1	2	1	1	Inf.
Inv.	$\mathbf{S}_{r_1,r_2\|h,t}$	$\mathbf{S}_{h\|r_1,r_2,t}$	$\mathbf{S}_{h,r_1\|r_2,t}$	$\mathbf{S}_{r_1,r_2\|h,t}$	$\mathbf{S}_{h\|r_1,r_2,t}$	$\mathbf{S}_{h,r_1\|r_2,t}$	$\mathbf{S}_{r_1,r_2\|h,t}$	$\mathbf{S}_{h\|r_1,r_2,t}$	$\mathbf{S}_{h,r_1\|r_2,t}$
	Inf	1	Inf	4	1	1	1	1	1

Note that solution space allows multiple dimensions, e.g. fixing head and having freedom in relation and tail, or any of the other combinations. For each relational pattern, the solution of each possible combination of vectors is provided. For example, a combination of three possible solutions $\mathbf{S}_{r|h,t}$, $\mathbf{S}_{h|r,t}$ and $\mathbf{S}_{h,r|t}$ is considered for symmetric relations. Thus, in case $S_{r|h,t} = Inf$ if for SpacE^{ss}; the solution space for RotatE, however is 2 i.e., $S_{r|h,t} = 2$. In the same way, SpacE^{ss} provides a bigger solution space for other relation patterns compared to TransComplEx and RotatE.

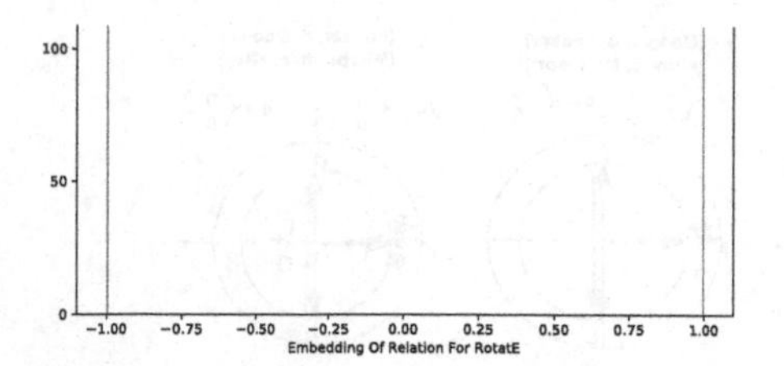

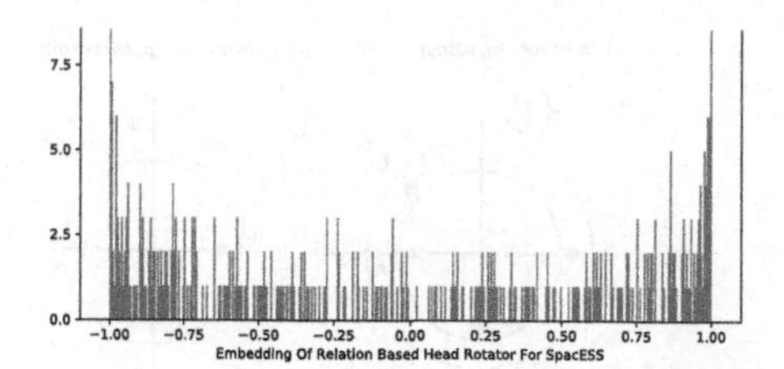

Fig. 4. Solution Space. The possible solutions for symmetric relation of "Similar To" in WN18 by RotatE (2) and SpacE^{ss} (Inf.) – compatible results in Table 2.

5 Experiments

The proposed model is evaluated on the link prediction problem using the filtered setting [3]. The task here is to predict whether a relation is likely to hold between two given entities. Here, we first generate a set of candidate triples by corrupting once the head h and once the tail entity t for each positive test triple (h, r, t). We remove any candidate triples constructed in this way if they appear in either validation, training, or the test set. Finally, we rank the remaining candidate triples against the original test triple (h, r, t). We use the standard evaluation methods: mean rank (MR), mean reciprocal rank (MRR) and hits at top N (Hits@N) for N = 1, 3, and 10 [24]. MR is the average rank of all the correct test triples; MRR is the average reciprocal rank of the correct triples and is defined as: $\sum_{j=1}^{n_t} \frac{1}{r_j}$, where r_j is the rank of the j-th (positive) test triple and n_t - the

Table 3. Evaluation 1. Results of models evaluated on FB15k and WN18. SpacE^{ss}+Pat is SpacE^{ss} model with pattern *Pat* explicitly injected. SpacE^{ss}-small is SpacE^{ss} model with 10 negative samples per one positive and dimension of 200. Results for models marked by ⋆ are reported from [19]; results for TuckER are from [1]; and results from TransComplEx are quoted from [16].

	FB15k					WN18				
	MR	MRR	Hits@1	Hits@3	Hits@10	MR	MRR	Hits@1	Hits@3	Hits@10
TransE⋆	–	.463	.297	.578	.749	–	.495	.113	.888	.943
DistMult⋆	42	**.798**	–	–	.893	655	.797	–	–	.946
HolE⋆	–	.524	.402	.613	.739	–	.938	.930	.945	.949
ComplEx⋆	–	.692	.599	.759	.840	–	.941	.936	.945	.947
ConvE⋆	51	.657	.588	.723	.831	374	.943	.935	.946	.956
RotatE⋆	40	.797	**.746**	.830	.884	309	.949	.944	.952	.959
TuckER	–	.795	.741	.833	.892	–	**.953**	**.949**	**.955**	.958
TransComplEx	38	.682	–	–	.875	284	.922	–	–	.955
SpacE^{ss}	34.5	.760	.667	.836	.895	197	.946	.936	.953	**.962**
SpacE^{ss}-small	41	.732	.630	.815	.884	228	.946	.936	.953	**.962**
SpacE^{ss}+Inverse	35.3	.774	.686	.845	**.898**	**141**	.939	.921	.953	**.962**
SpacE^{ss}+Implication	35	.765	.673	.839	.896	–	–	–	–	–
SpacE^{ss}+Symmetry	36	.768	.680	.838	.894	–	–	–	–	–
SpacE^{ss}+Equality	36	.773	.687	.845	.896	–	–	–	–	–
SpacE^{ss}+All	**33.7**	.789	.713	**.851**	**.898**	–	–	–	–	–

Table 4. Evaluation 2. Results of models evaluated on FB15k-237 and WN18RR. SpacE^{ss}+Pat is SpacE^{ss} model with pattern *Pat* explicitly injected. SpacE^{ss}-small is SpacE^{ss} model with 10 negative samples per one positive and dimension of 200. Results for models marked by ⋆ are reported from [19]; results for TuckER are from [1]; and results from TransComplEx are quoted from [16].

	FB15k-237					WN18RR				
	MR	MRR	HIT@1	HIT@3	HIT@10	MR	MRR	HIT@1	HIT@3	HIT@10
TransE⋆	357	.294	–	–	.465	3384	.226	–	–	.501
DistMult⋆	254	.241	.155	.263	.419	5110	.43	.39	.44	.49
ComplEx⋆	339	.247	.158	.275	.428	5261	.44	41	.46	.51
ConvE⋆	244	.325	.237	.356	.501	4187	.43	.40	.44	.52
RotatE⋆	177	.338	.241	.375	.533	3340	**.476**	.428	.492	.571
TuckER	–	**.358**	**.266**	**.394**	**.544**	–	.470	**.443**	.482	.526
TransComplEx	223	.317	–	–	.493	4081	.389	–	–	.498
SpacE^{ss}	167	.337	.238	.376	.539	**2959**	.457	.392	.488	**.583**
SpacE^{ss}-small	171	.333	.236	.369	.530	2986	.469	.412	**.493**	.577
SpacE^{ss}+Inverse	167	.340	.243	.375	.537	–	–	–	–	–
SpacE^{ss}+Implication	168	.338	.240	.374	.540	–	–	–	–	–
SpacE^{ss}+Equality	167	.337	.240	.376	.538	–	–	–	–	–
SpacE^{ss}+All	**163**	.335	.237	.372	.533	–	–	–	–	–

Table 5. Evaluation 3. Results with low Dimension equal to 10.

	FB15k					WN18				
	MR	MRR	Hits@1	Hits@3	Hits@10	MR	MRR	Hits@1	Hits@3	Hits@10
TransE⋆	3350	.023	.009	.022	.048	1355	.128	.066	.138	.246
DistMult⋆	3459	.021	.010	.019	.041	753	.403	.247	.475	.742
ComplEx⋆	876	.122	**.069**	.134	.220	**709**	.453	.304	.524	.769
RotatE⋆	748.7	.050	.018	.045	.105	891	.522	.403	.591	.748
TransComplEx	511	.115	.053	.132	.239	1700	.117	.065	.123	.221
SpacE^{ss}	**393**	**.130**	**.069**	**.136**	**.246**	805	**.569**	**.451**	**.647**	**.785**
	FB15k-237					WN18RR				
	MR	MRR	Hits@1	Hits@3	Hits@10	MR	MRR	Hits@1	Hits@3	Hits@10
TransE⋆	431	.159	.092	.170	.292	6207	.093	.009	.141	.249
DistMult⋆	432	.159	.089	.170	.302	8749	.100	.001	.180	.352
ComplEx⋆	**388**	.165	.094	.173	.314	8977	.203	.118	.266	.358
RotatE⋆	489	.132	.067	.139	.266	6358	.323	.245	.391	.430
TransComplEx	453	.154	.088	.163	.292	6645	.177	.119	.202	.291
SpacE^{ss}	390	**.183**	**.109**	**.197**	**.334**	**6115**	**.393**	**.368**	**.406**	**.437**

number of triples in the test set; and Hits@N is the percentage of the triples whose rank is equal or smaller than N.

Datasets. We evaluate our model on set of four widely used knowledge graphs: FB15k [3] FB15k-237 [20], WN18 [3], and WN18RR [4]. The relation patterns (rules) for FB15k and WN18 are adapted from [8] and [7] respectively. We only considered rules with confidence level of 0.8 or higher. The number of triples involved in symmetric, implication and inverse patterns both in FB15k and FB15k-237 are above $35k$ in each pattern category. The number of triples with inverse patterns in FB15k is above $390k$. The above statistics are based on triple

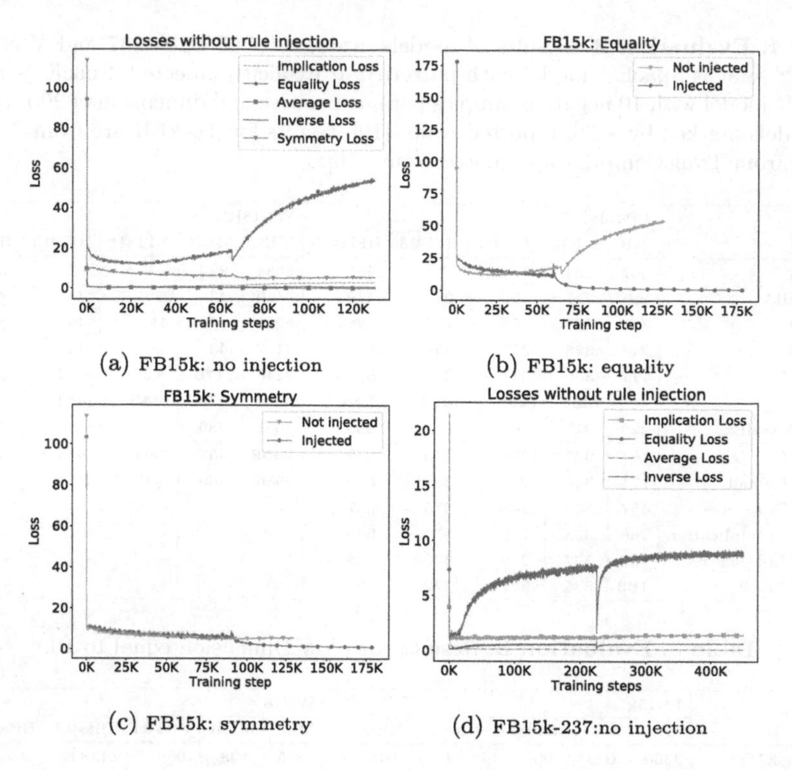

(a) FB15k: no injection (b) FB15k: equality

(c) FB15k: symmetry (d) FB15k-237:no injection

Fig. 5. Evaluation 4. Evolution of losses for relation patterns during optimization phase with/without injection: (a) shows the convergence of losses for main relation patterns in FB15K without injection. In (b), the equality patterns are shown with/without injection; (c) shows the same for symmetric patterns and (d) shows the convergence of losses for all patterns on FB15k-237 without injection.

counting, however, we follow [8] when constructing valid groundings: a grounding of a rule is considered valid if the triples appearing in its antecedent are present in the knowledge graph, while the triples in the consequent are not. Given an example pattern $p \Rightarrow q$ (e.g. inverse is $\forall X, Y : r(X,Y) \implies r'(Y,X)$), we refer to p as the antecedent and q as the consequent of the rule. Most of the groundings in both FB15k and WN18 are for inverse rule.

Experimental Setup. We train our model by using the RotatE loss [19]. We use Adagrad [5] as the optimizer of SpacE^{ss}. The hyper parameters were fine-tuned on the validation set, using grid search over the following ranges: batch size $\in \{200, 512, 1024\}$, embedding dimension dim $\in\{200, 500\}$, number of negative samples #neg $\in$ { 10, 20, 50 }, adversarial sampling temperature $\alpha \in \{0.5, 1.0\}$, $\gamma \in\{3, 9, 12, 18, 24\}$, learning rate $lr \in \{0.001, 0.01, 0.1\}$. γ is the hyper-parameter of the losses. Embedding dimension 500 and 20 negative samples are used as best hyper-parameters for our model.

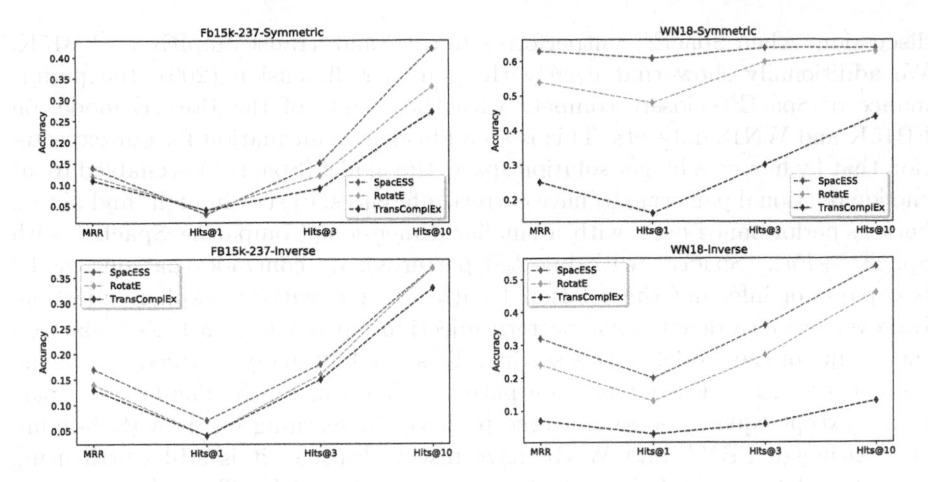

Fig. 6. Symmetric and Inverse Patterns. Practical investigation on the theories of Table 1 in low dimension 10 for FB15K-237 and 15 for WN18.

Results and Discussion. A comparison of SpacE^{ss} to TransE, DistMult, HolE, CompEx, ConvE, and RotatE is provided in Tables 3 and 4. We follow the steps introduced in [7, 15] for explicit pattern injecting such that: first, the loss function for the relational patterns is computed and then the results are added to the main loss function as a regularization term. For example, in order to inject a symmetric pattern, we add the regularization term $\|f_r(h,t) - f_r(t,h)\|$. We use following definitions to compute regularization terms for the other rules: we say that $A \iff B$ holds iff $A = B$ and $A \implies B$ iff $A \leq B$; (soft) truth value (or the score) of $A \wedge B$ is computed as $A \times B$, $A \vee B$ as $A + B - A \times B$, and $\neg A$ as $1 - A$. The loss terms for $A \leq B$ and $A = B$ are computed as $Relu(A - B)$ and $\|A - B\|$, respectively. We test our model both with and without explicitly injected relational patterns. We use SpacE^{ss}+Pat ("Pat" for a specific pattern that is injected) to denote that the model uses pattern regularization (one type of rule is injected at a time). For instance, SpacE^{ss}+Inverse refers to SpacE^{ss} with inverse relations injected explicitly via regularization terms. SpacE^{ss}+All refers to the results of injecting multiple (all) patterns.

According to [19], FB15K and WN18 datasets contain a significant amount of relational patterns (inverse and symmetric). Table 2 (which is derived from 1) shows the design and development of the SpacE^{ss} model have been done with the purpose of having a bigger solution space than RotatE and TransComplEx. Therefore, in two evaluation settings (with bigger and smaller dimension), the SpacE^{ss} model achieves: a) a better performance than the other distance-based models encoding relational patterns (with same dimension), b) same accuracy (in smaller dimension) due to expanded solution space for encoding pattern e.g. inverse relations in our experiments on FB15K and WN18.

As shown in Table 3, SpacE^{ss} obtains 89.8 Hits@10 while RotatE and TransComplEx get 88.4 and 87.5 respectively. These results confirm our theoretical discussions when SpacE^{ss} outperforms RotatE and TransComplEx on FB15K. We additionally show that even with a smaller dimension (200), the performance of SpacE^{ss} closely compete with the results of the RotatE model on FB15K and WN18 datasets. This is an additional confirmation for our expectation that by having a bigger solution space, the model (SpacE^{ss}) is enabled to: a) encode relational patterns, b) have correct inferences, c) stay in high (and obtain better) performance even with a smaller dimension. Comparing SpacE^{ss} with SpacE^{ss}+Pat, (SpacE^{ss} with injected patterns), we conclude that our model is capable of inferring the relational patterns even without explicit injection. However, we also denote that pattern injection did not have a high impact on the results of the model in this setting. This is additionally justified by tracing the convergence of loss for relation patterns shown in Fig. 5. The losses of patterns (except equality loss) converge properly by learning on data (Sub-figure 5a). Although FB15k and WN18 have testing leakage, it is still worth using these two datasets while investigating capacity of models. These datasets contain many inverse and symmetric patterns, therefore if the solution space of a model is limited, then the model cannot express those patterns and the accuracy is expected to be dropped substantially even with testing leakage.

As shown in Sub-figure 5b, injection enables the quality loss to converge. Using symmetry relation (Sub-figure 5c), we show even without injection, the model properly infers the pattern. Although with these two datasets (FB15K and WN18), our focus has been on showcasing relation patterns of type inverse and symmetric, encoding of relational patterns by SpacE^{ss} is not limited to these. This is proven by running SpacE^{ss} on FB15K-237 and WN18-RR datasets within which the inverse relational patterns have mostly been removed originally. The results are shown in Table 4 and Table 3 where our performance is closely competing with RotatE and TransComplEx. However, in comparison to TransComplEx with performance of 49.3, our model achieves a better performance of 53.9 in Hits@10. Tucker gets the state-of-the-art performance on FB15K-237. However, Tucker obtains these results by using much more parameters due to the design of its scoring function. Moreover, this performance is also due to the used boosting techniques such as data augmentation (adding reverse triples), and using $1-n$ scoring which is not applicable in large scale KGs. Using WN18RR, SpacE^{ss} outperforms all models considering Hits@10 and MR, even with a smaller dimension. Table 5 includes the results for dimension 10.

As said, the solution space of a model is heavily depending on the model formulation. However, one can increase it with the cost of getting high in the size of the embedding dimension. Since the evaluation in the state-of-the-art models have been done on relatively small standard KGs with big dimensions e.g. 500, 1000, the difference between models is not visible. Normally there would be two ways of highlighting the effect of solution space: 1) compare the embedding models with regard to their solution space in a very large scale of KGs e.g. millions of entities and billions of triples, 2) prototype it with toy KGs e.g. FB15k-237 in a very low dimension e.g. 5 or 10. Since the first approach is not feasible technically, we provided the results following the second way. Our extended evaluations using very low dimensions show that for FB15k-237, RotatE has 26.6 Hits@10, however SpacE^{ss} gets 33.4 with dimension 10. With dimension 5, the difference in performance is even more visible up to 15% (RotatE shows 3% and SpacE^{ss} 19% in Hits@10) of differences (complete results have been omitted from this paper for lack of space). Figure 6 shows the results for low dimensional of 15 over WN18 and 10 over FB15K-237. For symmetric patterns of WN18 in Hits@1, we gain 13% difference over RotatE (SpacE^{ss} = 61.01, RotatE = 48.3).

6 Conclusion and Future Work

In this paper, we introduced the concept of solution space as an approach towards overcoming the expressiveness problem of embedding models. It provides a fine-grained analysis on the capability of the models to express certain patterns. We introduced the SpacE^{ss} model that is designed based on the concept of solution space. We specifically provided a theoretical demonstration of the solution space for SpacE^{ss}, RotatE and TransComplEx models on reflexive, symmetric and inversion patterns. An experimental evaluation is provided that shows the performance of SpacE^{ss} in comparison to the state-of-the-art models which are able to encode a relational pattern. The experiments are done both in high and low dimensions in order to simulate their utilization over large-scale KGs. The results of the comparisons on high dimension show the performance improvements of SpacE^{ss} influenced by the concept of solution space. This is further visible in low dimensional embedding where the experiments show a surprising drop in the performance of all the considered models including SpacE^{ss}, even on FB15K which has leakage on patterns. However, the difference of performance demonstrated by SpacE^{ss} is yet another approval on the importance of solution space. In this work, we only investigated a few of the well-known embedding models. Our future work contains analysing more models in terms of their solution space and broaden our scope to find more factors that influence the expressiveness of models. We showcased the effect of solution space considering some of the relational patterns. We plan to extensively include other pattern types.

Acknowledgements. This work is supported by the EC Horizon 2020 grant LAMBDA (GA no. 809965), the CLEOPATRA project (GA no. 812997), the Vienna Science and Technology Fund (WWTF) grant VRG18-013, and the EPSRC grant EP/M025268/1.

References

1. Balažević, I., Allen, C., Hospedales, T.M.: TuckER: tensor factorization for knowledge graph completion. arXiv preprint arXiv:1901.09590 (2019)
2. Bollacker, K., Evans, C., Paritosh, P., Sturge, T., Taylor, J.: Freebase: a collaboratively created graph database for structuring human knowledge. In: ACM SIGMOD, pp. 1247–1250. ACM (2008)
3. Bordes, A., Usunier, N., Garcia-Duran, A., Weston, J., Yakhnenko, O.: Translating embeddings for modeling multi-relational data. In: NIPSm pp. 2787–2795 (2013)

4. Dettmers, T., Minervini, P., Stenetorp, P., Riedel, S.: Convolutional 2D knowledge graph embeddings. In: AAAI (2018)
5. Duchi, J., Hazan, E., Singer, Y.: Adaptive subgradient methods for online learning and stochastic optimization. JMLR **12**(7), 2121–2159 (2011)
6. Ebisu, T., Ichise, R.: TorusE: knowledge graph embedding on a lie group. In: Thirty-Second AAAI Conference on Artificial Intelligence (2018)
7. Guo, S., Wang, Q., Wang, L., Wang, B., Guo, L.: Jointly embedding knowledge graphs and logical rules. In: EMNLP, pp. 192–202 (2016)
8. Guo, S., Wang, Q., Wang, L., Wang, B., Guo, L.: Knowledge graph embedding with iterative guidance from soft rules. In: AAAI (2018)
9. Ji, G., He, S., Xu, L., Liu, K., Zhao, J.: Knowledge graph embedding via dynamic mapping matrix. In: ACL-IJCNLP, pp. 687–696 (2015)
10. Kazemi, S.M., Poole, D.: Simple embedding for link prediction in knowledge graphs. In: NIPS, pp. 4284–4295 (2018)
11. Lehmann, J., et al.: DBpedia - a large-scale, multilingual knowledge base extracted from wikipedia. Seman. Web J. **6**(2), 167–195 (2015). outstanding Paper Award (Best 2014 SWJ Paper)
12. Lin, Y., Liu, Z., Sun, M., Liu, Y., Zhu, X.: Learning entity and relation embeddings for knowledge graph completion. In: AAAI (2015)
13. Liu, H., Wu, Y., Yang, Y.: Analogical inference for multi-relational embeddings. In: ICML, pp. 2168–2178 (2017)
14. Miller, G.A.: Wordnet: a lexical database for english. CACM **38**(11), 39–41 (1995)
15. Minervini, P., Costabello, L., Muñoz, E., Nováček, V., Vandenbussche, P.-Y.: Regularizing knowledge graph embeddings via equivalence and inversion axioms. In: Ceci, M., Hollmén, J., Todorovski, L., Vens, C., Džeroski, S. (eds.) ECML PKDD 2017. LNCS (LNAI), vol. 10534, pp. 668–683. Springer, Cham (2017). https://doi.org/10.1007/978-3-319-71249-9_40
16. Nayyeri, M., Xu, C., Yaghoobzadeh, Y., Yazdi, H.S., Lehmann, J.: On the knowledge graph completion using translation based embedding: the loss is as important as the score. arXiv Preprint arXiv:1909.00519 (2019)
17. Nickel, M., Rosasco, L., Poggio, T.: Holographic embeddings of knowledge graphs. In: AAAI (2016)
18. Nie, B., Sun, S.: Knowledge graph embedding via reasoning over entities, relations, and text. Future Gener. Comput. Syst. **91**, 426–433 (2019)
19. Sun, Z., Deng, Z.H., Nie, J.Y., Tang, J.: Rotate: knowledge graph embedding by relational rotation in complex space. arXiv preprint arXiv:1902.10197 (2019)
20. Toutanova, K., Chen, D.: Observed versus latent features for knowledge base and text inference. In: Proceedings of the 3rd Workshop on Continuous Vector Space Models and their Compositionality, pp. 57–66 (2015)
21. Trouillon, T., Welbl, J., Riedel, S., Gaussier, É., Bouchard, G.: Complex embeddings for simple link prediction. In: ICML, pp. 2071–2080 (2016)
22. Tucker, L.R.: Some mathematical notes on three-mode factor analysis. Psychometrika **31**(3), 279–311 (1966)
23. Vrandečić, D., Krötzsch, M.: Wikidata: a free collaborative knowledgebase. CACM **57**(10), 78–85 (2014)
24. Wang, Q., Mao, Z., Wang, B., Guo, L.: Knowledge graph embedding: a survey of approaches and applications. IEEE Trans. Knowl. Data Eng. **29**(12), 2724–2743 (2017)
25. Wang, Y., Gemulla, R., Li, H.: On multi-relational link prediction with bilinear models. In: AAAI (2018)

26. Wang, Y., Ruffinelli, D., Broscheit, S., Gemulla, R.: On evaluating embedding models for knowledge base completion. arXiv preprint arXiv:1810.07180 (2018)
27. Wang, Z., Zhang, J., Feng, J., Chen, Z.: Knowledge graph embedding by translating on hyperplanes. In: AAAI (2014)
28. Yang, B., Yih, W.T., He, X., Gao, J., Deng, L.: Embedding entities and relations for learning and inference in knowledge bases. arXiv preprint arXiv:1412.6575 (2014)
29. Yoon, H.G., Song, H.J., Park, S.B., Park, S.Y.: A translation-based knowledge graph embedding preserving logical property of relations. In: NAACL - HLT (2016)

LM4KG: Improving Common Sense Knowledge Graphs with Language Models

Janna Omeliyanenko(✉), Albin Zehe, Lena Hettinger, and Andreas Hotho

Julius-Maximilians-University Würzburg, Am Hubland, 97074 Würzburg, Germany
{omeliyanenko,zehe,hettinger,hotho}@informatik.uni-wuerzburg.de

Abstract. Language Models (LMs) and Knowledge Graphs (KGs) are both active research areas in Machine Learning and Semantic Web. While LMs have brought great improvements for many downstream tasks on their own, they are often combined with KGs providing additionally aggregated, well structured knowledge. Usually, this is done by leveraging KGs to improve LMs. But what happens if we turn this around and use LMs to improve KGs?

In this paper, we propose a method enabling the use of the knowledge inherently encoded in LMs to automatically improve explicit knowledge represented in common sense KGs. Edges in these KGs represent relations between concepts, but the strength of the relations is often not clear. We propose to transform KG relations to natural language sentences, allowing us to utilize the information contained in large LMs to rate these sentences through a new perplexity-based measure, Refined Edge WEIGHTing (REWEIGHT). We test our scoring scheme REWEIGHT on the popular LM BERT to produce new weights for the edges in the well-known ConceptNet KG. By retrofitting existing word embeddings to our modified ConceptNet, we create ConceptNet NumBERTbatch embeddings and show that these outperform the original ConceptNet Numberbatch on multiple established semantic similarity datasets.

Keywords: Knowledge Graph · Language Model · Common Sense

1 Introduction

Knowledge Graphs (KG) are one of the core areas of research in the Semantic Web community [11]. Their creation and curation have long been tasks of great interest, since the resulting graphs are invaluable in a wide range of applications within the community, but also in Natural Language Processing, Information Retrieval and Machine Learning. Thus, KGs provide a natural link between the Semantic Web and Machine Learning, where they are being used to provide

Electronic supplementary material The online version of this chapter (https://doi.org/10.1007/978-3-030-62419-4_26) contains supplementary material, which is available to authorized users.

J. Z. Pan et al. (Eds.): ISWC 2020, LNCS 12506, pp. 456–473, 2020.
https://doi.org/10.1007/978-3-030-62419-4_26

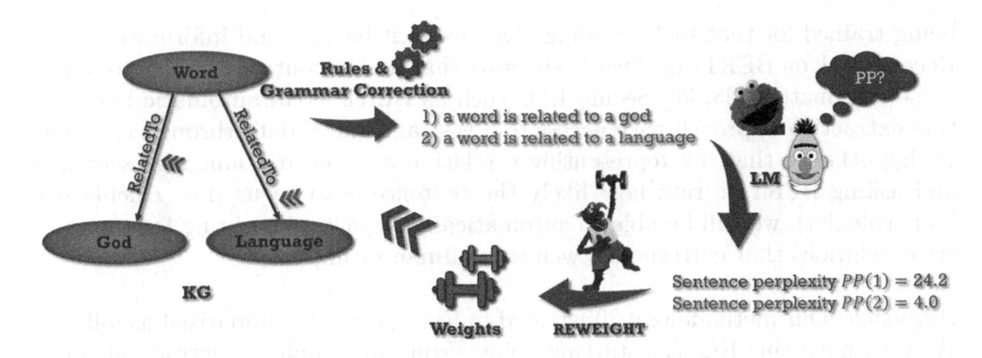

Fig. 1. Illustration of the REWEIGHT pipeline. A KG's relations are weighted through transforming them to sentences and obtaining perplexity scores with an LM.

explicit, structured background knowledge that may not be readily available in unstructured data sources. While the use of KGs in Machine Learning applications is very common [27,28,37], in this paper we propose to go in the opposite direction: We use a well-established model from the area of Natural Language Processing, the Language Model (LM) BERT [8] to improve the knowledge encoded in a widely used, state of the art KG, ConceptNet [28].

In order to supply a range of information that is as broad as possible, KGs are often constructed using (semi-)automatic methods, with ConceptNet combining multiple other knowledge bases (e.g., Wiktionary, DBPedia) as well as extracting additional information from plain text and games with a purpose [14,28,30]. While these sources are mostly reliable, there is no explicit information about the strength of the relations described therein. However, often it is crucial to know the strength of the relation between two words: For example, a search engine may want to perform a query expansion using a KG to look for related terms. When looking for terms related to "word", a KG like Wiktionary would return both "god" and "language". While both relations are correct, the second one is more prevalent in most situations and would usually be considered stronger, meaning that it will be the better choice for a query expansion in most contexts. However, Wiktionary contains no indication that there is a difference between both relations. ConceptNet partially deals with this issue by assigning reliability scores to different sources, but this does not help to distinguish between relations from the same source. Hence we are interested in automatically extracting this prevalence information from unstructured data and adding it as structured information to the graph by refining its edge weights.

Hypothesis. In this paper, we propose Refined Edge WEIGHTing (REWEIGHT), a novel approach towards automatically acquiring the prevalence information of relations in order to weight the edges in a KG using pretrained LMs such as BERT [8]. Recent research has shown that these models trained on enormous corpora contain a certain amount of world knowledge, in some cases even being able to perform limited question answering without ever being trained for that task or being given explicit background information [24]. Recent work on BERT specifically suggests that it may contain relevant common sense information [23,35]. Seeing LMs such as BERT as an automatic information extraction approach with access to a vast amount of data through training, we hypothesize that, by representing a relation as a natural language sentence and asking BERT to rate how likely the sentence is to occur (i.e., calculating its perplexity), we will be able to automatically extract a weighting for common sense relations that corresponds well to a human rating.

Approach. Our methodology, illustrated in Fig. 1, can be summarised as follows: We use an existing KG as a starting point. From this graph, we extract all edges (corresponding to relations between two words) and construct sentences from these edges by applying a manually defined set of rules and automated grammar correction. The resulting sentences are then used as input to a LM and their perplexity is calculated. We apply a transformation to the perplexity scores to map them to the range of the edge weights in the original graph, where high edge weights correspond to strong relations. Finally, we feed the edge weights back into the KG, yielding an enriched knowledge resource that contains information about the prevalence of its relations. While we utilize BERT's common sense knowledge in our pipeline, we formulate the approach in a general way to allow application on all types of KGs with different LMs.

To evaluate our approach, we show that REWEIGHT is capable of improving the already well suited ConceptNet KG on the task of refining existing word embeddings for semantic relatedness. We evaluate REWEIGHT by applying the same retrofitting [10] procedure as ConceptNet Numberbatch [28], showing that the enriched graph yields embeddings with improved performance on multiple semantic relatedness datasets.

Contribution. Our contribution in this paper is three-fold: 1. We propose a novel, general methodology for enriching KGs by weighting the edges in a KG according to their importance. 2. We update the weights of the common sense KG ConceptNet with the BERT LM, showing that our approach improves the semantic information encoded in the graph.[1] 3. We perform a detailed analysis, investigating different influence factors on our proposed approach.

Structure. The remainder of this paper is structured as follows: Sect. 2 gives an introduction to common sense KGs and retrofitting, while Sect. 3 describes work related to our paper. In Sect. 4 we describe our edge weighting scheme REWEIGHT. Section 5 describes the experimental setup of our evaluation. Our results are contained in Sect. 6, while we carry out deeper analysis in Sect. 7. Section 8 concludes our work.

[1] Code, updated KGs and embeddings are available under https://github.com/JohannaOm/REWEIGHT.

2 Background

In this section we describe the background setting of our paper. This includes a general overview of KGs for Common Sense Knowledge, where the most prominent representative is ConceptNet, and the Retrofitting algorithm that we use to derive word embeddings from our modified KG. Following previous work, we will later use these embeddings to evaluate the quality of our new weights.

2.1 Common Sense Knowledge Graphs

Common sense describes the most basic knowledge and information a human has at their disposal [28].

In our experiments we focus on one of the most prevalent common sense KGs, **ConceptNet** [28]. ConceptNet aggregates its information from sources like DBPedia, Wiktionary, Open Multilingual WordNet and "games with a purpose". It is a multilingual KG specifically designed as an information source for assessing semantic relatedness between concepts, setting a special focus on natural language expressions. For our experiments, we use version 5.7, which contains 30.6 million relations between 17.8 million concepts, out of which 2.3 million relations exist between 440.000 English concepts. The graphs original weights are distributed between 0.1 and $\gamma_{\max} = 50$, with mean 1.1 and median $\tilde{\gamma} = 1$.

Next to ConceptNet, we also take a look at other common sense KGs. **WebChild 2.0** [30] is an English common sense KG focusing on activities, properties, and their semantic relations. It contains 23 million relations between 450.000 concepts. **YAGO 3.1** [25] is an ontology extracted from multilingual Wikipedia. Wile YAGO, as a general knowledge base, contains many facts about specific real world entities, we use YAGO's taxonomy subgraph that contains more abstract information that more closely represents generally applicable common sense knowledge. The YAGO Taxonomy contains 1.7 million relations between 800.000 concepts.

2.2 Evaluation of KGs

Evaluating KGs is a non-trivial problem, since there is usually no ground truth available that can directly be used as an intrinsic evaluation target. One possible way of extrinsic evaluation is using the KG to enrich existing word embeddings and assess the quality improvement in the embeddings induced through the KG. We will adopt this way of evaluation by following [29] in applying Retrofitting (cf. Sect. 2.3) to enrich word embeddings using either the unmodified version of a KG or the modified version after applying REWEIGHT. Retrofitting uses the weights in the KG as indication of how close two words should be, making this a suitable method of evaluating whether REWEIGHT actually improves the weights in the KG: If the quality of the embeddings improves after applying REWEIGHT, we can conclude that we have improved the weights in the KG.

2.3 Retrofitting

Retrofitting [10] uses relational information of KGs to refine existing word embeddings. The main idea is to re-calibrate the embedding vector of each word, leaving it both close to the original embedding vector and close to the embeddings of all neighboring words in the KG.

Formally, retrofitting minimizes the objective function

$$\Psi(Q) = \sum_{i \in V} \left[\alpha_i ||q_i - \hat{q}_i||^2 + \sum_{(i,j) \in E} \beta_{i,j} ||q_i - q_j||^2 \right] \quad (1)$$

where q_i and $\hat{q}_i$ mark the new and original embeddings of word i out of vocabulary V respectively, and $\beta_{i,j}$ represents the weight of the edge $(i,j) \in E$ in the KG, which we want to improve with REWEIGHT. α_i is a hyper-parameter determining how close q_i should stay to $\hat{q}_i$.

[28] use an extended version of retrofitting that is capable of processing out-of-vocabulary words. In this work we also use the same extended version.

3 Related Work

KGs and (large) LMs have been investigated extensively in recent years. One of the best understood large **language models** is BERT. It performs on par with knowledge bases extracted from text [23] and substantially outperforms pretrained word embeddings when queried for relational common sense knowledge [4]. When compared to other recently introduced LMs, BERT outperformed GPT2 and XLnet on a series of common sense tasks [38]. BERT also offers enough clues to enable common sense reasoning for visual understanding, and more so than GloVe and ELMo embeddings [35]. Hence, we conclude that BERT is a fitting model to extract common sense knowledge for KG enhancement.

In general, **knowledge resources** can be a vital addition to any NLP task. There exist various methods to create knowledge bases, e.g. from web resources like Wikipedia or through crowdsourcing as in ConceptNet. So far, relations from KGs have mostly been used to enrich LMs: either during training [32,34] or by adapting the resulting embeddings afterwards (*retrofitting*) [10,18,29]. A prominent example is ERNIE [36], which aligns KG entities from WikiData with NEs to then train contextual word embeddings similar to BERT. Experimental results show that ERNIE significantly outperforms BERT on knowledge-driven tasks such as relation classification. It is also possible to learn an improved word embedding by integrating human feedback [22] or by jointly exploiting a text corpus and a KG [2].

To the best of our knowledge, we are the first to explore the usage of LMs to **enhance common sense knowledge** in a KG. We asses the validity of our method by producing word embeddings from our improved KG and evaluating them on several semantic similarity tasks, which stem from the primary ConceptNet papers [28] and [29] and hence provide direct comparison to the initial results. Additionally, we assume that semantic similarity of word representations is a good indicator of improvement, as it has been shown that it influences other tasks, e.g. named entity disambiguation [9].

A related setting for improving existing KGs is **graph completion**, or link prediction, in which the goal is to automatically create edges between existing and new nodes of a given KG [3,26]. There exist approaches which successfully utilize BERT for the task of graph completion on ConceptNet [20] as well as WordNet and Freebase [33]. While this is in principle similar to our method, we set ourselves a different task: Where KG completion allows for enriching existing KGs with new nodes and relations, this is only effective when the base graph used for training the completion approaches already contains facts of high quality. Our aim, however, is to further improve the information contained in existing edges in the base KG.

4 Methodology

To transfer knowledge from a LM to a KG, we propose REWEIGHT, which consists of a *sentence construction* and a *weight generation* step.

4.1 Sentence Construction

Relation-to-Sentence Mapping. We want to evaluate the information contained in a KG by means of an LM. Thus, we first transform every edge $e \in E$ from the graph into a natural language sentence. We manually define a set of rules, which map the relations between graph nodes to sentences. For example, a *"DefinedAs"* relation between nodes **A** and **B** in ConceptNet is transformed to the sentence "**A** *is defined as* **B**". For most relations, such a simple transcription of the relation is sufficient. For some relation types, however, we observe that the LM reacts poorly to the direct transcription. We assume that this is due to the sparsity of sentences explicitly mentioning words such as *"antonym"* in their training data. Hence, we manually create transcriptions to better reflect natural language. Similarly, we observe that sentences are rated as more likely if all concepts are preceded by the indefinite article "a". For the full mapping we employ for the ConceptNet KG, we refer to the Supplementary Material.

Sentence Correction. Due to the simple transformation rules, sentences generated in the previous step may not always be grammatically correct. LMs like BERT, however, have been shown to encode both syntactic and semantic information [17]. Since we aim to use the LM for assessing the semantic content of the sentence, we would like to discard any influence of syntax. To achieve this, we employ an additional LM trained to improve the grammatical quality of sentences. We feed our rule-generated sentences into the grammar correction model, obtaining semantically equivalent sentences with improved syntax. Further details on the specific implementation used in this work is given in Sect. 5.

4.2 Weight Generation

After constructing a sentence for every edge $e \in E$ in the KG, we need to measure the sentences' meaningfulness. We use the perplexity of a pre-trained LM to assess whether the sentence and thus the relation contains a probable fact, assuming that a well-trained LM will assign a high perplexity to sentences describing questionable or uncommon relations.

Perplexity in Bi-directional LMs. Since [7] has shown that the common definition of perplexity is not applicable to bi-directional LMs such as BERT, we use their approximation to compute a score for each edge $e \in E$ in the graph: the perplexity $pp(e)$ for each sentence $\mathbf{s}_e = \langle w_{e,1}, \dots, w_{e,n_e} \rangle$ can be approximated as

$$pp(e) = \exp\left(-\frac{1}{n_e}\sum_{j=1}^{n_e} \log p(w_{e,j} | \langle w_{e,k} : k \neq j \rangle)\right), \tag{2}$$

where $\langle w_{e,k} : k \neq j \rangle$ denotes the context of $w_{e,j}$ in sentence $\mathbf{s}_e$.

We will now introduce two approaches to transform the resulting perplexities from their original range of $[1, +\infty)$ to the range of original KG weights $[0, \gamma_{\max}]$, where $\gamma_{\max}$ is the maximum weight of the original KG and $\tilde{\gamma}$ its median.

REWEIGHT$_{light}$. For a light variant of the REWEIGHT scheme, we obtain the weight for an edge $e \in E$ in the KG through transforming the perplexities obtained by the LM into the range of the original KG edge weights through

$$\beta_{\mathrm{RWL}}(e) := \frac{\gamma_{\max}}{pp(e)} \tag{3}$$

where $\gamma_{\max}$ denotes the maximum weight in the original KG as noted above.

REWEIGHT$_{mod}$. Furthermore, we propose an adaptive version of REWEIGHT, making use of a parameter pp_b to separate sentences into reasonable and unreasonable ones. Let $pp_{\max}$ be the maximum perplexity obtained by feeding all edges $e \in E$ through the above pipeline, $pp_{\max} = \max_{e \in E} pp(e)$, and pp_b a parameter, which can be chosen freely. Then we define our REWEIGHT$_{\mathrm{mod}}$ weights as

$$\beta_{\mathrm{RWM}}(e) := \begin{cases} r(e), \text{ if } pp(e) < pp_b \\ u(e), \text{ otherwise} \end{cases} \tag{4}$$

with $r : [0, pp_b[\to]\tilde{\gamma}, \gamma_{\max}]$ producing new edge weights for reasonable sentences and $u : [pp_b, \infty[\to [0, \tilde{\gamma}]$ for uncommon relations. For both functions we will utilize an inverted perplexity, which limits the influence of very high values

$$pp^{\mathrm{inv}}(e) = \log_{10}\left(\frac{pp_{\max}}{pp(e)}\right). \tag{5}$$

We feed this inverted perplexity into a min-max-scaling scheme separately for $r(e)$ and $u(e)$, to distribute scores evenly for both partitions. Thus, we set

$$u(e) := \frac{\tilde{\gamma} \cdot pp^{\mathrm{inv}}(e)}{pp_b^{\mathrm{inv}}}, \tag{6}$$

where $pp_b^{\text{inv}} := \log_{10}(\frac{pp_{\max}}{pp_b})$. Note that while the lower bound for our new edge weights could be set to any value, we choose 0 as the retrofitting method used in our experiments treats relations with edge weight 0 as non-existent, allowing our rating scheme to effectively remove edges with very low reasonability scores. For reasonable sentences we use a similar min-max-scaling,

$$r(e) := \tilde{\gamma} + (\gamma_{\max} - \tilde{\gamma}) \cdot \frac{pp^{\text{inv}}(e) - \max_{e \in E}(pp^{\text{inv}}(e)) + log_{10}(pp_b)}{log_{10}(pp_b)}. \tag{7}$$

The resulting weights are then used to replace the edge weights of the KG, yielding a linear mapping with control over the reasonability border pp_b.

5 Experimental Setting

We use the following setup throughout all our experiments: We apply REWEIGHT to ConceptNet to derive a new weighting for all relations between English concepts, leaving all relations that involve at least one non-English concept unchanged. We additionally follow [28] by removing uncommon concepts with less than three neighbors, and concepts that are not in any way connected to those in the vocabulary of the word embeddings used during Retrofitting.

For the sentence correction step of our approach, we use the BERT-based language correction model PIE [1], a current model performing strongly on the CoNLL-2014 shared task on grammatical error correction [21]. We additionally chose the PIE grammar checker since it is specifically tuned to improve sentences towards what BERT would consider to be syntactically correct, fitting the aim of mitigating the syntactic signal of sentences. The model takes as input sentences for correction and iteratively improves their grammar. In our experiments we use three correction iterations over each sentence, after which no further changes to the sentences were observed.

To obtain the perplexity of each sentence, we then use an openly available BERT LM adaptation[2] that calculates sentence perplexities based on the perplexity approximation for bidirectional LMs described in Sect. 4.2. We specifically chose a BERT model, since next to its state-of-the-art performance on many natural language tasks, BERT has also been shown to contain a certain amount of world knowledge [31]. The BERT model used in our experiments is the BERT-large (whole word masked) model.

5.1 Evaluation Task

As highlighted in Sect. 2.2, we extrinsically evaluate the weights determined by REWEIGHT by deriving word embeddings from our modified ConceptNet using the expanded retrofitting algorithm described in Sect. 2.3. With retrofitting using all weights in the KG to transform the embedding space, we use the relatedness scores between many words in this space to measure how well the information

[2] https://github.com/xu-song/bert-as-language-model.

in the KG enriches the embedding space. Comparing the results to embeddings obtained through the base graph (with identical structure) then factors out the impact of the general graph structure and yields an automatic evaluation scheme that highlights the quality of the edge weights in the entire graph. In order to enable a direct comparison of our modified weights to the original ones, we use the same setup as [28], the only difference being that we apply Retrofitting to our REWEIGHTed ConceptNet instead of the original. Since the resulting embeddings are a combination of ConceptNet NumberBatch and BERT, we name them *ConceptNet NumBERTbatch*.

Where not otherwise noted, we employ $\text{REWEIGHT}_{\text{mod}}$ with the following parameters: For ConceptNet we find that the median and maximum of original weights is $\tilde{\gamma} = 1$ and $\gamma_{\max} = 50$, respectively (cf. Sect. 2). After inspecting perplexities of generated sentences, we set the perplexity border value to $pp_b = 100$, which will be validated later in Sect. 6.2. We also follow [28] in assessing the quality of the embeddings by calculating the cosine similarity of words in the embedding space and comparing the results to human intuition through Spearman correlation for several word similarity and relatedness datasets.

5.2 Evaluation Datasets

We use the following established semantic relatedness datasets for evaluation: **MEN3000** [5] consists of 3000 word pairs and their similarity scores collected through crowdsourcing. Scores of the dataset are distributed between 0–50. Additionally, this dataset contains a development- and test-split of 2000 and 1000 word pairs respectively. We report our main results on the full 3000 word pairs, while using only the development set for some additional experiments. **Rare Words** (RW) [19] contains 2034 word pairs of words with low occurrence counts in a Wikipedia text corpus. Each word pair is assigned a similarity score by ten human annotators. The pair scores are defined between 0 and 10. For ablation studies, we employ a development set of 1356 word pairs (RW_{dev}). **MTurk-771** [13] contains 771 word pairs with their relatedness scores. The dataset aims to cover different types of relatedness (e.g. synonymy, meronymy, etc.). The scores are defined between 1–5. **WS353** [12] consists of 353 word pairs with human relatedness scores distributed between 0 and 10. **Semeval17-2a** [6] consists of 500 word pairs, with scores ranging from 0 to 4. The pairs contain named entities and multi-word expressions. The dataset was designed to cover different domains (e.g. Biology, Education, etc.). **SimLex999** [16] contains 999 word pairs. Human annotators were instructed to differentiate between similarity and relatedness, rating word pairs purely on their similarity. SimLex999 has been created to evaluate how well models asses similarity of word pairs rather than relatedness.

On some of the described, widely used datasets, small sample size does not allow for showing significance when comparing to an already strong baseline. Hence, we follow [28] by calculating results on many different datasets, showing significance on the larger and the overall trend on all datasets.

5.3 Baselines

We evaluate our approach against two baselines. As a first baseline, we join several pretrained word embeddings (word2vec, GloVe, FastText) through truncated SVD [28], which achieves stronger performance than the base embeddings individually. The second baseline is provided by the ConceptNet NumberBatch embeddings [28], which are constructed from ConceptNet in the same procedure we use for our NumBERTbatch embeddings, joining several pretrained word embeddings (word2vec, GloVe, FastText) and Retrofitting them to ConceptNet.

Table 1. Spearman correlation of embeddings generated through retrofitting with different KGs on multiple word similarity datasets. Significant difference to NB_{orig} through Fischer's z-transformation with $^{\dagger}p < 0.01$, $^{\S}p < 0.05$.

Group	Embedding	MEN 3000	RW	MTurk	WS353	SemEval	SimLex	Average
Baseline	Joint	0.852	0.565	0.782	0.803	0.645	0.519	0.694
	NB_{orig}	0.872	0.630	0.822	0.833	0.779	**0.633**	0.762
Ours	$NBERT_{light}$	0.877	†**0.663**	0.827	0.840	0.783	**0.633**	**0.770**
	NBERT	†**0.881**	§0.651	**0.828**	**0.845**	0.780	0.618	0.767
Other LMs	$NBERT_{base}$	0.873	0.644	0.822	0.833	**0.784**	0.625	0.764
	w/o grammar	§0.879	§0.650	**0.828**	0.843	0.774	0.624	0.766

6 Results

In this section, we report our main experimental results in comparison to the two baselines, as well as an ablation study evaluating different variations of our proposed measure REWEIGHT. Table 1 contains all main results from this section, which we will address in the course of the section.

6.1 NumBERTbatch Embeddings

We compare the NumBERTbatch embeddings resulting from our REWEIGHTed KG to the performance of the original NumberBatch and the joint word embeddings without retrofitting. We additionally evaluate $REWEIGHT_{light}$, generating $NumBERTbatch_{light}$ embeddings. The results for these settings are shown in the first two blocks of Table 1. With both weighting schemes, we obtain consistent improvements over the already strong original NumberBatch on multiple datasets, especially showing significant improvements on the large MEN3000 and Rare Words (RW) datasets. This suggests that our method is capable of improving the knowledge aggregated in a KG. It is interesting to note that, while both schemes improve the overall performance over the baselines, they seem to present different focuses, with one improving more strongly on MEN3000 and the other on Rare Words. Another interesting observation is that on SimLex, a dataset tailored to semantic similarity (as opposed to relatedness), NumBERT-batch performs worse than the original. This is not unexpected, since we do not enforce a distinction between relatedness and similarity. It would be an interesting task for future work to evaluate whether the performance on SimLex can be improved by focusing on relations describing similarity, such as "SimilarTo".

6.2 Ablation Study

In order to gain further insights into the performance of our approach, we conduct a deeper investigation, analyzing the influence of different hyper-parameter choices and model variations on the performance of our method.

Varying the Perplexity Border pp_b. First, we investigate the influence of the perplexity border pp_b for REWEIGHT$_{\text{mod}}$ (the maximum perplexity of a sentence that is considered to be "reasonable"), varying pp_b in the range from 50 to 1000. We find that most values for pp_b do not have a large influence on the results and refer to the supplementary material for details. Choosing higher values of pp_b leads to slight loss of performance, while still consistently remaining above the original graph. This matches our intuition, since for very high values of pp_b even sentences that the LM deems improbable receive somewhat high scores. Thus the separation between more and less reasonable sentences is weakened.

Clipping Outliers. As a next step, we test the impact that possible outliers (i.e., sentences with extremely high perplexity) may have on our weighting scheme. For this, we define an upper bound pp_c for the perplexity of generated sentences, setting $pp_i = \min(pp_i, pp_c)$ for all sentences. Results of applying REWEIGHT$_{\text{mod}}$ to ConceptNet with different upper bounds show no statistically significant changes compared to not using any upper bound. For details, we again refer to the supplementary material.

Trimming Extreme Weights. To investigate how much information is contained within the edges that received particularly low (high) weights during our re-weighting, we experiment with setting all weights below (above) a given threshold to 0, thus removing the information of these edges during retrofitting. We expect removing edges with low weights to only have a small influence on the results (since these are not particularly important), while removing highly weighted edges having a more serious impact. The results of the experiment support our hypothesis: Removing edges with high weights has much more impact on the overall performance than removing edges with small weights. Details are provided in the supplementary material.

Changing the LM. In order to investigate the influence of the LM used during the REWEIGHT process, we experiment with using the smaller *BERT-base* model instead of *BERT-large*. With the *BERT-base* model containing 110M parameters, significantly fewer than the 340M parameters of *BERT-large*, we expect it to encode less knowledge, leading to a lower performance when used with

REWEIGHT$_{\text{mod}}$. The results in Table 1 under $NBERT_{base}$ show a considerable loss of performance with the use of the smaller LM, with performance on most datasets being only slightly above NB$_{\text{orig}}$, which uses the original ConceptNet.

Table 2. Spearman correlation of embeddings generated through retrofitting. Different KGs used for retrofitting, as well as KGs with shuffled and rescaled edge weights.

Group	Embedding	MEN 3000	RW	MTurk	WS353	SemEval	SimLex	Average
Scaling	lim = 10	0.877	0.612	0.824	0.839	0.779	0.617	0.758
	lim = 15	0.875	0.617	0.823	0.839	0.780	0.622	0.759
Shuffling	R-NB$_{orig}$	0.871	0.641	0.821	0.832	0.778	0.625	0.761
	R-EN NB$_{orig}$	0.870	0.643	0.821	0.831	0.780	0.631	0.763
	R-NBERT	0.867	0.628	0.814	0.829	0.768	0.608	0.752
	R-EN NBERT	0.871	0.617	0.816	0.833	0.774	0.605	0.753
Other KGs	WebChild	0.850	0.507	0.781	0.803	0.674	0.529	0.691
	WCBERT	0.847	0.514	0.770	0.805	0.678	0.510	0.687
	Yago	0.835	0.391	0.739	0.792	0.670	0.550	0.663
	YagoBERT	0.829	0.393	0.734	0.783	0.665	0.542	0.658

Removing Grammar Correction. As a final experiment, we want to show that the grammar correction step is necessary for our model. We therefore apply the REWEIGHT$_{\text{mod}}$ process without the PIE grammar checker. Results in the final column of Table 1 show a slight decrease in performance across all datasets. This suggests that the grammar correction step can indeed help to reduce the influence of *syntactical* signals on the performance, therefore increasing the weight of the *semantic* signals that we want to use for our REWEIGHTing process.

7 Analysis

In this section, we provide an extensive analysis of how our method influences the KG's weights. To this end, we verify that the improvements are not due to lucky rescaling or reshuffling of the original weights and provide insight into the weight changes from the original ConceptNet to our REWEIGHTed version.

7.1 Assessing Added Information

This section aims at showing that the improvements from our REWEIGHTed graph are not only due to changing the underlying distribution of the weights in the graph, but that the LM actually adds useful information. To this end, we conduct two experiments: rescaling the weights of the original CN and reshuffling our modified weights.

Rescaling the Original Weights. To make sure that our method's improvements are not simply due to amplifying the weights in the original graph, we experiment with manual rescaling. Specifically, the weights of all edges between English concepts are scaled linearly between 0 and 50 through min-max scaling as follows:

$$\gamma \rightarrow \begin{cases} [0, 45] & \text{if } \gamma \leq lim \\ (45, 50] & \text{else} \end{cases} \tag{8}$$

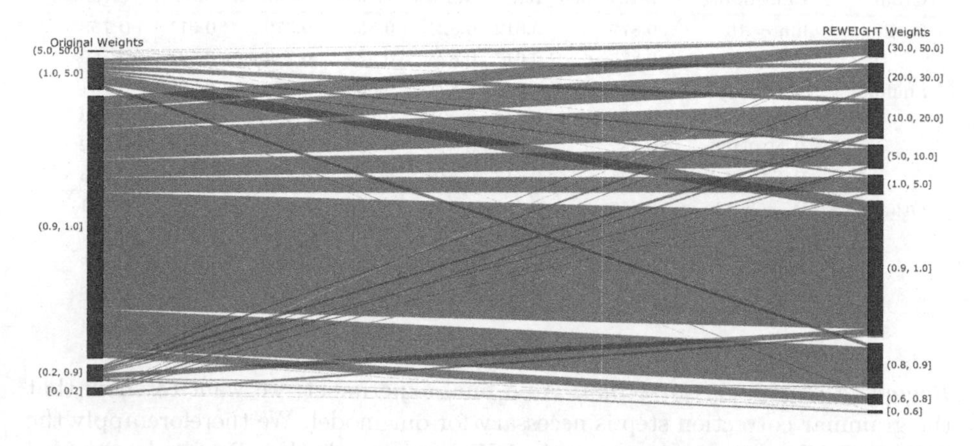

Fig. 2. ConceptNet weights before and after REWEIGHTing

where we try different values for lim in order to specifically highlight high scoring edges in the base KG. Results for the values $lim \in \{10, 15\}$ are reported in Table 2. While an increase in performance in comparison to the base graph is observable in most datasets for $lim = 10$, the results do not meet our weighted NumBERTbatch embeddings. Reasons for the improvement are further discussed when we investigate the changes made to the KG by our approach in Sect. 7.2.

Reshuffling the Modified Weights. This experiment serves as proof that our method does not simply change the distribution of the weights in a favorable way, without actually adding information from the LM to the graph. We take our improved KG and randomly shuffle the weights of either (a) all relations or (b) only English relations. If our method just luckily changed the distribution, this reshuffling would still lead to better results than the original KG weights. The resulting correlation coefficients after retrofitting can be observed in block *Shuffling* in Table 2. It can be seen that the randomized distribution of weights leads to lower performance on all datasets. Shuffling only the English part of the graph appears to retain a small amount of information from the remaining languages, yielding a slightly higher performance than shuffling the full graph. The strong decreases in performance indicate that the information contained in the edge weights of the graph are important for the task of semantic relatedness.

7.2 Changes to the KG

We further investigate the changes that REWEIGHT made to the KG. Figure 2 shows the transition of edge weights during the application of $\text{REWEIGHT}_{\text{mod}}$. We observe that $\text{REWEIGHT}_{\text{mod}}$ redistributes its weights more broadly over the value range, with considerably more high and low weights in comparison to the base graph. This might explain why additionally increasing the weight of important edges in the base graph leads to the improvements in correlation observed in Sect. 7.1. The major changes our approach appears to make to the weight distribution of the KG are increasing the weight of many relations in the interval $(0.9, 1]$, which shows an ability to highlight specific reasonable relations. $\text{REWEIGHT}_{\text{mod}}$ also slightly decreases the weight of many edges in the range $(1, 5]$, bringing e.g. "**mathematical** *SimilarTo* **unquestionable**" from 2.0 to 0.88. Additionally, for the edges that were rated very low in the original ConceptNet, we observe many slight weight increases, as well as many strong increases, with e.g. "**mathematics** *RelatedTo* **geometry**" being changed from very low (0.1) to very high (34.8) weights by $\text{REWEIGHT}_{\text{mod}}$.

On the other hand, we observe difficulties of the approach on relations that include highly specific concepts such as "anthrax". Since these concepts do not appear in the vocabulary of the BERT LM, they are assessed on character- and substring-level which causes higher perplexity scores than known concepts. Due to this, highly specific relations such as "**anthrax** *IsA* **disease**" are changed from high (2.8) to low scores (0.9) in spite of containing reasonable information. This suggests possible further improvements of the approach through assessing out-of-vocabulary concepts separately, which we leave as future work.

7.3 Choice of KG

REWEIGHT can be applied to improve the weights in any KG. Our previous experiments have focused on ConceptNet, one of the most prevalent common sense KGs being employed on a variety of application scenarios [27,28,37]. In this section, we evaluate the suitability of REWEIGHT to derive new weights for two other well-known KGs, YAGO and WebChild. As a preprocessing step, we aggregate all scores for relations that occur several times between the same concepts, creating a unique relation between the concepts with summed score. We then use the KGs with original weights for retrofitting, reporting our results in Table 2. We find that retrofitting with either WebChild or YAGO does not achieve an improvement over the original joint embeddings (*Joint* in Table 1). We evaluate both KGs further, but find that neither weighting their edges with REWEIGHT, nor any other modifications we tried (i.e., manually scaling edge weights, removing entire subgraphs, and removing uncommon concepts) manage to improve on our baselines.

We therefore conclude that the application of retrofitting to WebChild and YAGO does improve word embeddings on semantic relatedness. While this may be caused by the Retrofitting task itself, we also make the following observations concerning the structure of the graphs: WebChild strongly represents structured knowledge about activities (e.g. *drive a car*) and object properties (e.g. *hasSize*), while relations between concepts are only represented through part-whole relations (e.g. *isMemberOf*, *partOf*) and comparison relations (e.g. *largerThan*). The YAGO Taxonomy builds hierarchical information of *isA* relations between concepts. Although these relations contain important knowledge for word relatedness, the relations in both KGs are focused on hierarchical connections between concepts, which appear to carry less information for the semantic relatedness datasets compared to the rich relations in ConceptNet. Since our method only improves the weights of the edges and is not capable of changing the structure of the graph, it may thus be unsuitable to improve the performance of WebChild and YAGO for our semantic similarity tasks.

8 Conclusion

In this paper, we have proposed REWEIGHT, a pipeline for enriching structured common sense KGs with information contained in LMs through converting KG relations to natural language sentences and rating their reasonability. For this, we introduced a mapping of KG edges to natural sentences, and assessed the semantic reasonability of the sentences by calculating their perplexity with an LM. We then introduced a scheme for transforming the resulting perplexities to edge weights in the range of the original KG weights, yielding an enriched KG containing additional information through knowledge from an LM.

We applied REWEIGHT on the relatedness-oriented common sense KG ConceptNet, investigating whether the world knowledge contained in the BERT LM can be used to improve the information contained in the KG for the task of semantic relatedness. To evaluate the performance of the enriched KG, we employed the retrofitting setting of [28], using the KG as additional information to improve existing word embeddings and evaluating the resulting embeddings on multiple semantic relatedness datasets.

Our results show that the BERT LM can be used to further improve the already strongly performing ConceptNet NumberBatch across all evaluated relatedness datasets. In an extended investigation we found that BERT managed to assess the semantic reasonability of ConceptNet relations well, giving high weights to edges with essential information for use in improving existing word embeddings.

Overall, our results uncover promising opportunities for improving existing KGs with unstructured information contained in LMs. Through representing edges in KGs as natural sentences, many established techniques in Natural Language Processing (NLP) may be used to automatically improve the information contained in KGs. Additionally, it may be possible to add information from specialized LMs into a KG, which in turn can be used as a source of background knowledge for domain dependent tasks [15]. One further opportunity for future work may be the careful construction of sentences from edges, aiming to eliminate any biases the employed NLP approaches may have towards sentence construction, i.e. through employing different and varying sentence templates.

References

1. Awasthi, A., Sarawagi, S., Goyal, R., Ghosh, S., Piratla, V.: Parallel iterative edit models for local sequence transduction. In: 2019 EMNLP-IJCNLP (2019)
2. Bollegala, D., Alsuhaibani, M., Maehara, T., Kawarabayashi, K.I.: Joint word representation learning using a corpus and a semantic lexicon. In: Thirtieth AAAI Conference on Artificial Intelligence (2016)
3. Bosselut, A., Rashkin, H., Sap, M., Malaviya, C., Çelikyilmaz, A., Choi, Y.: COMET: commonsense transformers for automatic knowledge graph construction. In: ACL (2019)
4. Bouraoui, Z., Camacho-Collados, J., Schockaert, S.: Inducing relational knowledge from BERT. In: AAAI 2019 (2019)
5. Bruni, E., Tran, N.K., Baroni, M.: Multimodal distributional semantics. J. Artif. Intell. Res. **49**, 1–47 (2014)
6. Camacho-Collados, J., Pilehvar, M.T., Collier, N., Navigli, R.: Semeval-2017 task 2: multilingual and cross-lingual semantic word similarity. In: 11th International Workshop on Semantic Evaluation (SemEval-2017), pp. 15–26 (2017)
7. Chen, X., Liu, X., Ragni, A., Wang, Y., Gales, M.J.: Future word contexts in neural network language models. In: 2017 IEEE Automatic Speech Recognition and Understanding Workshop (ASRU), pp. 97–103. IEEE (2017)
8. Devlin, J., Chang, M.W., Lee, K., Toutanova, K.: BERT: pre-training of deep bidirectional transformers for language understanding. In: 2019 Conference of the North American Chapter of the Association for Computational Linguistics (2018)
9. Eshel, Y., Cohen, N., Radinsky, K., Markovitch, S., Yamada, I., Levy, O.: Named entity disambiguation for noisy text. In: Proceedings of the 21st Conference on Computational Natural Language Learning (CoNLL 2017), pp. 58–68 (2017)
10. Faruqui, M., Dodge, J., Jauhar, S.K., Dyer, C., Hovy, E., Smith, N.A.: Retrofitting word vectors to semantic lexicons. In: Proceedings of the 2015 Conference of the North American Chapter of the Association for Computational Linguistics: Human Language Technologies, pp. 1606–1615 (2015)
11. Fensel, D., et al.: Knowledge Graphs: Methodology, Tools and Selected Use Cases. Springer, Switzerland (2020). https://doi.org/10.1007/978-3-030-37439-6
12. Finkelstein, L., et al.: Placing search in context: the concept revisited. In: Proceedings of the 10th International Conference on World Wide Web, pp. 406–414 (2001)
13. Halawi, G., Dror, G., Gabrilovich, E., Koren, Y.: Large-scale learning of word relatedness with constraints. In: Proceedings of the 18th ACM SIGKDD International Conference on Knowledge Discovery and Data Mining, pp. 1406–1414 (2012)
14. Havasi, C., Speer, R., Alonso, J.: ConceptNet 3: a flexible, multilingual semantic network for common sense knowledge. In: Recent Advances in Natural Language Processing, pp. 27–29. Citeseer (2007)
15. Hettinger, L., Dallmann, A., Zehe, A., Niebler, T., Hotho, A.: Claire at SemEval-2018 task 7: classification of relations using embeddings. In: 12th International Workshop on Semantic Evaluation (2018)
16. Hill, F., Reichart, R., Korhonen, A.: SimLex-999: evaluating semantic models with (genuine) similarity estimation. Comput. Linguist. **41**(4), 665–695 (2015)
17. Jawahar, G., Sagot, B., Seddah, D.: What does BERT learn about the structure of language? In: Association for Computational Linguistics (2019)
18. Lengerich, B., Maas, A., Potts, C.: Retrofitting distributional embeddings to knowledge graphs with functional relations. In: Proceedings of the 27th International Conference on Computational Linguistics, pp. 2423–2436 (2018)

19. Luong, M.T., Socher, R., Manning, C.D.: Better word representations with recursive neural networks for morphology. In: Proceedings of the Seventeenth Conference on Computational Natural Language Learning, pp. 104–113 (2013)
20. Malaviya, C., Bhagavatula, C., Bosselut, A., Choi, Y.: Commonsense knowledge base completion with structural and semantic context. In: AAAI (2020)
21. Ng, H.T., Wu, S.M., Briscoe, T., Hadiwinoto, C., Susanto, R.H., Bryant, C.: The CoNLL-2014 shared task on grammatical error correction. In: 18th Conference on Computational Natural Language Learning: Shared Task, pp. 1–14 (2014)
22. Niebler, T., Becker, M., Pölitz, C., Hotho, A.: Learning semantic relatedness from human feedback using relative relatedness learning. In: 16th International Semantic Web Conference (ISWC) (2017)
23. Petroni, F., et al.: Language models as knowledge bases? In: 2019 Conference on Empirical Methods in Natural Language Processing (EMNLP), pp. 2463–2473, January 2019
24. Radford, A., Wu, J., Child, R., Luan, D., Amodei, D., Sutskever, I.: Language models are unsupervised multitask learners. OpenAI Blog **1**(8), 9 (2019)
25. Rebele, T., Suchanek, F., Hoffart, J., Biega, J., Kuzey, E., Weikum, G.: YAGO: a multilingual knowledge base from wikipedia, wordnet, and geonames. In: Groth, P., et al. (eds.) ISWC 2016. LNCS, vol. 9982, pp. 177–185. Springer, Cham (2016). https://doi.org/10.1007/978-3-319-46547-0_19
26. Sadeghi, A., Graux, D., Shariat Yazdi, H., Lehmann, J.: MDE: multiple distance embeddings for link prediction in knowledge graphs. In: ECAI (2020)
27. Sharifirad, S., Jafarpour, B., Matwin, S.: Boosting text classification performance on sexist tweets by text augmentation and text generation using a combination of knowledge graphs. In: 2nd Workshop on Abusive Language Online (ALW2) (2018)
28. Speer, R., Chin, J., Havasi, C.: ConceptNet 5.5: an open multilingual graph of general knowledge. In: Thirty-First AAAI Conference on Artificial Intelligence (2017)
29. Speer, R., Lowry-Duda, J.: ConceptNet at SemEval-2017 task 2: extending word embeddings with multilingual relational knowledge. In: Proceedings of the 11th International Workshop on Semantic Evaluation (SemEval-2017), pp. 85–89 (2017)
30. Tandon, N., De Melo, G., Weikum, G.: WebChild 2.0: fine-grained commonsense knowledge distillation. In: ACL 2017, System Demonstrations, pp. 115–120 (2017)
31. Xiong, W., Du, J., Wang, W.Y., Stoyanov, V.: Pretrained encyclopedia: weakly supervised knowledge-pretrained language model. In: International Conference on Learning Representations (2020)
32. Xu, C., et al.: RC-NET: a general framework for incorporating knowledge into word representations. In: 23rd ACM International Conference on Information and Knowledge Management, pp. 1219–1228 (2014)
33. Yao, L., Mao, C., Luo, Y.: KG-BERT: BERT for knowledge graph completion. In: arXiv preprint arXiv:1909.03193 (2019)
34. Yu, M., Dredze, M.: Improving lexical embeddings with semantic knowledge. In: Proceedings of the 52nd Annual Meeting of the Association for Computational Linguistics (Volume 2: Short Papers), pp. 545–550 (2014)
35. Zellers, R., Bisk, Y., Farhadi, A., Choi, Y.: From recognition to cognition: visual commonsense reasoning. In: Proceedings of the IEEE Conference on Computer Vision and Pattern Recognition, pp. 6720–6731 (2019)
36. Zhang, Z., Han, X., Liu, Z., Jiang, X., Sun, M., Liu, Q.: ERNIE: enhanced language representation with informative entities. In: Proceedings of the 57th Annual Meeting of the Association for Computational Linguistics, pp. 1441–1451 (2019)

37. Zhong, W., Tang, D., Duan, N., Zhou, M., Wang, J., Yin, J.: Improving question answering by commonsense-based pre-training. In: Natural Language Processing and Chinese Computing (2019)
38. Zhou, X., Zhang, Y., Cui, L., Huang, D.: Evaluating commonsense in pre-trained language models. In: AAAI (2020)

SHACL Satisfiability and Containment

Paolo Pareti[1(✉)], George Konstantinidis[1], Fabio Mogavero[2], and Timothy J. Norman[1]

[1] University of Southampton, Southampton, UK
{pp1v17,g.konstantinidis,t.j.norman}@soton.ac.uk
[2] Università degli Studi di Napoli Federico II, Napoli, Italy
fabio.mogavero@unina.it

Abstract. The *Shapes Constraint Language (SHACL)* is a recent W3C recommendation language for validating RDF data. Specifically, SHACL documents are collections of constraints that enforce particular shapes on an RDF graph. Previous work on the topic has provided theoretical and practical results for the validation problem, but did not consider the standard decision problems of *satisfiability* and *containment*, which are crucial for verifying the feasibility of the constraints and important for design and optimization purposes. In this paper, we undertake a thorough study of the different features of SHACL by providing a translation to a new first-order language, called **SCL**, that precisely captures the semantics of SHACL w.r.t. satisfiability and containment. We study the interaction of SHACL features in this logic and provide the detailed map of decidability and complexity results of the aforementioned decision problems for different SHACL sublanguages. Notably, we prove that both problems are undecidable for the full language, but we present decidable combinations of interesting features.

1 Introduction

The Shapes Constraint Language (SHACL) has been recently introduced as a W3C recommendation language for the validation of RDF graphs. A SHACL document is a collection of *shapes* which define particular constraints and specify which nodes in a graph should be validated against these constraints. The ability to validate data with respect to a set of constraints is of particular importance for RDF graphs, as they are schemaless by design. Validation can be used to detect problems in a dataset and it can provide data quality guarantees for the purpose of data exchange and interoperability.

Recent work has focused on defining precise semantics and implementations for validation of SHACL documents, in particular for the case of recursion [8]. In this paper, instead, we focus on the decision problems of satisfiability and containment for SHACL documents; problems which have not been previously investigated. Given a particular SHACL document, satisfiability is the problem of deciding whether there is an RDF graph which is validated by the document; we also investigate finite satisfiability, that is, whether there exists a valid graph

J. Z. Pan et al. (Eds.): ISWC 2020, LNCS 12506, pp. 474–493, 2020.
https://doi.org/10.1007/978-3-030-62419-4_27

of finite size. Containment studies whether a particular SHACL document is subsumed by a second one; that is, whether all graphs that are validated by the first are also validated by the second. We investigate whether these decision problems can be decided not only at the level of documents, but also for individual shapes (i.e. sets of constraints) within documents.

Satisfiability and containment are standard decision problems that have important applications in optimization and design. When integrating two datasets subject to two different SHACL documents, for example, it is important to know whether the two SHACL documents are in conflict with each other, or if one of them is subsumed by the other. At the level of shapes, an unsatisfiable shape constraint might not necessarily cause the unsatisfiability of a whole SHACL document, but it is likely an indication of a design error. Being able to decide containment for individual shapes offers more design choices to the author of a SHACL document, and it is a venue for optimization.

In this paper we focus on the *core constraint components* of SHACL [16] and we do not consider recursion. Validation under recursion is left unspecified in SHACL and, while different semantics have been proposed [8], we already show that even without it the language has undecidable satisfiability and containment. For a subset of the core constraint components and a restricted form of recursion (à la stratified negation), containment of individual shape constraints is shown to be decidable in [17]. This is achieved via reduction to description logic reasoning [3], reminiscent to our Theorem 5.

One of our main contributions is a comprehensive translation of SHACL into **SCL** , a new fragment of first-order logic extended with counting quantifiers and the transitive closure operator. To the best of our knowledge such a translation has not been attempted before. Our approach translates a SHACL document to an **SCL** equisatisfiable sentence, i.e., there is a valid RDF graph for the first iff there is a model for the second.

Distinct SHACL constructs translate to particular **SCL** features of different expressiveness. We identify eight such prominent features (such as counting quantifiers or transitive closure) that can be used on top of a base logic and study their interactions. On one hand, the full language is undecidable and, in fact, so are most fragments with just three or four features. On the other hand, our base language has decidable satisfiability and containment, and it is ExpTime-complete. We create a detailed map, in between these extremes, proving positive and negative results for many interesting combinations.

2 Background and Problem Definition

The core structure of the RDF data model is a graph whose nodes and edges are defined by a set of *triples*. A triple $\langle s, p, o \rangle$ identifies an edge with label p, called *predicate*, from a node s, called *subject*, to a node o, called *object*. The main type of entities that act as nodes and edges in RDF graphs are IRIs. We represent RDF graphs in Turtle syntax and by abbreviating IRIs using XML namespaces; the namespace sh refers to SHACL terms.

In an RDF graph, *literal* constants (representing datatype values) can only appear in the object position of a triple, while in *generalized* RDF [9] they can appear in any position. We will use the generalised model for simplicity. Most of our results apply to both data models and we will state clearly when this is not the case. We do not use variables in the predicate position in this paper and so we represent triples as binary relations in FOL. We use the atom $R(s, o)$ as a shorthand for $\langle s, R, o \rangle$. We use a minus sign to identify the *inverse* atom, namely $R^{-}(s, o) = R(o, s)$. We use the binary relation name isA to represent class membership triples $\langle s, \texttt{rdf:type}, o \rangle$ as isA(s, o).

```
:studentShape a sh:NodeShape ;
   sh:targetClass :Student ;
   sh:not :disjFacultyShape .
:disjFacultyShape a sh:PropertyShape ;
   sh:path (:hasSupervisor :hasFaculty);
   sh:disjoint :hasFaculty .
```

```
:Alex a :Student ;
   :hasFaculty :CS ;
   :hasSupervisor :Jane .
:Jane :hasFaculty :CS .
```

Fig. 1. A SHACL document (left) and a graph that validates it (right).

SHACL defines constraints that can validate RDF graphs [16]. A SHACL document is a set of *shapes*. A shape, denoted s:$\langle t, d \rangle$, has three main components: (1) a set of *constraints* which are used in conjunction, and hence referred to as a single constraint d; (2) a set of *target declarations*, referred to as *target definition* t, which provides a set of RDF nodes that are validated against d; and (3) a *shape name* s. One can think of t and d as unary queries over the nodes of G. Given a node n in a graph G, and a shape s:$\langle t, d \rangle$, we denote with $G \models t(n)$ the fact that node n that satisfies definition t, and $G \models d(n)$ denotes that a node n validates d in G. A graph G validates a shape s:$\langle t, d \rangle$, formally $G \models$ s:$\langle t, d \rangle$, iff every node in the target t validates the constraints d, that is, iff for all $n \in G$, if $G \models t(n)$ then $G \models d(n)$. An empty target definition is never satisfied while an empty constraint definition is always satisfied. A graph G validates a set of shape definitions, i.e. a SHACL document, M, formally $G \models M$, iff G validates all the shapes in M. Constraints might refer to other shapes. When a shape is referenced by another shape it can be handed down a set of *focus nodes* to validate, in addition to those from its own target definition. A shape is *recursive* when it references itself (directly or through other shapes). As mentioned, we focus on non-recursive SHACL documents using the SHACL core constraint components. Without loss of generality, we assume that shape names in a SHACL document do not occur in other SHACL documents or graphs.

The example SHACL document in Fig. 1 defines the constraint that, intuitively, all students must have at least one supervisor from the same faculty. The shape with name :studentShape has class :Student as a target, meaning that all members of this class must satisfy the constraint of the shape. The constraint definition of :studentShape requires the non-satisfaction of shape :disjFacultyShape, i.e., a node satisfies :studentShape if it does not satisfy

`:disjFacultyShape`. The `:disjFacultyShape` shape states that an entity has no faculty in common with any of their supervisors (the `sh:path` term defines a property chain, i.e., a composition of roles `:hasSupervisor` and `:hasFaculty`). A graph that validates these shapes is provided in Fig. 1. It can be made invalid by changing the faculty of `:Jane` in the last triple.

We now define the SHACL satisfiability and containment problems.

(i) **SHACL Satisfiability**: A SHACL document M is satisfiable iff there exists a graph G such that $G \models M$.
(ii) **Constraint Satisfiability**: A SHACL constraint d is satisfiable iff there exists a graph G and a node n such that $G \models d(n)$.
(iii) **SHACL Containment**: For all SHACL documents M_1, M_2, we say that M_1 is contained in M_2, denoted $M_1 \subseteq M_2$, iff for all graphs G, if $G \models M_1$ then $G \models M_2$.
(iv) **Constraint Containment**: For all SHACL constraints d_1 and d_2 we say that d_1 is contained in d_2, denoted by $d_1, \subseteq d_2$ iff for all graphs G and nodes n, if $G \models d_1(n)$ then $G \models d_2(n)$.

The satisfiability and containment problems for constraints can be reduced to SHACL satisfiability, as follows. A constraint d is satisfiable iff there exists a constant c, either occurring in d or a fresh one, such that the SHACL document corresponding to shape $\mathsf{s}{:}\langle t_\mathsf{c}, d\rangle$ is satisfiable, where t_c is the target definition that targets node c. Similarly, constraint d_1 is not contained in d_2 iff there exists a constant c, occurring in d_1, d_2 or a fresh one, such that the SHACL document corresponding to shape $\mathsf{s}{:}\langle t_\mathsf{c}, d'\rangle$ is satisfiable; $d'(x)$ is true whenever $d_1(x)$ is true and $d_2(x)$ if false. Thus, satisfiability and containment of constraints in a given SHACL fragment are decidable whenever SHACL satisfiability of that fragment is decidable, and have the same complexity upper bound. However, undecidability of SHACL satisfiability in a fragment does not necessarily imply undecidability for the two constraint problems; we leave this as an open problem.

3 A First Order Language for SHACL Documents

In this section we present a translation of SHACL into an equisatisfiable fragment of FOL extended with counting quantifiers and the transitive closure operator, called **SCL**. As discussed before, for a shape $\mathsf{s}{:}\langle t, d\rangle$ in a SHACL document M, t and d can be seen as unary queries. Intuitively, given a suitable translation q from SHACL into FOL, M is satisfiable iff the sentence $\bigwedge_{\mathsf{s}:\langle t,d\rangle \in M} \forall x.\ q(t(x)) \rightarrow q(d(x))$ is satisfiable, i.e., a node in the target definition of a shape needs to satisfy its constraint, for every shape. We subsequently present an approach that constructs such a sentence. This is reminiscent of [7], where a SHACL document M is translated into a SPARQL query that is true on graphs which however violate M. Intuitively, this query corresponds to sentence $\bigvee_{\mathsf{s}:\langle t,d\rangle \in M} \exists x.q(t(x)) \wedge \neg q(d(x))$, i.e. the negation of the sentence above. Nevertheless, several assumptions made in [7], such that ordering two values is not more complex than checking their equivalence, do not hold for the purposes of satisfiability and containment. We will use τ to denote the translation function from a SHACL document M to an **SCL** sentence $\tau(M)$, which is polynomial in the size of M and computable in polynomial time. We refer to our appendix[1] for the complete translations of τ and its inverse τ^-.

Next, we present our grammar of **SCL** in Definition 1. For simplicity, we assume that target definitions contain at most one target declaration, and that shapes referenced by other shapes have an empty target definition. This does not affect generality, as any shape can be trivially split in multiple copies: one per target declaration and one without any. Letters in square brackets in Definition 1 are annotations naming **SCL** features and thus are not part of the grammar. The top-level symbol φ in **SCL** corresponds to a SHACL document. This could be empty ($\top$), a conjunction of documents, or the translation of an individual shape. A sentence that corresponds to a single shape could have five different forms in **SCL**, depending on the target definition of the translated shape. These are summarized in Table 1, where $\tau_d(x)$ is the **SCL** translation of the constraint of the shape. In SHACL only four types of target declarations are allowed: (1) a particular constant c (node target), (2) instances of class c (class target), or (3)/(4) subjects/objects of a triple with predicate R (subject-of/object-of target). Our translation function gives explicit names to referenced shapes using the $\mathsf{hasShape}$ relation. We refer to the last component of the φ rule (i.e., $\forall x.\ \mathsf{hasShape}(x, \mathsf{s}) \leftrightarrow \psi(x)$) as a *referenced shape definition* and to its internal constant s as *referenced shape*.

Table 1. Translation of shape $\mathsf{s}{:}\langle t, d\rangle$ in SCL with respect to its target definition t.

Target declaration in t	Translation $\tau(\mathsf{s}{:}\langle t, d\rangle)$
Node target (node c)	$\tau_d(\mathsf{c})$ (equivalent form of: $\forall x.\ x = \mathsf{c} \rightarrow \tau_d(x)$)
Class target (class c)	$\forall x.\mathsf{isA}(x,\mathsf{c}) \rightarrow \tau_d(x)$
Subjects-of target (relation R)	$\forall x, y.R(x, y) \rightarrow \tau_d(x)$
Objects-of target (relation R)	$\forall x, y.R^-(x, y) \rightarrow \tau_d(x)$
No target declaration	$\forall x.\ \mathsf{hasShape}(x, \mathsf{s}) \leftrightarrow \tau_d(x)$

The non terminal symbol $\psi(x)$ corresponds to the subgrammar of the SHACL constraints. Within this subgrammar, $\top$ identifies an empty constraint, $x = \mathsf{c}$ a constant equivalence constraint and F a monadic filter relation (e.g. $F^{\mathrm{IRI}}(x)$, true iff x is an IRI). By *filters* we refer to the SHACL constraints about ordering, node-type, datatype, language tag, regular expressions and string length. Filters are captured by $F(x)$ and the O component. The C component captures qualified value shape cardinality constraints. The E, D and O components capture the equality, disjointedness and order property pair components. The $\pi(x, y)$ subgrammar models SHACL property paths. Within this subgrammar S denotes

[1] https://arxiv.org/abs/2009.09806.

sequence paths, A denotes alternate paths, Z denotes a zero-or-one path and T denotes a zero-or-more path.

Definition 1. The *SHACL* first-order language (**SCL**, for short) is the set of *sentences* (φ) and *one-variable formulas* ($\psi(x)$) built according to the following context-free grammar, where c and s are constants (from disjoint domains), F is a monadic-filter name, R is a binary-relation name, * indicates the transitive closure of the relation induced by $\pi(x, y)$, the superscript $\pm$ refers to a relation or its inverse, and $n \in \mathbb{N}$:

$$\begin{aligned}
\varphi &:= \top \mid \psi(\mathsf{c}) \mid \forall x\,.\, \mathsf{isA}(x, \mathsf{c}) \rightarrow \psi(x) \mid \forall x, y\,.\, R^{\pm}(x, y) \rightarrow \psi(x) \mid \varphi \wedge \varphi; \mid \\
&\quad \forall x.\ \mathsf{hasShape}(x, \mathsf{s}) \leftrightarrow \psi(x)\,; \\
\psi(x) &:= \top \mid x = \mathsf{c} \mid F(x) \mid \mathsf{hasShape}(x, \mathsf{s}) \mid \neg\psi(x) \mid \psi(x) \wedge \psi(x) \mid \\
&\quad \exists y.\, \pi(x, y) \wedge \psi(y) \mid \neg\exists y.\, \pi(x, y) \wedge R(x, y)\ \textbf{[D]} \mid \forall y.\, \pi(x, y) \leftrightarrow R(x, y)\ \textbf{[E]} \mid \\
&\quad \forall y, z\,.\, \pi(x, y) \wedge R(x, z) \rightarrow \sigma(y, z)\ \textbf{[O]} \mid \exists^{\geq n} y\,.\, \pi(x, y) \wedge \psi(y)\ \textbf{[C]}; \\
\pi(x, y) &:= R^{\pm}(x, y) \mid \exists z\,.\, \pi(x, z) \wedge \pi(z, y)\ \textbf{[S]} \mid x = y \vee \pi(x, y)\ \textbf{[Z]} \mid \pi(x, y) \vee \pi(x, y)\ \textbf{[A]} \mid \\
&\quad (\pi(x, y))^*\ \textbf{[T]}; \\
\sigma(x, y) &:= x <^{\pm} y \mid x \leq^{\pm} y.
\end{aligned}$$

To enhance readability, we define the following syntactic shortcuts:

(i) $\psi_1(x) \vee \psi_2(x) \doteq \neg(\neg\psi_1(x) \wedge \neg\psi_2(x))$;
(ii) $\pi(x, \mathsf{c}) \doteq \exists y.\pi(x, y) \wedge y = \mathsf{c}$;
(iii) $\forall y\,.\, \pi(x, y) \rightarrow \psi(y) \doteq \neg\exists y\,.\, \pi(x, y) \wedge \neg\psi(y)$.

```
select ?x where {
   ?x rdf:type :Student .
   filter not exists {
      ?x :hasSupervisor ?z .
      ?z :hasFaculty ?y .
      ?x :hasFaculty ?y . } }
```

$$\begin{aligned}
&(\forall x.\ \mathbf{isA}(x, \mathbf{:Student}) \rightarrow \\
&\quad \neg\mathbf{hasShape}(x, \mathbf{:disjFacultyShape})) \wedge \\
&(\forall x.\ \mathbf{hasShape}(x, \mathbf{:disjFacultyShape}) \leftrightarrow \\
&\quad \neg\exists y.\ (\ \exists z.\ R_{\mathbf{:hasSupervisor}}(x, z) \wedge \\
&\qquad R_{\mathbf{:hasFaculty}}(z, y) \wedge \\
&\qquad R_{\mathbf{:hasFaculty}}(x, y)\ )\ )
\end{aligned}$$

Fig. 2. Translation of the SHACL document from Fig. 1 into the SPARQL query that looks for violations (left) and into an **SCL** sentence (right).

Our translation τ results in a subset of **SCL** sentences, called *well-formed*. An **SCL** sentence is well-formed if for every occurrence of a referenced shape s there is a corresponding referenced shape definition sentence with the same s, and no referenced shape definitions are recursively defined. Figure 2 shows the translation of the document from Fig. 1, into a SPARQL query, via [7], and a well-formed **SCL** sentence, via τ.

To distinguish different fragments of **SCL**, Table 2 lists a number of *prominent* SHACL components, that is, important for the purpose of satisfiability. The language defined without any of these constructs is our *base* language, denoted

$\varnothing$. When using such an abbreviation of a prominent feature, we refer to the fragment of our logic that includes the base language together with that feature enabled. For example, SA identifies the fragment that only allows the base language, sequence paths and alternate paths.

The SHACL specification presents an unusual asymmetry in the fact that equality, disjointedness and order components forces one of their two path expressions to be an atomic relation. This can result in situations where the order constraints can be defined in just one direction, since only the less-than and less-than-or-equal property pair constraints are defined in SHACL. Our O fragment models a more natural order comparison that includes the $>$ and $\geq$ components. We instead denote with O' the fragment where the order relations in the $\sigma(x, y)$ subgrammar cannot be inverted.

Table 2. Relation between prominent SHACL components and **SCL** expressions.

Abbr	Name	SHACL component	Corresponding expression
S	Sequence paths	Sequence paths	$\exists z . \pi(x, z) \wedge \pi(z, y)$
Z	Zero-or-one paths	sh:zeroOrOnePath	$x = y \vee \pi(x, y)$
A	Alternative paths	sh:alternativePath	$\pi(x, y) \vee \pi(x, y)$
T	Transitive paths	sh:zeroOrMorePath sh:oneOrMorePath	$(\pi(x, y))^*$
D	Property Pair Disjointness	sh:disjoint	$\neg\exists y . \pi(x, y) \wedge R(x, y)$
E	Property pair equality	sh:equals	$\forall y . \pi(x, y) \leftrightarrow R(x, y)$
O	Property pair order	sh:lessThanOrEquals	$x \leq^{\pm} y$ and $x <^{\pm} y$
C	Cardinality constraints	sh:qualifiedValueShape sh:qualifiedMinCount sh:qualifiedMaxCount	$\exists^{\geq n} y . \pi(x, y) \wedge \psi(y)$ with $n \neq 1$

Relying on the standard FOL semantics, we define the satisfiability and containment for **SCL** sentences, as well as the closely related finite-model property, in the natural way.

SCL Sentence Satisfiability. An **SCL** sentence ϕ is satisfiable iff there exists a first-order structure Ω such that $\Omega \models \phi$.

SCL Sentence Containment. For all **SCL** sentences ϕ_1, ϕ_2, we say that ϕ_1 is contained in ϕ_1, denoted $\phi_1 \subseteq \phi_2$, iff, for all first-order structures Ω, if $\Omega \models \phi_1$ then $\Omega \models \phi_2$.

SCL Finite-model Property. An **SCL** sentence ϕ (resp. formula $\psi(x)$) enjoys the finite-model property iff whenever ϕ is satisfiable, it is so on a finite model.

In the following two subsections, we discuss SHACL-to-**SCL** satisfiability and containment. In this respect, we assume that filters are interpreted relations. In particular, we prove equisatisfiability of SHACL and **SCL** on models that we call *canonical*, that is, having the following properties: (1) the domain of the model is the set of RDF terms, (2) such a model contains built-in interpreted relations for filters, and (3) ordering relations $<^{\pm}$ and $\leq^{\pm}$ are the disjoint union of the total orders of the different comparison types allowed in SPARQL. In Sect. 3.3, we discuss an explicit axiomatization of the semantics of a particular set of filters in order to prove decidability of the satisfiability and containment problems for several **SCL** fragments in the face of these filters.

3.1 SHACL Satisfiability

A fine-grained analysis of the bidirectional translation between our grammar and SHACL, provided in the appendix, can lead to an inductive proof of equisatisfiability between the two languages. In particular, given a satisfiable SHACL document M which validates an RDF graph G, we can translate G and M into a canonical first-order structure I which models $\tau(M)$, thus proving the latter satisfiable, and vice versa. Intuitively, the structure I is composed of two substructures, Ω_G which corresponds to the translation of triples from G, and $\Omega_{G,M}$ which interprets the hasShape relation. These substructures, as explained below, have disjoint interpretations and we write $I = \Omega_G \cup \Omega_{G,M}$ to denote that I is the structure that considers the union of their domains and of their interpretations.

For any RDF predicate R in G, the structure Ω_G is a canonical structure that interprets the binary relation R as the set of all pairs $\langle s, o\rangle$ for which $\langle s, R, o\rangle$ is in G. The structure $\Omega_{G,M}$ interprets hasShape as the binary relation which, for all referenced shape definitions $\forall x.\ \mathsf{hasShape}(x, \mathsf{s}) \leftrightarrow \psi(x)$ in $\tau(M)$, it contains a pair $\langle c, s\rangle$ whenever Ω_G satisfies $\psi(c)$. We will call $\Omega_{G,M}$ the *shape definition model* of G and M. Since we do not address recursive shape definitions, this model always exists (corresponding to the *faithful total assignment* from [8]). Inversely, given a well-formed **SCL** sentence ϕ that is satisfiable and has a model I, by eliminating from I all references of hasShape and then transforming the elements of the relations to triples we get an RDF graph G that is valid w.r.t. the SHACL document $\tau^{-}(\phi)$.

Theorem 1. *For all SHACL documents M: (1) $\tau(M)$ is polynomially computable; (2) M is (finitely) satisfiable iff $\tau(M)$ is (finitely) satisfiable on a canonical model.*
For all well-formed **SCL** *sentences ϕ: (1) $\tau^{-}(\phi)$ is polynomially computable; (2) ϕ is (finitely) satisfiable on canonical models iff $\tau^{-}(\phi)$ is (finitely) satisfiable.*

3.2 SHACL Containment

Containment of two SHACL documents does not immediately correspond to the containment of their SCL translations. Given two SHACL documents M_1 and M_2 where M_1 is contained in M_2, there might exist a first-order structure I that models $\tau(M_1)$ but not $\tau(M_2)$. Notice, in fact, that structure $I = \Omega_G \cup \Omega_{G,M_1}$ models M_1, but that Ω_{G,M_1} does not necessarily model the referenced shape definitions of $\tau(M_2)$. Let $\delta(\phi)$ be the definitions of referenced shapes in an **SCL** sentence ϕ. Note that for a graph G and a SHACL document M the shape definition model $\Omega_{G,M}$ models $\delta(\tau(M))$. The reduction of SHACL containment into **SCL** is, therefore, as follows. This result also applies for containment over finite structures.

Theorem 2. *For all SHACL documents* M_1 *and* M_2*: (1)* $\delta(\tau(M_2))$ *is polynomially computable; (2)* $M_1 \subseteq M_2$ *iff* $\tau(M_1) \wedge \delta(\tau(M_2)) \subseteq \tau(M_2)$ *on all canonical models.*

Proof. ($\Rightarrow$) Let $M_1 \subseteq M_2$. If M_1 is not satisfiable the theorem holds. If M_1 is satisfiable, let G be any graph that validates M_1, and thus M_2. It holds that $\Omega_G \cup \Omega_{G,M_1}$ models $\tau(M_1)$ per Sect. 3.1, and $\Omega_G \cup \Omega_{G,M_2}$ models $\tau(M_2)$. It is easy to see that if $\Omega_G \cup \Omega_{G,M_1}$ models $\tau(M_1)$ the union of another hasShape interpretation over a disjoint set of shape names, i.e., $\Omega_G \cup \Omega_{G,M_1} \cup \Omega_{G,M_2}$ also models $\tau(M_1)$. Similarly $\Omega_G \cup \Omega_{G,M_1} \cup \Omega_{G,M_2}$ models $\tau(M_2)$ as well.

($\Leftarrow$) If M_1 is not contained in M_2, then there is a graph G that models M_1 but not M_2. Thus, $\Omega_G \cup \Omega_{G,M_1}$ models $\tau(M_1)$ but $\Omega_G \cup \Omega_{G,M_2}$ does not model $\tau(M_2)$. So we have that $\Omega_G \cup \Omega_{G,M_1} \cup \Omega_{G,M_2}$ models $\tau(M_1) \cup \delta(\tau(M_2))$ but not $\tau(M_2)$. □

Since our grammar is not closed under negation we cannot trivially reduce (finite) **SCL** containment to (finite) **SCL** satisfiability. Nevertheless, all positive (decidability and complexity) results are obtained by exhibiting inclusion of some **SCL** fragment into a particular (extension of a) fragment of first-order logic already studied in the literature that is closed under negation. Thus we can always solve the (finite) **SCL** containment problem for sentences $\phi_1 \subseteq \phi_2$ by deciding (finite) unsatisfiability of a sentence $\phi_1 \wedge \neg\phi_2$. Dually, the unsatisfiability of an **SCL** sentence ϕ is equivalent to $\phi \subseteq \bot$. Hence, containment and unsatisfiability have the same complexity.

3.3 Filter Axiomatization

Decidability of **SCL** satisfiability depends on the decidability of filters. In this section we present a decidable axiomatization that allows us to treat some filters as simple relations instead of interpreted ones. In particular, we do not consider `sh:pattern` which supports complex regular expressions, and the `sh:lessThanOrEquals` or `sh:lessThan` that are binary relations (the O and O' components of our grammar). All other features defined as filters in Sect. 3 are represented by monadic relations $F(x)$ of the **SCL** grammar.

The actual problem imposed by filters w.r.t. deciding satisfiability and containment is that each combination of filters might be satisfied by a limited number of elements (zero, if the combination is unsatisfiable). For example, the number of elements of datatype boolean is two, the number of elements that are literals is infinite and the number of elements of datatype integer that are greater than 0 and lesser than 5 is four.

Let a *filter combination* $\mathbb{F}(x)$ denote a conjunction of atoms of the form $x = \mathsf{c}$, $x \neq \mathsf{c}$, $F(x)$ or $\neg F(x)$, where c is a constant and F is a filter predicate. Given a filter combination, it is possible to compute the number of elements that can satisfy it. Let γ be the function from filter combinations to naturals returning this number. The computation of $\gamma(\mathbb{F}(x))$ for the monadic filters we consider is trivial as it boils down to determining: (1) the lexical space and compatibility of datatypes and node types (including those implied by language tag and order constraints); (2) the cardinality of intervals defined by order or string-length constraints; and (3) simple RDF-specific restrictions, e.g., the fact that each node has at most one datatype and language tag. Combinations of the previous three points are equally computable. Let $\mathbb{F}^{\varphi}$ be the set of filter combinations that can be constructed with the filters and constants occurring in a sentence φ. The filter axiomatization $\alpha(\varphi)$ of a sentence φ is the following conjunction (conjuncts where $\gamma(\mathbb{F}(x))$ is infinite are trivially simplified to $\top$).

$$\alpha(\varphi) = \bigwedge\nolimits_{\mathbb{F}(x) \in \mathbb{F}^{\varphi}} \exists^{\leq \gamma(\mathbb{F}(x))} x.\, \mathbb{F}(x)$$

Theorem 3. *An* **SCL** *sentence ϕ is satisfiable on a canonical model iff $\phi \wedge \alpha(\phi)$ is satisfiable on an uninterpreted model. Containment $\phi_1 \subseteq \phi_2$ of two* **SCL** *sentences on all canonical models holds iff $\phi_1 \wedge \alpha(\phi_1 \wedge \phi_2) \subseteq \phi_2$ holds on all uninterpreted models.*

Proof Sketch. We focus on satisfiability, since the proof for containment is similar. First notice that every canonical model I of φ is necessarily a model of $\phi \wedge \alpha(\phi)$. Indeed, by definition of the function γ, given a filter combination $\mathbb{F}(x)$, there cannot be more than $\gamma(\mathbb{F}(x))$ elements satisfying $\mathbb{F}(x)$, independently of the underlying canonical model. Thus, I satisfies $\alpha(\phi)$. Consider now a model I of $\phi \wedge \alpha(\phi)$ and let $I^{\star}$ be the structure obtained from I by replacing the interpretations of the monadic filter relations with their canonical ones. Obviously, for any filter combination $\mathbb{F}(x)$, there are exactly $\gamma(\mathbb{F}(x))$ elements in $I^{\star}$ satisfying $\mathbb{F}(x)$, since $I^{\star}$ is canonical. As a consequence, there exists a injection ι between the elements satisfying $\mathbb{F}(x)$ in I and those satisfying $\mathbb{F}(x)$ in $I^{\star}$. At this point, one can prove that $I^{\star}$ satisfies φ. Indeed, every time a value x, satisfying $\mathbb{F}(x)$ in I, is used to verify a subformula ψ of φ in I, one can use the value $\iota(x)$ to verify the same subformula ψ in $I^{\star}$. □

4 SCL Satisfiability

In this section we embark on a detailed analysis of the satisfiability problem for different fragments of **SCL**. Some of the proven and derived results are visualized in Fig. 3. The decidability results are proved via embedding into known decidable (extensions of) fragments of first-order logic, while the undecidability ones are obtained through reductions from the domino problem. Since we are not considering filters explicitly, but via axiomatization, the only interpreted relations are the equality and the orderings.

For the sake of space and readability, the map depicted in the figure is not complete *w.r.t.* two aspects. First, it misses few fragments whose decidability can be immediately derived via inclusion into a more expressive decidable fragment,

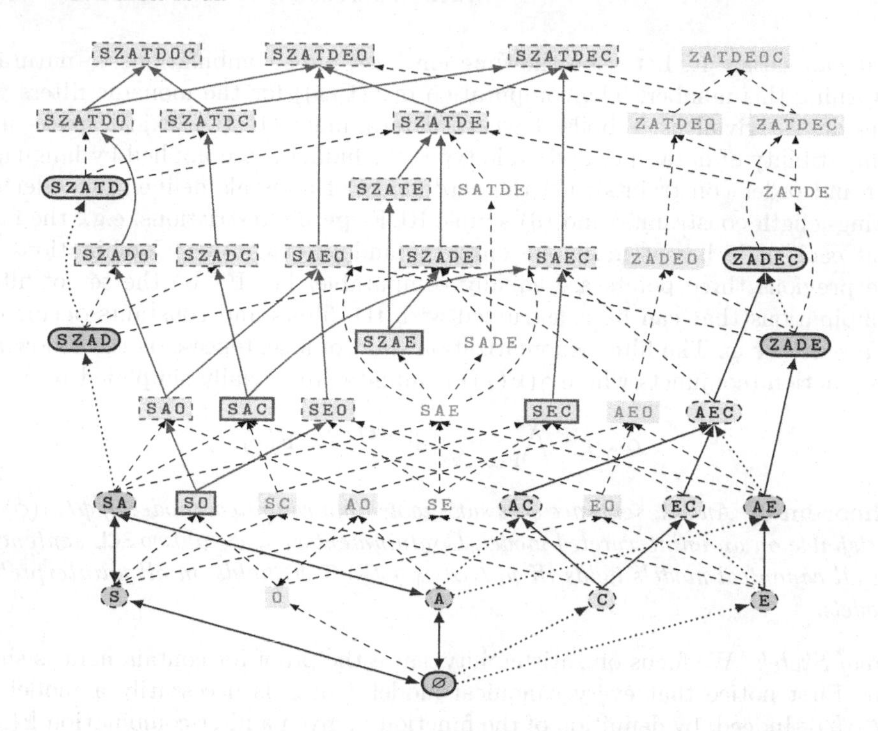

Fig. 3. Decidability and complexity map of **SCL**. Round (blue) and square (red) nodes denote decidable and undecidable fragments, respectively. Solid borders on nodes correspond to theorems in this paper, while dashed borders are implied results. Directed edges indicate inclusion of fragments, while bidirectional edges denote polynomial-time reducibility. Solid edges are preferred derivations to obtain tight results, while dotted ones leads to worst upper-bounds or model-theoretic properties. Finally, a light blue background indicates that the fragment enjoys the finite-model property, while those with a light red background do not satisfy this property. (Color figure online)

e.g., ZADEC or SZATD. Second, the rest of the missing cases have an open decidability problem. In particular, while there are several decidable fragments containing the T feature we do not know any decidable fragment with the O or O' feature. Notice that the undecidability results making use of the last two are only applicable to generalized RDF.

As first result, we show that the base language ∅ is already powerful enough to express properties writable by combining the S, Z, and A features. In particular, the latter one does not augment the expressiveness when the D and O features are considered alone.

Theorem 4. *There are semantic-preserving and polynomial-time finite-model-invariant satisfiability-preserving translations between the following* **SCL** *fragments: 1.* $\varnothing \equiv$ S $\equiv$ Z $\equiv$ A $\equiv$ SZ $\equiv$ SA $\equiv$ ZA $\equiv$ SZA*; 2.* D $\equiv$ AD*; 3.* O $\equiv$ AO*; 4.* DO $\equiv$ ADO.

Proof. To show the equivalences between the fourteen **SCL** fragments mentioned in the thesis, we consider the following first-order formula equivalences that represent few distributive properties enjoyed by the S, Z, and A features *w.r.t.* some of the other language constructs. The verification of their correctness only requires the application of standard properties of Boolean connectives and first-order quantifiers.

- **[S].** The sequence combination of two path formulas π_1 and π_2 in the body of an existential quantification is removed by nesting two quantifications, one for each π_i:

$$\exists y . (\exists z . \pi_1(x, z) \wedge \pi_2(z, y)) \wedge \psi(y) \equiv \exists z . \pi_1(x, z) \wedge (\exists y . \pi_2(z, y) \wedge \psi(y)).$$

- **[Z].** The Z path construct can be removed from the body of an existential quantification on a free variable x by verifying whether the formula ψ in its scope is already satisfied by the value bound to x itself:

$$\exists y . (x = y \vee \pi(x, y)) \wedge \psi(y) \equiv \psi(x) \vee \exists y . \pi(x, y) \wedge \psi(y).$$

- **[A].** The removal of the A path construct from the body of an existential quantifier or of the D and O constructs can be done by exploiting the following equivalences:

$$\exists y . (\pi_1(x, y) \vee \pi_2(x, y)) \wedge \psi(y) \equiv (\exists y . \pi_1(x, y) \wedge \psi(y)) \vee (\exists y . \pi_2(x, y) \wedge \psi(y));$$
$$\neg\exists y. (\pi_1(x, y) \vee \pi_2(x, y)) \wedge R(x, y) \equiv (\neg\exists y. \pi_1(x, y) \wedge R(x, y)) \wedge (\neg\exists y. \pi_2(x, y) \wedge R(x, y));$$
$$\forall y, z . (\pi_1(x, y) \vee \pi_2(x, y)) \wedge R(x, z) \rightarrow \sigma(y, z) \equiv (\forall y, z . \pi_1(x, y) \wedge R(x, z) \rightarrow \sigma(y, z)) \wedge (\forall y, z . \pi_2(x, y) \wedge R(x, z) \rightarrow \sigma(y, z)).$$

At this point, the equivalences between the fragments naturally follow by iteratively applying the discussed equivalences.

The removal of the Z and A constructs from an existential quantification might lead, however, to an exponential blow-up in the size of the formula due to the duplication of the body ψ of the quantification. To obtain polynomial-time finite-model-invariant satisfiability-preserving translations, we first construct from the given sentence φ a finite-model-invariant equisatisfiable sentence $\varphi^\star$. The latter has a linear size in the original one and all the bodies of its quantifications are just plain relations. Then, we apply the above described semantic-preserving translations to $\varphi^\star$ that, in the worst case, only leads to a doubling in the size. The sentence $\varphi^\star$ is obtained by iteratively applying to φ the following two rewriting operations, until no complex formula appears in the scope of an existential quantification. Let $\psi'(x) = \exists y . \pi(x, y) \wedge \psi(y)$ be a subformula, where $\psi(y)$ does not contain quantifiers other than possibly those of the S, D, and O features. Then: (i) replace $\psi'(x)$ with $\exists y . \pi(x, y) \wedge \mathsf{hasShape}(y, \mathsf{s})$, where s is a fresh constant; (ii) conjoin the resulting sentence with $\forall x.\ \mathsf{hasShape}(x, \mathsf{s}) \leftrightarrow \psi(x)$. The two rewriting operations only lead to a constant increase of the size and are applied only a linear number of times. □

It turns out that the base language ∅ resembles the description logic $\mathcal{ALC}$ extended with universal roles, inverse roles, and nominals [3]. This resemblance is exploited as the key observation at the core of the following result.

Theorem 5. *All* **SCL** *subfragments of* S Z A *enjoy the finite-model property. Moreover, the satisfiability problem is ExpTime-complete.*

Proof. The finite-model property follows from the fact that Theorem 8 states the same property for the subsuming language S Z A D. As far as the satisfiability problem is concerned, thanks to Item 1 of Theorem 4, we can focus on the base language $\varnothing$. It can be observed that the description logic $\mathcal{ALC}$ extended with inverse roles and nominals [3] and the language $\varnothing$ deprived of the universal quantifications at the level of sentences are linearly interreducible. Indeed, every existential modality $\exists R.C$ (*resp.*, $\exists R^{-}.C$) precisely corresponds to the **SCL** construct $\exists y \,.\, R(x, y) \wedge \psi_C(y)$ (*resp.*, $\exists y \,.\, R^{-}(x, y) \wedge \psi_C(y)$), where $\psi_C(y)$ represents the concept C. Moreover, every nominal n corresponds to the equality construct $x = \mathsf{c}_n$, where a natural bijection between nominals and constants is considered. Since the aforementioned description logic has an ExpTime-complete satisfiability problem [11,24], it holds that the same problem for all subfragments of S Z A is ExpTime-hard. Completeness follows by observing that the universal quantifications at the level of sentences can be encoded in the further extension of $\mathcal{ALC}$ with the universal roles [24], which has an ExpTime-complete satisfiability problem [23]. □

To derive properties of the Z A D E fragment, together with its sub-fragments (two of those – E and A E – are shown in Fig. 3), we leverage on the syntactic embedding into the two-variable fragment of first-order logic.

Theorem 6. *The* Z A D E*fragment of* **SCL** *enjoys the finite-model property. Moreover, the associated satisfiability problem is solvable in NExpTime.*

Proof. Via inspection of the **SCL** grammar one can notice that, by avoiding the S and O features of the language it is only possible to write formulas with at most two free variables [19]. For this reason, every Z A D E formula belongs to the two-variable fragment of first-order logic which is known to enjoy both the finite-model property and a NExpTime satisfiability problem [13]. □

The embedding used in the previous theorem can be generalized when the C feature is added to the picture. However, this additional expressive power does not come without a price since the complexity increases and the finite-model property is lost.

Theorem 7. *The* C *fragment of* **SCL** *does not enjoy the finite-model property and has a NExpTime-hard satisfiability problem. Nevertheless, the finite and unrestricted satisfiability problems for* Z A D E C *are NExpTime-complete.*

Proof. As for the proof of Theorem 6, one can observe that every Z A D E C formula belongs to the two-variable fragment of first-order logic extended with counting quantifiers. Such a logic does not enjoy the finite-model property [14], since it syntactically contains a sentence that encodes the existence of an injective non-surjective function from the domain of the model to itself. The C fragment of

SCL allows us to express the same property via the following sentence φ, thus implying the first part of the thesis:

$$\varphi \doteq \mathtt{isA}(0, \mathtt{c}) \wedge \neg\exists x \,.\, R^{-}(0, x) \wedge \forall x \,.\, \mathtt{isA}(x, \mathtt{c}) \rightarrow \psi(x);$$
$$\psi(x) \doteq \exists^{=1} y \,.\, (R(x, y) \wedge \mathtt{isA}(y, \mathtt{c})) \wedge \neg\exists^{\geq 2} y \,.\, R^{-}(x, y).$$

Intuitively, the first two conjuncts of φ force every model of the sentence to contain an element 0 that does not have any R-predecessor and that is related to c in the isA relation. In other words, 0 is not contained in the image of the relation R. The third conjunct of φ ensures that every element related to c *w.r.t.* isA has exactly one R-successor, also related to c in the same way, and at most one R-predecessor. Thus, a model of φ must contain an infinite chain of elements pairwise connected by the functional relation R.

By generalizing the proof of Theorem 5, one can notice that the C fragment of **SCL** semantically subsumes the description logic $\mathcal{ALC}$ extended with inverse roles, nominals, and cardinality restrictions [3]. Indeed, every qualified cardinality restriction $(\geq n\, R.C)$ (*resp.*, $(\leq n\, R.C)$) precisely corresponds to the **SCL** construct $\exists^{\geq n} y \,.\, R(x, y) \wedge \psi_C(y)$ (*resp.*, $\neg\exists^{\geq n+1} y \,.\, R(x, y) \wedge \psi_C(y)$), where $\psi_C(y)$ represents the concept C. Thus, the hardness result for C follows by recalling that the specific $\mathcal{ALC}$ language has a NExpTime-hard satisfiability problem [18,25]. On the positive side, however, the extension of the two-variable fragment of first-order logic with counting quantifiers has decidable finite and unrestricted satisfiability problems. Specifically, both can be solved in NExpTime, even in the case of binary encoding of the cardinality constants [20,21]. Hence, the second part of the thesis follows as well. □

Thanks to the axiomatization of (the subset of) filters given in Sect. 3.3, it is immediate to see that the ZADEC fragment extended with these filters is decidable as well. Indeed, although the sentence $\alpha(\varphi)$ is not immediately expressible in **SCL** it belongs to the two-variable fragment of FOL extended with counting quantifiers. Notice however that, since $\alpha(\varphi)$ might be exponential in the size of φ, this approach only leads to a (potentially) coarse upper bound. An attempt to prove a tight complexity result might exploit the SMT-like approach described in [2] for the LTL part of Strategy Logic. Indeed, one could think to extend the decision procedure for the above FOL fragment in such a way that the filter axiomatization is implicitly considered during the check for satisfiability.

For the S Z A D fragment, we obtain model-theoretic and complexity results via an embedding into the unary-negation fragment of first-order logic. When the T feature is considered, the same embedding can be adapted to rewrite S Z A T D into the extension of the above first-order fragment with regular path expressions. Unfortunately, as for the addition of the C feature to ZADE, we pay the price of losing the finite-model property. In this case, however, no increase of the complexity of the satisfiability problem occurs.

Theorem 8. *The* SZAD *fragment of* **SCL** *enjoys the finite-model property. The* STD *fragment does not enjoy the finite-model property. However, the finite and unrestricted satisfiability problems for* SZATD *are solvable in 2ExpTime.*

Proof. By inspecting the **SCL** grammar, one can notice that every formula that does not make use of the T, E, O, and C constructs can be translated into the standard first-order logic syntax, with conjunctions and disjunctions as unique binary Boolean connectives, where negation is only applied to formulas with at most one free variable. For this reason, every SZAD formula semantically belongs to the unary-negation fragment of first-order logic, which is known to enjoy the finite-model property [5,6].

Similarly every SZATD formula belongs to the unary-negation fragment of first-order logic extended with regular path expressions [15]. Indeed, the grammar rule $\pi(x, y)$ of **SCL**, precisely resembles the way the regular path expressions are constructed in the considered logic, when one avoids the test construct. Unfortunately, as for the two-variable fragment with counting quantifiers, this logic also fails to satisfy the finite-model property since it is able to encode the existence of a non-terminating path without cycles. The STD fragment of **SCL** allows us to express the same property, as described in the following. First of all, consider the ST path formula $\pi(x, y) \doteq \exists z \,.\, (R^{-}(x, z) \wedge (R^{-}(z, y))^{*})$. Obviously, $\pi(x, y)$ holds between two elements x and y of a model if and only if there exists a non-trivial R-path (of arbitrary positive length) that, starting in y, leads to x. Now, by writing the STD formula $\psi(x) \doteq \neg\exists y \,.\, (\pi(x, y) \wedge R(x, y))$, we express the fact that an element x does not belong to any R-cycle since, otherwise, there would be an R-successor y able to reach x itself. Thus, by ensuring that every element in the model has an R-successor, but does not belong to any R-cycle, we can enforce the existence of an infinite R-path. The STD sentence φ expresses exactly this property:

$$\varphi \doteq \mathtt{isA}(0, \mathtt{c}) \wedge \forall x \,.\, \mathtt{isA}(x, \mathtt{c}) \rightarrow (\psi(x) \wedge \exists y \,.\, (R(x, y) \wedge \mathtt{isA}(y, \mathtt{c}))).$$

On the positive side, however, the extension of the unary-negation fragment of first-order logic with arbitrary transitive relations or, more generally, with regular path expressions has decidable finite and unrestricted satisfiability problems. Specifically, both can be solved in 2ExpTime [1,10,15]. □

At this point, it is interesting to observe that the O feature allows us to express a very weak form of counting restriction which is, however, powerful enough to lose the finite-model property. For the proof of the following we refer to our appendix.

Theorem 9. **SCL** *fragments* O *and* EO' *do not satisfy the finite-model property.*

In the remaining part of this section, we show the undecidability of the satisfiability problem for five fragments of **SCL** through a semi-conservative reduction from the standard domino problem [4,22,26], whose solution is known to be Π_0^1-complete. A $\mathbb{N} \times \mathbb{N}$ tiling system $(T, \mathsf{H}, \mathsf{V})$ is a structure built on a non-empty set T of domino types, a.k.a. tiles, and two horizontal and vertical matching relations $\mathsf{H}, \mathsf{V} \subseteq T \times T$. The domino problem asks for a compatible tiling of the first quadrant $\mathbb{N} \times \mathbb{N}$ of the plane, *i.e.*, a solution mapping $\eth \colon \mathbb{N} \times \mathbb{N} \rightarrow T$ such that, for all $x, y \in \mathbb{N}$, both $(\eth(x, y), \eth(x+1, y)) \in \mathsf{H}$ and $(\eth(x, y), \eth(x, y+1)) \in \mathsf{V}$ hold true.

Theorem 10. *The satisfiability problems of the* SO, SAC, SEC, SEO', *and* SZAE *fragments of* **SCL** *are undecidable.*

Proof. The main idea behind the proof is to embed a tiling system into a model of a particular **SCL** sentence that is satisfiable if and only if the tiling system allows for an admissible tiling. The hardest part in the reduction consists in the definition of a satisfiable sentence all of whose models homomorphically contain the infinite grid of the tiling problem. In other words, this sentence should admit an infinite square grid graph as a minor of the model unwinding. Given that, the remaining part of the reduction can be completed in the base language $\varnothing$.

Independently of the fragment we are proving undecidable, consider the sentence

$$\varphi \doteq \bigvee_{t \in T} \mathtt{isA}(0, t) \wedge \bigwedge_{t \in T} \forall x \,.\, \mathtt{isA}(x, t) \rightarrow (\psi_T^t(x) \wedge \psi_G(x)).$$

Intuitively, this first states the existence of the point 0, the origin of the grid, labeled by some tile and then ensures the fact that all points x, that are labeled by some tile t, need to satisfy the two formulas $\psi_T^t(x)$ and $\psi_G(x)$. The first formula is used to ensure the admissibility of the tiling, while the second one forces the model to embed a grid.

$$\psi_T^t(x) \doteq \bigwedge_{t' \in T}^{t' \neq t} \neg \mathtt{isA}(x, t')$$
$$\wedge \left(\forall y \,.\, H(x, y) \rightarrow \bigvee_{(t,t') \in \mathsf{H}} \mathtt{isA}(y, t') \right) \wedge \left(\forall y \,.\, V(x, y) \rightarrow \bigvee_{(t,t') \in \mathsf{V}} \mathtt{isA}(y, t') \right)$$

The first conjunct of the $\varnothing$ formula $\psi_T^t(x)$ verifies that the point x is labeled by no other tile than t. The second part, instead, ensures that the points y on the right or above of x are labeled by some tile t' which is compatible with t, *w.r.t.* the constraints imposed by the horizontal H and vertical V relations, respectively.

At this point, we can focus on the formula $\psi_G(x)$ defined as follows:

$$\psi_G(x) \doteq (\exists y \,.\, H(x, y)) \wedge (\exists y \,.\, V(x, y)) \wedge \gamma(x).$$

The first two conjuncts guarantee the existence of an horizontal and vertical adjacent of the point x, while the subformula $\gamma(x)$, whose definition depends on the considered fragment of **SCL**, needs to enforce the fact that x is the origin of a square. That is, that going horizontally and then vertically or, vice versa, vertically and then horizontally the same point is reached. In order to do this, we make use of the two S path formulas $\pi_{HV}(x, y) \doteq \exists z \,.\, (H(x, z) \wedge V(z, y))$ and $\pi_{VH}(x, y) \doteq \exists z \,.\, (V(x, z) \wedge H(z, y))$. In some cases, we also use the SA path formula $\pi_D(x, y) \doteq \pi_{HV}(x, y) \vee \pi_{VH}(x, y)$ combining the previous ones. We now proceed by a case analysis on the specific fragments.

- **[SO]** By assuming the existence of a non-empty relation D connecting a point with its opposite in the square, *i.e.*, the diagonal point, we can say that all points reachable through π_{HV} or π_{VH} are, actually, the same unique point:

$$\gamma(x) \doteq \exists y \,.\, D(x,y) \\ \wedge \forall y, z \,.\, \pi_{HV}(x,y) \wedge D(x,z) \to y \le z \;\wedge\; \forall y, z \,.\, \pi_{HV}(x,y) \wedge D(x,z) \to y \ge z \\ \wedge \forall y, z \,.\, \pi_{VH}(x,y) \wedge D(x,z) \to y \le z \;\wedge\; \forall y, z \,.\, \pi_{VH}(x,y) \wedge D(x,z) \to y \ge z.$$

The S O formula $\gamma(x)$ ensures that relation D is non-empty and functional and that all points reachable via π_{HV} or π_{VH} are necessarily the one reachable through D.

- **[S A C]** By applying a counting quantifier to the formula π_D encoding the union of the points reachable through π_{HV} or π_{VH}, we can ensure the existence of a single diagonal point: $\gamma(x) \doteq \neg\exists^{\ge 2} y \,.\, \pi_D(x,y)$.
- **[S E C]** As for the S O fragment, here we use a diagonal relation D, which needs to contain all and only the points reachable via π_{HV} or π_{VH}. By means of the counting quantifier, we ensure its functionality:

$$\gamma(x) \doteq \neg\exists^{\ge 2} y.\, D(x,y) \wedge \forall y.\pi_{HV}(x,y) \leftrightarrow D(x,y) \wedge \forall y.\pi_{VH}(x,y) \leftrightarrow D(x,y).$$

- **[S E O']** This case is similar to the previous one, where the functionality of D is obtained by means of the O construct:

$$\gamma(x) \doteq \forall y, z \,.\, D(x,y) \wedge D(x,z) \to y \le z \\ \wedge \forall y \,.\, \pi_{HV}(x,y) \leftrightarrow D(x,y) \;\wedge\; \forall y \,.\, \pi_{VH}(x,y) \leftrightarrow D(x,y).$$

- **[S Z A E]** This proof is inspired by the one used for the undecidability of the guarded fragment extended with transitive closure [12]. This time, the functionality of the diagonal relation D is indirectly ensured by the conjunction of the four formulas $\gamma_1(x)$, $\gamma_2(x)$, $\gamma_3(x)$, and $\gamma_4(x)$ that exploit all the features of the fragment:

$$\gamma(x) \doteq \gamma_1(x) \wedge \gamma_2(x) \wedge \gamma_3(x) \wedge \gamma_4(x) \wedge \forall y \,.\, \pi_D(x,y) \leftrightarrow D(x,y), \text{ where}$$

$$\gamma_1(x) \doteq \forall y \,.\, \left(\bigvee_{i \in \{0,1\}} D_i(x,y) \right) \leftrightarrow D(x,y),$$

$$\gamma_2(x) \doteq \left(\bigvee_{i \in \{0,1\}} \neg\exists y.\, D_i(x,y) \right) \wedge \left(\bigwedge_{i \in \{0,1\}} \forall y.\, D_i(x,y) \to \exists z.\, D_{1-i}(y,z) \right),$$

$$\gamma_3(x) \doteq \bigwedge_{i \in \{0,1\}} \forall y \,.\, (x = y \vee D_i(x,y) \vee D_i^-(x,y)) \leftrightarrow E_i(x,y), \text{ and}$$

$$\gamma_4(x) \doteq \bigwedge_{i \in \{0,1\}} \forall y \,.\, (\exists z.(E_i(x,z) \wedge E_i(z,y))) \leftrightarrow E_i(x,y).$$

Intuitively, γ_1 asserts that D is the union of the two accessory relations D_0 and D_1, while γ_2 guarantees that a point can only have adjacents *w.r.t.* just one relation D_i and that these adjacents can only appear as first argument of the opposite relation D_{1-i}. In addition, γ_3 ensures that the additional relation E_i is the reflexive symmetric closure of D_i and γ_4 forces E_i to be transitive as well.

We can now prove that the relation D is functional. Suppose by contradiction that this is not case, *i.e.*, there exist values a, b, and c in the domain of the model of the sentence φ, with $b \neq c$ such that both $D(a,b)$ and $D(a,c)$ hold true. By the formula γ_1 and the first conjunct of γ_2, we have that $D_i(a,b)$ and $D_i(a,c)$ hold for exactly one index $i \in \{0,1\}$. Thanks to the full γ_2, we surely know that $a \neq b$, $a \neq c$, and neither $D_i(b,c)$ nor $D_i(c,b)$ can hold. Indeed, if $a = b$ then $D_i(a,a)$. This in turn implies $D_{1-i}(a,d)$ for some value d due to the second conjunct of γ_2. Hence, there would be pairs with the same first element in both relations, trivially violating the first conjunct of γ_2. Similarly, if $D_i(b,c)$ holds, then $D_{1-i}(c,d)$ needs to hold as well, for some value d, leading again to a contradiction. Now, by the formula γ_3, both $E_i(b,a)$ and $E_i(a,c)$ hold, but $E_i(b,c)$ does not. However, this clearly contradicts γ_4. As a consequence, D is necessarily functional.

Now, it is not hard to see that the above sentence φ (one for each fragment) is satisfiable if and only if the domino instance on which the reduction is based on is solvable. □

5 Conclusion

In this paper we define and study the decision problems of satisfiability and containment for SHACL documents and shape constraints. In order to do so, we introduce a complete translation between SHACL and **SCL**, a fragment of FOL extended with counting quantifiers and a transitive closure operator. Using these translations we lay out a map of SHACL fragments for which we are able to prove undecidability or decidability along with complexity results, for the satisfiability and containment problems. We also expose semantic properties and asymmetries within SHACL which might inform a future update of the specification. The satisfiability and containment problems are undecidable for the full SHACL specification. However, decidability can be achieved by restricting the usage of certain SHACL components, such as cardinality restrictions over property shapes or property paths. Nevertheless, the decidability of some fragments of SHACL remains an open question, worthy of further investigation.

References

1. Amarilli, A., Benedikt, M., Bourhis, P., Vanden Boom, M.: Query answering with transitive and linear-ordered data. In: IJCAI 2016, pp. 893–899 (2016)
2. Acar, E., Benerecetti, M., Mogavero, F.: Satisfiability in strategy logic can be easier than model checking. In: AAAI 2019, pp. 2638–2645 (2019)

3. Baader, F., Calvanese, D., McGuinness, D., Nardim, D., Patel-Scheider, P.: The Description Logic Handbook: Theory, Implementation, and Applications. Cambridge University Press, Cambridge (2003)
4. Berger, R.: The undecidability of the domino problem. MAMS **66**, 1–72 (1966)
5. ten Cate, B., Segoufin, L.: Unary negation. In: STACS 2011, pp. 344–355. LIPIcs 9, Leibniz-Zentrum fuer Informatik (2011)
6. ten Cate, B., Segoufin, L.: Unary negation. LMCS **9**(3), 1–46 (2013)
7. Corman, J., Florenzano, F., Reutter, J.L., Savković, O.: Validating SHACL constraints over a sparql endpoint. In: Ghidini, C., et al. (eds.) ISWC 2019. LNCS, vol. 11778, pp. 145–163. Springer, Cham (2019). https://doi.org/10.1007/978-3-030-30793-6_9
8. Corman, J., Reutter, J.L., Savković, O.: Semantics and validation of recursive SHACL. In: Vrandečić, D., et al. (eds.) ISWC 2018. LNCS, vol. 11136, pp. 318–336. Springer, Cham (2018). https://doi.org/10.1007/978-3-030-00671-6_19
9. Cyganiak, R., Wood, D., Markus Lanthaler, G.: RDF 1.1 concepts and abstract syntax. W3C Recommendation, W3C (2014). http://www.w3.org/TR/2014/REC-rdf11-concepts-20140225/
10. Danielski, D., Kieronski, E.: Finite satisfiability of unary negation fragment with transitivity. In: MFCS 2019, pp. 17:1–15. LIPIcs 138, Leibniz-Zentrum fuer Informatik (2019)
11. Donini, F., Massacci, F.: ExpTime tableaux for $\mathcal{ALC}$. AI **124**(1), 87–138 (2000)
12. Grädel, E.: On the restraining power of guards. JSL **64**(4), 1719–1742 (1999)
13. Grädel, E., Kolaitis, P., Vardi, M.: On the decision problem for two-variable first-order logic. BSL **3**(1), 53–69 (1997)
14. Grädel, E., Otto, M., Rosen, E.: Two-variable logic with counting is decidable. In: LICS 1997, pp. 306–317. IEEECS (1997)
15. Jung, J., Lutz, C., Martel, M., Schneider, T.: Querying the unary negation fragment with regular path expressions. In: ICDT 2018, pp. 15:1–15:18. OpenProceedings.org (2018)
16. Knublauch, H., Kontokostas, D.: Shapes constraint language (SHACL). W3C Recommendation, W3C (2017). https://www.w3.org/TR/shacl/
17. Leinberger, M., Seifer, P., Rienstra, T., Lämmel, R., Staab, S.: Deciding SHACL shape containment through description logics reasoning. In: Pan, J.Z., et al. (eds.) The Semantic Web - ISWC 2020, vol. 12506, pp. 366–383. Springer, Cham (2020)
18. Lutz, C.: An Improved NExpTime-Hardness Result for Description Logic $\mathcal{ALC}$ Extended with Inverse Roles, Nominals, and Counting. Technical Report, 05–05. Dresden University of Technology, Dresden, Germany (2005)
19. Mortimer, M.: On languages with two variables. MLQ **21**(1), 135–140 (1975)
20. Pratt-Hartmann, I.: Complexity of the two-variable fragment with counting quantifiers. JLLI **14**(3), 369–395 (2005)
21. Pratt-Hartmann, I.: The two-variable fragment with counting revisited. In: Dawar, A., de Queiroz, R. (eds.) WoLLIC 2010. LNCS (LNAI), vol. 6188, pp. 42–54. Springer, Heidelberg (2010). https://doi.org/10.1007/978-3-642-13824-9_4
22. Robinson, R.: Undecidability and nonperiodicity for tilings of the plane. IM **12**, 177–209 (1971)
23. Sattler, U., Vardi, M.Y.: The hybrid μ-calculus. In: Goré, R., Leitsch, A., Nipkow, T. (eds.) IJCAR 2001. LNCS, vol. 2083, pp. 76–91. Springer, Heidelberg (2001). https://doi.org/10.1007/3-540-45744-5_7
24. Schild, K.: A correspondence theory for terminological logics: preliminary report. In: IJCAI 1991, pp. 466–471 (1991)

25. Tobies, S.: The complexity of reasoning with cardinality restrictions and nominals in expressive description logics. JAIR **12**, 199–217 (2000)
26. Wang, H.: Proving theorems by pattern recognition II. BSTJ **40**, 1–41 (1961)

Contextual Propagation of Properties for Knowledge Graphs

A Sentence Embedding Based Approach

Pierre-Henri Paris[1(✉)], Fayçal Hamdi[1], Nobal Niraula[2], and Samira Si-said Cherfi[1]

[1] CEDRIC, Conservatoire National des Arts et Métiers, Paris, France
pierre-henri.paris@upmc.fr, {faycal.hamdi,samira.cherfi}@cnam.fr
[2] Nowa Lab, Madison, AL, USA
nobal@nowalab.com

Abstract. With the ever-increasing number of RDF-based knowledge graphs, the number of interconnections between these graphs using the *owl:sameAs* property has exploded. Moreover, as several works indicate, the identity as defined by the semantics of *owl:sameAs* could be too rigid, and this property is therefore often misused. Indeed, identity must be seen as context-dependent. These facts lead to poor quality data when using the *owl:sameAs* inference capabilities. Therefore, contextual identity could be a possible path to better quality knowledge. Unlike classical identity, with contextual identity, only certain properties can be propagated between contextually identical entities. Continuing this work on contextual identity, we propose an approach, based on sentence embedding, to find semi-automatically a set of properties, for a given identity context, that can be propagated between contextually identical entities. Quantitative experiments against a gold standard show that our approach achieved promising results. Besides, the use cases provided demonstrate that identifying the properties that can be propagated helps users achieve the desired results that meet their needs when querying a knowledge graph, i.e., more complete and accurate answers.

Keywords: RDF · Contextual identity · Property propagation · Knowledge graph · Linked data · Sentence embedding

1 Introduction

Open and RDF-based knowledge graphs (KGs), like prominent Wikidata[1] or DBpedia[2], are continuously growing in terms of size and usage. Consequently, the number of entities described in those KGs leads to a problem for both data publishers and data users: **how to know if two entities are the same or not?** According to Noy et al. [18], this question remains one of the top challenges

[1] https://www.wikidata.org.
[2] https://wiki.dbpedia.org/.

J. Z. Pan et al. (Eds.): ISWC 2020, LNCS 12506, pp. 494–510, 2020.
https://doi.org/10.1007/978-3-030-62419-4_28

in knowledge graphs industry. To interlink KGs, the *owl:sameAs* property has been defined by the W3C[3] in 2004 to link entities that are the same. Indeed, a (real world) object is described across several KGs, and those descriptions are linked thanks to the *owl:sameAs* property. However, the semantic definition of *owl:sameAs* is very strict. It is based on Leibniz's identity definition, i.e., the identity of indiscernibles: $\forall x, \forall y(\forall p, \forall o, (\langle x, p, o\rangle \textit{ and } \langle y, p, o\rangle) \rightarrow x = y)$. And its converse, the indiscernibility of identicals: $\forall x, \forall y(x = y \rightarrow \forall p, \forall o, (\langle x, p, o\rangle \rightarrow \langle y, p, o\rangle))$. Hence, two entities are considered identical if they share all their $\langle$*property, value*$\rangle$ pairs in all possible and imaginable contexts. In other words, two entities are identical if **all their properties are indiscernibles** for each value.

Once an identity link is stated between two entities, it is possible to use $\langle$*property, value*$\rangle$ pairs from one entity to another. However, it is a very strong assertion to state that two objects are the same whatever the context. From a philosophical point of view, there are multiple counterarguments to the definition of Leibniz's identity. For example, if we consider two glasses from the same set of glasses, they are indiscernible from each other and yet they are two different physical objects. Similarly, is a person the same as he or she was ten years ago?

It is also a technical problem because of the open-world assumption [6], on the one hand, and on the other hand, because of what a data publisher has in mind that could be different from what the user expects when using data. Besides, when data is published, it is "almost" impossible to know the **consensus** behind the decision of creating an *owl:sameAs* link. Several works such as [11] and [5] have demonstrated that the use of *owl:sameAs* was inadequate. Indeed, established links might be considered as true only in specific contexts.

As a first intuition, a contextual identity between two entities might be seen as a subset of properties Π for which these entities share the same values for each $p \in \Pi$.

Example 1. Two different generic drugs *Drug1* and *Drug2* can be identical when considering the active ingredient. If a KG contains the triples $\langle$*Drug1 activeIngredient Molecule1*$\rangle$ and $\langle Drug2\ activeIngredient\ Molecule1\rangle$, then $Drug1 \equiv_{activeIngredient} Drug2$ when the context is $activeIngredient$.

One of the core features of *owl:sameAs* is to be able to **propagate all properties** from an entity to other identical entities. Hence, *owl:sameAs* allows to discover more knowledge and to increase completeness. In the same way, contextual identity must help to discover **more knowledge and to increase completeness**, but only under specific circumstances. So, to be useful, a contextual identity must specify what is happening with properties that are not part of the context. In other words, **an identity context must have propagating properties**.

Example 2. Following the Example 1, stating only $Drug1 \equiv_{activeIngredient} Drug2$ has a limited interest, if we do not know what to do with other properties

[3] https://www.w3.org/TR/owl-ref/.

besides *activeIngredient*. Considering the context *activeIngredient*, the property *targetDisease* is propagating, and if the statement ⟨*Drug1 targetDisease Disease1*⟩ exists then we can state that ⟨*Drug2 targetDisease Disease1*⟩. But if we consider the property *excipient* as context, then the property *targetDisease* is not propagating.

Moreover, the ability to propagate a property between entities depends on the context, i.e., the same property might be propagating in a context C_1 and not propagating in a context C_2 as illustrated in Example 2.

Research Questions: With a given identity context between two entities, how to find properties that can be propagated? Is it possible to find propagating properties (semi-)automatically?

In this paper, based on the context definition of Idrissou et al. [14], we propose an approach to **find propagating properties** to facilitate knowledge discovery for users. Instead of manually listing the propagating properties as in Idrissou et al. [14], we automatically identify the propagating properties for a given context using semantic textual similarity, significantly reducing burden to users. The semantic similarity is based on the sentence embeddings corresponding to the textual descriptions of the properties. We validated our approach through quantitative and qualitative experiments.

The rest of the paper is organized as follows. In following section, we present the related work. In Sect. 4, we present our approach. In Sect. 5, we present the experiments we have conducted. Finally, we conclude and define the next directions for our future work in Sect. 6.

2 Related Work

In the first part of this section, we describe papers that pointed out the problems raised by the *owl:sameAs* usage. In the second part, we discuss the proposals that tackle these problems.

2.1 Identity Crisis

As early as 2002, Guarino and Welty [10] raised the issue of identity for ontologies. Especially when time is involved, stating that two things are identical became a philosophical problem. The authors proposed to involve in identity only essential properties, i.e., a property that cannot change. As described in Horrocks et al. [13], the *owl:sameAs* property purpose is to link two entities that are strictly the same, i.e., both entities are identical in every possible context. *owl:sameAs* has a strict semantics allowing to infer new information. Many existing tools produce such *owl:sameAs* links [9], and several surveys are available to this end [1,9,17].

However, none of these approaches consider contextual identity links. Their purpose is to discover identity links that allegedly always hold. This is, from a philosophical point of view, hard to obtain as underlined by Leibnitz's identity definition. Indeed, as stated for example in Halpin et al. [11] or Ding et al. [5], because of the strict semantic of *owl:sameAs*, the burden of data publishers might be too heavy. As a matter of fact, *owl:sameAs* links are not often adequately used. Some might be simply wrong, and, more insidiously, some might be context-dependent, i.e., the *owl:sameAs* link does not hold in every possible context because it is hard to obtain a consensus on the validity of a statement. What a data modeler means may not be what a data user expects. This misuse of *owl:sameAs* is often referred to as the "identity crisis" [11].

2.2 Contextual Identity

Beek et al. [2] addressed this issue by constructing a lattice of identity contexts where contexts are defined as sets of properties. All entities belonging to a context share the same values for each property of this context. Hence, a context is a set of indiscernible properties for an entity. However, the authors do not give indications about the usage of properties not belonging to such contexts. Raad et al. [19] proposed an algorithm named DECIDE to compute contexts, where identity contexts are defined as sub-ontologies. Nevertheless, as in the first work, properties of entities that are not in the sub-ontology are ignored. So, in both previous works, there is a limitation of properties that do not belong to a context. This limitation cripples the interest of using such approaches. Indeed, one of the goals of an identity context is to define an identity relation between two entities to use information about one on the other. The solution by Idrissou et al. [14] involves such propagation of properties, and thus, increases completeness of an entity according to a context. However, this proposal requires users to provide both the propagating and indiscernible properties as input. Hence, it leaves the burden to the user to identify and provide context and properties.

In this work, we propose to remove this burden partially from the user, i.e., to **semi-automatically compute the propagation set of properties given an indiscernibility set of properties**. For this, we will use sentence embedding (presented in Sect. 4.3) to compute the embeddings of properties using their descriptions to discover the **propagating properties** with respect to a given identity context (as defined in [14]).

3 Motivation

Sometimes, real-world entities may be close regarding their properties but not the same. For example, the French capital, Paris, is both a city and a department (an administrative subdivision of the French territory). While considering that the city and the department are the same concerning their geography, they are two distinct entities administratively (or legally) speaking, i.e., they are not considered the same per *owl:sameAs*. Now, suppose both Paris are represented in a KG as distinct entities, and both are linked to (possibly distinct) movie theaters. If one wants to retrieve movie theaters located in the city of Paris, results will not be complete if some of them are linked to the department (see Fig. 1).

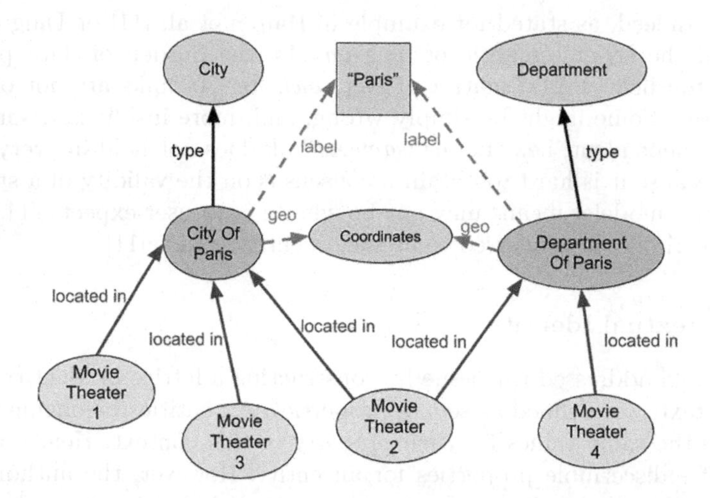

Fig. 1. Excerpt of a KG about Paris, France. The properties in red are indiscernible for both the city and the department. The properties in blue are propagating given the red properties are indiscernible. (Color figure online)

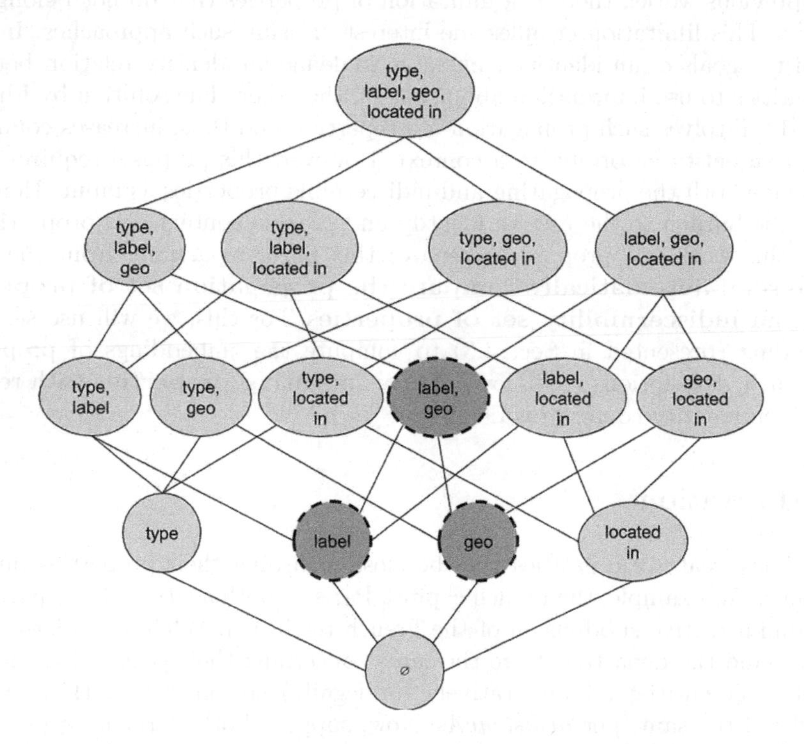

Fig. 2. Simplified identity lattice from Fig. 1: each node is an indiscernible set of properties. Only the red nodes have similar entities. (Color figure online)

A French citizen might know this ground truth, but how to allow an automated agent to discover this fact? Contextual identity is a possible answer to this question, i.e., a set of properties for which values are the same for both entities. Considering the present example, both Paris (city and department) are geographically the same and some properties related to geography might be **propagated**. In Fig. 1, the dotted red properties (*geo* and *label*) are indiscernible (have the same values) and the *located in* properties are propagating. Although the two entities do not share the same values for the *located in* property, this one is related to the geographic context. Indeed, for a human agent, the *located in* property might be obviously propagated between the two entities. While we expected to have the four movie theaters located in Paris, a query on the City of Paris will only return movie theaters 1, 2 and 3 (see Fig. 1).

Thus, discovering such contexts of identity between entities, might improve completeness of query results. Our intuition is inspired by Tobler's first law [23], that is: "*Everything is related to everything else, but near things are more related than distant things.*" Therefore, **we hypothesize that, from a semantic point of view, the closer a property is to the identity context, the more likely it could be a good candidate for propagation**. In the previous example, *located in* clearly refers to a geographic fact, and the context of identity is about geography since it is composed of geographical coordinates. So, the idea is to **compute a semantic distance between indiscernible properties** and **candidate properties for propagation**. Consequently, numbers, and in our case numerical vectors, are best suited to compute this distance. A numerical representation of the textual description of each property through its *rdfs:comment* or *schema:description* can provide a basis to get this vector. In most KGs, properties are described with such sentences. For example, 99% of properties in Wikidata have descriptions. Sentence embeddings of property descriptions output numerical vectors such that semantically similar descriptions appear closer in the vector space.

4 Approach

4.1 Preliminaries

As mentioned in Sect. 2, several proposals have been made to define an identity context. We choose the one from Idrissou et al. [14] since it is the only one that considers the propagation of properties. They give the following definition of the identity context:

Definition 1 ***(Identity Context).*** *An identity context $C = (\Pi, \Psi, \approx)$ is defined by two sets of properties (Π and Ψ) and an* ***alignment procedure*** *($\approx$). Π is the* ***indiscernibility set*** *of properties (Eq. 1) and Ψ is the* ***propagation set*** *of properties (Eq. 2). In the following, x and y are entities.*

$$\begin{aligned} x =_{(\Pi,\Psi,\approx)} y \leftrightarrow \forall(p_1,p_2) \in \Pi^2 \text{ with } p_1 \approx p_2 \\ \text{and } \forall v_1, v_2 \text{ with } v_1 \approx v_2 : \langle x, p_1, v_1 \rangle \leftrightarrow \langle y, p_2, v_2 \rangle \end{aligned} \tag{1}$$

$$x =_{(\Pi,\Psi,\approx)} y \rightarrow \forall (p_1, p_2) \in \Psi^2 \textit{ with } p_1 \approx p_2 \\ \textit{and } \forall v_1, v_2 \textit{ with } v_1 \approx v_2 : \langle x, p_1, v_1 \rangle \leftrightarrow \langle y, p_2, v_2 \rangle \quad (2)$$

Moreover, we define the ***level of a context*** $|\Pi_C|$ *as the number of its indiscernible properties.*

In the case where similar entities according to an identity context belong to the same KG, it is not necessary to have an alignment procedure.

An entity can have several identity contexts, depending on properties in the indiscernibility set Π. Indeed, two different combinations of properties can give different sets of similar entities. The identity lattice of all identity contexts of an entity e is defined as follow:

Definition 2 ***(Identity Lattice).*** *An identity lattice $\mathcal{L}$ is a lattice, where each element is an identity context. The set inclusion between indiscernibility set of properties of each context is the binary relation responsible for the partial order.*

The last notion is the seed of a lattice or a context that we define as follows:

Definition 3 ***(Seed of a lattice or a context).*** *Each context of a lattice is constructed from the* ***same entity*** *e. This entity e is called the seed of the lattice.*

As per Definition 2, to build an identity lattice, we need to start from a seed, despite the fact that the lattice could potentially be valid with another seed (see Fig. 2).

Now that we have defined the necessary concepts, we will explain the core of our approach.

4.2 Computation of Contexts

We present Algorithm 1 that computes an identity lattice. It takes as input the seed entity, the source KG to which the seed belongs, the target KG (possibly the same as the source KG) and an alignment procedure if the two KGs are distinct. The main idea is to start by computing level one identity contexts with each seed's property and finally combine those contexts to obtain upper-level identity contexts. When building a context, its first part is its indiscernibility set, from which we then get similar entities, to obtain candidate properties for propagation and, in the end, propagating properties.

The first step, line 3, is to compute all level 1 identity contexts (see Definition 1). Indeed, for each property p of the seed, there is exactly one identity context (its indiscernibility set is $\Pi = \{p\}$). Later, identity contexts with only one indiscernibility property will be merged to give identity contexts of higher-levels. Next, we retrieve similar entities $entities_p$ to the seed that have the same value(s) for the given property p. If p is multi-valuated, then entities in $entities_p$ are similar to the seed for all values o such that $\langle seed\ p\ o \rangle$. It is worth noting that, when filling $entities_p$, we search only entities that have the same type(s) with the seed. This is because we want to avoid absurd results, e.g., comparing

Data: $\mathcal{KG}_1$: the source KG, $\mathcal{KG}_2$: the target KG, *seed*: an entity of $\mathcal{KG}_1$, $\approx$: an alignment procedure between $\mathcal{KG}_1$ and $\mathcal{KG}_2$

Result: $\mathcal{L}$: a lattice of identity contexts between the seed and entities in the target KG

```
1  L = ∅;
   /* Get all explicit and implicit types of the seed                         */
2  T_seed = {t : ⟨seed rdf:type t⟩ ∈ KG1};
   /* the following will create all contexts of the level 1 (with only
      one indiscernible property)                                             */
3  for each property p of seed do
4      candidateEntities = ∅;
5      for each value o such as ⟨seed p o⟩ ∈ KG1 do
           /* entities_{p,o} is the set of indiscernible entities with seed
              with respect to the p, o pair                                   */
6          entities_{p,o} = {e : (∃(p', o'), p' ≈ p, o' ≈ o, ⟨e p' o'⟩ ∈ KG2) ∧ (∃t ∈
            T_seed, t' ≈ t, ⟨e rdf:type t'⟩ ∈ KG2)};
7          if entities_{p,o} ≠ ∅ then
8              candidateEntities = candidateEntities ∪ {entities_{p,o}};
9          end
10     end
       /* entities_p is the set of indiscernible entities with seed with
          respect to the property p                                           */
11     entities_p = ⋂ candidateEntities;
12     Ψ = getPropagationSet(seed, entities_p, {p});
13     if Ψ ≠ ∅ then
14         Π = {p};
15         C = (Π, Ψ, ≈);
16         L = L ∪ C;
17     end
18 end
   /* Now we can combine contexts of the same level                           */
19 return constructUpperLevels(L, KG1, KG2, seed, ≈)
```

Algorithm 1: createLattice: calculate identity lattice of an entity.

a person with an airplane. It also has the advantage of lowering the number of possible identity contexts to compute. Finally, based on $entities_p$, we compute the propagation set Ψ (line 8) as explained in the following section (Sect. 4.3).

The second step (see Algorithm 2) is to compute upper-level identity contexts based on those from level 1. The loop (line 2) of the algorithm calculates these upper-levels by combining contexts of the same level, and stops when it cannot construct new upper-level identity contexts. This calculation is based on an identity lattice operator, which is the set inclusion on indiscernibility sets. For example, a level 2 context is built on two contexts from level 1. Again, to lower the number of possible identity contexts to compute, if there is no similar entity to the seed for a given context C_i, there is no need to compute higher-level contexts based on C_i.

```
Data: 𝓛: the lattice with only level one contexts, 𝒦𝒢₁: the source KG, 𝒦𝒢₂: the
      target KG, seed: an entity of 𝒦𝒢₁, ≈: an alignment procedure between
      𝒦𝒢₁ and 𝒦𝒢₂
Result: 𝓛: a lattice of identity contexts between the seed and entities in the
        target KG
/* lvl is the current level in the lattice                              */
1  lvl = 1;
2  while ∅ ∉ 𝓛 do
3      contexts = ∅;
4      for (𝒞₁, 𝒞₂) ∈ {(𝒞ᵢ, 𝒞ⱼ) ∈ 𝓛 × 𝓛 : |Π_𝒞ᵢ| = |Π_𝒞ⱼ| = lvl, i > j} do
5          Π = Π_𝒞₁ ∪ Π_𝒞₂;
           /* getEntities function gives the set of entities that are
              similar under the given identity context in the given KG */
6          entities = getEntities(𝒞₁, 𝒦𝒢₂) ∩ getEntities(𝒞₂, 𝒦𝒢₂);
7          if entities ≠ ∅ and Π ∉ 𝓛 then
8              Ψ = getPropagationSet(seed, entities, Π);
               /* see Algo. 3                                           */
9              if Ψ ≠ ∅ then
10                 𝒞 = (Π, Ψ, ≈);
11                 contexts = contexts ∪ 𝒞;
12             end
13         end
14     end
15     𝓛 = 𝓛 ∪ contexts;
16     lvl = lvl + 1;
17 end
18 return 𝓛
```

Algorithm 2: constructUpperLevels: calculate upper-levels of the identity lattice of an entity.

4.3 Propagation Set Using Sentence Embedding

Our approach for computing propagation set (Line 8 in Algorithm 2) is elaborated in Algorithm 3. It is based on sentence embedding which maps a sentence to a numerical vector. Ideally, semantically close sentences appear nearby in the numerical vector space.

Sentence embedding is a technique that maps a sentence to a numerical vector. Ideally, semantically close sentences are represented by close vectors in the numerical space considered. The reasons behind using sentence embedding instead of a more classical distance measures, e.g., the edit distance, RDF graph embedding like RDF2Vec [20], or an ontological alignment technique are: *(i)* classical string distances ignore sentence semantics, *(ii)* RDF graph embedding techniques are not yet adapted to such task, and *(iii)* ontological alignment techniques align pairwise properties and not sets of properties. Sentence embedding is widely used in several tasks such as computing semantic similarities between two texts. An encoder derives sentence embeddings, to capture the semantics of a language, from a large text corpus. State-of-the-art encoders include Universal

```
Data: seed: the entity that generated Π,
entities: set of entities similar to seed with respect to Π,
Π: an indiscernibility set
Result: Ψ: a propagation set
/* computation of the embeddings of each property in Π by using one
   of the encoder                                                  */
1  indiscernibilityEmbeddings ← getEmbeddings(Π);
2  meanVector ← mean(indiscernibilityEmbeddings);
/* getCandidateProperties function returns the set of all candidate
   properties for propagation                                      */
3  candidates ← getCandidateProperties(Π, {seed} ∪ entities);
/* then compute their embeddings                                   */
4  candidatesEmbeddings ← getEmbeddings(candidates);
5  Ψ ← ∅;
6  for candidateVector in candidatesEmbeddings do
7  |   similarity ← cosineSimilarity(candidateVector, meanVector);
8  |   if similarity ≥ threshold then
9  |   |   Ψ ← Ψ ∪ {candidateVector};
10 |   end
11 end
12 return Ψ
```

Algorithm 3: getPropagationSet: calculate the propagation set.

Sentence Encoder [3], GenSen [22] and InferSent [4]. A lot of attention has been given to sentence embeddings lately.

As presented in Sect. 1, our intuition, based on Tobler's first law, is that a propagation set of properties can be found given an indiscernibility set, if vectors of descriptions of those two sets are close enough. In this work, we propose to use property descriptions (e.g., *rdfs:comment* or *schema:description* as "*standard plug type for mains electricity in a country*") to find properties that are semantically related and consequently good candidates for propagation for a given indiscernibility set Π. For example, in Wikidata, the property "director" has the follow description: "director(s) of film, TV-series, stageplay, video game or similar". Descriptions are mainly composed of one sentence. Most of the properties are described with such annotations, e.g., properties of Wikidata are annotated with an English *schema:description* at 98.9%. For the embedding computation, any of the previously described encoders can be used.

Algorithm 3 presents our proposal to compute Ψ given a Π. It takes as input three parameters: a seed (an entity), a set of property built from the seed (indiscernibility set Π), and a set of entities that are similar to the seed with respect to Π. The computation of Π is presented in the previous section (see Algorithm 1).

First, for each property in the indiscernibility set Π, we calculate its representational vector. Then, we compute the mean vector that represents the indiscernibility set. Similarly, we consider each property of the seed or its similar entities, and compute their representational vectors. Therefore, on the one hand, we have one vector that represents the set of indiscernibility and, on the other hand, we have n vectors for the n properties that are candidates for propagation. Properties of similar entities (with respect to the indiscernibility set Π) are also considered as candidates since possibly one of them can have a propagating property that the seed does not have.

Then we loop on each candidate property to compute a cosine similarity [21] between each candidate vector and the mean vector representing the indiscernibility set Π. If the cosine similarity is high enough (above a specified threshold as explained in the following section) the candidate property is considered as a propagating property.

5 Experimental Results

For evaluation, we first implemented our approach, and then we present several SPARQL queries that benefited from our approach.

5.1 Implementation and Set-Up

We implemented our approach in Python. For the sake of reproducibility, the code is made available on a GitHub repository[4]. As mentioned earlier, we used three sentence embedding approaches, namely *InferSent*[5], *GenSen*[6] and *Universal Sentence Encoder*[7]. We used an HDT file (see [16] and [8]) that contains a dump of the last version of Wikidata[8]. The computer we used had an i7 processor and 32 GB of RAM. As an indication, the complete calculation of the identity lattice for an entity such as the city of Paris, France takes about 1396 ms. It has more than 1000 property-object pairs and, in Wikidata, the mean number of property-object pairs is about 60. Thus, it is a rather large entity and this approach could scale well.

5.2 Quantitative Study

The goal of quantity study is to evaluate how well the proposed approach can retrieve the propagating properties specified in Ψ, given the indiscernibility set of properties Π for each identity context (Π, Ψ, $\equiv$). Since there is not a prior work or dataset that we can leverage to evaluate our algorithm, we manually constructed a gold standard dataset from the Wikidata KG that is known for its high data quality [7].

The dataset consists of 100 identity contexts where each context contains the indiscernibility set of properties Π and the propagation set of properties Ψ. We do not need an alignment procedure ($\equiv$) specified for identity contexts since

[4] https://github.com/PHParis/ConProKnow.
[5] https://github.com/facebookresearch/InferSent.
[6] https://github.com/Maluuba/gensen.
[7] https://tfhub.dev/google/universal-sentence-encoder/2.
[8] http://gaia.infor.uva.es/hdt/wikidata/wikidata2018_09_11.hdt.gz.

both source and target KGs are the same i.e., the Wikidata KG. To test the performance across different classes, identity contexts were constructed across five diverse class types: country, comics character, political party, literary work, and film. We randomly selected 20 entities from each class type and computed their identity lattices. One context was selected from each lattice. The propagation set of properties (Ψ) for each context was manually identified by looking at its indiscernibility set of properties Π.

Evaluation: We compared our algorithm with a baseline system that computes, using Jaccard index (JI) [15], a similarity score (range 0–1) between a candidate property and each property in Π of a given identity context. If the mean similarity score is above a specified threshold, we considered the candidate property as a propagating property for this context.

We evaluated the performance of a model using standard $Precision = \frac{tp}{tp+fp}$, $Recall = \frac{tp}{tp+fn}$, and $Fmeasure = \frac{2 \times Precision \times Recall}{Precision + Recall}$ where tp (true positive) is the number of predicted properties that are actually in Ψ, fp (false positive) is the number of predicted properties which are not in Ψ, and fn (false negative) is the number of predictive properties in Ψ not selected by the model.

We experimented with different sentence embeddings (namely InferSent, Universal Sentence Encoder, and GenSen) and with different thresholds (0 to 1). Due to space constraint, we only present the results in Table 1 corresponding to InferSent and thresholds of 0.1 and 0.9. The proposed approach outperformed the baseline for every threshold. This is expected because the baseline uses Jaccard Index, and thus it relies only on the exactly matching tokens between the property descriptions. Because our approach uses InferSent, it can obtain semantically similar descriptions even though the descriptions themselves do not contain the exact tokens. As we increased the similarity threshold, precision increased, but recall decreased. The threshold of 0.9 was a balance between precision and recall that yielded the F1 scores up to 0.69 (for film and literary work). In fact, F1 scores were above 0.60 for every class except for the country class, which had an F1 score of 0.36 due to overlapping descriptions among propagating and non-propagating properties. The overlapping descriptions for the country class appeared very close in the vector space, which reduced the precision and F1 scores. In addition, the performances were impacted by noisy descriptions, and thus, better preprocessing techniques can potentially improve these scores. In sum, we obtained an overall F1 score of 0.59 and validated our Tobler-inspired hypothesis, i.e., properties can be sorted using their descriptions obtaining the propagating properties at the top. Our result further provides a strong baseline for future research for this novel research problem.

5.3 Qualitative Study

In this section, we describe three different queries that could demonstrate the benefits of our approach by extending their results. To achieve our goal, we used *InferSent* and the threshold value equal to 0.9. All of these queries are simplified

Table 1. Baseline and InferSent results with thresholds of 0.1 and 0.9.

Class	Threshold	Precision		Recall		F1	
		Baseline	Approach	Baseline	Approach	Baseline	Approach
Comics character	0.1	0.40	0.39	0.1	1.00	0.16	0.54
	0.9	0.00	0.49	0.00	0.90	0.00	0.61
Country	0.1	0.05	0.15	0.01	1.00	0.01	0.23
	0.9	0.00	0.32	0.00	0.81	0.00	0.36
Film	0.1	0.15	0.34	0.03	1.00	0.05	0.49
	0.9	0.00	0.62	0.00	0.93	0.00	0.70
Literary work	0.1	0.03	0.50	0.01	1.00	0.01	0.65
	0.9	0.00	0.60	0.00	0.90	0.00	0.69
Political party	0.1	0.39	0.20	0.51	1.00	0.36	0.31
	0.9	0.00	0.55	0.00	0.87	0.00	0.62
Overall	0.1	0.20	0.32	0.13	1.00	0.12	0.44
	0.9	0.00	0.51	0.00	0.88	0.00	0.59

queries tested on Wikidata (for ease of reading). The original queries can be found on the GitHub repository (See footnote 4).

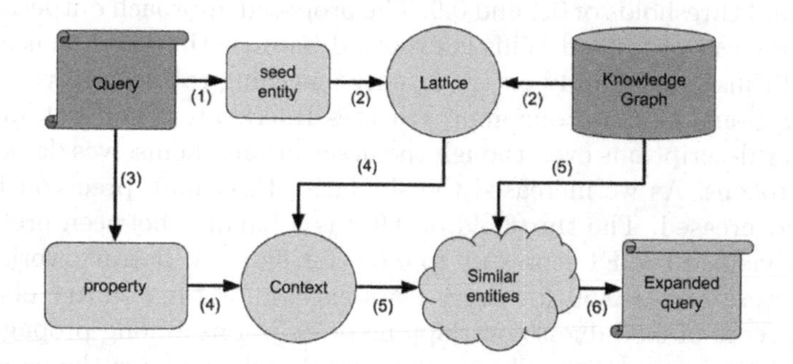

Fig. 3. Qualitative experiment workflow: the elements in red are the inputs and the element in green is the output. To simplify the diagram, we consider only one instantiated entity linked to one instantiated property in the query. (Color figure online)

Task Description: For each query, the goal is to find an identity context that will allow expanding the query with similar entities according to the user's objective. In this way, users can benefit from more complete results. The workflow is the following (see Fig. 3): first, from the query, we extract the instantiated entity (or entities) that will be the seed(s) (step 1). Second, for each seed, we compute its identity lattice (step 2) that will contain in each of its nodes an indiscernible and a propagating set of properties (cf. Algorithms 1 and 3). Third, with the instantiated property (or set of properties) linked to the seed in the query, we select from the lattice, the node having this property in its propagation set (step

4). This node will be considered as the identity context of the query. Indeed, if multiple identity contexts are possible, the user must choose the best suited for its task purpose. Finally, based on the selected identity context, we can get similar entities (step 5) and rewrite the query with both the seed and similar entities (step 6).

Queries: We tested our approach with three queries. The first query (Listing 1.1) is to retrieve all clinical trials of the drug "Paracetamol". An interesting expansion of this query could be to find all trials of similar legal drugs in terms of medical conditions treated and physical interactions. The second query is to retrieve all persons who once lead France. However, France has a complicated history and has changed its political regime several times (for example, during World War II, or the Napoleonian period). Thus, even if the French territory was almost always the same during the past centuries, each political regime has its own entity in Wikidata. Finally, the third query is to retrieve French politicians from The Republican party that have been convicted. The peculiarity here is that this major political party changed its name several times because of either political scandal or humiliating defeats. We only give details about the first query because of space limitation, the other two are available on the GitHub repository.

```
SELECT DISTINCT ?clinicalTrial WHERE {
  ?clinicalTrial :researchIntervention :Paracetamol .
}
```

Listing 1.1. SPARQL query retrieving all studies about the painkiller named Paracetamol.

Table 2. Identity context contribution to queries.

	Listing 1.1	See GitHub Repo	See GitHub Repo
Seed	Paracetamol	France	The Republicans
Ψ	research intervention	head of	member of political party
Π	condition treated, interacts with, legal status	capital, official language	country, political ideology
Similar entities	Ibuprofen Aspirin	French 2nd Republic, July Monarchy, ...	UMP, RPR, ...
# of results w/o context	586	12	2
# of results w/ context	860	99 (77)	13

Table 2 shows the additional results brought by our approach. Each column corresponds to a query. For the first query (and also for the next ones), there is only one seed "Paracetamol" ("France" and "the Republicans" in the second and the third columns respectively) as it is the only instantiated entity in the query. To fill this table, we first computed the lattice of the seed. Then, we selected a context containing the property "research intervention" in its Ψ since this property is instantiated in the query. Moreover, as explained, our goal is to retrieve trials of similar drugs in terms of the condition treated and legal status. Finally, the query is expanded with similar entities, as shown in Listing 1.2. The results show a 47% increase in the number of clinical trials for the considered context. For the second query, it should be noted that among the 99 results, 22 persons were not head of France. 14 were head of Paris City Council, and 8 were Grand Master of Masonic obedience in France. This is because the council and the obedience are misplaced in the Wikidata ontology. These errors cannot, therefore, be attributed to our approach. The results show a 542% increase in the number of France leaders for the considered context. The results of the third query show a 550% increase in the number of convicted politicians for the considered context.

```
SELECT DISTINCT ?clinicalTrial WHERE {
  VALUES (?drug) { (:Paracetamol) (:Ibuprofen)
     (:Aspirin) }
   ?clinicalTrial :researchIntervention ?drug .
}
```

Listing 1.2. Expanded SPARQL query retrieving all studies about Paracetamol similar entities.

5.4 Discussion

As we have seen, our approach allows for discovering propagating properties for a given indiscernibility set of properties Π. An identity context with its indiscernibility and propagation sets can provide more complete answers to queries through query expansion. The results are very promising but need to be confronted to more different kinds of KGs and to combination of distinct KGs. Also, our approach does not work when the property of an entity lacks property describing it (such as *rdfs:comment* or *schema:description*). Hence, the first step for future work is to circumvent this flaw with a multifaceted approach that can include other information than the descriptions alone. Moreover, sophisticated preprocessing and textual similarity techniques can be incorporated to further improve the results.

6 Conclusion and Future Work

In this paper, we demonstrated that propagating properties can be discovered semi-automatically. To this end, we presented an approach based on sentence embedding. Given an indiscernible set of properties, the proposed system discovers properties that could be propagated using semantic similarities between the properties. Our approach computes, for an entity, an identity lattice that represents all its possible identity contexts, i.e., both indiscernible and propagating properties. We validated using quantitative and qualitative evaluations that the proposed approach generates promising results for both discovering propagating properties and providing complete answers to the given queries.

Future work includes using other features to improve the results, like values of properties, number of property usage, or semantic features of the property should be tried. However, capturing ontological information of a property when embedding is still an open problem. Secondly, using only sentence embedding, combined with intuition from Tober's first law, might be naïve in some cases. Therefore, there is a need to challenge our work with a combination of distinct KGs. For the time being, we only considered in lattices the case where the entity is subject to a triple, and we should also consider cases where it is the value of a triple. Moreover, using SPARQL queries to help the user to select the best-suited identity context might be an interesting starting point for later work. Finally, to explore SPARQL queries expansion (presented in Sect. 5.3), a prototype should be implemented to allow users selecting the proper context according to an ordered list of contexts. Also, using RDF* and/or SPARQL* [12] to represent the context as defined in this paper should be investigated.

References

1. Achichi, M., Bellahsene, Z., Todorov, K.: A survey on web data linking. Revue des Sciences et Technologies de l'Information-Série ISI: Ingénierie des Systèmes d'Information (2015)
2. Beek, W., Schlobach, S., van Harmelen, F.: A contextualised semantics for `owl:sameAs`. In: Sack, H., Blomqvist, E., d'Aquin, M., Ghidini, C., Ponzetto, S.P., Lange, C. (eds.) ESWC 2016. LNCS, vol. 9678, pp. 405–419. Springer, Cham (2016). https://doi.org/10.1007/978-3-319-34129-3_25
3. Cer, D., et al.: Universal sentence encoder. CoRR abs/1803.11175 (2018)
4. Conneau, A., Kiela, D., Schwenk, H., Barrault, L., Bordes, A.: Supervised learning of universal sentence representations from natural language inference data. In: EMNLP, pp. 670–680. Association for Computational Linguistics (2017)
5. Ding, L., Shinavier, J., Finin, T., McGuinness, D.L.: owl: sameAs and Linked Data: An empirical study. In: Proceedings of the Second Web Science Conference, Raleigh, NC, USA, April 2010
6. Drummond, N., Shearer, R.: The open world assumption. In: eSI Workshop: The Closed World of Databases Meets the Open World of the Semantic Web, vol. 15 (2006)
7. Färber, M., Bartscherer, F., Menne, C., Rettinger, A.: Linked data quality of DBpedia, Freebase, OpenCyc, Wikidata, and YAGO. Semant. Web **9**(1), 77–129 (2018). https://doi.org/10.3233/SW-170275
8. Fernández, J.D., Martínez-Prieto, M.A., Gutiérrez, C., Polleres, A., Arias, M.: Binary RDF representation for publication and exchange (HDT). Web Semant. Sci. Serv. Agents World Wide Web **19**, 22–41 (2013). http://www.websemanticsjournal.org/index.php/ps/article/view/328
9. Ferrara, A., Nikolov, A., Scharffe, F.: Data linking for the semantic web. Int. J. Semant. Web Inf. Syst. (IJSWIS) **7**(3), 46–76 (2011)

10. Guarino, N., Welty, C.A.: Evaluating ontological decisions with OntoClean. Commun. ACM **45**(2), 61–65 (2002)
11. Halpin, H., Hayes, P.J., McCusker, J.P., McGuinness, D.L., Thompson, H.S.: When owl:sameAs isn't the same: an analysis of identity in linked data. In: Patel-Schneider, P.F., et al. (eds.) ISWC 2010. LNCS, vol. 6496, pp. 305–320. Springer, Heidelberg (2010). https://doi.org/10.1007/978-3-642-17746-0_20
12. Hartig, O., Thompson, B.: Foundations of an alternative approach to reification in RDF. arXiv abs/1406.3399 (2014)
13. Horrocks, I., Kutz, O., Sattler, U.: The even more irresistible SROIQ. In: KR, vol. 6, pp. 57–67 (2006)
14. Idrissou, A.K., Hoekstra, R., van Harmelen, F., Khalili, A., den Besselaar, P.V.: Is my: sameAs the same as your: sameAs?: Lenticular lenses for context-specific identity. In: K-CAP (2017)
15. Jaccard, P.: Nouvelles recherches sur la distribution florale. Bull. Soc. Vaud. Sci. Nat. **44**, 223–270 (1908)
16. Martínez-Prieto, M.A., Arias Gallego, M., Fernández, J.D.: Exchange and consumption of huge RDF data. In: Simperl, E., Cimiano, P., Polleres, A., Corcho, O., Presutti, V. (eds.) ESWC 2012. LNCS, vol. 7295, pp. 437–452. Springer, Heidelberg (2012). https://doi.org/10.1007/978-3-642-30284-8_36
17. Nentwig, M., Hartung, M., Ngonga Ngomo, A.C., Rahm, E.: A survey of current link discovery frameworks. Semant. Web **8**(3), 419–436 (2017)
18. Noy, N.F., Gao, Y., Jain, A., Narayanan, A., Patterson, A., Taylor, J.: Industry-scale knowledge graphs: lessons and challenges. Commun. ACM **62**(8), 36–43 (2019). https://doi.org/10.1145/3331166
19. Raad, J., Pernelle, N., Saïs, F.: Detection of contextual identity links in a knowledge base. In: K-CAP (2017)
20. Ristoski, P., Paulheim, H.: RDF2Vec: RDF graph embeddings for data mining. In: Groth, P., et al. (eds.) ISWC 2016. LNCS, vol. 9981, pp. 498–514. Springer, Cham (2016). https://doi.org/10.1007/978-3-319-46523-4_30
21. Singhal, A.: Modern information retrieval: a brief overview. IEEE Data Eng. Bull. **24**(4), 35–43 (2001)
22. Subramanian, S., Trischler, A., Bengio, Y., Pal, C.J.: Learning general purpose distributed sentence representations via large scale multi-task learning. CoRR abs/1804.00079 (2018)
23. Tobler, W.R.: A computer movie simulating urban growth in the Detroit region. Econ. Geogr. **46**(sup1), 234–240 (1970)

In-Database Graph Analytics with Recursive SPARQL

Aidan Hogan[1], Juan L. Reutter[2], and Adrián Soto[3(✉)]

[1] DCC, Universidad de Chile & IMFD, Santiago, Chile
[2] Pontificia Universidad Católica de Chile & IMFD, Santiago, Chile
[3] Faculty of Engineering and Sciences, Universidad Adolfo Ibáñez & Data Observatory Foundation & IMFD, Santiago, Chile
adrian.soto@uai.cl

Abstract. Works on knowledge graphs and graph-based data management often focus either on graph query languages or on frameworks for graph analytics, where there has been little work in trying to combine both approaches. However, many real-world tasks conceptually involve combinations of these approaches: a graph query can be used to select the appropriate data, which is then enriched with analytics, and then possibly filtered or combined again with other data by means of a query language. In this paper we propose a language that is well-suited for both graph querying and analytical tasks. We propose a minimalistic extension of SPARQL to allow for expressing analytical tasks over existing SPARQL infrastructure; in particular, we propose to extend SPARQL with recursive features, and provide a formal syntax and semantics for our language. We show that this language can express key analytical tasks on graphs (in fact, it is Turing complete). Moreover, queries in this language can also be compiled into sequences of iterations of SPARQL update statements. We show how procedures in our language can be implemented over off-the-shelf SPARQL engines, with a specialised client that can leverage database operations to improve the performance of queries. Results for our implementation show that procedures for popular analytics currently run in seconds or minutes for selective sub-graphs (our target use-case).

1 Introduction

Recent years have seen a surge in interest in graph data management, learning and analytics within different sub-communities, particularly under the title of "knowledge graphs" [1]. However, more work is needed to combine complementary techniques from different areas [2]. As a prominent example, while numerous query languages have been proposed for graph databases, and numerous frameworks have been proposed for graph analytics, few works aim to combine both: while some analytical frameworks support lightweight query features [3,4], and some query languages support lightweight analytical features [5–7], only specific types of queries or analytics are addressed.

Take, for example, the following seemingly simple task, which we wish to apply over Wikidata[1]: *find stations from which one can still reach Palermo metro station in*

[1] https://www.wikidata.org/, or see endpoint at https://query.wikidata.org/.

J. Z. Pan et al. (Eds.): ISWC 2020, LNCS 12506, pp. 511–528, 2020.
https://doi.org/10.1007/978-3-030-62419-4_29

Buenos Aires if Line C is closed. Although standard graph query languages such as SPARQL [5] or Cypher [6] support path expressions that capture reachability, they cannot express conditions on the nodes through which such paths pass, as is required by this task (i.e., that they are not on Line C). Consider a more complex example that again, in principle, can be answered over Wikidata: *find the top author of scientific articles about the Zika virus according to their p-index within the topic*. The *p*-index of authors is calculated by computing the PageRank of papers in the citation network, and then summing the scores of the papers for each respective author [8]. One way this could currently be achieved is to: (1) perform a SPARQL query to extract the citation graph of articles about the Zika virus; (2) load the graph or connect the database with an external tool to compute PageRank scores; (3) perform another query to extract the (bipartite) authorship graph for the articles; (4) load or connect again the authorship graph into the external tool to join authors with papers, aggregate the *p*-index score per author, sort by score, and output the top result. Here the user must ship data back and forth between different tools or languages to solve the task. Another strategy might be to load the Wikidata dump directly into a graph-analytics framework and address all tasks within it; in this case, we lose the convenience of a query language and database optimisations for extracting (only) the relevant data.

In this paper, we instead propose a general, (mostly) declarative language that supports *graph queralytics*: tasks that combine querying and analytics on graphs, allowing to interleave both arbitrarily. We coin the term "*queralytics*" to highlight that these tasks raise new challenges and are not well-supported by existing languages and tools that focus only on querying or analytics. Rather than extending a graph query language with support for specific, built-in analytics, we rather propose to extend a graph query language to be able to express any form of (computable) analytical task of interest to the user. Specifically, we explore the addition of recursive features to the SPARQL query language, proposing a concrete syntax and semantics for our language, showing examples of how it can combine querying and analytics for graphs. We call our language the *SPARQL Protocol and RDF Query & Analytics Language* (*SPARQAL*). We study the expressive power of SPARQAL with similar proposals found in the literature [9–12]. We then discuss the implementation of our language on top of a SPARQL query engine, introducing different evaluation strategies for our procedures. We present experiments to compare our proposed strategies on real-world datasets, for which we devise a set of benchmark queralytics over Wikidata. Our results provide insights into the scale and performance with which an existing SPARQL engine can perform standard graph analytics, showing that for queralytics wherein a selective sub-graph is extracted for analysis, interactive performance is feasible; on the other hand, the current implementation struggles for larger-scale graphs, opening avenues for future research.

Example 1. Suppose that there is a concert close to Palermo metro station in Buenos Aires; however, Line C of the metro is closed due to a strike. As mentioned in the introduction, we would like to know from which metro stations we can still reach Palermo. The data to answer this query are available on Wikidata [13]. We can express this request in our SPARQL-based language, as shown in Fig. 1. Two adjacent stations are given by the property `wdt:P197` and the metro line by `wdt:P81`; the entities `wd:Q3296629` and `wd:Q1157050` refer to Palermo metro station and Line C,

```
1  LET reachable = (      # stations directly adjacent to Palermo not on Line C
2    SELECT ?s WHERE {
3      wd:Q3296629 wdt:P197 ?s . MINUS { ?s wdt:P81 wd:Q1157050 }
4    }
5  );
6  DO (
7    LET adjacent = (   # stations adjacent to stations in variable reachable
8      SELECT (?adj AS ?s) WHERE {
9        ?s wdt:P197 ?adj . MINUS { ?adj wdt:P81 wd:Q1157050 } QVALUES(reachable)
10     }
11   );
12   LET reachable = (  # add stations in variable adjacent to variable reachable
13     SELECT DISTINCT ?s WHERE {
14       { QVALUES(adjacent) } UNION { QVALUES(reachable) }
15     }
16   );
17 ) UNTIL(FIXPOINT(reachable) );
18 RETURN(reachable);
```

Fig. 1. Procedure to find metro stations from which Palermo can be reached

respectively. From lines 1 to 5, we first define a *solution variable* called `reachable` whose value is the result of computing all stations directly adjacent to Palermo that are not on Line C. From lines 6 to 17 we have a loop that executes two instructions: the first, starting at line 7, computes all stations directly adjacent to the current reachable stations not on Line C; here the `QVALUES(reachable)` clause is used to invoke all solutions stored in variable `reachable`. The second, starting at line 12, adds the new adjacent stations to the list of known reachable stations with a union. The loop is finished when the set of solutions assigned to the variable `reachable` does not change from one iteration to another (a fixpoint is thus reached). Finally, on line 18, we return reachable stations. □

2 Related Work

We now discuss frameworks for applying graph analytics, proposals for combining graph querying and graph analytics, and recursive extensions of graph query languages.

Frameworks for Graph Analytics. Various frameworks have been proposed for performing graph analytics at large-scale, including GraphStep [14], Pregel [15], HipG [16], PowerGraph [17], GraphX [3], Giraph [18], Signal/Collect [19], etc. These frameworks operate on a computational model – sometimes called the systolic model [20], Gather/Apply/Scatter (GAS) model [17], graph-parallel framework [3], etc. – whereby each node in a graph recursively computes its state based on data available in its neighbourhood. However, implementing queries on such frameworks, selecting custom subgraphs to be analysed, etc., is not straightforward. Datalog variants also offer an interesting framework for graph analytics, especially when Datalog is extended with arithmetic features, as in, e.g., [12,21–24]. As we discuss in Sect. 4, SPARQAL can be seen as bridging existing RDF databases and SPARQL services with such frameworks.

Graph Queries and Analytics. Our work aims to combine graph queries and analytics for RDF/SPARQL. Along these lines, Trinity.RDF [25] stores RDF in a native graph format where nodes store inward and outward adjacency lists, allowing to traverse from a node to its neighbours without the need for index lookup; the system is then implemented in a distributed in-memory index, with query processing and optimisation components provided for basic graph patterns. Although the authors discuss how Trinity.RDF's storage scheme can also be useful for graph algorithms based on random walks, reachability, etc., experiments focus on SPARQL query evaluation from standard benchmarks [25]. Later work used the same infrastructure in a system called Trinity [26] to implement and perform experiments with respect to PageRank and Breadth-First Search, this time rather focusing on graph analytics without performing queries. Though such an infrastructure could be adapted to apply graph queralytics, the authors do not discuss the combination of queries and analytics, nor do they propose languages.

Most modern graph query languages offer some built-in analytical features. SPARQL 1.1 [5] introduced *property paths* [27] that allow for finding pairs of nodes connected by some path matching a regular expression, and some extensions allow for invoking specific extra analytical features [7]. The Cypher query language [6] (used by Neo4j [28]) also allows for querying on paths with limited regular expressions; however, it also supports shortest paths, returning paths, etc. The G-CORE query language [29] also supports features relating to paths, allowing to store and label paths, find weighted shortest paths, and more besides. In general, however, graph query languages tend to only support analytics relating to path finding and reachability [30].

Gremlin [4] is an imperative scripting language that can express analytical tasks through graph traversals. Per the Trinity.RDF system [25], graph traversals, when combined with variables, can be used to express and evaluate, for example, basic graph patterns [29]. Gremlin [4] also supports some standard query operators, such as union, projection, negation, path expressions, and so forth, along with recursion, which allows to capture general analytical tasks; in fact, the Gremlin language is Turing complete [4]. However, Gremlin is specifically designed to work under a property graph data model, and more importantly is missing practical RDF-specific features of SPARQL such as datatype ordering, built-in functions (e.g., `langMatches`, `isIRI`, `year`), named graphs, federation, etc. Thus, using Gremlin in the context of RDF databases would require porting these features between both systems, which is precisely what we want to avoid.

Recursive Graph Queries. Most graph query languages support recursively matching path expressions; however, per Example 1, more powerful forms of recursion are needed in order to support a more general class of analytics[2]. Later we will compare the expressive power of our proposal to recursive graph query languages, such as those proposed by Reutter et al. [9] for SPARQL, and by Urzua and Gutierrez [11] for G-CORE. We also highlight the LDScript language as proposed by Corby et al. [10], which also relates to our proposal, supporting the definition of functions using SPARQL expressions; local variables that can store individual values, lists or the results of queries; and iteration over lists of values using loops, as well as recursive function calls. We remark that LDScript does not include support for arbitrary do–until iteration, where applying a fixed number of iterations is insufficient for a broad range of analytical tasks.

[2] Though more complex forms of "navigational patterns" have been proposed in the literature, they are mostly limited to path-finding and reachability [30].

Novelty. Unlike graph analytics frameworks, we propose a language for combining queries and analytics on graphs. Unlike Gremlin and Datalog variants, we propose a language designed to extend SPARQL, thus benefiting from its built-in support for RDF. The closest proposals to ours are those that extend graph query languages with recursive features [9–11]. In comparison with the proposal of Reutter et al. [9] and Urzua and Gutierrez [11], we allow recursion over `SELECT` queries, which adds flexibility by not requiring to maintain intermediate results as (RDF) graphs: for example, allowing us to maintain multiple intermediate relations of arbitrary arity (without requiring some form of reification); we further allow for terminating a loop based on a boolean condition (an `ASK` query), which can more easily express termination conditions in cases where an analytics task is infinitary and/or requires approximation (e.g., PageRank). Unlike LDScript [10], our focus is on supporting graph analytics, adding features, such as fixpoint and do–until loops, that are essential for many forms of graph analytics.

3 Language

Recursion stands out in the literature as a key feature for supporting graph analytics. Our proposal – called SPARQAL – extends SPARQL (1.1) with recursion by allowing to iteratively evaluate queries (optionally) joined with solution sequences of prior queries until some condition is met. In order to support this form of iteration, we need two key operators. First, we extend SPARQL with *solution variables* to which the results of a `SELECT` query can be assigned, and which can then be used within other queries to join solutions. Second, we extend SPARQL with *do–until loops* to support iteratively repeating a sequence of SPARQL queries until some termination condition is met; this condition may satisfy a fixed number of iterations, a boolean `ASK` query, or a fixpoint on a solution variable (terminating when the set of solutions do not change).

We refer back to Example 1, which illustrates how our language can be used to address a relatively simple queralytic task. We now present the syntax of our language, and thereafter proceed to define the formal semantics. We finish the section with a second, more involved example for computing the *p*-index of authors in an area.

Preliminaries: To formally define our language and give our examples we assume familiarity with SPARQL and basic notions of graph analytics algorithms. We use the standard syntax and semantics of SPARQL in terms of mappings [5]. We recall the notion of a *solution sequence*, which is the result of a SPARQL query evaluated on a graph (or dataset), listing zero-or-more solutions for which the query matches the data. We assume use of the full SPARQL 1.1 query language as defined by the standard [5].

3.1 Syntax

SPARQAL aims to be a minimalistic extension of the SPARQL language that allows to express queralytic tasks. Specifically, a task is defined as a *procedure*, which is a sequence of *statements*. A statement can be an *assignment*, *loop* or *return* statement.

Assignment: Assigns the solution sequence of a query to a solution variable. The syntax of an assignment statement is **LET** var = (Q); where var is a variable name and Q is a SPARQL SELECT query that may use constructs of the form **QVALUES**(var).

Loop: Executes a sequence of statements until a termination condition holds. The syntax of a loop statement is **DO** (S) **UNTIL** (condition); where S is a sequence of statements and condition is one of the following three forms of termination condition: (1) **TIMES** t, where t is an integer greater than 0; (2) **FIXPOINT** (var), where var is a solution variable; (3) AQ, an ASK query that may use **QVALUES**.

Return: Specifies the solution sequence to be returned by the procedure. The syntax of a return statement is **RETURN** (var); where var is a solution variable.

Finally, a SPARQAL *procedure* is a sequence of statements satisfying the following two conditions: (1) the last statement, and only the last statement, is a return statement; (2) all solution variables used in **QVALUES**, **FIXPOINT** and **RETURN** have been assigned by **LET** in a previous statement (or a nested statement thereof).

Example 2. Figure 1 illustrated a SPARQAL procedure with three statements: an assignment statement (lines 1–5); a loop statement with a fixpoint termination condition and two nested assignments (lines 6–17); and a final return statement (line 18). □

3.2 Semantics

We now give the semantics of statements that form procedures in SPARQAL. More formally, let $P = s_1; \ldots; s_n$ be a sequence of statements, and let var_1, ..., var_k be all variables mentioned in any statement in P (including in nested statements). For a tuple $\mathrm{val}_0 = (r_1, \ldots, r_k)$ of initial assignments of (possibly empty) solution sequences to variables var_1, ..., var_k, we will construct a sequence $\mathrm{val}_0, \ldots, \mathrm{val}_n$ of k-tuples, where each val_i represents the value of all variables after executing statement s_i.

The construction is done inductively. Assume that $\mathrm{val}_{i-1} = (r_1, \ldots, r_k)$. The value of val_i depends on whether s_i is an assignment, loop or return statement.

First, if s_i is the assignment statement **LET** var_j = (Q);, then tuple val_i is constructed as follows. Define SPARQL query $Q[(\text{var\_1}, \ldots, \text{var\_k}) \mapsto (r_1, \ldots, r_k)]$ as the result of substituting each subquery {**QVALUES**(var_j)} in Q for the solution sequence r_j[3], and let r^* be the result of evaluating this extended query over the database. Then, substituting r_j for r^* in the tuple val_{i-1}, we define $\mathrm{val}_i = (r_1, \ldots, r_{j-1}, r^*, r_{j+1}, r_k)$.

Next, if s_i is the loop statement **DO** (S) **UNTIL** (condition); the tuple val_i is constructed as follows. Assume that S is the sequence $s'_1, \ldots, s'_\ell$ and notice that (by definition) S must use a subset of the k solution variables in P. Repeat the following steps until the terminating condition is met:

1. Initialise $\mathrm{val}'_0 :- \mathrm{val}_{i-1}$.
2. Compute the tuple val'_ℓ that represents the result of executing statements $s'_1, \ldots, s'_\ell$.

[3] A syntactic way of doing this is to use a **VALUES** command in SPARQL.

3. If val'_ℓ does not satisfy the condition, set val'_0 :– val'_ℓ and repeat step 2 above.
4. Otherwise finish, and set val_i :– val'_ℓ.

To define when a tuple val'_ℓ over k variables satisfies a condition, we have three cases:

– If the condition is **TIMES** t, then the condition is met once the loop above has repeated t times.
– If the condition is **FIXPOINT** (var_j), then the condition is met when the j-th component of val'_ℓ contains the same set of solutions as the j-th component of val'_0.
– If the condition is AQ, then the condition is met when the ASK query $AQ[(\text{var\_1}, \ldots, \text{var\_k}) \mapsto \text{val}'_\ell]$ evaluates to true.

```
1  LET zika = (                    # directed graph of citations between Zika articles
2    SELECT ?node ?cite WHERE {
3      ?node wdt:P31 wd:Q13442814 ; wdt:P921 wd:Q202864 ; wdt:P2860 ?cite .
4      ?cite wdt:P31 wd:Q13442814 ; wdt:P921 wd:Q202864 .
5    }
6  );
7  LET nodes = (                   # all nodes of Zika graph
8    SELECT DISTINCT ?node WHERE {
9      { QVALUES(zika) } UNION { SELECT (?cite AS ?node) WHERE { QVALUES(zika) } }
10   }
11 );
12 LET n = (                       # number of nodes in Zika graph
13   SELECT (COUNT(*) AS ?n) WHERE { QVALUES(nodes) }
14 );
15 LET degree = (                  # out-degree (>1) of nodes in Zika graph
16   SELECT ?node (COUNT(?cite) AS ?degree) WHERE { QVALUES(zika) } GROUP BY ?node
17 );
18 LET rank = (                    # initial rank
19   SELECT ?node (1.0/?n AS ?rank) WHERE { QVALUES(nodes) . QVALUES(n) }
20 );
21 DO (                            # begin 10 iterations of PageRank
22   LET rank_edge = (             # spread rank to neighbours via edges
23     SELECT (?cite AS ?node) (SUM(?rank*0.85/?degree) AS ?rankEdge) WHERE {
24       QVALUES(degree) . QVALUES(rank) . QVALUES(zika)
25     } GROUP BY ?cite
26   );
27   LET unshared = (              # compute total rank not shared via edges
28     SELECT (1-SUM(?rankEdge) AS ?unshared) WHERE { QVALUES(rank_edge) }
29   );
30   LET rank = (                  # split and add unshared rank to each node
31     SELECT ?node (COALESCE(?rankEdge,0)+(?unshared/?n) AS ?rank) WHERE {
32       QVALUES(nodes) . QVALUES(n) . QVALUES(unshared) . OPTIONAL { QVALUES(rank_edge) }
33     }
34   );
35 ) UNTIL (TIMES 10);
36 LET p_index_top = (             # compute p-index for authors, select top author
37   SELECT ?author (SUM(?rank) AS ?p_index) WHERE {
38     QVALUES(rank) . ?node wdt:P50 ?author .
39   } GROUP BY ?author ORDER BY DESC(?p_index) LIMIT 1
40 );
41 RETURN(p_index_top);
```

Fig. 2. Procedure to compute the top author in terms of p-index for articles about the Zika virus

Finally, if s_i is the return statement **RETURN**(var_j), then the program terminates and returns the solution sequence r_j that is the j-th component of val_i.

Note that we assume all solution variables to have a global scope as it makes the semantics simpler to define; one could define local solution variables analogously. Moreover, some SPARQAL statements may incur infinite loops; later we will discuss fragments for which every program can be shown to terminate (as in, e.g., Datalog or recursive SPARQL). Currently we do not consider blank nodes when checking **FIXPOINT** conditions; these could be supported in a future version using the labelling of [31], which has been shown to be efficient for a wide variety of graphs.

Example 3. We recall Example 1, this time to illustrate the semantics of SPARQAL. In the first **LET** statement, we assign the solution sequence of the given SPARQL query to the variable `reachable`. Then the procedure enters a loop. We assign `adjacent` to the results of a SPARQL query that embeds the current solutions of `reachable` as a sub-query, leading to a join between current `reachable` stations and pairs of adjacent stations not on Line C. We then update the `reachable` solutions, adding `adjacent` solutions; here we can use `reachable` in the **LET** and **QVALUES** of the same statement since it was assigned before (line 1). In each iteration the solutions for `reachable` will increase, discovering new stations adjacent to previous ones, until a fixpoint. Finally, the **RETURN** clause specifies the solutions to be given as a result of the procedure. □

3.3 Example with PageRank

We now illustrate a procedure for a more complex queralytic.

Example 4. Suppose we have the citation network of articles on a topic of interest and, we want to apply a centrality algorithm in order to know which articles of the network are the most important. Thereafter we wish to use these scores to find the most prominent authors in the area. We can express this task using SPARQAL. In this case we will consider the citation network of all the articles about the Zika virus on Wikidata, where we then encode and apply the PageRank algorithm over the citation network, using the resulting article scores to compute p-indexes for the respective authors. We show a procedure in our language for solving this task in Fig. 2.

In this procedure we start by defining a variable that contains a solution sequence with pairs (`?node`, `?cite`) such that both `?node` and `?cite` are instances of (`P31`) scientific articles (`Q13442814`) about (`P921`) the Zika virus (`Q202864`) and `?node` cites (`P2860`) `?cite`. The solutions for this query are assigned to `zika`. We can think of this variable as the representation of a directed subgraph extracted from Wikidata. We also define the variables `nodes` with all nodes in the subgraph, `n` with the number of nodes, and `degree` with the out-degree of all nodes in the graph (with some out-edge).

After extracting the graph and preparing some data structures for it, we then start the process of computing PageRank. First we assign the variable `rank` with initial ranks for all nodes of $\frac{1}{n}$. We then start a loop where we will execute 10 iterations of PageRank. In each iteration we will first compute and assign to `rank_edge` the PageRank that each node shares with its neighbours; here we assume a damping factor $d = 0.85$ as typical for PageRank [32], denoting the ratio of rank that a node shares with its neighbours. Next we compute and assign to `unshared` the total rank not shared with neighbours in the previous step (this arises from nodes with no out-edges and the $1 - d$ factor not used previously for other nodes). We conclude the iteration by allocating the unshared rank to each node equally, updating the results for `rank`. The loop is applied 10 times.

Subsequently, we join the PageRank scores for articles with their authors, and use aggregation to sum the scores for each author, applying ordering and a limit to select the top author according to that sum, assigning the solution to `p_index_top`. Finally, the procedure returns the solution for `p_index_top` denoting the top author. □

3.4 Graph Updates

Although there is a straightforward way to implement our language on top of any engine using the `VALUES` clause, this can generate long query strings that current engines struggle to process. Hence we define a recursive algebra for graphs that can also express queralytics. As a motivating example, consider the declaration of variables `zika` and `degree`, in lines 1 and 15 respectively of Fig. 2. These statements initialise these variables, but we can view them as queries constructing two graphs. More precisely, we use the graph `ex:zika` to store the result of the query:

```
1  CONSTRUCT { ?node ex:zikacites ?cite } WHERE {
2    ?node wdt:P31 wd:Q13442814; wdt:P921 wd:Q202864; wdt:P2860 ?cite .
3    ?cite wdt:P31 wd:Q13442814; wdt:P921 wd:Q202864 }
```

Thus, instead of storing pairs of values for <node> <cite> in a SPARQAL solution variable `zika`, we store them as triples of the form <node> `ex:zikacites` <cite> in a graph named `ex:zika`. Using this graph we can now store the result of `degree` in graph `ex:degree` by means of the following query:

```
1  CONSTRUCT { ?node ex:zikadegree ?degree } WHERE {
2    SELECT ?node (COUNT(?cite) AS ?degree) WHERE {
3      GRAPH ex:zika {?node ?p ? cite} }
4    GROUP BY ?node }
```

We remark that a general solution would involve reifying any SPARQAL variable using more than two SPARQL variables, possible generating new nodes.

Algebra of Updates. Let $\mathcal{G} = \{(n_1, G_1), \ldots, (n_k, G_k)\}$ be a set of named graphs with IRIs $\{n_1, \ldots, n_k\}$ and RDF graphs $\{G_1, \ldots, G_k\}$ such that $n_i = n_j$ if and only if $i = j$. Let Q be a `CONSTRUCT` query. Given an IRI n, we use $n \leftarrow Q$ to express the action of storing the result G of $Q(\mathcal{G})$ as the named graph (n, G) in $\mathcal{G}$, overwriting the graph previously named n if necessary. Our algebra of updates consists of (1) update expressions of the form $n \leftarrow Q$, for n an IRI and Q a `CONSTRUCT` query that may reference any of the existing graphs in $\mathcal{G}$, (2) loop expressions of the form **DO** A **UNTIL** (condition) where `A` is a sequence of expressions and `(condition)` is again one of **`TIMES`** `t`; **`FIXPOINT`** `n`, where `n` is a graph name in $\mathcal{G}$; or `AQ`, an `ASK` query that may reference graphs in $\mathcal{G}$.

With respect to the semantics of this algebra, starting with the initial set $\mathcal{G}$, an expression modifies graphs in $\mathcal{G}$ as follows. An assignment expression $n \leftarrow Q$ removes the graph (n, G) from $\mathcal{G}$ (if it exists), and adds $(n, Q(\mathcal{G}))$, where $Q(\mathcal{G})$ denotes the evaluation of Q over $\mathcal{G}$. A loop expression **DO** A **UNTIL** (condition) applies iteration, evaluating the sequence `A`: t times if `condition` is **`TIMES`** `t`, or until the named graph $(n, G) \in \mathcal{G}$ did not change at the end of two subsequent iterations if `condition` is **`FIXPOINT`** `n`, or until the evaluation of query `AQ` over $\mathcal{G}$ returns true if `condition` is `AQ`.

Given an expression A dealing with graphs in $\mathcal{G}$, we use $A(\mathcal{G})$ to denote the result of evaluating A over $\mathcal{G}$. Looking at our motivating example, one sees that transforming our procedural language into the graph algebra is not difficult, and neither is transforming graph algebra expressions into our procedural language. The following proposition, proven in an extended version of this paper available online [33], summarises the claim that both languages have the same expressive power.

Proposition 1. *Let P be a SPARQAL procedure, with v the solution variable returned by P. Then one can construct an expression A in the algebra of updates mentioning a set $\mathcal{G}$ of graphs, and a* `SELECT` *query Q, such that evaluating Q over $A(\mathcal{G})$ yields the same solutions as those stored by v after evaluating P over $\mathcal{G}$. Likewise, for an algebra expression A mentioning graphs $\mathcal{G}$, and any named graph $(n, G) \in \mathcal{G}$, one can construct a SPARQAL procedure P returning a solution variable v over $\mathcal{G}$, and a* `CONSTRUCT` *query Q, such that evaluating Q over the solutions stored by v yields the graph G.*

Thus, we now have two strategies for implementing SPARQAL procedures: we can implement them directly by translating **`QVALUES`** clauses as **`VALUES`** statements while running the procedures, or we can compile the procedure into an expression in our algebra of updates and implement this directly. We will analyse these two possibilities in Sect. 5.2, but first we study the expressive power of these formalisms.

4 Expressive Power

In this section we review the expressive power of procedures in SPARQAL. Our results come in two flavours: first we focus on what the language can do, showing Turing-completeness and complexity results, and then we turn to the comparison between our language and other related query languages extended with recursion.

4.1 Turing-Completeness

Although do–until loops may appear to be just a mild extension to a query language, our first result states that this is actually enough to achieve Turing-completeness. Formally, we say that a query language $\mathcal{L}$ is Turing-complete if for every Turing machine M over an alphabet Σ one can construct a query Q in $\mathcal{L}$ and define a computable function f that takes a word in Σ^* and produces an RDF graph, and such that a word $w \in \Sigma^*$ is accepted by M if and only if the evaluation of Q over the graph $f(w)$ produces a non-empty result. Along these lines, we prove the following result:

Theorem 1. *SPARQAL is Turing-complete*

The proof of this theorem (presented in the extended version of this paper [33]) relies on the combination of do–until loops and the ability to create new values in the base SPARQL language through **`BIND`** statements and algebraic functions [5]. Of course, for the proof one must assume that there is no limit on the memory used by the evaluation algorithm; however, the proof reveals a linear correspondence between the memory used by the query and the number of cells visited by the machine M.

Traditional theoretical results have tended to study languages assuming that the creation of new values is not possible, or, if possible, that there is a bound on the number of values that are created. But this is not the case with SPARQAL procedures; for starters, we can iterate and sum to create arbitrarily big numbers. However, for the purpose of comparing SPARQAL procedures against other traditional database languages, we ask, what would be its expressive power if one disallows the creation of new values? In fact, do–until loops have been studied previously in the literature, especially in the context of relational algebra (see e.g. [34]). In our context, we ask what happens if we disallow the invention of new values in the procedure: more formally, we say that a procedure P *does not invent new values* if for every graph G and every variable var defined in P, all mappings in any solution sequence associated to var always binds variables to values already present in G. In this case, there is a limit on the maximum number of mappings in the solution sequence of any variable at any point in time during evaluation of the procedure, and this limit depends polynomially on the size of the graph. This implies that the evaluation of this procedure can be performed in PSPACE (in data complexity), and we can also show that this bound is tight. To formally state this result, let P be a SPARQAL procedure. The evaluation problem for P receives a graph as an input, and asks whether the evaluation of P over G is not empty[4]. We can then state the following (the proposition is proven in the extended version of this paper [33]):

Proposition 2. *The evaluation problem for SPARQAL procedures that do not invent new values is PSPACE-complete.*

4.2 Comparison with Other Recursive Extensions to SPARQL

We base our comparison on the recursive extension proposed by Reutter et al. [9], but these results apply to similar languages, such as the (with) recursive operator in SQL. The first observation is that these languages only define semantics for monotone queries. For example, recursive SPARQL uses CONSTRUCT queries of the form:

```
1 WITH RECURSIVE G AS {Q_CONSTRUCT}
2 Q_SELECT
```

where G is an IRI used to denote a temporary graph, $Q_{\text{CONSTRUCT}}$ is a CONSTRUCT SPARQL query and Q_{SELECT} is a SELECT SPARQL query. The idea of this form of recursion is that $Q_{\text{CONSTRUCT}}$ defines a query meant to compute G in an iterative fashion (there may also be references to the graph G inside this same query). In other words, we can view $Q_{\text{CONSTRUCT}}$ as an operator $T_Q(G)$ that – as a single step – takes as input an RDF graph and produces as output an RDF graph. The final output graph then corresponds to the least fixed point of the sequence $T_Q(\emptyset)$, $T_Q(T_Q(\emptyset))$, ... Such a fixed point is only guaranteed when $Q_{\text{CONSTRUCT}}$ is *monotone*: where $G \subseteq G'$ implies that $T_Q(G) \subseteq T_Q(G')$. To guarantee monotonicity, Reutter et al. [9] impose major syntactic restrictions on the operands available for the $Q_{\text{CONSTRUCT}}$ query, forbidding, for example, the use of **BIND**, **NOT EXISTS**, **MINUS**, as well as **OPTIONAL** patterns that are not *well designed* [35].

[4] This corresponds to boolean evaluation. This is without loss of generality because the problem where one considers a tuple of values as an input can be simulated by means of filters.

So how does our language compare with these recursive variants? The first observation is that all of these queries can actually be expressed as a SPARQAL procedure: a query in the form above can be straightforwardly simulated by the following procedure:

```
1  DO ( LET graph = ( SELECT ?s ?p ?o WHERE P'_CONSTRUCT ) ) UNTIL ( FIXPOINT (graph) );
2  LET result = Q'_SELECT;
3  RETURN result;
```

Here $P'_{\text{CONSTRUCT}}$ is the graph pattern of the **WHERE** clause of $Q_{\text{CONSTRUCT}}$ from the recursive SPARQL query, but where we retrieve triples from `QVALUES(graph)` instead of from the temporary graph G. Query Q'_{SELECT} corresponds to Q_{SELECT} from the recursive SPARQL query, but where again we use `QVALUES(graph)` instead of G.

In the other direction, can recursive SPARQL simulate SPARQAL procedures? This depends on what sorts of queries we allow in $Q_{\text{CONSTRUCT}}$. If we take the language as originally defined by Reutter et al., so that queries $Q_{\text{CONSTRUCT}}$ must be monotone, then we know that the evaluation for recursive SPARQL queries is in PTIME [9]. Together with Proposition 2, this means that recursive SPARQL cannot simulate SPARQAL procedures unless PTIME = PSPACE, which is widely assumed to be false. A similar result was shown for similar extensions to relational algebra: relational algebra equipped with fixed point cannot simulate do–until queries unless PTIME = PSPACE [34].

Conversely, the semantics for recursive SPARQL is not defined when one allows to use operands such as **BIND** clauses. The standard solution for this case is to assign a partial fixed point semantics, which means that a query of the form above would retrieve a graph G which is the fixed point of the sequence $T_Q(\emptyset), T_Q(T_Q(\emptyset)), \ldots$, if it exists, or an empty graph otherwise (when the operator runs into an infinite loop). In this context, and if we allow full SPARQL 1.1 in $Q_{\text{CONSTRUCT}}$, one can show that both languages coincide, because recursive SPARQL becomes Turing-complete as well.

4.3 Comparison with the Datalog Framework

Our algebra of graph updates also gives us a way of comparing with Datalog variants for analytics tasks that have been proposed in the literature (for this discussion we assume familiarity with the Datalog language). Indeed, consider a set of named graphs $\mathcal{G} = \{(n_1, G_1), \ldots, (n_k, G_k)\}$, a sequence A of graph updates of the form $n \leftarrow Q$, for n one of $n_1, \ldots, n_k$ and Q a construct query over $\mathcal{G}$. If we assume that each Q is monotone, then an algebra expression **DO** A **UNTIL FIXPOINT** n_i can be understood as a Datalog program over k ternary predicates $T_1, \ldots, T_k$, each interpreted as the triples in graphs $n_1, \ldots, n_k$, given by the rules $\leftarrow T_1, \ldots, \leftarrow T_k$ and a rule $T_j \leftarrow Q$ for each update $n_j \leftarrow Q$ in A. We evaluate this program until the data for predicate T_i does not change.

Thus, for example, if we restrict queries in SPARQL so that they match the expressive power of the SociaLite language by Seo et al. [12], then we end up precisely with SociaLite. What SPARQAL adds on top of these Datalog variants is (1) native support for SPARQL, since the right-hand side of rules are actually stated in SPARQL, and (2) not having to depend on particular fixed point semantics[5]. As we remarked when comparing to recursive SPARQL, this does come with an increase in expressive power.

[5] Here we are not interested in languages with decidable containment, in part because we are not addressing how to do reasoning within SPARQAL, but this is a fertile area for future work.

5 Experiments

In this section we present our prototypical implementation of a queralytics engine based on the SPARQAL language, along with experiments over different datasets to ascertain its performance and limitations. The goals of this prototype are to demonstrate that the language can be used, in practice, to express in-database analytics, and to ascertain the performance achievable when operating over an off-the-shelf SPARQL query engine. The target use-case for our prototype is – per the scenarios outlined in Examples 1 and 4 – to run queralytics (near-)interactively on small-to-medium graphs projected from a larger graph using a query. Along these lines, the prototype was developed on top of the Apache Jena Framework, version 3.10 (for our second set of tests we also provide a version of the prototype mounted on top of Virtuoso). The implementation provides the following core functionalities: (1) it parses a SPARQAL procedure into a sequence of statements, which are evaluated according to their semantics by: (2a) maintaining a map of solution variables to solution sequences; (2b) replacing variables used within a **QVALUES** clause with a **VALUES** string with the respective solution sequence; (2c) evaluating SPARQL queries, and (2d) in order to handle **FIXPOINT** conditions, keeping the previous solution sequence of the respective variable in-memory to track changes. We also provide an initial prototype for the algebraic strategy defined in Sect. 3.4; this prototype creates the new graphs using CONSTRUCT statements, and deletes/adds new graphs using the native functionalities provided by SPARQL systems.

Table 1. Number of nodes and edges in graphs considered

	Q1	Q2	Q3	Q4	Q5	Q6
Nodes	93	3,057	480	266	7,194	627
Edges	172	38,738	766	211	8,719	996

Experiments were tested on a MacBook Pro with a 3.1 GHz Intel I5 processor and 16 GB of RAM. For our motivating scenarios, Example 1 took just 1.3 s to return 16 stations from which Palermo can be reached without using Line C, and Example 4 – running 10 iterations of PageRank on a graph of 38,738 edges (citations) and 3,057 nodes (articles) – took 53.1 seconds to find the top author (from 2,214 authors) by *p*-index in the citation network, which we consider to be reasonable, but improvable[6].

To further test our implementation, we design a benchmark based on Wikidata for running analytical tasks on sub-graphs extracted through queries. Finally, we stress-test our prototype for a graph analytics benchmark at a larger scale. In particular, we show that the algebraic approach may be better suited for handling large datasets.[7]

5.1 Wikidata: Queralytics Benchmark

To the best of our knowledge, there is no existing benchmark for queralytics along the lines discussed in this paper. This led us to design a novel benchmark for queralyt-

[6] For reference, the top such author is George Dick, with a *p*-index of 0.124.

[7] All sources and datasets are available at https://adriansoto.cl/files/SPARQAL.zip.

ics over the Wikidata knowledge graph. We took the "truthy" RDF dump of Wikidata as our benchmark graph [36]. Designing the queralytic tasks required collecting and combining two elements: queries that return results corresponding to graphs, and graph algorithms to apply analytics on these graphs. In terms of the queries returning graphs, we revised the list of use-case queries for the Wikidata Query Service[8]. From this list, we identified the following six queries returning graphs:

Q1 A graph of adjacent metro stations in Buenos Aires
Q2 A graph of citations for articles about the Zika virus
Q3 A graph of characters in the Marvel universe and the groups they belong to
Q4 A graph of firearm cartridges and the cartridges they are based on
Q5 A graph of horses and their lineage
Q6 A graph of drug–disease interactions on infectious diseases

These queries provide a mix of connected graphs, disconnected graphs, bipartite graphs, trees, DAGs, near-DAGs, and so forth. We provide the sizes of these graphs in Table 1.

Next we must define the analytics that we would like to apply on these graphs. For this, we adopted five of the six algorithms from the Graphalytics Benchmark [37]:

BFS Breadth-First Search
PR PageRank
LCC Local Clustering Coefficient
WCC Weakly Connected Components
SSSP Single-Source Shortest Path

We do not include the *Community Detection through Label Propagation* **CDLP** as it assumes data with initial labels. We implement these five algorithms as procedures in the SPARQAL language, prefixing each with the six different Wikidata graph queries, stored as solution variables. The result is a benchmark of $6 \times 5 = 30$ queralytic tasks.

In Fig. 3, we show the results for these 30 tasks using our in-memory implementation. First we remark that the Weakly Connected Components (**WCC**) algorithm timed-out in the case of the Zika graph after 10 min. While the cheapest algorithm in general was **BFS**, the most expensive was **WCC**. Although some of these tasks took over a

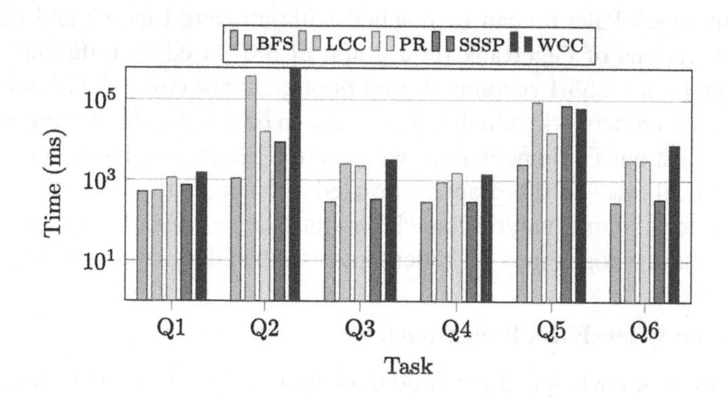

Fig. 3. Results for Wikidata queralytic benchmark

[8] https://www.wikidata.org/wiki/Wikidata:SPARQL_query_service/queries/examples.

minute in the case of graphs with thousands or tens of thousands of nodes (Zika/**Q1** and Horses/**Q5**), those with fewer than a thousand nodes/edges ran in under a second, and thus would be compatible with interactive use.

5.2 Graphalytics: Stress Test

The scale of the previous graphs is quite low and uses (mostly) the in-memory algorithm. Hence we use the Graphalytics Benchmark [37] to perform stress tests for our prototype at larger scale with the goal of identifying the choke points of the current implementation. We adopt the `cit-Patents` dataset: a directed graph with 3,774,768 vertices and 16,518,947 edges. We implement both alternatives for evaluating SPARQAL procedures: using **VALUES** and using Graph Updates. In order to try a different backend, we also implemented the Graph Updates alternative on top of Virtuoso.

The results of the Graphalytics benchmark are shown in Table 2. For the **VALUES** implementation, we identify two key choke points. An obvious choke-point is presented by the fact that solution sequences are stored in memory: this puts an upper-bound on scalability, leading to OOM errors for complex queralytics on larger graphs (with millions of nodes and tens of millions of edges). The other choke-point is the handling of **QVALUES** clauses using a **VALUES** clause with large solution sequences, yielding queries that are inefficient for Apache Jena. We view a number of possibilities for addressing these choke points in future work. Keeping with the in-database analytics scenario, the first choke point could be alleviated with compression and indexing techniques, while both choke points could be addressed by batch-at-a-time processing of **QVALUES** clauses.

The performance issues of the **VALUES** implementation are alleviated, to some extent, when we switch to the implementation based on graph updates. Intermediate graphs are stored in memory, but their sizes tend to be smaller than the size of solution sequences, as one avoids replication. Here, the main choke-point is the fact that constructed graphs are not currently indexed, and thus queries over them run slower. When comparing the Jena/Updates implementation against the one using Virtuoso, we see several differences. Both implementations handle BFS much better. We speculate that Virtuoso is better at SSSP because it is more efficient when dealing with strings representing paths. On the other hand, all of LCC, WCC and PR require large update operations on temporary graphs, something that transactional databases like Virtuoso are not designed for.

Looking to the future, we speculate that implementing lightweight indexes in constructed graphs would provide even faster times for our Updates implementation. Another in-database alternative would be using GPU-acceleration for parallelising

Table 2. Execution time (min) for Graphalytics benchmark. Here OOM is for out-of-memory error.

Algorithm	BFS	LCC	PR	SSSP	WCC
SPARQAL/Jena–Values	11	OOM	250	300	OOM
SPARQAL/Jena–Updates	2	26	112	127	13
SPARQAL/Virtuoso–Updates	1	TIMEOUT	244	5	310

batches. In general, however, in order to process larger graphs, an in-database solution may not be feasible, but rather SPARQAL procedures would need to be translated to tasks that can run on graph processing or Datalog frameworks, as discussed in Sect. 2.

6 Conclusion

We believe that the combination of graph queries and analytics is a natural one, in the sense that tasks of interest to users often involve interleaving both paradigms. The SPARQAL language provides a way to express such tasks, and makes initial steps towards a system to support them. We see this language as being useful for combining querying and analytical tasks specifically in an RDF/SPARQL setting.

We hope that our proposal ignites discussion on different ways for enriching SPARQL with graph analytics, and the best architecture to support them (see [38] for a related discussion). A key research challenge relates to the optimisation of SPARQAL procedures. We have investigated batch-at-a-time and also compilation into algebraic-like statements for evaluation within the database, but we still need support for indexing temporary graphs (perhaps as in [39]), and looking at whether or not traditional database optimisation tasks are likewise suitable for optimising SPARQAL procedures.

Acknowledgements. This work was supported by the Millennium Institute for Foundational Research on Data (IMFD) and by Fondecyt Grant No. 1181896.

References

1. Hogan, A., et al.: Knowledge Graphs. CoRR abs/2003.02320 (2020)
2. Bonatti, P.A., Decker, S., Polleres, A., Presutti, V.: Knowledge graphs: new directions for knowledge representation on the semantic web. Dagstuhl Rep. **8**(9), 29–111 (2018)
3. Xin, R.S., Gonzalez, J.E., Franklin, M.J., Stoica, I.: GraphX: a resilient distributed graph system on spark. In: International Workshop on Graph Data Management Experiences and Systems (GRADES). ACM Press (2013)
4. Rodriguez, M.A.: The Gremlin graph traversal machine and language. In: Symposium on Database Programming Languages (DBPL), pp. 1–10. ACM (2015)
5. Harris, S., Seaborne, A., Prud'hommeaux, E.: SPARQL 1.1 Query Language. W3C Recommendation (2013). https://www.w3.org/TR/sparql11-query/
6. Francis, N., et al.: Cypher: an evolving query language for property graphs. In: SIGMOD, pp. 1433–1445. ACM (2018)
7. Song, X., Chen, S., Zhang, X., Feng, Z.: A CONSTRUCT-based query for weighted RDF graph analytics. In: ISWC Satellites, pp. 25–28 (2019)
8. Senanayake, U., Piraveenan, M., Zomaya, A.: The pagerank-index: going beyond citation counts in quantifying scientific impact of researchers. PLOS ONE **10**(8), 1–34 (2015)
9. Reutter, J.L., Soto, A., Vrgoč, D.: Recursion in SPARQL. In: Arenas, M., et al. (eds.) ISWC 2015. LNCS, vol. 9366, pp. 19–35. Springer, Cham (2015). https://doi.org/10.1007/978-3-319-25007-6_2
10. Corby, O., Faron-Zucker, C., Gandon, F.: LDScript: a linked data script language. In: d'Amato, C., et al. (eds.) ISWC 2017. LNCS, vol. 10587, pp. 208–224. Springer, Cham (2017). https://doi.org/10.1007/978-3-319-68288-4_13

11. Urzua, V., Gutiérrez, C.: Linear recursion in G-CORE. In: Alberto Mendelzon International Workshop on Foundations of Data Management (AMW), vol. 2369. CEUR-WS.org (2019)
12. Seo, J., Guo, S., Lam, M.S.: SociaLite: datalog extensions for efficient social network analysis. In: International Conference on Data Engineering (ICDE), pp. 278–289
13. Vrandečić, D., Krötzsch, M.: Wikidata: a free collaborative knowledgebase. Commun. ACM **57**(10), 78–85 (2014)
14. DeLorimier, M., et al.: GraphStep: a system architecture for sparse-graph algorithms. In: IEEE Symposium on Field-Programmable Custom Computing Machines (FCCM), pp. 143–151. IEEE Computer Society (2006)
15. Malewicz, G., et al.: Pregel: a system for large-scale graph processing. In: SIGMOD, pp. 135–146. ACM Press (2010)
16. Krepska, E., Kielmann, T., Fokkink, W., Bal, H.E.: HipG: parallel processing of large-scale graphs. Oper. Syst. Rev. **45**(2), 3–13 (2011)
17. Gonzalez, J.E., Low, Y., Gu, H., Bickson, D., Guestrin, C.: PowerGraph: distributed graph-parallel computation on natural graphs. In: 10th USENIX Symposium on Operating Systems Design and Implementation, OSDI 2012, Hollywood, CA, USA, 8–10 October 2012, pp. 17–30. USENIX Association (2012)
18. Ching, A., Edunov, S., Kabiljo, M., Logothetis, D., Muthukrishnan, S.: One trillion edges: graph processing at facebook-scale. PVLDB **8**(12), 1804–1815 (2015)
19. Stutz, P., Strebel, D., Bernstein, A.: Signal/Collect12. Semant. Web J. **7**(2), 139–166 (2016)
20. Low, Y., Gonzalez, J.E., Kyrola, A., Bickson, D., Guestrin, C., Hellerstein, J.M.: Graphlab: a new framework for parallel machine learning. CoRR abs/1408.2041 (2014)
21. Kaminski, M., Grau, B.C., Kostylev, E.V., Motik, B., Horrocks, I.: Stratified negation in limit datalog programs. In: International Joint Conference on Artificial Intelligence, pp. 1875–1881. ijcai.org (2018)
22. Bellomarini, L., Gottlob, G., Pieris, A., Sallinger, E.: Vadalog: a language and system for knowledge graphs. In: Benzmüller, C., Ricca, F., Parent, X., Roman, D. (eds.) RuleML+RR 2018. LNCS, vol. 11092, pp. 3–8. Springer, Cham (2018). https://doi.org/10.1007/978-3-319-99906-7_1
23. Eisner, J., Filardo, N.W.: Dyna: extending datalog for modern AI. In: de Moor, O., Gottlob, G., Furche, T., Sellers, A. (eds.) Datalog 2.0 2010. LNCS, vol. 6702, pp. 181–220. Springer, Heidelberg (2011). https://doi.org/10.1007/978-3-642-24206-9_11
24. Carral, D., Dragoste, I., González, L., Jacobs, C., Krötzsch, M., Urbani, J.: VLog: a rule engine for knowledge graphs. In: Ghidini, C., et al. (eds.) ISWC 2019. LNCS, vol. 11779, pp. 19–35. Springer, Cham (2019). https://doi.org/10.1007/978-3-030-30796-7_2
25. Zeng, K., Yang, J., Wang, H., Shao, B., Wang, Z.: A distributed graph engine for web scale RDF data. PVLDB **6**(4), 265–276 (2013)
26. Shao, B., Wang, H., Li, Y.: Trinity: a distributed graph engine on a memory cloud. In: SIGMOD, pp. 505–516 (2013)
27. Kostylev, E.V., Reutter, J.L., Romero, M., Vrgoč, D.: SPARQL with property paths. In: Arenas, M., et al. (eds.) ISWC 2015. LNCS, vol. 9366, pp. 3–18. Springer, Cham (2015). https://doi.org/10.1007/978-3-319-25007-6_1
28. Miller, J.J.: Graph database applications and concepts with Neo4j. In: Southern Association for Information Systems Conference (SAIS). AIS eLibrary (2013)
29. Angles, R., et al.: G-CORE: a core for future graph query languages. In: SIGMOD, pp. 1421–1432 (2018)
30. Angles, R., Arenas, M., Barceló, P., Hogan, A., Reutter, J.L., Vrgoc, D.: Foundations of modern query languages for graph databases. ACM C. Surv. **50**(5), 68:1–68:40 (2017)
31. Hogan, A.: Canonical forms for isomorphic and equivalent RDF graphs: algorithms for leaning and labelling blank nodes. ACM TWEB **11**(4), 1–62 (2017)

32. Page, L., Brin, S., Motwani, R., Winograd, T.: The PageRank citation ranking: Bringing order to the Web. Technical report, Stanford InfoLab (1999)
33. Hogan, A., Reutter, J.L., Soto, A.: In-database graph anaytics with recursive SPARQL [Extended Version]. https://adriansoto.cl/pdf/SPARQAL-Extended.pdf
34. Abiteboul, S., Hull, R., Vianu, V.: Foundations of Databases, vol. 8. Addison-Wesley Reading, Boston (1995)
35. Pérez, J., Arenas, M., Gutierrez, C.: Semantics and complexity of SPARQL. ACM Trans. Database Syst. (TODS) **34**(3), 16 (2009)
36. Malyshev, S., Krötzsch, M., González, L., Gonsior, J., Bielefeldt, A.: Getting the most out of wikidata: semantic technology usage in wikipedia's knowledge graph. In: Vrandečić, D., et al. (eds.) ISWC 2018. LNCS, vol. 11137, pp. 376–394. Springer, Cham (2018). https://doi.org/10.1007/978-3-030-00668-6_23
37. LDBC: Graphalytics Benchmark Suite (2019). https://graphalytics.org/
38. Raasveldt, M., Mühleisen, H.: Data management for data science-towards embedded analytics. In: CIDR (2020)
39. Holanda, P., Raasveldt, M., Manegold, S., Mühleisen, H.: Progressive indexes: indexing for interactive data analysis. Proc. VLDB Endowment **12**(13), 2366–2378 (2019)

From Syntactic Structure to Semantic Relationship: Hypernym Extraction from Definitions by Recurrent Neural Networks Using the Part of Speech Information

Yixin Tan, Xiaomeng Wang(✉), and Tao Jia

College of Computer and Information Science, Southwest University, Chongqing 400715, People's Republic of China
tanyixin233@gmail.com, {wxm1706,tjia}@swu.edu.cn

Abstract. The hyponym-hypernym relation is an essential element in the semantic network. Identifying the hypernym from a definition is an important task in natural language processing and semantic analysis. While a public dictionary such as WordNet works for common words, its application in domain-specific scenarios is limited. Existing tools for hypernym extraction either rely on specific semantic patterns or focus on the word representation, which all demonstrate certain limitations. Here we propose a method by combining both the syntactic structure in definitions given by the word's part of speech, and the bidirectional gated recurrent unit network as the learning kernel. The output can be further tuned by including other features such as a word's centrality in the hypernym co-occurrence network. The method is tested in the corpus from Wikipedia featuring definition with high regularity, and the corpus from Stack-Overflow whose definition is usually irregular. It shows enhanced performance compared with other tools in both corpora. Taken together, our work not only provides a useful tool for hypernym extraction but also gives an example of utilizing syntactic structures to learn semantic relationships (Source code and data available at https://github.com/Res-Tan/Hypernym-Extraction).

Keywords: Hypernym extraction · Syntactic structure · Word representation · Part of speech · Gated recurrent units

1 Introduction

Hypernym, sometimes also known as hyperonym, is the term in linguistics referring to a word or a phrase whose semantic field covers that of its hyponym. The most common relationship between a hypernym and a hyponym is an "is-a" relationship. For example, "red is a color" provides the relationship between "red" and "color", where "color" is the hypernym of "red".

The hypernym-hyponym relation is an essential element in the semantic network and corresponding tasks related to semantic network analysis [1].

J. Z. Pan et al. (Eds.): ISWC 2020, LNCS 12506, pp. 529–546, 2020.
https://doi.org/10.1007/978-3-030-62419-4_30

The hypernym graph built on a collection of hyponym-hypernym relations can enhance the accuracy of taxonomy induction [2,3]. The linkage between the hyponym and the hypernym can be used to improve the performance of link prediction and network completion in the knowledge graph or semantic network [4,5]. In natural language processing (NLP), the hyponym-hypernym relation can help the named entity recognition [6], and the question-answering tasks for "what is" or "is a" [7,8]. The data mining, information search and retrieval can also benefit from the hyponym-hypernym relation [9,10].

Given the role and application of the hypernym-hyponym relation, it is essential to explore an automatic method to extract such the relation between two entities, which presents an important task in knowledge-driven NLP [11]. Following the landmark work focusing on lexico-syntactic patterns [12], several pattern-based methods are developed for hypernym extraction [8,13]. Then the feature-based classification methods are introduced [14,15], which applies machine learning tools to enhance the recall rate. Recently, distributional methods and hybrid distributional models are successfully applied to learn the embedding of words, based on which the hypernym-hyponym relation can be inferred [16–18]. The deep learning approach is also effective in many sequence labeling tasks including hypernym extraction [19,20].

While the extraction of hyponym-hypernym relation can be done in many different environments, in this work we focus on the hypernym extraction from definitions. More specifically, the definition refers to a short statement or description of a word. Take the word "red" as an example, whose definition on Wikipedia[1] is "Red is the color at the end of the visible spectrum of light, next to orange and opposite violet." The aim is to identify the word "color" as the hypernym of "red" from all the nouns in the definition. Intuitively, this task can be solved by general resources such as WordNet dictionary [21] or Wikipedia. But given a word's different meanings in different contexts, these resources can not sufficiently complete this task. As an example, the term "LDA" in Wikipedia denotes "Linear Discriminant Analysis" in machine learning, "Low dose allergens" in medicine, and "Landing distance available" in aviation. The combination of general resources and context identification would also fail in some domain-specific applications where the general resources do not cover the special or technical terms in that area. Moreover, existing technical approaches also demonstrate certain limitations in the task of hypernym extraction from definitions, which we summarize as follows:

1) Hypernym and hyponym are connected in many different ways. Even the "is a" pattern, which is usually considered typical, has many variations such as "is/was/are/were + a/an/the". It is impossible that one enumerates all different patterns. Consequently, despite high precision, the pattern selection method usually gives a low recall value.
2) The traditional feature-based classification method relies on manually selected features and the statistical machine learning models. It may work

[1] https://www.wikipedia.org/.

well in a class of formats, but in general, the performance can not be guaranteed once the data or the environment changes.

3) The distributional method, which relies on the similarity measure between two words to gauge the semantic relationship, is usually less precise in detecting a specific semantic relation like hypernym. Moreover, it needs a large training corpus to accurately learn the representation of words from their heterogeneous co-occurrence frequencies. In definitions, however, the appearance frequency of a word is usually low and the size of data is relatively small. The distributional method may not be directly applicable to this scenario.
4) The deep learning method, such as the recurrent neural network (RNN), can be used to process word sequences, which does not rely on particular features selected. To a great extent, it overcomes the limitation 2). However, current approaches usually take the word sequence as the input, or focus on the modification of RNN structures. Other features of the word, such as its part of speech, are not fully explored.

To briefly illustrate the difficulty, let us consider a definition from the Stack-Overflow[2] with an irregular format: "fetch-api: the fetch API is an improved replacement for XHR". The term "fetch-api" is not included in any common dictionary. While the definition has the "is an" pattern, it does not connect to the hypernym. The definition is very short and every distinct word in this definition appears just once, which makes it difficult to accurately learn the word representation. Overall, it is challenging to find a method that would accurately identify "API" as the correct hypernym.

The definition of a word represents a certain type of knowledge extracted and collected from disordered data. Indeed, there are tools capable of extracting definitions from the corpora with good accuracy [14,15,19,20,22]. Nevertheless, tools to extract hypernym from definitions remain limited. To cope with this issue, we propose a recurrent network method using syntactic features. Because the definition directly points to a noun, the hyponym is already given. Therefore, the hypernym extraction is to identify the correct hypernym from all words in the definition sentence. This task can be considered as a binary classification, in which the classifier judges if a candidate noun is a hypernym or not. In order to better learn the syntactic feature, we transfer the definition sentence into the part of speech (PoS) sequence after labeling the PoS of each word by a standard tool (Stanford-NLP [23]). The syntactic structure surrounding the candidate is learned by a bidirectional gated recurrent units (GRU) based model. To further fine tune the results, we use a set of features including the centrality of the word in the hypernym co-occurrence network. We use two corpora to evaluate our method. One is Wikipedia, featuring definitions with canonical syntax structure and intensively used by previous studies. The other is from Stack-Overflow, whose definition is domain-specific and usually with the irregular format. Our method is compared with several existing ones. Overall, it outperforms all others in both corpora, which demonstrates the advantage of combing both the tool of RNN and the PoS information in the task of hypernym extraction.

[2] https://stackoverflow.com/.

This paper is organized as follows. We review related works in Sect. 2 and introduce details of the method in Sect. 3. Experiments and evaluations of the proposed model are presented in Sect. 4. After that, we draw a conclusion about this research in Sect. 5.

2 Related Work

The existing methods in hypernym extraction generally fall into one of the following four categories: pattern-based method, feature-based classification method, distributional method and deep learning method.

2.1 Pattern-Based Method

The pattern-based method directly uses the syntactic patterns in definitions, such as "is-a", "is called", "is defined as" and more. This method is commonly applied in early works due to its simplicity and intuitiveness. The majority of these approaches apply the symbolic method that depends on lexico-syntactic patterns or features [12], which are manually crafted or semi-automatically learned. However, because only a small fraction of syntactic patterns can be included, these methods usually have a low recall value. In order to cover more patterns, [24] considers PoS tags instead of simple word sequences, which raises the recall rate. To improve the generalization of the pattern-based method, [8] starts to model the pattern matching as a probabilistic process that generates token sequences. Moreover, [22] proposes the three-step use of directed acyclic graphs, called Word-Class Lattices (WCLs), to classify definitions on Wikipedia. To better cluster definition sentences, the low-frequency words are replaced by their PoS. For a simple example, definitions that "Red is a color" and "English is a language" are in the same class that is characterized by a pattern "noun is a noun". In this way, more patterns can be characterized to identify the hypernym. In recent years, much research pay attention to extracting hypernyms from larger data resources via the high precise of pattern-based methods. [25] extract hypernymy relations from the CommonCrawl web corpus using lexico-syntactic patterns. In order to address the low recall of pattern-based method in large data resources, [18,26] integrate distributional methods and patterns to detect hypernym relations from several existing datasets.

Nevertheless, the pure pattern-based approaches are generally inefficient, given the fact that syntactic patterns are either noisy by nature or domain-specific. It is very difficult to further improve the performance in this direction.

2.2 Feature-Based Classification Method

To overcome the issue of generalization in the pattern-based method, the feature-based classification method is introduced. [27] proposes a method to learn the generalized lexico-syntactic pattern and assign scores to candidate hypernyms.

The scores are used to identify the true hypernym out of others. [28] uses conditional random fields to identify scientific terms and their accompanying definitions. Moreover, [14] uses the role of syntactic dependencies as the input feature for a support vector machine (SVM) based classifier. [15] explores the features in the dependency tree analysis.

These feature-based classification approaches heavily rely on manually specified features. Patterns learned from sentences or features analyzed from the NLP tools may not fully represent the syntactic structure. In addition, the NLP tools like dependency tree analysis are often time-consuming, and error at early steps may propagate which eventually leads to inaccurate final results.

2.3 Distributional Method

The distributional method is based on the Distributional Inclusion Hypothesis which suggests that a hypernym tends to have a broader context than its hyponyms [29,30]. If the similarity between two words can be accurately measured, then a hypernym should be associated with a similar but larger set of words than its hyponyms [30–32], [33] tests the Distributional Inclusion Hypothesis and find that hypothesis only holds when it is applied to relevant dimensions. Because word embedding can reflect the corresponding semantic relationship, [16] constructs semantic hierarchies based on the notion of word embedding. [34] uses linear classifiers to represent the target words by two vectors concatenation. [35] introduces a simple-to-implement unsupervised method to discover hypernym via per-word non-negative vector embeddings. [36] proposes a novel representation learning framework, which generates a term pair feature vectors based on bidirectional residuals of projections, reaches a state of the art performance in general resources.

Nevertheless, the application of the distributional method relies on a very large corpus to learn the word representation. Moreover, the Distributional Inclusion Hypothesis may not be always hold. In the task discussed in this paper, because many terminologies occur infrequently and the length of a definition is usually short, it can be very inefficient to learn word representation.

2.4 Deep Learning Method

The recurrent neural networks (RNN) [37] have been applied to handle many sequential prediction tasks. By taking a sentence as a sequence of tokens, RNN also works in a variety of NLP problems, such as spoken language understanding and machine translation. It is applied in hypernym extraction as well. [19] converts the task of definition extraction to sequence labeling. Using a top-N strategy (same as [22]), the infrequently appeared words are replaced by their corresponding PoS. The sequence mixed with words and PoS elements is fed to the long short-term memory (LSTM) [38] RNN to predict the definition. More recently, [20] proposes a two-phase neural network model with yields an enhanced performance compared with [19]. The first phase is constructed by a bi-directional LSTM to learn the sequence information. Then a CRF and a logistic regression are used to refine the classification results. Both of the two works focus on words. Although [19] considers the PoS information, the purpose is only to reduce the total number of words by grouping less frequent words together according to their PoS property. While they demonstrate improved performance compared with other methods, they are only tested in Wikipedia corpus, where the definition usually has a very regular format. The performance on other irregular definitions remains unknown.

3 Method

In our approach, a definition sentence is split into words. The words are further labeled according to their grammatical properties, which form a PoS sequence representing the syntactic structure of the definition. The nouns are selected as hypernym candidates which need to be classified. An illustration of this procedure is shown in Fig. 1. We particularly focus on the syntactic structure surrounding a noun. This feature is learned from the training set that helps the hypernym recognition in the testing set. Our model contains three phases (Fig. 2): syntactic feature representation, syntactic feature learning, and hypernym identification refinement.

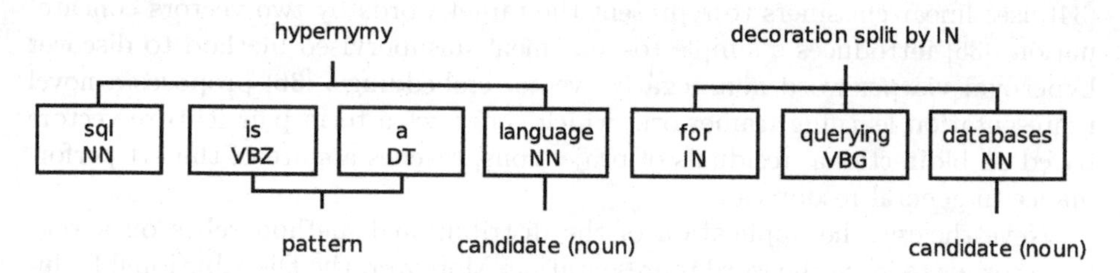

Fig. 1. An example of a hypernym-hyponym pair in a definition: "sql is a language for querying databases". The definition is split into units (words and the corresponding PoS) for analysis. The word "language" and "databases" are two hypernym candidates. The PoS elements surround "language" and "databases" are different. Our model learns such features and identifies "language" as the hypernym of "sql".

3.1 Syntactic Feature Representation

In the first phase of hypernym extraction, a definition sentence is converted into a context segment sequence which captures syntactic features of the definition. The context segment sequence is used as the input of the RNN at the second phase.

A definition sentence can be considered as a word sequence of N elements $W = [w_1, ..., w_i, ..., w_N]$, which further gives a PoS sequence $Q = [q_1, ..., q_i, ..., q_N]$. Assume that there are T nouns in the definition which are the hypernym candidates. These T nouns can be recorded as $C = \{c_i^j\}$, where

i is the position of the noun in the word sequence and j is its order in the T nouns. We use a window to extract the local syntactic feature around a noun from the PoS sequence Q, yielding T context segments as

$$s_i^j = [q_{i-L}, ..., q_{i-1}, q_{i+1}, ..., q_{i+L}], \tag{1}$$

where L is the window size which also determines the length of each context segment. To make each context segment equal length, we extend the sequence Q by adding the null element on its two ends when needed, i.e. $q_i = \varnothing$ for $i < 1$ and $i > N$.

Because the number of PoS types is limited and small, we can represent each q_i as a one-hot vector X_i, where the corresponding PoS type has the value 1 and others are with value 0. More specifically, in this work, we consider 15 PoS types and one null element $\varnothing$. Consequently, each q_i is represented by a 16-dimensional vector X_i and s_i^j is represented by Eq. 2, which is a 16 by $2L$ matrix.

$$s_i^j = [X_{i-L}, ..., X_{i-1}, X_{i+1}, ..., X_{i+L}], \tag{2}$$

3.2 Syntactic Feature Learning

We use the RNN to learn the local syntactic features. Because the original RNN model cannot effectively use the long sequential information due to the vanishing gradient problem [39], the long short-term memory (LSTM) architecture is proposed to solve this issue. In our input, a context segment s_i^j can be divided into two parts: the pre-sequence $[X_{i-L}, ..., X_{i-1}]$ and the post-sequence $[X_{i+1}, ..., X_{i+L}]$. Naturally, we adopt the gated recurrent unit (GRU) [40] architecture, which is a variant of LSTM, but simpler, and faster in training than LSTM. We use a bi-directional structure (Fig. 2(2)) containing a positive GRU and a negative GRU to learn the pre- and post-syntactic features separately from the above two sequences. The intermediate results Y_1 and Y_2 obtained through the two GRU modules are merged into $Y = [Y_1; Y_2]$ and fed into a feedforward

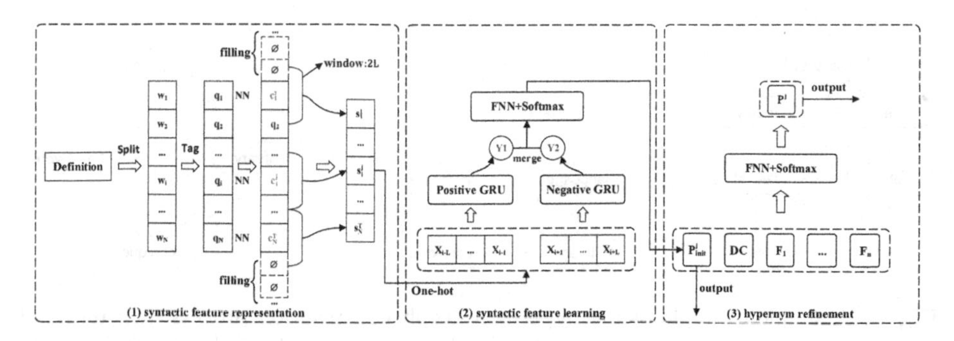

Fig. 2. The architecture of our model includes three phases: (1) syntactic feature representation (2) syntactic feature learning and (3) hypernym refinement.

neural network. The softmax layer outputs the probability P^j_{init} that c^j_i is the hypernym. P^j_{init} can be expressed as

$$P^j_{init} = p(c^j_i|s^j_i) = p(c^j_i|X_{i-L}, ..., X_{i-1}, X_{i+1}, ..., X_{i+L}) \tag{3}$$

3.3 Hypernym Refinement

The initial probability P^j_{init} obtained through the above steps can be used directly to identify the hypernym. Nevertheless, some other features of the words can be used to improve accuracy. The P^j_{init} and the selected features are fed into another feedforward neural network to compute the final probability P^j, which is presumably more optimal. The candidate with the maximum probability is selected as the hypernym of the target definition.

Features that can be included in this phase include a word's position in the sentence, whether it is capitalized, the frequency of usage, and so on. We encode these as a refinement feature vector $[F_1, F_2, ..., F_n]$. Besides these commonly known features, we also consider the degree centrality (DC) of a candidate in the hypernym co-occurrence network, following the intuition that a concept with higher centrality in a semantic network is more likely to be a hypernym. In the folksonomy, such as Stack-Overflow and Twitter, an item may be tagged by multiple labels [41]. A scientific paper may also be labeled with multiple keywords or other tags [42]. The fact that multiple entities simultaneously occur together tells some hidden relationship between them. To make use of this feature, we first extract the co-occurrence of hyponyms from the data, where multiple hyponyms are used as notations of a question or a statement. Using the hyponym-hypernym relationship in the training set, we further obtain the co-occurrence of the hypernym, based on which the hypernym co-occurrence network is built. Figure 3 gives an example of the hypernym co-occurrence network construction. The feature DC, which counts how many neighbors a hypernym has, can help identify hypernyms in several tricky cases. For example, the definition "fetch-api: the fetch API is an improved replacement for XHR, ...", P_{init} would predict "replacement" as the hypernym. The real hypernym "API" can only be revealed after taking the DC feature into consideration.

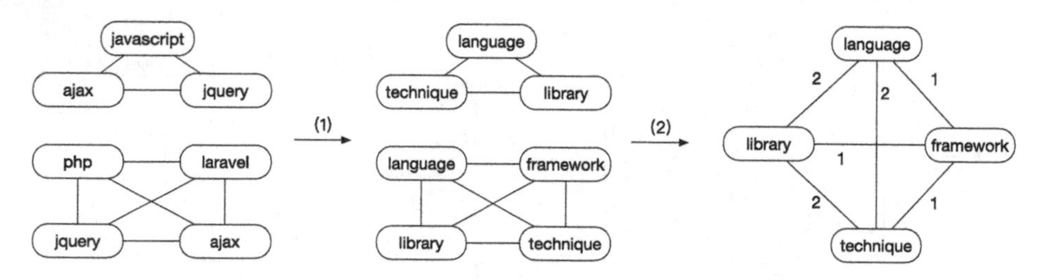

Fig. 3. A simple example of the hypernym graph construction process. (1): terms of co-occurrence are replaced by their corresponding hypernyms from the training set. (2): hypernym co-occurrence network is built based on the co-occurrence of the hypernym.

4 Experiment

We test and evaluate our method with both Wikipedia and Stack-Overflow data sets. Before the experiment, some details about data are introduced to explain the basis of feature selection. Then, we compare the performance of our method with other existing ones. Finally, we perform extended tests to confirm the advantage of using syntactic features and the RNN in hypernym extraction.

4.1 Dataset

Table 1. Details of annotation datasets from Wikipedia and Stack-Overflow.

Dataset	Definitons	Invalid-definitions	Total words	Total sentences	Average length
Wikipedia	1871	2847	21843	4718	12.05
Stack-Overflow	3750	1036	9921	4786	14.29

Two corpora are selected to train and test our method. One is the public Wikipedia corpus [27] and the other is the corpus from Stack-Overflow. The definition syntax in Wikipedia is very standardized. Hence the Wikipedia corpus is used in most existing works. However, besides common concepts, domain-specific concepts or terms are emerging from different fields. One typical example

Table 2. 15 PoS and their corresponding abbreviations in our experiment.

Abbreviation	PoS
DT	Determiner
EX	Existential *there*
IN	Preposition or subordinating conjunction
NN	Noun (singular or plural), Proper Noun (singular or plural)
TO	to
VB	Verb, base form
VBD	Verb, past tense
VBG	Verb, gerund or present participle
VBN	Verb, past participle
VBP	Verb, non-3rd person singular present
VBZ	Verb, 3rd person singular present
WDT	Wh-determiner
WP	Wh-pronoun
WP$	Possessive wh-pronoun
WRB	Wh-adverb

is computer science. In the online community Stack-Overflow, massive technical terms are discussed and organized, providing a rich body of definition corpus. In this work, we collect about 36,000 definitions from Stack-Overflow. The details of annotation datasets are shown in Table 1.

Some data pre-processing is performed. First, we use the definition extraction method [20] to filter out invalid definitions. Second, we remove words in the parentheses because they are usually used for explanations and no likely to contain the hypernym. For example, the sentence "Javascript (not be confused with Java) is a programming language ..." is simplified to "Javascript is a programming language ...". In addition, we remove some PoS such as adjectives and adverbs after PoS Tagging, which would not affect the meaning of a text. The 15 PoS types used in our methods are shown in Table 2.

4.2 PoS Position Comparison

To demonstrate that the syntactic structure captured by the PoS elements is a suitable feature for hypernym identification, we show the probability that a PoS element appears around a hypernym and a non-hypernym (Table 3). For simplicity, we only consider the closest word before and after the hypernym and the non-hypernym (equivalently window size $L = 1$ in our model). For non-hypernyms, except for WDT and DT, a PoS element appears on either side with roughly the same probability. In contrast, the appearance of the PoS element around the hypernym is very polarized. For example, for more than 99% of the time, a preposition appears after the hypernym. The clear difference in the syntactic structure surrounding the hypernym and non-hypernym provides a good basis for the classification task.

Table 3. The probability that a PoS element appears before (P_1) and after (P_2) a target. The probability is conditioned on the appearance of the PoS element hence $P_1 + P_2 = 1$. N represents the cases that the target is not a hypernym and H represents that the target is a hypernym.

PoS	$P_1(N)$	$P_2(N)$	$P_1(H)$	$P_2(H)$
WDT	0.065	0.935	0	1
IN	0.571	0.429	0.008	0.992
TO	0.540	0.460	0.028	0.972
VBP	0.539	0.461	0.033	0.967
VBZ	0.404	0.596	0.044	0.956
VBN	0.385	0.614	0.071	0.929
VBG	0.647	0.353	0.428	0.572
NN	0.416	0.584	0.963	0.037
DT	0.933	0.067	0.970	0.030

4.3 Method Comparison and Evaluation

Baseline Methods. To illustrate that the PoS based feature is more effective than the word-based feature, we separately take the one-hot code of PoS and the embedding of the word as input. The two models with different inputs are denoted by $\text{Model}_{\text{PoS}}$ and $\text{Model}_{\text{Word}}$. We also consider other existing methods for comparison, including **(1) WCLs**: An algorithm that learns a generalization of word-class lattices for modeling textual definitions and hypernym [22]. **(2) Dependencies**: A method that only uses syntactic dependencies features extracted from a syntactic parser to fed into the classifier and extract definitions and hypernyms [15]. **(3) Grammar**: A feature engineering model for hypernym extraction, using 8 handcrafted features which contain linguistic features, definitional features and graph-based features [15]. **(4) Two-Phase**: A deep learning model for sequence labeling hypernym extraction based on bidirectional LSTM and CRF [20].

Experimental Settings. (1) We use 80% of the total sample as the training set and another 20% as the testing set. (2) The performance of a method is measured by precision (P), recall (R), and F1-Score (F1) metric. (3) Extra-features for refinement including a word's position, capitalized, usage frequency, and degree centrality. (4) In $\text{Model}_{\text{Word}}$, we use the embedding layer to convert each word into a vector representation by looking up the embedding matrix $W^{\text{word}} \in \mathbb{R}^{d^w|V|}$, where V is a fixed-sized vocabulary, and d^w is the 100-dimensional embedding size. The matrix W^{word} is a parameter to be learned.

Table 4. Hypernym Extraction in Wikipedia corpus and Stack-Overflow corpus: the best results are shown in **black bold** and $\text{Model}_{\text{Word}}$ is used as comparison.

Dataset	Method	P %	R %	F1 %
Wikipedia	WCLs [22]	78.6	60.7	68.6
	Dependencies [14]	83.1	68.6	75.2
	Grammar [15]	84.0	76.1	79.9
	Two-Phase [20]	83.8	83.4	83.5
	$\text{Model}_{\text{Word}}$	82.1	76.8	79.4
	$\text{Model}_{\text{PoS}}$	**94.4**	**88.3**	**91.3**
Stack-Overflow	WCLs [22]	75.2	58.6	65.9
	Dependencies [14]	81.7	66.2	73.1
	Grammar [15]	82.8	71.4	76.7
	Two-Phase [20]	86.3	78.4	82.2
	$\text{Model}_{\text{Word}}$	76.1	72.9	74.5
	$\text{Model}_{\text{PoS}}$	**94.7**	**90.2**	**92.4**

We transform a word w_i into its word embedding e_i by using the matrix-vector product:

$$e_i = W^{\text{word}} v^i, \tag{4}$$

where v_i is a vector of size $|V|$ which has value 1 at index e_i and 0 in all other positions. (5) To prevent neural networks from over fitting, a dropout layer [43] is used. (6) The objective formulation is defined by Cross-Entropy, and the root mean square prop (RMSProp) [44] algorithm is used to train our model.

Empirical Results. The results (Table 4) show that the proposed method outperforms all existing ones. The different performance between $\text{Model}_{\text{PoS}}$ and $\text{Model}_{\text{Word}}$ confirms the advantage of using PoS feature in the hypernym extraction over the use of word embedding. It is noteworthy that the accuracy in PoS tagging would significantly affect the final outcome, given the role of PoS in our method. As an example, depending on the context, the word "control" can either be a verb or a noun. Therefore, for the definition "gridview: a control for displaying and manipulating data from ...", incorrectly tagging "control" as a verb will yield incorrect hypernym. For simplicity, the task of PoS tagging in our work is carried out by the Stanford-NLP tool. But its accuracy still has the potential for further improvement, which can eventually enhance the final performance of our method.

Hyper-Parameters Sensitivity. We show the Precision, Recall and F1-Score of our model with different hyper-parameters to analyze the model's sensitivity (Fig. 4). In general, the choice of hyper-parameters does not significantly affect the performance of our model.

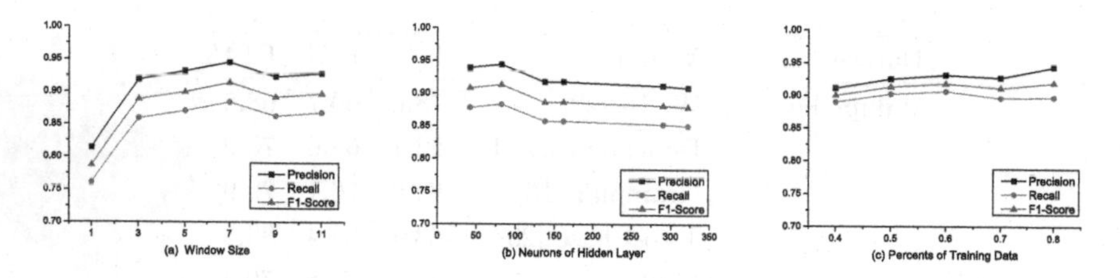

Fig. 4. The model performance (the Precision, Recall and F1-Score in the y-axis) with varying window sizes (a), neuron number in the hidden layer (b) and the ratio of training samples (c).

4.4 Word Feature and Learning Kernel Ablation

Hybrid Representation Strategy for Word Feature Ablation. The fact that the $\text{Model}_{\text{PoS}}$ outperforms the $\text{Model}_{\text{Word}}$ confirms the advantage of using PoS as the input feature. This, however, gives rise to another question: could the performance improve if the model combines both the PoS feature and word embedding? Indeed, the hybrid representation strategy was successfully applied in previous studies [19,22] to reach improved extraction results. For this reason, we analyze the performance of the hybrid strategy. For a definition sentence $W = [w_1, w_2, ..., w_N]$, we convert the word w_i into token t_i as follows:

$$t_i = \begin{cases} w_i & w_i \in W_{top} \\ PoS(w_i) & w_i \notin W_{top} \end{cases} \tag{5}$$

where W_{top} is a set of top-K words of appearance. In this way, a word w_i is left unchanged if it occurs frequently in the training corpus, or it is converted into its PoS. Eventually, we obtain a generalized definition $W' = [t_1, t_2, ..., t_N]$ with a mixture of words and PoS terms.

Table 5. The performance of our model after using the TOP-K strategy. In this table, K represents the hyper-parameter of TOP-K strategy, W represents the Wikipedia corpus and S represents the Stack-Overflow corpus. The best results are shown in **black bold**.

Representation	K	W (F1%)	S (F1%)
Word embeddings	25	88.3	89.6
	50	88.6	89.5
	100	89.0	91.0
	200	89.0	88.8
	400	89.7	89.1
	800	90.2	85.8
	2000	85.6	78.8
	4000	81.4	76.3
	8000	80.5	75.7
One-hot	10	82.7	83.8
	20	77.8	80.1
	30	72.4	77.9
	40	67.7	74.8
	50	61.9	69.3
$\text{Model}_{\text{PoS}}$		**91.2**	**92.4**

The W' is used to replace the PoS sequence Q in our method (Fig. 2) which further gives the context segment s_i^j. We consider two strategies to convert the token t_i into a high dimensional vector. One is to use the embedding layer to convert each term into a vector with dimension 100. The other is to use the one-hot vector to convert a top-K word into a vector with dimension $K + 16$. The s_i^j is then fed into the same GRU kernel as that in our model. The results are shown in Table 5. Overall, word embedding is more suitable for this mixed feature representation. The performance varies on the choice of top-K values and the best parameters differ in different data sets. Nevertheless, the best performance of the hybrid strategy is not as good as our original method, which further confirms the advantage of directly using only PoS information.

Table 6. The performances of hypernym extraction methods, which contain traditional classifiers using PoS distributional features and deep learning models using word and PoS representation. The best results are shown in **black bold**.

Dataset	Method	P %	R %	F1 %
Wikipedia	Naive bayes	85.8	81.7	83.7
	LDA	87.4	83.3	85.3
	Softmax regression	88.4	84.1	86.2
	SVM	87.3	83.2	85.2
	Decision tree	83.1	79.2	81.1
	Random forest	87.9	83.8	85.8
	CRF	88.9	77.0	82.5
	$\text{Model}_{\text{Word}}$	82.1	76.8	79.4
	$\text{Transformer}_{\text{Word}}$	86.6	81.9	84.2
	$\text{Bert}_{\text{Word}}$	87.3	83.6	85.4
	$\text{Model}_{\text{PoS}}$	94.4	88.3	91.3
	$\text{Transformer}_{\text{PoS}}$	94.8	88.7	91.6
	Bert_{PoS}	**95.2**	**89.1**	**92.0**
Stack-Overflow	Naive bayes	84.8	78.4	81.5
	LDA	86.0	81.9	83.9
	Softmax regression	87.2	82.3	84.7
	SVM	87.7	83.6	85.6
	Decision tree	83.2	78.2	80.6
	Random forest	88.4	83.7	86.0
	CRF	84.1	80.6	82.3
	$\text{Model}_{\text{Word}}$	76.1	72.9	74.5
	$\text{Transformer}_{\text{Word}}$	80.6	74.3	77.3
	$\text{Bert}_{\text{Word}}$	76.1	71.9	74.8
	$\text{Model}_{\text{PoS}}$	94.7	90.2	92.4
	$\text{Transformer}_{\text{PoS}}$	95.1	90.6	92.8
	Bert_{PoS}	**95.5**	**91.0**	**93.2**

Learning Kernel Ablation. While the RNN model adequately solves the problem, it is not the most up-to-date tool in sequence labeling. The recent pre-training language models such as Bert [45], which is based on the Transformer structure [46], has led to significant performance gains in many NLP applications [47]. Hence, it is of interest to analyze to what extend the final performance can be improved if the learning kernel is replaced by Transformer or by Bert. For this reason, we perform a learning kernel ablation experiment by applying the Transformer encoder and Bert encoder kernels in our model. We use the same input of word embedding and PoS feature as these used in $\text{Model}_{\text{Word}}$ and $\text{Model}_{\text{PoS}}$. Correspondingly, the results are recorded as $\text{Transformer}_{\text{Word}}$, $\text{Transformer}_{\text{PoS}}$, $\text{Bert}_{\text{Word}}$ and Bert_{PoS}.

In addition, to bring some insights on extent that our results benefit from the deep learning kernels, we apply some traditional classifiers and compare the results with deep learning kernels. For the traditional classifiers, we focus on the PoS feature captured by the context segment s_i^j which is extracted from the PoS sequence $Q = [q_1, ..., q_i, ..., q_N]$. In our RNN based method, each PoS element q_i is converted to a one-hot vector. Consequently, s_i^j becomes a 16 by $2L$ matrix where the number 16 corresponds to the 15 PoS elements and a and a null element $\varnothing$. To make the input compatible with traditional classifiers, we consider a slightly different representation of s_i^j. We use an integer I_q from 1 to 16 to represent each of the 16 possible values of q. To distinguish the complementary relationship that an element is before the noun and after the noun, we represent the pre-sequence $[q_{i-L}, ..., q_{i-1}]$ as $[I_{q_{i-L}}, ..., I_{q_{i-1}}]$ and the post-sequence $[q_{i+1}, ..., q_{i+L}]$ as $[33 - I_{q_{i+1}}, ..., 33 - I_{q_{i+L}}]$. In addition, we insert the same set of features $[F_1, ..., F_n]$ used in the refinement phase to the end of the sequence s_i^j. In this way, the s_i^j is converted into a one-dimensional vector as $[I_{q_{i-L}}, ..., I_{q_{i-1}}, 33 - I_{q_{i+1}} ..., 33 - I_{q_{i+L}}, DC, F_1, ..., F_n]$.

The results by different deep learning kernels and traditional classifiers are shown in Table 6. When fixing the PoS feature as the input, the use of RNN at least improves the F1 score by about 6 percentiles compared to traditional classifiers. The improvement by Transformer and Bert over RNN is relatively marginal, which is roughly 1 percentile. It is somewhat expected that Transformer and Bert will give better results, as these two kernels are more sophisticated. The magnitude of the improvement, however, implies that RNN might be a better balance between the performance and the computational complicity. Furthermore, the comparison between results by different types of input clearly demonstrates the advantage of using the PoS feature. Indeed, random forest, a very simple classifier but with PoS feature as the input, can easily outperform the deep learning kernels with the word embedding input ($\text{Model}_{\text{Word}}$, $\text{Transformer}_{\text{Word}}$ and $\text{Bert}_{\text{Word}}$) in both data sets. While the word representation is almost the by-default approach in related studies, the results presented in Table 6 shows that using the right choice of input can sometimes be more efficient than optimizing the architecture of the learning kernel.

5 Conclusion and Future Work

The hyponym-hypernym relationship plays an important role in many NLP tasks. Despite intensive studies on this topic, tools that can accurately extract hypernym from a definition is limited. The definition, representing a special type of summarized knowledge, is commonly observed, not only because some corpora such as Wikipedia or GitHub directly give the definition of a term, but also because there are tools capable of extracting definitions with good accuracy. Hence, it is useful to develop a capable tool for this task. Here we construct a bidirectional GRU model for patterns learning. We use the PoS tags of words surrounding the hypernym as the feature. Our model outperforms existing methods in both the general corpus (Wikipedia) and the domain-specific corpus (Stack-Overflow). It also demonstrates a good balance between the performance and complexity, if compared with the kernels by Transformer or Bert. More importantly, by the feature and kernel ablation, we show that the PoS feature is indeed the key element that guarantees the final performance.

The application of the tool we proposed in Stack-Overflow would help us understand the evolution of technology, group users for social network study, and build the semantic network in the domain of computer science. The performance of the tool is limited by the accuracy of PoS tagging. Hence, it would be useful to try or develop other methods other than the Stanford-NLP tool. The use of PoS feature may also have potential in other text sequence labeling tasks, which may have advantages over the word embedding. All these problems will be addressed in future studies.

Acknowledgments. This work is supported by the National Natural Science Foundation of China (NSFC) (No. 62006198).

References

1. Hertling, S., Paulheim, H.: WebIsALOD: providing hypernymy relations extracted from the web as linked open data. In: d'Amato, C., et al. (eds.) ISWC 2017. LNCS, vol. 10588, pp. 111–119. Springer, Cham (2017). https://doi.org/10.1007/978-3-319-68204-4_11
2. Navigli, R., Velardi, P., Faralli, S.: A graph-based algorithm for inducing lexical taxonomies from scratch. In: IJCAI (2011)
3. Gupta, A., Lebret, R., Harkous, H., Aberer, K.: Taxonomy induction using hypernym subsequences. In: Proceedings of the 2017 ACM on Conference on Information and Knowledge Management, pp. 1329–1338 (2017)
4. Dettmers, T., Minervini, P., Stenetorp, P., Riedel, S.: Convolutional 2D knowledge graph embeddings. In: AAAI Conference on Artificial Intelligence (2018)
5. Trouillon, T., Dance, C.R., Gaussier, E., Welbl, J., Riedel, S., Bouchard, G.: Knowledge graph completion via complex tensor factorization. J. Mach. Learn. Res. **18**(1), 4735–4772 (2017)
6. Torisawa, K., et al.: Exploiting wikipedia as external knowledge for named entity recognition. In: EMNLP-CoNLL, pp. 698–707 (2007)
7. Saggion, H., Gaizauskas, R.J.: Mining on-line sources for definition knowledge. In: FLAIRS Conference, pp. 61–66 (2004)
8. Cui, H., Kan, M.-Y., Chua, T.-S.: Soft pattern matching models for definitional question answering. TOIS **25**(2), 8 (2007)
9. Paulheim, H., Fümkranz, J.: Unsupervised generation of data mining features from linked open data. In: Proceedings of WIMS'12, pp. 1–12 (2012)
10. Chandramouli, K., Kliegr, T., Nemrava, J., Svátek, V., Izquierdo, E.: Query refinement and user relevance feedback for contextualized image retrieval (2008)

11. Zhang, Z., Han, X., Liu, Z., Jiang, X., Sun, M., Liu, Q.: Ernie: enhanced language representation with informative entities. arXiv preprint arXiv:1905.07129, 2019
12. Hearst, M.A.: Automatic acquisition of hyponyms from large text corpora. In COLING, pp. 539–545. Association for Computational Linguistics (1992)
13. Snow, R., Jurafsky, D., Ng, A.Y.: Learning syntactic patterns for automatic hypernym discovery. In: Advances in Neural Information Processing Systems, pp. 1297–1304 (2005)
14. Boella, G., Di Caro, L.: Extracting definitions and hypernym relations relying on syntactic dependencies and support vector machines. In: ACL, vol. 2, pp. 532–537. ACL (2013)
15. Espinosa-Anke, L., Ronzano, F., Saggion, H.: Hypernym extraction: combining machine-learning and dependency grammar. In: Gelbukh, A. (ed.) CICLing 2015. LNCS, vol. 9041, pp. 372–383. Springer, Cham (2015). https://doi.org/10.1007/978-3-319-18111-0_28
16. Fu, R., Guo, J., Qin, B., Che, W., Wang, H., Liu, T.: Learning semantic hierarchies via word embeddings. In: ACL, pp. 1199–1209 (2014)
17. Shwartz, V., Santus, E., Schlechtweg, D.: Hypernyms under siege: Linguistically-motivated artillery for hypernymy detection. arXiv preprint arXiv:1612.04460 (2016)
18. Shwartz, V., Goldberg, Y., Dagan, I.: Improving hypernymy detection with an integrated path-based and distributional method. arXiv preprint arXiv:1603.06076 (2016)
19. Li, S.L., Xu, B., Chung, T.L.: Definition extraction with LSTM recurrent neural networks. In: Sun, M., Huang, X., Lin, H., Liu, Z., Liu, Y. (eds.) CCL/NLP-NABD -2016. LNCS (LNAI), vol. 10035, pp. 177–189. Springer, Cham (2016). https://doi.org/10.1007/978-3-319-47674-2_16
20. Sun, Y., Liu, S., Wang, Y., Wang, W.: Extracting definitions and hypernyms with a two-phase framework. In: Li, G., Yang, J., Gama, J., Natwichai, J., Tong, Y. (eds.) DASFAA 2019. LNCS, vol. 11448, pp. 415–419. Springer, Cham (2019). https://doi.org/10.1007/978-3-030-18590-9_57
21. Christiane Fellbaum. Wordnet: An electronic lexical database and some of its applications, 1998
22. Navigli, R., Velardi, P.: Learning word-class lattices for definition and hypernym extraction. In ACL, pp. 1318–1327. Association for Computational Linguistics (2010)
23. Qi, P., Dozat, T., Zhang, Y., Manning, C.D.: Universal dependency parsing from scratch. In: CoNLL, Brussels, Belgium, pp. 160–170. Association for Computational Linguistics(2018)
24. Westerhout, E., Monachesi, P.: Extraction of dutch definitory contexts for elearning purposes. LOT Occas. Ser. **7**, 219–234 (2007)
25. Seitner, J., et al.: A large database of hypernymy relations extracted from the web. In: Proceedings of LREC 2016, pp. 360–367 (2016)
26. Bernier-Colborne, G., Barriere, C.: Crim at semeval-2018 task 9: a hybrid approach to hypernym discovery. In: Proceedings of The 12th International Workshop on Semantic Evaluation, pp. 725–731 (2018)
27. Navigli, R., Velardi, P., Ruiz-Martínez, J.M., et al.: An annotated dataset for extracting definitions and hypernyms from the web. In: LREC (2010)
28. Jin, Y., Kan, M.P., Ng, J.P., He, X.: Mining scientific terms and their definitions: a study of the ACL anthology. In: EMNLP, pp. 780–790 (2013)
29. Kotlerman, L., Dagan, I., Szpektor, I., Zhitomirsky-Geffet, M.: Directional distributional similarity for lexical inference. Nat. Lang. Eng. **16**(4), 359–389 (2010)

30. Lenci, A., Benotto, G.: Identifying hypernyms in distributional semantic spaces. In: ACL, pp. 75–79 (2012)
31. Lenci, A.: Distributional semantics in linguistic and cognitive research. IJL **20**(1), 1–31 (2008)
32. Yu, Z., Wang, H., Lin, X., Wang, M.: Learning term embeddings for hypernymy identification. In: IJCAI (2015)
33. Roller, S., Erk, K., Boleda, G.: Inclusive yet selective: supervised distributional hypernymy detection. In: COLING, pp. 1025–1036 (2014)
34. Roller, S., Erk, K.: Relations such as hypernymy: identifying and exploiting hearst patterns in distributional vectors for lexical entailment. arXiv preprint arXiv:1605.05433 (2016)
35. Chang, H.S., Wang, Z., Vilnis, L., McCallum, A.: Distributional inclusion vector embedding for unsupervised hypernymy detection. arXiv preprint arXiv:1710.00880 (2017)
36. Wang, C., He, X.: Birre: learning bidirectional residual relation embeddings for supervised hypernymy detection. In: ACL, pp. 3630–3640 (2020)
37. Elman, J.L.: Finding structure in time. Cogn. Sci. **14**(2), 179–211 (1990)
38. Hochreiter, S., Schmidhuber, J.: Long short-term memory. Neural Comput. **9**(8), 1735–1780 (1997)
39. Hochreiter, S., Bengio, Y., Frasconi, P., Schmidhuber, J.: Gradient flow in recurrent nets: the difficulty of learning long-term dependencies (2001)
40. Chung, J., Gulcehre, C., Cho, K., Bengio, Y.: Empirical evaluation of gated recurrent neural networks on sequence modeling. arXiv (2014)
41. Wang, X., Ran, Y., Jia, T.: Measuring similarity in co-occurrence data using egonetworks. Chaos Interdisc. J. Nonlinear Sci. **30**(1), 013101 (2020)
42. Jia, T., Wang, D., Szymanski, B.K.: Quantifying patterns of research-interest evolution. Nat. Hum. Behav. **1**(4), 1–7 (2017)
43. Srivastava, N., Hinton, G., Krizhevsky, A., Sutskever, I., Salakhutdinov, R.: Dropout: a simple way to prevent neural networks from overfitting. JMLR **15**(1), 1929–1958 (2014)
44. Tieleman, T., Hinton, G.: Lecture 6.5-rmsprop: divide the gradient by a running average of its recent magnitude. COURSERA Neural Netw. Mach. Learn. **4**(2), 26–31 (2012)
45. Devlin, J., Chang, M.W., Lee, K., Toutanova, K.: Bert: pre-training of deep bidirectional transformers for language understanding. arXiv preprint arXiv:1810.04805 (2018)
46. Vaswani, A., et al.: Attention is all you need. In: Advances in Neural Information Processing Systems, pp. 5998–6008 (2017)
47. Liu, Y., et al.: Roberta: a robustly optimized bert pretraining approach. arXiv preprint arXiv:1907.11692 (2019)

Focused Query Expansion with Entity Cores for Patient-Centric Health Search

Erisa Terolli[1(✉)], Patrick Ernst[2], and Gerhard Weikum[1]

[1] Max Planck Institute for Informatics, 66123 Saarbrücken, Germany
{eterolli,pernst,weikum}@mpi-inf.mpg.de
[2] Amazon, Berlin, Germany

Abstract. The Web provides a plethora of contents about diseases, symptoms and treatments. Most notably, users turn to health forums to seek advice from doctors and from peers with similar cases. However, the benefit of forums mostly lies in community QA and browsing. Expressive querying for patient-centric needs is poorly supported by search engines. This paper overcomes this issue by enriching user queries with judiciously chosen entities and classes from a large knowledge graph. Candidate entities are extracted from the full text of user posts. To counter topical drift that would arise from picking *all* entities, we devise ECO, a novel method that computes a *focused entity core* for query expansion. Experiments with contents from health forums and clinical trials demonstrate substantial gains that ECO achieves over state-of-the-art baselines.

1 Introduction

Motivation. The Internet provides a wealth of online content about health topics, including linked open data about drugs and diseases (e.g., drugbank.ca and disease-ontology.org), scientific articles about biomedical research in PubMed[1], online portals with encyclopedic entries to inform doctors and patients (e.g., mayoclinic.org and patient.info/health), all the way to online health communities (e.g., patient.info/forums and healthboards.com). All these contents are indexed by search engines, but the query result quality is fairly poor (compared to queries about music, movies, games etc.); it is often a tedious process to find relevant answers [1].

Advances on health search and QA [24] have mostly focused on specific kinds of information needs and content sources: short consumer queries that can tap health portals on topics such as "Alzheimer's treatments" or "Aricept side effects" (e.g., [18,46]), expert queries on scientific articles (e.g., [36,41]) such as "pancreatic cancer risk with DPP4 inhibitors", and specialized retrieval over electronic patient records or clinical notes (e.g., [7,25,44]). In contrast, *patient-centric* needs focusing on queries about individual health situations posed by patients themselves of general physicians on their behalf, have received little-to-no attention.

[1] https://pubmed.ncbi.nlm.nih.gov/.

J. Z. Pan et al. (Eds.): ISWC 2020, LNCS 12506, pp. 547–564, 2020.
https://doi.org/10.1007/978-3-030-62419-4_31

Aricept has made my mum worse!! #1

Hello All

My mum was diagnosed with early stages Alzheimers at the end of June but she has been suffering loss of memory for propably 3 years but as usual we put it down to 'old age'. My dad is 85 and in wonderful health, mum is 76 She had her first appointment with the local memory clinic and they prescribed 5mg Aricept. Day 1 she was fine, no side effects; day 2 she started feeling sick and then was very ill for the best part of 24 hours. She also hallucinated did not recognise her home, my dad, saw my gran (deceased) etc. We stopped the medication immediately, called the memory clinic (who didn't call back) so we have been trying to cope, for the first time, with my mum in a horrible state of confusion and anger, where she thinks we are poisoning her, trying to steal her money, not let her go home... the paranoia is endless. Can anyone please tell me how this has happened? How is she SO confused?

Fig. 1. Example of user post from forum.alzheimers.org.uk.

Example. Consider someone with Alzheimer's Disease who has taken specific drugs for years (e.g., Aricept or Risperidone) but starts to suffer from various forms of confusion. Looking up portal pages about Alzheimer's or Aricept, it is tiresome to find advice for the individual user's case, and searching PubMed is not useful either. The best source rather would be *online health forums*, where patients share experiences and doctors offer advice. The user has several options:

i) Post a question in the forum. Figure 1 shows an example with a post title and a description in the post body. Then, the user would wait for good replies by doctors or other patients in the QA community.
ii) Browse the forum, navigating over posts and topical links. This is tedious and time-consuming, but may eventually lead to helpful results such as the one shown in Fig. 2.
iii) Fill the forum's search box to query posts of other users. This faces the problem that the user's individual needs are not easily cast into a crisp set of keywords. Using the post title alone is too unspecific. Using the full post body leads to a long, verbose and diffuse query.

A general physician (GP) who searches on behalf of the patient may consider also tapping *clinical trials*: empirical studies of patient cohorts (e.g., clinicaltrials.gov). However, the GP would also struggle with the limitations of the search engine. The goal here is to find information that is *individually relevant* for the patient, taking into account the specific description in the user's post or the doctor's initial assessment.

Aricept

My mother went through a similar phase of accusing my father of affairs and she had paranoid delusions. These did get worse concurrently with being on Aricept, but it is simply impossible for me to say whether this was down to the Aricept or the progress of the disease. As FifiMo post indicates, Aricpet can make patients aggressive. As the delusions and paranoia persisted when she came off Aricept, I'm inclined to say it was probably mainly the progression of the disease in my mother's case. Risperidone has toned down the symptoms of paranoia, but it hasn't got rid of it altogether.

Fig. 2. Example of reply from forum.alzheimers.org.uk.

Problem. This paper addresses the case of *patient-centric* information needs over online contents of patient experiences. The primary source for this purpose is online health communities. Users are patients who are unhappy with their current treatment, because they have non-standard symptoms and the diagnosis is unclear, or because they suffer from adverse side effects of their therapies. The goal is to find, for an individual case, similar patients and specifically related advice by doctors. For the example post of Fig. 1, we aim to automatically retrieve the post of Fig. 2 as a highly related and useful result.

In addition to health forums, we also consider searching clinical trials for patient-centric needs, expecting that studies with similar cohorts can be helpful.

Design Space and Approach. We aim to aid users and doctors by automatically generating *user-specific* and *coherent* queries from the description that a user puts in a forum post. To this end, a number of design choices could be pursued.

An Information Retrieval (IR)-style approach would employ *query expansion* [6], by combining the user question with the terms in the full text of the post body, with term weights derived from forum statistics. However, this will lead to broad and noisy queries. A machine-learning approach could learn to classify relevant posts, with training data based on "thank you" indicators in the forum's threads. However, the *training data* will be *scarce and noisy*, and the approach would not work for highly individualized needs. A Semantic-Web approach could identify *named entities* in the user posts and link them to entries in a *knowledge graph* and other Linked-Data resources. The question could then be translated into a crisp entity-aware query (e.g., [38]). However, this provides no guarantee that the query keeps its focus, as user posts often contain cues for remotely related entities.

The design choice put forward in this paper is a combination of the IR and Semantic-Web paradigms. We build on query expansion, and use extracted named entities and a knowledge graph to generate expanded queries.

Contribution. To counter the dilution from adding too many entities, we devise a novel method to identify an *entity core* for each query, which is a compact subgraph of the knowledge graph. We utilize KnowLife[2] [12,13] which integrates various Semantic-Web resources like UMLS, DrugBank etc. Entities qualify for query expansion if and only if 1) they are highly *relevant* for the user post and 2) they are *coherent* with each other so that jointly they have a clear focus.

In the Alzheimer's example provided earlier, the list would include memory loss, aricept, feeling sick, hallucination, death, aggression, confusion, poisoning, and many more. Some of these are merely peripheral and misleading. A coherent core should focus on the key entities and classes: aricept, hallucination, dementia, and a few more. Our method, called ECO (for *E*ntity *Co*res), computes this entity core (EC) using advanced graph algorithms [17,20] and harnesses the EC for judicious query expansion.

[2] http://knowlife.mpi-inf.mpg.de/.

ECO is designed for patient-centric search over health contents, but can be carried over to other domains.

The salient contributions of this work are:

- A novel method for query expansion, by computing entity cores that identify the most relevant and coherent terms for focused expansion.
- Experimental studies with model patients for 20 different diseases, studying two cases: search over health forums and search over clinical trials. The results show the superiority of the ECO method over baselines of entity-aware query expansion.
- Data and code are accessible at: http://eco.mpi-inf.mpg.de/.

2 Related Work

Health Search. Early work on health search (e.g., [31,32]) focused on query rewriting based on the MeSH ontology and interactive user support for better recall and result diversification. Recent works (see the tutorial [24] and references therein) have mostly shifted the attention to clinical texts and leveraging domain knowledge for expert search. A major exception is [46] on consumer health search over general Web pages, which aims to bridge end-user and clinical vocabularies via knowledge bases like UMLS and dictionaries like CHV (Consumer Health Vocabulary).

Search over health forums has been addressed in few projects (e.g., [12,34]), with basic methods for retrieval and ranking. The demo paper [14] presented a system architecture for personalized search, but merely sketched a high-level methodology without technical detail. [43] analyzed health-related queries in large search engine logs. [21] investigated the quality of community-QA responses from health forums, finding that they are more useful than results from Web search. Studies on health forums investigated dimensions like misinformation or emotions (e.g., [22,33]). The work of [10] tackled the task of detecting narrative patient posts in health forums, by means of a supervised classifier. Topical classification for health content in Reddit discussion threads was investigated by [5], proposing word-embedding-based clustering methods. None of these works addresses the search problem.

Benchmark competitions like CLEF Consumer Health Search Task [42] and TREC Precision Medicine Track [36] focus on broad queries over general web pages and specialized search over scientific publications, respectively. Neither considers online health communities. CLEF addresses general queries such as "infectious disease prevention"; one of the tasks is personalization, but this is with regard to the user's level of expertise and comprehension of search results, not regarding the user's individual health situation.

Query Expansion. Query expansion is a classical IR topic (see, e.g., [6]). As sources for expansion terms, most works considered either initial search results assuming pseudo relevance feedback or background corpora for computing semantic relatedness measures between terms (see, e.g., [15,16]). A recent trend is to incorporate latent embeddings learned from large text collections into the relatedness scores for query expansion (e.g., [27,28]). The works of [9,40,45] studied query reformulation for medical search over clinical trials, health records and scientific articles. None of these considers the user's individual health situation. Recently, health-specific language embeddings, like Bio-BERT, and neural learning have been utilized to advance question answering over scientific PubMed articles [2,19,29].

Semantic Web and Knowledge Graphs. Semantic-Web research on health data has mostly addressed the horizontal integration of structured data. The iASiS project [26] pursues the goal of semantic data integration towards personalized precision medicine. The Horus.AI project [11] builds services for patient monitoring on specific conditions (e.g., diabetes). The Thalia project [41] provides a semantic search engine for PubMed articles, to support biomedical experts. SemEHR [44] harnesses semantic background knowledge to enhance search over clinical notes. In these and further projects of similar kind, online health communities are out of scope, and layperson queries is not an issue either.

Knowledge graphs (KGs) have been leveraged as a source of relevant entities and types for query expansion or query translation. A major focus here is on bridging the gap between user vocabulary, such as "high blood sugar", and biomedical terminology, such as "hyperglycemia" [24,35].

Entity-aware Query Expansion. Query expansion by including (appropriately weighted) terms from entities and types in general-purpose KGs, such as Freebase or Wikipedia-derived, has been investigated by [3,8,30,35,38] and others. Especially for entity-seeking queries [4] this has proven to be a powerful asset, in broad domains like searching for companies, products or entertainment works.

For health search, these approaches have been pursued to a lesser extent. Notable works, where the KG is constituted by domain-specific knowledge from MeSH, UMLS, CHS or health-centric parts of Wikipedia, include [12,23,46]. For consumer health search with short keyword queries, [46] conducted a systematic experimental study with a large variety of KG configurations. One of their findings is that it is crucial to configure all details properly for good performance, and identifying such good configurations is a difficult task by itself.

In our previously unexplored setting with forum contents and patient-centric queries, we expect these difficulties to be even more pronounced. In particular, unrestricted KG-based expansion with a large number of query-related entities and types as additional search terms, does not work at all. Even when term weights are carefully tuned, the expanded queries tend to be diluted and suffer from topical drifts. This is a key motivation for our approach of *focused* expansion using entity cores. In our experiments, we consider the prior works on KG-based expansion as baselines.

3 The ECO Method for Coherent Query Enrichment

3.1 Overview

ECO aims to answer patient-centric information needs consisting of

- an informational search query: a short phrase or few keywords, e.g., mentioning a disease or side effect;
- a patient-specific case description: free text about the user's individual health situation and anamnesis.

The post title *"Aricept has made my mum worse"* together with the case description in the post body, which are shown in Fig. 1, are a good example how a online forum post can cover such information needs comprehensively. Given such information, our approach is able to generate coherent queries, which are tailored to the information needs of the user. The generated queries are executed over health-forum contents or, alternatively, clinical trials. Figure 3 gives an overview of the ECO architecture. In the following, we discuss its key components.

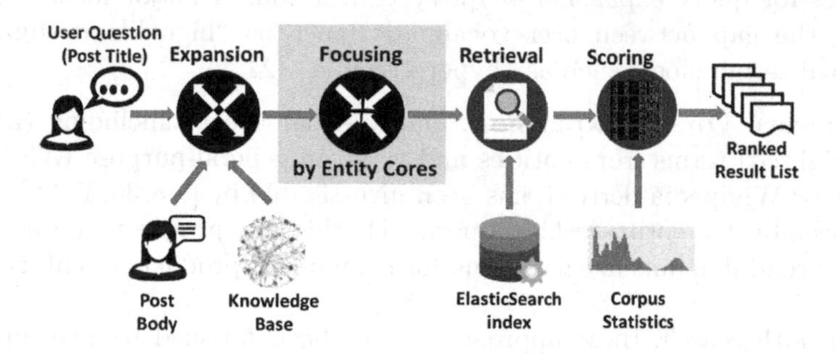

Fig. 3. ECO overview.

Health Corpus & Index. We retrieve search results from a corpus consisting of 1 million crawled and indexed forum threads and 100k clinical trials. A forum thread is a discussion starting with an initial post, having a short informational post title and an elaborate post body which contains a description of the user's individual situation (as shown in Fig. 1). We leverage such posts as starting point for generating queries, since they extensively cover patient-centric information needs as aforementioned. This post is followed by a sequence of replies by other users. Each thread belongs to a topical sub-forum. For instance, for the health forums we considered in Sect. 4.2, such sub-forums contain threads for a specific (family of) disease(s) or drug(s). For example, on healthboards.com most of the Thyroid-centered posts can be found in the *Endocrine > Thyroid Disorders* and *Endocrine > Hormone Problems* sub-forums. Even though this categorization is descriptive, relevant posts are often spread out across sub-forums, which can be inter-related.

Clinical trials are taken from clinicaltrials.gov and are semi-structured study records, which obey a fixed schema. This schema represents a broad-spectrum of patient-specific information in the form of semantic structures, such as medical conditions, genders and age-ranges considered within the trial and free-text fields, such as study description and summary.

All documents are semantically enriched by the components described in Sect. 3.2. In order to execute search queries, we store and index all free-texts and various semantic assets, such as extracted entities and categories, using ElasticSearch[3].

Knowledge Graph. We use the KnowLife resource as our knowledge graph (KG), comprising:

- entities from UMLS (Unified Medical Language System[4], together with basic relations from its source vocabularies (e.g. mereological properties over anatomical concepts or dosage forms of drugs),
- subject-property-object triples for relational statements compiled by KnowLife [13] from a variety of sources, capturing symptoms, treatments of diseases, side effects of drugs, etc.,
- types from the DeepLife project [12], containing general categories (e.g., *endocrine system disorders* subsuming *thyroid disease* among others) as well as categories derived form facts (e.g. *risk factors for thyroid disease*).

In total, the KG contains 3.2 million entities, 323,862 types, 2,170,660 property triples and is stored as RDF triples in a Neo4J graph database.

Query Processing. Given a patient-centric information in the form of initial forum posts, ECO starts with the few keywords stated in the post title and enriches it in two stages, by leveraging the knowledge graph as follows:

- **Expansion:** Information extraction is performed on the provided case descriptions, i.e. the body of health forum post, to identify entities in the KG that are specific for the medical situation of the patient. These entities are added to the query.
- **Focusing:** The expanded query is often too broad, with the risk of drifting away from the user's intent and needs. Therefore, we refocus the query by computing a coherent core of most relevant entities. This way, the expanded query is reduced into a more concise form, to ensure that query answers are focused on the user's individual needs.

The focused query, comprising the gathered information (i.e. keywords, entities and semantic categories), is executed on ElasticSearch using a custom scoring function to compute the final search result ranking as explained in Sect. 3.4.

[3] https://www.elastic.co.
[4] https://www.nlm.nih.gov/research/umls/.

3.2 Query Expansion

A case description usually contains crucial information which tailors a general medical condition to a individual situation. For instance, while the post title in Fig. 1 is about a patient's bad reaction to drug *Aricept*, the corresponding post body substantiates this medical condition with situation-specific symptoms, such as confusion, hallucination, etc. We incorporate such information by inferring the most important medical entities as follows:

Named Entity Recognition (NER). To extract entities we pre-process texts with StanfordCoreNLP[5] for tokenization and part-of-speech tagging, and then run the OpenNLP Chunker[6] to generate an initial set of noun phrase candidates. This set is extended by applying a small number of rules, like splitting or merging prepositional phrases, conjunctions, and proper/common nouns.

Named Entity Disambiguation (NED). To prune the set of candidates and link them to the KG, we use the algorithm proposed by [39]. This NED method is based on Locality Sensitive Hashing (LSH) with min-wise independent permutations for matching candidate phrases against entity names and their semantic types. We leverage type information from the KG to disambiguate between multiple entity candidates that match the same noun phrase. Whenever multiple entities have high matching scores, we pick the one with the more specific type. As the KG provides a ranked list of entities for each exactly-matching name (using information from UMLS), we further disambiguate by picking the highest ranked entity. If two entities share the same rank, the entity with the highest number of occurrences in different UMLS vocabularies is preferred.

Using the type hierarchy of the KG we prune out abstract entities of uninformative types such as *physical objects* or *concepts*, constraining the entity set to symptoms, diseases, medical findings, and pharmacological substances.

Category Expansion. For each entity in the expanded query, we retrieve its semantic categories from the KG. The categories do not only encode type information (e.g., the pharmacological class of a drug), but also relational facts harvested by KnowLife from large text corpora such as PubMed, Wikipedia articles, MayoClinic pages and more (e.g., the diseases for which a certain drug is prescribed). For instance, for *Alzheimer* we retrieve the categories *Mental or Behavioral Dysfunction* (a type category) and also *causes of memory impairment* (a fact category) among many others.

3.3 Query Focusing

Often, patient case descriptions are all but precise. They contain relevant information as well as peripheral or general information that digresses from the actual health issue. Therefore, the key focus is often buried under a substantial amount of secondary or irrelevant points. The expansion step alone cannot resolve this

---

[5] https://stanfordnlp.github.io/CoreNLP/.

[6] https://opennlp.apache.org/.

concern. This calls for a second step to re-focus the expanded query. In the second stage, we exploit the KG by considering the relationships between entities, this way enforcing:

- the coherence between entities in the query to counter topical drift, and
- the conciseness of the query itself by removing entities that are not in the core of the query intent.

This step does not only filter out irrelevant entities, but also produces a more comprehensive query. It discovers relevant semantic background knowledge for the patient's medical condition by exploring neighboring entities related to entities mentioned in the case description. We model this task as a graph-algorithmic problem. First, the KG excerpt under consideration defines a *Query Graph* as follows:

Definition 1. *A* ***Query Graph****, denoted by* $QG = (V, E)$*, is a directed graph with labeled vertices* V *and labeled edges* E*.* V *consists of the entities that appear in a patient's question's title and the full text of the corresponding post.* E *consists of the relational statements that exist between entities of* V *in the underlying knowledge graph.*

Our goal is to extract the *most informative* and *focused* sub-graph from the QG. This resembles the task of graph summarization, where summaries take the form of dense subgraphs, aiming to represent the gist of the query. On one hand, such a graph should be as comprehensive as possible, but on the other hand we also need to factor in the varying degrees of informativeness of the included entities. To incorporate these two requirements, the ECO method maps the task into a *Prize Collecting Steiner Tree (PCST)* problem [20]. The PCST problem is a generalization of Steiner Trees, which considers both edge and node weights and relaxes the requirement that all terminal nodes are included in the resulting subgraph. Our method for computing Entity Cores is based on a PCST algorithm.

Definition 2. *For a given query* q *posted in sub-forum* S*, let* $QG = (V, E)$ *be the Query Graph constructed from* q*, enhanced with node rewards* $r(u)$ *and edge costs* $c(u, v)$ *where* u *and* v *are nodes in* QG *as follows:*

- $r(u) =$ *term-frequency* (u, S) / *#sub-forums containing* u
- $c(u, v) = 1 - PMI^2 (e_u, e_v)$ *where* PMI^2 *is the squared pointwise mutual information between two entities [37].*

The ***Entity Core (EC)*** *for this query is a connected subgraph* $T' = (V', E')$ *of* QG *that maximizes* $f(T') = \sum_{v \in V'} r(v) - \sum_{u,v \in V'} c(u, v)$ *and satisfies the condition that* T' *contains the node for sub-forum* S*.*

An EC could be a general subgraph, but the nature of the objective function guarantees that only trees can be optimal. This is because including additional paths between already included nodes only increases the cost without improving the reward.

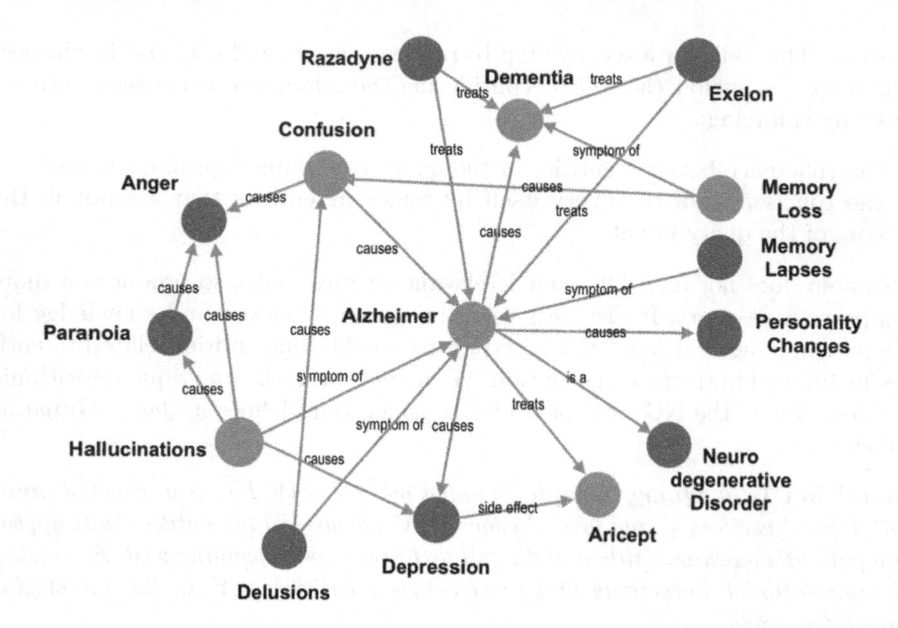

Fig. 4. Query Graph with Entity-Core Nodes Depicted in Green Color (Color figure online)

The output of ECO's focusing step is the Entity Core (EC). The final query consists of three parts: all terms from the original user question, entities in the EC, and their semantic categories.

Approximation Algorithm. Not surprisingly, computing EC's is NP-hard, but greedy methods are good approximations in many settings. We adopt the framework of [17], which consists of an iterative clustering method that groups nodes in the graph by merging existing clusters. More specifically, the algorithm can be divided in two stages: 1) growth and 2) pruning. During the growth stage, a set of active clusters and their respective spanning trees is maintained. The algorithm proceeds by iteratively merging or deactivating clusters until a desired number of active clusters is reached. In the pruning stage, unnecessary nodes are removed from the spanning trees of the last active clusters. This algorithm runs in nearly-linear time ($O(n \ \log^k n)$ with constant k) and has a factor-2 approximation guarantee.

As an illustration, Fig. 4 depicts a Query Graph for the example post in Fig. 1, with the computed Entity-Core nodes colored in green. As we can see, the EC reduces the overly broad Query Graph into a coherent and concise set of query terms.

3.4 Scoring and Ranking of Query Answers

Our scoring function for ranking query answers is based on a weighted linear combination of TF-IDF scores (tf = term frequency, idf = inverse document frequency). Weights are derived from corpus statistics, and hyper-parameters are determined using a withheld validation set. A query Q is a triple $Q = (T, E, C)$, where T is the set of keywords, E is the set of extracted entities, and C is the set of semantic categories for E. Correspondingly, all documents D are divided into three fields (D_t, D_e, D_c), i.e free-text, entities, and categories, which are indexed separately. With these representations we compute a ranking score s for a document and query as:

$$score(D,Q) = \lambda_T \sum_{t \in T} \frac{\mathbf{idf}(t)^2 * \mathbf{tf}(t, D_t)}{\sqrt{D_T}} + \lambda_C \sum_{c \in C} \frac{\mathbf{idf}(c)^2 * \mathbf{tf}(c, D_c)}{\sqrt{D_C}} + \lambda_E \sum_{e \in E} \frac{\mathbf{idf}(e)^2 * \mathbf{tf}(e, D_e)}{\sqrt{D_E}}$$

where $\sqrt{D_{\{T,E,C\}}}$ is a field-length normalization factor. Appropriate values for the hyper-parameters $\lambda_{\{T,E,C\}}$ are obtained by grid search (see Sect. 4.2).

Table 1. Health forum corpus

Source	Subforums	Users	Threads	Posts
healthboards.com	236	316,658	751,304	1,213,383
ehealthforum.com	285	338,079	297,356	4,251,533
patient.co.uk	800	18,326	44,618	151,583

4 Experimental Studies

To study the performance of the ECO method and compare it with state-of-the-art baselines, we conduct experiments with two different kinds of online contents: health forums and clinical trials. For the evaluation of the retrieved results, we use two kinds of assessments:

- relevance judgements by crowdsourcing workers
- authoritative judgements by two medical doctors, for a sub-set of the results.

The assessments by medical professionals primarily serve to validate the soundness of the crowdsourcing results. In addition, they reflect different perspectives for health forums where lay users and doctors may have different views on whether a reply is useful or not (not a point for clinical trials, though). Hence, we report on both settings separately.

4.1 Setup

Competitors. We compare a suite of strategies for generating queries:

- *Baseline - Title:* using all terms present in the post title, that is, in the user-question itself.
- *Baseline - Title+Post:* using all terms present in the title and full text of the post.
- *Baseline - Entity Expansion:* expanding the title-based query with biomedical entities from the full user post.
- *Baseline - Entity+Type Expansion:* expanding the title-based query with biomedical entities and their semantic types.
- *Baseline - Steiner Tree Expansion:* refining the title-based query with terms for all entities present in the Steiner Tree, computed over the Query Graph.
- *Entity Core Expansion (ECO):* enriching the title-based query with all entities present in the Entity Core as in Definition 2.

Note that the Steiner-Tree-based expansion is not really a prior-works baseline, as it already makes use of our KG-based query graph construction. However, it is simpler than ECO, hence considered as another point of comparison.

We evaluated the rankings of query results by Top-k Precision (PRE@k), Top-k Mean Average Precision (MAP@k), and Normalized Discounted Cumulative Gain (NDCG@k).

Hyper-Parameters. We perform grid search to set the hyper-parameters $\lambda_{T,E,C}$ of the answering scoring of Sect. 3.4, using a small validation set of 10 withheld queries. The resulting values are $\lambda_T = 1.0$, $\lambda_E = 0.6$ and $\lambda_C = 0.1$.

Crowdsourcing Assessments. For gathering human judgements, we conducted crowdsourcing tasks over the appen.com platform to assess the retrieval quality of the different query formulation strategies. To this end, crowd workers were asked to judge if a retrieved forum thread is relevant for a particular query along with the full user post (i.e., reflecting the individual health situation of the user whose post the query was derived from). The retrieved answer threads were presented to the worker as a combination of the root post that initiates the thread and the post with the highest word overlap measured by Jaccard similarity with the query post.

For quality assurance, we designed a set of test cases intermingled with the actual assessment tasks, and we cross-checked the workers' answers with our gold-standard results. The gold-standard set consisted of a set of 10 questions, that were evaluated by at least two experts that had perfect agreement between them for the relevance labels of the test cases. Poorly performing workers (2237 out of 14437) who failed to answer correctly the test question assigned to them were eliminated. We obtained 3 judgments for each query and paid 2.5 cent for each assessment. On average, trusted annotators needed 2.5 min to finish a task of 4 items. Overall, the inter-annotator agreement measured by Krippendorff's Alpha is 0.46.

Professional Assessments. To validate the relevance data obtained by crowdsourcing and to have authoritative judgements for evaluating our approach, we asked two professionals, both medical doctors, to label the results. A result is considered to be relevant, if both doctors label it as relevant. Due to the limited availability of the annotators, we reduce the evaluation set by randomly selecting 15 queries out of our 100 test queries.

4.2 Health Forums

Data. Our experimental data is obtained by crawling multiple health forums with a total of 1,048,428 discussion threads, from three main sources as given in Table 1. The forums are organized into sub-forums on more than 100 diseases, syndromes and drugs, from which we selected the following 20 topics with high coverage: Depression, Eating Disorders, Skin Cancer, Alzheimer Disease, Acid Reflux, Arthritis, Asthma, Back Pain, Carpal Tunnel Syndrome, Crohn Disease, Diabetes, Fibromyalgia, High Blood Pressure and Hypertension, Insect Bites, Low Blood Pressure and Hypotension, Meningitis, Multiple Sclerosis, Pancreas Disorders, Sinusitis, Vision and Eye Disorders. For each of these disorders, we identified 5 typical user posts which serve as queries in our experiments. As such, our test workload consists of 100 individual queries. To make our experiments transparent and reproducible for third parties, we release the datasets on both the forum-search and clinical-trials experiments at: http://eco.mpi-inf.mpg.de/.

Expansion Strategies. Table 2 compares the Title and Title+Post baselines with straightforward expansion strategies using Entities and Entities+Types. The first observation is that a simple expansion using Title+Post baseline degrades the results compared to Title only. This illustrates the difficulty of generating queries that capture specific user's situation yet stay focused and concise. Entity expansion outperforms the baseline in all evaluation metrics, where all results have statistical significance (with a p-value ≤ 0.01 for a paired t-test). Expansion with types and categories (in addition to entities), is significantly better than the baseline (with p-value ≤ 0.01) but does not improve over expanding merely with entities. Overall, we conclude that incorporating entities from the full text of user posts is crucial and significantly improves search result quality. The additional incorporation of entity types does not give notable benefits.

Focusing Strategies. For comparing ECO against the expansion-only strategies, we focus on the best-performing baselines using solely entities. Table 3 compares the results of two focusing strategies against the best expansion-only strategy *Entity Expansion*. The table clearly shows that focusing with Steiner Trees cannot improve the results, and actually loses against expansion-only by all metrics (with p-value<0.01). In contrast, the ECO method yields additional benefits in retrieval performance with significant gains. This underlines the need for judiciously re-focusing the expanded query, where Entity Cores turn out to

Table 2. Crowdsourcing evaluation of expansion baselines for health forums.

Approach	PRE		MAP		NDCG	
	@5	@10	@5	@10	@5	@10
Title	0.59	0.59	0.72	0.67	0.80	0.80
Title + Post	0.49	0.46	0.72	0.67	0.8	0.79
Entity expansion	**0.68**	**0.67**	**0.8**	**0.76**	**0.86**	**0.87**
Entity + Type expansion	0.66	0.64	0.79	0.75	0.86	0.87

Table 3. Crowdsourcing evaluation of focusing strategies for health forums.

Approach	PRE		MAP		NDCG	
	@5	@10	@5	@10	@5	@10
Entity expansion	0.68	0.67	0.8	0.76	0.86	0.87
Ex + ST	0.59	0.58	0.73	0.69	0.8	0.81
ECO	**0.75**	**0.74**	**0.81**	**0.79**	**0.87**	**0.88**

be much better than Steiner Trees. The superiority of ECO is confirmed also in the evaluation by medical professionals, as shown in Table 4. Here, too, ECO significantly outperforms both baselines.

Retrieval Time. Generating and executing focused expanded queries with ECO takes 1 to 5 s ($\mu = 1.86$, $\sigma = 0.97$). The analysis of posts for detecting entities takes 5 to 60 s, with high variance, as it is approximately proportional to the post length. Both entity markup and query processing could be sped up by more engineering.

4.3 Clinical Trials

To demonstrate the versatility of our approach, we also test its applicability for clinical trials, where doctors would search on behalf of a patient. Our experimental data consists of 97,390 clinical trials from clinicaltrials.gov. We evaluate ECO on the 15 randomly selected queries.

The crowdsourcing results in Table 5 demonstrate that ECO is able to achieve large performance gains across all metrics compared to the previously best baseline. The inter-annotator agreement between crowd workers is 0.49, far from perfect but remarkably high.

Since clinical trials are difficult to interpret for lay users, we also evaluate the results with judgements by medical professionals. Even though the doctors' assessments of relevance and utility tend to be more conservative than the crowdsourcing judgements, the ECO method significantly outperforms the baselines for all metrics (with p-value<0.01) as shown in Table 6. This shows that the judiciously re-focused use of KG entities and categories does successfully bridge the

Table 4. Medical doctor evaluation for health forums.

Approach	PRE		MAP		NDCG	
	@1	@5	@1	@5	@1	@5
Title	0.33	0.28	0.33	0.49	0.33	0.56
Entity expansion	0.33	0.31	0.33	0.54	0.33	0.63
ECO	**0.40**	**0.39**	**0.40**	**0.62**	**0.40**	**0.69**

Table 5. Crowdsourcing evaluation for clinical trials

Approach	PRE		MAP		NDCG	
	@1	@5	@1	@5	@1	@5
Title	0.67	0.63	0.67	0.79	0.67	0.86
Entity expansion	0.87	0.64	0.87	0.82	0.87	0.90
ECO	**0.93**	**0.87**	**0.93**	**0.91**	**0.93**	**0.95**

terminologies of users (in post titles as queries) and medical experts (in result documents). Altogether, this confirms that ECO is able to achieve large gains over the baselines also under the meticulous examination by professionals.

Table 6. Evaluation by medical professionals for clinical trials

Approach	PRE		MAP		NDCG	
	@1	@5	@1	@5	@1	@5
Title	0.40	0.40	0.40	0.50	0.40	0.53
Entity expansion	0.40	0.41	0.40	0.55	0.40	0.60
ECO	**0.60**	**0.69**	**0.60**	**0.74**	**0.60**	**0.81**

5 Conclusion

This work addressed the under-explored topic of supporting patient-centric information needs by search over health contents. Our experiments, with evaluation by both crowdsourcing users and medical professionals, demonstrated the viability of our ECO method. In comparison to state-of-the-art baselines with query expansion by entities and classes from a KG, the experimental results clearly showed that the re-focusing step, based on entity cores, is crucial for the superior performance of ECO.

We focused on two kinds of health contents: forums of online communities and reports on clinical trials, as these are the best sources on patient experiences. Nevertheless, we plan to explore the suitability of our approach for other kinds of health documents, such as PubMed articles or health news.

In this work, we have focused on searching health forums and clinical trials, as health is by itself an important domain with high impact. In general, our methodology can be adapted to other domains as well, such as finance, food or travel. For example, we could address a travel discussion forum where people ask about and exchange experiences about visa issues, sightseeing beaten paths, local food and culture, etc. These are subject to individual preferences, so that ranking answers by personal relevance is important. We would use travel-centric KGs, and use ECO for focused query expansion. This is left for future work.

References

1. Abrahamson, J.A., Fisher, K.E., Turner, A.G., Durrance, J.C., Turner, T.C.: Lay information mediary behavior uncovered: exploring how nonprofessionals seek health information for themselves and others online. J. Med. Library Assoc. JMLA **96**(4), 310 (2008)
2. Alsentzer, E., et al.: Publicly available clinical bert embeddings. arXiv preprint arXiv:1904.03323 (2019)
3. Balaneshinkordan, S., Kotov, A.: An empirical comparison of term association and knowledge graphs for query expansion. In: Ferro, N., et al. (eds.) ECIR 2016. LNCS, vol. 9626, pp. 761–767. Springer, Cham (2016). https://doi.org/10.1007/978-3-319-30671-1_65
4. Balog, K.: Entity-Oriented Search. Springer Nature, Cham (2018). https://doi.org/10.1007/978-3-319-93935-3
5. Barros, J.M., Buitelaar, P., Duggan, J., Rebholz-Schuhmann, D.: Unsupervised classification of health content on reddit. In: Proceedings of the 9th International Conference on Digital Public Health, pp. 85–89 (2019)
6. Carpineto, C., Romano, G.: A survey of automatic query expansion in information retrieval. ACM Comput. Surv. (CSUR) **44**(1), 1–50 (2012)
7. Chamberlin, S.R., et al.: A query taxonomy describes performance of patient-level retrieval from electronic health record data. medRxiv, p. 19012294 (2019)
8. Dalton, J., Dietz, L., Allan, J.: Entity query feature expansion using knowledge base links. In: Proceedings of the 37th International ACM SIGIR Conference on Research & Development in Information Retrieval, pp. 365–374 (2014)
9. De Vine, L., Zuccon, G., Koopman, B., Sitbon, L., Bruza, P.: Medical semantic similarity with a neural language model. In: Proceedings of the 23rd ACM International Conference on Conference on Information and Knowledge Management, pp. 1819–1822 (2014)
10. Dirkson, A., Verberne, S., Kraaij, W.: Narrative detection in online patient communities. In: Texts@ECIR, pp. 21–28 (2019)
11. Dragoni, M.: Semantic ai for healthcare: The horus. ai platform. In: Second International Workshop on Semantic Web Meets Health Data Management (SWH 2019) co-located with the 18th International Semantic Web Conference (ISWC 2019). vol. 2515, pp. 1–4. CEUR-WS. org (2019)
12. Ernst, P., et al.: DeepLife: an entity-aware search, analytics and exploration platform for health and life sciences. In: ACL, pp. 19–24 (2016)
13. Ernst, P., Siu, A., Weikum, G.: Knowlife: a versatile approach for constructing a large knowledge graph for biomedical sciences. BMC Bioinform. **16**(1), 157 (2015)

14. Ernst, P., Terolli, E., Weikum, G.: LongLife: a platform for personalized searchfor health and life sciences. In: 18th Semantic Web Conference, pp. 237–240. ceur-ws. org (2019)
15. Fang, H., Zhai, C.: Semantic term matching in axiomatic approaches to information retrieval. In: Proceedings of the 29th Annual International ACM SIGIR Conference on Research and Development in Information Retrieval, pp. 115–122 (2006)
16. Hazimeh, H., Zhai, C.: Axiomatic analysis of smoothing methods in language models for pseudo-relevance feedback. In: ICTIR, pp. 141–150. ACM (2015)
17. Hegde, C., Indyk, P., Schmidt, L.: A nearly-linear time framework for graph-structured sparsity. In: ICML (2015)
18. Jimmy, Zuccon, G., Palotti, J.R.M., Goeuriot, L., Kelly, L.: Overview of the CLEF 2018 consumer health search task. In: Working Notes of CLEF (2018)
19. Jin, Q., Dhingra, B., Liu, Z., Cohen, W.W., Lu, X.: PubMedQA: a dataset for biomedical research question answering. arXiv preprint arXiv:1909.06146 (2019)
20. Johnson, D.S., Minkoff, M., Phillips, S.: The prize collecting steiner tree problem: theory and practice. In: SODA, pp. 760–769 (2000)
21. Kanthawala, S., Vermeesch, A., Given, B., Huh, J.: Answers to health questions: internet search results versus online health community responses. J. Med. Internet Res. **18**(4), e95 (2016)
22. Khanpour, H., Caragea, C.: Fine-grained information identification in health related posts. In: The 41st International ACM SIGIR Conference on Research & Development in Information Retrieval, pp. 1001–1004 (2018)
23. Kondylakis, H., et al.: Semantically-enabled personal medical information recommender. In: ISWC (2015)
24. Koopman, B., Zuccon, G.: WSDM 2019 tutorial on health search (HS2019): a full-day from consumers to clinicians. In: WSDM, pp. 838–839 (2019)
25. Koopman, B., Zuccon, G., Bruza, P.: What makes an effective clinical query and querier? JASIST **68**(11), 2557–2571 (2017)
26. Krithara, A., et al.: iASiS: towards heterogeneous big data analysis for personalized medicine. In: 2019 IEEE 32nd International Symposium on Computer-Based Medical Systems (CBMS), pp. 106–111. IEEE (2019)
27. Kuzi, S., Carmel, D., Libov, A., Raviv, A.: Query expansion for email search. In: SIGIR, pp. 849–852. ACM (2017)
28. Kuzi, S., Shtok, A., Kurland, O.: Query expansion using word embeddings. In: Proceedings of the 25th ACM International on Conference on Information and Knowledge Management, pp. 1929–1932 (2016)
29. Lee, J., et al.: Biobert: a pre-trained biomedical language representation model for biomedical text mining. Bioinformatics **36**(4), 1234–1240 (2020)
30. Liu, X., Chen, F., Fang, H., Wang, M.: Exploiting entity relationship for query expansion in enterprise search. Inf. Retrieval **17**(3), 265–294 (2014)
31. Luo, G., Tang, C.: On iterative intelligent medical search. In: Proceedings of the 31st Annual International ACM SIGIR Conference on Research and Development in Information Retrieval, pp. 3–10 (2008)
32. Luo, G., Tang, C., Yang, H., Wei, X.: MedSearch: a specialized search engine for medical information retrieval. In: Proceedings of the 17th ACM Conference on Information and Knowledge Management, pp. 143–152 (2008)
33. Mukherjee, S., Weikum, G., Danescu-Niculescu-Mizil, C.: People on drugs: credibility of user statements in health communities. In: Proceedings of the 20th ACM SIGKDD International Conference on Knowledge Discovery and Data Mining, pp. 65–74 (2014)

34. Pang, P.C.I., Verspoor, K., Pearce, J., Chang, S.: Better health explorer: designing for health information seekers. In: OzCHI, pp. 588–597. ACM (2015)
35. Patel, C., et al.: Matching patient records to clinical trials using ontologies. In: Aberer, K., Choi, K.-S., Noy, N., Allemang, D., Lee, K.-I., Nixon, L., Golbeck, J., Mika, P., Maynard, D., Mizoguchi, R., Schreiber, G., Cudré-Mauroux, P. (eds.) ASWC/ISWC -2007. LNCS, vol. 4825, pp. 816–829. Springer, Heidelberg (2007). https://doi.org/10.1007/978-3-540-76298-0_59
36. Roberts, K., et al.: Overview of the trec 2017 precision medicine track. In: TREC (2017)
37. Role, F., Nadif, M.: Handling the impact of low frequency events on co-occurrence based measures of word similarity. In: Proceedings of the International Conference on Knowledge Discovery and Information Retrieval (KDIR-2011). Scitepress, pp. 218–223 (2011)
38. Rospocher, M., Corcoglioniti, F., Dragoni, M.: Boosting document retrieval with knowledge extraction and linked data. Semantic Web **10**(4), 753–778 (2019)
39. Siu, A., Nguyen, D.B., Weikum, G.: Fast entity recognition in biomedical text. In: Proceedings of Workshop on Data Mining for Healthcare (DMH) at Conference on Knowledge Discovery and Data Mining (KDD). ACM Press, New York (2013)
40. Soldaini, L., Yates, A., Goharian, N.: Learning to reformulate long queries for clinical decision support. JAIST **68**(11), 2602–2619 (2017)
41. Soto, A.J., Przybyla, P., Ananiadou, S.: Thalia: semantic search engine for biomedical abstracts. Bioinformatics **35**(10), 1799–1801 (2019)
42. Suominen, H., et al.: Overview of the CLEF eHealth evaluation lab 2018. In: Bellot, P., et al. (eds.) CLEF 2018. LNCS, pp. 286–301. Springer, Cham (2018). https://doi.org/10.1007/978-3-319-98932-7_26
43. White, R.W., Horvitz, E.: From health search to healthcare: explorations of intention and utilization via query logs and user surveys. JAMIA **21**(1), 49–55 (2013)
44. Wu, H., et al.: SemEHR: a general-purpose semantic search system to surface semantic data from clinical notes for tailored care, trial recruitment, and clinical research. J. Am. Med. Inform. Assoc. **25**(5), 530–537 (2018)
45. Zhu, D., Wu, S., Carterette, B., Liu, H.: Using large clinical corpora for query expansion in text-based cohort identification. J. Biomed. Inform. **49**, 275–281 (2014)
46. Zuccon, G., Koopman, B., et al.: Payoffs and pitfalls in using knowledge-bases for consumer health search. Inf. Retrieval J. **22**(3–4), 350–394 (2019)

Generating Expressive Correspondences: An Approach Based on User Knowledge Needs and A-Box Relation Discovery

Elodie Thiéblin, Ollivier Haemmerlé, and Cássia Trojahn[(✉)]

IRIT & Université de Toulouse 2 Jean Jaurès, Toulouse, France
elodie@thieblin.fr, {ollivier.haemmerle,cassia.trojahn}@irit.fr

Abstract. Ontology matching aims at making different ontologies interoperable. While most approaches have addressed the generation of simple correspondences, more expressiveness is required to better address the different kinds of ontology heterogeneities. This paper presents an approach for generating complex correspondences that relies on the notion of competency questions for alignment (CQA). A CQA expresses the user knowledge needs in terms of alignment and aims at reducing the alignment scope. The approach takes as input a set of CQAs as SPARQL queries over the source ontology. The generation of correspondences is performed by matching the subgraph from the source CQA to the lexically similar surroundings of the instances from the target ontology. Evaluation of the approach has been carried out on both synthetically generated and real-word datasets.

1 Introduction

Ontology matching aims at enabling interoperability between knowledge expressed in different ontologies. It is an active area with different solutions been proposed from various disciplines, e.g., databases, statistical, natural language processing, and machine learning. The matching process can be seen as the task of generating a set of correspondences (i.e., an alignment) between the entities of different ontologies, usually one source and one target ontologies [5]. Despite the variety of proposals, most of the matching approaches are still dedicated to the generation of simple correspondences (i.e., those linking one single entity of a source ontology to one single entity of a target ontology). This kind of correspondence is however not expressive enough for fully covering the different kinds of ontology heterogeneities (lexical, semantic, conceptual). Complex correspondences (i.e., those involving logical constructors or transformation functions) are rather required [27]. For example, the piece of knowledge expressing an accepted paper can be represented as a class IRI (e.g., *Accepted_Paper*) in a source ontology, or as a class expression representing the papers having acceptance as decision of type in a target ontology (e.g., $Paper \sqcap \exists$ *hasDecision.Acceptance*). Expressive correspondences are required for expressing these different representations. For citing some applications and domains requiring

J. Z. Pan et al. (Eds.): ISWC 2020, LNCS 12506, pp. 565–583, 2020.
https://doi.org/10.1007/978-3-030-62419-4_32

such kind of correspondences, in the cultural heritage domain, the need for complex correspondences has been identified for data integration or data translation applications [15]. In the agronomic domain, complex alignments help cross-query linked open data repositories [24]. In the biomedical domain, complex alignments have also been used to build a consensual model from heterogeneous terminologies [11].

While the matching space for generating complex correspondences is higher than $\mathcal{O}(2^{mn})$ (m and n being respectively the number of entities of the source and target ontologies), a space reduction strategy can be based upon on an assumption that, in practical, it may be the case that the user does not need the alignment to cover the full scope of the ontologies. This assumption goes in opposite to the existing complex alignment generation approaches which intend to cover the full common scope of the aligned ontologies. This has the side effect of neglecting the user needs. This also impacts the matching performance, in particular when dealing with large knowledge bases.

This paper presents an approach for generating complex correspondences that relies on competency questions for alignment (CQAs) as a way of expressing user knowledge needs in terms of alignment. This approach is based on the following hypothesis: (i) users are able to express their needs in terms of SPARQL queries; and (ii) for each knowledge need, the knowledge bases share at least one common instance.

Based on these hypothesis, the approach takes as input a set of CQAs translated into SPARQL queries over the source ontology. Each answer is a set of instances retrieved from a knowledge base described by the source ontology. At least one instance is common with respect to the target knowledge base. The generation of the correspondence is then performed by matching the subgraph from the source CQA to the lexically similar surroundings of the target instances.

The main contributions of this paper can be summarised as follows: (i) a novel notion of competency question for alignment is introduced as a way for reducing the matching scope (this notion can hence be applied on the generation of simple correspondences); (ii) a CQA based matching approach able to generate complex correspondences involving logical constructions[1]; (iii) a comparison of the proposed approach to state-of-the-art ones; and (iv) a discussion of their strengths and weaknesses.

The rest of the paper is organised as follows. Next section introduces ontology matching and CQA (Sect. 2), followed by the presentation of the approach (Sect. 3). The evaluation is presented (Sect. 4), followed by a discussion on the related work (Sect. 5). Finally, the conclusions and future work end the paper (Sect. 6).

[1] Complex correspondences with transformations functions are out of the scope of this paper.

2 Foundations

2.1 Complex Ontology Alignment

Ontology matching (as in [5]) is defined as the process of generating an alignment A between two ontologies: a source ontology o_1 and a target ontology o_2. A is a set of correspondences $\langle e_1, e_2, r, n \rangle$. Each correspondence expresses a relation r (e.g., equivalence ($\equiv$), subsumption ($\sqsupseteq$, $\sqsubseteq$)) between two members e_1 and e_2, and n expresses its level of confidence [0..1]. A member can be a single ontology entity (class, object property, data property, individual) of respectively o_1 and o_2 or a complex construction which is composed of entities using constructors. Two kinds of correspondences are considered depending on the type of their members:

- a correspondence is **simple** if both e_1 and e_2 are single entities (IRIs): $\langle o_1$:*Paper*, o_2:*Paper*, $\equiv$, *1*$\rangle$
- a correspondence is **complex** if at least one of e_1 or e_2 involves a constructor: $\langle o_1$:*Accepted_Paper*, $\exists o_2$:*hasDecision*.o_2:*Acceptance*, $\equiv$, *1*$\rangle$

A simple correspondence is usually noted (s:s), and a complex correspondence can be (s:c) if its source member is a single entity, (c:s) if its target member is a single entity or (c:c) if both members are complex entities. An approach which generates complex correspondences is referred as "complex approach" or "complex matcher" in the remainder of this paper.

2.2 Competency Questions for Alignment (CQAs)

In ontology authoring, in order to formalise the knowledge needs of an ontology, competency questions (CQs) have been introduced as *ontology's requirements in the form of questions the ontology must be able to answer* [8]. A competency question for alignment (CQA) is a competency question which should (in the best case) be covered by two or more ontologies, i.e., it expresses the knowledge that an alignment should cover in the best case (if both ontologies' scopes can answer the CQA). The first difference between CQA and CQ is that the scope of the CQA is limited by the intersection of its source and target ontologies' scopes. The second difference is that this maximal and ideal alignment's scope is not known *a priori* (as it is the purpose of the alignment). As the ontology authoring competency questions (CQs) [19], a CQA can be expressed in natural language or as SPARQL queries. Inspired [19], the notion of **question arity**, which represents the arity of the expected answers to a CQA is introduced:

- A *unary* question expects a set of instances, e.g., "Which are the accepted papers?" *(paper1), (paper2).*
- A *binary* question expects a set of instances or value pairs, e.g., "What is the decision on a paper?" *(paper1, accept), (paper2, reject).*
- A *n-ary* question expects a tuple of size ≥ 3, e.g., "What is the decision associated with the review of a given paper?" *(paper1, review1, weak accept), (paper1, review2, reject).*

CQAs for the approach are limited to *unary* and *binary* questions, of *select* type, and no modifier. This is a limitation in the sense that we do not deal with specific kinds of SPARQL queries, as the ones involving CONSTRUCT and ASK. The approach does not deal with transformation functions or filters inside the SPARQL queries and only accepts queries with one or two variables. However, as classes and properties are unary and binary predicates, these limitations still allow the approach to cover ontology expressiveness.

3 Matching Approach

The proposed approach takes as input a set of CQAs in the form of SPARQL SELECT queries over the source ontology. It requires that the source and target ontologies have an *Abox* with at least one common instance for each CQA. The answer to each input query is a set of instances, which are matched with those of a knowledge base described by the target ontology. The matching is performed by finding the surroundings of the target instances which are lexically similar to the CQA. The idea behind the approach is to rely on a few examples (answers) to find a generic rule which describes more instances. The overall approach is articulated in 11 steps (Fig. 1). It is based on **subgraphs** which are a **set of triples** for a unary CQA and a **property path** for a binary CQA. The implementation of the approach is publicly available[2].

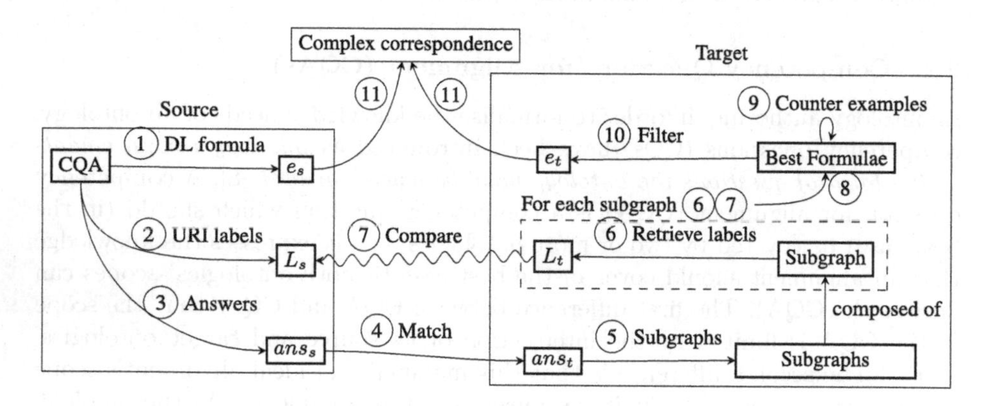

Fig. 1. Schema of the general approach.

In the remainder of the paper, the examples consider the knowledge bases in Fig. 2. They share common instances: o_1*:person1* and o_2*:person1*, o_1*:paper1* and o_2*:paper1*. Ontology o_1 represents the concept of *accepted paper* as a class while o_2 models the same knowledge with a *has decision* property. The property *paper written by* is represented by a single property in o_1 while in o_2, the property *writes* links a *person* to a *document.* A criticism to this example could be that

[2] https://framagit.org/IRIT_UT2J/ComplexAlignmentGenerator.

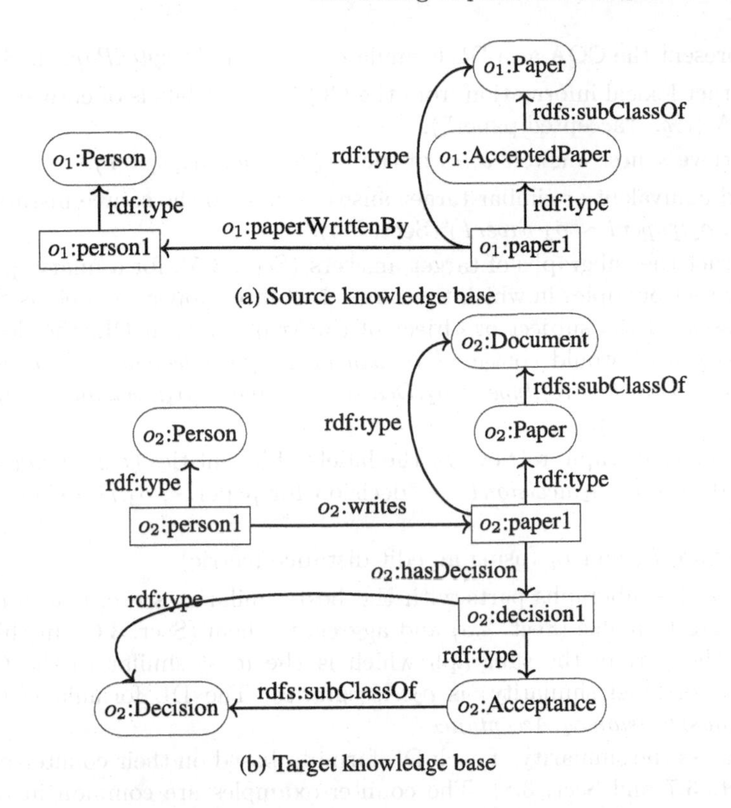

Fig. 2. Source and target knowledge bases.

two knowledge bases may not represent the same conference, therefore they may not share common paper instances. However, these bases may have a different but overlapping scope. For example o_1 could focus on the event organisation part of a conference and o_2 on reviewer management. Before detailing the main steps of the approach, we instantiate the overall approach to deal with unary and binary queries.

3.1 Approach over a Unary CQA

We instanciate Fig. 1 for a unary CQA. The SPARQL CQA is that of Fig. 3.

```
SELECT ?x WHERE {
  ?x a o1:AcceptedPaper.
}
```

Fig. 3. SPARQL SELECT query with one variable.

(1) Represent the CQA as a DL formula e_s (*e.g.*, o_1*:AcceptedPaper*) (Sect. 3.3).
(2) Extract lexical information from the CQA, L_s set labels of entities from the CQA (*e.g.*, "accepted paper").
(3) Retrieve source answers ans_s of the CQA (*e.g.*, o_1*:paper1*).
(4) Find equivalent or similar target answers ans_t to the source instances ans_s (*e.g.* o_1*:paper1* $\sim$ o_2*:paper1*) (Sect. 3.4).
(5) Extract the subgraphs of target answers (Sect. 3.5): for a unary query, this is the set of triples in which the target instances appear as well as the types (classes) of the subject or object of the triple (*e.g.* in DL, the description of o_2*:paper1* would contain $\langle$ o_2*:paper1* , o_2*:hasDecision* , o_2*:decision1* $\rangle$, $\langle$ o_2*:decision1* , *rdf:type* , o_2*:Decision* $\rangle$ *and* $\langle$ o_2*:decision1* , *rdf:type* , o_2*:Acceptance* $\rangle$.
(6) For each subgraph, retrieve L_t the labels of its entities (*e.g.*, o_2*:hasDecision* $\rightarrow$ "decision", o_2*:decision1* $\rightarrow$ "decision for paper1", o_2*:Decision* $\rightarrow$ "decision").
(7) Compare L_s and L_t (using an edit distance metric).
(8) Select the subgraphs parts with the best similarity score, transform them into DL formulae (Sect. 3.5) and aggregate them (Sect. 3.6). In this example, the part of the subgraph which is the most similar to the CQA (in terms of label similarity) is o_2*:Acceptance*. The DL formula is therefore $\exists o_2$*:hasDecision.*o_2*:Acceptance*.
(9) Reassess the similarity of each DL formula based on their counter-examples (Sect. 3.7 and Sect. 3.8). The counter-examples are common instances of the two knowledge bases which are described by the target DL formula but not by the original CQA.
(10) Filter the DL formulae based on their similarity score (if their similarity score is higher than a threshold) (Sect. 3.9).
(11) Put the DL formulae e_s and e_t together to form a correspondence (*e.g.*, $\langle$ o_1*:AcceptedPaper* , $\exists$ o_2*:hasDecision.*o_2*:Acceptance* , $\equiv$ $\rangle$) and express this correspondence in a reusable format (*e.g.*, EDOAL). The confidence assigned to a correspondence is the similarity score of the DL formula computed.

3.2 Approach over a Binary CQA

The main difference with the case of unary CQAs is in Step (4) because the two instances of the pair answer are matched instead of one, Step (5) and Step (8) which deal with the subgraph extraction and pruning.

```
SELECT ?x ?y WHERE {
  ?x o1:paperWrittenBy ?y.
}
```

Fig. 4. SPARQL SELECT query with two variables.

1. Extract source DL formula e_s (*e.g.*, o_1*:paperWrittenBy*) from SPARQL CQA (Fig. 4).
2. Extract lexical information from the CQA, L_s set labels of atoms from the DL formula (*e.g.*, "paper written by").
3. Extract source answers ans_s of the CQA (*e.g.*, a pair of instances (o_1*:paper1*, o_1*:person1*).
4. Find equivalent or similar target answers ans_t to the source instances ans_s (*e.g.* o_1*:paper1* $\sim$ o_2*:paper1* and o_1*:person1* $\sim$ o_2*:person1*).
5. Retrieve the subgraphs of target answers: for a binary query, it is the set of paths between two answer instances as well as the types of the instances appearing in the path (*e.g.*, a path of length 1 is found between o_2*:paper1* and o_2*:person1*). The path is composed of only one property and there are no other instances than o_2*:paper1* and o_2*:person1* in this path. Their respective types are retrieved: (o_2*:Paper*,o_2*:Document*) for o_2*:paper1* and (o_2*:Person*) for o_2*:person1*.
6. For each subgraph, retrieve L_t the labels of its entities (*e.g.*, o_2*:writes* $\rightarrow$ "writes", o_2*:Person* $\rightarrow$ "person", o_2*:Paper* $\rightarrow$ "paper", *etc.*).
7. Compare L_s and L_t.
8. Select the subgraph parts with the best score, transform them into DL formulae. Keep the best path variable types if their similarity is higher than a threshold. (*e.g.*, the best type for the instance o_2*:paper1* is o_2*:Paper* because its similarity with the CQA labels is higher than the similarity of o_2*:Document*).
9. Reassess the similarity of each DL formula based on their counter-examples.
10. Filter the DL formulae based on their similarity score (if their similarity score is higher than a threshold).
11. Put the DL formulae e_s and e_t together to form a correspondence (*e.g.*, $\langle$ o_1*:paperWrittenBy* , *dom*(o_2*:Paper*) $\sqcap$ o_2*:writes*$^-$, $\equiv$ $\rangle$ and express this correspondence in a reusable format (*e.g.*, EDOAL). The confidence assigned to a correspondence is the similarity score of the DL formula computed.

3.3 Translating SPARQL CQAs into DL Formulae

In Step (1), in order to translate a SPARQL query into a DL formula, the query is translated into a FOL formula and then transformed it into a DL formula. Here, a SPARQL SELECT query is composed of a SELECT clause containing variable names and a basic graph pattern, *i.e.*, a set of triples with variables sometimes with constructors (such as UNION or MINUS). First, the variables in the SELECT clause become the quantified variables of the formula. In unary CQAs, the SELECT clause contains one variable. In binary CQAs, the SELECT clause contains two variables. For instance, the SPARQL query of Fig. 3, *?x* becomes the quantified variable of our formula: $\forall x$. Then, the basic graph pattern is parsed in order to find what predicates apply to the quantified variables and add them to the formula. Each triple of the basic graph pattern is either a unary or a binary predicate. If new variables are added, an existential quantifier is used for them. In the example, the triple is find ⟨ *?x* , o_2:hasDecision , *?y* ⟩. The FOL formula becomes $\forall x, \exists y$, *o_2:hasDecision(x,y)*. It is then recursively keeping on exploring the basic graph pattern for each new variable introduced. After exploring the basic graph pattern for the variable *?y*, the FOL formula becomes $\forall x, \exists y$, *o_2:hasDecision(x,y)* $\wedge$ *o_2:Acceptance(y)*. At the end of the process, the basic graph pattern is transformed into a DL formula (also translated into an EDOAL[3]): $\forall x, \exists$ *y, o_2:hasDecision(x,y)* $\wedge$ *o_2:Acceptance(y)* becomes in DL: $\exists$ *o_2:hasDecision.o_2:Acceptance*. The FOL to DL equivalence is done as in [3].

3.4 Instance Matching

In Step (4), the answers of the CQA over the source knowledge base which have been retrieved are matched with the instances of the target knowledge base. This instance matching phase relies on existing links (*owl:sameAs, skos:exactMatch, skos:closeMatch, etc.*) if they exist. If no such link exists, an exact label match is performed. With binary CQAs, whose results are an instance-literal value pair, the instance is matched as before (existing links or exact labels), the literal value will be matched with an identical value in the path finding step, detailed next.

3.5 Retrieving and Pruning Subgraphs

The whole approach relies on subgraphs, which are sets of triples from a knowledge base. In Step (5), these subgraphs are found and then pruned and transformed into DL formulae in Step (8). The type of subgraphs is inspired from [33], which proposes an approach to find equivalent subgraphs within the same knowledge base.

A ***unary*** *CQA* expects a set of single instances as answer. The subgraph of a single instance is composed of a triple in which the instance is either the subject or the object, and the types (classes) of the object or subject of this triple. For example, *o_2:paper1* is the subject of the triple *o_2:paper1 o_2:hasDecision o_2:decision1* and *o_2:decision1* has types (classes) *o_2:Acceptance* and *o_2:Decision*. A subgraph of *o_2:paper1* is therefore composed of the following triples:

1. ⟨ *o_2:paper1* , *o_2:hasDecision* , *o_2:decision1* ⟩
2. ⟨ *o_2:decision1* , *rdf:type* , *o_2:Acceptance* ⟩
3. ⟨ *o_2:decision1* , *rdf:type* , *o_2:Decision* ⟩

When comparing the subgraph with the CQA labels, if the most similar object (resp. subject) type is more similar than the object (resp. subject) itself, the type is kept. Considering the *accepted paper* CQA, the most similar type of the triple of the object is *o_2:Acceptance*. Therefore, triple 3 is pruned. The object of triple 1 is *o_2:decision1* and the most similar object type to the CQA

[3] http://alignapi.gforge.inria.fr/edoal.html.

is o_2*:Acceptance*. o_2*:Acceptance* is more similar to the CQA than o_2*:decision1*. o_2*:decision1* becomes a variable and triple 2 stays in the subgraph.

In order to translate, a subgraph into a DL formula, firstly this subgraph is translated into a SPARQL query:

- The answer is transformed into a variable and put in the SELECT clause. In this example, o_2*:paper1* becomes a variable *?x* in the SELECT clause: *SELECT ?x WHERE*.
- The instances of the subgraphs which are not kept are transformed into variables. In the example, o_2*:decision1* becomes a variable *?y*.
- These transformations are applied to the selected triples of the subgraph which become the basic graph pattern of the SPARQL query. In this example, the SPARQL query is the one in Fig. 3.

Finally, the SPARQL query is transformed into a DL formula by using the same process as that described in Sect. 3.3: $\exists$$o_2$*:hasDecision.*$o_2$*:Acceptance*.

*A **binary** CQA* expects a set of pairs of instances (or pairs of instance-literal value) as answer. Finding a subgraph for a pair of instances consists in finding a path between the two instances. The shortest paths are considered more accurate. Because finding the shortest path between two entities is a complex problem, paths of length below a threshold are sought. First, paths of length 1 are sought, then if no path of length 1 is found, paths of length 2 are sought, *etc.* If more than one path of the same length are found, all of them go through the following process. When a path is found, the types of the instances forming the path are retrieved. If the similarity of the most similar type to the CQA is above a threshold, this type is kept in the final subgraph. For example, for a *"paper written by"* CQA with the answer (o_2*:paper1*,o_2*:person1*) in the target knowledge (Fig. 2), a subgraph containing the following triples is found: ⟨ o_2*:person1* , o_2*:writes* , o_2*:paper1* ⟩, ⟨ o_2*:paper1* , *rdf:type* , o_2*:Paper* ⟩, ⟨ o_2*:paper1* , *rdf:type* , o_2*:Document* ⟩, ⟨ o_2*:person1* , *rdf:type* , o_2*:Person* ⟩.

The most similar type of o_2*:person1* is o_2*:Person*, which is below the similarity threshold. The triple 4 is then removed from the subgraph. The most similar type of o_2*:paper1* is o_2*:Paper*. The triple 3 is therefore removed from the subgraph. o_2*:Paper*'s similarity is above the similarity threshold: triple 2 stays in the subgraph. The translation of a subgraph into a SPARQL query is the same for binary and unary CQAs. Therefore, the subgraph will be transformed into a SPARQL query and saved as the following DL formula: *dom(*o_2*:Paper)*[4] $\sqcap$ o_2*:writes*$^-$.

3.6 DL Formula Aggregation

In Step (8), when dealing with unary CQA, the DL formulae can be aggregated. It consists in transforming one or more formulae with a common predicate into a more generic formula. This aggregation only applies to formulae

[4] *dom* is introduced here for denoting the domain of a property.

which contain an instance or a literal value and which were kept in the subgraph selection step. For example, this step would apply for a formula such as $\exists$ o_2*:hasDecision.*$\{o_2$*:accept*$\}$.

In a first step, a first aggregated formula is created, called the **extension** formula. It consists in merging the instances or literal values of the formulae with the same predicate into one set of values. Considering that through various answers to a CQA (*e.g.*, o_2*:paper1*, o_2*:paper2*, *etc.*), the following formulae is extracted:

$\exists o_2$*:hasDecision.*$\{o_2$*:accept*$\}$,$\exists o_2$*:hasDecision.*$\{o_2$*:strongAccept*$\}$, $\exists o_2$*:hasDecision.*$\{o_2$*:weakAccept*$\}$.

The extension formula of these formulae is:

$\exists o_2$*:hasDecision.*$\{o_2$*:accept,*o_2*:strongAccept,*o_2*:weakAccept*$\}$.

The extension formula of a formula which does not share its predicate with any other is the formula itself. Then, an **intension** formula can be computed by replacing the set of values by the top class $\top$. It allows for fully abstracting the formula. The intension formula of the example formulae is: $\exists$ o_2*:hasDecision.*$\top$. Finally, a choice is made between the extension or intension formulae based on the predicate similarity to the CQA. If the predicate is more similar than the values, the intension formula is kept. Otherwise, the extension formula is kept. Applied to the examples of Table 1, o_2*:accept*, o_2*:strongAccept* and o_2*:weakAccept* are more similar to the CQA than o_2*:hasDecision*. The extension form is chosen.

3.7 Calculating Counter-Examples

In Step (9), the DL formula similarity score is refined by looking for counterexamples (details on the similarity score are given in Sect. 3.8). A **counterexample** is a common instance of the source and target ontologies which is described by the DL formula found by the approach in the target ontology but which is not described by the CQA in the source ontology.

For example, assuming that the target formula e_t is o_2*:Paper* for the "accepted paper" CQA. From the target ontology, the answers o_2*:paper1*, o_2*:paper2*, o_2*:paper3* and o_2*:paper4* are retrieved from e_t and matched to the source instances respectively o_1*:paper1*, o_1*:paper2*, o_1*:paper3* and o_1*:paper4*. However, only o_1*:paper1* and o_1*:paper2* are accepted papers (and are described by the CQA) in the source ontology, then o_1*:paper3* and o_1*:paper4* are counterexamples.

The percentage of counterexamples is computed as follows. The answers $ans_t^{e_t}$ described by the target subgraph (e_t) are retrieved from the target knowledge. These answers are matched to source instances: $ans_s^{e_t}$. The percentage of counterexamples is the proportion of common instances $ans_s^{e_t}$ which are not answers to the CQA ($\neg(ans_s^{cqa})$). The equation for the percentage of counterexamples is therefore:

$$percCounterExamples = \frac{|ans_s^{e_t} \sqcap \neg(ans_s^{cqa})|}{|ans_s^{e_t}|} \quad (1)$$

In the example, the percentage is $\frac{2}{4} = 50\%$.

3.8 DL Formula Similarity

In Step (10), the formulae are filtered based on their similarity score with the CQA. The similarity score is a combination of:

Label similarity *labelSim* is the sum of the label similarity of each entity of the formula with the CQA.

Structural similarity *structSim*. This similarity was introduced to enhance some structural aspects in a formula. In the implementation of the approach, this value is set to 0.5 for a path between the two instances of the answer, and 0 for a unary CQA subgraph. Indeed, if the label similarity of the path is 0, the structural similarity hints that the fact that a path was found is a clue in favour of the resulting DL formula.

Percentage of counterexamples *percCounterExamples* which is computed in Step (9) and detailed Sect. 3.7.

The similarity score is as following:

$$sim = (labelSim + strucSim) \times (1 - percCounterExamples) \quad (2)$$

In the example above, the similarity of $\exists o_2{:}hasDecision.o_2{:}Acceptance$ with the unary CQA *"accepted paper"* is calculated as follows:

- $labelSim = 0.8 + 0.0$ because
  - $sim(labels(CQA), labels(o_2{:}hasDecision)) = 0.0$
  - $sim(labels(CQA), labels(o_2{:}Acceptance)) = 0.8$
- $strucSim = 0.0$ because it is a unary CQA
- $percCounterExamples = 0.0$

The similarity of this DL formula is $sim = (0.8 + 0.0) \times (1 - 0) = 0.8$.

3.9 DL Formula Filtering

In Step (10), the formulae are filtered. Only the DL formulae with a similarity higher than a threshold are put in a correspondence with the CQA DL formula. If for a given CQA, there is no DL formula with a similarity higher than the threshold, only the best DL formulae with a non-zero similarity are put in the correspondence. The best DL formulae are the formulae with the highest similarity score. When putting the DL formula in a correspondence, if its similarity score is greater than 1, the correspondence confidence value is set to 1.

4 Experiments

4.1 Dataset and Metrics

Two evaluation settings have been considered here. First, an automatic evaluation was performed on the populated version of the OAEI Conference benchmark [28]. This dataset is composed of 5 ontologies, with 100 manually generated

CQAs. This evaluation measured the impact of various parameters on the approach. Second, a manual evaluation was carried out on the Taxon dataset about plant taxonomy, composed of 4 large populated ontologies: AgronomicTaxon [23], AgroVoc [4], DBpedia [2] and TaxRef-LD [13]. 6 CQAs from AgronomicTaxon have been manually generated. These two datasets are the populated ones used in the first OAEI complex track [25].

Table 1. Initial, extension, intension and final (in bold) formulae. The CQA considered is *"accepted papers"*.

Initial formulae	Extension	Intension
$\exists o_2{:}hasDecision.\{o_2{:}accept\}$ $\exists o_2{:}hasDecision.\{o_2{:}strongAccept\}$ $\exists o_2{:}hasDecision.\{o_2{:}weakAccept\}$	$\boldsymbol{\exists o_2{:}hasDecision.\{o_2{:}accept, o_2{:}strongAccept, o_2{:}weakAccept\}}$	$\exists o_2{:}hasDecision.\top$

The evaluation metrics used here are the ones adopted in the OAEI 2019 campaign[5]. These metrics are based on the comparison of instance sets. The generated alignment is used to rewrite a set of reference source CQAs whose results (set of instances) are compared to the ones returned by the corresponding target reference CQA. This metric shows the overall *coverage* of the alignment with respect to the knowledge needs and the best rewritten query[6]. A balancing strategy consists in calculating the intrinsic alignment *precision* based on common instances. Given an alignment A_{eval} to be evaluated, a set of CQA reference pairs cqa_{pairs} (composed of source cqa_s and target cqa_t), kb_s the source knowledge base, kb_t a target knowledge base, and f an instance set (I) comparison function:

$$coverage(A_{eval}, cqa_{pairs}, kb_s, kb_t, f) = \underset{\langle cqa_s, cqa_t \rangle \in cqa_{pairs}}{\text{average}} f(I^{kb_t}_{cqa_t}, I^{kb_t}_{bestq_t}) \quad (3)$$

Different functions f can be used for comparing instance sets (overlap, precision-oriented, recall-oriented etc.). Here, *coverage* is based on the *queryFmeasure* (also used for selecting the best rewritten query). This is motivated by the fact that it better balances precision and recall. Given a reference instance set I_{ref} and an evaluated instance set I_{eval}:

$$QP = \frac{|I_{eval} \cap I_{ref}|}{|I_{eval}|} \qquad QR = \frac{|I_{eval} \cap I_{ref}|}{|I_{ref}|} \quad (4)$$

$$queryFmeasure(I_{ref}, I_{eval}) = 2 \times \frac{QR \times QP}{QR + QP} \quad (5)$$

$$bestq_t = \underset{q_t \in rewrite(cqa_s, A_{eval}, kb_s)}{\text{argmax}} queryFmeasure(I^{kb_t}_{cqa_t}, I^{kb_t}_{q_t}) \quad (6)$$

[5] http://oaei.ontologymatching.org/2019/complex/index.html.

[6] The description of rewriting systems is out of the scope of this paper.

Balancing *coverage*, *precision* is based on classical (i.e., scoring 1 for same instance sets or 0 otherwise) or non-disjoint functions f:

$$precision(A_{eval}, kb_s, kb_t, f) = \underset{\langle e_1, e_2 \rangle \in A_{eval}}{\text{average}} f(I_{e_1}^{kb_s}, I_{e_2}^{kb_t}) \quad (7)$$

Such metrics have been used in the automatic evaluation on the controlled populated version of the Conference dataset. Given the uneven population of Taxon (*i.e.*, a same piece of knowledge can be represented in various ways within the same ontology and that all instances are not described identically), a manual evaluation has been carried out instead in order to avoid entailing noise in the instance-based comparison. The tool and evaluation have been executed on an Ubuntu 16.04 machine configured with 16 GB of RAM running under an i7-4790K118 CPU 4.00GHzx8 processors. The runtimes are given for a single run.

4.2 Results and Discussion

Impact of Parameters. The impact of the different matching parameters (Table 2) has been measured on the Conference dataset (for sake of space, only the results varying the CQAs and counterexamples are presented in Table 3). The Levenshtein edit distance has been used as similarity metric, with a path max length of 3 properties (empirically chosen) and formula filtering threshold confidence value of 0.6 or best formulae. The higher the Levenshtein threshold, the more formulae have been filtered out. When Levenshtein threshold increases, we observe: stagnation of runtime, decrease of number of correspondences, increase of precision, and decrease of coverage. The higher the number of support answers, more *accidental correspondences* appear, with satisfying results with 1 support answer. When the number of support answers increases: increase of runtime, increase of number of correspondences, decrease of precision, stagnation of coverage. With respect to impact of CQAs with respect to automatically generated queries, overall better results with CQAs both in terms of coverage and precision, as a higher number of correspondences are generated by using the queries (introducing noise). Finally, computing counterexamples increases precision (reducing the number of generated correspondences), keeping the coverage. However, the runtime increases considerably (from 2 h up to 46 h).

Comparison with Existing Approaches. The alignments generated by the proposed approach have been compared to the following ones (Table 4)[7]: (i) query rewriting (Rew), the query rewriting oriented alignment set from [26] - 10 pairs of ontologies; (ii) ontology merging (Mer), the ontology merging oriented alignment set from [26] - 10 pairs of ontologies; (iii) ra1, the reference simple alignment from the OAEI conference dataset - 10 pairs of ontologies; (iv) Ritze, the output alignment[8] from [21] - complex correspondences found on 4 pairs of ontologies; and (v) AMLC, the output alignment[9] from [6] - output alignments between 10

[7] The choice of these alignments was based on the fact that they were the publicly available complex matchers at the time of running the experiments.
[8] https://code.google.com/archive/p/generatingcomplexalignments/downloads/.
[9] http://oaei.ontologymatching.org/2018/results/complex/conference/.

Table 2. Variation of parameters.

Variant	Nb ans	Levesthein threshold	Counterexamples	CQAs
Baseline	10	0.4		√
Levenshtein	10	0.0–1.0		√
Support answers	1–100	0.4		√
Query	10	0.4		
Counterexamples	10	0.4	√	√

Table 3. Results with the variation of parameters.

	Impact CQA		Impact counterexamples	
	CQAs	queries	no counterexamples	counterexamples
Runtime	2 h	2 h	2 h	46 h
Number of correspondences	1,699	3,098	1,699	1,320
Precision	0.63	0.47	0.63	0.74
Coverage	0.76	0.64	0.76	0.76

pairs of ontologies. Our approach is the only one able to generate more expressive (c:c) correspondences. Overall our approach obtains the best coverage scores comparing to the all other approaches. With respect to precision, with classical instance comparison function, we obtain the worst results (0.4 with counterexamples). However, precision results should be considered carefully. First, the relation of the correspondence is not considered in this score. Merg. and Rew. alignments contain many correspondences with a subsumption relation, so their classical precision score is lower than the percentage of correct correspondences it contains. Second, the precision of the alignments is considered to be between the classical precision and the percentage of correspondences whose members are either overlapping or both empty (not disjoint) due to the way the ontologies were populated. In order to compensate these errors, we use the non-disjoint scoring metrics in the precision evaluation. The score for a correspondence is 1 when the members are overlapping or both empty, and 0 otherwise. With the non-disjoint precision, we outperform Ritze and AMLC, with equivalent values for ra1, Mer. and Rew. Comparing the systems between them, the Rew. alignment outperforms the Merg. in terms of CQA Coverage. In fact, in the Merg. alignments, unions of properties were separated into individual subsumptions which were usable by the rewriting system. Ritze only outputs equivalent or disjoint correspondences. Its precision score is therefore the same for all metrics. AMLC achieves a better classical precision than our baseline approach but contains a high number of disjoint correspondences. Overall, as expected, the precision scores of the reference alignments are higher than those output by the matchers. Moreover, Ritze and AMLC both rely on correspondence patterns which limit the types of correspondences they can generate.

Table 4. Comparative results. CQA is calculated with query Fmeasure and precision with classical and not disjoint instance comparison set functions (noted classical-non disjoint in the results).

	baseline	counterexamples	Ritze	AMLC	ral	Mer	Rew
Correspondence type	(c:c)	(c:c)	(s:c)	(s:c)	(s:s)	(s:c)	(s:c)
Runtime	2 h	46 h	1 h	0 h03			
Number of correspondences	1,699	1,320	360	441	348	628	842
Precision	0.3–1	0.4–1	0.8	0.4–0.6	0.6–1	0.4–1	0.4–1
Coverage	0.8	0.8	0.4	0.5	0.4	0.6	0.7

Table 5. Evaluation on the Taxon dataset.

	v1	v10
Runtime	28 h	32 h
Number of correspondences	134	328
Precision	0.3–1	0.3–1
Coverage	0.3–0.7	0.5-0.8

Manual Evaluation. A manual evaluation has been carried out on the Taxon dataset (Table 5). The baseline has been declined in two versions, using counterexamples: *v*1 with 1 support and *v*10 with 10 supports. In the lack of *owl:sameAs* links, then the links have been generated by a exact match on the instance labels. In this dataset, given the uneven population, more support instances entail a better coverage.

5 Related Work

Comparison to Other Matching Approaches. Earlier works in the ontology matching field have introduced the need for complex ontology alignments [12,30], and different approaches for generating them have been proposed in the literature afterwards (the reader can refer to [27] for a survey on them). These approaches involve different techniques such as relying on templates of correspondences (called patterns) and/or instance evidence. The approaches in [20,21] apply a set of matching conditions (label similarity, datatype compatibility, etc.) to detect correspondences that fit certain patterns. The approach of [22] uses the linguistic frames defined in FrameBase to find correspondences between object properties and the frames. KAOM [10] relies on *knowledge rules* which can be interpreted as probable axioms. The approaches in [16,17,31] use statistical information based on the linked instances to find correspondences fitting a given pattern. The approach in [14] uses genetic programming on instances to find correspondences with value transformation functions between two knowledge bases. The one in [18] uses a path-finding algorithm to find correspondences between two knowledge bases with common instances. The one in [9] iteratively constructs correspondences based on the information gain from matched instances between the two knowledge-bases. More recently, [6] relies on lexical similarity and structural conditions to detect correspondence patterns, close to [20]. Comparing our proposal to those described above, none of the complex approaches involve the user before or during the matching process. Like the ones in [9,16–18,31], we rely on the hypothesis that the knowledge bases contain common instances. Furthermore, as for the matching processing in general, in particular for the complex matching approaches in [20,21], we rely on the hypothesis that the ontologies in the knowledge base have a relevant lexical layer. Differently from most of them, the proposed does not rely on correspondence patterns. Finally, competency questions have not been adapted nor used for ontology matching.

SPARQL CQA. In our approach, CQA are used as basic pieces of information which will be transformed as source members of correspondences. Their formulation in a SPARQL query over the source ontology is a limitation of the approach as a user would need to be familiar with SPARQL and the source ontology. However, in the scenario where someone wants to publish and link a knowledge base he or she created on the LOD cloud, this person is already familiar with the source ontology and can reuse the CQ of their own ontology. In other cases, one could rely on question answering systems which generate a SPARQL query from a question in natural language. This kind of system is evaluated in the QALD open challenge [29].

Generalisation Process. Ontology matching approaches relying on the *Abox* of ontologies infer general statements from the instances, *i.e.*, they perform a generalisation[10]. This is the principle of *machine learning* in general and methods such as *Formal Concept Analysis* [7] or *association rule mining* [1]. These generalisation processes however require a considerable amount of data (or instances). Approaches such as the ones from [9,16,17,31] rely on large amounts of common ontology instances for finding complex correspondences. Few exceptions in ontology matching rely on few examples. For instance, the matcher of [32] relies on example instances given by a user. With this information, the generalisation can be performed on few examples. The idea behind our approach is to rely on a few examples to find general rules which would apply to more instances. In particular, the generalisation phase of our approach is guided by the CQA labels. Thanks to that, only one instance is sufficient for finding a correspondence. This would apply to knowledge bases which represent different contexts or points of view but whose ontologies are overlapping.

6 Conclusions and Future Work

This paper has presented a complex alignment generation approach based on CQAs. The CQA define the knowledge needs of a user over two or more ontologies. The use of CQAs is both a strength of the approach as it allows for a

[10] 'They infer general statements or concepts from specific cases' (Oxford Dictionary, "Generalisation" Retrieved June 3 2019 from https://en.oxforddictionaries.com/definition/generalization.

generalisation over few instances and a limitation as it requires users to be able to express her or his needs as SPARQL queries in terms of the source vocabulary (this is however the only manual effort required for the user). The approach depends as well on the quality of the instance matches. The approach can be extended in several directions: one could consider exploring more sophisticated instance-based matching approaches and, alternatively, conditional or link keys (systems generating keys could also benefit from complex correspondences to improve their results); designing a purely T-Box strategy based on both linguistic and semantic properties of the ontologies and CQAs; taking into account specialization/generalization relations; or still dividing the problem in sub-tasks through ontology partitioning (given the inherent high search space in this task). Last but not least, incoherence resolution systems for complex alignments are scarce.

References

1. Agrawal, R., Imieliński, T., Swami, A.: Mining association rules between sets of items in large databases. In: ACM SIGMOD Conference, pp. 207–216 (1993)
2. Auer, S., Bizer, C., Kobilarov, G., Lehmann, J., Cyganiak, R., Ives, Z.: DBpedia: a nucleus for a web of open data. In: Aberer, K., et al. (eds.) ASWC/ISWC -2007. LNCS, vol. 4825, pp. 722–735. Springer, Heidelberg (2007). https://doi.org/10.1007/978-3-540-76298-0_52
3. Borgida, A.: On the relative expressiveness of description logics and predicate logics. Artif. Intell. **82**(1–2), 353–367 (1996)
4. Caracciolo, C., et al.: Thesaurus maintenance, alignment and publication as linked data: the AGROVOC use case. Int. J. Metadata Semant. Ontol. **7**(1), 65 (2012)
5. Euzenat, J., Shvaiko, P.: Conclusions. Ontology Matching, pp. 399–405. Springer, Heidelberg (2013). https://doi.org/10.1007/978-3-642-38721-0_13
6. Faria, D.: Results of AML in OAEI. In: OM Workshop, pp. 125–131 (2018)
7. Ganter, B., Stumme, G., Wille, R. (eds.): Formal Concept Analysis. LNCS (LNAI), vol. 3626. Springer, Heidelberg (2005). https://doi.org/10.1007/978-3-540-31881-1
8. Grüninger, M., Fox, M.S.: Methodology for the design and evaluation of ontologies. In: Workshop on Basic Ontological Issues in Knowledge Sharing (1995)
9. Hu, W., Chen, J., Zhang, H., Qu, Y.: Learning complex mappings between ontologies. In: Pan, J.Z., et al. (eds.) JIST 2011. LNCS, vol. 7185, pp. 350–357. Springer, Heidelberg (2012). https://doi.org/10.1007/978-3-642-29923-0_24
10. Jiang, S., Lowd, D., Kafle, S., Dou, D.: Ontology matching with knowledge rules. In: Hameurlain, A., Küng, J., Wagner, R., Chen, Q. (eds.) Transactions on Large-Scale Data- and Knowledge-Centered Systems XXVIII. LNCS, vol. 9940, pp. 75–95. Springer, Heidelberg (2016). https://doi.org/10.1007/978-3-662-53455-7_4
11. Jouhet, V., Mougin, F., Bréchat, B., Thiessard, F.: Building a model for disease classification integration in oncology, an approach based on the national cancer institute thesaurus. J. Biomed. Semant. **8**(1), 6:1–6:12 (2017)
12. Maedche, A., Motik, B., Silva, N., Volz, R.: MAFRA — A MApping FRAmework for distributed ontologies. In: Gómez-Pérez, A., Benjamins, V.R. (eds.) EKAW 2002. LNCS (LNAI), vol. 2473, pp. 235–250. Springer, Heidelberg (2002). https://doi.org/10.1007/3-540-45810-7_23

13. Michel, F., Gargominy, O., Tercerie, S., Faron-Zucker, C.: A model to represent nomenclatural and taxonomic information as linked data. Application to the French Taxonomic Register, TAXREF. In: 2nd International Workshop on Semantics for Biodiversity (2017)
14. Pereira Nunes, B., Mera, A., Casanova, M.A., Fetahu, B., P. Paes Leme, L.A., Dietze, S.: Complex matching of RDF datatype properties. In: Decker, H., Lhotská, L., Link, S., Basl, J., Tjoa, A.M. (eds.) DEXA 2013. LNCS, vol. 8055, pp. 195–208. Springer, Heidelberg (2013). https://doi.org/10.1007/978-3-642-40285-2_18
15. Nurmikko-Fuller, T., et al.: Building complex research collections in digital libraries: a survey of ontology implications. In: Proceedings of the 15th ACM/IEEE-CE Joint Conference on Digital Libraries, pp. 169–172. ACM (2015)
16. Parundekar, R., Knoblock, C.A., Ambite, J.L.: Linking and building ontologies of linked data. In: Patel-Schneider, P.F., et al. (eds.) ISWC 2010. LNCS, vol. 6496, pp. 598–614. Springer, Heidelberg (2010). https://doi.org/10.1007/978-3-642-17746-0_38
17. Parundekar, R., Knoblock, C.A., Ambite, J.L.: Discovering concept coverings in ontologies of linked data sources. In: Cudré-Mauroux, P., et al. (eds.) ISWC 2012. LNCS, vol. 7649, pp. 427–443. Springer, Heidelberg (2012). https://doi.org/10.1007/978-3-642-35176-1_27
18. Meersman, R., Tari, Z. (eds.): OTM 2007. LNCS, vol. 4803. Springer, Heidelberg (2007). https://doi.org/10.1007/978-3-540-76848-7
19. Ren, Y., Parvizi, A., Mellish, C., Pan, J.Z., van Deemter, K., Stevens, R.: Towards competency question-driven ontology authoring. In: Presutti, V., d'Amato, C., Gandon, F., d'Aquin, M., Staab, S., Tordai, A. (eds.) ESWC 2014. LNCS, vol. 8465, pp. 752–767. Springer, Cham (2014). https://doi.org/10.1007/978-3-319-07443-6_50
20. Ritze, D., Meilicke, C., Šváb Zamazal, O., Stuckenschmidt, H.: A pattern-based ontology matching approach for detecting complex correspondences. In: OM Workshop (2009)
21. Ritze, D., Völker, J., Meilicke, C., Šváb Zamazal, O.: Linguistic analysis for complex ontology matching. In: OM Workshop (2010)
22. Rouces, J., de Melo, G., Hose, K.: Complex schema mapping and linking data: beyond binary predicates. In: Workshop on Linked Data on the Web (2016)
23. Roussey, C., Chanet, J., Cellier, V., Amarger, F.: Agronomic taxon. In: Workshop on Open Data, pp. 5:1–5:4 (2013)
24. Thiéblin, E., Amarger, F., Hernandez, N., Roussey, C., Trojahn Dos Santos, C.: Cross-querying LOD datasets using complex alignments: an application to agronomic taxa. In: Garoufallou, E., Virkus, S., Siatri, R., Koutsomiha, D. (eds.) MTSR 2017. CCIS, vol. 755, pp. 25–37. Springer, Cham (2017). https://doi.org/10.1007/978-3-319-70863-8_3
25. Thiéblin, E., Cheatham, M., dos Santos, C.T., Zamazal, O., Zhou, L.: The first version of the OAEI complex alignment benchmark. In: ISWC Poster Track (2018)
26. Thiéblin, É., Haemmerlé, O., Hernandez, N., Trojahn, C.: Task-oriented complex ontology alignment: two alignment evaluation sets. In: Gangemi, A., et al. (eds.) ESWC 2018. LNCS, vol. 10843, pp. 655–670. Springer, Cham (2018). https://doi.org/10.1007/978-3-319-93417-4_42
27. Thiéblin, E., Haemmerlé, O., Hernandez, N., Trojahn, C.: Survey on complex ontology matching. Semant. Web J. (2019)
28. Thiéblin, É., Trojahn, C.: Conference v3.0 : a populated version of the conference dataset. In: ISWC Poster Track (2019)

29. Unger, C., et al.: Question answering over linked data (QALD-4). In: Working Notes for CLEF, pp. 1172–1180 (2014)
30. Visser, P.R., Jones, D.M., Bench-Capon, T.J., Shave, M.: An analysis of ontology mismatches: heterogeneity versus interoperability. In: AAAI, pp. 164–172 (1997)
31. Walshe, B., Brennan, R., O'Sullivan, D.: Bayes-ReCCE: a Bayesian model for detecting restriction class correspondences in linked open data knowledge bases. Int. J. Semant. Web Inf. Syst. **12**(2), 25–52 (2016)
32. Wu, B., Knoblock, C.A.: An iterative approach to synthesize data transformation programs. In: IJCAI, pp. 1726–1732 (2015)
33. Zheng, W., Zou, L., Peng, W., Yan, X., Song, S., Zhao, D.: Semantic SPARQL similarity search over RDF knowledge graphs. VLDB Endowment **9**(11), 840–851 (2016)

Weakly Supervised Short Text Categorization Using World Knowledge

Rima Türker[1,2(✉)], Lei Zhang[1], Mehwish Alam[1,2], and Harald Sack[1,2]

[1] FIZ Karlsruhe – Leibniz Institute for Information Infrastructure, Eggenstein-Leopoldshafen, Germany
{rima.tuerker,lei.zhang,mehwish.alam,harald.sack}@fiz-karlsruhe.de

[2] Karlsruhe Institute of Technology, Institute AIFB, Karlsruhe, Germany
{rima.tuerker,mehwish.alam,harald.sack}@kit.edu

Abstract. Short text categorization is an important task in many NLP applications, such as sentiment analysis, news feed categorization, etc. Due to the sparsity and shortness of the text, many traditional classification models perform poorly if they are directly applied to short text. Moreover, supervised approaches require large amounts of manually labeled data, which is a costly, labor intensive, and time-consuming task. This paper proposes a weakly supervised short text categorization approach, which does not require any manually labeled data. The proposed model consists of two main modules: (1) a data labeling module, which leverages an external Knowledge Base (KB) to compute probabilistic labels for a given unlabeled training data set, and (2) a classification model based on a Wide & Deep learning approach. The effectiveness of the proposed method is validated via evaluation on multiple datasets. The experimental results show that the proposed approach outperforms unsupervised state-of-the-art classification approaches and achieves comparable performance to supervised approaches.

Keywords: Short text categorization · Weakly supervised short text categorization · Wide & Deep model

1 Introduction

Due to rapid growth of the Web content, short text data such as search snippets, news feeds, short messages, etc. is drastically multiplying online [3]. Hence, short text categorization has become a crucial task for a wide range of applications including sentiment analysis and news feed categorization [14]. While conventional text classification methods such as Support Vector Machines (SVMs) have demonstrated their success in classifying long and well structured text, as e.g., news articles, in case of short text they seem to have a substandard performance [33]. Moreover, due to the main characteristics of short text, i.e., limited context, sparsity and ambiguity, the traditional classification methods based on Bag of Words (BOW) [31] or approaches that utilize word embeddings perform poorly

J. Z. Pan et al. (Eds.): ISWC 2020, LNCS 12506, pp. 584–600, 2020.
https://doi.org/10.1007/978-3-030-62419-4_33

if directly applied to short text. Besides, such approaches often lead to inaccurate results on new and rare words. Thus, to overcome these challenges, it is indispensable to use external sources such as Knowledge Bases (KBs) to enrich and obtain more advanced text representations [30].

Recently, several deep learning approaches have been proposed for short text classification, which demonstrated remarkable performance in this task [4,15]. The two main advantages of these models for the classification task are that minimum effort is required for feature engineering and their classification performance is better in comparison to traditional text classification approaches [16]. However, the requirement of large amounts of labeled data remains the main bottleneck for neural network based approaches [16]. Acquiring labeled data for the classification task is costly and time-consuming. Especially, if the data to be labeled is of a specific domain then only a limited number of domain experts are able to label them correctly, which makes it a labor intensive task.

To overcome this bottleneck several *dataless* [9,12], *semi supervised* [19,32], and *weakly supervised* [16,17] classification algorithms have been proposed. The *dataless classification* algorithms do not require any labeled data to perform text categorization. Instead, they project each predefined label and document into a common vector space by exploiting the words present in the labels and the documents. As a second step, based on the vector similarity a label is assigned to each document. However, the most prominent dataless classification methods are designed for long text, e.g., news article classification [12]. In addition, for addressing the labeled data scarcity problem, *semi supervised* text classification algorithms have been proposed. However, they also require some set of labeled data. Yet, generating small training sets for semi supervised methods still remains an expensive process due to the diversity of the documents in many applications. Furthermore, there has been a considerable amount of studies in *weakly supervised* text classification approaches. Most of these methods require user-given weak supervision sources such as some labeled documents, class related keywords, etc. for the classification task. Besides, existing weakly supervised text classification solutions mostly rely on hard-coded heuristics, such as looking for specific keywords or syntactical patterns in text, which still requires domain expertise and is especially prone to noise. Moreover, the most well-known weakly supervised methods are designed for long text classification.

Motivated by the aforementioned challenges, this paper proposes a novel model for **We**akly **S**upervised **S**hort **Te**xt **C**ategorization using World Knowledge[1] (WESSTEC). The proposed approach does not require any labeled data for short text categorization. It exploits Knowledge Bases and embedding models such as Doc2Vec [10], LINE [26], Word2Vec [18] etc. as weak supervision sources without requiring any manual effort. Instead, given a list of labels and unlabeled short text documents, the proposed method first associates each text with its relevant concepts in a KB to enhance the semantic representation of short texts and then generates labels for each document by utilizing the aforementioned embedding models. In the second step, words and concepts from the

[1] https://github.com/ISE-FIZKarlsruhe/WESSTEC.

labeled documents are exploited for training a Wide & Deep learning based classification model [5]. Finally, the trained model is used to categorize new short text documents. Overall, the main contributions of the paper are as follows:

- a new paradigm for short text categorization, based on a knowledge based weak supervision;
- a method to combine weak supervision sources to generate labeled data which can be used for any arbitrary classification model;
- adaptation of a Wide & Deep model for weakly supervised short text categorization;
- utilizing multiple features, i.e., both words and entities present in a given short text and their combination for the Wide & Deep model;
- an experimental evaluation using four different standard datasets for short text categorization.

The rest of this paper is structured as follows: Sect. 2 provides a review of the related work. In Sect. 3, the proposed approach for short text categorization is explained. Section 4 presents the experimental setup for the evaluation of the proposed approach and the discussion of the achieved results. Finally, Section 5 concludes the paper with open issues and future work.

2 Related Work

The aim of this study is to categorize short text documents under a weak supervision setting without requiring any manually labeled data. Hence, this section presents prior related studies on *Short Text Classification*, *Weakly Supervised Text Classification* as well as *Dataless Text Classification.*

Short Text Classification. Recent works [2,30,31] have proposed deep neural network based models to overcome the problem of data sparsity that arises when dealing with short text classification. The main characteristic of short text is the insufficient text length, which is no longer than 200 characters [24]. While [2,13,30] utilize an external knowledge to enrich the representation of short text, [31] exploits word embedding models and Convolutional Neural Network (CNN) to expand the information contained in short text. On the other hand, instead of focusing on expanding the representation of short text, [33] proposes topic memory networks which aim to encode latent topic representation of class labels for short text classification. In addition, recently, more sophisticated deep neural network based short text classification methods [4,15] have been proposed for sentiment analysis. Although the aforementioned approaches have demonstrated superior performance in text classification, they require huge amounts of labeled data. Conversely, the proposed method in this study does not require any manually labeled data for short text categorization.

Weakly Supervised Text Classification. There has been a considerable amount of studies related to weakly supervised text classification to address the problem of missing labeled data [16,17,21]. Most of these methods require user-given weak supervision sources such as class related key words, small amount of labeled data, etc. Hence, the requirement of domain expertise is still inevitable. On the contrary, the proposed approach does not require such manually designed weak supervision sources for the categorization task. Instead, it utilizes unsupervised embedding models such as Word2Vec, Doc2Vec and LINE as weak supervision sources.

Dataless Text Classification. To address the problem of missing labeled data, [1] introduced a dataless text classification method by representing documents and labels into a common semantic space. Then, the classification is performed by considering the vector similarity between the documents and the labels. The most prominent dataless classification methods [1,9,12] utilize only words present in documents for the classification task and they ignore the entities. However, entities carry much more information than the words. Moreover, aforementioned studies are designed for the classification of long and well structured documents such as news articles. Such methods use traditional supervised approaches i.e., Naive Bayes (NB), Support Vector Machine (SVM), etc. with the features calculated based on the term frequency and the inverse document frequency to perform classification. In contrast to these studies, the proposed approach aims to categorize short text documents without requiring any labeled data and it utilizes entities as well as words present in documents for the classification task. Further, our approach exploits the Wide & Deep model for short text classification in the dataless scenario. The Wide & Deep model has been proposed by [5] for Recommendation Systems with the goal of jointly training a wide linear model (for memorization) alongside a deep neural network (for generalization).

The most recent work related with ours is Knowledge-Based Short Text Categorization (KBSTC) [29], which is a probabilistic model and does not require any labeled training data to perform short text categorization. Instead, the category of the given text is derived based on the semantic similarity between the entities present in the text and the set of predefined categories. KBSTC utilizes only entities and ignores the words. However, WESSTEC exploits words as well as entities. In addition, the proposed model leverages both textual information (in Doc2Vec model) and structural information (in LINE model) from KBs to better capture the semantic representation of entities, however, KBSTC uses only structural information of entities. Further, while KBSTC labels the input text only based on the heuristics of semantic similarity, WESSTEC adapts an additional classification model using Wide & Deep learning.

Last but not least, all previous approaches rely on a single model (e.g., [1] utilizes only word2vec, [29] utilizes only entity-and-category embedding) to categorize text data, while WESSTEC combines different embedding models to increase the accuracy and coverage.

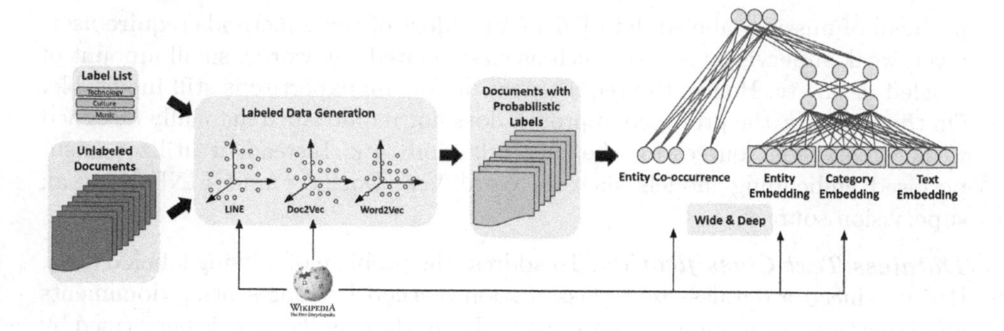

Fig. 1. The workflow of WESSTEC

3 Weakly Supervised Short Text Categorization

This section provides a formal definition of the short text classification task, followed by the description of the proposed approach.

Problem Formulation. Given an input short text t and n predefined labels $L = \{l_1, l_2, .., l_n\}$, the output is the most relevant label $l_i \in L$ for the given short text t, i.e., we compute the label function $f_{lab}(t) = l_i$, where $l_i \in L$.

Method Overview. The general workflow of WESSTEC is shown in Fig. 1. Given a list of labels and a set of unlabeled short text documents, the *Labeled Data Generation* module is responsible for generating *probabilistic training labels* for each document. In other words, it utilizes three different embedding models, i.e., LINE [26], Doc2Vec [10] and Word2Vec [18] to estimate the probability of each predefined label for a given document. This module generates documents with probabilistic labels as training data.

The second main module of the workflow is a Wide & Deep learning based classification model [5], which utilizes the documents with the probabilistic labels for training. Several different feature sets are extracted from the documents to train the Wide & Deep model. Note that in this work we have utilized Wikipedia as a KB.

Section 3.1 and Sect. 3.2 provide a detailed description of each module and the feature sets that have been utilized by each module.

3.1 Labeled Data Generation

The aim of this module is to generate labeled documents from a given label list and unlabeled set of documents (see Fig. 1). In other words, given a short text t and n labels $L = \{l_1, l_2, .., l_n\}$, the goal of this module is to produce a probabilistic label for t as $\mathbf{y_t} = [p_1, p_2, ..., p_n]$ where $p_i \in [0, 1]$, and p_i is the corresponding probability of l_i for t. To this end, this module utilizes three different embedding models, namely, LINE, Doc2Vec and pre-trained Word2Vec to capture the semantic correlations between the predefined labels and the words as well as entities present in a short text. First, each document and label is projected into common vector spaces, then the probabilistic labels of given texts are calculated based on the cosine similarity between documents and the set of predefined labels.

LINE is a network embedding model, which is designed to learn embedding of arbitrary types of large-scale networks (weighted, directed, undirected, etc.). The model has been trained by utilizing Wikipedia hyperlink structure to obtain a vector representation of each entity from Wikipedia. In other words, from Wikipedia hyperlink structure, an *entity-network* has been constructed to be utilized by this model. More technical details about the construction of the *entity-network* can be found in [29]. To obtain a document vector with the help of LINE, we simply take the average of entity vectors present in that document. To extract entities from a document an *anchor text dictionary* [27–29] is used. The anchor text dictionary is constructed by leveraging the anchor texts of hyperlinks of Wikipedia, which are pointing to any article in Wikipedia. The anchor texts are considered as entity mentions and the links refer to the corresponding entities.

Doc2Vec creates the distributed representation of documents by utilizing the context words present in the corresponding documents. This model has been trained on Wikipedia articles and contains a vector representation of each entity of Wikipedia. Note that we consider each Wikipedia article page as an entity. To form a document vector for a given text, the average of entity vectors present in that text is considered.

Word2Vec learns the low dimensional distributed representation of words. We use the pre-trained Word2Vec model[2] for our approach. To create document vectors with Word2Vec, the average of the word vectors in that document is considered.

Moreover, each given label is also mapped to its corresponding vector in the respective vector space, e.g., the label *Music* is mapped to the word vector of *Music* from Word2Vec and it is also mapped to the entity vector of *Music* from Doc2Vec and LINE.

After embedding each text and label into common vector spaces, each embedding model assigns the most similar label to each text based on the vector similarity between the text and the labels. As there are three embedding models, for each given text three labels are generated. These labels can overlap or conflict. Then, the goal of the remaining process of this module is to convert the outputs of the embedding measures into *probabilistic training labels*. In order to achieve that a heuristic approach has been employed.

Based on outputs of each embedding measure for all texts, the heuristic approach estimates the *confidence* of each embedding model by considering the output label agreement and disagreement rates. The *confidence* of an embedding model EM_i is defined as follows:

[2] https://code.google.com/archive/p/word2vec/.

$$C_{EM_i} = \frac{Agg_{EM_i} + noneAgg}{TotalAgg + noneAgg}, \tag{1}$$

where Agg_{EM_i} is the number of documents, on which the model EM_i agreed for a label with at least one of the other embeddings, $noneAgg$ is the number of documents, on which none of the embedding models agreed for the assigned label and $TotalAgg$ is the number of documents which at least two embedding models agreed on their labels (i.e., $TotalAgg = \#TotalDocuments - noneAgg$).

The confidence values are exploited to convert the generated labels into probabilistic training labels $\mathbf{y_t}$. For each text, the preferred label from each embedding measure will be weighted using its confidence and then all three weighted labels are combined together, which could result in three probabilistic labels when three measures disagree with each other or two probabilistic labels when two measures agree or one label when all agree on it. Finally, these values are normalized to produce the probabilistic training labels $\mathbf{y_t}$.

Given a short text t and n labels $L = \{l_1, l_2, .., l_n\}$, let $\mathbf{y_t} = [p_1, p_2, ..., p_n]$ denote t's probabilistic training labels, where $p_i \in [0, 1]$. To calculate the probability p_i of the label l_i for t, we define the following formula:

$$p_i(t) = \frac{\sum_{j=1}^{e} C_{EM_j} I^i_{EM_j}(t)}{\sum_{k=1}^{n} \sum_{j=1}^{e} C_{EM_j} I^k_{EM_j}(t)}, \tag{2}$$

where e is the total number of embedding models that are utilized in *labeled data generation* module, C_{EM_j} is the confidence of embedding model EM_j, n is the total number of predefined labels and $I^i_{EM_j}$ is defined as

$$I^i_{EM_j}(t) = \begin{cases} 1 & \text{if } EM_j \text{ assigns } l_i \text{ to } t\,, \\ 0 & \text{otherwise}\,. \end{cases} \tag{3}$$

3.2 Wide and Deep Model for Short Text Categorization

The second main module of our workflow is a Wide & Deep learning based classification model which was proposed in [5] for Recommender Systems. We adapt this approach for the short text categorization task. To the best of our knowledge, this is the first attempt of utilizing the Wide & Deep model for short text categorization.

The model consists of two main components i.e., Wide Component and Deep Component. Moreover, the model has the ability of memorizing feature interactions and generalizing feature combinations by jointly training the wide and deep components as shown in Fig. 1 (right).

In the following, we first introduce the Wide model and Deep model separately and then present the joint Wide & Deep model.

Wide Model: The wide part has the ability of memorizing feature interactions. In other words, it is able to learn the frequent co-occurrence of features.

Hence, we design this model to be able to capture the correlation between the co-occurrence of features and the target labels. In our approach, ***Entity co-occurrence*** information of each document is used as a feature for the wide part (see Fig. 1). Given a short text t let $\mathbf{x_t} = [x_1, x_2, x_3, ..., x_m]$ denote the m entities present in t. To construct the d dimensional *Entity co-occurrence* feature vector we apply cross-product transformation [5] as:

$$\phi_k(\mathbf{x_t}) = \prod_{i=1}^{m} x_i^{c_{ki}} \quad c_{ki} \in \{0, 1\}, \tag{4}$$

where c_{ki} is a boolean variable that is 1 if the i-th feature is part of the k-th transformation ϕ_k, and 0 otherwise. The wide part is a model of the form as:

$$P(Y = l_i|t) = softmax(\mathbf{w}_i^T \phi(\mathbf{x_t}) + b_i), \tag{5}$$

where t is a given short text, $\phi(\mathbf{x_t}) = [\phi_1(\mathbf{x_t}), \phi_2(\mathbf{x_t}), ..., \phi_d(\mathbf{x_t})]$ is the cross product transformations of $\mathbf{x_t}$, $\mathbf{w}_i = [w_1, w_2, ..., w_d]$ and b_i are the model parameters corresponding to the i-th label l_i. The *softmax* function is defined as:

$$softmax(z_i) = \frac{e^{z_i}}{\sum_{z_j \in \mathbf{z}} e^{z_j}}, \tag{6}$$

for $i = 1, 2, .., n$ and $\mathbf{z} = (z_1, z_2, ..., z_n) \in \mathbb{R}^n$.

We give the following example to illustrate how an *Entity co-occurrence* feature vector can be formed. Given a short text *"Motorola and HP in Linux tie-up"*, the extracted entities are $E' = \{Motorola, HP, Linux\}$ and the possible entity pairs are $E'_p = \{(Motorola, HP), (Motorola, Linux), (HP, Linux)\}$. The dimension of the vector is the number of all the possible entity pairs of the dataset and each dimension corresponds to an entity pair. For each entity pair $e_{p_i} \in E'_p$, the value of the corresponding dimension of the vector would be 1 and the rest would be 0.

Deep Model: The deep part is a neural network, which is capable of generalization of feature combinations through low-dimensional dense embeddings. In our approach, three different embedding vectors, i.e., ***Entity Embedding***, ***Category Embedding*** and ***Text Embedding*** are utilized as an input to the deep part (see Fig. 1).

To construct each feature vector, different embedding models are utilized, i.e., for *Entity Embedding* LINE, for *Category Embedding* the joint entity and category embedding model [29] and for *Text Embedding* Word2Vec. The joint entity and category embedding model has been proposed by [29] to capture the semantic relations between entities and categories from a KB. This model first constructs a weighted network of entities and categories, and then jointly learns their embeddings from the network.

In order to form an *Entity Embedding* vector for a given text, entities present in the document are extracted with the help of a prefabricated Anchor-Text dictionary [29] and then the average of the vector representations of these entities is taken. For the *Category Embedding* feature vector, all the categories that are directly associated with the entities appearing in the text are collected from Wikipedia, then the average of the category vector representations is taken. Finally, for a given text a *Text Embedding* feature vector is constructed by taking the average of the word vector representations in that document.

The deep part is a feed forward neural network, which takes low-dimensional embedding vectors as an input i.e., $[\mathbf{e}_t^e, \mathbf{e}_t^c, \mathbf{e}_t^t]$, where $\mathbf{e}_t^e$ is the entity embedding, $\mathbf{e}_t^c$ is the category embedding and $\mathbf{e}_t^t$ is the text embedding.
The deep part is the model of the form as:

$$P(Y = l_i|t) = softmax(\mathbf{w}_i^T a^{(lf)} + b), \tag{7}$$

where $\mathbf{w}_i$ are the weights that are applied on the final activation $a^{(lf)}$ for the i-th label l_i, l is the layer number and f is the activation function which is ReLU.

We have built 3-layer feed forward neural network for the deep part and each hidden layer of this model performs the following computation [5]:

$$a^{(l+1)} = f(W^{(l)} a^{(l)} + b^{(l)}), \tag{8}$$

$a^{(l)}$ is activations, $b^{(l)}$ is bias and $W^{(l)}$ is model weights at l-th layer.

Wide & Deep Model: The wide and the deep components are combined for joint training by back propagating the gradients from the output of both wide and deep parts simultaneously. The combined model is illustrated in Fig. 1 (right). For a given short text t the prediction of Wide & Deep model is:

$$P(Y = l_i|t) = softmax(\mathbf{w}_{wide_i}^T \phi(\mathbf{x}_t) + \mathbf{w}_{deep_i}^T a^{(lf)} + b_i). \tag{9}$$

In order to deal with the probabilistic training labels, we configure our model to train with a noise-aware loss function, i.e., cross-entropy between the probability of each training label and the output of the softmax function, which is defined as:

$$H(p, q) = -\sum_n p_i(t) * log(P(Y = l_i|t)) \tag{10}$$

Note that the reason of exploiting different feature sets in Labeled Data Generation and Wide & Deep modules is mainly two-fold: (1) Combining different features into Labeled Data Generation module requires much more feature engineering efforts. In other words, the Wide & Deep model can automatically learn the weights of the feature sets, however, it is not the same case with the proposed heuristic model designed for labeled data generation. (2) There are some features (e.g., entity co-occurrence) that cannot be straightforwardly integrated into heuristic algorithms to help calculate semantic similarity between input text and labels and do the labeling. However, such "non-heuristic" features can be transferred into the final classification model trained on labeled data generated by the heuristic algorithms using other features. Overall, we expect the trained model to provide performance gains over the heuristics that it is trained on both by applying to "non-heuristic" features (e.g., entity co-occurrence), and by learning to generalize beyond heuristics, i.e., putting weights on more subtle features that each individual heuristic algorithm cannot cover.

4 Experimental Results

This section provides a description of the datasets and the baselines, followed by the experimental results and a comparison to the state-of-the-art text categorization approaches.

4.1 Datasets

Four different real-world datasets have been used to evaluate the performance of the proposed approach: **AG News** [34], which contains the title and a short description of the news articles, **Snippets** [20], which contains short snippets from Google search results, **DBpedia Ontology** classification dataset [11], which is constructed by selecting 14 non-overlapping classes from DBpedia 2014 and **Twitter**[3] topic categorization dataset contains tweets belong to 6 different categories. The Twitter dataset is preprocessed, in other words, the dataset does not contain hash symbols, emoticons, user mentions, etc. Besides, the special characters and numbers present in each dataset have been removed, further, each sample has been converted to lower case. Table 1 shows the distribution of the datasets, the average number of entities and words as well as the standard deviation of entities and words per text in each dataset.

Furthermore, as WESSTEC does not require any labeled training data, the training datasets of AG News, Snippets, DBpedia and Twitter have been used without their labels. In other words, the training set of each dataset without their labels have been utilized as an input to *Labeled Data Generation* module of the WESSTEC framework (see Fig. 1) to generate the training labels.

Table 1. Statistics for the short text datasets

Dataset	#Category	#Train	#Test	Avg. #Ent	Avg. #Word	SD Ent	SD Word
AG News	4	120,000	7,600	11.83	38.65	3.80	9.8
Snippets	8	10,060	2,280	8.90	17.97	3.56	4.84
DBpedia	14	560,000	70,000	15.30	46.49	6.9	21.57
Twitter	6	9,879	3,697	4.31	12.36	2.29	5.13

[3] https://github.com/madhasri/Twitter-Trending-Topic-Classification/tree/master/data.

4.2 Baseline Approaches

To demonstrate the performance of the proposed approach, the following models have been selected as baselines:

- **Dataless ESA and Dataless Word2Vec:** Two variants of the state-of-the-art dataless approach [25] are considered as baselines, which are based on different methods to compute word similarity, i.e., ESA [8] and Word2Vec [18].
- **KBSTC** [29]**:** Knowledge-based short text categorization, which does not require any labeled data for short text categorization. Instead it relies on the semantic similarity between the given short text and predefined labels to categorize a given short text.
- **SVM+tf-idf:** In this model, the term frequency-inverse document frequency (tf-idf) is calculated as features for a subsequent Support Vector Machine (SVM) classifier.
- **CNN** [35]**+Word2Vec, CNN+Ent and CNN+Category:** A Convolutional Neural Network (CNN) is applied on text, entity and category matrices separately. These matrices are constructed by using Word2Vec, LINE, joint entity and category embedding model [29] respectively.
- **LSTM:** The standard LSTM model is composed of a single LSTM layer followed by a dense output layer.
- **charCNN** [34]**:** This model learns character embeddings using "one-hot" encoding. Subsequently, CNN is applied for the classification process.
- **BERT** [6]**:** The state-of-the-art language representation model[4] have been commonly leveraged to derive sentence embeddings. To produce BERT embeddings, first, each sentence has been passed through pre-trained BERT, then the outputs of the model have been averaged, which is the most common way of obtaining sentence embeddings from BERT [23]. In the experiments, the BERT embeddings have been generated as features for the subsequent 3-layer feed forward neural network.

4.3 Feature Sets

This section describes the feature sets that have been extracted from the *Documents with Probabilistic Labels* (see Fig. 1) and utilized to train the Wide & Deep model. To construct feature sets, words and entities present in texts as well as parent categories of entities from Wikipedia have been leveraged.

As shown in Fig. 1, the wide part exploits the **Entity Co-occurrence (Ent Co)** information as a feature and the deep part utilizes three different feature sets, namely, **Text Embedding (Text)**, **Entity Embedding (Entity)** and **Category Embedding (Category)** vectors as well as their combinations, such as Text+Entity (see Table 2) refers to the concatenation of text embeddings and entity embeddings. The detailed construction of the feature sets is explained in Sect. 3.2.

[4] https://github.com/google-research/bert.

Table 2. The classification accuracy of different models with different features

Model	Feature	AG News	Snippets	DBpedia	Twitter
Wide	Entity Co-occurance (Ent Co)	0.561	0.447	0.499	0.278
Deep	Text	0.802	0.795	0.786	0.555
	Entity	0.790	0.764	0.775	0.521
	Category	0.773	0.698	0.754	0.444
	Text+Entity	0.793	0.785	0.779	0.524
	Text+Category	0.801	0.794	0.786	0.554
	Entity+Category	0.792	0.771	0.771	0.534
	Text+Entity+Category	0.792	0.786	0.785	0.529
Wide & Deep	Ent Co+Text	0.807	0.792	0.786	0.556
	Ent Co+Entity	0.791	0.774	0.768	0.520
	Ent Co+Category	0.792	0.693	0.774	0.446
	Ent Co+Text+Entity	0.787	0.802	0.776	0.53
	Ent Co+Text+Category	**0.814**	0.803	**0.792**	**0.581**
	Ent Co+Entity+Category	0.791	0.770	0.766	0.544
	Ent Co+Text+Entity+Category	0.790	**0.805**	0.778	0.572

4.4 Evaluation of WESSTEC

Table 2 depicts the classification accuracy of the Wide & Deep model of WESSTEC, in comparison to individual Wide-only and Deep-only models with different features on AG News, Snippets, DBpedia and Twitter datasets.

It has been observed that the jointly trained Wide & Deep model outperforms the individual Wide-only and Deep-only models on each datasets. The reason here can be attributed to the benefit of utilizing the Wide & Deep model to achieve both memorization and generalization of features for short text classification. In addition, we have observed that some of the wrongly classified samples with the Deep part, have been correctly classified after combining the Wide part and jointly training the model.

Wide model performs best on the AG News dataset. This dataset has the least number of categories and the length of the samples are not as limited as Twitter dataset, therefore, it is easier for the Wide model to handle this dataset in comparison to other datasets. The reason of the general low accuracy of the Wide model (in comparison to the Deep model and Wide & Deep model) is that a very sparse set of features have been used to train the model. It is a well known fact that the Deep Neural Networks (DNNs) can be much more powerful than the linear models. Therefore, the Deep model always outperforms the Wide model on each dataset. Similar to the Wide model, with the Deep model the best classification accuracy has been obtained on the AG news.

On the other hand, despite the specific properties of Tweets (e.g., out-of-vocabulary words) WESSTEC can still obtain reasonable accuracy on the Twitter dataset. To illustrate the difficulty of categorizing tweets, we give the following tweet from the Twitter dataset as an example: *"BSE NSE Stock*

Tip HINDUSZI", which is labeled as *"Business"*. The categorization of such tweets is rather difficult for many standard categorization models, which rely on only words. However, WESSTEC enriches text representations by leveraging entities present in texts and their associated categories with the help of a KB. For the given example the detected entities are `Bombay_Stock_Exchange`, `National_Stock_Exchange_of_India` and `Stock`, which capture very useful information for categorization of the tweet. Further, even for out-of-vocabulary words such as *"BSE"*, WESSTEC can still detect entities, which are crucial for the categorization task.

This study has also investigated the impact of each feature combination on the classification performance. The Deep model performs the best when utilizing only words. Whereas, the Wide & Deep model enjoys the combination of the feature sets. However, it has been observed that using entity features in both wide and deep parts could result in a bias of the whole model towards entity information, which might not reflect the entire semantics of text, especially when the text is longer such that there could be some more words that cannot be detected as entities (e.g., in AG News and DBpedia). This suggests that our Wide & Deep model (Ent-Co+Text+Category) using Entity Co-occurrence (Ent-Co) as a feature in the wide part as well as Text Embedding (Text) and Category Embedding (Category) as features in the deep part could be the most promising combination. The results in Table 2 also shows that (Ent-Co+Text+Category) clearly yields best results on AG News, DBpedia and Twitter datasets and performs only slightly worse than (Ent-Co+Text+Entity+Category) on Snippets dataset (with the difference of 0.002 for accuracy).

Overall, the experiments show that, firstly, it is possible to perform short text categorization with a high accuracy in the complete absence of labeled data with our proposed approach and secondly, the Wide & Deep model can be successfully applied for the short text categorization problem.

Since WESSTEC achieves almost the best performance with the combination of Ent-Co+Text+Category features, we use the results of this model for the comparison between WESSTEC and other approaches in the rest of the experiments.

4.5 Comparison of WESSTEC with the Unsupervised Approaches

Table 3 presents the classification accuracy of WESSTEC in comparison to the text classification approaches that do not require any labeled data.

It is observed that the proposed approach based on the Wide & Deep model considerably outperforms the dataless approaches as well as KBSTC. Although the dataless approaches achieved promising results in case of longer news articles in [25], they cannot perform well on short text due to the data sparsity problem.

KBSTC is a probabilistic model which does not require any training phase and it utilizes entities and categories from a KB for the categorization process. Whereas, WESSTEC first generates documents with probabilistic labels from a given unlabeled document set, then it utilizes those documents to train a Wide & Deep model to classify new documents. Moreover, WESSTEC exploits words present in text as well as entities and their directly associated categories from a KB for categorization. Hence, the proposed model is much more sophisticated and utilizes more features than the KBSTC model. Therefore, as expected the classification performance has been improved with the proposed approach.

Table 3. The classification accuracy against the unsupervised baselines

Model	AG News	Snippets	DBpedia	Twitter
Dataless ESA [25]	0.641	0.485	0.551	0.317
Dataless Word2Vec [25]	0.527	0.524	0.679	0.5
KBSTC [29]	0.805	0.720	0.460	0.359
WESSTEC	**0.814**	**0.803**	**0.792**	**0.581**

4.6 Comparison of WESSTEC with the Supervised Approaches

In order to show the effectiveness of the Wide & Deep Module (see Sect. 3.2), its performance has been compared with the supervised baselines. The generated training sets of respective datasets (see Sect. 3.1) have been utilized to train Wide & Deep as well as the baseline models. The respective original test datasets have been used for evaluating the trained models. Table 4 reports the classification performance.

The results show that the proposed Wide & Deep model can yield better accuracy in comparison to the baselines. This is due to the fact that in contrast to other approaches, the Wide & Deep model is capable of both memorization and generalization of features and thus it performs the best among all the approaches. Moreover, especially on the Snippets dataset, Wide & Deep model significantly outperforms all the baselines. The reason here can be attributed to the different characteristics of this dataset. The Snippets dataset has less average number of entities, words per text and the size of the training set is much smaller in comparison to AG News and DBpedia (see Table 1). In contrast to baselines, the proposed Wide & Deep model utilizes different resources from a KB to enrich the semantic representations of texts. Thus, it is capable of categorizing of such a dataset with a high accuracy.

Another advantage of the Wide & Deep model over the baselines is different feature combinations (e.g., entity co-occurrence, text embedding, entity embedding, etc.) can be easily exploited by the model for the categorization task.

Furthermore, a statistical significance test, namely, the 5×2cv paired t-test [7] has been also performed to compare the results of Wide & Deep and BERT. This test has been proposed to overcome the drawbacks of other significance tests (e.g., resampled paired t-test) and it is based on five iterations of two-fold cross validation. According to 5×2cv paired t-test, the experimental results are significantly different at 95% level of significance with 5 degrees of freedom.

Overall, the obtained results in Table 4 suggest that in comparison to the baselines the Wide & Deep model is better suited for the short text categorization task by utilizing the generated labeled data for training.

Table 4. The classification accuracy against the supervised baselines. The baselines have been trained with the generated training sets (see Sect. 3.1) of respective datasets.

Model	AG	Snippets	DBpedia	Twitter
SVM+tf-idf	0.808	0.696	0.784	0.513
CNN+W2V	0.796	0.787	0.784	0.542
CNN+Ent	0.794	0.703	78.24	0.456
CNN+Category	0.779	0.656	0.762	0.449
LSTM	0.786	0.693	0.796	0.473
charCNN	0.773	0.497	0.760	0.472
BERT	0.806	0.801	**0.804**	0.560
Wide & Deep	**0.814**	**0.803**	0.792	**0.581**

4.7 Evaluation of the Generated Labeled Data

To evaluate the performance of each embedding model, i.e., Word2Vec, Doc2Vec and LINE in the context of labeling the training data, we have conducted a set of experiments. First, each of the unlabeled documents and predefined labels has been projected into common vector spaces. Then each embedding model has assigned the most similar label to the documents based on the vector similarity. Additionally, by considering a simple majority vote of all the embedding models each document has also been labeled. The accuracy of labeled datasets has been calculated by comparing them with the original hand-labeled data. Table 5 presents the accuracy of the labeled training data based on the individual embedding models and the majority vote. The results suggest that considering all the embedding models for the labeling task can help in assigning more accurate labels. Therefore, to estimate the probabilistic labels for each training sample, all the embedding models have been used in the *Labeled Data Generation* module (see Sect. 3.1).

Further experiments have been conducted to asses the performance of the Wide & Deep model when it is trained on the training samples that are labeled based on majority vote. Table 6 presents the classification accuracy. The results show that using probabilistic labels in WESSTEC leads to higher-quality supervision for training the end classification model.

Table 5. The accuracy of generated training data based on the embedding models

Model	AG News	Snippets	DBpedia	Twitter
Vector Similarity LINE	0.776	0.657	0.708	0.536
Vector Similarity Doc2Vec	0.651	0.644	0.672	0.479
Vector Similarity Word2Vec	0.612	0.692	0.702	0.527
Vector Similarity (Majority)	**0.778**	**0.709**	**0.757**	**0.555**

Table 6. The classification accuracy of WESSTEC against the Wide & Deep model trained on majority vote based training set

Model	AG News	Snippets	DBpedia	Twitter
Wide & Deep (Majority)	0.812	0.799	0.772	0.559
WESSTEC	**0.814**	**0.803**	**0.792**	**0.581**

5 Conclusion and Future Work

In this study we have proposed WESSTEC, a new paradigm for weakly supervised short text categorization using world knowledge. The proposed model does not require any labeled data for categorizing documents. Instead, it first generates labeled training data from unlabeled documents by utilizing three different embedding models, i.e., Word2Vec, LINE, Doc2Vec. Several features are extracted from the labeled documents to train the Wide & Deep classification model. Finally, the new documents are classified with the help of this model. The experimental results have proven that WESSTEC is capable of categorizing short text documents with a high accuracy without requiring any labeled data and it significantly outperforms the classification approaches which do not require any labeled data. As for future work, we aim to (1) improve the labeled data generation process by exploiting advanced weak supervision approaches such as Snorkel [22]; (2) adopt WESSTEC with different KBs; (3) evaluate the performance of WESSTEC on more text classification benchmarks.

References

1. Chang, M.W., Ratinov, L.A., Roth, D., Srikumar, V.: Importance of semantic representation: dataless classification. In: AAAI (2008)
2. Chen, J., Hu, Y., Liu, J., Xiao, Y., Jiang, H.: Deep short text classification with knowledge powered attention. In: AAAI (2019)
3. Chen, M., Jin, X., Shen, D.: Short text classification improved by learning multi-granularity topics. In: IJCAI (2011)
4. Chen, P., Sun, Z., Bing, L., Yang, W.: Recurrent attention network on memory for aspect sentiment analysis. In: EMNLP (2017)
5. Cheng, H., et al.: Wide & deep learning for recommender systems. In: DLRS@RecSys (2016)
6. Devlin, J., Chang, M., Lee, K., Toutanova, K.: BERT: pre-training of deep bidirectional transformers for language understanding. In: NAACL-HLT (2019)
7. Dietterich, T.G.: Approximate statistical tests for comparing supervised classification learning algorithms. Neural Comput. **10**, 1895–1923 (1998)
8. Gabrilovich, E., Markovitch, S.: Computing semantic relatedness using wikipedia-based explicit semantic analysis. In: IJCAI (2007)
9. Hingmire, S., Chougule, S., Palshikar, G.K., Chakraborti, S.: Document classification by topic labeling. In: SIGIR (2013)
10. Le, Q.V., Mikolov, T.: Distributed representations of sentences and documents. In: ICML (2014)

11. Lehmann, J., et al.: DBpedia - a large-scale, multilingual knowledge base extracted from wikipedia. Semant. Web **6**, 167–195 (2015)
12. Li, C., Xing, J., Sun, A., Ma, Z.: Effective document labeling with very few seed words: a topic model approach. In: CIKM (2016)
13. Li, M., Clinton, G., Miao, Y., Gao, F.: Short text classification via knowledge powered attention with similarity matrix based CNN. CoRR (2020)
14. Linmei, H., Yang, T., Shi, C., Ji, H., Li, X.: Heterogeneous graph attention networks for semi-supervised short text classification. In: EMNLP-IJCNLP (2019)
15. Ma, Y., Peng, H., Cambria, E.: Targeted aspect-based sentiment analysis via embedding commonsense knowledge into an attentive LSTM. In: AAAI (2018)
16. Meng, Y., Shen, J., Zhang, C., Han, J.: Weakly-supervised neural text classification. In: CIKM (2018)
17. Meng, Y., Shen, J., Zhang, C., Han, J.: Weakly-supervised hierarchical text classification. In: AAAI (2019)
18. Mikolov, T., Sutskever, I., Chen, K., Corrado, G.S., Dean, J.: Distributed representations of words and phrases and their compositionality. In: NIPS (2013)
19. Nigam, K., McCallum, A., Thrun, S., Mitchell, T.M.: Text classification from labeled and unlabeled documents using EM. Mach. Learn. **39**, 103–134 (2000)
20. Phan, X.H., Nguyen, L.M., Horiguchi, S.: Learning to classify short and sparse text & web with hidden topics from large-scale data collections. In: WWW (2008)
21. Rabinovich, E., et al.: Learning concept abstractness using weak supervision. In: EMNLP (2018)
22. Ratner, A., Bach, S.H., Ehrenberg, H.R., Fries, J.A., Wu, S., Ré, C.: Snorkel: rapid training data creation with weak supervision. In: PVLDB (2017)
23. Reimers, N., Gurevych, I.: Sentence-bert: sentence embeddings using siamese BERT-networks. In: EMNLP-IJCNLP (2019)
24. Song, G., Ye, Y., Du, X., Huang, X., Bie, S.: Short text classification: a survey. J. Multimedia **9**, 635 (2014)
25. Song, Y., Roth, D.: On dataless hierarchical text classification. In: AAAI (2014)
26. Tang, J., Qu, M., Wang, M., Zhang, M., Yan, J., Mei, Q.: LINE: large-scale information network embedding. In: WWW (2015)
27. Türker, R., Zhang, L., Koutraki, M., Sack, H.: TECNE: knowledge based text classification using network embeddings. In: EKAW (2018)
28. Türker, R., Zhang, L., Koutraki, M., Sack, H.: "The less is more" for text classification. In: SEMANTiCS (2018)
29. Türker, R., Zhang, L., Koutraki, M., Sack, H.: Knowledge-based short text categorization using entity and category embedding. In: ESWC (2019)
30. Wang, J., Wang, Z., Zhang, D., Yan, J.: Combining knowledge with deep convolutional neural networks for short text classification. In: IJCAI (2017)
31. Wang, P., Xu, B., Xu, J., Tian, G., Liu, C.L., Hao, H.: Semantic expansion using word embedding clustering and convolutional neural network for improving short text classification. Neurocomputing **174**, 806–814 (2016)
32. Xuan, J., Jiang, H., Ren, Z., Yan, J., Luo, Z.: Automatic bug triage using semi-supervised text classification. In: SEKE (2010)
33. Zeng, J., Li, J., Song, Y., Gao, C., Lyu, M.R., King, I.: Topic memory networks for short text classification. In: EMNLP (2018)
34. Zhang, X., LeCun, Y.: Text understanding from scratch. CoRR (2015)
35. Zhang, Y., Wallace, B.C.: A sensitivity analysis of (and practitioners' guide to) convolutional neural networks for sentence classification. CoRR (2015)

PreFace: Faceted Retrieval of Prerequisites Using Domain-Specific Knowledge Bases

Prajna Upadhyay(✉) and Maya Ramanath

IIT Delhi, Hauz Khas, New Delhi 110016, India
{prajna.upadhyay,ramanath}@cse.iitd.ac.in

Abstract. While learning new technical material, a user faces difficulty encountering new concepts for which she does not have the necessary prerequisite knowledge. Determining the right set of prerequisites is challenging because it involves multiple searches on the web. Although a number of techniques have been proposed to retrieve prerequisites, none of them consider grouping prerequisites into interesting facets. To address this issue, we have developed a system called **PreFace** that (i) automatically determines interesting facets for a given concept of interest, and, (ii) determines prerequisites for the concept and facet. The key component of PreFace is a retrieval model that balances the trade-off between the relevance of the facets and their diversity. We achieve this by representing each facet as a language model estimated using a domain-specific knowledge base and a large corpus of research papers, and ranking them using a risk-minimization framework. Our evaluation of the results over a benchmark set of queries shows that PreFace retrieves better facets and prerequisites than state-of-the-art facet extraction techniques.

Keywords: Facets · Prerequisite · Knowledge base

1 Introduction

When reading new technical material, a common problem faced by readers is encountering new and unknown concepts, to understand which the reader does not have the required prerequisite knowledge. A prerequisite for a concept `a` is another concept `b` that can be suggested for study before `a` for better understanding of `a`. For example, to understand `artificial_neural_network`, one needs to have a prerequisite knowledge of `perceptron` and `activation_function`. Also, a knowledge of a programming language, such as `matlab`, will help the user in implementing `artificial_neural_network`, and a knowledge of `phoneme` will help her understand applications of `artificial_neural_network`, because `phoneme_recognition` is an application of `artificial_neural_network`. So, a prerequisite also includes concepts that help the user understand the multiple factes of a queried concept. Identifying the right set of prerequisite concepts is challenging because retrieval systems only return relevant documents that may or

J. Z. Pan et al. (Eds.): ISWC 2020, LNCS 12506, pp. 601–618, 2020.
https://doi.org/10.1007/978-3-030-62419-4_34

Table 1. Example of 4 facets and prerequisites retrieved by **PreFace** for artificial_neural_network

Facets
neural_network, perceptron
binary_classification, medical_classification, phoneme
backpropagation, optimization_algorithm, gradient_descent,
octave, matlab

may not contain prerequisites in them. Even if they do, the user may need to further refer to the prerequisite's prerequisite. This leads to a chain of searches and is time-consuming for the user. It would be helpful to have a retrieval system that, given an input concept, returns exactly the prerequisite concepts required to understand it. A number of techniques to determine prerequisites for a concept have been proposed over the years. Most of them address this problem by constructing prerequisite functions that take in a pair of concepts and determine whether one is a prerequisite of the other [21,22,28] or by constructing prerequisite graphs [39], [31,41]. These techniques have typically relied on features from textual sources, structure of textbooks and learning from training examples to construct or learn prerequisite relationships.

The main issue with these techniques is that they ignore the multiple facets of understanding of a query. Consequently, the prerequisites returned by these techniques are not grouped into facets. For example, for artificial_neural_network, along with concepts such as perceptron, concepts such as matlab, octave or phoneme are returned together. matlab and octave are relevant if the user is interested in implementing artificial_neural_network. So, instead of returning them together, it is desirable if they are returned as facets. Table 1 shows four facets for prerequisites for artificial_neural_network, 1) neural_network and perceptron, which are related to neural_networks 2) binary_classification, medical_classification, and phoneme, which help the user understand *applications* of artificial_neural_network, 3) backpropagation, optimization_algorithm, and gradient_descent, which help the user understand *algorithms* related to the query, and 4) octave and matlab, which help the user implement the query. All four of them are important towards an overall understanding of the concept. So, instead of returning all of them together, it is desirable to have a system that returns them as facets or groups.

One way to build such a system is to use existing techniques to solve the two sub-problems separately, namely facet extraction [9,18,32] and prerequisite determination [4,22] i.e. we can first extract facets for a query and then only retain concepts that are prerequisites to the query in each facet. However, this approach does not guarantee good results. There are two main reasons for this. Firstly, query-based facets are generally extracted using entities and relationships from open-domain knowledge bases like Freebase [18]. Using Freebase to retrieve facets for queries in Computer Science retrieves little or no results because the domain-specific relationships and entities are under-represented in them [37]. So, there is a need to use domain-specific knowledge bases such as TeKnowbase [36,37]. The second reason is that the proposed techniques assume that the knowledge base is sufficient to extract facets from FreeBase [9,18]. The key challenge they address is the efficient ranking of facets because they generate a large number of candidate facets in the open domain. This assumption does not hold for domain specific knowledge bases such as TeKnowbase because they are sparse. Moreover, these techniques retrieve poor quality facets when the knowledge base is from a different domain. We need a new technique to automatically extract more and better quality facets.

To address these issues, we introduce the novel problem of faceted prerequisite extraction and develop **PreFace**[1], which solves the problem of facet extraction and prerequisite determination for a query. We formulate this as a retrieval problem where we first generate high quality facets using TeKnowbase and the Open Research Corpus [1]. The facets and the query are then represented as language models [29], and ranked balancing the trade-off between the relevance and diversity of retrieved facets. Our evaluation over a standard benchmark set of queries shows that PreFace extracts better facets and prerequisites than state-of-the-art facet and pre-requisite extraction systems.

Contributions. The salient contributions of this paper are:

- Introduction of the novel problem of faceted retrieval of prerequisites
- Development of PreFace, which is a language model framework to retrieve interesting facets as well as prerequisites for a query of interest using a domain-specific knowledge base and a corpus of research papers.
- Demonstrating that PreFace can retrieve better facets and prerequisites together than separately retrieving them using state-of-the art techniques.
- PreFace is designed to work with *any* prerequisite function.

This paper is organized as follows. Section 2 describes the retrieval model for PreFace and the estimation techniques. Section 3 describes the experimental setup and results are discussed in Sect. 4. Section 5 discusses the related work.

2 Framework for PreFace

Figure 1 shows the architecture of PreFace. It takes a query and returns a ranked list of facets containing prerequisites. The terminologies are as follows:

Concept. A concept is any technical topic that can be studied and understood. In our case, a concept is an entity in the domain of Computer Science.

Query. A query is a concept about which the user wishes to study. For example `artificial_neural_network` is a query.

[1] The code and dataset for PreFace is available at http://www.cse.iitd.ac.in/~prajna/preface.html.

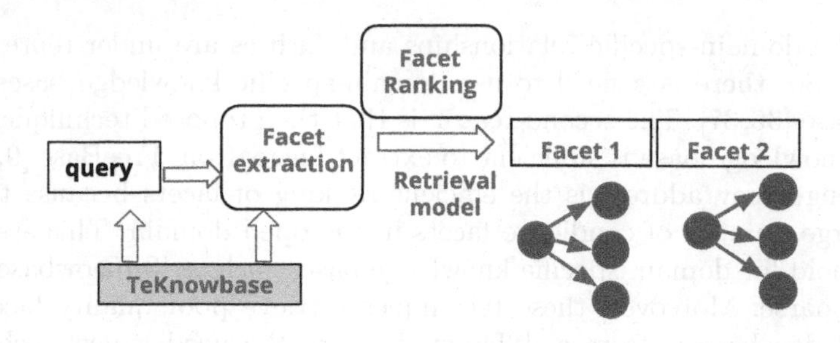

Fig. 1. Components of PreFace. It takes a query and returns a ranked list of facets containing pre-requisites for the query.

Aspect. An aspect describes some subtopic of the query that the user is interested in. For example, *application* or *implementation* are aspects of interest for `artificial_neural_network`.

Prerequisite. A prerequisite of a concept `a` is another concept `b` that can be suggested to be studied before `a` for better understanding of `a`. For example, `perceptron` is a prerequisite for `artificial_neural_network`. It also includes concepts such as `matlab` or `phoneme`, which helps the user understand different aspects of the query, such as *implementation* or *application* respectively.

Facet. A facet is a set of prerequisites to the query that describe an aspect of the query. For example, facet number 4 in Table 1 consists of `matlab` and `octave` which are pre-requisites for the *implementation* aspect for `artificial_neural_network`.

An overview of the main components of PreFace is described as follows:

Facet Extraction. This component generates candidate facets using TeKnowbase and a corpus of research papers.

Ranking of Facets. The extracted facets as well as the query are represented as language models. The language model for the query is estimated using TeKnowbase. The candidate facets are ranked balancing the trade-off between the similarity of their language model with the query language model, and the diversity of the retrieved facets.

TeKnowbase. TeKnowbase is the backbone of PreFace. It helps in the extraction as well as the modeling of the relevance of the facets. All these components are described in details in the following subsection.

2.1 Facet Extraction

A facet is a group of prerequisites for the query that describes some aspect of the query. We used the relevant documents returned in the top positions for the query to generate candidate facets. The key idea used is to extract frequently occurring key-phrases from these documents and cluster them to generate facets. Below we describe in detail these two steps:

Extracting Key-Phrases from Documents. We indexed the Open Research Corpus dataset[2] on Galago[3] and retrieved top-1000 documents for a query. We then used Rake[4], a tool to extract and score essential phrases from a document. To further clean the list of extracted phrases, we performed two data cleaning operations as follows – i) we retained only those phrases that had a length of at most 5, and ii) phrases with a score (returned by Rake) less than 5 were removed from the set of candidate phrases. The main reason for using phrases instead of entities or terms is because phrases capture the context better than entities. For example, consider the phrase `applications like robot navigation` and `robots using new camera technologies` retrieved for query `computer vision`. The phrases mention entities from TeKnowbase such as `robot navigation` or `camera`. Additionally, presence of terms, which are not entities in TeKnowbase, such as `applications` and `using` indicate that these phrases are relevant for the *application* aspect for `computer vision`, because they are modeled by our aspect-based retrieval model [38].

Clustering Key-Phrases into Facets. The next step is to cluster these phrases and obtain candidate facets. To generate semantically related clusters, we used a bag of entities representation for the key-phrases along with bag of words. The phrases were tagged with entities from TeKnowbase. Additionally, this set was expanded by adding entities situated at a 1-hop distance from already tagged entities in TeKnowbase. This was done to capture better context. Consider the phrase `using backpropagation` extracted for `artificial neural network`. The triple ⟨`backpropagation, type, algorithm`⟩ exists in TeKnowbase, so `algorithm` exists in its 1-hop neighborhood and will be added to its feature set. So, it will have high similarity to other phrases containing `algorithm`, and will likely appear in the same cluster as them. Having such a representation, these phrases were clustered into semantically related groups using agglomerative clustering algorithm with complete linkage. The distance between the phrases was measured using cosine distance.

2.2 Ranking of Facets

Modelling Facet Relevance. Given a query q, we address this problem by defining a language model for the query as well as the facet. As already defined in Sect. 2, a facet consists of prerequisites relevant for some aspect of the query. So, it should contain terms that are found in prerequisites of the query, as well as terms relevant for the query and the aspect. The challenge lies in identifying the pre-requisites and the aspects for the query, and then modeling the relevance for the query and the aspect. The facets should also contain items that are highly similar to each other. So, the relevance is modeled by two components:

---

[2] https://allenai.org/data/s2orc.
[3] https://www.lemurproject.org/galago.php.
[4] https://pypi.org/project/rake-nltk/.

1) Query dependant facet relevance. This is denoted by $PreFace(w|q)$.

$$PreFace(w|q) = \lambda Preq(w|q) + (1-\lambda)\sum_i P(q_i|q)P(w|q,q_i), \quad (1)$$

It consists of two components, $Preq(w|q)$ and $\sum_i P(q_i|q)P(w|q,q_i)$, which are mixed using λ. These two components are described as follows:

i) Prerequisite probability. $Preq(w|q)$ models the probability of a word w appearing in a prerequisite for the query.
ii) Query and aspect probability. To be able to retrieve other concepts that help understand other aspects of the query, we first have to identify these aspects.

After identifying the set of aspects A with $q_i \in A$, the relevance of a term w for q and q_i is modeled using the technique proposed by us in [38]. The query and the aspect component is represented by $P(w|q,q_i)$ and is modeled as follows:

$$P(w|q,q_i) = \gamma P_{ind}(w|q_i) + (1-\gamma)P_{dep}(w|q,q_i) \quad (2)$$

where $P_{ind}(w|q_i)$ is the component determined by the aspect alone and $P_{dep}(w|q,q_i)$ is the query dependent component, determined by both the query and the aspect. γ is used to mix these two components.

2) Query independent facet relevance. The query independent facet relevance models the relevance of the facet independent of the query. This is determined by the quality of facet, dependent on the size of the facet and the strength of the similarity between its items. A facet that contains a large number of similar entities is more important than one that contains lesser number of entities, provided the strength of similarity between the two is the same. So, we first apply a similarity threshold on the facets, and then use the size of the facet as a measure of its quality. The query independent facet relevance is denoted by $Q(f)$.

Algorithm 1: Probabilistic framework for PreFace (λ, τ, F, q)

$S = \emptyset$;
$PreFace(w|q) = \lambda Preq(w|q) + (1-\lambda)\sum_i P(q_i|q)P(w|q,q_i)$;
$f* = \text{argmax}_{f\in F} Q(f) * \frac{1}{D_{KL}(PreFace||M_f)}$;
$S = S \cup \{f*\}$;
while $|S| < \tau - 1$ **do**
  $f* = \text{argmax}_{f\in F\setminus S} Q(f) * \frac{D_{KL}(M_f||M_S)}{D_{KL}(PreFace||M_f)}$;
  $F = F \setminus \{f*\}$;
  $S = S \cup \{f*\}$;
end
return S

Modeling Facet Diversity. Algorithm 1 describes the procedure for the ranking of facets. It takes a query (q), the number of facets to be returned (τ), the mixing parameter to combine the two components of Eq. 1 (λ), and the set of candidate facets (F) as input and returns a ranked list of facets S. It greedily selects the best facet at each iteration that balances the trade-off between its relevance to the query and dissimilarity to the facets already retrieved. The user should be recommended facets that are diverse to one another. This means that if a facet describing the algorithms for understanding `artificial_neural_network` appears in the top-k position, it is desirable that it is not suggested again. This is done by returning facets whose language model diverges the most from the language model of already retrieved facets and least from the query. Each facet is scored according to the following equation:

$$\frac{D_{KL}(M_f||M_S)}{D_{KL}(PreFace||M_f)} = \frac{\sum_w M_f(w) log \frac{M_f(w)}{M_s(w)}}{\sum_w PreFace(w) log \frac{PreFace(w)}{M_f(w)}} \quad (3)$$

where M_f is the language model of a facet f and M_S is the language model representation of the set of facets already retrieved. $D_{KL}(M_f||M_S)$ is the KL divergence between facet language model and the language model for the set of facets already retrieved. $D_{KL}(PreFace||M_f)$ is the KL divergence between the language model for the query $(PreFace(q))$ and the language model for the facet. The language model of a facet f and set S is described by the following equations. These models are smoothed using additive smoothing techniques.

$$M_f(w) = \frac{tf(w,f)+1}{length(f)+|V|} \quad (4) \qquad M_S(w) = \frac{\sum_{f_i \in S} tf(w,f_i)+1}{\sum_{f_i \in S} length(f_i)+|V|} \quad (5)$$

where $tf(w,f)$ and $length(f)$ is the frequency of w in f and number of terms in f, respectively. In other words, greater the divergence between the language model of the facet and language model of S, better is the facet and lower the divergence between the query language model and the facet language model, better the facet. The facets are re-ranked at each iteration, until the desirable number (τ) of facets are retrieved using the following equation:

$$f* = \text{argmax}_{f \in F \setminus S} Q(f) * \frac{D_{KL}(M_f||M_S)}{D_{KL}(PreFace||M_f)} \quad (6)$$

where $Q(f)$ is the quality of a facet. The facet retrieved at this position is removed from the pool of candidate facets and added to S.

Estimation of Components. In this section, we describe the techniques to estimate the probabilities that are used in our probabilistic framework.

Estimating $Preq(w|q)$. This component models the probability of words likely to appear in prerequisites of the query. To estimate this component, we can use any standard prerequisite function from the literature. For our work, we used the well-known prerequisite function, $RefD$ (or reference distance) [22], because it is a simple, unsupervised metric and gives good results. $RefD$ takes two concepts as input and returns a score denoting the strength of the pre-requisite relationship between them. We further identified the set of siblings $Siblings(q)$ of q (entities in TeKnowbase that share same parent in its taxonomy) and also their pre-requisites to estimate $Preq(w|q)$. At first, we computed $Preq_s(w|s_i)$ for each sibling s_i of q in $Siblings(q)$.

$$Preq_s(w|s_i) = \frac{\sum_{e_k \in ent(w)} RefD(e_k, s_i)}{\sum_{e_k \in C} RefD(e_k, s_i)}, RefD(e_k, s_i) > thresh \quad (7)$$

Then, $Preq(w|q)$ is estimated as follows:

$$Preq(w|q) = \frac{1}{|Siblings(q)|} \sum_{s_i \in Siblings(q)} Preq_s(w|s_i) \quad (8)$$

where C is the concept space and $ent(w) \subset C$ is the set of entities that contain the term w in TeKnowbase. The intuition behind using a mixture of $Preq_s(w|s_i)$, where s_i is an entity that shares the same parent as q is that siblings in TeKnowbase taxonomy have similar prerequisites, and we can make our distribution more accurate by including concepts that were not returned as prerequisites for q.

Estimating Query and Aspect Probability. The second component in Eq. 1 models the query and the aspect probability. To estimate this component, we first have to identify the set A of aspects for q. As already described in Sect. 2, aspects describe some subtopic for the query, which can be entities or relationships in TeKnowbase. The key-idea used is to acquire entities from key-phrases and cluster them into groups based on the graph structure of TeKnowbase and identify a representative from each group to be used as the aspect. The procedure to generate A is described as follows:

1) Acquiring set of entities. We tagged entities from TeKnowbase in the set of key-phrases retrieved using the procedure described in Sect. 2.1 and obtained the set of relevant entities E. Each $e \in E$ was scored using the following formula:

$$score(e) = co\_occ(e, q) RefD(e, q), RefD(e, q) > thresh \quad (9)$$

where $co\_occ(e, q)$ counts the number of times e and q have appeared together in a document across the top-1000 relevant documents retrieved for q. An entity that frequently co-occurs with the query in relevant documents should be more important to the query, so is assigned a higher score using this formula.

2) Using TeKnowbase entities as aspects. Having a set of entities E, we have to partition it into groups such that each group is highly relevant to the query as well as is semantically similar to each other. We can then choose a representative from each group as an aspect for q. To do this, we used the links in TeKnowbase and created an induced sub-graph G on TeKnowbase using the set of entities in E and then applied the star clustering algorithm [2] on G to cluster entities into groups. Star Clustering algorithm works on a graph and takes a similarity threshold σ as input. It retains edges that have strength greater than

σ and then clusters the nodes of the graph into groups. It is a greedy algorithm that chooses the node with the highest degree first and assigns all its adjacent nodes to its cluster. It repeats the procedure with other nodes that have not yet been assigned to any cluster. In TeKnowbase, all links are assumed to have a strength of 1, so σ was set to 1. We scored each cluster using the sum of scores of its entities, given by: $\sum_{c_i \in C} score(c_i)$, where $score(c_i)$ is the score of each entity calculated using Eq. 9. From every top-10 scored clusters, we chose the highest scored entity to be added to A.

3) Using TeKnowbase relationships as aspects. Apart from using entities in TeKnowbase as aspects, we expanded the set by adding relationships from TeKnowbase as aspects. We used the aspects that were used in [38] for query q, namely *algorithm*, *application* and *implementation*. We also added *type* and *technique* to the set of aspects A.

After generating the set of aspects A, we have to estimate $P(q, q_i)$ for each $q_i \in A$. As already described in Sect. 2.2, we used our previously proposed aspect based retrieval [38] technique to model this component. The query independent and dependent components of this model were estimated as follows:

1) Estimating $P_{ind}(w|q_i)$. We estimated the query-independent aspect probability by explicitly querying for the aspect term alone and retrieving the top documents. To further make our estimation accurate, we retained only those documents that mention the aspect term in the title or abstract. Having this set of documents D, we estimated the query independent aspect probability as follows:

$$P_{ind}(w|q_i) = \frac{1}{|D|} \sum_{d \in D} \frac{tf(w,d)}{\sum_{w' \in d} tf(w',d)} \tag{10}$$

where $tf(w,d)$ is the frequency of w in a document d.

2) Estimating $P_{dep}(w|q, q_i)$. We estimated this component from both the search results and TeKnowbase. To estimate this component from search results, we explicitly queried for q and q_i together and retrieved top ranked documents. To further make our estimation accurate, we only retained those documents that contained both the query and aspect terms in either the title or the abstract. This probability was estimated as follows:

$$P_{docs}(w|q, q_i) = \frac{1}{|D'|} \sum_{d \in D'} \frac{tf(w,d)}{\sum_{w' \in d} tf(w',d)} \tag{11}$$

where $tf(w,d)$ is the frequency of w in a document d and D' is the set of documents with each document containing the query and the aspect term both. We also used TeKnowbase to further improve the accuracy of estimation. TeKnowbase consists of entities connected to q via relation described by the aspect q_i. So, the words appearing in entities connected to the q via q_i should also be considered for estimation. For example, TeKnowbase consists of the triple ⟨`activity_recognition, application, hidden_markov_model`⟩, which implies that `activity_recognition` can be suggested as a prerequisite for the application aspect. However, TeKnowbase is sparse and only using those links to estimate this probability will not result in an accurate estimation. So, we used the approach adopted in [38] for improving the estimation using meta-paths [34] in TeKnowbase, which computes the probability $DI_{e_i}(e_j)$ of two entities being connected via the relation described by the aspect q_i. This is used to estimate $P_{KB}(w|q, q_i)$ as follows:

$$P_{KB}(w|q, q_i) = \sum_{e \in ent(w)} DI_e(q) \quad (12)$$

We then computed the query and aspect probability by mixing the probability distributions given by Eq. 11 and Eq. 12. The final probability for query and aspect, both, is given as follows:

$$P_{dep}(w|q, q_i) = \alpha P_{docs}(w|q, q_i) + (1 - \alpha) P_{KB}(w|q, q_i) \quad (13)$$

3) Estimating $P(q_i|q)$. This models how important is the aspect q_i to q. All the aspects can be given equal probability or the probability can be proportional to $score(q_i)$, described by Eq. 9. Given A, the set of aspects, the second component of the final relevance equation is a linear combination of the query and aspect probabilities, described as follows:

$$\sum_i P(q_i|q) P(w|q, q_i) \quad (14)$$

The final relevance equation is a mixture of Eq. 14 and Eq. 8.

4) Ranking of facets. After estimating the query dependent probability of terms given a query, we rank the facets according to Algorithm 1.

Item Ranking. After the facets have been ranked, we have to rank the entities in the facet to be shown as pre-requisites to the user. To do so, we first identified a representative element re for each facet. We tagged entities in the facet and chose the most frequently occurring entity as the representative. After choosing the representative, we computed the score for each entity e tagged in the facet as follows: $freq(e)sim(e, re)$, where $sim(e, re)$ is the normalized cosine similarity between the vector representations of entities e and re. These vector representations were obtained by training Node2Vec algorithm on TeKnowbase. The entities in each facet are then ranked in decreasing order of this score.

3 Experiments

3.1 Setup

We experimented with the Wikipedia and the Open Research Corpus datasets. The values of λ, γ and α were set to 0.5. *thresh* was set to 0. For every baseline, we retrieved the top-5 facets for each query. Then, in each facet, the top 3 items were shown to the users for evaluation.

```
artificial neural network , backpropagation, collaborative filtering,
computer vision, conditional random field, context-sensitive grammar,
cross entropy, dimensionality reduction, generative adversarial networks,
genetic algorithm, gradient descent, hidden markov model, latent
dirichlet allocation, linear regression, logistic regression, optical
character recognition, pagerank, probabilistic context-free grammar,
question answering, recursive neural network, regular expression,
reinforcement learning, sentiment analysis, shallow parsing, singular
value decomposition, spectral clustering, speech recognition, statistical
machine translation, word-sense disambiguation, word2vec
```

Fig. 2. Benchmark queries

3.2 Benchmark Queries

We chose 30 queries from the set of topics released by [21] (listed in Fig. 2), which is a set of concepts annotated with their prerequisites. We used these annotations to measure the precision of prerequisites retrieved by our technique as well as the baselines. We additionally conducted user-studies to evaluate the precision of concepts that were retrieved but not already in that dataset. We restricted ourselves to queries that have a Wikipedia page because the prerequisite function $RefD$ uses Wikipedia to compute reference distance between concepts.

3.3 Baselines

As already stated in Sect. 1, we can solve the two sub-problems separately using existing state-of-the-art techniques, as in the baselines mentioned below:

1) QDMKB + RefD. QDMKB [18] is a state-of-the art facet retrieval technique for extracting facets from knowledge bases and search results. It improves upon the results of its predecessor, QDMiner [8] and other state-of-the-art techniques QF-I and QF-J [19]. QDMKB extracts first and second-hop properties (or relationships the query participates in) for the query from the knowledge base, assuming that each property is a candidate facet. It ranks them according to the frequency of the entities appearing in the relevant documents. $RefD$ is a state-of-the-art prerequisite function already described in Sect. 2.2. We implemented QDMKB and extracted facets for a query from TeKnowbase. Then, for each facet, we retained only those entities that were returned as prerequisites for the query according to $RefD$.

2) RefD + TKB. We can also retrieve facets for prerequisites of a query by clustering them into groups. We used the links in TeKnowbase to cluster the candidate prerequisites into meaningful groups. We tagged entities from TeKnowbase in the top-1000 results. We then constructed an induced sub-graph from these entities on TeKnowbase and applied star clustering algorithm [2] on it, as described in Sect. 2.2. Each cluster was scored according to the following equation. The clusters were then ranked according to $score(C)$ (Eq. 15).

$$score(C) = \sum_{c_i \in C} RefD(c_i, q), RefD(c_i, q) > thresh \quad (15)$$

3) PreFace. This is our technique that extractes facets using TeKnowbase and a corpus of research papers and then ranks them by representing them as language models using Algorithm 1.

3.4 Evaluation Scheme

There are two components to evaluate – 1) quality of facets 2) quality of prerequisites. Owing to the lack of a standard dataset for evaluation, we used human evaluators (computer science researchers) to evaluate the generated facets. Top 5 facets with 3 items in each facet were shown to two evaluators (computer science researchers) who evaluated it for its quality.

Evaluation of Facet Quality. To evaluate the quality of facets retrieved, we conducted the following experiments. Each facet was evaluated for the quality of clustering and ranking of facets. We used semantic similarity to measure the quality of clusters retrieved by each technique and DCG (Discounted Cumulative Gain) to measure the ranking of facets. The methodology to evaluate both the qualities is described as follows:

Ranking of Facets. To evaluate the ranking quality, each user was shown a representative item from each facet and asked if that item was relevant to the query. For Preface, the entity that was most frequently occurring in the facet was shown as the representative. For RefD + TKB, the representative was the star centre of each cluster generated by the star clustering algorithm. For QDMKB + RefD, we chose the item in the facet that obtained the highest score for RefD. The relevance scores could be 0: not relevant at all, 1: somewhat relevant, and 2: very relevant. We then used these scores to compute DCG values.

Clustering Quality. We have to evaluate the quality of facets generated by our technique as well as the baselines. To judge the clustering quality, we asked the user to score the similarity between other entities in the facet to the representative of the facet. The score could be 2: very similar, 1: somewhat similar, and 0: not similar at all. For example, `quadratic_convex_function` and `general_smooth_nonlinear_function_approximator` are similar to each other because both are functions, whereas `algorithm` and `integer` are not similar to each other. For PreFace, we showed the top-3 items ranked according to the approach described in Sect. 2.2. For RefD + TKB, we showed the top-3 entities scored according to *RefD* scores that were added to the clusters after their star centres were chosen. For QDMKB, top 3 entities ranked in decreasing order of their *RefD* scores were shown. We computed the score for each pair and normalised the similarity score so that it lies between 0 and 1.

Evaluation of Prerequisites. Apart from evaluating the quality of facets, we also have to evaluate the prerequisites retrieved by our technique. We used the set of prerequisite concept pairs released by [21] as the ground truth. The same items that were shown to the user for evaluating the quality of facets were shown to be evaluated as prerequisites. Since the definition of our prerequisites is broader than in earlier work, we performed a user study to judge the relevance of prerequisites not present in the dataset. The top 5 facets were used for evaluation of prerequisite concept. Each prerequisite was annotated by 2 evaluators (computer science researchers) with scores of 0 or 1. A score of 1 was assigned if the prerequisite was judged to be relevant for the aspect described by the representative item of that facet. In other cases, a score of 0 is assigned.

4 Results and Discussion

4.1 Results

Facet Quality. Table 2(a) shows the values for facet quality for all 3 techniques. Our technique outperforms the baselines in retrieving better quality facets.

Table 2. Tables showing results for a) DCG and cluster similarity values for facet ranking and facet quality, respectively, for all 3 techniques b) Precision of prerequisites retrieved by PreFace and competing techniques.

Techniques	DCG @5	Cluster similarity
PreFace	**5.80**	**0.95**
QDMKB + RefD	4.26	0.80
RefD + TKB	5.56	0.77

Techniques	Precision
PreFace	**0.76**
QDMKB + RefD	0.636
RefD + TKB	0.68

Clustering Quality. The average cluster similarity for our technique was 0.95, which is very high and the highest among other techniques. This was possible because of the bag-of-words and entities representation of items using TeKnowbase. QDMKB + RefD obtains a cluster similarity score of 0.8. The reason for it performing worse than PreFace is that not all the facets returned by QDMKB + RefD contain semantically similar items with respect to the query. For example, Table 3 shows the facets retrieved for `artificial_neural_network` by all the techniques. QDMKB + RefD returns a facet consisting of items `machine_learning`, `probability`, `hidden_markov_models` and `decision_tree`. This facet was returned because all the items in the facet are related to `artificial_neural_network` via the sequence ⟨`research(relatedTo)`, `artificial_intelligence`, `techniquein_inverse`⟩. Amongst these items, `probability` is not semantically similar to `machine_learning`. So, all the second hop properties may not lead to good quality facets. RefD + TKB obtains a cluster similarity score of 0.77. The reason for the lower similarity value is that the semantics of relations are not considered while clustering the entities. For example, for the same query, a facet retrieved at 3rd position consists of computer_science and matlab. Both these items are not similar to each other, but have appeared together because they participate in the following triples with programming_language: ⟨matlab, typeof, programming_language⟩ and ⟨programming_language, issoftware_notations_and_tools(relatedto), computer_science⟩ in TeKnowbase.

Ranking Quality. The ranking quality of the facets is measured using DCG. Our technique outperforms the baselines in ranking of facets. QDMKB + RefD performs worse because it fails to retrieve at least 5 facets for all the queries. RefD + TKB performs better than QDMKB + RefD. Overall, PreFace generates much better facets as compared to its competitors.

Quality of Prerequisites. Table 2(b) shows the precision of retrieved prerequisites. PreFace outperforms both the baselines by obtaining a precision of 0.76 across all queries. RefD + TKB comes second in retrieving prerequisites to our technique because it uses *RefD* to construct facets. It obtains a precision of 0.68. QDMKB + RefD performs the worst because it returns few prerequisites in each facet and the facet is also not relevant to the query. This shows that our retrieval system is able to return better prerequisites than other techniques.

Table 3. Prerequisites retrieved for artificial_neural_network by PreFace, QDMKB + RefD and RefD + TKB for top 6 facets

PreFace	RefD + TKB	QDMKB + RefD
neural_network, network_model, perceptron, backpropagation	integer, turing_machine, information_theory, differential_equation	software, theorem
genetic_algorithm, backpropagation, optimization_algorithm, gradient_descent	mathematics, statistics, regression_analysis, statistical_inference	machine_learning, probability, hidden_markov_models, decision_tree
transfer_function, activation_function, linear, basis_function	computer_science, matlab, fortran, natural	metaheuristic, syntactic_pattern_recognition
computer_security, program, laptop_computer, quantum_computer	continuous_function, transfer_function, computable_function, integral	
binary_classification, medical_classification, tumor, phoneme	probability_distribution, multiplication, linear_system, impulse_response	
statistical_software, system_software, octave, matlab	machine_learning, artificial_intelligence, statistical_estimation	

5 Related Work

While ours is the first attempt at retrieving faceted pre-requisites, both of these techniques i.e., facet extraction and prerequisite determination have been independently explored. Below we review both the approaches.

5.1 Facet Extraction

Extracting facets has been studied over a long time, using knowledge graphs and/or search results. Below we list related work in each of these areas.

Facets are either pre-defined categories on the corpus or are built dynamically based on the query. Among existing work that use static facet categories are Ontogator [26] and mSpace [32] that use RDF graphs to annotate images to facilitate faceted browsing. [27] developed BrowseRDF, that helps the user browse an RDF graph by providing constraints to be applied on graph properties. They also proposed metrics to measure the quality of facets and rank them. [14] helps a user answer complex queries using faceted search on Wikipedia. The properties are extracted from Wikipedia info-boxes and displayed to the user for further refining the results. gFacet [16] and VisiNav [15] are tools that provide visualization of web of data supported with faceted filtering techniques using RDF graphs and properties. [6] proposed a system to construct facet hierarchies for a text corpus and then assign the documents to each of these facets. This is different from our facets which are co-ordinate and not hierarchies.

Among the systems that generate facets dynamically are those that build SPARQL queries on the fly to be executed on the respective SPARQL endpoints. [10] and [9] have used these approaches to build facets for a query. The authors proposed QDMiner [8] to retrieve facets from search results by extracting frequently occurring lists in relevant documents. These lists were extracted from structured data in the documents, like HTML lists or tables. [18] proposed QDMKB that improved the results generated by [8] by using FreeBase. Another extension to QDMiner was done by [19] where they improved the quality of facets generated by using a probabilistic graphical model. Both QDMiner and QDMKB assume that the corpus is rich in meta-data, which is not always true. The techniques that use knowledge bases to generate facets assume that they are sufficient, which may not be the case for domain-specific graphs.

In the context of academic search, [11] built *Scienstein* that allows users to search for papers using authors or reference lists apart from the usual keyword-query search. These tools make use of the underlying structure of the citation graph as well as machine learning techniques on the document text. [7] made an effort to provide faceted retrieval for research papers in computer science. The facets were – publication years, authors or conferences. These facets are different from aspects in our scenario. [3] proposed techniques to further categorise the relationships between the query paper and the recommended paper. These relationships are expressed in the form of facets like `background`, `alternative_approaches`, `methods` and `comparisons`. [5] used similar facets to summarize scientific papers. These facets are extracted by identifying the context of the text surrounding the citation.

5.2 Prerequisite Determination

Among the techniques that determine prerequisites between a pair of concepts, [35] used crowd-sourcing to create a gold standard dataset that was used to train a classifier using features from Wikipedia. In [22], the authors proposed *RefD* using frame semantics to compute prerequisites between concepts using Wikipedia. In [31], the authors make use of Wikipedia clickstream data to build the classifier. In [23], the authors used *RefD* to infer concept prerequisite relationships from course prerequisite pairs. They later proposed active learning techniques to reduce the amount of training data in [24]. [12] proposed information theoretic measures to determine dependencies between concepts in a scientific corpus. In [28], authors trained classifier using lecture transcripts from MOOCs to improve the prediction of prerequisite pairs. [41] proposed an optimization framework to model prerequisite links among concepts as latent links which can be used to infer prerequisite links between course pairs across universities. [30] proposed a neural model using siamese networks to improve prediction of prerequisite relations. Supervised learning model has been used in [25] to determine prerequisite relations by extracting high quality phrases from educational data.

A number of techniques have been proposed to present information in an organized manner. These include generating hierarchies over document collections [20] or ordering documents in a sequence. [33] proposed metro-maps to show the developments between research papers. [40] proposed methods to generate reading orders for a concept of interest in the domain of physics. [13] and [17] proposed techniques to generate reading lists of research papers for a query.

Although a number of techniques exist that solve the two sub-problems independently, to the best of our knowledge, there exists no other system that solves both of these problems together.

6 Conclusion

In this paper, we developed PreFace, a system to automatically extract facets together with prerequisites for a concept of interest. To the best of our knowledge, ours is the first system that solves this problem. PreFace extracts facets using TeKnowbase and a corpus of research papers and represents them as language models. It then ranks them by balancing the trade-off between their relevance and diversity. Our evaluation of the results shows that PreFace retrieves better facets and prerequisites than state-of-the art techniques.

References

1. Ammar, W., et al.: Construction of the literature graph in semantic scholar. In: NAACL (2018)

2. Aslam, J.A., Pelekhov, E., Rus, D.: The star clustering algorithm for static and dynamic information organization. J. Graph Algorithms Appl. **8**(1), 95–129 (2004)
3. Chakraborty, T., et al.: FeRoSa: a faceted recommendation system for scientific articles. In: PAKDD (2016)
4. Chen, Y., Wuillemin, P.H., Labat, J.M.: Discovering prerequisite structure of skills through probabilistic association rules mining. In: EDM (2015)
5. Cohan, A., Goharian, N.: Scientific document summarization via citation contextualization and scientific discourse. Int. J. Digit. Libr. **19**(2–3), 287–303 (2018)
6. Dakka, W., Ipeirotis, P.G.: Automatic extraction of useful facet hierarchies from text databases. In: ICDE (2008)
7. Diederich, J., et al.: Demonstrating the semantic growBag: automatically creating topic facets for FacetedDBLP. In: JCDL (2007)
8. Dou, Z., et al.: Finding dimensions for queries. In: CIKM (2011)
9. Feddoul, L., Schindler, S., Löffler, F.: Automatic facet generation and selection over knowledge graphs. In: Acosta, M., Cudré-Mauroux, P., Maleshkova, M., Pellegrini, T., Sack, H., Sure-Vetter, Y. (eds.) SEMANTiCS 2019. LNCS, vol. 11702, pp. 310–325. Springer, Cham (2019). https://doi.org/10.1007/978-3-030-33220-4_23
10. Ferré, S.: Expressive and scalable query-based faceted search over SPARQL endpoints. In: Mika, P., et al. (eds.) ISWC 2014. LNCS, vol. 8797, pp. 438–453. Springer, Cham (2014). https://doi.org/10.1007/978-3-319-11915-1_28
11. Gipp, B., et al.: Scienstein: a research paper recommender system. In: ICETCCT (2009)
12. Gordon, J., et al.: Modeling concept dependencies in a scientific corpus. In: ACL (2016)
13. Gordon, J., et al.: Structured generation of technical reading lists. In: BEA@NAACL (2017)
14. Hahn, R., et al.: Faceted wikipedia search. In: Abramowicz, W., Tolksdorf, R. (eds.) BIS 2010. LNBIP, vol. 47, pp. 1–11. Springer, Heidelberg (2010). https://doi.org/10.1007/978-3-642-12814-1_1
15. Harth, A.: VisiNav: a system for visual search and navigation on web data. J. Web Sem. **8**, 348–354 (2010)
16. Heim, P., Ziegler, J., Lohmann, S.: gFacet: a browser for the web of data. In: IMC-SSW@SAMT, vol. 417 (2008)
17. Jardine, J.G.: Automatically generating reading lists. Ph.D. thesis, University of Cambridge, UK (2014)
18. Jiang, Z., Dou, Z., Wen, J.: Generating query facets using knowledge bases. IEEE Trans. Knowl. Data Eng. **29**(2), 315–329 (2017)
19. Kong, W., Allan, J.: Extracting query facets from search results. In: SIGIR (2013)
20. Koutrika, G., Liu, L., Simske, S.: Generating reading orders over document collections. In: ICDE (2015)
21. Li, I., et al.: What should i learn first: introducing lecturebank for NLP education and prerequisite chain learning. In: AAAI (2019)
22. Liang, C., et al.: Measuring prerequisite relations among concepts. In: EMNLP (2015)
23. Liang, C., et al.: Recovering concept prerequisite relations from university course dependencies. In: AAAI (2017)
24. Liang, C., et al.: Investigating active learning for concept prerequisite learning. In: EAAI (2018)
25. Lu, W., et al.: Concept extraction and prerequisite relation learning from educational data. In: AAAI (2019)

26. Mäkelä, E., Hyvönen, E., Saarela, S.: Ontogator—a semantic view-based search engine service for web applications. In: Cruz, I., et al. (eds.) ISWC 2006. LNCS, vol. 4273, pp. 847–860. Springer, Heidelberg (2006). https://doi.org/10.1007/11926078_61
27. Oren, E., Delbru, R., Decker, S.: Extending faceted navigation for RDF data. In: Cruz, I., et al. (eds.) ISWC 2006. LNCS, vol. 4273, pp. 559–572. Springer, Heidelberg (2006). https://doi.org/10.1007/11926078_40
28. Pan, L., et al.: Prerequisite relation learning for concepts in MOOCs. In: ACL (2017)
29. Ponte, J.M., Croft, W.B.: A language modeling approach to information retrieval. In: SIGIR (1998)
30. Roy, S., et al.: Inferring concept prerequisite relations from online educational resources. In: AAAI (2019)
31. Sayyadiharikandeh, M., et al.: Finding prerequisite relations using the wikipedia clickstream. In: WWW Companion (2019)
32. Schraefel, M.C., et al.: The evolving mspace platform: leveraging the semantic web on the trail of the memex. In: Hypertext (2005)
33. Shahaf, D., Guestrin, C., Horvitz, E.: Metro maps of science. In: KDD (2012)
34. Sun, Y., Han, J.: Mining Heterogeneous Information Networks: Principles and Methodologies. Morgan & Claypool (2012)
35. Talukdar, P. P. and Cohen, W.: Crowdsourced comprehension: predicting prerequisite structure in wikipedia. In: BEA@NAACL (2012)
36. Upadhyay, P., et al.: TeKnowbase: towards construction of knowledge-base of technical concepts. Technical report. http://arxiv.org/abs/1612.04988 (2016)
37. Upadhyay, P., et al.: Construction and applications of teknowbase: a knowledge base of computer science concepts. In: WWW Companion (2018)
38. Upadhyay, P., Bedathur, S., Chakraborty, T., Ramanath, M.: Aspect-based academic search using domain-specific KB. In: Jose, J.M., et al. (eds.) ECIR 2020. LNCS, vol. 12036, pp. 418–424. Springer, Cham (2020). https://doi.org/10.1007/978-3-030-45442-5_52
39. Wang, S. and Liu, L.: Prerequisite concept maps extraction for automatic assessment. In: WWW Companion (2016)
40. Wohlgenannt, G., et al.: Dynamic integration of multiple evidence sources for ontology learning. JIDM **3**(3), 243–254 (2012)
41. Yang, Y., et al.: Concept graph learning from educational data. In: WSDM (2015)

Detecting Different Forms of Semantic Shift in Word Embeddings via Paradigmatic and Syntagmatic Association Changes

Anna Wegmann[1(✉)], Florian Lemmerich[1], and Markus Strohmaier[1,2]

[1] RWTH Aachen University, 52062 Aachen, Germany
anna.wegmann@rwth-aachen.de,
{florian.lemmerich,markus.strohmaier}@cssh.rwth-aachen.de
[2] GESIS - Leibniz Institute for the Social Sciences, 50667 Cologne, Germany

Abstract. Automatically detecting semantic shifts (i.e., meaning changes) of single words has recently received strong research attention, e.g., to quantify the impact of real-world events on online communities. These computational approaches have introduced various measures, which are intended to capture the somewhat elusive and undifferentiated concept of semantic shift. On the other hand, there is a longstanding and well established distinction in linguistics between a word's *paradigmatic* (i.e., terms that can replace a word) and *syntagmatic* associations (i.e., terms that typically occur next to a word). In this work, we join these two lines of research by introducing a method that captures a measure's sensitivity for paradigmatic and/or syntagmatic (association) shifts. For this purpose, we perform synthetic distortions on textual corpora that in turn induce shifts in word embeddings trained on them. We find that the *Local Neighborhood* is sensitive to paradigmatic and the *Global Semantic Displacement* is sensitive to syntagmatic shift in word embeddings. By applying the newly validated paradigmatic and syntagmatic measures on three real-world datasets (Amazon, Reddit and Wikipedia) we find examples of words that undergo paradigmatic and syntagmatic shift both separately and at the same time. With this more nuanced understanding of semantic shift on word embeddings, we hope to analyze a similar concept of semantic shift on RDF graph embeddings in the future.

Keywords: Semantic shift detection · Paradigmatic associations · Syntagmatic associations · RDF embedding shift

1 Introduction

In the context of word meaning, linguistic theory has long since distinguished between two fundamentally different types of word relations (e.g., [25,26]) that even have been claimed to correspond to basic operations in the brain, cf. [6, 29]: *Paradigmatic* associations of a word w are terms that occur with the same

J. Z. Pan et al. (Eds.): ISWC 2020, LNCS 12506, pp. 619–635, 2020.
https://doi.org/10.1007/978-3-030-62419-4_35

context words as w (i.e., which can substitute w without changing the sentence's grammatical structure), e.g., "cat" and "dog". *Syntagmatic* associations of a word w are terms that co-occur with w, e.g., "cat" and "wild". This notion is transferable to knowledge representations such as RDF graphs: Paradigmatically related entities would be those that can be replaced by each other (e.g., "cold" by "sniffles" in a symptom-disease network). Syntagmatically related entities, would be those that connect to each other in a network (e.g., "cold" and "coughs").

On the other hand, popular methods for densely encoding word meaning for computational use are word embeddings (e.g., word2vec or GloVe), which also form the basis for important algorithms for knowledge graph embeddings [4,22]. When words or RDF graph entities change their meaning over time, text corpora (resp. RDF graphs) from these time periods – and consequently the embeddings trained on them – encode these semantic shifts. Several measures of semantic (in-)stability, which can be used to infer meaning shifts from changes in word embeddings, have been proposed in literature [11,12,16,17,30]. However, it is currently unclear what exactly they are measuring in relation to paradigmatic and syntagmatic associations. Thus, we evaluate different computational approaches for detecting *semantic shift* in this paper. We define the semantic shift of a word or entity as anything that affects its paradigmatic and syntagmatic associations. While we focus on word embeddings in this paper, we see our work also as a step towards analyzing changing knowledge graph embeddings in the future [10,15].

Research Questions. In particular, we aim to investigate the following research questions regarding word embeddings: (i) How can the sensitivity of semantic shift measures to paradigmatic and syntagmatic shift be evaluated? (ii) What are the differences in the measures' sensitivity? (iii) Can both types of shift be observed in real-world datasets and do they always co-occur with each other?

Approach. Based on theoretical considerations we perform a series of experiments in which we synthetically modify a text corpus (similar to [28]) to induce paradigmatic and/or syntagmatic shift. Then, we calculate word embeddings on these corpora and check whether the measures detect the different types of introduced shifts. We compare the performance of the different measures to identify those that are best at detecting paradigmatic (syntagmatic) shift. We apply those measures to detect words that underwent association shifts on three real-world datasets and evaluate the relation between the two forms of shift on them.

Results. By and large, our findings suggest that the *Local Neighborhood* is sensitive to paradigmatic, and the *Global Semantic Displacement* is sensitive to syntagmatic shift (both defined in [11]). Both types of shift occur in real-world datasets. We find examples of simultaneous paradigmatic and syntagmatic shift, paradigmatic without syntagmatic and syntagmatic without paradigmatic shift.

Contribution. We develop an evaluation framework of general semantic shift measures on the basis of the longstanding linguistic distinction between different forms of word associations. We demonstrate that the resulting forms of shift can

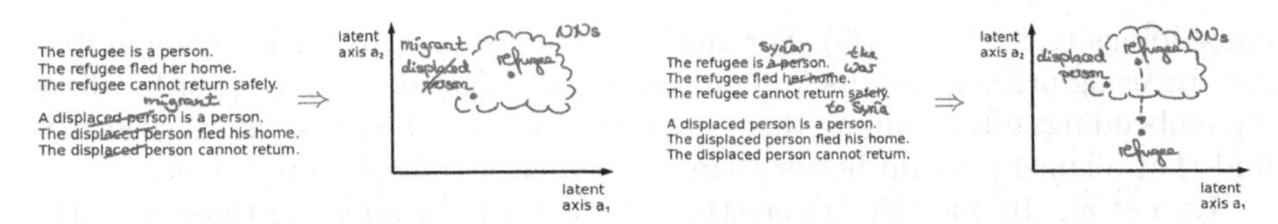

(a) Paradigmatic distortion of the text (left) and the resulting embedding shift

(b) Syntagmatic distortion of the text (left) and the resulting embedding shift

Fig. 1. *Examples of paradigmatic and syntagmatic shift.* (a) illustrates a paradigmatic shift of the word "refugee": In the text, its paradigmatic association "displaced person" is replaced by "migrant". As a result, its nearest neighbors (NNs) in the embedding change accordingly. On the other hand, the text in (b) demonstrates a syntagmatic shift. Modifications of words co-occurring with "refugee" (e.g., "Syrian") lead to a shift in its embedding vector.

be inherently different. This contributes to a more nuanced understanding of semantic shift mechanisms. This will enable future work to improve the explainability of automatically detected semantic shift in word and RDF embeddings.

2 Related Work

This section discusses existing literature with respect to paradigmatic and syntagmatic relations in computational approaches, the definition of semantic shift, approaches to measuring semantic shift, and the performance of such measures.

For word space models, several considerations have been made with regard to paradigmatic and syntagmatic relations (see [25,27,31]): Sahlgren concludes that word space models based on either paradigmatic or syntagmatic relations capture different semantic properties. Sun et al. [31] also emphasize that it is important to capture both relations to represent linguistic properties. To our knowledge, association *shifts* have not been considered before. In this work, we provide empirical evidence for Hamilton et al. [11]'s theory that the Local Neighborhood is more sensitive to shifts in a word's paradigmatic than syntagmatic relations.

To our knowledge there exists no unambiguous definition of semantic shift (for computational use). Most previous work on automatic semantic shift detection does not define semantic shift (e.g., [11,12,24,32]) or defines it circularly (e.g., in [9,18,28]). Linguists seem to use a similar approach (e.g., [1,2,33]). There are some attempts at further isolating this elusive concept by giving explicit examples of what a semantic shift should not be (e.g., non-seasonality in [28]).

Regarding the quantification of semantic shift, the state-of-the-art methods are based on word embeddings (e.g., [19]), which are subject to some inherent drawbacks (c.f. [32]). Several detection approaches are utilized on them (c.f. [18]): Neighborhood-based approaches compare the nearest neighbors of a word between two time steps (e.g., [8,11,21]). Another group of common measures calculate the cosine similarities between the word vectors of different embeddings (e.g., [11,14,16]). For this, embeddings are first made comparable, e.g., by using previous results for embedding initialization (e.g., [16]) or by aligning embeddings after training them individually (e.g., [17]). Shoemark et al. [28] find that aligned perform better than continuously trained embeddings.

Kim et al. [16] identify "interesting" shift words by selecting those with the lowest similarity between the first and last embedding of the series. Others make use of different correlation measures (e.g., [12,28]). Kulkarni et al. [17] search for the words with the biggest mean similarity shift before and after a detected shift point. Jatowt et al. [14] include word frequency in this consideration.

With respect to evaluating the performance of semantic measures, quantifying the effect of noise (see [20,34]) can be a first step (e.g., [7,17,28]). Others rely on human-annotated lists or qualitative human evaluation (e.g., [11,12,16,23]). An increasingly popular approach is to use a form of synthetic evaluation (e.g., [17,24,28]). Rosenfeld et al. [24] expand the *donor-receptor approach* (see [17]) by modeling a gradual change from one meaning to another. Shoemark et al. [28] validate the measures in separate experiments - those where the measure should not and those where they should detect semantic shift.

3 Semantic Shift

Next, we define semantic shift, semantic measures for comparing two embeddings and an approach for detecting interesting shifts on diachronic embeddings.

3.1 Paradigmatic and Syntagmatic Shift

The *contextual normality* approach, cf. [5], expresses that anything that affects the way a word is normally used contributes to its meaning. According to structuralist theories, the only types of relations between words are syntagmatic and paradigmatic (cf. [25,26]). Consequently, we define a semantic shift of a word as anything that affects its syntagmatic or paradigmatic associations (see Fig. 1).

General Problem Definition. The goal of semantic shift detection is usually generalized as studying a word w over several texts $T_1, ..., T_k$ in time sensitive order. For this, we use word embedding algorithms to train dense d-dimensional representations of words. For a text T_i, we denote the word embeddings obtained this way as E_i. Intuitively, the vector for word w in embedding E_i (i.e., a single column in the embedding matrix) represents semantic properties of the word w in text T_i. In this paper, we want to identify measures that can quantify paradigmatic (syntagmatic) shifts. For an arbitrary word w and two texts T_1 and T_2, an *ideal measure of paradigmatic (syntagmatic) shift* satisfies the following: (i) Its range is $[0, 1]$. (ii) At a value of 0 the paradigmatic (syntagmatic) associations of w in T_1 and T_2 have nothing in common. (iii) At a value of 1 the paradigmatic (syntagmatic) associations are the same. (iv) The values between these extremes change linearly with the shift in the paradigmatic (syntagmatic) associations.

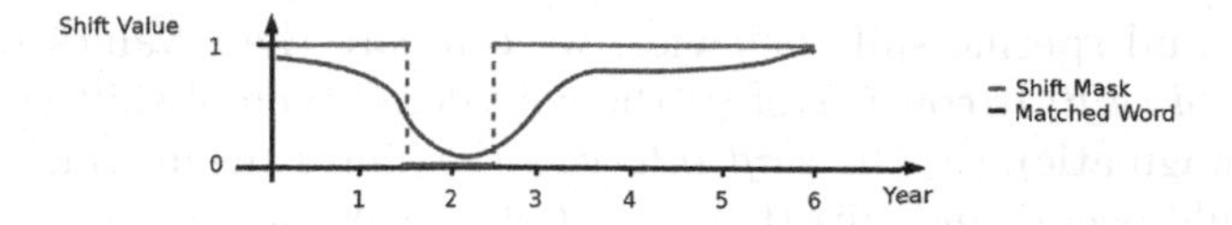

Fig. 2. *Illustration of a Shift Mask.* The Shift Mask [1, 0, 1, 1, 1, 1] for years 0–6 is displayed. Here, we would be interested in words that undergo a significant change in year 2, and only in year 2. The words that match this mask most closely might have consecutive measure values that are similar to the blue curve.

3.2 Measuring Semantic Shift

To identify approximations of such an ideal measure, we investigate measures from literature and introduce adaptations thereof. Different to the cited literature, we use cosine similarities and not cosine distances (i.e., 1 - cosine similarity).

Global Semantic Displacement. Hamilton et al. [12] define the *Global Semantic Displacement* (SD). They use an embedding alignment approach by solving the Orthogonal Procrustes Problem. Then, the cosine similarity between the aligned word vectors of the word w is calculated.

Local Neighborhood. Another approach to this task is the *Local Neighborhood* (LN) (see [11]). It computes semantic shift via the k nearest neighbors of the word. More precisely, it is defined as the cosine similarity of the vector of cosine similarities between w and its k nearest neighbors in E_1 and E_2 respectively. As suggested, we use $k = 25$ throughout this work (cf. [11]).

Angle-Transitioned Local Neighborhood and Semantic Displacement. The Global Semantic Displacement and the Local Neighborhood both utilize the cosine similarity between word vectors. As a result, they are not linear with regard to the change in the included angle. Still, the included angle might change linearly with the paradigmatic (syntagmatic) shift. We propose the *angle-transitioned Semantic Displacement* (f(SD)) and the *angle-transitioned Local Neighborhood* (f(LN)). These can be computed by the function $f(x) = 1 - \frac{1}{90} \cdot \arccos(\max(x, 0))$. It computes the relative size of the angle, when x is the cosine similarity of the vectors. We assume that every angle over 90° already indicates a maximal semantic distance between two word vectors.

3.3 Detecting Diachronic Semantic Shift

Let us assume that we know an ideal paradigmatic (syntagmatic) measure. Then, in a diachronic embedding series E_1,...,E_k, we want to detect words that underwent an "interesting" shift:

First, we define (a) the *consecutive measure* values for a word w as all the measure values for w between two subsequent embeddings of the diachronic series, i.e., E_i and E_{i+1} for an $i \in \{1, ..., k-1\}$ and (b) the *reference measure* values for a word w as all the measure values for w between the first and every other embedding of the diachronic series, i.e., E_1 and E_i for $i \in \{2, ..., k\}$.

Then, to find specific shift behavior, we compare these values with a user-defined *desired shift*: It consists of (i) the considered type of shift (i.e., paradigmatic or syntagmatic), (ii) the *shift intervals* (i.e., intervals in which the semantic shift should occur) and (iii) the *desired shift development* (i.e., whether the words should develop towards a new or back towards their original meaning). (ii) is given by a *Shift Mask* (i.e., a series of $k-1$ values that are 0 for the shift interval and 1 otherwise), see Fig. 2. The comparison of the desired shift with the actual paradigmatic (syntagmatic) measure behavior of every word w takes place in two steps: (1) comparing the consecutive measure values of w and the shift mask (see Fig. 2) and (2) comparing the reference measure values of w and the desired shift development. The comparisons could, for example, take place via a mean squared error, a Pearson Correlation or a threshold.

4 Simulating Semantic Shift

This section introduces a framework for simulating semantic shifts via five different types of synthetic corpus distortions, which we will call attacks. The core idea is based on the *donor-receptor* approach, where the *donor* "donates" its place in the corpus to the *receptor* word with a given probability (cf. [17]). We compare three different semantic (*Paradigmatic Attack*, *Syntagmatic Attack*, *Combined Attack*) and two baseline attacks (*Baseline - No Change*, *Baseline - Random Attack*). We give an overview of the semantic attacks (cf. Table 1) and the expected embedding change (cf. Fig. 3), where p signifies the extent of the distortion.

Table 1. *Overview of semantic attacks.* For every attack, we summarize the words affected by the introduced shift and what an ideal measure would detect.

Attack	simulates shift	on words	ideal measure
Baseline - No	no	any	constant at 1.0
Baseline - Random	no	donor	constant at 1.0
Combined	parad. and syntag	receptor	linear with $\frac{1}{1+p}$
Parad	parad	donor	linear with $\frac{1}{1+p}$
Syntag	syntag	receptor	linear with $1-p$

4.1 Baseline

No Attack. As a simple baseline, we train multiple embeddings on the same corpus. Variations result from the inherent instability of the embedding algorithms.

Random Attack. Additionally, we test robustness of measures under no association shift for the considered word but significant shift in other words:

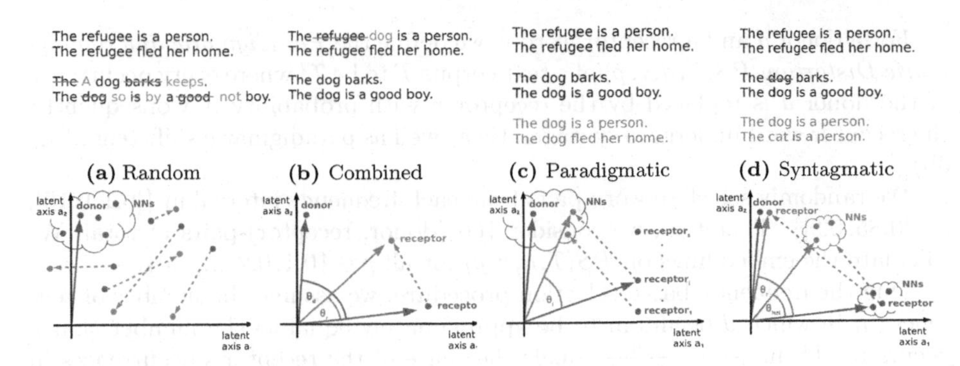

Fig. 3. *Textual distortions and the expected embedding change resulting from different attacks.* In the first row examples of textual distortions with $p = 1/2$ are displayed. For this purpose, "refugee" refers to the donor and if necessary, "dog" to the receptor with "cat" being its only paradigmatic association. In the second row, the expected embedding changes are displayed. These are the result of our intuitive understanding of the mechanisms behind word embeddings and purely displayed for illustrational purposes. Here, NNs refers to the nearest neighbors to the donor or receptor word. In *Baseline - Random Attack*, only sentences with the donor and the paradigmatic associations of the donor stay the same. In *Combined Attack*, the occurrences of the donor are replaced by the receptor. In *Paradigmatic Attack*, the receptors increasingly occur with the context words of the donor. In *Syntagmatic Attack*, the original co-occurrences of the receptor and its paradigmatic associations are replaced by the donor's.

For a donor (word) d and a bijection B : *Vocabulary* $\rightarrow$ *Vocabulary*, we define the *Random Distortion* $R(T, d, k, p, B)$ of a text corpus T to be T' where each word v is replaced by $B(v)$ with probability p. We additionally restrict the distortion to only those sentences where neither d nor any of its k closest paradigmatic associations occur (we denote this set of words as W). Consequently, the distortion induces no syntagmatic or paradigmatic shift for d (e.g., Fig. 3a).

We arrange every word in the corpus in an interval between 0 and 1 according to frequency. We select 10 donor words per *frequency interval* in $\{[0.1, 0.2],$ $..., [0.8, 0.9]\}$, leaving out the 10% most frequent and least frequent words. The bijection B is chosen randomly on $V \backslash W$. We set $k = 50$ as we assume all paradigmatic associations to be among the first 50 paradigmatically related words. We calculate the embeddings on $R(T, d, k, p, B)$ for all $p \in \{0.1, 0.2, ..., 1.0\}$.

In the resulting embedding series, the position of the donor and its nearest neighbors is expected to stay the same as, by design, their co-occurrences do not change. With increasing p, every other word should be subject to substantial position change (cf. Fig. 3a).

4.2 Combined Attack

We test whether the measures can detect any, syntagmatic or paradigmatic, shift:

For a donor d and a receptor word r, we define the *Paradigmatic and Syntagmatic Distortion* $PS(T, d, r, p)$ of a text corpus T to be T' where every occurrence of the donor d is replaced by the receptor r with probability p. Consequently, the receptor word undergoes syntagmatic as well as paradigmatic shift (e.g., Fig. 3b).

We randomly select 10 word pairs from each frequency interval in $\{[0.1, 0.15]$, ..., $[0.85, 0.9]\}$. Therefore, we consider 160 (donor, receptor)-pairs in total. We calculate the embeddings on $PS(T, d, r, p)$ for all $p \in \{0.1, 0.2, ..., 1.0\}$.

Due the frequency-based selection procedure, we assume the number of sentences n in which d occurs in to be approximately equal to the number that r occurs in. Then, $\frac{1}{1+p} = \frac{n}{n+p \cdot n}$ equals the share of the receptor's occurrences in its original sentences (i.e., with its original paradigmatic/syntagmatic associations). The reference values of an ideal measure of paradigmatic (syntagmatic) shift should be linear with this fraction for the receptor. The donor word should undergo minor syntagmatic shift up until a point from which it drastically deteriorates to 0 as it does not occur in $PS(T, d, r, p)$ for $p = 1$. Its paradigmatic change might be significant with the function $\frac{1}{1+p}$. The paradigmatic associations of the donor and receptor word could also undergo some minor change with the shift of the receptor and donor word. This could lead to a worse performance in the altered words prediction of a paradigmatic compared to a syntagmatic measure.

In the resulting embedding series, we expect the receptor representation to develop towards the original donor representation with increasing p (cf. Fig. 3b).

4.3 Paradigmatic Attack

We test whether the measures can pick up on paradigmatic association changes:

For a donor word d, l receptor words $(r_1, ..., r_l) =: r$ and probabilities $p := p_1, ..., p_l \in [0, 1]$, we define the *Paradigmatic Distortion* $P(T, d, r, p)$ of a text corpus T to T'. In T', for every sentence d occurs in and for each receptor word r_i, a new sentence is added with probability p_i in which every occurrence of d is replaced by r_i. Consequently, we induce a paradigmatic but no syntagmatic shift of the donor by adding sentences (e.g., Fig. 3c).

We randomly select 10 (donor, receptors)-pairs per 0.05 frequency interval from 0.1 to 0.9, i.e., 160 donor words in total. We set $l = 10$ as we assume the changes in the 10 closest paradigmatic associations to be significant for d. We introduce increasing changes in 10 consecutive steps i. We set p_j in step i to $\delta_{j,min(i,j)}$, where δ is the Kronecker Delta. As a result, the 10 receptor words successively become the new closest paradigmatic associations of the donor word. For consistency, we will also refer to the different steps with $p = i/10$ for $p \in \{0.1, ..., 1.0\}$. We calculate the embeddings on $P(T, d, r, p)$ for all $p \in \{0.1, 0.2, ..., 1.0\}$.

The paradigmatic change of the donor as well as the receptor words should be linear with $\frac{1}{1+p} = \frac{1}{1+i \cdot (1:l)} = \frac{nl}{nl+n \cdot i}$ for step i. This formula represents the share of occurrences of the $l = 10$ receptor words in their original sentences.

In the resulting embedding series, we expect the receptor representations to successively develop towards the donor representation, therefore altering the donor's nearest neighbors (cf. Fig. 3c).

4.4 Syntagmatic Attack

Finally, we describe a test for whether measures can detect syntagmatic changes. Here, we aim to distort the corpus such that the syntagmatic shift is significant for the considered word, while the paradigmatic shift for the same word is smaller or non-distinguishable from a larger set of words:

For a probability $p \in [0,1]$, a donor d, and a receptor r, we define the *Syntagmatic Distortion* $S(T,d,r,p,k)$ of the text corpus T to be T' where, for every sentence d occurs in, the sentence is added $k+1$ times with probability p. Here, d is replaced by r or its ith paradigmatic association n_i respectively for $i \leq k$. Moreover, for each original sentence r occurs in, r is deleted from the sentence with probability p, leaving it "incomplete". Similarly, for each original sentence where n_i occurs in, it is deleted with probability $p/2$. Thus, we introduce a syntagmatic as well as a substantially less pronounced paradigmatic shift for r by adding and altering sentences d, r or n_i occur in (cf. Fig. 3d).

This is done for overall 32 donors – 4 out of each frequency interval in $\{[0.1, 0.2], \ldots, [0.8, 0.9]\}$. We set $k = 25$ as we assume that the 25 closest paradigmatic associations include the most relevant. We chose to use significantly less pairs and $k < 50$ as for each donor word $k+1$ new sentences are added and, additionally, any sentence where r or n_i occur in are altered. This changes the original corpus exponentially more than before. We calculate the embeddings on $S(T,d,r,p,k)$ for all $p \in \{0.1, 0.2, ..., 1.0\}$.

r undergoes the greatest syntagmatic shift among all words, since its original occurrences decrease with $1-p$. As a result, the syntagmatic change of r is the most correlated with $1-p$. The syntagmatic shift of its original k paradigmatic associations is also related to $1-p$. d, r as well as the n_i undergo paradigmatic shift. However, the paradigmatic shift for r should be considerably smaller than its syntagmatic shift as we perform similar changes for its paradigmatic associations.

The position of the receptor representation is expected to shift to the previous donor position (see Fig. 3d). The nearest neighbors of the receptor word should shift towards it as well but also stay between the original donor and receptor representation.

5 Experiments

This section describes our experimental setup and results.

5.1 Datasets and Training

We work with three different datasets: Firstly, the *Reddit* comments and submissions from 2012–2018[1]. Secondly, the "aggressively deduplicated" *Amazon* reviews data from May 1996 - July 2014 (cf. [13]). Thirdly, the *Wikipedia* snapshots from 2014–2018[2]. We converted each character to lowercase and filtered out URLs. We removed each non-alphanumeric symbol and treated them as separation between words, i.e., conversion of "i've" to "i" and "ve". We assume that, simple tokenization works comparably well (cf. [3]). For all experiments, we use the 2012 Reddit corpus with about 8.8 billion words, the 2014 Amazon review corpus with about 1 billion words and the 2016 Wikipedia snapshot with about 2.5 billion words as a basis. We call these corpora the *basis corpora*.

We use the multi-threaded Python framework *gensim* to train word2vec embeddings in the faster CBOW variant and negative sampling at 5 (cf. [19]). CBOW and negative sampling perform better for frequent than infrequent words[3]. We use 300 dimensions and a general min_count of 60. The number of epochs is chosen at 4. All other parameters are left at their default values.

5.2 Approach

We test whether the synthetically distorted words (see Sect. 4) can be detected by the different measures. As the words consistently change more with increasing p, we skip (1) of the approach detailed in Sect. 3.3. Consequently, we assume that (1) returned all words as candidates that could match the induced form of shift. In (2), for every measure, we predict the synthetically altered words by identifying those that have the highest Pearson Correlation with the expected shift (i.e., $\frac{1}{1+p}$ or $1-p$, cf. Table 1). We perform the evaluation via an *accuracy curve*, i.e., the share of the correctly predicted words out of the actually changed words (cf. [17,28]).

5.3 Outcome

Representative results on the Reddit data for this approach are shown in Fig. 4. Results for the other datasets were equivalent. Key observations (in bold) include:

All measures detect a form of paradigmatic or syntagmatic shift. The results of the Combined Attack show that all measures detect a form of paradigmatic and/or syntagmatic shift (see Fig. 4c). SD and f(SD) are even behaving

---

[1] Baumgartner, J.: Reddit dataset, https://files.pushshift.io/reddit/, (accessed on 2019-09-25.

[2] wikimedia: wikipedia snapshots on archive.org, https://archive.org/download/enwiki-20150112, https://archive.org/download/enwiki-20160113, https://archive.org/download/enwiki-20170101, https://archive.org/download/enwiki-20180101, https://archive.org/details/enwiki-20190120, (accessed on 2019-09-25).

[3] google: word2vec documentation, https://code.google.com/archive/p/word2vec/, (accessed on 2019-09-25).

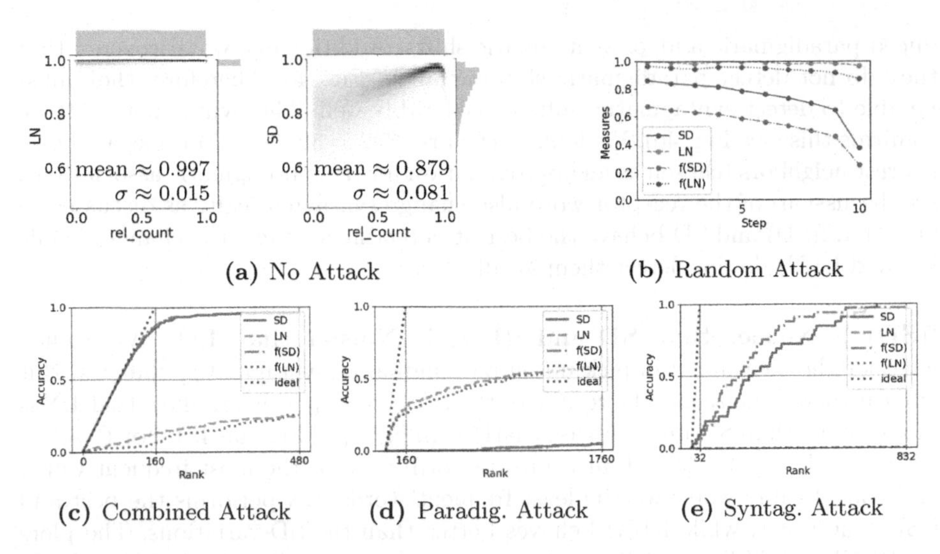

(a) No Attack (b) Random Attack

(c) Combined Attack (d) Paradig. Attack (e) Syntag. Attack

Fig. 4. *Experimental results on Reddit data.* (a) shows heatmaps of the relative sorted frequency for every word (rel_count, where 1 is most frequent) and its mean semantic shift according to LN and SD. Overall distributions are shown at the side and the top of the plot. (b) displays the average measure values over the unchanged words for each step. LN stays closest to the ideal constant value of 1.0. For the semantic attacks (c,d,e), the accuracy curve shows the share of the altered words that were correctly predicted by the Pearson Correlation. The dotted black line shows the ideal measure behavior. All measures are able to measure syntagmatic and/or paradigmatic shift but to a varying extent. For the Combined Attack and Syntagmatic Attack (c,d), SD and its angle-transitioned variation f(SD) perform the best. By contrast in d), LN and its angle-transitioned variation f(LN) are the best at detecting the induced paradigmatic shifts.

close to linear with the expected paradigmatic and syntagmatic change of $\frac{1}{1+p}$. In Sect. 4.2, we expected the paradigmatic shift to correlate with more than just the receptors. Therefore, LN and f(LN) could be less accurate because they are more paradigmatic measures.

The LN-Measures Perform Best at Detecting Paradigmatic Shift. f(LN) and LN are the best at detecting paradigmatic shift (see Fig. 4d). f(SD) and SD do not pick up on paradigmatic shift at all. The upper limit of the x-axis is at $160 \cdot (1 + 10) = 1760$ as not only the donor but also the receptors change paradigmatically (cf. Sect. 4.3). Surprisingly, for LN-based measures, there is a plateau reached after the first 160 predicted words. A potential reason for this is that the measures cannot detect finer paradigmatic changes for some (donor, receptors)-pairs that had a lower starting angle.

The SD-Measures Perform Best at Detecting Syntagmatic Shift. As seen in Fig. 4c, the SD-based measures seem to change linearly with the introduced paradigmatic and/or syntagmatic shifts. Additionally, we discovered that they do not detect paradigmatic shifts at all in Fig. 4d. Therefore, they must be able to detect syntagmatic shifts considerably well. The Syntagmatic Attack confirms this (see Fig. 4e). We look at the first $832 = 32 \cdot (1+25)$ ranks as the 25 nearest neighbors (chosen as an approximation for the paradigmatic associations, see discussion) of the receptor word also change syntagmatically as discussed in Sect. 4.4. f(SD) and SD behave the best at detecting syntagmatic changes, while LN and f(LN) do not detect them at all.

f(SD) is Noisier than SD and f(LN) is Noisier than LN. We studied whether the measures can pick up on paradigmatic (syntagmatic) changes. But what if there is neither? The results of the Baseline experiments show that LN is more robust than SD under no association changes (cf. Fig. 4a–4b). For Baseline - No Attack (in Fig. 4a), all measures perform well for the most frequent words and considerably worse for the least frequent words. LN performs the best and f(SD) the worst, while f(LN) behaves better than the SD-variations. The plots for f(LN) and f(SD) are left out as they are monotone distortions LN and SD. Due to the chosen linearization approach, they are a lot more sensitive to the random differences between word embeddings trained on the same corpus. This noise seems not to be worth the small advantage (see Fig. 4e) of having a linear change measure. The results for Baseline - Random Attack (see Fig. 4b) are comparable.

Overall, we conclude that SD is the best measure for detecting syntagmatic and LN is the best measure to detect paradigmatic shift.

Table 2. *Top 3 syntagmatic and paradigmatic shift words.* The overlap specifies the number of the top 5 most changed words according to one measure that are contained in the top 25 words of to the other. Words do not undergo paradigmatic and syntagmatic shift to the same extent.

Shift in	Top-3 syn. shift words	Top-3 para. shift words	overlap	
never	songs, get, story	1991, 1975, 1973	0	0
2007	kindle, plastics, leopard	kindle, hg, reroute	2	1
2012	insurgent, vita, g5	vita, bared, marquee	2	4
Amazon reviews from 2005 to 2014				
never	cdotas, pidamente, abdomen	01100011, 01100100, 01110101	0	0
2014	braum, oras, 20ex	w33, triche, oras	2	1
2016	ladybonersgw, nougat, trumper	grubbin, coolheaded, tdil	1	1
Reddit from 2012 to 2018				
never	jeandat, subsidiaries, migrate	1885, 1842, 13	0	0
2016	attd, andp, binaria	sanep, thrret, wk14	4	2
2017	vlindernet, 14px, dcrj	intret, kilmainemore, pastorally	2	0
Wikipedia from 2014 to 2018				

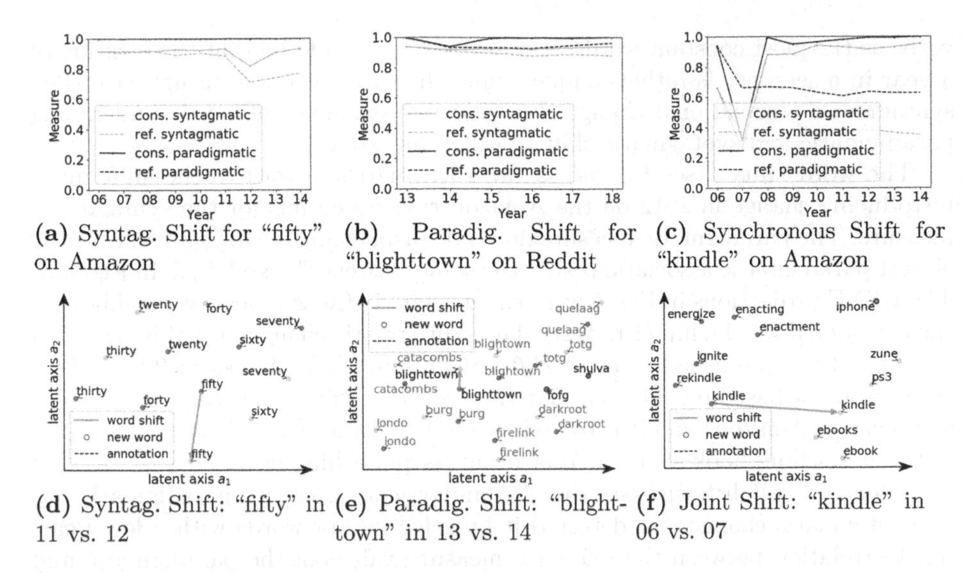

(a) Syntag. Shift for "fifty" on Amazon (b) Paradig. Shift for "blighttown" on Reddit (c) Synchronous Shift for "kindle" on Amazon

(d) Syntag. Shift: "fifty" in 11 vs. 12 (e) Paradig. Shift: "blighttown" in 13 vs. 14 (f) Joint Shift: "kindle" in 06 vs. 07

Fig. 5. *Conflicting and synchronous behavior of the paradigmatic and syntagmatic measures.* Plots in the first row display consecutive (continuous line) and reference (dashed line) point values of the paradig. and the syntag. measure. Plots in the lower row show the t-SNE projection of embeddings before (grey) and after the shift (blue dots). Green words were not present in the previous year. "fifty" has a syntagmatic but no paradigmatic shift point in 2012. The nearest neighbors of "fifty" stay the same, the vector however moves away from its original position (blue arrow) similar to Fig. 1b The word "blighttown" exhibits a paradigmatic shift between 2013 and 2014. "blighttown" and its former nearest neighbors stay at a similar position, but new words appear. The measures synchronously detect a change for "kindle". The "kindle" vector moves out of the previous nearest neighbors in 2006 towards new nearest neighbors in 2007. (Color figure online)

6 Application Examples

We use the our new insights to detect paradigmatic and syntagmatic shifts in real world data, i.e., the Amazon, Reddit, and Wikipedia corpora. Based on our previous results, we utilize LN as the paradigmatic and SD as the syntagmatic measure. We define the shift interval of the *desired shift* (cf. Sect. 3.3) as an empty or one point interval (i.e., words with one shift point or none at all). We detect the most interesting words as those with the lowest mean squared error to the desired shift mask. We observe the following key findings:

A Word Can Undergo Paradigmatic and Syntagmatic Shift to Different Extent. For example, the number of words that were among most shifting words in a given year according to the paradigmatic (syntagmatic) measure and also are within the most shifting 25 according to the syntagmatic (paradigmatic) measure is consistently less than 5 (cf. *overlap* in Table 2). The overlap is 0 for no shift points: LN mostly detects (year) numbers and SD detects nouns and verbs as the most constant words. A reason for this could be that the position of a year in a sentence is rather unique, while the exact words it occurs with (i.e., syntagmatic associations) change. We give two examples of words undergoing paradigmatic and syntagmatic shift to different extent:

The word "fifty" (see Fig. 5a) is the 16th matched word to the shift mask introducing change in 2012 on the Amazon reviews corpus for the syntagmatic measure. The paradigmatic measure does not display any meaningful shift as the closest paradigmatic associations stay the same ("twenty", "sixty", ... in Fig. 5d). The t-SNE projections in Fig. 5 were calculated via the 200 nearest neighbors of the considered word (similar to [12]). The syntagmatic change probably occurred because of the published print of *Fifty Shades* by E. L. James in 2012[4]. This assumption is based on the fact that the search of "fifty" returns Fifty Shades products on Amazon[5] and it is to be expected that there have been many copies of the bestselling book sold via Amazon in its publishing year.

The word "blighttown" (see Fig. 5b) underwent significant paradigmatic but no syntagmatic change. We detected it by selecting for words with a low Pearson Correlation between the reference measure values of the paradigmatic and syntagmatic measure. The paradigmatic curve shows a shift in 2014, the syntagmatic measure does not. "blighttown" is the name of an area in the video game *Dark Souls*. In 2014, *Dark Souls II* was released with the new areas "shulva"[6] and "fofg" (short for "Forest of Fallen Giants"[7]), which correspond to new nearest neighbors of "blighttown". The position of "blighttown" and the other nearest neighbors did not change (cf. Fig. 5e).

Words with an Extreme Shift in One Measure Follow a Similar Trend in the Other. The Pearson Correlation of the paradigmatic and syntagmatic reference measure values for the words in the top 25 is mostly moderate to high (above 0.2). Therefore, although different words are predicted for the greatest paradigmatic vs. syntagmatic changes, it is still likely that words with an extreme shift in one measure also undergo a shift in the other. For example, the word "kindle" is the first predicted word for the shift point in 2007 for both measures (plot see Fig. 5c). The Amazon kindle was introduced in 2007.

7 Discussion

In the following, we address potential criticism and limitations of our work:

"Paradigmatic (syntagmatic) shifts are not necessarily semantic shifts according to common understanding" Words like "christmas" are talked about differently

[4] Wikipedia: Fifty shades of grey, https://en.wikipedia.org/wiki/Fifty_Shades_of_Grey (accessed on 2019-10-14).

[5] Amazon: amazon search for "fifty", https://www.amazon.com/s?k=fifty&ref=nb_sb_noss (accessed on 2019-09-18).

[6] Darksouls.fandom.com: Shulva, Sanctum City, https://darksouls.fandom.com/wiki/Shulva,_Sanctum_City (accessed on 2019-09-30).

[7] Darksouls.fandom.com: Forest of fallen giants, https://darksouls.fandom.com/wiki/Forest_of_Fallen_Giants (accessed on 2019-09-30).

in December than in April due to seasonal variations. Arguably there has also been a shift in the way people use "refugee" after 2015. Are those types of shifts semantic shifts? According to our approach they are. According to the common rather fuzzy understanding, they are probably not. We still decided for those types of changes to be defined as semantic shift as they describe interesting societal dynamics and changes in the way people think about different concepts. *"Measure shifts do not necessarily occur due to paradigmatic or syntagmatic shift"* We showed that paradigmatic (syntagmatic) shifts lead to measure shifts. We partly evaluate the reverse with the baseline experiments. We recommend the addition of further experiments (e.g., for word frequency as done in [28]).

"There are regularities in the types of words that are changing the most." We did not statistically evaluate which word types are prevalent. However, LN is more sensitive to changes in nouns than SD (see [11]). This could be connected to the paradigmatic vs. syntagmatic association distinction: Nouns are more likely to undergo "cultural shift" (see [11]). As a result their paradigmatic associations might be completely replaced while syntagmatic associations stay more constant (due to, e.g., co-occurring verbs and grammatical forms).

"Paradigmatic associations in texts might not be the same as the nearest neighbors in embeddings" In (a) Baseline - Random Attack and (b) Syntagmatic Attack, we assume that the closest paradigmatic associations of a word have a significant overlap with its nearest neighbors in the embedding. This is an intuitive assumption since the positions of the word vectors should mostly be determined by their syntagmatic associations. The results from the Paradigmatic Attack, which was performed independently from (a) and (b), also make this assumption reasonable: LN, which calculates shifts via nearest neighbor changes, performed the best at detecting paradigmatic association changes.

"There is not only syntagmatic shift introduced in the Syntagmatic Attack" In designing the Syntagmatic Attack, we found no simple method to synthetically introduce the same kind of syntagmatic shift for a group of words without introducing similar paradigmatic shift for a subset of this group as well. This is because as soon as a syntagmatic change to a word w is introduced, the previous paradigmatic associations are less strongly related to w than before. Altering those paradigmatic associations again introduces syntagmatic change.

"The synthetic corpus changes might introduce unwanted association shifts" We add several sentences with nearly the same words or remove single words from sentences in the Paradigmatic and the Syntagmatic Attack. Here, we want to only introduce syntagmatic change to one word. The other words in the added sentences also undergo syntagmatic change. However, we assume this effect to be negligible since most co-occurrences stay the same.

8 Conclusion

In this work, we introduced an operationalization of semantic shift via paradigmatic and syntagmatic associations. We studied a variety of measures in their abilities for detecting and discerning between paradigmatic and syntagmatic shifts. We evaluated them on word embeddings trained on corpora that were synthetically distorted. We observed that the *Local Neighborhood* captures paradigmatic shift, while the *Global Semantic Displacement* captures syntagmatic shift. We showed examples where those measures are behaving differently. The main contributions are (i) the differentiation of semantic shift with the help of a well-established linguistic approach, (ii) the introduction of an evaluation framework of semantic shift measures via synthetic experiments, (iii) the identification of the best paradigmatic and syntagmatic measure and (iv) a demonstration that the two associations shifts can be inherently different. Future work will include the application of the paradigmatic (syntagmatic) measure for the analysis of diachronic shift in RDF graphs. Then, thresholding of our approach could give a clear signal for when a public RDF graph or embedding should be updated.

Acknowledgments. Part of the simulations were performed with computing resources granted by RWTH Aachen University. We thank Dong Nguyen for providing advise regarding this work and our (meta-) reviewers for their constructive feedback.

References

1. Bloomfield, L.: Language. Allen & Unwin, London (1933)
2. Bréal, M.: Essai de sémantique. Lambert-Lucas (1897)
3. Camacho-Collados, J., Pilehvar, M.T.: On the role of text preprocessing in neural network architectures: an evaluation study on text categorization and sentiment analysis. In: EMNLP Workshop, pp. 40–46 (2018)
4. Cochez, M., Ristoski, P., Ponzetto, S.P., Paulheim, H.: Global RDF vector space embeddings. In: d'Amato, C., et al. (eds.) ISWC 2017. LNCS, vol. 10587, pp. 190–207. Springer, Cham (2017). https://doi.org/10.1007/978-3-319-68288-4_12
5. Cruse, A.: Meaning in Language. Oxford Linguistics (2004)
6. Dell, G.S., Oppenheim, G.M., Kittredge, A.K.: Saying the right word at the right time: syntagmatic and paradigmatic interference in sentence production. Lang. Cogn. Processes **23**(4), 583–608 (2008)
7. Dubossarsky, H., Grossman, E., Weinshal, D.: Outta control: laws of semantic change and inherent biases in word representation models. In: EMNLP, pp. 1136–1145 (2017)
8. Eger, S., Mehler, A.: On the linearity of semantic change: investigating meaning variation via dynamic graph models. In: ACL, pp. 52–58 (2016)
9. Frermann, L., Lapata, M.: A Bayesian model of diachronic meaning change. In: ACL, pp. 31–45 (2016)
10. Gutierrez, C., Hurtado, C., Vaisman, A.: Temporal RDF. In: Gómez-Pérez, A., Euzenat, J. (eds.) ESWC 2005. LNCS, vol. 3532, pp. 93–107. Springer, Heidelberg (2005). https://doi.org/10.1007/11431053_7
11. Hamilton, W.L., Leskovec, J., Jurafsky, D.: Cultural shift or linguistic drift? Comparing two computational measures of semantic change. In: EMNLP, pp. 2116–2121 (2016)
12. Hamilton, W.L., Leskovec, J., Jurafsky, D.: Diachronic word embeddings reveal statistical laws of semantic change. In: ACL, pp. 1489–1501 (2016)

13. He, R., McAuley, J.: Ups and downs: modeling the visual evolution of fashion trends with one-class collaborative filtering. In: WWW, pp. 507–517 (2016)
14. Jatowt, A., Duh, K.: A framework for analyzing semantic change of words across time. In: JCDL, pp. 229–238 (2014)
15. Khurana, U., Deshpande, A.: Efficient snapshot retrieval over historical graph data. In: ICDE, pp. 997–1008 (2005)
16. Kim, Y., Chiu, Y., Hanaki, K., Hegde, D., Petrov, S.: Temporal analysis of language through neural language models. In: ACL Workshop, pp. 61–65 (2014)
17. Kulkarni, V., Al-Rfou, R., Perozzi, B., Skiena, S.: Statistically significant detection of linguistic change. In: WWW, pp. 625–635 (2015)
18. Kutuzov, A., Øvrelid, L., Szymanski, T., Velldal, E.: Diachronic word embeddings and semantic shifts: a survey. In: COLING, pp. 1384–1397 (2018)
19. Mikolov, T., Sutskever, I., Chen, K., Corradom, G., Dean, J.: Distributed representations of words and phrases and their compositionality. In: NIPS, pp. 3111–3119 (2013)
20. Pierrejean, B., Tanguy, L.: Predicting word embeddings variability. In: SEM, pp. 154–159 (2018)
21. del Prado Martin, F., Brendel, C.: Case and cause in Icelandic: reconstructing causal networks of cascaded language changes. In: ACL, pp. 2421–2430 (2016)
22. Ristoski, P., Rosati, J., Di Noia, T., De Leone, R., Paulheim, H.: RDF2Vec: RDF graph embeddings and their applications. Semant. Web J. **10**, 721–752 (2019)
23. Rohrdantz, C., Hautli, A., Mayer, T., Butt, M., Keim, D., Plank, F.: Towards tracking semantic change by visual analytics. In: ACL, pp. 305–310 (2011)
24. Rosenfeld, A., Erk, K.: Deep neural models of semantic shift. In: NAACL-HLT, pp. 474–484 (2018)
25. Sahlgren, M.: The word-space model: Using distributional analysis to represent syntagmatic and paradigmatic relations between words in high-dimensional vector spaces. Ph.D. dissertation (2006)
26. de Saussure, F.: Cours de linguistique generale. Payot, Paris (1916)
27. Schütze, H., Pedersen, J.: A vector model for syntagmatic and paradigmatic relatedness. In: Conference of the UW Centre for the New OED and Text Research, pp. 104–113 (1993)
28. Shoemark, P., Liza, F.F., Nguyen, D., Hale, S.A., McGillivray, B.: Room to Glo: a systematic comparison of semantic change detection approaches with word embeddings. In: EMNLP and IJCNLP, pp. 66–76 (2019)
29. Sokolova, L.V., Cherkasova, A.S.: Spatiotemporal organization of bioelectrical brain activity during reading of syntagmatic and paradigmatic collocations by students with different foreign language proficiency. Hum. Physiol. **41**(6), 583–592 (2015). https://doi.org/10.1134/S0362119715060092
30. Stewart, I., Arendt, D., Bell, E., Volkova, S.: Measuring, predicting and visualizing short-term change in word representation and usage in VKontakte social network. In: ICWSM, pp. 672–675 (2017)
31. Sun, F., Guo, J., Lan, Y., Xu, J., Cheng, X.: Learning word representations by jointly modeling syntagmatic and paradigmatic relations. In: ACL and IJCNLP, pp. 136–145 (2015)
32. Tahmasebi, N., Borin, L., Jatowt, A.: Survey of computational approaches to lexical semantic change detection. In: ACL, pp. 31–45 (2018)
33. Traugott, E.C., Dasher, R.B.: Regularity in Semantic Change. Cambridge University Press, Cambridge (2001)
34. Wendlandt, L., Kummerfeld, J.K., Mihalcea, R.: Factors influencing the surprising instability of word embeddings. In: NAACL-HLT, pp. 2092–2102 (2018)

BCRL: Long Text Friendly Knowledge Graph Representation Learning

Gang Wu[1,2](✉), Wenfang Wu[1], Leilei Li[1], Guodong Zhao[1], Donghong Han[1,2], and Baiyou Qiao[1,2]

[1] School of Computer Science and Engineering, Northeastern University, Shenyang, China
wugang@mail.neu.edu.cn, 389446497@qq.com, leilei-li@foxmail.com, gdzhao@stumail.neu.edu.cn, {handonghong,qiaobaiyou}@mail.neu.edu.cn

[2] Key Laboratory of Intelligent Computing in Medical Image, Ministry of Education, Northeastern University, Shenyang, China

Abstract. The sparse data and large computational overhead in the use of large-scale knowledge graphs have caused widespread attention to Knowledge Representation Learning (KRL) technology. Although many KRL models have been proposed to embed structure information, their ability to accurately represent newly added entities or entities with few relations is significantly insufficient. In some studies, the introduction of textual information has partially solved this problem. However, most existing text-enhanced models only consider the shallow description information of the entities, and ignore the relation mention information between entities, and deep semantic information between sentences and words, which is not optimized for long texts supplementary information like Wikipedia.

In this paper, we proposed a long text friendly structure-text joint KRL model, named BCRL (BERT and CNN Representation Learning), which can effectively explore rich semantics embedded in entity description and relation mention text taking Wikipedia as supplementary information. For the obtained text of entity description and relation mention, the model first uses the BERT model to generate sentence vector representation respectively. Then it uses a convolutional neural network with an attention mechanism to select valid information in the text and obtain the overall vector representation of the text. Finally, the gate mechanism is used to combine the structure-based and the text-based vectors to generate the final joint representation. We evaluated the performance of our BCRL model on link prediction tasks using FB15K and WN18 datasets. The experimental results show that BCRL outperforms structure-only models and text-enhanced models in most cases, and has significant advantages in complex relation representation.

Keywords: Knowledge Representation Learning · Long text · BERT · Convolutional neural network

Supported by the National Key R&D Program of China (Grant No. 2019YFB1405302) and the NSFC (Grant No. 61872072 and No. 61672144).

J. Z. Pan et al. (Eds.): ISWC 2020, LNCS 12506, pp. 636–653, 2020.
https://doi.org/10.1007/978-3-030-62419-4_36

1 Introduction

In recent years, the Knowledge Graph (KG) has received extensive attention from academia and industry for its powerful semantic expression capabilities, and has been widely used in fields such as question answering [5,21] systems and web search. In order to solve the problems of low computing efficiency and sparse data, KRL technology has been widely concerned. Its main goal is to represent the entities and relations of a KG in a low-dimensional dense real-valued vector space. In this way, it improves the efficiency of complex semantic relationship computation within entities, relations, and between them.

The translation models typified by TransE (Translating Embedding) [3] are recent research hotspots of KRL. They are not only simple in model, high in computational efficiency, but also can guarantee good knowledge expression ability. However, their ability to accurately represent newly added entities or entities with few relationships is insufficient because only the structural information of triples is taken into consideration in such models. To tackle this problem, some work began to introduce textual information [1,16] to help improve knowledge representation. Entity description is the most common type of such textual information. As exemplified in Fig. 1, the head entity and the tail entity of a triple from the Freebase KG are each associated with a piece of textual description.

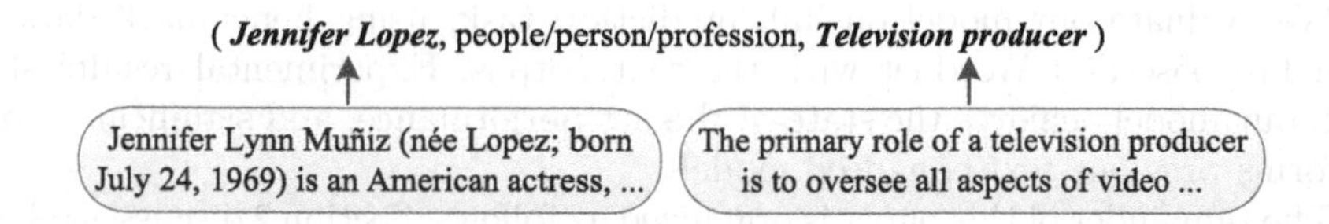

Fig. 1. An example of entity descriptions in Freebase

However, the existing text-enhanced KRL methods are still facing challenges.

i) It is difficult to capture the exact meaning of relations in context text. A typical situation is how to distinguish multiple different semantics of the same relation. For example, the relation "parentOf" can mean either "being the father of" or "being the mother of" depending on the entities in triples.

ii) The representation of entity description is not comprehensive enough. For example, the semantics between sentences (or words) in the case of long description texts are usually ignored. And the reflection of the semantic difference of the same entity in different triple contexts is generally lacking.

One of the possible reasons behind these problems is that existing methods do not make full use of the rich semantics in long texts, i.e. multiple sentences. Therefore, we proposed a long text friendly structure-text joint KRL model, named BCRL, which can effectively explore rich semantics embedded in entity description and relation mention texts that are obtained from Wikipedia as supplementary information. Firstly, the model obtains accurate text information of entities and relations through lemmatization, stop words removal, and similarity calculations for relation mentions. Secondly, the BERT model is used to obtain the sentence vector and learn the semantic information between words in the sentence. Furthermore, the CNN with sentence-level positional information coding is employed to learn the semantic information between sentences to obtain the overall vector representation of the text. Finally, the gate mechanism is introduced to realize the joint representation of structural information and textual information on top of the TransE framework. In addition, for the entity description text, a relation-related attention mechanism is added to further enhance the text embedding of the entity.

In summary, the contributions of this paper are as follows:

1. The proposed model achieves long text friendly by introducing BERT and CNN to gradually capture the semantics of different granularities (word level and sentence level) in the text.
2. To meet the first challenge, relation mention information is introduced in the model to enhance the knowledge representation as well, which is obtained from all entity descriptions in the triples involved by the relation.
3. To meet the second challenge, the model makes the representation of entity description more comprehensive by introducing a relation-oriented attention mechanism that captures the most relevant information in the entity description in different contexts through a triple-relation text vector.

We evaluate our model on link prediction task, using benchmark datasets from Freebase and Wordnet with the text corpus. Experimental results show that, our model achieves the state-of-the-art performance, and significantly outperforms previous text-enhanced models.

The remainder of this paper is organized as follows. Section 2 discusses related work. Section 3 presents the long text friendly text representation model in detail. Section 4 presents the structure-text joint learning. Empirical evaluation of the proposed model and comparison with other state-of-the art models are presented in Sect. 5. Finally, Sect. 6 summarises the whole paper and points out some future work.

2 Related Work

2.1 Translation-Based Models

In recent years, there has been a great deal of work on KRL, and most studies concentrate on translation-based models. This kind of models propose to embed both entities and relations into a continuous low-dimensional vector space according to some distance-based scoring functions.

One of the most representative translation models is TransE which regards the relationships in the KG as some kind of translation vector between entities. Specifically, for each fact triple (h, r, t), it represents entities and relationships in the same vector space, and considers the relationship vector r as the translation between the head entity vector h and the tail entity vector t, *i.e.*, "$h + r \approx t$".

Thus, the scoring function is defined as $f_r(h,t) = \|h + r - t\|_{L1/L2}$. Where h, r and t represent the vectors of head entity h, relation r and tail entity t, respectively. And $L1$ and $L2$ represent 1-norm and 2-norm respectively. If the fact (h, r, t) is true, the score $f_r(h, t)$ tends to be close to zero.

Though TransE is an effective KRL model for representing 1-to-1 relation, its rough translation idea has flaws in dealing with more complicated relations like 1-to-N, N-to-1 and N-to-N. This motivates the proposal of subsequent improvements such as TransH [17], TransR [9], TransD [8], etc., which allow entities to have different representations when different relationships are involved. TransE is a simple and efficient method for KRL.

2.2 Introducing Text Information

In order to improve the KRL, many research works have been proposed to embed text information to improve the knowledge representation.

Embedding KGs with textual information to improve the knowledge representation can be traced back to the neural tensor network model (NTN) proposed by Socher et al. [13], where textual information is simply used to initialize the entity representation. Specifically, NTN first learns word embeddings from the auxiliary news corpus, and then initializes the representation of each entity by averaging the vectors of words contained in its name. For example, the embedding of AlfredHitchcock is initialized by the average word embeddings of Alfred and Hitchcock. Since this method separates text information from KG facts, it cannot effectively utilize the interactive information between fact triple entities. Moreover, the method initializes the representation only on the basis of the entity name, which makes it impossible to make full use of textual information.

Wang et al. [17] proposed a joint model, which aligns the entity name and the Wikipedia anchor text to project KG's knowledge and Wikipedia text into the same space, which can better use text information in the embedding process and improve the accuracy of fact prediction.

Toutanova et al. [14] used convolutional neural networks to derive continuous representations for text relations, which has greatly improved entities with text representations. Xu et al. [19] learns the joint representation of structure and text through LSTM network with gate mechanism.

Xie et al. [18] proposed a text-enhanced TransE model which uses continuous bag-of-words model and CNN to encode the entity description information. The model jointly represents the structure-based and description-based two parts. The former captures the structural information of the facts of the KGs, and the latter captures the textual information of the entity description. Although CNN is used to encode text information, it only includes convolutional layers and pooling layers, and cannot learn semantic information between multiple sentences of text. In addition, the method has not considered the filtering and screening of textual information and the effective form of joint representation.

3 Long Text Friendly Text Representation

As stated in the introduction, effective use of long texts may be one of the possible ways to better meet the novel challenges of KRL. In this section, we first present the preparation of long texts for entities and relations respectively, and then focus on the long text friendly text representation model.

3.1 Long Text Friendly Text Information Extraction

Entity Description Extraction. The sparseness and staleness of entity description information is very common in a single KG. Taking Freebase as an example, due to the premature establishment of the knowledge base, a lot of information is out of date, and the length of different entity description varies widely, from 350 words to several words. Linking Wikipedia information for KG entities is a commonly used solution for this case. For example, Freebase provides entity mapping files on Wikipedia[1]. In this paper, the abstract text of the linked Wikipedia entry is taken as the supplementary of the entity description in this way. General entity link tools can also be used to obtain the corresponding supplementary information, such as TAGME [6] and AIDA [20].

Relation Mention Extraction. For the relation in a triple, it is acceptable to supplement text information with the entities mentioned in the triple. To this end, a corpus is built with all the text corresponding to the Wikipedia entries linked in the entity linking process. Then the text of a relation mention can be extracted from the corpus. The relation dataset is made available on GitHub[2]. Specifically, given a relation r of the triple (h, r, t), all sentences containing both the head entity h and the tail entity t in the triple are extracted from the corpus as candidate relation mentions [1].

Obviously, this will involve a lot of noise that is not actually related to the relation r, which will affect subsequent textual representations. In order to effectively filter noise, similarity calculations are performed between relations and their candidate mentions from the lexical level and the semantic level respectively.

For the lexical-level, a candidate mention sentence s is determined to be similar to the relation r if any of the synonyms and superordinate words of r in WordNet are found in s. For example, for a triple (Pain,/medicine/disease/prevention_factors, Capsicum), a sentence can be regarded as an accurate relation only if the sentence contains the triple head and tail entities and at least one synonym or superordinate word about the relation Mention. In the example, *medicine* and *disease* are the hypernyms of *prevention_factors*, *drug* is a synonym of *medicine* in WordNet, and the relationship set is (prevention_factors, disease, medicine, drug).

---

[1] http://storage.googleapis.com/freebase-public/fb2w.nt.gz.
[2] https://github.com/BoBoManTou/KG.

Hence, its similarity can be calculated by the vector space model. For example, the sentence "Many capsicum medicines have been used in the management of pain in various traditional systems" is processed into text to obtain a set of words medicine, manage, tradition, system. Each word represents a dimension, and its value is 0 or 1, indicating whether the word appears in the current text. Take {prevention_factors, disease, medicine, drug, manage, tradition, system} as the dimension to get mention and relationship. The two vector representations are $0, 0, 1, 0, 1, 1, 1, 1$ and $1, 1, 1, 1, 0, 0, 0$. Suppose m represents the candidate relation mention set, r is the corresponding relation set, V_m represents the space vector representation of the mention set, and V_r represents the vector representation of the relation set. Then the similarity between the two can be expressed by the cosine distance. The calculation method is shown in Eq. 1.

$$\cos(V_m, V_r) = \frac{V_m \cdot V_r}{|V_m||V_r|} \tag{1}$$

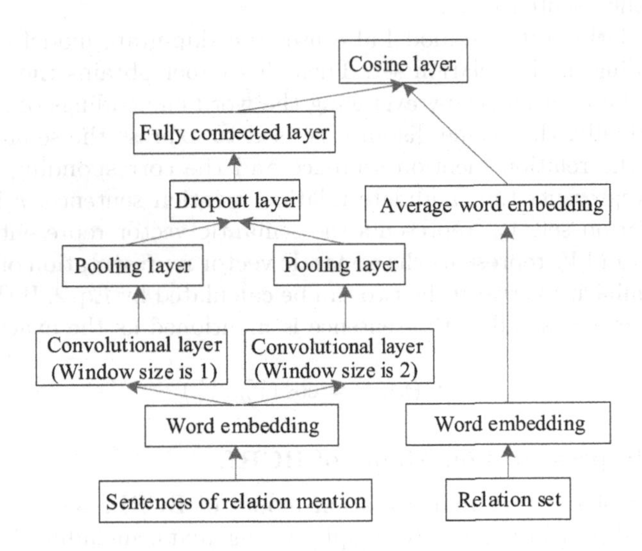

Fig. 2. Semantic level similarity calculation

Further filtering from the semantic level similarity is necessary especially when the relation mention sentence does not contain any superordinate words or synonyms of the corresponding relation. Here, a combination of CNN and Skip-gram [11] is developed to model candidate relation mention sentences in semantic vectors, and the vector space model can be used to calculate the similarity to the word embedding of the relation. As shown in Fig. 2, two parallel CNN models are used to learn the vector representation of the sentence mentioned in the candidate relations, and the average word embedding method is used to learn the vector representation of the relation.

For relation-mentioned sentences, the beginning of the model is to use the Skip-gram [11] model to obtain the word embedding of the relation-mentioned sentences based on the corpus in the previous article. Two convolution kernels with different window sizes of 1 and 2 are used in the convolution layer to extract local features with different granularities to maximize information utilization. In this paper, the activation function in the convolutional layer uses ReLU. The pooling layer after the convolutional layer is used to select a variety of semantic combinations, extract the main features, and change the variable-length input into a fixed-length output. The pooling layer adopts Max-pooling operation, and selects the strongest value of the input vector in each window to form a new vector. The output after the pooling operation passes through a Dropout layer. Dropout sets each feature extracted by the pooling layer to 0 with a certain probability. This can avoid overfitting caused by the model's excessive dependence on certain features, thereby improving the generalization ability of the model. For the extracted main features, the non-linear recombination is performed through the fully connected layer to obtain the semantic vector representation of the input mentioned sentence.

For the relation set, the model also uses the skip-gram model to obtain the word embedding of the relation set. Then this paper obtains the vector representation of the relation set by averaging the word embeddings of all the words in the set. Finally, the cosine distance is used to express the semantic similarity between the relation mention sentence and the corresponding relation set. Suppose m represents the candidate relation mention sentence, r is the corresponding relation set, V_m represents the semantic vector representation of the reference set, and V_r represents the semantic vector representation of the relation set, so the similarity between the two can be calculated by Eq. 2. If the similarity exceeds the set threshold ε, the sentence is mentioned as the exact text of the relationship.

$$sim(m, r) = \cos\left(V_m, V_r\right) \tag{2}$$

3.2 Text Representation Model of BCRL

In the design of the text representation model of BCRL, several technologies are introduced and integrated to adapt to long texts, including BERT, CNN, attention mechanism, and sentence position coding. Figure 3 shows the overall framework of the text-enhanced representation model. The function of each part of the model is explained in detail below.

The Overall Framework of Text Representation Model
The above entity description and relation mention extraction methods bring more accurate long text information. In order to embed as much semantic information as possible within and between sentences into the text representation, we propose to combine the BERT language model and the CNN. Sentence sequence vectors are first generated by the BERT model, and then these sentence-level feature vectors are input into a convolutional neural network to form final overall text vector. In addition, the attention mechanism and position coding are added to CNN to further enrich textual representation of the entity description.

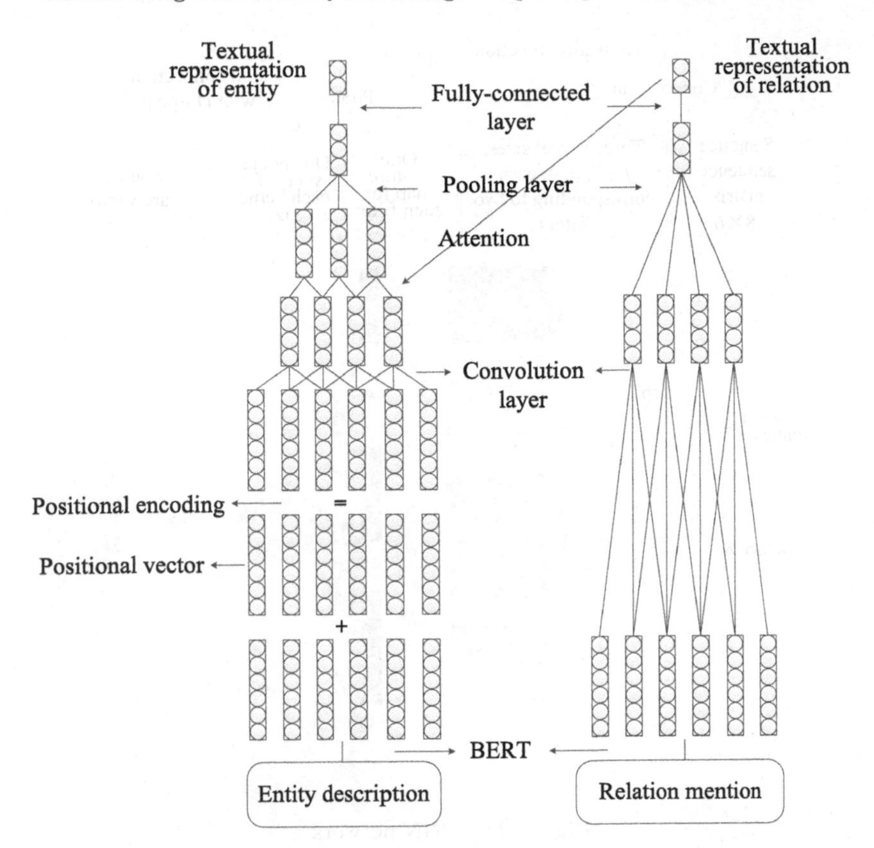

Fig. 3. The overall framework of text representation model

BERT. The BERT model is derived from the paper [4], which is a language model based on two-way Transformer proposed by Google. This paper uses the BERT model to obtain the sentence vector representation of the text. In order to achieve this, the value of BERT's parameter *max_seq_len* should be increased. Hence, we set the value of max_seq_len to be the average length of the entity description texts. Although theoretically the output value of any layer of the transformer can be used as a sentence vector, the experimental results show that the value of the penultimate layer is better. The input of the BERT model is a sequence of preprocessed sentences d where the sequence length is n and each sentence contains m words. Thus, the input is defined as $d_1 : n = d_1, d_2, \cdots, d_n$. Where $d_i \in D^m$ representing m words of the ith sentence of an entity description text. For the sentence sequence d, in order to prevent overfitting problems in text processing, the output value of the penultimate layer with a dimension of 768 is selected as the output sentence vector v.

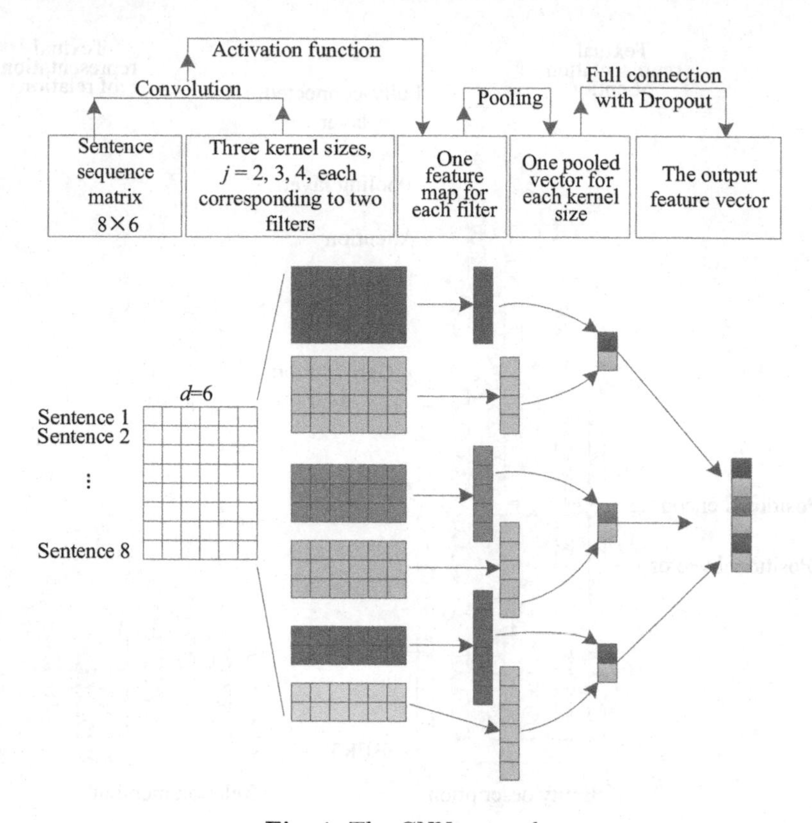

Fig. 4. The CNN network

CNN. The CNN network consists of a convolutional layer, a pooling layer, a Dropout layer, and a fully connected layer. Figure 4 illustrates an example that takes a sequence of 8 sentence vectors as input. Each sentence dimension is 6. For each convolution kernel size $j = 2$, 3, and 4, the convolution operation, pooling operation, and full connection are performed in sequence.

Specifically, in our model, the input of the CNN convolutional layer are n sentence vectors v obtained by previous BERT where each sentence dimension is 768. The convolution layer performs convolution operation on these n sentence vectors with a sliding window of size j, and outputs the feature map q. The sentence vector sequence processed by the sliding window is defined as $v_{i:i+j-1} = v_i, v_{i+1}, \dots, v_{i+j-1}$. The i-th output feature vector after convolution is shown in Eq. 3, where $w \in R^{j \times m}$ is the filter, $b \in R$ is the bias term, and f is the activation function. In this paper, RELU is selected as the activation function.

$$q_i = f(w \cdot v_{i,i+j-1} + b) \tag{3}$$

The first k maximum pooling (K-Max Pooling) is used here, i.e., the first k maximum values are selected for the input vectors in each window to form a new vector. The i-th vector output by the pooling layer with a window size of

n_p can be calculated by using Eq. 4. When the number of filters is l, the output of the pooling layer is $p = [p_1, \dots, p_l]$.

$$p_i = \max_k (q_{n_p \cdot i}, \dots, q_{n_p \cdot (i+1)-1}) \tag{4}$$

The model also provides a Dropout layer working in a Bernoulli process to further prevent overfitting. As shown in Eq. 5, the output of the Dropout layer is $\tilde{p}$ where vector $\hat{\beta} \sim \text{Bernoulli}(\rho)$ with probability ρ.

$$\tilde{p} = \hat{\beta} * p \tag{5}$$

The output of the CNN fully connected layer is defined as Eq. 6 where w_o is a parameter matrix and b_o is an optional bias term.

$$e_d = w_o \cdot \tilde{p} + b_o \tag{6}$$

Relation-Based Attention for Entity Text Representation
As we know, in addition to the common 1-1 relations, there are also complex relations such as 1-N, N-1, and N-N in a knowledge graph. For the entity description information, CNN semantically encodes the entire text, without considering that the description information contains the different semantics of the entity under multiple relations. This means that given a triple, the relationship is given, which will cause some interference for the entity description to contain information about other relations. In order to make CNN sensitive to the different semantics of the entity under various relations, an attention mechanism is integrated between the convolutional layer and the pooling layer. In this way, the most relevant relations between entities can be effectively captured with the help of generated relation mention vectors.

Given the sentence vector sequence $v_{1:n} = v_1, v_2, \dots, v_n$ of an entity and a relation $r \in R^m$, the textual representation r_d of the relation r is believed to be closely related to the relationship mention information. Therefore, the relation-based attention of entity description is defined as Eq. 7. Suppose the output of the convolution layer is q, then the output with the relation-based attention is defined to be $\tilde{q} = q\alpha(r)$, which can be used as the input of the pooling layer.

$$\alpha(r) = Softmax(v_{1:n} r_d) \tag{7}$$

Sentence Level Positional Encoding for Entity Text Representation
Another useful but overlooked feature is the sentence order information in the sentence sequence. Although BERT considers the order information of the words in the sentence, CNN does not include the order feature of the sentence when encoding the whole text, and part of the semantics may be lost. Therefore, to make effective use of this information, the sentence position is encoded as position vector γ_i and then combined with the sentence vector v_i into a new vector C_i by addition.

The position vector γ_i is generated by using the sine and cosine functions on position *pos* at different frequencies according to Vaswani's method, expressed as

Eqs. 8 and 9. Here, pos corresponds to the input position, and d is the dimension of the position vector.

$$\gamma_{(pos,2i)} = \sin pos/10000^{2i/d} \tag{8}$$

$$\gamma_{(pos,2i+1)} = \cos pos/10000^{2i/d} \tag{9}$$

Given a sentence sequence vector $v_{1:n} = v_1, \cdots, v_n$, its position vector $\gamma_{1:n} = (\gamma_1, \cdots, \gamma_n)$, the new input of CNN after adding location information is $C_{1:n} = (v_1 + \gamma_1, \cdots, v_n + \gamma_n)$.

4 Structure-Text Joint Knowledge Graph Learning

4.1 TransE-Based Structural Representation

TransE-based representation models perform well in tasks such as knowledge reasoning and relationship extraction, and have become a research hotspot for knowledge representation.

Given a triple (head entity, relation, tail entity), express it as (h, r, t). The corresponding vector of the triple (h, r, t) is represented as $(\mathbf{h}, \mathbf{r}, \mathbf{t})$. TransE aims to express entities and relationships as low-dimensional continuous vectors. The legal triple vector should satisfy the formula $\mathbf{h} + \mathbf{r} \approx \mathbf{t}$, and the wrong triple does not. Therefore, TransE defines the following score function to measure the quality of the triple, as shown in Eq. 10.

$$\begin{aligned} f_r(h,t) &= \|\mathbf{h} + \mathbf{r} - \mathbf{t}\|_{L_1/L_2}, \\ s.t. : \|\mathbf{h}\|_2^2 &\leq 1; \|\mathbf{t}\|_2^2 \leq 1 \end{aligned} \tag{10}$$

Equation 10 is the L1 or L2 distance between vectors $\mathbf{h}+\mathbf{r}$ and $\mathbf{t}$. For a reasonable scoring function, the score of the legal triple is lower than the score of the wrong triple.

4.2 Structure-Text Joint Representation

As shown in Fig. 5, the model jointly expresses structure information and text information through a gate mechanism.

In this paper, the gate mechanism proposed by Xu et al. [19] is used for the fusion of the learned textual representation and the structural representation from TransE. As defined in Eq. 11 and 12, it means that the joint representation V_j is regarded as the result of the weighted sum of the textual representation V_d and the structural representation V_s. Here, g_s and g_d are the gates that balance the two information sources, and $\odot$ is the element multiplication.

$$V_j = g_s \odot V_s + g_d \odot V_d \tag{11}$$

$$s.t.\ g_d = 1 - g_s; g_s, g_d \in [0, 1] \tag{12}$$

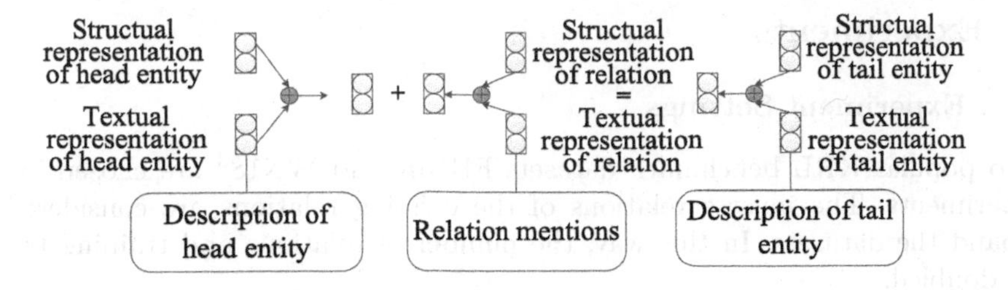

Fig. 5. Structure-text joint representation

The gate g is defined as $g = Softmax(\hat{g})$, where $\hat{g} \sim$ uniform$(0,1)$ is a real-valued vector initialized randomly in a uniform distribution. Softmax function is employed here to constrain the value of the gate control to [0, 1]. Note that the Sigmoid function is also applicable for computing the gate as stated in [19].

Similar to the TransE series model, the structure-text joint representation score function is defined as shown in Eq. 13.

$$f(h,r,t;d_h,d_r,d_t) = ||(g_{hs} \odot h_s + g_{hd} \odot h_d) + (g_{rs} \odot r_s + g_{rd} \odot r_d) \\ - (g_{ts} \odot t_s + g_{td} \odot t_d)||_{L1/L2} \tag{13}$$

Among them, g_{hs} and g_{hd} are the doors of the head entity, g_{rs} and g_{rd} are the door of the relation, and g_{ts} and g_{td} are the door of the tail entity.

4.3 Model Training

According to the TransE, the maximum interval method [3] is utilized to train the model. The loss function of the triples (h,r,t) is described in Eq. 14 where f is the score function of our model, $\gamma > 0$ is the margin between golden tuples and negative tuples, D is the set of valid triples in the KG, and $\hat{D}$ is the set of invalid triples not in the KG.

$$L = \sum\nolimits_{(h,r,t)\in D} \sum\nolimits_{(\hat{h},\hat{r},\hat{t})\in \hat{D}} \left[f\left(h,r,t\right) + \gamma - f\left(\hat{h},\hat{r},\hat{t}\right)\right]_+ \tag{14}$$

This paper uses the method proposed by Wang et al. [17] to set different probabilities to replace the head or tail entities according to the Bernoulli distribution, which divides the relations into four different types according to the number of connected entities at both ends: 1-1, 1-N, N-1, and N-N. If it is a 1-N relation, it increases the chance of replacing the head entity, and if it is an N-1 relation, it increases the chance of replacing the tail entity, which can effectively improve the model training effect. For each triple, a valid triple (h,r,t) is defined as $\hat{D} = \left\{\left(\hat{h},r,t\right)\right\} \cup \{(h,\hat{r},t)\} \cup \left\{\left(h,r,\hat{t}\right)\right\}$.

5 Experiments

5.1 Experiment Settings

Two popular KRL benchmark datasets FB15K and WN18[3] are chosen in the experiments. The inverse relations of the existing relations are considered to expand the datasets. In this way, the number of relations and training triples are doubled.

Initial entity descriptions are available from GitHub[4]. A simplified corpus was then built on the existing entities by performing entity linking with the English Wikipedia[5] data (May 16, 2019) which is about 15.5G in size and contains more than 1.2 billion words. The entity description representation and relation mention representation in the experiments are all based on this corpus.

In order to accelerate the convergence, the vectors and matrices of BCRL are initialized through the RTransE [7] model. The entity/relation vector dimension $d \in \{50, 100\}$, the learning rate $\alpha \in \{0.01, 0.001, 0.0001, 0.0005\}$, and the maximum interval $\gamma \in \{0.1, 1, 2, 4, 4.5, 5, 5.5, 6\}$. The pre-trained BERT in the text representation model is BERT-Base-Uncased. The window size of the convolutional layer $j \in \{2, 3, 4, 5\}$, the number of filters $l \in \{50, 100\}$, and the drop rate is set to 0.5. The L1 normal form is used in the scoring function. The training process iterates the MBGD (mini-batch gradient descent method) algorithm 2000 times.

In order to better compare with other knowledge representation learning models such as TransE, the same evaluation criteria as TransE are used, i.e., Mean Rank and Hits@10. The smaller the Mean Rank is, the better the Hits@10 is.

In addition, in order to better analyze the impact of text information on knowledge graph representation learning, we divide the relations into four types: 1-1, 1-N, N-1, and N-N. Compare the results of Hits@10 (Filtered) on the dataset.

5.2 Experiment Introduction

Link prediction refers to the task of predicting entities that may have specific relations with a given entity. Specifically, for a triple (h, r, t), it means to predict tail t when given head h and relation r, and to predict head h when given relation r and tail t. The former can be denoted as $(?, r, t)$, and the latter can be denoted as $(h, r, ?)$. The candidate prediction result entities are returned as a ranked set.

Two sets of comparative experiments were performed on the link prediction task to evaluate the performance of the proposed BCRL model. The comparison models can be divided into two categories.

- Structure-only models: SME [2], TransE [3], TransH [17], TransR [9], TransD [8], HolE [12], ANALOGY [10], CompleEx [15].

[3] https://everest.hds.utc.fr/doku.php?id=en:transe.
[4] https://github.com/xrb92/DKRL.
[5] https://dumps.wikimedia.org/enwiki/latest/enwiki-latest-pages-articles.xml.bz2.

– Text-enhanced model: Jointly(LSTM) [19], Jointly(A-LSTM) [19], TEKE_E [1], AATE_E [1], CNN+TransE [18].

Experiment 1. Compare the BCRL model with other representation learning models such as that those use only structural information and that those introduce textual information, and evaluate the relative accuracy of the model in the average ranking and the top ten rankings. In order to investigate the effect of attention mechanism and position information introduced in BCRL on the ability of model representation, BCRL-A (add attention mechanism), BCRL-PA (add location and attention mechanism) and BCRL (neither of them are added) were also added for comparative experiments.

Experiment 2. In order to specifically analyze the impact of text information on different relations, BCRL, BCRL-A, BCRL-PA, TransE, and other representation learning models that introduce textual information were compared experimentally for 1-1, 1-N, N-1 and N-N four relations. This part of the experiment was only done on the FB15K data set.

5.3 Experiment Results

Table 1. The result of the experiment about BCRL on the task of link prediction.

Method	WN18				FB15K			
	MeanRank		Hits@10		MeanRank		Hits@10	
	Raw	Filt	Raw	Filt	Raw	Filt	Raw	Filt
SME	545	533	65.1	74.1	274	154	30.7	40.8
TransE	263	251	75.4	89.2	243	125	34.9	47.1
TransH	401	388	73.0	82.3	212	87	45.7	64.4
TransR	238	225	79.8	92.0	198	77	48.2	68.7
TransD	224	212	79.6	92.2	194	91	53.4	77.3
HolE	–	–	–	**94.9**	-	65	–	81.0
ANALOGY	–	–	–	94.7	–	–	–	**85.4**
CompleEx	–	–	–	94.7	–	–	–	84.0
CNN+TransE	–	–	–	–	181	91	49.6	67.4
Jointly (LSTM)	117	95	79.5	91.6	179	90	49.3	69.7
Jointly (A-LSTM)	134	123	78.6	90.9	167	73	52.9	75.5
TEKE_E	–	127	–	93.8	–	79	-	67.6
AATE_E	–	123	–	94.1	–	76	-	76.1
TransE (our)	304	291	72.4	82.5	211	75	49.1	65.0
BCRL	110	97	77.7	92.3	165	67	53.6	83.5
BCRL-A	107	92	78.7	94.5	**159**	**63**	**55.3**	84.7
BCRL-PA	**106**	**90**	**80.7**	**94.9**	164	67	52.9	82.3

Experiment 1. In order to exhibit the performance under the same environment, we implemented both the TransE model and the BCRL model. The performance of our TransE is significantly different from that of the original paper TransE system on the FB15K dataset. All the results of Experiment 1 are listed in Table 1. The best result values in each group of experiments are highlighted in bold, and the underlined ones indicate the suboptimal values. The result values of the baseline evaluations are from their original work. The "–"s in the table indicate those results not reported in previous work. The same applies to the following experimental result table.

The following conclusions can be drawn according to Table 1.

- The performance of the BCRL-A model in this paper is significantly better than the TransE model (TransE is a baseline KRL model). For the WN18 and FB15K datasets, the average ranking effect has improved by 64.8%, 68.4%, 8.7%, and 14.5%, and the top ten rankings have increased by 24.6%, 16.0%, 12.6%, and 30.3%. They are also superior to the other structure-based models TransH, TransR, and TransD. The results confirm that textual information is beneficial to a structure-based knowledge graph representation learning model.
- The metrics of the BCRL-A model on the WN18 and FB15K datasets are similar to those of the current best semantic matching model ANALOGY, and the MeanRank on the FB15k dataset has achieved the best results so far. Since our BCRL model is simply based on the TransE framework, there is still much room for improvement.
- Compared with the typical text representation model Jointly (A-LSTM), most of the metrics value of the BCRL-A model are superior, which indicates that our BCRL model can effectively capture the semantics in textual information, and has certain effects in joint representation of textual information and structural information.
- Comparing three variants of our model, BCRL-A is significantly better than BCRL, which means that introducing relation-based attention mechanism can strengthen the semantic difference of entity description information and further improve the discrimination of entity representation. On the FB15k dataset, BCRL-PA with additional position-coding information performs worse than BCRL-A with only the attention mechanism. This may be due to the differences in the number of description sentences and the length between different entities in the dataset. Position-coded information cannot effectively reflect such difference, and even becomes interference information. However, BCRL-PA performs better than BCRL-A on the WN18 dataset. A possible reason is that the sentence length of the WN18 dataset is short and the difference in sentence length is not large. Thus, the position coding is more suitable in this case.

Table 2. Hit@10 of link prediction on different type of relations on FB15k dataset.

Task	Head entity prediction				Tail entity prediction			
Relationship type	1-1	1-N	N-1	N-N	1-1	1-N	N-1	N-N
Jointly(A-LSTM)	83.8	95.1	21.1	47.9	83.0	30.8	94.7	53.1
TransE	43.7	65.7	18.2	47.2	43.7	19.7	66.7	50.0
BCRL	<u>85.9</u>	95.2	36.9	<u>81.8</u>	85.1	46.5	<u>95.6</u>	84.3
BCRL-A	**87.8**	**96.9**	**40.7**	**83.5**	**87.8**	**50.4**	**95.7**	**85.6**
BCRL-PA	85.4	<u>95.7</u>	<u>37.8</u>	81.2	<u>85.8</u>	<u>46.7</u>	95.3	<u>84.4</u>

Experiment 2. From Table 2, we can see that our BCRL model has better performance than the basic model on all types of relations (1-1, 1-N, N-1, and N-N). In addition, the BCRL-A model has better results than the Jointly (A-LSTM) model, especially for the head entity prediction under the N-1, N-N relation and the tail entity prediction under 1-N, N-N. Since BCRL-A and Joint (A-LSTM) are both based on TransE, we conclude that the introduction of relation mention text is very meaningful for improving overall knowledge representation.

6 Conclusions

In this paper, we propose a text-enhanced knowledge graph representation model, named BCRL, which utilizes entity description and relation mention to enhance the knowledge representations of a triple. It tackles the challenges of incomprehensive entity description representation, and inaccurate relation mention representation from the perspective of text-sentence representation. The experimental results show that BCRL can capture the semantic information of text more effectively than the previous textual information based model, and has significant improvements on the link prediction task compared with the baseline systems.

References

1. An, B., Chen, B., Han, X., Sun, L.: Accurate text-enhanced knowledge graph representation learning. In: Proceedings of the 2018 Conference of the North American Chapter of the Association for Computational Linguistics: Human Language Technologies, Volume 1 (Long Papers), pp. 745–755, June 2018
2. Bordes, A., Glorot, X., Weston, J., Bengio, Y.: A semantic matching energy function for learning with multi-relational data. Mach. Learn. **94**(2), 233–259 (2013). https://doi.org/10.1007/s10994-013-5363-6
3. Bordes, A., Usunier, N., Garcia-Durán, A., Weston, J., Yakhnenko, O.: Translating embeddings for modeling multi-relational data. In: Proceedings of the 26th International Conference on Neural Information Processing Systems - Volume 2, NIPS 2013, pp. 2787–2795 (2013)

4. Devlin, J., Chang, M.W., Lee, K., Toutanova, K.: BERT: pre-training of deep bidirectional transformers for language understanding. arXiv preprint arXiv:1810.04805 (2018)
5. Dubey, M., Banerjee, D., Abdelkawi, A., Lehmann, J.: LC-QuAD 2.0: a large dataset for complex question answering over Wikidata and DBpedia. In: Ghidini, C., et al. (eds.) ISWC 2019. LNCS, vol. 11779, pp. 69–78. Springer, Cham (2019). https://doi.org/10.1007/978-3-030-30796-7_5
6. Ferragina, P., Scaiella, U.: TAGME: on-the-fly annotation of short text fragments (by Wikipedia entities). In: Proceedings of the 19th ACM International Conference on Information and Knowledge Management, CIKM 2010, pp. 1625–1628 (2010)
7. García-Durán, A., Bordes, A., Usunier, N.: Composing relationships with translations. In: Proceedings of the 2015 Conference on Empirical Methods in Natural Language Processing, pp. 286–290, September 2015
8. Ji, G., He, S., Xu, L., Liu, K., Zhao, J.: Knowledge graph embedding via dynamic mapping matrix. In: Proceedings of the 53rd Annual Meeting of the Association for Computational Linguistics and the 7th International Joint Conference on Natural Language Processing (Volume 1: Long Papers), pp. 687–696, July 2015
9. Lin, Y., Liu, Z., Sun, M., Liu, Y., Zhu, X.: Learning entity and relation embeddings for knowledge graph completion. In: Proceedings of the Twenty-Ninth AAAI Conference on Artificial Intelligence, AAAI 2015, pp. 2181–2187. AAAI Press (2015)
10. Liu, H., Wu, Y., Yang, Y.: Analogical inference for multi-relational embeddings. arXiv: Learning (2017)
11. Mikolov, T., Chen, K., Corrado, G., Dean, J.: Efficient estimation of word representations in vector space. In: 1st International Conference on Learning Representations, ICLR 2013, Scottsdale, Arizona, USA, 2–4 May 2013, Workshop Track Proceedings (2013)
12. Nickel, M., Rosasco, L., Poggio, T.: Holographic embeddings of knowledge graphs. arXiv: Artificial Intelligence (2015)
13. Socher, R., Chen, D., Manning, C.D., Ng, A.Y.: Reasoning with neural tensor networks for knowledge base completion. In: Proceedings of the 26th International Conference on Neural Information Processing Systems - Volume 1, NIPS 2013, pp. 926–934 (2013)
14. Toutanova, K., Chen, D., Pantel, P., Poon, H., Choudhury, P., Gamon, M.: Representing text for joint embedding of text and knowledge bases. In: Proceedings of the 2015 Conference on Empirical Methods in Natural Language Processing, pp. 1499–1509, September 2015
15. Trouillon, T., Welbl, J., Riedel, S., Gaussier, É., Bouchard, G.: Complex embeddings for simple link prediction. In: Proceedings of the 33nd International Conference on Machine Learning, ICML 2016, New York City, NY, USA, 19–24 June 2016, JMLR Workshop and Conference Proceedings, vol. 48, pp. 2071–2080 (2016)
16. Wang, Q., Mao, Z., Wang, B., Guo, L.: Knowledge graph embedding: a survey of approaches and applications. IEEE Trans. Knowl. Data Eng. **29**(12), 2724–2743 (2017)
17. Wang, Z., Zhang, J., Feng, J., Chen, Z.: Knowledge graph and text jointly embedding. In: Proceedings of the 2014 Conference on Empirical Methods in Natural Language Processing (EMNLP), pp. 1591–1601. Association for Computational Linguistics, October 2014
18. Xie, R., Liu, Z., Jia, J., Luan, H., Sun, M.: Representation learning of knowledge graphs with entity descriptions. In: Proceedings of the Thirtieth AAAI Conference on Artificial Intelligence, AAAI 2016, pp. 2659–2665 (2016)

19. Xu, J., Chen, K., Qiu, X., Huang, X.: Knowledge graph representation with jointly structural and textual encoding. arXiv: Computation and Language (2016)
20. Yosef, M.A., Hoffart, J., Bordino, I., Spaniol, M., Weikum, G.: AIDA: an online tool for accurate disambiguation of named entities in text and tables. Proc. VLDB Endow. **4**(12), 1450–1453 (2011)
21. Zhu, S., Cheng, X., Su, S.: Knowledge-based question answering by tree-to-sequence learning. Neurocomputing **372**, 64–72 (2020)

Temporal Knowledge Graph Completion Based on Time Series Gaussian Embedding

Chenjin Xu[1(✉)], Mojtaba Nayyeri[1], Fouad Alkhoury[1], Hamed Yazdi[1], and Jens Lehmann[1,2]

[1] Smart Data Analytics Group, University of Bonn, Bonn, Germany
{xuc,nayyeri,shariat,jens.lehmann}@cs.uni-bonn.de

[2] Enterprise Information Systems Department, Fraunhofer IAIS, Sankt Augustin, Germany
jens.lehmann@iais.fraunhofer.de
https://sda.tech/

Abstract. Knowledge Graph (KG) embedding has attracted more attention in recent years. Most KG embedding models learn from time-unaware triples. However, the inclusion of temporal information besides triples would further improve the performance of a KGE model. In this regard, we propose **ATiSE**, a temporal KG embedding model which incorporates time information into entity/relation representations by using **A**dditive **Ti**me **Se**ries decomposition. Moreover, considering the temporal uncertainty during the evolution of entity/relation representations over time, we map the representations of temporal KGs into the space of multi-dimensional Gaussian distributions. The mean of each entity/relation embedding at a time step shows the current expected position, whereas its covariance (which is temporally stationary) represents its temporal uncertainty. Experimental results show that ATiSE significantly outperforms the state-of-the-art KGE models and the existing temporal KGE models on link prediction over four temporal KGs.

Keywords: Temporal knowledge graph · Knowledge representation and reasoning · Time series decomposition

1 Introduction

Knowledge Graphs (KGs) are being used for gathering and organizing scattered human knowledge into structured knowledge systems. YAGO [22], DBpedia [1], WordNet [18] and Freebase [3] are among existing KGs that have been successfully used in various applications including question answering, assistant systems, information retrieval, etc. In these KGs, knowledge can be represented as RDF triples (s, p, o) in which s (subject) and o (object) are entities (nodes), and p (predicate) is the relation (edge) between them.

J. Z. Pan et al. (Eds.): ISWC 2020, LNCS 12506, pp. 654–671, 2020.
https://doi.org/10.1007/978-3-030-62419-4_37

KG embedding attempts to learn the representations of entities and relations in high-dimensional latent feature spaces while preserving certain properties of the original graph. Recently, KG embedding has become a very active research topic due to the wide ranges of downstream applications. Different KG embedding models have been proposed so far to efficiently learn the representations of KGs and perform KG completion as well as inferencing [4,9,23,25,28,30].

We notice that most of existing KG embedding models solely learn from time-unknown facts and ignore the useful temporal information in the KBs. In fact, there are many time-aware facts (or events) in some temporal KBs. For example, (*Obama, wasBornIn, Hawaii*) happened at August 4, 1961. (*Obama, presidentOf, USA*) was true from 2009 to 2017. These temporal KGs, e.g. Integrated Crisis Early Warning System (ICEWS) [14], Global Database of Events, Language, and Tone (GDELT) [16], YAGO3 [17] and Wikidata [6], store such temporal information either explicitly or implicitly. Traditional KBE models such as TransE learn only from time-unknown facts. Therefore, they cannot distinguish entities with similar semantic meaning. For instance, they often confuse entities such as *Barack Obama* and *Bill Clinton* when predicting (?, *presidentOf*, *USA*, 2010).

To tackle this problem, temporal KGE models [5,7,15] encode time information in their embeddings. TKGE models outperform traditional KGE models on link prediction over temporal KGs. It justifies that incorporation of time information can further improve the performance of a KGE model. Most existing TKGE models embed time information into a latent space, e.g. representing time as a vector. These models cannot capture some properties of time information such as the length of time interval as well as order of two time points. Moreover, these models ignore the uncertainty during the temporal evolution. We argue that the evolution of entity representations has randomness, because the features of an entity at a certain time are not completely determined by the past information. For example, (*Steve Jobs, diedIn, California*) happened on 2011-10-05. The semantic characteristics of this entity should have a sudden change at this time point. However, due to the incompleteness of knowledge in KGs, this change can not be predicted only according to its past evolutionary trend. Therefore, the representation of *Steve Jobs* is supposed to include some random components to handle this uncertainty, e.g. a Gaussian noise component.

In order to address the above problems, in this paper, we propose a temporal KG embedding model, ATiSE[1], which uses additive time series decomposition to capture the evolution process of KG representations. ATiSE fits the evolution process of an entity or relation as a multi-dimensional additive time series which composes of a trend component, a seasonal component and a random component. Our approach represents each entity and relation as a multi-dimensional Gaussian distribution at each time step to introduce a random component. The mean of an entity/relation representation at a certain time step indicates its current expected position, which is obtained from its initial representation, its linear change term, and its seasonality term. The covariance which describes

[1] The code is available at https://github.com/soledad921/ATISE.

the temporal uncertainty during its evolution, is denoted as a constant diagonal matrix for computing efficiency. Our contributions are as follows.

- Learning the representations for temporal KGs is a relatively unexplored problem because most existing KG embedding models only learn from time-unknown facts. We propose ATiSE, a new KG embedding model to incorporate time information into the KG representations.
- We specially consider the temporal uncertainty during the evolution process of KG representations. Thus, we model each entity/relation as a Gaussian distribution at each time step. As shown in Fig. 1, the mean vectors of multi-dimensional Gaussian distributions of entities and relations indicate their position which changes over time and the covariance matrices indicate the corresponding temporal uncertainty. A symmetric KL-divergence between two Gaussian distributions is designed to compute the scores of facts for optimization.
- Different from the previous temporal KG embedding models which use time embedding to incorporate time information, ATiSE fits the evolution process of KG representations as a multi-dimensional additive time series. Our work establishes a previously unexplored connection between relational processes and time series analysis with a potential to open a new direction of research on reasoning over time.
- Our experimental results show that ATiSE significantly outperforms other TKG models and some state-of-the-art static KGE on link prediction over four TKG datasets.

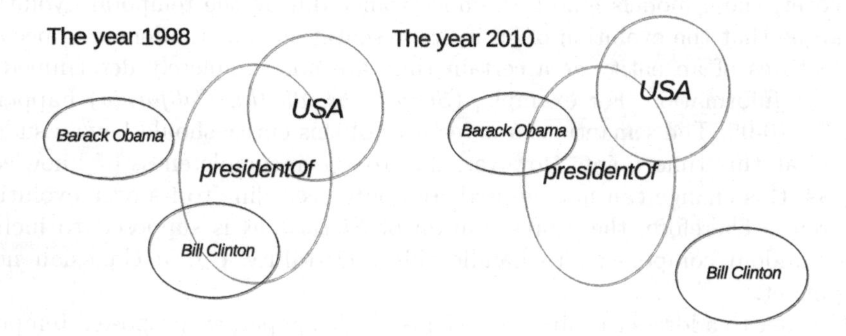

Fig. 1. Illustration of the means and (diagonal) variances of entities and relations in a temporal Gaussian Embedding Space. The labels indicate their position. In the representations, we might infer that *Bill Clinton* was *presidentOf USA* in 1998 and *Barack Obama* was *presidentOf USA* in 2010.

The rest of the paper is organized as follows: In the Sect. 2, we first review related works; in the Sect. 3, we introduce the architecture and the learning process of our proposed models; in the Sect. 4, we compare the performance of our models with the state-of-the-art models; in the Sect. 5, we make a conclusion in the end of this paper.

2 Related Work

A large amount of research has been done in KG embeddings [26]. A few examples of state-of-the-art KGE models include TransE [4], TransH [27], TransComplEx [20], RotatE [23], DistMult [28], ComplEx [25], ComplEx-N3 [13] and QuatE [30].

The above methods achieve good results on link prediction in KGs. However, these time-unaware KGE models have limitations on reasoning over TKGs. More concretely, given two quadruples with the same subjects, predicates, objects and different time stamps, i.e., (*Barack Obama*, *presidentOf*, *USA*, 2010) and (*Barack Obama*, *presidentOf*, *USA*, 2020), static KGE models will model them with the same scores due to their ignorance of time information, while the validities of these two quadruples might be different.

Recent researches illustrate that the performances of KG embedding models can be further improved by incorporating time information in temporal KGs.

TAE [11] captures the temporal ordering that exists between some relation types as well as additional common-sense constraints to generate more accurate link predictions.

TTransE [15] and HyTE [5] adopt translational distance score functions and encode time information in the entity-relation low dimensional spaces with time embeddings and temporal hyperplanes.

Know-Evolve [24] models the occurrence of a fact as a temporal point process. However, this method is built on a problematic formulation when dealing with concurrent events, as shown in Sect. 4.3.

TA-TransE and TA-DistMult [7] utilize recurrent neural networks to learn time-aware representations of relations and use standard scoring functions from TransE and DistMult. These models can model time information in the form of time points with or without some particular temporal modifiers, i.e., '*occursSince*' and '*occursUntil*'.

DE-SimplE [8] incorporates time information into diachronic entity embeddings and achieves the state of the art results on event-based TKGs. However, same as TA-TransE and TA-DistMult, DE-SimplE can not model facts involving time intervals shaped like [2005, 2008].

Moreover, TEE [2] encodes representations of years into entity embeddings by aggregating the representations of the entities that occur in event-based descriptions of the years.

3 Our Method

In this section, we present a detailed description of our proposed method, ATiSE, which not only uses relational properties between entities in triples but also incorporates the associated temporal meta-data by using additive time series decomposition.

3.1 Additive Time Series Embedding Model

A time series is a series of time-oriented data. Time series analysis is widely used in many fields, ranging from economics and finance to managing production operations, to the analysis of political and social policy sessions [19]. An important technique for time series analysis is additive time series decomposition. This technique decomposes a time series Y_t into three components as follows,

$$Y_t = T_t + S_t + R_t. \tag{1}$$

where T_t, S_t and R_t denote the trend component, the seasonal component and the random component (i.e. "noise"), respectively. Figure 2 shows an instance of the additive time series decomposition of a time series.

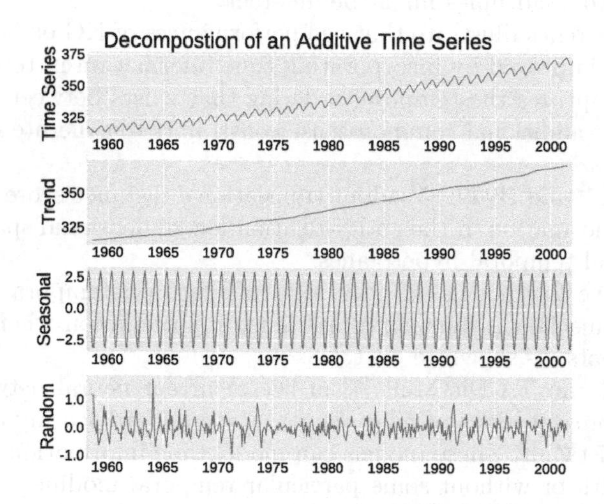

Fig. 2. Illustration of additive time series decomposition.

In our method, we regard the evolution of an entity/relation representation as an additive time series. For each entity/relation, we use a linear function and a Sine function to fit the trend component and the seasonal component respectively due to their simplicity. Considering the efficiency of model training, we model the irregular term by using a Gaussian noise instead of a moving average model (MA model) [10], since training an MA model requires a global optimization algorithm which will lead to more computation consumption.

To incorporate temporal information into traditional KGs, a new temporal dimension is added to fact triples, denoted as a quadruple (s, p, o, t). It represents the creation of relationship edge p between subject entity s, and object entity o at time step t. The score term $x_{spot} = f_t(e_s, r_p, e_o)$ can represent the conditional probability or the confidence value of this event x_{spot}, where $e_s, e_o \in \mathbf{R}^{L_e}$, $r_p \in \mathbf{R}^{L_r}$ are representations of s, o and p. In term of a long-term fact $(s, p, o, [t_s, t_e])$, we consider it to be a positive triple for each time step between t_s and t_e. t_s and t_e denote the start and end time during which the triple (s, p, o) is valid.

At each time step, the time-specific representations of an entity e_i or a relation r_p should be updated as $e_{i,t}$ or $r_{p,t}$. Thus, the score of a quadruple (s,p,o,t) can be represented as $x_{spot} = f_e(e_{s,t}, r_{p,t}, e_{o,t})$ or $x_{spot} = f_r(e_s, r_{p,t}, e_o)$. We utilize additive time series decomposition to fit the evolution processes of each entity/relation representation as:

$$\begin{aligned} e_{i,t} &= e_i + \alpha_{e,i} w_{e,i} t + \beta_{e,i} \sin(2\pi\omega_{e,i} t) + \mathcal{N}(0, \Sigma_{e,i}) \\ r_{p,t} &= r_p + \alpha_{r,p} w_{r,p} t + \beta_{r,p} \sin(2\pi\omega_{r,p} t) + \mathcal{N}(0, \Sigma_{r,p}) \end{aligned} \tag{2}$$

where the e_i and r_p are the time-independent latent representations of the ith entity which is subjected to $||e_i||_2 = 1$ and the pth relation which is subjected to $||r_p||_2 = 1$. $e_i + \alpha_{e,i} w_{e,i} t$ and $r_p + \alpha_{r,p} w_{r,p} t$ are the trend components where the coefficients $|\alpha_{e,i}|$ and $|\alpha_{r,p}|$ denote the evolutionary rates of $e_{i,t}$ and $r_{p,t}$, the vectors $w_{e,i}$ and $w_{r,p}$ represents the corresponding evolutionary directions which are restricted to $||w_{e,i}||_2 = ||w_{r,p}||_2 = 1$. $\beta_{e,i}\sin(2\pi\omega_{e,i}t)$ and $\beta_{r,p}\sin(2\pi\omega_{r,p}t)$ are the corresponding seasonal components where $|\beta_{e,i}|$ and $|\beta_{r,p}|$ denote the amplitude vectors, $|\omega_{e,i}|$ and $|\omega_{r,p}|$ denote the frequency vectors. The Gaussian noise terms $\mathcal{N}(0, \Sigma_{e,i})$ and $\mathcal{N}(0, \Sigma_{r,p})$ are the random components, where $\Sigma_{e,i}$ and $\Sigma_{r,p}$ denote the corresponding diagonal covariance matrices.

In other words, for a fact (s,p,o,t), entity embeddings $e_{s,t}$ and $e_{o,t}$ obey Gaussian probability distributions: $\mathcal{P}_{s,t} \sim \mathcal{N}(\overline{e}_{s,t}, \Sigma_s)$ and $\mathcal{P}_{o,t} \sim \mathcal{N}(\overline{e}_{o,t}, \Sigma_o)$, where $\overline{e}_{s,t}$ and $\overline{e}_{o,t}$ are the mean vectors of $e_{s,t}$ and $e_{o,t}$, which do not include the random components. Similarly, the predicate is represented as $\mathcal{P}_{r,t} \sim \mathcal{N}(r_p, \Sigma_r)$.

Similar to translation-based KGE models, we consider the transformation result of ATiSE from the subject to the object to be akin to the predicate in a positive fact. We use the following formula to express this transformation: $\mathcal{P}_{s,t} - \mathcal{P}_{o,t}$, which corresponds to the probability distribution $\mathcal{P}_{e,t} \sim \mathcal{N}(\mu_{e,t}, \Sigma_e)$. Here, $\mu_{e,t} = \overline{e}_{s,t} - \overline{e}_{o,t}$ and $\Sigma_e = \Sigma_s + \Sigma_o$. Combined with the probability of relation $\mathcal{P}_{r,t} \sim \mathcal{N}(r_{p,t}, \Sigma_r)$, we measure the similarity between $\mathcal{P}_{e,t}$ and $\mathcal{P}_r$ to score the fact.

KL divergence is a straightforward method of measuring the similarity of two probability distributions. We optimize the following score function based on the KL divergence between the entity-transformed distribution and relation distribution [29].

$$\begin{aligned} x_{spot} &= f_t(e_s, r_p, e_o) = \mathcal{D}_{\mathcal{KL}}(P_{r,t}, P_{e,t}) \\ &= \int_{x \in \mathcal{R}^{k_e}} \mathcal{N}(x; r_{p,t}, \Sigma_r) \log \frac{\mathcal{N}(x; \mu_{e,t}, \Sigma_e)}{\mathcal{N}(x; r_{p,t}, \Sigma_r)} dx \\ &= \frac{1}{2} \Big\{ tr(\Sigma_r^{-1}\Sigma_e) + (r_{p,t} - \mu_{e,t})^T \Sigma_r^{-1} (r_{p,t} - \mu_{e,t}) \\ &\quad - \log \frac{det(\Sigma_e)}{det(\Sigma_r)} - k_e \Big\} \end{aligned} \tag{3}$$

where, $tr(\Sigma)$ and Σ^{-1} indicate the trace and inverse of the diagonal covariance matrix, respectively.

Since the computation of the determinants of the covariance matrices in Eq. 3 is time consuming, we define a symmetric similarity measure based on KL divergence to simplify the computation of the score function.

$$f_t(e_s, r_p, e_o) = \frac{1}{2}(\mathcal{D}_{\mathcal{KL}}(P_{r,t}, P_{e,t}) + \mathcal{D}_{\mathcal{KL}}(P_{e,t}, P_{r,t})) \tag{4}$$

Considering the simplified diagonal covariance, we can compute the trace and inverse of the matrix simply and effectively for ATiSE. The gradient of log determinant is $\frac{\partial logdet A}{\partial A} = A^{-1}$, the gradient $\frac{\partial x^T A^{-1} y}{\partial A} = -A^{-T} x y^T A^{-T}$, and the gradient $\frac{\partial tr(X^T A^{-1} Y)}{\partial A} = -(A^{-1} Y X^T A^{-1})^T$ [21].

3.2 Complexity

In Table 1, we summarize the scoring functions of several existing (T)KGE approaches and our models and compare their space complexities. n_e, n_r, n_t and n_{token} are numbers of entities, relations, time steps and temporal tokens used in [7]; d is the dimensionality of embeddings. $\langle x, y, z\rangle = \sum_i x_i y_i z_i$ denotes the tri-linear dot product; $\mathrm{Re}(\cdot)$ denotes the real part of the complex embedding [25]; $\otimes$ denotes the Hamilton product between quaternion embeddings; $\triangleleft$ denotes the normalization of the quaternion embedding. $\mathcal{P}_t$ denotes the temporal projection for embeddings [5]; LSTM$(\cdot)$ denotes an LSTM neural network; $[r_p; t_{seq}]$ denotes the concatenation of the relation embedding and the sequence of temporal tokens [7]; $\overrightarrow{e}$ and $\overleftarrow{e}$ denote the temporal part and untemporal part of a time-specific diachronic entity embedding e^t [8]; p^{-1} denotes the inverse relation of p, i.e., $(s, p, o, t) \leftrightarrow (o, p^{-1}, s, t)$.

Table 1. Comparison of our models with several baseline models for space complexity.

Model	Scoring function	Space complexity	Time complexity
TransE	$\|\|e_s + r_p - e_o\|\|$	$\mathcal{O}(n_e d + n_r d)$	$\mathcal{O}(d)$
DistMult	$\langle e_s, r_p, e_o\rangle$	$\mathcal{O}(n_e d + n_r d)$	$\mathcal{O}(d)$
ComplEx	$\mathrm{Re}(\langle e_s, r_p, \overline{e}_o\rangle)$	$\mathcal{O}(n_e d + n_r d)$	$\mathcal{O}(d)$
RotatE	$\|\|e_s \circ r_p - e_o\|\|$	$\mathcal{O}(n_e d + n_r d)$	$\mathcal{O}(d)$
QuatE	$e_s \otimes r_p^{\triangleleft} \cdot e_o$	$\mathcal{O}(n_e d + n_r d)$	$\mathcal{O}(d)$
TTransE	$\|\|e_s + r_p + w_t - e_o\|\|$	$\mathcal{O}(n_e d + n_r d + n_t d)$	$\mathcal{O}(d)$
HyTE	$\|\|P_t(e_s) + P_t(r_p) - P_t(e_o)\|\|$	$\mathcal{O}(n_e d + n_r d + n_t d)$	$\mathcal{O}(d)$
TA-TransE	$\|\|e_s + \mathrm{LSTM}([r_p; t_{seq}]) - e_o\|\|$	$\mathcal{O}(n_e d + n_r d + n_{token} d)$	$\mathcal{O}(d)$
TA-DistMult	$\langle e_s, \mathrm{LSTM}([r_p; t_{seq}]), e_o\rangle$	$\mathcal{O}(n_e d + n_r d + n_{token} d)$	$\mathcal{O}(d)$
DE-SimplE	$\frac{1}{2}(\langle \overrightarrow{e}_s^t, r_p, \overleftarrow{e}_o^t\rangle + \langle \overrightarrow{e}_o^t, r_{p^{-1}}, \overleftarrow{e}_s^t\rangle)$	$\mathcal{O}(n_e d + n_r d)$	$\mathcal{O}(d)$
ATiSE	$\mathcal{D}_{\mathcal{KL}}(\mathcal{P}_{e,t}, \mathcal{P}_{r,t})$	$\mathcal{O}(n_e d + n_r d)$	$\mathcal{O}(d)$

As shown in Sect. 3.2, our model has the same space complexity and time complexity as static KGE models listed in Sect. 3.2 as well as DE-SimplE. On the other hand, the space complexities of TTransE, HyTE, TA-TransE or TA-DistMult will be higher than our models if n_t or n_{token} is much larger than n_e and n_r.

3.3 Learning

In this paper, we use the same loss function as the negative sampling loss proposed in [23] for optimizing ATiSE. This loss function has been proved to be more effective than the margin rank loss function proposed in [4] on optimizing translation-based KGE models.

$$\mathcal{L} = \sum_{t \in [T]} \sum_{\xi \in \mathcal{D}_t^+} \sum_{\xi' \in \mathcal{D}_t^-} -\log \sigma(\gamma - f_t(\xi)) - \log \sigma(f_t(\xi') - \gamma) \tag{5}$$

where, $[T]$ is the set of time steps in the temporal KG, $\mathcal{D}_t^+$ is the set of positive triples with time stamp t, and $\mathcal{D}_t^-$ is the set of negative sample corresponding to $\mathcal{D}_t^+$. In this paper, we generate negative samples by randomly corrupting subjects or objects of the positives such as (s', p, o, t) and (s, p, o', t). Moreover, we adopt self-adversarial training proposed in [23] and reciprocal learning used in [8,13,30] to further enhance the performances of our model. To avoid overfitting, we add some regularizations while learning ATiSE. As described in the Sect. 3.1, the norms of the original representations of entities and relations, as well as the norms of all evolutionary direction vectors, are restricted by 1. Besides, the following constraint is used for guaranteeing that the covariance matrices are positive definite and of appropriate size when we minimize the loss:

$$\forall l \in \mathcal{E} \cup \mathcal{R}, c_{min} I \le \Sigma_l \le c_{max} I \tag{6}$$

where, $\mathcal{E}$ and $\mathcal{R}$ are the set of entities and relations respectively, c_{min} and c_{max} are two positive constants. We use $\Sigma_l \leftarrow \max(c_{min}, \min(c_{max}, \Sigma_l))$ to achieve this regularization for diagonal covariance matrices. This constraint 6 for the covariance is considered during both the initialization and training process.

Algorithm: The learning algorithm of **ATiSE**

input: The training set $\mathcal{D}^+ = \{(s,p,o,t)\}$, entity set $\mathcal{E}$, relation set $\mathcal{R}$, embedding dimensionality d, margin γ, batch size b, the ratio of negative samples over the positives η, learning rate lr, restriction values c_{min} and c_{max} for covariance, and a score function $f_t(e_s, r_p, e_o)$ where $s, o \in \mathcal{E}$, $p \in \mathcal{R}$.

output: Time-independent embeddings for each entity e_i and relation r_j (the mean vectors and the covariance matrices), the evolutionary rate $\alpha_i$and the evolutionary direction vector w_i for each entity, where $i \in \mathcal{E}$, $j \in \mathcal{R}$.

1. **initialize** $e_i, r_j \leftarrow$ uniform $(-\frac{6}{\sqrt{d}}, \frac{6}{\sqrt{d}})$, $i \in \mathcal{E}$, $j \in \mathcal{R}$
2. $w_{e,i}, w_{r,j} \leftarrow$ uniform $(-\frac{6}{\sqrt{d}}, \frac{6}{\sqrt{d}})$, $i \in \mathcal{E}$, $j \in \mathcal{R}$
3. $\Sigma_{e,i}, \Sigma_{r,j} \leftarrow$ uniform (c_{min}, c_{max}), $i \in \mathcal{E}$, $j \in \mathcal{R}$
4. $\omega_{e,i}, \omega_{r,j} \leftarrow$ uniform (c_{min}, c_{max}), $i \in \mathcal{E}$, $j \in \mathcal{R}$
5. $\alpha_{e,i}, \alpha_{r,j} \leftarrow$ uniform $(0,0)$, $i \in \mathcal{E}$, $j \in \mathcal{R}$
6. $\beta_{e,i}, \beta r, j \leftarrow$ uniform $(0,0)$, $i \in \mathcal{E}$, $j \in \mathcal{R}$
7. **loop**
8. $e_i \leftarrow e_i/||e_i||_2$, $i \in \mathcal{E}$
9. $r_j \leftarrow r_j/||r_j||_2$, $j \in \mathcal{R}$
10. $w_{e,i} \leftarrow w_{e,i}/||w_{e,i}||_2$, $i \in \mathcal{E}$
11. $w_{r,j} \leftarrow w_{r,j}/||w_{r,j}||_2$, $j \in \mathcal{R}$
12. $\mathcal{D}_b^+ \leftarrow$ sample$(\mathcal{D}^+, b)$ // sample a minibatch
13. **for** $(s,p,o,t) \in \mathcal{D}_b^+$ **do**
14. $\mathcal{D}_b^- = \{(s_k', p, o_k', t)\}_{k=1\ldots\eta}$ // generate η negative samples
15. **end for**
16. Update e_i, w_i, α_i and r_j based on Equation 4 and 5 w.r.t. $\mathcal{L} = \sum_{\xi \in \mathcal{D}_b^+} \sum_{\xi' \in \mathcal{D}_b^-} -\log \sigma(\gamma - f_t(\xi)) - \log \sigma(f_t(\xi') - \gamma)$
17. regularize the covariances for each entity and relation based on Constraint 6, $\Sigma_{e,i} \leftarrow max(cmin, min(cmax, \Sigma_{e,i}))$, $i \in \mathcal{E}$ $\Sigma_{r,j} \leftarrow max(cmin, min(cmax, \Sigma_{r,j}))$, $j \in \mathcal{R}$
18. **end loop**

4 Experiment

To show the capability of ATiSE, we compared it with some state-of-the-art KGE models and the existing TKGE models on link prediction over four TKG datasets. Particularly, we also did an ablation study to analyze the effect of the dimensionality of entity/relation embeddings and various components of the additive time series decomposition.

4.1 Datasets

As mentioned in Sect. 1, common TKGs include ICEWS [14], Wikidata [6] and YAGO3 [17]. Four subsets of these TKGs are used as datasets in [7], i.e., ICEWS14, ICEWS05-15, YAGO15k and Wikidata11k. However, all of time intervals in YAGO15k and Wikidata11k only contain either start dates or end dates, shaped like *'occursSince 2003'* or *'occursUntil 2005'* while most of time intervals in Wikidata and YAGO are presented by both start dates and end dates. -Thus, we prefer using YAGO11k and Wikidata12k released in [5] instead of YAGO15k and Wikidta12k. The statistics of the datasets used in this paper are listed in Table 2.

Table 2. Statistics of datasets.

	#Entities	#Relations	#Time steps	Time span	#Training	#Validation	#Test
ICEWS14	6,869	230	365	2014	72,826	8,941	8,963
ICEWS05-15	10,094	251	4,017	2005–2015	368,962	46,275	46,092
YAGO11k	10,623	10	70	−453–2844	16,408	2,050	2,051
Wikidata12k	12,554	24	81	1709–2018	32,497	4,062	4,062

Table 3. Statistics of long-term facts

	#Long-term relations	#Training	#Validation	#Test
YAGO11k	8	12,579	1,470	1,442
Wikidata12k	20	18,398	2,194	2,200

ICEWS is a repository that contains political events with specific time annotations, e.g., (*Barack Obama*, *visits*, *Ukraine*, *2014-07-08*). ICEWS14 and ICEWS05-15 are subsets of ICEWS [14], which correspond to the facts in 2014 and the facts between 2005 to 2015. These two datasets are filtered by only selecting the most frequently occurring entities in the graph [7]. It is noteworthy that all of time annotations in ICEWS datasets are time points.

YAGO11k is a subset of YAGO3 [17]. Different from ICEWS, a part of time annotations in YAGO3 are represented as time intervals, e.g. (*Paul Konchesky*, *playsFor*, *England national football team*, [2003-##-##, 2005-##-##]). Following the setting used in HyTE [5], we only deal with year level granularity by dropping the month and date information and treat timestamps as 70 different time steps in the consideration of the balance about numbers of triples in different time steps. For a time interval with the missing start date or end date, e.g., [2003-##-##, ####-##-##] representing 'since 2003', we use the first timestep or the last timestep to represent the missing start time or end time.

Wikidata12k is a subset of Wikidata [6]. Similar to YAGO11k, Wikidata12k contains some facts involving time intervals. We treat timestamps as 81 different time steps by using the same setting as YAGO11k.

As shown in Table 3, most of facts in YAGO11k and Wikidata12k involve time intervals. For TKGE models, we discretized such facts $(s, p, o, [t_s, t_e])$ involving multiple timesteps into multiple quadruples which only involve single timesteps, i.e., $\{(s, p, o, t_s), (s, p, o, t_{s+1}), \cdots, (s, p, o, t_e)\}$, where t_s and t_e denote the start time and the end time.

4.2 Evaluation Metrics

We evaluate our model by testing the performances of our model on link prediction task over TKGs. This task is to complete a time-wise fact with a missing entity. For a test quadruple (s, p, o, t), we generate corrupted triples by replacing

s or o with all possible entities. We sort scores of all the quadruples including corrupted quadruples and the test quadruples and obtain the ranks of the test quadruples. For a test fact involving multiple time steps, e.g., $(s, p, o, [t_s, t_e])$, the score of one corrupted fact $(s, p, o', [t_s, t_e])$ is the sum of scores of multiple discreet quadruples, $\{(s, p, o', t_s), (s, p, o', t_{s+1}), \cdots, (s, p, o', t_e)\}$.

Two evaluation metrics are used here, i.e., Mean Reciprocal Rank and Hits@k. The Mean Reciprocal Rank (MRR) is the means of the reciprocal values of all computed ranks. And the fraction of test quadruples ranking in the top k is called Hits@k. We adopt the time-wise filtered setting used in source code released by [8]. Different from the original filtered setting proposed in [4], for a test fact (s, p, o, t) or $(s, p, o, [t_s, t_e])$, instead of removing all the triples that appear either in the training, validation or test set from the list of corrupted facts, we only filter the triples that occur at the time point t or throughout the time interval $[t_s, t_e]$ from the list of corrupted facts. This ensures that the facts that do not appear at t or throughout $[t_s, t_e]$ are still considered as corrupted triplets for evaluating the given test fact.

4.3 Baselines

We compare our approach with several state-of-the-art KGE approaches and existing TKGE approaches, including TransE [4], DistMult [28], ComplEx-N3 [13], RotatE [23], QuatE^2 [30], TTransE [15], TA-TransE, TA-DistMult [7] and DE-SimplE [8]. ComplEx-N3 has been proven to have better performance than ComplEx [25] on FreeBase and WordNet datasets. And QuatE^2 has the best performances among all variants of QuatE as reported in [30].

As mentioned in Sect. 2, TA-TransE, TA-DistMult and DE-SimplE mainly focus on modeling temporal facts involving time points with or without some particular temporal modifiers, *'occursSince'* and *'occursUntil'*, and cannot model time intervals shaped like [2003-##-##, 2005-##-##]. Besides, DE-SimplE needs specific date information including year, month and day to score temporal facts, while most of time annotations in YAGO and Wikidataset only contain year-level information. Thus, we cannot test these three models on YAGO11k and Wikidataset15k.

We do not take Know-Evolve [24] as baseline model due to its problematic formulation and implementation issues. Know-Evolve uses the temporal point process to model the temporal evolution of each entity. The intensity function of Know-Evolve (equation 3 in [24]) is defined as $\lambda_r^{s,o}(t|\bar{t}) = f(g_r^{s,o}(\bar{t}))(t - \bar{t})$, where $g(\cdot)$ is a score function, t is current time, and $\bar{t}$ is the most recent time point when either subject or object entity was involved in an event. This intensity function is used in inference to rank entity candidates. However, they don't consider concurrent event at the same time stamps, and thus $\bar{t}$ will become t after one event. For example, we have events $event_1 = (s, r, o_1, t_1)$, $event_2 = (s, r, o_2, t_1)$. After $event_1$, $\bar{t}$ will become t (subject s's most recent time point), and thus the value of intensity function for $event_2$ will be 0. This is problematic in inference since if $t = \bar{t}$, then the intensity function will always be 0 regardless of entity candidates. In their code, they give the highest ranks (first rank) for all entities including the ground truth object in this case, which we think is unfair since the scores of many entity candidates including the ground truth object might be 0 due to their formulation. It has been proven that the performances of Know-Evolve on ICEWS datasets drop down to almost zero after this issue fixed [12].

4.4 Experimental Setup

We used Adam optimizer to train our model and selected the optimal hyper-parameters by early validation stopping according to MRR on the validation set. We restricted the maximum epoch to 5000. We fixed the mini-batch size b as 512. We tuned the embedding dimensionalities d in $\{100, 200, 300, 400, 500\}$, the ratio of negatives over positive training samples η in $\{1, 3, 5, 10\}$ and the learning rate lr in $\{0.00003, 0.0001, 0.0003, 0.001\}$. The margins γ were varied in the range $\{1, 2, 3, 5, 10, 20, \cdots, 120\}$. We selected the pair of restriction values c_{min} and c_{max} for covariance among $\{(0.0001, 0.1), (0.003, 0.3), (0.005, 0.5), (0.01, 1)\}$. The default configuration for ATiSE is as follows: $lr = 0.00003$, $d = 500$, $\eta = 10$, $\gamma = 1$, $(c_{min}, c_{max}) = (0.005, 0.5)$. Below, we only list the non-default parameters: $\gamma = 120$, $(c_{min}, c_{max}) = (0.003, 0.3)$ on ICEWS14; $\gamma = 100$, $(c_{min}, c_{max}) = (0.003, 0.3)$ on ICEWS05-15.

4.5 Experimental Results

Table 4 and 5 show the results for link prediction task. On ICEWS14 and ICEWS05-15, ATiSE outperformed all baseline models, considering MR, MRR, Hits@10 and Hits@1. Compared to DE-SimplE which is a very recent state-of-the-art TKGE model, ATiSE got improvement of 4% on both datasets regarding MRR, and improved Hits@10 by 4% and 6% on ICEWS14 and ICEWS05-15 respectively. On YAGO11k and Wikidata12k where time annotations in facts are time intervals, ATiSE surpassed baseline models regarding MRR, Hits@1, Hits@3. Regarding Hits@10, ATiSE achieved the state-of-the-art results on Wikidata12k and the second best results on YAGO11k. As mentioned in Sect. 4.3, the results of TA-TransE, TA-DistMult and DE-SimplE on YAGO11k and Wikidata12k are unobtainable since they have difficulties in modeling facts involving time intervals in these two datasets.

A part of results listed on Table 4 and 5 are obtained based on the implementations released in [5,13,23]. We list the implementation details of some baseline models as follows:

- We used the implementation released in [23] to test RotatE on all four datasets, and DistMult on YAGO11k and Wikidata12k. The source code was revised to adopt the time-wise filtered setting. To search the optimal configurations for RotatE and DistMult, we followed the experimental setups reported in [23] except setting the maximum dimensionality as 500 and the maximum negative sampling ratio as 10. The default optimal configuration for RotatE and DistMult is as follows: $lr = 0.0001$, $b = 1024$, $d = 500$, $\eta = 10$.

Table 4. Link prediction results on ICEWS14 and ICEWS05-15. *: results are taken from [7]. ◇: results are taken from [8]. Dashes: results are unobtainable. The best results among all models are written bold.

	ICEWS14				ICEWS05-15			
Metrics	MRR	Hits@1	Hits@3	Hits@10	MRR	Hits@1	Hits@3	Hits@10
TransE*	.280	.094	–	.637	.294	.090	–	.663
DistMult*	.439	.323	–	.672	.456	.337	–	.691
ComplEx-N3	.467	.347	.527	.716	.481	.362	.535	.729
RotatE	.418	.291	.478	.690	.304	.164	.355	.595
QuatE^2	.471	.353	.530	.712	.482	.370	.529	.727
TTransE◇	.255	.074	–	.601	.271	.084	–	.616
HyTE◇	.297	.108	.416	.655	.316	.116	.445	.681
TA-TransE*	.275	.095	–	.625	.299	.096	–	.668
TA-DistMult*	.477	.363	–	.686	.474	.346	–	.728
DE-SimplE◇	.526	.418	.592	.725	.513	.392	.578	.748
ATiSE	**.545**	**.423**	**.632**	**.757**	**.533**	**.394**	**.623**	**.803**

Table 5. Link prediction results on YAGO11k and Wikidata12k. The best results among all models are written bold.

	YAGO11k				Wikidata12k			
Metrics	MRR	Hits@1	Hits@3	Hits@10	MRR	Hits@1	Hits@3	Hits@10
TransE	.100	.015	.138	.244	.178	.100	.192	.339
DistMult	.158	.107	.161	.268	.222	.119	.238	.460
ComplEx-N3	.167	.106	.154	.282	.233	.123	.253	.436
RotatE	.177	.113	.177	**.315**	.221	.116	.236	.461
QuatE^2	.164	.107	.148	.270	.230	.125	.243	.416
TTransE	.108	.020	.150	.251	.172	.096	.184	.329
HyTE	.105	.015	.143	.272	.180	.098	.197	.333
ATiSE	**.185**	**.126**	**.189**	.301	**.252**	**.148**	**.288**	**.462**

Below, we only list the non-default parameters: for RotatE, the optimal margins are $\gamma = 36$ on ICEWS14, $\gamma = 48$ on ICEWS05-15, $\gamma = 3$ on YAGO11k and $\gamma = 6$ on Wikidata12k; for DistMult, the optimal regularizer weights are $r = 0.00001$ on YAGO11k and Wikidata12k.

- We used the implementation released in [13] to test ComplEx-N3 and QuatE^2 on all four datasets. The source code was revised to adopt the time-wise filtered setting. To search the optimal configurations for ComplEx-N3 and QuatE^2, we followed the experimental setups reported in [13] except setting the maximum dimensionality as 500. The default optimal configuration for ComplEx-N3 and QuatE^2 is as follows: $lr = 0.1$, $d = 500$, $b = 1000$. Below, we list the optimal regularizer weights: for ComplEx-N3, $r = 0.01$ on ICEWS14 and ICEWS05-15, $r = 0.1$ on YAGO11k and Wikidata12k; for QuatE^2, $r = 0.01$ on ICEWS14 and YAGO11k, $r = 0.05$ on ICEWS05-15, $r = 0.1$ on Wikidata.

- We used the implementation released in [5] to test TransE, TTransE and HyTE on YAGO11k and Wikidata12k for obtaining their performances regarding MRR, Hits@1 and Hits@3. We followed the optimal configurations reported in [5]. As shown in Table 5, Hits@10s of TransE and TTransE we got were better than those reported in [5].
- As shown in Table 4, other baseline results are taken from [7,8].

4.6 Ablation Study

In this work, we analyze the effects of the dimensionality and various components of entity/relation embeddings.

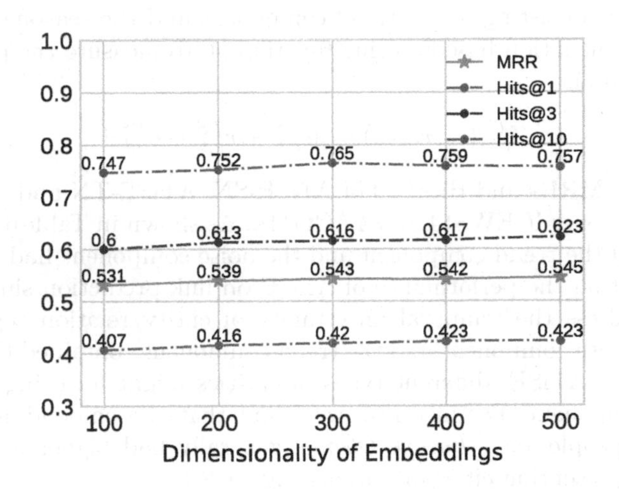

Fig. 3. Results for ATiSE with different embedding dimensionalities on ICEWS14.

The embedding dimensionality is an important hyperparameter for each (T)KGE model. A high embedding dimensionality might be beneficial to boost the performance of a (T)KGE model. For instance, ComplEx-N3 and QuatE^2 achieved the state-of-the-art results on link prediction over static KGs with 2000-dimensional embeddings [13,30]. On the other hand, a lower embedding dimensionality will lead to less consumption on training time and memory space, which is quite important for the applications of (T)KGE models on large-scale datasets. Figure 3 shows the performances of ATiSE with different embedding dimensionalities on ICEWS14. With a same embedding dimensionality of 100 as DE-SimplE [8], ATiSE still achieved the state-of-the-art results on ICEWS14. An ATiSE model with an embedding dimensionality of 100 trained on ICEWS14 had a memory size of 14.2 Mb while a DE-SimplE model and a QuatE^2 model with the same embedding dimensionality had memory sizes of 13.3 Mb and 12.4 Mb. And the memory size of an ATiSE model increases linearly with its embedding dimensionality. Moreover, training an ATiSE model with an embedding dimensionality of 100 took 2.8 s per epoch on a single GeForce RTX2080, and an ATiSE with 500-dimensional embeddings took 3.7 s per epoch.

To analyze the effects of different components of entity/relation representation in ATiSE, we developed three comparison models, namely, ATiSE-SN, ATiSE-TN and ATiSE-TS, which exclude the trend component, seasonal component and the noise component respectively. The entity representations of these three comparison models are as follows:

$$\begin{aligned} e_{i,t}^{SN} &= e_i + \beta_{e,i}\sin(2\pi\omega_{e,i}t) + \mathcal{N}(0, \Sigma_{e,i}) \\ e_{i,t}^{TN} &= e_i + \alpha_{e,i}w_{e,i}t + \mathcal{N}(0, \Sigma_{e,i}) \\ e_{i,t}^{TS} &= e_i + \alpha_{e,i}w_{e,i}t + \beta_{e,i}\sin(2\pi\omega_{e,i}t) \end{aligned} \tag{7}$$

For ATiSE-TS consisting of the trend component and the seasonal component, we used the translation-based scoring function [4] to measure the plausibility of the fact (s, p, o, t).

$$f_t^{TS}(e_s, r_p, e_o) = ||e_{s,t}^{TS} + r_{p,t}^{TS} - e_{o,t}^{TS}|| \tag{8}$$

We report the MRRs and Hits@10 of ATiSE-SN, ATiSE-TN and ATiSE-TS on link prediction over ICEWS14 and YAGO11k. As shown in Table 6, we find that the removal of the trend component and the noise component had a remarkable negative effect on the performance of ATiSE on link prediction since the model could not address the temporal uncertainty of entity/relation representations without the noise component and the trend component contained the main time information. In ATiSE, different types of entities might have big difference in the trend component. For instance, we found that the embeddings of entities representing people, e.g., *Barack Obama*, generally had higher evolution rates than those representing cities or nations, e.g., *USA*.

Table 6. Link prediction results of ablation experiments.

Datasets	ICEWS14				YAGO11K$_D$			
Metrics	MRR	Hits@1	Hits@3	Hits@10	MRR	Hits@1	Hits@3	Hits@10
ATiSE-SN	.405	.284	.488	.710	.139	.095	.143	.249
ATiSE-TN	.536	.407	.626	.771	.167	.115	.171	.292
ATiSE-TS	.323	.127	.429	.676	.115	.023	.145	.274
ATiSE	**.545**	**.423**	**.632**	**.757**	**.185**	**.126**	**.189**	**301**

ATiSE-TN performed worse than ATiSE on YAGO11k where facts involve time intervals. Different from ICEWS14 dataset which is an event-based dataset where all relations or predicates are instantaneous, there exist both short-term relations and long-term relations in YAGO11k. Adding seasonal components into evolving entity/relation representations is helpful to distinguish short-term patterns and long-term patterns in YAGO11k. It can be seen from Table 7 that short-term relations learned by ATiSE, e.g., *wasBornIn*, generally had higher evolutionary rates, and their seasonal components had smaller amplitudes and higher frequencies than long-term relations, e.g., *isMarriedTo*.

Table 7. Relations in YAGO11k and the mean step numbers of their duration time (TS), as well as the corresponding parameters learned from ATiSE, including the evolutionary rate $|\alpha_r|$, the mean amplitude $\overline{|\beta_r|}$ and the mean frequency $\overline{|\omega_r|}$ of the seasonal component for each relation.

Relations	#TS	$\lvert\alpha_r\rvert$	$\overline{\lvert\beta_r\rvert}$	$\overline{\lvert\omega_r\rvert}$
wasBornIn	1.0	0.142	0.000	1.032
worksAt	18.7	0.046	0.058	0.294
playsFor	4.7	0.071	0.046	0.766
hasWonPrize	28.6	0.010	0.107	0.041
isMarriedTo	16.5	0.049	0.076	0.090
owns	24.9	0.017	0.088	0.101
graduatedFrom	38.1	0.016	0.104	0.029
deadIn	1.0	0.249	0.006	0.897
isAffliatedTo	25.8	0.014	0.049	0.126
created	27.1	0.011	0.040	0.087

5 Conclusion

We introduce ATiSE, a temporal KGE model that incorporates time information into KG representations by fitting the temporal evolution of entity/relation representations over time as additive time series. Considering the uncertainty during the temporal evolution of KG representations, ATiSE maps the representations of temporal KGs into the space of multi-dimensional Gaussian distributions. The covariance of an entity/relation representation represents its randomness component. Experimental results demonstrate that our method significantly outperforms the state-of-the-art methods on link prediction over four TKG benchmarks.

Our work establishes a previously unexplored connection between relational processes and time series analysis with a potential to open a new direction of research on reasoning over time. In the future, we will explore to use more sophisticated models to model different components of relation/entity representations, e.g., an ARIMA model for the noise component and a polynomial model for the trend component.

Acknowledgements. This work is supported by the CLEOPATRA project (GA no. 812997), the German national funded BmBF project MLwin and the BOOST project.

References

1. Auer, S., Bizer, C., Kobilarov, G., Lehmann, J., Cyganiak, R., Ives, Z.: DBpedia: a nucleus for a web of open data. In: Aberer, K., et al. (eds.) ASWC/ISWC 2007. LNCS, vol. 4825, pp. 722–735. Springer, Heidelberg (2007). https://doi.org/10.1007/978-3-540-76298-0_52
2. Bianchi, F., Palmonari, M., Nozza, D.: Towards encoding time in text-based entity embeddings. In: Vrandečić, D., et al. (eds.) ISWC 2018. LNCS, vol. 11136, pp. 56–71. Springer, Cham (2018). https://doi.org/10.1007/978-3-030-00671-6_4
3. Bollacker, K., Evans, C., Paritosh, P., Sturge, T., Taylor, J.: Freebase: a collaboratively created graph database for structuring human knowledge. In: Proceedings of the 2008 ACM SIGMOD International Conference on Management of Data, pp. 1247–1250. ACM (2008)
4. Bordes, A., Usunier, N., Garcia-Duran, A., Weston, J., Yakhnenko, O.: Translating embeddings for modeling multi-relational data. In: Advances in Neural Information Processing Systems, pp. 2787–2795 (2013)
5. Dasgupta, S.S., Ray, S.N., Talukdar, P.: HyTE: hyperplane-based temporally aware knowledge graph embedding. In: Proceedings of the 2018 Conference on Empirical Methods in Natural Language Processing, pp. 2001–2011 (2018)
6. Erxleben, F., Günther, M., Krötzsch, M., Mendez, J., Vrandečić, D.: Introducing Wikidata to the linked data web. In: Mika, P., et al. (eds.) ISWC 2014. LNCS, vol. 8796, pp. 50–65. Springer, Cham (2014). https://doi.org/10.1007/978-3-319-11964-9_4
7. García-Durán, A., Dumančić, S., Niepert, M.: Learning sequence encoders for temporal knowledge graph completion. In: EMNLP (2018)
8. Goel, R., Kazemi, S.M., Brubaker, M., Poupart, P.: Diachronic embedding for temporal knowledge graph completion. In: AAAI (2020)
9. He, S., Liu, K., Ji, G., Zhao, J.: Learning to represent knowledge graphs with Gaussian embedding. In: Proceedings of the 24th ACM International on Conference on Information and Knowledge Management, pp. 623–632. ACM (2015)
10. Ho, S., Xie, M.: The use of ARIMA models for reliability forecasting and analysis. Comput. Ind. Eng. **35**(1–2), 213–216 (1998)
11. Jiang, T., et al.: Towards time-aware knowledge graph completion. In: Proceedings of COLING 2016, the 26th International Conference on Computational Linguistics: Technical Papers, pp. 1715–1724 (2016)
12. Jin, W., et al.: Recurrent event network: global structure inference over temporal knowledge graph. arXiv:1904.05530 (2019)
13. Lacroix, T., Usunier, N., Obozinski, G.: Canonical tensor decomposition for knowledge base completion. In: International Conference on Machine Learning, pp. 2869–2878 (2018)
14. Lautenschlager, J., Shellman, S., Ward, M.: ICEWS event aggregations (2015). https://doi.org/10.7910/DVN/28117
15. Leblay, J., Chekol, M.W.: Deriving validity time in knowledge graph. In: Companion of the The Web Conference 2018 on The Web Conference 2018, pp. 1771–1776. International World Wide Web Conferences Steering Committee (2018)

16. Leetaru, K., Schrodt, P.A.: GDELT: global data on events, location, and tone, 1979–2012. In: ISA Annual Convention, vol. 2, pp. 1–49. Citeseer (2013)
17. Mahdisoltani, F., Biega, J., Suchanek, F.M.: YAGO3: a knowledge base from multilingual Wikipedias. In: CIDR (2013)
18. Miller, G.A.: WordNet: An Electronic Lexical Database. MIT Press, Cambridge (1998)
19. Montgomery, D.C., Jennings, C.L., Kulahci, M.: Introduction to Time Series Analysis and Forecasting. Wiley, Hoboken (2015)
20. Nayyeri, M., Xu, C., Yaghoobzadeh, Y., Yazdi, H.S., Lehmann, J.: Toward understanding the effect of loss function on the performance of knowledge graph embedding (2019)
21. Petersen, K.B., Pedersen, M.S., et al.: The matrix cookbook. Tech. Univ. Denmark **7**(15), 510 (2008)
22. Suchanek, F.M., Kasneci, G., Weikum, G.: YAGO: a core of semantic knowledge. In: Proceedings of the 16th International Conference on World Wide Web, pp. 697–706. ACM (2007)
23. Sun, Z., Deng, Z.H., Nie, J.Y., Tang, J.: RotatE: knowledge graph embedding by relational rotation in complex space. In: ICLR (2019)
24. Trivedi, R., Dai, H., Wang, Y., Song, L.: Know-Evolve: deep temporal reasoning for dynamic knowledge graphs. In: ICML (2017)
25. Trouillon, T., Welbl, J., Riedel, S., Gaussier, É., Bouchard, G.: Complex embeddings for simple link prediction. In: Proceedings of ICML (2016)
26. Wang, Q., Mao, Z., Wang, B., Guo, L.: Knowledge graph embedding: a survey of approaches and applications. IEEE Trans. Knowl. Data Eng. **29**(12), 2724–2743 (2017)
27. Wang, Z., Zhang, J., Feng, J., Chen, Z.: Knowledge graph embedding by translating on hyperplanes. In: AAAI, pp. 1112–1119. Citeseer (2014)
28. Yang, B., Yih, W.t., He, X., Gao, J., Deng, L.: Embedding entities and relations for learning and inference in knowledge bases. In: ICLR, p. 12 (2015)
29. Yu, D., Yao, K., Su, H., Li, G., Seide, F.: KL-divergence regularized deep neural network adaptation for improved large vocabulary speech recognition. In: 2013 IEEE International Conference on Acoustics, Speech and Signal Processing, pp. 7893–7897. IEEE (2013)
30. Zhang, S., Tay, Y., Yao, L., Liu, Q.: Quaternion knowledge graph embeddings. In: Advances in Neural Information Processing Systems, pp. 2731–2741 (2019)

Revealing Secrets in SPARQL Session Level

Xinyue Zhang[1], Meng Wang[1,2(✉)], Muhammad Saleem[3], Axel-Cyrille Ngonga Ngomo[4], Guilin Qi[1,2], and Haofen Wang[5]

[1] Southeast University, Nanjing, China
{zhangxy216,meng.wang,gqi}@seu.edu.cn

[2] Key Laboratory of Computer Network and Information Integration (Southeast University), Ministry of Education, Nanjing, China

[3] AKSW, Leipzig University, Leipzig, Germany
saleem@informatik.uni-leipzig.de

[4] University of Paderborn, Paderborn, Germany
axel.ngonga@upb.de

[5] Intelligent Big Data Visualization Lab, Tongji University, Shanghai, China
carter.whfcarter@gmail.com

Abstract. Based on Semantic Web technologies, knowledge graphs help users to discover information of interest by using live SPARQL services. Answer-seekers often examine intermediate results iteratively and modify SPARQL queries repeatedly in a search session. In this context, understanding user behaviors is critical for effective intention prediction and query optimization. However, these behaviors have not yet been researched systematically at the SPARQL session level. This paper reveals secrets of session-level user search behaviors by conducting a comprehensive investigation over massive real-world SPARQL query logs. In particular, we thoroughly assess query changes made by users w.r.t. *structural* and *data-driven* features of SPARQL queries. To illustrate the potentiality of our findings, we employ an application example of how to use our findings, which might be valuable to devise efficient SPARQL caching, auto-completion, query suggestion, approximation, and relaxation techniques in the future (Code and data are available at: https://github.com/seu-kse/SparqlSession.).

1 Introduction

Semantic Web technologies enable an increasing amount of data to be published as knowledge graphs using RDF. SPARQL endpoints have emerged as useful platforms for accessing knowledge graphs via live SPARQL querying. Currently, there are billions of RDF triples available from hundreds of SPARQL endpoints[1]. However, users often fail to express their information needs in one succinct query. This is due to their unfamiliarity with the ontology underlying the endpoints

[1] https://sparqles.ai.wu.ac.at/availability, accessed on October 22, 2020.

J. Z. Pan et al. (Eds.): ISWC 2020, LNCS 12506, pp. 672–690, 2020.
https://doi.org/10.1007/978-3-030-62419-4_38

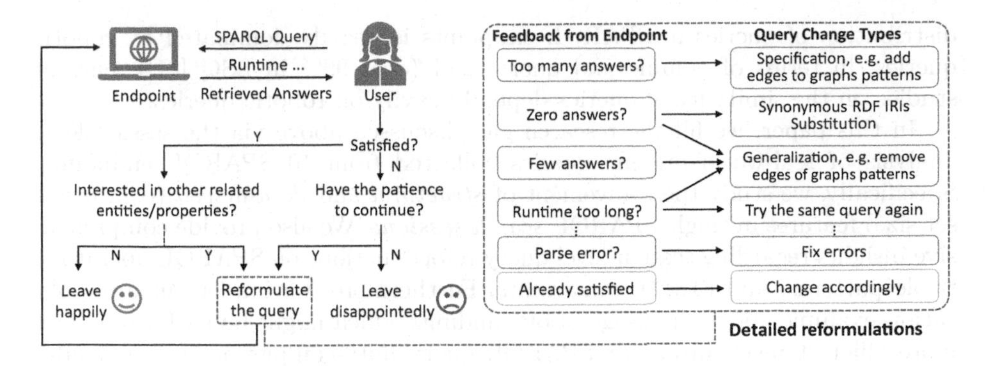

Fig. 1. A typical SPARQL search session

they query, or with SPARQL's syntax. This finding has been corroborated by an analysis on the LSQ dataset [21], where 31.70% of the real-world queries posted to 4 different SPARQL endpoints contain parse errors and 21.42% of the queries produce zero answers. Therefore, SPARQL queries are continuously refined to retrieve satisfying results in practice. We can use techniques based on information about underlying data or query sequence history to assist users. The underlying data is informative and useful, but in some cases, historical queries are the main source of information that is available, e.g., where we do not have access to data. In this paper, we provide session-level query analysis to enhance techniques based on query sequence history.

In the field of Information Retrieval (IR), the continuous query reformulation process is called a *search session* and has been well-studied to generate query suggestions and enhance user satisfaction by utilizing implicit (e.g., query changes [11], clicks and dwell time in a certain website [15]), and explicit (e.g., relevance scores [11]) user feedback. In a SPARQL *search session*, feedback from users is generally only revealed in query changes, which makes it more challenging to understand drifting user intentions. Fortunately, SPARQL queries contain richer information in query *change types* (Fig. 1) compared to the keyword queries in IR. Thus, a more detailed session-level analysis of the real-world SPARQL queries posted by users is both possible and of central importance for devising efficient caching mechanisms [16], query relaxation [12,27], query approximation [13], query auto-completion [9], and query suggestion [14].

Prior SPARQL query log analyses [2,18,21,26] have focused on analyzing the *structural* features (e.g., usage of different SPARQL operators, triple patterns, types of joins) of queries in isolation. The potential correlations between queries in a search session have not been fully investigated. Similarities between queries within the same session have been reported [7,19]. This property has been used in query augmentation [16] to retrieve closely related results. However, these works do not provide deeper insight into query changes within the search session. In addition, there has been no distinction made between robotic queries (i.e., machine-generated) and organic (i.e., human-generated) queries. Given that the distribution of queries in SPARQL endpoints is heavily dominated by robotic queries, in terms of volume and query load (over 99% in LSQ [21]), current studies on the similarity of queries depend heavily on robotic queries.

In this paper, we fill the research gap discussed above via the session-level analysis of real-world organic queries collected from 10 SPARQL endpoints. Specifically, we study the evolvement of *structural* and *data-driven* (e.g., result set size) features in single SPARQL *search sessions*. We also provide comprehensive insights regarding session-level query reformulations on SPARQL operators, triple patterns, and `FILTER` constraints. Furthermore, we implement an application example about the usage of our findings which might be useful to devise more efficient mechanisms for SPARQL query auto-completion, recommendations, caching, etc. Our contributions can be summarized as follows:

- We port the concept of sessions to SPARQL queries and give a specification of SPARQL *search sessions*.
- We are the first, to the best of our knowledge, to investigate potential correlations between SPARQL queries and provide a comprehensive analysis of query reformulations in a given search session.
- We provide an application example of how our findings can be used to illustrate the potentiality of utilizing user behaviors in a search session.

2 Preliminaries

This section briefly introduces datasets and the pre-processing we use, followed by a formal definition of the SPARQL *search session*, as well as *structural* and *data-driven* features of SPARQL queries.

2.1 Datasets and Pre-processing

The difficulties of formulating a SPARQL query depend on the complexity of schema of knowledge graphs. Also, SPARQL queries that are used to query knowledge graphs from different domains have different features. Therefore, we selected 10 LSQ datasets [21] (version 2, 15 from Bio2RDF and 3 others), containing real-world SPARQL queries collected from public SPARQL endpoints of these datasets. The selected datasets include 7/15 diverse datasets from Bio2RDF [4] (a compendium of bioinformatics datasets in RDF), i.e., NCBI Gene (Ncbigene), National Drug Code Directory (Ndc), Orphanet, Saccharomyces Genome Database (Sgd), Side Effect Resource (Sider), Affymetrix, Gene Ontology Annotation (Goa), and the remaining 3 datasets: DBpedia [6] (extracted from Wikipedia), SWDF [17] (Semantic Web Dog Food about conferences metadata), and LinkedGeoData (LGD) [25] (a spatial RDF dataset).

Table 1 gives an overview of the selected datasets in terms of the number of queries (`#Queries`) and their total number of executions (`#Executions`[2]) executed by different users (`#Users`) within a time frame. The basic distribution of

[2] A query can be executed multiple times on the same dataset.

Table 1. Statistics of SPARQL query log datasets. (The "/" is used to show the number of queries (executions) *excluding/including* parse errors, while colors are for different domains.)

Dataset	#Queries	#Executions	Begin time	End time	#Users
LGD	651,251/667,856	1,586,660/1,607,821	2015/11/22	2016/11/20	26,211
SWDF	520,740/521,250	1,415,438/1,415,993	2014/5/15	2014/11/12	936
DBpedia	3,001,541/4,196,762	3,552,212/6,248,139	2015/10/24	2016/2/11	39,922
Affymetrix	618,796/630,499	1,782,776/1,818,020	2013/5/5	2015/9/18	1,159
Goa	630,934/638,570	2,345,460/2,377,718	2013/5/5	2015/9/18	1,190
Ncbigene	679,586/689,885	1,561,592/1,593,958	2014/5/14	2015/9/18	417
Ndc	707,579/720,838	2,354,808/2,411,232	2013/5/16	2015/9/18	1,286
Sgd	618,670/630,891	1,992,800/2,038,097	2013/5/5	2015/9/18	1,304
Sider	186,122/187,976	677,950/681,247	2015/5/31	2015/9/18	216
Orphanet	476,603/477,036	1,521,797/1,523,459	2014/6/11	2015/9/18	171

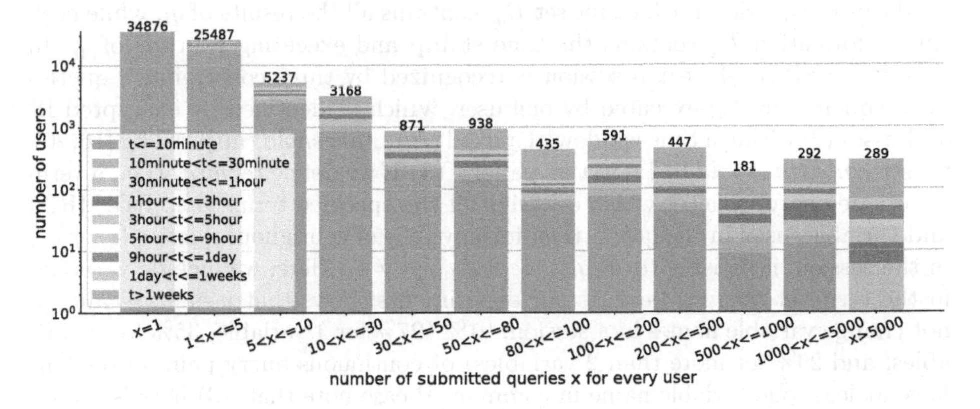

Fig. 2. Distribution of the number of submitted queries x and time-span t of the submitted queries for each user. The X-axis indicates different intervals of submitted query numbers; The Y-axis indicates the number of users in the interval. Different colors indicate different time-spans.

the number and time-span of the submitted queries for each user is presented in Fig. 2. This figure shows the existence of robotic queries that are submitted in a short period. These robotic queries do not show clear trends in individual human usage [5] but easily cause analytic biases due to their sheer size. Therefore, we need to remove robotic queries. There are generally three characteristics that can be used to recognize them: (1) special agent names (e.g. Java) [5,19] (2) relatively high query request frequency [19] (3) loop patterns existing in query sequences submitted by one user [19], where the SPARQL structures remain the same in contiguous queries, while only IRIs, literals, or variables change. However, due to the privacy policy, agent names are usually unavailable in practice. Therefore, we combine (2) and (3) to design a two-step process: (a) filtering out users who submit queries with a high-request frequency, i.e., users who submit more than

30 times in a 30 minutes sliding window. This threshold is a relatively high frequency in our dataset. We use it to compute the average frequency. Also, to make sure this is not a rigorous cut-off rule, we supplement the second step: (b) examining every query sequence submitted by one user. Those sequences with loop patterns are excluded. After robotic query removal process, there are 51,575 (0.64%) likely organic queries and 67,594 (0.36%) executions in our datasets. These executions come from 7,718 (10.60%) users, each having submitted 8.76 queries on average.

2.2 Definitions

Formally, a **SPARQL search session** $s = \{Q, R, T\}$ consists of a sequence of queries $Q = \{q_1, \cdots, q_i, \cdots, q_n\}$, retrieved result sets $R = \{R_{q_1}, \cdots, R_{q_i}, \cdots, R_{q_n}\}$, and time information $T = \{T_{q_1}, \cdots, T_{q_i}, \cdots, T_{q_n}\}$, where n is the number of queries in the session (i.e., the session length) and i indexes the queries. Each result set R_{q_i} contains all the results of q_i, while each time information T_{q_i} contains the time stamp and executing runtime of q_i. In practice, a SPARQL search session is recognized by three constraints[3]: queries in a sequence are (1) executed by one user, which is identified by encrypted IP addresses (2) within a time window of a fixed *time_threshold* (inspired by [16,20], we set *time_threshold* to 1 h in this paper). (3) If we define $term(q)$ (i.e., a term set of one query) as a set which contains all the specified terms (i.e., RDF IRIs) and variables used in the query, then for any pair of contiguous queries (q_i, q_{i+1}) in the session, it satisfies $term(q_i) \cap term(q_{i+1}) \neq \varnothing$. Here, we include variables in the term set $term(q)$ because our experiments shows that users typically do not change variable names in a session: 91% (27% for 1 variable, 35% for 2 variables, and 29% for more than 2 variables) of continuous query pairs in sessions have at least one variable name in common. Please note that, (3) here is a minimum requirement for sessions, while the one user and 1-hour threshold setting can ensure the topic continuity to a large extent, which can be evaluated by the number of common variable names and high similarity score of IRI terms in Fig. 7 (introduce later). Furthermore, although we acknowledge that there could be other ways to identify sessions, the method we present here is reasonable. Based on these constraints of sessions, we extract 14,039 sessions from organic queries in our dataset. The distribution of the organic session length is presented in Fig. 3.

We follow [1,22–24] to define two types of SPARQL query features, i.e., *structural* and *data-driven* features, for the SPARQL session-level analysis.

Structural Features: The basic graph patterns (BGPs) in SPARQL queries organize a set of triple patterns into different types of structures. We represent each BGP of a SPARQL query as a directed hypergraph to easily compare the structural changes between different queries in a search session. The hypergraph

[3] We remove the queries with parse errors and the contiguous same queries before the recognition. For example, q_1, q_2, q_2, q_3 is processed into q_1, q_2, q_3.

representation [24] contains nodes for all three components of the triple patterns <*s*,*p*,*o*>. A hyperedge $e = (s, (p, o)) \in E \subseteq V^3$ connects the head vertex s and the tail hypervertex (p, o), where E is the set of all hyperedges and V is the set of all vertices in the hypergraph. The hypergraph of a complete SPARQL query (consider BGPs only) is the union of hypergraph representations of all BGPs in the query. An example is illustrated in Fig. 4. We define the following *structural* features based on the hypergraph representation.

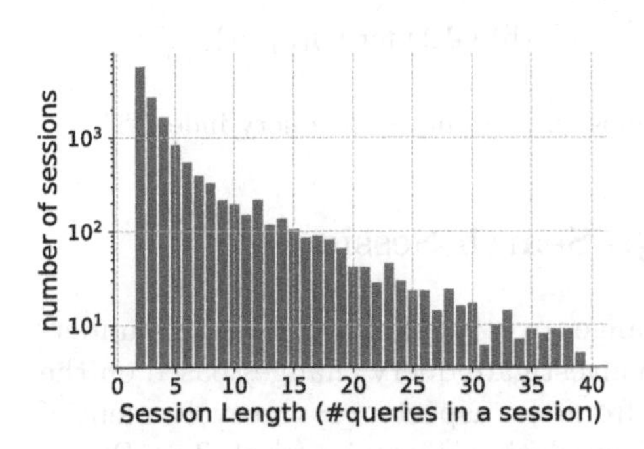

Fig. 3. Organic session length.

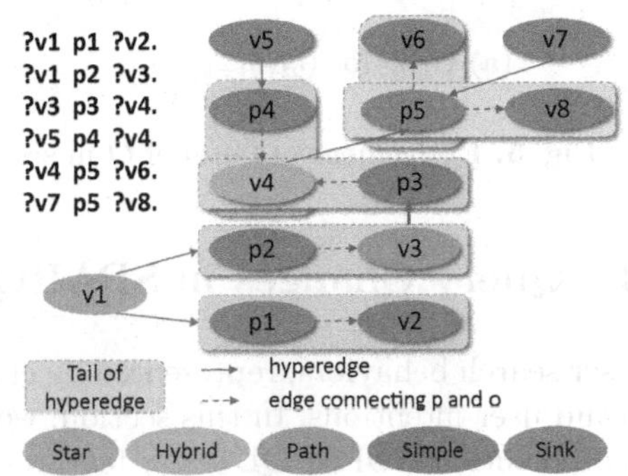

Fig. 4. Hypergraph of a BGP.

- The **triple pattern count** refers to the number of triple patterns in a BGP, which distinguishes between simple and structural complex queries.
- The **join vertex type** is characterized by in-degrees and out-degrees for vertices in BGPs. A *star* vertex only has (multiple) outgoing edges. A *sink* vertex only has (multiple) incoming edges. There is only one in-degree and one out-degree for a *path* vertex. The in-degree (or out-degree) of a *hybrid* vertex is more than one while out-degree (or in-degree) is at least one.
- The **join vertex degree** indicates the summation of the in-degree and out-degree of a join vertex. For a SPARQL query, we use the minimum, mean, and maximum of join vertex degrees in the query to represent this feature.
- The **projection variable count** is the number of selected variables that form the solution sequences in the `SELECT` query form.
- The **IRI term set** is the collection of used IRI terms in a SPARQL query. This feature presents the information that users are interested in.

Data-Driven Features: We mainly consider the **result size**, i.e., $|R_{q_i}|$, the number of solutions for SPARQL queries in this paper. The change of result size (decrease or increase) generally reflects whether users want more specific or more general answers, and as a result, is an important feature to capture the drifting query intentions.

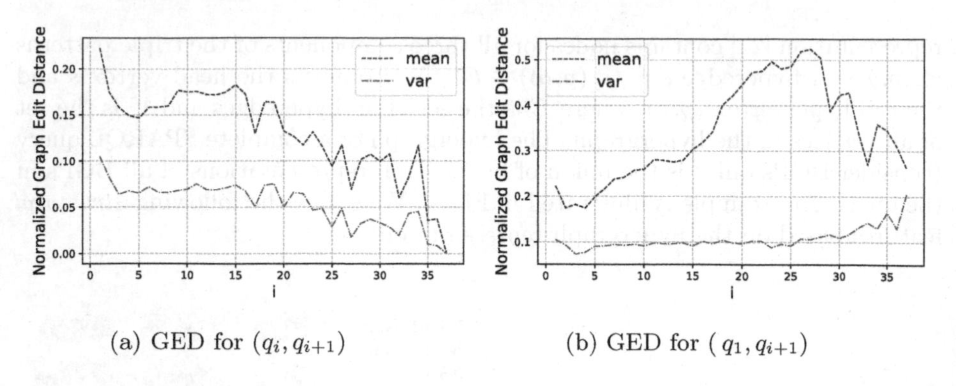

Fig. 5. Evolvement of GED of Q in sessions. X-axis shows the query index "i".

3 Query Changes in SPARQL Search Session

User search behaviors, represented by changes over queries, are the key to understand user intentions. In this section, we investigate query changes based on the aforementioned SPARQL query features from two aspects: (1) the evolvement of query changes (Sect. 3.1); (2) detailed reformulation strategies (Sect. 3.2). Please note that due to the space limitation, we only provide individual dataset-level results when different datasets show very different results. More rudimentary dataset analysis are provided in [21].

3.1 Evolvement of Query Changes

We study the query evolvement in terms of three structural aspects (i.e., graph edit distance, graph pattern similarity, and IRI term similarity), as well as one data-driven aspect, i.e., changes of result size.

Graph Edit Distance (GED): Given a query sequence Q of a session s, we represent each BGP of queries as a directed hypergraph and utilize the normalized GED to measure differences between hypergraphs. The GED between two hypergraphs is normalized by dividing the maximum of the number of edges and vertices in two hypergraphs. On this basis, the GED between two queries is accessed by the average of GEDs between hypergraphs in different operator blocks of the two queries. A GED numeric value ranges from 0 (no change), to 1 (complete change), indicating the degree of changes between two queries. We conduct two types of comparisons: (1) GED between two contiguous queries, i.e., (q_i, q_{i+1}), (2) GED between the initial query and the other query in a given session, i.e., (q_1, q_{i+1}). Consider the sequence $\{q_1, q_2, q_3\}$ as an example: we calculate GED values of (1) (q_1, q_2),(q_2, q_3), and (2) (q_1, q_2),(q_1, q_3). The average

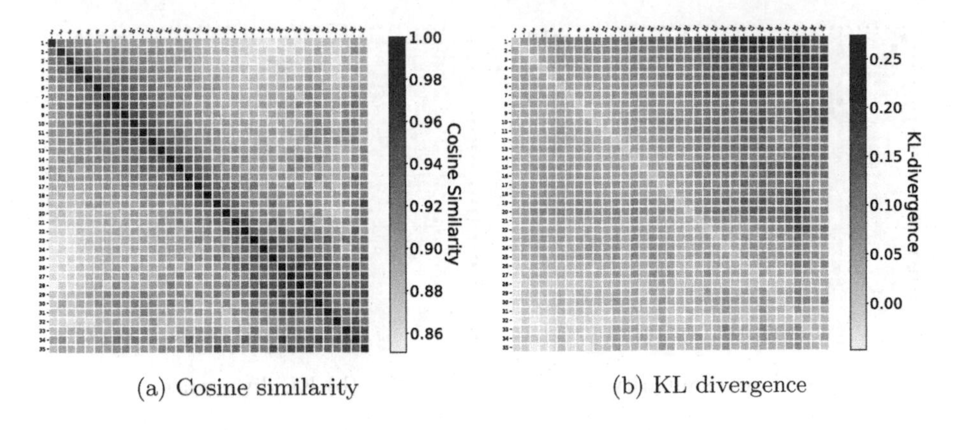

(a) Cosine similarity (b) KL divergence

Fig. 6. Graph pattern similarity of query sequence Q in sessions.

and variance of GEDs (given by *mean* and *var* respectively) in single search sessions on our 10 datasets[4] are presented in Fig. 5.

Graph Pattern Similarity: Based on [1,24], we select the following 10 structural features to form a feature vector[5,6]:

$$\begin{aligned} V = [&\&\#triplePatterns,\ \#BGP,\ \#Projection,\ \#SinkJoinVertex, \\ &\#StarJoinVertex,\ \#HybridJoinVertex,\ \#PathJoinVertex, \\ &MaxJoinDegree,\ MinJoinDegree,\ MeanJoinDegree\ ]. \end{aligned} \tag{1}$$

For a query sequence $Q = \{q_1, q_2 \cdots q_n\}$ in a single search session s, we initialize vectors $\{\mathbf{V_{q_1}}, \mathbf{V_{q_2}} \cdots \mathbf{V_{q_n}}\}$ according to Eq. 1. Then, we normalize every item (k indexes the item) in a vector by

$$\hat{\mathbf{V}}_{\mathbf{q_i}}(k) = \frac{\mathbf{V_{q_i}}(k)}{\max_{j=1,\cdots,n} \mathbf{V_{q_j}}(k)}. \tag{2}$$

We use two metrics to measure graph pattern similarity between two queries: (1) cosine distance, which is a symmetric measurement defined as $Cosine(\hat{\mathbf{V}}_{\mathbf{q_1}}, \hat{\mathbf{V}}_{\mathbf{q_2}}) = Cosine(\hat{\mathbf{V}}_{\mathbf{q_2}}, \hat{\mathbf{V}}_{\mathbf{q_1}})$ and performed by:

$$Cosine(\hat{\mathbf{V}}_{\mathbf{q_1}}, \hat{\mathbf{V}}_{\mathbf{q_2}}) = \frac{\hat{\mathbf{V}}_{\mathbf{q_1}} \cdot \hat{\mathbf{V}}_{\mathbf{q_2}}}{\left\|\hat{\mathbf{V}}_{\mathbf{q_1}}\right\| \left\|\hat{\mathbf{V}}_{\mathbf{q_2}}\right\|} \tag{3}$$

(2) KL divergence, which is asymmetric, and performed by:

$$D_{KL}(\hat{\mathbf{V}}_{\mathbf{q_1}} || \hat{\mathbf{V}}_{\mathbf{q_2}}) = \sum \hat{\mathbf{V}}_{\mathbf{q_1}}(k) \log \frac{\hat{\mathbf{V}}_{\mathbf{q_1}}(k)}{\hat{\mathbf{V}}_{\mathbf{q_2}}(k)}. \tag{4}$$

[4] We use randomly selected sessions in DBpedia because the GED computation on such large-scale data is NP-hard and time-consuming.

[5] We append a 1 to vectors to avoid all-zero vectors.

[6] Features in this vector can also be extended to more dimensions or features.

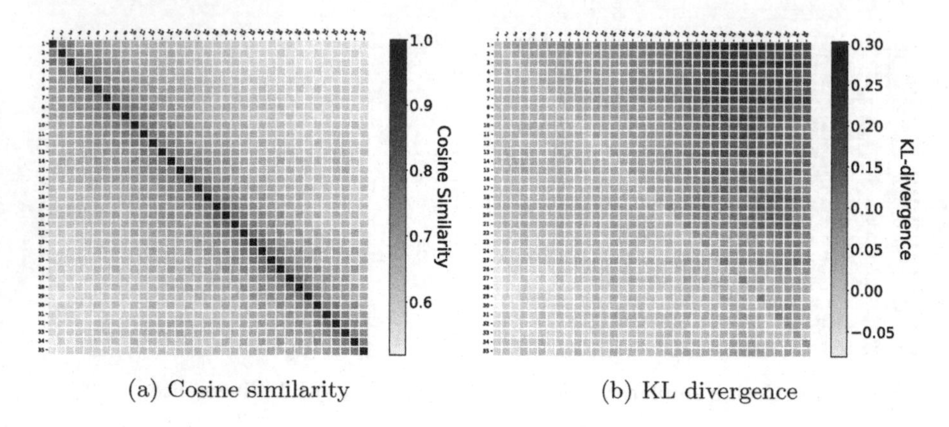

(a) Cosine similarity (b) KL divergence

Fig. 7. IRI term similarity of query sequence Q in sessions.

Cosine similarity between two vectors ranges from 0 (complete change) to 1 (constant). Original KL divergence ranges from 0 (constant) to $+\infty$. The $+\infty$ is caused by zeros in denominators. To prevent this problem, we only calculate $D_{KL}(\hat{\mathbf{V}}_{\mathbf{q_1}}||\hat{\mathbf{V}}_{\mathbf{q_2}})$ when $\hat{\mathbf{V}}_{\mathbf{q_1}}(k) \neq 0$ *and* $\hat{\mathbf{V}}_{\mathbf{q_2}}(k) \neq 0$ here. The minus, zero, and positive result of $D_{KL}(\hat{\mathbf{V}}_{\mathbf{q_1}}||\hat{\mathbf{V}}_{\mathbf{q_2}})$ indicate that distribution of $\hat{\mathbf{V}}_{\mathbf{q_2}}$ is more concentrated than, equal to, or more scattered than distribution of $\hat{\mathbf{V}}_{\mathbf{q_1}}$, respectively. Results are presented in Fig. 6 as a $m \times m$ matrix M, where m is the longest length of sessions. The rows and columns of M are indexed by the query q_i in a session. M_{ij} in M presents the average cosine similarity (or KL divergence) between vectors of q_i and q_j in single search sessions, i.e., $\hat{\mathbf{V}}_{\mathbf{q_i}}$ and $\hat{\mathbf{V}}_{\mathbf{q_j}}$.

IRI Term Similarity: We construct a query-term matrix D which is a $x \times y$ matrix for every dataset. x is the number of queries and y is the number of terms used in queries of a certain dataset. The rows of D are indexed by queries q_i and columns are indexed by terms t_j. D_{ij} in this matrix represents whether the term t_j is used in query q_i. If t_j is used, D_{ij} is 1. If not, D_{ij} is 0. Query q_i can be represented by a vector $\mathbf{V}_{\mathbf{q_i}}$ which is constituted by row i in this query-term matrix D. The vector $\mathbf{V}_{\mathbf{q_i}}$ indicates the IRI term distribution in q_i[7]. Then, we use cosine similarity and KL divergence to visualize the evolvement of IRI term similarity in single search sessions, as shown in Fig. 7. Please note that the analyses and visualizations of Fig. 5, 6, 7 are based on raw data. Lengths of sessions are not normalized. The motivation is to find different user behaviors by session position, which is normally used in log analysis of web searching fields.

Change of Result Size: For the *data-driven* feature, we investigate the transition probability between three result size change states, i.e., decrease, remain

[7] The query representation method can be replaced by other distributed representations such as trained embedding. We do not use embedding here because training embeddings for 10 datasets is highly resource and time-consuming.

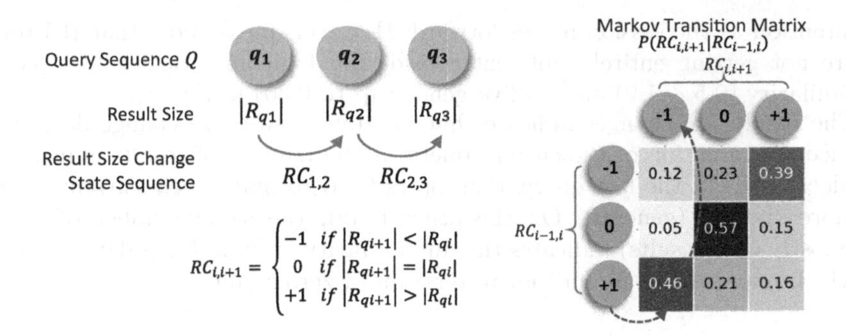

Fig. 8. Markov transition matrix of result size change states.

unchanged, and increase[8], presented as -1, 0, $+1$ respectively. For a single query sequence $Q = \{q_1, q_2, \cdots, q_{n-1}, q_n\}$, we generate a *result size change state sequence* $\{RC_{1,2}, \cdots, RC_{n-1,n}\}$ which is then used to calculate the Markov transition matrix between three types of RC states, i.e., $-1, 0$, and $+1$. A Markov transition matrix is a square matrix describing the probabilities of transferring from one state to another. The state transition probability is formulated by $P(RC_{i,i+1}|RC_{i-1,i}) = \frac{\#(RC_{i-1,i}, RC_{i,i+1})}{\#RC_{i-1,i}}$. The state transition probabilities in single search sessions on our 10 datasets are shown in Fig. 8. The probability of transferring from $RC_{i-1,i}$ to $RC_{i,i+1}$ can be determined by the intersections of the corresponding row and column in the Markov transition matrix. For example, as shown in Fig. 8, the number 0.46 in row $+1$, column -1 indicates the probability of moving from a result size increase state to a decrease state, i.e., $P(-1|+1)$, is 0.46.

Key Findings: The above results allow us to make the following observations.

1. The GEDs between (q_i, q_{i+1}) decrease gradually in a session (as shown in Fig. 5a), which indicates that query change between two contiguous queries is increasingly indistinct as users getting closer to their information needs. Interestingly, the GEDs between (q_1, q_{i+1}) increase consistently at first, then decrease (Fig. 5b). Combining with key findings.3 (below), this suggests that users may use prior query structures to explore other related information.
2. The graph patterns of queries in the same session are broadly similar, as illustrated by the $0.78 \sim 1$ cosine similarity and $-0.07 \sim 0.46$ KL divergence in Fig. 6. This indicates that users usually change the structure of graph patterns slightly in a SPARQL search session. The GEDs in Fig. 5 show this conclusion as well.
3. The IRI term similarity is less and less similar, as shown in Fig. 7. In more detail, the distribution of IRI terms used in queries is more scattered, which indicates that users tend to include more IRI terms and express a clearer

[8] We eliminate the processing error state here.

intention as the session moves forward. However, please note that IRI terms are not getting entirely different considering high numerical values (cosine similarity ($0.5 \sim 1.0$) and kl-divergence (up to 0.30) in Fig. 7).

4. The result size changes indicate that previous result size change does influence the intention of the current query: if the number of results is increased (decreased) in the last query, then users tend to make their current queries more specific (general). On the other hand, the same number of results (mostly zero results) indicates the unfamiliarity of underlying data for users, which may lead to an additional iteration of zero results.

3.2 Query Reformulations in Single SPARQL Sessions

We explore different types of reformulations over query sequences in single SPARQL search sessions as discussed in detail below. Please note that we have not considered semantically equivalent rewritings for now. We only track user reformulations and try to find valuable findings about user behaviours.

Reformulations of SPARQL Operators: We first investigate reformulations in terms of operators for contiguous query pairs. The usage of operators generally reflects the query intent. For instance, the addition of `Distinct` may occur when a user checks answers with many duplicates. For SPARQL query forms (i.e., `SELECT, CONSTRUCT, ASK, DESCRIBE`), only 2.51% SPARQL query pairs have such changes. Among these changes, the most common one (49.26% relative to the number of changes on query forms) is between `SELECT` and `CONSTRUCT`. This indicates that users first check the underlying data in knowledge graphs by `SELECT`, then construct a graph using `CONSTRUCT`. The second most frequent change (22.60%) of the query form is between `SELECT` and `ASK`. In this scenario, users may issue an `ASK` query to examine whether a specific solution exists, followed by the `SELECT` query to get the desired results. Table 2 shows the percentage-wise distribution of the different operators in terms of their usage (i.e., presence of an operator) and reformulations (addition or removal) in the query logs. Please note that *removals* and *additions* are relative to the total *usage* of the operators in the query logs. The results show that a majority of the selected operators are frequently reformulated in the query logs.

Reformulations of Triple Patterns: Given a contiguous query pair (q_i, q_{i+1}) in a search session, there are three formulations possible pertaining to the triple patterns used in the query pair: (1) new triple pattern(s) is added, (2) existing triple pattern(s) is deleted, (3) some changes (*substitutions*) are made in the individual elements (*subject, predicate, object*) of the triple patterns. In this section, we show reformulations of triple patterns within different SPARQL operator blocks (e.g.., `Union`, `Optional`) and the substitutions made on different join vertex types and their connecting edges and nodes.

(1) Operator Block-wise Reformulations: There are 78.24% pairs of contiguous queries that show changes in triple patterns. We list the triple pattern reformulations that occur in the top-6 most frequent SPARQL operator

Table 2. Percentages (%) of the total usage and reformulations (removals and additions) of operators over all query logs. Coloring is used to show different groups of operators, namely, graph patterns, property paths, aggregations, and solution modifiers.

Operator	Total-usage	Removals	Additions	Operator	Total-usage	Removals	Additions
Filter	64.67	11.13	10.99	Count	2.64	38.06	31.00
Union	23.42	9.63	9.56	Sample	0.17	27.19	32.46
Optional	15.14	18.62	19.02	GroupConcat	0.10	23.19	20.29
Graph	1.71	25.33	26.45	Sum	0.03	50.00	50.00
Bind	0.98	24.55	25.00	Min	0.06	12.50	15.00
Minus	0.37	52.63	42.91	Max	0.02	45.45	27.27
Service	0.33	17.49	21.08	Avg	0.02	14.29	28.57
Values	<0.01	0	100	Distinct	50.63	4.08	3.73
SeqPath	2.22	4.20	5.93	Limit	21.84	13.58	14.00
MulPath	0.67	11.62	12.06	OrderBy	7.97	25.83	24.29
AltPath	0.30	7.43	26.73	Offset	2.60	16.06	21.58
InvPath	0.05	14.29	8.57	GroupBy	1.35	23.85	26.04
Projection	67.77	3.29	3.34	Having	0.22	18.00	26.67

blocks in Table 3. In addition, we show reformulations in the `Main` block which does not contain any of the operator blocks. An example of the `Main` block is the body of the SPARQL `SELECT` query, which only contains a set of triple patterns as the BGP. The triple patterns in the `Graph Template` operator block represent the graph templates used in the `CONSTRUCT` queries. The *combined substitutions* represent the made-in-one or more-than-one elements of the triple patterns. The percentages reported in this table are relative to the total usage of certain operator blocks in query logs. Note that the reformulations on triple patterns are only considered when the corresponding operator block exists both in q_i and q_{i+1}. The additions and removals of operators are not included in Table 3.

The results suggest that reformulations are very common in different operator blocks. In most operator blocks, substitutions are more frequent than additions and removals. This indicates that users first make changes in the elements of the existing triple patterns, rather than inserting or deleting new triple patterns. Substitutions happening in *subject, predicate* and *object* are mostly evenly distributed.

(2) Substitutions on Different Join Vertex Types and Neighbors: To further study user preferences on substitutions, we investigate the elements in hypergraphs of the queries in which substitutions appear most frequently. To this end, we consider the join vertex (the center), the direct *subjects* and *objects* this vertex connects to (neighbor nodes), and the direct *predicates* this vertex connects to (neighbor edges). Also, for *hybrid* vertices, we divide their neighbors into incoming and outgoing types. The distribution of substitutions on different positions is shown in Table 4. These percentages are relative to the occurrence of join vertex types and the neighbors of centers. We use *red* to indicate the highest value in each column. The results indicate that most ssubstitutions happen on

Table 3. Percentages (%) of reformulations (additions, removals, and substitutions) on triple patterns in 6 most frequent operator blocks, as well as percentages (%) of substitutions occurring in different elements of triple patterns. (Template = Graph Template).

	Main	Template	Union	Optional	Service	Graph	Subquery
Addition	21.92	42.00	7.79	4.30	6.87	4.21	79.95
Removal	21.28	26.33	8.30	3.00	7.63	3.31	80.06
Combined Substitution	61.10	55.92	43.16	17.76	9.16	8.93	1.21
Subject substitution	37.97	28.95	49.81	40.41	54.55	18.66	73.88
Predicate substitution	28.06	36.44	18.49	9.56	18.18	36.27	5.22
Object substitution	33.97	34.61	31.70	50.02	27.27	45.07	20.90

Table 4. Percentages (%) of substitutions on join vertex types and neighbors. (neigh = neighbor, in = incoming, out = outgoing)

		Ncbigene	Ndc	Orphanet	Sgd	Sider	Affymetrix	Goa	SWDF	LGD	DBpedia
Star	center	20.51	12.50	11.40	1.98	20.37	2.08	1.96	6.93	28.48	29.38
	neigh edges	3.20	2.37	3.35	11.44	0.77	3.75	2.88	3.77	8.63	7.11
	neigh nodes	12.32	9.34	14.13	13.14	35.00	20.13	18.86	6.40	9.38	12.67
Sink	center	5.26	5.88	3.70	8.68	45.75	2.94	0.64	7.41	0.64	15.52
	neigh edges	0	5.88	0	4.25	0.08	22.73	0	4.00	0.27	11.96
	neigh nodes	19.51	10.73	22.22	51.73	11.18	65.24	61.83	6.62	26.06	22.12
Path	center	26.67	22.81	21.43	6.19	6.28	17.13	24.53	7.91	29.04	27.28
	neigh edges	1.67	5.26	7.14	13.84	0.88	7.69	8.49	4.73	14.31	5.42
Hybrid	center	18.75	0	0	90.88	13.04	87.53	68.84	11.51	43.92	45.54
	in edges	0	0	0	0	0	0	0	0.66	0.80	15.19
	in nodes	0	0	0	37.15	2.94	36.06	28.70	5.81	18.73	24.41
	out edges	23.81	19.23	30.00	0.38	0	0.18	1.27	1.12	0.27	5.72
	out nodes	47.62	41.67	60.00	2.62	16.83	1.68	7.84	4.45	18.31	13.66

incoming nodes of the *hybrid* vertex. This is because the hybrid node has the highest connectivity with other nodes in the query hypergraph. As such, it is likely to be changed more frequently by the users.

Reformulations of FILTER Constraints: A constraint, expressed by the keyword `FILTER`, is a restriction on solutions over the whole group in which the `FILTER` appears[9]. Similar to reformulations of triple patterns, there are three reformulations for `FILTER` constraints: addition(s), removal(s), and substitutions on elements of `FILTER` constraints. But unlike the triple pattern, which has three elements, a `FILTER` constraint can have different elements that are used inside its body. Therefore, we express `FILTER` constraints as parse trees (see Fig. 9). On this basis, we compare two parse trees of `FILTER` constraints in contiguous queries, i.e., q_i and q_{i+1}, and find changes in corresponding elements (*substitutions*). For example, the elements with the same patterns in Fig. 9 are compared.

[9] https://www.w3.org/TR/sparql11-query/#scopeFilters.

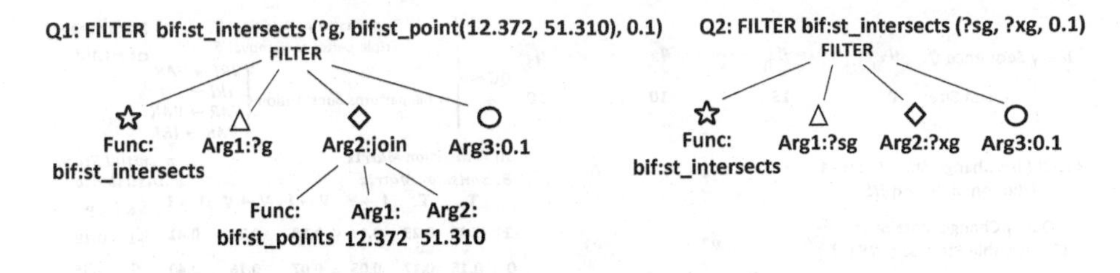

Fig. 9. Example of corresponding elements of two FILTER constraints.

Table 5. Substitutions on FILTER constraints.

Dataset	Ncbigene	Ndc	Orphanet	Sgd	Sider	Affymetrix	Goa	SWDF	LGD	DBpedia
Block Subs	0	20	8	121	3	94	7	34	11,787	3,155
Specific Subs	4	69	52	67	32	97	17	137	5,017	5,702
variable	25.00	24.64	21.15	17.91	0	39.18	11.76	19.71	3.41	21.43
IRI	0	59.42	5.77	74.63	0	20.62	35.29	8.03	1.14	30.90
string	75.00	15.94	73.08	7.46	100	38.14	29.41	64.96	3.37	28.20
number	0	0	0	0	0	0	0	0.73	90.53	7.33

Please note that corresponding elements are not only between single values, i.e., *specific substitutions*, which can be compared directly, but also between one single value and another constraint function or between constraint functions i.e., *block substitutions*. The *Arg2* in Fig. 9 is an example of *block substitution*.

Among all the contiguous query pairs in the same session, 37.68% have reformulations about FILTER constraints. Again, the majority of the reformulations (92.17%) are substitutions. We present distributions of *block* and *specific substitutions* in different datasets in Table 5. The first two rows present the number of *block* and *specific substitutions*. For *specific substitutions*, we also list the percentage of *specific substitutions* on different data types: variable, IRI, string, and number. Substitutions on FILTER constraints show very different distributions in different datasets, especially in the LGD. The LGD is a knowledge graph that contains spatial datasets [25]. Geometry data types and functions embedded in GEOSPARQL [3] are used to satisfy the needs for representing and retrieving spatially related data. Functions like *intersects, overlaps* involve many numeric calculations, which makes *numbers-specific substitutions* more dominant (90.53%) compared to other substitutions. Furthermore, FILTER constraints in the LGD are more complex than other datasets: the number of *block substitutions* is twice the number of *specific substitutions*. For other datasets, substitutions usually happen in strings, which serve as an argument in functions of strings.

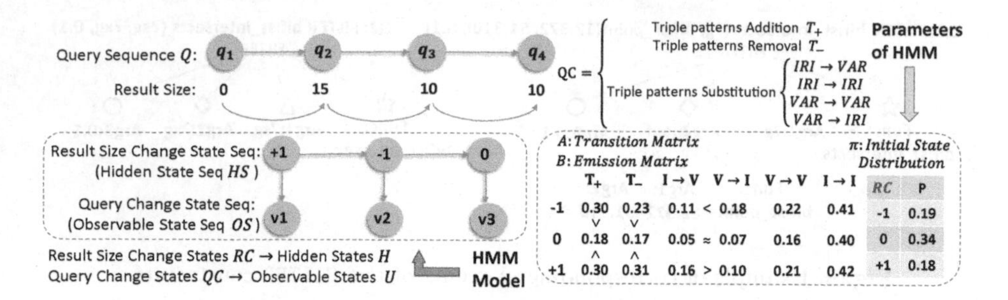

Fig. 10. HMM model of the SPARQL search session.

4 An Application Example of Findings

To show the potentiality of our findings, we use a simple model to predict user intentions of a given session and give reformulation suggestions based on the predicted intention. In single sessions, continuous query reformulations can be captured, while the drifting user intentions are abstract and can not be observed directly. We utilize a Hidden Markov Model (HMM) to characterize this process, and model the intention sequence as an unobservable sequence, the reformulation sequence as an observable sequence. We assume that $H=\{h_1, h_2 \cdots h_e\}$ is the set of hidden states and $U=\{u_1, u_2 \cdots u_f\}$ is the set of observable states (e and f are the number of corresponding states), while $HS=(hs_1, hs_2 \cdots hs_t)$ and $OS=(os_1, os_2 \cdots os_t)$ are the sequence of hidden states and observable states, respectively. We use result size changes to model drifting intentions, i.e., the hidden states H, and consider changes in triple patterns as observable states U. We employ the maximum likelihood estimation to calculate parameters of the HMM model, i.e., initial state distribution π, transition probability matrix A for hidden states, and the emission probability matrix B. The matrix A is the Markov transition matrix in Fig. 8. The details and parameters of the model are presented in Fig. 10. In summary, our model is capable of (1) inferring user intentions based on the observable query change sequence, i.e., a decoding problem: given $\lambda=(A, B, \pi)$ and $OS=(os_1, os_2 \cdots os_t)$, calculate a sequence $HS=(hs_1, hs_2 \cdots hs_t)$ that maximizes $P(HS|OS)$; (2) suggesting reformulation strategies by the possibility of subsequent reformulation strategies, i.e., an evaluation problem: given parameters of HMM $\lambda=(A, B, \pi)$, calculate $p(OS|\lambda)$.

Case Study: We use a session shown in Fig. 11 to illustrate how our model works. In this session, the user use 6 queries in total to find the locations of the *conferenceEvent*. By recommending adding a generic triple pattern to impose a restriction on the variable a first, then making it specific according to the retrieved results, we assist this user omitting a few inefficient reformulations.

Discussions: Here are some possible directions to update the model: (1) More comprehensive ways to model states in HMM. (2) Consider correlations between

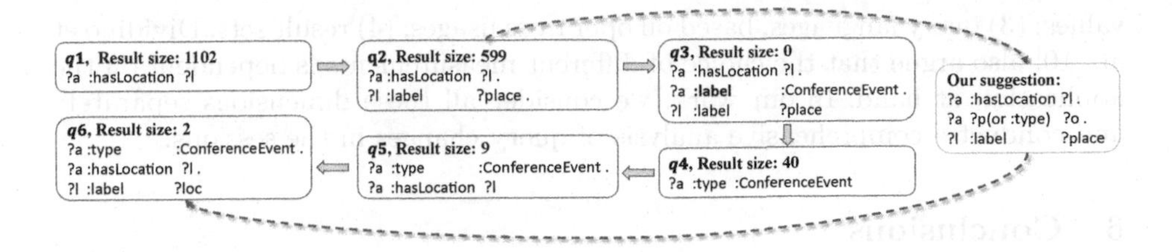

Fig. 11. A session (only BGPs without prefixes) from SWDF log dataset.

queries in query sequences, not just correlations of contiguous query pairs. (3) Combination with techniques based on the underlying data.

5 Related Work

SPARQL Query Log Analysis in Session Level: Previous SPARQL query log analyses have given a comprehensive analysis of SPARQL queries in terms of *structural* features in isolation, such as the most frequent patterns [26], topological structures [7] and the join vertex types [2] etc. However, the analysis of potential correlations between queries is limited. Raghuveer et al. [19] first define the query sequence executed by the same user as a *SPARQL user session*. On this basis, they introduce the important feature of robotic queries, the loop patterns, to describe the repetitive patterns of sessions. Bonifati et al. [7] illustrate the similarity of queries in a query sequence as per the distribution of the length of so-called *streaks*. However, the similarity property introduced in these studies [7,19] applies more to robotic queries from which organic queries are not separated. Bonifati et al. [8] analyze robotic and organic queries separately, but not at the session level. In this paper, we seek a more specific definition of the *search session*, and comprehensively analyze the evolvements of *structure* and *data-driven* features of the organic queries in sessions.

Applications Based on Session-Level Analysis: The similarity property proposed by previous researchers [7,19] has been utilized in query augmentation [16] to retrieve more related results. Lorey et al. [16] focus on retrieving SPARQL queries with high similarity with current queries, but fail to capture the drifting intentions behind queries in single search sessions. Utilizing explicit user feedback directly, Lehmann et al. [14] use active learning to determine different reformulation strategies, which is similar to the example we conduct in this study. However, explicit feedback is usually unavailable in most search scenarios. We utilize reformulations between queries as implicit user feedback.

SPARQL Similarity: Different SPARQL similarity measures have been used in this paper to capture the query changes in sessions. Dividino et al. [10] classify SPARQL similarity measures into 4 categories: (1) query structure, where SPARQL queries are expressed as strings or graph structures; (2) query content, where triple patterns are expressed as strings, ontological terms, or numerical values; (3) query languages, based on operators usages; (4) result sets. Dividino et al. [10] also argue that the choice of different measurements is dependent on the application at hand. In our work, we consider all these dimensions separately and conduct a comprehensive analysis of query changes in the sessions.

6 Conclusions

This paper reveals secrets of user search behaviors in SPARQL search sessions by investigating 10 real-world SPARQL query logs. Specifically, we analyze the evolvement of query changes, w.r.t. *structural* and *data-driven* features of SPARQL queries in sessions, and reach a series of novel findings. We thoroughly investigate reformulations in terms of SPARQL operators, triple patterns, and `FILTER` constraints. Furthermore, we provide an application example about the usage of our findings. We hope results presented here will serve as a basis for future SPARQL caching, auto-completion, suggestion, and relaxation techniques.

Acknowledgements. This work has been supported by by National Natural Science Foundation of China with Grant Nos. 61906037 and U1736204; the German Federal Ministry for Economic Affairs and Energy (BMWi) within the project RAKI under the grant no 01MD19012D, by the German Federal Ministry of Education and Research (BMBF) within the project DAIKIRI under the grant no 01IS19085B, and by the EU H2020 Marie Skłodowska-Curie project KnowGraphs under the grant agreement no 860801; National Key Research and Development Program of China with Grant Nos. 2018YFC0830201 and 2017YFB1002801; the Fundamental Research Funds for the Central Universities.

References

1. Aluç, G., Hartig, O., Özsu, M.T., Daudjee, K.: Diversified stress testing of RDF data management systems. In: Mika, P., et al. (eds.) ISWC 2014. LNCS, vol. 8796, pp. 197–212. Springer, Cham (2014). https://doi.org/10.1007/978-3-319-11964-9_13
2. Arias, M., Fernández, J.D., Martínez-Prieto, M.A., de la Fuente, P.: An empirical study of real-world SPARQL queries. arXiv preprint arXiv:1103.5043 (2011)
3. Battle, R., Kolas, D.: Enabling the geospatial semantic web with parliament and GeoSPARQL. Semant. Web **3**(4), 355–370 (2012)
4. Belleau, F., Nolin, M.-A., Tourigny, N., Rigault, P., Morissette, J.: Bio2RDF: towards a mashup to build bioinformatics knowledge systems. J. Biomed. Inform. **41**(5), 706–716 (2008)
5. Bielefeldt, A., Gonsior, J., Krötzsch, M.: Practical linked data access via SPARQL: the case of Wikidata. In: LDOW Workshop, pp. 1–10 (2018)
6. Bizer, C., et al.: DBpedia-a crystallization point for the web of data. JWS **7**(3), 154–165 (2009)
7. Bonifati, A., Martens, W., Timm, T.: An analytical study of large SPARQL query logs. VLDB J. **29**(2), 655–679 (2019). https://doi.org/10.1007/s00778-019-00558-9

8. Bonifati, A., Martens, W., Timm, T.: Navigating the maze of Wikidata query logs. In: The World Wide Web Conference, pp. 127–138 (2019)
9. Campinas, S., Perry, T.E., Ceccarelli, D., Delbru, R., Tummarello, G.: Introducing RDF graph summary with application to assisted SPARQL formulation. In: DEXA, pp. 261–266 (2012)
10. Dividino, R., Gröner, G.: Which of the following SPARQL queries are similar? Why? In: Linked Data for Information Extraction, pp. 2–13. CEUR-WS.org (2013)
11. Guan, D., Zhang, S., Yang, H.: Utilizing query change for session search. In: ACM SIGIR, pp. 453–462 (2013)
12. Hogan, A., Mellotte, M., Powell, G., Stampouli, D.: Towards fuzzy query-relaxation for RDF. In: Simperl, E., Cimiano, P., Polleres, A., Corcho, O., Presutti, V. (eds.) ESWC 2012. LNCS, vol. 7295, pp. 687–702. Springer, Heidelberg (2012). https://doi.org/10.1007/978-3-642-30284-8_53
13. Kiefer, C., Bernstein, A., Stocker, M.: The fundamentals of iSPARQL: a virtual triple approach for similarity-based semantic web tasks. In: Aberer, K., et al. (eds.) ASWC/ISWC -2007. LNCS, vol. 4825, pp. 295–309. Springer, Heidelberg (2007). https://doi.org/10.1007/978-3-540-76298-0_22
14. Lehmann, J., Bühmann, L.: AutoSPARQL: let users query your knowledge base. In: Antoniou, G., et al. (eds.) ESWC 2011. LNCS, vol. 6643, pp. 63–79. Springer, Heidelberg (2011). https://doi.org/10.1007/978-3-642-21034-1_5
15. Liu, M., Mao, J., Liu, Y., Zhang, M., Ma, S.: Investigating cognitive effects in session-level search user satisfaction. In: ACM SIGKDD, pp. 923–931 (2019)
16. Lorey, J., Naumann, F.: Detecting SPARQL query templates for data prefetching. In: Cimiano, P., Corcho, O., Presutti, V., Hollink, L., Rudolph, S. (eds.) ESWC 2013. LNCS, vol. 7882, pp. 124–139. Springer, Heidelberg (2013). https://doi.org/10.1007/978-3-642-38288-8_9
17. Möller, K., Heath, T., Handschuh, S., Domingue, J.: Recipes for semantic web dog food — the ESWC and ISWC metadata projects. In: Aberer, K., et al. (eds.) ASWC/ISWC -2007. LNCS, vol. 4825, pp. 802–815. Springer, Heidelberg (2007). https://doi.org/10.1007/978-3-540-76298-0_58
18. Picalausa, F., Vansummeren, S.: What are real SPARQL queries like? In: The International Workshop on Semantic Web Information Management, pp. 1–6 (2011)
19. Raghuveer, A.: Characterizing machine agent behavior through SPARQL query mining. In: USEWOD, pp. 1–8 (2012)
20. Rico, M., Touma, R., Queralt Calafat, A., Pérez, M.S.: Machine learning-based query augmentation for SPARQL endpoints. In: The 14th International Conference on Web Information Systems and Technologies, pp. 57–67 (2018)
21. Saleem, M., Ali, M.I., Hogan, A., Mehmood, Q., Ngomo, A.-C.N.: LSQ: the linked SPARQL queries dataset. In: Arenas, M., et al. (eds.) ISWC 2015. LNCS, vol. 9367, pp. 261–269. Springer, Cham (2015). https://doi.org/10.1007/978-3-319-25010-6_15
22. Saleem, M., Hasnain, A., Ngomo, A.C.N.: LargeRDFBench: a billion triples benchmark for SPARQL endpoint federation. J. Web Semant. **48**, 85–125 (2018)
23. Saleem, M., Mehmood, Q., Ngonga Ngomo, A.-C.: FEASIBLE: a feature-based SPARQL benchmark generation framework. In: Arenas, M., et al. (eds.) ISWC 2015. LNCS, vol. 9366, pp. 52–69. Springer, Cham (2015). https://doi.org/10.1007/978-3-319-25007-6_4
24. Saleem, M., Szárnyas, G., Conrads, F., Bukhari, S.A.C., Mehmood, Q., Ngonga Ngomo, A.C.: How representative is a SPARQL benchmark? An analysis of RDF Triplestore benchmarks. In: TheWebConf, pp. 1623–1633 (2019)

25. Stadler, C., Lehmann, J., Höffner, K., Auer, S.: LinkedGeoData: a core for a web of spatial open data. Semant. Web **3**(4), 333–354 (2012)
26. Stegemann, T., Ziegler, J.: Pattern-based analysis of SPARQL queries from the LSQ dataset. In: ISWC (Posters, Demos & Industry Tracks), pp. 1–4 (2017)
27. Wang, M., Wang, R., Liu, J., Chen, Y., Zhang, L., Qi, G.: Towards empty answers in SPARQL: approximating querying with RDF embedding. In: Vrandečić, D., et al. (eds.) ISWC 2018. LNCS, vol. 11136, pp. 513–529. Springer, Cham (2018). https://doi.org/10.1007/978-3-030-00671-6_30

Author Index

Printed in the United States
By Bookmasters